Santillana USA is proud to announce the University of Salamanca's endorsement

D1271799

VNiVERSiDAD ÐSALAMANCA
CAMPUS DE EXCELENCIA INTERNACIONAL

CURSOS *Internacionales*

A Message to Educators and Parents:

Since its inception in 1218, *Universidad de Salamanca* has been linked to the teaching, learning, and dissemination of the Spanish language. It was in Salamanca where the first grammar of the language was published in 1492, and where, at the beginning of the XX Century, Spanish as a foreign language studies were first and fully integrated into the academic programs of a university.

Throughout its historical dedication to the teaching of the Spanish language and culture, *Universidad de Salamanca* has nurtured a tradition of sharing its knowledge and efforts with select educational institutions and organizations. This pedagogical philosophy has led *Cursos Internacionales de la Universidad de Salamanca* to reach an agreement with Editorial Santillana — leader in the publication of instructional materials throughout the world — to carry out a study of Santillana's Spanish as a world language program in order to accredit the program's suitability for educational use in the United States.

Cursos Internacionales de la Universidad de Salamanca, after carefully evaluating **Español Santillana**, has endorsed the linguistic and cultural excellence of this program based on the following findings:

- Reflects the latest pedagogical and methodological research-based approaches that current investigations deem appropriate to the teaching and learning of Spanish as a second language
- Is linguistically and grammatically accurate, and reflects the current use of Spanish around the world
- Presents authentic culture in meaningful contexts to support language instruction
- Aligns to the U.S. National Language Standards, preparing students to become college and career ready
- Fosters progressive Spanish language acquisition to achieve the highest possible level of communicative proficiency

In order to continue to support the further spread and study of the Spanish language, *Cursos Internacionales de la Universidad de Salamanca* is pleased to collaborate with Santillana in its efforts to promote the Spanish language in the United States with quality materials, and appreciates the confidence that Santillana has placed in our institution to evaluate **Español Santillana**.

José Miguel Sánchez Llorente
Consejero Delegado
Cursos Internacionales de la Universidad de Salamanca

Teacher's Edition

High School

Español
Santillana

SANTILLANA USA
Language Education Experts

Español Santillana is a collaborative effort by two teams specializing in the design of Spanish-language educational materials. One team is located in the United States and the other in Spain.

Santillana USA Publishing Company, Inc.
2023 NW 84th Avenue, Doral, FL 33122

Español Santillana
Teacher's Edition Level 2
ISBN-13: 978-1-61605-255-3

Illustrator: **Bartolomé Seguí**
Picture Coordinator: **Carlos Aguilera**

Cartographers: **José Luis Gil, Tania López**
Cartographic Coordinator: **Ana Isabel Calvo**

Production Manager: **Jacqueline Rivera**

Production Coordinator: **Julio Hernández**

Design and Layout: **Jorge Borrego**

Proofreaders: **Nuria del Peso, Elizabeth A. Pease, Marta López**

Photo Researchers: **Mercedes Barcenilla, Amparo Rodríguez**

Printed in the United States of America by Worzalla Publishing Co.

2 3 4 5 6 7 8 9 10   19 18 17 16

Editorial Staff in the United States
Anne Silva
Ana Isabel Antón

Editorial Staff in Spain
Susana Gómez
Belén Saiz
Clara Alarcón

Linguistic and Cultural Advisers in Latin America and in the United States

Antonio Moreno
Editorial Director, Santillana México

Mayra Méndez
Editorial Director, Santillana Puerto Rico

Luis Guillermo Bernal
Editorial Director, Santillana Guatemala

Cecilia Mejía
Editorial Director, Santillana Perú

Graciela Pérez de Lois
Editorial Director, Santillana Argentina

Manuel José Rojas
Editorial Director, Santillana Chile

Mario Núñez
Director of Professional Development, Santillana USA

Reviewers

Lorrie Ann Button-Edelson
Katy, TX

Yvonne Davault
Mansfield, TX

Frances S. Hoch
Raleigh, NC

Rita Oleksak
Glastonbury, CT

Nieves Pérez-Knapp
Provo, UT

Ana Sainz de la Peña
Allentown, PA

Eugenia Sarmiento
Centennial, CO

Maritza Sloan
Plano, TX

Carlos Soler Montes
Calgary, AB, Canada

Alan Svidal
San Diego, CA

Thomasina White
Philadelphia, PA

Writers (Teacher's Edition)

Paloma Lapuerta
New Britain, CT

María Á. Pérez
Tenerife, Spain

María Lourdes Casas
New Haven, CT

María Inés García
Austin, TX

Lisa Berliner
Farmington, CT

Elizabeth Millán
Highland Park, IL

Jan Ferrier Sands
North Granby, CT

Andrea Roberson
Miami, FL

Writers (Student Book)

Paloma Lapuerta
teaches Spanish Language, Literature and Culture at Central Connecticut State University. She graduated from the University of Salamanca, Spain, and received her PhD from the University of Geneva, Switzerland. She has taught in different countries and is co-author of several Spanish textbooks.

María Lourdes Casas
received her Masters of Arts and PhD in Spanish at the University of Wisconsin-Madison. Dr. Casas has taught Spanish Language and Literature at the University of Wisconsin-Madison, Connecticut College, and Southern Connecticut State University. Currently she is an Assistant Professor at Central Connecticut State University.

Lisa Berliner
received her MA in Educational Leadership from Central Connecticut State University. She is currently pursuing a Masters degree in Spanish. She teaches Spanish at the secondary level in Simsbury, CT.

Jan Ferrier Sands
received her BS in Spanish and MS in Curriculum and Supervision from Central Connecticut State University. She is a career teacher of Spanish at Simsbury High School, Simsbury, CT. From 2005 to 2008, she served as the World Languages Teacher-in-Residence at the Connecticut State Department of Education.

María Á. Pérez
received her MA in Spanish from Portland State University. She was the assistant director for the Spanish Basic Language Program at the University of Illinois in Chicago. She has taught college-level Spanish at several institutions, and has worked as an editor and writer for various publishers.

Contributing Writers

Ana Isabel Antón
Miami, FL

Clara Alarcón
Madrid, Spain

Susana Gómez
Madrid, Spain

Íñigo Javaloyes
Newton, MA

Andrea Roberson
Miami, FL

Belén Saiz
Madrid, Spain

Contributors

Janet L. Glass
Dwight-Englewood School
Englewood, NJ

Jan Kucerik
Pinellas County Schools
Largo, FL

Carol McKenna Semonsky
Georgia State University
Atlanta, GA

Anne Nerenz
Eastern Michigan University
Ypsilanti, MI

Gerardo Piña-Rosales
North American Academy of the Spanish Language
The City University of New York, New York, NY

Paul Sandrock
ACTFL
Madison, WI

Emily Spinelli
AATSP
University of Michigan-Dearborn, Dearborn, MI

Brandon Zaslow
Occidental College
Los Angeles, CA

Advisers

Paula Hirsch
Windward School, Los Angeles, CA

María Orta
Kennedy High School, Chicago, IL

Developmental Editor

Belén Saiz and María Á. Pérez

Editorial Coordinator

Anne Silva

Editorial Director

Enrique Ferro

Índice

Español Santillana. Presentation

Scope and Sequence

Key Ideas for Today's Language Classroom

Unidad preliminar. Vamos a recordar

Unidad 1. Centroamérica

Unidad 2. Las Antillas

Unidad 3. Andes centrales

Unidad 4. Norteamérica

Unidad 5. España

Unidad 6. Caribe continental

Unidad 7. Río de la Plata

Unidad 8. La Panamericana

Appendices

Español Santillana

1. A motivating story

1. *Español Santillana* tells a story of travels and challenges.

Four pairs of enthusiasts of the Spanish language and Hispanic culture want to explore the Spanish-speaking world: its people, its cities, its regions, and its cultures. Because of this, they have decided to create the *Fans del español* website and to travel to different countries in order to discover and show unique aspects of each place. In each country, the four teams compete, taking on different *desafíos*, or challenges, that they must complete.

The community of *Fans* has grown, and in Levels 3 and 4, new fans will take on all-new challenges with the same objective: to get to know the places, the cultures, and the lifestyles of Spanish-speaking countries.

2. The challenges present exceptionally motivating situations and fascinating places.

Each unit presents several challenges (four in Levels 1 and 2; three in Levels 3 and 4) related to the people, the regions, or the cultures of a country or geographic area. For example, the teams participate in the ritual of the *voladores de Papantla* in Mexico (Level 1), act in a *telenovela* in Buenos Aires (Level 2), prepare a typical dish of *ropa vieja* with a recipe from the Canary Islands (Level 3), and participate in the ritual of preparing and drinking *mate* (Level 4).

3. The students decide which team wins the challenge in each unit.

In Levels 1 and 2, students discuss the challenges at the beginning of each unit, and make predictions about which pair will win. At the end of the unit, students take a vote to decide the winners of the challenge according to a previously established criterion: the most original, the most fun, the most relevant, and so on.

In Levels 3 and 4, students get to choose one of the pairs' challenges in order to perform a task related to it.

Active participation in the storyline promotes student involvement and motivation.

⚑→ TU DESAFÍO

The *Tu desafío* section that appears on certain pages of Levels 1 and 2 is intended to motivate students and promote independent work. Upon accessing the *Fans del español* website to do the proposed activity, students earn points, which they can accumulate throughout the year.

In Levels 3 and 4, the students' challenges are linked to the challenges that the three pairs take on in each unit.

¿Quién ganará?

4 Los desafíos

▶ **Habla.** What will be the challenge for each pair? Think about this question and discuss it with your classmates.

DESAFÍO 1
La máscara de jade

Diana y Rita

DESAFÍO 2
Vamos de compras

Patricia y Tess

DESAFÍO 3
Tres trajes típicos

Mack y Tim

DESAFÍO 4
Un mercado especial

Janet y Andy

5 Las votaciones

▶ **Decide.** You decide. You will vote to choose the most interesting challenge. Who do you think will win?

Interesante

Tu desafío

88 Los desafíos

¿Recuerdas los desafíos que Andy y Tess les plantearon a los personajes? ¿Cuál te gusta más? Elige una de estas opciones y resuelve tu desafío.

DESAFÍO A

Escribe y dibuja una historieta gráfica. Incluye adjetivos de descripción física o de personalidad. Si quieres, puedes hacerla sobre uno de estos personajes de autores hispanos.

Mot (Nacho y Azpiri)
Este simpático monstruo, capaz de viajar a otras dimensiones, apareció en 1988 en un suplemento para niños del diario español El País. Sus historietas se adaptaron después a la televisión y a los videojuegos.

Máximo Chambónez (Themo Lobos)
Según el diccionario, Chambón significa «persona de poca habilidad en el juego». Esta definición retrata bien a este personaje inocente y de buenas intenciones, al que nada le sale bien.

¡YA METÍ LA PATA!

DESAFÍO B

Elige uno de estos dos cuadros, busca información en Internet y elabora una audioguía. Debes describir el cuadro e incluir algo de información sobre el pintor.

Pablo Picasso (España). La familia de saltimbanquis.

Diego Rivera (México). Baile en Tehuantepec.

DESAFÍO C

Inventa y escribe una leyenda utilizando los tiempos de pasado. Debes incluir alguno de estos elementos:

• Personajes: una princesa, un rey, un monstruo, un mago.

• Acontecimientos: una boda, una muerte, un viaje, una mentira.

• Lugares: un bosque, una selva, un desierto, un país muy lejano.

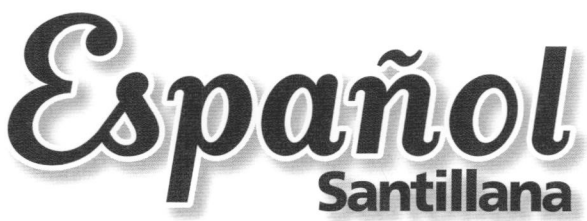

Español Santillana

Key Ideas

2. The integration of culture into the units

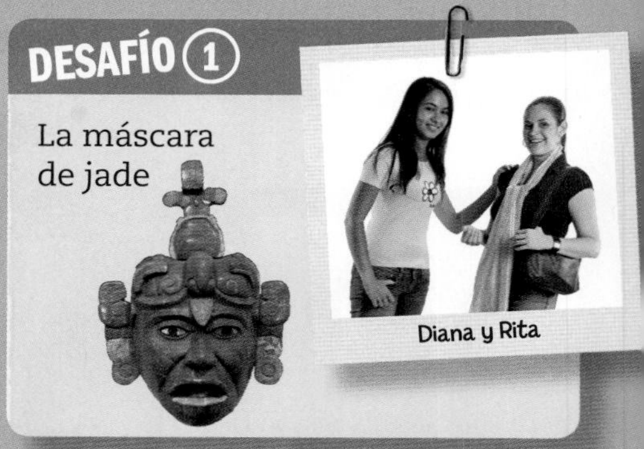
DESAFÍO 1
La máscara de jade
Diana y Rita

Find a jade mask in Antigua.

1. Culture is the framework for learning Spanish.

Culture is present throughout the unit: in the challenges, in the boxes that feature the five Cs of language learning, in the section titled *Mapa cultural*, in the readings, and in the final project.

Culture is also present in the practice activities: students analyze the cultural perspectives, practices, and products of a country or cultural area, compare it with their own country, and transfer what they have learned to their own reality.

2. Culture is presented in an original way.

Each challenge features a **cultural element** related to the theme of the unit. For example, *Desafío 1* in Guatemala (Level 1) showcases an element of traditional Guatemalan culture: jade masks.

Elements of the culture related to the theme of the unit are also presented in an organized way in the *Mapa cultural* section.

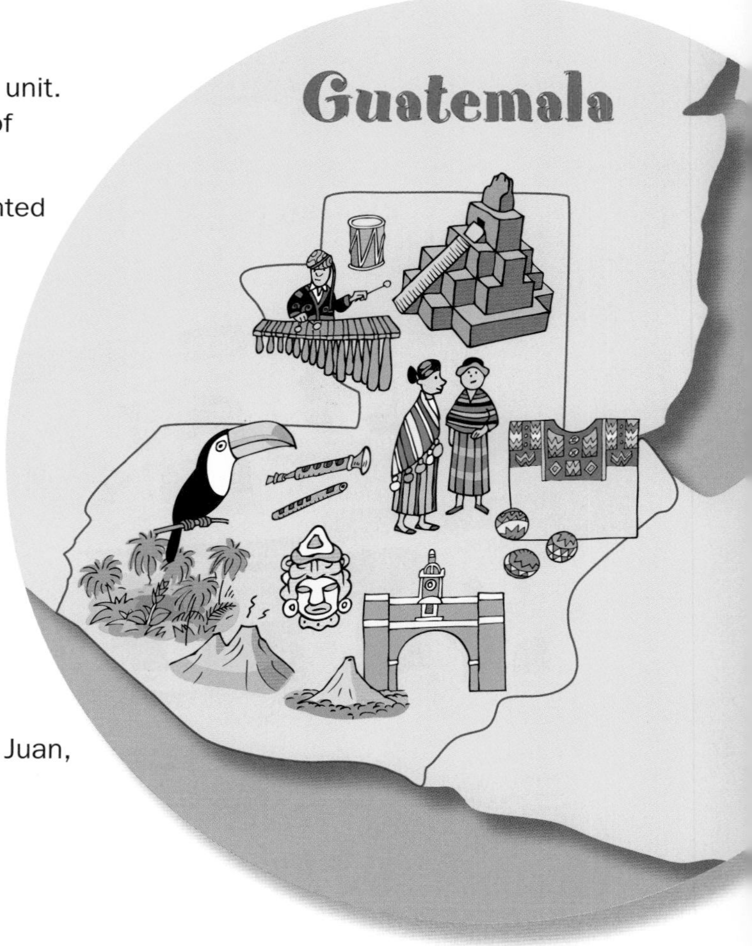
Guatemala

3. Culture is recognized in all its richness.

Culture is explored as a perspective, a practice, and a product. For example, students reflect about the festivals, customs, traditions, family dynamics, table manners, courtesy expressions, dances, foods, etc.

Culture is exhibited from a variety of angles:

- Major cities such as Mexico City, San Juan in Puerto Rico, Antigua in Guatemala, Santo Domingo, Cartagena de Indias, Buenos Aires, Seville, etc.
- Archeology, architecture, and the fine arts: Teotihuacan, Tikal, Machu Picchu, the Zócalo in Mexico City, the El Morro fortress in San Juan, the Alhambra, Frida Kahlo, Diego Rivera, Pablo Picasso, Fernando Botero, etc.
- Customs such as festivals, traditional clothing, foods, and sports.
- Youth culture, such as music and fashion.
- Social relationships and societal organization.

An example of the integration of culture

Level: 1   **Country:** Guatemala   **Theme:** Shopping and clothing

DESAFÍO ②

Vamos de compras

Patricia y Tess

Buy articles of clothing in a mall in Guatemala.

DESAFÍO ③

Tres trajes típicos

Mack y Tim

Acquire three traditional garments in Tikal.

DESAFÍO ④

Un mercado especial

Janet y Andy

Locate a bag of worry dolls in the Chichicastenango market.

Mar Caribe

MAPA CULTURAL

Guatemala

¿Qué significa Guatemala?

México

Chichicastenango
Sololá
Guatemala
Antigua Guatemala

Honduras

El Salvador

OCÉANO PACÍFICO

Guatemala es una república de Centroamérica. Por el norte limita con México. Es un país más pequeño que el estado de Tennessee y tiene más de 13 millones de habitantes.

La capital de Guatemala es la ciudad de Guatemala, el núcleo más grande de Centroamérica.

98 Proporciones

▶ **Escribe.** Use the map to correct these sentences.
1. México es un país menos ancho que Guatemala.
2. Honduras es un país más estrecho que Belice.
3. Guatemala es un país más grande que Nicaragua.
4. Guatemala es un país más pequeño que Belice.

190 ciento noventa

1. La gran ciudad maya de Tikal
The region of flatlands in the northern part of Guatemala is called Peten. Here is located Tikal, an immense Mayan city. The Tikal National Park covers an area of 576 km² (222 square miles). This is equivalent to the area occupied by the city of Chicago, Illinois.

(1) Ruinas de la ciudad de Tikal (Petén).

2. El quetzal: el ave de Guatemala
The quetzal is the bird represented on the Guatemalan flag. It symbolizes freedom. Because the quetzal is in danger of extinction, it has been declared a protected species.

The quetzal played an important role in many Mayan myths.

(2) Un quetzal.

99 Mensajes desde Guatemala

▶ **Investiga y escribe.** Choose one of these topics to research.
1. El centro histórico. Describe the buildings (size, color) and the types of shops.
2. El cantante. Describe his appearance. Compare him with a singer you like.
3. La Quema del Diablo. Compare this festival with one you know.

① El centro histórico de la ciudad de Guatemala.

② El cantante Ricardo Arjona.

③ La tradición de la Quema del Diablo.

▶ **Escribe.** Use two of the most important facts to write an e-mail to a friend.

ciento noventa y uno 191

Tikal

México

Belice

Chichicastenango

Sololá

Guatemala

Antigua Guatemala

Honduras

OCÉANO PACÍFICO

El Salvador

0	25	50
millas

0	25	50
kilómetros

3. An organization based on motivation and learning

1. The units are organized around *Desafíos.*

The units are organized by sections called *Desafíos.* Each *Desafío* presents a challenge that a pair of characters must resolve. In this way, the *Desafíos* contextualize learning in a motivating, meaningful storyline.

The *Desafío* is the cultural and communicative context in which language learning happens.

▶ Each *Desafío* revolves around a **cultural topic** that is related to the theme of the unit: living spaces, clothing, food, health, work, free time, nature, history, politics, society, etc. Culture is the core of each *Desafío.*

▶ Each *Desafío* is focused on a certain **communicative function**: identifying oneself, describing people, describing places, expressing states and feelings, expressing obligation, giving orders or advice, etc.

2. Vocabulary and grammar are presented in context within the framework of each *Desafío.*

Vocabulary and grammar are presented in short, well-defined sections within each *Desafío.* This system facilitates focus on the topic being studied.

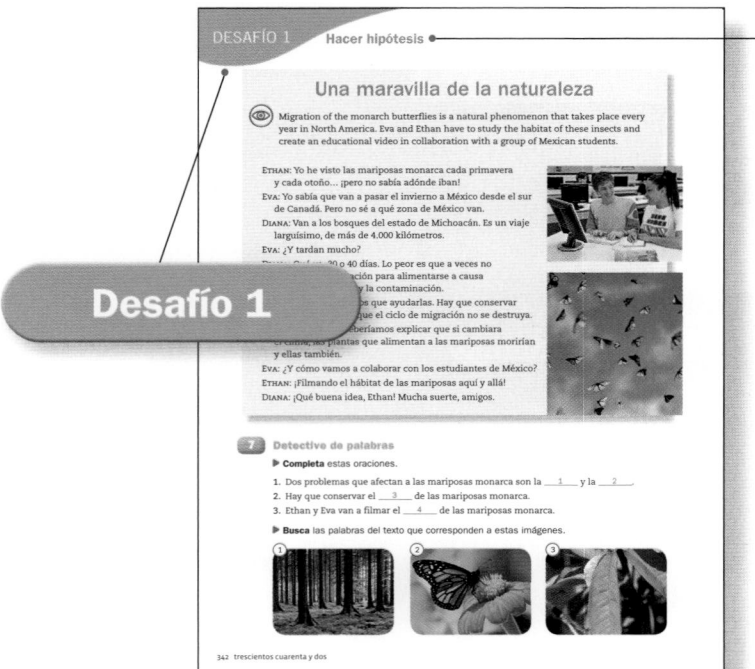

Communicative function

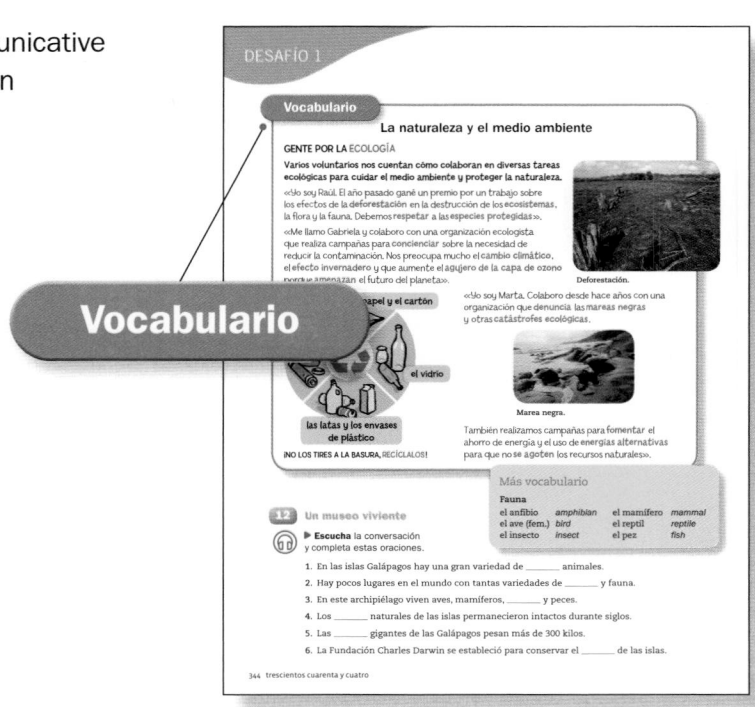

Some of the characters' challenges

Level 1

- Dress like Frida Kahlo (Mexico).
- Perform as a Papantla Flyer (Mexico).
- Find the most colorful house in Old San Juan (Puerto Rico).
- Find an ancient Mayan jade mask (Guatemala).
- Buy worry dolls in a market in Guatemala.
- Prepare Peruvian *ceviche*.
- Get the autograph of the leader in the Tour of Spain bicycle race.
- Play a game of dominoes on Calle 8 in Miami.
- Spend the night in the Hispanic Society of America Museum in New York.
- Take a trip on the Train to the Clouds in Salta, Argentina.
- Find the fake *moai* on Easter Island (Chile).
- Participate in the Stairs Marathon in Valparaiso, Chile.

Level 2

- Find the tallest woman in León, Nicaragua.
- Find Sir Francis Drake's scale in Santo Domingo, Dominican Republic.
- Participate in a serenade in Ponce, Puerto Rico.
- Participate in the Oruro Carnival (Bolivia).
- Prepare Day of the Dead bread (Mexico).
- Participate in a chili contest in San Antonio, Texas.
- Find a *margarita cubista* in the Picasso Museum in Barcelona, Spain.
- Find *El Dorado* in Colombia.
- Drive a bus through the streets of Caracas, Venezuela.
- Act in a *telenovela* (Argentina).
- Cross the Panama Canal in a kayak.
- Help baby sea turtles in Tortuguero National Park (Costa Rica).

The tasks

In Levels 3 and 4, the *Desafíos* propose tasks that the characters and students have to complete: create a comic strip, write a legend, make an audio guide about a painting, compose an invitation, write an e-mail, design a flag, describe an Andalusian patio, present a typical dish, design a webpage, prepare an interview, present a character, respond to an ad, write a report, make a poster, write an essay, create a brochure, etc.

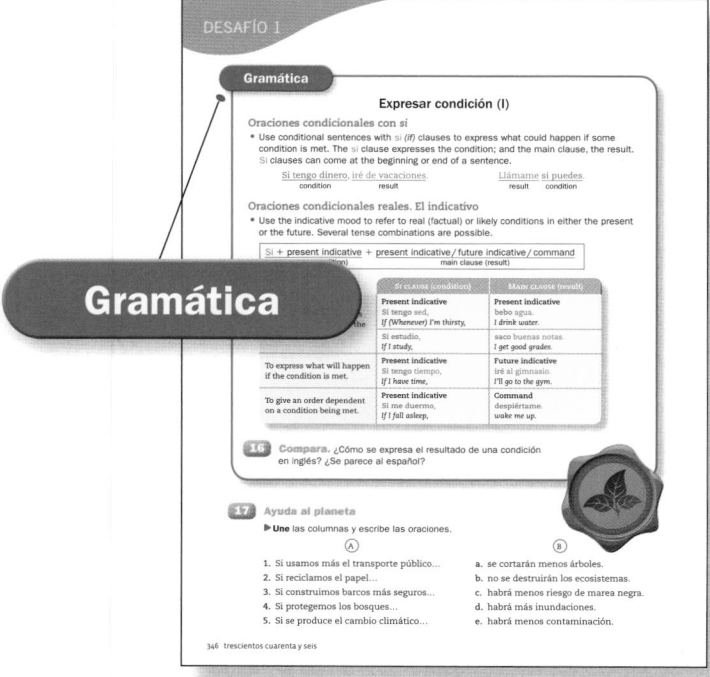

Gramática

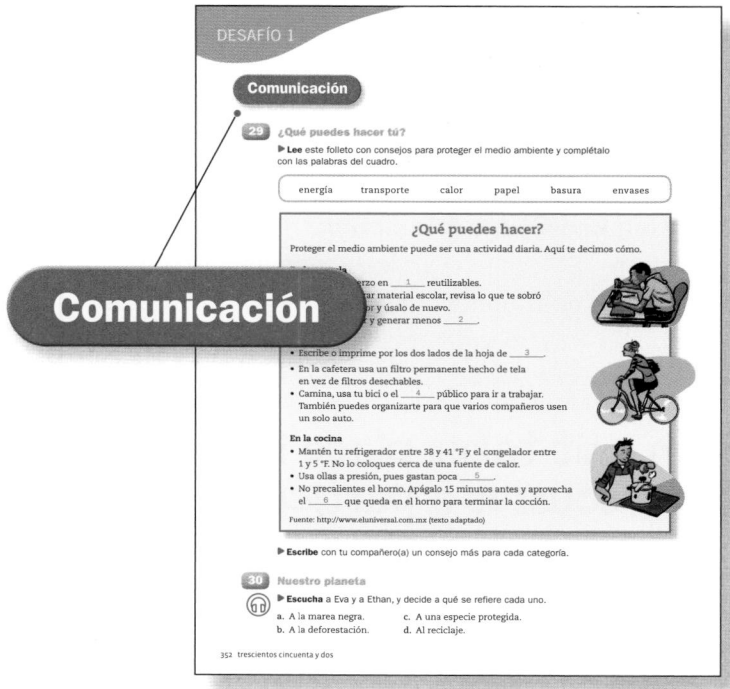

Comunicación

The Unit: Levels 1 and 2

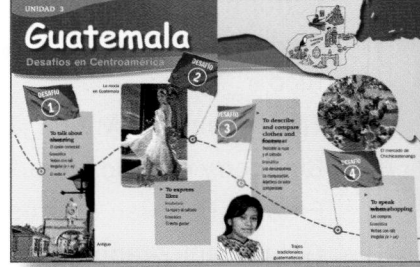

The units are organized in three major blocks.

1. **The linguistic nucleus.** This is the fundamental and most extensive part of the unit. It is centered around the vocabulary, the grammar, and the practice of communication in the context of the travels and the challenges. It contains these sections:

   ▶ **La llegada.** The characters arrive at the destination, which serves as the geographic framework of the unit. This section presents the unit's target vocabulary and grammar in context, as well as some *expresiones útiles* (useful expressions).

   ▶ **Los Desafíos.** Each pair of characters receives a challenge. In this section, the vocabulary and grammar are presented in detail. Following the *Desafíos* is a section called ***Todo junto***, with culminating communicative activities.

   ▶ **El encuentro.** The pairs are reunited to discuss the tasks they have completed, and students choose the winning team.

2. **An in-depth look into culture.** This has as its core the ***Mapa cultural***. This section presents some of the characteristic cultural aspects of a country (Level 1) or a region (Level 2).

   The *Mapa cultural* is complemented by a ***Lectura*** section, in which students learn about a cultural aspect while practicing reading comprehension skills and strategies.

3. **Putting knowledge into action:** the ***Repaso*** pages and the ***Proyecto.*** Students review the vocabulary and grammar of the unit, then do a project in which they integrate the unit's key linguistic and cultural concepts in a communicative way.

Each unit takes place in a country or region and discusses a particular theme.

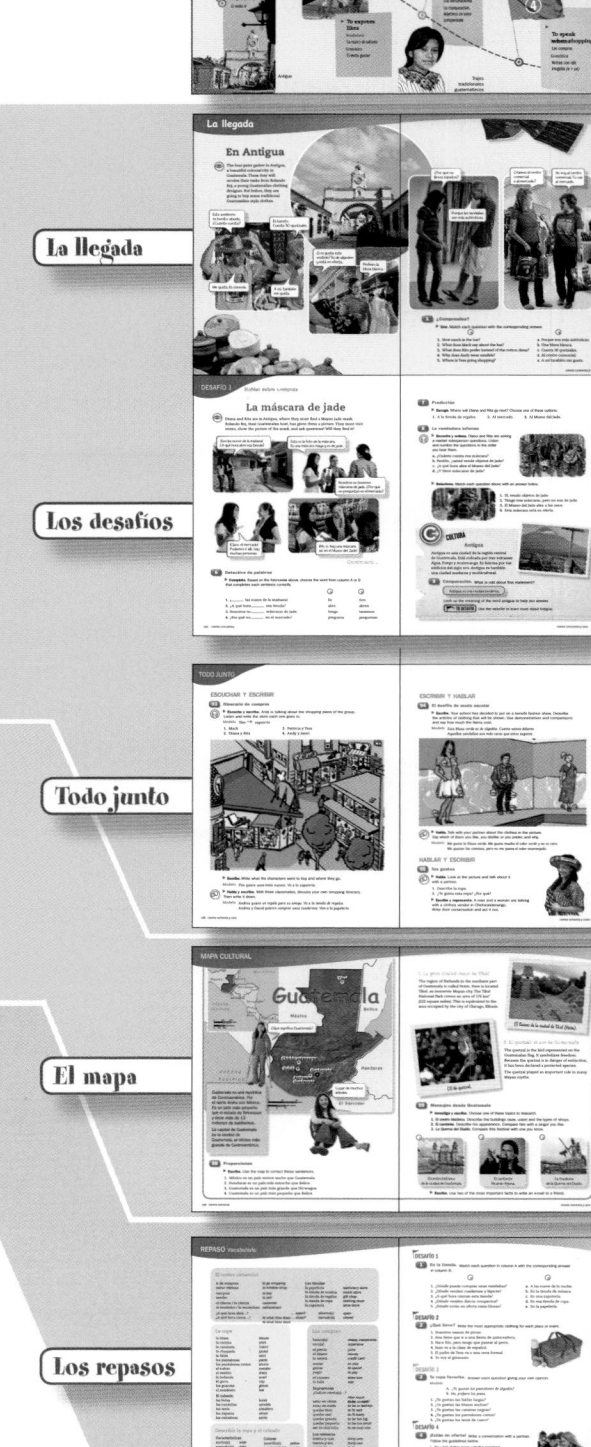

La llegada

Los desafíos

Todo junto

El mapa

Los repasos

El encuentro

Interesante

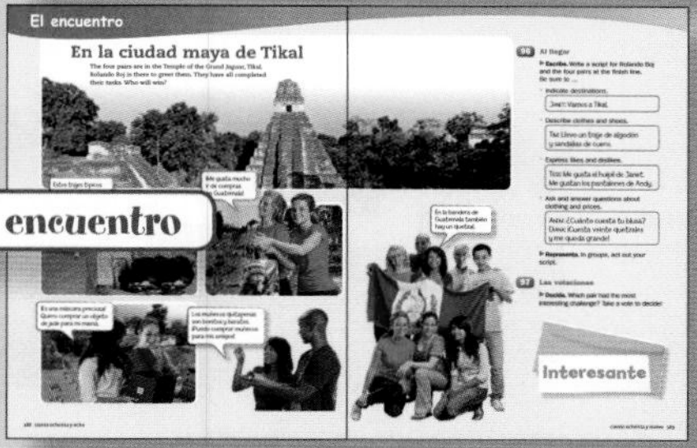

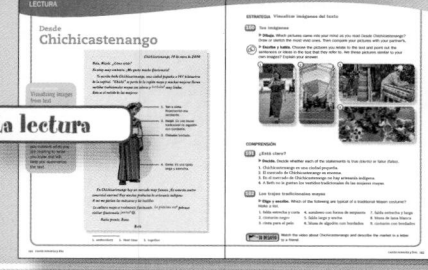

La lectura

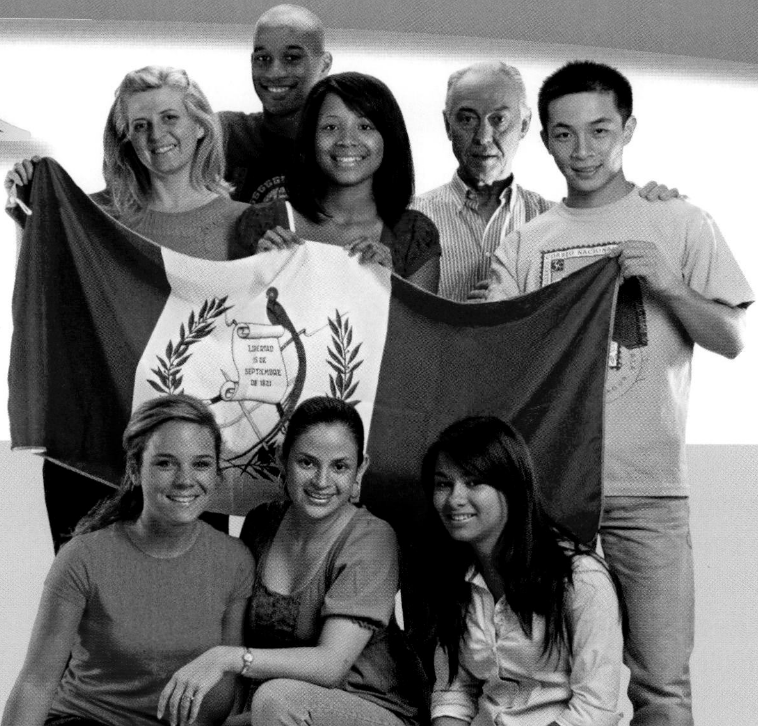

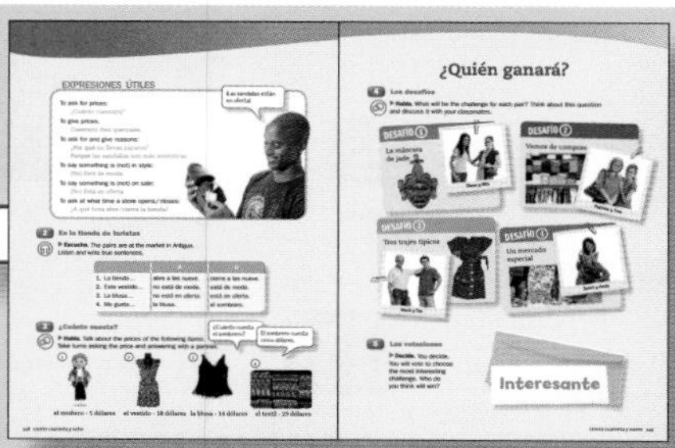

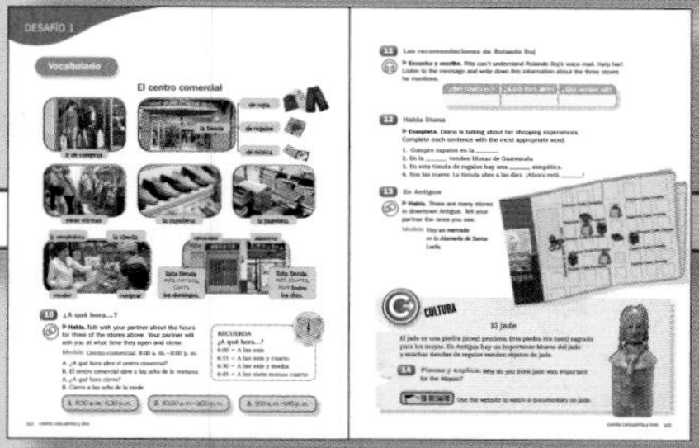

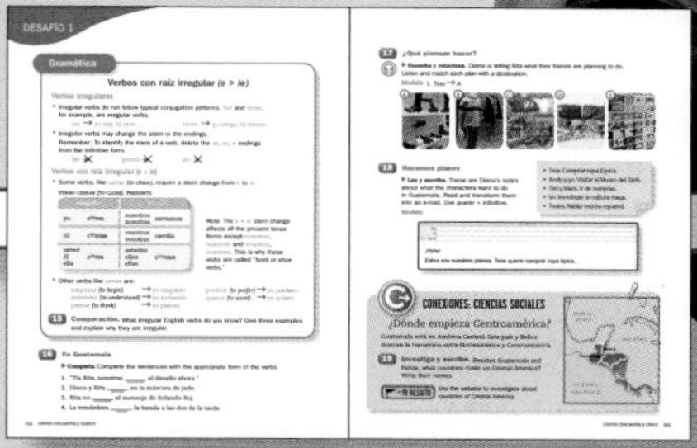

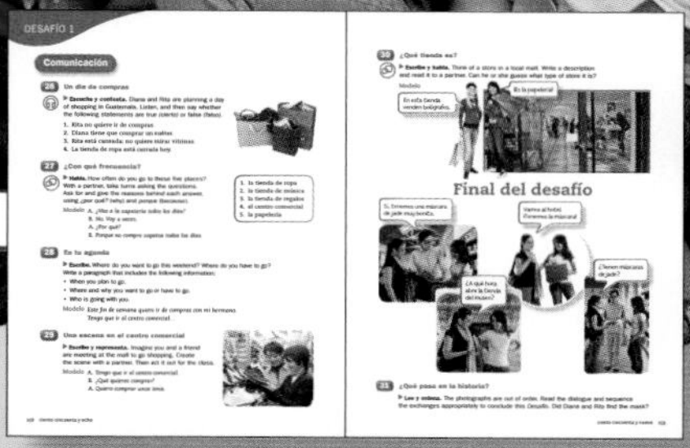

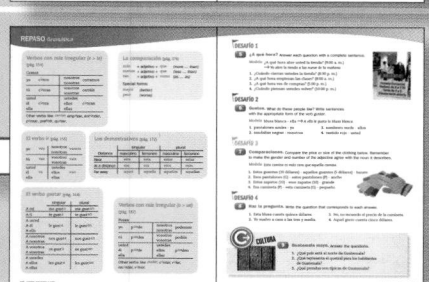

El proyecto

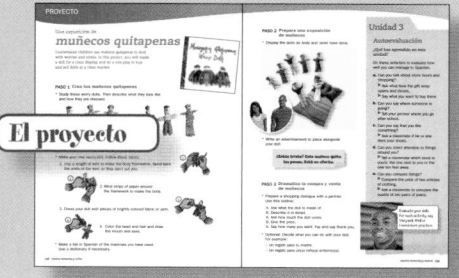

The Unit: Levels 3 and 4

The units maintain the organization in three major blocks.

1. **The linguistic nucleus.** It is centered around the vocabulary, the grammar, and the practice of communication in the context of the *Desafíos*. It contains these sections:

   - **Las tareas.** The characters receive the tasks they will complete throughout the unit. This section presents the unit's target vocabulary and grammar in context, introduces some *expresiones útiles* (useful expressions), and reviews previously learned vocabulary related to the theme.

   - **Los Desafíos.** In addition to the Vocabulary and Grammar, this part includes a **Lectura** section that systematically alternates between a dialogue, an informative text, or a literary text.

   - **Para terminar.** Includes **Todo junto** and **Tu desafío**. In this last part, the students must complete one of the challenges presented to the characters.

2. **An in-depth look into culture.** The **Mapa cultural** presents different practices, products, and perspectives of the Spanish-speaking world, related to the theme of the unit.

   The *Mapa cultural* is complemented by an **Escritura** section. In this section, students practice and extend their writing skills, and apply the vocabulary and grammar they have learned in the unit.

3. **Putting knowledge into action:** the **Repaso** pages and the **Proyecto.** Students review the vocabulary and grammar of the unit, then do a project in which they integrate the unit's key linguistic and cultural concepts in a communicative way.

The unit closes with preparation for the AP* Spanish Language and Culture Exam.

In Level 4, each unit focuses on one specific portion of the AP* Exam.

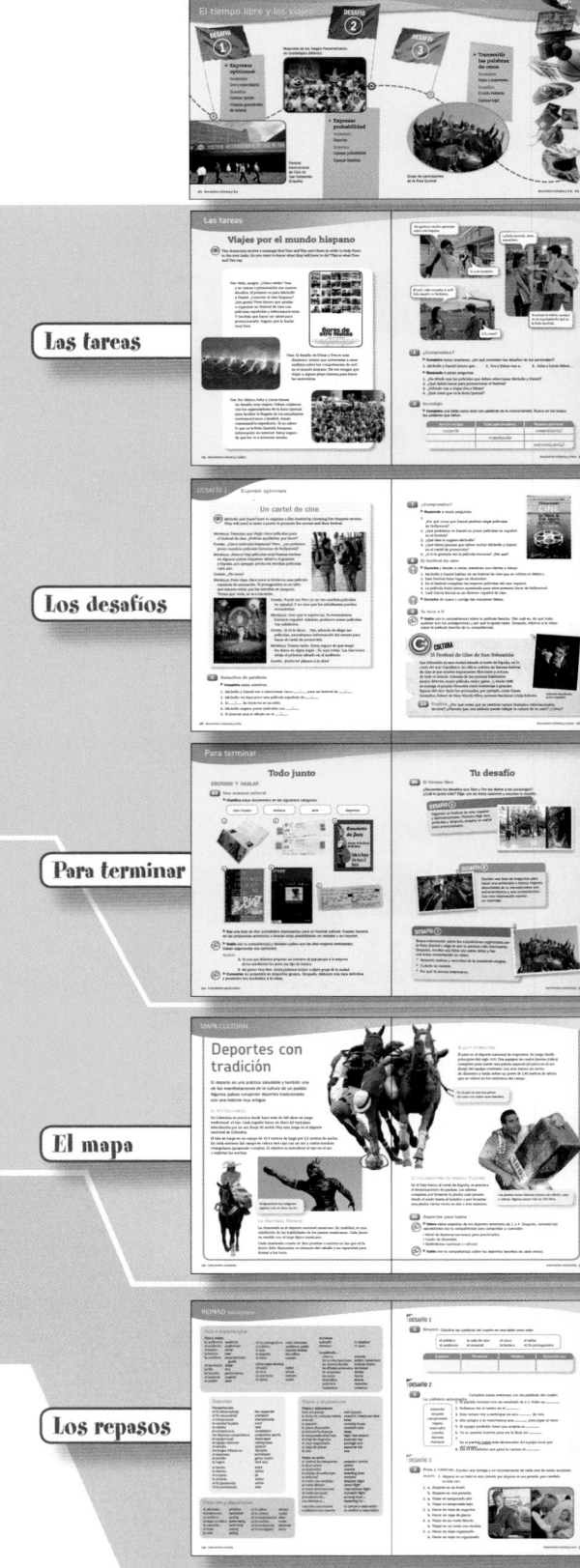

Las tareas

Los desafíos

Para terminar

El mapa

Los repasos

In Levels 3 and 4, there are three *desafíos* per unit.

La escritura

El proyecto

* AP is a registered trademark of the College Board, which was not involved in the production of, and does not endorse, this product.

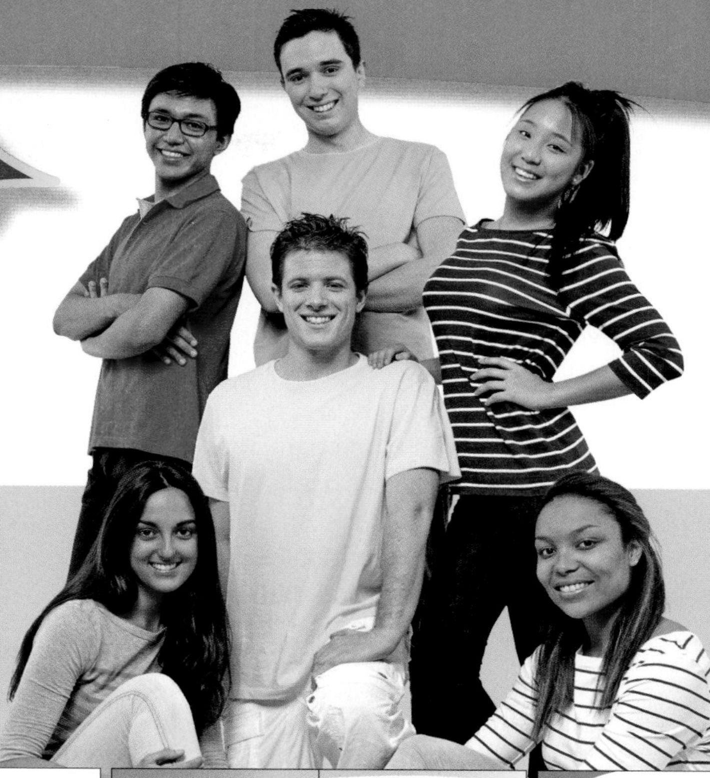

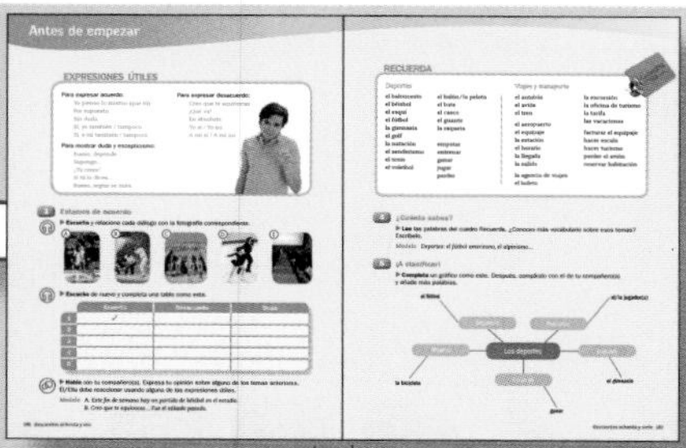

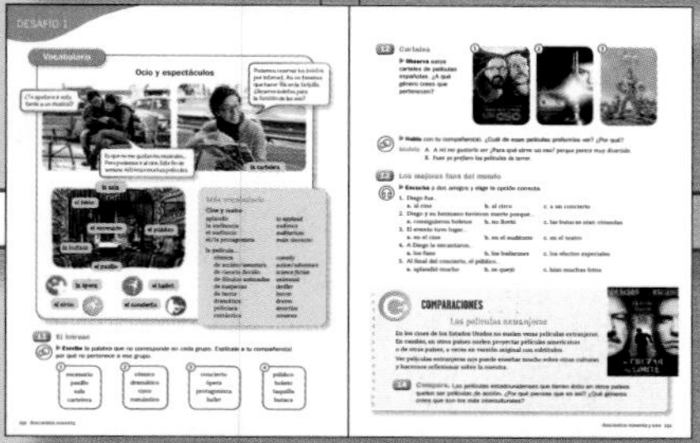

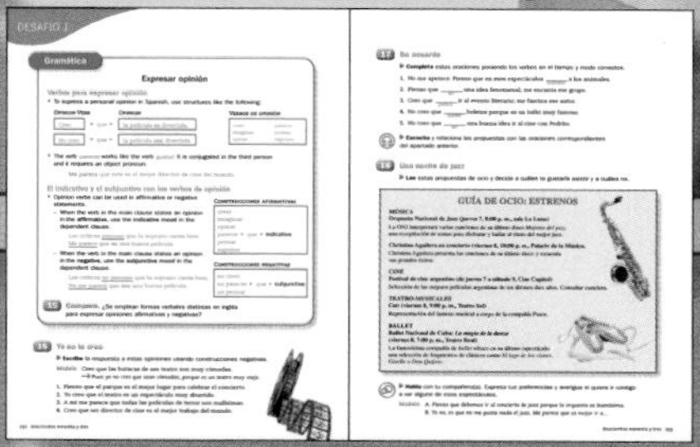

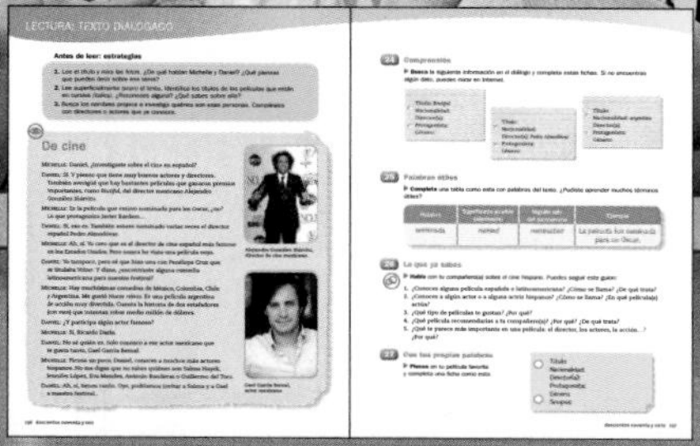

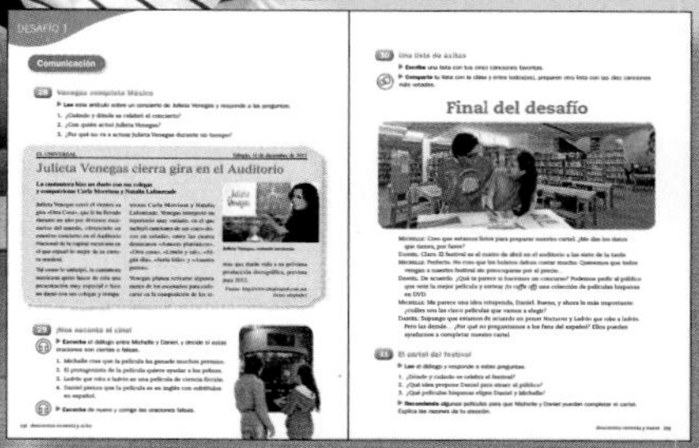

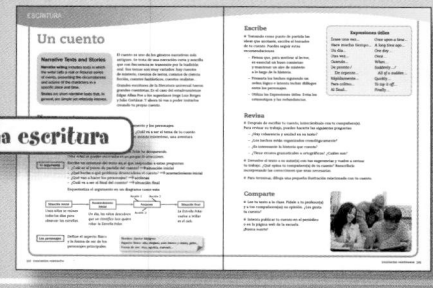

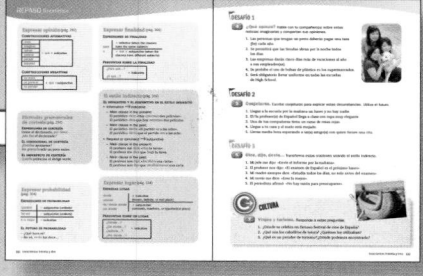

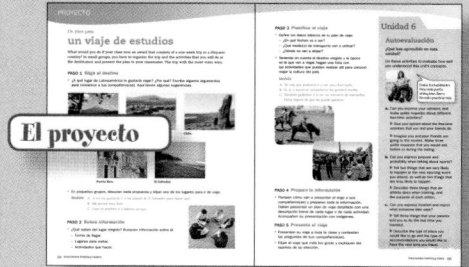

Organization of the Unit: The Structure of a *Desafío*

Each *Desafío* consists of culture, vocabulary, and grammar.

The *Desafío* is the story of each team's challenge, and is therefore the basis of the storyline. It also develops key vocabulary and grammar around a communicative function in a cutural setting.

1. *El desafío* (presentation)

The **Desafío** begins with a text in which the characters talk about their challenge using the target vocabulary and grammar in a context. The context allows the students to become familiar with the new words and structures, and to make hypotheses about their meaning and their usage.

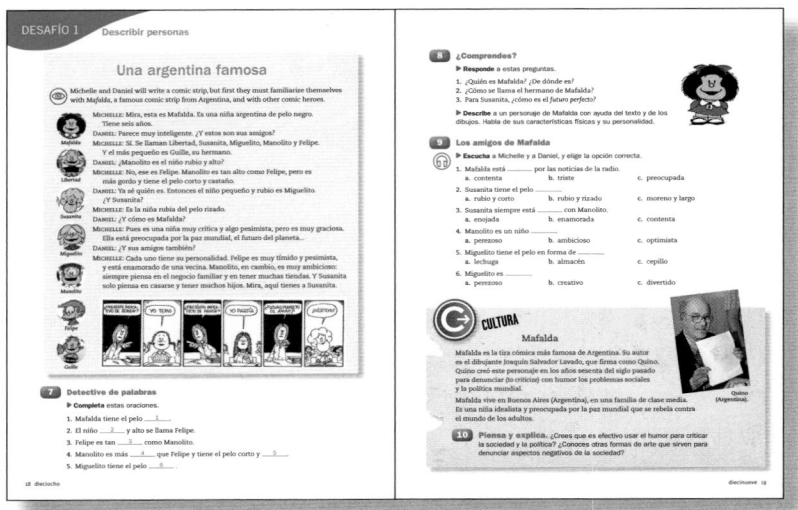

2. *El vocabulario*

On the **vocabulary** pages, the new words and phrases are presented with the support of images and language context. Students use the vocabulary in follow-up activities.

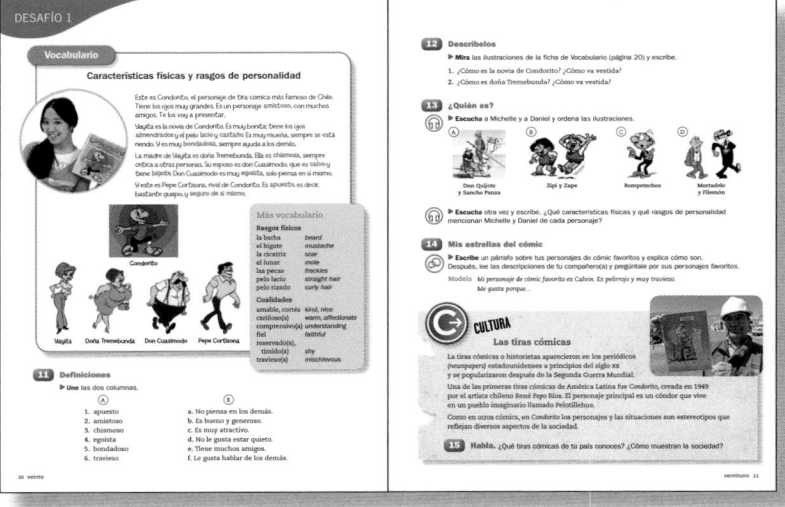

3. *La gramática*

On the **grammar** pages, students are given explanations of key structures, which are practiced along with the key vocabulary.

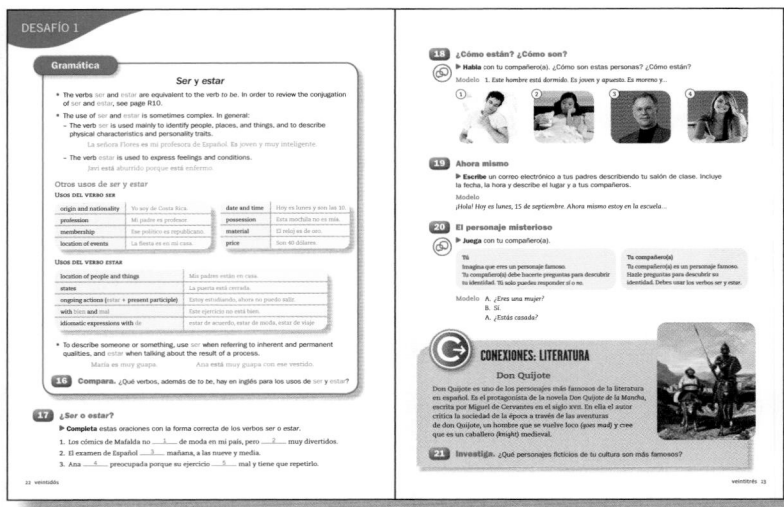

4. *La lectura*

In Levels 3 and 4, **reading** is practiced in each *Desafío* via a written dialogue, an informative text, or a literary text.

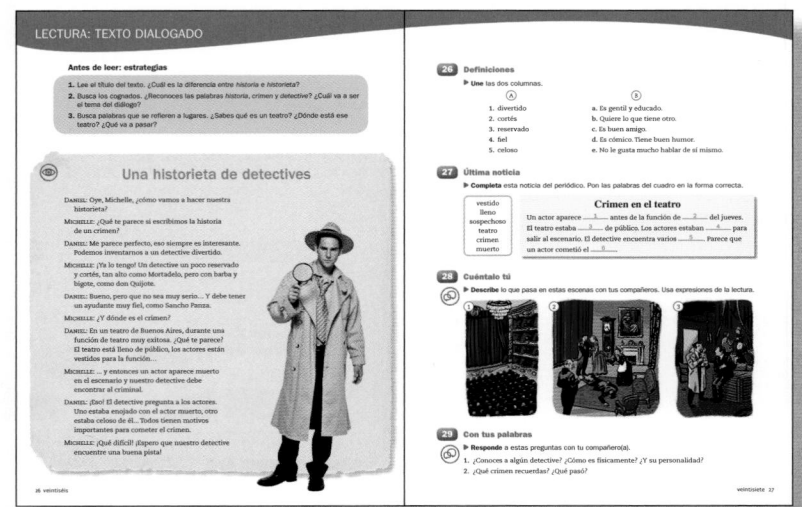

5. *La comunicación*

On the **communication** pages, there are progressively more open-ended activities that allow students to apply the key vocabulary and grammar in communicative situations.

6. *Final del desafío*

The *Desafío* ends with a *fotonovela*, which is a continuation of, and a conclusion to, the initial text.

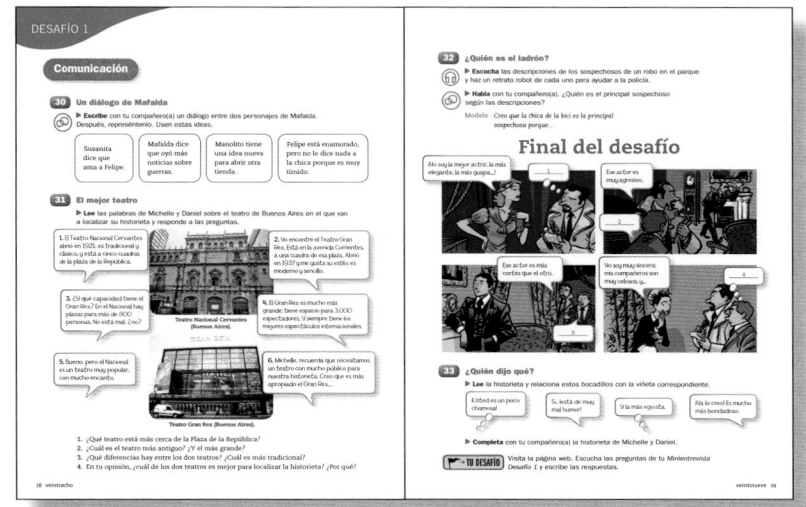

The "C-Boxes"

In each *Desafío*, there are informative segments about **Culture**, **Connections, Comparisons**, and **Communities**. These boxes complement the **Communication** skills that are developed throughout the *Fotonovela*, Vocabulary, Grammar, and *Comunicación* pages.

CULTURA

No más preocupaciones

Los muñecos qui
Estos muñecos re
preocupaciones (*wo*
Por la mañana, tus

59 Compara.

COMPARACIONES

El costo de la vida

El costo de la vi
en una ciudad o
¿Son iguales los
ciudad? ¿Qué tie
o las pequeñas?
de los centros co
(*neighborhoods*)?

87 Investig
and at a
this is the

→ TU DESAFÍ

COMUNIDADES

MO

Los trajes tradicional
de un país. En Guate
una especie de blusa
común a muchas cor

39 Piensa y ex
1. Is there a t
your count
2. How do the
heritage of

→ TU DESAFÍO   Use the website to watch how *huipiles* are made.

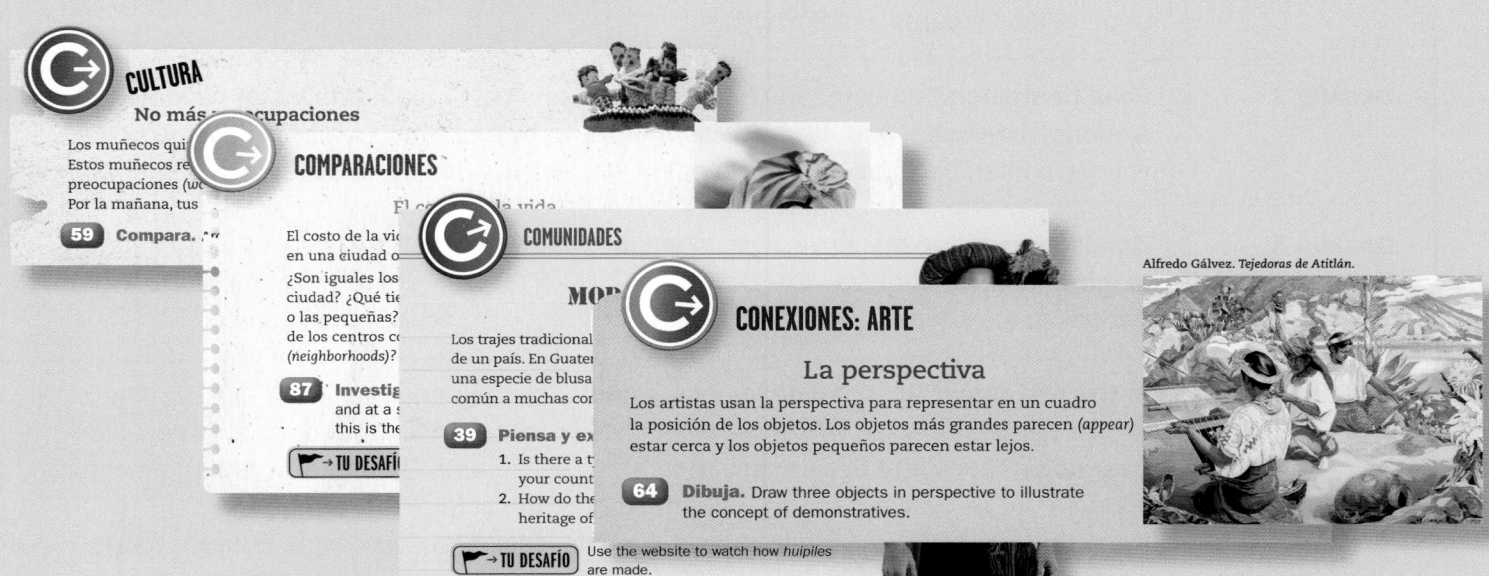

Alfredo Gálvez. *Tejedoras de Atitlán.*

CONEXIONES: ARTE

La perspectiva

Los artistas usan la perspectiva para representar en un cuadro la posición de los objetos. Los objetos más grandes parecen (*appear*) estar cerca y los objetos pequeños parecen estar lejos.

64 **Dibuja.** Draw three objects in perspective to illustrate the concept of demonstratives.

The Vocabulary

A careful selection.

Key vocabulary has been selected, considering the specifications of organizations dedicated to the instruction and evaluation of Spanish, including the *Instituto Cervantes* and the American Association of Teachers of Spanish and Portuguese (AATSP) and the course themes of the AP* Exam.

In general, the most commonly used and standard Spanish terms have been chosen, rather than regional variants. Whenever possible, words close to their English counterparts (cognates) have been included.

The basic criteria for the selection of vocabulary were frequency of use and relevance to students' everyday life, interests, and needs.

Organization by topic or situations.

The vocabulary is organized by topic or by situations related to the theme of the unit. For example, a unit dedicated to the theme of food includes words relating to foods and beverages, meals, and food stores.

Level 2, Unit 4. Theme: Food

Desafío 1	**Foods**: los pescados, los mariscos, el salmón, los camarones, el atún, los cereales, el pan, la pasta, el arroz, la carne, los frijoles, las lentejas, los guisantes, los lácteos, el queso, la leche, el yogur, la mantequilla, las frutas, las fresas, las uvas, la sandía, el melón, la piña, la pera, las verduras, las hortalizas…
Desafío 2	**Food containers**: un bote, una lata, una caja, una bolsa, una botella, un paquete. **Actions, measures, and other words related to buying food**: comprar, hacer la compra, vender, costar, pedir, pensar, hacer cola / fila; un kilo, un litro; la lista de la compra, el precio.
Desafío 3	**Condiments**: el aceite, el vinagre, la sal, la pimienta, el azúcar, la salsa de tomate, la mayonesa, la mostaza. **Actions in the kitchen**: pelar, cortar, echar, mezclar, batir, cocer, hervir, freír, asar.
Desafío 4	**In the restaurant**: el menú del día, de primero, de segundo. **At the table**: el mantel, la servilleta, el cuchillo, el tenedor, el vaso, la cuchara. **Describing foods and beverages**: agrio(a), dulce, picante, salado(a), soso(a), amargo(a), bueno(a), malo(a), delicioso(a), caliente, frío(a), fresco(a). **Preparing food**: frito(a), asado(a), a la plancha, cocido(a), hervido(a), empanado(a).

The instructional focus: work on many levels.

1. *Fotonovelas* and *Desafío* presentation texts

These include new vocabulary words and expressions that students can understand through their visual or verbal context. The activities help students focus on the lexical items and formulate hypotheses about their meaning.

2. *Vocabulario*

The new words and expressions are presented on the vocabulary pages in each *Desafío* with the support of images and/or language contexts.

Students practice the vocabulary first in closed-ended activities (less difficult) and then in open-ended activities (more difficult), where they can apply the vocabulary in real-life situations.

3. *Gramática*, *Comunicación*, and *Todo junto*

Key vocabulary is reinforced and used in different contexts, along with recycled vocabulary from previous units.

4. *Repaso*

At the end of the unit, vocabulary is reviewed and pre-assessment activities are included.

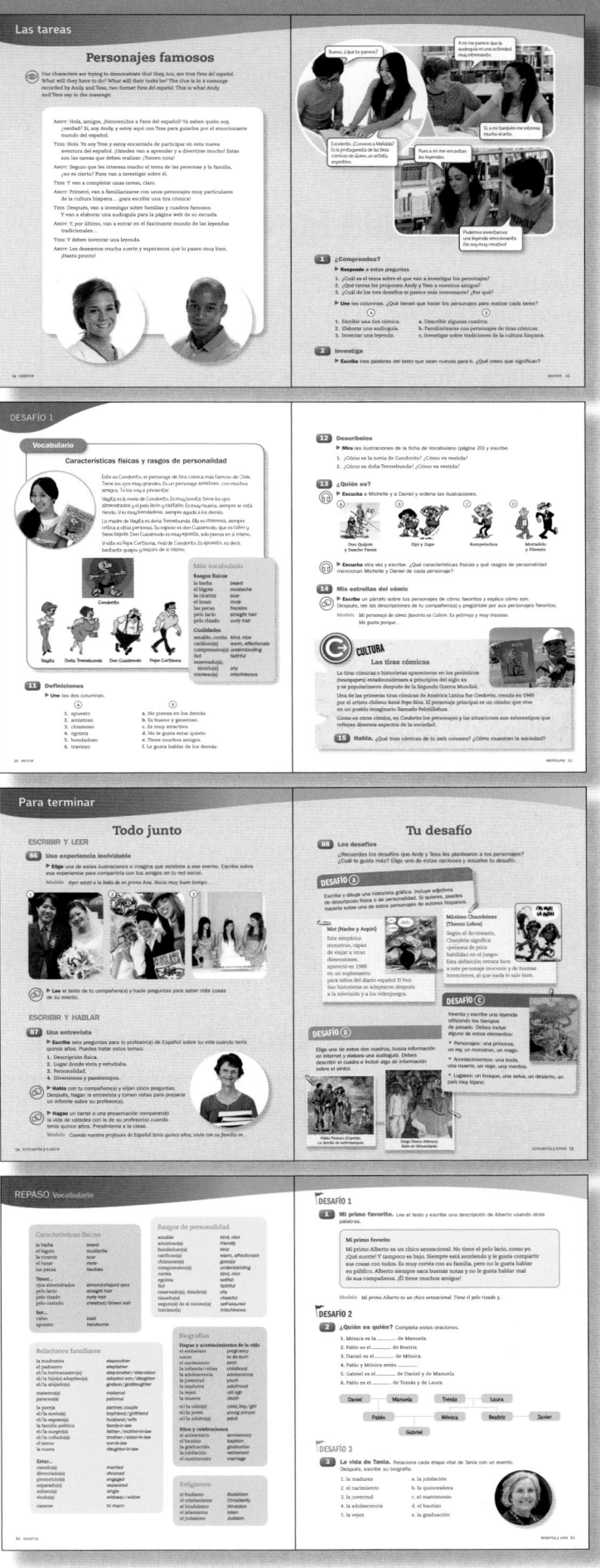

The Grammar

A decision guided by experience.

The selection and sequence of the grammatical elements was determined keeping three fundamental criteria in mind: the use of the structures, their productivity in communicative contexts, and their difficulty.

For example, the verbs *ser*, *estar*, and *tener* are presented before the verb *gustar* because they are more frequently used, they are more productive, and they present fewer difficulties for English speakers than the verb *gustar*.

Organization: grammar linked to communicative functions.

In general, the presentation of grammar is linked to a communicative function. For example, in Level 2, Unit 1, dedicated to the theme of personal life, the following functions and structures are learned:

Gramática

Verbos con raíz irregular (e > ie)

Verbos irregulares

- Irregular verbs do not follow typical conjugation patterns. Ser and tener, for example, are irregular verbs.

    ser → yo soy, tú eres...   tener → yo tengo, tú tienes...

- Irregular verbs may change the stem or the endings.
  Remember: To identify the stem of a verb, delete the -ar, -er, -ir endings from the infinitive form.

    lav -ar̶   prend -er̶   abr -ir̶

Verbos con raíz irregular *(e > ie)*

- Some verbs, like cerrar (to close), require a stem change from e to ie.

VERBO CERRAR (TO CLOSE). PRESENTE

Singular		Plural	
yo	cierro	nosotros nosotras	cerramos
tú	cierras	vosotros vosotras	cerráis
usted él ella	cierra	ustedes ellos ellas	cierran

Note: The e > ie stem change affects all the present tense forms except nosotros, nosotras and vosotros, vosotras. This is why these verbs are called "boot or shoe verbs."

- Other verbs like cerrar are:

    empezar *(to begin)*   → yo empiezo
    entender *(to understand)* → yo entiendo   preferir *(to prefer)* → yo prefiero
    pensar *(to think)*   → yo pienso   querer *(to want)* → yo quiero

15 **Comparación.** What irregular English verbs do you know? Give three examples and explain why they are irregular.

Level 2, Unit 1. Theme: Personal Life

Desafío 1 Identifying yourself and others	Possessive adjectives and pronouns
Desafío 2 Describing people	Adjectives and nouns
Desafío 3 Expressing states and feelings	Comparison and superlatives
Desafío 4 Asking questions	Interrogatives

Didactic focus: the use of concise and organized information.

1. *Fotonovelas* and *Desafío* presentation texts

The beginning texts of each *Desafío* include new structures that students can comprehend by their visual or linguistic context. The activities help students to focus on these structures and to formulate hypotheses about their meaning and usage.

2. *Gramática*

The grammar boxes contain explicit information about the structures presented in the initial text. They present the information supported by concise, visually organized graphics, tables, and diagrams. Each grammar box concludes with a comparison between Spanish and English.

The grammar activities are sequenced according to difficulty, from closed-ended activities to open-ended and personalized activities.

3. *Comunicación* and *Todo junto*

Key grammatical structures are reinforced by their application in open-ended, communicative activities.

4. *Repaso*

Key grammar is reviewed at the end of the unit by means of pre-assessment activities.

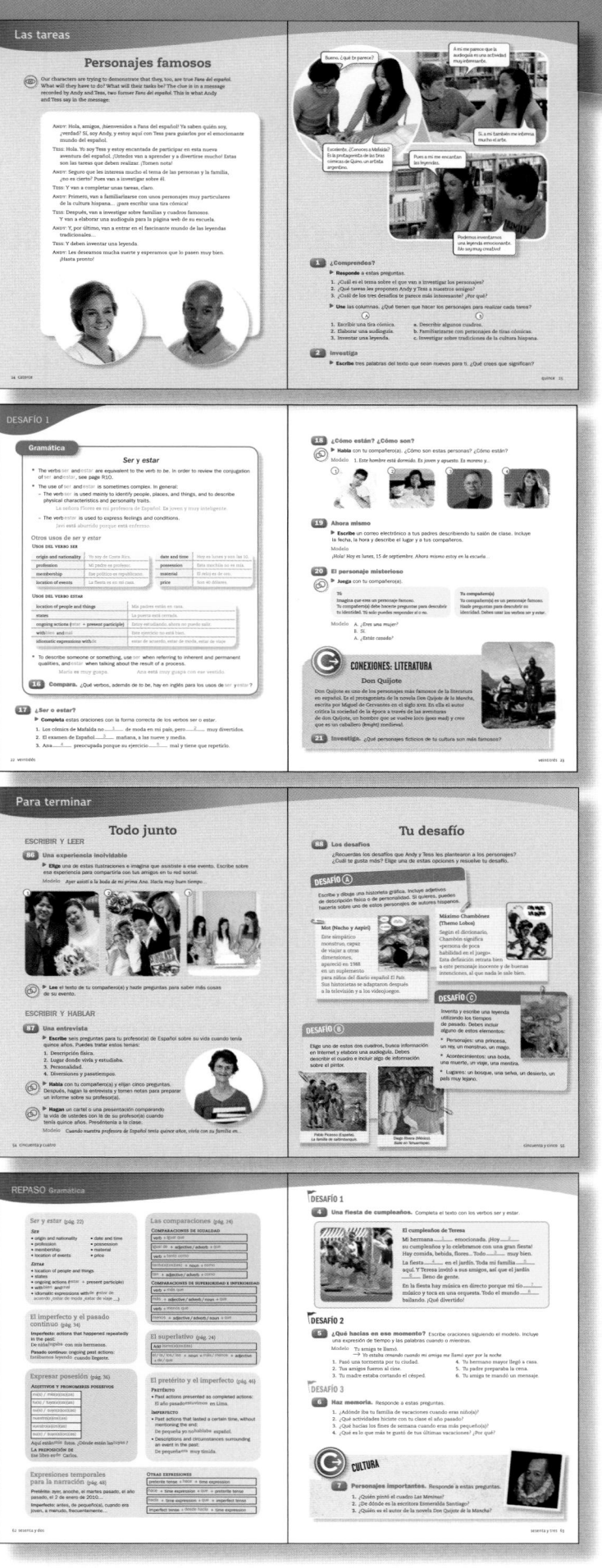

The *Mapas Culturales*

The *Mapas culturales* propose a systematic study.

The *Mapa cultural* is the section in which students study Hispanic cultures in an organized and systematic way.

In Levels 1 and 2, the *Mapa cultural* is based on the study of a country (Mexico, Puerto Rico, Spain, etc.) or a geographical region with cultural similarities (Central America, the Antilles, the Río de la Plata region, etc).

The first page contains **general information** about the country or cultural area which is being studied: its location, size, the countries in this region, main cities, etc.

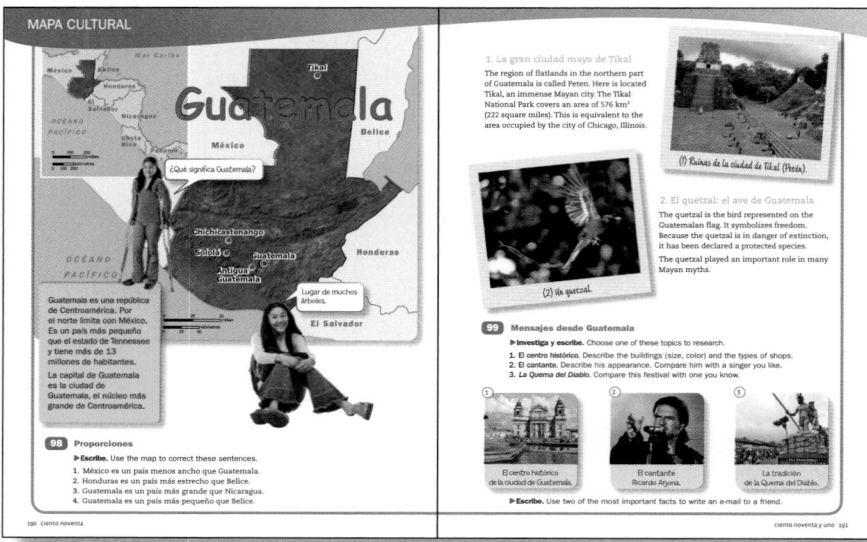

The *Mapa cultural* offers a selection of representative cultural aspects: places, people, traditions, customs, and folklore.

In Levels 3 and 4, the *Mapa cultural* compares a cultural practice or product in different Spanish-speaking countries: the festivals (the *Desfile de Llamadas* in Uruguay, the *Grito de Dolores* in Mexico, the *castells* in Spain), the traditional sports (*tejo* in Colombia, the *charreada* in Mexico, *pato* in Argentina, stone lifting in Spain), urbanism in colonial cities, the universities, etc.
The integrated thematic structure allows students to make comparisons and to appreciate the richness and diversity of the Spanish-speaking world.

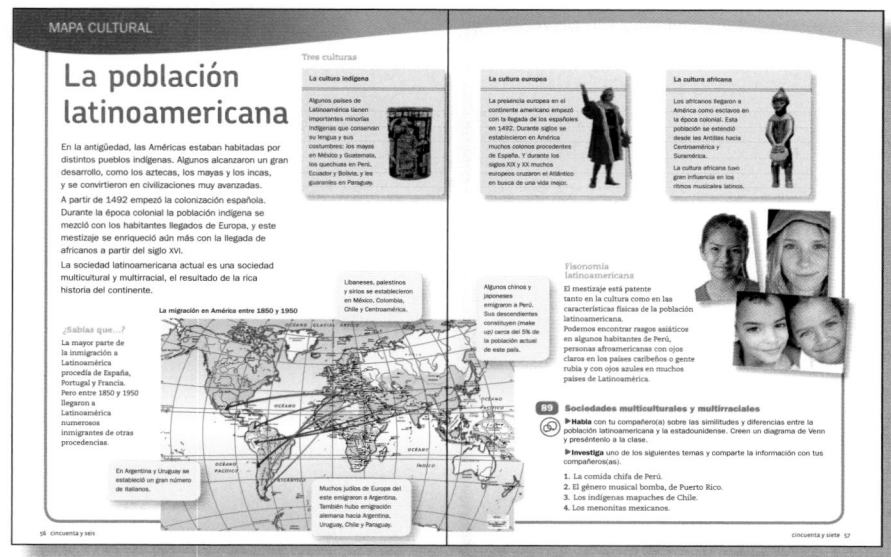

Level 1

México	La antigua Tenochtitlán El sur: la población indígena
Puerto Rico	El Viejo San Juan La salsa, la esencia de Puerto Rico
Guatemala	La gran ciudad maya de Tikal El quetzal: el ave de Guatemala
Perú	Los incas, reyes de las montañas Las líneas de Nazca
España	Madrid: paraíso de pintores El sur: la herencia árabe
Estados Unidos	Huellas hispanas en los Estados Unidos Estados con historia hispana Concentración hispana en las ciudades
Argentina	El tango Buenos Aires
Chile	La Isla de Pascua Pablo Neruda Los chinchineros

Level 2

Centroamérica	Mestizaje y cultura Riqueza natural
Las Antillas	Barrios coloniales Música caribeña
Andes centrales	Quechuas y aymaras Los equecos Las islas Galápagos
Norteamérica	El Camino Real de Tierra Adentro Los chicanos
España	Paisaje mediterráneo La Noche de San Juan Las lenguas romances
Caribe continental	Símbolos nacionales El mestizaje y los bailes Cocina del Caribe: color y sabor
Río de la Plata	Influencia italiana Cultura rioplatense El chipá
La Panamericana	Variedad geográfica El mundo hispano

Level 3

La población latinoamericana	Indígenas, europeos, africanos El mestizaje
La fiesta: expresión comunitaria	El Desfile de Llamadas (Uruguay) El Grito de Dolores (México) Los castells (España)
La ciudad colonial	El modelo urbanístico de las ciudades coloniales
Alimentos básicos en el mundo hispano	El maíz (México y Centroamérica), el trigo (España), la papa (Perú), la yuca (Paraguay)
Universidades hispanas	Universidad de Chile Universidad de Alcalá (España) Universidad Autónoma de México
Deportes con tradición	El tejo (Colombia), la charreada (México), el pato (Argentina), el levantamiento de piedras (España)
Espacios naturales singulares	Cabo de Hornos (Chile) Lanzarote (España) Las Yungas (Argentina) Arrecife Alacranes (México)
Una ciudad con historia: Barcelona	La antigua Barcino La Barcelona medieval La Barcelona moderna La Barcelona actual

Level 4

Unidad y variedad del español	Variaciones léxicas Variaciones gramaticales
Sistemas de salud en el mundo hispano	Cobertura sanitaria en México Turismo sanitario en Costa Rica El sistema de salud en España
La economía de Latinoamérica	Los países de clima tropical Los países de clima templado Los países extractores
El turismo en Latinoamérica	Riviera Maya Bariloche y la Patagonia argentina Santo Domingo
La inmigración hispana en los Estados Unidos	Los mexicanos Los cubanos Los dominicanos
El «boom» de la novela latinoamericana	Gabriel García Márquez Mario Vargas Llosa Carlos Fuentes

Reading

Reading materials, linked to a comprehension strategy, build competency for reading in Spanish.

The reading materials present an opportunity to practice the given vocabulary and grammatical structures, while improving students' ability to interpret new vocabulary and grammatical structures in context. The use of numerous cognates makes the context more understandable and helps students to increase their vocabulary.

In Levels 1 and 2, each unit focuses on a specific reading strategy to understand Spanish texts: identifying cognates, identifying key concepts, making inferences, and so on.

Level 1

Theme	Type of Text
• Teotihuacán	An informative text.
• El Morro	A travel blog.
• Desde Chichicastenango	A letter.
• Festividad inca del Inti Raymi	A travel brochure.
• El *Guernica*, de Pablo Picasso	An art catalog.
• Celebramos la Herencia Hispana	An invitation.
• *La vuelta al mundo de Cinthia Scoch*	A short story.
• *Oda a la manzana,* de Pablo Neruda	A poem.

Level 2

Theme	Type of Text
• El blog de Ichxel	A personal blog.
• Estilo de vida caribeño	A travel magazine.
• Textiles andinos bolivianos	A museum brochure.
• La receta del guacamole	An instructional text.
• *Figura en una ventana,* de Salvador Dalí	A descriptive text.
• El Dorado, ecos de una leyenda	An informative text.
• Un cuento de Benedetti	A narrative text.
• El Tapón de Darién	An argumentative text.

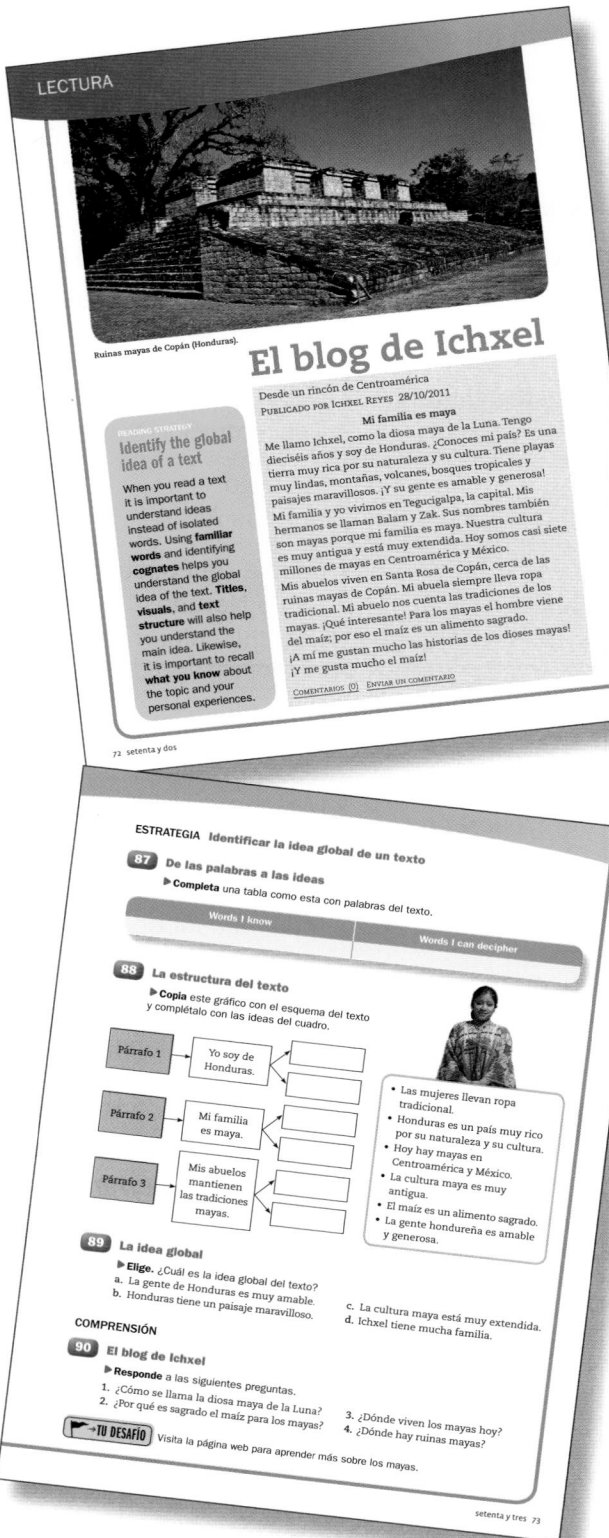

The readings work with different types of texts.

In Levels 1 and 2, the readings are linked to the culture of a country or cultural area, or with the theme of the unit, and represent different writing genres: narrative, descriptive, instructional, literary texts, etc.

In Levels 3 and 4, reading is practiced systematically in each unit with three types of texts: a written dialogue, an informative text, and a literary text.

Level 3

Textos informativos	Textos literarios
• Una breve biografía de Frida Kahlo	• *Los hermanos Ayar* (leyenda inca)
• Juegos precolombinos	• *El mensaje*
• Guía de viajeros: un hotel inolvidable	• *La casa de muñecas*
• El blog personal de Sara	• *La leyenda del maíz* (leyenda azteca)
• Manuel Jalón, un inventor humanista (reportaje)	• *Música*, de Ana María Matute
• Historia de los Juegos Panamericanos	• *Galletitas*, de Jorge Bucay
• Las tradiciones del Sol	• *El eclipse*, de Augusto Monterroso
• Entrevista a Debra McKeon	• *La muralla*, de Nicolás Guillén

Level 4

Textos informativos	Textos literarios
• *El oficio más romántico: escribir cartas de amor por encargo*	• *El diario a diario*, de Julio Cortázar
• *El cáncer y su prevención*	• *La piedra mágica* (cuento popular)
• *La globalización económica* (artículo de economía)	• *El constructor de ecuaciones*, de Juan Bonilla
• *Como la vida misma*, de Rosa Montero	• *Vivir para contarla*, de Gabriel García Márquez
• *María Eva Duarte de Perón* (biografía)	• *El exiliado,* de Cristina Peri Rossi
• *Rafael Moneo* (entrevista)	• *El sur,* de Jorge Luis Borges

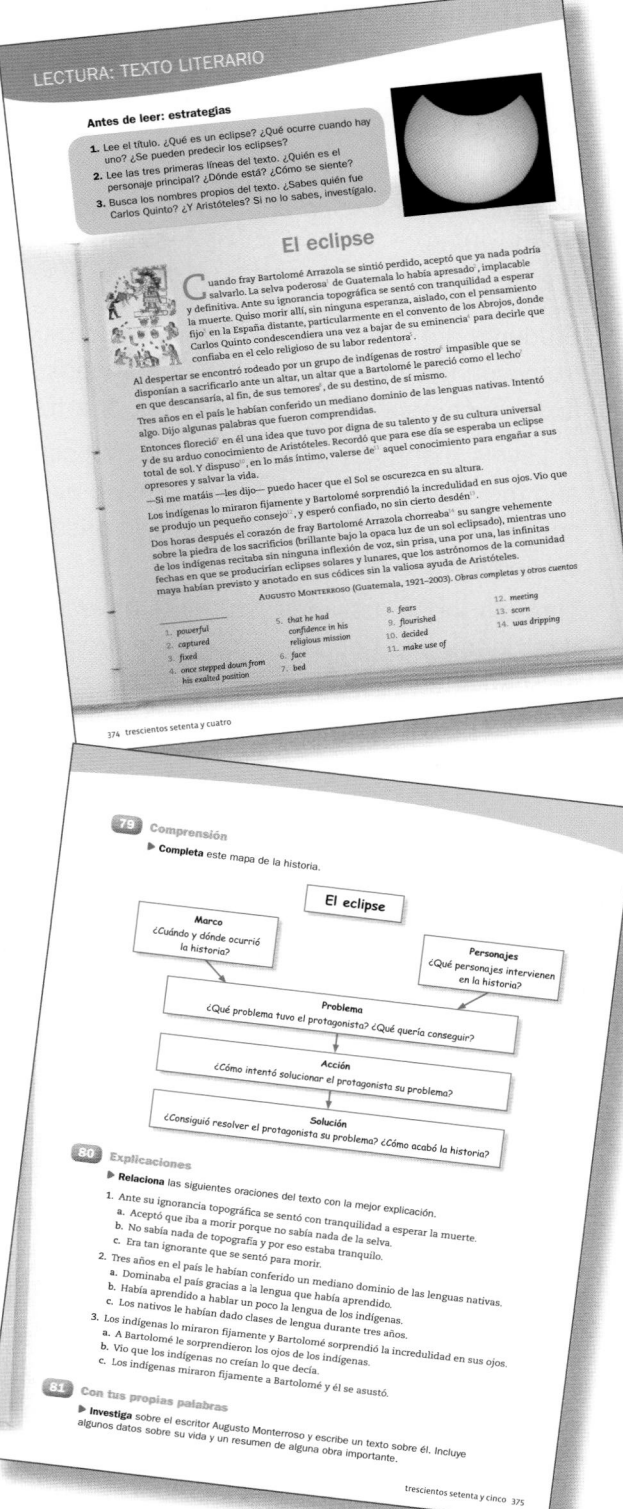

Writing

Writing moves toward the production of more complex texts.

In Levels 1 and 2, writing is practiced at several points throughout the unit:

▶ In the *Comunicación* and *Todo junto* pages within the framework of the *Desafíos*.

▶ In the project.

Students are faced with increasingly more complex texts, which range from writing simple lists (such as a shopping list), to more elaborate texts, such as a diary entry, a script, or a travelogue.

In Levels 3 and 4, there is an additional composition included and the students are required to create somewhat more complex compositions: a character sketch, an essay, a short story, a report, an opinion article, etc.

Through these activities, students have the opportunity to express their ideas and become accustomed to formal and creative writing in Spanish.

Writing Tasks. Examples

Level 1

- Describe people or places.
- Write an Instant Messenger conversation with a classmate.
- Write a post to introduce oneself.
- Make lists with different items.
- Write a postcard to a friend.
- Write informal and formal e-mails.
- Write a radio ad.
- Write a review of a restaurant.
- Write a note.
- Write a blog entry.
- Narrate actions or events.
- Write a plan for a vacation.
- Write a summary of a story.
- Write a travelogue.

Level 2

- Write a menu.
- Write dialogues.
- Write a summary of events.
- Write a poem.
- Write a short story.
- Write a newspaper ad.
- Write a shopping list.
- Write a diary entry.
- Write a chat conversation.
- Write slogans.
- Write a recipe.
- Write a news article.
- Write a script.
- Write a post in a travel blog.
- Write an e-mail or a letter.
- Write a weather report.

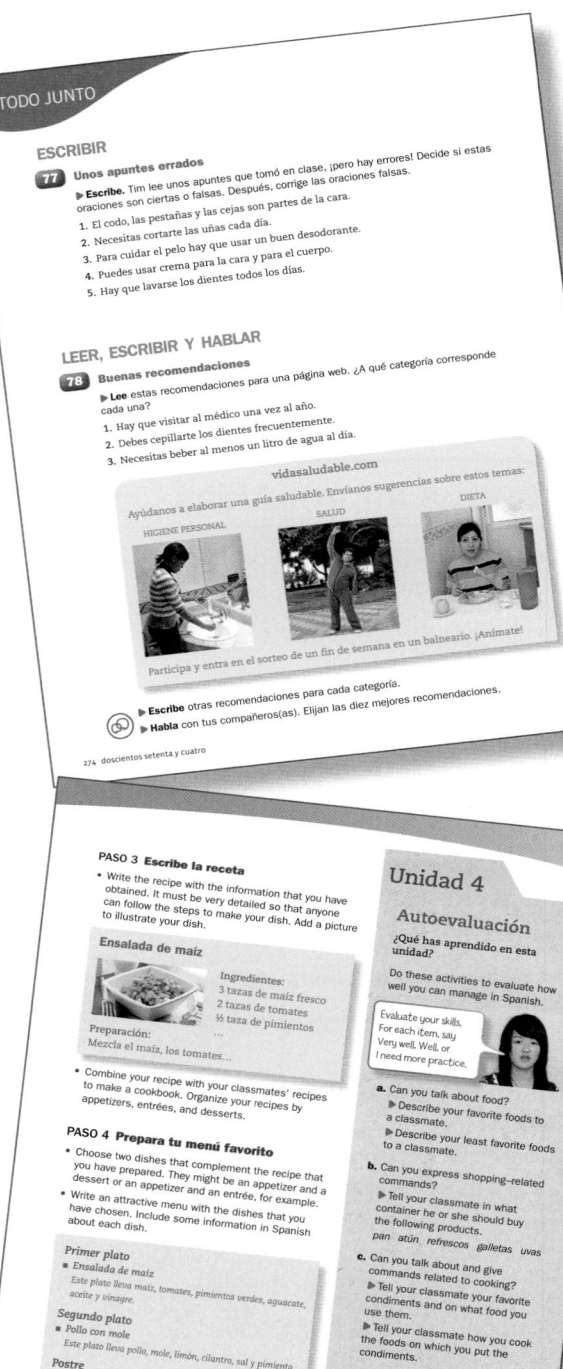

Compositions are developed within the framework of the writing process.

In Levels 3 and 4, writing is developed in a four-step process:

1 *Piensa* **2** *Escribe* **3** *Revisa* **4** *Comparte*

In this process, students frequently exchange their writing with their peers in the tasks of planning and revision, thus taking full advantage of collaborative work.

Writing Program

Level 3

- Un personaje interesante (bosquejo biográfico)
- ¿Un poema o un dibujo? ¡Un caligrama!
- Un ensayo de moda
- Una receta típica
- Una carta formal
- Un cuento
- Un reportaje medioambiental
- Y tú, ¿qué opinas? (un texto de opinión)

Level 4

- Un correo de presentación
- Recomendaciones de viajes
- Un currículum vítae
- Un blog de viajes
- Un ensayo
- Una reseña

Information about the type of writing being practiced.

Steps to the writing process.

Graphic organizers as a planning tool.

Useful vocabulary.

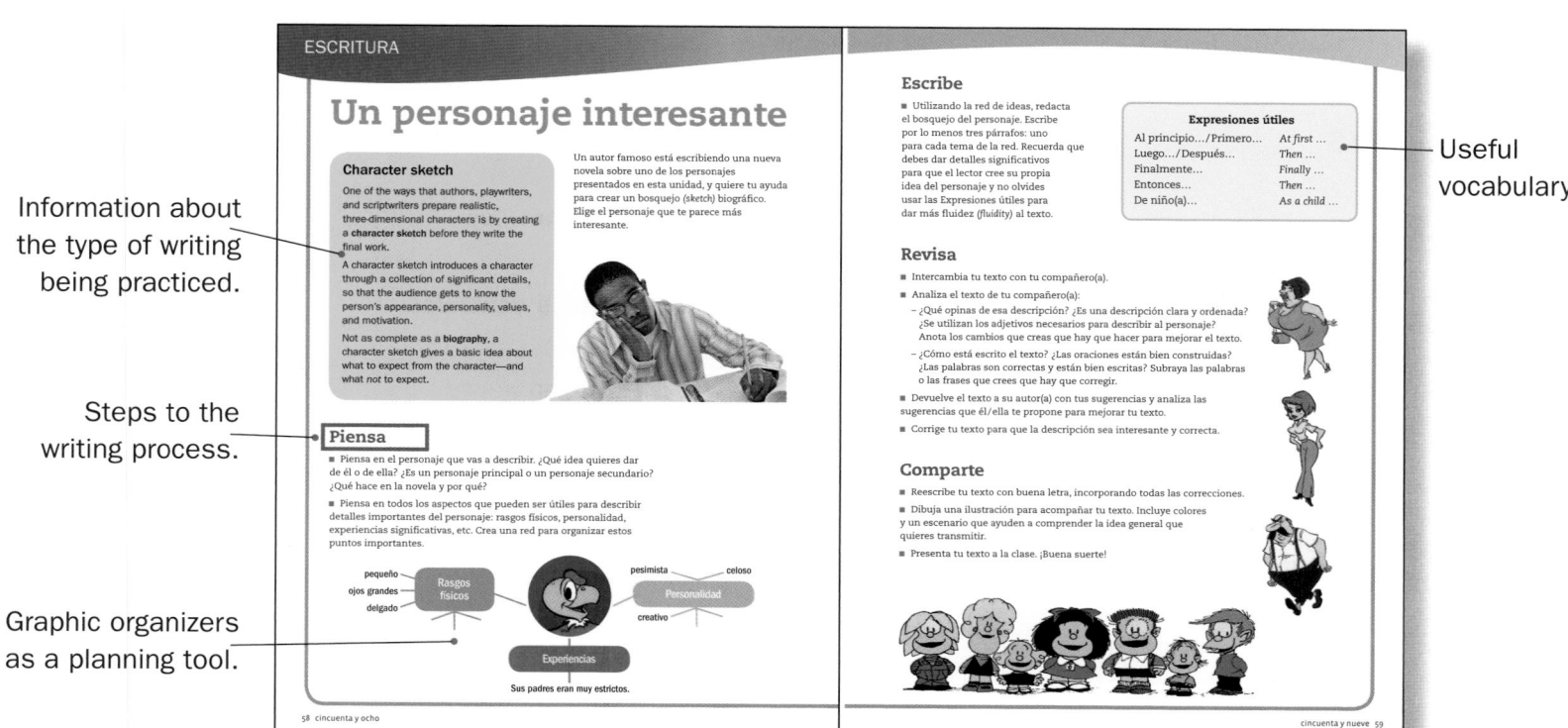

The Project

The project provides an opportunity for integrating and applying knowledge.

Each unit closes with a project that encourages students' creativity and communicative capacity, while activating vocabulary and grammatical structures that students have learned. Each project develops a communicative activity that integrates cultural and linguistic information.

The activities are separated into steps.

Each project develops from a set of activities presented sequentially in separate steps. Each step is clearly defined and includes guidelines to help students complete the activities.

Una exposición de muñecos quitapenas

PASO 1   **Crea tus muñecos quitapenas**

PASO 2   **Prepara una exposición de muñecos**

PASO 3   **Dramatiza la compra y venta de muñecos**

Project Tasks
Level 1

México	Una presentación sobre Diego Rivera
Puerto Rico	Una visita guiada por la Casa Blanca
Guatemala	Una exposición de muñecos quitapenas
Perú	Nuestros restaurantes
España	Un póster sobre hábitos de higiene
Estados Unidos	Un cartel sobre un hispano famoso
Argentina	Crónica de un viaje
Chile	Un póster sobre animales en peligro

Project: *Una exposición de muñecos quitapenas*

Vocabulary	• Clothing. Characteristics, materials, and colors of clothing • Shopping
Grammar	• The verb *gustar* • Demonstrative adjectives • Comparisons • Present tense of irregular verbs
Culture	• Indigenous traditions • Traditional handicrafts from Guatemala

Level 2

Centroamérica	Una historia sobre personajes de Guatemala
Las Antillas	Un juego en las calles de Santo Domingo
Andes centrales	Una revista sobre moda andina
Norteamérica	Un menú con ingredientes americanos
España	Una presentación sobre hábitos de alimentación
Caribe continental	Un folleto sobre la laguna de Guatavita
Río de la Plata	Un guión para una telenovela
La Panamericana	Un boletín sobre la predicción meteorológica

Level 3

Las personas y la familia	Un álbum de fotos de tu vida
Vida social	Un plan de actividades con tus amigos
La ropa y la vivienda	Una feria sobre ciudades coloniales hispanas
La alimentación y la salud	Una guía para una vida saludable
El trabajo y las profesiones	Un proyecto de una organización solidaria
El tiempo libre y los viajes	Un plan para un viaje de estudios
La naturaleza y el medio ambiente	Una campaña publicitaria en favor del medio ambiente
Historia, política y sociedad	Una presentación sobre un país de Latinoamérica

Level 4

Relaciones sociales y comunicación	Una página web de nuestra clase de Español
Los alimentos y la salud	Un cómic sobre la salud
Los estudios y el trabajo	Un premio a la empresa hispana del año
El ocio y los viajes	Un anuncio para promocionar un país
Historia y sociedad	Un manifiesto para solucionar un problema de tu comunidad
Arte y literatura	Una exposición de las obras de arte favoritas

The unit closes with a self-evaluation.

At the end of each unit is a self-evaluation section with questions that correspond to the unit objectives, so that students can reflect upon their progress.

Presentation of the task.

Steps.

Project instructions.

Self-evaluation.

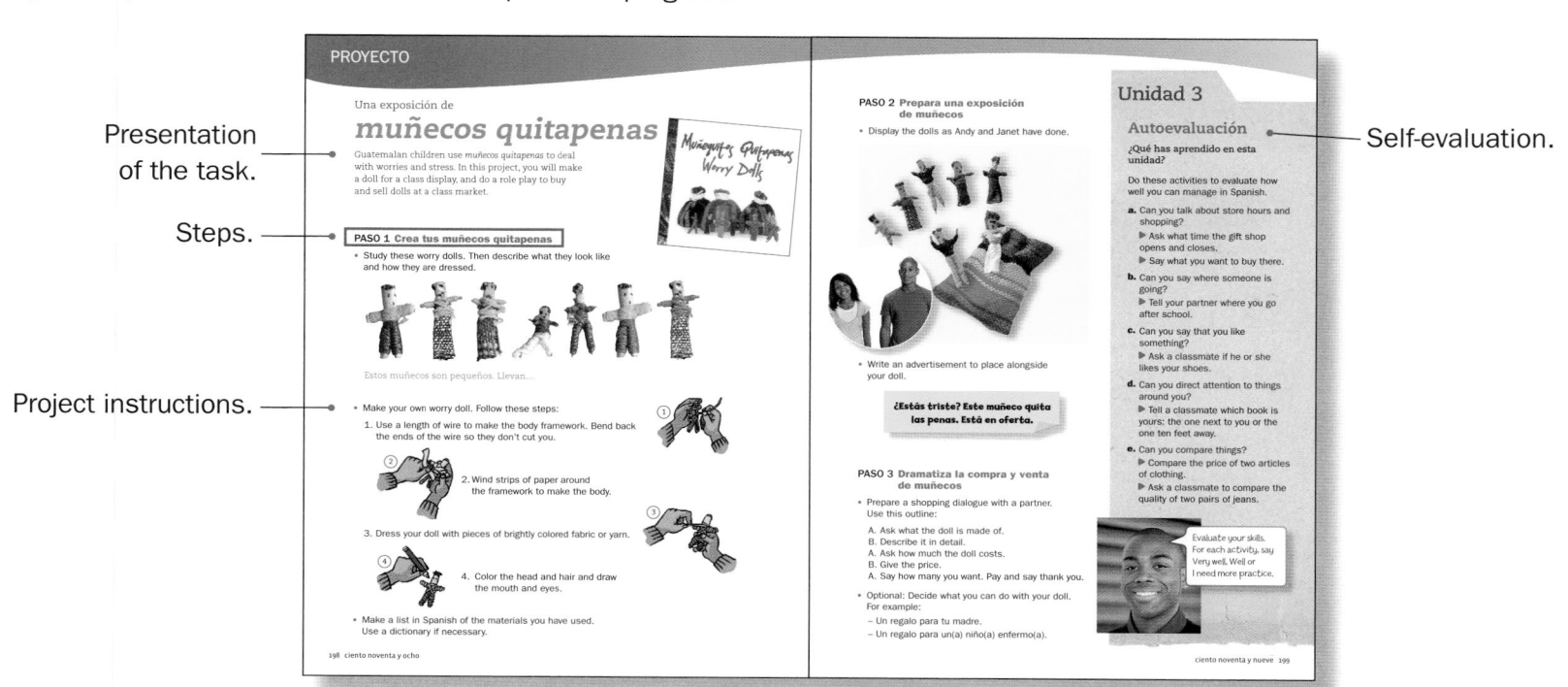

Instruction is centered around the development of communicative skills.

Español Santillana places heavy emphasis on communicative aspects of language. Beginning in the first unit of Level 1, students undertake activities that strengthen the development of speaking, listening, reading, writing, and interacting skills. These activities are the springboard by which students can reach the level of excellence in Spanish required by the AP* Exam.

The Level 4 Student Book offers preparation specifically geared toward the AP* Exam.

Each unit in Level 4 ends with a section called *Hacia el AP* Exam*, which is designed specifically to prepare students for the test. In this section, students learn about the structure of the test and the characteristics of each activity type, as well as strategies for performing well in each section. It also contains a sample exercise so that students can practice taking each type of activity on the exam.

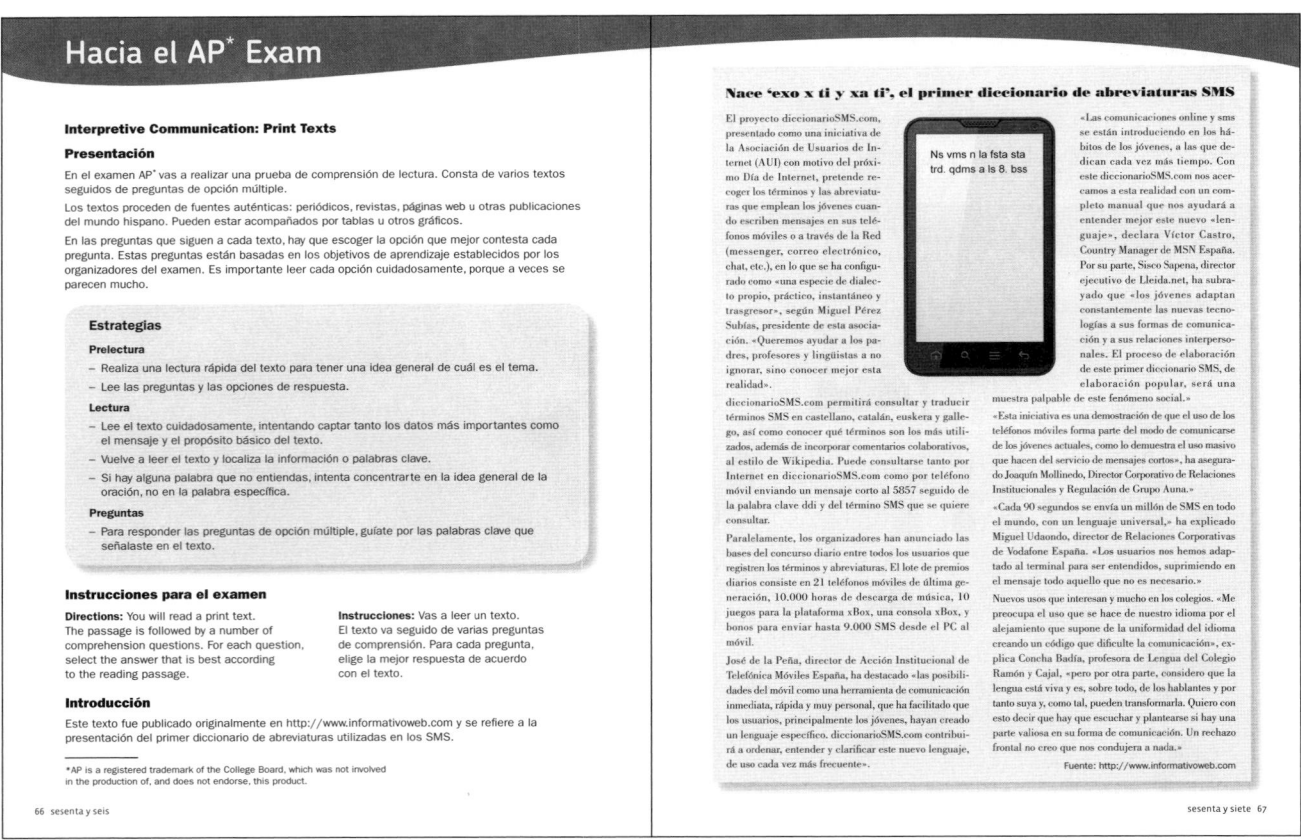

Hacia el AP* Exam

Interpretive Communication: Print Texts

Presentación

En el examen AP* vas a realizar una prueba de comprensión de lectura. Consta de varios textos seguidos de preguntas de opción múltiple.

Los textos proceden de fuentes auténticas: periódicos, revistas, páginas web u otras publicaciones del mundo hispano. Pueden estar acompañados por tablas u otros gráficos.

En las preguntas que siguen a cada texto, hay que escoger la opción que mejor contesta cada pregunta. Estas preguntas están basadas en los objetivos de aprendizaje establecidos por los organizadores del examen. Es importante leer cada opción cuidadosamente, porque a veces se parecen mucho.

Estrategias

Prelectura
- Realiza una lectura rápida del texto para tener una idea general de cuál es el tema.
- Lee las preguntas y las opciones de respuesta.

Lectura
- Lee el texto cuidadosamente, intentando captar tanto los datos más importantes como el mensaje y el propósito básico del texto.
- Vuelve a leer el texto y localiza la información o palabras clave.
- Si hay alguna palabra que no entiendas, intenta concentrarte en la idea general de la oración, no en la palabra específica.

Preguntas
- Para responder las preguntas de opción múltiple, guíate por las palabras clave que señalaste en el texto.

Instrucciones para el examen

Directions: You will read a print text. The passage is followed by a number of comprehension questions. For each question, select the answer that is best according to the reading passage.

Instrucciones: Vas a leer un texto. El texto va seguido de varias preguntas de comprensión. Para cada pregunta, elige la mejor respuesta de acuerdo con el texto.

Introducción

Este texto fue publicado originalmente en http://www.informativoweb.com y se refiere a la presentación del primer diccionario de abreviaturas utilizadas en los SMS.

*AP is a registered trademark of the College Board, which was not involved in the production of, and does not endorse, this product.

66 sesenta y seis

Nace 'exo x ti y xa ti', el primer diccionario de abreviaturas SMS

El proyecto diccionarioSMS.com, presentado como una iniciativa de la Asociación de Usuarios de Internet (AUI) con motivo del próximo Día de Internet, pretende recoger los términos y las abreviaturas que emplean los jóvenes cuando escriben mensajes en sus teléfonos móviles o a través de la Red (messenger, correo electrónico, chat, etc.), en lo que se ha configurado como «una especie de dialecto propio, práctico, instantáneo y trasgresor», según Miguel Pérez Subías, presidente de esta asociación. «Queremos ayudar a los padres, profesores y lingüistas a no ignorar, sino conocer mejor esta realidad».

diccionarioSMS.com permitirá consultar y traducir términos SMS en castellano, catalán, euskera y gallego, así como conocer qué términos son los más utilizados, además de incorporar comentarios colaborativos, al estilo de Wikipedia. Puede consultarse tanto por Internet en diccionarioSMS.com como por teléfono móvil enviando un mensaje corto al 5857 seguido de la palabra clave ddi y del término SMS que se quiere consultar.

Paralelamente, los organizadores han anunciado las bases del concurso diario entre todos los usuarios que registren los términos y abreviaturas. El lote de premios diarios consiste en 21 teléfonos móviles de última generación, 10.000 horas de descarga de música, 10 juegos para la plataforma xBox, una consola xBox, y bonos para enviar hasta 9.000 SMS desde el PC al móvil.

José de la Peña, director de Acción Institucional de Telefónica Móviles España, ha destacado «las posibilidades del móvil como una herramienta de comunicación inmediata, rápida y muy personal, que ha facilitado que los usuarios, principalmente los jóvenes, hayan creado un lenguaje específico. diccionarioSMS.com contribuirá a ordenar, entender y clarificar este nuevo lenguaje, de uso cada vez más frecuente».

«Las comunicaciones online y sms se están introduciendo en los hábitos de los jóvenes, a las que dedican cada vez más tiempo. Con este diccionarioSMS.com nos acercamos a esta realidad con un completo manual que nos ayudará a entender mejor este nuevo «lenguaje», declara Víctor Castro, Country Manager de MSN España. Por su parte, Sisco Sapena, director ejecutivo de Lleida.net, ha subrayado que «los jóvenes adaptan constantemente las nuevas tecnologías a sus formas de comunicación y a sus relaciones interpersonales. El proceso de elaboración de este primer diccionario SMS, de elaboración popular, será una muestra palpable de este fenómeno social.»

«Esta iniciativa es una demostración de que el uso de los teléfonos móviles forma parte del modo de comunicarse de los jóvenes actuales, como lo demuestra el uso masivo que hacen del servicio de mensajes cortos», ha asegurado Joaquín Mollinedo, Director Corporativo de Relaciones Institucionales y Regulación de Grupo Auna.»

«Cada 90 segundos se envía un millón de SMS en todo el mundo, con un lenguaje universal,» ha explicado Miguel Udaondo, director de Relaciones Corporativas de Vodafone España. «Los usuarios nos hemos adaptado al terminal para ser entendidos, suprimiendo en el mensaje todo aquello que no es necesario.»

Nuevos usos que interesan y mucho en los colegios. «Me preocupa el uso que se hace de nuestro idioma por el alejamiento que supone de la uniformidad del idioma creando un código que dificulte la comunicación», explica Concha Badía, profesora de Lengua del Colegio Ramón y Cajal, «pero por otra parte, considero que la lengua está viva y es, sobre todo, de los hablantes y por tanto suya y, como tal, pueden transformarla. Quiero con esto decir que hay que escuchar y plantearse si hay una parte valiosa en su forma de comunicación. Un rechazo frontal no creo que nos condujera a nada.»

Fuente: http://www.informativoweb.com

sesenta y siete 67

A targeted workbook.

The series is complemented with a *Preparation Workbook for AP*,* which systematically practices each one of the skills measured by the AP* Exam:

Interpretive Communication	Print Texts.
Interpretive Communication	Print and Audio Texts (combined).
Interpretive Communication	Audio Texts.
Interpersonal Writing	E-mail Reply.
Presentational Writing	Persuasive Essay.
Interpersonal Speaking	Conversation.
Presentational Speaking	Cultural Comparison.

The workbook provides strategies for taking each portion of the test, sample answers, and practice activities.

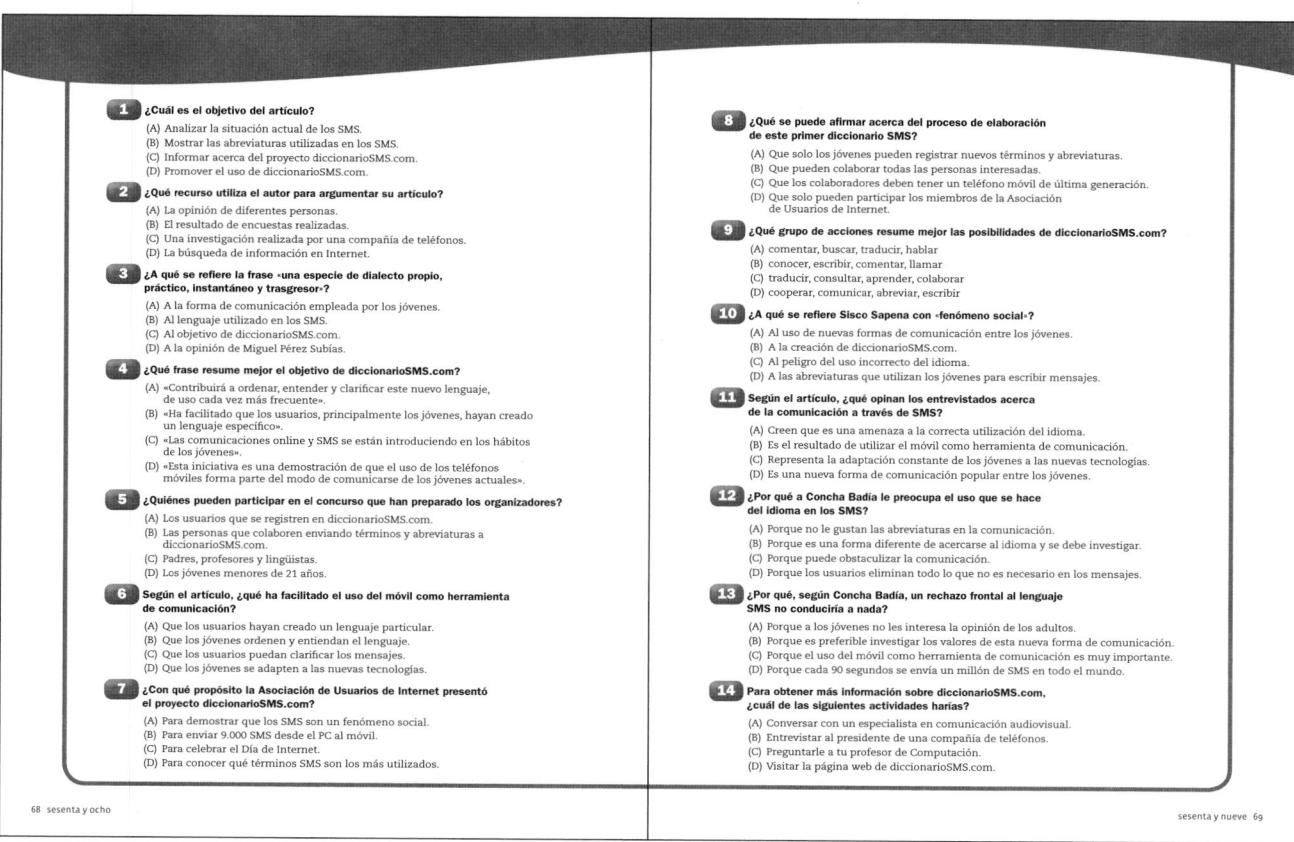

1 ¿Cuál es el objetivo del artículo?

(A) Analizar la situación actual de los SMS.
(B) Mostrar las abreviaturas utilizadas en los SMS.
(C) Informar acerca del proyecto diccionarioSMS.com.
(D) Promover el uso de diccionarioSMS.com.

2 ¿Qué recurso utiliza el autor para argumentar su artículo?

(A) La opinión de diferentes personas.
(B) El resultado de encuestas realizadas.
(C) Una investigación realizada por una compañía de teléfonos.
(D) La búsqueda de información en Internet.

3 ¿A qué se refiere la frase «una especie de dialecto propio, práctico, instantáneo y trasgresor»?

(A) A la forma de comunicación empleada por los jóvenes.
(B) Al lenguaje utilizado en los SMS.
(C) Al objetivo de diccionarioSMS.com.
(D) A la opinión de Miguel Pérez Subías.

4 ¿Qué frase resume mejor el objetivo de diccionarioSMS.com?

(A) «Contribuirá a ordenar, entender y clarificar este nuevo lenguaje, de uso cada vez más frecuente».
(B) «Ha facilitado que los usuarios, principalmente los jóvenes, hayan creado un lenguaje específico».
(C) «Las comunicaciones online y SMS se están introduciendo en los hábitos de los jóvenes».
(D) «Esta iniciativa es una demostración de que el uso de los teléfonos móviles forma parte del modo de comunicarse de los jóvenes actuales».

5 ¿Quiénes pueden participar en el concurso que han preparado los organizadores?

(A) Los usuarios que se registren en diccionarioSMS.com.
(B) Las personas que colaboren enviando términos y abreviaturas a diccionarioSMS.com.
(C) Padres, profesores y lingüistas.
(D) Los jóvenes menores de 21 años.

6 Según el artículo, ¿qué ha facilitado el uso del móvil como herramienta de comunicación?

(A) Que los usuarios hayan creado un lenguaje particular.
(B) Que los jóvenes ordenen y entiendan el lenguaje.
(C) Que los usuarios puedan clarificar los mensajes.
(D) Que los jóvenes se adapten a las nuevas tecnologías.

7 ¿Con qué propósito la Asociación de Usuarios de Internet presentó el proyecto diccionarioSMS.com?

(A) Para demostrar que los SMS son un fenómeno social.
(B) Para enviar 9.000 SMS desde el PC al móvil.
(C) Para celebrar el Día de Internet.
(D) Para conocer qué términos SMS son los más utilizados.

8 ¿Qué se puede afirmar acerca del proceso de elaboración de este primer diccionario SMS?

(A) Que solo los jóvenes pueden registrar nuevos términos y abreviaturas.
(B) Que pueden colaborar todas las personas interesadas.
(C) Que los colaboradores deben tener un teléfono móvil de última generación.
(D) Que solo pueden participar los miembros de la Asociación de Usuarios de Internet.

9 ¿Qué grupo de acciones resume mejor las posibilidades de diccionarioSMS.com?

(A) comentar, buscar, traducir, hablar
(B) conocer, escribir, comentar, llamar
(C) traducir, consultar, aprender, colaborar
(D) cooperar, comunicar, abreviar, escribir

10 ¿A qué se refiere Sisco Sapena con «fenómeno social»?

(A) Al uso de nuevas formas de comunicación entre los jóvenes.
(B) A la creación de diccionarioSMS.com.
(C) Al peligro del uso incorrecto del idioma.
(D) A las abreviaturas que utilizan los jóvenes para escribir mensajes.

11 Según el artículo, ¿qué opinan los entrevistados acerca de la comunicación a través de SMS?

(A) Creen que es una amenaza a la correcta utilización del idioma.
(B) Es el resultado de utilizar el móvil como herramienta de comunicación.
(C) Representa la adaptación constante de los jóvenes a las nuevas tecnologías.
(D) Es una nueva forma de comunicación popular entre los jóvenes.

12 ¿Por qué a Concha Badía le preocupa el uso que se hace del idioma en los SMS?

(A) Porque no le gustan las abreviaturas en la comunicación.
(B) Porque es una forma diferente de acercarse al idioma y se debe investigar.
(C) Porque puede obstaculizar la comunicación.
(D) Porque los usuarios eliminan todo lo que no es necesario en los mensajes.

13 ¿Por qué, según Concha Badía, un rechazo frontal al lenguaje SMS no conduciría a nada?

(A) Porque a los jóvenes no les interesa la opinión de los adultos.
(B) Porque es preferible investigar los valores de esta nueva forma de comunicación.
(C) Porque el uso del móvil como herramienta de comunicación es muy importante.
(D) Porque cada 90 segundos se envía un millón de SMS en todo el mundo.

14 Para obtener más información sobre diccionarioSMS.com, ¿cuál de las siguientes actividades harías?

(A) Conversar con un especialista en comunicación audiovisual.
(B) Entrevistar al presidente de una compañía de teléfonos.
(C) Preguntarle a tu profesor de Computación.
(D) Visitar la página web de diccionarioSMS.com.

The *Teacher's Edition*

Keys for teaching and learning.

The pages at the beginning of each unit offer a broad overview as well as tools for the organization and planning of school activities.

Objectives, contents, and evaluation criteria.

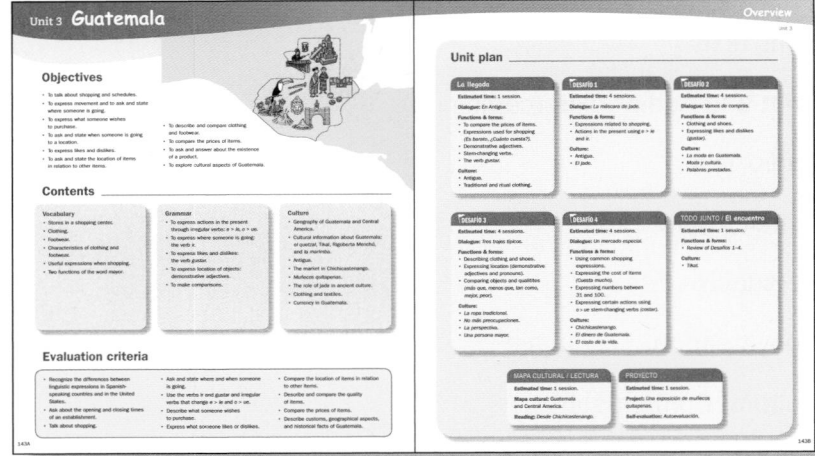

Outline of the unit and estimated time for completing each section.

Detailed description of the standards for learning Spanish in the unit.

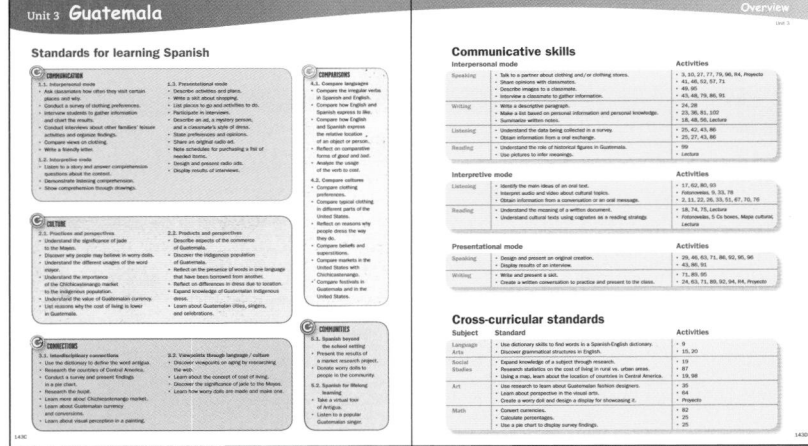

Communicative abilities practiced in the unit classified by skill (speaking, writing, listening, and reading) and by use (interpersonal, interpretative, and presentational).

Standards for other areas also discussed.

Detailed lesson plans for 50- and 90-minute classes.

Audio scripts.

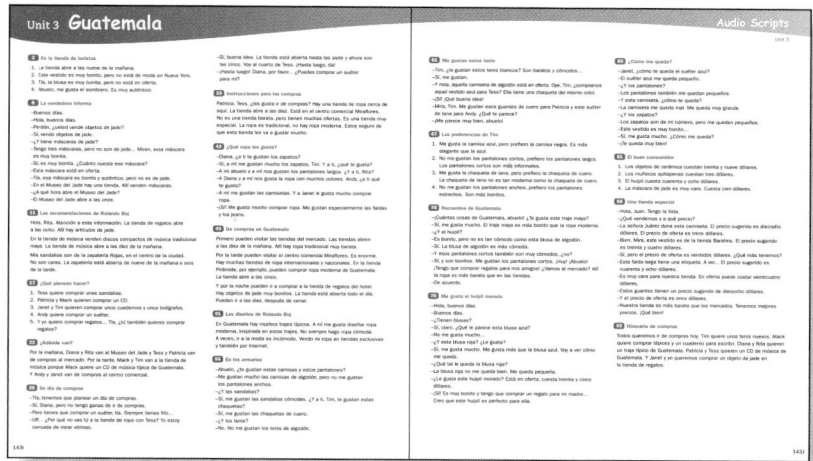

The instructional guides offer numerous resources for making the teacher's job easier.

General overview of the section.

Explanation of key educational and methodological solutions for interpreting the material.

Additional information about the cultural topics discussed.

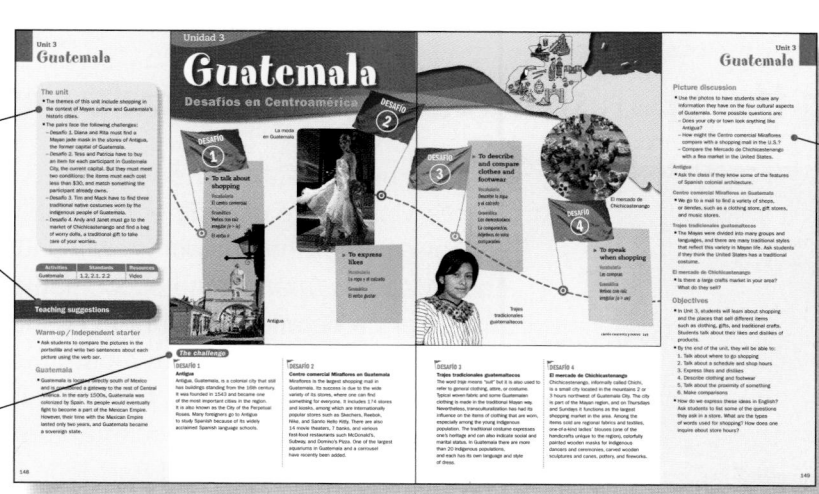

Methodological proposals and suggestions: how to present the material, what to do with the class, how to prevent common errors, etc.

Differentiated instruction: developing learners, expanding learners, heritage language learners, special-needs learners, cooperative learning, multiple intelligences, critical thinking, etc.

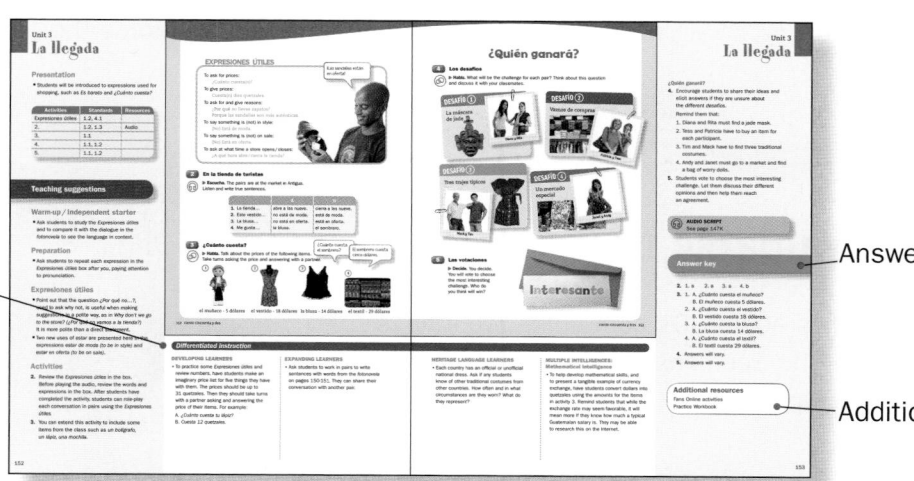

Answer key.

Additional resources.

Technology

A wide variety of technological resources.

Español Santillana relies on broad technological support, including digital versions of print materials (books, workbooks, and teacher's guides), plus an extensive offering of specific resources: visual presentations, videos, audio materials, a webpage, and more.

Visual presentations in the *fotonovelas* and the challenges.

The *fotonovelas* that present the characters' arrival in the country and their challenges are supported by visual presentations that replicate the dialogues and the story. The visual presentations offer an excellent method for improving students' listening comprehension ability.

Videos for enjoying the Spanish-speaking world's cultures.

The unit begins with a video that gives students an overview of the country or cultural area and the challenges that the characters will undertake. Each *Mapa cultural* is also accompanied by a video that offers a detailed view of the country or cultural area, its landscapes, and its most outstanding characteristics. In addition, each unit includes two other videos on significant cultural topics: the house of Frida Kahlo (Mexico), Old San Juan (Puerto Rico), the market of Chichicastenango (Guatemala), and so on. The videos are highly evocative, serving to motivate students and reinforce their listening skills while promoting learning.

The audios, an invaluable tool.

The books are accompanied by Audio CDs containing recordings of all the listening activities. The *Speaking and Listening Workbook* (see page T37) is also accompanied by Audio CDs.

The webpages are a fundamental element of *Español Santillana.*

The webpage **Fans del español** (www.fansdelespañol.com) features the basic plot of the story. The characters decide to create the website *Fans del español* in order to share what they know about the Spanish-speaking world. Characters post information about themselves and about challenges that students can access on this webpage. In this manner, fiction becomes reality.

Additionally, the **Español Santillana** series is supported by the **eLearning Center**, which offers countless activities, photogalleries, games, and other resources for the student, as well as an extensive bank of assessment activities for the teacher to use (Online Assessments).

The digital versions provide a complete multimedia experience.

Both the Student Book and Teacher's Edition are available in an interactive digital format:

▶ The **Interactive Student Book** contains numerous multimedia resources that enhance and complement learning Spanish: videos, visual presentations, audios, photogalleries, flashcards, etc. Students can listen to the pronunciation of the dialogues and vocabulary words, and can also use interactive tools such as highlighters and sticky notes.

▶ The **All-in-One Digital Teacher's Edition** brings together all of the elements that the teacher needs to plan and teach a class:

- The *Interactive Student Book* and its multimedia resources. This version of the *Student Book* is designed so that the teacher can project the pages onto a screen and can also activate the videos, the visual presentations, the audios, and other features.
- The *Teacher's Edition* pages.
- The *Teacher's Annotated Edition* of the *Practice Workbook* and the *Speaking and Listening Workbook*, with its corresponding audio tracks.
- The Assessment Program, with answer keys for the teacher.
- An editable version of the Lesson Plans, so that the teacher can personalize the lesson plans to his or her needs.

The workbooks are also available in digital format.

The Workbooks

Three workbooks to practice with.

Español Santillana features three student workbooks for each level: the *Practice Workbook*, the *Speaking and Listening Workbook*, and the workbook for heritage Spanish speakers (the *Cuaderno para hispanohablantes*). Additionally, High School Level 4 is complemented by the *Preparation Workbook for AP** (see page T31).

The *Practice Workbook* deepens the study of the language independently.

This is the perfect complement to the Student Book. Here students will find many opportunities to work with the linguistic and cultural contents of the series. It contains all the information (word glossaries and grammar summaries) that students need, and the activities have been designed so that students can work them out without having to consult other sources.

The *Speaking and Listening Workbook* consolidates two fundamental skills.

This workbook deals specifically with comprehension and verbal expression.

The listening activities can be used in the classroom or at home. The Audio CD that accompanies the workbook allows the students to work independently. In contrast, the speaking activities are designed to be used in the classroom.

The speaking and listening activities allow students to practice the key vocabulary and grammatical structures presented in the books.

The workbook for heritage Spanish speakers improves their reading comprehension and writing ability.

This workbook complements the *Español Santillana* textbook and is for heritage Spanish speakers capable of completing an activity in Spanish by themselves.
The workbook maintains the themes and structures of the Student Book, allowing heritage Spanish speakers to work with the textbook in class while completing tasks appropriate to their language level in the workbook.

The objectives of the workbook are the following:

- To develop reading comprehension (Reading).
- To expand students' vocabulary (Vocabulary).
- To improve students' handling of written expression for various purposes (Spelling, Writing).
- To encourage understanding of and appreciation for differences in cultural origins (Connections, Communities).

Scope and Sequence High School 1

Contents

Unidad	Vocabulario
Unit 1 **México** 30–85	• People • Physical characteristics • Personality traits • Family • States and conditions
Unit 2 **Puerto Rico** 86–143	• The house • Furniture and objects in a house • Household chores • Leisure activities
Unit 3 **Guatemala** 144–199	• The shopping center • Clothing and footwear • Describing clothing and footwear • Shopping
Unit 4 **Perú** 200–255	• Foods and beverages • Food stores • At the table • Describing food
Unit 5 **España** 256–309	• Parts of the body • Personal hygiene • Symptoms and illnesses • Basic remedies • Healthy habits
Unit 6 **Estados Unidos** 310–363	• The world of work • Hobbies • Free time • Sports
Unit 7 **Argentina** 364–417	• Transportation • Travel • Destinations and lodging • The city. Location and directions
Unit 8 **Chile** 418–471	• The universe • Geography • Political divisions • Numbers from 101 to 1,000 • Nature and the environment

Gramática		Cultura	

• Subject pronouns
• The verb *ser*
• Adjectives
• The verb *tener*
	• Expressing possession:
	  – Possessive adjectives
	  – The preposition *de*
	• The verb *estar*
		• *Mapa cultural:* Mexico
		  • Mexico City: Tenochtitlan
		  • The south: the indigenous population
			• *Lectura: Teotihuacán, ciudad de los dioses*

• Nouns
• Articles. Agreement with nouns
• Expressing existence. The verb *haber*
• Expressing location
• Regular *-ar* verbs, present tense
	• Regular *-er* and *-ir* verbs, present tense
	• Expressing obligation:
	  – *Tener que* + infinitive
	  – *Hay que* + infinitive
	• Adverbs of frequency
		• *Mapa cultural:* Puerto Rico
		  • Old San Juan
		  • Salsa, the essence of Puerto Rico
			• *Lectura: El Morro: Blog de viajes*

• Stem-changing verbs (*e > ie*)
• The verb *ir*
• The verb *gustar*
• Demonstratives
	• Comparison. Comparative adjectives
	• Stem-changing verbs (*o > ue*)
		• *Mapa cultural:* Guatemala
		  • The great Mayan city of Tikal
		  • The quetzal, national bird of Guatemala
			• *Lectura: Desde Chichicastenango*

• Adverbs of quantity
• Expressing want, preference, and rejection. The verbs *querer* and *preferir*
	• Irregular verbs in the *yo* form
	• Direct object pronouns
	• Indirect object pronouns
	• Stem-changing verbs (*e > i*)
		• *Mapa cultural:* Peru
		  • The Incas, kings of the mountains
		  • The Nazca lines
			• *Lectura: Festividad inca del Inti Raymi*

• The verbs *ver, oír, oler,* and *decir*
• Reflexive verbs
• The verb *doler*
	• The verb *sentirse*
	• Affirmative *tú* commands. Regular verbs
		• *Mapa cultural:* Spain
		  • Madrid: a painter's paradise
		  • The south: an Arabic heritage
			• *Lectura: El* Guernica*, de Pablo Picasso*

• Affirmative commands. Irregular verbs
• *Ir a* + infinitive. Time markers in the future
• The present progressive
	• The present participle
	• Stem-changing verbs (*u > ue*)
		• *Mapa cultural:* United States
		  • Hispanic influence in the United States
		  • States with Hispanic history
			• Concentration of Hispanic people in cities
			• *Lectura: Celebramos la Herencia Hispana*

• The preterite tense of regular *-ar* verbs
• The preterite tense of regular *-er* and *-ir* verbs
	• Time markers in the past
	• The preterite tense of the verbs *ser* and *ir*
	• Negative commands
		• *Mapa cultural:* Argentina
		  • The tango
		  • Buenos Aires
			• *Lectura: La vuelta al mundo de Cinthia Scoch*

• Expressing cause: *porque* and *por*
• Expressing quantity. Indefinites
• Irregular verbs in the preterite. *Decir* and *hacer*
	• Irregular verbs in the preterite. *Estar* and *tener*
	• Expressing permission and prohibition
		• *Mapa cultural:* Chile
		  • Easter Island
		  • Pablo Neruda
		  • The chinchineros
			• *Lectura: Oda a la manzana*

Scope and Sequence High School 2

Contents

Unidad	Vocabulario
Unit 1 **Centroamérica** 28–79	• Personal and family relationships • Physical characteristics and personality traits • Emotional states and feelings • Personal information
Unit 2 **Las Antillas** 80–131	• The house. Household chores • Furniture and objects in a house • Electrical appliances • The neighborhood. Places and services
Unit 3 **Andes centrales** 132–183	• Clothing and accessories • Describing clothes • Stores and establishments • Shopping
Unit 4 **Norteamérica** 184–235	• Foods • Buying food • In the kitchen • In the restaurant
Unit 5 **España** 236–287	• Parts of the body • Personal hygiene • Health: symptoms and illnesses • Healthy habits
Unit 6 **Caribe continental** 288–339	• Trips and excursions • On the train and on the plane • The car • The hotel. The bank
Unit 7 **Río de la Plata** 340–391	• The school • Professions • Hobbies, free time activities, and entertainment • Sports
Unit 8 **La Panamericana** 392–443	• Geography • Countries • The weather • Nature and environment

Gramática		Cultura	

• Possessives
• Adjectives and nouns
	• Comparisons and superlatives
	• Interrogatives
		• *Mapa cultural:* Centroamérica
		  ◦ Mestizaje y cultura
		  ◦ Riqueza natural
			• *Lectura: El blog de Ichxel*

• The present progressive
• Direct object pronouns
	• Indirect object pronouns
	• Demonstratives
		• *Mapa cultural:* Las Antillas
		  ◦ Barrios coloniales
		  ◦ Música caribeña
			• *Lectura: Estilo de vida caribeño*

• The preterite tense of regular
  -*ar* verbs
• The preterite tense of regular
  -*er* and -*ir* verbs
	• The preterite tense of the verbs *ser, ir,*
	  decir, tener, estar, and *hacer.*
	• The preterite tense of
	  stem-changing -*ir* verbs
		• *Mapa cultural:* Andes centrales
		  ◦ Quechuas y aymaras
		  ◦ Los equecos
		  ◦ Las islas Galápagos
			• *Lectura: Textiles andinos bolivianos*

• Expressing amount. Indefinites
• Singular affirmative commands
	• Plural affirmative commands
	• Negative commands
		• *Mapa cultural:* Norteamérica
		  ◦ El Camino Real de Tierra Adentro
		  ◦ Los chicanos
			• *Lectura: La receta
			  del guacamole*

• The past participle
• Adverbs ending in -*mente*
	• *Por* and *para*
	• Making recommendations
		• *Mapa cultural:* España
		  y el Mediterráneo
		  ◦ Paisaje mediterráneo
		  ◦ La Noche de San Juan
		  ◦ Las lenguas romances
			• *Lectura:* Figura en una ventana,
			  de Salvador Dalí

• The imperfect tense
• The preterite tense of the verbs
  dar, poder, poner, querer, saber,
  and *venir*
	• Talking about past actions. The preterite
	  and imperfect tenses
	• Talking about past actions and describing
	  in the past. The preterite and imperfect
	  tenses
		• *Mapa cultural:* Caribe continental
		  ◦ Símbolos nacionales
		  ◦ El mestizaje y los bailes
		  ◦ Cocina del Caribe: color
		  y sabor
			• *Lectura: El Dorado, ecos
			  de una leyenda*

• Expressing existence. Indefinites
• The present subjunctive
  of regular verbs
	• The present subjunctive of
	  stem-changing verbs
	• The present subjunctive of
	  irregular verbs
		• *Mapa cultural:* El río de la Plata
		  ◦ Influencia italiana
		  ◦ Cultura rioplatense
		  ◦ El chipá
			• *Lectura: Un cuento de Benedetti*

• The relative superlative
• Expressing plans
  and intentions
	• The future tense
	• Hiding the agent. The pronoun *se*
		• *Mapa cultural:* La ruta Panamericana
		  ◦ Variedad geográfica
		  ◦ El mundo hispano: unidad
		  y diversidad
			• *Lectura: El Tapón de Darién:
			  un corte en la ruta Panamericana*

Scope and Sequence High School 3

Contents

Unidad	Vocabulario
Unit 1 **¿Cómo eres?** 12–65	• Physical characteristics and personality traits • Family relationships • Biographies
Unit 2 **Entre amigos** 66–119	• Personal relationships • Introductions. Expressions to invite, accept, and reject an invitation • Phone calls
Unit 3 **Tus cosas** 120–173	• Clothing • Describing objects • Household chores and professions
Unit 4 **Vida sana** 174–227	• Foods • Healthy habits • The doctor's office. The human body
Unit 5 **¿Trabajas?** 228–281	• Jobs and professions • Work and technology • Volunteering and community service
Unit 6 **Tus aficiones** 282–335	• Free time and events • Sports • Travel and lodging
Unit 7 **Nuestro planeta** 336–389	• Nature and the environment • The weather. The universe • Natural disasters. Natural resources
Unit 8 **En sociedad** 390–443	• Historical figures, events, civilizations • Politics and government • Society

Gramática		Cultura		Escritura
• *Ser* and *estar* • Comparatives and superlatives • The imperfect and the past progressive	• Expressing possession • The preterite and the imperfect tenses • Time expressions for narration	• Lectura informativa: *Una breve biografía* • Lectura literaria: *Los hermanos Ayar* (leyenda inca)	• Mapa cultural: La población latinoamericana	Un bosquejo biográfico
• Direct object and indirect object pronouns • Reflexive and reciprocal verbs • Expressing wishes, likes, and preferences	• Non-reflexive verbs used with pronouns • Expressing need and obligation • Speaking about the future	• Lectura informativa: *Juegos precolombinos* • Lectura literaria: *El mensaje*	• Mapa cultural: La fiesta: expresión comunitaria	Un caligrama
• The past participle • Talking about recent actions. The present perfect tense • Indefinites	• Impersonal constructions. The pronoun *se* • The past perfect tense • Demonstratives	• Lectura informativa: *Guía de viajeros: un hotel inolvidable* • Lectura literaria: *La casa de muñecas*	• Mapa cultural: La ciudad colonial	Un ensayo
• Commands • Verbs that express change • *Para* and *por*	• Making value statements • The conditional tense • Giving advice and recommendations	• Lectura informativa: *El blog personal de Sara* • Lectura literaria: *La leyenda del maíz* (leyenda azteca)	• Mapa cultural: Alimentos básicos en el mundo hispano	Una receta
• Expressing certainty and doubt • The imperfect subjunctive • Giving details. The relative pronoun *que*	• The gender of nouns • Expressing feelings • Expressing difficulty	• Lectura informativa: *Manuel Jalón, un inventor humanista* • Lectura literaria: *Música* (Ana María Matute)	• Mapa cultural: Universidades hispanas	Una carta formal
• Expressing opinion • Grammatical forms of courtesy • Expressing probability	• Expressing purpose • Indirect speech • Expressing place	• Lectura informativa: *Historia de los Juegos Panamericanos* • Lectura literaria: *Galletitas* (Jorge Bucay)	• Mapa cultural: Deportes con tradición	Un cuento
• Expressing condition (I) • Expressing condition (II) • Expressing time	• The present perfect subjunctive • Expressing cause and consequence • The personal *a*	• Lectura informativa: *Las tradiciones del Sol* • Lectura literaria: *El eclipse* (Augusto Monterroso)	• Mapa cultural: Espacios naturales singulares	Un reportaje
• The passive voice • The past tenses (review) • Referring to the stages of an action	• Uses of the indicative (review) • Articles • Uses of the subjunctive (review)	• Lectura informativa: *Entrevista a Debra McKeon* • Lectura literaria: *La muralla* (Nicolás Guillén)	• Mapa cultural: Una ciudad con historia: Barcelona	Un texto de opinión

Contenidos

Unidad	Vocabulario
Unidad 1 ## Nos relacionamos 12–69	• Características físicas y rasgos de personalidad • La oficina de correos • Los medios de comunicación
Unidad 2 ## Nos cuidamos 70–127	• En el restaurante • La sala de urgencias • Estados físicos y anímicos
Unidad 3 ## Trabajamos 128–183	• La escuela • La economía • Trabajo y profesiones
Unidad 4 ## Nos divertimos 184–239	• Ocio y espectáculos. Deportes y tiempo libre • Los viajes • El alojamiento. El tiempo meteorológico
Unidad 5 ## Participamos 240–297	• Historia • Política y gobierno • Problemas sociales y medioambientales
Unidad 6 ## Creamos 298–353	• Arte y pintura • Arquitectura y escultura • Literatura

Gramática		Cultura		Escritura	Hacia el AP* Exam
• Expresar gustos, intereses, sentimientos y emociones • Los adjetivos • Los verbos pronominales	• Los verbos reflexivos y recíprocos • Hablar de acciones en curso • Expresar cantidad	• Lectura informativa: *El oficio más romántico: escribir cartas de amor por encargo* (reportaje) • Lectura literaria: *El diario a diario* (Julio Cortázar)	• Mapa cultural: Unidad y variedad del español	Un correo de presentación	Interpretación de textos escritos
• Las construcciones impersonales. El pronombre *se* • Los pronombres de OD y OI • Los verbos con preposición	• Los artículos • La voz pasiva • *Ser y estar*	• Lectura informativa: *El cáncer y su prevención* (artículo científico) • Lectura literaria: *La piedra mágica* (cuento popular)	• Mapa cultural: Sistemas de salud en el mundo hispano	Recomendaciones de viajes	Interpretación de textos orales
• El participio pasado • El presente perfecto y el pluscuamperfecto • Los pronombres relativos	• El futuro perfecto • Expresar deseos • Expresar condición	• Lectura informativa: *La globalización económica* (artículo de economía) • Lectura literaria: *Un constructor de ecuaciones* (Juan Bonilla)	• Mapa cultural: La economía de Latinoamérica	Tu currículum ideal	Interacción escrita
• Expresar frecuencia • Expresar probabilidad (I) • Expresar probabilidad (II)	• El presente perfecto de subjuntivo • Expresar causa • Expresar consecuencia	• Lectura informativa: *Como la vida misma* (Rosa Montero; columna periodística) • Lectura literaria: *Vivir para contarla* (Gabriel García Márquez)	• Mapa cultural: El turismo en Latinoamérica	Un blog de viajes	Interacción oral
• Los numerales ordinales • Expresar certeza y duda • Expresar finalidad	• Expresar dificultad • Expresar condición. El pluscuamperfecto de subjuntivo • Expresar tiempo	• Lectura informativa: *María Eva Duarte de Perón* (biografía) • Lectura literaria: *El exiliado* (Cristina Peri Rossi)	• Mapa cultural: La inmigración hispana en los Estados Unidos	Un ensayo	Presentación escrita
• Las comparaciones • El artículo neutro *lo* • Expresar opinión	• Hacer valoraciones • Los diminutivos • Dar consejos y hacer recomendaciones	• Lectura informativa: *Rafael Moneo* (entrevista) • Lectura literaria: *El Sur* (Jorge Luis Borges)	• Mapa cultural: El «boom» de la literatura latinoamericana	Una reseña	Presentación oral

The Spanish Language of the United States

Gerardo Piña-Rosales The North American Academy of the Spanish Language

First of all, dear reader, let us focus on the title of this essay: "The Spanish Language *of* the United States" instead of "The Spanish Language *in* the United States." The difference between these two prepositions is an essential one: it implies that we have begun to speak of a United States Spanish with its own characteristics, as one more of the multiple variants of the Spanish language spoken around the world.

Spanish Speakers in the United States

It is estimated that there are some 45 million Spanish-speaking people in the United States, which translates into 15 percent of the nation's population, and it is expected that this figure will rise to more than 150 million Spanish speakers by 2050. In other words, it is highly probable that the United States will become the country with the largest number of Spanish-speaking inhabitants on our planet. More than half of the 45 million Spanish speakers were born in this country, and they make up a younger-than-average portion of the overall population: 48 percent of Hispanics are younger than 25 years of age. Whether or not a minority language replaces the language spoken by the majority depends, above all, on the new generations; thus, the relative youth of the Hispanic population will undoubtedly influence the future of the Spanish language in the United States.

Spanish Variants

When we speak of the Spanish language of the United States, it is important to point out that we are not referring to a monolithic, uniform language, but to one that encompasses a number of variants. In this regard, we can divide the country into several linguistic areas, each with its own distinct characteristics. In the West and Southwest, where 60 percent of Hispanics reside, a *chicano* variant of Spanish is spoken; in Florida, and especially in Miami, a Cuban variant of Spanish is heard. In the Northeast, including New York, New Jersey, and Connecticut, a Caribbean form of Spanish is spoken. Furthermore, one can hear *isleño* Spanish in Louisiana and a distinctive form of Spanish spoken in the region of the Sabine River (Louisiana and Texas).

English Influences

The massive influence of English has imparted a unique imprint on the Spanish language of the United States, which contrasts with that of other Spanish-speaking countries. This particular influence is manifested in new vocabulary, much of it based on "borrowed" words, which have contributed to the incorporation of *anglicisms* into the Spanish spoken in those countries.

English Influence at Work

Hispanic immigrants try to learn and speak English at their workplace and in their associations with Americans. This effort to communicate tends to facilitate the use of *Spanglish*. In time, if they have a certain level of education, they learn both languages well and become bilingual. There is a desire to acquire a better knowledge not only of English but also of the Spanish of their heritage.

Spanglish

A distinctive characteristic of the Spanish language of the United States is the so-called "code-switching," which consists of a speaker's use of both languages during a conversation. Since this means of communication has not been methodically studied until recently, a certain notion exists—both among the general public and among certain educators—that it is a random mixture of languages, i.e., *Spanglish*. In fact it is a process with its own structural conventions, one that also plays a unique role among bilingual Spanish speakers, precisely as an alternative to communicating in a single language. The economic importance of the Spanish language of the United States is greater than that of any other Spanish-speaking country. The Spanish language would survive if only for the United States.

Bibliography

Amastae, Jon and Lucía Elías-Olivares. *Spanish in the United States: Sociolinguistic Aspects.* Cambridge: Cambridge University Press, 1982.

Elías-Olivares, Lucía, ed. *Spanish in the U.S. Setting: Beyond the Southwest.* Rosslyn, VA: National Clearinghouse for Bilingual Education, 1983.

Lipski, John M. *Varieties of Spanish in the United States.* Washington DC: Georgetown University Press, 2008.

López-Morales, Humberto, ed. *Enciclopedia del español en los Estados Unidos.* Madrid: Instituto Cervantes/Santillana, 2008.

Teaching and Learning: Language and Culture

Janet Glass Dwight Englewood School, Englewood, New Jersey, Rutgers University

Alfred Nobel's Peace Prize wished to reward "the person who shall have done the most or the best work for fraternity between nations." What could be more critical today? As teachers of world languages, our medium is language, but our message is one of cultural ambassador. Besides, what is more intriguing to a student than to learn how to make a new friend from another culture, to enter another world? This motivation is what stimulates our students' curiosity and helps them master the language. But once hooked, how can we make the most of their interest?

Five-Senses Culture

We can start by integrating culture into the whole language instruction process, making sure that culture underscores every language activity and is at the core of the unit. We can go beyond cultural "awareness" and try to experience the target culture in the classroom with smells, touches, simulations, tastes, rhythms, and video clips. Learning is enhanced when exchanges with people from the target culture happen early and often. As Byram et al. say in "Developing Intercultural Competence in Practice," "the task is rather to facilitate learners' interactions with some small part of another society and its cultures … and encouraging them to investigate for themselves the otherness around them." Let's lift it off the page!

Measuring Culture

When it comes to culture, students are always asking, "Does it *count*?" Although we have currently come a long way in measuring the language proficiency of our students, we are challenged to do as well with testing cultural appropriateness. Culture has to be taught systematically and then, assessed. How powerful it is to show students evidence of their own cultural competence, yet more exploration of how to best assess cultural competence is needed.

Seeing Our Own Culture with New Eyes

As language teachers, we also make the most of students' interest when we show how language shapes our thoughts, and leads to how we behave. Most of us don't become aware of our own cultural assumptions until confronted by another world view. When I was in Japan, for example, people frequently apologized as part of their daily conversation. They said, "Sorry I disturbed you" when calling someone on the phone. How does this habit of polite language reflect its culture? Accepting responsibility is a very high priority in Japan. As a result, we find it is a culture that discourages blame and is relatively free of lawsuits. Cultural instincts become internal, hidden, and subconscious. Through the target language, we strive to have our students uncover these influences, empathize with the people, and be able to interact in culturally appropriate ways.

Research Says

Meanwhile, research has confirmed what we have sensed. In a survey of young students studying language and culture, their responses to "People from other countries are scary" and "Hearing a language that's not English makes me nervous" was a resounding "No!" Students not in the program answered "Maybe" and "Yes."

So, as we make the foreign become familiar, the familiar will become a bit more foreign. By bringing cultural experiences into the classroom, measuring the outcomes, aiming for deep understanding and exchanges, we put linguistic and cultural abilities together and at the forefront of our shrinking world. *¡Sí, se puede!*

Bibliography

Byram, Michael, A. Nichols, and D. Stevens. "Developing Intercultural Competence in Practice." *Multilingual Matters Ltd*. 3 (2001).

Kennedy, Teresa, et al. "The FLES Attitudinal Inventory." *Foreign Language Annals*, ACTFL 33(3), May/June 2000: 278–289.

Wright, David A. "Culture as Information and Culture as Affective Process: A Comparative Study." *Foreign Language Annals*, ACTFL 33(3), May/June 2000: 330–341.

The Integration of Language, Culture, and Content in the Three Modes of Communication

Brandon Zaslow Site Director, California Foreign Language Project, Department of Education, Occidental College, Los Angeles, California

Work with teachers who are implementing a standards-based instructional approach shows that the integration of language, culture, and content is the area of greatest challenge and the aspect of standards-based practice that has the most transformative effect on student learning.

Preparing students to use language for real-world purposes in culturally appropriate ways requires that teachers specify the tasks students will need to carry out in order to function in target-language communities. The most efficient way to gain access to language, culture, and content is through the use of authentic materials, those that are designed for individuals who speak the language and share the culture and its perspectives on content. Semi-authentic video, audio, or print media are often used to ensure that all of the language, culture, and content necessary for successful real-world language use are available for learning.

Interpretive Mode

Teachers use a variety of strategies for making language, culture, and content comprehensible. They prepare students for interpretation by interesting them in the theme of the lesson, building on previous knowledge, and previewing key language, culture, and content. They ask students to make predictions, provide non-linguistic supports to meaning, and work with texts multiple times using different interpretive tasks that focus student attention on language, culture, or content. Often teachers break up texts into smaller segments in order to help students skim for main ideas and then scan for supporting details. Texts with storylines or content that can be divided into logical parts are easier to understand and recall.

Interpersonal Mode

When learners understand the materials used during interpretive communication, they need a great deal of practice to use the language, content, and cultural knowledge and skills to participate in real-world tasks. In order to gain proficiency in interpersonal communication, learners need to practice carrying out real-world tasks in multiple settings combining various elements of language, culture, and content. Recycling communicative elements that will occur in culminating tasks ensures that students will be successful in spontaneous, unrehearsed interpersonal communication.

gain proficiency using their language in a variety of ... uthentic settings, teachers integrate language, culture, ... t in more demanding simulations or real-world ... nal tasks.

Presentational Mode

When students have had an opportunity to practice with others and carry out a number of interpersonal tasks using language, culture, and content, they will have developed the skills necessary to carry out real-world presentational tasks with sufficient clarity and accuracy to be successfully understood by a target-culture audience. Presentational tasks can be oral or written or combine both speech and writing. It is important when constructing presentational tasks to focus learner attention on culturally appropriate behavior and target-culture audiences. In written presentational tasks, rubrics are useful to guide the many drafts that may be necessary to produce a clear and accurate text that communicates effectively with the target audience.

Conclusion

Although challenging, the integration of language, culture, and content in interpretive, interpersonal, and presentational communication will transform world language classrooms and prepare students to function effectively in target-language communities.

Bibliography

National Standards in Foreign Language Education Project. *Standards for Foreign Language Learning in the 21st Century*. Lawrence, KS: Allen Press, Inc., 1999.

Anderson, Nancy, ed. *Spanish for Native Speakers*. AATSP, 2000.

Ballman, Terry L., Judith E. Liskin Gasparro, and Paul B. Mandell, eds. *The Communicative Classroom*. AATSP, 2001.

Birckbichler, Diane W. and Robert M. Terry, eds. *Reflecting on the Past to Shape the Future*. ACTFL, 2000.

Galloway, Vicky, ed. *Teaching Cultures of the Hispanic World: Products and Practices in Perspective*. AATSP, 2001.

Gunterman, Gail, ed. *Teaching Spanish with the Five C's: A Blueprint for Success*. ACTFL, 2000.

Heining-Boynton, Audrey L., ed. *2005-2015: Realizing Our Vision of Languages for All*. ACTFL, 2006.

Lafayette, Robert C., ed. *National Standards: A Catalyst for Reform*. ACTFL, 1996.

Omaggio-Hadley, Alice. *Teaching Language in Context*, 3rd ed. Boston: Heinle and Heinle, 2001.

Shrum, Judith L. and Eileen W. Glisan, *Teacher's Handbook: Contextualized Language Instruction*, 4th ed. Boston: Heinle and Heinle, 2010.

Teaching Vocabulary and Grammar Using Authentic Literary Texts and Other Reading Selections

Emily Spinelli Executive Director, American Association of Teachers of Spanish and Portuguese. Professor Emerita of Spanish, University of Michigan-Dearborn

For many years the foreign language profession viewed the teaching of language and the teaching of literature as two very separate and distinct activities. At all educational levels the reading of literary texts was often seen as a task that only very advanced students could undertake. As a result, the early years of instruction were generally devoted to learning the language so that students could study literature in upper-level courses.

Authentic Texts Defined

In the 1970s this separation of language and literature teaching was challenged as researchers in language acquisition advocated for the use of authentic texts and materials in the language classroom. Widdowson pointed out that the language presented to students does not need to be simplified for easy access. He further stated that, "Nowadays there are recommendations that the language presented should be authentic." Wallace later defined authentic language as that found in "…real-life texts, not written for pedagogic purposes." Soon thereafter, authentic materials gradually made their way into textbooks in the form of advertisements, brochures, menus, schedules, and other items utilized in daily life. However, literature was still not viewed as suitable material for language learning.

Contemporary View of Literary Texts

Recently, a report from the Modern Language Association called for an end to the separation of language courses and literature courses and recommended a curriculum "in which language, culture, and literature are taught as a continuous whole." This contemporary view of the role of literature reinforces the notion that literary texts can be used to teach language beginning at the earliest levels. In addition to providing language models for students, literary selections also provide authentic cultural information, help critical thinking skills, and emphasize historical and literary traditions.

Reading Strategies and Activities to Promote Comprehension

It is now generally accepted that literary and other authentic texts should not be simplified or modified in order to help students comprehend them. Rather, students should be provided with reading strategies and activities prior to reading the selection. In turn, these strategies and activities will help students comprehend the authentic material.

Pre-reading, During-reading, and Post-reading Activities

Generally the strategies, explanations, and activities related to a reading selection fall into three categories called pre-reading, during-reading, and post-reading activities, depending on when they are used in relation to reading the selection. Pre-reading strategies provide students with reading techniques such as reading for gist, understanding the genre of the text, or forming hypotheses about the theme or topic of the text. Pre-reading activities can involve a presentation or review of vocabulary or grammar structures used within the literary selection. Vocabulary activities typically focus on cognate recognition, word families, prefixes and suffixes and other information designed to assist students with comprehending individual words. Grammar activities generally focus on recognition of parts of speech, verb forms and tenses, and word order. Other pre-reading activities focus on cultural information that have students compare or contrast cultural products, practices or perspectives found in the text with those found in their own cultures. During-reading activities generally help students focus on the pre-reading strategies and other information taught or reviewed in the pre-reading phase. Finally, the post-reading activities focus on comprehension and ask students to demonstrate what they learned while reading.

By helping students comprehend authentic texts through the use of pre-reading strategies and activities, we expand their language capabilities while strengthening their cross-cultural and literacy skills.

Bibliography

Bernardo, Sacha Anthony. "The Use of Authentic Materials in the Teaching of Reading." *The Reading Matrix* 6 (2006): 60–69.

Foreign Languages and Higher Education: New Structures for a Changed World. New York: Modern Language Association, 2006.

Wallace, Catherine. *Reading.* Oxford: Oxford University Press, 1992.

Widdowson, Henry G. *Aspects of Language Teaching.* Oxford: Oxford University Press, 1990.

Motivation

Jan Kucerik Pinellas County Public Schools, Pinellas County, Florida

A seventh grade student known to his Spanish teacher as "Juanito" ambles reluctantly into his beginning Spanish classroom. He greets the teacher, not with an enthusiastic "Buenos días, señora," but instead with the question on the mind of many of his classmates, "What are we doing in here today?" Although we would like to believe that the question has been posed out of genuine interest in the classroom activities, we realize that Juanito's question is motivated by self-preservation. He worries that he might be unprepared for, or embarrassed by, the activities Señora has planned for the day.

What Motivates Our Students

Motivation is crucial to teaching and learning. Whenever we feel a desire or need for something, we are in a state of motivation. Juanito is motivated to survive the class period, and his teacher wants him to thrive and share her passion for the Spanish language and Hispanic culture. He has a need to feel safe, yet his teacher understands that he must take risks in order to acquire language. He wants to avoid struggle, and she knows that great effort is involved in negotiating meaning and learning from mistakes. Although human beings are motivated to learn from birth, students are often not motivated to learn what we want them to learn in the way that we want them to learn it. They do, however, select information and learning experiences that are important to them every day. Teachers continue to work tirelessly to motivate their students, but most focus on extrinsic motivators, which may not be enough to truly engage students in the long term. How do we make students feel connected to learning? How do we make them feel as if the learning could not happen without them? How do we create excitement for learning, resulting in students eagerly entering our classrooms each day?

Relationships Are Key

We rely on the standards and performance guidelines to articulate authentic tasks and clear goals. We persevere in our commitment to adjust the learning environment and the content to attract students. Most importantly, we recognize that our relationships with our students and their relationship with the learning process are crucial. Students must believe that they can be successful and experience incremental growth through ___ experiences carefully designed around small chunks ___ ful language, leading to purposeful communication. ___ ust be fun. Students are more likely to retain the ___ hey acquire in a learning context that they enjoy.

They must feel that they are part of the learning environment, that they belong to the target culture, while they are acquiring their new language. They must understand the purpose of the lesson and have the freedom to select language that is important to them along the way.

Motivation and Learning

Students are motivated to take part in Spanish class when the context through which the language is presented and practiced is meaningful, serves a purpose, and relies on the students to bring it to life. Effective teachers understand the link between motivation and learning, and select language and cultural contexts that rely on the students to tell the story. "What are we doing in here today, Señora?" "We need you, Juanito, to help guide us on our learning journey."

Bibliography

Blaz, Deborah. *Foreign Language Teacher's Guide to Active Learning.* Larchmont, NY: Eye on Education, Inc., 1999.
———. *Bringing the Standards for Foreign Language Learning to Life.* NY: Eye on Education, Inc., 2002.
Curtain, Helena, and Carol A. Dahlberg. *Languages and Children—Making the Match.* Boston: Allyn and Bacon, 2004.
High, Julie. *Second Language Learning through Cooperative Learning.* San Clemente, CA: Kagan Publishing, 1993.
Marzano, Robert J., Debra J. Pickering, and Jane E. Pollock. *Classroom Instruction that Works.* Baltimore: ASCD, 2001.
Omaggio, Alice H. *Teaching Language in Context.* Florence, KY: Cengage and Heinle, 2000.
Patrick, Paula. *The Keys to the Classroom.* Alexandria, VA: The American Council on the Teaching of Foreign Languages, 2007.
Rogers, Spence. *21 Building Blocks Critical to Leaving No Child Left Behind.* Evergreen, CO: PEAK Learning Systems, Inc., 2003.
Rogers, Spence, Jim Ludington, and Becky Graf. *Teaching and Training Techniques: Lighting the Way to Performance Excellence.* Evergreen, CO: PEAK Learning Systems, Inc., 2003.
Rogers, Spence, Jim Ludington, and Shari Graham. *Motivation and Learning: A Teacher's Guide to Building Excitement for Learning and Igniting the Drive for Quality.* Evergreen, CO: PEAK Learning Systems, Inc., 1999.
Shrum, Judith L., and Eileen W. Glisan. *Teacher's Handbook: Contextualized Language Instruction.* Florence, KY: Cengage and Heinle, 2005.

Features of Backwards Design Found in *Español Santillana*

Carol McKenna Semonsky Associate Professor Emerita, Georgia State University

Principles of Backwards Design

Backwards Design, developed by Grant Wiggins and Jay McTighe, is an approach to unit development that puts the emphasis on big ideas and enduring understandings rather than on discrete skills and coverage. It has three main steps: 1) identify desired results; 2) determine acceptable evidence; and 3) plan learning experiences and instruction. Assessments are performance-based, reflect the big ideas, and are designed before the instructional activities.

Step One: Identify Desired Results

In step one, teachers define the unit's goals, its essential questions and enduring understandings, as well as the key language skills students will acquire as a result of the unit. Enduring understandings are those that have value in real life beyond the classroom, that have a potential for engaging students, and that include core tasks that are essential and integral to the subject matter. For world language teachers, national, state, and local standards as well as thematic planning provide essential guidelines and contexts when defining desired results.

Español Santillana's overall format, that of thematic units centered around young people traveling in various Spanish-speaking countries, addresses enduring understandings, such as, "Who are the Spanish-speaking peoples of the world and how do they live?" and "How are our lives similar and different?" The themes are broad and reflect cultural perspectives. For instance, in Level 1, *Unidad 3*, the stated theme is "shopping in the context of Mayan cultures and Guatemala's historic cities."

Step Two: Determine Acceptable Evidence

In step two, teachers decide which evidence will show that students have a grasp of the big ideas and enduring understandings. Wiggins and McTighe suggest that performance tasks provide the best evidence. For world language teachers, performance-based assessments, focused on student use of extended, communicative language in authentic situations, are recommended. However, the use of extended language requires initial skill building where core vocabulary and structures are mastered first.

Español Santillana offers a wide selection of contextualized formative assessments centered on these core skills as well as summative assessments that prompt extended and authentic language. Students are given an opportunity to reflect on their accomplishment of the goals by using the *Autoevaluación* at the end of each unit.

Step Three: Plan Learning Experiences and Instructions

It is in step three, in the planning for learning experiences, where *Español Santillana* excels. Both the textbook and ancillaries offer plentiful and contextualized practice of essential skills that form the building blocks necessary for meaningful communication. Practice exercises represent real-life situations. Daily plans found in the Teacher's Edition facilitate planning for both regular and block scheduling. The Teacher's Edition directly links unit content to standards and offers many ideas to address individual differences, including suggestions for reaching all learners via multiple intelligences and differentiated instruction. *Español Santillana* has a selection of ancillary materials, including websites, DVDs, and other multimedia from which teachers may choose in order to design the most effective instruction, matching both their initial desired results and their students' individual needs.

Bibliography

Center for Advanced Research on Language Acquisition. *Creating an Assessment Unit Process: Backwards Design.* University of Minnesota. July, 2010. <http://www.carla.umn.edu/assessment/vac/CreateUnit/p_1.html>.

National Standards in Foreign Language Education Project. *Standards for Foreign Language Learning in the 21st Century*. Lawrence, KS: Allen Press, Inc., 1999.

Wiggins, Grant and Jay McTighe. *Understanding by Design*. Power Point presentation. Winter 2004. <http://www.grantwiggins.org/documents/mtuniontalk.pdf>.

———. *Understanding by Design, Expanded 2nd Edition*. Alexandria, VA: Association for Supervision and Curriculum Development, 2005.

Contextualization in the Language Classroom

Anne Nerenz, Eastern Michigan University

American educator John Dewey wrote: "We only think when we are confronted with a problem." In some subject areas, students have difficulty connecting what they are learning with real-life situations in which the knowledge and skills are needed. When taught as a collection of isolated bits and pieces, vocabulary and grammar rules are meaningless abstractions to be "covered" in class but never used. In contrast, contextualized learning sets each new word or grammatical structure in an age-appropriate, relevant situation and highlights its usefulness. Knowing what to say, when, and to whom can only be acquired through practice in carrying out increasingly complex real-world tasks. Research shows that by contextualizing learning, students can more easily acquire knowledge and skills and transfer their knowledge and skills to new and different situations.

Making Learning Meaningful

There are several ways to contextualize learning. First, we can make learning meaningful simply by stating at the beginning of each lesson why and for what purpose the vocabulary and grammar will be needed. Instead of saying: "Today, we'll be learning about adjective agreement," we make learning relevant by saying: "By the end of class today, you'll be able to describe someone's appearance." Contextualized learning focuses students' attention on the tasks they will be able to complete.

Emphasizing the Cultural Context

In addition to stating our lesson objective as a communication task, we can also make learning meaningful by emphasizing cultural situations in which vocabulary and grammar would be needed. Rather than teaching vocabulary for fruits, vegetables, meat or desserts in an alphabetical list, in one lesson we could teach only the items that would typically be sold in a single store. For example, the communication task might be "asking for and stating a price;" the cultural context might be "at the bakery." In addition to learning about culturally specific products that are sold in a bakery and the expressions and cultural practices used to purchase something in a bakery, students can compare this daily life situation with the way in which they complete a similar task in their own communities (Standards 2.1, 2.2, and 4.2).

Making Connections to Other Disciplines

One final way to contextualize what students learn is to incorporate content from other academic disciplines. Using art as an example, when learning articles of clothing and colors, students might focus on the tasks "asking for a description" and "identifying and describing clothing" by analyzing clothing items and painting styles from the target culture. In addition to learning to accomplish meaningful language tasks and learning about important cultural products, students also make connections to art as they observe artists' use of color, light, background, and detail (Standards 3.1 and 3.2).

Teaching in Context

By focusing instruction on meaningful language tasks, situating lessons in engaging cultural contexts, and making connections to other disciplines, we capture students' attention and make learning relevant for them. Teaching in context helps all students to move seamlessly from *acquiring* skills to *applying* those skills as they work their way more and more smoothly through the business of life in the target culture.

Bibliography

American Council on the Teaching of Foreign Languages (ACTFL). *Standards for Language Learning.* Yonkers, NY: Author, 1999.

Bransford, John D., Ann L. Brown, and Rodney R. Cocking, eds. *How People Learn: Brain, Mind, Experience, and School*. Washington, DC: National Academy Press, 1999.

Glaser, Robert. "Expert Knowledge and Processes of Thinking." *Enhancing Thinking Skills in the Sciences and Mathematics*. Ed. Diane F. Halpern. Hillsdale, NJ: Erlbaum, 1992. 63–75.

Greeno, James G., Lauren Resnick, and Allan Collins. "Cognition and Learning." *Handbook of Educational Psychology*. Eds. David Berliner and Robert Calfee. New York: Simon & Schuster Macmillan, 1997. 15–46.

Hartman, Hope J., ed. *Metacognition in Learning and Instruction: Theory, Research and Practice*. Norwell, MA: Kluwer Academic Publishers, 2001.

Merrifield, Juliet. *Equipped for the Future Research Report: Building the Framework*, 1993–1997. Washington, DC: National Institute for Literacy, 2000.

Pressley, Michael, and Vera Woloshyn. *Cognitive Strategy Instruction That Really Improves Children's Academic Performance*. Cambridge, MA: Brookline Books, 1995.

Wenger, Etienne. *Communities of Practice: Learning, Meaning, and Identity*. New York: Cambridge University Press, 1998.

Learning Languages: Pathway to Common Core Literacy

Paul Sandrock Director of Education. American Council on the Teaching of Foreign Languages

The *Common Core State Standards for English Language Arts and Literacy* describe a pathway to develop college- and career-ready high school graduates. The building blocks of that pathway are the four strands of reading, writing, speaking and listening, and language.

Common Core and World Languages

Language educators also have a set of national standards that form a core common across most states' standards: the five C goal areas of Communication, Cultures, Connections, Comparisons, and Communities. The standards that describe Communication match the strands of the Common Core State Standards, not just superficially, but at a deeper conceptual level and with many commonalities for implementation:

- Reading corresponds to the Interpretive Mode
- Writing corresponds to the Presentational Mode
- Speaking and Listening correspond to the Interpersonal Mode, and also to the Presentational (speaking) and Interpretive (listening) modes

By emphasizing the purpose behind the communication, the language learning standards move away from isolated skill building and situate the development of language usage in that purpose. When these standards guide curriculum, assessment, and instruction, learners are on a pathway to literacy.

The fourth strand of the Common Core—Language—corresponds to the overarching description of how proficiency develops. How learners improve their language performance (increasing their vocabulary, awareness of language conventions, and control of language functions) is captured in the ACTFL Proficiency Levels: Novice, Intermediate, Advanced, Superior, and Distinguished. Making this conceptual link of language standards with Common Core is easy. To actually put this into practice implies important changes in our assessment and instruction. The Common Core State Standards, just like the national language standards, do not describe content to teach but rather outline the competencies that need to be developed in a standards-based program.

National Standards and the AP* Program

The National Standards for Learning Languages are now the framework for the Advanced Placement* language and culture courses and exams. With this common emphasis on the three communication modes (interpersonal, interpretive, and presentational) and an engaging context through the other four Cs, the AP* language and culture course connects to the vertical development of the same language performance across every grade level and learning experience.

The Common Core Standards and *Español Santillana*

The Santillana materials supporting language learning and Advanced Placement* follow this approach to developing literacy:

- **Interpersonal mode.** Language learners develop Common Core literacy in listening and speaking when they practice strategies to initiate and maintain a conversation, negotiate meaning, ask follow-up questions, ask for clarification, and come to agreement. This requires creating a need to engage in conversation, find out information, exchange ideas, and come to consensus.
- **Interpretive mode.** Language learners develop Common Core literacy in listening and reading when they practice strategies to figure out what the writer, speaker, or producer wants them to understand. Learners need to acquire a variety of strategies to access meaning, including skimming and scanning for key words and phrases, predicting what might be in the "text," looking for clues from the context, verifying if potentially true statements are logical, and hypothesizing about the meaning and then verifying as more evidence emerges.
- **Presentational mode.** Language learners develop Common Core literacy in speaking and writing when they practice strategies to plan and organize their content, self-correct and peer-edit, research and present findings, and develop and carefully construct an argument.

Conclusion

Using the Standards for Learning Languages as a guide, language educators are poised to support the development of learners' literacy as described in the Common Core State Standards, simultaneously helping students acquire and practice the strategies that will improve their use of both native and target languages.

Bibliography

Aligning the National Standards for Learning Languages with the Common Core State Standards. 2012. <http://cort.as/6WMd>.

American Council on the Teaching of Foreign Languages. *ACTFL Proficiency Guidelines.* 2012. <http://actflproficiencyguidelines2012.org/>.

Common Core State Standards for English Language Arts & Literacy in History/Social Studies, Science, and Technical Subjects. 2010. <http://www.corestandards.org/ELA-Literacy>.

National Standards in Foreign Language Education Project. *Standards for Foreign Language Learning in the 21st Century.* Lawrence, KS: Allen Press, Inc., 2006.

Santillana USA. *The Common Core State Standards & World Languages.* 2013. <http://cort.as/6WMv>.

Español
Santillana

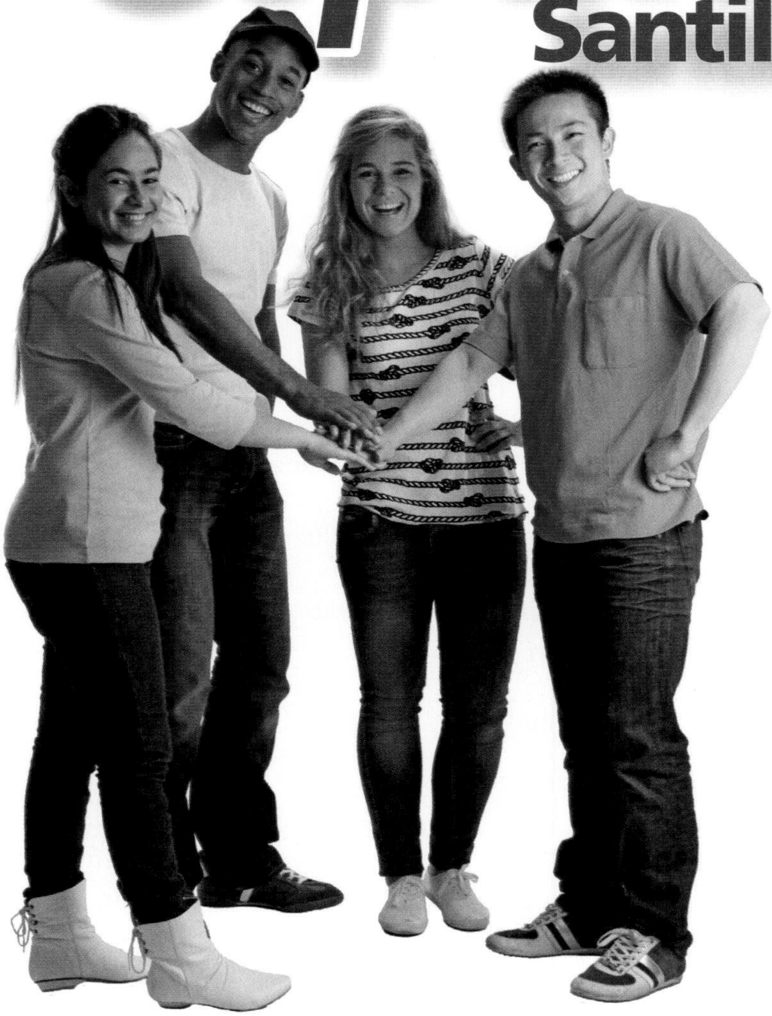

fans del Español

SANTILLANA USA

Español Santillana is a collaborative effort by two teams specializing in the design of Spanish-language educational materials. One team is located in the United States and the other in Spain.

Español Santillana
Student Book Level 2
ISBN-13: 978-1-61605-256-0
ISBN-10: 1-61605-256-2

Illustrator: **Bartolomé Seguí**
Picture Coordinator: **Carlos Aguilera**

Cartographer: **José Luis Gil, Tania López**
Cartographic Coordinator: **Ana Isabel Calvo**

Production Manager: **Ángel García Encinar**

Production Coordinator: **Julio Hernández**

Design and Layout: **Jorge Borrego, Luis González, Hilario Simón**

Proofreaders: **María A. Pérez, Elizabeth A. Pease, Marta López**

Photo Researchers: **Mercedes Barcenilla, Amparo Rodríguez**

Santillana USA Publishing Company, Inc.
2023 NW 84th Avenue, Doral, FL 33122

1 2 3 4 5 6 7 8 9 10   19 18 17 16 15 14

Editorial Staff in the United States

Anne Silva
Ana Isabel Antón

Editorial Staff in Spain

Susana Gómez
Clara Alarcón
Belén Saiz

Linguistic and Cultural Advisers in Latin America and in the United States

Antonio Moreno
Editorial Director, Santillana México

Mayra Méndez
Editorial Director, Santillana Puerto Rico

Luis Guillermo Bernal
Editorial Director, Santillana Guatemala

Cecilia Mejía
Editorial Director, Santillana Perú

Graciela Pérez de Lois
Editorial Director, Santillana Argentina

Manuel José Rojas
Editorial Director, Santillana Chile

Mario Núñez
Director of Professional Development, Santillana USA

Reviewers

Lorrie Ann Button-Edelson
Katy, TX

Yvonne Davault
Mansfield, TX

Frances S. Hoch
Raleigh, NC

Rita Oleksak
Glastonbury, CT

Nieves Pérez-Knapp
Provo, UT

Ana Sainz de la Peña
Allentown, PA

Eugenia Sarmiento
Centennial, CO

Maritza Sloan
Plano, TX

Carlos Soler Montes
Calgary, AB, Canada

Alan Svidal
San Diego, CA

Thomasina White
Philadelphia, PA

Writers

Paloma Lapuerta
teaches Spanish Language, Literature and Culture at Central Connecticut State University. She graduated from the University of Salamanca, Spain, and received her PhD from the University of Geneva, Switzerland. She has taught in different countries and is co-author of several Spanish textbooks.

María Lourdes Casas
received her Masters of Arts and PhD in Spanish at the University of Wisconsin-Madison. Dr. Casas has taught Spanish Language and Literature at the University of Wisconsin-Madison, Connecticut College, and Southern Connecticut State University. Currently she is an Assistant Professor at Central Connecticut State University.

Lisa Berliner
received her MA in Educational Leadership from Central Connecticut State University. She is currently pursuing a Masters degree in Spanish. She teaches Spanish at the secondary level in Simsbury, CT.

Jan Ferrier Sands
received her BS in Spanish and MS in Curriculum and Supervision from Central Connecticut State University. She is a career teacher of Spanish at Simsbury High School, Simsbury, CT. From 2005 to 2008, she served as the World Languages Teacher-in-Residence at the Connecticut State Department of Education.

María Á. Pérez
received her MA in Spanish from Portland State University. She was the assistant director for the Spanish Basic Language Program at the University of Illinois in Chicago. She has taught college-level Spanish at several institutions, and has worked as an editor and writer for various publishers.

Contributing Writers

Ana Isabel Antón
Miami, FL

Clara Alarcón
Madrid, Spain

Susana Gómez
Madrid, Spain

Íñigo Javaloyes
Newton, MA

Andrea Roberson
Miami, FL

Belén Saiz
Madrid, Spain

Contributors

Janet L. Glass
Dwight-Englewood School
Englewood, NJ

Jan Kucerik
Pinellas County Schools
Largo, FL

Carol McKenna Semonsky
Georgia State University
Atlanta, GA

Anne Nerenz
Eastern Michigan University
Ypsilanti, MI

Gerardo Piña-Rosales
North American Academy of the Spanish Language
The City University of New York, New York, NY

Paul Sandrock
ACTFL
Madison, WI

Emily Spinelli
AATSP
University of Michigan-Dearborn, Dearborn, MI

Brandon Zaslow
Occidental College
Los Angeles, CA

Advisers

Paula Hirsch
Windward School, Los Angeles, CA

María Orta
Kennedy High School, Chicago, IL

Developmental Editor
Susana Gómez

Editorial Coordinator
Anne Silva

Editorial Director
Enrique Ferro

Welcome to

The pairs

Andy Douglas y Janet Douglas

Nosotros somos fans del español por la música. La música latina es muy divertida.

Tess Williams y Patricia Williams

Hay lugares fantásticos en el mundo hispano.

Español Santillana

Who we are

We are four pairs of fans of the Spanish language and of Hispanic cultures. Our objective is to get to know the Spanish-speaking world: its people, its landscapes, its cities, its customs, and its traditions. That's why we've created the website Fans del Español.

What we do

To reach our goal, we are going to travel to different Spanish-speaking countries with special missions: to find the most surprising place, the most fun customs and traditions, the most original recipe, and so on. In each country, we will take on Desafíos (challenges) that each pair will try to complete. Will we succeed?

You can follow our adventures through this book and on the website www.fansdelespañol.com.

Rita Delgado y Diana Robles

Tim Taylor y Mack Taylor

(1) Puente de las Américas
(Panamá)

(2) Barrio de La Boca
(Buenos Aires, Argentina)

(3) Mercado de Otavalo
(Ecuador)

The geographic regions of the challenges

What geographic regions are the pairs going to visit? Let's find out. Look at the map and answer these questions:

Centroamérica

1. ¿Qué siete países forman Centroamérica? ¿En cuáles se habla español?

Las Antillas

2. ¿Entre qué océano y qué mar está situado el archipiélago de las Antillas? ¿En qué países de las Antillas se habla español?

Andes centrales

3. ¿Qué cordillera atraviesa Ecuador, Perú y Bolivia?

Norteamérica

4. ¿Qué países forman Norteamérica? ¿En qué país se habla español? ¿En qué país de habla inglesa hay muchos hispanos?

España

5. ¿En qué continente está situado España?

Caribe continental

6. ¿Qué países de Suramérica tienen costa en el mar Caribe?

Río de la Plata

7. ¿Qué países están en el estuario del Río de la Plata?

Your participation counts!

1. Your vote decides the winner

In these challenges, you are going to play an important role. Pay close attention, because you are going to form part of the judging panel. In each unit, you will evaluate which pair has done the best job. Each time, you will help to decide the winning team.

2. Your challenge

You will also have your own challenge: TU DESAFÍO. During the course of the year, you will be able to accumulate points visiting the *Fans del español* website. To do this, go to the website when you see this symbol in the Student Book:

Just by participating, you will earn points for your own challenge.

CANADÁ

ESTADOS UNIDOS

OCÉANO ATLÁNTICO

BAHAMAS

CUBA

REPÚBLICA DOMINICANA

HAITÍ

JAMAICA

PUERTO RICO

MÉXICO

BELICE

GUATEMALA

HONDURAS

EL SALVADOR

NICARAGUA

COSTA RICA

PANAMÁ

Mar Caribe

VENEZUELA

GUYANA

Guayana Francesa

SURINAM

COLOMBIA

ECUADOR

PERÚ

BRASIL

OCÉANO PACÍFICO

BOLIVIA

PARAGUAY

CHILE

URUGUAY

ARGENTINA

Río de la Plata

OCÉANO ATLÁNTICO

España

Mar Mediterráneo

0   375   750 millas

0   375   750 kilómetros

0   500   1.000 millas

0   500   1.000 kilómetros

Contents

Unidad	Vocabulario
Unit 1 **Centroamérica** 28–79	• Personal and family relationships • Physical characteristics and personality traits • Emotional states and feelings • Personal information
Unit 2 **Las Antillas** 80–131	• The house. Household chores • Furniture and objects in a house • Electrical appliances • The neighborhood. Places and services
Unit 3 **Andes centrales** 132–183	• Clothing and accessories • Describing clothes • Stores and establishments • Shopping
Unit 4 **Norteamérica** 184–235	• Foods • Buying food • In the kitchen • In the restaurant
Unit 5 **España** 236–287	• Parts of the body • Personal hygiene • Health: symptoms and illnesses • Healthy habits
Unit 6 **Caribe continental** 288–339	• Trips and excursions • On the train and on the plane • The car • The hotel. The bank
Unit 7 **Río de la Plata** 340–391	• The school • Professions • Hobbies, free-time activities, and entertainment • Sports
Unit 8 **La Panamericana** 392–443	• Geography • Countries • The weather • Nature and environment

Gramática		Cultura	

• Possessives
• Adjectives and nouns
	• Comparisons and superlatives
	• Interrogatives
		• *Mapa cultural:* Centroamérica
		  • Mestizaje y cultura
		  • Riqueza natural
			• Lectura: *El blog de Ichxel*

• The present progressive
• Direct object pronouns
	• Indirect object pronouns
	• Demonstratives
		• *Mapa cultural:* Las Antillas
		  • Barrios coloniales
		  • Música caribeña
			• Lectura: *Estilo de vida caribeño*

• The preterite tense of regular *-ar* verbs
• The preterite tense of regular *-er* and *-ir* verbs
	• The preterite tense of the verbs *ser, ir, decir, tener, estar,* and *hacer*
	• The preterite tense of stem-changing *-ir* verbs
		• *Mapa cultural:*
		Andes centrales
		  • Quechuas y aymaras
		  • Los equecos
		  • Las islas Galápagos
			• Lectura: *Textiles andinos bolivianos*

• Expressing amount. Indefinites
• Singular affirmative commands
	• Plural affirmative commands
	• Negative commands
		• *Mapa cultural:* Norteamérica
		  • El Camino Real de Tierra Adentro
		  • Los chicanos
			• Lectura: *La receta del guacamole*

• The past participle
• Adverbs ending in *-mente*
	• *Por* and *para*
	• Making recommendations
		• *Mapa cultural:* España y el Mediterráneo
		  • Paisaje mediterráneo
		  • La Noche de San Juan
		  • Las lenguas romances
			• Lectura: Figura en una ventana, *de Salvador Dalí*

• The imperfect tense
• The preterite tense of the verbs *dar, poder, poner, querer, saber,* and *venir*
	• Talking about past actions. The preterite and imperfect tenses
	• Talking about past actions and describing in the past. The preterite and imperfect tenses
		• *Mapa cultural:* Caribe continental
		  • Símbolos nacionales
		  • El mestizaje y los bailes
		  • Cocina del Caribe: color y sabor
			• Lectura: *El Dorado, ecos de una leyenda*

• Expressing existence. Indefinites
• The present subjunctive of regular verbs
	• The present subjunctive of stem-changing verbs
	• The present subjunctive of irregular verbs
		• *Mapa cultural:* Río de la Plata
		  • Influencia italiana
		  • Cultura rioplatense
		  • El chipá
			• Lectura: *Un cuento de Benedetti*

• The relative superlative
• Expressing plans and intentions
	• The future tense
	• Hiding the agent. The pronoun *se*
		• *Mapa cultural:* La ruta Panamericana
		  • Variedad geográfica
		  • El mundo hispano: unidad y diversidad
			• Lectura: *El Tapón de Darién: un corte en la ruta Panamericana*

UNIDAD 1

Centroamérica

En tierras mayas

Video Program

Videos

- Centroamérica. En tierras mayas
- Atitlán
- Personajes populares
- Mapa cultural de Centroamérica

Audiovisuales

 *En Managua*

 *El gigante maya de Atitlán*

 *Un garífuna peculiar*

 *La mujer más alta de León*

 *Un viaje arbóreo*

www.fansdelespañol.com

UNIDAD 2

Las Antillas

Por las islas del Caribe

Video Program

Videos

- Las Antillas. Por las islas del Caribe
- La Casa del Cordón
- La ciudad de las flores
- Mapa cultural de Las Antillas

Audiovisuales

 *En Santo Domingo*

 *La balanza del pirata Drake*

 *Un mosquito del Jurásico*

 *Una serenata en Ponce*

 *El Festival de las flores*

www.fansdelespañol.com

UNIDAD 3

Andes centrales

Entre las altas montañas

DESAFÍO ①

DESAFÍO ②

Video Program

Videos

- Andes centrales. Entre las altas montañas
- La Avenida de los volcanes
- El carnaval de Oruro
- Mapa cultural de los Andes centrales

Audiovisuales

 *En Guayaquil*

 *Un sorbete de volcán*

 *Una carrera de llamas*

 *El carnaval de Oruro*

 *La montaña de plata*

www.fansdelespañol.com

UNIDAD 4

Norteamérica

La herencia hispana

Video Program

Videos

- Norteamérica.
  La herencia hispana
- El Día de Muertos
- Tierra de misiones
- Mapa cultural
  de Norteamérica

Audiovisuales

 En Santa Fe

 ¿Un pan de muerto?

 La moneda más antigua de América

 Un concurso de chile en San Antonio

 El ingrediente secreto de Cholula

www.fansdelespañol.com

UNIDAD 5

España

Entre el Atlántico y el Mediterráneo

Video Program

Videos

- España. Entre el Atlántico y el Mediterráneo
- Salamanca
- Los sanfermines
- Mapa cultural de España

Audiovisuales

 *En Sevilla*

 *Una margarita cubista*

 *La rana de la suerte*

 *Los encierros de Pamplona*

 *Gazpacho para todos*

www.fansdelespañol.com

UNIDAD 6

Caribe continental

En busca de El Dorado

DESAFÍO ③

DESAFÍO ④

Video Program

Videos

- Caribe continental
  En busca de El Dorado
- El salto Ángel
- Las haciendas cafeteras
- Mapa cultural del Caribe
  continental

Audiovisuales

 *En Cartagena de Indias*

 *El tesoro más valioso de Colombia*

 *El salto Ángel*

 *Un paseo en bus*

 *El mejor café del mundo*

www.fansdelespañol.com

fans del Español

UNIDAD 7

Río de la Plata

Por la cuenca del Paraná

Video Program

Videos

- Río de la Plata. Por la cuenca del Paraná
- Montevideo
- La pasión por los colores
- Mapa cultural del Río de la Plata

Audiovisuales

En Córdoba

¿Un idioma imposible?

¡Ojalá encontremos a Bruno!

Estrellas de telenovela

El clásico y el Aconcagua

www.fansdelespañol.com

La Panamericana

De vuelta a casa

Video Program

Videos

- La Panamericana. De vuelta a casa
- El canal de Panamá
- Costa Rica, paraíso natural
- Mapa cultural de la ruta Panamericana

Audiovisuales

 En Santiago de Chile

 Una obra de gigantes

 La mitad del mundo

 Aire frío y agua caliente

 El paraíso de las tortugas

www.fansdelespañol.com

Vamos a recordar

Objectives

- To describe and identify people.
- To express likes and dislikes.
- To talk about habitual actions.
- To express place and existence.
- To introduce yourself and others.
- To say goodbye.
- To talk about feelings.
- To describe physical characteristics and personality traits.
- To identify different rooms in the home and their contents.

- To talk about food preferences.
- To simulate a shopping experience.
- To describe daily routines.
- To talk about body parts.
- To identify the symptoms of illness.
- To discuss common remedies.
- To talk about travel and transportation.
- To give directions to places in the community.
- To describe nature.

Contents

Vocabulary

- Greetings and goodbyes.
- Classroom items.
- Physical characteristics and personality traits.
- Emotional states.
- Household items.
- Foods and drinks.
- Clothing and colors.
- Body parts.
- Symptoms and illnesses.
- Healthy habits and routines.
- Sports and leisure activities.
- Travel and transportation.
- City landmarks.
- Nature.

Grammar

- *Ser* and *estar.*
- Adjectives.
- Nouns.
- Articles.
- The verb *gustar.*
- Adverbs of quantity.
- Regular verbs in the present tense.
- Reflexive verbs.
- Adverbs that express frequency.
- Irregular verbs in the present tense.
- *Estar* + *en* to express location.
- Adverbs that express location.
- To express existence with the verb *haber.*
- First-person irregular verbs.
- The verb *ir.*

Evaluation Criteria

- Greet others and introduce yourself.
- Describe classroom items.
- Talk about someone's physical characteristics and personality traits.
- Express feelings.
- Describe a home.
- Express likes and dislikes.
- Talk about food.

- Simulate a shopping experience.
- Identify body parts and their potential aches and pains.
- Describe healthy hygiene habits and daily routines.
- Simulate a visit to the doctor due to a minor illness.
- Talk about sports and leisure activities.

- Recognize and use the adverbs that express frequency.
- Describe a trip and the modes of transportation used.
- Identify places in a city.
- Recognize and use verbs in the present tense.

Unit Plan _____

Páginas preliminares

Estimated time: 1 session.

Functions & forms:
- *Vamos a recordar*.

1. DESCRIBIR E IDENTIFICAR

Estimated time: 2 sessions.

Functions & forms:
- Greetings and goodbyes.
- Classroom items.
- Physical characteristics and personality traits.
- Emotional states.
- The verbs *ser* and *estar*.
- Adjectives.
- Nouns.
- Articles.

2. EXPRESAR GUSTOS Y ACCIONES HABITUALES

Estimated time: 2 sessions.

Functions & forms:
- Household items.
- Foods and drinks.
- Clothing and colors.
- The verb *gustar*.
- Adverbs of quantity.
- Regular verbs in the present tense.

3. EXPRESAR ACCIONES HABITUALES

Estimated time: 2 sessions.

Functions & forms:
- Body parts.
- Symptoms and illnesses.
- Healthy habits and routines.
- Sports and leisure activities.
- Reflexive verbs.
- Adverbs that express frequency.
- Irregular verbs in the present tense: Stem-changing verbs.

4. EXPRESAR LUGAR Y EXISTENCIA

Estimated time: 2 sessions.

Functions & forms:
- Travel and transportation.
- City landmarks.
- Nature.
- To express location: *Estar + en*.
- Adverbs that express location.
- To express existence: The verb *haber*.
- First-person irregular verbs.
- To express movement: The verb *ir*.

REPASO Y EVALUACIÓN

Estimated time: 1 session.

Functions & forms:
- Review of Overviews 1–4.

Standards for Learning Spanish

 COMMUNICATION

1.1. Interpersonal mode

- Discuss the topics learned in the previous course.
- Discuss what students will learn in this course.
- Interview students on a selected topic.
- Discuss a recommended treatment for an illness.
- Read and respond to an e-mail.

1.2. Interpretive mode

- Listen to a conversation about recipes.
- Listen to an oral text and take notes.

1.3. Presentational mode

- Draw conclusions based on collected data.
- Write a babysitting schedule.
- Write instructions on how to get to a certain location.
- Describe personal uses of mass transportation.
- Organize survey results and present.
- Write a menu.
- Write a text.

 CULTURE

2.1. Practices and perspectives

- Greetings and introductions.
- Leave-taking and common courtesies.

 CONNECTIONS

3.1. Interdisciplinary connections

- Reinforce grammatical concepts.

 COMPARISONS

4.1. Compare languages

- Understand the difference between the structure of nouns in English and their structures in Spanish.
- Understand the difference between the infinitive form of verbs in English and in Spanish.
- Compare the construction of prepositional phrases in English and in Spanish.

4.2. Compare cultures

- Compare the favorite foods of people from other cultures.
- Compare formal versus informal letter-writing styles of native Spanish speakers and native English speakers.

 COMMUNITIES

5.1. Spanish within and beyond the school setting

- Play a guessing game.

5.2. Spanish for lifelong learning

- Design an advertisement.

Communicative Skills

Interpersonal Mode | Activities

Speaking	• Compare information with a classmate. • Initiate a guessing game with another student. • Ask and answer guided questions. • Interview a classmate. • Engage in conversation with a classmate. • Describe people based on a picture.	• 14, 29 • 37, 38 • 40 • 32 • 3, 6, 19, 20, 23, 25, 26, 42 • 11
Writing	• Write descriptive sentences or texts. • Use personal information to respond to an e-mail.	• 5, 10, 23 • 7
Listening	• Interpret a classmate's answers. • Understand simple oral descriptions. • Extract pertinent information from a classmates' oral description.	• 3, 10, 19 • 25, 30, 34, 36 • 2, 35
Reading	• Understand simple texts that describe people. • Understand the key concepts of a written conversation.	• 7, 31 • *Vocabulario* sections

Interpretive Mode | Activities

Listening	• Obtain information from a conversation.	• 13, 17, 25, 28, 39
Reading	• Understand and make inferences from brief written exchanges. • Understand descriptive texts.	• 1, 12 • 10, 31, 40

Presentational Mode | Activities

Speaking	• Present the results of a survey to the class.	• 19, 26, 29, 32
Writing	• Summarize information. • Write descriptions or narratives based on a picture.	• 19, 27 • 11

Cross-Curricular Standards

Subject | Standard | Activities

Language Arts	• Summarize grammatical concepts covered in previous textbook. • Write a descriptive paragraph. • Create a Venn diagram to organize information.	• *Gramática* sections • 10 • 17, 28

Lesson Plans (50-Minute Classes)

Day	Objectives	Sessions	Activities	Time	Standards	Resources / Homework
1	To introduce Level 2 and the *Unidad preliminar*	**Introduction** • Warm-Up: Book orientation • Functions and forms		5 m. 45 m.	1.1, 1.2	
2	To greet and say goodbye, and to identify people and things	**1. Describir e identificar – Vocabulario** (2–3) • Warm-Up: Independent Starter • Vocabulary: *Las personas*	1–3	5 m. 45 m.	1.1, 1.2, 1.3, 2.1, 5.1	Audio Practice Workbook
3	To describe people and states of being and to identify people and things	**1. Describir e identificar – Gramática** (4–7) • Warm-Up: Independent Starter • Grammar: *Describir personas y estados de ánimo* • Grammar: *Identificar personas y cosas*	4–7 8–11	5 m. 25 m. 20 m.	1.1, 1.2, 1.3, 3.1, 5.1	Audio Practice Workbook
4	To talk about the home, shopping, and food	**2. Expresar gustos y acciones habituales – Vocabulario** (8–9) • Warm-Up: Independent Starter • Vocabulary: *Un sábado típico*	12–15	5 m. 45 m.	1.1, 1.2, 1.3, 2.1, 5.1	Audio Practice Workbook
5	To express different degrees of liking and to express habitual actions in the present tense	**2. Expresar gustos y acciones habituales – Gramática** (10–13) • Warm-Up: Independent Starter • Grammar: *Expresar gustos en distinto grado* • Grammar: *Expresar acciones habituales en el presente*	16–19 20–23	5 m. 25 m. 20 m.	1.1, 1.2, 1.3, 3.1, 5.1	Audio Practice Workbook
6	To talk about minor illness	**3. Expresar acciones habituales – Vocabulario** (14–15) • Warm-Up: Independent Starter • Vocabulary: *Ausente por enfermedad*	24–26	5 m. 45 m.	1.1, 1.2, 1.3	Audio Practice Workbook
7	To talk about daily routines and to talk about habitual actions in the present tense	**3. Expresar acciones habituales – Gramática** (16–19) • Warm-Up: Independent Starter • Grammar: *Expresar las rutinas diarias* • Grammar: *Expresar acciones habituales en el presente*	27–29 30–32	5 m. 25 m. 20 m.	1.1, 1.2, 1.3, 3.1, 5.1	Audio Practice Workbook
8	To talk about nature, travel, and transportation	**4. Expresar lugar y existencia – Vocabulario** (20–21) • Warm-Up: Independent Starter • Vocabulary: *Un viaje de fin de semana*	33–35	5 m. 45 m.	1.1, 1.2, 1.3, 2.1, 3.1, 3.2, 5.1	Audio Practice Workbook
9	To express place and existence and to express habitual actions in the present tense	**4. Expresar lugar y existencia – Gramática** (22–25) • Warm-Up: Independent Starter • Grammar: *Expresar lugar y existencia* • Grammar: *Expresar acciones habituales en el presente*	36–38 34–42	5 m. 25 m. 20 m.	1.2, 1.3, 3.1, 5.1	Audio Practice Workbook
10	To integrate vocabulary and grammar and to assess student proficiency	**Repaso/Assessment** (26–27) • Warm-Up: Independent Starter • *Repaso* • Test	1–8	5 m. 25 m. 20 m.	1.2, 1.3, 3.1, 5.2	

Lesson Plans (90-Minute Classes)

Day	Objectives	Sessions	Activities	Time	Standards	Resources / Homework
1	To introduce Level 2 and the *Unidad preliminar*, to greet and say goodbye, and to identify people and things	**Introduction / 1. Describir e identificar – Vocabulario** (1–3) • Warm-Up: Book orientation • Functions and forms • Vocabulary: *Las personas*	1–3	5 m. 40 m. 45 m.	1.1, 1.2, 1.3, 2.1, 5.1	Audio Practice Workbook
2	To describe people and states of being and to identify people and things	**1. Describir e identificar – Gramática** (4–7) • Warm-Up: Independent Starter • Grammar: *Describir personas y estados de ánimo* • Grammar: *Identificar personas y cosas*	4–7 8–11	5 m. 45 m. 40 m.	1.1, 1.2, 1.3, 3.1, 5.1	Audio Practice Workbook
3	To talk about the home, shopping, and food, to express different degress of liking, and to express habitual actions in the present tense	**2. Expresar gustos y acciones habituales – Vocabulario/Gramática** (8–13) • Warm-Up: Independent Starter • Vocabulary: *Un sábado típico* • Grammar: *Expresar gustos en distinto grado* • Grammar: *Expresar acciones habituales en el presente*	12–15 16–19 20–23	5 m. 25 m. 30 m. 30 m.	1.1, 1.2, 1.3, 2.1, 3.1, 5.1	Audio Practice Workbook
4	To talk about minor illness, to talk about daily routines, and to talk about habitual actions in the present tense	**3. Expresar acciones habituales – Vocabulario/Gramática** (14–19) • Warm-Up: Independent Starter • Vocabulary: *Ausente por enfermedad* • Grammar: *Expresar las rutinas diarias* • Grammar: *Expresar acciones habituales en el presente*	24–26 27–29 30–32	5 m. 25 m. 30 m. 30 m.	1.1, 1.2, 1.3, 3.1, 5.1	Audio Practice Workbook
5	To talk about nature, travel, and transportation, to express place and existence, and to express habitual actions in the present tense	**4. Expresar lugar y existencia – Vocabulario/Gramática** (20–25) • Warm-Up: Independent Starter • Vocabulary: *Un viaje de fin de semana* • Grammar: *Expresar lugar y existencia* • Grammar: *Expresar acciones habituales en el presente*	33–35 36–38 39–42	5 m. 25 m. 30 m. 30 m.	1.1, 1.2, 1.3, 2.1, 3.1, 3.2, 5.1	Audio Practice Workbook
6	To integrate vocabulary and grammar and to assess student proficiency	**Repaso / Assessment** (26–27) • Warm-Up: Independent Starter • *Repaso* • Test	1–8	5 m. 55 m. 30 m.	1.2, 1.3, 3.1, 5.2	

Audio Scripts

Icons

The (🎧) symbol is used to refer to audio activities.
The audio scripts for these activities are found in each unit at the end of the Overview section.

The (👁) symbol is used to refer to activities that are accompanied by a visual presentation. The scripts for these presentations are identical to the dialogues found in the fotonovelas in the Student Book.

The (🗨) symbol is used to refer to speaking activities. These activities require spoken expression by the student and do not follow any particular script.

2 ¿Qué hay en el salón de clase?

1. ¿Dónde está mi cuaderno?
2. Necesito un bolígrafo.
3. ¿Es esta tu mochila?
4. Ese es mi lápiz.
5. ¿Usamos la computadora?

4 Mi familia

1. Mi padre es pelirrojo.
2. Mis primos son antipáticos.
3. Mi abuela Silvia es muy mayor.
4. Mi madre es muy bonita.

8 En el salón de clase

1. un
2. los
3. la
4. unos

13 ¡Me gustan las ensaladas!

–Uno de mis platos preferidos es la ensaladilla de verano.
–¿Cómo se prepara?
–Debes cocinar unos guisantes, dos papas...
–Espera. Unos guisantes, dos papas... ¿Y qué más?
–Después debes cortar una cebolla y un tomate.
–Cebolla y tomate.

–Sí. Y al final debes mezclar todo con salsa mayonesa.
–¡Perfecto!
–Y otro plato que me gusta mucho es la macedonia de frutas.
–¿Qué lleva?
–Pues lleva muchas frutas. Debes cortar una manzana, una naranja, un kiwi...
–¡Un momento! Manzana, naranja, kiwi. ¿Y qué más?
–Un poco de jugo de limón y un poco de azúcar.
–¡Qué rico! Gracias, Liz.

17 ¿Qué alimentos les gustan?

–A ver, ¿qué comemos? A mí me gustan mucho los frijoles. ¿Y a ti?
–No, a mí los frijoles no me gustan nada. A mí me gusta el arroz.
–Hum... A mí el arroz no me gusta mucho. ¿Te gustan las ensaladas? A mí, sí.
–Sí, son muy ricas. También me gusta el maíz.
–A mí el maíz no me gusta, pero sí me gustan las tortillas de maíz.
–¡A mí no! Bueno, pues... ¿qué te parece un bistec?
–¡Buena idea! La carne es mi comida favorita. Vamos a comer un bistec con ensalada.

21 ¿Qué hacen?

1. Elisa bebe un vaso de leche.
2. Yo subo las escaleras.
3. Nosotros abrimos la puerta.
4. Ellos hablan mucho.
5. Tú comes a la una.
6. Ustedes llaman por teléfono.

25 No me siento bien

1. –Buenos días. ¿Cómo te sientes?
   –Mal, doctora. Me duele la garganta y me duelen mucho los oídos.
   –Vamos a ver si tienes fiebre. A ver... No, no tienes fiebre.
   –Pero sí tengo tos.
   –Sí, tienes un resfriado. Debes beber mucha agua y descansar.
   –Gracias, doctora.
2. –¡Hola! ¿Cómo estás?
   –Pues no muy bien. Me duelen mucho las piernas. Y también me duele la espalda.
   –¿Te duele la cabeza?
   –No, pero me duele un poco el estómago.
   –¿Haces deporte normalmente?
   –Sí, entreno para participar en un maratón.
   –Bueno, pues te voy a dar unos medicamentos para el dolor.
   –De acuerdo, doctora.

28 **¿Qué hacen?**

–Beatriz, ¿qué haces cuando estás enferma?

–Pues me quedo en casa. Y normalmente me levanto tarde.

–Sí, yo también. Y después, me ducho.

–Yo no me ducho.

–¿No te duchas?

–No, prefiero bañarme.

–Ah, ya veo. Luego me visto con ropa cómoda.

–¿No te peinas?

–No, y tampoco me afeito. ¿Y tú?

–Yo sí me peino, pero no me afeito.

–¿Y te vistes con ropa cómoda?

–Sí, claro.

30 **¿Quién habla?**

1. Yo pido la cuenta a la mesera.
2. Las clases empiezan a las nueve.
3. Yo vuelvo a casa a las seis.
4. Yo me visto con ropa cómoda.
5. Yo cierro la puerta de la escuela.

34 **¿Dónde está?**

1. Ahí tengo toda la ropa para mi viaje.
2. No puedo viajar a otro país sin él. Tengo que enseñarlo en el aeropuerto.

3. Ahí hay recomendaciones de los lugares que debo visitar. Tiene información de hoteles, restaurantes...
4. Lo necesito para subir al avión.

36 **¿Dónde está la bolsa?**

1. Está debajo de la mesa.
2. Está lejos de la mesa.
3. Está al lado de la mesa.
4. Está encima de la mesa.

39 **¡Llegamos tarde!**

–Carlos, ¿estás ahí? ¿Cuándo sales del baño?

–Ya salgo.

–¡Uf, es muy tarde! ¿Quién hace la maleta?

–Yo la hago.

–Muy bien, yo pongo el pasaporte y el boleto en la bolsa.

–Oye, ¿tienes tú la guía turística?

–Sí, ahora la traigo.

–Perfecto. La maleta ya casi está.

–¡Ay! ¿Dónde está la reserva del hotel?

–Ahí.

–¿Dónde? No la veo.

–Encima de la mesa.

–Ah, sí, gracias. Pues ya estamos listos.

–¡Vamos al aeropuerto!

The Unit

- This unit is a review of the main objectives of Spanish Level 1. Students will review the following topics:
  - Identifications and descriptions, expressing likes and dislikes, habitual actions, place, and existence.
  - Vocabulary relating to greetings and farewells, classroom items, people, the home, food, clothing, the human body, health, free-time activities, sports, travel, transportation, places in the city, and nature.
  - Expressing physical characteristics and personality traits (*ser*), feelings and temporary conditions (*estar*), likes (*gustar*), daily personal routine (reflexive verbs), location (*estar en*), existence (*haber*), and movement (*ir*).

Activities	Standards	Resources
Vamos a recordar	1.2	

Teaching Suggestions

Warm-Up / Independent Starter

- Ask students to write the names of the participants shown on this page. Can they remember everyone's name? Do they know the family relationships between each of the pairs?
- Have students look at the objectives for this unit. Then divide the class into small groups and assign each group one of the objectives. Ask the groups to come up with an example for their assigned objective. Have students share their examples with the rest of the class.

Preparation

- In order to assess your students' proficiencies, give them this performance pre-test. If students are not able to perform certain tasks, this will be a good indication that you might need to spend some extra class time reviewing the corresponding structures or vocabulary.

¡¡Hola, fan del español!! ¡¡Bienvenido(a) a segundo!!

Tú ya eres un(a) experto(a) y sabes hacer muchas cosas en español: sabes presentarte, decir cómo te sientes, hablar de lo que haces habitualmente, decir qué cosas te gustan... Y puedes usar el español para comunicarte en una tienda, en un restaurante, en una agencia de viajes...

Este año vas a aprender a hacer muchas cosas más en español: contar recuerdos, narrar anécdotas, expresar deseos y sentimientos, hablar del futuro, describir lugares... Y vas a recorrer muchos países siguiendo los desafíos de Andy, Tess, Diana, Tim y todos nuestros(as) fans del español.

> ¡¡¡Ven con nosotros!!! Vamos a vivir grandes desafíos.

¿Estás preparado(a) para el viaje? Pues antes de empezar, vamos a recordar lo que sabes.

Preview

ANDY AND JANET DOUGLAS
Relationship: brother and sister
Ages: 17 and 25 years old
Hometown: Atlanta, GA
Team Motto: Games are to be played and we play well.

DIANA ROBLES AND RITA DELGADO
Relationship: niece and aunt
Ages: 15 and 29 years old
Hometown: Lawrenceville, NJ
Team Motto: There is no I in TEAM.

TESS AND PATRICIA WILLIAMS
Relationship: daughter and mother
Ages: 16 and 47 years old
Hometown: San Antonio, TX
Team Motto: When life hands you lemons, make lemonade!

TIM AND MACK TAYLOR
Relationship: grandson and grandfather
Ages: 15 and 62 years old
Hometown: San Francisco, CA
Team Motto: Be the change you want to see in the world.

1. Describir e identificar

Vocabulario

Saludos y despedidas
Objetos del aula
Características físicas y rasgos de personalidad
Estados de ánimo

Gramática

Los verbos *ser* y *estar*
Los adjetivos
Los nombres
Los artículos

2. Expresar gustos y acciones habituales

Vocabulario

La casa
Comidas y bebidas
Ropa
Colores

Gramática

El verbo *gustar*
Adverbios de cantidad
Verbos regulares. Presente

3. Expresar acciones habituales

Vocabulario

Partes del cuerpo
Síntomas y enfermedades
Hábitos saludables
Deportes y actividades de ocio y tiempo libre

Gramática

Los verbos reflexivos
Adverbios de frecuencia
Verbos con raíz irregular. Presente

4. Expresar lugar y existencia

Vocabulario

Viajes
Medios de transporte
Lugares en la ciudad
Naturaleza

Gramática

La construcción *estar en*
Adverbios y expresiones de lugar
El verbo *haber*
Verbos irregulares en la primera persona. Presente
El verbo *ir*

uno 1

1. Describir e identificar

- Have students
  - Introduce themselves and introduce a friend to another student.
  - Describe the physical characteristics of another student.
  - Talk about the emotions and temporary conditions of another student.

2. Expresar gustos y acciones habituales

- Have students
  - Describe their ideal house.
  - Talk about their likes and dislikes regarding food.
  - Describe the clothing two of their classmates are wearing.

3. Expresar acciones habituales

- Have students
  - Identify the main symptoms of some common illnesses.
  - Describe their daily personal routines.
  - Describe what they do in their leisure time and how frequently they do these activities.

4. Expresar lugar y existencia

- Have students
  - Talk about their preferred travel destinations, accommodations, and modes of transportation.
  - Describe places in the city, say where they are located, and give directions.
  - Describe nature and the environment in their community or state.

Objectives

- In this unit, students will
  - Greet people and introduce friends.
  - Describe and identify people and things.
  - Express habitual actions in the present tense.
  - Express likes and dislikes.
  - Talk about the home, food, clothing, health, free-time activities, travel, and nature.
  - Express place, movement, and existence.
- By the end of this unit, students will have reviewed
  - Vocabulary relating to greetings and farewells, classroom items, people, the home, food, clothing, the human body, health, free-time activities, sports, travel, transportation, places in the city, and nature.
  - The verbs *ser, estar, gustar, haber, ir.*
  - Regular and stem-changing irregular verbs in the present tense, and reflexive verbs.
  - Adverbs of quantity, frequency, and place.

CENTRAL AMERICA, THE ANTILLES, THE ANDES, NORTH AMERICA

Students will learn in the upcoming units about Central America, where the participants will visit Guatemala, Honduras, Nicaragua, and Costa Rica. Students will then explore the Spanish-speaking islands of the Antilles —Cuba, the Dominican Republic, and Puerto Rico—, which the participants will visit. From the Caribbean, the participants will travel to the Central Andes, where students will learn about Ecuador, Peru, and Bolivia. Students will then come closer to home to learn about North America, with special emphasis on Mexico and the United States.

SPAIN, THE CONTINENTAL CARIBBEAN, THE RIVER PLATE REGION, THE PAN-AMERICAN HIGHWAY

In the last four units of this book, students will learn about Spain, the birthplace of the Spanish language. From Spain, the participants will cross the Atlantic Ocean to visit Colombia and Venezuela, where students will learn about El Dorado. Students will then learn about the River Plate Region and the three countries that comprise this region: Paraguay, Uruguay, and Argentina. Finally, students will learn about the Pan-American Highway—a network of highways that extends from Chile to Alaska and connects South and North America.

1

1. DESCRIBIR E IDENTIFICAR

Vocabulario – Las personas

Presentation

- In this section, students will review:
  - Greetings, introductions, and farewells.
  - Physical characteristics and personality traits.
  - Classroom items.
  - Feelings and temporary conditions.

Activities	Standards	Resources
Vocabulario	1.2, 2.1	
1.	1.2	
2.	1.1, 1.2	Audio
3.	1.1, 1.2	

Teaching Suggestions

Warm-Up / Independent Starter

- Ask students to list as many words and expressions used to introduce oneself, greet someone, and say goodbye as they recall.

Preparation

- Have students work in groups of three to greet and introduce each other, and then say goodbye before they switch places with students in another group. Repeat the activity until all of the students have met everybody in the class.

- Ask students to write a brief self-description on a slip of paper, including two or three physical characteristics and personality traits, as well as a statement about how they are feeling. For example: *Soy baja y pelirroja. Soy espontánea y creativa. Ahora estoy emocionada.* Have students turn over the slips of paper and mix them up in a bag. Then ask each student to pick one slip of paper from the bag, read the statement aloud, and try to guess who is being described.

- Point out that the word *excited* is a false cognate in Spanish. To express *I am excited*, we say *Estoy emocionado(a)*. Similarly, the word *gracioso* is a false cognate in English. To express *Ella es graciosa*, we say *She is funny*. You may also want to emphasize the importance of careful pronunciation. For instance, *cansado* (tired) and *casado* (married) are different words.

2 dos

Differentiated Instruction

DEVELOPING LEARNERS

- Ask students to divide a sheet of paper lengthwise and title the left section *¿Cómo es?* and the right section *¿Cómo está?* Have students list words for physical characteristics and personality traits in the left column, and words to express feelings and temporary conditions in the right column.

- Ask students to work with a partner to come up with a list of four well-known people in four different situations (e.g., Salma Hayek winning an Oscar). Have students take turns answering the questions *¿Cómo es?* and *¿Cómo está?* for each person.

EXPANDING LEARNERS

- Ask students to choose one of the people pictured in activity 3 and write a description that is the opposite of what this person looks like. Students should also add a statement describing the opposite of what the person's feelings and temporary condition seem to be. Ask students to read their description to a partner. The partner should correct the description. For example: *No, ella no es alta, es baja. Tampoco es morena, es rubia. No está emocionada, creo que está nerviosa y tiene miedo.*

1 Presentaciones y despedidas

▶ **Une.** Match the two columns to complete the dialogues.

 (A)   (B)

1. Te presento a mi amigo Luis.
2. ¿Cuántos años tienes?
3. ¡Adiós!
4. ¿Cómo te llamas?

a. Tengo quince años.
b. Elena. ¿Y tú?
c. Mucho gusto.
d. Hasta luego.

2 ¿Qué hay en el salón de clase?

 ▶ **Escucha e identifica.** Listen and identify the item being mentioned.

(A)    (B) 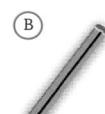   (C)    (D) 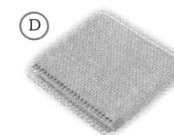   (E)

 ▶ **Habla.** With a partner, identify ten more items in your classroom.

3 Descripciones

 ▶ **Escribe.** Look at the image and write a detailed description of two people. Then read your description to your partner and have him or her guess which two people you are describing.

Modelo   *Es alta, morena y delgada. También es muy simpática.*

 ▶ **Habla.** Discuss with your partner how each person in the picture might be feeling. Use appropriate words from the boxes.

estar...	
emocionado	contento
nervioso	enojado
cansado	triste

tener...	
calor	hambre
sed	frío
miedo	sueño

tres 3

---

1. DESCRIBIR E IDENTIFICAR

Vocabulario – Las personas

Activities

1. Once students have completed this activity individually, pair them up to act out the dialogues. Invite volunteer pairs to role-play some of the dialogues in front of the class.

2. For additional practice with this vocabulary, have one of the partners call out a classroom item and the other point to it in the classroom. Ask partners to rotate the caller.

3. Ask pairs of students to describe another person in the room and see if the partner can guess who is being described. For example: *Es alto y rubio. También es serio.* Once the partner has guessed, have both partners discuss how they think the person being described is feeling. For example:
   A. *Creo que está contento.*
   B. *Yo creo que está nervioso.*

 AUDIO SCRIPT
See page XXVG.

Answer Key

1. 1. c   2. a   3. d   4. b
2. 1. D   2. E   3. A   4. B   5. C
   ▶ Answers will vary.
3. Answers will vary.
   ▶ Answers will vary. Sample answer: Está cansada y tiene sueño.

Additional Resources

Fans Online activities
Practice Workbook

3

HERITAGE LANGUAGE LEARNERS

- Ask pairs of students to go over the differences in Spanish between greeting and introducing themselves to a classmate and doing so in a more formal situation. Have students visualize several formal situations (e.g., greeting their school's principal, meeting their parents' friends, etc.), and have them create a brief dialogue to exemplify each situation.

- Invite volunteer pairs to role-play these more formal introductions and greetings in front of the class.

MULTIPLE INTELLIGENCES:
Visual-Spatial Intelligence

- Have students work in small groups. Assign different classroom items to each group and have students create labels in Spanish for their assigned items. Then ask students to label the items.

- Students may know other words for some classroom items. They can also create alternative labels for these other words.
  El salón de clase: el aula, la sala de clase.
  El bolígrafo: la pluma, el esfero, el boli.
  La pizarra: el pizarrón, el tablero, el encerado.
  La computadora: el computador, el ordenador.

1. DESCRIBIR E IDENTIFICAR

Gramática – Describir personas y estados de ánimo

Presentation

- In this section, students will review:
  - Conjugations of the verbs *ser* and *estar* in the present tense.
  - Adjectives and adjective/noun agreement.

Activities	Standards	Resources
Gramática	1.2, 3.1, 4.1	
4.	1.2	Audio
5.	1.2	
6.	1.1, 1.2	
7.	1.1, 1.2, 1.3	

Teaching Suggestions

Warm-Up / Independent Starter

- Write the following sentences on the board and have students complete them with the correct forms of the verbs *ser* and *estar*.
  1. *Nosotros … muy inteligentes y creativos.* (somos)
  2. *Luis … enojado con su hermano.* (está)
  3. *Yo … baja y simpática.* (soy)
  4. *Mis amigos … tristes hoy.* (están)

Preparation

- Tell students not to worry if they occasionally confuse these two verbs. Using *ser* and *estar* correctly takes time and practice. Encourage students to pay attention to how these verbs are used when they read texts in Spanish and watch Spanish TV channels or hear Spanish speakers talk with each other.

- Show students the painting *Las Meninas* by Diego Velázquez. (You will find it in the online gallery of the Prado Museum at http://www.museodelprado.es). Have students work in pairs to write a brief description of each character's physique, as well as his or her personality, based on what they can infer from the image. Students should also add a statement describing how they think each character is feeling. Invite volunteers to share their descriptions with the class. Compare and contrast the students' descriptions for some of the characters.

Gramática

Describir personas y estados de ánimo

Los verbos *ser* y *estar*

VERBO SER (TO BE). PRESENTE

Singular		Plural	
yo	soy	nosotros nosotras	somos
tú	eres	vosotros vosotras	sois
usted él ella	es	ustedes ellos ellas	son

VERBO ESTAR (TO BE). PRESENTE

Singular		Plural	
yo	estoy	nosotros nosotras	estamos
tú	estás	vosotros vosotras	estáis
usted él ella	está	ustedes ellos ellas	están

- The verb *ser* is used mainly to identify people, places, and things, and to describe physical characteristics and personality traits.

  La señora Flores **es** mi profesora de Español. Ella **es** joven y muy inteligente.

- The verb *estar* is used to express feelings and conditions.

  Ellos **están** tristes porque **están** enfermos.

Los adjetivos

- Spanish adjectives can be masculine or feminine, singular or plural.
- The **feminine** form is developed from the masculine form:

Masculine form	Feminine form	Examples
Ends in -o.	Changes -o to -a.	El niño es rubio. ⟶ La niña es rubia.
Ends in -e or in a consonant.	Does not change.	Mi tío es mayor. ⟶ Mi tía es mayor.

- The **plural** form is developed from the singular form:

Singular form	Plural form	Examples
Ends in a vowel.	Adds -s.	Ella es simpática. ⟶ Ellas son simpáticas.
Ends in a consonant.	Adds -es.	Mi tío es joven. ⟶ Mis tíos son jóvenes.

4 Mi familia

 ▶ **Escucha y elige.** Choose the adjective that corresponds to each description you hear.
  1. pelirroja/pelirrojo
  2. antipáticos/antipáticas
  3. mayores/mayor
  4. bonito/bonita

Differentiated Instruction

DEVELOPING LEARNERS

- Ask students to use the following prompts to form sentences.
  1. *Ella / enfermo*
  2. *Los chicas / estudioso*
  3. *Elisa y Samuel / moreno*
  4. *Mi abuela / mayor*
- Once students have finished their sentences, ask them to explain their decisions regarding their verb choices (*ser* vs. *estar*) and adjective/noun agreement.

EXPANDING LEARNERS

- Some adjectives can express both an emotion and a personality trait. In these cases, the use of the verbs *estar* and *ser* changes the meaning of the adjective. For example: *Amanda está aburrida* (emotion: Amanda is bored) and *Amanda es aburrida* (personality trait: Amanda is boring). Similarly, some adjectives can express a physical trait (with the verb *ser*) and a temporary condition (with the verb *estar*).
- Have students explain the difference between these sentences:
  – *Ernesto es delgado. Ernesto está delgado.*
  – *Laura es guapa. Laura está guapa.*

5 **Personas diferentes**

▶ **Escribe.** Describe the following people, referring to their physical characteristics and personalities. Use some of the words in the box.

atlético	delgado	serio	moreno	alto	joven
tímido	gracioso	rubio	delgado	bajo	estudioso

Modelo 1. la niña → *La niña es baja, delgada y tímida.*

la niña

el chico

la chica

la mujer

las estudiantes

6 **¿Un día difícil?**

▶ **Habla.** Talk to a partner about how each of you is feeling today.

Modelo A. *¿Cómo estás, Paula?*
B. *Estoy emocionada y muy contenta. ¿Y tú?*
A. *Estoy cansado.*

7 **Mi nueva amiga**

▶ **Escribe.** Patricia wrote an e-mail describing her new friend at school. Read her e-mail and answer by describing your new friend.

Mensaje nuevo

Para:
Cc:
Asunto:

Hola. ¿Qué tal? Hoy es mi primer día en la escuela. Estoy emocionada porque tengo una nueva amiga. Se llama Jennifer y es muy simpática. Es baja y pelirroja. Siempre está contenta y es muy graciosa.

¿Y tú? ¿Tienes un nuevo amigo o amiga?

Un abrazo,

Patricia

Gramática – Describir personas y estados de ánimo

Activities

5. Have students come up with two additional descriptions: one for themselves and one for a family member. Ask students to share their descriptions with a classmate.

6. Have pairs scan this unit and describe how some of the people pictured might be feeling based on their facial expressions and body language.

7. Verify that students' descriptions have the correct agreements and that the verbs *ser* and *estar* are used correctly. Then invite volunteers to read their descriptions aloud.

AUDIO SCRIPT
See page XXVG.

Answer Key

4. 1. pelirrojo
2. antipáticos
3. mayor
4. bonita

5. Answers will vary. Sample answers:
2. El chico es joven y gracioso.
3. La chica es rubia y atlética.
4. La mujer es mayor y seria.
5. Las estudiantes son morenas y estudiosas.

6. Answers will vary.

7. Answers will vary.

Additional Resources

Fans Online activities
Practice Workbook

HERITAGE LANGUAGE LEARNERS

• Have students think of the usage of the verbs *ser* and *estar* in each of the following cases. Ask them to come up with an example for each case.
– dates (*Hoy es lunes, 7 de septiembre.*)
– location (*Estoy en el salón de clase.*)
– nationality (*Salma Hayek es mexicana.*)
– occupation (*Marta y Sonia son arquitectas.*)

TOTAL PHYSICAL RESPONSE (TPR)

• Distribute index cards to students and ask half of them to write the verb *ser* in their cards and the other half to write *estar*. Tell students you will read aloud several incomplete sentences. The students who have the card for the verb that completes each sentence should stand and hold up their card after you read the sentence.
1. *Yo ... el/la profesor(a) de español.* (ser)
2. *Mi mejor amiga ... muy simpática.* (ser)
3. *¿Por qué ... triste?* (estar)
4. *Los deportistas ... atléticos.* (ser)
5. *Carlos ... enojado.* (estar)

1. DESCRIBIR E IDENTIFICAR

Gramática – Identificar personas y cosas

Presentation

- In this section, students will review:
  - Nouns.
  - Masculine and feminine noun endings.
  - Definite and indefinite articles.

Activities	Standards	Resources
Gramática	1.2, 3.1, 4.1	
8.	1.2	Audio
9.	1.2	
10.	1.1, 1.2, 1.3	
11.	1.1, 1.2	

Teaching Suggestions

Warm-Up / Independent Starter

- Ask students to list ten classroom items: five in the singular and five in the plural. For example: *bandera, libros, cuadernos, lápiz*.

Preparation

- Remind students that Spanish is one of many languages that assign grammatical gender to nouns. Students may not know that Old English nouns had grammatical gender too, but English gradually lost the gender system. There are, however, some cases in modern English in which a gender is assigned to inanimate objects. For example: a boat → she, a country → she.

- Ask students to classify the nouns they listed in the Independent Starter section in a table like the one below. Then invite students to think about how this table would look in English.

el / un	la / una	los / unos	las / unas

- Write the following nouns on the board: *casa, carro, bicicleta, parque, pintor, escuela, papel*. Have students give you the correct definite and indefinite articles for each noun. Then ask students to give you the plural forms for both the nouns and the articles. Finally, ask students to classify these nouns and their plural forms in a table like the one above.

6

Gramática

Identificar personas y cosas

Los nombres

- Nouns are words for people, animals, places, and things. Spanish nouns can be **masculine** or **feminine**. Almost all nouns that end in -o are masculine, and those that end in -a are usually feminine.
- Nouns that refer to people usually have a masculine and a feminine form. The feminine form is developed from the masculine form:

Masculine form	Feminine form	Examples
Ends in -o.	Changes -o to -a.	el niño ⟶ la niña
Ends in a consonant.	Adds -a.	el profesor ⟶ la profesora

- Most Spanish nouns can be **singular** (one) or **plural** (more than one). The plural form is developed from the singular form:

Singular form	Plural form	Examples
Ends in a vowel.	Adds -s.	el primo ⟶ los primos
Ends in a consonant.	Adds -es.	el director ⟶ los directores

Los artículos

- Spanish nouns are usually used with a **definite** (el) or **indefinite** (un) article.

ARTÍCULOS DEFINIDOS E INDEFINIDOS

	SINGULAR		PLURAL	
	Masculine	Feminine	Masculine	Feminine
Definite articles	el	la	los	las
Indefinite articles	un	una	unos	unas

- Articles, like adjectives, agree in **gender** and **number** with the noun they accompany. That is, they show the same gender and number as the noun.

El chico es delgado.   Es **una** señora muy creativa.
Los chicos son delgados.   Son **unas** señoras muy creativas.

8   En el salón de clase

▶ **Escucha y elige.** Choose the noun that agrees with the article you hear.

1. reloj/computadora   2. cuaderno/libros   3. pizarra/libro   4. borradores/bandera

6   seis

Differentiated Instruction

DEVELOPING LEARNERS

- Ask students to complete the following sentences with the correct definite article:
  1. ... *reloj da la hora. (El)*
  2. *Nos sentamos en ... silla. (la)*
  3. *Cuando hace calor, abrimos ... ventanas. (las)*

- Ask students to complete the following sentences with the correct indefinite article:
  1. *Tengo ... bolígrafos en la mochila. (unos)*
  2. *Hay ... bandera en el salón. (una)*
  3. *Necesito ... cuaderno. (un)*

EXPANDING LEARNERS

- Explain to students that captions give the writer an opportunity to explain the pictures and summarize the story they accompany. Good captions pull the reader in and provide context for the image.

- Have pairs of students leaf through magazines and books that are available in the classroom. Ask them to choose four images and write descriptive captions. Remind them to be careful about the use of articles and gender and number agreement. Invite volunteer pairs to present their pictures and captions to the rest of the class.

9 Mi escuela

▶ **Une y escribe.** Complete the sentences using each article in the box once. Then match the columns and write the completed sentences.

Ⓐ

un
unas
la
una ✓
los

1. El salón de clase tiene
2. Los profesores hablan con
3. En la cafetería trabajan
4. Los estudiantes leen
5. Esa mujer es

Ⓑ

a. _____ señoras de Honduras.
b. _____ libro.
c. _____ profesora de Música.
d. _____ bandera.
e. _____ estudiantes.

Modelo 1. *El salón de clase tiene una bandera.*

10 Primeras impresiones

▶ **Lee y completa.** Use the words in the box to complete this description, changing the words as needed for gender and number agreement.

computadora
estudiante
profesor
salón
amigo
escuela

Estoy contento. La ___1___ es grande y mis ___2___ son muy simpáticos. Tenemos varias ___3___ en todos los ___4___ de clase. Los ___5___ son muy inteligentes. Tengo una nueva ___6___; se llama Laura.

 ▶ **Escribe y habla.** Write a similar paragraph with a description of your school and share it with a classmate. Are your descriptions and first impressions similar?

11 Descripciones de fotos

▶ **Escribe.** Write the captions for these photos using the appropriate form of the indefinite article (*un, una, unos, unas*).

Modelo *Un hombre y una niña.*

 ▶ **Habla.** With a partner, describe the people in the photos using the appropriate definite articles (*el, la, los, las*).

Modelo *El hombre es alto y simpático. Está emocionado.*

HERITAGE LANGUAGE LEARNERS

- Have students think of Spanish nouns that exemplify the following exceptions:
  1. masculine nouns that end in *-a* (e.g., *el día, el mapa, el programa, el sofá*);
  2. feminine nouns that end in *-o* (e.g., *la mano, la moto* [from *la motocicleta*], *la foto* [from *la fotografía*]). Ask students to list these nouns in a two-column chart.

- Have students work with a partner to choose the nouns from their lists that are most commonly used in daily speech. Then ask them to make a list of these nouns to be used as reference by other students in the class.

CRITICAL THINKING

- Ask students to think of advantages for assigning gender to nouns. Have them consider the following:
  - What additional information is provided by the Spanish sentence *Voy al cine con una amiga*? (*amiga*: female friend)
  - What would be the English translation for *La gata toma leche*? (*gata*: female cat)
  - There are a few Spanish nouns whose meanings change depending on their gender. For example: *el capital* (the capital —money) and *la capital* (the capital—city); *el policía* (the police officer) and *la policía* (the police force).

Gramática – Identificar personas y cosas

Activities

8. You can extend this activity by asking students to add the appropriate article to the other noun in each pair. For example: 1. *un reloj / una computadora*, 2. *el cuaderno / los libros*.

10. Have partners use a chart like the one below to classify the nouns in this activity.

Masculino singular	Masculino plural	Femenino singular	Femenino plural
		escuela	

11. Ask students to choose one of the three pictures and write a brief story to describe the scene. Encourage students to include a description of the people, who they might be, what they are like, and how they might be feeling.

 AUDIO SCRIPT
See page XXVG.

Answer Key

8.
1. (un) reloj
2. (los) libros
3. (la) pizarra
4. (unos) borradores

9.
1. d (una)
2. e (los)
3. a (unas)
4. b (un)
5. c (la)

10.
1. escuela
2. profesoras
3. computadoras
4. salones
5. estudiantes
6. amiga
▶ Answers will vary.

11. Answers will vary. Sample answers:
1. Un chico.
2. Una madre y una hija.
3. Un hombre y una niña.
▶ Answers will vary.

Additional Resources

Fans Online activities
Practice Workbook

7

2. EXPRESAR GUSTOS Y ACCIONES HABITUALES

Vocabulario – Un sábado típico

Presentation

- In this section, students will review:
  - Rooms, appliances, and furniture in the house.
  - Food and beverage.
  - Shopping and clothing.

Activities	Standards	Resources
Vocabulario	1.2	
12.	1.2	
13.	1.1, 1,2, 2.2	Audio
14.	1.1, 1.2, 1.1, 5.1	
15.	1.1, 1.2, 5.2	

Teaching Suggestions

Warm-Up / Independent Starter

- Give students two minutes to list, in a chart like the one below, all the words they can recall that are related to each of these three topics.

La casa	La comida	La ropa

Preparation

- Have students compare their Independent Starter chart with those of two other students. Ask them to add to their list words their classmates had listed that they did not have.

- Ask students to circle the cognate words they have in each category (e.g., *sofá, refrigerador, garaje, sopa, frutas, blusa, tenis,* etc.). Remind students that recognizing cognates is a very good reading and listening strategy. There are hundreds of Spanish-English cognates.

- Ask students to look up the etymology (i.e., origin and history of a word) of each cognate they circled. If they have access to the Internet, they may use the following online dictionaries: http://www.merriam-webster.com for English and http://www.rae.es/rae.html for Spanish. Invite students to share some of their findings with the rest of the class. If time allows, discuss with students why different languages might have adopted some of these cognate words.

Vocabulario

Un sábado típico

Tess visita por primera vez a su amigo Dani. Él vive en una casa de dos **plantas**.

¡Bienvenida, Tess! Esta es mi casa.

¡Hola, Dani!

La sala y el comedor

el televisor
el sofá
la mesa
la silla

El dormitorio y el baño

la puerta
el lavabo
el armario
la cama

Tess y Dani pasan a la **cocina** para preparar el **almuerzo**.

¿Pido una pizza?

No sé.

Humm... prefiero huevos con pan. No, mejor pollo con verduras, un vaso de jugo y algo dulce de postre. No, mejor una manzana de postre y...

Después de comer, Tess y Dani **van de compras** al **centro comercial**. Tess mira la **ropa** y Dani unos **zapatos**.

Me gusta este vestido negro.

¿Cuánto cuesta?

Son cómodos, y me quedan bien. Pero son muy caros.

Está en oferta. El precio es $ 65. ¿Te gusta?

8 ocho

Differentiated Instruction

DEVELOPING LEARNERS

- Have students write a description of their typical Saturday. Ask them to specify in which areas of the house they spend more time on Saturdays, what they usually eat, and whether they go shopping. If they go shopping, ask them to say where they go (e.g., the supermarket, the mall) and what they usually buy.

- Ask students to compare their typical Saturday with that of a classmate. What do they have in common? What is different?

EXPANDING LEARNERS

- Discuss with students how fashion influences the way we dress, what we eat, and even how we decorate our homes. Have students work in pairs to come up with a list of clothing items and shoes that are fashionable now. Then have students compare today's fashions with what was fashionable when their parents were young. What is no longer fashionable?

- Ask students to repeat this activity with food. What are some of the most popular foods today? Have students changed the way they eat and what they eat since they were children?

12 Decoración de interiores

▶ **Une.** Match each item with the room in the house where it belongs.

Ⓐ
1. la estantería
2. la mesa y las sillas
3. el inodoro
4. la estufa
5. la mesita de noche

Ⓑ
a. el dormitorio
b. la cocina
c. la sala
d. el baño
e. el comedor

13 ¡Me gustan las ensaladas!

 ▶ **Escucha y escribe.** Liz is sharing the recipes for two of her favorite dishes with her friend Paul. Listen and write the list of ingredients for each dish.

Ensaladilla de verano
guisantes   2
        1   mayonesa
cebolla

Macedonia de frutas
        3   5
        4   6
kiwi

 ▶ **Habla.** Share one of your favorite recipes with a partner.

14 ¡Señores, aquí tienen la carta!

▶ **Escribe.** You have been hired to design the menu for a new café in your neighborhood. Include foods and beverages for breakfast and lunch.

Almuerzo
12:00 - 2:00 p. m.
Sándwich de pollo.
Pescado con papas.

▶ **Lee, habla y compara.** Exchange your menu with a partner. Read each other's menus and compare them. Whose restaurant do you think will be more successful?

15 ¿Qué lleva?

▶ **Habla.** Choose a classmmate and describe what he or she is wearing. Your partner guesses who the person is.

Lleva unos pantalones azules, unos tenis blancos, un...

¡Es Lisa!

HERITAGE LANGUAGE LEARNERS

• Food is quite varied throughout the Spanish-speaking world. Each country's indigenous traditions, history, and weather contribute to this variety. Have students think of some dishes from their country of origin. Invite volunteers to share with the class some of these culinary traditions and to detail the ingredients. Do they know where some of these ingredients can be purchased in their community? Is there a restaurant in the community that serves some of these dishes?

SPECIAL-NEEDS LEARNERS

• For students with organizational or information-processing difficulties, the amount of vocabulary presented in a review lesson may be overwhelming. To assist these students, encourage them to draw three concept webs and organize this lesson's vocabulary in these webs. Have students write the following in the central circle of each of the three webs: *La casa, La comida, La ropa.* Then ask students to write the vocabulary related to each category in the circles branching out from the central circle in each of the webs.

---

2. EXPRESAR GUSTOS Y ACCIONES HABITUALES

Vocabulario – Un sábado típico

Activities

12. Have students draw a floor plan for their ideal house. Ask them to label each room and draw and label some furniture and appliances. Have students exchange their floor plans with a classmate and compare their houses.

14. Ask the class to imagine that the school cafeteria is choosing a new menu. Have students present the menus they created for this activity to the class, and have the class vote on the menu they like best for their school cafeteria.

15. Have partners talk about how they dress for different occasions and in different seasons. Ask them to describe in detail the kinds of outfits they wear. Then have partners compare what they wear. Do they have similar tastes in fashion? Would they have fun going shopping together?

 AUDIO SCRIPT
See page XXVG.

Answer Key

12. 1. c   2. e   3. d   4. b   5. a
13. 1. papas   4. naranja
     2. tomate   5. jugo de limón
     3. manzana   6. azúcar
     ▶ Answers will vary.
14. Answers will vary.
     ▶ Answers will vary.
15. Answers will vary.

Additional Resources

Fans Online activities
Practice Workbook

2. EXPRESAR GUSTOS Y ACCIONES HABITUALES

Gramática – Expresar gustos en distinto grado

Presentation

■ In this section, students will review:
  – The verb *gustar*.
  – Adverbs of quantity.

Activities	Standards	Resources
Gramática	1.2, 3.1, 4.1	
16.	1.2	
17.	1.2	Audio
18.	1.2	
19.	1.1, 1.2, 1.3, 3.1, 5.1	

Teaching Suggestions

Warm-Up/Independent Starter

■ Ask students to make a list of six foods and two drinks. Have them include in their list things they like and things they dislike.

Preparation

■ Go over the grammar presentation with the class. Remind students that in sentences like *No me gustan nada las verduras*, there are two negative words: *no* and *nada*. When a Spanish sentence is negative, a negative word must be placed in front of the verb. Any other word in the sentence that has a negative version will be in the negative. In contrast, English negative sentences use a negative word first and then an affirmative one.

■ Ask students to rank, using the verb *gustar* and adverbs of quantity, the foods and drinks they listed in their Independent Starter. Have students share their lists with the class and tally the class's results on the board. Do certain foods seem to be more popular than others?

Activities

17. Ask students to share with a partner their opinion about the foods mentioned in this activity, adding adverbs of quantity. For example:

A. *A mí me gustan bastante los frijoles.*

B. *A mí no me gustan mucho los frijoles.*

Gramática

Expresar gustos en distinto grado

El verbo *gustar*

● To express likes or dislikes, use the verb *gustar*.

Me gusta el helado.   **No me gustan** los refrescos.

● The verb *gustar* is a regular verb, but usually only two of its forms are used:
  1. To speak about one thing or an action, use the **singular form** *gusta*.

  A Marta le **gusta** la fruta.   A Carlos le **gusta** cocinar.

  2. To speak about two or more things, use the **plural form** *gustan*.

  A mí me **gustan** los jugos de frutas.

● The verb *gustar* does not require a subject pronoun. Instead, these object pronouns are used: me, te, le, nos, os, les.

VERBO *GUSTAR* (*TO LIKE*). PRESENTE

	Singular		Plural		
(A mí)	me	gusta	me	gustan	*I like*
(A ti)	te	gusta	te	gustan	*you like*
(A usted) (A él/a ella)	le	gusta	le	gustan	*you like* *he/she likes*
(A nosotros/as)	nos	gusta	nos	gustan	*we like*
(A vosotros/as)	os	gusta	os	gustan	*you like*
(A ustedes) (A ellos/a ellas)	les	gusta	les	gustan	*you like* *they like*

Note: The meaning of the pronouns can be clarified with the prepositional phrases a mí, a ti, a usted, a él, a ella, a nosotros, a nosotras, a vosotros, a vosotras, a ustedes, a ellos, a ellas.

Adverbios de cantidad

● Some verbs can be modified by a word that expresses quantity. These words are called adverbs of quantity.

  nada   **poco**   **bastante**   **mucho**

  No me gustan **nada** las verduras, pero me gusta **mucho** el pollo.

16   Los gustos de mi familia

▶ **Une y escribe.** Match the two columns. Then write the sentences.

Ⓐ
1. A mi hermano y a mí
2. A mis padres
3. A mi prima Lupe

Ⓑ
a. les gusta desayunar un café con leche.
b. no le gustan nada los frijoles.
c. nos gustan mucho las papas fritas.

Differentiated Instruction

DEVELOPING LEARNERS

● To help reinforce the structure of sentences with the verb *gustar*, discuss with students the following two examples.

  – *A nosotros nos gusta la escuela.*
    (a nosotros → nos; singular → gusta)
  – *A ella no le gustan las tiendas de ropa.*
    (a ella → le; plural → gustan)

● Then have students complete the following sentences.
  1. *A ti … las frutas.* (te gustan)
  2. *A mis amigos no … el café.* (les gusta)
  3. *A usted … las papas fritas.* (le gustan)

EXPANDING LEARNERS

● Have students work in pairs to describe foods and drinks to each other. Encourage them to describe how the food tastes (i.e., *dulce, salado, picante, agrio,* and *amargo*) Partners then guess what is being described. For example:
  Es picante. Algunos son verdes y otros rojos.
  (el chile, ají o pimiento)

● Once the partners have guessed, ask them to say how much they like or dislike the food and why.
  Me gusta poco el chile. Si es muy picante, no me gusta nada porque no puedo comer picante.

17 **¿Qué alimentos les gustan?**

 ▶ **Escucha y completa.** Two friends are trying to decide what to eat. Listen and complete the Venn diagram by writing the foods they like.

A él   los frijoles   A ella

▶ **Escribe.** Write five sentences using the information above and the correct form of the verb *gustar*.

Modelo   *A él le gustan los frijoles.*

18 **Cuestión de gustos**

▶ **Escribe.** Use the correct form of the verb *gustar* and the adverbs to say what the people in the photos like or dislike, and how much they like or dislike it.

Modelo   1. *A ellos les gusta bastante la casa.*

ellos – bastante   ella – nada   él – mucho   nosotros – poco

19 **¿Tenemos hábitos saludables?**

 ▶ **Habla.** Do students in your class have healthy eating habits? Ask four classmates how much they like or dislike the foods below and tally their responses in a chart.

Modelo
A. *¿Te gustan los refrescos?*
B. *No, no me gustan nada.*

	nada	poco	bastante	mucho
refrescos	✔			✔✔✔

▶ **Escribe.** Summarize the results and draw a conclusion about your classmates' eating habits.

Modelo   *A tres estudiantes les gustan mucho los refrescos y a uno no le gustan nada.*

---

2. EXPRESAR GUSTOS Y ACCIONES HABITUALES

Gramática – Expresar gustos en distinto grado

18. Ask students to image a young couple in a restaurant. Have them come up with three sentences describing what this couple likes and dislikes. Ask students to use the verb *gustar* and adverbs of quantity. For example: *A él le gustan mucho las verduras. A ella le gustan bastante las ensaladas. A ellos no les gustan nada los frijoles.*

19. Have pairs of students speculate on what foods and beverages their same-age peers in Mexico might like and dislike. For example: *Creo que les gustan mucho los frijoles. Pienso que les gusta poco el pescado.* Do students think Mexico's proximity to the United States influences what people on both sides of the border eat?

 AUDIO SCRIPT
See page XXVG.

Answer Key

16. 1. c   2. a   3. b

17. A él: los frijoles, las tortillas de maíz
A ella: el arroz, el maíz
A los dos: las ensaladas, la carne
▶ Answers will vary. Sample answers:
A él le gustan las tortillas de maíz.
A ella le gusta el arroz.
A ella le gusta el maíz.
A los dos les gustan las ensaladas.
A los dos les gusta la carne.

18. 2. A ella no le gusta nada la sopa.
3. A él le gusta mucho el helado.
4. A nosotros nos gusta poco lavar los platos.

19. Answers will vary.
▶ Answers will vary.

Additional Resources

Fans Online activities
Practice Workbook

HERITAGE LANGUAGE LEARNERS

- Heritage language learners probably know and use several more adverbs of quantity to express different degrees of preference (e.g., *algo, apenas, casi, demasiado*). Ask students to make a list of these adverbs. If they don't know what adverbs of quantity are, explain that these words would answer the question *¿Cuánto te gusta?*

- Then have students create a drawing that shows different levels of intensity (e.g., a thermometer, a 1–10 scale, etc.). Ask students to write these adverbs in the appropriate areas of their diagram.

MULTIPLE INTELLIGENCES:
Visual-Spatial Intelligence

- Ask students to bring supermarket flyers to class and have them select a variety of foods and beverages from different departments (e.g., produce, bakery, meat, seafood, etc.). Then have students cut out the images of the products they chose.

- Ask students to use the cutout images to make a poster that expresses their preferences. To express different degrees of preference, students could color code four areas of the poster to indicate *mucho, bastante, poco,* and *nada*. Have students compare their posters.

11

2. EXPRESAR GUSTOS Y ACCIONES HABITUALES

Gramática – Expresar acciones habituales en el presente

Presentation

- In this section, students will review present tense regular verb conjugations.

Activities	Standards	Resources
Gramática	1.2, 3.1, 4.1.	
20.	1.1, 1.2	
21.	1.2	Audio
22.	1.2	
23.	1.1, 1.2	

Teaching Suggestions

Warm-Up / Independent Starter

- Have students think of five things they do around the house on Saturdays. Ask them to write five sentences listing these activities in the order in which they usually do them. For example: *Preparo el desayuno. Leo mi correo.*

Preparation

- Have students walk around the room to find out which classmates do some of the same things on Saturdays. Have students ask yes / no questions. For example: *¿Preparas el desayuno? ¿Lees tu correo?*

- Ask students to list, in a chart like the one below, the infinitive form of the verbs as well as the two conjugated forms they used (*yo* and *tú*).

Infinitive	yo	tú
preparar	preparo	preparas
leer	leo	lees

- Go over the grammar presentation in the book. Then ask students to complete the chart with the rest of the conjugations.

él / ella usted	nosotros / nosotras	vosotros / vosotras	ellos / ellas ustedes
prepara			
lee			

Gramática

Expresar acciones habituales en el presente

Verbos regulares. Presente

- In English, an infinitive is the verb form that uses the word *to*: *to buy, to sell, to open*. In Spanish, the infinitive always ends in *-ar, -er,* or *-ir*:

  -AR comprar   -ER vender   -IR abrir

- Regular verbs in Spanish have a stem that is used with all subjects. They also have a set of endings that are added to the stem to identify the subject. To find the stem of a verb, remove the *-ar, -er,* or *-ir* ending.

  compr -a̶r̶   vend -e̶r̶   abr -i̶r̶

- Regular *-ar, -er,* and *-ir* verbs are conjugated in the following ways:

VERBOS COMPRAR (TO BUY), VENDER (TO SELL) Y ABRIR (TO OPEN). PRESENTE

		Comprar	Vender	Abrir
Singular	yo	compro	vendo	abro
	tú	compras	vendes	abres
	usted, él, ella	compra	vende	abre
Plural	nosotros, nosotras	compramos	vendemos	abrimos
	vosotros, vosotras	compráis	vendéis	abrís
	ustedes, ellos, ellas	compran	venden	abren

20 **En la tienda de ropa**

▶ **Une y escribe.** Match the two columns and write the sentences.

Modelo 1. *El vendedor recibe el dinero de la clienta.*

(A)
1. El vendedor
2. Un cliente
3. Dos chicas
4. Todos nosotros
5. Un niño
6. Yo

(B)
a. compramos ropa.
b. corre por la tienda.
c. miro un vestido.
d. paga con tarjeta de crédito.
e. leen los carteles de las ofertas.
f. recibe el dinero de la clienta.

▶ **Habla.** Talk with a partner to find out whether he or she does some of these things when he or she is at a store.

Modelo A. *¿Tú pagas con tarjeta de crédito?*
B. *No, yo pago en efectivo.*

12 doce

Differentiated Instruction

DEVELOPING LEARNERS

- Go over the conjugation chart with students and discuss some of the patterns they notice (e.g., *-er* and *-ir* verbs have the same endings, except for the *nosotros* form; also the *yo* form is the same for the three conjugations, etc.).

- Have students close their books. Write the following on the board: *escuchar, aprender, vivir.* Then ask students to write the conjugations for these verbs, adding the endings in a different color. Finally, have students write a sentence for each verb.

EXPANDING LEARNERS

- Have pairs of students play a game of association. One partner calls out a part of the house or furniture and the other partner creates a complete sentence saying something that happens there. Then partners switch roles. For example:
  A. *La cocina.*
  B. *Mi hermano y yo comemos en la cocina.*
  B. *Las escaleras.*
  A. *Tú subes las escaleras.*

21 **¿Qué hacen?**

 ▶ **Completa y escucha.** Complete these sentences with the correct form of the verbs. Then listen and check your answers.

1. Elisa _____ un vaso de leche.
   <u>beber</u>

2. Yo _____ las escaleras.
   <u>subir</u>

3. Nosotros _____ la puerta.
   <u>abrir</u>

4. Ellos _____ mucho.
   <u>hablar</u>

5. Tú _____ a la una.
   <u>comer</u>

6. Ustedes _____ por teléfono.
   <u>llamar</u>

22 **Todos trabajan**

▶ **Lee y completa.** Sally and her family have a busy weekend at home. She wrote what they are doing each day and posted the notes on the refrigerator. Complete her notes using the correct form of the verbs in the box.

sacudir
preparar
escribir
ordenar
barrer
lavar

Sábado
- Mi padre y yo __1__ el suelo de la casa.
- Mi madre __2__ en su blog.
- Mis padres __3__ el carro.

Domingo
- Yo __4__ el desayuno.
- Mi hermano __5__ los muebles.
- Mi hermano y yo __6__ el garaje.

23 **Descripciones**

▶ **Escribe.** Write a sentence to describe what each person is doing.

Modelo 1. *Los jóvenes ven la televisión.*

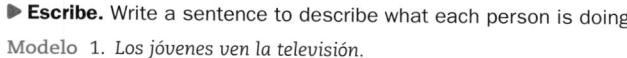

  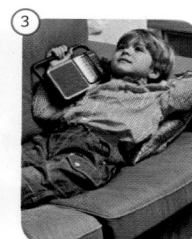 

 ▶ **Habla.** Talk with two classmates to find out if they do the activities above and what they think about them.

Modelo A. *¿Ves la televisión?*
       B. *Sí, veo la televisión. ¡Me gusta mucho!*
       C. *No, no veo la televisión. Es aburrido.*

trece 13

2. EXPRESAR GUSTOS Y ACCIONES HABITUALES

Gramática – Expresar acciones habituales en el presente

Activities

20. To extend this activity, have students think of a busy day in Spanish class. Then ask them to write five sentences describing what different people do. For example:
 – *Nosotros abrimos los libros.*
 – *Natalie pregunta algo.*

22. After students complete this activity, have them substitute the characters with members of their household and use the verbs to tell who does each of these activities at home. If there is something that nobody does, they should say so (e.g., *Nadie escribe en un blog*).

23. Ask students to remain in the same groups and talk about their chores at home. Do they have similar chores or not?

AUDIO SCRIPT
See page XXVG.

Answer Key

20. 1. f   2. d   3. e   4. a   5. b   6. c
 ▶ Answers will vary.

21. 1. bebe   4. hablan
   2. subo   5. comes
   3. abrimos   6. llaman

22. 1. barremos   4. preparo
   2. escribe   5. sacude
   3. lavan   6. ordenamos

23. 2. Los señores corren.
   3. El chico escucha la radio.
   4. El hombre y la niña leen.
   ▶ Answers will vary.

Additional Resources

Fans Online activities
Practice Workbook

HERITAGE LANGUAGE LEARNERS

- In parts of South and Central America, *vos* is used instead of *tú* for informal situations. This is called *voseo*, and the verb endings employed with *vos* are different from those used with *tú* (e.g., *-ar* > *-ás, vos hablás;* *-er* > *-és, vos comés; -ir* > *-ís, vos escribís*). Some heritage language learners in your class may be familiar with *voseo*.

- Ask students to practice the *vos* form of the *-ar, -er,* and *-ir* verbs by writing one sentence for each. For example: *Vos comprás zapatos en la zapatería.*

COOPERATIVE LEARNING

- Have students work in groups of four. Ask them to prepare cards for the verbs *leer, escribir, comprar, vender, recibir,* and *mirar*, and the nouns *dinero, tarjeta de crédito, tienda, ropa, camiseta,* and *mesa.* Have students mix up each set of cards and place them face down in two piles.

- Partners draw a card from each pile. They have one minute to form a complete and grammatically correct sentence, even if it is a silly one. They earn a point for each correct sentence and lose a turn if they do not form a correct sentence.

3. EXPRESAR ACCIONES HABITUALES

Vocabulario – Ausente por enfermedad

Presentation

- In this section, students will review:
  - Vocabulary for symptoms, illnesses, and basic remedies.
  - Free-time activities and sports.

Activities	Standards	Resources
Vocabulario	1.2	
24.	1.2	
25.	1.1, 1.2	Audio
26.	1.1, 1.2, 1.3, 5.1	

Teaching Suggestions

Warm-Up / Independent Starter

- Write this activity on the board. Students will match the two columns to complete the dialogues.
  1. ¿Cómo te sientes?
  2. ¿Comes alimentos sanos?
  3. ¿Qué haces en tu tiempo libre?
  4. ¿Estás en forma?

  a. Voy al cine.
  b. Sí, hago mucho ejercicio.
  c. Me duele la garganta.
  d. A veces.

Preparation

- Have students interview three classmates using the questions from the Independent Starter. Ask them to present their findings to the class. Once the students have reported to the class, discuss any patterns or trends they found. Are certain free-time activities more popular than others? Do students, in general, seem to have healthy habits? Are they feeling well today? Etc.

- Go over the vocabulary presentation. Then have different students read the speech bubbles. Assign a narrator to read the introductory passages. Model pronunciation as needed.

- Point to the last scene and ask students for the name of the sport (baloncesto). Give students two minutes to compile a list of other sports for which they know the names in Spanish. Then invite different volunteers to share their list with the class.

Vocabulario

Ausente por enfermedad

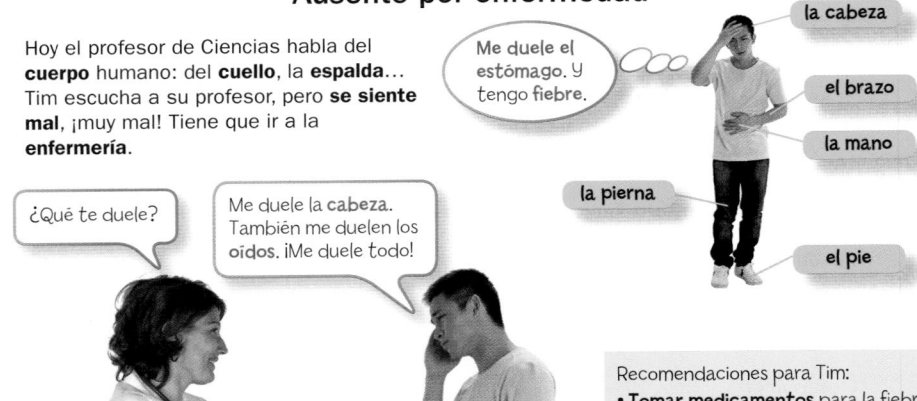

Hoy el profesor de Ciencias habla del **cuerpo** humano: del **cuello**, la **espalda**... Tim escucha a su profesor, pero **se siente mal**, ¡muy mal! Tiene que ir a la **enfermería**.

> Me duele el estómago. Y tengo fiebre.

> la cabeza
> el brazo
> la mano
> la pierna
> el pie

> ¿Qué te duele?

> Me duele la **cabeza**. También me duelen los oídos. ¡Me duele todo!

Recomendaciones para Tim:
- **Tomar medicamentos** para la fiebre.
- **Descansar**.
- **Comer** bien.
- **Beber** mucha agua.

> Tienes un **resfriado**.

Al día siguiente, Tim no va a la escuela. Tiene que seguir los consejos de la **enfermera** y **cuidarse**. ¿Qué puede hacer en casa?

> ¿Qué hago para no aburrirme? Puedo **leer** un libro y escuchar música. No... mejor juego a los videojuegos y después veo una película.

Dos días después, Tim vuelve a la escuela. Ya no **está enfermo**, pero **se siente** un poco **débil**.

> No, todavía no estoy en forma. Solo voy a jugar con el **balón**.

> Hola, Tim. ¿Listo para un **partido de baloncesto**?

Differentiated Instruction

DEVELOPING LEARNERS

- Ask students to complete each of the following phrases with two different possibilities.
  1. Me duele... (la cabeza, el estómago)
  2. Me duelen... (las piernas, los oídos)
  3. Uso una cámara para... (tomar fotos, grabar)
  4. ¿Quieres jugar un partido de...? (tenis, béisbol)
  5. En mi tiempo libre me gusta... (bailar, jugar a los videojuegos)
  6. Para tocar usamos... (los dedos, las manos)

EXPANDING LEARNERS

- Have students create a five W's chart for three of their favorite free-time activities and sports. They should answer the following questions: ¿Qué actividad es? ¿Dónde la practicas? ¿Cuándo la practicas? ¿Con quién la practicas? ¿Por qué la practicas?

- Ask students to write a paragraph with the information from the chart. Invite volunteers to share their paragraph with the class. Are there other students in class who practice the same activities?

24 Todo tiene una función

▶ **Corrige y escribe.** Answer the questions, correcting the mistakes. Use each word in the boxes once.

Modelo ¿Caminas con **los ojos**? → *No, camino con los pies.*

1. ¿Ves con **la cabeza**?
2. ¿Hueles con **los dientes**?
3. ¿Tocas con **las orejas**?
4. ¿Saboreas con **el pelo**?

los dedos	la boca
la nariz	los ojos

25 No me siento bien

 ▶ **Escucha y elige.** Listen to the conversation between a doctor and two patients. Select the problems each patient has.

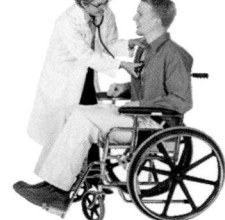

Paciente 1
1. Tiene fiebre.
2. Le duelen los oídos.
3. Tiene tos.
4. Le duele la espalda.
5. Le duele la garganta.

Paciente 2
1. Le duele el estómago.
2. Le duele la cabeza.
3. Le duelen los brazos.
4. Le duele la espalda.
5. Le duelen las piernas.

 ▶**Habla.** In small groups, discuss what the doctor recommended for each patient and say whether you agree or disagree with her. What else would you recommend?

26 Unos niños muy activos

▶ **Escribe.** This Saturday you are babysitting your neighbor's very active children, Ted and Jenny. Your neighbor has asked you for a schedule of activities you plan to do with them. Complete the table below using the expressions in the box.

montar en bicicleta	nadar en la piscina	leer un libro	jugar al béisbol
tomar fotos	usar la computadora	pintar	bailar
jugar al fútbol	ver una película	escuchar música	cantar

Hora	Ted	Jenny	Los dos
3:00 p. m.			leer un libro
4:00 p. m.			
5:00 p. m.			
6:00 p. m.			

 ▶**Habla.** Now share your schedule with a partner. Are the activities your partner chose suitable? What would you change?

HERITAGE LANGUAGE LEARNERS

• Have students think about free-time activities and sports that are popular in their countries of origin. They may ask a family member if they do not have enough information. Ask students to write a description of some of these activities. When and by whom are these activities practiced? How did these activities originate? Do they think some of these activities could become popular in the United States? Ask students to read their description to the class and encourage a discussion about some of the activities.

MULTIPLE INTELLIGENCES:
Bodily-Kinesthetic Intelligence

• Have students work in small groups of four to play a game of charades. Two students choose a vocabulary word or phrase from this lesson and act it out.

• Ask groups that show a good command of the vocabulary to work on more sophisticated scenes that guessers would need to describe with two or three complete sentences. For example: *Es un paciente y un dentista. Al paciente le duelen las muelas. El dentista le pone anestesia.*

---

3. EXPRESAR ACCIONES HABITUALES

Vocabulario – Ausente por enfermedad

Activities

24. Have students work in pairs to practice this vocabulary. One partner calls out a body part and the other points to it. Ask students to pay attention to plural and singular forms. For instance, if they hear *el dedo*, they should point to one of their fingers.

25. Remind students that the verb *doler* follows the same rules as the verb *gustar*. To extend this activity, have students work in pairs. One of the partners acts out a scenario of someone in pain and the other partner guesses what the person is feeling.

26. Ask students to rate the activities in terms of how much they like and practice them. Students may add two more activities that they practice often if these activities were not included in the list. Have students write their names on sticky notes. Then create a bar graph on the board using the students' sticky notes. Which activities are the most popular?

 AUDIO SCRIPT
See page XXVG.

Answer Key

24. 1. No, veo con los ojos.
2. No, huelo con la nariz.
3. No, toco con los dedos.
4. No, saboreo con la boca.

25. Paciente 1: 2, 3, 5
Paciente 2: 1, 4, 5
▶ Answers will vary.

26. Answers will vary.
▶ Answers will vary.

Additional Resources

Fans Online activities
Practice Workbook

3. EXPRESAR ACCIONES HABITUALES

Gramática – Expresar las rutinas diarias

Presentation

- In this section, students will review:
  - Reflexive verbs associated with personal daily routines.
  - Adverbs of frequency.

Activities	Standards	Resources
Gramática	1.2, 3.1, 4.1	
27.	1.2	
28.	1.2, 3.1	Audio
29.	1.1, 1.2, 1.3, 5.1	

Teaching Suggestions

Warm-Up / Independent Starter

- Ask students to list, in chronological order, five things they do every morning before coming to school. Remind them to use reflexive verbs. For example:
  1. *Me levanto.*
  2. *Me ducho.*
  3. *Me visto. …*

Preparation

- Write the following sentences on the board and discuss with students the functions of the different elements in each sentence.
  - *Yo baño al perro. (yo → sujeto, baño → verbo, perro → objeto)*
  - *Yo me baño. (yo → sujeto, baño → verbo, me → objeto)*
  Point out that, in a reflexive sentence, the subject and object are the same.
- Go over the grammar presentation with students. To practice reflexive verb conjugation, write different infinitives on the board. Then call out a subject pronoun and have students conjugate the verb. For example: *afeitarse, él → se afeita; ducharse, nosotros → nos duchamos.* Ask students to write sentences saying how often they do these things. For example: *Nunca me afeito. Me ducho todos los días.*

Gramática

Expresar las rutinas diarias

Los verbos reflexivos

- Sometimes an action is reflected back onto the subject. In Spanish, this idea is expressed with a reflexive verb.

  Rocío se peina. (Rocío performs the action, and she receives the effects of the action.)

  The verbs afeitarse, bañarse, ducharse, lavarse, maquillarse, and vestirse are reflexive verbs.

- Reflexive verbs are conjugated with a reflexive pronoun: me, te, se, nos, os, se. The pronoun is placed as follows:
  - In front of the conjugated verb: Yo me peino.
  - Attached to the end of the infinitive or commands: Quiero peinarme. Péiname.

VERBO PEINARSE (TO COMB ONE'S HAIR). PRESENTE

Singular		Plural	
yo	me **pein**o	nosotros nosotras	nos **pein**amos
tú	te **pein**as	vosotros vosotras	os **pein**áis
usted él ella	se **pein**a	ustedes ellos ellas	se **pein**an

- Many verbs related to habits are reflexive verbs.
  - despertarse *(ie)* *(to wake up)* ⟶ Yo me despierto a las siete de la mañana.
  - levantarse *(to get up)* ⟶ Yo me levanto a las siete y media.
  - acostarse *(ue)* *(to go to bed)* ⟶ Ellos se acuestan a las once.
  - dormirse *(ue)* *(to fall asleep)* ⟶ Tú te duermes pronto.

Adverbios de frecuencia

- These adverbs and adverbial phrases express how often something is done.

nunca   casi nunca/rara vez   a veces   muchas veces   casi siempre   siempre/todos los días

Ella se peina **todos los días**.   Yo me acuesto **siempre** a las once.

Differentiated Instruction

DEVELOPING LEARNERS

- Ask students to classify the following sentences as *reflexivas* or *no reflexivas*.
  1. *Nosotros nos levantamos de la silla.* (reflexiva)
  2. *Yo lavo la ropa.* (no reflexiva)
  3. *El papá duerme al bebé.* (no reflexiva)
  4. *El bebé se duerme.* (reflexiva)
  5. *Tú te acuestas tarde.* (reflexiva)
  6. *La música despierta a los vecinos.* (no reflexiva)
  7. *Ellas se peinan antes de salir.* (reflexiva)

EXPANDING LEARNERS

- In a reflexive sentence, the reflexive pronoun indicates that the subject of the sentence is doing the action of the verb to him or herself. It is, therefore, redundant to use a possessive adjective in front of the body parts. We use a definite article.
- Have students translate the following sentences into Spanish.
  1. You shave your beard. (*Tú te afeitas la barba.*)
  2. We apply makeup to our eyes. (*Nosotras nos maquillamos los ojos.*)
  3. They brush their teeth. (*Ellos se cepillan los dientes.*)

27 La rutina de Michelle

▶ **Ordena y escribe.** Put Michelle's routine in chronological order and write a brief paragraph to summarize what she does.

____ a. Me levanto.

____ b. Me visto.

____ c. Me baño.

__1__ d. Me despierto temprano.

____ e. Me acuesto tarde.

____ f. Me maquillo.

Modelo   Michelle se despierta temprano. Después…

28 ¿Qué hacen?

▶ **Escucha y clasifica.** Listen to Beatriz's and Raúl's routines when they feel sick and stay home. Then organize their routines in a Venn diagram.

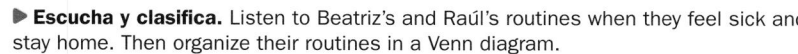

Beatriz   Los dos   Raúl

se levantan tarde

29 La rutina del fin de semana

▶ **Escribe.** Describe your weekend routine. Indicate the frequency of each activity.

Modelo   Casi siempre me despierto temprano. Rara vez me baño, pero siempre me ducho…

▶ **Habla.** Compare your routine with a partner's and report your findings to the class using a chart similar to the one below.

	Yo	Mi compañero(a)	Los dos
nunca			
casi nunca / rara vez		Se despierta temprano.	
a veces			
muchas veces			
casi siempre	Me despierto temprano.		
siempre / todos los días			

3. EXPRESAR ACCIONES HABITUALES

Gramática – Expresar las rutinas diarias

Activities

27. Have students list their own daily routine out of order on a slip of paper, and have them exchange it with a classmate. The classmate puts the routine in chronological order. Did they get the correct order?

28. After students have completed this activity, have them get together with a partner and talk about their routines when they feel sick and stay home. Ask them to create a Venn diagram like the one for this activity summarizing their routines.

29. Review the grammar presentation on adverbs of frequency with students before they complete this activity.

 AUDIO SCRIPT
See page XXVH.

Answer Key

27. 1. d   2. a   3. c   4. b   5. f   6. e
Answers will vary. Sample answer:
Michelle se despierta temprano. Después se levanta, se baña y se viste. Luego se maquilla. Al final del día se acuesta tarde.

28. Beatriz: se baña, se peina
Raúl: se ducha, no se peina, no se afeita
Los dos: se levantan tarde, se visten con ropa cómoda

29. Answers will vary.
▶ Answers will vary.

Additional Resources

Fans Online activities
Practice Workbook

HERITAGE LANGUAGE LEARNERS

• Have students discuss similarities and differences between people's personal daily routines in their country of origin and in the United States. Do people in their country of origin get up earlier or later than people in the United States? Do they usually shower in the morning or in the evening? Do women wear makeup every day? Etc.

• If students are not familiar with personal routines in their country of origin, they may ask their relatives. Encourage students to find out if their parents or family members changed their personal routines when they moved to the United States.

CRITICAL THINKING

• Ask students to think of different factors that might account for variations in people's daily personal routines. Cultural background and religious norms, for instance, might be some of the reasons for women not to wear makeup and men not to shave their beards. Weather may also influence daily routines.

• Divide the class into small groups and have them come up with a list of factors that affect personal routines and how they affect these routines. Ask them to write complete sentences. Have students compare their work with that of other groups.

3. EXPRESAR ACCIONES HABITUALES

Gramática – Expresar acciones habituales en el presente

Presentation

- In this section, students will review stem-changing verbs: *e > ie*, *o > ue*, and *e > i*.

Activities	Standards	Resources
Gramática	1.2, 3.1, 4.1	
30.	1.2	Audio
31.	1.2	
32.	1.1, 1.2, 1.3	

Teaching Suggestions

Warm-Up / Independent Starter

- Ask students to write three sentences telling one thing they want to do but cannot do, one thing they do not want to do but can do, and one thing they always ask for when they go to a restaurant. For example:
  1. *Quiero volar pero no puedo.*
  2. *No quiero limpiar el baño pero puedo hacerlo.*
  3. *Siempre pido agua.*

Preparation

- Remind students that they already know three groups of stem-changing verbs in the present tense. The stem of these verbs changes in a predictable way in all forms except *nosotros* and *vosotros*. The endings are the same for regular verbs and stem-changing verbs.

- Go over the grammar presentation with students. Model pronunciation and ask students to read aloud all the forms in the three conjugation charts. Tell students that by listening for these verbs whenever they hear Spanish as well as repeating them to themselves, they will develop a feel for what sounds right.

- Ask students to go around the room sharing with their classmates their sentences from the Independent Starter. Have students read their sentences aloud. If the listener does not understand, he or she should ask for clarification. Then invite volunteers to share with the class some of the answers they considered most original.

Gramática

Expresar acciones habituales en el presente

Verbos irregulares

- Irregular verbs do not follow typical conjugation patterns. These verbs may be irregular in the stem or in the endings.

Verbos con raíz irregular: *e > ie*
VERBO QUERER (TO WANT). PRESENTE

Singular		Plural	
yo	**quiero**	nosotros nosotras	**queremos**
tú	**quieres**	vosotros vosotras	**queréis**
usted él ella	**quiere**	ustedes ellos ellas	**quieren**

- Other *e > ie* verbs:
  cerrar *(to close)* ⟶ yo cierro
  empezar *(to begin)* ⟶ yo empiezo
  entender *(to understand)* ⟶ yo entiendo
  pensar *(to think)* ⟶ yo pienso
  preferir *(to prefer)* ⟶ yo prefiero

Verbos con raíz irregular: *o > ue*
VERBO PODER (TO BE ABLE). PRESENTE

Singular		Plural	
yo	**puedo**	nosotros nosotras	**podemos**
tú	**puedes**	vosotros vosotras	**podéis**
usted él ella	**puede**	ustedes ellos ellas	**pueden**

- Other *o > ue* verbs:
  contar *(to count)* ⟶ yo cuento
  costar *(to cost)* ⟶ cuesta(n)
  recordar *(to remember)* ⟶ yo recuerdo
  volar *(to fly)* ⟶ yo vuelo
  volver *(to return)* ⟶ yo vuelvo

Verbos con raíz irregular: *e > i*
VERBO PEDIR (TO ASK FOR). PRESENTE

Singular		Plural	
yo	**pido**	nosotros nosotras	**pedimos**
tú	**pides**	vosotros vosotras	**pedís**
usted él ella	**pide**	ustedes ellos ellas	**piden**

- Other *e > i* verbs:
  competir *(to compete)* ⟶ yo compito
  medir *(to measure)* ⟶ yo mido
  repetir *(to repeat)* ⟶ yo repito
  servir *(to serve)* ⟶ yo sirvo
  vestir *(to dress)* ⟶ yo visto

Note: The *e > ie*, *o > ue*, and *e > i* stem changes affect all the present tense forms except nosotros(as) and vosotros(as).

Differentiated Instruction

DEVELOPING LEARNERS

- Clarify that the stem of a verb is the part of the verb that is left once you take away the *-ar*, *-er*, or *-ir* ending. In regular verbs, the stem does not change. In some irregular verbs, however, the stem changes in a predictable way.

- Ask students to create verb flashcards for the following verbs: *pensar, volver, repetir*. Have students use three differently colored markers: one color for the letters that do not change, another for stem changes, and a third color for the verb endings.

EXPANDING LEARNERS

- Have pairs of students create three short dialogues using stem-changing verbs from the three groups listed on page 18. For example:

  A. *¿Quieres ir al cine esta tarde?*
  B. *Lo siento, pero esta tarde no puedo.*

- Have pairs act out their dialogues in front of other pairs. Ask the "audience" to suggest one more line to add to one of the dialogues.

30 **¿Quién habla?**

 ▶ **Escucha y relaciona.** Listen and match each sentence with the corresponding picture.

31 **Este trabajo es para mí**

▶ **Lee y completa.** Lorena sent her résumé and a cover letter for a job at a restaurant. Read her letter and complete it with the appropriate form of the verbs.

empezar   pensar

servir   volver

poder   pedir

> Estimada Sra. García:
>
> ¡Soy la candidata ideal! Cuando los clientes me **piden** algo, yo les ___1___ con una sonrisa. Por eso, ellos siempre ___2___. Mis amigos ___3___ que soy muy simpática y una buena vendedora. Yo ___4___ las clases esta semana, pero ___5___ trabajar los fines de semana.
> Atentamente,
> Lorena Suárez

32 **Te recomiendo…**

 ▶ **Habla.** You are a camp counselor and need to plan free-time activities for a group of students. Interview four classmates to find out their preferences. Use the verbs *querer*, *preferir*, *poder*, *competir,* and *pensar*.

Modelo A. *¿Compites en deportes de equipo?*
B. *No. Prefiero hacer ejercicio solo.*

▶ **Completa y habla.** Organize the results of your survey in a table, write recommendations for your classmates, and present them to the people you interviewed.

Nombre	Preferencias	Recomendación
John Smith	Prefiere hacer ejercicio solo.	Puede nadar en la piscina.

---

3. EXPRESAR ACCIONES HABITUALES

Gramática – Expresar acciones habituales en el presente

Activities

31. Have students write their own cover letter for a job as a salesperson in a clothing store. Ask them to use some of the stem-changing verbs listed on page 18 and to follow the same format as the letter in this activity. Then have students share their letter with a classmate for peer review.

32. Before students interview their classmates, have them take a few minutes to organize their thoughts and write down the questions for their survey. Ask them to pay attention to their verb conjugations. Once students finish their interviews and present their recommendations to the people they interviewed, have the interviewees comment on the recommendations. Do they agree with the recommendations? Is there something else that they would prefer doing?

 AUDIO SCRIPT
See page XXVH.

Answer Key

30. 1. B   2. A   3. E   4. C   5. D

31. 1. sirvo   4. empiezo
2. vuelven   5. puedo
3. piensan

32. Answers will vary.
▶ Answers will vary.

Additional Resources

Fans Online activities
Practice Workbook

19

HERITAGE LANGUAGE LEARNERS

• Most heritage language learners in your class may not use the *vosotros* form—the second person plural familiar form of the verb. Explain to students that *vosotros* is mostly used in mainland Spain and if they ever speak with someone from Spain or watch a film, read a newspaper, or listen to Spanish music, they would need to be familiar with it.

• Have students imagine that they and their friends are planning what to do on Saturday. Ask them to create a dialogue in which they use *vosotros*. Invite volunteer groups to perform their dialogue for the class.

SPECIAL-NEEDS LEARNERS

• Provide the script for activity 30 to students with hearing disabilities. Have them read the script once or twice before listening to the recording. You may also wish to read the script to them before playing the recording. Then play the recording and have students track the text with their fingers. Have them look at the pictures and play the recording again so that students can complete the activity.

4. EXPRESAR LUGAR Y EXISTENCIA

Vocabulario – Un viaje de fin de semana

Presentation

- In this section, students will review:
  - Travel and transportation vocabulary.
  - Places in the city and directions vocabulary.
  - Nature and ecology vocabulary.

Activities	Standards	Resources
Vocabulario	1.2	
33.	1.1, 1.2	
34.	1.2	Audio
35.	1.1, 1.2, 1.3	

Teaching Suggestions

Warm-Up / Independent Starter

- Have students complete these sentences with information about their ideal trip.
  - *Quiero ir a...* (travel destination)
  - *Voy en...* (mode of transportation)
  - *Voy a llevar...* (travel item)
  - *Me quedo en...* (accommodations)
  - *Pienso visitar...* (places)

Preparation

- Ask students to share their answers for the Independent Starter with the class. You may organize the students' answers in a five-column chart. Classify the different destinations students mention by the geographic features that each represent (e.g., *las montañas, la costa, el bosque,* etc.) instead of listing the actual place name.

- Encourage the class to analyze the results of this survey. What are the most popular destinations and the preferred modes of transportation? Do students prefer far-away destinations or places closer to home? What type of accommodations does the majority of the class perceive as ideal? To encourage critical thinking, ask students to think of reasons for these answers. How big a role do they think the media have in our travel choices?

- Proceed to introduce the story on page 20. Invite volunteers to read the different sections.

Vocabulario

Un viaje de fin de semana

 Andyviajero
Hoy decidimos adónde vamos este fin de semana. Yo quiero **viajar** en **avión**, ir a una gran **ciudad**, salir del **campo**. Pero Janet nunca me escucha.

Yo prefiero ir a la **costa** y tomar un **barco** para hacer un crucero.

Vamos en **tren** a la **capital**.

 Andyviajero
¡Increíble! Estoy en el **aeropuerto**. Por una vez hacemos lo que yo quiero.

Tengo que **facturar** el **equipaje**. ¿Dónde está Janet?

el boleto

el mostrador de información

la maleta

la bolsa

 Andyviajero
Hoy nos espera un gran día de **turismo a pie** por la ciudad. Tengo una **guía turística** con recomendaciones de **cafés, museos**...

Perdón, ¿hay una **biblioteca** por aquí?

Sí. Tienen que **seguir recto** hasta la **plaza** y allí **doblar a la izquierda**.

¿Tenemos que **cruzar la calle**?

No, no es necesario.

 Andyviajero
Mi hermana insiste en ver **naturaleza**: **lagos, ríos, bosques, aire** puro... Es un poco aburrido, pero hoy es su día, así que vamos a ir a un **parque**.

Aquí hay **insectos**...

Aquel **árbol** es un **roble**. En el otoño las **hojas** son rojas.

20 veinte

Differentiated Instruction

DEVELOPING LEARNERS

- Ask students to re-read the vocabulary presentation and dialogues on page 20. To assess reading comprehension, have students tell whether the following statements are true (*cierto*) or false (*falso*). Ask students to correct the false statements.
  1. *Andy quiere ir al campo.* (*falso*)
  2. *En el aeropuerto no nos dan información.* (*falso*)
  3. *Andy piensa que la guía turística es útil.* (*cierto*)
  4. *A Andy no le gusta la naturaleza.* (*cierto*)
  5. *Asociamos el aire puro con la ciudad.* (*falso*)

EXPANDING LEARNERS

- Have students work in small groups to expand on the story on page 20. They may, for instance, come up with an additional scene at the end of the story in which the characters participate in a recycling drive at the park. Or, they may add a scene in the middle, when the characters arrive at their destination. Allow students time to rehearse. Then have them act out the new story without a script for the class.

Hay muchas maneras de viajar

▶ **Lee y decide.** Read what each person says and decide which mode of transportation he or she is referring to.

Ⓐ

1. Cuando voy a Nueva York siempre lo uso.
2. Es la mejor opción para los viajes largos.
3. Es necesario para visitar la isla.
4. Es una buena forma de viajar por todo el estado.
5. No es rápido, pero a mí me gusta caminar.

Ⓑ

a. el avión
b. el barco
c. a pie
d. el metro
e. el coche

 ▶ **Habla.** Tell a classmate which modes of transportation you use and when you use them.

Modelo *Yo uso el autobús para venir a la escuela.*

34 **¿Dónde está?**

 ▶ **Escucha y elige.** These people have lost something right before leaving on vacation. Listen and select the items they are looking for.

1. a. la maleta
   b. la guía turística
2. a. el equipaje
   b. el pasaporte
3. a. la guía turística
   b. la bolsa
4. a. el boleto
   b. el recuerdo

35 **Direcciones para no perderse**

▶ **Escribe.** Write instructions telling how to get from one place to another in this city. Specify the starting point.

Modelo *Estás en la iglesia. Para llegar a tu destino tienes que seguir recto…*

 ▶ **Lee y habla.** Now, read your instructions to a partner. If necessary, help him or her along the way.

Did your partner arrive at the right place?

Vocabulario – Un viaje de fin de semana

Activities

33. Ask students to talk about the pros and cons of each mode of transportation. Have students also include in their discussion other modes of transportation not mentioned in the activity (e.g., *bicicleta, autobús, taxi*). Suggest that they organize their comments in a chart like the one below.

Medio de transporte	Ventajas	Desventajas
avión	rápido	contamina, caro

34. In pairs, have students come up with a list of five things these people can do on their vacation. For example: *ir a la oficina de turismo, comprar recuerdos, visitar museos,* etc.

35. For additional practice, ask students to give instructions to a classmate telling him or her how to get from one place or area in the school to another. For example: *Estás en la cafetería. Para llegar a tu destino debes doblar a la derecha al salir de la cafetería…*

 AUDIO SCRIPT
See page XXVH.

Answer Key

33. 1. d   2. a   3. b   4. e   5. c
▶ Answers will vary.

34. 1. a   2. b   3. a   4. a

35. Answers will vary.
▶ Answers will vary.

Additional Resources

Fans Online activities
Practice Workbook

HERITAGE LANGUAGE LEARNERS

• Ask heritage language learners in your class to create a presentation to promote their country of origin—or a region in their country of origin—as a travel destination. For instance, they can create a brochure or a poster with photos and drawings. They can also create a slideshow or a PowerPoint presentation.

• Encourage students to include their recommendations regarding what to bring and information about places to visit, geographical features, cities, etc. Have students present their destination to the class. If time allows, you may have a question and answer session at the end of each presentation.

MULTIPLE INTELLIGENCES:
Naturalist Intelligence

• Have students research environmental issues in their community or in their state and create a report about those issues. Encourage students to describe the problems and discuss proposed solutions. They can create a poster or an audiovisual presentation. Be sure students cite their sources.

4. EXPRESAR LUGAR Y EXISTENCIA

Gramática – Expresar lugar y existencia

Presentation

- In this section, students will review:
  – Adverbs of place.
  – The verbs *estar* and *haber*.

Activities	Standards	Resources
Gramática	1.2, 3.1, 4.1	
36.	1.2	Audio
37.	1.1, 1.2, 5.1	
38.	1.1	

Teaching Suggestions

Warm-Up / Independent Starter

- Have students answer the following questions describing the location of these objects and persons. Ask students to use words such as *encima de, al lado de, cerca de, ahí,* and so on.
  1. *¿Dónde está tu libro de Español?*
  2. *¿Dónde está tu teléfono celular?*
  3. *¿Dónde está tu cuaderno?*
  4. *¿Dónde está el/la profesor(a)?*

Preparation

- Ask for volunteers to share some of their answers from the Independent Starter with the class. Write on the board the adverbs of place students used in their answers and go over the grammar presentation with the class.

- Pass a coin or other small object around and tell students it stands for a frog. Have the student who receives the frog choose a location for it (e.g., under his or her desk, far away from him or her, etc.). Have the student ask a classmate at the other end of the room, *¿Dónde está la rana?* Then the student who answered the question gets the frog and continues with the activity.

- Once the "frog" has gone around the room, take it and place it on your desk. Ask students, *¿Qué hay en mi escritorio?* (*Hay una rana.*) Then remove it from your desk and ask, *¿Hay ranas en mi escritorio?* (*No, no hay ranas en su escritorio.*)

Gramática

Expresar lugar y existencia

La construcción *estar en*

- To say where things are, use the verb estar followed by words that express place. The preposition en expresses location. It is equivalent to the English words *at, in, on,* and *inside.*

  La rana **está en el bosque.**

Adverbios y expresiones de lugar

- Many other words and phrases are used to show location.

¿Dónde está la rana?

aquí · ahí · allí · al lado de la flor · lejos de la flor · cerca de la flor · detrás de la flor · encima de la flor · a la izquierda de la flor · delante de la flor · debajo de la flor · a la derecha de la flor

Expresar existencia. El verbo *haber*

- To say that someone or something exists, use the form hay (*there is, there are*).

  Hay una rana en la flor.   **Hay** muchas ranas en la flor.

- To ask about the existence of something, use hay.

  ¿Hay un río en el bosque?   **¿Hay** pájaros en el árbol?

- The Spanish phrase equivalent to *there isn't* or *there aren't* is no hay.

  No hay un río en el bosque.   **No hay** pájaros en el árbol.

Differentiated Instruction

DEVELOPING LEARNERS

- Ask students to look around and write six sentences telling the location of different items in the room in relation to other items. Have them use the following adverbs of place:
  – *encima de*
  – *al lado de*
  – *lejos de*
  – *debajo de*
  – *detrás de*
  – *a la derecha de*

EXPANDING LEARNERS

- Have students visualize a place (e.g., a forest, a beach, a park). Ask them to write a detailed description specifying how many of each thing there are and where they are located. For example: *Es un parque y hay un árbol cerca de la entrada. Encima del árbol hay dos pájaros. Al lado del árbol hay una ardilla. Etc.*

- Ask students to read their description to a partner, who will then draw the scene. Once students have finished their drawings ask them to show them to their partners. Does the drawing depict the scene the other student had visualized?

36 ¿Dondé está la bolsa?

 ▶ **Escucha y elige.** Choose the image that describes each location you hear about.

 A 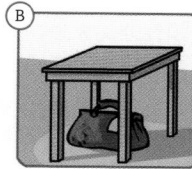 B  C  D

37 ¿Qué lugar es?

▶ **Escribe.** Choose five buildings or places from this picture and write sentences telling where each one is.

Modelo *La plaza está delante del hotel.*

 ▶ **Habla.** Tell a partner the location of each building or place. Your partner will guess what building or place it is.

Modelo A. *Está delante del hotel.*
B. *Es la plaza.*

38 Lo que hay a tu alrededor

 ▶ **Habla.** Tell a partner how many of a certain item there is in your classroom. Your partner will try to guess the item by saying where he or she thinks it is located.

Modelo A. *Hay veinte.*
B. *[Looks around.] ¿Están encima de las mesas?*
A. *Sí.*
B. *Son los libros de Español.*
A. *¡Sí! ¡Muy bien!*

4. EXPRESAR LUGAR Y EXISTENCIA

Gramática – Expresar lugar y existencia

Activities

36. For additional practice with adverbs of place, have students work in pairs. One student puts an object in different places and the other student describes the object's locations. For example: *El libro está debajo de la silla.* If they get a location wrong, they lose their turn to the other student.

37. Have students continue the conversation by describing the location of well-known landmarks in their town. The partner will guess what building it is. For example:
A. *Está a la derecha de la biblioteca.*
B. *Es el café Coffee Time.*

38. To extend this activity, have students ask where in school certain items are located. Then they should ask for the location of the place the partner mentions. For example:
A. *¿Dónde hay balones de baloncesto?*
B. *En el gimnasio.*
A. *¿Y dónde está el gimnasio?*
B. *Está al lado de las oficinas.*

 AUDIO SCRIPT
See page XXVH.

Answer Key

36. 1. B   2. D   3. C   4. A
37. Answers will vary.
▶ Answers will vary.
38. Answers will vary.

Additional Resources

Fans Online activities
Practice Workbook

HERITAGE LANGUAGE LEARNERS

• Heritage language learners probably know and use more adverbs of place than those listed in this lesson (e.g., *alrededor, enfrente, dentro, fuera, arriba, abajo,* etc.). Ask students to make a list of these adverbs and use them to describe the location of different objects and persons in the classroom.

• Explain to students that possessive adjectives should not be used with adverbs of place to describe a person's location. For example:
La maestra está detrás mío. (incorrect)
La maestra está detrás de mí. (correct)

TOTAL PHYSICAL RESPONSE (TPR)

• Have students take out a pencil or other small object. Give them verbal instructions for where to put the pencil. For example:
– *El lápiz está encima de la mesa.* (Students place their pencils on their desks.)
– *El lápiz está aquí, debajo de mi mesa.* (Students move towards the teacher's desk.)
– *El lápiz está detrás del libro.* (Students place their pencils behind their books.)

23

4. EXPRESAR LUGAR Y EXISTENCIA

Gramática – Expresar acciones habituales en el presente. Expresar movimiento

Presentation

- In this section, students will review:
  – First-person irregular verbs.
  – The verb *ir*.

Activities	Standards	Resources
Gramática	1.2, 3.1, 4.1	
39.	1.2	Audio
40.	1.1, 1.2, 3.1	
41.	1.1, 1.2, 1.3	
42.	1.1, 5.1	

Teaching Suggestions

Warm-Up / Independent Starter

- Ask students to write seven sentences describing some of the things they do and don't do when they are on vacation. Have them use the verbs *hacer, salir, traer, poner, conocer, ir,* and *ver.* For example: *Salgo con mis amigos. No voy a la escuela.*

Preparation

- Have students talk with a partner about their statements from the Independent Starter. Do they have similar routines when they are on vacation?
- Go over the verbs in the grammar lesson. Explain that the verb *poner* is also used reflexively (*ponerse*), in which case it means "to put on." For example: *Me pongo una camisa roja.*
- Write the following sentences on the board:
  1. *Sé hablar español.*
  2. *Mi padre se levanta temprano.*
  Clarify that *sé*, the first person singular form of the verb *saber*, has an accent mark to distinguish it from the reflexive pronoun *se*.

Activities

39. To enhance comprehension, have students read the verbs before listening to the audio. Ask them to imagine the scene. What might the characters bring on their trip? What documents might they need and where would they carry them?

Gramática

Expresar acciones habituales en el presente

Verbos irregulares en la primera persona

- Some verbs are irregular in the present tense only in the first person (the *yo* form). The rest of the forms follow the same pattern as the regular verbs.

VERBOS HACER (TO MAKE, TO DO), PONER (TO PUT), TRAER (TO BRING) Y SALIR (TO LEAVE). PRESENTE

		Hacer	Poner	Traer	Salir
Singular	yo	hago	pongo	traigo	salgo
	tú	haces	pones	traes	sales
	usted, él, ella	hace	pone	trae	sale
Plural	nosotros, nosotras	hacemos	ponemos	traemos	salimos
	vosotros, vosotras	hacéis	ponéis	traéis	salís
	ustedes, ellos, ellas	hacen	ponen	traen	salen

- These verbs are also irregular only in the first person:

  conocer *(to be acquainted with)* → yo **conozco**, tú conoces, él conoce…
  saber *(to know)* → yo **sé**, tú sabes, él sabe…
  ver *(to see)* → yo **veo**, tú ves, él ve…

Expresar movimiento

El verbo *ir*

- *Ir* is an irregular verb.
- To say where someone is going, use the verb *ir (to go)* and this formula:

  | *ir a* + place | → **Voy** al lago.

- The verb *ir* is commonly used in combination with other verbs.

  Tengo que ir a la biblioteca.
  Quiero ir al campo.

VERBO IR (TO GO). PRESENTE

Singular		Plural	
yo	voy	nosotros nosotras	vamos
tú	vas	vosotros vosotras	vais
usted él ella	va	ustedes ellos ellas	van

39 ¡Llegamos tarde!

 ▶ **Escucha.** Listen as Carlos and Rosie rush to get ready for a trip, and write the name of the person who does each of the following actions.

1. salir → Carlos
2. hacer
3. poner
4. traer
5. ver
6. ir a

Differentiated Instruction

DEVELOPING LEARNERS

- Before the grammar presentation, review with students the present tense regular *-ar, -er,* and *-ir* conjugations. Point out that there are verbs that follow these conjugations except for the first person singular form (*yo*).
- Explain that the verb *ir* has a very irregular conjugation. Have students answer the following questions in complete sentences:
  1. *¿Adónde vas los fines de semana?*
  2. *¿Adónde tienen que ir tus amigos de lunes a viernes?*
  3. *¿Adónde quieres ir de vacaciones?*

EXPANDING LEARNERS

- Explain that there are many expressions with the verb *ir* in Spanish. Students are probably familiar with most of the following:
  – *ir en* + means of transport: to travel by
  – *ir de compras*: to go shopping
  – *ir de vacaciones / excursión*: to go on vacation / on a field trip
  – *ir con*: to match
  – *ir bien*: to do well
- Ask students to think of situations in which these expressions might be used. Then ask them to work in pairs to come up with sentences illustrating each of these expressions.

40 **Cuando estoy de vacaciones**

▶ **Completa.** Isabel describes her routine when she is on vacation at the beach. Complete her description with the appropriate verbs from the box.

ver
saber
salir ✓
conocer
poner
traer
ir

Un día en la playa

Cuando estoy de vacaciones en la costa, yo _salgo_ temprano del hotel y ___1___ a la playa. Miro a mi alrededor y ___2___ a muchas personas que no se cuidan la piel. No lo entiendo. Yo me ___3___ crema con filtro solar porque yo ___4___ que tomar mucho el sol es peligroso.

Yo no ___5___ a nadie en la playa, así que ___6___ un libro en mi bolsa para leer. A veces también paseo por la playa.

 ▶ **Habla.** Ask two classmates whether they do some of these things when they are on their summer vacation.

Modelo   A. ¿Sales temprano del hotel cuando estás de vacaciones?
          B. No, yo salgo tarde.
          C. Yo también salgo tarde. ¡Me gusta dormir!

 41 **Viajes de fin de semana**

▶ **Escribe.** Answer the following questions in writing regarding your most recent weekend trips.

1. ¿A qué lugares vas?
2. ¿Cómo vas?
3. ¿Haces turismo por el lugar?
4. ¿Conoces gente nueva?
5. ¿Traes recuerdos del lugar?

42 **En mi tiempo libre**

 ▶ **Habla.** Which of these things do you do when you have a few days off? And your partner? Tell each other what you do and when you do it.

1. hacer cámping
2. salir de la ciudad
3. ir de excursión
4. conocer nuevos lugares

¿Vas de excursión en tu tiempo libre?

Sí, me gusta ir al campo.

---

4. EXPRESAR LUGAR Y EXISTENCIA

Gramática – Expresar acciones habituales en el presente. Expresar movimiento

40. Have students write a travel blog entry describing a typical day at their favorite vacation spot. Ask them to use some of the verbs on page 24. Then have students erase or white-out some of those verbs and give their entry to a partner. Can their partner guess the missing verbs?

42. Ask students to write a paragraph comparing what they do with what their partners do when they have time off. For example: *John sale de la ciudad y va de excursión al campo. Yo no salgo de la ciudad. Por lo general voy con mis amigos al cine…* Invite volunteers to read their paragraphs aloud and have the class give a thumbs-up signal to partners who could spend their time off together and a thumbs-down signal to partners who are not compatible.

 AUDIO SCRIPT
See page XXVH.

Answer Key

39.
1. Carlos	4. Rosie
2. Carlos	5. Carlos
3. Rosie	6. Rosie y Carlos

40.
1. voy	4. sé
2. veo	5. conozco
3. pongo	6. traigo

▶ Answers will vary.

41. Answers will vary. Sample answers:
1. Voy a la playa y a la montaña.
2. Voy en coche.
3. Sí, casi siempre hago turismo por el lugar.
4. Sí, conozco a mucha gente.
5. No, nunca traigo recuerdos.

42. Answers will vary.

Additional Resources

Fans Online activities
Practice Workbook

HERITAGE LANGUAGE LEARNERS

• There are many expressions in Spanish with *poner*. For example:
– *poner la mesa*: to set the table
– *poner en duda*: to doubt
– *poner peros:* to find fault
– *poner en peligro*: to endanger
– *ponerse rojo*: to blush

• Have heritage learners create a list of different expressions they know with *poner*. Ask them to include an example of usage for each expression. Then have students combine all their expressions into one big class list to post in the classroom.

MULTIPLE INTELLIGENCES:
Verbal-Linguistic Intelligence

• Have students work in small groups to create a short poem in which they use the first-person irregular verbs from this lesson. They may, for instance, describe a typical day when they are on vacation. For example:
Me pongo crema en la piel
y salgo pronto del hotel.
Traigo un libro para leer,
y más tarde voy a comer.

• Ask students to read their poem aloud in their groups and listen for rhyme and rhythm. Then invite volunteers to recite their poems in front of the class.

REPASO

Presentation

- In this section, students will review the contents of this Preliminary Unit.

Activities	Standards	Resources
1.	1.2	
2.	1.2	
3.	1.3	
4.	1.3	
5.	1.3	
6.	1.3	
7.	1.2, 1.3	
8.	1.2	

Teaching Suggestions

Warm-Up / Independent Starter

- Have students work in pairs. Ask them to read the objectives for this unit and then come up with an example for each objective. If time allows, have students share their examples with the rest of the class.

Preparation

- Ask students to use this review section as a mock test to measure how well they know the material reviewed in this unit. They should mark the questions for which they do not know the answers before going back into the unit to review.

Activities

1. To extend this activity, ask students to list all the phrases that they know for saying goodbye. Then have students create a dialogue using two of the phrases they listed.

3. Have students choose two people from the picture and add a personality description for each one.

5. Ask students to include information in their ads about price, materials (e.g., *lana, algodón, cuero*), available sizes and colors, etc.

8. Have students choose three of these activities and ask them to write sentences describing how often they do them. For example: *En el verano nado en el lago todos los días. Casi nunca voy de excursión al campo.*

26

Repaso

1 **Completa.** Complete these dialogues with appropriate words from the box.

gusto	llamas	tengo	presento	llamo	años	días

1. – Buenos ____1____.
   – ¡Hola!
2. – Te ____2____ a Carlos.
   – Mucho ____3____.

3. – ¿Cómo te ____4____?
   – Me ____5____ Paula.
4. – ¿Cuántos ____6____ tienes?
   – ____7____ catorce años.

2 **Une.** Match each action with the appropriate item.

(A)
1. Hablo con
2. Escribo con
3. Leo
4. Veo la hora en
5. Llevo los libros en

(B)
a. un reloj.
b. una mochila.
c. mis compañeros.
d. un bolígrafo.
e. un libro.

3 **Escribe.** Look at the picture and write a description of each person, referring to their physical characteristics and how you think they are feeling in the picture.

Alfonso
Jaime
Sonia
Eva

4 **Escribe y ordena.** Express how much you like or dislike each of these foods. Then organize them from the least to the most liked.

1 2 3 4 5 6

Differentiated Instruction

DEVELOPING LEARNERS

- If students were not able to perform certain tasks, this will be a good indication that they need to spend additional time reviewing the corresponding structures and vocabulary. Ask students to list the areas in which they need improvement.

- Review with students different learning strategies (e.g., creating flashcards and verb charts, looking for cognates, using multimedia, etc.). Then ask them to choose the strategies that work best for them and have them apply these strategies to review the areas in which they need reinforcement.

EXPANDING LEARNERS

- Ask students to prepare their own short mock quiz for this unit. Have them develop questions and activities for each of the topics reviewed. Encourage students to come up with different types of activities. They should also prepare an Answer Key. You may wish to check students' quizzes before they give them to classmates.

- Have students exchange their quizzes with a classmate and test each other. Once they have finished ask them to give the quiz back to the author for correction. Have students discuss their results.

5 **Decide y diseña.** Decide who would wear each of these clothing items, and in what situation he or she would wear it. Then design an ad with a description of two items.

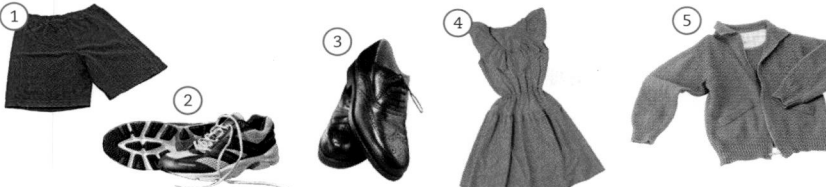
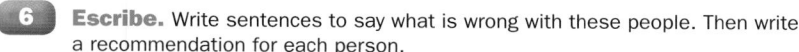

6 **Escribe.** Write sentences to say what is wrong with these people. Then write a recommendation for each person.

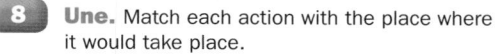

7 **Contesta.** Answer the following questions in complete sentences. Then say which of these activities you like and how often you do each of them.

1. ¿Qué actividades de ocio te gusta hacer en tu tiempo libre? Escribe cuatro.
2. ¿Qué aparato usamos normalmente para tomar fotos? ¿Y para grabar un video?
3. ¿Adónde van las personas a ver una película?
4. ¿Qué necesitas para jugar al tenis? ¿Y para jugar al béisbol?
5. ¿Qué deportes puedes practicar solo? Escribe tres.

8 **Une.** Match each action with the place where it would take place.

A	B
1. ir de excursión	a. la agencia de viajes
2. nadar	b. la tienda
3. cruzar la calle	c. el campo
4. facturar el equipaje	d. el lago
5. comprar un boleto	e. la estación de tren
6. reservar habitación	f. la ciudad
7. comprar recuerdos	g. el aeropuerto

veintisiete **27**

Answer Key

1.
1. días
2. presento
3. gusto
4. llamas
5. llamo
6. años
7. Tengo

2. 1. c   2. d   3. e   4. a   5. b

3. Answers will vary. Sample answer:
Jaime es rubio, alto, delgado y joven. Él está contento y emocionado.

4. Answers will vary. Sample answers:
1. Me gustan bastante las verduras.
2. No me gusta nada el pescado.
3. Me gustan poco los huevos.
4. Me gustan mucho las papas.
5. Me gustan mucho las frutas.
6. Me gusta bastante el pollo.

5. Answers will vary. Sample answers:
1. Un hombre lleva estos pantalones cortos cuando hace deporte.
2. Un chico lleva estos tenis cuando sale a jugar o a caminar, o cuando va a la escuela.
3. Un hombre lleva estos zapatos para ir a trabajar o a una fiesta.
4. Una mujer lleva este vestido cuando va a una fiesta.
5. Una mujer o un hombre llevan esta chaqueta en invierno cuando hace frío.

6. Answers will vary. Sample answers:
1. Le duele la espalda. Debe descansar.
2. Le duele la cabeza. Debe tomar medicamentos.
3. Le duele el estómago. Debe comer alimentos saludables.
4. Tiene fiebre. Debe ir al médico.
5. Le duelen los pies. Debe descansar.

7. Answers will vary.

8.
1. c
2. d
3. f
4. g
5. e
6. a
7. b

Additional Resources

Fans Online activities
Practice Workbook

Unit 1 Centroamérica

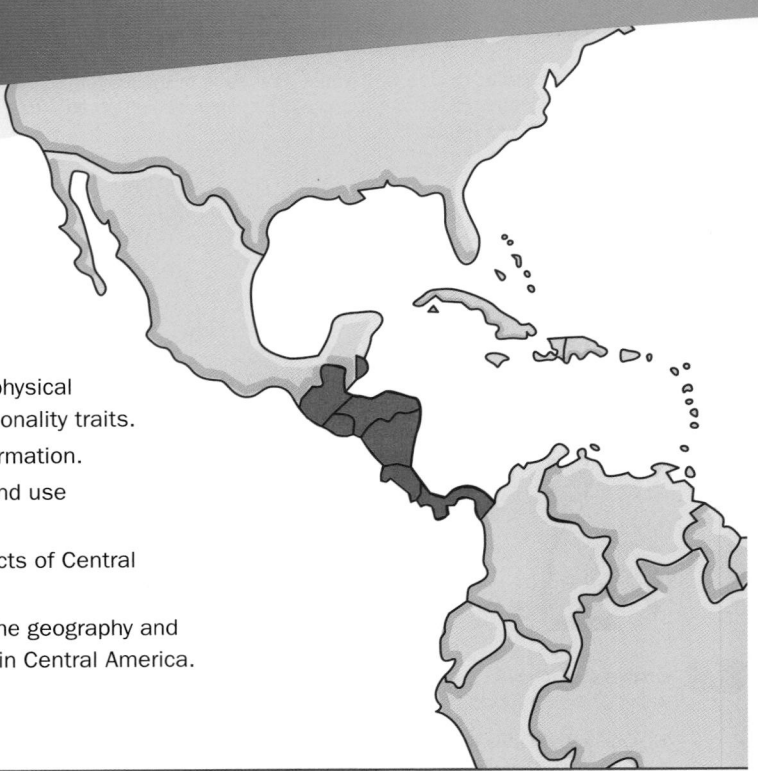

Objectives

- To identify yourself and others.
- To describe people.
- To express states of being and feelings.
- To ask questions.
- To use expressions to introduce oneself, to express admiration of someone and to express joy and fun.
- To describe family members and personal relationships.

- To describe a person's physical characteristics and personality traits.
- To provide personal information.
- To make comparisons and use superlatives.
- To explore cultural aspects of Central America.
- To acquire facts about the geography and history of the countries in Central America.

Contents

Vocabulary
- Personal introductions, expressing admiration, expressing feelings and emotions.
- Family members and personal relationships.
- Physical characteristics and personality traits.
- Emotional states and feelings.
- Personal information.

Grammar
- Possessive adjectives and pronouns.
- Adjectives and nouns.
- Comparisons and superlatives.
- To ask questions: Interrogatives.

Culture
- Central American geography and cultures.
- Lake Atitlán.
- Godparents.
- *Los garífunas*.
- International System of Measurement.
- Honduran linguistic diversity.
- *La gigantona y el enano cabezón*.
- *Popol Vuh*.
- *Rincón de la Vieja* National Park.
- Surnames.
- National Palace of Culture in Managua.

Evaluation Criteria

- Introduce oneself and others.
- Express admiration of someone's traits.
- Express personal feelings and emotions.
- Identify family members.
- Describe someone's physical characteristics and personality traits.
- Express states of being and feeling.
- Provide personal information.
- Recognize and use possessive adjectives and pronouns.

- Recognize and use adjectives that agree in gender and number with the nouns they modify.
- Compare people and things to express equality, inequality, and extreme degrees of an adjective.
- Recognize and use interrogatives when asking and responding to questions.
- Express understanding of the role of *padrinos*.

- Express understanding of selected Central American customs, geographical aspects, and historical facts.
- Calculate height and weight using the International System of Measurement.
- Write a poem to describe yourself.
- Identify the main idea of a text.
- Write a short story about an imaginary character.

Unit Plan

La llegada

Estimated time: 1 session.

Dialogue: *En Managua.*

Functions & forms:
- To introduce oneself.
- To express admiration of someone.
- To express feelings and emotions.

Culture:
- Managua, Nicaragua.
- *Parque Rubén Darío.*

DESAFÍO 1

Estimated time: 4 sessions.

Dialogue: *El gigante maya de Atitlán.*

Functions & forms:
- Family and personal relationships.
- Possessive adjectives and pronouns.

Culture:
- *El lago de Atitlán.*
- *Los padrinos.*

DESAFÍO 2

Estimated time: 4 sessions.

Dialogue: *Un garífuna peculiar.*

Functions & forms:
- Physical characteristics and personality traits.
- Adjectives.

Culture:
- *Los garífunas.*
- *El Sistema Internacional de Medidas.*
- *Diversidad lingüística.*

DESAFÍO 3

Estimated time: 4 sessions.

Dialogue: *La mujer más alta de León.*

Functions & forms:
- Emotional states and feelings.
- Comparisons and superlatives.

Culture:
- *La gigantona y el enano cabezón.*
- *Popol Vuh.*
- *Rubén Darío.*

DESAFÍO 4

Estimated time: 4 sessions.

Dialogue: *Un viaje arbóreo.*

Functions & forms:
- Personal information.
- To ask questions: Interrogatives.

Culture:
- *Rincón de la Vieja.*
- *Los apellidos.*

TODO JUNTO/El encuentro

Estimated time: 1 session.

Dialogue: *En el Palacio Nacional de Cultura.*

Functions & forms:
- Review of *Desafíos 1–4.*

Culture:
- National Palace of Culture in Managua, Nicaragua.

MAPA CULTURAL/LECTURA

Estimated time: 1 session.

Mapa cultural: *Centroamérica.*

Reading: *El blog de Ichxel.*

PROYECTO

Estimated time: 1 session.

Project: *Una historia sobre personajes de Guatemala.*

Unit 1 Centroamérica

Standards for Learning Spanish

COMMUNICATION

1.1 Interpersonal mode
- Discuss the challenge for each team in Central America.
- Speculate on which pair will win the challenge.
- Discuss what students know about Central America.
- Talk about the geographical features included in a legend.
- Interview a classmate.
- Play a guessing game with a classmate.
- Survey the class on a particular subject.

1.2. Interpretive mode
- Take notes from an audio recording.
- Read a cultural text and extract pertinent information.
- Summarize information in a written text.
- Read a poem and summarize from the web.

1.3. Presentational mode
- Write a postcard to a friend.
- Write a poem.
- Write a summary of a pair's challenge.
- Present an original short story based on characters in a painting.
- Develop a personal profile.
- Develop a diagram around the five critical questions of a familiar story.

CULTURE

2.1. Practices and perspectives
- Discuss prior knowledge of Central America.
- Read about the Mayan legend of creation.
- Read about the use of surnames.
- Research the influence of Mestizos on Central American cuisine.

2.2. Products and perspectives
- Discuss the impact of a Nicaraguan poem.
- Research the influence of Mestizos on Central American clothing.

CONNECTIONS

3.1. Interdisciplinary connections
- Acquire knowledge of Central American geography.
- Work on a Venn diagram.
- Convert meters and kilos into feet and pounds.
- Discuss the auxiliary verb in English.
- Identify the main idea of a text.
- Write a short story.

3.2. Viewpoints through language / culture
- Read a cultural text in Spanish.
- Read a postcard from a foreign friend.
- Read a Rubén Darío poem.
- Read the blog of a Mayan teenager.

COMPARISONS

4.1. Compare languages
- Compare possessives in English and Spanish.
- Compare the position of adjectives in English and Spanish.
- Compare irregular comparative adjectives.
- Compare interrogative sentence patterns in English and in Spanish.

4.2. Compare cultures
- Discuss cultural sharing.
- Discuss festivals which use street puppets in the United States and in other countries.
- Compare myths and legends from different cultures.
- Discuss ecotourism.

COMMUNITIES

5.1. Spanish within and beyond the school setting
- Create a relationship web using photos and clippings.
- Discuss languages spoken in the student's community.
- Based on two personality profiles, determine the best person suited to be class president.

5.2. Spanish for lifelong learners
- Plan an ecotourism trip.
- Write a poem.
- Research Central American topics.

Communicative Skills

Interpersonal Mode

		Activities
Speaking	• Engage in conversation with a classmate. • Describe people. • Interview a classmate. • Initiate a guessing game with another student. • Tell a story to a classmate.	• 4, 12, 34, 38, 42, 62, 82 • 17, 24, 33 • 12, 56, 66, 73, 77, 82 • 39, 53 • 76
Writing	• Write a paragraph to describe people. • Write dialogues.	• 37 • 57, 59
Listening	• Understand questions and sentences and respond appropriately. • Understand simple descriptions.	• 77, 82 • 23, 36
Reading	• Understand the information in a blog, e-mail, or postcard. • Understand simple texts that describe people and/or feelings.	• 19, 58, 80, 81, *Lectura* • 19, 34, 58, 80, 81

Interpretive Mode

		Activities
Listening	• Understand and obtain basic information from a conversation. • Understand oral descriptions. • Interpret audio and video about culture.	• 2, 12, 16, 46, 51, 55, 61, 74 • 10, 18, 23, 26, 36, 43, 55, 79 • *Tu desafío, videos*
Reading	• Understand brief written exchanges. • Infer meanings based on a cultural text. • Demonstrate comprehension of the main ideas of a text. • Reflect on and explain cultural topics in relation to personal experience. • Understand cultural texts by identifying the global idea of a text.	• 1, 6, 11, 21, 22, 41, 60 • 9, 13, 25, 30, 35, 44, 49, 54, 63 • 8, 19, 22, 28, 34, 40, 41, 42, 58, 60, 80, 81, 85, 90 • 9, 13, 25, 35, 44, 49, 54, 63, 67 • *Lectura*

Presentational Mode

		Activities
Speaking	• Act out a short skit aloud. • Present or represent emotion by acting. • Present information to the class.	• 21, 57, 75, 78 • 45, 48, 57 • 12, 20, 77, 82, *Proyecto*
Writing	• Write descriptive sentences or texts. • Write a story or a summary of events. • Write questions or answers about personal information. • Write a list of personality traits. • Summarize the results of a survey.	• 37, 47, 53, 81 • 83, *Proyecto* • 61, 66, 75 • 59 • 56

Cross-Curricular Standards

Subject	Standard	Activities
Language Arts	• Compare elements of English grammar with Spanish equivalents. • Write a poem.	• 14, 31, 50, 68 • 84
Social Studies	• Read and research about the geography and cultural topics of Central American countries.	• 85, 86
Art History	• Study a work by a Guatemalan artist.	• *Proyecto*
Math	• Convert meters and kilos into feet and pounds.	• 30

Lesson Plans (50-Minute Classes)

Day	Objectives	Sessions	Activities	Time	Standards	Resources / Homework
1	To introduce Central America and to discuss the pairs' challenges	**Centroamérica / La llegada** (28–33) • Warm-Up: Region orientation • *Centroamérica* • Images and functions • Presentation: *En Managua* • *Expresiones útiles* and *¿Quién ganará?*	 1 2–5	5 m. 5 m. 10 m. 10 m. 20 m.	1.1, 1.2, 1.3, 2.1, 2.2, 3.1, 3.2, 4.1	Visual Presentation Audio Video Practice Workbook
2	To identify oneself and others	**Desafío 1 – El gigante maya de Atitlán** (34–35) • Warm-Up: Independent Starter • *Fotonovela: El gigante maya de Atitlán* • *Cultura: El lago de Atitlán*	 6–8 9	 5 m. 35 m. 10 m.	1.1, 1.2, 1.3, 2.1, 3.1, 3.2, 4.1, 5.1, 5.2	Visual Presentation Audio Video *Tu desafío*
3	To talk about family and personal relationships	**Desafío 1 – Vocabulario** (36–37) • Warm-Up: Independent Starter • *Vocabulary: Relaciones familiares y personales* • *Cultura: Los padrinos*	 10–12 13	 5 m. 35 m. 10 m.	1.1, 1.2, 1.3, 3.1, 3.2, 4.2	Audio Practice Workbook
4	To learn and use possessive adjectives and pronouns	**Desafío 1 – Gramática** (38–39) • Warm-Up: Independent Starter • *Grammar: Los posesivos*	 14–17	 5 m. 45 m.	1.1, 1.2, 1.3, 3.1, 4.1	Audio Practice Workbook
5	To integrate vocabulary and grammar and to assess student proficiency	**Desafío 1 – Comunicación / Evaluación** (40–41) • Warm-Up: Independent Starter • *Comunicación:* Review • *Final del desafío* • Quiz on *Desafío 1*	 18–20 21	 5 m. 20 m. 10 m. 15 m.	1.2, 1.3, 2.2, 5.1	Audio Practice Workbook
6	To describe people	**Desafío 2 – Un garífuna peculiar** (42–43) • Warm-Up: Independent Starter • *Fotonovela: Un garífuna peculiar* • *Cultura: Los garífunas*	 22–24 25	 5 m. 35 m. 10 m.	1.1, 1.2, 1.3, 2.2, 3.1, 3.2, 4.2	Visual Presentation Audio *Tu desafío*
7	To speak about physical characteristics and personality traits	**Desafío 2 – Vocabulario** (44–45) • Warm-Up: Independent Starter • *Vocabulary: Características físicas y rasgos de personalidad* • *Conexiones: El Sistema Internacional de Medidas*	 26–29 30	 5 m. 35 m. 10 m.	1.1, 1.2, 1.3, 2.1, 3.1, 3.2	Audio Practice Workbook
8	To learn and use adjectives and nouns	**Desafío 2 – Gramática** (46–47) • Warm-Up: Independent Starter • *Grammar: Los adjetivos y el nombre* • *Comunidades: Diversidad lingüística*	 31–34 35	 5 m. 35 m. 10 m.	1.1, 1.2, 1.3, 2.1, 3.2, 4.1, 4.2, 5.1	Practice Workbook
9	To integrate vocabulary and grammar and to assess student proficiency	**Desafío 2 – Comunicación / Evaluación** (48–49) • Warm-Up: Independent Starter • *Comunicación:* Review • *Final del desafío* • Quiz on *Desafío 2*	 36–39 40	 5 m. 20 m. 10 m. 15 m.	1.1, 1.2, 1.3, 2.1, 5.1, 5.2	Audio Practice Workbook *Tu desafío*

Day	Objectives	Sessions	Activities	Time	Standards	Resources / Homework
10	To express emotional states and feelings and to make comparisons and use superlatives	**Desafío 3 – *La mujer más alta de León*** (50–51) • Warm-Up: Independent Starter • *Fotonovela: La mujer más alta de León* • *Cultura: La gigantona y el enano cabezón*	41–43 44	5 m. 35 m. 10 m.	1.1, 1.2, 1.3, 2.1, 2.2, 3.2, 4.2, 5.1	Visual Presentation Audio Video
11	To talk about emotional states and feelings	**Desafío 3 – *Vocabulario*** (52–53) • Warm-Up: Independent Starter • *Vocabulary: Estados de ánimo y sentimientos* • *Cultura: Popol Vuh*	45–48 49	5 m. 35 m. 10 m.	1.1, 1.2, 1.3, 2.1, 3.1, 3.2, 5.1	Audio Practice Workbook
12	To make comparisons and to use superlatives	**Desafío 3 – *Gramática*** (54–55) • Warm-Up: Independent Starter • *Grammar: Las comparaciones y el superlativo* • *Conexiones: Rubén Darío*	50–53 54	5 m. 35 m. 10 m.	1.1, 1.2, 1.3, 2.2, 3.1, 3.2, 4.1, 5.1	Audio Practice Workbook *Tu desafío*
13	To integrate vocabulary and grammar and to assess student proficiency	**Desafío 3 – *Comunicación / Evaluación*** (56–57) • Warm-Up: Independent Starter • *Comunicación: Review* • *Final del desafío* • Quiz on *Desafío 3*	55–58 59	5 m. 20 m. 10 m. 15 m.	1.1, 1.2, 1.3, 2.2, 5.1	Audio Practice Workbook
14	To ask questions	**Desafío 4 – *Un viaje arbóreo*** (58–59) • Warm-Up: Independent Starter • *Fotonovela: Un viaje arbóreo* • *Conexiones: Rincón de la Vieja*	60–62 63	5 m. 35 m. 10 m.	1.1, 1.2, 1.3, 2.1, 2.2, 3.1, 3.2, 4.2, 5.1, 5.2	Visual Presentation Audio
15	To ask for and give personal information	**Desafío 4 – *Vocabulario*** (60–61) • Warm-Up: Independent Starter • *Vocabulary: Información personal* • *Cultura: Los apellidos*	64–66 67	5 m. 35 m. 10 m.	1.1, 1.2, 1.3, 2.1, 3.2	Practice Workbook
16	To learn and use interrogatives	**Desafío 4 – *Gramática*** (62–63) • Warm-Up: Independent Starter • *Grammar: Los interrogativos*	68–73	5 m. 45 m.	1.1, 1.2, 1.3, 3.1, 4.1	Audio Practice Workbook
17	To integrate vocabulary and grammar and to assess student proficiency	**Desafío 4 – *Comunicación / Evaluación*** (64–65) • Warm-Up: Independent Starter • *Comunicación: Review* • *Final del desafío* • Quiz on *Desafío 4*	74–77 78	5 m. 20 m. 10 m. 15 m.	1.1, 1.2, 1.3, 3.1, 5.1	Audio Practice Workbook *Tu desafío*
18	To integrate language in context	**Todo junto / El encuentro** (66–69) • Warm-Up: Independent Starter • *Todo junto* • *El encuentro: En el Palacio Nacional de Cultura*	79–82 83–84	5 m. 20 m. 25 m.	1.1, 1.2, 1.3, 2.1, 2.2, 3.2, 5.1, 5.2	Audio Practice Workbook
19	To learn about Central American customs and traditions	**Mapa cultural / Lectura** (70–73) • Warm-Up: Independent Starter • *Mapa cultural: Centroamérica* • *Lectura: El blog de Ichxel*	85–86 87–90	5 m. 20 m. 25 m.	1.2, 1.3, 2.1, 2.2, 3.1, 3.2, 5.2	Video Practice Workbook *Tu desafío* Project work
20	To write a short story	**Proyecto** (78–79) • Warm-Up: Prepare project presentations • Project presentations		10 m. 40 m.	1.1, 1.2, 1.3, 2.1, 2.2, 3.1, 5.1	Practice Workbook **Repaso – *Vocabulario*** (74–75) **Repaso – *Gramática*** (76–77) **Autoevaluación** (79)

Lesson Plans (90-Minute Classes)

Day	Objectives	Sessions	Activities	Time	Standards	Resources / Homework
1	To introduce Central America and to identify oneself and others	***Centroamérica / La llegada*** (28–33) • Warm-Up: Region orientation • *Centroamérica* / Images and functions • Presentation: *En Managua* • *Expresiones útiles* and *¿Quién ganará?*	 1 2–5	10 m. 15 m. 30 m. 35 m.	1.1, 1.2, 1.3, 2.1, 2.2, 3.1, 3.2, 4.1	Visual Presentation Audio Video Practice Workbook
2	To talk about family and personal relationships	***Desafío 1 – El gigante maya de Atitlán / Vocabulario*** (34–37) • Warm-Up: Independent Starter • *Fotonovela: El gigante maya de Atitlán* • *Cultura: El lago de Atitlán* • Vocabulary: *Relaciones familiares y personales* • *Cultura: Los padrinos*	 6–8 9 10–12 13	 5 m. 30 m. 10 m. 35 m. 10 m.	1.1, 1.2, 1.3, 2.1, 3.1, 3.2, 4.2, 5.1, 5.2	Visual Presentation Audio Video Practice Workbook *Tu desafío*
3	To learn and use possessive adjectives and pronouns, to integrate vocabulary and grammar, and to assess student proficiency	***Desafío 1 – Gramática / Comunicación / Evaluación*** (38–41) • Warm-Up: Independent Starter • Grammar: *Los posesivos* • *Comunicación:* Review • *Final del desafío* • Quiz on *Desafío 1*	 14–17 18–20 21	 5 m. 30 m. 30 m. 10 m. 15 m.	1.1, 1.2, 1.3, 2.2, 3.1, 4.1, 5.1	Audio Practice Workbook
4	To describe people and to talk about physical characteristics and personality traits	***Desafío 2 – Un garífuna peculiar / Vocabulario*** (42–45) • Warm-Up: Independent Starter • *Fotonovela: Un garífuna peculiar* • *Cultura: Los garífunas* • Vocabulary: *Características físicas y rasgos de personalidad* • *Conexiones: El Sistema Internacional de Medidas*	 22–24 25 26–29 30	 5 m. 30 m. 10 m. 35 m. 10 m.	1.1, 1.2, 1.3, 2.1, 2.2, 3.1, 3.2, 4.2	Visual Presentation Audio Practice Workbook *Tu desafío*
5	To learn and use adjectives, to integrate vocabulary and grammar, and to assess student proficiency	***Desafío 2 – Gramática / Comunicación / Evaluación*** (46–49) • Warm-Up: Independent Starter • Grammar: *Los adjetivos y el nombre* • *Comunidades: Diversidad lingüística* • *Comunicación:* Review • *Final del desafío* • Quiz on *Desafío 2*	 31–34 35 36–39 40	 5 m. 25 m. 10 m. 25 m. 10 m. 15 m.	1.1, 1.2, 1.3, 2.1, 3.2, 4.1, 5.1, 5.2	Audio Practice Workbook *Tu desafío*
6	To talk about emotional states and feelings	***Desafío 3 – La mujer más alta de León / Vocabulario*** (50–53) • Warm-Up: Independent Starter • *Fotonovela: La mujer más alta de León* • *Cultura: La gigantona y el enano cabezón* • Vocabulary: *Estados de ánimo y sentimientos* • *Cultura: Popol Vuh*	 41–43 44 45–48 49	 5 m. 35 m. 10 m. 30 m. 10 m.	1.1, 1.2, 1.3, 2.1, 2.2, 3.1, 3.2, 4.2, 5.1	Visual Presentation Audio Video Practice Workbook

Day	Objectives	Sessions	Activities	Time	Standards	Resources / Homework
7	To make comparisons, to use superlatives, to integrate vocabulary and grammar, and to assess student proficiency	**Desafío 3 – Gramática / Comunicación / Evaluación** (54–57) • Warm-Up: Independent Starter • Grammar: *Las comparaciones y el superlativo* • *Conexiones: Rubén Darío* • *Comunicación:* Review • *Final del desafío* • Quiz on *Desafío* 3	 50–53 54 55–58 59	 5 m. 25 m. 10 m. 25 m. 10 m. 15 m.	1.1, 1.2, 1.3, 2.2, 3.1, 3.2, 4.1, 5.1	Audio Practice Workbook *Tu desafío*
8	To ask questions and ask for and give personal information	**Desafío 4 – Un viaje arbóreo / Vocabulario** (58–61) • Warm-Up: Independent Starter • *Fotonovela: Un viaje arbóreo* • *Conexiones: Rincón de la Vieja* • Vocabulary: *Información personal* • *Cultura: Los apellidos*	 60–62 63 64–66 67	 5 m. 35 m. 10 m. 30 m. 10 m.	1.1, 1.2, 1.3, 2.1, 2.2, 3.1, 3.2, 4.2, 5.1, 5.2	Visual presentation Audio Practice Workbook
9	To learn and use interrogatives, to integrate vocabulary and grammar, and to assess student proficiency	**Desafío 4 – Gramática / Comunicación / Evaluación / Todo junto** (62–67) • Warm-Up: Independent Starter • Grammar: *Los interrogativos* • *Comunicación:* Review • *Final del desafío* • Quiz on *Desafío* 4 • *Todo junto*	 68–73 74–77 78 79–82	 5 m. 20 m. 25 m. 5 m. 15 m. 20 m.	1.1, 1.2, 1.3, 3.1, 4.1, 5.1	Audio Practice Workbook *Tu desafío*
10	To integrate language in context and to learn about Central American customs and traditions	**El encuentro / Mapa cultural / Lectura** (68–73) • Warm-Up: Independent Starter • *El encuentro: En el Palacio Nacional de Cultura* • *Mapa cultural: Centroamérica* • *Lectura: El blog de Ichxel*	 83–84 85–86 87–90	 5 m. 30 m. 25 m. 30 m.	1.2, 1.3, 2.1, 2.2, 3.1, 3.2, 5.1, 5.2	Audio Video Practice Workbook *Tu desafío* **Repaso – Vocabulario** (74–75) **Repaso – Gramática** (76–77) Project work
11	To write a short story and to assess student proficiency	**Proyecto / Assessment** (78–79) • Warm-Up: Prepare project presentations • Project presentations • *Autoevaluación* • Test		 10 m. 40 m. 10 m. 30 m.	1.1, 1.2, 1.3, 2.1, 2.2, 3.1, 5.1	

Unit 1 Centroamérica

2 Conversaciones

1. Mi hermana es ingeniera y habla inglés, francés y español.
2. Ustedes tienen que viajar a Costa Rica.
3. ¿Eres Jonás?
4. Mira, este es un actor muy famoso.

7 ¿Quién habla?

1. Mi hermano y yo estamos muy emocionados de estar en Guatemala. ¡Qué maravilla!
2. El lago es un lugar mágico. Mi esposa y yo vivimos aquí.
3. Mi hermana dice que estamos cerca del gigante. Yo digo que los gigantes no existen, pero no me gusta discutir.
4. Y cuentan que aquí vive una serpiente enorme.

10 La familia de Andy

Hola, soy Andy y tengo dieciocho años. Soy de los Estados Unidos; de Atlanta, Georgia. Tengo una hermana mayor. Se llama Janet y tiene veintiséis años. Janet no está casada y no tiene hijos, pero ella es la madrina de Alison, nuestra prima. Alison tiene cuatro años. Mi padre se llama Gary; es profesor de Matemáticas. Y mi madre, Marcela; es profesora de Música. ¡Ellos están casados desde hace casi treinta años!

16 Los preparativos

1. –¿De quién es esta mochila? ¿Es tuya, Janet?
   –No, la mía es roja. Esa mochila es de Andy.
2. –Ese es el pasaporte de Mack, ¿no?
   –Sí, ese es su pasaporte.
3. –Tess, Patricia, ¿estas son sus chaquetas?
   –Sí, son las nuestras, gracias.
4. –¿Esta cámara es tuya, Diana?
   –No, no es mía.
   –¿Es tuya, Rita?
   –Sí, es mi cámara. ¡Gracias!
5. –¿Dónde están nuestros tenis, abuelo?
   –Los míos están en la maleta y los tuyos son estos.

18 Relaciones familiares

1. Mi abuelo tiene 68 años. Él es muy simpático y siempre hacemos cosas juntos. Me ayuda con mi tarea y me compra regalos para mi cumpleaños.
2. Mi hermana y yo discutimos por todo. No nos llevamos muy bien.
3. Mi mamá y mi papá están casados hace veinte años. Ellos se quieren mucho. Somos una familia muy feliz.

23 ¿Cómo es?

1. Mira, te presento a Juan Carlos. Él es un músico garífuna de Honduras.
2. Estas son sus hijas, Elena y María. Son jóvenes y bonitas.

3. Esta es su esposa. Se llama Flora y también es garífuna. Es profesora.
4. Y estos son los padres de Flora. Son mayores, pero muy activos.

26 Descripciones

1. Es un chico joven, fuerte, muy alto y calvo.
2. Es una chica rubia, un poco tímida. No es ni alta ni baja.
3. Es una señora rubia muy simpática.
4. Es un señor mayor muy gracioso. Lleva gafas y no tiene bigote.
5. Ella es morena y tiene el pelo largo. Es muy trabajadora.

36 Gente de Honduras

1. María es rubia y tiene el pelo corto. Lleva gafas.
2. Tomás es alto y fuerte. Tiene barba.
3. Miguel es alto y calvo. No es muy mayor.
4. Lina es rubia. Tiene el pelo largo.

43 Comparaciones

Tess y Patricia son rubias, pero Tess es más rubia que Patricia y tiene el pelo más largo. Las dos son altas, pero Patricia es más alta que Tess. Normalmente Tess está más contenta que Patricia, pero hoy no. Hoy Tess está menos contenta porque está más frustrada. ¡No encuentran a la mujer más alta de León! Patricia está muy nerviosa. ¡Más nerviosa que Tess!

46 ¿Cómo están hoy?

1. –¿Qué tal, Nico, cómo te va?
   –¡Genial! Tenemos un partido de fútbol esta tarde, ¡y vamos a ganar!
2. –Hola, Ana, ¿qué tal estás?
   –Estoy a punto de acostarme. Todos los días me levanto muy temprano para ir a trabajar.
3. –Hola, Luis, ¿qué tal tu hermano?
   –No me hables de mi hermano… Discutimos todo el tiempo.
4. –¿Cómo estás, María?
   –No sé… Mañana es el examen de Matemáticas y tengo mucho que estudiar. Quiero sacar buenas notas, ¡pero estudié poco!

51 Muy cansadas

–Tess, nuestro desafío es muy difícil. Tú estás muy cansada. Creo que estás más cansada que yo.
–No, mamá. Tú también estás muy cansada. Siempre corres por la mañana. Por eso yo estoy menos cansada que tú.
–Bueno, no importa. ¡Las dos estamos cansadísimas!

55 El día de Tess

–Hola, John, soy Tess.
–Hola, Tess, ¿cómo estás?
–No me siento bien, estoy enferma. Por eso no puedo ir al cine contigo. Quiero ir, pero no puedo.
–¡Pobrecita! ¿Qué tienes?

–No sé, pero estoy muy cansada y aburrida.

–Entonces tienes que descansar. Nos vemos mañana. ¡Cuídate!

–Sí, gracias. Hasta mañana.

61 **En una oficina**

–Hola. Buenos días.

–Buenos días, señor. ¿En qué puedo ayudarlo?

–Quiero inscribirme para hacer un *tour*.

–Muy bien. ¿Cuál es su nombre?

–Me llamo Mack.

–¿Y sus apellidos?

–Mi apellido es Taylor.

–Muy bien. ¿Me dice su fecha de nacimiento?

–El siete de marzo.

–Perfecto, gracias.

70 **Preguntas y respuestas**

1. Me llamo Isabel.
2. Ahora vivo en California.
3. Soy de El Salvador.
4. Estudio Economía.

74 **Una entrevista por televisión**

–Tenemos aquí al señor Mack Taylor, que está con su nieto Tim en Costa Rica en un desafío cultural. Bienvenido, Mack.

–Gracias, muy amable.

–Dígame, señor Taylor, ¿es la primera vez que viene usted a Costa Rica?

–No, no es la primera vez. Es la segunda. Estuve aquí el año pasado.

–¿Y le gusta Costa Rica?

–Sí, me gusta mucho. Es un país muy bonito.

–Muchas gracias, qué amable. Ustedes están aquí para completar un desafío para Fans del español, ¿no es cierto?

–Sí, eso es.

–¿Es un desafío difícil?

–No, no es difícil. Tengo que montar en tirolina.

–¿Y no tiene usted miedo?

–No.

–Estupendo. ¿Participa su nieto también en el desafío?

–Sí. Mi nieto Tim y yo hacemos juntos todos los desafíos.

–Pues mucha suerte.

–Gracias.

79 **¿Quién habla?**

1. Esta es mi familia. Mi esposa, Carmen, es rubia, está un poco gordita y es muy bonita. Tenemos dos hijos, una chica y un chico. Se llaman Cristina y Félix. Cristina es rubia, como su madre. Félix es alto y delgado y lleva gafas.

2. Les voy a presentar a mi familia. Mis papás son Manuel y Elena. Los dos son morenos. Mi papá tiene bigote. Yo también soy moreno, pero mi hermana Silvia no. Ella es rubia.

3. ¿Quieren conocer a mi familia? Mi esposo se llama Roberto. Es bastante alto, moreno y muy guapo. Todos en la familia somos bastante altos. Roberto y yo tenemos dos hijos: Javi y Tania. Javi es muy delgado y Tania es rubia y delgada.

4. ¡Hola! Me llamo Teresa. En casa somos cuatro. Tengo un hermano mayor. Se llama Agustín y es un chico muy fuerte. Mi papá es también muy fuerte y tiene barba. Mi mamá es pelirroja, como yo.

Unit 1
Centroamérica

The Unit

- The theme for Unit 1 is personal and family life in the context of Central America.
- The pairs meet their host, the poet Felipe Santos, in Managua, Nicaragua, to receive their tasks in Central America.
  - *Desafío 1.* Andy and Janet will travel to San Pedro de Atitlán, a village in Guatemala, in search of a giant.
  - *Desafío 2.* Diana and Rita will travel to Travesía, Honduras, where they will visit a Garífuna community in search of a musician with a gift for them.
  - *Desafío 3.* Tess and Patricia will travel to León, Nicaragua. They must find the tallest woman in a community of over 100,000 people.
  - *Desafío 4.* Tim and Mack will travel to Rincón de la Vieja National Park in Costa Rica, where they must ride a zip line over the jungle.

Activities	Standards	Resources
Centroamérica	1.2, 2.1, 2.2, 3.1, 3.2	Video

Teaching Suggestions

Warm-Up / Independent Starter

- Ask students to look at a map and list all of the countries that constitute Central America and their capital cities. Then ask students to take note of the places to which the four pairs will travel. Have students describe the location of the challenges in relation to the capital cities in complete sentences in Spanish.

Central America

- Central America consists, from north to south, of Belize, Guatemala, El Salvador, Honduras, Nicaragua, Costa Rica, and Panama. This part of the Western Hemisphere is located between the Pacific Ocean and the Caribbean Sea, an arm of the Atlantic Ocean. Central America is bordered by Mexico to the north and Colombia to the south.

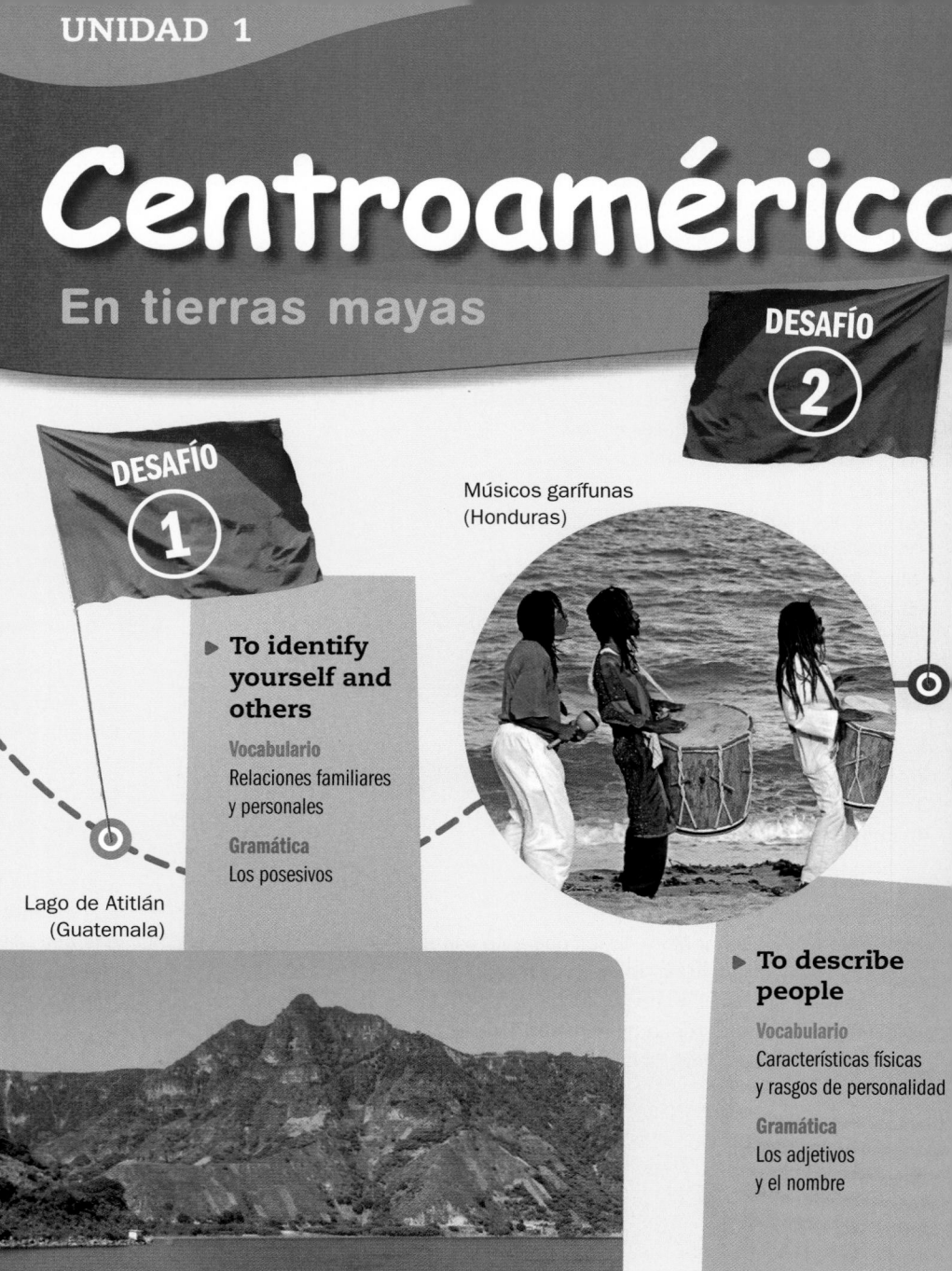

UNIDAD 1

Centroamérica
En tierras mayas

DESAFÍO 1

▶ **To identify yourself and others**

Vocabulario
Relaciones familiares y personales

Gramática
Los posesivos

Lago de Atitlán (Guatemala)

DESAFÍO 2

Músicos garífunas (Honduras)

▶ **To describe people**

Vocabulario
Características físicas y rasgos de personalidad

Gramática
Los adjetivos y el nombre

The Challenge

DESAFÍO 1

Lago Atitlán

Lake Atitlán is a large lake located in the Guatemalan highlands. It is recognized as the deepest lake in Central America, and is also one of the main sources of income for the region due to its role as a major tourist attraction. The lake is shaped by the deep slopes that surround it and by three volcanoes on its southern shore: Atitlán, Tolimán, and San Pedro. One of the unique characteristics of Lake Atitlán is a strong wind known as Xocomil, which is generally felt around noon.

DESAFÍO 2

Músicos garífunas

The Garinagu, or Garifuna people, are descendants of the Carib and Arawak indigenous populations of the Caribbean and African slaves. They were expelled from Saint Vincent, in the Lesser Antilles, in the 18th century for fighting the British, and settled on the island of Roatán, in Honduras. Today they live primarily along the Caribbean coast, in Belize, Guatemala, Honduras, and Nicaragua. There are also Garifuna communities in the United States.

Centroamérica

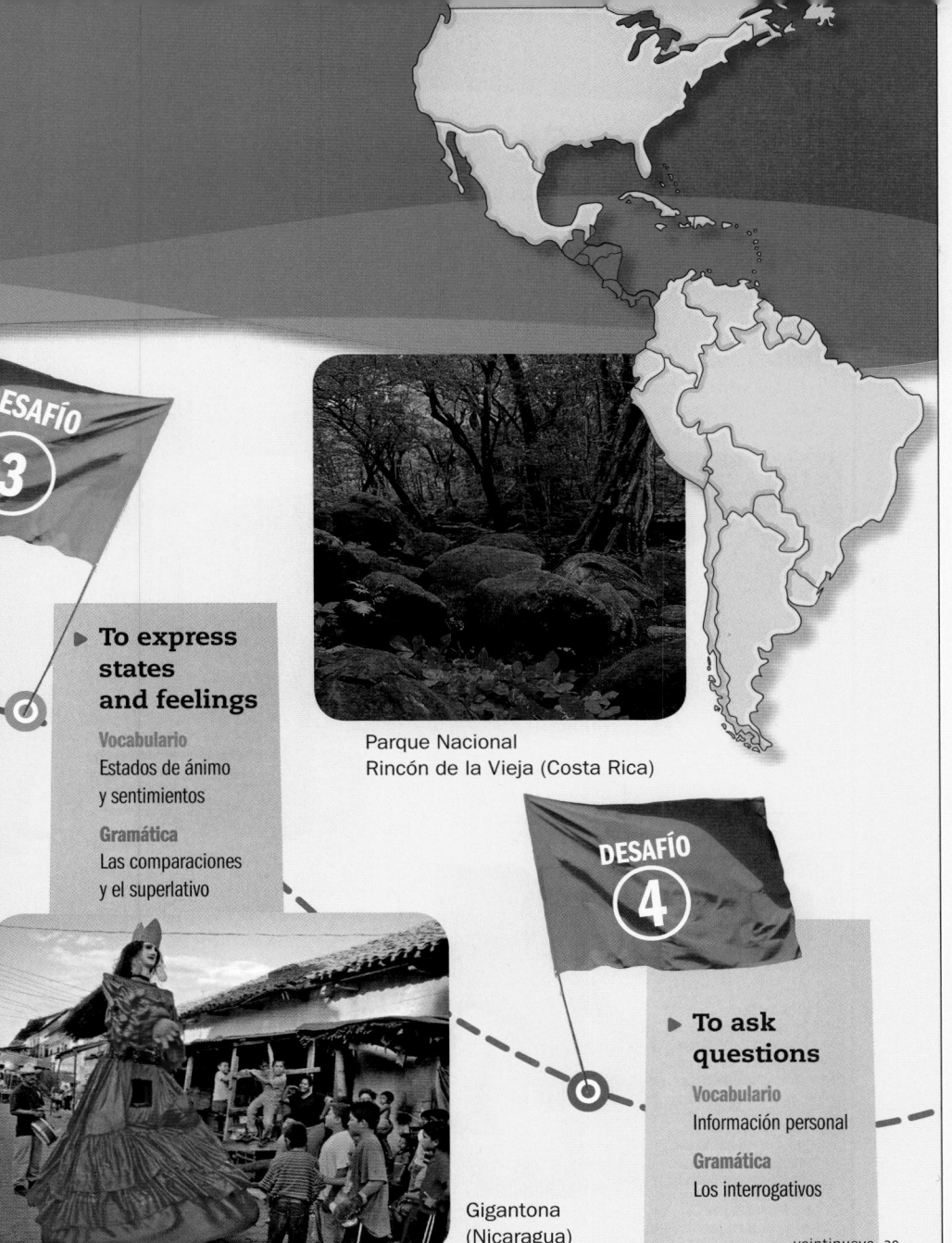

DESAFÍO

3

▶ **To express states and feelings**

Vocabulario
Estados de ánimo y sentimientos

Gramática
Las comparaciones y el superlativo

Parque Nacional
Rincón de la Vieja (Costa Rica)

DESAFÍO

4

▶ **To ask questions**

Vocabulario
Información personal

Gramática
Los interrogativos

Gigantona
(Nicaragua)

veintinueve **29**

- Focus students' attention on the map on the top of the page. Ask them to comment about other characteristics of Central America. For example, size and nearby islands (Cuba, the Dominican Republic, Haiti, Jamaica, and Puerto Rico).

Picture Discussion

- Ask students to look at the pictures. Has anyone in the class ever been to any of the places pictured or participated in any of the activities? Encourage students to share their experiences.

Lago Atitlán (Guatemala)

- Ask the class to look closely at the mountain. Do students notice anything special about the mountain? Does it look like a mountain in the United States that they know of?

Músicos garífunas (Honduras)

- Ask students if by looking at this picture they would immediately think of Honduras. There are several groups of Spanish-speaking people of African descent in Central America. Ask students why they think that is and where most of these descendants live. To guide students in answering this question, have them observe the map of Central America, paying special attention to the Caribbean coast of Belize, Guatemala, Honduras, and Nicaragua.

Gigantona (Nicaragua)

- Draw students' attention to the height of the *gigantona*. Ask students how they think she can stand that tall. Then discuss what students think this figure represents. Call their attention to the figure's dress and hairstyle to guide the discussion.

Parque Nacional Rincón de la Vieja (Costa Rica)

- The themes for this *Desafío* are personal information and question words. Ask students how they think a national park would apply to these themes. This picture gives us insight into what the grounds of the park look like, but do students think the view would be the same if it were from above the trees?

Objectives

- By the end of Unit 1, students will be able to
  - Identify themselves and others.
  - Describe people.
  - Express states and feelings.
  - Ask questions.
  - Understand and talk about different cultural aspects of Central America.

DESAFÍO 3

Gigantona

The city of León is an important center of commerce and industry in Nicaragua. The *gigantona* and the *enano cabezón* are representations of people from colonial times who make appearances at León's festivals. The *gigantona* is a three-meter (almost ten feet) tall figure who represents a Spanish lady, complete with dress and jewelry. Her height represents the power the Spaniards had over the indigenous population. The *enano cabezón* represents the indigenous people, short in stature yet very intelligent.

DESAFÍO 4

Parque Nacional Rincón de la Vieja

The Rincón de la Vieja Volcano National Park lies in the northwestern part of Costa Rica. Visitors can take advantage of thermal mud pools, freshwater lakes, and waterfall swimming areas. The park has a large variety of wildlife, including over 300 species of birds, such as the crested guan, military macaw, laughing falcon, emerald toucanet, and various quetzals and eagles. Mammals seen in the park include spider and howler monkeys, jaguars, collared anteaters, margays (a spotted cat), peccaries, and many more.

Unit 1
La llegada

Presentation

- This section presents the pairs' arrival in Central America. They will meet their host, poet Felipe Santos, at the *Rubén Darío Park* in Managua, Nicaragua.

- Students will see vocabulary in context, with pictures and illustrations. Presenting new words in this manner helps students develop their Spanish vocabulary with background knowledge while engaging them with the context.

Activities	Standards	Resources
Fotonovela	1.2, 2.2	Vis. Pres.
1.	1.2, 3.1	

Teaching Suggestions

Warm-Up / Independent Starter

- Ask students to read through the *fotonovela* and classify the words as noun (*nombre*), verb (*verbo*), and adjective (*adjetivo*). Copy the following chart on the board for students to use as a template.

Nombre	Verbo	Adjetivo
Felipe Santos	soy	guapo

Preparation

- Acquaint or reacquaint students with the four pairs.
  - Andy and Janet Douglas are a brother and sister pair from Atlanta, GA.
  - Diana Robles and Rita Delgado are a niece and aunt pair from Lawrenceville, NJ.
  - Tess and Patricia Williams are a daughter and mother pair from San Antonio, TX.
  - Tim and Mack Taylor are a grandson and grandfather pair from San Francisco, CA.

- All four pairs are *fans del español* and have traveled to Mexico, Puerto Rico, Guatemala, Peru, Spain, the United States, Argentina, and Chile seeking to further their knowledge of the Spanish language and the different cultures associated with the people who speak Spanish. This year the pairs have decided to travel to different regions throughout the Spanish-speaking world. The first region they will visit is Central America.

30

En Managua

 The pairs gather at *Parque Rubén Darío*, in Managua, the capital city of Nicaragua. The park is named after a famous Nicaraguan poet who lived in the early twentieth century. Their host, Felipe Santos, is a poet himself.

30 treinta

Differentiated Instruction

DEVELOPING LEARNERS

- Have students go through the dialogue and write the words they do not know in their notebook. Then students will look up these words in a Spanish-English dictionary. After students have finished looking up these words, have them re-read the dialogue to see if they understand it better the second time.

EXPANDING LEARNERS

- Ask students to choose a scene from the *fotonovela* and rewrite it as if they were present in the scene. They must introduce themselves and add a line to the dialogue.

Y ustedes son...

Yo soy Diana y ella es Rita. Soy su sobrina.

Ustedes tienen que encontrar a un músico garífuna en Honduras. Él es moreno y lleva gafas.

Gari... ¿qué?

Ustedes son Tess y Patricia, ¿verdad? Tienen que buscar a una mujer altísima de León, aquí, en Nicaragua.

¿Cómo es ella?

Y ustedes son los famosos Mack y Tim. Su misión es en Costa Rica.

¡Qué bien! ¡Estoy emocionado!

Ah, y todos tienen que traer un poema sobre su desafío. ¡Buena suerte!

1 **¿Comprendes?**

▶ **Elige** la palabra correcta.

1. Managua es la capital de **Nicaragua / Honduras**.
2. El **nombre / apellido** de dos personajes es Douglas.
3. Mack está **emocionado / frustrado**.
4. El músico garífuna es **moreno / rubio** y lleva gafas.
5. Tess y Patricia tienen que encontrar a una mujer muy **alta / morena**.
6. La misión de Mack y Tim es en **Costa Rica / Nicaragua**.

treinta y uno **31**

◉ La fotonovela

Before Viewing

- Ask a volunteer to read the introduction to the *fotonovela*. Then ask students why they believe it is significant for Felipe Santos to ask the pairs to meet him at the *Rubén Darío Park*. The answer is that Felipe Santos is a Nicaraguan poet, as was Rubén Darío.

- Remind students of some of the reading and listening strategies from Level 1, which are to look for cognates, to recognize prefixes and suffixes, and to check the dictionary for unknown words.

After Viewing

- With a show of hands, ask students if they understood the main ideas of the *fotonovela*. Ask a volunteer to summarize what happened at the park in Managua.

Activities

1. Once students have finished this activity, have them rewrite the sentences with the correct answer. For example:
   1. *Managua es la capital de Nicaragua.*

Answer Key

1. 1. Managua es la capital de <u>Nicaragua</u>.
2. El <u>apellido</u> de dos personajes es Douglas.
3. Mack está <u>emocionado</u>.
4. El músico garífuna es <u>moreno</u> y lleva gafas.
5. Tess y Patricia tienen que encontrar a una mujer muy <u>alta</u>.
6. La misión de Mack y Tim es en <u>Costa Rica</u>.

Additional Resources

Fans Online activities
Practice Workbook

HERITAGE LANGUAGE LEARNERS

- Rubén Darío is a famous Nicaraguan poet. Ask students to research famous poets from the other countries the pairs will visit in Central America (Guatemala, Honduras, and Costa Rica). Have them answer the following questions in a brief paragraph.
  – *¿Cuándo nació / murió?*
  – *¿Cuál es su país de origen?*
  – *¿Cuáles son los temas de su poesía?*

CRITICAL THINKING

- Ask students why they believe the pairs changed from all visiting the same country to all visiting different countries within a region. Write all the students' theories on the board and vote on one theory for the class.

Unit 1
La llegada

Presentation

- In this section, students will learn useful expressions to introduce themselves, to express admiration of someone, and to express feelings and emotions.

Activities	Standards	Resources
Expresiones útiles	1.2, 1.3, 4.1	
2.	1.2, 1.3	Audio
3.	1.2, 1.3	
4.	1.2, 1.2, 2.1	
5.	1.1, 1.3	

Teaching Suggestions

Warm-Up / Independent Starter

- Have students look at the *expresiones útiles*, and relate each *expresión* to an expression they already know. For example: *Yo soy...* → *Me llamo...*

Preparation

- Go over the *Expresiones útiles* section with students. Be sure to enunciate each word, as some have more than three syllables.
- Have students get into pairs to create a six-line conversation using the *expresiones útiles*. Ask students to practice their conversations and invite volunteer pairs to role-play their dialogue.

Activities

2. Play the audio two times. Tell students to simply listen for the correct answers the first time and mark their answers the second time.

3. Ask students to write all the other expressions that would apply to each photo. Then have students write a scenario that would go along with each photo. For example: *A la chica le gusta mucho el actor Robert Pattinson. ¡Qué guapo!*

¿Quién ganará?

4. Have students get into small groups and discuss the pairs' challenges. Ask groups to look at the pictures, read the captions, and write a brief paragraph about what they believe the pairs will do in their challenges. They must also come to a consensus on which challenge will be the group's favorite and where this challenge will take place. Have each group read their paragraph aloud.

32

EXPRESIONES ÚTILES

Estoy emocionado.
¡Qué maravilla!

To introduce oneself:
Yo soy...   Mi nombre es...
Nosotros somos... Nuestro apellido es...

To express admiration of someone:
¡Qué guapo!   ¡Qué inteligente!
¡Qué alta!   ¡Qué simpático!

To express joy and fun:
¡Qué bien!   ¡Qué emocionante!
¡Qué maravilla!   ¡Qué divertido(a)!

2 **Conversaciones**

▶ **Escucha** y decide. ¿Qué respuesta *(answer)* es más apropiada en cada caso?

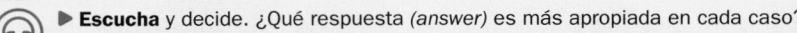

a. ¡Qué maravilla! **b.** Sí. Mi apellido es Brown. **c.** ¡Qué inteligente! **d.** ¡Qué guapo!

3 **¿Qué dicen?**

▶ **Relaciona** las expresiones con las fotografías.

 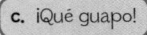

a. ¡Qué divertido!   **b.** ¡Qué estudioso!   **c.** ¡Qué guapo!

Differentiated Instruction

DEVELOPING LEARNERS

- Ask students to look through old magazines to find photos or illustrations of people and situations that represent the expressions with *¡Qué!* in the *Expresiones útiles* section. Have students paste the images on sheets of paper and label them with a sentence using the appropriate expression. Then ask students to read their sentences aloud. Students may refer to these illustrated expressions whenever needed.

EXPANDING LEARNERS

- Give students more practice with the expressions in the *Expresiones útiles* section by having them work with a partner to develop a dialogue. In their conversation, they should introduce themselves, make at least two statements of admiration toward each other, and express feelings and emotions appropriate to the context of the dialogue. Encourage students to go beyond the vocabulary presented on the page, and use words from previous lessons.

¿Quién ganará?

4 **Los desafíos**

▶ **Habla.** ¿Cuál será el desafío de cada pareja? Piénsalo y coméntalo con tus compañeros(as).
What will the challenge be for each pair? Think about this question and discuss it with your classmates.

DESAFÍO ①
El gigante maya de Atitlán
Andy y Janet

DESAFÍO ②
Un garífuna peculiar
Diana y Rita

DESAFÍO ③
La mujer más alta de León
Tess y Patricia

DESAFÍO ④
Un viaje arbóreo
Tim y Mack

▶ **Habla.** ¿En qué países son los desafíos? ¿Qué sabes de esos lugares? Coméntalo con tus compañeros(as).
Which countries will the challenges be in? What do you know about those places? Talk to your classmates.

5 **La tarea final**

▶ **Decide.** ¿Qué tarea tienen que hacer los personajes al final? ¿Qué pareja crees que ganará?
What task do the characters have to do? Who do you think will win?

LA TAREA
Un poema

---

5. Students have been provided a clue as to what the pairs will have to do to win the *Desafío* in Central America. The clue is *un poema*. As a class, have students discuss what they think the challenge in Central America entails. Invite volunteers to share with the class what they know about poetry and writing poems. Which do they think is more complex, writing prose or poetry? Based on the class discussion, have students vote for the pair they feel will win the challenge. Tally the results of the vote.

 AUDIO SCRIPT
See page 271.

Answer Key

2. 1. c   2. a   3. b   4. d
3. 1. c   2. a   3. b
4. Answers will vary.
   ▶ Answers will vary.
5. Answers will vary.

Additional Resources

Fans Online activities
Practice Workbook

HERITAGE LANGUAGE LEARNERS

• Ask students to describe situations in which they would use each of the following expressions: *¡Qué emocionante! ¡Qué bien! ¡Qué maravilla! ¡Qué divertido! ¡Qué amable!* They should write or say their descriptions in one or two complete sentences. Encourage students to add two or three more expressions with *¡Qué!*, and to describe the situation in which they would use each one.

MULTIPLE INTELLIGENCES:
Intrapersonal Intelligence

• Ask students to write journal entries that reflect their moods and feelings during the past few days. They should describe situations that they experienced during this time and then use the appropriate expressions with *¡Qué!* to summarize the emotions they felt.

33

Unit 1
DESAFÍO 1
Identificarte e identificar a otros

Presentation

- In *Desafío 1*, Andy and Janet are in San Pedro de Atitlán, in Guatemala. They have to find a Mayan giant along the shores of Lake Atitlán.

- In this section, students will preview:
  - Words for family members.
  - Relationships within the family.
  - Possessive adjectives and pronouns.

Activities	Standards	Resources
Fotonovela	1.2, 3.1, 3.2	Vis. Pres.
6.	1.2	
7.	1.2	Audio
8.	1.2, 1.3, 2.1, 3.2	
9. Cultura	1.1, 1.2, 2.1, 3.1, 3.2	Video
Tu desafío	1.2, 3.2, 5.1, 5.2	

Teaching Suggestions

Warm-Up / Independent Starter

- Have students read the following situations and write the *expresión útil* that best describes the situation.
  1. *Tu hermano cumple 16 años.*
  2. *El actor más guapo del mundo visita tu escuela.*
  3. *Vas a montar en bicicleta con tus amigos.*
  4. *Te presentas a un nuevo estudiante.*
  5. *Sacas una A en un examen muy difícil.*

Preparation

- Read the introduction to the *fotonovela* aloud to the class. Ask students if that was what they thought the challenge was going to be when they saw the picture on the *¿Quién ganará?* page. Ask students if they think this challenge is more or less interesting now that they know what it is.

 La fotonovela

Before Viewing

- Ask for a male and a female volunteer to read the parts of Andy and Janet in the *fotonovela*.

After Viewing

- Have students write a short paragraph to summarize what happened in the *fotonovela* based on what they heard from their peers and they saw in the visual presentation. Ask for volunteers to share their summary with the class.

34

El gigante maya de Atitlán

Andy and Janet are in San Pedro de Atitlán, a village in Guatemala on the shores of the deepest lake in Central America. They must walk along the shore of the lake and find a Mayan giant.

> Este lugar es mágico para los mayas. Lo dicen la señora del hotel y su esposo.

> Los padres mayas cuentan a sus hijos que en el lago hay una serpiente enorme.

> Sí, pero aquí no hay gigantes. El desafío nuestro es imposib[le].

> No hay nada imposible, hermano. Creo que estamos cerca del gigante.

> No, Janet, no hay gigantes. Los gigantes no existen.

> ¡Mira las montañas! Voy a tomar una foto con mi cámara.

> Sí existen, Andy.

> Si tú lo dices, hermana... No me gusta discutir.

6 **Detective de palabras**

Continuará...

▶ **Completa** estas oraciones.

1. Los _____ mayas hablan de una serpiente enorme.
2. Los _____ mayas escuchan leyendas (*legends*) sobre el lago.
3. La señora del hotel y su _____ dicen que el lago es mágico.
4. Al _____ de Janet no le gusta discutir.

34   treinta y cuatro

Differentiated Instruction

DEVELOPING LEARNERS

- Ask students to work with a partner and role-play the characters in the speech bubbles from the *fotonovela*. Be sure students use proper intonation and tone to match each character's point of view. Call on some pairs to present their dramatizations in front of the class.

EXPANDING LEARNERS

- Ask students to role-play Janet's and Andy's points of view with respect to the legend surrounding Lake Atitlán in the form of a debate. One student (Janet) will defend the legend of the giant. The other (Andy), will dismiss the legend and argue that giants do not exist. You might want to give each speaker two minutes to present his or her arguments and another minute or two for rebuttal.

7 **¿Quién habla?**

 ▶ **Escucha** y decide. ¿Quién está hablando?

Ⓐ

Ⓑ

Ⓒ

Ⓓ

8 **Los misterios de Atitlán**

▶ **Responde** a estas preguntas.
1. ¿A quiénes cuentan historias sobre el lago los padres mayas?
2. ¿Quién dice que el lago es mágico?
3. ¿Qué dice Andy sobre su desafío?
4. ¿Qué quiere fotografiar Janet?

 **CULTURA**

El lago de Atitlán

El lago de Atitlán está en Guatemala, en una zona donde viven muchos mayas. Es un lago muy profundo de origen volcánico.

Hay muchos cuentos y leyendas antiguas sobre la historia y el origen de este lago.

Volcán Tolimán y lago de Atitlán.

9 **Piensa y explica.** ¿Por qué crees que el lago de Atitlán y otros lugares similares son el origen de tantas leyendas?

 **→ TU DESAFÍO** Visita la página web para aprender más sobre el lago de Atitlán.

HERITAGE LANGUAGE LEARNERS

• Ask students to imagine they are TV reporters at the scene by Lake Atitlán. They have been hearing rumors that a giant has been sighted at the lake, and they are there to investigate. They will need to interview a few residents and tourists, and then make a presentation of their findings to their local television station. Students will work in groups, playing the part of reporter(s), residents, and tourists. Encourage students to use expressions with *¡Qué!* to reflect their emotions.

CRITICAL THINKING

• Invite all students to participate in a discussion about why they think legends are often used to describe the origins of things, why they have survived through the centuries, and why they continue to interest so many people. Encourage all students to share what else they know about legends.

Identificarte e identificar a otros

Activities

8. Ask students to cover up the *fotonovela* as they answer the questions.

9. Have students think about the urban legends that surround the bodies of water that are nearest to your town. When and where do students think these legends began? If students don't know of any, then pose this question: If you began to circulate a story about a lake, how long would it take for it to become an urban legend?

 AUDIO SCRIPT
See page 271.

 CULTURA

El lago de Atitlán

Lake Atitlán occupies a caldera, formed by a voluminous volcanic eruption and the subsequent collapse of the volcanic cone thousands of years ago. There are numerous small towns, mainly inhabited by Mayas, on the perimeter of this lake. Each of these towns has its own character. Santiago, for instance, is known for its local artist community and San Pedro La Laguna is famous with backpackers who appreciate its natural beauty and low-key lifestyle.

Answer Key

6. 1. padres 2. hijos 3. esposo 4. hermano

7. 1. C 2. A 3. D 4. B

8. 1. Los padres mayas les cuentan historias sobre el lago a sus hijos.
2. La señora del hotel y su esposo dicen que el lago es mágico.
3. Dice que el desafío es imposible.
4. Janet quiere fotografiar las montañas.

9. Answers will vary.

Additional Resources

Fans Online activities

Unit 1
DESAFÍO 1

Vocabulario – Relaciones familiares y personales

Presentation

■ In this section, students will learn words for family members and relationships within the family.

Activities	Standards	Resources
Vocabulario	1.2	
10.	1.2	Audio
11.	1.2	
12.	1.1, 1.3	
13. Cultura	1.1, 1.2, 1.3, 2.1, 3.2, 4.2	

Teaching Suggestions

Warm-Up / Independent Starter

■ Have students answer the following questions about Andy and Janet.
  1. *¿Dónde están Andy y Janet ahora?*
  2. *¿Qué tienen que hacer en ese lugar?*
  3. *¿Qué relación de familia tienen Andy y Janet?*

Preparation

■ Say the words in the vocabulary presentation aloud and ask students to repeat after you. Listen carefully for students' pronunciation of the words. If they do not repeat a word correctly, then repeat it again before moving on.

■ As you read the words, ask students to raise their right hand every time they hear a review word, their left hand every time they hear a new word, or not to raise either hand if they are unsure.

■ Have students write the Spanish words for family members along with the names of the people in their families that fit the words. For example, *la prima* → cousin Mary.

Activities

10. If the statement is true, have students add an extra detail about that person to the sentence. For example: 2. *Janet está soltera y es la hermana de Andy.*

12. Have students interview more than one classmate. See how many classmates each student can interview in 10 minutes. The student with the most information about his or her classmates wins.

36

Vocabulario

Relaciones familiares y personales

Este es mi abuelo Mack.

Sí, Tim es mi nieto.

Andy y yo somos hermanos. A veces discutimos, pero nos llevamos bien.

Yo soy Rita. Mi sobrina y yo somos de New Jersey.

Esta chica es mi hija.

Sí, Patricia es mi madre. Mi padre está en San Antonio.

la madre
el padrino
la madrina
el bebé
el padre

Estado civil

Nosotros estamos casados.

estar **soltero**
estar **casado**

el esposo
la esposa

10 **La familia de Andy**

 ▶ **Escucha** y decide si estas oraciones sobre la familia de Andy son ciertas *(true)* o falsas *(false)*. Si son falsas, corrígelas.
1. Andy es el hermano de Janet.
2. Janet está soltera.
3. Alison es la sobrina de Janet.
4. La esposa de Gary se llama Marcela.
5. La madre de Andy y Janet es profesora de Matemáticas.

Differentiated Instruction

DEVELOPING LEARNERS

• To reinforce the vocabulary, ask students the following questions.
  1. *¿Quién es el nieto de Mack?* (Tim)
  2. *¿Quién es el hermano mayor de Janet?* (Andy)
  3. *¿Quién es la hija de Patricia?* (Tess)
  4. *¿Quién es la sobrina de Rita?* (Diana)
  5. *¿Quién es el abuelo de Tim?* (Mack)
  6. *¿Cuál es el estado civil de Janet?* (soltera)
  7. *¿Quién es el esposo de la señora Santos?* (Felipe Santos)
  8. *¿Quién es la madre de Tess?* (Patricia)

EXPANDING LEARNERS

• Ask students to create a fictitious family, based on the relationships introduced in this lesson. Have them assign names to each member, and draw a portrait of each one. Then have students work with a partner to ask and answer questions about their fictitious families. For example:
  A. *¿Quién es José?*
  B. *José es el abuelo de Marta. Marta es su nieta.*
  A. *¿Quién es la madrina de Marta?*
  B. *Julia es su madrina.*

11 **Relaciones**

▶ **Completa** estas oraciones.

1. Andy y Janet son ___hermanos___. Se llevan ___1___.
2. Patricia es la ___2___ de Tess.
3. El señor Santos no está soltero, está ___3___.
4. Tim es el ___4___ de Mack.
5. Diana es la ___5___ de Rita.
6. El ___6___ de Patricia está en San Antonio.

▶ **Escribe** oraciones similares sobre tu familia.

Modelo *Mi hermano se llama Frank. Nos llevamos mal.*

12 **Encuesta familiar**

▶ **Pregunta** a tu compañero(a) sobre su familia. Toma notas para presentar la información a tus compañeros(as).

Modelo

> ¿Cuántos hermanos tienes?

> Tres: dos hermanas y un hermano.

- número de hermanos
- nombre de los abuelos
- número de primos
- lugar donde viven los tíos favoritos

- número de sobrinos
- nombre del familiar favorito
- nombre del familiar con quien discutes más

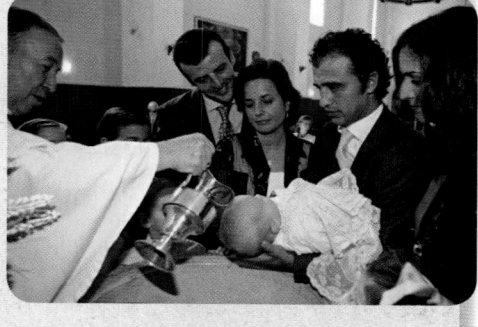

CULTURA
Los padrinos

En los países hispanos las familias cristianas celebran el bautizo (*baptism*) de los bebés.
Para la ceremonia los padres eligen a dos familiares o dos buenos amigos como padrinos del bebé.
Los padrinos actúan como «padres simbólicos» y son una parte importante en la vida del niño.

13 **Piensa y explica.** ¿Tienes padrinos? ¿A quiénes elegirías (*would you choose*) tú como padrinos? ¿Por qué?

HERITAGE LANGUAGE LEARNERS

- Ask students to describe the special relationship young people in Spanish-speaking countries might have with their godparents. Students should be prepared to describe the ceremonies the *padrinos* attend for their *ahijado* or *ahijada*, the traditions they observe, and the relationship they have with the parents of their godchildren.

SPECIAL-NEEDS LEARNERS

- For students with receptive language problems, have them classify all the nouns, along with their definite articles, in a two-column chart. Ask students to label the first column *Masculino* and the second, *Femenino*. Then guide them as they complete each column with the corresponding article and noun. For example, in the first column: *el abuelo, el nieto, los hermanos, el padre, el padrino, el bebé, el esposo*; in the second column: *la sobrina, la chica, la hija, la madre, la madrina, la esposa.*

DESAFÍO 1

Vocabulario – Relaciones familiares y personales

13. The idea of having godparents is not just a religious rite. Ask students what other functions godparents might have. Although some answers may be comical, such as "to buy me gifts for my birthday," other answers may include "to take care of me in case something happens to my parents," or "to give me advice when I don't want to talk to my parents."

 AUDIO SCRIPT
See page 271.

 CULTURA

Los padrinos

In certain Christian denominations, a child's parents select godparents as witnesses to the child's baptism. In Judaism, godparents serve as witnesses to the male child's circumcision ceremony. In Chinese tradition, a child is matched with a godparent who cannot have children of his or her own. Regardless of the nature of the godparents' duties, each child has a loving extended family that will be an important part of his or her life.

Answer Key

10. 1. Falso   4. Cierto
2. Cierto   5. Falso
3. Falso

11. 1. bien   4. nieto
2. madre   5. sobrina
3. casado   6. esposo
▶ Answers will vary.

12. Answers will vary.

13. Answers will vary.

Additional Resources

Fans Online activities
Practice Workbook

DESAFÍO 1

Gramática – Los posesivos

Presentation

- In this section, students will learn to express ownership with possessive adjectives and pronouns.

Activities	Standards	Resources
Gramática	3.1	
14.	1.3, 3.1, 4.1	
15.	1.2, 1.3	
16.	1.2	Audio
17.	1.1, 1.3	

Teaching Suggestions

Warm-Up / Independent Starter

- Ask students to write a five-sentence paragraph about the people they live with in their household and how they get along.

Preparation

- Read over the grammar presentation with students.
- Play a game with students. Hold up your pen, and ask one student, *¿De quién es este bolígrafo?* The student should say, *Es tu (su) bolígrafo.* Then pass the pen to him or her and say, *Ahora es el tuyo.* Now that student needs to continue the process with your pen. He or she may add one of his or her own pens to make the answer plural. See how many times you can go around the room without stopping the chain.
- Write the possessive adjectives in English on the board in a chart similar to this one. Have students compare the chart on the board to the Spanish chart in the textbook.

Personal Pronouns	Possessive Adjectives	Possessive Pronouns
I	my	mine
you	your	yours
he	his	his
she	her	hers
it	its	its
we	our	ours
you	your	yours
they	their	theirs

38

Gramática

Los posesivos

Los adjetivos posesivos

- Possessives (adjectives and pronouns) are used to show ownership.

  Esta es **mi** mochila.   Esa es **mi** escuela.

- Possessive adjectives can be placed before or after the noun they accompany, but some forms change depending on their position.

  Carlos es **mi** primo.   Carlos es un primo **mío**.

ADJETIVOS POSESIVOS

	ANTES DEL NOMBRE (mi tío)				DESPUÉS DEL NOMBRE (un tío mío)			
	Singular		Plural		Singular		Plural	
	Masculino	Femenino	Masculino	Femenino	Masculino	Femenino	Masculino	Femenino
my	mi		mis		mío	mía	míos	mías
your (inf.)	tu		tus		tuyo	tuya	tuyos	tuyas
his, her your	su		sus		suyo	suya	suyos	suyas
our	nuestro	nuestra	nuestros	nuestras	nuestro	nuestra	nuestros	nuestras
your (inf.)	vuestro	vuestra	vuestros	vuestras	vuestro	vuestra	vuestros	vuestras
their, your	su		sus		suyo	suya	suyos	suyas

- Possessive adjectives agree in number with the noun they accompany. They agree with the thing possessed, not with the owner. Nuestro and vuestro also agree in gender with the item possessed.

  Estas son nuestras primas, Ana y Lucía.

Los pronombres posesivos

- Possessive pronouns are used instead of a noun. The forms are the same as those of the possessive adjectives after the noun.

  Ese libro es mío.

- When the possessive pronoun is used to identify, it is preceded by an article.

  Estos son nuestros profesores y aquellos son los vuestros.

14 **Compara.** ¿Qué semejanzas y diferencias hay entre los posesivos en inglés y en español?

15 **Comparar familias**

▶ **Completa** estas oraciones sobre las familias de Tess y de Janet.

1. ___1___ mamá se llama Patricia y la ___2___ se llama Marcela.
   Mi/Mía   su/suya

2. ___3___ abuelos son de California, pero los ___4___ son de Connecticut.
   Sus/Suyos   mis/míos

38   treinta y ocho

Differentiated Instruction

DEVELOPING LEARNERS

- Review with students the usage and forms of the possessive adjectives that are placed after the noun. Then give them the following sentence starters to complete.
  1. *Yo tengo una cámara. La cámara es...* (mía)
  2. *Tú tienes dos perros. Los perros son...* (tuyos)
  3. *Este es el pasaporte de mi padre. El pasaporte es...* (suyo)
  4. *Nosotros tenemos una casa. La casa es...* (nuestra)
  5. *Ustedes tienen cinco bolígrafos. Los bolígrafos son...* (suyos)

EXPANDING LEARNERS

- Give students more practice by having them choose the correct form of the possessive adjective or pronoun.
  1. *Esta no es nuestra mochila, porque nuestra/la nuestra es nueva.* (la nuestra)
  2. *¿Son los tuyos/tuyos estos cuadernos?* (tuyos)
  3. *Ustedes tienen seis hermanos; su familia es más grande que los míos/la mía.* (la mía)
  4. *Mis sobrinas son de México, pero tuyas/las tuyas son de California.* (las tuyas)
  5. *Este libro es de un hermano mi/mío.* (mío)

16 Los preparativos

 ▶ **Escucha** y relaciona los personajes con las fotografías correspondientes.

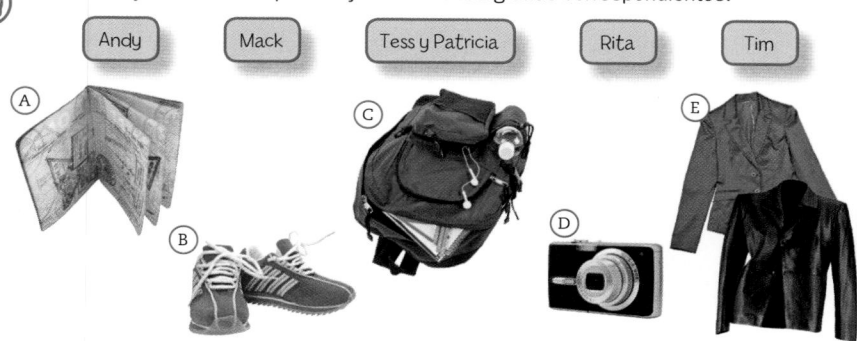

| Andy | Mack | Tess y Patricia | Rita | Tim |

 ▶ **Escucha** de nuevo y completa las respuestas con el posesivo correcto.

1. No, la ___1___ es roja. Esa mochila es de Andy.
2. Sí, ese es ___2___ pasaporte.
3. Sí, son las ___3___, gracias.
4. No, no es ___4___.
5. Los ___5___ están en la maleta y los ___6___ son estos.

17 Fotos de familia

 ▶ **Imagina** que estas son tu familia y la de tu compañero(a). Explícale quiénes son y cómo se llevan.

Modelo   A. *Estos son mis tíos. Tienen dos hijos. Ellos se llevan bien.*
                B. *Los míos...*

Mi familia.

La familia de mi compañero.

Gramática – Los posesivos

Activities

14. Refer students to the English possessive chart on the board. Remind them that the Spanish personal pronouns *él, ella,* and *usted* share the same possessive pronoun. The same applies for the personal pronouns *ellos, ellas,* and *ustedes*. Ask students if this is the case with English pronouns.

16. Play the audio three times in a row. Tell students to simply listen to the audio the first time, to complete the matching section the second time, and to complete the fill-in section the third time.

17. If students have a picture of their family with them in class, then they may use their family.

> **AUDIO SCRIPT**
> See page 27l.

Answer Key

14. Answers will vary. Sample answer: Los posesivos, tanto en inglés como en español, indican posesión. Los posesivos en español concuerdan con el objeto poseído, mientras que en inglés concuerdan con el dueño del objeto.

15. 1. Mi   2. suya   3. Sus   4. míos

16. A. Mack   D. Rita
     B. Tim   E. Tess y Patricia
     C. Andy
     ▶ 1. mía   4. mía
       2. su   5. míos
       3. nuestras 6. tuyos

17. Answers will vary. Sample answer:
A. Estos somos mis padres, mis tíos, mis primos y yo. Mis tíos tienen dos hijos: mi primo Luis y mi prima Marta. Nos llevamos bien.

> ### Additional Resources
> Fans Online activities
> Practice Workbook

HERITAGE LANGUAGE LEARNERS

- Ask students to describe when they would use the different forms of *tuyo, suyo,* or *vuestro*. Have them name the form they would use for their *padres, hermanos, primos, abuelos, padrinos,* and *tíos*. Then have them explain which form they would use while talking to a teacher or the principal. Which form would they use for talking to a new friend, a friend of their parents, or a stranger? And what form would they use if they were talking to their pets?

TOTAL PHYSICAL RESPONSE (TPR)

- Write each form of the possessive adjectives and pronouns on small index cards and place them in a bag. Have students select a card, walk over to another student or place in the classroom, point to an object, and say a sentence using the corresponding possessive adjective or pronoun. For example: A student picks *tuyo* from the bag. He or she walks to another student, points to that student's notebook, and says, *El cuaderno es tuyo*.

DESAFÍO 1

Comunicación

Presentation

- In this section, students will integrate the vocabulary and grammar from *Desafío 1* in order to describe family members, relationships within the family, and possessions.

Activities	Standards	Resources
18.	1.2, 1.3	Audio
19.	1.2, 1.3, 5.1	
20.	1.3, 5.1	
21. Final del desafío	1.2, 1.3, 2.2	

Teaching Suggestions

Warm-Up / Independent Starter

- Have students use the following words to form sentences.
  1. *mi / es / Esta / camisa*
  2. *abuelos / son / Mis / fantásticos*
  3. *papel / Este / es / suyo / el*
  4. *Ellas / nuestras / primas / son*

Preparation

- Take 10 minutes to review the vocabulary and grammar themes of *Desafío 1*.
- Refer students back to the *fotonovela* for *Desafío 1*. Have them find all of the words for family members, relationships within the family, and possessive adjectives within the dialogue. Do students understand the dialogue better now that they have gone through the vocabulary and grammar from the *Desafío*?

Activities

18. Ask students to think of their same family members and say if they get along well or not. If they do not get along, then have students say a different family member who does get along with that person. For example: *Mis hermanos discuten mucho, pero mi hermana y yo nos llevamos bien.*

19. Have students work in pairs to complete this activity. One student will classify the information into two columns and the other will answer the questions. Once students have finished their part, they will share the answers with their partner.

Comunicación

18 **Relaciones familiares**

 ▶ **Escucha** y decide si estas personas se llevan bien o mal con su familia.

	Se lleva bien	Se lleva mal
1		
2		
3		

19 **Familias diferentes**

▶ **Lee** el blog de Andy y clasifica la información en dos columnas.

Nuestras familias

Publicado por Andy, 24 de septiembre

La familia de Roberto y la mía son muy diferentes, pero se llevan muy bien. A nuestras familias les gusta hacer cosas juntas, como ir de excursión los fines de semana.

Mi familia es pequeña, la suya es grande. Yo tengo una hermana, pero él tiene siete. Un hermano suyo vive en los Estados Unidos. Yo solo tengo dos primas, Alison y Eloísa, pero él tiene... ¡veinte primos y cinco sobrinos! Un sobrino suyo está casado con nuestra amiga Ana.

COMENTARIOS (0) ENVIAR UN COMENTARIO

Mi familia	La familia de Roberto
Es pequeña.	

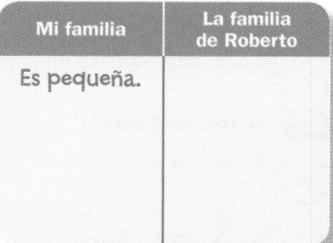

▶ **Responde** a las siguientes preguntas.
1. ¿Cómo se llevan las dos familias?
2. ¿Cómo es la familia de Andy?
3. ¿Cuántos hermanos tiene Roberto?
4. ¿Dónde vive un hermano de Roberto?
5. ¿Con quién está casada Ana?
6. ¿Qué hacen las familias los fines de semana?

Differentiated Instruction

DEVELOPING LEARNERS

- Give students the following words and have them say what the opposite is.
  1. *la madrina (el padrino)*
  2. *el esposo (la esposa)*
  3. *casado (soltero)*
  4. *la nieta (el nieto)*
  5. *el hijo (la hija)*
  6. *el chico (la chica)*
  7. *la abuela (el abuelo)*
  8. *el sobrino (la sobrina)*
  9. *la madre (el padre)*
  10. *el hermano (la hermana)*

EXPANDING LEARNERS

- Ask students to work with a partner and describe their families to one another. They should include as many family members as they can name, how they get along with each other, and any additional details, such as where they live, what they do for a living, what pets they have, and what activities they enjoy doing. Then, using the paragraphs in activity 19 as a guide, have students write at least two paragraphs comparing both families.

20 Una red de relaciones

▶ **Crea** una red de relaciones imaginarias con fotos de revistas y descríbela.
Create a fictional relationship web using photos and clippings. Describe it.

Modelo *Él es mi hermano. Se llama Orlando. Está casado con mi amiga Sarah.*

▶ **Presenta** tu familia imaginaria a la clase.

Final del desafío

a. JANET: Sí, aquí está su nariz.

b. JANET: ¡Mira, Andy! ¿Qué ves aquí?

c. ANDY: Claro. ¡El gigante maya de Atitlán es una montaña!

d. ANDY: ¡Parece la silueta de nuestro padre!

e. JANET: Ayer la esposa de Felipe y su madrina me hablaron del Rostro Maya.

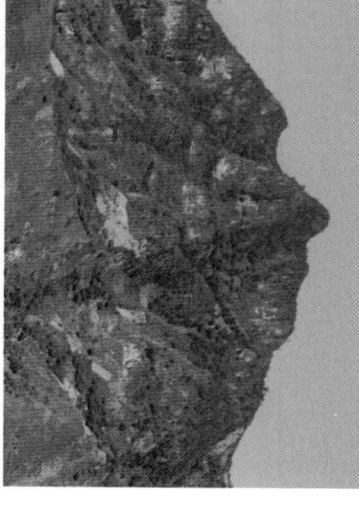

21 ¿Qué pasa en la historia?

▶ **Ordena** los bocadillos *(speech bubbles)* del final del desafío. Después, representa el diálogo con tu compañero(a).

HERITAGE LANGUAGE LEARNERS

- Point out that the verb *discutir* means "to discuss," as well as "to argue." The context will clarify its meaning. Ask students to list other verbs that mean "to argue" (e.g., *pelearse, reñir, alegar*) and nouns that mean "argument" (e.g., *discusión, pelea, riña*). Have them use these words in sentences.

- Then ask students to come up with other ways "getting along" is expressed in Spanish. For example, *le va muy bien en la escuela* (he's getting along well in school); *nos las arreglamos durante meses sin teléfono* (we got along for months without a telephone).

COOPERATIVE LEARNING

- Have students work in groups and imagine they are members of the same family. Groups will assign students a role to play, and determine who will get along well or badly with other family members, which may include those from their extended family (*primos, abuelos,* etc.). Each family member will make a short oral presentation of his or her family and explain how each one gets along with the others.

DESAFÍO 1
Comunicación

20. As an alternative to doing this activity in class, have students take this assignment home as homework. Ask students to use poster board for a sturdier work surface and a glue stick for less mess.

21. To extend this activity, ask students to imagine that, at first, Andy cannot see a human face in the mountain. Have pairs come up with two or three additional lines of dialogue in which Janet tells his brother how to look at the picture. Andy is skeptical, but eventually sees the face.

 AUDIO SCRIPT
See page 271.

Answer Key

18. Se lleva bien: 1, 3
Se lleva mal: 2

19. Mi familia: Es pequeña. Tengo una hermana. Tengo dos primas.
La familia de Roberto: Es grande. Él tiene siete hermanos. Él tiene veinte primos y cinco sobrinos.
  ▶ 1. Las dos familias se llevan bien.
  2. La familia de Andy es pequeña.
  3. Roberto tiene siete hermanos.
  4. Un hermano de Roberto vive en los Estados Unidos.
  5. Ana está casada con un sobrino de Roberto.
  6. Los fines de semana van de excursión las dos familias juntas.

20. Answers will vary.
  ▶ Answers will vary.

21. b, d, a, e, c

Additional Resources

Fans Online activities
Practice Workbook

Unit 1
DESAFÍO 2

Describir personas

Presentation

- In *Desafío 2*, Diana and Rita are in Travesía, Honduras. They must find a Garifuna musician who will give them a special gift.
- In this section, students will preview:
  - Physical characteristics.
  - Personality traits.
  - Noun and adjective agreement.

Activities	Standards	Resources
Fotonovela	1.2, 3.1, 3.2	Vis. Pres.
22.	1.2	
23.	1.2	Audio
24.	1.3	
25. Cultura	1.1, 1.2, 2.2, 3.2, 4.2	
Tu desafío	1.2, 3.1, 3.2	

Teaching Suggestions

Warm-Up / Independent Starter

- Ask students to read the introduction to the *fotonovela* individually. Then have them write a short paragraph about how they feel this task compares to the task Andy and Janet had to perform in the first *Desafío*.

Preparation

- Ask a volunteer to read the introduction to the *fotonovela* aloud. While he or she is reading, have the rest of the class look at the pictures in the *fotonovela*. When the volunteer has finished, ask the class to imagine what this Garifuna man looks like.

La fotonovela

Before Viewing

- Read the *fotonovela* aloud to students, changing your voice for each character.

After Viewing

- Now that students have a description of the Garifuna man, ask them if they have a better idea of what he looks like. Have students draw a picture of what they think this man looks like and share it with the class.

Un garífuna peculiar

 Diana and her aunt are going to Travesía, a Garifuna community on the Honduran coast. They must find a musician who will give them a special gift—a traditional Garifuna instrument made out of a turtle shell.

Diana, vamos, date prisa.

¡Qué impaciente eres, tía!

¿Cómo vamos a encontrar al músico?

Felipe Santos dijo que es moreno y lleva gafas.

Pero tía, todos los garifunas son morenos.

Hola. Buscamos a un músico moreno y con gafas. ¿Lo conoce?

Sí, conozco a un músico moreno y con gafas. Tiene el pelo corto. Y tiene barba y bigote. Se llama Marcos Esteban. Es espontáneo y muy gracioso.

¡Qué música más alegre! ¿La oyes?

Sí. ¡Seguro que ahí está Marcos Esteban!

Continuará...

22 **Detective de palabras**

▶ **Completa** estas oraciones.

1. Rita es _____.
2. Los garífunas son _____.
3. El músico es moreno y lleva _____.
4. Marcos Esteban tiene barba y _____.
5. Marcos Esteban es espontáneo y muy _____.

42 cuarenta y dos

Differentiated Instruction

DEVELOPING LEARNERS

- Help students identify the cognates in the cultural note about the Garifuna. Cognates include: *grupo, étnico, regiones, Centroamérica, Caribe, africanos, zona, escaparon, indígenas, cultura, música*. Encourage students to add these words to their notebooks for vocabulary enrichment.

EXPANDING LEARNERS

- Ask students to use some of the physical characteristics and personality traits mentioned in this lesson and apply them to friends, celebrities, or themselves. Students will then write a paragraph with these descriptive words or phrases and develop a profile of the person selected.

23 ¿Cómo es?

 ▶ **Escucha.** Rita nos presenta a algunas personas que conoce en Honduras.
Elige la oración relacionada con cada persona o grupo de personas.
Listen to Rita introduce some of the people she meets in Honduras. Choose the sentence related to each person or group.

    a. Es profesora. **b.** Es un músico garífuna. **c.** Son jóvenes y bonitas. **d.** Son mayores.

24 Descripciones

▶ **Describe** a estas personas.

moreno	rubio	bajo	alto	joven	mayor	tiene bigote
lleva gafas		tiene el pelo largo		tiene los ojos azules		tiene los ojos marrones

1. La señora…   2. Diana…   3. El hombre…

CULTURA

Los garífunas

Los garífunas son un grupo étnico que vive en varias regiones de Centroamérica, el Caribe y los Estados Unidos. Descienden de los africanos que fueron llevados *(were taken)* a la zona como esclavos *(slaves)* entre los siglos XVI y XVII, escaparon y fueron a vivir con los pueblos indígenas.

Los garífunas de Centroamérica hablan garífuna y español. Tienen una cultura muy rica en música y baile.

25   **Piensa y explica.** ¿Qué ocurre cuando dos culturas totalmente diferentes se encuentran *(meet)*? ¿Qué elementos culturales se comparten *(share)* primero?

▶ **TU DESAFÍO**   Visita la página web para aprender más sobre los garífunas y su música.

HERITAGE LANGUAGE LEARNERS

- Explain that there are many forms of music throughout the Spanish-speaking world. Invite students to share what they know about the music of their family's native country, or of a Hispanic country they have visited. Encourage them to bring in recordings of both traditional and contemporary music, and play some for the class. Ask them to explain the lyrics and describe the instruments that are used in this music. Have them share what they know about some of the performers.

CRITICAL THINKING

- Have a classroom discussion on the role music has had and continues to have on culture. Ask students what music means to them, and why they think people create music. Ask why they think some music has survived over the centuries, and to share what kind of music they enjoy listening to. Ask if there is such a thing as "good" music and "bad" music, and why.

Activities

22. Have students complete this activity by memory. If they can't remember the word, have them add a word they think works as well.

24. Let students know that there may be more than one response for each person. They must write each correct answer in complete sentences.

25. Ask students if they know of any other instances where cultures mixed, resulting in a beautiful product. (jazz, salsa)

 AUDIO SCRIPT
See page 271.

 CULTURA

Los garífunas

Today, the Garifuna live mainly in Central America, the Caribbean islands, and in the United States. In fact, the Garifuna population in the United States is second only to that of Honduras. Ethnic discrimination and lack of economic prospects are some of the factors that threaten the survival of the Garifuna culture in Central America. Several organizations are making efforts to ensure the survival of this unique culture.

Answer Key

22. 1. impaciente   4. bigote
     2. morenos   5. gracioso
     3. gafas

23. 1. a   2. c   3. b   4. d

24. Answers will vary. Sample answer:
     1. La señora es morena y baja. Es mayor. Tiene los ojos marrones.

25. Answers will vary.

Additional Resources

Fans Online activities

Unit 1
DESAFÍO 2

Vocabulario – Características físicas y rasgos de personalidad

Presentation

- In this section, students will learn physical characteristics and personality traits.

Activities	Standards	Resources
Vocabulario	1.2	
26.	1.2	Audio
27.	1.2, 1.3	
28.	1.1, 1.3, 2.1	
29.	1.3	
30. Conexiones	1.2, 3.1, 3.2	

Teaching Suggestions

Warm-Up / Independent Starter

- Ask students to think about what characteristics and traits they would want in a boyfriend or girlfriend and write them in their notebooks.

Preparation

- Go over the vocabulary presentation with students. Have them write down the Spanish words for the traits they chose for their boyfriend or girlfriend from the Independent Starter. If there are some characteristics or traits that are not on the vocabulary list, have students look them up in a Spanish-English dictionary.

- Have students choose three words from the vocabulary presentation that describe them best. Ask for volunteers to share their three words, then ask the rest of the class if they agree with each student's description.

- Have students write a description of what they believe the Garifuna people are like, based on what students have learned about the Garifuna and the information in the vocabulary presentation.

Activities

26. Have students write the name of a person they know who fits each description Diana gives.

27. Have students choose six more vocabulary words from the presentation to define.

29. Ask students to create a second Venn diagram to compare themselves with a sibling, or with a cousin or friend if they are an only child.

44

Vocabulario

Características físicas y rasgos de personalidad

¿Cómo son físicamente?

Yo soy rubia y alta, mido 1,78.

Yo soy pelirroja y llevo gafas.

Yo soy calvo y fuerte. Peso 80 kg.

Yo no soy gordo y tengo barba.

¿Cómo es su personalidad?

Nosotros no somos perezosos, somos trabajadores.

Ellas no son tacañas, son generosas.

Él no es serio, es gracioso.

creativo(a)	espontáneo(a)	estudioso(a)	sincero(a)	tímido(a)
inteligente	paciente	impaciente	optimista	pesimista

26 Descripciones

▶ **Escucha** las descripciones y ordena las fotografías.

Ⓐ  Ⓑ  Ⓒ  Ⓓ  Ⓔ

Differentiated Instruction

DEVELOPING LEARNERS

- For practice with noun-adjective agreement, have students choose the correct adjective for each of the following sentences.
  1. *Los chicos son generosos/generosas.* (generosos)
  2. *Ustedes son serias/seria.* (serias)
  3. *Nosotras somos trabajadores/trabajadoras.* (trabajadoras)
  4. *El chico es alto y pelirroja/alto y pelirrojo.* (alto y pelirrojo)
  5. *Ellos no son tacaños/tacañas.* (tacaños)
  6. *Yo soy impaciente/impacientes, pero generosos/generosa.* (impaciente, generosa)

EXPANDING LEARNERS

- Ask students to use the postcard from the lesson as a model, and have them write an e-mail to a fan in Honduras. Students should explain who they are, where they're from, give some personal information such as age, some physical characteristics, and personality traits. They should also include some information about what they are studying in school and how they like to spend their free time.

27 Dos columnas

▶ **Une** las dos columnas.

Ⓐ

1. Ana es graciosa.
2. Luis es estudioso.
3. María es impaciente.
4. Fernando es sincero.

Ⓑ

a. Siempre dice la verdad.
b. Sus amigos se ríen.
c. Va mucho a la biblioteca.
d. No le gusta esperar.

28 Un fan de Honduras

▶ **Responde** a estas preguntas sobre la carta de un fan hondureño de Diana.

Diana received a letter from a Honduran fan. Read it and answer the questions.

1. ¿Cómo es Héctor?
2. ¿Cómo es su esposa?
3. ¿Cómo es el hijo de Héctor?

> *Hola, Diana:*
>
> *Me llamo Héctor y soy de Honduras. ¡Bienvenida a mi país!*
>
> *Tengo treinta y cuatro años y estoy casado. Mi esposa se llama Luisa. Yo soy sincero y optimista y ella es fuerte y muy trabajadora. Tenemos un hijo, Julián. Él es moreno y lleva gafas. También es fan de ustedes.*
>
> *Los hondureños son generosos y espontáneos. Bueno, eso pienso yo... ¿Te gusta mi país? ¿Y la gente?*
>
> *Un saludo.*
>
> *Héctor*

29 ¿Es bueno o malo?

▶ **Clasifica** los adjetivos de personalidad del Vocabulario (página 44) en un diagrama.

bueno   malo

estudioso

CONEXIONES: MATEMÁTICAS

El Sistema Internacional de Medidas

En muchos países del mundo se usa el Sistema Internacional de Medidas o Sistema Métrico. Estas son algunas conversiones muy comunes:

1 kilogramo (kg) = 2,21 libras (lbs)
1 metro (m) = 3,28 pies (ft)
1 kilómetro (km) = 0,62 millas (mi)

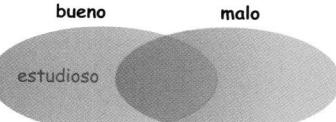

30 Calcula. ¿Cuánto pesa *(weighs)* en libras y cuánto mide *(measures)* en pies el futbolista hondureño Wilson Palacios?

Peso: 76 kilos   Altura: 1,76 metros

HERITAGE LANGUAGE LEARNERS

- There are synonyms as well as many regional variants for some of the vocabulary presented here. For example, some Spanish speakers might say *güero* (Mexico), *mono* (Colombia), *catire* (Venezuela), *chele* (Central America), or *fulo* (Panama) for *rubio*, and *lentes, anteojos,* or *espejuelos* for *gafas*. Ask students to come up with other words for *perezoso, tacaño,* and *gracioso*, or any other words presented here that might have synonyms or regional variants.

MULTIPLE INTELLIGENCES:
Logical-Mathematical Intelligence

- Have students work with a partner and use a standard ruler to measure some common classroom objects, such as the width of a student desk, the height of the teacher's desk, the length of the chalkboard, the door width, a pencil or pen, and their Spanish textbook. Then have them convert the results to the metric system.

- You might have partners also research the height and weight of several athletes, and then convert the results to the metric system.

Vocabulario – Características físicas y rasgos de personalidad

30. Have students convert their own height and weight from feet to meters, and pounds to kilos. You may ask for volunteers to read their converted height and weight aloud. In order to avoid sensitivity issues, do not call on anyone who did not raise his or her hand.

 AUDIO SCRIPT
See page 271.

 CONEXIONES: MATEMÁTICAS

El Sistema Internacional de Medidas

The International System of Units, abbreviated SI, was developed in 1960 from what we know as the metric system. This system uses meters for length, kilograms for mass, seconds for time, amps for electrical currents, and kelvin for temperature; however, the Celsius temperature scale is more frequently used. Although the International System of Units is not common in the United States, it is the most commonly used measurement system in the world.

Answer Key

26. 1. C   2. D   3. B   4. A   5. E

27. 1. b   2. c   3. d   4. a

28. 1. Es sincero y optimista.
    2. Es fuerte y muy trabajadora.
    3. Es moreno y lleva gafas.

29. Answers will vary.

30. 5.77 ft. and 167.55 Lbs.

Additional Resources

Fans Online activities
Practice Workbook

DESAFÍO 2

Gramática – Los adjetivos y el nombre

Presentation

- In this section, students will learn noun and adjective agreement.

Activities	Standards	Resources
Gramática	3.1	
31.	1.1, 3.1, 4.1	
32.	1.2	
33.	1.3	
34.	1.1, 1.2, 1.3, 3.2	
35. Comunidades	1.1, 1.2, 2.1, 3.2, 4.2, 5.1	

Teaching Suggestions

Warm-Up / Independent Starter

- Ask students to draw a picture that represents their English teacher. They must include three representations of their teacher's physical characteristics and three representations of their teacher's personality traits.

Preparation

- Read over the grammar presentation with students. Write the words *rubio, moreno*, and *pelirrojo* on the board. Ask students what form these adjectives are in right now (masculine, singular). Then, one adjective at a time, have students call out the other three forms (*rubia, rubios*, and *rubias*, etc.). Be sure to clarify the form each adjective is in as you go over them (i.e., feminine, singular; masculine, plural; feminine, plural).
- Although it is not mentioned in the grammar presentation, let students know that a person from the United States is *estadounidense* or *(norte)americano*.

Activities

33. As an alternative to this activity, have students write the opposite physical characteristics and personality traits of the Honduran women.

34. Allow students to create a Venn diagram to compare themselves to Antonio and Lula. If poster board is available, have students create a poster with their Venn diagram.

Gramática

Los adjetivos y el nombre

La posición del adjetivo

- Adjectives in Spanish usually follow the noun.

  el músico calvo   la cantante morena

Concordancia del adjetivo

- In Spanish, adjectives reflect the gender and number of the noun they refer to.

Adjetivos que terminan en -o: tienen 4 formas	el chico simpático la chica simpática	los chicos simpáticos las chicas simpáticas
Adjetivos que terminan en -e: tienen 2 formas	el niño inteligente la niña inteligente	los niños inteligentes las niñas inteligentes
Adjetivos que terminan en consonante: tienen generalmente 2 formas	el señor débil la señora débil	los señores débiles las señoras débiles

Los adjetivos de nacionalidad

- Adjectives that express nationality also have variation of gender and number.

Adjetivos que terminan en -o o en consonante: tienen 4 formas	el chico hondureño la chica hondureña	los chicos hondureños las chicas hondureñas
	el niño español la niña española	los niños españoles las niñas españolas
Adjetivos que terminan en -e: tienen 2 formas	el señor canadiense la señora canadiense	los señores canadienses las señoras canadienses

31 **Compara.** ¿Qué posición tienen los adjetivos en español y en inglés? ¿Hay diferencias?

32 **Ustedes también**

▶ **Completa** estas oraciones.

1. Yo soy tímido. Clara también es _____.
2. Elena es inteligente. Su hermano también es muy _____.
3. Nosotras somos mexicanas. Ustedes también son _____.
4. Ellos son alemanes. Las chicas también son _____.
5. Ese chico es popular. Esas chicas también son _____.

46 cuarenta y seis

Differentiated Instruction

DEVELOPING LEARNERS

- To help reinforce noun-adjective agreement, ask students to use the correct form of an adjective that ends in -o to describe Diana, Andy, Mack and Tim, and Rita and Diana. Then have them use the correct form of an adjective that ends in -e to describe the same people. Finally, ask them to use the adjective of nationality, *español*, to describe *un libro, una chica, dos primos,* and *tres maestras*.

EXPANDING LEARNERS

- Ask students to write a list of additional adjectives that have to do with physical characteristics, personality traits, and nationalities in their notebooks. Ask them to look up their Spanish equivalents in a bilingual dictionary, and to use them in sentences to describe *un chico, una chica, dos chicos,* and *dos chicas.* Ask them to share their new words with the rest of the class.

33 **Mujeres hondureñas**

 ▶ **Describe** a estas mujeres hondureñas.
Incluye rasgos físicos y de personalidad.

Modelo *Una es morena y...*

 34 **¡Somos iguales!**

▶ **Lee** el texto y describe a la hermana
melliza *(twin)* de Antonio. Recuerda: Antonio y su hermana son muy parecidos *(similar)*.

> ¡Hola! Me llamo Antonio. Tengo dieciséis
> años y soy hondureño, de Tegucigalpa.
> Tengo una hermana melliza. Se llama
> Lula.
>
> Yo soy un chico joven, alto, delgado y
> moreno. Llevo gafas. Mido 1,75 metros y
> peso 70 kilos. Soy un chico inteligente y
> serio. Además, soy estudioso y trabajador.
> Soy muy generoso y me gusta pasar
> tiempo con mis mejores amigos.
>
> ¿Cómo es mi hermana Lula?

 ▶ **Habla** con tu compañero(a). ¿Son ustedes como Antonio y Lula?

Modelo A. *Ellos son altos y morenos. Nosotras dos somos altas.*
B. *Sí, pero tú no eres morena. Eres rubia.*

 COMUNIDADES

DIVERSIDAD LINGÜÍSTICA

En Honduras viven casi ocho millones de personas.
La mayoría de sus habitantes son mestizos *(of mixed
ancestry)* descendientes de europeos e indígenas. La mayor
parte habla español, pero algunos hablan también
garífuna u otras lenguas nativas.

35 **Piensa y explica.** ¿En tu comunidad se hablan
varias lenguas? ¿Sabes por qué y desde cuándo?

cuarenta y siete 47

Gramática – Los adjetivos
y el nombre

35. Ask students if they have ever been to a
community within your city or state that speaks
a language other than English. Invite students
to share their experiences with the class.

 COMUNIDADES

Diversidad lingüística

Central America shares the same origins as
the United States. Indigenous peoples
inhabited both Central America and the United
States before the European colonization.
Today, millions of descendants of these pre-
Columbian Americans still live in the United
States and Central America, and many still
speak the language of their ancestors.

Answer Key

31. Por lo general, los adjetivos en español van
después del nombre, y en inglés, delante.

32. 1. tímida   4. alemanas
2. inteligente   5. populares
3. mexicanas(os)

33. Answers will vary. Sample answer:
Una chica es rubia y la otra es morena. Las
dos tienen el pelo largo y rizado. No llevan
gafas. Son espontáneas e inteligentes.

34. Answers will vary. Sample answer:
La hermana es joven, alta, morena
y delgada. Tiene el pelo largo y también
lleva gafas. Es simpática.
▶ Answers will vary.

35. Answers will vary.

Additional Resources

Fans Online activities
Practice Workbook

HERITAGE LANGUAGE LEARNERS

• Ask students to research what other
languages are spoken in Honduras,
Guatemala, Costa Rica, and Nicaragua.
Additionally, have students research the
noun-adjective agreement in each language.
Have students write the similarities and
differences between those languages in this
grammatical function.

TOTAL PHYSICAL RESPONSE (TPR)

• Divide the class into two teams and play a
talking variation of "Charades." Team
members will take turns describing a student
in their class, their teacher, or someone in
the news. The other team members must
guess the person's identity after hearing a
clue. If no one guesses correctly, another
clue may be given. A total of three clues may
be given. Correct answers score 3 points
after the first clue, 2 after the second clue,
and 1 after the third. Clues should include
sentences such as, *Es una chica alta y rubia.
Es muy trabajadora. Es impaciente.*

DESAFÍO 2

Comunicación

Presentation

- In this section, students will integrate the vocabulary and grammar from *Desafío 2* in order to describe one's physical characteristics and personality traits, as well as to discuss noun and adjective agreement.

Activities	Standards	Resources
36.	1.2	Audio
37.	1.2, 1.3	
38.	1.1, 1.3, 5.1	
39.	1.1, 5.2	
40. Final del desafío	1.2, 2.1, 5.2	
Tu desafío	1.2, 1.3	

Teaching Suggestions

Warm-Up / Independent Starter

- Have students describe the physical characteristics and personality traits of the following people:
  1. *tu mejor amigo(a)*
  2. *tus abuelos*
  3. *tu profesor(a) de Matemáticas*

Preparation

- Take 10 minutes to review the vocabulary and grammar themes of *Desafío 2*.
- Refer students back to the *fotonovela* for *Desafío 2*. Have them find all of the physical characteristics, personality traits, and noun and adjective agreements within the dialogue. Do students understand the dialogue better now that they have gone through the vocabulary and grammar from the *Desafío*?
- Have students work in small groups on the *Comunicación* activities. Choose the members of each group, and try to include students of all skill levels and learning styles in each group. Monitor students to stay on task and use only Spanish in the speaking activities. Once students have finished the activities, have them describe each group member's physical characteristics and personality traits. Students should base the personality description on how each group member worked and interacted with the rest of the group.

48

Comunicación

36 **Gente de Honduras**

 ▶ **Escucha** y relaciona cada oración con la fotografía correspondiente.

37 **¿Cómo eres?**

▶ **Escribe** un párrafo describiendo tus rasgos físicos e incluye un dato falso. Luego dáselo a tu compañero(a). Él o ella tiene que encontrar el dato falso.
Write a paragraph about your physical traits, including one false statement. Your partner should identify the false information.

38 **El mejor presidente**

▶ **Escribe** la lista de rasgos de personalidad que debe tener un buen presidente del curso.
Write a list of the personality traits that a good class president should have.

 ▶ **Compara** tu lista con tu compañero(a). ¿Son similares? ¿Quién de ustedes piensa que puede ser mejor presidente del curso?
Compare your list with a partner. Are they similar? Which of you would make a better class president?

Modelo A. *Un buen presidente del curso tiene que ser estudioso y trabajador.*
B. *Sí. Y también tiene que ser espontáneo.*

> **EL PRESIDENTE DEL CURSO**
>
> estudioso
>
> trabajador
>
> ...

48 cuarenta y ocho

Differentiated Instruction

DEVELOPING LEARNERS

- Bring in magazine cutouts of people with various physical characteristics, as well as some obvious personality traits. Display the pictures to students and ask them to make up at least two sentences about the people pictured.

EXPANDING LEARNERS

- Have students imagine that they have an alter ego who is their complete opposite; that is, someone with totally different physical characteristics and personality traits. Ask students to write a brief description of themselves, and then another one of their alter ego. Encourage students to be as descriptive and creative as they can.

39 «10 preguntas»

▶ **Juega** con tu compañero(a). Escribe el nombre de una persona famosa. Él o ella tiene que adivinar (*must guess*) la identidad de esa persona.

Modelo   A. *¿Es un hombre o una mujer?*
B. *Es un hombre.*
A. *¿Es joven o viejo?*
B. *Es joven.*

Final del desafío

RITA: ¿Crees que este músico es Marcos Esteban?
DIANA: No, Marcos Esteban tiene barba y bigote.

DIANA: Este músico es moreno y tiene barba y bigote.
RITA: Sí, pero no lleva gafas. Además es muy serio, y Marcos Esteban es espontáneo y gracioso.
DIANA: Sí, es cierto. Y él no tiene nuestro regalo.

40 ¿Quién es Marcos Esteban?

▶ **Decide.** Usando las descripciones de la fotonovela y del final del desafío, decide cuál de los músicos es Marcos Esteban.

 → TU DESAFÍO   Visita la página web. Escucha las preguntas de tu *Minientrevista Desafío 2* y escribe las respuestas.

cuarenta y nueve   49

Activities

37. Have students organize the information in their paragraphs in a chart like the one below.

Introducción	Rasgos físicos y dato falso	Conclusión

38. If you already have a class president, have students compare their lists of personality traits to those of the current class president. Does the current president meet their expectations? How so or how not?

39. Limit the number of questions a student can ask in order to facilitate this activity. Allow students to ask five questions before they have to guess a celebrity name. Then allow students two guesses before they must move on.

40. Complete the *Final de desafío* as a class. Ask for volunteers to read the parts of Diana and Rita, then as a class, pick Marcos Esteban out of the people in the photos.

 AUDIO SCRIPT
See page 271.

Answer Key

36. 1. D   2. A   3. B   4. C

37. Answers will vary.

38. Answers will vary. Sample answer: Un buen presidente del curso debe ser trabajador, creativo y paciente. También debe ser inteligente y optimista.
▶ Answers will vary.

39. Answers will vary.

40. Answers will vary.

Additional Resources

Fans Online activities
Practice Workbook

HERITAGE LANGUAGE LEARNERS

• Diana and Rita describe the Garifuna people in this lesson. Ask students how they would describe their favorite Hispanic musician. Encourage them to find a photograph of the musician in a magazine, attach it to a sheet of paper, and then write a description of the person as well as of his or her music. Encourage students to share their information with the rest of the class.

CRITICAL THINKING

• Ask students to describe their personality traits. Lead a classroom discussion as to how students come to a decision about their personality traits. After the discussion, you might want to take a class vote to see which trait is the most commonly used and which one is the least commonly used.

49

Unit 1
DESAFÍO 3

Expresar estados de ánimo y sentimientos

Presentation

- In *Desafío 3*, Tess and Patricia are in León, Nicaragua. There they must find the tallest woman in the city and dress like her.
- In this section, students will preview:
  – Words to express emotional states.
  – How to make comparisons.
  – How to use superlatives.

Activities	Standards	Resources
Fotonovela	1.2, 2.1, 2.2	Vis. Pres.
41.	1.2	
42.	1.2, 1.3	
43.	1.2	Audio
44. Cultura	1.1, 1.2, 3.2, 4.2	Video
Tu desafío	1.2, 2.2, 3.2, 5.1	

Teaching Suggestions

Warm-Up / Independent Starter

- Ask students to write three sentences in Spanish about their feelings. One sentence should be about how they felt yesterday, one sentence about how they feel right now, and one sentence about how they will feel this weekend.

Preparation

- Have volunteers share their Independent Starter sentences with the class. Allow students to dive further into their feelings by asking, *¿Por qué?*

La fotonovela

Before Viewing

- Have students read the introduction to the *fotonovela* silently. Tell them not to read any of the dialogue on the page.
- Play the visual presentation for students two times. Students will simply watch the visual presentation the first time, and then follow along with the words in the textbook the second time.

After Viewing

- Ask students which way of viewing the *fotonovela* was better. Take a vote to find out how your students prefer to study this section.

50

La mujer más alta de León

Tess and Patricia are in León, on the Pacific coast of Nicaragua. In a city of over 100,000 people, they must find the tallest woman and dress like her!

Estoy emocionada. León es una ciudad maravillosa.

Sí, es una ciudad muy importante.

Estas mujeres no son muy altas.

Es cierto. Pero allí hay una mujer más alta que estas.

¿Tú crees que es ella?

No, tiene que ser una mujer altísima.

Estoy muy frustrada. ¿Qué podemos hacer?

Tranquila, Tess. Vamos a encontrarla.

¡Mira ese cartel!

CONCURSO ANUAL DE GIGANTONAS DE LA CIUDAD DE LEÓN

Continuará...

41 Detective de palabras

▶ **Completa** estas oraciones.

1. León es una ciudad ___muy___ __1__.
2. Estas mujeres no son __2__ __3__.
3. Allí hay una mujer __4__ __5__ que estas.
4. Tiene que ser una mujer __6__.
5. Tess está __7__ __8__.

Differentiated Instruction

DEVELOPING LEARNERS

- To reinforce students' comprehension of the *fotonovela*, have them work with a partner to memorize and practice the dialogue. Monitor their pronunciation and intonation as they read. Allow them time to rehearse and then have them present their skits to the class.

EXPANDING LEARNERS

- Ask students to work with a partner and prepare an alternative dialogue to the *fotonovela*. They do not have to follow the same story line, but their new plot needs to make use of the photographs shown. They should change how the two characters express their emotions and what they are going to do next. Encourage creativity, and if there is time, ask student pairs to present their new dialogues to the class.

42 **¿Comprendes?**

▶ **Responde** a estas preguntas.

1. ¿Dónde están Tess y Patricia?
2. ¿Cómo es la mujer que buscan?
3. ¿Por qué crees que Tess está frustrada?
4. ¿Qué piensas que es una *gigantona*?

43 **Comparaciones**

▶ **Escucha** la descripción de Tess y Patricia y completa una tabla como esta.

	Tess	Patricia
¿Quién es más rubia?	✓	
¿Quién es más alta?		
¿Quién está más contenta?		
¿Quién está más frustrada?		
¿Quién está más nerviosa?		

 **CULTURA**

La gigantona y el enano cabezón

La gigantona y el enano cabezón son dos personajes típicos del folclore nicaragüense. Los dos personajes intervienen en muchas fiestas populares.

La gigantona es un muñeco de tres metros de altura. Representa a una mujer española y lleva vestidos y joyas (*jewelry*) antiguos. El enano cabezón acompaña a la gigantona. Es bajo e inteligente y canta canciones criticando los problemas sociales. El enano cabezón representa al indígena. Los dos personajes bailan por las calles y alegran las fiestas.

En León hay todos los años un concurso (*contest*) para premiar las mejores figuras callejeras (*street puppets*).

44 **Compara.** ¿Conoces alguna otra fiesta en tu país o en otro lugar con figuras callejeras? ¿Qué representan?

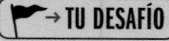 **→ TU DESAFÍO** | Visita la página web para aprender más sobre los personajes del folclore nicaragüense.

HERITAGE LANGUAGE LEARNERS

• Spanish speakers often add suffixes to nouns or adjectives to indicate admiration, affection, or disrespect. For example, *-ona* added to *gigante* conveys the meaning of an extremely large giant and *-ón* added to *cabeza* means someone with a very big head (and often someone who is extremely stubborn). Diminutives such as *-ito* and *-illo* convey the meaning of small, or affection toward the person or thing cited: *mi abuelito, mi casita*. Ask students to name some other examples of words that have different shades of meaning after adding one of these, or other, suffixes.

MULTIPLE INTELLIGENCES:
Visual-Spatial Intelligence

• Students will create their own *gigantonas*. First, they need to decide what personality traits this character represents in their community. The *gigantona* must represent positive or negative traits. Then they will draw her accordingly on poster board. Students will also identify the kind of celebration the character takes part in and represent this in their drawings. Finally, students should be prepared to present their posters to the rest of the class, and answer any questions their classmates may have.

DESAFÍO 3

Expresar estados de ánimo y sentimientos

Activities

42. As an alternative to this activity, have students answer the questions by themselves, then get into pairs to check their answers.

43. Have students get into pairs and use these questions to compare themselves to each other. They must create a table like the one in the book.

AUDIO SCRIPT
See page 271.

CULTURA

La gigantona y el enano cabezón

These characters are brought out during the festivities of December in León, Nicaragua. A band of drum players, or *tamborileros*, accompanies the *gigantona* and her page, the *enano*. The *gigantona* dances to the rhythm of the drums, which stop from time to time to allow the *enano* to recite his verses to her.

Answer Key

41.
1. importante
2. muy
3. altas
4. más
5. alta
6. altísima
7. muy
8. frustrada

42.
1. Están en la ciudad de León, en Nicaragua.
2. Es altísima.
4. No encuentra a la mujer más alta de León.
5. Una mujer gigante.

43. Tess: más rubia; más frustrada.
Patricia: más alta; más contenta; más nerviosa.

44. Answers will vary.

Additional Resources

Fans Online activities

51

DESAFÍO 3

Vocabulario – Estados de ánimo y sentimientos

Presentation

- In this section, students will learn how to express emotional states by using the verb *estar* followed by a descriptive adjective.

Activities	Standards	Resources
Vocabulario	1.2	
45.	1.1	
46.	1.2	Audio
47.	1.3	
48.	1.1	
49. Cultura	1.2, 2.1, 3.1, 3.2, 5.1	

Teaching Suggestions

Warm-Up / Independent Starter

- Ask students to look at the review words (the ones not pictured). Have them describe these terms. For example, *aburrido: no está haciendo nada...*

Preparation

- Go over the pictured part of the vocabulary presentation. Draw students' attention to the fact that the verb *estar* is used before every adjective.
- Ask volunteers to read their Independent Starters. After each one has read, ask the class if anyone else has the same description.

Activities

45. Turn this activity into a game, and complete it as a class. Write each emotion on a slip of paper, then fold the slips and place them in a hat. Split the class into four teams. Each team sends one person to pick a slip out of the hat and act out that emotion for their team only. If their team guesses correctly on the first try, they win a point. Then the next team repeats the process. The team with the most points after the last slip of paper is gone wins.

49. Allow students to discuss this topic among themselves. Have students research information on the *Popol Vuh* if they are not familiar with this book. You may facilitate the conversation, but be careful not to input personal beliefs in this discussion.

Vocabulario

Estados de ánimo y sentimientos

Está tranquila

Está nervioso

Están enamorados

Está celoso

Está confundida

Están sorprendidos

Está furiosa

aburrido(a)   contento(a)   emocionado(a)   enojado(a)   frustrado(a)   triste

45 **Estados de ánimo**

▶ **Representa** dos estados de ánimo *(emotions)*. Tus compañeros(as) tienen que adivinar *(must guess)* cómo te sientes.

46 **¿Cómo están hoy?**

 ▶ **Escucha** los diálogos. ¿Cómo se sienten los amigos de Tess? ¿Por qué?

Modelo Samantha → *Samantha está triste porque su gato está enfermo.*

1. Nico   2. Ana   3. Luis   4. María

Differentiated Instruction

DEVELOPING LEARNERS

- Using the illustrations of the new vocabulary as a guide, ask students to find abstract pictures on the Internet to describe each emotion. Then, and according to the items pictured, have students write or say a sentence that uses the correct form of the appropriate adjective. Remind students that they should use the verb *estar* when describing emotions.

EXPANDING LEARNERS

- Ask students to write five or more sentences about their emotional states and the events or circumstances that provoked these feelings. You might give them examples such as:

  1. *Estoy furioso(a) porque mi equipo favorito de fútbol americano perdió el partido.*
  2. *Estoy muy contento(a) porque hoy es fiesta.*
  3. *Estoy emocionado(a) porque mis padres y yo vamos a visitar Centroamérica.*
  4. *Estoy frustrado(a) porque no entiendo los pronombres posesivos en español.*
  5. *Estoy aburrido(a) porque no tengo nada que hacer.*

47 Emociones

▶ **Escribe** ¿Cómo están estas personas?

Modelo 1. *Los chicos están tristes y frustrados.*

48 ¿Cómo estás?

▶ **Dibuja** dos emoticonos para representar emociones y habla con tu compañero(a).
Draw two emoticons (smileys) to represent emotions. Then, talk to your partner.

Modelo A. *¿Cómo estás?* (shows enojado icon)
B. *Estoy enojada.*

CULTURA

Popol Vuh

Los mayas crearon muchas leyendas sobre el mundo, la naturaleza y los dioses. Estas leyendas están recogidas en un libro muy antiguo: el *Popol Vuh*.

Según los mayas, los dioses crearon primero hombres de barro (mud) y después hombres de madera (wood). Por fin crearon hombres de maíz (corn), el alimento principal de los mayas, y les dieron sentimientos.

49 Compara. ¿Conoces otras teorías sobre el origen del mundo? Compara y contrasta esas ideas con las de los mayas.

HERITAGE LANGUAGE LEARNERS

• Have students explain the difference between *ser aburrido* and *estar aburrido,* and between *ser triste* and *estar triste*. Ask them to provide other examples of adjectives of emotion with *ser* and *estar*, and explain the difference in their meanings depending on the verb used.

SPECIAL-NEEDS LEARNERS

• For students with visual impairment, enlarge the vocabulary page so they are able to easily see and identify the emotions and words shown. Go over each word with them to ensure their comprehension of both the new and review vocabulary. As you say each emotion, ask students to point to and say the corresponding sentence.

DESAFÍO 3

Vocabulario – Estados de ánimo y sentimientos

AUDIO SCRIPT
See page 271.

CULTURA

Popol Vuh

The *Popol Vuh* was written between 1554 and 1558 in the Maya Quiché language, but using the Spanish alphabet. The book seeks to answer some of life's questions, such as the creation of the world and its beings, and the history of their ancestors. It also tells mythical tales, exemplifying the epic battles of good versus evil. At the beginning of the 18th century, Father Francisco Ximénez, a parish priest of Chichicastenango, discovered the original book. He copied the original Quiché text and did a side-by-side translation into Spanish. Father Ximénez's manuscript is in the Newberry Library in Chicago, Illinois.

Answer Key

45. Answers will vary.

46. Answers will vary. Sample answers:
1. Nico está muy contento porque tiene un partido de fútbol y piensa ganar.
2. Ana está cansada porque se levanta muy temprano para ir a trabajar.
3. Luis está enojado con su hermano. No se llevan bien.
4. María está nerviosa porque tiene un examen.

47. Answers will vary.

48. Answers will vary.

49. Answers will vary.

Additional Resources

Fans Online activities
Practice Workbook

DESAFÍO 3

Gramática – Las comparaciones y el superlativo

Presentation

- In this section, students will learn:
  - How to make comparisons.
  - How to express the extreme of an adjective by using superlatives.

Activities	Standards	Resources
Gramática	3.1	
50.	1.3, 3.1, 4.1	
51.	1.2	Audio
52.	1.3	
53.	1.1, 1.3	
54. Conexiones	1.2, 2.2, 3.1, 3.2	
Tu desafío	1.2, 3.1, 3.2, 5.1	

Teaching Suggestions

Warm-Up / Independent Starter

- Ask students to page through a magazine and determine how each person in the photos feels. Have students write about at least five people in complete sentences.

Preparation

- Go over the grammar presentation with students. Let them know that there are two ways to compare nouns. The first way is to compare nouns to one another using *más... que, menos... que,* and *tan... como.* The second way is to use the extreme. It would be equivalent to using the term *most* or the suffix *-est* (most popular, happiest, etc.).
- Have students use the vocabulary from this *Desafío* to practice comparatives and superlatives. Tell students to select six classmates to use for inspiration.

Activities

51. Ask students to try to guess what Tess and Patricia are saying before listening to the audio recording.

52. Once students have finished this activity, ask them whether they agree or disagree with each statement. If they disagree, have them rewrite the sentences according to their opinions.

Gramática

Las comparaciones y el superlativo

Las comparaciones

- Things and people may be compared with respect to their characteristics and feelings.
- To express equality, use:

tan + adjective + como	*as ... as*

Pedro está **tan** aburrido **como** Luis.

verb + tanto como	*... as much as ...*

Yo estudio **tanto como** tú.

- To express inequality, use:

más / menos + adjective + que	*more/less ... than*

Antonia está **más** triste **que** Lola.
Ellos discuten **más que** nosotros.

verb + más que / menos que	*... more/less than*

Roberto está **menos** contento **que** Carlos.
Elena habla **menos que** yo.

El superlativo

- The superlative is used to express an extreme degree of an adjective.
- When the adjective ends in a consonant, add -ísimo, -ísima, -ísimos, -ísimas to form the superlative.

popular > + > ísimo   Carlos es popular**ísimo**.

- If the adjective ends in a vowel, drop the vowel before adding the superlative ending.

trist~~e~~ > + > ísimo   Pablo está trist**ísimo**.

- You can also use adverbs like *muy* before the adjective to express the same idea.
  Estamos **muy** tristes.

50 **Compara.** En español algunos adjetivos tienen formas de comparación irregulares, como *mejor* y *peor.* ¿Qué adjetivos tienen en inglés formas de comparación irregulares?

51 **Muy cansadas**

 ▶ **Escucha** a Tess y Patricia, y completa el diálogo.

PATRICIA: Tú estás ___1___ cansada ___2___ yo.
TESS: No, mamá. Yo estoy ___3___ cansada ___4___ tú.
PATRICIA: ¡Las dos estamos ___5___!

Differentiated Instruction

DEVELOPING LEARNERS

- Show students emoticons that exhibit the following emotions: nervous, happy, sad, angry, surprised, and in love. Ask students to compare two or more emoticons, by making statements such as, *La cara de la izquierda está tan nerviosa como la cara de la derecha.*

EXPANDING LEARNERS

- Ask students to imagine a person who is always competing with everyone. Have them rewrite the following sentences from this person's point of view.
  1. *Marta está tranquila. (Yo estoy tranquilísimo/a.)*
  2. *Marcos está aburrido. (Yo estoy aburridísimo/a.)*
  3. *Ana está sorprendida. (Yo estoy sorprendidísimo/a.)*
  4. *Estamos enojados. (Yo estoy enojadísimo/a.)*
  5. *Los chicos están enamorados. (Yo estoy enamoradísimo/a.)*

52 **¿Más o menos?**

▶ **Escribe** oraciones comparando el estado de ánimo de los personajes.

Modelo 1. *Patricia está más cansada que Tess.*

1. Patricia - (+ cansada) - Tess
2. Diana - (– tranquila) - Rita
3. Janet - (– contenta) - Diana
4. Andy - (+ aburrido) - Janet
5. Tim - (= emocionado) - Mack
6. Patricia - (= sorprendida) - Andy

53 **¿Quién es?**

 ▶ **Escribe** oraciones sobre los personajes. Utiliza el superlativo. Tu compañero(a) tiene que adivinar *(must guess)* a quién te refieres.

Modelo A. *Está contentísima.*
B. *¿Es Belén?*

Julieta　　Diego　　Alberto　　Belén　　Martín

 **CONEXIONES: LITERATURA**

Rubén Darío

Uno de los principales poetas en español es el nicaragüense Rubén Darío (1867–1916). A Darío le llaman «el padre del Modernismo» porque fue uno de los máximos representantes de este movimiento literario.

A los poetas modernistas les gusta describir los estados de ánimo, los sentimientos y el amor.

Sonatina

La princesa está triste... ¿Qué tendrá la princesa?
Los suspiros se escapan de su boca de fresa,
que ha perdido la risa, que ha perdido el color.
[...]
La princesa no ríe, la princesa no siente;
la princesa persigue por el cielo de Oriente
la libélula vaga de una vaga ilusión.

RUBÉN DARÍO

54 **Piensa y explica.** ¿Puede un poema afectar a tu estado de ánimo o solo lo puede describir?

⚑→ TU DESAFÍO Visita la página web para leer un poema de Rubén Darío. ¿Qué sentimientos describe?

HERITAGE LANGUAGE LEARNERS

- Ask students to explain or research some irregular forms of the superlative. For example, have them say what the superlative is for the following: *rico, simpático, antiguo,* and *feliz (riquísimo, simpatiquísimo, antiquísimo, felicísimo).* Then ask students to identify the irregular superlatives for these adjectives: *pobre, áspero, cierto, fiel, célebre,* and *valiente (paupérrimo, aspérrimo, certísimo, fidelísimo, celebérrimo, valentísimo).* Verify that students understand what these words mean.

- Have students write sentences with some of these superlatives.

MULTIPLE INTELLIGENCES:
Verbal-Linguistic Intelligence

- This section ends with an often-quoted poem by Rubén Darío. Ask students to think of an emotion or emotions they would like to express, and write a short poem to describe them. Encourage them to make at least one comparison in their work, or include one superlative. The poem does not need to rhyme, and students may use a dictionary to look up unfamiliar terms. They may add their own drawings or computer-generated graphic designs to their work. Ask volunteers to read their poetry to the class.

Gramática – Las comparaciones y el superlativo

54. Pose this question aloud to the class. If students say that a poem can affect your feelings, then encourage them to find an age-appropriate poem that they believe can do so.

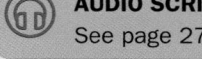 **AUDIO SCRIPT**
See page 271.

CONEXIONES: LITERATURA

Rubén Darío

Rubén Darío was born in Metapa, Nicaragua, in 1867. The town was later renamed Ciudad Darío after Rubén became a world-renowned poet. He was raised by his great-aunt and -uncle in León, Nicaragua. It is said that by age four he was reading and writing his first lines of poetry. By 13, he was a published poet. Darío has influenced poets across Central and South America, as well as Europe.

Answer Key

50. Ejemplos de formas irregulares en inglés: good → better; bad → worse; far → further, farther.

51.
1. más
2. que
3. menos
4. que
5. cansadísimas

52.
1. Patricia está más cansada que Tess.
2. Diana está menos tranquila que Rita.
3. Janet está menos contenta que Diana.
4. Andy está más aburrido que Janet.
5. Tim está tan emocionado como Mack.
6. Patricia está tan sorprendida como Andy.

53. Answers will vary.

54. Answers will vary.

Additional Resources

Fans Online activities
Practice Workbook

Unit 1
DESAFÍO 3
Comunicación

Presentation

- In this section, students will integrate the vocabulary and grammar from *Desafío 3* in order to express emotional states, to make comparisons, and to express the extreme of an adjective by using superlatives.

Activities	Standards	Resources
55.	1.2	Audio
56.	1.1, 1.3, 5.1	
57.	1.1, 1.3, 5.1	
58.	1.2	
59. Final del desafío	1.3, 2.2, 5.1	

Teaching Suggestions

Warm-Up / Independent Starter

- Have students create a list of superlatives for the students in their class. Ask students to pick categories like the funniest, the most popular, and the most studious.

Preparation

- Ask students to get into small groups and discuss their picks for the superlatives. If students have a different answer for a particular category, ask them to compare their picks. For example:
  A. *Mark Sánchez es graciosísimo.*
  B. *No, Michele Green es graciosísima.*
  A. *Sí, estoy de acuerdo. Michelle es más graciosa que Mark.*
  Or: *No, no estoy de acuerdo. Michelle es menos graciosa que Mark.*
- Take 10 minutes to review the vocabulary and grammar themes of the *Desafío*.
- Refer students back to the *fotonovela* for *Desafío 3*. Have them find all of the emotional states, comparisons, and superlatives within the dialogue. Do students understand the dialogue better now that they have gone through the vocabulary and grammar from the *Desafío*?
- Complete the *Comunicación* activities as a class. Choose four volunteers, one to lead each of the four activities on the double page. Do not assign the *Final del desafío* activity.

DESAFÍO 3

Comunicación

55 **El día de Tess**

 ▶ **Escucha** y decide. ¿Cómo se siente hoy Tess?

| cansada | contenta | aburrida | enferma | triste |

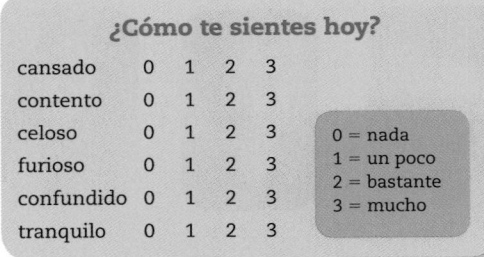

56 **¿Cómo estamos?**

▶ **Completa** esta encuesta *(survey)* sobre tu estado de ánimo.

¿Cómo te sientes hoy?

cansado	0	1	2	3
contento	0	1	2	3
celoso	0	1	2	3
furioso	0	1	2	3
confundido	0	1	2	3
tranquilo	0	1	2	3

0 = nada
1 = un poco
2 = bastante
3 = mucho

▶ **Pregunta** a tus compañeros(as) cómo se sienten hoy. Toma nota de sus respuestas.

Modelo

¿Estás cansado hoy, Juan?

Sí, bastante.

▶ **Escribe** seis comparaciones entre tu estado de ánimo y el de tus compañeros(as).

Modelo *Hoy yo estoy más cansado que Amy y Marta, pero estoy menos cansado que Juan.*

57 **Diálogos**

▶ **Escribe** diálogos con tu compañero(a) expresando los siguientes estados de ánimo.

1. frustradísimo(a)
2. nerviosísimo(a)
3. tranquilísimo(a)
4. aburridísimo(a)
5. tristísimo(a)
6. cansadísimo(a)

▶ **Representa** dos de tus diálogos con tu compañero(a).

—¿Qué te pasa?
—Estoy aburridísimo.
—¿Por qué? ¿No te gusta la película?
—No, no me gustan nada las películas de amor.

Differentiated Instruction

DEVELOPING LEARNERS

- Help students to understand that while the superlative in Spanish is similar to adding "very" before an adjective in English, it stresses the degree of the adjective. "I'm very tired" could be expressed by *Estoy muy cansado.* "I'm extremely tired" or "I'm really, really tired" might be better expressed by *Estoy cansadísimo.*
- Clarify for students that *tan* is used only before an adjective that is followed by *como*, and that *tanto como* is used after a verb. Ask students to say one or two sentences with *tan... como* and *tanto como*.

EXPANDING LEARNERS

- Using Tess and Lucía's e-mails as a model, ask students to compose a letter or e-mail to a friend. In the body, students should describe what they are doing at present, and what emotional states they are experiencing. They should be sure to make at least one comparison and use one superlative form of an adjective.

58 El mensaje de correo de Tess

▶ **Lee** los mensajes de correo de Tess y su amiga Lucía. Decide si las siguientes oraciones son ciertas o falsas.

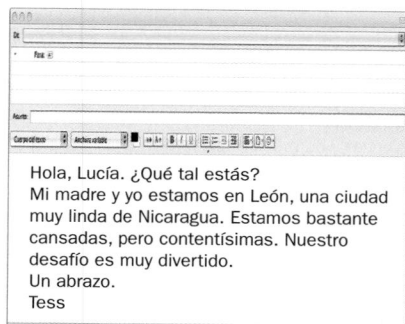

Hola, Lucía. ¿Qué tal estás?
Mi madre y yo estamos en León, una ciudad muy linda de Nicaragua. Estamos bastante cansadas, pero contentísimas. Nuestro desafío es muy divertido.
Un abrazo.
Tess

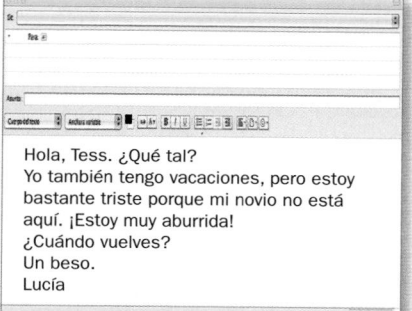

Hola, Tess. ¿Qué tal?
Yo también tengo vacaciones, pero estoy bastante triste porque mi novio no está aquí. ¡Estoy muy aburrida!
¿Cuándo vuelves?
Un beso.
Lucía

1. Tess está más cansada que Lucía.
2. Lucía está tan contenta como Tess.
3. Tess está más aburrida que Lucía.
4. Lucía está menos triste que Tess.

Final del desafío

59 Muchas gigantonas

▶ **Escribe** el diálogo entre Tess y Patricia. Luego represéntalo con tu compañero(a).

Activities

55. Have the audio recording ready for the volunteer in charge of this activity. Tell this volunteer to read the instructions, then play the audio recording two times. After he or she has finished playing the recording a second time, have him or her go over the answers aloud.

56. Ask this volunteer to read the instructions, then pair students in order to complete the survey and the writing exercise. Once students have finished, have the volunteer call on students to read their answers aloud.

57. Ask this volunteer to read the instructions, then pair students with a different partner than in the previous activity. Once students have finished, have the volunteer call on students to perform their skits for the class.

58. Ask the volunteer for this activity to read the instructions, then choose two students to read the two e-mails. Have the volunteer read the items to the class, and the class will answer with *cierto* or *falso*.

59. Thank your volunteers, then divide the class into small groups to complete the *Final del desafío*.

 AUDIO SCRIPT
See page 271.

Answer Key

55. Tess está enferma, aburrida y cansada.

56. Answers will vary.
▶ Answers will vary.
▶ Answers will vary.

57. Answers will vary.
▶ Answers will vary.

58. 1. Cierto   3. Falso
     2. Falso   4. Falso

59. Answers will vary.

Additional Resources

Fans Online activities
Practice Workbook

HERITAGE LANGUAGE LEARNERS

• Help students increase their vocabulary by asking them to write the corresponding nouns for the adjectives that appear on page 52. For example: *tranquila → tranquilidad; nervioso → nervios; enamorados → amor; celoso → celos; confundida → confusión; sorprendidos → sorpresa; furiosa → furia; aburrido → aburrimiento; contento → contento; emocionado → emoción; enojado → enojo; frustrado → frustración; triste → tristeza.*

• Have students add these words to their notebooks.

COOPERATIVE LEARNING

• Ask students to work with a partner to create a dialogue to compare their emotional states. Student A will express how he or she feels, and student B will respond by stating *Yo estoy tan* (adjective) *como tú* or *Yo estoy más/menos* (adjective) *que tú.* Ask each partner to make at least three statements.

DESAFÍO 4

Hacer preguntas

Presentation

- In *Desafío 4*, Tim and Mack are at the Rincón de la Vieja National Park in Costa Rica. There they must register and ride a zip line over the rainforest.

- In this section, students will preview how to ask and answer questions in order to give and obtain personal information.

Activities	Standards	Resources
Fotonovela	1.2, 2.1, 3.1	Vis. Pres.
60.	1.2	
61.	1.2, 1.3	Audio
62.	1.1, 5.2	
63. Conexiones	1.2, 2.2, 3.1, 3.2, 4.2, 5.1	

Teaching Suggestions

Warm-Up / Independent Starter

- Ask students to cover up the introduction to the *fotonovela* and write a short paragraph about what they think Tim and Mack have to do.

Preparation

- Read the introduction to the *fotonovela* aloud. Ask students if they or anyone in their family have ever been on a zip line. Then ask students what the physical characteristics and personality traits of a person who enjoys this type of activity might be.

- Ask students if they remember what Tim and Mack had to do in the Unit 1 of Level 1 that was risky. (They had to participate in the dance of the Papantla Flyers.) Ask students how that task compares to this one.

La fotonovela

Before Viewing

- Have students read the *fotonovela*. Ask them to write five sentences describing and comparing Tim and Mack based on what they've read.

- Now ask students what information Tim and Mack will need to register for their zip line session. Why is this information important? Elicit that the administrators of the zip line session need to know this information for the clients' safety and to assess their ability to perform the task at hand.

Un viaje arbóreo

 Tim and Mack are at the *Parque Nacional Rincón de la Vieja*, in the Costa Rican rainforest. They must put on a harness and glide through the top of the jungle attached to a cable. But first, they must register.

Mira, abuelo, nosotros tenemos que hacer eso. ¡Qué miedo!

Abuelo, tú no vas a montar, ¿verdad?

No te preocupes, Tim. Estas personas son profesionales.

¡Claro que sí! La edad es solo un número. Vamos a inscribirnos en la oficina.

¿Me dicen su nombre y sus apellidos?

Yo tengo dieciséis años y mi abuelo, sesenta y dos.

¿Y sus edades, por favor?

Me llamo Mack Taylor. Este es mi nieto Tim. Su apellido también es Taylor.

¿De dónde son?

Somos de San Francisco, California.

Continuará...

60 **Detective de palabras**

▶ **Completa** las oraciones.

1. La _____ es solo un número.
2. ¿Me dicen su _____ y sus apellidos?
3. El _____ de Tim también es Taylor.
4. Tim tiene dieciséis _____.
5. ¿De _____ son?

Differentiated Instruction

DEVELOPING LEARNERS

- To make sure students understood the information in the *fotonovela*, ask the following questions:
  1. *¿Dónde están Mack y Tim?* (en el Parque Nacional Rincón de la Vieja)
  2. *¿Qué van a hacer?* (montar en tirolina, o zip line)
  3. *¿Cuál es el apellido de Mack y Tim?* (Taylor)
  4. *¿De dónde son Mack y Tim?* (de San Francisco)
  5. *¿Cuántos años tiene Mack? ¿Y Tim?* (sesenta y dos; dieciséis)

EXPANDING LEARNERS

- Ask students to work in groups of three and imagine that they are going to take a zip line tour of the Costa Rican forests with a family member or friend. Students will decide who plays the part of the zip tour employee and those of the tourists. They may base their dialogues on the *fotonovela*, or create something entirely new. After groups have had a chance to practice, call on some to role-play their dialogues in front of the class.

61 En una oficina

▶ **Escucha** el diálogo entre Mack y un oficinista. Selecciona cuáles de estos datos le pide.
Listen to the dialogue and select the information that they need to provide.

Nombre	Fecha de nacimiento
Apellidos	Edad
Domicilio	Lugar de nacimiento

▶ **Escucha** otra vez y escribe la información que da Mack.

▶ **Escribe** tu propia información para los datos que pide la agencia.

Modelo *Nombre: Me llamo Carla.*

62 Planes de viaje

▶ **Habla** con tu compañero(a) para planear *(to plan)* un viaje. Hazle preguntas sobre los detalles del viaje con estos interrogativos.

¿Quién?   ¿Qué?   ¿Dónde?   ¿Cuándo?   ¿Cómo?

Modelo *¿Quién va con nosotros?*

CONEXIONES: CIENCIAS

Rincón de la Vieja

En Costa Rica hay muchos parques naturales. Uno de ellos es el Parque Nacional Rincón de la Vieja, en el norte del país. Este parque es un gran destino para practicar el ecoturismo. Allí hay selva, volcanes, ríos, lagos y aguas termales *(hot springs)*.

La mejor forma de admirar la gran variedad de plantas y animales es a caballo o montando en tirolina *(zip line)*.

63 **Compara.** ¿Conoces algún lugar en tu país para hacer ecoturismo? ¿Cuáles son las ventajas *(advantages)* y desventajas *(disadvantages)* del ecoturismo?

HERITAGE LANGUAGE LEARNERS

- Have students compare and contrast attitudes on aging in Hispanic cultures and in the United States. Do students think that "senior citizens" like Mack would be more respected in a Spanish-speaking country than in the States? What evidence do they have to support or refute this? How do the younger members of their families view the elderly? What kind of relationships do they have with their much older relatives? Conduct a classroom discussion to talk about these issues.

CRITICAL THINKING

- Mack states: *La edad es solo un número.* Ask students what they think he means by this remark. Do students feel that people in the United States discriminate against the elderly, and believe they are incapable of "keeping up" with younger men and women? Or do they think that younger people, especially teenagers, are discriminated against? Conduct a classroom discussion on the age discrimination topic.

After Viewing

- Take a vote of the number of students that think Tim and Mack will actually go through with this task. Ask students to explain why or why not.

Activities

61. Due to privacy concerns, it may be better for students to keep their addresses and other personal information private. This is a great opportunity for students to give themselves an address that they would like.

62. Once students have finished answering the questions, have them turn the information into an official invitation for an ecotourism trip. Have students share their invitations with the class.

AUDIO SCRIPT
See page 27J.

CONEXIONES: CIENCIAS

Rincón de la Vieja

This National Park is located in the state of Guanacaste, in Costa Rica. It was created in 1973 and includes the Rincón de la Vieja Volcano. The forests in this park are among the most pristine in Central America. A good way to tour the 34,800 acres of park is on horseback.

Answer Key

60.
1. edad	4. años
2. nombre	5. dónde
3. apellido	

61. Nombre, apellidos y fecha de nacimiento.
▶ Mack Taylor; 7 de marzo.
▶ Answers will vary.

62. Answers will vary.

63. Answers will vary.

Additional Resources

Fans Online activities

DESAFÍO 4

Vocabulario – Información personal

Presentation

- In this section, students will learn to ask for and give personal information.

Activities	Standards	Resources
Vocabulario	1.2	
64.	1.2, 1.3	
65.	1.2, 1.3	
66.	1.1, 1.3	
67. Cultura	1.2, 1.3, 2.1, 3.2	

Teaching Suggestions

Warm-Up / Independent Starter

- Have students write a list of places in which they will need to provide their personal information.

Preparation

- Ask for volunteers to call out the places on their lists. One place that many students will have on their lists is the Department (or Bureau) of Motor Vehicles.

- Take this opportunity to remind students not to share their personal information with strangers. For privacy purposes, have students make up an address and a passport or identification number for today's activities.

- Go over the vocabulary presentation with students. Point out the fact that an address is written differently in Spanish than it is in English, and may vary by country. Draw students' attention to the part of the *Hoja de inscripción* that says *Domicilio actual*. The c/ Zola stands for *calle* Zola or in English, Zola Street. These words are inverted just as the adjectives are inverted. Also tell students that in this case, the house number comes after the street name. Give students the example 1600 Pennsylvania Avenue (*avenida*), and have them practice writing this in a different format in their notebooks.

Activities

66. Complete the questions portion of this activity as a class. See if students can come up with different questions for each clue. For example: *Nombre – ¿Cómo te llamas? ¿Cuál es tu nombre? ¿Quién eres?*

Vocabulario

Información personal

> ¿Cómo te llamas?
>
> Me llamo Peter Wolcott.
>
> ¿De dónde eres?
>
> Soy de los Estados Unidos.
>
> ¿Cuál es tu fecha de nacimiento?
>
> El cuatro de mayo de 1995.
>
> ¿Dónde vives ahora?
>
> Vivo en la calle Zola, número 35.
>
> ¿Cuál es tu número de pasaporte o de identidad?
>
> El 1367890.

HOJA DE INSCRIPCIÓN

NOMBRE: Peter

APELLIDOS: Wolcott

FECHA DE NACIMIENTO: 4/5/95

LUGAR DE NACIMIENTO: Estados Unidos

DOMICILIO ACTUAL: c/ Zola, 35, San José

ESTADO CIVIL: soltero

N.º DE IDENTIDAD
O PASAPORTE: 1367890

64 Datos personales

▶ **Une** la información con la pregunta correspondiente.

Ⓐ

1. Domicilio actual
2. Nombre
3. Lugar de origen
4. Número de pasaporte
5. Fecha de nacimiento

Ⓑ

a. ¿Cómo te llamas?
b. ¿Cuál es tu número de pasaporte?
c. ¿De dónde eres?
d. ¿Cuándo es tu cumpleaños?
e. ¿Dónde vives ahora?

▶ **Completa** una hoja de inscripción con tus datos.

Differentiated Instruction

DEVELOPING LEARNERS

- Ask students to complete an *Hoja de inscripción* like the one on page 86 for each of the characters in this *Desafío*. Students may need to make up some of the information like their addresses and I.D. numbers, but they should keep in mind their ages to determine their birthdates.

EXPANDING LEARNERS

- Have students use the subheads from the *Hoja de inscripción* on page 60, but include information about a Hispanic celebrity. They may make up some of the data, but they should write the address and the dates as if they were in a Spanish-speaking country, where it is common to write the day first, then the month, and finally the year. May 10, 2012 would be written 10/5/12 (or 10/V/12). Then have students exchange their papers with a partner and take turns asking each other relevant questions in order to obtain the information from the *Hoja*.

65 Una hoja de inscripción

▶ **Completa** los datos de la hoja de inscripción *(registration form)* con la información de Carlos.

Yo me llamo Carlos Sánchez Mora. Vivo en la calle 32 en San José, pero soy de Puerto Limón (Costa Rica).

HOJA DE INSCRIPCIÓN

Nombre:

Apellidos:

Domicilio:

Lugar de nacimiento:

66 Preguntas y respuestas

▶ **Escribe** la pregunta apropiada para pedir los siguientes datos.

1. Nombre
2. Apellidos
3. Domicilio
4. Lugar de nacimiento
5. Fecha de nacimiento

▶ **Pregunta** a dos compañeros(as) para obtener *(to obtain)* información.

Modelo 1. Nombre: *¿Cómo te llamas?*

CULTURA

Los apellidos

En los países hispanos se usan dos apellidos. Normalmente el primer apellido es el apellido del padre y el segundo es el apellido de la madre. En general, las mujeres no cambian su apellido cuando se casan.

Ejemplo: Carlos   López   Sánchez
                              (apellido   (apellido
                              del padre)   de la madre)

67 Piensa. Imagina que vives en un país hispano. ¿Cuáles serían tus apellidos?

HERITAGE LANGUAGE LEARNERS

- Ask students to provide alternative ways of asking the same questions on page 60 by using the formal *usted* rather than the informal *tú*. For example, they might ask: *¿Cómo se llama usted? ¿De dónde es? ¿Cuál es su fecha de nacimiento? ¿Dónde vive ahora? ¿Cuál es su número de pasaporte o de identidad?*
- Have students discuss when speakers might address each other with *tú* and when only *usted* would be appropriate.

COOPERATIVE LEARNING

- In groups of five or six, students will play a version of "Jeopardy." You will give them answers and they will need to supply the corresponding questions by standing up and being the first to ask them.
  1. *Soy de Nueva York. (¿De dónde eres?)*
  2. *El 20 de noviembre. (¿Cuál es tu fecha de nacimiento?)*
  3. *Tres hermanos. (¿Cuántos hermanos tienes?)*
  4. *Dieciséis. (¿Cuántos años tienes?)*
  5. *Belmonte. (¿Cuál es tu apellido?)*

DESAFÍO 4

Vocabulario – Información personal

67. Ask students to think about the following situation. Mario López García marries Luisa Pérez Martín. What would their child's last names be? (López Pérez) The child takes the first surname of each parent.

CULTURA

Los apellidos

Sometimes you may see the word *de* in someone's last name. In the case of married women, it could be that the person has decided to take on her husband's last name, using *de* to differentiate it from her own (e.g., Ana García de Hernández). There are also some last names in which *de* is simply part of the last name (e.g., Carlos de la Vega Sánchez). A good rule of thumb is to say that a child takes on the first last name of each of his or her parents, and that women generally do not change their name when they get married.

Answer Key

64. 1. e   2. a   3. c   4. b   5. d
   ▶ Answers will vary.

65. Nombre: Carlos
   Apellidos: Sánchez Mora
   Domicilio: calle 32, San José
   Lugar de origen: Puerto Limón (Costa Rica)

66. Answers will vary. Sample answers:
   1. ¿Cómo te llamas?
   2. ¿Cuáles son tus apellidos?
   3. ¿Dónde vives?
   4. ¿De dónde eres?
   5. ¿Cuál es tu fecha de nacimiento?
   ▶ Answers will vary.

67. Answers will vary.

Additional Resources

Fans Online activities
Practice Workbook

DESAFÍO 4

Gramática – Los interrogativos

Presentation

- In this section, students will learn to ask for and give personal information.

Activities	Standards	Resources
Gramática	3.1	
68.	1.3, 3.1, 4.1	
69.	1.2	
70.	1.2	Audio
71.	1.3	
72.	1.3	
73.	1.1, 1.2, 1.3	

Teaching Suggestions

Warm-Up / Independent Starter

- Have students design a job application. First, they must create their company's name and the job title for which they are hiring. Then they must create the actual application. Tell students to leave enough space for someone to fill in the required information.

Preparation

- Have students go around the room and see which company and job title they think will best suit them. Once they find a job they like, have students fill out the application. Remind students to use their fake addresses and identification numbers.

- Go over the grammar presentation with students. Remind them that the interrogatives in Spanish have a question mark at the beginning and the end of the question.

- Ask student to create one question for each of the interrogatives. Ask for volunteers to read their questions aloud.

Activities

69. Ask students what the difference is between *cuál* and *cuáles*. (The difference is that *cuál* is singular and *cuáles* is plural.) Remind students to look at the verb in the sentence to make sure that the interrogative word and the verb agree in number.

70. After students put the questions in order, play the audio again and have students write the answers next to the questions. That way, students can have a record of how to answer questions.

Gramática

Los interrogativos

Hacer preguntas

- Interrogatives are words that are used to ask questions. Normally, interrogatives go at the beginning of a sentence.

  ¿Cómo te llamas?   ¿Dónde vives?

PRINCIPALES INTERROGATIVOS

¿Qué?	What?		¿Cuándo?	When?
¿Cuál(es)?	Which?		¿Cómo?	How?
¿Quién(es)?	Who?		¿Por qué?	Why?
¿Cuánto(a)?	How much?		¿Para qué?	What for?
¿Cuántos(as)?	How many?		¿Adónde?	Where to?
¿Dónde?	Where?		¿De dónde?	Where from?

- Cuál, cuáles are used to ask about one or more elements in a group. They are always followed by a verb, never by a noun.

  Aquí hay muchos libros. ¿Cuál es el tuyo?

- To ask where someone is from, use de dónde. Use adónde to ask where someone is going.

  ¿De dónde eres?   ¿Adónde va Juan?

Responder preguntas

- If the question begins with a question word, it is answered with the information that question word refers to.

  –¿Cómo te llamas?
  –Me llamo Alicia.

- If the question does not have a question word, it is answered with sí or no. To answer a question in the negative form, use double negation—once to answer, and once before the verb.

  –¿Eres española?
  –Sí. soy española / No, no soy española. Soy hondureña.

68 **Compara.** En español no se usa un verbo auxiliar para hacer preguntas. ¿Qué verbo se usa en inglés?

69 **¿Cuál o cuáles?**

▶ **Completa** estas oraciones con *cuál* o *cuáles*.

1. ¿ _____ es tu clase favorita?
2. ¿ _____ son tus mejores amigos?
3. ¿ _____ es tu país de origen?
4. ¿ _____ es tu número de teléfono?
5. ¿ _____ son los libros para la clase de Español?
6. ¿ _____ son tus profesores?

Differentiated Instruction

DEVELOPING LEARNERS

- Give students more practice with interrogatives by asking them to choose the correct word to complete the following questions.

1. ¿Qué / Cuál es tu nombre? (Cuál)
2. ¿Adónde / De dónde vas? (Adónde)
3. ¿Qué / Cuál idioma hablas? (Qué)
4. ¿Quiénes / Quién son tus profesores? (Quiénes)
5. ¿De dónde / Adónde es tu profesor de Español? (De dónde)
6. ¿Cuántos / Cuántas hermanas tienes? (Cuántas)

EXPANDING LEARNERS

- Ask students which historical figure they would like to interview, including individuals like Cleopatra, Christopher Columbus, or Montezuma, who all lived many years ago. They need to identify the person, and then write ten questions using a variety of interrogatives. If time permits, have other students play the role of the interviewee and, working in pairs, deliver the historical interview before the class.

70 **Preguntas y respuestas**

▶ **Escucha** las respuestas y ordena las preguntas que le hace Tim a su amiga.

A ¿Dónde vives?

B ¿De dónde eres?

C ¿Cómo te llamas?

D ¿Qué estudias?

71 **Interrogaciones**

▶ **Completa** estas oraciones con un interrogativo. Hay varias respuestas posibles.

1. ¿_____ es la profesora de Español?
2. ¿_____ es tu clase favorita?
3. ¿_____ vives?
4. ¿_____ lenguas hablas?

72 **Formas negativas**

▶ **Responde** a estas preguntas en forma negativa.

Modelo ¿Estudias español?
→ *No, no estudio español.*

1. ¿Vives en El Salvador?
2. ¿Eres de Costa Rica?
3. ¿Te llamas Pedro?
4. ¿Tienes hermanos?
5. ¿Estás casado?
6. ¿Eres perezoso?

73 **Una entrevista importante**

▶ **Escribe** seis preguntas para entrevistar *(to interview)* a un personaje importante.

Modelo *¿Cuál es tu película favorita?*

▶ **Responde** a las preguntas de tu compañero(a). Imagina que eres ese personaje importante.

sesenta y tres 63

Gramática – Los interrogativos

72. Now have students work with a partner to answer these questions with the real answer. For example:
A. *¿Vives en El Salvador?*
B. *No, no vivo en El Salvador. Vivo en Richmond, VA.*

73. Have students organize their interview. First, they must pick the position of the person they want to interview. Is this person a celebrity, the First Lady of the United States, the CEO of a company, etc.? Second, students must figure out the questions that are most relevant to this person's position. Finally, have students explain the person to their partner before they interview each other.

AUDIO SCRIPT
See page 27J.

Answer Key

68. En inglés se usa el verbo auxiliar *do.*

69.
1. Cuál	4. Cuál
2. Cuáles	5. Cuáles
3. Cuál	6. Cuáles

70. 1. c 2. a 3. b 4. d

71. Answers will vary. Sample answers:
1. Quién	3. Dónde
2. Cuál	4. Cuántas

72.
1. No, no vivo en El Salvador.
2. No, no soy de Costa Rica.
3. No, no me llamo Pedro.
4. No, no tengo hermanos.
5. No, no estoy casado(a).
6. No, no soy perezoso(a).

73. Answers will vary.
▶ Answers will vary.

Additional Resources

Fans Online activities
Practice Workbook

HERITAGE LANGUAGE LEARNERS

• Divide the class into two teams to play a word game. One player from each team chooses an interrogative (for example, *¿dónde?*) and writes it on the board for his or her team only. By turns, teammates will say a word that starts with each letter in *dónde* (*divertido, otoño, niño, día, enero*). For every correct word, the team scores a point. If a player fails to name a word, one point is subtracted from the team's score.

TOTAL PHYSICAL RESPONSE (TPR)

• Ask students to look at the photo of Tim making a gesture of "no" with his hand. Have them think of other gestures that are commonly used by Spanish speakers to emphasize something they are saying or as a substitute for words. They will then work with a partner or in small groups and come up with several typical (and polite!) gestures. Ask them to use these gestures in front of the class, and have classmates try to guess what they mean.

Unit 1
DESAFÍO 4
Comunicación

Presentation

- In this section, students will integrate the vocabulary and grammar from *Desafío 4* in order to ask questions and to give and obtain personal information.

Activities	Standards	Resources
74.	1.2	Audio
75.	1.1, 1.3	
76.	1.3, 5.1	
77.	1.1, 1.2, 1.3, 3.1, 5.1	
78. Final del desafío	1.2, 1.3	
Tu desafío	1.2, 1.3	

Teaching Suggestions

Warm-Up / Independent Starter

- Have students answer the following questions in complete sentences.
  1. *¿Cuándo es la clase de Español?*
  2. *¿Dónde está el salón de clase de Español?*
  3. *¿De dónde vienes antes de la clase de Español?*
  4. *¿Quién es el profesor / la profesora de Español?*
  5. *¿Cuántos estudiantes hay en la clase de Español?*

Preparation

- Ask students to imagine they work for a pizza delivery chain. In pairs, have them role-play the scenario. One student will play the role of the person answering the phone and the other student will play the role of the customer. Tell the person answering the phone to ask all the questions necessary to deliver the customer's pizza.

- Take 10 minutes to review the vocabulary and grammar themes of *Desafío 4*.

- Refer students back to the *fotonovela*. Have them find all of the personal information and interrogatives within the dialogue. Do students understand the dialogue better now that they have gone through the vocabulary and grammar from the *Desafío*?

- Make the *Comunicación* activities a competition. Divide the class into small groups. Have each group complete activities 74–77. The first group to finish and have all answers correct, wins. Remind students that they should focus on speed and accuracy at the same time.

64

Comunicación

74 **Una entrevista por televisión**

▶ **Escucha** la entrevista de la televisión local a Mack y decide si responde de forma afirmativa o negativa a estas preguntas.

1. ¿Es la primera vez que viene usted a Costa Rica?
2. ¿Le gusta Costa Rica?
3. Ustedes están aquí para completar un desafío para Fans del español, ¿no es cierto?
4. ¿Es un desafío difícil?
5. ¿No tiene usted miedo?
6. ¿Participa su nieto también en el desafío?

75 **Presentaciones**

▶ **Escribe** las preguntas que corresponden a la información de Sara y Alberto, dos amigos de Mack y Tim.

Modelo   1. *¿Cómo te llamas?*

Hola. (1) Me llamo Sara. (2) Soy de Nicaragua. (3) Mi clase favorita es Geografía. (4) Soy una buena estudiante y no soy perezosa. (5) Tengo 17 años.

(6) Yo soy Alberto. (7) Tengo dos hermanos y una hermana. (8) Mi deporte favorito es el tenis. (9) Vivo en los Estados Unidos. (10) Soy de Nicaragua.

76 **Una historia**

▶ **Haz** un diagrama sobre una historia real o ficticia para organizar tus ideas. Después, utilízalo para contar la historia a tu compañero(a).

Make a story map for a story you know or have made up. Use question words to organize your thoughts. Then, tell the story to your classmates.

¿Dónde?
¿Cómo?   ¿Quién es?   ¿Por qué?
¿Qué?   ¿Cuándo?

Differentiated Instruction

DEVELOPING LEARNERS

- Ask students to write a list of five questions using the interrogatives presented in this *Desafío*. Then have them get together with a partner, exchange lists, and answer each other's questions in writing. Be sure students use correct punctuation and include accents on all interrogatives.

EXPANDING LEARNERS

- Have students work with a partner and imagine that they have just completed a tour of the Costa Rican jungle via zip line. Ask them to record their reactions to the experience in a short dialogue. They should describe their emotions and what they observe during their ride. The dialogue should also indicate whether or not they would like to repeat the experience.

77 **Personajes**

▶ **Busca** información sobre un personaje famoso y prepara una presentación. Incluye (include) estos datos: nombre y apellidos, lugar de origen, edad, descripción física y características personales.

▶ **Prepara** algunas preguntas sobre los personajes de las presentaciones de tus compañeros(as).

Modelo ¿Qué lenguas habla?

Final del desafío

¿Están listos?

¡Sí! ¿ __1__ distancia hay desde aquí hasta el final?

¿ __2__ termina el Zip Tour?

¡¡¡Aaaaahhhhhh!!!

¡Qué maravilla! ¿ __3__ cuesta repetir?

¿Repetir? Huy, no. ¿ __4__ está la salida?

78 **¿Qué pasa en la historia?**

▶ **Completa** el diálogo con las palabras que faltan (missing words). Después, represéntalo con tus compañeros(as).

→ TU DESAFÍO Visita la página web. Escucha las preguntas de tu *Minientrevista Desafío 4* y escribe las respuestas.

Activities

76. If students are having a hard time choosing a story to use, recommend some childhood favorites, such as *Goldilocks and the Three Bears*, *Hansel and Gretel*, or *Cinderella*. All of these options talk about the themes of this unit: families, physical characteristics, personality traits, emotional states, and personal information.

78. Now that students have finished the competition, do the *Final del desafío* as a class. Ask for three volunteers to play the roles of the zip line coordinator, Tim, and Mack. Tell the volunteers to stop reading when they get to a blank to allow the rest of the class to call out the answer. Then have the volunteers read the dialogue again with the correct answers included.

AUDIO SCRIPT
See page 27J.

Answer Key

74. 1. negativa 4. negativa
2. afirmativa 5. negativa
3. afirmativa 6. afirmativa

75. Answers will vary. Sample answers:
1. ¿Cómo te llamas?
2. ¿De dónde eres?
3. ¿Cuál es tu clase favorita?
4. ¿Eres perezosa?
5. ¿Cuántos años tienes?
6. ¿Quién eres?
7. ¿Cuántos hermanos tienes?
8. ¿Cuál es tu deporte favorito?
9. ¿Dónde vives ahora?
10. ¿De dónde eres?

76. Answers will vary.

77. Answers will vary.
▶ Answers will vary.

78. 1. Qué 2. Cuándo 3. Cuánto 4. Dónde

Additional Resources

Fans Online activities
Practice Workbook

HERITAGE LANGUAGE LEARNERS

• Tim uses the expression *¡Guau!* to indicate "Wow!" Ask students to think of other expressions that might be used to express wonder or amazement and have them share these with the entire class. They should be prepared to say in which countries, or regions of a country, these expressions might be heard. Some examples include: *¡Ah!, ¡caramba!, ¡caray!, ¡genial!,* and *¡soberbio!*

COOPERATIVE LEARNING

• Ask students to work in small groups and imagine they are the owners of a zip tour business in Costa Rica. They want to promote their business by distributing some brochures. First, they will need to work together to agree on a name, location, prices, and questions they will need to ask potential customers on the brochures. Then they will design their brochures to appeal to the public. Finally, members of the group will distribute the brochures to passersby (fellow classmates) to advertise their services.

65

Unit 1
TODO JUNTO

Presentation

- In this section, students will review the unit objectives and put them into practice.

Activities	Standards	Resources
79.	1.2	Audio
80.	1.2, 1.3	
81.	1.1, 1.2, 1.3	
82.	1.1, 1.3, 5.1	

Teaching Suggestions

Warm-Up / Independent Starter

- Ask students to flip back to the vocabulary and grammar presentations in this unit. Have students create a quick reference guide to the information in these presentations on the front and back of a postcard. This will serve as a study guide for the unit test, midterm examination, and final examination. Ask students to keep this study guide for future use throughout the academic year.

Preparation

- Ask students to choose two family members that do not live in their household. Then have students use the following prompts to write a four-paragraph composition. They should include one introductory paragraph, one paragraph about each family member and one paragraph comparing the two family members.
  1. Describe their physical characteristics and personality traits.
  2. Describe their usual demeanor.
  3. Give any personal information you know.
  4. Compare the two family members.

Activities

79. Before you play the audio, have students describe the people in each picture with a partner. Tell students to be sure to include their family relationships and physical descriptions.

80. Tell students to compare themselves with Paula. They may create a Venn diagram for the comparison. Then have students write an e-mail to Tess, comparing themselves to Paula.

ESCUCHAR

79 **¿Quién habla?**

▶ **Escucha** las descripciones y relaciona cada una con la ilustración correspondiente.

LEER

80 **Todo sobre Paula**

▶ **Lee** el mensaje de Tess sobre su amiga Paula y completa una tabla como esta.

Mi amiga Paula

Paula vive en Honduras. Tiene 16 años y estudia en la escuela secundaria. Es morena, lleva gafas y mide 1,68 metros. Es muy trabajadora y muy simpática. Tiene muchos amigos. Paula no tiene hermanos, pero tiene una prima de 15 años. Ellas se llevan muy bien. Paula está muy contenta hoy porque... ¡está de vacaciones!

Información personal	Características físicas	Personalidad	Relaciones familiares	Estado de ánimo

Differentiated instruction

DEVELOPING LEARNERS

- Ask students to work with several magazine cutouts of people with different physical characteristics and obvious personality traits or emotional states. Have them attach the image to a sheet of paper and then write questions using interrogatives to ask about their appearance, personality, and emotions. Have them answer their questions. Then they should make comparisons between the people in the images.

EXPANDING LEARNERS

- Ask students to review the illustrations in activity 79. Based on the characters' physical characteristics, ask students to compare and contrast the people shown. Have students assign various personality traits and emotional states to the characters and compare and contrast these, too. In addition, students should use the superlative form of some adjectives when describing these individuals.

LEER Y ESCRIBIR

 81 **Te presento a mi familia**

▶ **Lee** la carta *(letter)* de Marisol y decide si las afirmaciones son ciertas o falsas.

> ¡Hola! Soy Marisol, la amiga de Tess.
>
> Tengo tres hermanos. Mi hermana mayor está casada. Ella y su esposo tienen un bebé. Es una niña preciosa, se llama Lucía. Mi hermano Pepe está soltero, pero tiene novia. Ella se llama Patricia. Es un poco tímida, pero muy inteligente, más inteligente que él. Y mi hermana pequeña, Eva, es muy graciosa. Mis padres se llaman Javier y Telma.
>
> A mis hermanos les gusta jugar al voleibol. A mí también me gusta, pero ellos son mejores que yo y siempre ganan.
>
> Hoy estoy muy emocionada. Mi familia y yo estamos de vacaciones en la playa. Es muy divertido porque somos una familia muy grande y todos nos llevamos bien. También están con nosotros mis abuelos. Son mayores, pero los dos son fuertes y están sanos. Y mañana viene mi tío Julio. Es mi padrino. Es más serio que mi papá, pero me llevo muy bien con él.
>
> ¿Qué haces tú en tus vacaciones? ¿También estás con tu familia? Escríbeme. Hasta pronto.
>
> Marisol

1. La sobrina de Marisol se llama Lucía.
2. Patricia no es tan inteligente como Pepe.
3. Marisol juega mejor al voleibol que sus hermanos.
4. Hoy Marisol no está contenta.
5. El padrino de Marisol es más serio que su padre.
6. Marisol se lleva bien con su familia.

▶ **Escribe** una postal a Marisol.

HABLAR

 82 **Presentaciones**

 ▶ **Habla** con tu compañero(a) de la información que necesitan para crear un perfil *online*. Después, intercambia información para crear un perfil ficticio.

With a classmate, exchange information to create a fictitious profile online for each other.

Modelo A. ¿Cuál es tu nombre?
B. Mi nombre es Anita Márquez.
A. ¿De dónde eres?
B. Soy de Nicaragua.

Anita Márquez

Nacionalidad: nicaragüense

Edad: 16

Dirección:

Estado civil:

Personalidad:

Actividad favorita:

---

81. Tell students to correct all of the false statements. If the statement is true, then have students add another piece of true information from the postcard about that person.

82. Remind students to use their fake information when doing this activity. If time allows, have students create a poster with the information they obtained from their classmate. They may use a picture from a magazine of a celebrity look-a-like as the picture for the profile.

 **AUDIO SCRIPT**
See page 27J.

Answer Key

79. 1. A   2. C   3. D   4. B

80. Answers will vary. Sample answers:
- Información personal: Vive en Honduras. Tiene 16 años y estudia en la escuela secundaria.
- Características físicas: Es morena, lleva gafas y mide 1,68.
- Personalidad: Es muy trabajadora y muy simpática.
- Relaciones familiares: Paula no tiene hermanos, pero tiene una prima de 15 años con quien se lleva bien.
- Estado de ánimo: Está muy contenta.

81. 1. Cierto   4. Falso
2. Falso   5. Cierto
3. Falso   6. Cierto

▶ Answers will vary.

82. Answers will vary.

Additional Resources
Fans Online activities
Practice Workbook

HERITAGE LANGUAGE LEARNERS

- Ask students to write a note to a friend of one of the characters in the *Desafíos*. They should describe some of their own physical characteristics and personality traits, as well as those of some family members. In their descriptions, they should also make some comparisons between family members, including the use of the superlative. Remind students to use interrogatives by asking their new friend several questions.

CRITICAL THINKING

- Considering the four *desafíos* the pairs had to complete, ask students what each challenge taught them about the culture and heritage of the countries they were visiting. Do they think that these tasks could be interchangeable among all four countries? Do they think that any of the *Desafíos* could have been carried out in the United States? If so, which ones, and why? If not, why not?

Unit 1

El encuentro

Presentation

- The four pairs meet in front of the National Palace of Culture in Managua, Nicaragua. There they must read their poems to their host and judge, Felipe Santos.

- Students will vote for the winner of the *Desafíos* in Central America.

Activities	Standards	Resources
Fotonovela	1.2, 2.1, 2.2	
83.	1.3	
84.	1.2, 1.3, 3.2, 5.1, 5.2	

Teaching Suggestions

Warm-Up / Independent Starter

- Tell students to close their textbooks and write a summary of each pair's challenge in Central America. Ask students to use the vocabulary and grammar they learned in this unit to represent the *Desafío* in each description.

Preparation

- Remind students that in *Desafío 1*, Andy and Janet went to San Pedro de Atitlán, in Guatemala, to look for a giant. In *Desafío 2*, Diana and Rita went to Travesía, Honduras, to search for a Garífuna musician with a gift for them. In *Desafío 3*, Tess and Patricia went to Léon, Nicaragua, to find the tallest woman in town and dress like her. And in *Desafío 4*, Tim and Mack went to Rincón de la Vieja National Park in Costa Rica, to ride a zip line over the jungle.

La fotonovela

- Have students look at the pictures. Ask them to describe how each pair is related, their physical characteristics and personality traits, and how they feel in the pictures.

- Ask for volunteers to read each pair's poem. Remind the volunteers that they are reading poems, and should try to keep the rhythm while reading. If time allows, have the volunteers practice before performing in front of the class.

El encuentro

En el Palacio Nacional de Cultura

The pairs meet in front of the National Palace of Culture in Managua. The four pairs have all completed their tasks, and they have written poems to document their experience.

Hola, chicos. ¿Qué tal? ¿Completaron sus desafíos?

«Andy busca y busca al gigante...

... y Janet le dice que está delante».

«Marcos siempre está contento...

... porque sabe tocar un instrumento».

«Como las famosas gigantonas de León...

... nos vemos bonitas ¡y medimos un montón!»

«Mack es mi nombre, Taylor mi apellido...

... mi abuelo y yo somos muy atrevidos.»

Differentiated Instruction

DEVELOPING LEARNERS

- Ask students to imagine that they are tourists and are standing by the National Palace of Culture when the participants of the *Desafíos* appear. Have them say or write observations about the characters' physical traits, their personalities, and their emotional states when they arrive. Encourage students to make comparisons between the pairs.

EXPANDING LEARNERS

- Ask students which *desafío* they would have liked to take part in, and why. Did the challenge take place in a country they would like to visit? Or was the challenge something that has always interested them or something they have thought about doing? They should also include the name of a family member or friend with whom they would have liked to participate, and why they chose this person.

El encuentro

83 **Al llegar**

▶ **Escribe** un resumen *(summary)* sobre el desafío de una pareja. Incluye esta información.

• Quiénes son y qué relación hay entre ellos.

> Los personajes son Andy y Janet. Son hermanos y se llevan muy bien.

• Cómo son (aspecto físico y personalidad).

> Andy es alto y atlético. Es calvo y...

• Dónde están y qué tienen que hacer allí.

> Están en San Pedro de Atitlán, un pequeño pueblo de Guatemala. Allí tienen que encontrar...

• Cómo se sienten.

> Janet está emocionada porque...

• Cómo resuelven su desafío.

> Andy no ve el gigante, pero Janet mira la fotografía de la montaña y entonces...

84 **Las votaciones**

▶ **Lee** los poemas de los personajes en la página 68. ¿Cuál te gusta más? ¿Por qué?

▶ **Escribe** tu propio poema. Estas preguntas te pueden ayudar.
Write your own poem. The following questions may serve as a guide.

> Un poema debe tener rima *(rhyme)* al final de los versos.

1. ¿Quién eres? ¿Cómo eres?
2. ¿Cómo te sientes? ¿Por qué?
3. ¿Quiénes son tus familiares? ¿Y tus amigos(as)?
4. ¿Cómo están ellos(as)?

▶ **Lee** el poema de tu compañero(a) y ayúdale a escribir dos líneas más.
Read your classmate's poem. Help him or her to add two more lines to his or her poem.

sesenta y nueve 69

- Ask students what they notice about the poems. Did students notice that all of the poems have two verses, or lines, and that one person of each pair read a verse? Did students notice that all of the poems rhymed? Did students notice that the unit's vocabulary and grammar were integrated in the text? You may want to write some examples on the board for the benefit of students who are visual learners.

Activities

83. You can complete activity 84 before completing this activity. Put students in groups based on who they voted for. Students will complete this activity on behalf of the pair they voted for. Once each group has finished, go over each group's answers so that all of the pairs are represented.

84. Remind students that the poems the pairs wrote rhymed. Tell students to try not to translate the poems from English into Spanish. Although it may rhyme in one language, the translation may not. Have students write their poems only in Spanish and use a Spanish-English dictionary if necessary.

Answer Key

83. Answers will vary.
84. Answers will vary.
   ▶ Answers will vary.
   ▶ Answers will vary.

HERITAGE LANGUAGE LEARNERS

• Ask students to describe another *desafío* that the characters could face. To do this, students should research some additional cultural aspects of the countries featured in this unit, or include El Salvador and Panama. They will then make their suggestions to the class, which will vote on the best one.

COOPERATIVE LEARNING

• Ask students to get into groups and discuss what they have learned in this unit and what new information has proven to be the most valuable. Encourage one group member to ask questions about the vocabulary, another student to ask questions about the grammar, and one student to ask questions about the cultural items that they may not fully comprehend.

Unit 1

MAPA CULTURAL

Centroamérica

Presentation

■ This section presents Central America through facts and physical features so learners can see the region from other perspectives. The map serves as a reference point for additional cultural readings and activities that expand on the skills students learned in this unit.

Activities	Standards	Resources
Mapa cultural	1.2, 2.1, 2.2, 3.1, 3.2	Video
85.	1.2, 1.3, 3.1	
86.	1.2, 2.1, 2.2, 3.1, 3.2, 5.2	

Cultural Topics

■ **Mestizaje y cultura.** Before the colonization period, distinct indigenous groups were already coexisting in the Americas. During colonization, the Europeans brought slaves from Africa, and through the years, these three groups began to intermarry and share cultural experiences. The fusion of European, African, and indigenous cultures has spawned an amazing mix of traditional and modern civilizations in Central America.

■ **Riqueza natural.** Central America is part of the Mesoamerican Biodiversity Hotspot. A biodiversity hotspot is an area with exceptional levels of endemic species. Vertebrates endemic to the Mesoamerican Hotspot include black howler and spider monkeys, jaguars, quetzals, horned guans, and a large variety of amphibians. Many of these species are seriously threatened by habitat loss, climate change, and human impact.

Central America's diverse and complex topography is partly responsible for the rich biodiversity of this region. Its location, between North and South America, creates a north-south corridor through which species move in both directions between the continents.

Teaching Suggestions

Warm-Up / Independent Starter

■ Ask students to look at the map of Central America. Have them list the countries that the pairs did not visit and where these countries are located in relation to the ones the pairs did visit.

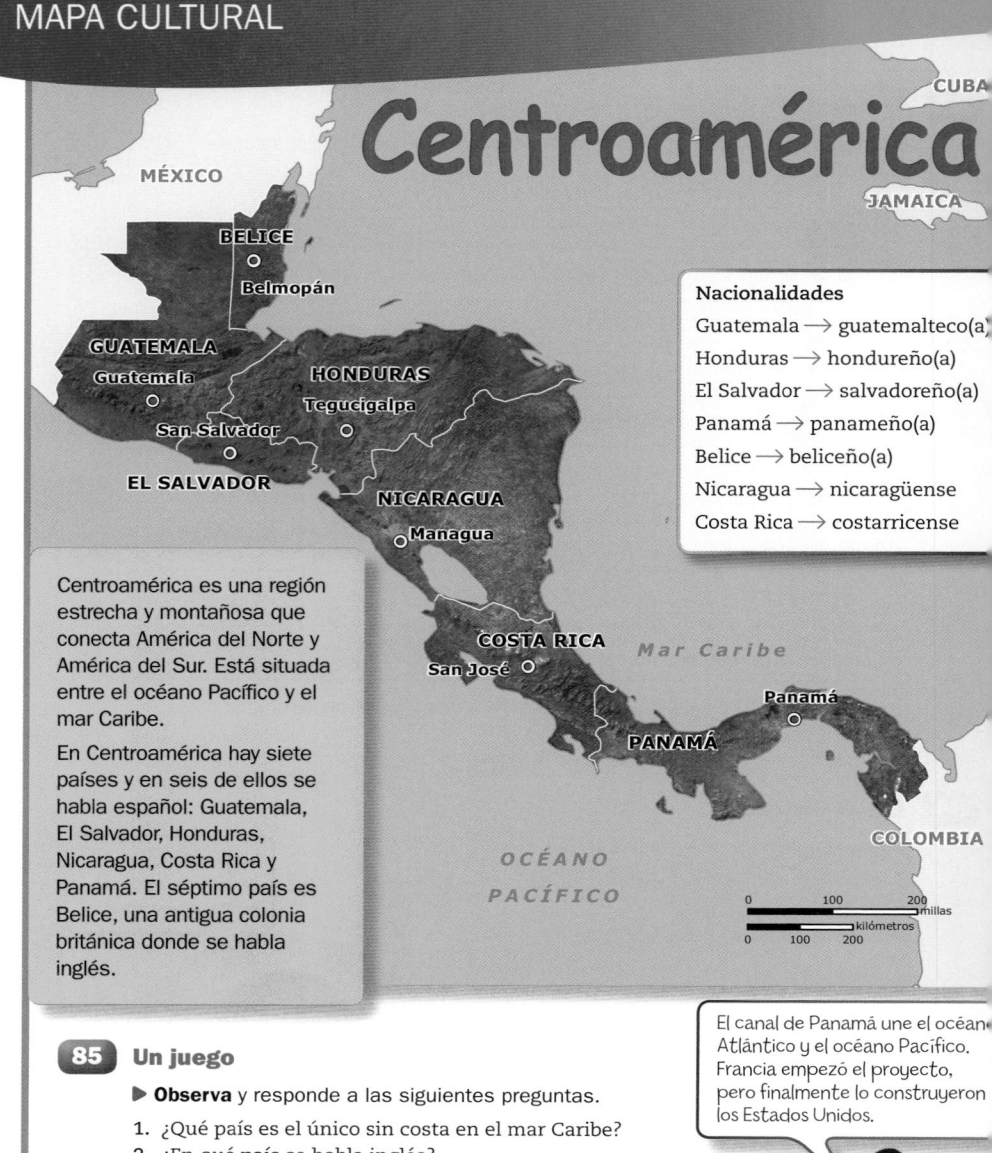

MAPA CULTURAL

Centroamérica

Nacionalidades
Guatemala → guatemalteco(a)
Honduras → hondureño(a)
El Salvador → salvadoreño(a)
Panamá → panameño(a)
Belice → beliceño(a)
Nicaragua → nicaragüense
Costa Rica → costarricense

Centroamérica es una región estrecha y montañosa que conecta América del Norte y América del Sur. Está situada entre el océano Pacífico y el mar Caribe.

En Centroamérica hay siete países y en seis de ellos se habla español: Guatemala, El Salvador, Honduras, Nicaragua, Costa Rica y Panamá. El séptimo país es Belice, una antigua colonia británica donde se habla inglés.

85 **Un juego**

▶ **Observa** y responde a las siguientes preguntas.

1. ¿Qué país es el único sin costa en el mar Caribe?
2. ¿En qué país se habla inglés?
3. ¿Qué país es el más largo y estrecho?
4. ¿Con qué país de Suramérica limita Panamá?

▶ **Escribe** el nombre de los países de Centroamérica y de sus capitales.

El canal de Panamá une el océano Atlántico y el océano Pacífico. Francia empezó el proyecto, pero finalmente lo construyeron los Estados Unidos.

70 setenta

Differentiated Instruction

DEVELOPING LEARNERS

• Ask students to trace the map of Central America from their book onto a blank sheet of paper. Have them label each country and shade the countries in different colors. Then have students answer the following questions about each country.

– ¿Dónde está el país con relación a otros países de Centroamérica?
– ¿Cómo es el país?
– ¿Cómo son las personas que viven en el país?

EXPANDING LEARNERS

• Ask students to trace the map of Central America from their book onto a blank sheet of paper. Have them label each country and shade the countries in different colors. Then have students answer the following questions. They may research the answers if necessary.

– ¿En qué se parecen y en qué se diferencian la topografía de Panamá y El Salvador?
– ¿En qué se diferencian Guatemala y Belice?
– ¿Hay algunos rasgos comunes a todos los países de Centroamérica? ¿Cuáles son?

1. Mestizaje y cultura

La palabra *mestizaje* se refiere a la mezcla o fusión de razas. Centroamérica es una región con mezcla de indígenas, europeos y africanos. Algunos grupos étnicos que proceden de esta fusión son los *garífunas* (Guatemala y Honduras) y los *misquitos* (Nicaragua y Honduras).

El mestizaje tiene una importante influencia en la cultura de Centroamérica. Los ritmos africanos, por ejemplo, son la base de la música y las danzas populares centroamericanas. Entre los instrumentos musicales, los tambores y la marimba (muy popular en Guatemala) son también de origen africano; la guitarra, el violín y el acordeón proceden de Europa; y las flautas de caña tienen origen indígena.

(1) *Músicos tocando la marimba.*

2. Riqueza natural

Guatemala significa en lengua náhuatl «tierra de muchos árboles». Realmente, esa descripción es común a toda Centroamérica. Se trata de un territorio montañoso, atravesado por la Cordillera Centroamericana, donde abundan los grandes ríos, los lagos, los volcanes y la vegetación. Además, hay selvas y manglares propios del clima tropical.

En estos entornos la fauna y la flora son muy ricas. En Costa Rica, por ejemplo, viven 91.000 especies de animales y de plantas, el 4,5 % de las que hay en todo el mundo. A causa de esta riqueza, varias zonas de Centroamérica están declaradas Reserva de la Biosfera.

(2) *Volcán de Santa Ana (El Salvador).*

86 **Centroamérica: rica en cultura y naturaleza**

▶ **Investiga y escribe.** Busca información sobre una de estas cuestiones *(topics).*

- Influencia del mestizaje en la cocina de Centroamérica.
- Influencia del mestizaje en la ropa de Centroamérica.
- Los volcanes activos de Centroamérica.
- Reservas de la Biosfera en Centroamérica.

setenta y uno 71

Preparation

- Explain that Central America is comprised of Guatemala, Belize, El Salvador, Honduras, Nicaragua, Costa Rica, and Panama. This region is located between the Pacific Ocean and the Caribbean Sea. Its narrowest point, the Isthmus of Darien in Panama, is only 30 miles wide. The highest peak is Tajumulco Volcano (13,845 feet), located in Guatemala.

- Almost 42 million people occupy the 201,700 square miles that is Central America. Nicaragua is the largest country, but Guatemala is the most populous, with 13,550,440 inhabitants (2010 est.). The most-widely spoken languages in Central America are Spanish, Mayan languages, and English.

- Ask for volunteers to read each section of the *Mapa cultural* aloud. Have students follow the map on the page as their classmates read.

Activities

85. Ask students to cover the map at the top of the page while they answer the questions. You may also split the class in half to form two teams. Ask two people, one from each team, to face off as you ask one of the questions from this activity. The person who answers the question correctly will win a point for his or her team.

86. Have students work in groups of four. Each group member will be responsible for one of the four topics.

Answer Key

85. 1. El Salvador.   3. Panamá.
　　 2. En Belice.   4. Con Colombia.
　　▶ Guatemala: Ciudad de Guatemala; Belice: Belmopán; El Salvador: San Salvador; Honduras: Tegucigalpa; Nicaragua: Managua; Costa Rica: San José; Panamá: Ciudad de Panamá.

86. Answers will vary.

Additional Resources

Fans Online activities
Practice Workbook

HERITAGE LANGUAGE LEARNERS

- Central America was first a colony of Spain and then—when Mexico gained its independence from Spain—Guatemala, El Salvador, Honduras, Nicaragua, and Costa Rica were part of the Mexican Empire for a few years before gaining total independence. Panama was part of Colombia until 1903.

- Ask students to choose one of the countries of Central America to research. Have them write a paragraph about the country's process of independence. Students may choose their country of origin if they or their family are from Central America.

CRITICAL THINKING

- Ask students how they believe the peoples like the Garifunas and the Miskitos came into existence. Have students research these Central American peoples and discuss their theories of how each began. Then invite students to compare these Central American peoples with the Louisiana Creole people. Do they see parallels?

LECTURA

El blog de Ichxel

Presentation

- In this section, students will practice and extend their reading skills by reading a blog by a 16-year-old Honduran girl. In addition, students will focus on identifying cognates, looking at the text structure, and using what they already know about the topic to understand the global idea of the reading.

Activities	Standards	Resources
Lectura	1.2, 2.1, 2.2, 3.1, 3.2	
87.	1.2, 1.3, 3.1, 3.2	
88.	1.2, 1.3, 2.1, 2.2, 3.1	
89.	1.3, 2.1	
90.	1.2, 1.3, 2.1, 2.2	
Tu desafío	1.2, 3.1, 5.2	

Teaching Suggestions

Warm-Up / Independent Starter

- Ask students to scan the reading, focusing on the images, headings, subheadings, and familiar words. Can they predict the topic and the general idea of the reading?

Preparation

- Before reading the text, point out the Reading Strategy box and ask a volunteer to read it aloud. Ask students how these strategies help them understand their reading. Invite volunteers to share with the class their predictions from the Independent Starter section.

- To introduce the topic, ask students to create a two-column chart. Have them list what they know about Honduras and its peoples in a column titled *Honduras y su gente*, and what they know about the Maya in a column titled *El pueblo maya*.

- Go over the photo and explain to students that the Maya were the most important pre-Hispanic civilization in Honduras. Copan, near the Guatemalan border, became an agricultural center and a large Mayan city during the Classic Period (AD 250–900). At its peak, Copan had about 20,000 inhabitants. Although we don't have precise information about Copan's decline, food shortages, wars, and diseases played an important role in the city's collapse and abandonment in the early 10th century AD.

Ruinas mayas de Copán (Honduras).

El blog de Ichxel

READING STRATEGY
Identify the global idea of a text

When you read a text it is important to understand ideas instead of isolated words. Using **familiar words** and identifying **cognates** helps you understand the global idea of the text. **Titles**, **visuals**, and **text structure** will also help you understand the main idea. Likewise, it is important to recall **what you know** about the topic and your personal experiences.

Desde un rincón de Centroamérica
PUBLICADO POR ICHXEL REYES 28/10/2011

Mi familia es maya

Me llamo Ichxel, como la diosa maya de la Luna. Tengo dieciséis años y soy de Honduras. ¿Conoces mi país? Es una tierra muy rica por su naturaleza y su cultura. Tiene playas muy lindas, montañas, volcanes, bosques tropicales y paisajes maravillosos. ¡Y su gente es amable y generosa!

Mi familia y yo vivimos en Tegucigalpa, la capital. Mis hermanos se llaman Balam y Zak. Sus nombres también son mayas porque mi familia es maya. Nuestra cultura es muy antigua y está muy extendida. Hoy somos casi siete millones de mayas en Centroamérica y México.

Mis abuelos viven en Santa Rosa de Copán, cerca de las ruinas mayas de Copán. Mi abuela siempre lleva ropa tradicional. Mi abuelo nos cuenta las tradiciones de los mayas. ¡Qué interesante! Para los mayas el hombre viene del maíz; por eso el maíz es un alimento sagrado.

¡A mí me gustan mucho las historias de los dioses mayas! ¡Y me gusta mucho el maíz!

COMENTARIOS (0) ENVIAR UN COMENTARIO

Differentiated Instruction

DEVELOPING LEARNERS

- Have students review the reading and write down the following in a three-column chart: 1. people identified in the reading, including their personal information and the family relationship between them; 2. descriptions of Honduras, the author's family, and the Mayan people; 3. opinions, as well as likes or dislikes, expressed by the author.

- Use the information students gathered from the reading to ask them yes / no questions. For example: *¿Es tacaña la gente de Honduras? ¿La autora tiene dos hermanos?*

EXPANDING LEARNERS

- Explain to students that recent studies suggest that corn was first domesticated in Mexico about 8,700 years ago. It would eventually become the most important crop in the Americas.

- Have students work in small groups to research and discuss the importance of corn in Mayan life. Why might the Maya consider themselves to have descended from corn? Is corn still an important part of the Central American diet? You may suggest this source: http://www.pbs.org/wnet/nature/spirits/html/maya.html.

ESTRATEGIA Identificar la idea global de un texto

87 De las palabras a las ideas

▶ **Completa** una tabla como esta con palabras del texto.

Words I know	Words I can decipher

88 La estructura del texto

▶ **Copia** este gráfico con el esquema del texto y complétalo con las ideas del cuadro.

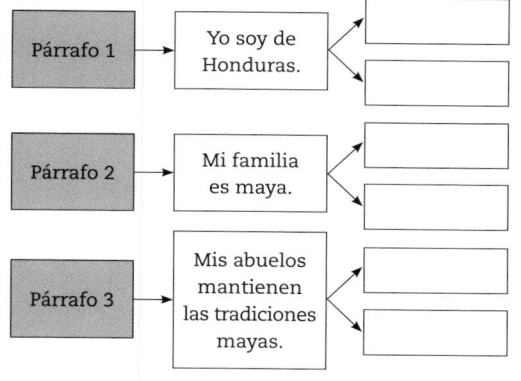

Párrafo 1 → Yo soy de Honduras. → [ ] [ ]

Párrafo 2 → Mi familia es maya. → [ ] [ ]

Párrafo 3 → Mis abuelos mantienen las tradiciones mayas. → [ ] [ ]

- Las mujeres llevan ropa tradicional.
- Honduras es un país muy rico por su naturaleza y su cultura.
- Hoy hay mayas en Centroamérica y México.
- La cultura maya es muy antigua.
- El maíz es un alimento sagrado.
- La gente hondureña es amable y generosa.

89 La idea global

▶ **Elige.** ¿Cuál es la idea global del texto?
a. La gente de Honduras es muy amable.
b. Honduras tiene un paisaje maravilloso.
c. La cultura maya está muy extendida.
d. Ichxel tiene mucha familia.

COMPRENSIÓN

90 El blog de Ichxel

▶ **Responde** a las siguientes preguntas.
1. ¿Cómo se llama la diosa maya de la Luna?
2. ¿Por qué es sagrado el maíz para los mayas?
3. ¿Dónde viven los mayas hoy?
4. ¿Dónde hay ruinas mayas?

▶ TU DESAFÍO Visita la página web para aprender más sobre los mayas.

El blog de Ichxel

Activities

87. Explain to students that cognate words can help them understand the meaning of a text. There are, however, many false cognates, or words that look alike but don't have the same meaning. You may want to point out, as an example, that the word *historias* at the end of the reading doesn't mean "histories" in this context, but rather "stories." Remind students that it is important to look at contextual clues.

89. Ask students to use the graphic organizer from activity 88 to help them come up with the global idea of the reading. Focus their attention on the main idea of each of the three paragraphs.

Answer Key

87. Answers will vary. Sample answers:
Words I know: Centroamérica, familia, país, montañas…
Words I can decipher: maya, cultura, volcanes, tropicales…

88. Párrafo 1 • Honduras es un país muy rico por su naturaleza y su cultura.
• La gente hondureña es amable y generosa.
Párrafo 2 • La cultura maya es muy antigua.
• Hoy hay mayas en Centroamérica y México.
Párrafo 3 • Las mujeres llevan ropa tradicional.
• El maíz es un alimento sagrado.

89. La cultura maya está muy extendida.

90. 1. La diosa maya de la Luna se llama Ichxel.
2. Porque para los mayas el ser humano viene del maíz.
3. Hoy en día los mayas viven en Centroamérica y México.
4. En Copán hay unas famosas ruinas mayas.

Additional Resources

Fans Online activities

HERITAGE LANGUAGE LEARNERS

- What's in a name? The blog's author tells us that her name is Ichxel, which is the moon goddess in Mayan mythology. She also mentions that her brothers have Mayan names: Balam (the "jaguar") and Zak (the "jaguar of the west").

- Have students research names of pre-Hispanic origin from their country of origin. For instance, Xóchitl in Mexico from the Nahuatl word for flower and Inti in Peru for the name of the Sun god. Ask students to compile the names they have all found on a large list to share with the class.

MULTIPLE INTELLIGENCES
Visual-Spatial Intelligence

- Explain that the Maya used a complex hieroglyphic script system consisting of hundreds of signs depicting animals, gods, humans, objects, and geometric designs. Students may look at some samples on http://www.pbs.org/wgbh/nova/maya/glyphs.html.

- Have students devise their own "hieroglyphic" script, using drawings and designs, to represent some of the information contained in the reading. Invite students to share some of their "writings" with the class.

REPASO

Vocabulario

Presentation

- In this section, students will review all key vocabulary from the unit, organized by themes, to prepare for an assessment. Students will complete practice activities for each of the four *Desafíos*.

Activities	Standards	Resources
1.	1.3	
2.	1.3	
3.	1.2, 1.3	
4.	1.3, 5.1	

Teaching Suggestions

Warm-Up / Independent Starter

- Ask students to draw a quick sketch of two family members or friends. Then have them write two sentences on the back of their drawings describing some of the most salient physical characteristics and personality traits of these two people.
- Once they have finished, have students sketch themselves and add a description, also on the back of the drawing, indicating how they are feeling today.

Preparation

- Have students work with a partner. Ask partners to exchange their sketches from the Independent Starter activity. First, they look at the drawings of the family members or friends and verbally describe these people in terms of physical characteristics and personality traits. Then, they look at the written descriptions on the back of the drawings. How accurate were their descriptions?
- Ask students to observe their partner and say how they think he or she is feeling at this very moment. Then have students look at the drawing their partner made of himself or herself and have them read the description their partner wrote. Has their partner's mood changed?
- Go over the vocabulary list with the class and model pronunciation. Encourage students to find connections between words. For example: *optimista* and *pesimista* are opposites, *furioso* and *enojado* have a similar meaning, etc.

REPASO Vocabulario

Relaciones familiares y personales

La familia

el padre	father
la madre	mother
los padres	parents
el hijo	son
la hija	daughter
los hijos	children
el hermano	brother
la hermana	sister
los hermanos	siblings
el abuelo	grandfather
la abuela	grandmother
los abuelos	grandparents
el nieto	grandson
la nieta	granddaughter
el tío	uncle
la tía	aunt
el sobrino	nephew
la sobrina	niece

el/la primo(a)	cousin
el padrino	godfather
la madrina	godmother
el/la bebé	baby

Estado civil

estar soltero(a)	to be single
estar casado(a)	to be married
el esposo	husband
la esposa	wife

Relaciones personales

discutir	to argue
llevarse bien	to get along well
llevarse mal	to get along badly

Características físicas

Aspecto

alto(a)	tall
bajo(a)	short
calvo(a)	bald
delgado(a)	thin
fuerte	strong
gordo(a)	fat
llevar gafas	to wear glasses
tener barba	to have a beard
tener bigote	to have a moustache
medir	to measure
pesar	to weigh

Color de pelo

moreno(a)	brunet(te)
pelirrojo(a)	red-haired
rubio(a)	blond(e)

Rasgos de personalidad

trabajador(a)	hard-working	creativo(a)	creative
perezoso(a)	lazy	espontáneo(a)	spontaneous
generoso(a)	generous	estudioso(a)	studious
tacaño(a)	stingy	inteligente	intelligent
serio(a)	serious	sincero(a)	sincere
gracioso(a)	funny	tímido(a)	shy
optimista	optimistic		
pesimista	pessimistic		
paciente	patient		
impaciente	impatient		

Estados de ánimo y sentimientos

aburrido(a)	bored
celoso(a)	jealous
confundido(a)	confused
contento(a)	happy
emocionado(a)	excited
enamorado(a)	in love
enojado(a)	angry
frustrado(a)	frustrated
furioso(a)	furious
nervioso(a)	nervous
sorprendido(a)	surprised
tranquilo(a)	calm
triste	sad

Información personal

nombre	first name	domicilio actual	present address
apellido	last name	estado civil	marital status
fecha de nacimiento	date of birth	número de identidad	ID number
lugar de nacimiento	birthplace	número de pasaporte	passport number

---

Differentiated Instruction

DEVELOPING LEARNERS

- Ask students to create a five-column chart and label each column: 1. *Relaciones familiares y personales*, 2. *Características físicas*, 3. *Rasgos de personalidad*, 4. *Estados de ánimo*, 5. *Información personal*. Allow them three minutes to list as many words as they can in each category without using the book.
- When time is up, have students check their charts against the vocabulary on page 74. How many words do they know? Do they need additional practice with some categories? Have students use this information to do a customized review of the vocabulary.

EXPANDING LEARNERS

- Ask students to work with a partner for about two to three minutes to quiz each other on the vocabulary. For example:
  A. *Es la mamá de mi primo. ¿Quién es?*
  B. *Es tu tía.*
- Have students switch partners and continue the review. For example:
  A. *¿Cómo estás si recibes una buena noticia?*
  B. *Estoy contento.*

DESAFÍO 1

1 **Mi familia.** Escribe las relaciones familiares de estas personas.

Modelo Leo y Adam → *Leo es el abuelo de Adam.*

1. Ana y Juan
2. Carla y José
3. Juan y yo
4. Dora y yo
5. Linn y Nina

DESAFÍO 2

2 **¿Cómo es?** Decide si estas oraciones son ciertas (C) o falsas (F). Después, corrige las falsas.

1. Pedro es moreno y tiene bigote. Su hijo César es calvo y es muy creativo. Los dos llevan gafas.

2. Ann y Kate estudian juntas. Ann es rubia y Kate es morena. Son muy trabajadoras.

DESAFÍO 3

3 **Detective.** Lee estas oraciones y escribe cómo se siente cada persona.

1. Alberto solo piensa en Valeria y quiere verla todos los días. → *Está enamorado.*
2. Mariana tiene una entrevista de trabajo hoy y no está tranquila.
3. A Laura no le gusta cuando su novio habla con otras chicas.
4. Gabriel no está contento porque su equipo pierde el partido.
5. Elena ve un programa de televisión poco interesante.

DESAFÍO 4

4 **Inscríbete.** Imagina que vas a un viaje con tus compañeros(as). Completa la hoja de inscripción con tus datos.

HOJA DE INSCRIPCIÓN

Nombre:
Apellidos:
Fecha de nacimiento:
Lugar de nacimiento:

Domicilio actual:
Estado civil:
N.º de identidad
o pasaporte:

HERITAGE LANGUAGE LEARNERS

• Explain what false cognates are and tell students that there are some false cognates in the vocabulary list. Ask them to embark on a search mission to find these *falsos amigos*. Some examples include, *familiares* —relatives, not "familiar" in this context; *discutir*—to argue, not "to discuss;" *fuerte* —strong, not "fort" in this context; *contento*—happy, not "content;" excited —*emocionado*, not "excitado." Invite students to share their lists with the rest of the class.

COOPERATIVE LEARNING

• Ask students to sit in a circle to play a vocabulary game. A student begins the game by saying a word from the vocabulary. The student to his or her right forms a meaningful sentence with the word, and then says another word for the next student. If a student is unable to make a meaningful sentence, the next student in the circle starts the sentence and then asks the previous student to complete it.

• After the game is over, discuss with students whether there are vocabulary categories that are causing them difficulties.

REPASO
Vocabulario

Activities

1. To extend this activity, have students determine, based on the information they have, whether the person is single, married, husband, or wife.

3. After students have completed this activity, have them think of an opposite situation for each case (e.g., Alberto doesn't like Valeria any longer, Mariana had the interview already and things went well, Laura is the one talking to other boys, etc.). Have students write down new sentences for this activity reflecting these new circumstances. Then ask students to swap papers with a classmate and have his or her partner describe how each person is feeling now.

4. Remind students that in most Spanish-speaking countries people use two last names: their father's last name followed by their mother's maiden name. Ask students to consider advantages and disadvantages to this system. Hold a brief class discussion in which students get to present both sides of the argument.

Answer Key

1. 1. Ana es la abuela de Juan.
2. Carla es la esposa de José.
3. Juan es mi primo.
4. Dora es mi tía.
5. Linn es hija de Nina.

2. 1. Falso. Pedro no es moreno, es calvo y tiene barba. César no es calvo, es moreno.
2. Falso. Ann es morena y Kate es rubia.

3. Answers will vary. Sample answers:
1. Alberto está enamorado.
2. Mariana está nerviosa.
3. Laura está celosa.
4. Gabriel está triste.
5. Elena está aburrida.

4. Answers will vary.

Additional Resources

Fans Online activities
Practice Workbook

75

REPASO

Gramática

Presentation

- Students will review grammatical structures presented in the unit. Each grammar point is cross-referenced to the corresponding page in which it was introduced. The activities here provide systematic practice by *Desafío*.

Activities	Standards	Resources
5.	1.2	
6.	1.3	
7.	1.2	
8.	1.2	
9. Cultura	1.3, 2.1, 2.2, 5.2	

Teaching Suggestions

Warm-Up / Independent Starter

- Ask students to focus on two of their classmates and have them write a two-sentence description of each of those students. The description should include physical characteristics as well as feelings. Then have students write another two sentences comparing the two students they described.

Preparation

- Invite volunteer students to read their descriptions from the Independent Starter section without specifying the names of the persons being described. Ask the rest of the class to guess who these two persons might be. Then have the volunteer student read his or her comparison sentences and ask the rest of the class whether they agree with the comparisons or not.

- Go over the *Repaso* with the class. Remind students that possessives in Spanish agree in gender and number with the thing possessed or owned and not with the possessor. To illustrate this point, you may want to compare and contrast the following sentences: *Luisa cuida sus libros.* – *Luisa takes care of her books.*

- Ask students to preview the review activities on page 77 and have them identify the grammar concept that is key to completing each activity. This will help them focus on the appropriate concept as they complete each activity.

Los posesivos (pág. 38)

	ADJETIVOS POSESIVOS							
	ANTES del nombre (mi tío)				DESPUÉS del nombre (un tío mío)			
	Singular		Plural		Singular		Plural	
	Masculino	Femenino	Masculino	Femenino	Masculino	Femenino	Masculino	Femenino
my	mi		mis		mío	mía	míos	mías
your (inf.)	tu		tus		tuyo	tuya	tuyos	tuyas
his, her, your	su		sus		suyo	suya	suyos	suyas
our	nuestro	nuestra	nuestros	nuestras	nuestro	nuestra	nuestros	nuestras
your (inf.)	vuestro	vuestra	vuestros	vuestras	vuestro	vuestra	vuestros	vuestras
their, your	su		sus		suyo	suya	suyos	suyas

Possessive pronouns have the same form as the possessive adjectives after the noun.

Los adjetivos y el nombre (pág. 46)

▶ In Spanish, adjectives reflect the gender and number of the noun they refer to.

End in -o: 4 forms	simpático	simpáticos
	simpática	simpáticas
End in -e: 2 forms	inteligente	inteligentes
End in a consonant: usually, 2 forms	débil	débiles

▶ Adjectives that express nationality also have variation of gender and number.

End in -o or in a consonant: 4 forms	español	españoles
	española	españolas
End in -e: 2 forms	canadiense	canadienses

Las comparaciones (pág. 54)

▶ To express equality, use:

tan + adj. + como	as … as

verb + tanto como	… as much as …

▶ To express inequality, use:

más / menos + adj. + que	more/less … than

verb + más / menos que	… more/less than …

El superlativo (pág. 54)

Adjectives ending in a consonant	Add -ísimo, -ísima, -ísimos, -ísimas. popular → popularísimo
Adjectives ending in a vowel	Drop the vowel and add the superlative ending. triste → tristísimo

Los interrogativos (pág. 62)

¿Qué?	What?	¿Cuántos(as)?	How many?	¿Por qué?	Why?
¿Cuál(es)?	Which?	¿Dónde?	Where?	¿Para qué?	What for?
¿Quién(es)?	Who?	¿Cuándo?	When?	¿Adónde?	Where to?
¿Cuánto(a)?	How much?	¿Cómo?	How?	¿De dónde?	Where from?

Differentiated Instruction

DEVELOPING LEARNERS

- Have students think of a family member or friend they admire. Ask them to create a six-column question chart about this person. Some possible questions are: *¿Quién es? ¿Dónde vive? ¿Cuántos años tiene? ¿Qué hace? ¿Cómo es? ¿Por qué la / lo admiro?*

- Have students fill in the chart using complete sentences and focusing on the information. Then ask them to go over the grammar review on page 76 and check the statements they wrote focusing on grammar this time. Look at their charts and point out things students might have overlooked in their revision.

EXPANDING LEARNERS

- In groups of three, ask students to write a brief description of their group partners. They should also include some comparisons and superlatives in their descriptions, as well as some wrong information.

- Have students share their descriptions with the rest of the group. When group partners hear incorrect information, they should correct it. For example:

A. *Jim es más alto que yo. También es delgado y calvo.*

B. *No, Jim es más bajo que tú.*

C. *Yo no soy calvo, ¡tengo mucho pelo!*

DESAFÍO 1

5 **Alicia y el orden.** Completa el texto con las formas correctas de los posesivos.

Alicia es mi única hermana. Ella no es muy organizada. _____ lápices
_{Su/Sus}
siempre están debajo del sofá. Los _____ están en _____
_{míos/mis} _{mi/mía}
mochila. _____ madre se enoja un poco, pero _____ abuelos
_{Nuestra/Nuestro} _{nuestro/nuestros}
siempre la ayudan a buscar _____ cosas.
_{su/sus}

DESAFÍO 2

6 **¡Son iguales!** Completa estas oraciones con el adjetivo correspondiente.

1. Vero es muy paciente. Luis también es muy _____.
2. Braulio y Saúl son generosos. Su hermana también es _____.
3. Cecilia es tacaña. Antonio y su padre también son _____.
4. Nuestro tío es optimista. Mi hermano y yo también somos _____.

DESAFÍO 3

7 **¿Es lógico o no?** ¿Son lógicas estas oraciones? Corrígelas.

1. Juan es altísimo. Él es más bajo que sus compañeros.
2. Glenda es perezosa. Es menos estudiosa que sus hermanas.
3. Amparo y Clara son muy graciosas. Ellas son aburridísimas.
4. A Pablo no le gusta nada el regalo de Paula. Está emocionadísimo.

DESAFÍO 4

8 **Preguntas.** Completa estas oraciones y une las dos columnas.

1. ¿__Cuándo__ es tu cumpleaños?   a. Están en mi mochila.
2. ¿_____ están tus libros?   b. Es el 2 de agosto.
3. ¿_____ es la chica rubia?   c. Mi deporte favorito es el tenis.
4. ¿_____ es tu deporte favorito?   d. Es Patricia, la hija de mi madrina.

CULTURA

9 **¡En Centroamérica!** Responde a estas preguntas.

1. ¿Qué sabes de los garífunas?
2. ¿Qué es el *Popol Vuh*?
3. ¿Quién es Rubén Darío?

Activities

6. Once students have completed this activity, ask them to change the second sentence to express the opposite of the first sentence. For example: *Vero es muy paciente. Luis no es paciente, es impaciente.*

7. Have students correct the second sentence to make it logical in each case that it is not logical.

8. Have students prepare a five-question questionnaire they would like to administer to a famous person they would like to know better. Then have students give the questionnaire to a classmate and have the classmate answer as if he or she were the famous person.

9. Ask students to complete this activity without referring back to their textbooks. Once they have answered the questions, have them verify their answers. Did they get a perfect score?

Answer Key

5. sus; míos; mi; Nuestra; nuestros; sus

6. 1. paciente   3. tacaños
    2. generosa   4. optimistas

7. 1. No es lógica.   3. No es lógica.
    2. Es lógica.   4. No es lógica.

8. 1. Cuándo – b   3. Quién – d
    2. Dónde – a   4. Cuál – c

9. Answers will vary. Sample answers:
1. Los garífunas viven en varias regiones de Centroamérica, el Caribe y los Estados Unidos. Los garífunas descienden de los esclavos africanos que se fueron a vivir con los pueblos indígenas.
2. El *Popol Vuh* es un libro muy antiguo. Recoge las leyendas mayas sobre el mundo y la naturaleza.
3. Rubén Darío es un poeta nicaragüense. Fue uno de los máximos representantes del Modernismo literario.

Additional Resources

Fans Online activities
Practice Workbook

HERITAGE LANGUAGE LEARNERS

• Heritage learners are probably familiar with the relative superlatives (e.g., *el/la más alto(a), el/la mejor/peor, el/la mayor/menor*). These superlatives describe a noun within the context of a group.

• Have students work with a partner to come up with the names of five famous people they both know. These people should be different in terms of their physical characteristics, gender, what they do for a living, and personality. Ask students to use the relative superlatives to compare these people. For example: *Salma Hayek es la más baja.*

SPECIAL-NEEDS LEARNERS

• Most students with learning disabilities benefit from the incorporation of multi-sensory support. Distribute four index cards and red, yellow, green, and blue stickers to students. Have them place a sticker on each index card and label each card with a *Desafío* (e.g., red – *Desafío 1*, yellow – *Desafío 2*, green – *Desafío 3*, blue – *Desafío 4*).

• Have students copy examples of the main grammar topic for each *Desafío* on the appropriate card. Then ask them to use the cards as reference when they complete the activities on page 77.

Unit 1

PROYECTO

Personajes de Guatemala

Presentation

- In this section, students will apply the vocabulary, grammar, and cultural information they have learned in this unit to complete a project about the Guatemalan painter Juan Sisay. Students will follow step-by-step instructions.

Activities	Standards	Resources
Paso 1	1.3, 2.2, 3.1	
Paso 2	1.3,	
Paso 3	1.3, 2.1	
Paso 4	1.2, 3.1	
Paso 5	1.1, 1.3, 5.1	

Teaching Suggestions

Warm-Up / Independent Starter

- Have students read the introduction to the project. Then ask them to observe the painting and jot down their impressions, thoughts, and feelings.

Preparation

- Explain to students that Juan Sisay, a self-taught Mayan artist from Guatemala, was born in 1921 in the town of Santiago Atitlán, on the shores of Lake Atitlán. He captured in his work the people and scenes from the daily life of the towns and villages of the Guatemalan highlands. He became known outside of Guatemala and his work was exhibited in Europe and the United States. In 1989, Juan Sisay was assassinated during a period of political unrest and civil war that took a heavy toll on the indigenous population of Guatemala. His style has been classified as *primitivista*, or naive art.

Step-by-Step Instructions

Paso 1

- Ask students to pull out their notes from the Independent Starter and read them as they observe the painting again. Have students pay special attention to the characters' eyes and their facial expressions. If they have something to add to their notes, ask them to do so now. Then have them read the instructions for *Paso 1*, choose the characters they want to describe, and answer the questions in writing.

78

Una historia sobre

personajes de Guatemala

You will write a short story based on a painting by famous Guatemalan artist Juan Sisay. In this project, you will need to pick a main character from the painting and bring him or her to life. Invent the reasons why he or she is in this setting, what is his or her relationship with other characters, and what is happening in the painting.

PASO 1 Decide quiénes van a ser los personajes de tu historia

- Look at the painting and choose a main character that will be the focus of your story. Then answer the following questions to develop your character's profile.

Juan Sisay. *Vendedoras de fruta.*

- ¿Es hombre o mujer? ¿Cómo se llama?
- ¿Cuántos años tiene?
- ¿De dónde es?
- ¿Cuáles son sus rasgos físicos y personales?
- ¿Cómo es su familia?
- ¿Dónde vive?
- ¿Cuál es su estado civil?
- ¿Cuál es su profesión?

- Choose a secondary character. These questions will help you create his or her profile.
  - ¿Quién es?
  - ¿Cuál es su profesión?
  - ¿Cómo es?
  - ¿Ese personaje conoce al personaje principal?

Rubric for Evaluation

	Content	Organization	Presentation
1 point	Limited relevance. Information is incomplete or not based on research. Little Spanish is used.	Inefficient use of class time. Information is disorganized or unclear. Main points are not explicit.	Communication is unclear. Delivery is not fluent. Many errors in vocabulary and grammar.
3 points	Basic information is correct. Relevant information but lacks significance. Spanish is used most of the time.	Class time is used well. Information and content are mostly organized but lack some clarity. Main points are clearly stated.	Good communication. Fluent delivery. Mostly correct vocabulary and grammar.

PASO 2 Cuenta qué pasa en el cuadro

- Focus your attention on the characters that you chose and the things that are happening right now. Ask yourself questions like these to help you focus your comments.
  - ¿Qué hacen los personajes?
  - ¿Por qué están allí?
  - ¿De qué hablan? ¿Cómo se sienten?
  - ¿Qué ocurre? ¿Qué van a hacer?

- Prepare a card for each character using the information that you developed.

Personaje	María
¿Qué hace?	Habla con su hermana.
¿Por qué está allí?	Quiere vender fruta.
¿Cómo se siente?	Está contenta.

PASO 3 Escribe la historia

- Organize all your information and write a short story. Your main character will tell the story, therefore, use his or her point of view. Develop your story in three or four paragraphs.

  Modelo Me llamo María. Tengo 20 años y soy de Guatemala. Soy morena, delgada y trabajadora. Hoy estoy en…

PASO 4 Corrige tu historia

- Read your story and proofread your work.
  - ¿Las frases son claras y están escritas correctamente?
  - ¿La ortografía y la puntuación son correctas?
  - ¿La información está bien organizada?

PASO 5 Presenta tu trabajo

- Present your story to the class. When you have finished, ask your classmates if they can guess who is your main character.

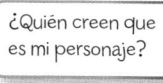

¿Quién creen que es mi personaje?

Unidad 1

Autoevaluación

¿Qué has aprendido en esta unidad?

Do the following activities to evaluate how well you understood this unit's concepts.

Evaluate your skills. For each item, say Very well, Well, or I need more practice.

a. Can you identify yourself and others?
  ▶ Talk about your family relationships and say how well you all get along.

b. Can you describe people?
  ▶ Look at pictures in a magazine and describe each person's physical characteristics, including your estimation of his or her height and weight.
  ▶ Using the same pictures, describe each person's personality.

c. Can you express states and feelings?
  ▶ With a classmate, play a guessing game. One person will make faces to represent emotional states and the other person guesses which emotion each person feels.
  ▶ Look around the classroom and compare how your classmates feel.

d. Can you ask questions?
  ▶ In groups, find out as much about your group members as you can. You will only have one minute per member. The group with the most information wins.

	Content	Organization	Presentation
5 points	Relevant, interesting information. Many details and significance are highlighted. Spanish is used exclusively.	Class time is used wisely. Information and content are clearly organized visually and logically. Hierarchy of main and secondary points clear.	Clear communication. Correct and complete vocabulary and grammar. Very motivating upbeat delivery.

Unit 1

PROYECTO

Personajes de Guatemala

Paso 2

- Invite students to consider, in their analyses of the characters, the civil war affecting Guatemala at the time Juan Sisay painted this picture. How might the killing of indigenous people and the infighting that was taking place in their towns have affected the people's daily lives and their relationships with one another?

- Have students exchange their impressions of the characters with a classmate. Do they have similar interpretations? Is there something that they missed in their observations?

Paso 3

- Remind students that the first person point of view brings the reader up close with the narrator. Have students pay attention to the text structure to make their message clear and powerful.

Paso 4

- Explain that grammar and vocabulary errors interfere with comprehension and rob their writing of precision and clarity.

Paso 5

- Rehearsals should enable students to present confidently and fluently. If possible, allow for rehearsal time.

Evaluation

- Distribute copies of the rubric to students. Discuss the evaluation criteria and explain how this project will be graded. Encourage students to refer to the rubric as they prepare their projects.

Content

- Emphasize the importance of including detailed and vivid descriptions. Ask students to imagine that they are describing the characters to a group of listeners who have not seen the painting.

Organization

- Remind students that each paragraph should start with a leading sentence so that the listener can immediately predict the paragraph's direction and purpose.

Presentation

- Students should use as much Spanish as possible. Encourage creativity and a presentation style that will hold their classmates' attention.

Unit 2 Las Antillas

Objectives

- To express the progress of an action.
- To identify and describe places.
- To express habitual actions.
- To describe a neighborhood.
- To use expressions that confirm information, express surprise or astonishment and approval or disapproval.
- To talk about household chores.

- To describe the rooms in a house.
- To identify the furnishings and fixtures in a room.
- To list the appliances and electronics in a house.
- To explore cultural aspects of the Caribbean.
- To acquire facts about the geography and history of the Caribbean.

Contents

Vocabulary

- Expressions used to confirm information.
- Expressions used to express surprise or astonishment.
- Expressions used to express approval and disapproval.
- The house.
- Household chores.
- Home furnishings and accessories.
- Home appliances.
- The city.
- The neighborhood.

Grammar

- Present progressive tense.
- Present participles.
- Direct object pronouns.
- Indirect object pronouns.
- Demonstratives.

Culture

- Sir Francis Drake.
- *La Casa del Cordón.*
- Buildings from the colonial period.
- Puerto Plata, Dominican Republic.
- *El Museo del Ámbar.*
- Hospitality.
- *Serenatas.*
- *Las tunas.*
- *El Festival de las flores de Aibonito.*
- Neighborhoods.
- *La Plaza de Armas.*
- Tourism in the Caribbean.
- The Antilles.
- The Caribbean lifestyle.

Evaluation Criteria

- Use an expression that confirms information.
- Use an expression that registers surprise or astonishment.
- Use expressions that denote approval or disapproval.
- Describe the various rooms of a house and its composition.
- Identify the furniture and fixtures in a house.

- List household chores.
- Describe the appliances and electronic devices in a household.
- Describe a neighborhood or city.
- Talk about actions that are happening.
- Recognize and use the present progressive.
- Use direct objects and direct object pronouns.

- Use indirect objects and indirect object pronouns.
- Express the location of places or persons in relation to other places or persons.
- Express understanding of selected Caribbean customs, geographical aspects, and historical facts.
- Express understanding of the Caribbean lifestyle.

Unit Plan

La llegada

Estimated time: 1 session.

Dialogue: *En Santo Domingo.*

Functions & forms:
- To confirm information.
- To express surprise or incredulity.
- To ask someone's opinion and to express approval and disapproval.

Culture:
- The *Alcázar de don Diego Colón,* Santo Domingo, the Dominican Republic.

DESAFÍO 1

Estimated time: 4 sessions.

Dialogue: *La balanza del pirata Drake.*

Functions & forms:
- Rooms and composition of a house.
- Present progressive tense.

Culture:
- *Sir Francis Drake.*
- *La Casa del Cordón.*
- *Las casas coloniales.*

DESAFÍO 2

Estimated time: 4 sessions.

Dialogue: *Un mosquito del Jurásico.*

Functions & forms:
- Furnishings and fixtures.
- Direct object pronouns.

Culture:
- *El Museo del Ámbar.*
- *Mi casa es tu casa.*

DESAFÍO 3

Estimated time: 4 sessions.

Dialogue: *Una serenata en Ponce.*

Functions & forms:
- Household appliances and electronics.
- Indirect object pronouns.

Culture:
- *Las serenatas.*
- *Las tunas.*

DESAFÍO 4

Estimated time: 4 sessions.

Dialogue: *El Festival de las Flores.*

Functions & forms:
- The neighborhood and public services.
- Demonstratives.

Culture:
- *El Festival de Flores de Aibonito.*
- *El barrio.*
- *La Plaza de Armas.*

TODO JUNTO/El encuentro

Estimated time: 1 session.

Dialogue: *En la fortaleza Ozama.*

Functions & forms:
- Review of *Desafíos 1–4.*

Culture:
- *El turismo en el Caribe.*
- Santo Domingo, the Dominican Republic.

MAPA CULTURAL/LECTURA

Estimated time: 1 session.

Mapa cultural: *Las Antillas.*

Reading: *Estilo de vida caribeño.*

PROYECTO/EVALUACIÓN

Estimated time: 2 sessions.

Project: *Un juego en las calles de Santo Domingo.*

Self-evaluation: *Autoevaluación.*

Standards for Learning Spanish

COMMUNICATION

1.1. Interpersonal mode
- Discuss the challenge for each pair in the Antilles.
- Discuss what students know about the Caribbean.
- Speculate on which team will win the challenge.
- Interview a classmate.
- Play a guessing game.
- Survey the class on a question.

1.2. Interpretive mode
- Take notes from an oral text.
- Read a cultural text.
- Summarize information in a written text.

- Research cultural topics.
- Listen to Caribbean music on the Internet.

1.3. Presentational mode
- Write a postcard to a friend.
- Write a summary of a pair's challenge.
- Write captions for photographs.
- Write a real estate advertisement.
- Develop a floor plan of an ideal house and describe it to someone.
- Develop interview questions.

CULTURE

2.1. Practices and perspectives
- Discuss prior knowledge of the Caribbean.
- Read about traditions of hospitality.
- Read about the tradition of the *serenata*.
- Research Caribbean music.
- Read about the naming of *barrios*.
- Read about the *Plazas de Armas*.

2.2. Products and perspectives
- Discuss the impact of amber on the Caribbean.
- Research colonial buildings in the Caribbean.

CONNECTIONS

3.1. Interdisciplinary connections
- Acquire knowledge of Caribbean geography.
- Research Sir Francis Drake.
- Research historical buildings in the area.
- Read about the formation of and uses for amber.
- Discuss direct objects and direct object pronouns.
- Identify the main idea and supporting details of a text.
- Design and create a board game.

3.2. Viewpoints through language / culture
- Read a *fotonovela* in Spanish.
- Read a cultural text in Spanish.
- Read about Caribbean musical instruments on the Internet.
- Read a letter from a member of one of the teams.
- Read and respond to an e-mail about Caribbean life.

COMPARISONS

4.1. Compare languages
- Compare direct object pronouns in English and in Spanish.
- Compare the position of indirect object pronouns in English and in Spanish.
- Compare demonstratives in English and in Spanish.

4.2. Compare cultures
- Compare natural resources near the student's home town and in other countries.
- Reflect on places of interest to tourists near the student's city.
- Discuss city planning.
- Compare the formation and naming of neighborhoods.
- Discuss practices in hospitality.
- Discuss common elements of folk music.
- Discuss the preservation of historical buildings.

COMMUNITIES

5.1. Spanish within and beyond the school setting
- Discuss historical buildings in the student's community.
- Discuss tourist sites in the student's community.
- Discuss natural materials used for artistic purposes in the student's community.

5.2. Spanish for lifelong learning
- Play a memory game.
- Design a board game.
- Research Caribbean area topics.

Communicative Skills

Interpersonal Mode | Activities

Speaking	• Engage in a basic conversation with a partner.	• 4, 5, 28, 39, 58, 80, 85
	• Ask and answer questions about the home and household items.	• 13, 19, 23, 24, 32, 35, 50
	• Talk to a partner about household tasks.	• 24, 82
	• Relate the cultural topics to personal experiences with a classmate.	• 46, 64, 81
	• Ask and answer questions about preferences.	• 38, 56, 85
	• Describe the elements of a picture to a classmate.	• 40, 41, 76, 80
Writing	• Write a conversation.	• 3, 42, 60
	• Make a list of household items or tasks.	• 30, 45
	• Write questions to ask a partner.	• 31
	• Write a responsive e-mail.	• 55
Listening	• Understand oral descriptions.	• 28, 31, 39, 45, 49, 72, 74
	• Obtain information from an oral exchange.	• 24, 80
	• Demonstrate comprehension of a conversation.	• 8, 21, 54, 56, 66, 78
	• Understand a partner's clues to play a guessing game.	• 32
Reading	• Understand simple texts about the home.	• 22, 55

Interpretive Mode | Activities

Listening	• Obtain information from a conversation.	• 8, 21, 28, 39, 54, 56, 74
	• Understand simple descriptions from an audio recording.	• 11, 18, 45, 49, 66, 72, 78
	• Interpret audio and video about culture.	• *Tu desafío, videos*
Reading	• Understand brief written exchanges.	• 1, 2, 6, 26, 27, 36, 44, 61, 62, 63, 71, 77, R6
	• Obtain basic information from a letter.	• 75, 79, 82
	• Infer meanings based on a text.	• 9, 14, 20, 29, 33, 43, 46, 51, 64, 68, 73, 81
	• Understand cultural texts by reading for detailed information.	• *Lectura*
	• Reflect on and explain cultural elements related to personal experience.	• 14, 20, 29, 33, 46, 51, 64, 68, 73, 81

Presentational Mode | Activities

Speaking	• Act out a short skit aloud.	• 3, 25, 42, 60, 77
	• Present the results of a survey or interview.	• 24, 50
Writing	• Write a short skit.	• 3, 42
	• Write a paragraph to summarize results.	• 24, 88
	• Write descriptive sentences or texts.	• 40, 41, 67, 76, 79, 80
	• Write a note.	• 83
	• Create a game for your classmates to play.	• *Proyecto*

Cross-Curricular Standards

Subject	Standard	Activities
Language Arts	• Compare elements of English grammar with Spanish equivalents.	• 34, 52, 69
Art	• Design and implement a board game.	• *Proyecto*
World History	• Read about a historical figure.	• 9

Lesson Plans (50-Minute Classes)

Day	Objectives	Sessions	Activities	Time	Standards	Resources / Homework
1	To introduce the Antilles and to discuss the pairs' challenges	**Las Antillas / La llegada** (80–85) • Warm-Up: Region orientation • *Las Antillas* • Images and functions • Presentation: *En Santo Domingo* • *Expresiones útiles* and *¿Quién ganará?*	 1 2–5	 5 m. 5 m. 10 m. 10 m. 20 m.	1.1, 1.2, 1.3, 2.1, 3.1, 3.2, 5.1	Visual Presentation Video Practice Workbook
2	To express the progress of an action	**Desafío 1 – La balanza del pirata Drake** (86–87) • Warm-Up: Independent Starter • *Fotonovela: La balanza del pirata Drake* • *Conexiones: Sir Francis Drake*	 6–8 9	 5 m. 35 m. 10 m.	1.1, 1.2, 1.3, 2.2, 3.1, 3.2, 5.1, 5.2	Visual Presentation Audio *Tu desafío*
3	To talk about the house and chores	**Desafío 1 – Vocabulario** (88–89) • Warm-Up: Independent Starter • Vocabulary: *La vivienda* • *Comparaciones: La Casa del Cordón*	 10–13 14	 5 m. 35 m. 10 m.	1.1, 1.2, 1.3, 2.2, 3.2, 4.2, 5.1, 5.2	Audio Video Practice Workbook *Tu desafío*
4	To learn and use the present progressive and present participle	**Desafío 1 – Gramática** (90–91) • Warm-Up: Independent Starter • Grammar: *El presente continuo* • *Comparaciones: Las casas coloniales*	 15–19 20	 5 m. 35 m. 10 m.	1.1, 1.2, 1.3, 2.1, 3.1, 3.2, 4.1, 4.2, 5.1	Audio Practice Workbook
5	To integrate vocabulary and grammar and to assess student proficiency	**Desafío 1 – Comunicación / Evaluación** (92–93) • Warm-Up: Independent Starter • *Comunicación:* Review • *Final del desafío* • Quiz on *Desafío 1*	 21–24 25	 5 m. 20 m. 10 m. 15 m.	1.1, 1.2, 1.3, 3.1	Audio Practice Workbook *Tu desafío*
6	To identify and describe places	**Desafío 2 – Un mosquito del Jurásico** (94–95) • Warm-Up: Independent Starter • *Fotonovela: Un mosquito del Jurásico* • *Cultura: El Museo del Ámbar*	 26–28 29	 5 m. 35 m. 10 m.	1.1, 1.2, 1.3, 2.2, 3.1, 3.2, 5.1, 5.2	Visual Presentation Audio *Tu desafío*
7	To talk about household furnishings and accessories	**Desafío 2 – Vocabulario** (96–97) • Warm-Up: Independent Starter • Vocabulary: *Muebles y accesorios para la casa* • *Comunidades: Mi casa es tu casa*	 30–32 33	 5 m. 35 m. 10 m.	1.1, 1.2, 1.3, 2.1, 4.2, 5.1	Audio Practice Workbook
8	To learn and use direct object pronouns	**Desafío 2 – Gramática** (98–99) • Warm-Up: Independent Starter • Grammar: *Los pronombres de objeto directo*	 34–38	 5 m. 45 m.	1.1, 1.2, 1.3, 3.1, 4.1	Practice Workbook
9	To integrate vocabulary and grammar and to assess student proficiency	**Desafío 2 – Comunicación / Evaluación** (100–101) • Warm-Up: Independent Starter • *Comunicación:* Review • *Final del desafío* • Quiz on *Desafío 2*	 39–41 42	 5 m. 20 m. 10 m. 15 m.	1.1, 1.2, 1.3, 2.2	Audio Practice Workbook
10	To express habitual actions	**Desafío 3 – Una serenata en Ponce** (102–103) • Warm-Up: Independent Starter • *Fotonovela: Una serenata en Ponce* • *Cultura: Las serenatas*	 43–45 46	 5 m. 35 m. 10 m.	1.1, 1.2, 1.3, 2.1, 3.2, 4.2, 5.1	Visual Presentation Audio *Tu desafío*

Day	Objectives	Sessions	Activities	Time	Standards	Resources / Homework
11	To talk about appliances and electronics	**Desafío 3 – Vocabulario** (104–105) • Warm-Up: Independent Starter • Vocabulary: *Los electrodomésticos* • *Cultura: Las tunas*	47–50 51	5 m. 35 m. 10 m.	1.1, 1.2, 1.3, 2.2, 3.2, 4.2, 5.1	Audio Practice Workbook *Tu desafío*
12	To learn and use indirect object pronouns	**Desafío 3 – Gramática** (106–107) • Warm-Up: Independent Starter • Grammar: *Los pronombres de objeto indirecto*	52–55	5 m. 45 m.	1.2, 1.3, 3.1, 4.1	Audio Practice Workbook
13	To integrate vocabulary and grammar and to assess student proficiency	**Desafío 3 – Comunicación / Evaluación** (108–109) • Warm-Up: Independent Starter • *Comunicación:* Review • Final del desafío • Quiz on *Desafío 3*	56–59 60	5 m. 20 m. 10 m. 15 m.	1.1, 1.2, 1.3, 2.1	Audio Practice Workbook *Tu desafío*
14	To describe the neighborhood	**Desafío 4 – El Festival de las flores** (110–111) • Warm-Up: Independent Starter • *Fotonovela: El Festival de las flores* • *Cultura: El Festival de las flores de Aibonito*	61–63 64	5 m. 35 m. 10 m.	1.1, 1.2, 1.3, 2.1, 2.2, 4,2, 5.1, 5.2	Visual Presentation Video *Tu desafío*
15	To talk about areas of a city	**Desafío 4 – Vocabulario** (112–113) • Warm-Up: Independent Starter • Vocabulary: *El barrio. Lugares y servicios* • *Comunidades: El barrio*	65–67 68	5 m. 35 m. 10 m.	1.1, 1.2, 1.3, 3.2, 4.2, 5.1	Audio Practice Workbook
16	To learn and use demonstratives	**Desafío 4 – Gramática** (114–115) • Warm-Up: Independent Starter • Grammar: *Los demostrativos* • *Cultura: La Plaza de Armas*	69–72 73	5 m. 35 m. 10 m.	1.1, 1.2, 1.3, 2.1, 3.1, 3.2, 4.1, 4.2, 5.1, 5.2	Audio Practice Workbook *Tu desafío*
17	To integrate vocabulary and grammar and to assess student proficiency	**Desafío 4 – Comunicación / Evaluación** (116–117) • Warm-Up: Independent Starter • *Comunicación:* Review • *Final del desafío* • Quiz on *Desafío 4*	74–76 77	5 m. 20 m. 10 m. 15 m.	1.1, 1.2, 1.3, 2.1, 2.2	Audio Practice Workbook
18	To integrate language in context	**Todo junto / El encuentro** (118–121) • Warm-Up: Independent Starter • *Todo junto* • *Cultura: El turismo en el Caribe* • *El encuentro: En la fortaleza Ozama*	78–80 81 82–83	5 m. 25 m. 5 m. 15 m.	1.1, 1.2, 1.3, 2.1, 2.2, 3.1, 3.2, 4.2, 5.1	Audio Practice Workbook
19	To learn about Caribbean customs and traditions	**Mapa cultural / Lectura** (122–125) • Warm-Up: Independent Starter • *Mapa cultural: Las Antillas* • *Lectura: Estilo de vida caribeño*	84–85 86–88	5 m. 20 m. 25 m.	1.1, 1.2, 1.3, 2.1, 2.2, 3.1, 3.2, 5.2	Audio Video Practice Workbook *Tu desafío* Project work
20	To create a board game	**Proyecto** (130–131) • Warm-Up: Prepare project presentations • Project presentations		10 m. 40 m.	1.1, 1.2, 1.3, 3.1, 5.2	Practice Workbook **Repaso – Vocabulario** (126–127) **Repaso – Gramática** (128–129)
21	To assess student proficiency	**Assessment** • *Autoevaluación* (131) • Test		10 m. 40 m.		

Lesson Plans (90-Minute Classes)

Day	Objectives	Sessions	Activities	Time	Standards	Resources / Homework
1	To introduce the Antilles and to discuss the pairs' challenges	**Las Antillas / La llegada** (80–85) • Warm-Up: Region orientation • *Las Antillas*/Images and functions • *Presentation: En Santo Domingo* • *Expresiones útiles* and *¿Quién ganará?*	 1 2–5	10 m. 15 m. 30 m. 35 m.	1.1, 1.2, 1.3, 2.1, 3.1, 3.2, 5.1	Visual Presentation Video Practice Workbook
2	To express the progress of an action and to talk about the house and chores	**Desafío 1 – La balanza del pirata Drake / Vocabulario** (86–89) • Warm-Up: Independent Starter • *Fotonovela: La balanza del pirata Drake* • *Conexiones: Sir Francis Drake* • Vocabulary: *La vivienda* • *Comparaciones: La Casa del Cordón*	 6–8 9 10–13 14	 5 m. 30 m. 10 m. 35 m. 10 m.	1.1, 1.2, 1.3, 2.2, 3.1, 3.2, 4.2, 5.1	Visual Presentation Audio Video Practice Workbook *Tu desafío*
3	To learn and use the present progressive and present participle, to integrate vocabulary and grammar, and to assess student proficiency	**Desafío 1 – Gramática / Comunicación / Evaluación** (90–93) • Warm-Up: Independent Starter • Grammar: *El presente continuo* • *Comparaciones: Las casas coloniales* • *Comunicación:* Review • *Final del desafío* • Quiz on *Desafío 1*	 15–19 20 21–24 25	 5 m. 25 m. 5 m. 25 m. 15 m. 15 m.	1.1, 1.2, 1.3, 2.1, 3.1, 3.2, 4.1, 4.2, 5.1	Audio Practice Workbook *Tu desafío*
4	To identify and describe places and to talk about household furnishings and accessories	**Desafío 2 – Un mosquito del Jurásico / Vocabulario** (94–97) • Warm-Up: Independent Starter • *Fotonovela: Un mosquito del Jurásico* • *Cultura: El Museo del Ámbar* • Vocabulary: *Muebles y accesorios para la casa* • *Comunidades: Mi casa es tu casa*	 26–28 29 30–32 33	 5 m. 30 m. 10 m. 35 m. 10 m.	1.1, 1.2, 1.3, 2.1, 3.1, 3.2, 4.2, 5.1, 5.2	Visual Presentation Audio Practice Workbook *Tu desafío*
5	To learn and use direct object pronouns, to integrate vocabulary and grammar, and to assess student proficiency	**Desafío 2 – Gramática / Comunicación / Evaluación** (98–101) • Warm-Up: Independent Starter • Grammar: *Los pronombres de objeto directo* • *Comunicación:* Review • *Final del desafío* • Quiz on *Desafío 2*	 34–38 39–41 42	 5 m. 30 m. 25 m. 15 m. 15 m.	1.1, 1.2, 1.3, 2.2, 3.1, 4.1	Audio Practice Workbook
6	To express habitual actions and to talk about appliances and electronics	**Desafío 3 – Una serenata en Ponce / Vocabulario** (102–105) • Warm-Up: Independent Starter • *Fotonovela: Una serenata en Ponce* • *Cultura: Las serenatas* • Vocabulary: *Los electrodomésticos* • *Cultura: Las tunas*	 43–45 46 47–50 51	 5 m. 35 m. 10 m. 30 m. 10 m.	1.1, 1.2, 1.3, 2.1, 2.2, 3.2, 4.2, 5.1	Visual Presentation Audio Practice Workbook *Tu desafío*

Day	Objectives	Sessions	Activities	Time	Standards	Resources / Homework
7	To learn and use indirect object pronouns, to integrate vocabulary and grammar, and to assess student proficiency	**Desafío 3 – Gramática / Comunicación / Evaluación** (106–109) • Warm-Up: Independent Starter • Grammar: *Los pronombres de objeto indirecto* • *Comunicación:* Review • *Final del desafío* • Quiz on *Desafío 3*	 52–55 56–59 60	5 m. 35 m. 25 m. 10 m. 15 m.	1.1, 1.2, 1.3, 2.1, 3.1, 4.1	Audio Practice Workbook *Tu desafío*
8	To describe the neighborhood and to talk about areas of a city	**Desafío 4 – El Festival de las flores / Vocabulario** (110–113) • Warm-Up: Independent Starter • *Fotonovela: El Festival de las flores* • *Cultura: El Festival de las flores de Aibonito* • Vocabulary: *El barrio. Lugares y servicios* • *Comunidades: El barrio*	 61–63 64 65–67 68	5 m. 35 m. 10 m. 30 m. 10 m.	1.1, 1.2, 1.3, 2.1, 2.2, 3.2, 4.2, 5.1, 5.2	Visual Presentation Audio Video Practice Workbook *Tu desafío*
9	To learn and use demonstratives, to integrate vocabulary and grammar, and to assess student proficiency	**Desafío 4 – Gramática / Comunicación / Evaluación / Todo junto** (114–119) • Warm-Up: Independent Starter • Grammar: *Los demostrativos* • *Cultura: La Plaza de Armas* • *Comunicación:* Review • *Final del desafío* • Quiz on *Desafío 4* • *Todo junto* • *Cultura: El turismo en el Caribe*	 69–72 73 74–76 77 78–80 81	5 m. 15 m. 5 m. 20 m. 10 m. 15 m. 15 m. 5 m.	1.1, 1.2, 1.3, 2.1, 2.2, 3.1, 3.2, 4.1, 4.2, 5.1, 5.2	Audio Practice Workbook *Tu desafío*
10	To integrate language in context and to learn about Caribbean customs and traditions	**El encuentro / Mapa cultural / Lectura** (120–125) • Warm-Up: Independent Starter • *El encuentro: En la fortaleza Ozama* • *Mapa cultural: Las Antillas* • *Lectura: Estilo de vida caribeño*	 82–83 84–85 86–88	5 m. 30 m. 25 m. 30 m.	1.1, 1.2, 1.3, 2.1, 2.2, 3.1, 3.2, 5.1, 5.2	Audio Video Practice Workbook **Repaso – Vocabulario** (126–127) **Repaso – Gramática** (128–129) Project work
11	To create a board game and to assess student proficiency	**Proyecto / Assessment** (130–131) • Warm-Up: Prepare project presentations • Project presentations • *Autoevaluación* • Test		10 m. 40 m. 10 m. 30 m.	1.1, 1.2, 1.3, 3.1, 5.2	

Unit 2 Las Antillas

8 ¿Cierto o falso?

–Andy, ¿qué piensas de Santo Domingo?

–¡Me encanta! Santo Domingo es una ciudad muy antigua, ¿verdad?

–Sí, tiene mucha historia. ¡Mira, un barco antiguo! ¡Qué bonito!

–Aquí llegaron hace tiempo muchos exploradores españoles. Y oí que también vinieron unos piratas.

–¿Piratas? ¿En serio? ¡Qué bien!

–Vamos a aprender mucho sobre ellos después de visitar el museo de la Casa del Cordón.

–¿Dónde está ese museo?

–No lo sé, pero creo que es fácil encontrarlo. Es una casa antigua de piedra, de dos pisos. Tenemos que buscar el cordón en la fachada.

–De acuerdo. ¡Vamos!

11 La Casa del Cordón

1. La Casa del Cordón tiene dos pisos.
2. La casa es de piedra.
3. Sobre la puerta hay una ventana.
4. La Casa del Cordón tiene balcones.

18 ¿Qué está pasando?

1. La chica está sacudiendo el polvo.
2. El hombre está planchando la ropa.
3. La mujer está colocando la comida en la despensa.
4. El chico está lavando los platos.

21 ¿Qué están haciendo?

–Dime, mamá, ¿qué está haciendo mi primo Ronaldo?

–Ronaldo está leyendo un libro muy interesante sobre Francis Drake.

–¿Y mis hermanos?

–Pues Sergio y Alán están nadando en la playa con sus amigos.

–¿Y qué están haciendo papá y tú?

–Tu papá está descargando el lavaplatos y yo estoy preparando la comida.

–OK, dale un beso de mi parte. Mañana te llamo, mamá.

–Bien, hija. Un beso.

28 De compras

–Tía, me encantan los muebles que hay en esta tienda. ¿Vamos a comprar algo para nuestra casa?

–Claro que sí, es una idea excelente.

–Mira, esta lámpara es muy linda. ¿Dónde podemos colocarla?

–Podemos ponerla en el estante de la sala. ¿Qué te parece?

–¡Muy bien! Y este espejo, ¿te gusta?

–No mucho, es un poco grande. Y no lo necesitamos.

–Tienes razón, tía.

–¿Y este florero? Lo podemos poner en la mesa de la sala.

–Sí, me gusta. ¿Lo compramos también?

–Sí, vamos a buscar al vendedor.

31 ¿Dónde están?

1. A mi mamá le gustan mucho las plantas. Tenemos floreros y plantas en toda la casa.

2. En mi dormitorio tengo una lámpara muy linda de color azul. Está sobre la mesita de noche.
3. También tengo unos estantes llenos de libros en mi dormitorio.
4. Todos los cuartos de mi casa tienen cortinas, pero en el comedor hay unas cortinas verdes muy bonitas.

39 Un apartamento en venta

–¿Qué tal el apartamento, Rosa? ¿Te gustó?

–Sí, bastante.

–¿Cómo es?

–Pues no es muy grande, pero para mí está bien. Tiene una sala, un comedor, dos dormitorios, la cocina y un baño.

–¿Hay muebles en la sala?

–Sí, hay un sofá grande y una alfombra.

–¿Y qué tal el baño y la cocina?

–Muy bien, todos los muebles de la cocina y del baño son nuevos.

–¿Entonces tienes todos los muebles necesarios en el apartamento?

–No. Hay bastantes muebles, pero tengo que comprar algunos. Por ejemplo, en los dormitorios hay un armario y una cama, pero no hay mesitas de noche.

–Pero ¿te quedas con el apartamento?

–Sí, creo que sí.

45 ¿Qué necesito?

1. ¡Qué sed! Voy a beber un refresco frío.
2. Tengo hambre. ¿Preparamos carne y unas papas fritas?
3. Estoy aburrido. ¿Vemos una película?
4. Voy a beber un vaso de leche caliente. ¿Quieres uno?

49 El apartamento de Pedro

Hola, soy Pedro. Vivo con mis padres y mis hermanos en un apartamento muy pequeño en el centro de San Juan. Tenemos bastantes electrodomésticos. En la cocina tenemos lavadora, pero no tenemos secadora. También tenemos una estufa, claro, y un horno, pero no tenemos microondas. No tenemos calefacción porque aquí no hace mucho frío. Pero sí tenemos aire acondicionado.

54 Todos trabajan para todos

–Sonia, ¿ustedes comparten las tareas en casa?

–Sí, claro. Todos ayudamos. Todas las mañanas, mi madre le prepara la comida a mi hermano.

–¿Y tu padre también hace tareas en la casa?

–Sí. Él nos lava la ropa y nos la plancha a todos.

–¿Y tú qué haces?

–Yo me hago mi cama. Y mi abuelo también ayuda. Él le coloca la ropa en el armario a mi hermana pequeña.

–Mi abuelo y yo también hacemos las tareas juntos.

56 ¿Qué prefieres?

1. A mí me encanta la música. Tengo un reproductor de MP3, pero mi electrodoméstico preferido es mi equipo de música.

2. A mí me parece muy importante la lavadora porque me gusta tener la ropa siempre limpia.
3. Yo prefiero el microondas porque sirve para calentar la comida preparada... ¡y yo no sé cocinar!

66 **En la ciudad**

1. Roberto compra tomates para hacer una ensalada.
2. Sara y Natalia le envían cartas a su abuela.
3. Jorge y Juan Miguel beben un café.
4. Rebeca se relaja y lee sentada en un banco.
5. Tomás va a sacar dinero para ir al cine.
6. Marcos va a clase de Ciencias.

72 **El barrio de Luisa**

1. Vivo en un barrio muy popular. Tengo un banco a dos cuadras de mi casa. En ese banco trabaja mi mamá.
2. Un poco más lejos hay una oficina de correos, pero a aquella oficina no voy muy frecuentemente.
3. En mi barrio también hay un parque. Es un parque muy popular y siempre hay mucha gente. Me gusta ir allí a pasear y a leer.
4. Pero lo mejor es que mi casa está en la plaza. Esta plaza es muy linda, ¿verdad?

74 **Mi lugar favorito**

Estoy en un lugar muy turístico de esta ciudad. Aquí se reúne la gente para hablar y pasear. Las calles son estrechas, de piedra, pero muy bonitas, llenas de casas de colores. En este barrio hay muchos monumentos, iglesias y lugares interesantes para visitar. Y también hay plazas muy lindas donde puedes pasear y sentarte en un banco a leer o a descansar.
¿Dónde estoy?

78 **Están muy ocupadas**

–Hola, Rita, ¿cómo estás?
–Hola, Patricia. Bien, ¿qué tal? ¿Qué haces?
–Bien... Bueno, Tess y yo estamos haciendo las tareas de la casa.
–¿Qué están haciendo?
–Yo estoy planchando.
–¡Qué aburrido!
–Sí, pero Tess también hace muchas cosas. Ahora está cargando el lavaplatos y también va a poner la lavadora. ¿Tú qué tal?
–Un poco aburrida. Es que yo también estoy limpiando.
–Ja, ja. ¿Qué estás haciendo?
–Estoy sacudiendo el polvo y luego voy a pasar la aspiradora.
–Uff, yo tengo que limpiar el baño. ¡Estamos todas muy ocupadas!
–Sí, claro.

Unit 2
Las Antillas

The Unit

- The theme for Unit 2 is home living in the context of the Antilles islands.
- The pairs meet in Santo Domingo, Dominican Republic, to receive their tasks from their hostess, Dolores Santiago.
  - *Desafío 1.* Andy and Janet will stay in Santo Domingo, where they must find the scale Sir Francis Drake used to weigh the gold he pirated from the townspeople.
  - *Desafío 2.* Diana and Rita travel to Puerto Plata, in the Dominican Republic, where they must find a 200-million-year-old insect that is preserved in amber and in the home of amber collector María Luisa Ayala.
  - *Desafío 3.* Tim and Mack will travel to the University of Puerto Rico in Ponce, Puerto Rico. There, they must learn and sing the words to a traditional *serenata* to serenade a student.
  - *Desafío 4.* Tess and Patricia will travel to Aibonito, Puerto Rico. There, they have to serve as judges in the Festival of Aibonito.

Activities	Standards	Resources
Las Antillas	1.2, 3.1, 3.2	Video

Teaching Suggestions

Warm-Up / Independent Starter

- Ask students to look at a map and list all of the countries that constitute the Greater Antilles and their capital cities. Then have them take notes of the places to which the four pairs will travel.

The Antilles Islands

- The Antilles are split into two major groups. The first group is called the Greater Antilles, which includes Cuba, Hispaniola (Haiti and Dominican Republic), Jamaica, and Puerto Rico. The second group is called the Lesser Antilles, which includes the rest of the islands, except the Bahamas, which are not usually included among the Antilles islands.

UNIDAD 2
Las Antillas
Por las islas del Caribe

DESAFÍO 1

To express the progress of an action

Vocabulario
La vivienda
Las tareas domésticas

Gramática
El presente continuo

Puerto Plata (República Dominicana)

Zona colonial de Santo Domingo

DESAFÍO 2

To identify and describe places

Vocabulario
Muebles y accesorios para la casa

Gramática
Los pronombres de objeto directo

80 ochenta

The Challenge

DESAFÍO 1
Zona colonial de Santo Domingo
The colonial zone of Santo Domingo was inscribed as a UNESCO World Heritage Site in 1990. This city, founded in 1496, boasts the first cathedral and the first hospital in the New World. Other famous colonial buildings include the Ozama Fortress, the oldest military construction still standing in the Americas, and the *Alcázar de Colón,* the oldest viceroy residence in the New World. Santo Domingo also claims the oldest university in the Western Hemisphere. The Columbus Plaza, where a large statue of Christopher Columbus stands, is at the heart of the colonial city.

DESAFÍO 2
Puerto Plata
Puerto Plata is one of the 31 provinces of the Dominican Republic. It is situated in the north of the country and includes many interesting places. La Isabela, one of the first European towns in the Americas, was founded by Christopher Columbus in the province of Puerto Plata in 1493. The city of San Felipe de Puerto Plata (commonly called Puerto Plata) is the capital of the province. Also known as the "Amber Coast" because it contains the largest amount of amber in the region, this area also features a museum dedicated to the stone.

Las Antillas

Ponce
(Puerto Rico)

DESAFÍO 3

▶ **To express habitual actions**

Vocabulario
Los electrodomésticos

Gramática
Los pronombres de objeto indirecto

DESAFÍO 4

▶ **To describe a neighborhood**

Vocabulario
El barrio.
Lugares y servicios

Gramática
Los demostrativos

BIENVENIDOS A AIBONITO
PUEBLO DE LAS FLORES

Aibonito (Puerto Rico)

ochenta y uno 81

- Focus students' attention on the map on the top of the page. Ask them how they would classify the Antilles geographically (i.e., North, Central, or South America) and culturally. Are several classifications possible?

Picture Discussion

- Ask students to look at the pictures. Has anyone in the class ever been to any of these places? Encourage students to share their experiences.

Zona colonial de Santo Domingo

- Invite students to share what they know about colonial architecture in the Spanish-speaking countries of the Americas. Do they know who the first European to arrive in the Dominican Republic was? Invite students to observe the picture and talk about who they think the statue represents.

Puerto Plata (República Dominicana)

- Have students locate Puerto Plata on a map of the Dominican Republic. Based on the picture and this city's location, what is the weather like? Explain that tourism is an important industry in Puerto Plata. Is it apparent to students why people would want to visit Puerto Plata?

Ponce (Puerto Rico)

- Explain that Ponce is a southern city. Have students discuss the characteristics they usually associate with southern cities in the United States (e.g., hospitality, warmer weather, a laid-back lifestyle, etc.). Do they think some of these characteristics would also apply to Ponce?

Aibonito (Puerto Rico)

- Discuss with students what in the picture supports Aibonito's nickname: "The City of Flowers." Do students know of cities in the United States that are also known for their flowers and gardens? (e.g., Portland, OR and Pasadena, CA: "City of Roses;" Macon, GA: "Cherry Blossom Capital of the World"). What kind of climate is best for growing flowers?

Objectives

- By the end of Unit 2, students will be able to
  - Express the progress of an action.
  - Identify and describe places.
  - Express habitual actions.
  - Describe a neighborhood.
  - Talk about different cultural aspects of the Antilles islands.

DESAFÍO 3

Ponce

Ponce is located in southern Puerto Rico. The colonial settlement of Ponce was granted the status of town in 1692. Today, it is the second most populous urban center after the San Juan metropolitan area. Ponce is located at about 3 miles from the coast. The city preserves its colonial center, which is comprised of several churches, plazas, fountains, and colonial homes. The University of Puerto Rico has a campus in Ponce to serve the local student population.

DESAFÍO 4

Aibonito

Aibonito is a small mountain town located on the Central Mountain Range on the island of Puerto Rico. Due to Aibonito's relatively high elevation, the climate is fairly rainy and cool all year long, so many flowers and plants are cultivated there and its gardens are spectacular. For this reason, Aibonito is called "Puerto Rico's Garden" or "The City of Flowers." One example of the importance that flowers have for Aibonito is the Festival of Flowers, or *Festival de las Flores*. This festival is celebrated every year at the end of June and beginning of July.

Unit 2
La llegada

Presentation

- This section presents the pairs' arrival in the Antilles islands. They will meet their hostess, Dolores Santiago, at the *Alcázar de don Diego Colón* in Santo Domingo, Dominican Republic.

- Students will see vocabulary in context, with pictures and illustrations. Presenting new words in this manner helps students develop their Spanish vocabulary with background knowledge while engaging them with the context.

Activities	Standards	Resources
Fotonovela	1.2, 3.1, 3.2	Vis. Pres.
1.	1.2, 2.1, 3.1, 3.2	

Teaching Suggestions

Warm-Up / Independent Starter

- Ask students to read the introduction to the *fotonovela*, then look at the pictures. Have them create a short story about Dolores Santiago. They must include a description of Dolores' physical characteristics and personality traits, as well as a short storyline.

Preparation

- Have students read the *fotonovela* silently. Remind them of some reading and listening Strategies from Level 1, such as looking for cognates, recognizing prefixes and suffixes, and checking the dictionary for unknown words. Students can also use the reading strategy from Unit 1, which is to identify the overall theme of the text.

La fotonovela

Before Viewing

- Ask for volunteers to read each speech bubble. There are many historical and informational facts within the dialogues. Have students create a "fun facts" sheet about the Antilles and their cultures.

- Encourage students to decorate their fun facts sheet and place it in their notebook where they can add more interesting information as the unit progresses. This sheet may also serve as a culture review.

La llegada

En Santo Domingo

The pairs gather in Santo Domingo, Dominican Republic, in front of the *Alcázar de don Diego Colón*. The *Alcázar* was the palace of Christopher Columbus's son, who was the first European ruler of the Dominican Republic. Dolores Santiago greets the pairs and hands them their challenges in the Caribbean islands.

Hola, yo soy Dolores Santiago. Bienvenidos a Santo Domingo.

Esta es la primera ciudad importante fundada por europeos en América. La fundó Bartolomé Colón, hermano de Cristóbal Colón.

¿En serio?

Las islas Antillas tienen muchas sorpresas para ustedes.

Differentiated Instruction

DEVELOPING LEARNERS

- To reinforce comprehension of the vocabulary in the *fotonovela*, ask students to match the words in the first column with their corresponding synonyms in the second column.

  1. *amor*   a. *establecer*   (g)
  2. *serenata*   b. *conocido*   (d)
  3. *fundar*   c. *deber*   (a)
  4. *tener que*   d. *canción de amor*   (c)
  5. *contar*   e. *población*   (f)
  6. *famoso*   f. *decir*   (b)
  7. *ciudad*   g. *cariño*   (e)

EXPANDING LEARNERS

- Ask students to write their own responses or reactions to each of the *desafíos*. For example, Janet might ask: *¿Quién es Francis Drake?* Rita might say: *¡Un mosquito no puede vivir doscientos millones de años!* Mack could ask: *¿A quién vamos a cantar la serenata?* And Tess might comment: *¡Estupendo! ¡Nos encantan las flores!* Encourage creativity and explain that they may also add comments from the character's partners.

- Ask students to read the entire dialogue with their new lines.

La llegada

ndy, Janet, ustedes tienen que investigar una aventura de Francis Drake en Santo Domingo.

El famoso pirata Francis Drake, ¿verdad?

Ustedes tienen que encontrar un mosquito de doscientos millones de años.

¿Un mosquito de doscientos millones de años? ¿Y dónde hay que buscarlo?

Ustedes tienen que ir a Puerto Rico y cantar una serenata.

¿Una serenata?

Y ustedes tienen que dar un premio en el Festival de las flores de Aibonito. ¿Qué les parece?

¡Qué buena idea!

Sí, una canción de amor.

Ah, y tienen que escribir una nota contando sus desafíos. ¡Buena suerte!

1 ¿Comprendes?

▶ **Une** cada pregunta con la respuesta adecuada.

 (A)

1. ¿Quién fundó Santo Domingo?
2. ¿Qué pirata famoso estuvo en Santo Domingo?
3. ¿Qué es una serenata?
4. ¿Cuántos años tiene el mosquito?
5. ¿Dónde se celebra el Festival de las flores?

 (B)

a. Doscientos millones.
b. En Aibonito.
c. Una canción de amor.
d. Bartolomé Colón.
e. Francis Drake.

After Viewing

- Now that students have read what the challenges in this unit will be, ask them what they think about the challenges. Encourage them to use the descriptive adjectives from Unit 1.

- Ask students to work in small groups to summarize the plot of the *fotonovela*. Then have them create a summarized version of the dialogue. Invite volunteer groups to role-play their dialogues in front of the class. Did they capture the essence of the *fotonovela*?

Activities

1. Once students have completed this activity, have them rewrite the correct answers in complete sentences. Then go over the answers as a class. Read the question, then call on a volunteer to read his or her complete answer to the class.

Answer Key

1. 1. d   4. a
     2. e   5. b
     3. c

Additional Resources

Fans Online activities
Practice Workbook

HERITAGE LANGUAGE LEARNERS

- Ask students to work in small groups and research the lives of Diego Colón, Bartolomé Colón, or their more famous relative, Cristóbal Colón. In addition to biographical information, such as date and place of birth, family data, and education, ask students to find some interesting anecdotal facts.

- Invite students to share their information with the rest of the class.

TOTAL PHYSICAL RESPONSE (TPR)

- Divide the class into teams and have them play "Charades." Write the challenges the characters were assigned, as well as some vocabulary items from the dialogue, on slips of paper and place them in a bag (one bag for each team). Team members will take turns pantomiming the *desafíos* or the related vocabulary. The only clue they can give their team is the number of words they are pantomiming. Examples of single item vocabulary include: *sorpresa, pirata, mosquito, amor, flores, nota*. Set a time limit per student and per game and award a point for every correct answer.

Unit 2
La llegada

Presentation

- In this section, students will learn useful expressions to ask for confirmation of a fact, to express surprise, to ask for someone's opinion, and to express approval and disapproval.

Activities	Standards	Resources
Expresiones útiles	1.2, 4.1	
2.	1.2	
3.	1.3	
4.	1.1, 3.1, 5.1	
5.	1.1, 5.1	

Teaching Suggestions

Warm-Up / Independent Starter

- Have students look at the *Expresiones útiles* section and relate each *expresión* with an expression they know in English. For example, ... *¿verdad?* → ... right?

Preparation

- Go over the *Expresiones útiles* section with students. Let them know that the question ... *¿no?* is used for positive confirmation, not for a negative response. Also, be sure to go over the English translation for each expression so students can equate the expression to something they would use in their everyday speech. For example, *¿De verdad?* would translate to "Really?". Use intonation and facial expressions to emphasize your point.

- Have students work with a partner to write several sentences followed by an *expresión útil*. Then ask volunteer pairs to read their sentences aloud. For example:
  A. *La profesora tiene tres gatos.*
  B. *¿De verdad?*

Activities

2. There is more than one possible answer for each item. Have students write all the possible answers. Then ask them which expression(s) will not work for each.

84

EXPRESIONES ÚTILES

Me parece muy bien.

To ask for confirmation of information:
    ... ¿no?   ... ¿verdad?

To express surprise and astonishment:
    ¿En serio?   ¿De verdad?

To ask someone's opinion:
    ¿Qué te parece?   ¿Qué opinas?

To express approval and disapproval:
    Me parece (muy) bien.   Me parece (muy) mal.
    ¡Qué bien!   ¡Qué mal!
    ¡Qué buena idea!   ¡Qué mala idea!

2   ¿Qué expresión usas?

▶ **Completa** estos diálogos con una de las expresiones útiles.

La capital de Puerto Rico es Santo Domingo, ___1___.

No, la capital de Puerto Rico es San Juan.

Este es mi coche nuevo. ___2___.

Me encanta, es muy bonito.

Julia tiene un televisor en el cuarto de baño.

___3___. ¡Qué extraño!

¿Hacemos una fiesta para celebrar tu cumpleaños?

¡Sí! ___4___.

3   Diálogos

▶ **Escribe** dos diálogos utilizando expresiones útiles. Después, representa uno con tu compañero(a).

84 ochenta y cuatro

Differentiated Instruction

DEVELOPING LEARNERS

- Provide additional practice with the expressions by having students choose the best expression to complete the following sentences.
  1. *Te llamas Miguel, ¿qué opinas?/¿verdad?* (¿verdad?)
  2. *—Acabo de recibir una buena nota. —¡Qué mal!/¡Qué bien!* (¡Qué bien!)
  3. *Vienes conmigo al partido de fútbol, ¿de verdad?/¿no?* (¿no?)
  4. *—No voy a estudiar para los exámenes. —Me parece mal./¡Qué bien!* (Me parece mal.)

EXPANDING LEARNERS

- Have students work with a partner to come up with short dialogues in which one or more of the expressions in the *Expresiones útiles* section could be used. For example:
  A. *Hoy tenemos un examen de Español.*
  B. *¿En serio?*
  B. *Voy a pintar el dormitorio de rojo. ¿Qué opinas?*
  A. *¡Qué buena idea!*
  A. *Mira, este es mi nuevo teléfono celular. ¿Qué te parece?*
  B. *¡Qué bonito!*

¿Quién ganará?

 4 **Los desafíos**

 ▶ **Habla.** ¿Cuál será *(will be)* el desafío para cada pareja? Piénsalo y coméntalo con tus compañeros(as).

DESAFÍO ①

La balanza del pirata Drake

Andy y Janet

DESAFÍO ②

Un mosquito del Jurásico

Diana y Rita

DESAFÍO ③

Una serenata en Ponce

Tim y Mack

DESAFÍO ④

El Festival de las flores

Patricia y Tess

 ▶ **Habla.** Las parejas viajan a la República Dominicana y a Puerto Rico. ¿Qué sabes de esos países? Coméntalo con tus compañeros(as).

5 **La tarea final**

▶ **Decide.** ¿Qué tarea tienen que hacer los personajes al final?
¿Qué pareja crees que ganará *(will win)*?

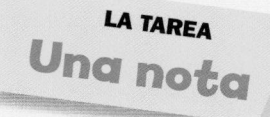
LA TAREA
Una nota

---

3. You can also have students write one dialogue individually, then share their dialogue with a classmate. Students may choose the dialogue they like best, and perform it for the class.

¿Quién ganará?

4. Have students get into small groups and discuss the pairs' challenges. Ask groups to look at the pictures, read the captions, and write a brief paragraph about what they believe the pairs will do in their challenges. They must also include in the paragraph any information they know about the Dominican Republic and Puerto Rico. Remind students that in the pairs' last adventure in Puerto Rico, they visited Old San Juan, Ana Garcia's home, the Bioluminescent Bay, and the Camuy Caves, and learned about the *coquí* frog. Have each group read their paragraph aloud.

5. Students have been provided a clue as to what the pairs will have to do to win their *desafío* in the Antilles. The clue is *una nota*. As a class, discuss examples of notes (e.g., social etiquette notes, routine notes, sympathy notes) and their characteristics (e.g., short, clear, readable). Ask students what kind of note they think the pairs will need to write in order to win their *desafío* in the Antilles.

Answer Key

2. Answers will vary. Sample answers:
   1. ¿verdad?
   2. ¿Qué te parece?
   3. ¿En serio?
   4. ¡Qué buena idea!
3. Answers will vary.
4. Answers will vary.
   ▶ Answers will vary.
5. Answers will vary.

Additional Resources

Fans Online activities
Practice Workbook

HERITAGE LANGUAGE LEARNERS

- Ask students to research information about the Dominican Republic or Puerto Rico, including more information about the topics mentioned for the *desafíos*. In addition, have students share any information they may have from family members who are from either the Dominican Republic or Puerto Rico, or who have traveled to one of these islands.

- Ask students to present their findings to the rest of the class.

MULTIPLE INTELLIGENCES:
Intrapersonal Intelligence

- Ask students to assess their own strengths and weaknesses, and then determine which one of the *desafíos* would be the best suited to them and which one would be the least suited. In addition, students also need to keep in mind their own interests and describe the ideal partner with whom to carry out the challenge. Students should write their responses in two or more paragraphs. Be sure they provide details to support their choices.

85

Unit 2
DESAFÍO 1

Expresar el desarrollo de una acción

Presentation

- In *Desafío 1*, Andy and Janet are in Santo Domingo, Dominican Republic. There they must find the scale that Sir Francis Drake used to weigh the gold he demanded to spare the city.

- In this section, students will preview:
  - Vocabulary for parts of the house.
  - Words for materials used to make a house.
  - Household chores.
  - The present progressive tense.

Activities	Standards	Resources
Fotonovela	1.2, 2.2, 3.1	Vis. Pres.
6.	1.2, 2.2	
7.	1.3, 2.2	
8.	1.2	Audio
9. Conexiones	1.1, 1.2, 3.1, 3.2, 5.1	
Tu desafío	1.2, 3.1, 3.2, 5.2	

Teaching Suggestions

Warm-Up / Independent Starter

- Ask students to read over the *fotonovela*. Then have them rewrite it adding in some of the *expresiones útiles* (e.g., *Estas casas son muy modernas, ¿no?*).

Preparation

- Read the introduction to the *fotonovela* aloud. Then ask for volunteers to read their *fotonovelas*.
- Draw students' attention to the words *ladrillo* and *piedra*. Ask them what other stories they know of that include different building materials (e.g., *The Three Little Pigs*).

 La fotonovela

Before Viewing

- Have students predict the main theme of this *desafío* based on the *fotonovela* (the home).

After Viewing

- Have students devise a strategy for Andy and Janet to find a stone house among brick houses.

La balanza del pirata Drake

 Andy and Janet are in the colonial area of Santo Domingo. They know that the English pirate Sir Francis Drake, took the city by storm in 1586. They must find out information about the pirate, and bring proof of his presence in the city—the scale he used to weigh the gold he demanded in order to spare the town from destruction.

6 **Detective de palabras**

▶ **Completa** estas oraciones.

1. En Santo Domingo hay _____ antiguas.
   - a. edificios
   - b. casas
2. La Casa del Cordón es _____.
   - a. de ladrillo
   - b. de piedra
3. La casa tiene _____ pequeñas.
   - a. puertas
   - b. ventanas
4. En la _____ hay un cordón.
   - a. ventana
   - b. pared

Continuará...

86   ochenta y seis

Differentiated Instruction

DEVELOPING LEARNERS

- To verify that students understand the information in the *fotonovela*, ask the following questions.
  1. *¿Qué están buscando Andy y Janet?* (*Información sobre el pirata Drake.*)
  2. *¿Cómo es la Casa del Cordón?* (*Es una casa de piedra muy antigua.*)
  3. *¿Es fácil o difícil reconocer la casa?* (*Fácil.*)
  4. *¿De qué son las casas modernas?* (*Son de ladrillo.*)
  5. *¿Cómo son las ventanas de la Casa del Cordón?* (*Son muy pequeñas.*)
  6. *¿Qué hay en la pared de la casa?* (*Hay un cordón.*)

EXPANDING LEARNERS

- Ask students to write a narrative of what is happening in the dialogue. Remind them that when they write a narrative, they are writing in the third person and are not including any direct speech. Encourage students to be creative and add additional information to their paragraphs.

7 **¿Comprendes?**

▶ **Habla** con tu compañero(a). Por turnos, pregunten y respondan.

1. ¿Dónde están Janet y Andy?
2. ¿Qué buscan?
3. ¿Cómo es la Casa del Cordón?
4. ¿Quién es Sir Francis Drake?

 8 **¿Cierto o falso?**

▶ **Escucha** la conversación de Andy y Janet y decide si estas oraciones son ciertas o falsas.

1. Janet y Andy están en la capital de Puerto Rico.
2. Ven un barco antiguo.
3. A Janet le gustan los piratas.
4. Andy y Janet van a visitar un museo.
5. En la Casa del Cordón hay un museo.
6. La Casa del Cordón tiene cuatro pisos.

 **CONEXIONES: HISTORIA**

Sir Francis Drake

Sir Francis Drake (1543–1596) fue un pirata inglés, explorador y navegante. Perteneció a la Marina Real Británica y dirigió varias expediciones contra los españoles en América.

En 1586 Sir Francis Drake ocupó Santo Domingo y pidió un rescate (*ransom*) para liberar la ciudad. En la Casa del Cordón puso una balanza para pesar el oro (*gold*) y las joyas (*jewelry*) que los ciudadanos tenían que llevar para pagar el rescate.

Retrato de Francis Drake.

9 **Piensa y explica.** Sir Francis Drake es un personaje polémico (*controversial figure*). Para algunas personas es un pirata y para otras es un héroe (*hero*) y un gran explorador (*explorer*). ¿Por qué crees que es así?

→ TU DESAFÍO Visita la página web para aprender más sobre Sir Francis Drake.

Activities

7. Ask pairs to discuss the significance of pirating in the 16th and 21st centuries, and the similarities and differences between pirates back then and modern-day pirates.

8. Have students read each item carefully, and then play the audio once. Did they get the information on the first try?

 AUDIO SCRIPT
See page 791.

 CONEXIONES: HISTORIA

Sir Francis Drake

Sir Francis Drake was a Vice Admiral in Queen Elizabeth I's army. He led many expeditions to the Americas in the Queen's name. To the Spaniards, Drake was a pirate looking to steal gold, land, and slaves. The English, however, regarded him as a legendary navigator and explorer. During one of his first voyages, Drake was attacked by the Spanish Armada off the coast of Mexico. He narrowly escaped, but he decided to wreak havoc on the Spanish Armada. But it wasn't the Armada that led to his demise; it was a preventable intestinal disease that killed him.

Answer Key

6. 1. b   2. b   3. b   4. b

7. Answers will vary. Sample answers:
   1. Están en Santo Domingo.
   2. Ellos buscan la Casa del Cordón.
   3. Es una casa de piedra muy antigua.
   4. Sir Francis Drake es un pirata inglés.

8. 1. F   2. C   3. C   4. C   5. F   6. F

9. Answers will vary.

Additional Resources

Fans Online activities

HERITAGE LANGUAGE LEARNERS

• Ask students to imagine that Sir Francis Drake has been apprehended by the authorities in Santo Domingo and that they are lawyers: some will defend the notorious pirate, and others will prosecute him. Have students decide who will play some of the other roles, such as Drake, the judge, witnesses, victims, etc. Ask "defense lawyers" and "prosecutors" to prepare opening statements, key questions they will ask Drake, witnesses, and victims; and closing remarks. Remind the judge to keep order in the "court." Have the class act as jury and decide Drake's fate: *culpable* or *no culpable*.

CRITICAL THINKING

• Ask students to discuss the role museums play in our lives. Have them talk about what they believe motivates people to visit museums, the importance of preserving history through artifacts collected and displayed in museums, and the impact museums have on society. Encourage students to discuss different types of museums, from art and anthropology to science, and those that represent different cultures.

• You might also have students talk about museums they have visited and what they have learned from their visits.

Unit 2
DESAFÍO 1
Vocabulario – La vivienda

Presentation

- In this section, students will learn:
  - Vocabulary for parts of the house.
  - Words for materials used to make a house.
  - Household chores.

Activities	Standards	Resources
Vocabulario	1.2	
10.	1.3	
11.	1.2	Audio
12.	1.2, 1.3	
13.	1.1	
14. Comparaciones	1.1, 1.2, 2.2, 3.2, 4.2, 5.1	Video
Tu desafío	1.2, 2.2, 3.2, 5.2	

Teaching Suggestions

Warm-Up / Independent Starter

- Have students write five sentences to describe Sir Francis Drake and Santo Domingo.

Preparation

- Have students write all of the vocabulary words on note cards. On one side they will write the Spanish word, and the English translation on the other side. This will serve as a review.
- Ask students to put a star next to the vocabulary words that apply to their homes. Have students compare their stars with those of a classmate.

Activities

10. Have students add the remaining vocabulary words to this list and classify them as well.

13. Have students write a paragraph to summarize their classmates' answers. Then have them present their paragraphs to the class. Their presentations should include an introduction of their classmates.

14. Ask students why the builders of the *Casa del Cordón* would use stone as their primary material. One potential answer could be that stone would stand up against the tropical storms that pass through the area.

88

Vocabulario

La vivienda

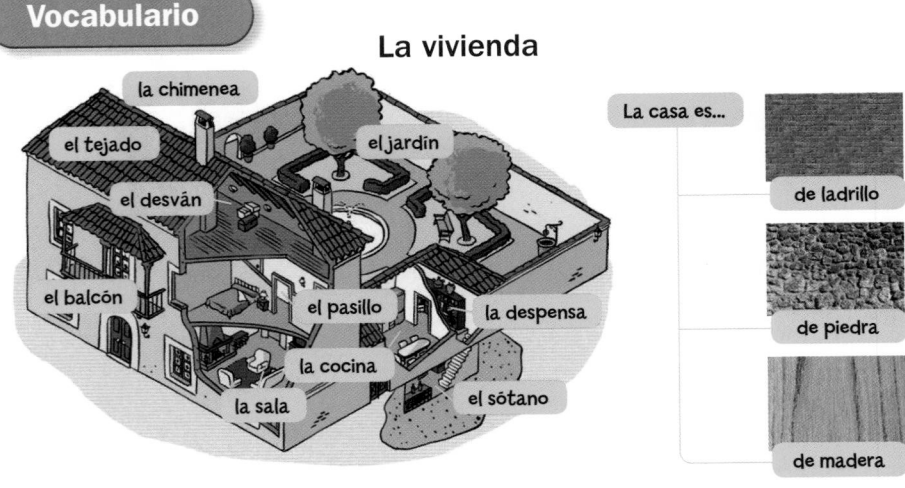

Las tareas domésticas

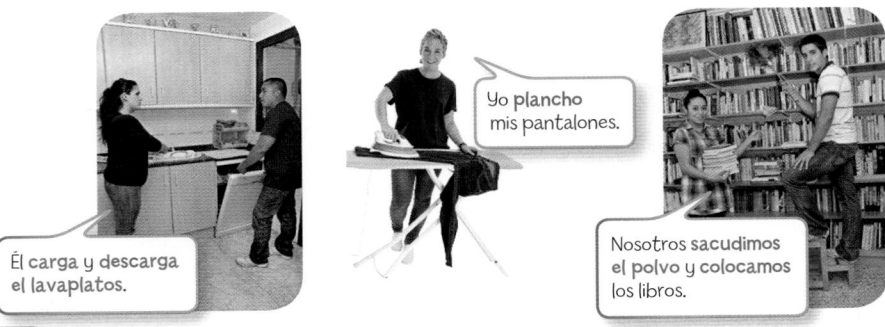

Yo plancho mis pantalones.

Él carga y descarga el lavaplatos.

Nosotros sacudimos el polvo y colocamos los libros.

10 **Cosas de casa**

▶ **Clasifica** estas palabras.

sótano	balcón	armario
tejado	lavaplatos	pasillo
plancha	despensa	jardín

Objetos	Partes dentro de la vivienda	Partes fuera de la vivienda

88   ochenta y ocho

Differentiated Instruction

DEVELOPING LEARNERS

- Have students work with a partner and ask each one to draw a sketch of a house, without revealing it to their partner, and include as many of the elements that are introduced on this page as possible. Then have partners take turns describing their house to each other. Encourage them to use adjectives of size and color. As one partner describes, the other will make a sketch of the house, according to what the partner says. When the description is complete, have partners compare the sketch made from descriptions with the original.

EXPANDING LEARNERS

- Ask students to correct the following statements by substituting the underlined word(s) with one from the list.

1. *Preparo la comida en el balcón.* (b)
2. *Laura sacude el lavaplatos.* (d)
3. *Yo descargo la chimenea.* (e)
4. *El desván está en la sala.* (c)
5. *El pasillo de esa cocina es grande.* (a)

   a. *la despensa*
   b. *la cocina*
   c. *la chimenea*
   d. *el polvo*
   e. *el lavaplatos*

11 La Casa del Cordón

 ▶ **Escucha** y decide si estas oraciones son ciertas o falsas.

1. La Casa del Cordón tiene tres pisos.
2. La casa es de madera.
3. Hay una ventana sobre la puerta.
4. La casa tiene balcones.

 12 Problemas domésticos

▶ **Lee** estas oraciones y escribe lo que tiene que hacer tu hermano Pablo.

Modelo Hay muchos platos sucios en la cocina.
   ⟶ *Pablo tiene que cargar el lavaplatos.*

1. El suelo (*floor*) no está muy limpio.
2. Las blusas están muy arrugadas (*wrinkled*).
3. Hay mucho polvo en la sala.
4. Hay mucha ropa desordenada en el dormitorio de Pablo.
5. El lavaplatos está lleno y los platos están limpios.

 13 ¿Cómo es tu casa?

▶ **Pregunta** a tu compañero(a).

1. ¿Tu casa es de ladrillo, de piedra o de madera?
2. ¿Hay una despensa en tu casa? ¿Dónde está? ¿Qué tienes en la despensa?
3. ¿Hay un desván en tu casa? ¿Qué tienes en el desván?
4. ¿Hay un armario en tu dormitorio? ¿Qué tienes en el armario?

 COMPARACIONES

La Casa del Cordón

La Casa del Cordón es la primera casa de piedra del Nuevo Mundo y, probablemente, la primera casa con dos pisos. Está en Santo Domingo y es del siglo XVI. Se llama así por el cordón (*cord*) que hay en su fachada (*front*).

Fachada de la Casa del Cordón.

14 **Explica.** ¿Hay casas de piedra donde tú vives? ¿Cuál es el edificio más antiguo (*oldest building*)?

 → **TU DESAFÍO** Visita la página web para aprender más sobre la Casa del Cordón.

 AUDIO SCRIPT
See page 791.

COMPARACIONES

La Casa del Cordón

The Cord House, or *La Casa del Cordón*, is the first known house made entirely of stone in the Americas. Francisco de Garay ordered its construction around 1502. This is where Christopher Columbus's son, Diego, and his wife lived temporarily until their permanent home was built. It is also the site used by Sir Frances Drake to collect the ransom for the liberation of the city. The name of the house comes from the symbol of the Franciscan friars: a rope belt carved into the façade. The house is currently occupied by the Cultural Center and a bank, but visitors are allowed into the courtyard and some of the interiors.

Answer Key

10. Objetos: plancha, lavaplatos, armario
Partes dentro de la vivienda: sótano, despensa, pasillo
Partes fuera de la vivienda: tejado, balcón, jardín

11. 1. Falso   3. Cierto
2. Falso   4. Cierto

12. 1. Pablo tiene que barrer el suelo.
2. Pablo tiene que planchar las blusas.
3. Pablo tiene que sacudir el polvo.
4. Pablo tiene que ordenar su dormitorio.
5. Pablo tiene que descargar el lavaplatos.

13. Answers will vary.

14. Answers will vary.

Additional Resources

Fans Online activities
Practice Workbook

HERITAGE LANGUAGE LEARNERS

• Ask students to research one or two other historical buildings or structures in the Dominican Republic. Some of these might include: *Casa de Bastidas*, *Fuerte de San Felipe*, *Catedral de Santa María*, *Alcázar de Colón*, and *Casa de Tostado*. After students gather the information, ask them to share it with the rest of the class. Be sure they mention the historical importance of each building or structure.

SPECIAL–NEEDS LEARNERS

• For students with visual impairments, enlarge the vocabulary page or write each of the words on large index cards so students can easily see and identify them. Then say each word, and as you say each one, ask students to point to the corresponding expression or pick up the correct index card and repeat the word after you.

• Once students have identified the words, ask them to make a simple sketch of a building and label it with as many of the new vocabulary words as they can.

DESAFÍO 1

Gramática – El presente continuo

Presentation

- In this section, students will learn the present progressive tense.

Activities	Standards	Resources
Gramática	3.1	
15.	1.3, 4.1	
16.	1.3	
17.	1.3	
18.	1.2	Audio
19.	1.1	
20. Comparaciones	1.1, 1.2, 2.1, 3.2, 4.2, 5.1	

Teaching Suggestions

Warm-Up / Independent Starter

- Ask students to imagine they are preparing for a presentation, but the outfit they want to wear is dirty and very wrinkled. Ask students to write a step-by-step guide to getting their outfit ready. Most students don't have a washer, dryer, and iron in their room, so they need to mention where they go in the house to take care of their washing, drying, and ironing needs.

Preparation

- Go over the grammar presentation with students. Remind them that only the verb *estar* changes and the present participle will always remain the same no matter which pronoun precedes it.

- Ask for a volunteer to pantomime an activity such as bicycling or running. Then have the rest of the class guess what he or she is doing in the present progressive tense. For example, a male student is running. Students will respond, *Él está corriendo*.

Activities

15. Have students read the words *creer*, *leer*, and *oír* with the *-iendo* ending aloud, then read the words with the *-yendo* ending. Then have students answer this critical thinking question.

17. Have two volunteers read the parts of Andy and Pedro. Ask them to pause when they get to a blank so the class can call out the answer.

Gramática

El presente continuo

- In Spanish we use the presente continuo (present progressive) to talk about actions that are happening at the moment of speaking.

- The present progressive is formed with the verb estar plus the gerundio:

  estar + gerundio

  –¿Qué **estás haciendo**, Pablo?
  –**Estoy cargando** el lavaplatos.

VERBO LAVAR. PRESENTE CONTINUO

yo	estoy lavando	nosotros nosotras	estamos lavando
tú	estás lavando	vosotros vosotras	estáis lavando
usted él, ella	está lavando	ustedes ellos, ellas	están lavando

El gerundio

- The gerundio (present participle) is formed by adding these endings to the verb stem:
  - -ando (-ar verbs):   lavar → lavando
  - -iendo (-er, -ir verbs):   hacer → haciendo; sacudir → sacudiendo

- Most present participles are regular. The only irregular ones occur in verbs that have these stem changes:

  e > i   o > u

decir → diciendo	preferir → prefiriendo	dormir → durmiendo
mentir → mintiendo	sentir → sintiendo	morir → muriendo
pedir → pidiendo	servir → sirviendo	

- When the stem of an -er or -ir verb ends in a vowel, the ending -iendo is written -yendo.

  creer → creyendo   leer → leyendo   oír → oyendo

15 **Piensa.** ¿Por qué la terminación *(ending)* del gerundio -iendo se transforma en *(becomes)* -yendo cuando la raíz *(stem)* de un verbo termina en vocal?

16 **Atareados**

▶ **Escribe.** ¿Qué están haciendo?

1. Yo _____ el desván.
   ordenar

2. Nosotros _____ los platos.
   lavar

3. Tú _____ una casa nueva.
   construir

4. Él _____ el almuerzo en la cocina.
   servir

Differentiated Instruction

DEVELOPING LEARNERS

- Ask students to close their books. Then have them choose the correct form of the present participle to complete each sentence.

  1. *El mesero está serviendo / sirviendo la comida.* (sirviendo)
  2. *Mi hermano está durmiendo / dormiendo.* (durmiendo)
  3. *¿Qué estás leiendo / leyendo?* (leyendo)
  4. *El hombre está pidiendo / pediendo la comida.* (pidiendo)
  5. *Ese niño está mentiendo / mintiendo.* (mintiendo)

- Ask students to open their books and check their answers.

EXPANDING LEARNERS

- Ask students to write or say sentences using the following verbs in the *presente continuo*: *dormir, sentir, competir, repetir, ir, venir, traer, vestir, seguir,* and *medir.* You might want to introduce the verbs *caer* (to fall) and *huir* (to run away), and ask students to first identify the present participle for each verb and then say or write a sentence for both verbs in the *presente continuo*.

17 Una conversación

▶ **Completa** la conversación entre Andy y un amigo.

ANDY: Hola, Pedro. ¿Qué <u>estás haciendo</u> ?
                           _{hacer}

PEDRO: Mis hermanos y yo <u> 1 </u> la casa porque tenemos una fiesta.
                               _{limpiar}

ANDY: ¿Y qué tareas domésticas <u> 2 </u> ustedes?
                                      _{hacer}

PEDRO: Yo <u> 3 </u> la aspiradora y mi hermana Alicia <u> 4 </u> el lavaplatos.
         _{pasar}   _{descargar}

ANDY: Ay, ustedes <u> 5 </u> mucho. ¿Y sus padres?
                       _{trabajar}

PEDRO: Mi padre <u> 6 </u> el césped y mi madre <u> 7 </u> el polvo.
              _{cortar}   _{sacudir}

ANDY: Bueno. Llámame después de completar tus tareas. Hasta luego.

18 ¿Qué está pasando?

▶ **Escucha** y ordena los dibujos.

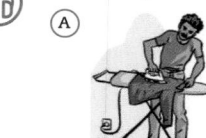 Ⓐ
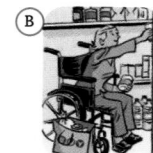 Ⓑ
 Ⓒ
 Ⓓ

19 Adivina

▶ **Representa** una tarea doméstica. Tus compañeros(as) tienen que adivinar *(guess)* cuál es.

Modelo *¡Estás planchando!*

COMPARACIONES

Las casas coloniales

La parte antigua de Santo Domingo tiene muchos edificios coloniales y monumentos muy bien conservados. Las construcciones de estilo colonial están hechas de piedra y ladrillo. Las casas se organizan en torno a un patio *(courtyard)* al que dan las habitaciones. Estos patios están decorados con fuentes, plantas y azulejos *(tiles)*.

La zona colonial de Santo Domingo fue declarada Patrimonio de la Humanidad por la UNESCO en 1990.

20 Piensa y explica. ¿En tu comunidad hay edificios antiguos? ¿Cómo son?

HERITAGE LANGUAGE LEARNERS

• Have students name other household chores, and then write or say a sentence using the *presente continuo* and stating who is doing that chore right now. For example:

1. *fregar los platos → Mi hermana y yo estamos fregando los platos.*
2. *trapear el suelo → Mi hermano está trapeando el suelo.*
3. *sacar la basura → Mi padre está sacando la basura.*
4. *limpiar las ventanas → Yo estoy limpiando las ventanas.*
5. *regar las plantas → Mi abuela está regando las plantas.*

MULTIPLE INTELLIGENCES:
Visual-Spatial Intelligence

• Ask students to imagine they are architects and have been commissioned to build a house for Sir Francis Drake. What kind of house do they think would suit him? Would it be *de piedra, de ladrillo,* or *de madera*? Would the windows be small so enemies could not enter? Would there be *balcones,* even though these might facilitate entry into the house? And what about *la cocina*? Would it have a huge *despensa* in order to store the food needed to feed Drake's many fellow sailors? Have students draw a diagram of their house and describe it to the class.

Gramática – El presente continuo

18. Play the audio for students two times. Have them close their eyes while they listen the first time. When they hear each action, have them act out that action while their eyes are still closed. Then students can put the actions in order the second time they hear them.

> 🎧 **AUDIO SCRIPT**
> See page 791.

COMPARACIONES

Las casas coloniales

The colonial zone in Santo Domingo was laid out on a grid pattern, which would become the model for other cities in the New World. Most of the landmarks in the colonial zone were built between the 16th and 19th centuries. This area is lined with cobblestone streets and buildings that include palaces, schools, and houses. The heart of this zone is *Parque Colón*, which has a large statue of Christopher Columbus.

Answer Key

15. Para facilitar la pronunciación al tener una vocal cerrada entre dos abiertas.

16.
1. estoy ordenando
2. estamos lavando
3. estás construyendo
4. está sirviendo

17.
1. estamos limpiando
2. están haciendo
3. estoy pasando
4. está descargando
5. están trabajando
6. está cortando
7. está sacudiendo

18. 1. C   2. A   3. B   4. D

19. Answers will vary.

20. Answers will vary.

Additional Resources

Fans Online activities
Practice Workbook

DESAFÍO 1

Comunicación

Presentation

- In this section, students will integrate the vocabulary and grammar from *Desafío 1* in order to talk about houses, household chores, and actions in progress.

Activities	Standards	Resources
21.	1.2, 1.3	Audio
22.	1.2, 1.3	
23.	1.1	
24.	1.3	
25. Final del desafío	1.3, 3.1	
Tu desafío	1.2, 1.3	

Teaching Suggestions

Warm-Up / Independent Starter

- Have students write five sentences about what they are doing in the different rooms of the house. For example: *Yo estoy planchando mi camisa en el dormitorio.*

Preparation

- Take 10 minutes to review the vocabulary and grammar themes from *Desafío 1*.
- Refer students back to the *fotonovela* for *Desafío 1*. Have them find all of the materials used to make a house, household chores, and the present progressive tense within the dialogue. Do students understand the dialogue better now that they have gone through the vocabulary and grammar from the *Desafío*?
- Tell students that this page is the last opportunity for them to ask questions about this *Desafío's* contents before beginning the *Comunicación* activities.

Activities

21. Have students guess what their same family members are doing at this very moment. Ask students to write in complete sentences.

22. Ask students to draw a picture of the inside and outside of the house described in the ad. Have them share their interpretation of the house with the class.

DESAFÍO 1

Comunicación

21 **¿Qué están haciendo?**

▶ **Escucha** la conversación entre Diana y su madre. ¿Qué está haciendo cada familiar? Completa.

1. Su primo Ronaldo _____.
2. Sus hermanos Sergio y Alán _____.
3. Su papá _____.
4. Su mamá _____.

22 **Un anuncio**

▶ **Lee** el anuncio *(ad)* y elige la opción correcta.

1. La casa es _____.   a. antigua   b. nueva
2. La casa es _____.   a. grande   b. pequeña
3. La casa tiene _____.   a. jardín   b. balcones
4. El precio es _____.   a. alto   b. bajo

▶ **Escribe** con tu compañero(a) un anuncio de una casa para el periódico *(newspaper)* local.

> **¡Fantástica oportunidad!**
> Casa del siglo XVI, de ladrillo y piedra. Cinco cuartos, desván y sótano. Dos pisos, escalera de madera. Grandes balcones a la calle. Muy buen precio.

23 **Una casa en Santo Domingo**

▶ **Imagina** que eres un agente inmobiliario *(realtor)* y tu compañero(a) es un(a) cliente *(client)*. Hablen sobre esta casa.

Modelo

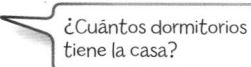
¿Cuántos dormitorios tiene la casa?

Tiene tres dormitorios.

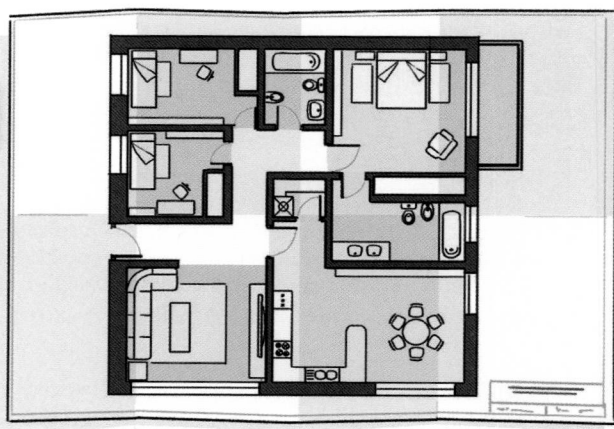

Differentiated Instruction

DEVELOPING LEARNERS

- Bring in magazine cutouts of different styles of homes and other buildings as well as those that depict some household chores and ask students questions about them, such as:
  1. *¿Tiene muchas ventanas o pocas?*
  2. *¿Hay balcones?*
  3. *¿De qué material es?*
  4. *¿Es el sótano o el desván?*
  5. *¿Qué está haciendo esta señora?*
  6. *¿Qué está haciendo con la aspiradora?*
- Encourage students to respond in complete sentences.

EXPANDING LEARNERS

- Ask pairs of students to write a dialogue in which one student asks the other to do a household chore. The student who is asked to do the chore responds in the negative because he or she is doing something else at the moment.
  A. *Sacude el polvo, por favor.*
  B. *No puedo. Estoy leyendo una revista.*
  A. *Saca la basura.*
  B. *No puedo. Estoy estudiando para el examen de Español.*
- See which pairs come up with the most household chores as well as the most inventive excuses.

24 **Tus tareas domésticas**

 ▶ **Pregunta** a tres compañeros(as) sobre sus tareas domésticas y toma nota.

1. ¿Quién plancha la ropa en tu casa?
2. ¿Quién pasa la aspiradora?
3. ¿Quién prepara la comida?
4. ¿Quién saca la basura?
5. ¿Quién carga y descarga el lavaplatos?
6. ¿Quién sacude el polvo?
7. ¿Qué haces tú?

▶ **Escribe** un párrafo *(paragraph)* con los resultados. Después, preséntaselos a la clase.

Final del desafío

Sí. Sir Francis Drake estuvo en esta casa. En 1586 atacó la isla y pidió un importante rescate.

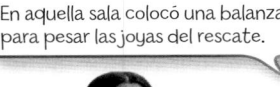

En aquella sala colocó una balanza para pesar las joyas del rescate.

  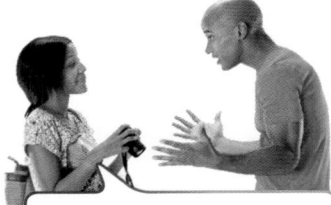

Andy, haz una foto y vamos a comprar una réplica de la balanza en una tienda de recuerdos.

 25 **¿Qué pasa en la historia?**

 ▶ **Lee** el diálogo. Después, representa el final del desafío con dos compañeros(as).

→ TU DESAFÍO Visita la página web. Escucha las preguntas de tu *Minientrevista Desafío 1* y escribe las respuestas.

HERITAGE LANGUAGE LEARNERS

- Point out how the prefix *des-* changes the meaning of the word *cargar*. Then ask students to make a list of other words whose meaning is changed by adding the prefix *des-*. You might start them out by writing the following words on the board: *cuidar, obedecer, conocer, ocupar, ordenar, mentir, hacer, organizar*. Call on students to read their lists, define both words, and then write or say a sentence with one of the pairs.

CRITICAL THINKING

- Ask students to imagine that they are one of the residents of Santo Domingo, and have been requested to turn over their gold and jewels to Sir Francis Drake in order to liberate their city. How would they react to this order? Would they turn over all of their possessions, or would they attempt to keep some of them? Would they consider trying to overturn the pirate and his men? Have students explain what they would do and why.

Comunicación

24. Complete this activity as a class. Have students interview their classmates, then return to their seats. Ask volunteers to reveal their answers to the class. As they reveal their answers, you will write them in a chart on the board. See if there is a pattern of who does each chore.

ropa	
aspiradora	
comida	
basura	
lavaplatos	
polvo	

25. As a class talk about what is happening in each photo. Then have students write their captions. Call on three volunteers to read a caption for each photo.

AUDIO SCRIPT
See page 791.

Answer Key

21. 1. está leyendo un libro
2. están nadando en la playa
3. está descargando el lavaplatos
4. está preparando la comida

22. 1. a   2. a   3. b   4. b
▶ Answers will vary.

23. Answers will vary.

24. Answers will vary.
▶ Answers will vary. Sample answer:
En la casa de Brad, su hermana plancha la ropa. En la casa de Lisa, no planchan la ropa, pero todos ayudan a limpiar la casa y preparar la comida. En la casa de Jenn, su padre carga y descarga el lavaplatos, su hermano saca la basura y ella sacude el polvo. Yo lavo la ropa.

25. Answers will vary.

Additional Resources

Fans Online activities
Practice Workbook

Unit 2
DESAFÍO 2
Identificar y describir lugares

Presentation

- In *Desafío 2*, Diana and Rita are in Puerto Plata, Dominican Republic. They must find a 200-million-year-old insect preserved in amber at the home of María Luisa Ayala.
- In this section, students will preview:
  – Words for household furniture and accessories.
  – Direct objects and direct object pronouns.

Activities	Standards	Resources
Fotonovela	1.2, 2.2, 3.1, 3.2	Vis. Pres.
26.	1.2, 1.3	
27.	1.2	
28.	1.2	Audio
29. Cultura	1.1, 1.2, 2.2, 3.1, 3.2, 5.1	
Tu desafío	1.2, 2.2, 3.1, 3.2, 5.2	

Teaching Suggestions

Warm-Up / Independent Starter

- Have students look at the pictures in the *fotonovela* and write five sentences about what Diana and Rita are doing.

Preparation

- Ask a volunteer to read the introduction to the *fotonovela* aloud.
- Ask students if they have seen amber before. Display a picture of amber on the board so students can see what it looks like. Have students describe the amber you displayed.

La fotonovela

Before Viewing

- Ask two volunteers to read the parts of Diana and Rita in the *fotonovela*. Once they have finished, ask the class why Diana and Rita were so frantic about a mosquito. Discuss the effects of mosquito bites.

After Viewing

- Remind students that the mosquito Diana and Rita are looking for is 200 million years old. Ask students how they think amber can preserve the body of a once-living being for so many years. Do they think maple sap would have the same effect?

Un mosquito del Jurásico

Diana and Rita are in Puerto Plata, Dominican Republic, one of the first European settlements in the Americas, and one of the largest sources of amber in the world. Together, they must find a 200–million–year–old insect! The ancient six–legged creature is somewhere in the home of María Luisa Ayala, a local amber collector.

26 Detective de palabras

▶ **Completa** estas oraciones. ¿Dónde está el mosquito?

1. Primero el mosquito está en el _____.
2. Luego el mosquito está encima de la _____.
3. Finalmente el mosquito está sobre el _____.

Continuará...

Differentiated Instruction

DEVELOPING LEARNERS

- Help students identify the cognates in the *fotonovela* in order to facilitate their comprehension. The cognates are: *mosquito, lámpara, millones, fósil, costa, ámbar, contiene, insectos*. Then ask students to make a list of the words they do not understand. If the context does not help them to decode these words, ask them to look up their meaning in a dictionary. They should write these new words in their notebook, along with the English translations.

EXPANDING LEARNERS

- Have students choose the appropriate word(s) to complete these sentences.
  1. *La tienda está en la cuadra siguiente. Está lejos / cerca de aquí.* (cerca)
  2. *La lámpara está debajo / encima de la mesa.* (encima)
  3. *Los mosquitos pueden estar dentro de / sobre un espejo.* (sobre)
  4. *Santo Domingo está al lado / lejos de San Juan.* (lejos)
  5. *La mesita de noche está junto a / encima de la cama.* (junto a)
  6. *El sótano está sobre / debajo de la sala.* (debajo de)

27 **¿Comprendes?**

▶ **Decide** si estas afirmaciones son ciertas o falsas.
Si son falsas, corrígelas.

1. Rita está oyendo un mosquito.
2. Diana rompe el florero.
3. Diana y Rita tienen que encontrar un espejo.
4. Rita y Diana están delante del Museo del Ámbar en Puerto Plata.
5. Diana y Rita van a pedir información a una señora.

28 **De compras**

 ▶ **Escucha.** Diana y Rita compran dos objetos para su casa. ¿Cuáles son?

① ② ③ ④

 ▶ **Habla** con tu compañero(a). ¿Cuáles de esos objetos hay en tu casa? ¿Dónde están?

Modelo   *En mi casa hay un florero en el pasillo.*

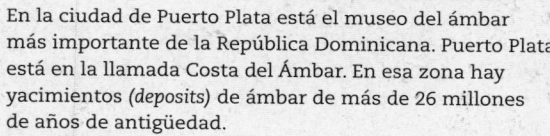

CULTURA

El Museo del Ámbar

En la ciudad de Puerto Plata está el museo del ámbar más importante de la República Dominicana. Puerto Plata está en la llamada Costa del Ámbar. En esa zona hay yacimientos *(deposits)* de ámbar de más de 26 millones de años de antigüedad.

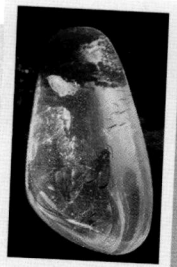

El ámbar dominicano es famoso por su gran variedad de colores. Se utiliza para hacer piezas de adorno y joyas *(jewelry)*. A veces contiene insectos porque el ámbar se forma a partir de la resina *(resin)* fosilizada de los árboles.

29 **Compara.** ¿Qué recursos naturales *(natural resources)* hay cerca de tu lugar de origen? ¿Alguno se usa para hacer adornos *(ornaments)*?

⚑→ TU DESAFÍO Visita la página web para aprender más sobre el Museo del Ámbar.

HERITAGE LANGUAGE LEARNERS

• The mosquito mentioned in Rita and Diana's *desafío* is very old, but there are other archaeological findings that might not be nearly as old but nonetheless offer a window into ancient civilizations. Ask students to investigate some of these, such as the prehistoric paintings in the Altamira caves in Spain, the mysterious Nazca lines in Peru, and some of the pre-Columbian cultures in the Americas, such as the Caral-Supe civilization in central Peru. You may wish to have students prepare a written report or make an oral presentation in front of the class.

SPECIAL-NEEDS LEARNERS

• Help those students with an auditory processing disorder by having them read the directions to all of the activities and repeat the directions back to you. Having them do this will reinforce their comprehension of the tasks at hand. You might also provide them with the audio script to read for any recorded material.

Activities

26. Ask students to rewrite the sentences with the correct answers included and circle the adverbs of place in each sentence. Then have them list all of the adverbs of place they remember.

28. Ask students which items they would like to buy for their bedroom and why.

 AUDIO SCRIPT
See page 791.

 CULTURA

El Museo del Ámbar

The Amber Museum wasn't always the modern marvel it is today. In the middle of the 20th century, the Victorian mansion where the museum is currently housed was an abandoned building. It wasn't until the late 1970s that the building was restored to its original beauty by Mr. Aldo Costa and his wife Didi, and turned into a museum, which opened its doors in 1982. Now the Amber Museum houses artifacts from as long as 30 million years ago.

Answer Key

26. 1. florero   2. lámpara   3. espejo

27. 1. Falso. Diana está oyendo un mosquito.
   2. Falso. Diana no rompe el florero.
   3. Falso. Diana y Rita tienen que encontrar un fósil de mosquito.
   4. Falso. Diana y Rita están delante de una tienda de ámbar.
   5. Cierto.

28. 1 y 4.
   ▶ Answers will vary.

29. Answers will vary.

Additional Resources

Fans Online activities

DESAFÍO 2

Vocabulario – Muebles y accesorios para la casa

Presentation

- In this section, students will learn vocabulary for household furniture and accessories.

Activities	Standards	Resources
Vocabulario	1.2	
30.	1.1, 1.2, 1.3	
31.	1.1, 1.2, 1.3	Audio
32.	1.1, 1.2, 1.3	
33. Comunidades	1.1, 1.2, 2.1, 4.2, 5.1	

Teaching Suggestions

Warm-Up / Independent Starter

- Ask students to think about what they would like to preserve for people to uncover 200 million years from now. Have students write a paragraph to describe the item they would preserve and why.

Preparation

- Go over the vocabulary presentation with students.
- Have students cut out the furniture they would like to have in their home from a catalog. Ask them to organize their pictures by rooms, and label each one.
- Ask volunteers to share their newly furnished home with the class. Take a vote for the student that came up with the most unique arrangement.

Activities

30. Some of these items can be found in non-traditional rooms of the house. Have students think of all of the other places they can find each item. For example, *el refrigerador* can also be found in *el sótano* and *el sofá* can also be found in *el desván*.

31. Do students agree on where Diana puts each accessory? Ask students where they would put each item.

32. Have students work in pairs to come up with the clues. Then have each pair exchange papers with another pair to figure out what is needed.

Vocabulario

Muebles y accesorios para la casa

el cuadro · el espejo · las cortinas · el estante · la lámpara · la cama · la mesita de noche · el sillón · el sofá · la mesa · el florero · la alfombra

30 **Un poco de orden**

▶ **Une** las dos columnas. ¿Dónde están estos objetos?

Ⓐ
1. el refrigerador
2. la bañera
3. la mesa
4. el sofá
5. la mesita de noche
6. la cama
7. el inodoro

Ⓑ
a. en la sala
b. en el comedor
c. en el baño
d. en el dormitorio
e. en la cocina

▶ **Escribe** el nombre de tres muebles o accesorios que hay normalmente en las partes de la casa de la columna B. Después, compara tu lista con la de tu compañero(a) y complétala.

Differentiated Instruction

DEVELOPING LEARNERS

- Prepare a worksheet with the words you would like students to practice or review from this lesson, but omit several of the letters. Ask students to complete each word and include the definite article. For example: *__orm__t__ri__: el dormitorio.*

EXPANDING LEARNERS

- Give students more practice with the vocabulary as well as adverbs of place by having them describe where several things are in a room of a house. Find images from home decorating magazines that depict many objects. Ask students to first identify the room and the objects, and then describe where the objects are in relation to one another. For example: *Esta es la sala y hay un sofá, una alfombra, dos mesas, dos sillones y tres lámparas. La alfombra está debajo de una de las mesas, y esa mesa está delante del sofá.*

31 **¿Dónde están?**

 ▶ **Escucha** a Diana y escribe. ¿Dónde está cada objeto?

 Ⓐ 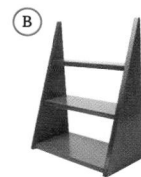 Ⓑ  Ⓒ  Ⓓ

▶ **Habla** con tu compañero(a). Por turnos, piensa en un objeto de la casa y descríbelo. Tu compañero(a) tiene que adivinar cuál es.

Modelo A. *Normalmente está al lado de la cama.*
B. *¿La mesita de noche?*
A. *No.*

 32 **¡Ayuda!**

▶ **Responde** a estas preguntas para ayudar a Rita.

1. Quiero un mueble para poner mis libros, mis gafas y mi reloj al lado de la cama. ¿Qué necesito?
2. Quiero luz para leer en la cama. ¿Qué necesito?
3. ¿Qué necesito para mirarme en el baño?
4. ¿Qué necesito para guardar la ropa en el dormitorio?
5. Quiero poner flores en la sala. ¿Qué necesito?

▶ **Habla.** Piensa en tres accesorios o muebles y escribe preguntas similares para tu compañero(a). ¿Sabe qué necesitas?

 **COMUNIDADES**

MI CASA ES TU CASA

En los países hispanos, cuando una persona tiene invitados *(guests)* en casa, es habitual enseñársela.

Los invitados suelen hacer comentarios positivos sobre las habitaciones o sobre algún mueble (*¡Qué grande! ¡Qué lámpara tan bonita!*).

33 **Piensa y explica.** ¿Alguna vez has mostrado *(have you ever shown)* tu casa a los invitados? ¿Qué opinas de esta costumbre?

noventa y siete **97**

Vocabulario – Muebles y accesorios para la casa

33. Ask students if they have ever moved from one house to another. Did they visit the house before moving in? Was there furniture in the house when they visited it or was it empty? Share your personal experiences with students and / or have students share with you.

 AUDIO SCRIPT
See page 791.

 COMUNIDADES

Mi casa es tu casa

In the United States there are several instances when guests would come to your house, including for holidays, special occasions, and religious celebrations. Most guests stay only in the common areas of the home such as the living room, kitchen, dining room, and patio. It would be considered rude if a guest invited him- or herself to look around, and the host is under no obligation to give a tour of the house.

Answer Key

30. 1. e   5. d
2. c   6. d
3. b   7. c
4. a
▶ Answers will vary.

31. 1. D   2. A   3. B   4. C
▶ Answers will vary.

32. 1. una mesita de noche   4. un armario
2. una lámpara   5. un florero
3. un espejo
▶ Answers will vary.

33. Answers will vary.

Additional Resources

Fans Online activities
Practice Workbook

97

HERITAGE LANGUAGE LEARNERS

• Have students review the vocabulary for rooms of a house, furniture, appliances, and accessories, and then come up with other words that are synonyms or regional variants for them. For example, *la bañera* could be *la tina* or *la bañadera*; *el refrigerador* could be *el frigorífico*, *la heladera*, or *la nevera*. Other words for *el dormitorio* are *la habitación, el cuarto, la recámara,* or *la pieza*. Ask students what other words they know that name rooms of a house, furniture, appliances, or accessories and share these words with the rest of the class.

CRITICAL THINKING

• Ask students what differences, if any, they perceive between a house and a home. What makes a house a home, and why do we have such expressions as "home sweet home" and not "house sweet house"? You might have students brainstorm other expressions with "home" and "house" (e.g., homecoming, going home, homeless, homework, homeland, house-hunting, housewarming, household, houseguest, housework). Invite the heritage speakers in the classroom to share differences between *casa, hogar,* and *vivienda* in their family's country of origin.

DESAFÍO 2

Gramática – Los pronombres de objeto directo

Presentation

- In this section, students will learn:
  - Direct objects and direct object pronouns.
  - Direct object pronoun placement.

Activities	Standards	Resources
Gramática	3.1	
34.	1.1, 3.1, 4.1	
35.	1.3	
36.	1.2	
37.	1.2	
38.	1.1	

Teaching Suggestions

Warm-Up / Independent Starter

- Have students draw a picture of their bedroom and label the furniture and accessories in it.

Preparation

- Read over the grammar presentation with students. Write the following questions on the board and have different volunteers answer them using the appropriate direct object pronouns.
  1. ¿Dónde compro una lámpara?
  2. ¿Dónde compramos un sofá?
  3. ¿Dónde compran las mesitas de noche?
  4. ¿Dónde compras los floreros?

Activities

34. This activity is meant to draw students' attention to the "personal a." If necessary, remind students that this word precedes people and pets when they are used as the object of a verb.

35. Have students add one more line to the conversation to ask their partner why they answered the way they did. For example:

    A. ¿Quieres una alfombra para tu dormitorio?
    B. No, no la quiero./Sí, la quiero.
    A. ¿Por qué no la quieres?/¿Por qué la quieres?
    B. No la quiero porque no me gustan las alfombras./La quiero porque las alfombras son bonitas.

Gramática

Los pronombres de objeto directo

El objeto directo

- Many verbs have a complement that indicates who or what receives the action of the verb. This complement is the direct object.

  Juan compra **un cuadro**.

- When the direct object refers to people or pets, it is preceded by the personal a:

  Yo llamo **a Juan** por teléfono.

Los pronombres de objeto directo

- Sometimes, the direct object is replaced with a direct object pronoun.

  –¿Hay **un sofá** en la sala?
  –Sí, **lo** hay.

  –¿Tienes **los libros** en el estante?
  –Sí, **los** tengo allí.

PRONOMBRES DE OBJETO DIRECTO

Singular		Plural	
me	me	nos	us
te	you (informal)	os	you (informal)
lo	you (formal), him, it	los	you, them
la	you (formal), her, it	las	you, them

Posición de los pronombres de objeto directo

- Direct object pronouns are placed before the conjugated verb, or attached to the infinitive, the present participle, or the command.

  Hay que planchar esa camisa. Plánchala.
  Me gusta ese cuadro. Lo quiero comprar. / Quiero comprarlo.
  La ropa está sobre la cama. La estoy colocando. / Estoy colocándola.

34 **Compara.** ¿Cómo dices en inglés Llamo a Juan por teléfono? ¿Usas una preposición, como en español?

35 **¿Qué quieres?**

▶ **Pregunta** a tu compañero(a).

Modelo A. ¿Quieres una alfombra para tu dormitorio?
B. No, no la quiero./Sí, la quiero.

 ① ② ③   ④  ⑤

Differentiated Instruction

DEVELOPING LEARNERS

- Have students go back to the *fotonovela* on page 94 and help them recognize the direct object pronoun in the second scene (¿*Lo* tienes?). Ask them what Diana is referring to here. Then ask them what Rita is referring to in the last scene when she says, *No los veo.* Then have students answer the following questions using the direct object pronoun.
  1. ¿Tienes los libros? (los)
  2. ¿Ves la mesa? (la)
  3. ¿Quieres a tu perrito? (lo)
  4. ¿Conoces a mis amigas? (las)

EXPANDING LEARNERS

- Have students work with a partner and take turns asking and answering questions to practice the placement of the direct object pronouns. Students answering the question should place the direct object pronouns both before and attached to the verb, when applicable. For example:
  A. ¿Estás planchando las camisas?
  B. Sí, /No, no las estoy planchando.
     Or: Sí, estoy planchándolas.
  A. ¿Vas a poner esta alfombra en el dormitorio?
  B. Sí, /No la voy a poner.
     Or: Sí, voy a ponerla.

36 ¡Ayuda!

▶ **Completa** la conversación con pronombres de objeto directo.

DIANA: ¿Tía, me escuchas?

RITA: Sí, sí, ___1___ escucho. ¿Qué quieres?

DIANA: No encuentro mis gafas. ¿___2___ ves tú por allí?

RITA: Creo que ___3___ tienes en tu mesita de noche.

DIANA: Tampoco veo mi chaqueta.

RITA: Está sobre tu cama. ¿No ___4___ ves?

DIANA: Ah, sí. ¿Y mis pantalones nuevos?

RITA: ___5___ tienes en el armario.

DIANA: Gracias, tía.

37 Todos están trabajando

▶ **Responde** a estas preguntas.

Modelo ¿Quién coloca el florero sobre la mesa?

→ *Andy lo coloca.*

1. ¿Quién pone la lámpara sobre la mesita de noche?
2. ¿Quién limpia el baño?
3. ¿Quién coloca la ropa en el armario?
4. ¿Quién cuelga el cuadro?

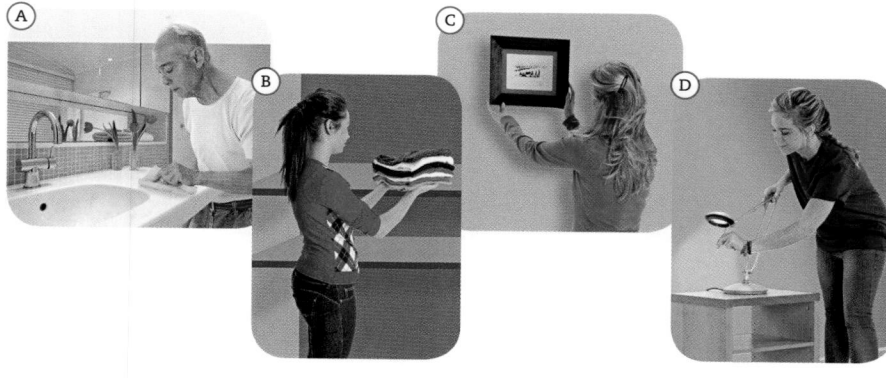

38 Tu dormitorio

▶ **Pregunta** a tu compañero(a) cómo va a decorar su dormitorio.

Modelo A. *¿Vas a comprar una alfombra para tu dormitorio?*
B. *No, no la voy a comprar. No la necesito.*

Gramática – Los pronombres de objeto directo

36. Once students have finished filling in the blanks, have them read the conversation with a partner.

38. Tell students that as their partner describes what he or she needs, the person listening should draw the item and present it to their partner. If the partner likes it, then they will move on to the next item. If the partner does not like it, then they will describe what they would like to change while the student re-draws the item.

Answer Key

34. *I call Juan on the phone.* En la frase en inglés no se usa la preposición *a.*

35. Answers will vary. Sample answers:
1. ¿Quieres un florero para la mesa?
   No, no lo quiero.
2. ¿Quieres un espejo para el baño?
   Sí, lo quiero.
3. ¿Quieres una lámpara para el dormitorio?
   Sí, la quiero.
4. ¿Quieres una cortina para la ventana?
   No, no la quiero.
5. ¿Quieres un cuadro para la sala?
   Sí, lo quiero.

36. 1. te   4. la
    2. Las   5. Los
    3. las

37. 1. Tess la pone.
    2. Mack lo limpia.
    3. Diana la coloca.
    4. Patricia lo cuelga.

38. Answers will vary.

Additional Resources

Fans Online activities

Practice Workbook

HERITAGE LANGUAGE LEARNERS

- Ask students to work with a partner to prepare a dialogue that makes use of direct object pronouns. They may use the dialogue in activity 36 as a model, but should create a new scene with different characters.

TOTAL PHYSICAL RESPONSE (TPR)

- Have students count off from 1 to 5 and assign a different room of the house to each number. Then say the name of a piece of furniture, appliance, or any other object that would typically be found in one of these rooms. As you say each word, students who represent the room will stand and complete the following phrase: [Direct object pronoun] *encuentras en* [room of the house]. For example: *la bañera* → *La encuentras en el baño; el sofá* → *Lo encuentras en la sala; las mesitas de noche* → *Las encuentras en el dormitorio,* etc.

DESAFÍO 2

Comunicación

Presentation

- In this section, students will integrate the vocabulary and grammar from *Desafío 2* in order to describe household furniture and accessories and use direct object pronouns.

Activities	Standards	Resources
39.	1.1, 1.2, 1.3	Audio
40.	1.1, 1.3	
41.	1.3	
42. Final del desafío	1.3, 2.2	

Teaching Suggestions

Warm-Up / Independent Starter

- Ask students to create a ten-question quiz with the vocabulary for household furniture and accessories and direct object pronouns. The quiz may only be matching or multiple choice.

Preparation

- Take 10 minutes to review the vocabulary and grammar themes from *Desafío 2*.
- Refer students back to the *fotonovela* for *Desafío 2*. Have them find all of the household furniture and accessories, and direct object pronouns within the dialogue. Do students understand the dialogue better now that they have gone through the vocabulary and grammar from the *Desafío*?
- Have students exchange and take their classmates' quizzes from the Independent Starter. Once students have finished, have them return the quiz to its creator for grading. Did everyone get 100%?

Activities

39. Ask for two volunteers to read the parts of the two friends from the audio script. Once they have finished, have students decide if the statements are true or false. If the statement is false, have students make it true.

40. Have students compare the two bedrooms using the words *más... que, menos... que,* and *tan... como*. For example: *La cama del dormitorio A es más grande que las camas del dormitorio B.*

Comunicación

39 **Un apartamento en venta**

 ▶ **Escucha.** Dos amigas hablan sobre un apartamento en venta. Decide si estas oraciones son ciertas o falsas.

1. El apartamento tiene dos baños.
2. En la sala hay un sofá y una alfombra pequeños.
3. Los muebles del baño son nuevos.
4. Los dormitorios tienen un armario, una cama, una mesita de noche y una lámpara.

 ▶ **Escucha** otra vez y toma nota de los detalles del apartamento. ¿Te parece un buen lugar para vivir? Habla con tu compañero(a).

Modelo

> A mí me parece un buen lugar para vivir porque tiene dos dormitorios.

> A mí también, porque...

40 **Habitaciones diferentes**

 ▶ **Describe** los dormitorios de las fotos con tu compañero(a).

Modelo A. ¿Hay una cama grande en ese dormitorio?
B. No, no la hay, pero hay dos camas pequeñas.

▶ **Escribe** un texto comparando uno de los dormitorios con el tuyo.

Modelo *El dormitorio de la fotografía B tiene dos camas, pero el mío tiene una.*

100 cien

Differentiated Instruction

DEVELOPING LEARNERS

- Give students more practice with direct object pronouns by having them re-state these sentences with the correct direct object pronoun.
  1. *Mis vecinos van a comprar una mesita de noche. (La van a comprar./Van a comprarla.)*
  2. *La profesora sacude el polvo del escritorio. (Lo sacude.)*
  3. *Mi padre está arreglando el inodoro y la lámpara. (Los está arreglando./Está arreglándolos.)*
  4. *Estoy pintando la sala. (La estoy pintando./Estoy pintándola.)*

EXPANDING LEARNERS

- Ask students to imagine that they have just moved into a new house. The movers have all their belongings, but are putting them in the wrong rooms! Ask students to first describe what the movers are doing and then tell the movers where they should put each thing. Be sure they use direct object pronouns whenever possible.
- You might offer this model: *Están colocando el refrigerador en el baño. Lo deben colocar en la cocina.*

41 Mi casa ideal

▶ **Dibuja** el plano *(floor plan)* de tu casa ideal y descríbesela a tu compañero(a).

Modelo *Aquí está la sala y este es el jardín…*

▶ **Escribe** un texto describiendo tu casa ideal. Explica cómo están decoradas las habitaciones.

Modelo *Mi casa ideal es grande. En la sala hay una lámpara y un florero antiguo.*

Final del desafío

Sí, yo vendo ámbar. Y también soy coleccionista.

Vamos a mi casa. Les voy a mostrar algunas piezas únicas.

42 ¿Dónde está el fósil de mosquito?

▶ **Escribe y representa.** ¿Qué pasa en la casa de María Luisa? Escribe el diálogo. Después, represéntalo con tu compañero(a).

41. If students are unable or unwilling to draw, then have them find their ideal home on the Internet. This home must have a picture of both the outside and inside so students can describe the entire home.

42. Have students organize their dialogues before they begin writing. First, they should look at the pictures. Second, they should read the speech bubbles. Third, they should brainstorm what they would say in the situation represented by the picture. Finally, they should write the dialogue for each picture. Ask students to remember to use grammar and vocabulary from this *Desafío* while writing the dialogue.

 AUDIO SCRIPT
See page 791.

Answer Key

39. 1. Falso
2. Falso
3. Cierto
4. Falso
▶ Answers will vary.

40. Answers will vary.
▶ Answers will vary. Sample answer:
El dormitorio de la fotografía A tiene una cama, igual que el mío, pero mi cama es más pequeña. En este dormitorio hay dos mesitas de noche con dos lámparas, pero en mi dormitorio solo hay una mesita con una lámpara.

41. Answers will vary.
▶ Answers will vary.

42. Answers will vary.

Additional Resources

Fans Online activities
Practice Workbook

HERITAGE LANGUAGE LEARNERS

- Invite students who have traveled or lived in a Spanish-speaking country to show-and-tell photographs of homes they have lived in, visited, or that belong to a family member. Have them point out the main features of the houses and how they differ from the ones in their present community.

MULTIPLE INTELLIGENCES:
Visual-Spatial Intelligence

- Have students imagine that they need to sell some property. Ask them to write and design an ad to sell a furnished house or apartment in the Dominican Republic. They should accompany their ads with an image of the property, either computer-generated, a magazine cutout, or hand-drawn, and also include a description of both the exterior and interior, as well as the selling price. Exhibit their ads in the classroom and have students vote for their favorite in the following categories: most original, best furnished, best value.

Unit 2
DESAFÍO 3

Expresar acciones habituales

Presentation

- In *Desafío* 3, Tim and Mack are at the University of Puerto Rico in Ponce. There they must perform a traditional *serenata*, or serenade.
- In this section, students will preview:
  – Words for household appliances and consumer electronics.
  – Indirect object pronouns.

Activities	Standards	Resources
Fotonovela	1.2, 2.1, 3.2	Vis. Pres.
43.	1.3	
44.	1.2	
45.	1.2, 1.3	Audio
46. Cultura	1.1, 1.2, 2.1, 3.2, 4.2, 5.1	
Tu desafío	1.2, 2.1, 3.2, 5.2	

Teaching Suggestions

Warm-Up / Independent Starter

- Have students think of their favorite love song in English and ask them to translate two stanzas.

Preparation

- Have volunteers share their translated stanzas with the class. Ask the class if they think these songs sound as pretty in Spanish as they do in English. Why or why not? Usually words that rhyme in one language don't carry the same rhythm or rhyme when translated into another language. Will this be an issue for Tim and Mack?

La fotonovela

Before Viewing

- Read the introduction to the *fotonovela*. With a show of hands, how many students in your class could learn a Spanish serenade to sing?

After Viewing

- Ask students to predict what is going to happen. Will Tim's shirt get cleaned and dried in time for the performance, or will they give up and go buy a new one, or will they miss the performance? Have the class vote for one of the three options, then say what they would do in this situation.

102

Una serenata en Ponce

 Tim and Mack arrive at the *Universidad de Puerto Rico* in Ponce, a southern city named after the first governor of Puerto Rico, Juan Ponce de León. They must memorize a traditional *serenata* (a type of song to express one's devotion for a loved one) and sing it to a student with the *tuna* (a musical group made up of university students).

43 Detective de palabras

Continuará...

▶ **Relaciona.** ¿Qué palabra de la fotonovela corresponde a cada imagen?

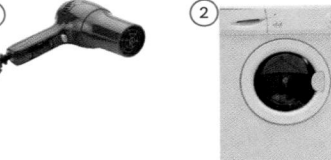

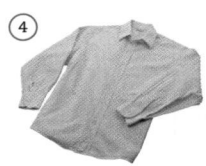

Differentiated Instruction

DEVELOPING LEARNERS

- To confirm comprehension of the *fotonovela*, and to practice some of the new vocabulary as well as the *presente continuo* from the previous *Desafío*, ask students to answer the following questions.
  1. ¿Quién está cantando? (Mack.)
  2. ¿Quién va a lavar la camisa? (Mack.)
  3. ¿Quién está mirando el reloj? (Tim.)
  4. ¿Quién está secando la camisa? (Mack.)
  5. ¿Con qué la está secando? (Con el secador de pelo.)
  6. ¿Quién va a planchar la camisa? (Tim.)

EXPANDING LEARNERS

- Ask students to close their books and put the steps of the *fotonovela* in order. Encourage them to use the *presente continuo* whenever they can. A sample summary might be: *Mack está cantando y tocando las maracas y Tim está vistiéndose. Mack derrama el café encima de la camisa de Tim, pero dice que la va a lavar. Tim está preocupado porque no tienen mucho tiempo. Mack está secando la camisa con el secador de pelo, pero Tim está muy impaciente y tiene la plancha en la mano.*

 **44** **¿Comprendes?**

▶ **Decide** si estas oraciones son ciertas o falsas. Si son falsas, corrígelas.

1. La camisa de Tim es vieja.
2. Mack lava la camisa en una lavadora.
3. Mack seca la camisa con un secador de pelo.
4. Mack y Tim tienen una plancha.

45 **¿Qué necesito?**

 ▶ **Escucha** y decide. ¿A qué electrodoméstico *(appliance)* se refiere cada oración?

 (A) 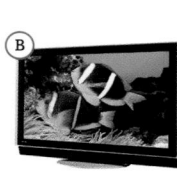 (B) (C)  (D)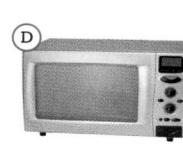

▶ **Escribe.** Con tu compañero(a), haz una lista de tareas domésticas *(household chores)* y de electrodomésticos para hacerlas.

Modelo *Para cocinar necesito una estufa, un horno…*

 **CULTURA**

Las serenatas

En muchos países latinos existe la tradición de las serenatas. Esta tradición tiene su origen en la costumbre de cantar baladas a la mujer amada bajo el balcón de su casa. El enamorado va normalmente con un pequeño grupo de músicos, como una tuna o un mariachi en el caso de México, para cantar a la mujer y expresar sus sentimientos de amor.

46 **Explica.** ¿Qué opinas *(do you think)* de la tradición de cantar serenatas? ¿Conoces alguna tradición similar? Explica en qué consiste.

🏁→ **TU DESAFÍO** Visita la página web para aprender más sobre las serenatas.

HERITAGE LANGUAGE LEARNERS

• Ask students to bring to class recordings of serenades or romantic *boleros* that they or their families have, and play one or two of the selections. They should be prepared to give their classmates a general idea of the lyrics, not a detailed translation. If they have any additional information about the composer or singers, have them share this with the class.

MULTIPLE INTELLIGENCES:
Musical-Rhythmic Intelligence

• Hold a song festival in your class. Have students work in small groups to write the lyrics of a *serenata*. They should identify the person or persons to whom the song is dedicated. Encourage creativity; students may choose a person in the news, their Spanish teacher, or their favorite sports team. Some of the more musically inclined should decide on an appropriate melody. Ask each group to sing their song before the class. If any members of the group play a musical instrument, have them accompany the singers.

Expresar acciones habituales

Activities

43. Have students use their finger to draw a line from each numbered item in this activity to the picture in the *fotonovela*. Then have students look at the text in the speech bubbles to scan for the words that relate to the picture.

44. Read each item aloud and have students call out *cierto* or *falso*. If the statement is false, then call on a volunteer to correct it.

 AUDIO SCRIPT
See page 791.

 CULTURA

Las serenatas

Serenades are songs traditionally sung by a man to the woman he is in love with. Traditionally, the man would sing a love song through a window while the woman listened at the windowsill. In some cases he would play an instrument such as a guitar, and sing until she turned off the light. That was a sign that either she loved him back and was coming downstairs or that she did not love him and went to bed. Generally, all serenades are done outside because the voices and instruments are too loud to be played indoors.

Answer Key

43. 1. secador de pelo 3. plancha
2. lavadora 4. camisa

44. 1. Falso. La camisa de Tim es nueva.
2. Cierto
3. Cierto
4. Falso. Tim tiene una plancha.

45. 1. C 2. A 3. B 4. D
▶ Answers will vary.

46. Answers will vary.

Additional Resources

Fans Online activities

DESAFÍO 3

Vocabulario – Los electrodomésticos

Presentation

- In this section, students will learn vocabulary for household appliances and consumer electronics.

Activities	Standards	Resources
Vocabulario	1.2	
47.	1.2, 1.3	
48.	1.2, 1.3	
49.	1.2, 1.3	Audio
50.	1.1, 1.3	
51. Cultura	1.1, 1.2, 2.2, 3.2, 4.2, 5.1	
Tu desafío	1.2, 2.1, 2.2, 3.2, 5.2	

Teaching Suggestions

Warm-Up / Independent Starter

- Ask students to memorize the following excerpt from the traditional Mexican serenade, "Las mañanitas." *Qué linda está la mañana / en que vengo a saludarte, / venimos todos con gusto / y placer a felicitarte. / El día en que tú naciste / nacieron todas las flores / y en la pila del bautismo / cantaron los ruiseñores.*

Preparation

- Ask for volunteers to sing or recite the lyrics to the class. Ask students to put themselves in Tim and Mack's shoes. They have the option to perform it, but Tim and Mack don't. That's what makes the *desafíos* so challenging—the fact that the pairs are taken outside of their comfort zones so they can totally immerse themselves in the Spanish language and its different cultures.
- Have students associate a household chore with each consumer electronic, appliance, and room of the house in the vocabulary presentation.

Activities

49. Ask students where they would go to use the items that Pedro does not have.

51. Have students think about university bands and choruses. How are they similar and different from a *tuna*?

104

Vocabulario

Los electrodomésticos

el refrigerador · el microondas · la estufa · el congelador · el lavaplatos · el horno · la cocina · la secadora · la plancha · la lavadora · el cuarto de lavar · el aire acondicionado · el equipo de música · el despertador · la caldera de calefacción

47 Organizamos la casa

▶ **Escribe.** ¿En qué parte de la casa están habitualmente estos electrodomésticos?

Modelo el televisor: *en la sala y en el dormitorio.*

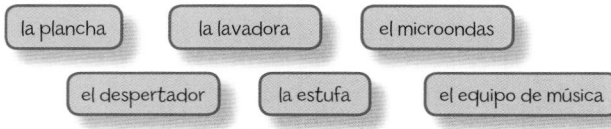

la plancha · la lavadora · el microondas · el despertador · la estufa · el equipo de música

▶ **Elige.** ¿Qué palabra no corresponde a cada grupo?

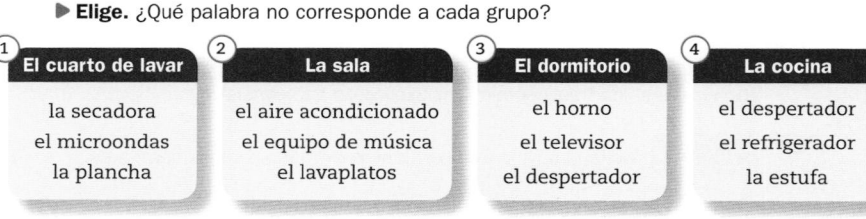

1 El cuarto de lavar	2 La sala	3 El dormitorio	4 La cocina
la secadora	el aire acondicionado	el horno	el despertador
el microondas	el equipo de música	el televisor	el refrigerador
la plancha	el lavaplatos	el despertador	la estufa

Differentiated Instruction

DEVELOPING LEARNERS

- Ask students which appliance would be the favorite of the following people.
  1. Your aunt who likes to cook: a. *el horno* b. *el despertador* (a)
  2. Your brother whose chore is to wash the dishes: a. *la plancha* b. *el lavaplatos* (b)
  3. Your sister who is in charge of washing clothes: a. *la lavadora* b. *la estufa* (a)
  4. Your father who needs to wake up early: a. *el congelador* b. *el despertador* (b)
  5. Your mother who needs to iron a skirt: a. *la secadora* b. *la plancha* (b)

EXPANDING LEARNERS

- Ask students to create a word family for some of the new vocabulary. Using what they know or a bilingual dictionary, ask students to list as many related words as they can for the following vocabulary words: *congelador, cocina, lavadora, plancha, despertador, música.* Examples include: *congelador → congelar, congelado, congelación; cocina → cocinar, cocinero(a); lavadora → lavar, lavado, lavandería; plancha → planchar, planchador(a), planchada; despertador → despertar, despierto(a); música → musical, músico(a).*

48 **¿Para qué sirven?**

▶ **Une** las dos columnas y escribe oraciones.

(A)

1. la lavadora
2. el refrigerador
3. el equipo de música
4. el despertador
5. la plancha
6. la estufa

(B)

a. cocinar
b. planchar la ropa
c. despertarse por la mañana
d. lavar la ropa
e. conservar la comida
f. escuchar música

Modelo   1. *La lavadora sirve para lavar la ropa.*

49 **El apartamento de Pedro**

▶ **Escucha** a Pedro y escribe qué electrodomésticos tiene y cuáles no.

Tiene	No tiene
una lavadora	

50 **En tu casa**

▶ **Habla** con tu compañero(a). ¿Qué aparatos eléctricos tiene en casa? Toma notas y presenta la información a la clase.

Modelo   A. *¿Qué aparatos eléctricos tienes en tu dormitorio?*
B. *Tengo un despertador y un televisor.*
A. *¡Yo también!*

CULTURA

Las tunas

Las tunas son grupos de estudiantes universitarios que interpretan temas tradicionales y serenatas. Llevan una capa negra con cintas (*ribbons*) de colores y emplean instrumentos como la bandurria, el laúd (*lute*), la guitarra o la pandereta (*tambourine*).

Las tunas nacieron en las universidades españolas en la Edad Media y con el tiempo llegaron a otros países europeos e hispanoamericanos. En Puerto Rico hay varias, como Tunamérica, la Tuna Bardos o la Tuna Interamericana.

51 **Compara.** ¿Existe algo similar a las tunas en tu país?

**→ TU DESAFÍO** Visita la página web para aprender más sobre las tunas.

ciento cinco   105

Unit 2
DESAFÍO 3

Vocabulario –
Los electrodomésticos

AUDIO SCRIPT
See page 791.

CULTURA

Las tunas

The *tunas* started in Spain at about the same time that the main universities were founded in the 13th century. Some students, whose families lacked the means to finance their studies, formed music groups and sang for a bowl of soup and some extra money to help pay for their room and board. For this reason, they were called *sopistas*, or soup-eaters, at first. The costume *tunos* wear today is similar to the clothing the *sopistas* used to wear centuries ago.

Answer Key

47. ▶ Answers will vary.
   1. el microondas   3. el horno
   2. el lavaplatos   4. el despertador

48. 2. e. El refrigerador sirve para conservar la comida.
   3. f. El equipo de música sirve para escuchar música.
   4. c. El despertador sirve para despertarse.
   5. b. La plancha sirve para planchar.
   6. a. La estufa sirve para cocinar.

49. Tiene: una lavadora, una estufa, un horno, aire acondicionado
   No tiene: una secadora, un microondas, calefacción

50. Answers will vary.

51. Answers will vary.

Additional Resources

Fans Online activities
Practice Workbook

HERITAGE LANGUAGE LEARNERS

• In the *fotonovela*, Tim uses the verb *poner* to say that he is going to turn on the washing machine. Ask students to make a list of other verbs that mean "turn on" and what device one typically turns on with each verb. Some examples include: *encender, prender* (the lights, TV, oven); *abrir* (faucet / tap); *dejar correr* (water); *conectar* (electricity). You might want to ask students to include words that mean "turn off," such as *apagar* (the lights, radio, heating); *cerrar* (faucet / water); *cortar* (water); *desconectar* (electricity).

COOPERATIVE LEARNER

• Ask students to work in small groups to create a crossword puzzle using some of the words from this lesson's vocabulary. Some students will select the words, others will write the clues, and others will create the grid for the puzzle, but all must work together to finalize the project.

• Ask groups to exchange puzzles and try to solve them.

DESAFÍO 3

Gramática – Los pronombres de objeto indirecto

Presentation

- In this section, students will learn:
  - Indirect objects.
  - Indirect object pronouns.
  - Indirect object pronoun placement.

Activities	Standards	Resources
Gramática	3.1	
52.	1.3, 3.1, 4.1	
53.	1.2	
54.	1.2, 1.3	Audio
55.	1.2, 1.3	

Teaching Suggestions

Warm-Up / Independent Starter

- Ask students to look at this grammar presentation and the grammar presentation for *Desafío 2*. Have students note the similarities and differences between direct and indirect objects pronouns.

Preparation

- Go over the grammar presentation with students. Copy the direct and the indirect object pronouns into a table like the one below and discuss the similarities and differences with students.

Singular Object Pronoun		Plural Object Pronoun	
Direct	Indirect	Direct	Indirect
me	*me*	*nos*	*nos*
te	*te*	*os*	*os*
la, lo	*le*	*las, los*	*les*

- Have students practice using both direct and indirect object pronouns in one sentence. Ask questions such as, *¿Quién va a comprarte una cama nueva?* Answers include, *Mi padre me la va a comprar*, or *Mi padre va a comprármela*.

Activities

52. The direct object in English answers the question who or what is "verbed" in the sentence—the same as in Spanish. The indirect object answers for whom or for what is the action of the verb intended.

Gramática

Los pronombres de objeto indirecto

El objeto indirecto

- The indirect object indicates for whom an action is performed or who benefits from it. The indirect object can be a noun with the preposition a (a su hijo) or a pronoun (le).

  Luis compra un despertador **a su hijo**. También **le** compra un equipo de música.

  PRONOMBRES DE OBJETO INDIRECTO

Singular		Plural	
me	to/for me	nos	to/for us
te	to/for you (informal)	os	to/for you (informal)
le	to/for you (formal), him, her	les	to/for you, them

- Sometimes for emphasis or for clarification, we use two indirect objects in the same sentence—an expression with the preposition a and a noun or pronoun (a Carlos, a mí) as well as a pronoun.

  A Luis le gustan los despertadores negros.

Posición de los pronombres de objeto indirecto

- Indirect object pronouns are placed before the conjugated verb, or attached to the infinitive, the present participle, or the command, like direct object pronouns.

  Le voy a regalar un CD a Pedro. / Voy a regalar**le** un CD a Pedro.

- Direct and indirect object pronouns may be used in the same sentence. In this case, the indirect object pronoun goes before the direct object pronoun.

  Patricia **me** compra un libro. → Patricia **me lo** compra.

- Le and les become se when placed in front of a direct object pronoun.

  Le compro un libro. → **Se lo** compro.

52 **Compara.** ¿Cuáles son los pronombres de objeto directo e indirecto en inglés? ¿Funcionan *(do they work)* igual que en español?

53 **¿A quién?**

▶ **Une** las dos columnas.

(A)	(B)
1. **Le** doy un libro	a. a mí
2. Voy a comprar**te** un disco	b. a él
3. **Me** regalas una flor	c. a ti
4. **Les** hago la cama todos los días	d. a ellas

Differentiated Instruction

DEVELOPING LEARNERS

- Have students choose the correct option to complete the following sentences for practice with placement of direct and indirect object pronouns.

  1. *Juan me prepara la comida. Juan me la / la me prepara. (me la)*
  2. *Les pido el equipo de música a ellos. Lo se / Se lo pido. (Se lo)*
  3. *Le lavo la ropa a Marta. Se la / La se lavo. (Se la)*
  4. *También le seco los pantalones. Se los / Los se seco. (Se los)*
  5. *Te plancho las camisas. Las te / Te las plancho. (Te las)*

EXPANDING LEARNERS

- Have students answer these questions with both the direct and indirect object pronouns.

  1. *¿Les limpias la casa a tus abuelos? (Sí, se la limpio.)*
  2. *¿Le lees un cuento a tu hermana? (Sí, se lo leo.)*
  3. *¿Me vas a regalar un equipo de música? (Sí, te lo voy a regalar / voy a regalártelo.)*
  4. *¿Les haces la cama a tus hermanitos? (Sí, se la hago.)*
  5. *¿Nos estás planchando las camisas? (Sí, se las estoy planchando / estoy planchándoselas.)*

54 **Todos trabajan para todos**

 ▶ **Escucha** la conversación de Tim y su amiga Sonia, y ordena las fotografías.

 Ⓐ  Ⓑ 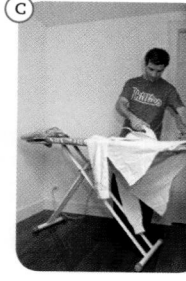 Ⓒ  Ⓓ

▶ **Completa** estas oraciones. Después, escucha otra vez y comprueba *(check your answers)*.

1. Mi madre ___1___ prepara la comida a mi hermano todas las mañanas.
   _me/le_

2. Mi padre ___2___ lava la ropa y ___3___ la plancha a todos nosotros.
   les/nos   _nos/se_

3. Yo siempre ___4___ hago mi cama.
   me/les

4. Mi abuelo ___5___ coloca la ropa en el armario a mi hermana pequeña.
   _te/le_

55 **Los regalos**

▶ **Lee** el mensaje de correo de Janet y complétalo.

> Mensaje nuevo
>
> Para:
> Cc:
> Asunto:
>
> ¡Hola, Paula! ¿Qué tal? Yo estoy comprando regalos para
> todos. Y también ___1___ compro ropa para mí, claro.
> A mi hermano Andy ___2___ compro un disco. A mis abuelos
> ___3___ compro unos libros y a ti ___4___ voy a regalar
> una sorpresa. ¿___5___ escribes un mensaje pronto?
> Un beso.
> Janet

▶ **Transforma** las oraciones anteriores con pronombres de objeto directo e indirecto.

Modelo 1. Me compro ropa para mí. → *Me la compro.*

▶ **Escribe** la respuesta de Paula a Janet.

DESAFÍO 3

Gramática – Los pronombres de objeto indirecto

54. To extend this activity, ask students to say if they do the same tasks as Sonia and in what order they do them. Have students write a paragraph to compare themselves with Sonia.

55. Once students have rewritten the e-mail, have them imagine they are Paula, and reply to Janet's e-mail. Tell students to greet Janet, answer her questions, and then reply with some personal information.

 AUDIO SCRIPT
See page 79I.

Answer Key

52. Los pronombres en inglés son los mismos para el objeto directo y para el indirecto: *me, you, him, her, us, them*. Funcionan de manera parecida, pero la posición de los pronombres es distinta en español.

53. 1. b   2. c   3. a   4. d

54. B, C, A, D

▶ 1. le   4. me
  2. nos   5. le
  3. nos

55. 1. me   4. te
  2. le   5. Me
  3. les

▶ 2. Se lo compro.
  3. Se los compro.
  4. Te la regalo.
  5. ¿Me lo escribes?

▶ Answers will vary.

Additional Resources

Fans Online activities
Practice Workbook

HERITAGE LANGUAGE LEARNERS

• Point out that in the *fotonovela*, Mack uses *un secador de pelo* to dry Tim's shirt, but he would normally use *una secadora* to dry clothes. Changes in the gender of a word alter the meaning, not only in words such as *el maestro/la maestra*, but in words such as *el cuento* (story) and *la cuenta* (bill), *el orden* (order) and *la orden* (command). Ask students to make a list of such words and explain the difference in meaning. Examples include: *el/la coma, el/la capital, el/la cometa, el/la mañana, el puerto/la puerta, el punto/la punta*. Have students share their list with the class.

MULTIPLE INTELLIGENCES:
Verbal-Linguistic Intelligence

• Write the infinitive of several verbs and a combination of two nouns on separate index cards. Put each category in a bag and have students pick one card from each. Ask them to make up a sentence using all the elements, plus a subject and an indirect object pronoun. For instance, if they picked *planchar, perro, camisas*, they might end up with a silly sentence such as, *Mi hermano le plancha las camisas al perro.* Then ask students to substitute the direct and indirect objects with the corresponding pronouns: *Mi hermano se las plancha.*

DESAFÍO 3

Comunicación

Presentation

- In this section, students will integrate the vocabulary and grammar from *Desafío 3* in order to talk about consumer electronics, household appliances, and indirect object pronouns.

Activities	Standards	Resources
56.	1.1, 1.2, 1.3	Audio
57.	1.3	
58.	1.3	
59.	1.3	
60. Final del desafío	1.3, 2.1	
Tu desafío	1.2, 1.3	

Teaching Suggestions

Warm-Up / Independent Starter

- Have students look at the *Final del desafío*. Ask them to write what is happening in the pictures.

Preparation

- Take 10 minutes to review the main vocabulary and grammar themes from *Desafío* 3.
- Refer students back to the *fotonovela* for *Desafío* 3. Have them find all of the household appliances and electronics as well as indirect object pronouns within the dialogue. Do students understand the dialogue better now that they have gone through the vocabulary and grammar from the *Desafío*?
- Make the *Comunicación* page a competition. Have students compete to see who can finish the activities first and with all correct answers. The first five students to finish all the activities correctly win. The competition begins after you play the audio for activity 56.
- Mark the incorrect answers for the students who finish first, so they can correct their responses and continue in the competition. Once the five winners have been chosen, have those five help their classmates to complete the activities.

Activities

56. Ask students to add their three least favorite appliances and explain why.

Comunicación

56 ¿Qué prefieres?

 ▶ **Escucha** y completa una tabla como esta.

	Electrodoméstico preferido	¿Por qué?
Tim		
Mack		
Andy		

 ▶ **Pregunta** a tres compañeros(as) cuál es su electrodoméstico preferido y por qué.

Modelo *Mi electrodoméstico preferido es el microondas porque calienta la comida muy rápido. Es muy cómodo.*

57 ¿Para quién?

▶ **Escribe** cinco oraciones con estos elementos. Usa pronombres de objeto indirecto.

Modelo *Le regalo flores a mi mamá.*

① regalar

② planchar

③ preparar

④ comprar

⑤ dar

¿A quién?
mi mejor amigo(a)
mi novio(a)
mi profesor(a)
mis compañeros(as)
mi papá / mi mamá

58 Entrega de regalos

 ▶ **Habla** con tu compañero(a). Una librería le da estos objetos a tu escuela. ¿A quién van a regalar cada objeto?

Modelo *El diccionario se lo damos a Willy.*

 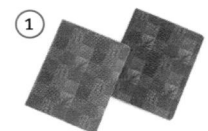   

① ② ③ ④

Differentiated Instruction

DEVELOPING LEARNERS

- Write several sentences with both direct and indirect object pronouns and cut them so that each word is on a separate piece of paper or index card. Then distribute the pieces for one sentence to each student. Have students put the sentence in the correct order. For example:
la – me – plancha – Juan
(Juan me la plancha.)

EXPANDING LEARNERS

- Ask students to imagine that they have a friend who is always giving away her household electronics and appliances. Have them write five sentences describing what their friend is giving away and to whom. Then have them use the same sentences and rewrite them using direct and indirect object pronouns. For example: *Marta está regalando el microondas a sus primos.* → *Marta está regalándoselo. / Se lo está regalando.*

59 Buenas intenciones

▶ **Lee** este texto. ¿A quién va a ayudar *(help)* Víctor la semana que viene? Escríbelo.

Modelo

¿A quién le va a ordenar el dormitorio?
→ Se lo va a ordenar a su hermana.

1. ¿A quién le va a planchar la ropa?
2. ¿A quién le va a hacer la cama?
3. ¿A quién le va a lavar el coche?
4. ¿A quién le va a preparar el almuerzo?

En casa, todos ayudamos con las tareas. Pero la semana que viene yo tengo muchas cosas que hacer.

Normalmente, mi hermana mayor y yo ordenamos nuestros dormitorios, pero la semana que viene la voy a ayudar. Ella tiene exámenes y está muy ocupada.

También voy a planchar la ropa a mi mamá porque ella tiene mucho trabajo. Y voy a hacer la cama al abuelo.

Ah, también quiero lavar el coche a mi papá. Y voy a preparar el almuerzo a toda la familia. ¡Cuántas cosas!

Víctor

Final del desafío

Espera, te la voy a planchar.

¿Y ahora qué me pongo?

No sé. No hay tiempo para arreglarla.

¡Date prisa, por favor!

60 ¿Qué pasa en la historia?

▶ **Escribe** el final del desafío. Después, represéntalo con tu compañero(a).

→ TU DESAFÍO Visita la página web. Escucha las preguntas de tu *Minientrevista Desafío 3* y escribe las respuestas.

ciento nueve 109

HERITAGE LANGUAGE LEARNERS

• Ask students to play the roles of Mack, Tim, and a journalist who is interviewing them for their hometown newspaper. The interviewer wants to know how their evening serenade went and whether they would like to repeat the experience in the United States. They might ask questions like: *¿Estaban nerviosos? ¿Tienen alguna anécdota interesante que contar? ¿Les gustaría tener esta costumbre de la serenata en los Estados Unidos? ¿A quién les gustaría cantar?*

CRITICAL THINKING

• Of all the household electronics and appliances mentioned in this *Desafío*, which ones do students think have been the most and the least beneficial to society in general? Is there one that was not mentioned, but deserves to be considered? Are there any that students think our culture could eliminate? Which one(s)? Students need to justify their opinions.

---

57. Make sure students know each of the items they are giving away. Ask students to say the words in Spanish before continuing with this activity.

58. Let students know they cannot choose themselves as the recipient of the items, but they can choose people other than their classmates.

60. Ask students to use their descriptions from the Independent Starter to complete this activity. Pair the students who correctly finish their *Comunicación* activities to perform their dialogues.

 AUDIO SCRIPT
See page 791.

Answer Key

56. Tim: el equipo de música. Porque le encanta la música.
    Mack: la lavadora. Porque le gusta tener la ropa limpia.
    Andy: el microondas. Porque no sabe cocinar.
    ▶ Answers will vary.

57. Answers will vary. Sample answers:
    1. Le regalo flores a mi mamá.
    2. Le plancho las camisas a mi hermano.
    3. Le preparo una comida a mi mejor amiga.
    4. Le compro un CD a mi profesora.
    5. Les doy un diccionario a mis compañeros.

58. Answers will vary.

59. 1. Se la va a planchar a su mamá.
    2. Se la va a hacer al abuelo.
    3. Se lo va a lavar a su papá.
    4. Se lo va a preparar a toda la familia.

60. Answers will vary.

Additional Resources

Fans Online activities
Practice Workbook

Unit 2
DESAFÍO 4

Describir el barrio

Presentation

- In *Desafío 4*, Tess and Patricia are at the Flower Festival in Aibonito, Puerto Rico. There they must serve as judges.
- In this section, students will preview:
  - Words associated with the neighborhood.
  - Places in the city.
  - Demonstrative adjectives.
  - Demonstrative pronouns.

Activities	Standards	Resources
Fotonovela	1.2, 2.1, 2.2	Vis. Pres.
61.	1.3	
62.	1.3	
63.	1.2, 1.3	
64. Cultura	1.1, 1.2, 2.1, 2.2, 4.2, 5.1	Video
Tu desafío	1.2, 2.1, 2.2, 5.2	

Teaching Suggestions

Warm-Up / Independent Starter

- Ask students to classify the following appliances by room: *el despertador, la plancha, la estufa, el televisor*.

Preparation

- Have students read the introduction to the *fotonovela* silently. Ask them to give some of the reasons for having festivals. One possible answer is that festivals combine music, arts and crafts, food, and entertainment. They generally feature something for all members of the family.

La fotonovela

Before Viewing

- Ask students what they think Tess and Patricia will be judging at the festival. Call on volunteers to share their theories with the class. Come up with a class conclusion.

After Viewing

- Reread the *fotonovela* to the class. Patricia sneezes at the end of the *fotonovela*. Ask students if they think that allergies will prevent Tess and Patricia from completing their *desafío*.

110

El Festival de las flores

Tess and Patricia have to serve as judges at the *Festival de las flores* in Aibonito, Puerto Rico. Will they make it to the judging booth on time?

Continuará...

61 **Detective de palabras**

▶ **Completa** estas oraciones.

1. ¿Vamos por aquella _____ de allí?
2. En Aibonito hay nueve _____ .
3. Aibonito Pueblo está en el _____ , no en las _____ .
4. Es mejor ir por esa _____ .
5. El parque está a tres _____ .

110 ciento diez

Differentiated Instruction

DEVELOPING LEARNERS

- To make sure students understand what is happening in the *fotonovela*, ask the following questions:
  1. ¿Qué empieza a las nueve? *(El concurso de flores.)*
  2. ¿Adónde tienen que ir Tess y su madre? *(Tienen que ir al parque.)*
  3. ¿En qué barrio es el concurso? *(En Aibonito Pueblo.)*
  4. ¿Van en taxi o van a pie? *(Van a pie.)*
  5. ¿Qué ven en el parque? *(Ven muchas flores.)*

EXPANDING LEARNERS

- The *fotonovela* gives students practice with both *ser* and *estar*. Ask students to write one sentence using *ser* for each of the following: to identify and describe physical characteristics or personality traits, with an expression of time; and one sentence using *estar* for each of the following: to describe location, to describe conditions or feelings. Also ask students to write two sentences that show a difference in meaning by using the same adjective with *ser* and *estar*; for example, *ser aburrido* and *estar aburrido*.

62 Por aquí, por allí

▶ **Clasifica** las palabras del cuadro de acuerdo con la fotonovela.

calle	ciudad	taxi	avenida	parque

AQUÍ (cerca de Tess y de Patricia)	AHÍ (a una distancia media de Tess y de Patricia)	ALLÍ (lejos de Tess y de Patricia)
		aquella calle

63 ¿Comprendes?

▶ **Responde** a estas preguntas.

1. ¿Dónde están Tess y Patricia?
2. ¿Cuándo es el concurso de flores?
3. ¿Dónde se celebra el festival?
4. ¿Cómo quiere ir Tess al festival?
5. ¿Cómo prefiere ir Patricia?
6. ¿Qué problema tiene Patricia en el festival?

 CULTURA

El Festival de las flores de Aibonito

Aibonito es una pequeña ciudad de Puerto Rico conocida como la ciudad de las flores o el jardín de Puerto Rico. Desde 1969 se celebra allí el famoso Festival de las flores. En junio o julio, miles de personas van a Aibonito para ver una gran exhibición de flores y plantas de todo tipo. Durante el festival hay actuaciones musicales, concursos (contests) y otras atracciones para los visitantes.

64 **Explica.** ¿Qué festivales celebra tu comunidad? ¿Qué aspectos culturales o históricos representan esos festivales?

 **TU DESAFÍO** Visita la página web para aprender más sobre Aibonito, la ciudad de las flores.

ciento once **111**

Activities

62. Call students' attention to the adverbs presented here: *aquí* (here), *ahí* (there), and *allí* (over there). Have students look at the *fotonovela* and classify the words in the box according to their relative distance from Tess and Patricia. You may want to mimic these distances before beginning this activity.

64. Call on volunteers to tell you the festivals they know of in your city or town. Then ask students the names and locations of the festivals they have attended or heard of outside your city.

 CULTURA

El Festival de las flores de Aibonito

The Festival has been celebrated every year since 1969, lasting from the last weekend in June to the first weekend in July. More than 50 flower vendors gather on 25 acres of land just outside the *Coliseo los Polluelos* in Aibonito, Puerto Rico. In addition to plants, flowers, and vegetables, this festival includes games, rides, food, live music, and arts and crafts. It is the largest and most popular plant festival on the island.

Answer Key

61. 1. calle   4. avenida
2. barrios   5. cuadras
3. centro, afueras

62. aquí: esta ciudad, este parque
ahí: esa avenida
allí: aquella calle, aquel taxi

63. 1. Están en Aibonito, en Puerto Rico.
2. Es a las nueve.
3. Se celebra en Aibonito Pueblo.
4. Quiere ir en taxi.
5. Patricia prefiere ir a pie.
6. Patricia tiene alergia a las flores.

64. Answers will vary.

Additional Resources

Fans Online activities

111

HERITAGE LANGUAGE LEARNERS

- Ask students to research and then talk about some festivals or fairs that are held in some Spanish-speaking countries. You might suggest those that celebrate food or the harvest, arts and crafts, and the many forms of music. Encourage students to also address book fairs, and festivals that celebrate topics as diverse as Spanish-language films, fashion, and technology.

COOPERATIVE LEARNING

- Have students work in small groups to plan a festival for their community. Be sure every member plays an active role. Students will need to decide what kind of festival would be appropriate for the community. What is the festival celebrating? When does it take place? Is it held every year? Will there be a parade? Students should describe the music, contests, and other attractions the festival offers. Have groups make their presentations to the class.

DESAFÍO 4

Vocabulario – El barrio. Lugares y servicios

Presentation

- In this section, students will learn:
  - Words associated with the neighborhood.
  - Places in the city.

Activities	Standards	Resources
Vocabulario	1.2	
65.	1.2	
66.	1.2, 1.3	Audio
67.	1.3	
68. Comunidades	1.1, 1.2, 3.2, 4.2, 5.1	

Teaching Suggestions

Warm-Up / Independent Starter

- Ask students to draw a picture to describe their neighborhood as well as the downtown area of your city.

Preparation

- As you go over the vocabulary presentation with students, have them label the parts of the neighborhood they drew in the Independent Starter.
- Tell students to name the parts of the city on their way home from school today and on their way to school tomorrow. The more they associate their vocabulary to everyday living, the better they will be at remembering their vocabulary words.
- Display an image of a city in Puerto Rico on the board. You can find one by typing the words "cities in Puerto Rico" in your favorite search engine, then click on the images tab.
- Ask students to look at the picture they drew and compare it to the city that is on the board. Have students discuss the similarities and differences.

Activities

65. Have students write an example of each of these parts of the city from your city or town. For example: *avenida → avenida Westwood*.

66. Let students know they will use the verb *estar*. Remember, the verb *estar* is used to indicate location.

Vocabulario

El barrio

> Perdone, señora. ¿El zoológico está en el centro?
>
> No. Está un poco lejos, en las afueras de la ciudad.

la cuadra
la avenida
la esquina
el semáforo
la acera
la plaza
el paso de cebra
la señal de pare
el banco
la calle

Lugares y servicios

la tienda de comestibles	la escuela	el parque	la biblioteca
la oficina de correos	la iglesia	el café	el banco

65 ¿Qué es?

▶ **Une** las dos columnas.

(A)

1. semáforo
2. esquina
3. avenida
4. paso de cebra
5. acera

(B)

a. Lugar de la calle para los peatones (*pedestrians*).
b. Lugar donde se cruzan dos calles.
c. Señal de luces para controlar el tráfico.
d. Lugar para cruzar la calle.
e. Calle principal, ancha y larga.

112 ciento doce

Differentiated Instruction

DEVELOPING LEARNERS

- Ask students to make two lists and label them, *En el centro* and *En las afueras*. Then have students think about their own community and classify the places in the image and those that appear in the word bank under one of these headings. Encourage students to add the names for other places in the community that they may already know.

EXPANDING LEARNERS

- Have students expand activity 65 by writing clues to other vocabulary words from this *Desafío*. These words might include: *festival, concurso, barrio, parque, plaza, banco, calle, señal de pare, cuadra, centro, las afueras*, as well as those places listed in the word bank, *Lugares y servicios*. After students have written their list of words and clues, ask them to exchange papers with a partner and answer each other's questions.

66 En la ciudad

▶ **Escucha** y escribe. ¿En qué lugar de la ciudad están estas personas?

Modelo *Roberto está en la tienda de comestibles.*

1. Roberto
2. Sara y Natalia
3. Jorge y Juan Miguel
4. Rebeca
5. Tomás
6. Marcos

67 ¿Qué pasa en la calle?

▶ **Describe** estas fotografías.

Modelo *En la calle hay una señal de pare.*

COMUNIDADES

EL BARRIO

Los barrios (*neighborhoods*) son las zonas en las que se divide una ciudad o un pueblo.

El origen de un barrio puede deberse a razones administrativas, históricas o urbanísticas.

En muchos casos, el nombre de un barrio está relacionado con su origen o con sus características. Por ejemplo, San Juan Antiguo (en San Juan de Puerto Rico) o Playa (en Ponce).

68 Compara. ¿Cómo son los barrios de tu ciudad? ¿Sabes por qué se llaman así?

Vocabulario – El barrio. Lugares y servicios

67. Ask students to use the places photographed to write how long it would take them to get from school to that place. For example: *El semáforo está en la esquina, cerca de la escuela.*

AUDIO SCRIPT
See page 79J.

COMUNIDADES

El barrio

Most neighborhoods, whether in the United States or abroad, are defined by one of two characteristics, the people or the physical location. For example, a neighborhood might have been formed by its location between a highway and a river, or by a particular group of people who chose to live there ("Little Italy," for example).

Answer Key

65. 1. c   2. b   3. e   4. d   5. a

66. 2. Sara y Natalia están en la oficina de correos.
3. Jorge y Juan Miguel están en la cafetería.
4. Rebeca está en el parque.
5. Tomás está en el banco.
6. Marcos está en la escuela.

67. Answers will vary. Sample answers:
2. En la avenida hay un paso de cebra. El semáforo está en rojo para los coches y la gente está cruzando la calle.
3. En la acera hay gente y en la esquina hay una oficina. Un chico va en bicicleta por la calle.
4. En la plaza hay gente sentada en los bancos. También hay un café.

68. Answers will vary.

Additional Resources

Fans Online activities
Practice Workbook

113

HERITAGE LANGUAGE LEARNERS

- Ask students what other words they know for some of the items on page 112. For example, some Spanish speakers say *la manzana* instead of *la cuadra*; *el paso de peatones* instead of *el paso de cebra*; *la vereda, la banqueta,* or *el andén* for *la acera*; and *la bodega, la tienda de abarrotes / ultramarinos,* or *el almacén* instead of *la tienda de comestibles.*

- Ask students to share these words with their classmates, who may want to write them in their notebooks.

CRITICAL THINKING

- Lead students in a discussion on the influence their neighborhood has on them, and the impact neighborhoods have on the rest of the community. Encourage students to come up with their own definitions of *barrio*.

DESAFÍO 4

Gramática – Los demostrativos

Presentation

- In this section, students will learn demonstrative adjectives and demonstrative pronouns.

Activities	Standards	Resources
Gramática	3.1	
69.	4.1	
70.	1.2	
71.	1.3	
72.	1.2, 1.3	Audio
73. Cultura	1.1, 1.2, 2.1, 3.1, 3.2, 4.2, 5.1	
Tu desafío	1.2, 2.2, 3.1, 3.2, 5.2	

Teaching Suggestions

Warm-Up / Independent Starter

- Have students imagine that they are the mayors of a small town named in their honor. Ask them to write ten sentences to describe their town.

Preparation

- Ask volunteers to share their town's description with the class. Take a vote on the best description to see who will be the classroom mayor for the day. Allow the "mayor" to help you.

- Go over the grammar presentation with students. Remind them that demonstrative adjectives and pronouns are relative to the speaker. Two people can have the same conversation about an object, but the relativity of the object is to the person talking, not the other person participating in the conversation.

Activities

69. Remind students that *ese* and *esa* correspond to "that" in English, while *aquel* and *aquella* are used to talk about something that is at a distance, generally outside arm's reach at least. In English, we would generally say "(way) over there" to represent *aquel* and *aquella*.

70. Remind students that the demonstrative adjectives and pronouns are gender and number specific, and they should keep this in mind.

Gramática

Los demostrativos

- To indicate where something or someone is located in relation to the person speaking, use demonstratives.

  ¿Quieres entrar en **este** café? Yo prefiero ir a **aquel** de allí.

- Demonstrative adjectives and pronouns show gender and number.

  En **esta** calle hay un café y en **aquella** hay un restaurante.

ADJETIVOS Y PRONOMBRES DEMOSTRATIVOS

Distance from speaker	Singular		Plural	
	Masculino	Femenino	Masculino	Femenino
Near	este	esta	estos	estas
At a distance	ese	esa	esos	esas
Far away	aquel	aquella	aquellos	aquellas

Los pronombres demostrativos

- Demonstrative pronouns can be used to point or to avoid repetition. They mean *this one/that one* or *these/those*.

  –¿Tú vives en **esa** plaza?
  –No, vivo en **aquella** de allí.

- Neutral forms *esto*, *eso*, and *aquello* are always pronouns. They are used in these cases:
  - To refer to situations or facts:

    Hoy voy al cine y **eso** me gusta.

  - To present or to refer to unknown objects:

    –¿Qué es **eso**?
    –**Eso** es una biblioteca.

69 **Compara.** ¿Cómo se expresa la distancia media (*ese*, *esa*, *eso*) en inglés?

70 **¿Dónde están?**

▶ **Une** las dos columnas.

A	B
1. Mis amigos están allí, sentados en aquellos	a. calles.
2. Te espero aquí, en este	b. parque.
3. Me gusta comprar ropa en esa	c. tienda.
4. Hay muchos cafés en estas	d. biblioteca.
5. Voy a estudiar a aquella	e. bancos.

114 ciento catorce

Differentiated Instruction

DEVELOPING LEARNERS

- To help students build confidence with the demonstratives, have them decide which demonstrative should be used with the following nouns:

1. *aquellos/estas bancos* (aquellos)
2. *este/esta plaza* (esta)
3. *esa/aquel acera* (esa)
4. *eso/ese semáforo* (ese)
5. *esto/esta calle* (esta)
6. *aquel/aquella esquina* (aquella)
7. *aquel/aquello paso de peatones* (aquel)

EXPANDING LEARNERS

- Remind students that the use of *este, ese,* and *aquel* depends on the speaker's perception. To give students practice with this, have two students come to the front of the class. Place an object in the hand of one of them. Then place an item far from both students. Ask both of the students to talk about the objects, using the correct form of *este, ese,* or *aquel.* For example:

A. *¿De qué color es este bolígrafo?*
B. *Ese bolígrafo es azul.*
B. *¿Es tuya aquella mochila?*
A. *No, aquella mochila es de Jack.*

71 En la plaza

▶ **Completa** los bocadillos con los demostrativos apropiados.

Perdone, ¿es ___1___ la Plaza de la Fuente?

No, pero está cerca. Tiene que cruzar ___2___ plaza y seguir por ___3___ avenida.

No, es ___5___ de allí.

Por favor, ¿la Plaza de la Fuente es ___4___?

72 El barrio de Luisa

▶ **Escucha** a Luisa, una amiga de Tess, y decide. ¿Dónde están estos lugares: cerca *(aquí)*, a media distancia *(ahí)* o lejos *(allí)*?

Modelo *Esa biblioteca está cerrada. → media distancia (ahí)*

1. el banco   2. la oficina de correos   3. el parque   4. la plaza

CULTURA

La Plaza de Armas

En el centro de muchas ciudades coloniales de América Latina –La Habana, Santiago de Chile, Quito, Cuzco, Lima– hay una plaza que se llama Plaza de Armas. En estas plazas se construyeron palacios, catedrales y otros edificios importantes de la ciudad.

Plaza de Armas de San Juan (Puerto Rico).

73 **Piensa y explica.** ¿Cuál es el centro de tu ciudad o de tu barrio? ¿Sabes si en el pasado fue otro lugar distinto?

▶→ **TU DESAFÍO** Visita la página web para aprender más sobre las Plazas de Armas.

ciento quince 115

Gramática – Los demostrativos

71. Once students have finished, ask for volunteers to read the speech bubbles aloud to the class.

73. Let students know that most cities and towns changed considerably during the 20th century, as people moved from the countryside to the cities. Have students research what your city or town looked like 100 years ago, and compare it to the current city.

 AUDIO SCRIPT
See page 79J.

 CULTURA

La Plaza de Armas

The main square of a town is sometimes known as the *Plaza de Armas*, especially in the Americas. During the Spanish colonization of the Americas, this plaza was the meeting point for the townspeople during an attack, so the town's ammunition supplies were stored in the main public buildings nearby.

Answer Key

69. Se expresa con la palabra *that*.

70. 1. e   4. a
2. b   5. d
3. c

71. 1. esta   4. esta
2. esa   5. aquella
3. aquella

72. 1. ese banco → ahí
2. aquella oficina → allí
3. ese parque → ahí
4. esta plaza → aquí

73. Answers will vary.

Additional Resources

Fans Online activities
Practice Workbook

HERITAGE LANGUAGE LEARNERS

• Have students create clues for a crossword puzzle to practice the different forms of the demonstratives, as well as *aquí, ahí,* and *allí*. Ask the technologically adept students to use computer-generated software to create the crossword grid. When they complete their task, ask volunteers from among the other students to try to solve the puzzle.

TOTAL PHYSICAL RESPONSE (TPR)

• Provide additional practice with demonstrative adjectives by giving students commands. Have several classroom objects prepared and placed beforehand. Then give students commands such as:

– [Name of student], *toma ese libro azul y ponlo en aquella mesa.*

– [Name of student], *cubre ese cuaderno con esta hoja de papel.*

– [Name of student], *pon estos lápices en esa mochila.*

115

Unit 2
DESAFÍO 4

Comunicación

Presentation

- In this section, students will integrate the vocabulary and grammar from *Desafío* 4 to use words associated with the neighborhood, to talk about places in the city, and to use demonstrative adjectives and pronouns.

Activities	Standards	Resources
74.	1.2, 2.2	Audio
75.	1.2, 2.1, 2.2	
76.	1.1, 1.3	
77. Final del desafío	1.2, 1.3, 2.2	

Teaching Suggestions

Warm-Up / Independent Starter

- Place up to ten of the same item in obvious places around the classroom. You can use pencils or dry erase markers, for example. Then have students look around the room and write where three of these items are in relation to their seats. Remind them to use the demonstratives *este*, *ese*, and *aquel* and the adverbs *aquí*, *ahí*, and *allí*. For example: *Ese lápiz está ahí.*

Preparation

- Have students point out where different classroom items are in the classroom. Point to one of the items and ask a student where it is in relation to his or her seat. Repeat this process several times with different students and items.

- Take 10 minutes to review the vocabulary and grammar themes from *Desafío* 4.

- Refer students back to the *fotonovela* for *Desafío* 4. Have them find all of the words associated with the neighborhood, places in the city, and demonstrative adjectives and pronouns within the dialogue. Do students understand the dialogue better now that they have gone through the vocabulary and grammar from the *Desafío*?

- Alternatively, ask students to complete the *Comunicación* activities individually and silently. Even the speaking activities can be written down. Tell students to pay close attention to the topics in which they need more practice.

116

Comunicación

74 **Mi lugar favorito**

 ▶ **Escucha** y decide. ¿De qué fotografía hablan?

Avenida Muñoz Rivera (San Juan de Puerto Rico).

Calle en el Viejo San Juan (San Juan de Puerto Rico).

 ▶ **Escucha** otra vez y escribe las palabras que mencionan.

monumentos	iglesias	hoteles	restaurantes
bibliotecas	cafés	calles	avenidas

75 **Una carta desde Ponce**

▶ **Lee** la carta de Tess y decide si estas oraciones son ciertas o falsas.

> ¡Hola, Ana! ¿Qué tal?
> Yo estoy en Ponce (Puerto Rico). Es una ciudad con mucha historia y tradición. Las calles son muy estrechas porque en el pasado sirvieron como protección contra los piratas.
> Esta ciudad es muy interesante. La gente puede visitar un museo, pasear en el Parque de la Ceiba, ver una obra de teatro en el Teatro La Perla o visitar el Museo de Arte de Ponce.
> Cerca del centro hay varias iglesias y una catedral. También hay muchos restaurantes y cafés.
> Mañana volvemos a Aibonito. Un beso.
>   Tess

1. Ponce es una ciudad histórica.
2. En el centro, las calles son anchas.
3. Hay muchos lugares de interés.
4. Tess va a visitar una catedral.
5. A Tess no le gusta mucho Ponce.

Differentiated Instruction

DEVELOPING LEARNERS

- For activity 76, have students exchange their written comparisons between their neighborhood and that of their partner with students who possess advanced language skills. These students will check spelling, punctuation, written accent marks, agreement, and correct use of vocabulary and expressions. They will mark any errors but not correct them, and add one or more suggestions for their classmates before returning their work to them.

- After receiving their work, students should correct the errors and incorporate the changes as they deem appropriate.

EXPANDING LEARNERS

- Have students work with a partner and ask them to think of another ending to this *desafío*. They might consider that Tess and Patricia get lost and miss the festival, or that Patricia's allergies prevent her from taking part in the contest. Perhaps the festival was canceled due to bad weather, or Tess and her mother were confused about the dates. Encourage creativity in plot and dialogue, and invite students to present their skits before the class.

76 **¿Conoces mi barrio?**

▶ **Dibuja** un mapa de tu barrio *(neighborhood)* y descríbeselo a tu compañero(a).

Modelo *En mi barrio hay un parque grande en el centro. A la izquierda del parque hay…*

▶ **Escribe** un texto comparando tu barrio con otro barrio de tu ciudad.

Final del desafío

① ¿Qué jardín te gusta más, mamá, este o __1__ de allí?

¡ACHÍIIS! ¡Uf!

② ¡Mira, qué bonito! Me gusta __2__ jardín de ahí.

Mamá..., __3__ jardín no es bonito. __4__ de aquí sí es bonito.

 ③ ¡Felicidades! Su jardín ganó el primer premio del año.

77 **El jardín ganador**

▶ **Escribe y representa.** Completa el diálogo con adjetivos y pronombres demostrativos. Después, representa la escena con tu compañero(a).

Activities

74. Of the words not mentioned, have students decide in which picture they would fit best.

75. Have students correct the false statements. Then have them write a response to Tess's letter with a description of their city or town.

76. Alternatively, have students write a one-paragraph description of their neighborhood instead of speaking to a classmate.

77. It appears that getting lost and having allergies did not affect Tess and Patricia's completion of this *desafío*. Once students have finished their *Comunicación* activities, have them reenact the *Final del desafío* in small groups.

AUDIO SCRIPT
See page 79 J.

Answer Key

74. Fotografía B.
  ▶ calles, monumentos, iglesias

75. 1. Cierto   4. Falso
   2. Falso   5. Falso
   3. Cierto

76. Answers will vary.
  ▶ Answers will vary.

77. 1. aquel   3. ese
   2. ese   4. este

Additional Resources

Fans Online activities
Practice Workbook

HERITAGE LANGUAGE LEARNERS

- Patricia uses the verb *¡Mira!* in the second scene of the *Final del desafío* to get her daughter's attention. There are many other verbs and expressions that Spanish speakers use for this end (e.g., *¡Fíjate!* and *¡Oye!*). Ask students to name other expressions that Spanish speakers use to get someone's attention, and ask them to share them with the class.

MULTIPLE INTELLIGENCES:
Naturalist Intelligence

- Address the importance of plants to life on Earth. Not only do they provide the air we breathe, they give us food, shelter, and are a source of medicine. Ninety percent of all plant and animal species live in the tropics, so it would be no surprise that a large variety of plants are exhibited in the *Festival de las flores* in Aibonito. Ask students to research some of the plant species that might be found at this fair, as well as others that thrive in the tropics. Ask them to describe some of these plants, especially those that are used for medical purposes.

117

Unit 2
TODO JUNTO

Presentation

- In this section, students will review the unit objectives and put them into practice.

Activities	Standards	Resources
78.	1.2	Audio
79.	1.2, 1.3, 2.2	
80.	1.1, 1.3	
81. Cultura	1.1, 1.2, 2.1, 2.2, 4.2, 5.1	

Teaching Suggestions

Warm-Up / Independent Starter

- Ask students to turn back to the vocabulary and grammar presentations in this unit. Have them create a quick reference guide to the information in these presentations on the front and back of a note card. This will serve as a study guide. Be sure students add this study guide to the one from Unit 1.

Preparation

- Have students imagine that they are working as commentators for the Household Chore Olympics in Santo Domingo, Dominican Republic. The competition begins inside a home at one end of the city and concludes with a race to the other end of the city.
- Tell students to write three paragraphs about what they see happening during the competition. They must include the chore and the room in which the chore is being performed. They must also include the furniture, accessories, and appliances that are in the room. Finally, they must describe the race across the city. What do the contestants pass as they run through the city? Have volunteers share their commentary with the class.

Activities

78. Have students write sentences to summarize the audio recording. *Tess está... Patricia está...*

79. Ask students if they have ever visited a house from another century (Monticello in Virginia, for example.) Have them compare the house Diana describes with the house they visited.

118

TODO JUNTO

ESCUCHAR

78 **Están muy ocupadas**

 ▶ **Escucha** y decide. ¿Quién hace cada tarea doméstica?

	Tess	Patricia	Rita
1. pasar la aspiradora			
2. cargar el lavaplatos			
3. limpiar el baño			
4. sacudir el polvo			
5. poner la lavadora			
6. planchar			

LEER Y ESCRIBIR

79 **La casa de mis sueños**

▶ **Lee** el mensaje de correo de Diana y responde a las preguntas.

Mensaje nuevo

Para:
Cc:
Asunto:

Hola, Luisa. ¿Qué tal?

Mi tía y yo estamos en Santo Domingo. Hay muchas casas antiguas y muy bonitas.

Ayer vi la casa de mis sueños, en el centro histórico. Es de piedra y tiene dos balcones. No es muy grande; tiene dos dormitorios, una sala, un cuarto de baño, un patio y un desván.

En la casa hay muebles de madera muy antiguos y muy bonitos. Y la decoración me gusta mucho; hay espejos, floreros y cuadros. Y unas alfombras espectaculares, con muchos colores.

Te mando unas fotos, quiero saber tu opinión.

Un abrazo de tu amiga.

Diana

1. ¿Dónde está la casa?
2. ¿Cómo es la casa?
3. ¿Cómo son los muebles?
4. ¿Qué accesorios tiene?

▶ **Escribe.** Imagina cómo es una habitación de esa casa y descríbela.

Differentiated Instruction

DEVELOPING LEARNERS

- Have students draw a picture of Diana's dream house according to her description in the e-mail. Then ask students to describe the house, according to their drawing.

EXPANDING LEARNERS

- Ask students to think about the following characters in this unit: Sir Francis Drake, *el arquitecto de la Casa del Cordón,* María Luisa Ayala *(la coleccionista de ámbar), los tunos, el jardinero ganador del Festival de las flores en Aibonito.* Then have students think of the ideal household chore for three of these characters. It might be a chore they are ideally suited for, or a chore as punishment! Ask students to make their assignments and then explain why they made these choices.

ESCRIBIR Y HABLAR

80 **Memoriza**

▶ **Escribe.** Mira esta fotografía del álbum de Tess durante un minuto. Después, cierra el libro y escribe un texto describiéndola.

 ▶ **Lee** tu descripción a tu compañero(a) y habla con él/ella de las cosas que recuerdas *(remember)* o no recuerdas de la foto.

 **CULTURA**

El turismo en el Caribe

El Caribe es uno de los principales destinos turísticos internacionales. Muchos turistas eligen esta zona por la arquitectura colonial. Hay varios lugares declarados Patrimonio de la Humanidad por la UNESCO: el centro histórico de La Habana (Cuba), la ciudad colonial de Santo Domingo (República Dominicana) o el Viejo San Juan (Puerto Rico), entre otros.

Castillo de San Felipe del Morro. San Juan (Puerto Rico).

81 **Piensa y explica.** ¿Qué lugares turísticos hay cerca de tu ciudad? ¿Por qué son famosos?

---

81. Ask students to give a tour of the neighborhood in which the tourist places are located, based on what they learned in *Desafío 4*.

 AUDIO SCRIPT
See page 79J.

 CULTURA

El turismo en el Caribe

One appealing way to travel to the Caribbean is by cruise ship. Tourists can travel to several different islands during one trip and take tours of the historical sites on each island. Festivals are another way to attract tourists to the Caribbean. Festivals such as *carnaval*, or carnival, take place on almost every island. Since most of these countries rely on tourists to fuel their economy, hosting a *carnaval* or other festival is a great way to attract tourists, as well as to celebrate the heritage and history of the people.

Answer Key

78. Tess: 2, 5
Patricia: 3, 6
Rita: 1, 4

79. 1. Está en el centro histórico de Santo Domingo.
2. Es de piedra y tiene dos balcones. También tiene dos cuartos, una sala, un cuarto de baño, un patio y un desván.
3. Son de madera, muy antiguos y bonitos.
4. Tiene espejos, floreros, cuadros y alfombras.
▶ Answers will vary.
80. Answers will vary.
▶ Answers will vary.
81. Answers will vary.

Additional Resources

Fans Online activities
Practice Workbook

HERITAGE LANGUAGE LEARNERS

- Ask students to research some other cultural aspects of the Dominican Republic and Puerto Rico and suggest another *desafío* that would be ideally suited to one of the pairs of participants. They should describe the challenge, its cultural significance, and why the selected partners are the ideal candidates to complete the task.

MULTIPLE INTELLIGENCES:
Visual-Spatial Intelligence

- Ask students to describe their dream house. They should state what country it is located in, and where in that country it is (city, countryside, beach, mountains, etc.). They should describe both the exterior and the interior and mention as many materials, sizes, and colors as they can. Students should be sure to name the rooms as well as the furniture and appliances in each one. Then ask students to accompany their descriptions with a drawing of their house.

Unit 2
El encuentro

Presentation

- The four pairs meet in front of the Ozama fortress in Santo Domingo, Dominican Republic. There they must read their notes to their hostess and judge, Dolores Santiago.
- Students will vote for the winner of the *Desafíos* in the Antilles islands.

Activities	Standards	Resources
Fotonovela	1.2, 2.2, 3.1	
82.	1.1, 1.2, 1.3	
83.	1.1, 1.2, 1.3	

Teaching Suggestions

Warm-Up / Independent Starter

- Ask students to close their textbooks and write a summary of each pair's challenge in the Antilles. Have them use the vocabulary and grammar from the *Desafío* in each description.

Preparation

- Remind students that in *Desafío 1*, Andy and Janet stayed in Santo Domingo to find the scale used by Sir Francis Drake. In *Desafío 2*, Diana and Rita went to Puerto Plata, in the Dominican Republic, to find a 200-million-year-old insect. In *Desafío 3*, Tim and Mack went to Ponce, Puerto Rico, to learn and sing a traditional *serenata*. And in *Desafío 4*, Tess and Patricia went to Aibonito, in Puerto Rico, to judge the *Festival de las flores de Aibonito*.

La fotonovela

- Read the introduction to *El encuentro* aloud.
- Have students look at the pictures. Ask them to describe what each pair is doing, the items they have in their hands, the clothes they are wearing, and any other details that might indicate how well they did in their *desafío*.
- Ask for volunteers to read each pair's note. Remind students that notes are a brief summary of a theme. Notes are very short, clear, and concise. Have the rest of the class pay close attention to the notes as the volunteers read. Did each pair write a short, clear, and concise note?

El encuentro

En la fortaleza Ozama

The pairs gather in front of the Ozama fortress, in Santo Domingo. This 1508 castle has defended the flags of Spain, France, Great Britain, the United States and, of course, the Dominican Republic. The pairs show the notes requested by Dolores.

> ¡Bienvenidos! ¿Consiguieron sus desafíos?

> El pirata Drake estuvo en la Casa del Cordón y usó una balanza como esta para pesar el oro del rescate.

> Este mosquito es en una roca de c y tiene más de 2 millones de años

> Te doy mi corazón... ♪

> Después de muchos problemas, conseguimos cantar una serenata con la tuna.

> Caminamos muchas cuadras y por muchos barrios, pero al fin llegamos al Festival de las flores.

120 ciento veinte

Differentiated Instruction

DEVELOPING LEARNERS

- Have students go back to the *Final del desafío* for all the challenges in order to review what the participants were doing. Ask students to copy any words or grammar items that are still challenging for them and include these in their notebook. Then ask them to do the same with the words and grammar in *El encuentro*. Encourage students to review these terms to help them prepare for tests and exams.

EXPANDING LEARNERS

- Ask students to work with a partner and imagine that they are one of the pairs of participants in this unit's *desafíos*. Ask them to elaborate on the notes the original participants presented. They may add more details, such as describing what they were thinking as they carried out the challenge, and what they most and least liked about their *desafío*.

120

El encuentro

82 **Al llegar**

▶ **Lee.** Los participantes se quedan en una casa histórica de Santo Domingo. Lee la nota del dueño y responde a estas preguntas.

The characters stay in a historic house in Santo Domingo. The owner leaves a note with some instructions. Read it and answer the questions.

> ¡Bienvenidos, amigos!
>
> La casa tiene seis dormitorios con cuarto de baño, un comedor y una sala muy grande con televisión, equipo de música y todos los muebles necesarios. Creo que les va a gustar.
>
> En la cocina hay estufa, horno, microondas, lavaplatos... En la despensa hay algunos alimentos básicos (leche, azúcar, arroz...), pero el refrigerador está vacío. En la plaza hay una pequeña tienda de comestibles y también hay un supermercado en el barrio.
>
> Finalmente, en el cuarto de lavar tienen lavadora, plancha y secadora. Allí también están la aspiradora y los productos para limpiar la casa.
>
> Disfruten de su estancia. Un saludo.
>
> Alberto Moncayo

1. ¿Cuántos cuartos de baño hay en la casa?
2. ¿Hay muebles en la sala y en los dormitorios?
3. ¿La cocina tiene electrodomésticos?
4. ¿En la casa hay comida?
5. ¿Hay tiendas de alimentación cerca de la casa?
6. ¿Quién tiene que hacer las tareas domésticas?

▶ **Habla** con tu compañero(a). ¿Qué tareas domésticas tienen que hacer los participantes? Decidan quién hace cada cosa.

Modelo *Andy y Janet ponen la lavadora y planchan la ropa.*

> Una nota debe ser muy clara y no muy larga.

83 **Las votaciones**

▶ **Compara** las notas de los personajes de la página 120. ¿Cuál es mejor? ¿Por qué?

▶ **Escribe** una nota para alguien de tu familia. Estas preguntas te pueden ayudar.

1. ¿Qué tareas domésticas tiene que hacer?
2. ¿Tiene que utilizar algún electrodoméstico?
3. ¿Tiene que hacer algo fuera de casa, como ir a la biblioteca o salir a comprar algo?

ciento veintiuno 121

Activities

82. Ask students to read Alberto Moncayo's note silently. Once they have finished, ask them to describe the difference between the notes the pairs had to write and Mr. Moncayo's note. The answer is that Moncayo's note is significantly longer and more detailed. Alberto Moncayo is describing the historical home in which the pairs are staying. Answer the questions as a class to ensure comprehension of the note. Then ask students to help you assign chores to the participants. Create a table on the board with four columns with each pair as the head of a column. Call on students to assign a chore to each pair. From the table on the board, have students write sentences to summarize the chores that each pair has to do.

Answer Key

82.
1. Hay seis cuartos de baño.
2. Sí, hay muebles en la sala y en los dormitorios.
3. Sí, en la cocina hay estufa, horno, microondas, lavaplatos y refrigerador.
4. Sí, en la despensa hay algunos alimentos básicos (leche, azúcar, arroz…), pero el refrigerador está vacío.
5. Sí, hay una pequeña tienda de comestibles en la plaza y un supermercado en el barrio.
6. Los participantes tienen que hacer las tareas domésticas.
▶ Answers will vary.

83. Answers will vary.
▶ Answers will vary.

HERITAGE LANGUAGE LEARNERS

• Ask students to describe in a four-paragraph composition what they have learned about the history and contemporary culture of the Dominican Republic and Puerto Rico after studying this unit.

CRITICAL THINKING

• Now that students know the outcome of the four *desafíos*, ask them to describe which one they would have liked to participate in and why. Do they think they would have done a better job at completing it than the original participants? Or do they think that the original participants could have fared better had they been given one of the other *desafíos* to carry out? Have students explain their answers.

Unit 2

MAPA CULTURAL

Las Antillas

Presentation

- This section presents Cuba, the Dominican Republic, and Puerto Rico through facts and physical features so learners can see these Caribbean islands from other perspectives. The map serves as a reference point for additional cultural readings and activities.

Activities	Standards	Resources
Mapa cultural	1.2, 2.2, 3.1, 3.2	Video
84.	1.3, 3.1, 3.2, 5.2	
85.	1.1, 1.3, 2.1, 2.2	

Cultural Topics

- **Barrios coloniales.** The following is a sample of the many well-preserved colonial structures in the Antilles that amaze today's visitors.
  - *El Morro*, in Puerto Rico, is one of the largest forts built by the Spaniards in the Americas. Construction began in 1539 and lasted until 1787.
  - The *Plaza de Armas* is the first-known public square in Havana, Cuba. It was the center of city life during colonial times and still is one of the most visited spots in Old Havana.
  - The *Alcantarilla colonial,* buried beneath the city of Santo Domingo, is comprised of two stretches of the original city sewer system built between 1502 and 1509. This was the first hydraulic sewage system in the Americas.
- **Música caribeña.** Afro-Cuban rhythms and Caribbean sounds became an international phenomenon in the 20th century. Some of most influential artists include the percussionist Tito Puente and the trombonist Willie Colón, both born in New York of Puerto Rican descent; Dámaso Pérez Prado, from Cuba, who specialized in mambo music; salsa singer Celia Cruz, also from Cuba; and merengue singer Johnny Ventura from the Dominican Republic.

Teaching Suggestions

Warm-Up / Independent Starter

- Have students look at the map of the Caribbean and note the location of the Antilles in relation to the United States. Then have them list two facts they have learned in this unit about each of the following Antilles: *Cuba, República Dominicana, Puerto Rico.*

122

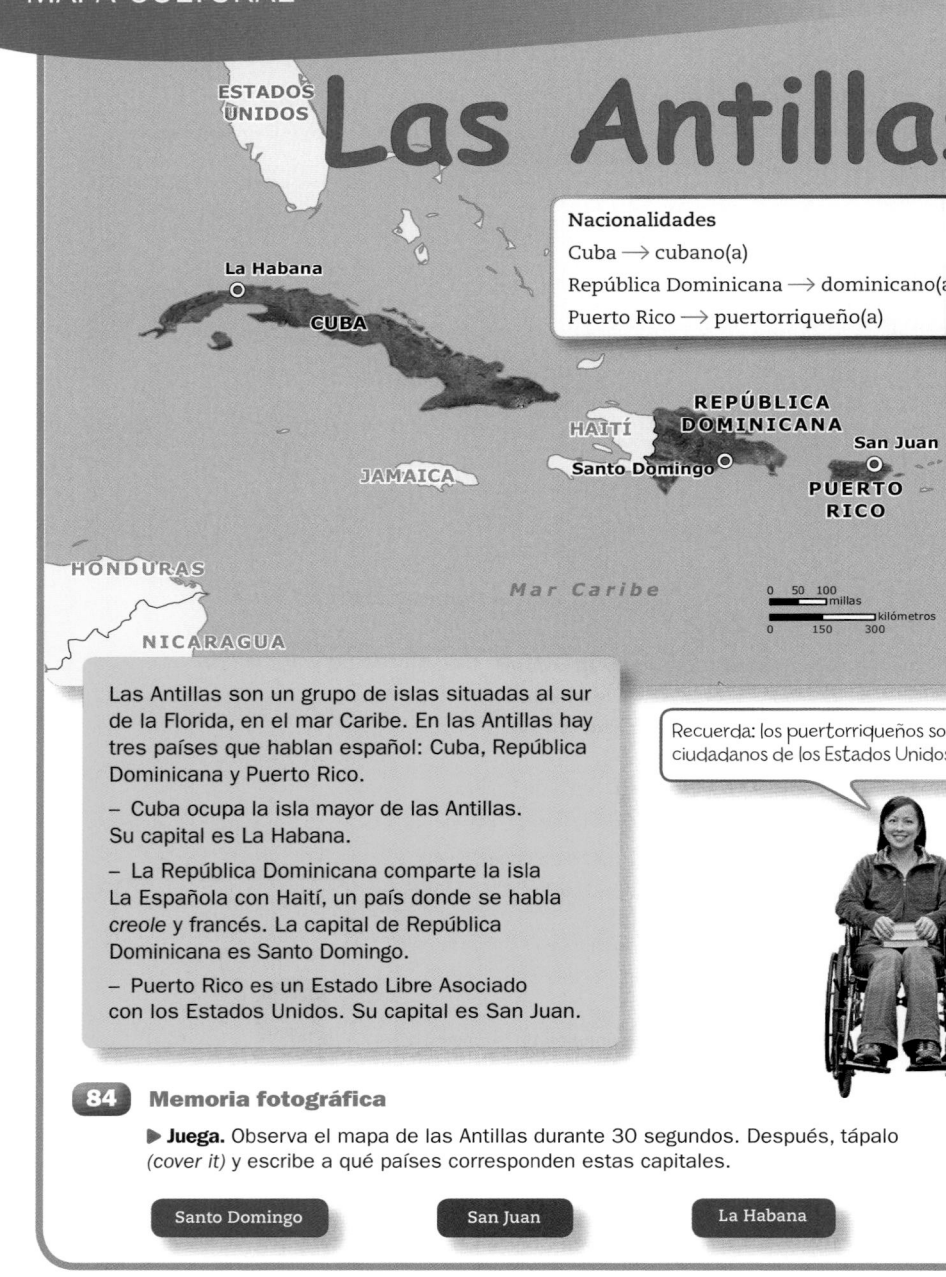

MAPA CULTURAL

Las Antillas

Nacionalidades
Cuba → cubano(a)
República Dominicana → dominicano(a)
Puerto Rico → puertorriqueño(a)

ESTADOS UNIDOS
La Habana
CUBA
REPÚBLICA DOMINICANA
HAITÍ
San Juan
JAMAICA
Santo Domingo
PUERTO RICO
HONDURAS
Mar Caribe
NICARAGUA

0 50 100 millas
0 150 300 kilómetros

Las Antillas son un grupo de islas situadas al sur de la Florida, en el mar Caribe. En las Antillas hay tres países que hablan español: Cuba, República Dominicana y Puerto Rico.

- Cuba ocupa la isla mayor de las Antillas. Su capital es La Habana.
- La República Dominicana comparte la isla La Española con Haití, un país donde se habla *creole* y francés. La capital de República Dominicana es Santo Domingo.
- Puerto Rico es un Estado Libre Asociado con los Estados Unidos. Su capital es San Juan.

Recuerda: los puertorriqueños son ciudadanos de los Estados Unidos.

84 **Memoria fotográfica**

▶ **Juega.** Observa el mapa de las Antillas durante 30 segundos. Después, tápalo *(cover it)* y escribe a qué países corresponden estas capitales.

Santo Domingo   San Juan   La Habana

122 ciento veintidós

Differentiated Instruction

DEVELOPING LEARNERS

- To help students organize the information presented in the *Mapa cultural*, have them create a three-column chart, one column for each island (i.e., Puerto Rico, Dominican Republic, Cuba). Ask them to summarize, in a bulleted list, information about each island. The first bullet should include geographic information; the second, historical information (including architectural style and famous buildings); the third, cultural information (including music); the fourth, any other miscellaneous data and information they have learned about the place.

EXPANDING LEARNERS

- Ask students to relate what they have learned about the architecture and music of the Antilles with what they know about the United States.
  - How does the colonial architecture of the Spanish-speaking Antilles compare with the colonial architecture of New England in the Northeast of the United States?
  - Are there similarities in the origin, development, and rhythms of Afro-Caribbean music and Afro-American music such as jazz and blues?

1. Barrios coloniales

Muchas ciudades de Cuba, República Dominicana y Puerto Rico tienen origen español y conservan hermosos barrios coloniales con calles empedradas (*stone-paved*), casas de colores y fortalezas defensivas. Son famosos los barrios coloniales de La Habana, Santo Domingo y San Juan.

Una de las calles coloniales más antiguas está en Santo Domingo. Se llama *calle de las Damas* por la costumbre de las damas de dar paseos por allí.

(1) Calle de las Damas (Santo Domingo).

(2) Bailarinas de salsa.

2. Música caribeña

La música y la danza son elementos característicos de la cultura del Caribe.

Hay muchos géneros de música caribeña. El más representativo es la salsa, que tiene influencia de los ritmos africanos y del jazz. Nació en los años 60 y fue una creación de la comunidad caribeña en Nueva York. Otros tipos de música muy conocidos son el merengue y la bachata, de la República Dominicana, y el son cubano.

85 ¡Ven a las islas del Caribe!

▶ **Elige** un país del Caribe y escribe qué sabes sobre él y qué te resulta más interesante.

▶ **Habla** con tu compañero(a). ¿Qué cosas pueden hacer en las islas del Caribe?

> Anne, ¿qué podemos hacer en las islas del Caribe?

> Pues... bailar salsa.

MAPA CULTURAL

Las Antillas

Preparation

- Invite different volunteers to share with the class the facts they listed in the Independent Starter. Then add the information below.

- The Antilles are divided into *Antillas Mayores* (Greater Antilles) and *Antillas Menores* (Lesser Antilles). The three Spanish-speaking islands in the Caribbean Sea are part of the Greater Antilles. Cuba, with a total area of 42,427 square miles and a population of 11,477,459 (2010 est.), is the largest island in the Caribbean. It is located about 90 miles south of Florida. The largest capital city in the Caribbean is Santo Domingo, in the Dominican Republic. It is also the oldest permanent city established by Europeans in the Western Hemisphere. Puerto Rico is the smallest of the Greater Antilles. It is a self-governing commonwealth in association with the United States. San Juan, Puerto Rico's capital, has one of the biggest and best natural harbors in the Caribbean.

- Ask for volunteers to read each section of the *Mapa cultural*. Have students follow the map on the page.

Activities

85. Ask students to choose one of the elements that they, as tourists in the Caribbean, would be most interested in, and summarize what they have learned throughout the unit about that element.

Answer Key

84. República Dominicana; Puerto Rico; Cuba

85. Answers will vary.
  ▶ Answers will vary.

Additional Resources

Fans Online activities
Practice Workbook

HERITAGE LANGUAGE LEARNERS

- Encourage students to describe the musical heritage of their country of origin. Ask them to research the history, influences, and famous interpreters of this music. Then have them summarize their findings to do a brief presentation in front of the class. They may bring samples of the most representative musical pieces to play in class.

MULTIPLE INTELLIGENCES:
Musical Intelligence

- Explain that the Cuban *son* originated in the eastern province of Santiago, around the end of the 19th century. The *son* was a precursor of other musical genres such as salsa.

- Have students listen to the songs "Son de la loma" and "Hueso na' ma" by the Trío Matamoros, one of the earliest Cuban *son* groups. (They can find the original recordings of these songs on the Internet.) Ask students to pay attention to the instruments, rhythms, and harmonies to see if they can place some of these elements in current Latin music.

123

LECTURA

Estilo de vida caribeño

Presentation

- In this section, students will increase their understanding of Caribbean culture by reading about the Caribbean way of life. In addition, students will focus on identifying the main idea and the most important details in the text they are reading in order to understand and summarize the information presented in the text.

Activities	Standards	Resources
Lectura	1.2, 2.1, 3.2	
86.	1.2, 2.1, 2.2	
87.	1.3, 2.1, 2.2	
88.	1.3, 2.1, 2.2	
Tu desafío	1.2, 2.1, 2.2, 3.2, 5.1	

Teaching Suggestions

Warm-Up / Independent Starter

- Ask students to look at the image on this page and the title of the reading. Then have them write down in their notebooks the first sentence of each of the four paragraphs.

Preparation

- Ask students what the reading strategy was in the previous unit. (To identify the global idea of a text.) Then point out the Reading Strategy box and ask a volunteer to read it aloud. Ask students how these strategies help them understand their reading.

- Ask for volunteers to read their sentences from the Independent Starter aloud. Ask students to make an informed guess about the content of this reading based on the photos, the text structure, and the first sentence from each paragraph.

- To introduce the reading, ask students to think for a few seconds about the information they have and what they know about the Spanish-speaking islands of the Caribbean. What are the weather, the music, and the people like? Then ask volunteer students to share with the class the images that come to their mind regarding life on these islands. Ask students to think of these images as they read the text. At the end of the reading, have them decide whether or not the text confirmed their assumptions about the Caribbean way of life.

Isla Saona. Punta Cana (República Dominicana).

Estilo de vida caribeño

READING STRATEGY

Read for detailed information

When you read a text for specific information, it is helpful to underline or make sticky notes of main ideas or important information. As you read each paragraph, write down the **main idea** and the most important **details**. You can then use your notes to summarize what you have read.

En las islas del Caribe, la vida tiene otro ritmo, otro color. El Caribe es sol, mar, abundante naturaleza y una cultura muy rica de orígenes diversos.

Las islas del Caribe tienen un colorido muy especial. El intenso azul del cielo, el color turquesa[1] del mar y el verde de la vegetación marcan su paisaje. Y en los barrios antiguos de Santo Domingo, el Viejo San Juan y otras ciudades coloniales, las casas tienen fachadas con vivos colores.

Vivir la vida con alegría es una característica esencial del carácter caribeño. La gente del Caribe es hospitalaria[2] y sociable. Los vecinos conversan en la puerta del colmado[3] o del café, o juegan al dominó en la calle.

La gran pasión de los caribeños es la música y el baile. Los ritmos y los músicos caribeños son famosos en todo el mundo. La salsa, el mambo, el merengue y la bachata son algunos de los ritmos más populares.

---

1. *turquoise blue*   2. *hospitable*   3. *grocery store*

Differentiated Instruction

DEVELOPING LEARNERS

- Have students complete the table for activity 87 as they read. Suggest, for instance, that they read each paragraph once for meaning. Then they should read it a second time focusing on the information the paragraph contains. At this point, they should point out the important information, or take notes on a sticky note. Then, have them fill in the main idea and details for that paragraph in the table in activity 87.

EXPANDING LEARNERS

- Have students write an opinion paragraph to express and explain what they think about the Caribbean lifestyle. What might some advantages and disadvantages to this way of life be? Overall, do they think this is a better approach to life?

- Remind students that they should start their paragraph with a topic sentence that states the main idea. Then they should add details to support or illustrate the main idea. They should finish with a concluding sentence that restates or summarizes the topic sentence.

COMPRENSIÓN

86 **¿Estilo de vida caribeño?**

▶ **Decide** si las siguientes afirmaciones son ciertas o falsas.

1. El Caribe tiene una cultura muy rica y diversa.
2. En Santo Domingo hay casas coloniales.
3. Los caribeños son melancólicos y aburridos.
4. A los caribeños no les gusta la música.

ESTRATEGIA **Buscar información específica en un texto**

87 **¿Qué dice el texto?**

▶ **Completa** una tabla como esta para recopilar *(to gather)* la información del texto. Puedes reformularla con tus propias palabras.

Ideas principales	Detalles importantes
1. La vida en el Caribe es diferente (tiene otro ritmo, otro color).	– El Caribe tiene una naturaleza abundante. – El Caribe tiene una cultura muy rica y muy diversa.

88 **En resumen**

▶ **Escribe** un resumen del texto. Usa tu tabla de la actividad 87 y las siguientes imágenes.

 **TU DESAFÍO** Visita la página web para aprender más sobre los músicos del Caribe.

HERITAGE LANGUAGE LEARNERS

• Discuss with students that people in every nation have their own distinctive way of life. Have them think of what characterizes the way of life in their country of origin. If they don't know, have them talk with an older member of their family.

• Have students present a brief summary of the most salient characteristics of the way of life in their countries of origin. Is music an important part of the culture? Do people get together often? Is food a key element in the celebrations? Do people enjoy going out or do they prefer to meet at home?

CRITICAL THINKING

• Explain that celebrations in the Caribbean are very important. For instance, Christmas season in Puerto Rico starts right after Thanksgiving and lasts until January 6th. Friends and family have impromptu parties, usually outdoors, where they sing and dance.

• Ask students if the weather in their state would allow for such celebrations in the midst of winter. What influence do they think the weather has on the way of life? Are there differences between the different regions in the United States? Can some of these differences be attributed to the weather?

LECTURA

Estilo de vida caribeño

Activities

86. Once students have finished this activity, ask them to rewrite the false statements to make them true. Then have students think of a detail that supports each true statement.

87. Before students begin this activity, explain that paragraphs usually start with a topic sentence that presents the main idea of the paragraph. Details or evidence to support what was said in the topic sentence usually follow. Tell students they will use the information in this table to summarize the reading.

88. Remind students to use transitions and connectors so that their summary is not just a series of disconnected sentences. The following are some examples of transition words and connectors in Spanish: *además* (moreover, furthermore), *también* (also, too, as well), *después* or *luego* (then), *por último* (finally).

Answer Key

86. 1. Cierto   3. Falso
2. Cierto   4. Falso

87. Answers will vary. Sample answers:
2. Idea principal: Las islas del Caribe tienen un colorido único.
Detalles: – Los colores de la naturaleza del Caribe son muy intensos y variados.
– Las casas del Caribe reflejan los colores de la naturaleza.
3. Idea principal: La alegría es un rasgo de la personalidad del caribeño.
Detalles: – Los caribeños son hospitalarios y sociables.
– Los vecinos se relacionan en la calle.
4. Idea principal: La música y el baile son muy importantes para los caribeños.
Detalles: – La música del Caribe es conocida en todo el mundo.
– Hay diversos ritmos caribeños.

88. Answers will vary.

Additional Resources

Fans Online activities

125

Unit 2
REPASO

Vocabulario

Presentation

- In this section, students will review all key vocabulary from the unit, organized by themes, to prepare for an assessment. Students will complete practice activities for each of the four *Desafíos*.

Activities	Standards	Resources
1.	1.2	
2.	1.2	
3.	1.3	
4.	1.3	

Teaching Suggestions

Warm-Up / Independent Starter

- Ask students to imagine that they are real estate agents who have a property for sale. The property has historical value and is fully furnished. Have students write a detailed description of the property, its contents, and the surrounding neighborhood for an ad on the Internet. They should write legibly. If time allows it, ask students to sketch a floor plan of the house or use a floor plan maker on the Internet to create a layout.

Preparation

- Collect the ads from the Independent Starter and mix them in a bag. Have students pick at random an ad from the bag. (If they get their ad, they should pick a different one from the bag.) Then ask them to analyze the ad as if they were a potential buyer. What do they like about the property? What do they need that the house doesn't have? What do they want to change? Etc. Ask students to jot down their thoughts about the property to help them in their decision process.
- Once students have analyzed the pros and cons of the property they picked, ask them to decide whether or not they would buy it. Have students sign their names on the ad if they want to buy the property. Then give the ads back to the "agents" who have these properties and tally the properties sold. Ask students who sold their property to read their descriptions. What seemed to be the deciding factors for selling these properties?

126

La vivienda

el balcón	balcony	**Material**		
la chimenea	fireplace	de ladrillo	brick	
la cocina	kitchen	de madera	wooden	
la despensa	pantry	de piedra	stone	
el desván	attic			
el jardín	garden			
el pasillo	hallway			
la sala	living room			
el sótano	basement			
el tejado	roof			

Las tareas domésticas

cargar el lavaplatos	to load the dishwasher
descargar el lavaplatos	to unload the dishwasher
colocar los libros	to arrange the books
planchar	to iron
sacudir el polvo	to dust

Los electrodomésticos

el aire acondicionado	air conditioning
la caldera de calefacción	furnace
el equipo de música	stereo
el despertador	alarm clock

El cuarto de lavar

la lavadora	washing machine
la plancha	iron
la secadora	clothes dryer

La cocina

el congelador	freezer
la estufa	stove
el horno	oven
el lavaplatos	dishwasher
el microondas	microwave
el refrigerador	refrigerator

Muebles y accesorios para la casa

la cama	bed	**Accesorios**	
el estante	shelf	la alfombra	rug
la mesa	table	las cortinas	curtains
la mesita		el cuadro	painting
de noche	nightstand	el espejo	mirror
el sillón	armchair	el florero	vase
el sofá	sofa	la lámpara	lamp

El barrio

la acera	sidewalk	**Lugares y servicios**	
la avenida	avenue	el banco	bank
el banco	bench	la biblioteca	library
la calle	street	el café	café
la cuadra	block	la escuela	school
la esquina	corner	la iglesia	church
la plaza	square/plaza	la oficina de correos	post office
el paso de cebra	crosswalk	el parque	park
el semáforo	stoplight	la tienda de comestibles	grocery store
la señal de pare	stop sign	en las afueras	on the outskirts
		en el centro	downtown

126 ciento veintiséis

Differentiated Instruction

DEVELOPING LEARNERS

- Ask students to draw a floor plan of their house. Have them also draw some of the furniture and accessories in each area of the house. Ask students to label the different parts of the house, as well as the furniture and accessories they drew. Have them include the definite article with each noun to reinforce acquisition of noun gender.
- In pairs, have students talk about their house.
  A. ¿Hay una sala en tu casa?
  B. Sí.
  A. ¿Y qué hay en la sala de tu casa?
  B. Hay...

EXPANDING LEARNERS

- Ask students to choose 20 words from the vocabulary list. Then have them draw a two-column chart like the one shown below. Have them write the vocabulary word in the left column and an action associated with it in the right column. For example:

Objeto o lugar	Acción
el paso de cebra	cruzar
la estufa	cocinar

- Have students choose five vocabulary words from their chart to write five sentences using the word and the verb they listed for the word.

DESAFÍO 1

1 **Partes de la casa.** Completa estas oraciones.

balcón
despensa
sótano
pasillo
chimenea

1. El _____ de mi casa es largo.
2. No me gusta bajar al _____ porque está muy oscuro.
3. Todos los dulces están guardados en la _____.
4. A Celia le gusta sentarse frente a la _____ en el invierno.
5. El dormitorio de Ana tiene un _____ muy grande.

DESAFÍO 2

2 **¿Qué hay en la sala?** Mira la fotografía y corrige los nombres de los muebles y accesorios.

1. lámpara → sofá
2. sofá
3. cuadro
4. florero
5. mesa

DESAFÍO 3

3 **¿Cómo se llaman?** Escribe el nombre de estos electrodomésticos.

DESAFÍO 4

4 **Mi camino a la escuela.** Completa el texto.

avenida   esquina   cuadras   paso de cebra   acera

Mi camino a la escuela

¡Para llegar a mi escuela tengo que caminar seis ___1___! Siempre voy por la ___2___ derecha de la ___3___ principal. Al llegar a la ___4___, cruzo por el ___5___. Mi escuela está al lado de la biblioteca.

Activities

3. After students have completed this activity, have them list one household chore that is usually done with each of these appliances. Then ask students to get together with a partner to talk about who does each of these chores at home. For example:

A. *Yo descargo el lavaplatos en casa.*

B. *Mi hermano descarga el lavaplatos. Yo lavo la ropa en la lavadora.*

4. Have students write a similar description for the route they take to get to school. If they or their parents drive them to school, have them describe the car's route. (For privacy reasons, ask students not to talk about the actual route they take. Have them imagine that they live on a different street and take a different route.) Then pair students up with a classmate they don't know and have them read their description of the route they take to their classmate. Have classmates guess where in town the other person lives. They should be as specific as possible. For example:

A. *¿Vives en la calle Washington, detrás de la oficina de correos?*

B. *No exactamente. Vivo en la calle Washington, pero en otra cuadra.*

A. *¿Vives en la cuadra del parque?*

B. *¡Sí!*

Answer Key

1.
1. pasillo
2. sótano
3. despensa
4. chimenea
5. balcón

2.
2. cuadro
3. lámpara
4. mesa
5. florero

3.
1. el lavaplatos
2. el refrigerador
3. el horno
4. la lavadora
5. la estufa

4.
1. cuadras
2. acera
3. avenida
4. esquina
5. paso de cebra

Additional Resources

Fans Online activities
Practice Workbook

HERITAGE LANGUAGE LEARNERS

- There are variations of words used to describe parts of the house, accessories, and furniture in the Spanish-speaking world. For example, the words *cuarto, habitación,* and *recámara* are used in some countries, instead of *dormitorio,* to refer to bedroom.

- Ask students to list the words that they use, or have heard their family use, that are variations from the words used in this *Desafío.*

MULTIPLE INTELLIGENCES:
Logical-Mathematical Intelligence

- Explain to students that most Spanish-speaking countries use the metric system. Measurements for the different parts of the house are given in square meters instead of square feet. One square foot is equal to approximately 0.093 square meters.

- Ask students to convert the average sizes of different parts of a house in the United States into square meters. For example: *El dormitorio tiene 120 pies cuadrados, es decir, 11,15 metros cuadrados.*

REPASO

Gramática

Presentation

- Students will review grammatical structures presented in the unit. Each grammar point is cross-referenced to the corresponding page in which it was introduced. The activities here provide systematic practice by *Desafío*.

Activities	Standards	Resources
5.	1.3	
6.	1.3	
7.	1.3	
8.	1.3	
9. Cultura	1.3, 2.1, 2.2, 5.2	

Teaching Suggestions

Warm-Up / Independent Starter

- Ask students to look around them and focus on a classmate. Have them observe this classmate in a non-obvious manner and write down what the classmate does in the next couple of minutes (e.g., *Monique está mirando a un compañero. Ahora está buscando algo en el libro…*).

Preparation

- Invite volunteers to read their sentences from the Independent Starter. Use one of the sentences students read as a source and write on the board two sentences similar to the following: *Monique está buscando algo en el libro. Ahora lo cierra y mira a aquel compañero de allí.*

- Review the *Repaso* presentation with the class. Use the sentences you wrote on the board as examples of some of the grammar points being reviewed.

Activities

5. Remind students that the present progressive is used in Spanish to talk about something that is in the process of taking place. To express what is going on in general or habitual actions, the simple present tense is used rather than the present progressive. Ask students to explain what each of the following sentences expresses:
   – *Amalia está escuchando música en la sala.*
   – *Amalia escucha música en la sala.*

El presente continuo (pág. 90)

▶ The present progressive is formed this way:

> estar + gerundio

Estoy cargando el lavaplatos.

▶ The **gerundio** is formed by adding these endings to the verb stem:

Verbs ending in -ar	Add -ando. lavar ⟶ lavando
Verbs ending in -er and -ir	Add -iendo. hacer ⟶ haciendo sacudir ⟶ sacudiendo

El gerundio (pág. 90)

decir ⟶ diciendo
mentir ⟶ mintiendo
pedir ⟶ pidiendo
preferir ⟶ prefiriendo
sentir ⟶ sintiendo
servir ⟶ sirviendo
dormir ⟶ durmiendo
morir ⟶ muriendo
creer ⟶ creyendo
leer ⟶ leyendo
oír ⟶ oyendo

Los pronombres de objeto directo (pág. 98)

Singular		Plural	
me	*me*	nos	*us*
te	*you (inf.)*	os	*you (inf.)*
lo	*you (formal), him, it*	los	*you, them*
la	*you (formal), her, it*	las	*you, them*

Los pronombres de objeto indirecto (pág. 106)

Singular		Plural	
me	*to/for me*	nos	*to/for us*
te	*to/for you (inf.)*	os	*to/for you (inf.)*
le	*to/for you (formal), him, her*	les	*to/for you, them*

Le and les become se when placed in front of a direct object pronoun.

Le compro un libro. ⟶ Se lo compro.

Los demostrativos (pág. 114)

| Distance from speaker | SINGULAR | | | PLURAL | |
	Masculino	Femenino	Neutro	Masculino	Femenino
Near	este	esta	esto	estos	estas
At a distance	ese	esa	eso	esos	esas
Far away	aquel	aquella	aquello	aquellos	aquellas

Differentiated Instruction

DEVELOPING LEARNERS

- Some students may have trouble locating the direct object of a sentence. Before they attempt to complete activity 6, have them analyze what or whom is the object of conversation in each dialogue. For instance, in the first case, Luis is talking about his *carpetas*, or folders. Ask students to point to the direct object in each sentence and then determine whether it is singular or plural, feminine or masculine. Students can then choose the appropriate direct object pronoun to complete the dialogue.

EXPANDING LEARNERS

- Have students complete the following dialogues with the appropriate question or answer. Ask students to use these words: *novia, mesero, hermanita.*
  A. ¿A quién le vas a regalar esas flores?
  B. … (*Se las voy a regalar a mi novia.*)
  A. … (*¿A quién le vas a pedir la sal?*)
  B. Se la voy a pedir al mesero.
  A. ¿A quién le vas a leer este cuento?
  B. … (*Se lo voy a leer a mi hermanita.*)

DESAFÍO 1

5 **¿Qué están haciendo?** Completa estas oraciones con una forma del presente continuo. Usa los verbos de la caja.

> leer
> cocinar
> planchar
> servir

1. Paloma _____ arroz y pescado para el almuerzo.
2. Susana _____ su vestido rojo para la fiesta.
3. Mariela y yo _____ una revista.
4. Tú _____ la cena en el comedor.

DESAFÍO 2

6 **Un poco de orden.** Completa con pronombres de objeto directo.

1. LUIS: No encuentro mis carpetas.
   BEATRIZ: ¡_____ tienes ahí!

2. LUIS: ¿Me das un lápiz?
   BEATRIZ: Sí, te _____ doy.

3. LUIS: No veo mi cuaderno de Español.
   BEATRIZ: Siempre _____ pierdes.

4. BEATRIZ: Mamá nos está llamando.
   LUIS: Sí, _____ escucho. ¡Ya estoy listo!

DESAFÍO 3

7 **¿A quién?** Decide a qué persona se refiere cada oración.

1. ¿Me preparas un sándwich?
2. Voy a ayudarte con las tareas.
3. Les compro un CD de música.
4. Le doy un vaso de agua.

> a ti   a ellas   a mí   a ella

DESAFÍO 4

8 **En la plaza.** Une las dos columnas.

Ⓐ

1. Yo vivo en esa calle.
2. Mis padres están en aquel restaurante.
3. Voy a beber algo en este café.
4. ¿Vamos a estudiar a aquella biblioteca?
5. Mi padre trabaja en ese banco.

Ⓑ

AQUÍ

AHÍ

ALLÍ

 CULTURA

9 **En las islas del Caribe.** Responde.

1. ¿Qué ciudad ocupó Francis Drake?
2. ¿Qué ciudades del Caribe conoces?
3. ¿Por qué el Caribe es un importante destino turístico?

ciento veintinueve **129**

---

8. Have students work with a partner to create a short dialogue in which they use direct and indirect object pronouns. They should use one of the sentences from this activity as the starting point for their dialogue. Invite pairs to act out their dialogue in front of the class. For example:
A. *¿Vamos a estudiar a aquella biblioteca?*
B. *No tengo los libros.*
A. *Yo los tengo.*
B. *Pero no tengo tiempo. Le tengo que comprar un regalo a mi novia.*

9. Once students have answered these questions, ask them what their main reason for visiting the Caribbean would be. Invite students to share their answer with the class and tally their responses. What is the top reason for visiting the Caribbean?

Answer Key

5. 1. está cocinando   3. estamos leyendo
    2. está planchando   4. estás sirviendo

6. 1. Las   3. lo
    2. lo   4. la

7. 1. a mí   3. a ellas
    2. a ti   4. a ella

8. 1. ahí   4. allí
    2. allí   5. ahí
    3. aquí

9. 1. La ciudad de Santo Domingo, en la República Dominicana.
    2. Answers will vary.
    3. El Caribe es un importante destino turístico por sus playas, su historia y la arquitectura colonial de sus ciudades.

Additional Resources

Fans Online activities
Practice Workbook

HERITAGE LANGUAGE LEARNERS

- Explain to students that lack of number agreement between the indirect object pronoun and the indirect object is a common error Spanish speakers make. For example, many people would say *Nunca le pido dinero a mis amigos*. However, the indirect object in this case is plural (i.e., *a mis amigos*), so the indirect object pronoun should also be plural (i.e., *les*).

- Ask students to correct the following sentences.
  – *Andrés siempre le pide a sus padres dinero para salir.*
  – *Siempre le digo la verdad a mis amigas.*
  – *El mesero le sirve la comida a los clientes.*

CRITICAL THINKING

- Explain to students that when two or more items are in a series we use only one demonstrative adjective in English (e.g., Helen is buying those pants and shirts). However, in Spanish, demonstrative adjectives must be repeated before each noun they modify (e.g., *Helen está comprando esos pantalones y esas camisas*). Ask students to think about why this might be the case in Spanish.

129

Unit 2

PROYECTO

Santo Domingo

Presentation

- In this section, students will apply the vocabulary, grammar, and cultural information they have learned in this unit to create a board game based on the city of Santo Domingo in the Dominican Republic. Students will follow step-by-step instructions.

Activities	Standards	Resources
Paso 1	2.2, 3.1	
Paso 2	1.3	
Paso 3	1.1, 3.1	
Paso 4	1.1, 1.2, 1.3, 5.2	

Teaching Suggestions

Warm-Up / Independent Starter

- Have students take a few minutes to review the cultural information learned in this unit as well as the vocabulary and grammar structures studied. Then have them read the project instructions silently.

Preparation

- Ask students to brainstorm all they know about the city of Santo Domingo. Explain that the colonial zone of Santo Domingo was declared a World Heritage Site by UNESCO in 1990. It was the first Spanish colonial city in the New World and it served as a model for the development of other Spanish cities in the Americas.

Step-by-Step Instructions

Paso 1

- Discuss with students the importance of using reliable sources of information. Dependable sources on the Internet include government sites (ending in .gov), education sites (ending in .edu), and international organizations (e.g., UNESCO, World Wildlife Fund, United Nations, etc.) whose addresses end in .org. There are also reputable online journals and newspapers that publish reliable information.

- For this particular section of their project, students will find a list of monuments, information, photos, and maps of Santo Domingo's colonial zone at: http://rsta.pucmm.edu.do/ciudad_colonial/monumentos1.htm.

Un juego en las calles de

Santo Domingo

In this project you will create a board game set in Santo Domingo, Dominican Republic. You will use images of this city and create cards and rules for your board game.

PASO 1 Localiza imágenes de Santo Domingo

- Get pictures on the Internet of houses, streets and neighborhoods in Santo Domingo. These are some ideas for your search:
  - Zona colonial de Santo Domingo.
  - Casas típicas de Santo Domingo.
  - Monumentos de Santo Domingo.
  - Plano de Santo Domingo.

- Save your favorite images; they will serve as the background for your board.

Rubric for Evaluation

	Content	Organization	Presentation
1 point	Some incorrect information. Questions are not well formulated and not leveled correctly. Little Spanish is used.	Inefficient use of class time. Information is disorganized or unclear.	Communication is unclear. Delivery is not fluent. Many errors in vocabulary and grammar. Many incorrect answers.
3 points	Information is correct. Questions are mostly well formulated and leveled. Spanish is used most of the time.	Class time is used well. Information and content are mostly organized but lack some clarity.	Good communication. Fluent delivery. Mostly correct vocabulary and grammar. Mostly correct answers.

PASO 2 Prepara las fichas y las instrucciones

- Write questions on twelve cards about the culture, the vocabulary, and the grammar that you learned in this unit. Write the question and the correct answer. Try to prepare four easy questions, four average questions and four difficult questions.
- On each card, write the number of squares that the player gets to advance if they get the answer right, using this scale:
  - Preguntas fáciles: 1 casilla
  - Preguntas normales: 3 casillas
  - Preguntas difíciles: 5 casillas

Pregunta: ¿Para qué sirve la lavadora?

Respuesta: Para lavar la ropa.

Avanza 3 casillas.

PASO 3 Diseña el tablero

- With your group, glue your favorite images of Santo Domingo on a large poster board (tabloid size or larger) in order to make the background for your board.
- With your group, design a path with fifty spaces over the images for people to move around on your board. Decide where the start and the finish lines are. You may include shortcuts and obstacles.

PASO 4 Junta las cartas con las de tus compañeros(as) y... ¡a jugar!

- Game rules: place all cards face down in a deck. One player takes a card and reads the question to the next player to the left. If the answer is not correct, the player has to go back one space. Take turns.
- Put the cards back into the deck because you will use them until one player arrives at the finish line.

Unidad 2

Autoevaluación

¿Qué has aprendido en esta unidad?

Complete these activities to evaluate how well you can communicate in Spanish.

Evaluate your skills. For each item, say Very well, Well, or I need more practice.

a. Can you express present activity in a home?
  ▶ Tell a classmate what chores you do at home and where in the home you do them.
  ▶ Tell the same classmate what your family members are doing while you are doing your chores.

b. Can you identify and describe rooms and furniture?
  ▶ Draw and label the furniture and the accessories in your room.
  ▶ Ask and answer questions about the things in your room.

c. Can you talk about household appliances and accessories?
  ▶ Tell a classmate what appliances you have in each room of your house and say for whom each appliance was purchased.

d. Can you describe a neighborhood?
  ▶ Take your classmate on a blind tour of your neighborhood. Have him or her close their eyes as you describe your neighborhood.

PROYECTO

Santo Domingo

Paso 2

- The *Repaso de vocabulario* section is a good source for the vocabulary questions. The *Mapa cultural* and the *Cultura* boxes are good sources for the culture questions. Explain to students that their questions should be about information learned in this unit. They cannot expect their classmates to know additional vocabulary or cultural information. Remind students to check their cards for clarity and grammar accuracy.

Paso 3

- Explain that this part of the project is to be done together with their group. They look at the images their group members selected in *Paso 1* and decide, as a group, which images they will include on the board. Ask them to add a brief photo caption identifying each image they will use.

Paso 4

- As students play, ask them to speak exclusively in Spanish and to do so clearly and slowly.

Evaluation

- Distribute copies of the rubric to students. Discuss the evaluation criteria and explain how this project will be graded. Encourage students to refer to the rubric as they prepare their projects.

Content

- Explain the importance of leveling their questions. If they are unsure about the level of difficulty of some of their questions, they may consult with a classmate from a different group to see what he or she thinks.
- To develop research skills, ask students to include a list of sources for the images they used on their board.

Organization

- Students should make sure that they are not repeating a question or asking twice about a particular piece of information. Their questions should be well balanced and reflect the unit's vocabulary and cultural content.

Presentation

- Students should speak exclusively in Spanish and do so clearly and slowly so that their classmates can understand the questions.

	Content	Organization	Presentation
5 points	Relevant, interesting, and correct information. Questions are well formulated and leveled appropriately. Spanish is used exclusively.	Class time is used wisely. Information and content are clearly organized.	Clear communication and fluent delivery. Correct and complete vocabulary and grammar. Correct answers.

Objectives

- To talk about past actions.
- To describe clothes.
- To talk about places in the community.
- To talk about past shopping experiences.
- To use expressions that ask about and express knowledge of a fact, expressions that express the order of actions, and expressions to wish somebody luck.
- To list articles of clothing and accessories.

- To list stores and businesses.
- To explore cultural aspects of the Andean region.
- To acquire facts about the geography and history of the countries in the Andean region.

Contents

Vocabulary

- Clothing and accessories.
- Fabric and fit.
- Colors and patterns.
- Stores and businesses.
- Shopping.
- Expressions used to ask about and to express knowledge of a fact.
- Expressions used to express the order of actions.
- Expressions to wish somebody luck.

Grammar

- Regular *-ar* verbs in the preterite tense.
- Regular *-er* and *-ir* verbs in the preterite tense.
- Irregular verbs *ser*, *ir*, *decir*, *tener*, *estar*, and *hacer* in the preterite tense.
- Irregular stem-changing *-ir* verbs in the preterite tense.

Culture

- *La Avenida de los volcanes.*
- Traditional clothing and textiles from the Andes
- *Huancavelica.*
- *Los camélidos andinos.*
- *El carnaval de Oruro.*
- *El aguayo, un textil tradicional.*
- *El mal de altura.*
- *Potosí.*
- *Los mercadillos.*
- *Vale un potosí.*
- The Andean region.

Evaluation Criteria

- Use an expression that asks about a fact.
- Use expressions that put actions in order.
- Use an expression to wish someone luck.
- Describe various articles of clothing and accessories.
- Describe the pattern, fit, and color of clothing and accessories.
- List stores and businesses.
- Talk about shopping experiences.

- Recognize and use regular *-ar* verbs in the preterite tense.
- Recognize and use regular *-er* and *-ir* verbs in the preterite tense.
- Recognize and use irregular verbs *ser*, *ir*, *decir*, *tener*, *estar*, and *hacer* in the preterite tense.
- Recognize and use stem-changing *-ir* verbs in the preterite tense.

- Express understanding of selected Andean region customs, geography, and historical facts.
- Express understanding of the role of textiles in the Andean region.
- Make inferences in a text.
- Develop and illustrate a spread in a fashion magazine.

Unit Plan

La llegada

Estimated time: 1 session.

Dialogue: *En Guayaquil.*

Functions & forms:
- Expressions used to ask about and to express knowledge of a fact.
- To express the order of actions.
- To wish somebody luck.

Culture:
- The Malecón of Guayaquil, Ecuador.

DESAFÍO 1

Estimated time: 4 sessions.

Dialogue: *Un sorbete de volcán.*

Functions & forms:
- Clothing and accessories.
- Preterite tense of regular *-ar* verbs.

Culture:
- *La Avenida de los volcanes.*
- *La ropa tradicional andina.*

DESAFÍO 2

Estimated time: 4 sessions.

Dialogue: *Una carrera de llamas.*

Functions & forms:
- Descriptions of clothing.
- Preterite tense of regular *-er* and *-ir* verbs.

Culture:
- *Huancavelica.*
- *Los camélidos andinos.*

DESAFÍO 3

Estimated time: 4 sessions.

Dialogue: *El carnaval de Oruro.*

Functions & forms:
- Stores and businesses.
- Preterite tense of the irregular verbs *ser, ir, decir, tener, estar,* and *hacer.*

Culture:
- *El carnaval de Oruro.*
- *El aguayo, un textil tradicional.*
- *El mal de altura.*

DESAFÍO 4

Estimated time: 4 sessions.

Dialogue: *La montaña de plata.*

Functions & forms:
- Shopping.
- Preterite tense of irregular *-ir* verbs.

Culture:
- *Potosí.*
- *Los mercadillos.*
- *Vale un potosí.*

TODO JUNTO/**El encuentro**

Estimated time: 1 session.

Dialogue: *En la avenida Olmedo de Guayaquil.*

Functions & forms:
- Review of *Desafíos 1–4.*

Culture:
- The *avenida Olmedo* in *Guayaquil,* Ecuador.

MAPA CULTURAL/LECTURA

Estimated time: 1 session.

Mapa cultural: *Andes centrales.*

Reading: *Textiles andinos bolivianos.*

PROYECTO

Estimated time: 1 session.

Project: *Una revista sobre moda andina.*

Standards for Learning Spanish

COMMUNICATION

1.1. Interpersonal mode
- Discuss the challenge for each pair in the Andean Region.
- Discuss what students know about the Andean Region.
- Speculate on which pair will win the challenge.
- Discuss how global warming affects the people of the Andean Region.
- Interview a classmate.
- Play a guessing game.
- Survey the class on a question.

1.2. Interpretive mode
- Take notes from an oral text.
- Read a cultural text.

- Summarize information in a written text.
- Research cultural topics.
- Read about the inhabitants of the Andes on the Internet.

1.3. Presentational mode
- Write a description of an original costume.
- Write captions for photographs.
- Write a page of a diary.
- Write the ending to a story.
- Write a conversation.
- Develop interview questions.

CULTURE

2.1. Practices and perspectives
- Discuss prior knowledge of the Andean Region.
- Discuss the impact of global warming on the Andes.
- Read about the role of the *mercadillos*.
- Read about the *carnaval de Oruro*.

2.2. Products and perspectives
- Read about the fleece-producing animals of the Andean Region.
- Research Andean fashion.
- Read about colonial era churches.
- Discover and understand the importance of geography of the Andes region for its inhabitants.

 CONNECTIONS

3.1. Interdisciplinary connections
- Acquire knowledge of Andean geography.
- Research altitude sickness.
- Research colonial buildings in the area.
- Read about two camel-like animals from the Andes.
- Discuss verb endings in English and in Spanish.
- Make inferences about certain words in a text.

3.2. Viewpoints through language / culture
- Read a picture story in Spanish.
- Read a cultural text in Spanish.
- Read about Andean culture on the Internet.
- Read an informational text.
- Read a recipe.

COMPARISONS

4.1. Compare languages
- Compare the irregular verbs in English and in Spanish.

4.2. Compare cultures
- Compare festivals like a carnival in the Andean region and in other countries.
- Compare clothing items in the Andean region and in other countries.
- Discuss clothing choices due to the climate.
- Compare mineral zones and resources in Bolivia and in the United States.
- Compare the preservation of the colonial past.
- Compare traditional markets from the Hispanic world with flea markets and outlet shops in the United States.
- Compare landlocked states and countries.

COMMUNITIES

5.1. Spanish within and beyond the school setting
- Discuss the impact of global warming.
- Discuss the vestiges of colonialism in the student's community.
- Discuss celebrations in the student's community where costumes are featured.

5.2. Spanish for lifelong learning
- Play a guessing game.
- Design a magazine story on Andean fashion.
- Research traditional costumes from the Andes and prepare a visual presentation.

Communicative Skills

Interpersonal Mode

Mode		Activities
Speaking	• Engage in conversation with a classmate. • Describe clothing. • Initiate a guessing game with another student. • Talk to a classmate about your likes. • Participate in a guided conversation with a classmate.	• 4, 13, 18, 21, 52, 64, 73, 76, 77 • 29, 77 • 30 • 13, 76 • 35, 39, 46, 67, 77
Writing	• Write a narrative summary. • Make a list. • Take notes on the pertinent information in a text. • Write dialogues.	• 18 • 20 • 73 • 71, 78
Listening	• Understand verbal questions and respond appropriately. • Infer meaning from an oral description.	• *Minientrevistas* • 12, 17, 20, 27, 34, 42, 63
Reading	• Understand the information in a blog, a diary entry, an e-mail, or an Instant Messenger conversation.	• 19, 25, 54, 71

Interpretive Mode

Mode		Activities
Listening	• Understand and obtain basic information from a conversation. • Understand oral descriptions or narratives. • Interpret audio and video about culture.	• 12, 17, 42, 51, 60, 78 • 27, 28, 36 • *Tu desafío, videos*
Reading	• Understand brief written exchanges. • Infer meanings based on a cultural text. • Demonstrate an understanding of the factual information in a text. • Comprehend a cultural text by making inferences. • Reflect on and explain cultural topics in relation to personal experience.	• 6, 23, 40, 74 • 9, 14, 26, 31, 43, 47, 53, 61 • 9, 53 • *Lectura* • 4, 14, 26, 31, 43, 47, 53, 61, 65

Presentational Mode

Mode		Activities
Speaking	• Act out a short skit aloud.	• 74, 78, *Proyecto*
Writing	• Write a summary of events or a narrative text. • Write a description. • Write a diary entry. • Summarize information. • Write a skit.	• 3, 8, 17, 19, 36, 72 • 30, 38, 77 • 25, 55, 79 • 73 • 74

Cross-Curricular Standards

Subject	Standard	Activities
Language Arts	• Compare elements of English grammar with Spanish equivalents. • Compare idiomatic expressions in English and Spanish.	• 48, 66 • 70
World History	• Read about a colonial Peruvian town.	• 26
Geography	• Read about the tallest volcano in Ecuador.	• 9
Science	• Read about camel-like animals from the Andes. • Read about "altitude sickness."	• 31 • 53

Unit 3 Andes centrales

Lesson Plans (50-Minute Classes)

Day	Objectives	Sessions	Activities	Time	Standards	Resources / Homework
1	To introduce the Andes region and to discuss the pairs' challenges	**Andes centrales / La llegada** (132–137) • Warm-Up: Region orientation • *Andes centrales* • Images and functions • Presentation: *En Guayaquil* • *Expresiones útiles* and *¿Quién ganará?*	 1 2–5	 5 m. 5 m. 10 m. 10 m. 20 m.	1.1, 1.2, 1.3, 2.1, 2.2, 4.1	Visual Presentation Video Practice Workbook
2	To talk about past actions	**Desafío 1 – Un sorbete de volcán** (138–139) • Warm-Up: Independent Starter • *Fotonovela: Un sorbete de volcán* • *Cultura: La Avenida de los volcanes*	 6–8 9	 5 m. 35 m. 10 m.	1.1, 1.2, 1.3, 2.1, 2.2, 3.1, 3.2, 5.1	Visual Presentation Video *Tu desafío*
3	To talk about clothing and accessories	**Desafío 1 – Vocabulario** (140–141) • Warm-Up: Independent Starter • Vocabulary: *La ropa y los complementos* • *Comparaciones: La ropa tradicional andina*	 10–13 14	 5 m. 35 m. 10 m.	1.1, 1.2, 1.3, 2.1, 2.2, 3.1, 3.2, 5.1	Audio Practice Workbook *Tu desafío*
4	To learn and use regular -ar verbs in the preterite tense	**Desafío 1 – Gramática** (142–143) • Warm-Up: Independent Starter • Grammar: *Verbos regulares en '-ar'. Pretérito*	 15–18	 5 m. 45 m.	1.1, 1.2, 1.3, 3.1, 4.1	Audio Practice Workbook
5	To integrate vocabulary and grammar and to assess student proficiency	**Desafío 1 – Comunicación / Evaluación** (144–145) • Warm-Up: Independent Starter • *Comunicación:* Review • *Final del desafío* • Quiz on *Desafío 1*	 19–21 22	 5 m. 20 m. 10 m. 15 m.	1.1, 1.2, 1.3, 2.1. 2.2	Audio Practice Workbook
6	To describe clothing	**Desafío 2 – Una carrera de llamas** (146–147) • Warm-Up: Independent Starter • *Fotonovela: Una carrera de llamas* • *Cultura: Huancavelica*	 23–25 26	 5 m. 35 m. 10 m.	1.1, 1.2, 1.3, 2.1, 2.2, 3.1, 3.2, 4.2, 5.1	Visual Presentation *Tu desafío*
7	To describe clothing	**Desafío 2 – Vocabulario** (148–149) • Warm-Up: Independent Starter • Vocabulary: *Describir la ropa* • *Conexiones: Los camélidos andinos*	 27–30 31	 5 m. 35 m. 10 m.	1.1, 1.2, 1.3, 2.2, 3.1, 3.2, 4.2, 5.1	Audio Practice Workbook
8	To learn and use regular -er and -ir verbs in the preterite tense	**Desafío 2 – Gramática** (150–151) • Warm-Up: Independent Starter • Grammar: *Verbos regulares en '-er' y en '-ir'. Pretérito*	 32–35	 5 m. 45 m.	1.1, 1.2, 1.3, 3.1, 4.1	Audio Practice Workbook
9	To integrate vocabulary and grammar and to assess student proficiency	**Desafío 2 – Comunicación / Evaluación** (152–153) • Warm-Up: Independent Starter • *Comunicación:* Review • *Final del desafío* • Quiz on *Desafío 2*	 36–38 39	 5 m. 20 m. 10 m. 15 m.	1.1, 1.2, 1.3, 2.1, 5.2	Audio Practice Workbook *Tu desafío*
10	To talk about places in the community	**Desafío 3 – El carnaval de Oruro** (154–155) • Warm-Up: Independent Starter • *Fotonovela: El carnaval de Oruro* • *Cultura: El carnaval de Oruro*	 40–42 43	 5 m. 35 m. 10 m.	1.1, 1.2, 1.3, 2.1, 3.2, 4.2, 5.1, 5.2	Visual Presentation Audio Video *Tu desafío*

Day	Objectives	Sessions	Activities	Time	Standards	Resources / Homework
11	To talk about stores and commercial establishments	**Desafío 3 – Vocabulario** (156–157) • Warm-Up: Independent Starter • Vocabulary: *Tiendas y establecimientos* • *Comparaciones: El aguayo, un textil tradicional*	 44–46 47	5 m. 35 m. 10 m.	1.1, 1.2, 1.3, 2.2, 3.2, 4.2, 5.1	Audio Practice Workbook
12	To learn and use verbs *ser, ir, decir, tener, estar,* and *hacer* in the preterite tense	**Desafío 3 – Gramática** (158–159) • Warm-Up: Independent Starter • Grammar: *Verbos irregulares en el pretérito. 'Ser', 'ir', 'decir', 'tener', 'estar' y 'hacer'* • *Conexiones: El mal de altura*	 48–52 53	5 m. 35 m. 10 m.	1.1, 1.2, 1.3, 3.1, 4.1, 5.1	Audio Practice Workbook
13	To integrate vocabulary and grammar and to assess student proficiency	**Desafío 3 – Comunicación / Evaluación** (160–161) • Warm-Up: Independent Starter • *Comunicación:* Review • *Final del desafío* • Quiz on *Desafío 3*	 54–56 57	5 m. 20 m. 10 m. 15 m.	1.2, 1.3, 5.1	Audio Practice Workbook
14	To talk about past shopping experiences	**Desafío 4 – La montaña de plata** (162–163) • Warm-Up: Independent Starter • *Fotonovela: La montaña de plata* • *Cultura: Potosí*	 58–60 61	5 m. 35 m. 10 m.	1.1, 1.2, 1.3, 2.2, 3.1, 3.2, 4.2, 5.1	Visual Presentation Audio
15	To talk about shopping	**Desafío 4 – Vocabulario** (164–165) • Warm-Up: Independent Starter • Vocabulary: *Las compras* • *Comunidades: Los mercadillos*	 62–64 65	5 m. 35 m. 10 m.	1.1, 1.2, 1.3, 2.1, 3.2, 4.2, 5.1	Audio Practice Workbook
16	To learn and use irregular stem-changing -ir verbs in the preterite tense	**Desafío 4 – Gramática** (166–167) • Warm-Up: Independent Starter • Grammar: *Verbos en '-ir' con raíz irregular en el pretérito* • *Conexiones: Vale un potosí*	 66–69 70	5 m. 35 m. 10 m.	1.1, 1.2, 1.3, 2.2, 3.1, 3.2, 4.1, 5.1	Audio Practice Workbook
17	To integrate vocabulary and grammar and to assess student proficiency	**Desafío 4 – Comunicación / Evaluación** (168–169) • Warm-Up: Independent Starter • *Comunicación:* Review • *Final del desafío* • Quiz on *Desafío 4*	 71–73 74	5 m. 20 m. 10 m. 15 m.	1.1, 1.2, 1.3, 2.2, 5.1	Audio Practice Workbook *Tu desafío*
18	To integrate language in context	**Todo junto / El encuentro** (170–173) • Warm-Up: Independent Starter • *Todo junto* • *El encuentro: En la avenida Olmedo de Guayaquil*	 75–77 78–79	5 m. 20 m. 25 m.	1.1,1.2, 1.3, 2.1, 2.2, 3,1 4.2, 5.1, 5.2	Audio Practice Workbook
19	To learn about the Andes region, customs, and traditions	**Mapa cultural / Lectura** (174–177) • Warm-Up: Independent Starter • *Mapa cultural: Andes centrales* • *Lectura: Textiles andinos bolivianos*	 80–81 82–84	5 m. 20 m. 25 m.	1.1, 1.2, 1.3, 2.1, 2.2, 3.1, 3.2, 4.2, 5.2	Video Practice Workbook *Tu desafío* Project work
20	To develop and illustrate a spread in a fashion magazine	**Proyecto** (182–183) • Warm-Up: Prepare project presentations • Project presentations		10 m. 40 m.	1.1, 1.2, 1.3, 2.2, 3.1, 5.2	Practice Workbook **Repaso – Vocabulario** (178–179) **Repaso – Gramática** (180–181) **Autoevaluación** (183)

Lesson Plans (90-Minute Classes)

Day	Objectives	Sessions	Activities	Time	Standards	Resources / Homework
1	To introduce the Andes region and to discuss the pairs' challenges	***Andes centrales / La llegada*** (132–137) • Warm-Up: Region orientation • *Andes centrales* / Images and functions • Presentation: *En Guayaquil* • *Expresiones útiles* and *¿Quién ganará?*	 1 2–5	 10 m. 15 m. 30 m. 35 m.	1.1, 1.2, 1.3, 2.1, 2.2, 4.1	Visual Presentation Video Practice Workbook
2	To talk about clothing and accessories	***Desafío 1 – Un sorbete de volcán / Vocabulario*** (138–141) • Warm-Up: Independent Starter • *Fotonovela: Un sorbete de volcán* • *Cultura: La Avenida de los volcanes* • Vocabulary: *La ropa y los complementos* • *Comparaciones: La ropa tradicional andina*	 6–8 9 10–13 14	 5 m. 30 m. 10 m. 35 m. 10 m.	1.1, 1.2, 1.3, 2.1, 2.2, 3.1, 3.2, 5.1	Visual Presentation Audio Video Practice Workbook *Tu desafío*
3	To learn and use regular -ar verbs in the preterite tense, to integrate vocabulary and grammar, and to assess student proficiency	***Desafío 1 – Gramática / Comunicación / Evaluación*** (142–145) • Warm-Up: Independent Starter • Grammar: *Verbos regulares en '-ar'. Pretérito* • *Comunicación:* Review • *Final del desafío* • Quiz on *Desafío 1*	 15–18 19–21 22	 5 m. 30 m. 30 m. 10 m. 15 m.	1.1, 1.2, 1.3, 2.1, 2.2, 3.1, 4.1	Audio Practice Workbook
4	To describe clothing	***Desafío 2 – Una carrera de llamas / Vocabulario*** (146–149) • Warm-Up: Independent Starter • *Fotonovela: Una carrera de llamas* • *Cultura: Huancavelica* • Vocabulary: *Describir la ropa* • *Conexiones: Los camélidos andinos*	 23–25 26 27–30 31	 5 m. 30 m. 10 m. 35 m. 10 m.	1.1, 1.2, 1.3, 2.1, 2.2, 3.1, 3.2, 4.2, 5.1	Visual Presentation Audio Practice Workbook *Tu desafío*
5	To learn and use regular -er and -ir verbs in the preterite tense, to integrate vocabulary and grammar, and to assess student proficiency	***Desafío 2 – Gramática / Comunicación / Evaluación*** (150–153) • Warm-Up: Independent Starter • Grammar: *Verbos regulares en '-er' y en '-ir'. Pretérito* • *Comunicación:* Review • *Final del desafío* • Quiz on *Desafío 2*	 32–35 36–38 39	 5 m. 30 m. 30 m. 10 m. 15 m.	1.1, 1.2, 1.3, 2.1, 3.1, 4.1, 5.2	Audio Practice Workbook *Tu desafío*
6	To talk about places in the community and to talk about stores and commercial establishments	***Desafío 3 – El carnaval de Oruro / Vocabulario*** (154–157) • Warm-Up: Independent Starter • *Fotonovela: El carnaval de Oruro* • *Cultura: El carnaval de Oruro* • Vocabulary: *Tiendas y establecimientos* • *Comparaciones: El aguayo, un textil tradicional*	 40–42 43 44–46 47	 5 m. 35 m. 10 m. 30 m. 10 m.	1.1, 1.2, 1.3, 2.1, 2.2, 3.2, 4.2, 5.1	Visual Presentation Audio Video Practice Workbook *Tu desafío*

Day	Objectives	Sessions	Activities	Time	Standards	Resources / Homework
7	To learn and use verbs *ser, ir, decir, tener, estar,* and *hacer* in the preterite tense, to integrate vocabulary and grammar, and to assess student proficiency	**Desafío 3 – Gramática / Comunicación / Evaluación** (158–161) • Warm-Up: Independent Starter • Grammar: *Verbos irregulares en el pretérito. 'Ser', 'ir', 'decir', 'tener', 'estar' y 'hacer'* • *Conexiones: El mal de altura* • *Comunicación:* Review • *Final del desafío* • Quiz on *Desafío 3*	 48–52 53 54–56 57	 5 m. 25 m. 10 m. 25 m. 10 m. 15 m.	1.1, 1.2, 1.3, 3.1, 4.1, 5.1	Audio Practice Workbook
8	To talk about past shopping experiences and to talk about shopping	**Desafío 4 – La montaña de plata / Vocabulario** (162–165) • Warm-Up: Independent Starter • *Fotonovela: La montaña de plata* • *Cultura: Potosí* • Vocabulary: *Las compras* • *Comunidades: Los mercadillos*	 58–60 61 62–64 65	 5 m. 35 m. 10 m. 30 m. 10 m.	1.1, 1.2, 1.3, 2.1, 2.2, 3.1, 3.2, 4.2, 5.1	Visual Presentation Audio Practice Workbook
9	To learn and use irregular stem-changing *-ir* verbs in the preterite tense, to integrate vocabulary and grammar, and to assess student proficiency	**Desafío 4 – Gramática / Comunicación / Evaluación / Todo junto** (166–171) • Warm-Up: Independent Starter • Grammar: *Verbos en '-ir' con raíz irregular en el pretérito* • *Conexiones: Vale un potosí* • *Comunicación:* Review • *Final del desafío* • Quiz on *Desafío 4* • *Todo junto*	 66–69 70 71–73 74 75–77	 5 m. 20 m. 5 m. 20 m. 5 m. 15 m. 20 m.	1.1, 1.2, 1.3, 2.1, 2.2, 4.1, 5.1	Audio Practice Workbook *Tu desafío*
10	To integrate language in context and to learn about Andean region customs and traditions	**El encuentro / Mapa cultural / Lectura** (172–177) • Warm-Up: Independent Starter • *El encuentro: En la avenida Olmedo de Guayaquil* • *Mapa cultural: Andes centrales* • *Lectura: Textiles andinos bolivianos*	 78–79 80–81 82–84	 5 m. 30 m. 25 m. 30 m.	1.1, 1.2, 1.3, 2.1, 2.2, 3.1, 3.2, 4.2, 5.1, 5.2	Video Practice Workbook *Tu desafío* **Repaso – Vocabulario** (178–179) **Repaso – Gramática** (180–181) Project work
11	To develop and illustrate a spread in a fashion magazine and to assess student proficiency	**Proyecto / Assessment** (182–183) • Warm-Up: Prepare project presentations • Project presentations • *Autoevaluación* (183) • Test		10 m. 40 m. 10 m. 30 m.	1.1, 1.2, 1.3, 2.2, 3.1, 5.2	

12 Una cena elegante

–¡Hola, tía! ¿Qué tal estás?

–¡Hola, Janet! Estoy bien. Me estoy preparando para esta noche.

–¿Adónde vas?

–Tu tío y yo vamos a cenar en un restaurante muy elegante. Hoy es nuestro aniversario.

–¡Qué emocionante! ¡Feliz aniversario! ¿Y qué vas a llevar?

–Una falda y una blusa. También unos aretes y un collar. Ah, y unos zapatos nuevos. Son muy bonitos.

–¿Y mi tío?

–Él se va a poner su traje favorito y una corbata azul. Y también un abrigo y un reloj nuevo.

–¿Y mi prima? ¿Qué hace?

–Tu prima está lista para dormir. Ahora mismo lleva el pijama y unas zapatillas. Janet, tengo que dejarte. Tu tío está impaciente.

–Hasta luego. ¡Diviértanse!

–¡Dale un beso a Andy! ¡Hasta luego!

17 Actividades

–Oye, Janet, ¿revisamos nuestra lista de tareas?

–Sí, a ver... Anteayer llegamos a Riobamba y buscamos un hotel.

–Sí.

–Tú hablaste con mamá y papá ayer, ¿cierto?

–Sí, los llamé por la noche. Están bien.

–Yo compré un impermeable.

–Sí, y yo preparé la mochila para el camino.

–Y los dos practicamos deporte para estar en forma. ¡Este desafío no va a ser fácil! ¿Ya caminaste por las montañas alguna vez?

–No... ¿y tú?

–No, yo tampoco. ¡Tenemos que entrenar más!

19 El blog de Janet

1. Janet y yo llegamos ayer a Riobamba.
2. Los dos nos preparamos para nuestro desafío.
3. Janet habló mucho con el guía.
4. El guía nos explicó muy poco de la geografía de la región.
5. El guía nos buscó ropa de abrigo porque en las montañas hace mucho frío.
6. Janet lo pasó muy bien en Ecuador.

20 ¿Qué anuncian?

Disfrute de nuestros precios especiales esta semana. En la planta baja, en la sección de complementos, pueden encontrar grandes ofertas en bolsos. En la primera planta hay descuentos en todo tipo de ropa de señora: vestidos, faldas, blusas... Y en la segunda planta hay trajes de caballero en oferta.

27 Los regalos

Ya tengo algunos regalos para guardar en la maleta. Vamos a ver... Para mi mamá compré un gorro de lana de color gris. Para mi mejor amiga compré un suéter de rayas de muchos colores. Para mi compañera de trabajo compré un collar dorado y un anillo plateado. Para mi esposo compré una camisa de cuadros de color café. Y para Tess compré una falda de lunares. ¡Cuántos regalos!

28 Las compras

1. Me gustan estas botas azules, pero son muy incómodas.
2. A mí me gustan mucho estas botas, pero me quedan pequeñas. Creo que no son de mi número.
3. Este suéter de rayas me queda muy bien, ¿verdad?
4. Uff, estos pantalones negros de cuero me quedan muy mal, no me gustan nada.
5. ¡Qué bonita es esa falda gris de lana! Me la voy a comprar.

34 Final del día

1. Todos los días paseamos por las calles de Huancavelica.
2. Anoche comimos en un restaurante donde sirven una comida deliciosa.
3. La semana pasada vimos una carrera de llamas. ¡Fue fascinante!
4. Ayer olvidé llamar a Tess y perdimos el autobús para ir a ver unas ruinas.
5. Ahora escribo en mi diario mis impresiones sobre nuestro viaje.
6. El mes pasado Tess y yo decidimos hacer ejercicio con más frecuencia.

36 ¿Qué pasó?

Hola, Tess. Hola, Patricia. ¡Perdónenme! Llego tarde porque tuve un problema. Perdí mis llaves, las del carro y las de mi casa. Las busqué por todas partes, pero no las encontré. Entonces, volví a mi casa para buscar otras llaves. Toqué a la puerta, pero no respondió nadie. Entonces llamé por teléfono a mi esposa, pero tampoco contestó. Salí a la calle de nuevo y escribí un mensaje a mi hija con mi celular. Ella contestó rápido. ¡Menos mal! Me abrió la puerta de casa, yo conseguí mis llaves y salí corriendo para aquí. ¡Qué carrera!

42 ¿Estuviste en el carnaval?

–Rita, ¿es la primera vez que viene al carnaval de Oruro?

–Sí. Y me gusta mucho, es muy interesante.

–Todos los años viene gente de todo el mundo a verlo.

–¿Tú participaste alguna vez en el desfile del carnaval?

–Sí, el año pasado. Fui con un disfraz muy original.

–¡Qué suerte! Yo también quiero participar.

–¿Viste algún desfile?

–Sí, esta mañana estuve en uno con mi sobrina. Hice muchas fotos para mostrárselas a mis amigos.

–¡Qué bien! Yo no fui al desfile porque tuve que trabajar. Oye, ¿y tu sobrina también compró un disfraz?

–No lo sé. Ella fue a una tienda de bisutería a comprar unos complementos y no sé dónde está.

45 Las compras de Rita y Diana

Esta mañana mi tía y yo nos levantamos temprano para empezar nuestra visita a Oruro. A las nueve de la mañana salimos del hotel.

Primero compramos unas revistas en un quiosco. Después fuimos a una tienda de bisutería para comprar unos complementos. Yo me compré unos aretes y un collar. Luego visitamos una tienda de artesanía para comprar recuerdos. Compramos una máscara muy bonita. Y antes de volver al hotel, fuimos a un supermercado para comprar un poco de fruta. Volvimos al hotel a las ocho de la tarde. ¡Qué día tan largo!

51 ¿Recuerdas?

–Diana, estoy escribiendo una carta a casa. ¿Recuerdas qué hicieron todos anteayer?

–Sí, tía. Creo que sí.

–¿Qué hizo Mack?

–Mack fue a cenar a un restaurante.

–¿Y Tim?

–Tim no fue con él. Él fue a una fiesta.

–Y Janet estuvo enferma, ¿no?

–Sí, se sintió mal. Por eso no estuvo con nosotras en la asociación indígena. ¿Te gustó ser trabajadora voluntaria?

–Sí, fue muy interesante. Y me divertí mucho. Oye, ¿y qué hizo Andy?

–Compró ropa de abrigo para él y para Janet.

–¿Ah, sí?

–Sí. Y Tess y Patricia hicieron muchas fotos con su cámara nueva.

–Bueno, pues ya está todo. Voy a escribir la carta.

56 Los lugares de la comunidad

1. Andy estuvo en un quiosco para comprar una revista y unos periódicos.
2. Rita fue a una librería para comprar un libro.
3. Tim fue a una tienda de complementos para comprar unas gafas de sol.
4. Diana visitó una joyería para comprar unos aretes y un collar.
5. Janet fue a un centro comercial para comprarse un suéter de lana y un abrigo de color azul.
6. Mack estuvo en una tienda de artesanía. Compró regalos para su familia.

60 ¿De qué están hablando?

–¿Y cómo es, abuelo?

–Es roja, amarilla y verde. Y tiene un escudo en el centro.

–Ah, ya… Y el escudo tiene una montaña y un pájaro en el centro, ¿cierto?

–Sí, pero no es un simple pájaro, Tim. Es un cóndor, el ave de los Andes.

–Ah. La bandera boliviana es muy original, ¿verdad?

63 ¿Qué pasa en la tienda?

1. Luz va a pagar sus compras en efectivo.
2. En esta tienda no hay descuentos.
3. Puedes comprar un balón de fútbol en esta tienda.
4. Este chico está en la caja porque quiere probarse unos pantalones.

68 La fiesta sorpresa

La fiesta sorpresa para nuestro guía boliviano fue excelente. Todos nuestros amigos ayudaron y salió todo perfecto. Mi abuelo Mack consiguió refrescos y bebidas deliciosas. Tess y Patricia se vistieron con ropa típica de Bolivia. Rita pidió ayuda para preparar la comida… ¡una comida buenísima! Yo serví los postres. Andy y Janet eligieron un regalo para Juan. Y, finalmente, Diana se despidió de todos los invitados.

72 Un mensaje en el contestador

Hola, mamá. El abuelo y yo estamos en Bolivia. Llegamos aquí hace un mes y nos estamos divirtiendo mucho. Hoy tuve tiempo para llamarte porque ayer conseguimos nuestro desafío. Anteayer buscamos y buscamos la moneda, pero no encontramos nada. La encontramos ayer. Mamá, te voy a llevar un regalo genial: un poncho de lana de Bolivia para el invierno. Lo elegí la semana pasada en un mercadillo de artesanía. Hablamos luego. ¡Un beso!

75 ¡Rebajas!

¡Bienvenidos al Centro Comercial Quito! Hoy tenemos grandes rebajas en las secciones de ropa y bisutería. ¡Comprueben los precios! Pantalones de hombre de todas las tallas; faldas de todos los colores; ropa para todos: mujeres, hombres y niños. Además, tenemos fantásticos collares y aretes con importantes descuentos. ¡Aprovechen nuestras rebajas!

78 Recuerdos de Ecuador

–Yo compré unas botas negras muy cómodas. Mira.

–¡Qué bonitas!

–¿Y tú?

–Yo compré un gorro y una bufanda de lana de muchos colores.

–¿Y encontraste regalos originales?

–Sí, miré muchas cosas y al final elegí una muñeca vestida con ropa tradicional andina.

–¡Yo también! ¿Dónde compraste todo eso?

–El gorro y la bufanda en un centro comercial. Y la muñeca en una tienda de artesanía. ¿Y tú?

–Yo compré las botas en una zapatería del centro de Guayaquil. Y la muñeca en un mercado.

–¿Cuánto te costó?

–Tres dólares.

Unit 3
Andes centrales

The Unit

- The themes for Unit 3 are fashion and shopping in the context of the Andes region.
- The pairs meet in Guayaquil, Ecuador, to receive their tasks in the Andes, but first they must find out what José Joaquín Olmedo is wearing.
  - *Desafío 1.* Andy and Janet will travel to Riobamba, Ecuador, where they must climb one of the glaciers on Mount Chimborazo and collect some snow to make an iced drink.
  - *Desafío 2.* Tess and Patricia travel to Huancavelica, Peru, where they meet the mayor, Héctor Gonzáles. They must take part in the town's annual llama race.
  - *Desafío 3.* Diana and Rita will travel to Oruro, Bolivia, where they must dress in a traditional costume and participate in the most famous carnival in the Andean region.
  - *Desafío 4.* Tim and Mack will travel to Potosí, Bolivia, where they must decode the coat of arms on the Bolivian flag to find the location of a valuable coin.

Activities	Standards	Resources
Andes centrales	1.2, 3.1, 3.2	Video

Teaching Suggestions

Warm-Up / Independent Starter

- Ask students to look at a map of South America and list all of the countries that make up the central Andes region and their capital cities. Then ask students to locate on the map the places to which the four pairs will travel.

The Central Andes

- The Andes are the longest and second highest mountain range in the world. The range extends into seven different countries: Argentina, Bolivia, Chile, Colombia, Ecuador, Peru, and Venezuela. Valleys, rich mineral deposits, volcanoes, and wildlife surround this mountain range, which also played home to the extensive Inca Empire in the 15th century.

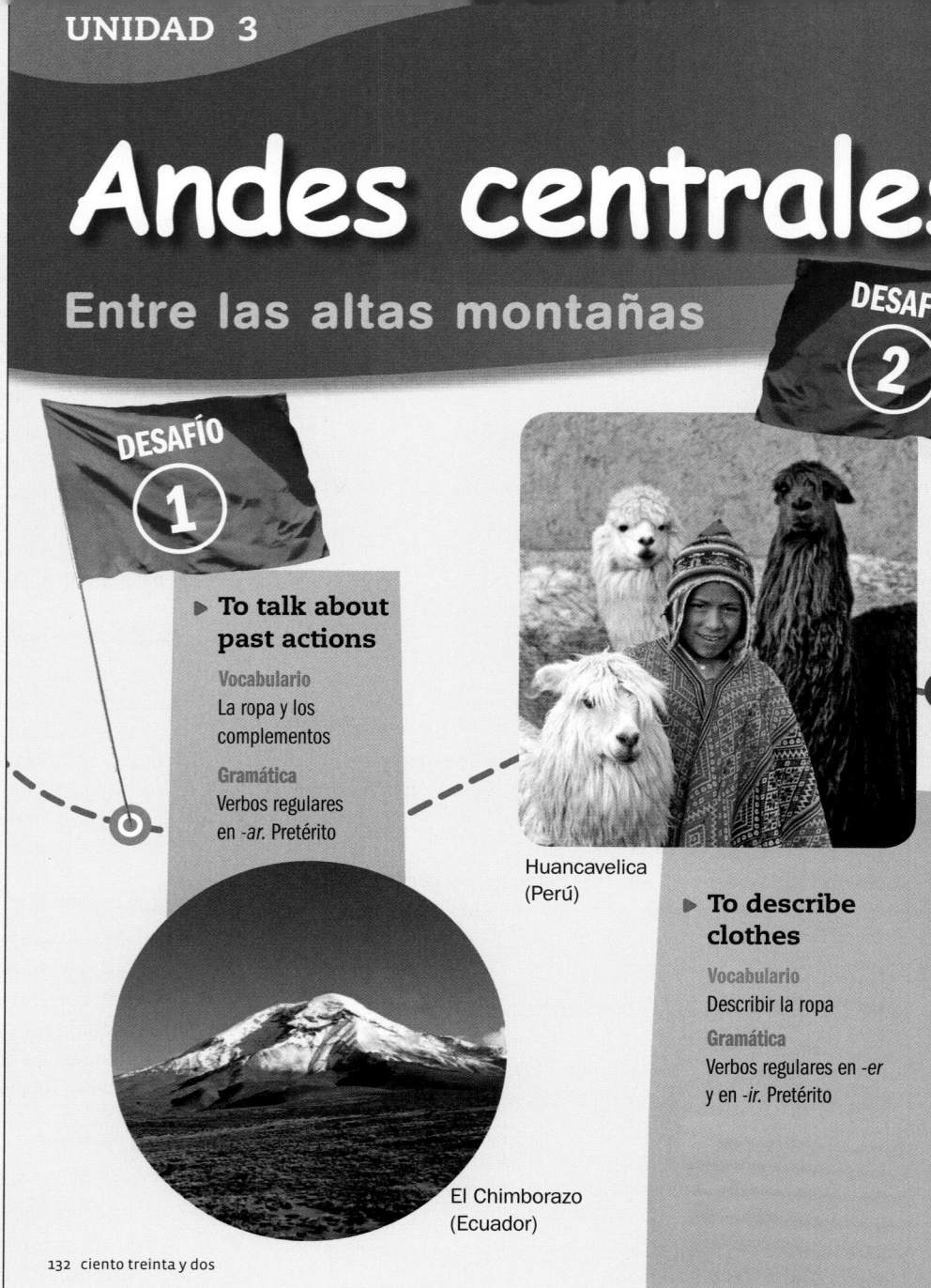

Andes centrales
Entre las altas montañas

DESAFÍO 1

▶ **To talk about past actions**

Vocabulario
La ropa y los complementos

Gramática
Verbos regulares en -ar. Pretérito

El Chimborazo (Ecuador)

DESAFÍO 2

Huancavelica (Perú)

▶ **To describe clothes**

Vocabulario
Describir la ropa

Gramática
Verbos regulares en -er y en -ir. Pretérito

132 ciento treinta y dos

The Challenge

DESAFÍO 1

El Chimborazo

Mount Chimborazo is the highest peak in Ecuador, but not in the Andes when measured from sea level. It is, however, the point farthest away from the center of the Earth. This is due to the equatorial bulge caused by the spin of the Earth. Mount Chimborazo is an inactive volcano located approximately 18 miles from the city of Riobamba in Ecuador. It rises to 20,702 feet above sea level and is heavily glaciated. In 1880, the British mountaineer Edward Whymper became the first known person to reach the summit.

DESAFÍO 2

Huancavelica

The town of Huancavelica is located at an elevation of about 12,000 feet in central Peru. Each June, people from all over the world descend on Huancavelica to watch the famous llama race. In this race, llama herders make their llamas run for close to 1.9 miles. This race is part of a week-long regional agricultural fair and expo. Llamas have been important pack animals in the Andes since pre-Columbian times, and are still used by the local population for this purpose and as a source of wool.

Andes centrales

arnaval
Oruro
livia)

▶ **To talk about places in the community**

DESAFÍO 3

Vocabulario
Tiendas
y establecimientos

Gramática
Verbos irregulares
en el pretérito.
*Ser, ir, decir, tener,
estar y hacer.*

otosí (Bolivia)

DESAFÍO 4

▶ **To talk about past shopping experiences**

Vocabulario
Las compras

Gramática
Verbos en -*ir* con raíz
irregular en el pretérito

ciento treinta y tres 133

■ Focus students' attention on the map and ask them to comment on the region's location, bordering the Pacific coast and the Andes. Ask students if they think a person who lives in the high plateaus would dress the same as a person who lives on the coast. Why or why not?

Picture Discussion

■ Ask students to look at the pictures. Has anyone in the class ever been to any of the these places? Encourage students to share their experiences.

El Chimborazo (Ecuador)

■ Explain that the Chimborazo lies in the Pacific Ring of Fire which extends from Alaska to Chile in the Americas. Have students discuss which states of the United States are part of this Ring of Fire and which volcanoes in these states would be comparable to Chimborazo.

Huancavelica (Perú)

■ Ask students if they have ever seen a llama or an alpaca. Have them share what they know about these Andean animals. Invite students to think about what these animal provide (e.g., wool, transportation, meat) and their importance to the economy of towns at altitudes above 9,000 feet.

El carnaval de Oruro (Bolivia)

■ Have students describe the costumes people are wearing in the picture. What do the masks represent? Have students ever attended a carnival or a parade? You may want to discuss, as a class, the reason(s) for the existence of these festivals and communal celebrations.

Potosí (Bolivia)

■ Explain that at one point in history Potosí was the most important mining city in the world, but once the mines were depleted, the city declined. Do we have similar examples in the United States? Can places rich in natural resources avoid this fate? Invite students to discuss ways in which we can manage resources more responsibly and efficiently.

Objectives

■ By the end of Unit 3, students will be able to
  – Talk about past actions.
  – Describe clothes.
  – Talk about places in the community.
  – Talk about past shopping experiences.
  – Talk about different cultural aspects of the central Andes region.

DESAFÍO 3
El carnaval de Oruro

Oruro has been a mining center for much of the past 400 years. During the Spanish colonial period, it was a rich silver-producing region. At the end of the 19th century and for part of the 20th century, it was a tin mining center. Mining has since declined and today Oruro is better known for its carnival, which takes place 40 days before Easter Sunday. The main event is a ceremonial parade that lasts 20 hours and involves dances performed by more than 20,000 dancers and accompanied by about 10,000 musicians.

DESAFÍO 4
Potosí

Potosí, in southern Bolivia, is one of the world's highest cities, located at 13,290 feet above sea level on the Bolivian *altiplano*, or high plateau. At one point during the Spanish colonial period, it was the largest city in the Americas. Potosí owed this prosperity to its large deposits of silver ore, which were mined intensively during the 16th and 17th centuries. Mining has greatly declined since then, but the city of Potosí has preserved its colonial architecture. It was declared a UNESCO World Heritage Site in 1987.

133

Unit 3
La llegada

Presentation

- This section presents the pairs' arrival in the central Andes region. They meet in Guayaquil, Ecuador, at the Malecón walkway. There the participants must find out what José Joaquín Olmedo is wearing before they can receive their challenges for this unit.

- Students will see vocabulary in context, with pictures and illustrations. Presenting new words in this manner helps students develop their Spanish vocabulary with background knowledge while engaging them with the context.

Activities	Standards	Resources
Fotonovela	1.2, 2.1, 2.2	Vis. Pres.
1.	1.2, 2.1, 2.2	

Teaching Suggestions

Warm-Up / Independent Starter

- Ask students to read the introduction to the *fotonovela*, without looking at the dialogue or the pictures. Ask them to write a short paragraph about who they think José Joaquín Olmedo is and why his clothes are so important.

Preparation

- Ask students to share their Independent Starter. Write some of their predictions on the board. Keep a tally of the most popular predictions.

- Have students read the *fotonovela* silently. Remind them of some reading and listening Strategies from Level 1, such as looking for cognates, recognizing prefixes and suffixes, and checking the dictionary for unknown words. Students can also use the reading strategies from Units 1 and 2, which are identifying the overall theme of the text and noting the details.

La fotonovela

Before Viewing

- Now that students have read the dialogues, check the board to see if anyone had the right idea about José Joaquín Olmedo's importance and clothing. Have a class discussion about the similarities and differences in students' predictions and the actual facts.

134

En Guayaquil

The pairs gather at the Malecón, a long walkway overlooking the Guayas River in the Ecuadorian port city of Guayaquil. They must find out what a man named José Joaquín Olmedo is wearing before they can receive their tasks, which will take place thousands of feet high, in the Andean region.

¿Usted sabe quién es José Joaquín Olmedo?

Bueno, sé quién fue.

¿Fue? ¿Él está muerto?

Claro, murió hace más de 150 años.

134 ciento treinta y cuatro

Differentiated Instruction

DEVELOPING LEARNERS

- After students have read the dialogues, have them write out, in two separate columns, the words they recognize and those they do not recognize. Then have them classify the words into three groups: "Recycled Vocabulary," "New Vocabulary," and "Verbs." Ask students to analyze whether the words in each category help them understand the dialogue. Discuss this as a class.

EXPANDING LEARNERS

- Have students change the subject of the dialogue to Theodore "Teddy" Roosevelt, the 26th president of the United States. Ask students to get into pairs and rewrite the dialogue using the questions already presented, changing the answers to accommodate the new subject. Then have pairs perform their dialogue aloud to the class. As they read, have the rest of the class take notes on the information they learned about Teddy Roosevelt, and about which pair provided the best dialogue on the new subject. Take a class vote for the pair with the best dialogue.

No sé cómo vamos a encontrar a José Joaquín Olmedo.

No sabemos si lleva traje y corbata...

¿Cuándo te compraste ese celular?

Lo compré ayer en el centro comercial. Quiero ver qué ropa lleva Olmedo y cómo es.

¡O una camiseta y pantalones cortos!

Lo siento, Tim, pero no se puede mirar en Internet.

José Joaquín Olmedo fue un héroe nacional de Ecuador.

Bienvenidos a Guayaquil. Me llamo José Joaquín Olmedo. Nací en esta ciudad en 1780. Fui poeta y líder de la independencia de Ecuador. ¡Buena suerte!

¡Ahora lo entiendo!

Primero deben completar sus desafíos y al final tienen que escribir un diario de sus experiencias.

---

1  **¿Comprendes?**

▶ **Une** las dos columnas.

(A)

1. ¿Quién compró ayer un celular?
2. ¿Dónde lo compró?
3. ¿Quién fue un héroe nacional de Ecuador?
4. ¿Dónde nació José Joaquín Olmedo?
5. ¿Cuándo murió?

(B)

a. En Guayaquil.
b. Hace 150 años.
c. Tim.
d. En el centro comercial.
e. José Joaquín Olmedo.

After Viewing

- Ask students who was talking in the last frame of the dialogue. We have already established that José Joaquín Olmedo was born over 200 years ago, so who do students think is the voice of Mr. Olmedo? Discuss this as a class.

- Go over the dialogue again. Have different pairs of students read the participants' dialogue aloud. Then invite students to observe the clothes both the pairs and Mr. Olmedo are wearing. The differences are obvious, but are there similarities? Challenge students to find at least five common elements between what people were wearing 150 years ago and what people wear now.

Activities

1. Have students work in pairs to complete this activity. Have one partner ask the question and the other answer it. Tell students to be sure to alternate the person asking and the person answering the question.

Answer Key

1. 1. c   4. a
         2. d   5. b
         3. e

Additional Resources

Fans Online activities
Practice Workbook

 HERITAGE LANGUAGE LEARNERS

- The *malecón* is a boardwalk that runs alongside the Guayas River. Ask students to name and describe any other *malecones* or boardwalks that they know of, including those in the United States. Tell students to be sure to describe the purpose of the boardwalk and any activities that normally take place there. Have volunteers share this information with their classmates.

COOPERATIVE LEARNING

- Pair developing learners with an expanding or heritage learner. Ask the expanding or heritage learner to read the dialogue aloud to the developing learner. After each speech bubble, have the expanding or heritage learner pause to allow the developing learner time to summarize what he or she just heard. This will assist with reading comprehension and will allow students immediate clarification if needed.

Unit 3
La llegada

Presentation

- In this section, students will learn useful expressions to ask about and to express knowledge of a fact, to express the order of actions, and to wish someone luck.

Activities	Standards	Resources
Expresiones útiles	1.2, 1.3, 4.1	
2.	1.2, 1.3	
3.	1.3	
4.	1.1, 2.1	
5.	1.1	

Teaching Suggestions

Warm-Up / Independent Starter

- Ask students to close their textbooks and write down all of the information they can remember from the previous page about José Joaquín Olmedo and what he was wearing.

Preparation

- Go over the *Expresiones útiles* section with students. Then have them get into groups of four to write an impromptu story using the expressions for the order of actions. Ask students to use the template below as an example.
  A. *Primero me levanté.*
  B. *Después...*
  C. *Entonces...*
  D. *Al final...*
- Have students read their impromptu story to the class. Ask the class to vote for the most interesting story.

Activities

2. Ask students to add four more questions of their own to this activity. You may suggest a topic about which students can ask questions (e.g., historical figures, the *fotonovela*). Students will take turns asking their partner the questions.

3. Have students choose the four sequence expressions they would like to use for this activity. Then ask them to write their complete sentences using the sequence expressions they chose.

136

EXPRESIONES ÚTILES

¡Yo lo sé!

To ask about and to express knowledge of a fact:
–¿Sabes dónde está Guayaquil?
–Sí, está en Ecuador. / No, no lo sé.

To express the order of actions:
Primero
Luego / Después / A continuación
Al final / Por fin / Finalmente

To wish somebody luck:
¡Buena suerte!

2 **¿Sabes o no sabes?**

▶ **Pregunta** a tu compañero(a) los siguientes datos. Usa el verbo *saber*.

Modelo A. *¿Sabes cuál es la capital de Perú?*
B. *¡Sí, lo sé! Es Lima. / No, no lo sé.*

1. Cuándo es el cumpleaños de tu profesor(a).
2. Cuál es la capital de Ecuador.
3. Cuánto cuesta un celular.
4. Dónde está Guayaquil.

3 **Fotos desordenadas**

▶ **Ordena** las fotografías y escribe lo que hace Patricia.

Modelo *Primero Patricia...*

  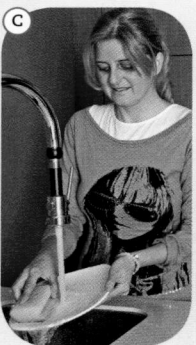 

136 ciento treinta y seis

Differentiated Instruction

DEVELOPING LEARNERS

- Ask students to write the body of an e-mail to a friend in Ecuador about their plans for this weekend. Tell students to begin with Friday after school and end at bedtime on Sunday night. Encourage students to use the expressions of order to tell their story sequentially. If students don't have any plans, then have them write about their ideal weekend.

EXPANDING LEARNERS

- Have students work in small groups to play a game of "¿Sabes?" using the *expresiones útiles*. Each student in the group tells a story. The story can be either true or false, but it must begin with *primero* and end with *al final*, *por fin*, or *finalmente*. Once each storyteller finishes, he or she asks, *¿Sabes?* The rest of the group answers *¡Yo lo sé!* if they think the story is true and *¡No lo sé!* if they think it is false. The student with the most correct guesses after everyone has had a turn telling a story wins.

¿Quién ganará?

4 Los desafíos

Habla. ¿Cuál será el desafío para cada pareja? Piénsalo y coméntalo con tus compañeros(as).

DESAFÍO ①

Un sorbete de volcán

Andy y Janet

DESAFÍO ②

Una carrera de llamas

DESAFÍO ③

El carnaval de Oruro

Diana y Rita

DESAFÍO ④

La montaña de plata

Tim y Mack

Habla. Las parejas viajan a Ecuador, Perú y Bolivia. ¿Qué sabes de esos países? Coméntalo con tus compañeros(as).

5 La tarea final

Decide. ¿Qué tarea tienen que hacer los personajes al final?
¿Qué pareja crees que ganará?

LA TAREA
Un diario

ciento treinta y siete 137

¿Quién ganará?

4. Have students get into small groups and discuss the pairs' challenges. Ask groups to look at the pictures, read the captions, and write a brief paragraph about what they believe the pairs will do in their challenges. They must also include in their paragraph any information they know about the different places or events mentioned in the captions.

5. Students have been provided a clue as to what the pairs will have to do to win their *desafío* in the Andes region. The clue is *un diario*. As a class, have students discuss what kind of diary the pairs will need in order to win the *Desafío* in the Andes.

Answer Key

2. Answers will vary. Sample answers:
1. A. ¿Sabes cuándo es el cumpleaños de tu profesor?
   B. No, no lo sé.
2. A. ¿Sabes cuál es la capital de Ecuador?
   B. ¡Sí, lo sé! Es Quito.
3. A. ¿Sabes cuánto cuesta un celular?
   B. ¡Sí, lo sé! Hay buenos modelos por $150.
4. A. ¿Sabes dónde está Guayaquil?
   B. ¡Sí, lo sé! Está en Ecuador.

3. B, D, A, C
Answers will vary. Sample answer:
Primero Patricia saca el pan. Después ella prepara un sándwich. Luego lo come. Al final Patricia lava el plato sucio.

4. Answers will vary.
   ▶ Answers will vary.

5. Answers will vary.

Additional Resources

Fans Online activities
Practice Workbook

HERITAGE LANGUAGE LEARNERS

• There are several ways to talk about luck in Spanish. Have students answer the following questions about luck.
1. *¿Cómo se llama una persona que siempre tiene suerte?* (afortunado, suertudo)
2. *¿Cómo se llama una persona que nunca tiene suerte?* (desafortunado)
3. *¿Sabes algún dicho sobre la suerte?* (Más confío en el trabajo que en la suerte, La suerte favorece a la mente preparada, etc.)
4. *¿Qué símbolos representan la suerte?* (El trébol de cuatro hojas, la herradura, etc.)

CRITICAL THINKING

• Most language arts teachers ask students to organize their compositions sequentially. Ask students if they think the same rules apply in Spanish compositions as in English compositions. Do students think the sequence expressions should only be used as a way to get organized, or can they be used within the composition?

137

Unit 3
DESAFÍO 1
Hablar de acciones pasadas

Presentation

- In *Desafío 1*, Andy and Janet are in Riobamba, Ecuador. They must climb one of the glaciers on Mount Chimborazo and collect snow to make a frozen drink.

- In this section, students will preview:
  - Vocabulary for clothes, shoes, and accessories.
  - Regular *-ar* verbs in the preterite tense.

Activities	Standards	Resources
Fotonovela	1.2, 2.2	Vis. Pres.
6.	1.2, 2.2	
7.	1.2	
8.	1.2, 1.3	
9. Cultura	1.1, 1.2, 2.1, 3.1, 3.2, 5.1	Video
Tu desafío	1.2, 3.1, 5.1	

Teaching Suggestions

Warm-Up / Independent Starter

- Have students read the introduction to the *fotonovela*. Ask them to write their theories of how Andy and Janet could get the snow from the top of the glacier to a place where they can blend it into a frozen drink.

Preparation

- Have students share their theories from the Independent Starter. Remind them that once the temperature rises above the freezing point, the snow will begin to melt. Knowing this, do any of your students want to change their theories?

La fotonovela

Before Viewing

- Have students look at the pictures of the *fotonovela* and take note of what each person is wearing from head to toe.

After Viewing

- Ask students how it could be that Andy and Janet aren't dressed appropriately for the climb. One possible answer is that the ground temperature could potentially be much warmer than the temperature at higher elevations.

138

Un sorbete de volcán

 Andy and Janet are in the town of Riobamba, the starting point for their arduous hike. The siblings will have to climb to one of the glaciers of Chimborazo, the highest volcano in Ecuador. Their task is to collect some snow from the glacier, and use it to make an iced drink called *sorbete*.

> ¡Ay, ayer compré estas botas en una zapatería, pero me quedan pequeñas!

> Pues hay que caminar diez millas. ¡Qué problema!

> ¿Solo llevas esa ropa?

> ¿Hace mucho frío allí? ¡No compramos abrigos! ¡Qué desastre!

> Janet, ¿seguro que ese sombrero combina con esas gafas de sol?

> No pasa nada. Aquí tenemos ropa y calzado apropiados para ustedes: calcetines, pantalones, botas...

> ¡Perfecto! ¡Estas botas me hacen daño!

> Las mujeres de los Andes llevan este tipo de sombrero, Andy.

Continuará...

6 **Detective de palabras**

▶ **Escribe.** ¿Qué palabra de la fotonovela corresponde a cada foto?

① 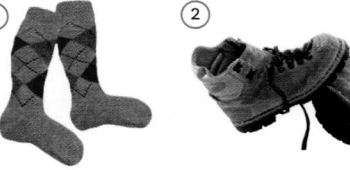 ②  ③ ④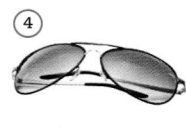

Differentiated Instruction

DEVELOPING LEARNERS

- In a reading of more than a few sentences, students may feel overwhelmed if they don't know every word, and get stuck or distracted by single words rather than focusing on the overall meaning. When reading a *fotonovela* or a culture passage, have students use small scraps of paper to cover up any words that they truly have no idea about, and then see if they can understand the overall message of the passage even without those words.

EXPANDING LEARNERS

- Have students analyze Andy and Janet's preparedness for their challenge. Do students think they would be better prepared for the task than Andy and Janet? Ask students to rewrite the speech bubbles to correct all of Andy and Janet's mistakes, and to add the things they will need to be better prepared to climb Chimborazo. Have volunteers share their new dialogue with the class.

7 ¿Comprendes?

▶ **Decide** si estas oraciones son ciertas o falsas. Si son falsas, corrígelas.

Modelo Andy y Janet viajan a la capital de Ecuador.
→ *Falso. Andy y Janet viajan a la ciudad de Riobamba.*

1. A Andy le quedan pequeñas las botas.
2. Janet lleva ropa para el frío.
3. Janet compró abrigos para el frío.
4. El guía tiene ropa y calzado para Andy y Janet.
5. Janet lleva un sombrero típico.

8 Buscando la nieve del Chimborazo

▶ **Ordena** estas oraciones sobre la fotonovela con tu compañero(a).

a. Janet compra unas botas en la zapatería.
b. Andy y Janet llegan a Riobamba.
c. Andy le pregunta al guía si hace mucho frío.
d. Janet se pone un sombrero típico de los Andes.
e. Andy, Janet y el guía empiezan a caminar.

▶ **Escribe** lo que pasa en la fotonovela. Usa estas expresiones.

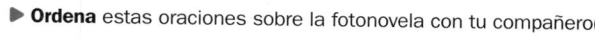

primero · luego · después · a continuación · y · finalmente

CULTURA

La Avenida de los volcanes

La cordillera de los Andes atraviesa Ecuador de norte a sur con montañas y volcanes de 5.000 y 6.000 metros de altitud. Muchos volcanes están agrupados en un área de más de 300 kilómetros de longitud llamada Avenida de los volcanes. Allí está el Chimborazo, el volcán más alto de Ecuador (6.310 metros).

El Chimborazo.

Todavía hay personas que suben por hielo *(ice)* al Chimborazo para venderlo en los mercados de las ciudades cercanas. En esos mercados venden jugos y sorbetes preparados con el hielo del Chimborazo.

9 Piensa y explica.
El calentamiento global *(global warming)* está produciendo el deshielo *(melting)* de los glaciares. ¿Cómo crees que puede afectar esto a los habitantes de los Andes?

→ **TU DESAFÍO** Visita la página web para aprender más sobre la Avenida de los volcanes.

Activities

7. Turn this activity into a speaking activity. Have students work with a classmate. One student will read a statement. If the statement is true, their partner will say, *Sí, es cierto.* If the statement is false, their partner will correct it. Tell students to be sure to alternate reading and answering each item.

9. Lead a discussion about some of the other effects of global warming besides the glaciers melting. You may also want to discuss ways students can preserve our planet and reverse the effects of global warming.

CULTURA

La Avenida de los volcanes

The Ecuadorian Andes split into two mountain ranges: the *Cordillera Occidental* (the western range) and *Cordillera Central* (the central range). The western range is geologically more recent and has a line of 19 volcanoes, including Chimborazo. Twenty volcanoes stand on the older and higher central range. The fertile valleys located between these mountain ranges have fed the inhabitants of this region for thousands of years.

Answer Key

6. 1. calcetines   3. sombrero
    2. botas   4. gafas de sol

7. 1. Falso. A Janet le quedan pequeñas las botas.
    2. Falso. Janet no lleva ropa para el frío.
    3. Falso. Janet no compró abrigos.
    4. Cierto.
    5. Cierto.

8. b, a, c, d, e
    ▶ Answers will vary.

9. Answers will vary.

Additional Resources
Fans Online activities

HERITAGE LANGUAGE LEARNERS

• Ask students to get into pairs and to imagine that they are going to climb one of the glaciers of Mount Chimborazo with Andy and Janet. Tell students to add themselves to the conversation by adding two speech bubbles to every scene. Once students have finished, have two pairs join together to read their scenes. The first time, one pair will read the parts of Andy and Janet while the other pair reads their added lines. Then the pairs will switch roles to allow the other pair to read their added lines.

TOTAL PHYSICAL RESPONSE (TPR)

• Help students identify the clothing items and stores mentioned on this page. Read through each speech bubble. As students hear a clothing item or store, have them point to the clothing item or body part that it refers to. For instance, when you read *Ay, ayer compré estas botas en una zapatería del pueblo*, students will point to their feet.

Unit 3

DESAFÍO 1

Vocabulario – La ropa y los complementos

Presentation

- In this section, students will learn about clothing, shoes, and accessories.

Activities	Standards	Resources
Vocabulario	1.2	
10.	1.2	
11.	1.2	
12.	1.2, 1.3	Audio
13.	1.1	
14. Comparaciones	1.1, 1.2, 2.1, 2.2, 3.1, 3.2	
Tu desafío	1.2, 3.1, 3.2, 5.2	

Teaching Suggestions

Warm-Up / Independent Starter

- Have students look at the picture of Andy and Janet at the end of the *fotonovela* and label their clothing based on the vocabulary from this page.

Preparation

- Go over the vocabulary presentation. Then have students close their eyes and describe what different students in the class are wearing. As you describe each person, write his or her name on the board. With their eyes still closed, ask students whom you are describing. Then have students open their eyes and see if they got any of the names correct.

- Ask students what clothes they need to wear in each case.
  1. *Sales al patio de la casa en traje de baño y está haciendo mucho frío.*
  2. *Estás en pijama y tocan a la puerta.*
  3. *Un amigo te lleva a una fiesta muy elegante y tú tienes puestos unos pantalones cortos.*

Activities

10. Ask students to replace the item that does not belong with an item that does belong.

12. Once students have finished, have them write three to five sentences to summarize what each person is wearing.

140

Vocabulario

La ropa y los complementos

- la corbata
- el traje
- el abrigo
- la gorra
- la sudadera
- el impermeable
- la bata
- el pijama
- las zapatillas
- el traje de baño
- las gafas de sol
- el reloj
- el bolso
- el collar
- los aretes
- la pulsera
- el anillo

10 **Palabras mezcladas**

▶ **Decide** qué palabra no corresponde a cada grupo.

Ropa de invierno	Ropa de verano	Complementos
suéter	abrigo	bufanda
traje de baño	pantalón corto	sombrero
guantes	camiseta	bolso
bufanda	sandalias	vestido

140 ciento cuarenta

Differentiated Instruction

DEVELOPING LEARNERS

- Ask students to cut out an example of each clothing item listed in the vocabulary presentation from old magazines or advertisement catalogues. Have students write the vocabulary word on the back of each picture. Then have them work with a partner to quiz each other on the vocabulary. One student will hold up a clothing item and the other person will say what the item is. Tell students to alternate asking and answering the words.

EXPANDING LEARNERS

- Have students study the vocabulary for two or three minutes in silence. Then ask them to close their books and describe from head to toe what the following people usually wear:
  – *un hombre de negocios*
  – *una mujer de negocios*
  – *un surfista*
  – *una maestra*
  – *un deportista*
  – *una actriz la noche del Oscar*

11. ¿Qué llevan?

▶ **Escribe.** ¿Qué llevan estas personas?

 (A)  (B)  (C)  (D)

12. Una cena elegante

▶ **Escucha** la conversación de Janet y su tía. ¿Qué lleva cada uno? Completa una tabla como esta.

	Ropa	Calzado y complementos
Su tía	Una falda y _____1_____	Unos aretes, _____2_____ y unos zapatos.
Su tío	_____3_____, una corbata y un abrigo.	_____4_____
Su prima	_____5_____	_____6_____

13. ¿Qué les gusta llevar?

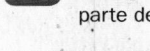

▶ **Habla** con tres compañeros(as). ¿Qué les gusta llevar en estas situaciones?

Modelo A. *¿Qué te gusta llevar cuando vas a un concierto?*
B. *Me gusta llevar unos jeans y una camiseta.*

- ir a una fiesta
- ir a la escuela
- ir a un restaurante
- ir a hacer deporte
- ir de excursión al campo

COMPARACIONES

La ropa tradicional andina

El poncho y el chullo –un tipo de gorro– son dos prendas típicas de los habitantes de los Andes. Estas prendas se fabrican con la lana de las llamas y las alpacas de los Andes. Sirven para protegerse del frío y de la lluvia.

14 **Compara.** ¿Qué prendas sueles llevar? ¿Hay alguna parte del país donde se usa otro tipo de ropa? ¿Por qué?

Poncho andino.

→ TU DESAFÍO Visita la página web para aprender más sobre los habitantes de los Andes.

HERITAGE LANGUAGE LEARNERS

- There are many other words that students could use for these clothing items. Have them come up with the regional clothing vocabulary from their country of origin. Ask students to draw the clothing items and write the label underneath. Have students share their regional vocabulary with the class. You may want to make a class list with all the regional terms.

MULTIPLE INTELLIGENCES:
Visual-Spatial Intelligence

- Bring in or ask students to bring in old but clean clothing items such as pants, shirts, skirts, dresses, etc. Divide the class into small groups and distribute the clothing items among the groups. Ask one student in each group to put on a clothing item on top of his or her clothes. The rest of the group will say what he or she is wearing in a complete sentence. For example: *Ella lleva una camisa.*

DESAFÍO 1

Vocabulario – La ropa y los complementos

13. As each person describes his or her ideal outfits, one student in the group will draw a picture to try to match the description. Then the artist will reveal his or her drawing. Did the artist capture the description?

14. Ask students to think of the clothing, shoes, and accessories that they do not need to purchase where they live.

 AUDIO SCRIPT
See page 131I.

 COMPARACIONES

La ropa tradicional andina

The weather in the Andean highlands is usually cold. For this reason, local people have used the wool of llamas and alpacas since pre-Columbian times to make the durable and warm clothing they wear. But clothing also serves as a cultural identifier and, as such, each region has its unique style of clothing and color combinations.

Answer Key

10. Ropa de invierno: traje de baño
Ropa de verano: abrigo
Complementos: vestido

11. A. Una chaqueta, una camisa y unos pantalones.
B. Un vestido y un collar.
C. Un traje y una corbata.
D. Una sudadera y unos pantalones largos.

12. 1. una blusa 4. un reloj
2. un collar 5. un pijama
3. un traje 6. unas zapatillas

13. Answers will vary.

14. Answers will vary.

Additional Resources

Fans Online activities
Practice Workbook

DESAFÍO 1

Gramática – Verbos regulares en -*ar*. Pretérito

Presentation

- In this section, students will learn to conjugate regular -*ar* verbs in the preterite tense.

Activities	Standards	Resources
Gramática	3.1	
15.	1.1, 3.1, 4.1	
16.	1.3	
17.	1.2, 1.3	Audio
18.	1.1, 1.3	

Teaching Suggestions

Warm-Up / Independent Starter

- Have students conjugate the following -*ar* verbs in the present tense. Ask them to write these verbs one under the other, and to leave space to the right of each verb for the conjugations.

hablar	comprar	sacar
llevar	pagar	comenzar

Preparation

- Go over the grammar presentation with students. Pay close attention to the -*car*, -*gar*, and -*zar* verbs. Let students know that all -*car*, -*gar*, and -*zar* verbs have a spelling change in the preterite tense, so they should pay close attention to these verbs.

- Now that students know how to conjugate -*ar* verbs in the preterite tense, have them conjugate the verbs from the Independent Starter in the preterite tense, next to the present-tense conjugations. Discuss the similarities and differences with students. For instance, the *nosotros* form does not change.

Activities

15. Before students answer this question, ask them to take the verbs *buscar*, *llegar*, and *empezar* and say them using the spelling for the regular yo form of -*ar* verbs in the preterite (i.e., **buscé, *llegé, *empezé*). Then have students say the verbs with the irregular spelling (i.e., *busqué, llegué, empecé*). Then ask students to answer the question.

Gramática

Verbos regulares en -*ar*. Pretérito

- To talk about actions completed in the past, we use the preterite tense.

  Ayer **compré** una gorra nueva en el centro comercial.

- These are the preterite tense endings of -ar verbs.

VERBO COMPRAR. PRETÉRITO

Singular		Plural	
yo	**compré**	nosotros nosotras	**compramos**
tú	**compraste**	vosotros vosotras	**comprasteis**
usted él ella	**compró**	ustedes ellos ellas	**compraron**

Note: The nosotros form is the same in the preterite as in the present. Context will clarify the tense.

PRESENTE
Todos los días **almorzamos** a la una.

PRETÉRITO
Ayer **almorzamos** a las doce.

Verbos con cambios ortográficos

- Verbs ending in -car, -gar, and -zar require a change of spelling in the yo form of the preterite tense.

-car → -qué	buscar → yo bus**qué**, tú buscaste
-gar → -gué	llegar → yo lle**gué**, tú llegaste
-zar → -cé	empezar → yo empe**cé**, tú empezaste

15 **Piensa.** ¿Por qué hay un cambio ortográfico en la forma yo del pretérito de los verbos terminados en -car, -gar y -zar?

16 **¿Qué hicieron?**

▶ **Escribe.** ¿Cómo se prepararon Andy y Janet para su desafío?

comprar

preparar

viajar

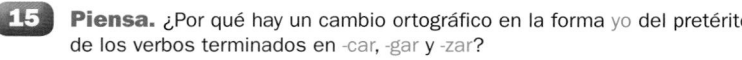
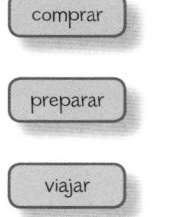

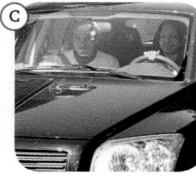

Differentiated Instruction

DEVELOPING LEARNERS

- Have students continue to practice the -*ar* verb conjugations in the preterite tense. Be sure they use a different color for the verb endings, as they see in the grammar presentation.

– cenar	– pensar
– jugar	– abrigar
– clasificar	– tocar
– utilizar	– organizar

EXPANDING LEARNERS

- Using as many -*car*, -*gar*, and -*zar* verbs as possible, have students write a short paragraph in the present tense describing an unusual event. Then have them rewrite this paragraph in the past tense, using the preterite forms of these verbs. They should try to use a few different subjects within the paragraph, but especially the yo form.

17 **Actividades**

 ▶ **Escucha** a Andy y a Janet, y completa una tabla como esta.

Tarea	¿Sí o no?	¿Quién?
llegar a Riobamba		
buscar un hotel		
hablar con mamá y papá		
comprar un impermeable		
preparar la mochila		
practicar deporte		

▶ **Escribe** un texto con la información anterior.

Modelo   *Andy y Janet llegaron a Riobamba. Andy habló con…*

18 ¿Qué pasó?

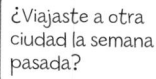 ▶ **Pregunta** a tu compañero(a). ¿Qué hizo la semana pasada?

Modelo

¿Viajaste a otra ciudad la semana pasada?

No, no viajé a otra ciudad la semana pasada.

1. viajar a otra ciudad
2. comprar ropa
3. almorzar con sus amigos(as)
4. pasear por el parque
5. hablar con su mejor amigo(a)
6. buscar un libro en la biblioteca
7. visitar un museo
8. llegar tarde a la escuela

▶ **Escribe** un resumen de lo que tu compañero(a) y tú hicieron la semana pasada.

Modelo

La semana pasada Sally y yo compramos ropa y almorzamos con nuestros amigos. Ella visitó un museo y yo...

ciento cuarenta y tres   143

Unit 3
DESAFÍO 1
Gramática – Verbos regulares en -*ar*. Pretérito

16. First, have students match the verbs to the pictures. Then have them conjugate the verbs according to who is in the picture. Finally, have students write sentences to say how Andy and Janet prepared for this *desafío*.

17. Before you play the audio recording, explain to students that the first column, *Tarea*, is a possible action performed by either Andy or Janet. The second column, *¿Sí o no?*, is whether Andy or Janet actually performed the action. The third column, *¿Quién?*, is to tell who performed the action if it was completed.

18. Once students have completed this activity, have volunteers read the summary. Then divide the class in half, and have each half draw a series of scenes to represent all of the experiences on a long piece of construction paper.

 AUDIO SCRIPT
See page 131I.

Answer Key

15. Para conservar el mismo sonido de la última consonante. Por ejemplo, con *busqué* en lugar de **buscé* se conserva el sonido /k/ de la *c* en *buscar*.

16. Answers will vary. Sample answers:
   A. Janet compró unas botas.
   B. Andy preparó el equipaje.
   C. Andy y Janet viajaron a Riobamba.

17. llegar a Riobamba: sí; Andy y Janet
   buscar un hotel: sí; Andy y Janet
   hablar con mamá y papá: sí; Andy
   comprar un impermeable: sí; Janet
   preparar la mochila: sí; Andy
   practicar deporte: sí; Andy y Janet
   ▶ Answers will vary.

18. Answers will vary.
   ▶ Answers will vary.

Additional Resources

Fans Online activities
Practice Workbook

143

HERITAGE LANGUAGE LEARNERS

• Have students make a list of all of the *-car*, *-gar*, and *-zar* verbs they can think of and can research on the Internet. Then have them create a decorative poster to hang in your room as a "cheat sheet" for themselves and the rest of the class. Mark any verbs that are also stem-changing or have other irregularities.

SPECIAL-NEEDS LEARNERS

• To focus students' attention more effectively, have them focus on one verb at a time. Ask them to conjugate the verb *hablar* in the preterite tense just as they see it done in the grammar presentation with the verb *comprar*. Then have these students act out the action of speaking. Then have them draw a picture of a person speaking, with the speech bubble *Yo hablé en español ayer*. Repeat the process with the verb *cenar* and any other verbs they have trouble with.

Unit 3
DESAFÍO 1
Comunicación

Presentation

- In this section, students will integrate the vocabulary and grammar from *Desafío 1* in order to talk about clothes, shoes, accessories, and past actions using *-ar* verbs.

Activities	Standards	Resources
19.	1.2, 1.3	Audio
20.	1.1, 1.2, 1.3, 2.1	Audio
21.	1.1, 1.3	
22. Final del desafío	1.2, 1.3, 2.2	

Teaching Suggestions

Warm-Up / Independent Starter

- Ask students to think about the clothes, shoes, and accessories that the mannequins in their favorite store were wearing the last time they were there. Then have students think about what the mannequins wore the time before that. Have students write a comparison between the clothing from their last two visits.

Preparation

- Take 10 minutes to review the vocabulary and grammar themes trom *Desafío 1*.
- Refer students back to the *fotonovela* for *Desafío 1*. Have them find all of the clothes, shoes, accessories, and past actions with *-ar* verbs within the dialogue. Do students understand the dialogue better now that they have gone through the vocabulary and grammar from the *Desafío*?
- Display a weekly calendar and call on one student for each day of the week to write what they wore on that day. Do students see a pattern of what is popular to wear among students, or is everyone's style completely different?

Activities

20. Once students have finished this activity, have them research a local department store or an online store and write the same information for the store they researched. Then ask students to talk to a classmate about what floor or area they would spend the most time in and why.

144

Comunicación

19 **El blog de Janet**

▶ **Lee** el blog de Janet y escribe. ¿Qué hizo en Ecuador? Utiliza el pretérito.

Modelo *Andy y Janet llegaron ayer a...*

Riobamba, 15 de octubre

Andy y yo llegamos ayer a Riobamba. Los dos nos preparamos para nuestro desafío.

Andy habla mucho con el guía. Él nos explica muchas cosas de la geografía de esta región y nos ayuda mucho. Busca unos ponchos y unos gorros porque nosotros necesitamos ropa para el frío.

Andy y yo lo pasamos muy bien en Ecuador.

Continuará...

 ▶ **Escucha** a Andy y decide. ¿Está de acuerdo con lo que dice Janet en su blog?

20 **¿Qué anuncian?**

 ▶ **Escucha** este anuncio de unos grandes almacenes y completa una tabla como esta.

	Productos en oferta
Planta baja	
Primera planta	
Segunda planta	

▶ **Escribe.** ¿Qué otros productos puede haber en cada planta de estos grandes almacenes? Haz una lista con tu compañero(a).

Complementos

Ropa de señora

Ropa de caballero

144 ciento cuarenta y cuatro

Differentiated Instruction

DEVELOPING LEARNERS

- Ask students to think about their wardrobe for the last week. Have them write what they wore in complete sentences using the verb *llevar* and words for clothes, shoes, and accessories from the vocabulary presentation. Tell students to illustrate their sentences with pictures or drawings of their wardrobe.

EXPANDING LEARNERS

- Have students talk about the clothes, shoes, and accessories their mothers used to wear when they were teenagers. Then have students talk about the clothes, shoes, and accessories their mothers currently wear. Finally, have students compare the two styles. Ask them if some of the fashion trends have repeated themselves or if the styles are completely different.

21 **¿Qué llevaste?**

▶ **Escribe.** ¿Qué ropa llevaste en estas situaciones?

Modelo *Cuando fui a la fiesta de cumpleaños de mi mejor amiga, llevé un vestido nuevo.*

| Cuando fuiste a una fiesta. | Cuando fuiste a hacer deporte. | Cuando fuiste de excursión. |

▶ **Habla** con tu compañero(a). ¿Llevaron ropa similar?

Final del desafío

Andy y Janet ___1___ ropa de abrigo y ___2___ un té caliente para no tener frío.

Andy ___3___ fotografías de la nieve.

Luego Andy y Janet ___4___ a Riobamba.

Finalmente, ___5___ la nieve con jugo de limón. ¡Y ___6___ de un auténtico sorbete de volcán!

 22 **Hielo junto al volcán**

▶ **Lee** el final del desafío y completa los pies de foto con la forma correcta del pretérito de estos verbos.

| mezclar | disfrutar | llegar | llevar | comprar | sacar |

ciento cuarenta y cinco **145**

HERITAGE LANGUAGE LEARNERS

• Ask students to discuss the clothes, shoes, and accessories people wear to special events in their country of origin; this may include the United States. Ask students from different countries of origin to illustrate or find pictures on the Internet of their special-occasion attire for the rest of the class to compare.

MULTIPLE INTELLIGENCES:
Intrapersonal Intelligence

• Ask students to write a diary entry about their sense of style, where it comes from, and what it represents. Although this may be difficult for some students to do in Spanish, encourage students to try to the best of their abilities. Have volunteers share their diary entries with the class.

---

21. Tell students to go a step further and describe with whom they went and what this other person was wearing. You may also have students find pictures of the scenes in a magazine or on the Internet to illustrate the scene and what they were wearing at the time.

22. Remind students that they will need to conjugate each verb according to the subject in the sentence. Also remind them to pay close attention to the *-car, -gar,* and *-zar* verbs in order to spell the words correctly.

 AUDIO SCRIPT
See page 131l.

Answer Key

19. Answers will vary. Sample answer: Andy y Janet llegaron ayer a Riobamba. Los dos se prepararon para su desafío. Andy habló mucho con el guía. Éste les explicó muchas cosas y los ayudó. El guía también les buscó ponchos y gorros. Andy y Janet lo pasaron muy bien en Ecuador.

▶ 1. Sí. 3. No. 5. Sí.
2. Sí. 4. No. 6. Sí.

20. Planta baja: bolsos y carteras
Primera planta: ropa de mujer
Segunda planta: trajes de caballero
▶ Answers will vary.

21. Answers will vary. Sample answers:
Cuando fui a una fiesta de la escuela llevé una camisa y unos pantalones nuevos. Cuando fui a hacer deporte llevé una sudadera, pantalones cortos y tenis. Cuando fui de excursión llevé unas botas para caminar y unos pantalones largos.
▶ Answers will vary.

22. 1. llevaron   4. llegaron
2. compraron   5. mezclaron
3. sacó   6. disfrutaron

Additional Resources

Fans Online activities
Practice Workbook

DESAFÍO 2

Describir la ropa

Presentation

- In *Desafío* 2, Tess and Patricia are in Peru to run in the annual llama race in Huancavelica.
- In this section, students will preview:
  - Words for colors, materials, and patterns of clothing.
  - Describing the look and fit of clothing.
  - Regular -*er* and -*ir* verbs in the preterite.
  - Time expressions to talk about the past.

Activities	Standards	Resources
Fotonovela	1.2, 2.1, 3.1, 3.2	Vis. Pres.
23.	1.3	
24.	1.2, 1.3, 2.1, 2.2	
25.	1.2, 1.3, 2.1	
26. Cultura	1.1, 1.2, 2.2, 3.1, 3.2, 4.2, 5.1	
Tu desafío	1.2, 3.1, 3.2, 5.1	

Teaching Suggestions

Warm-Up / Independent Starter

- Have students make a list of all of the unusual marathons they've heard of from around the world.

Preparation

- Start with the number 5 and see how many students have five unusual marathons. Increase your number in increments of five until you find a winner. Have the winner read off his or her list.

La fotonovela

Before Viewing

- Ask a volunteer to read the introduction to the *fotonovela* aloud. Point out the town of Huancavelica on a map of Peru.

After Viewing

- Ask students what Tess's confusion was about the race. A lama is another name for a monk from Tibet, but a llama is an animal. The double l (*ll*) is pronounced /ya/ in Spanish; therefore, a *carrera de llamas* is a llama race and a *carrera de lamas* would be a Tibetan monk race. Ask students if they understood the word play in the *fotonovela*.

Una carrera de llamas

Tess and Patricia are in Huancavelica, a village in the Peruvian Andes. Héctor Gonzáles, the town's mayor, has arrived to welcome them. The pair will take part in the town's annual llama race, which is three kilometers (1.9 miles) long.

Mamá, ¿tenemos que vestirnos de color anaranjado como los lamas del Tíbet?

Claro, como los monjes de las montañas.

¿Como los lamas del Tíbet?

¡Nooo! No es una carrera de lamas. Es una carrera de llamas, con elle.

Las llamas son esos animales de color blanco y café. Esto no es el Himalaya. ¡Estamos en los Andes!

Tienen que correr tres kilómetros detrás de los animales.

¡Yo ya corrí esta mañana!

¡Ah, claro! La lana de las llamas es muy suave.

Continuará...

23 **Detective de palabras**

▶ **Completa** estas oraciones.

1. Los monjes del Tíbet visten de color _____1_____.
2. Las llamas son animales de color _____2_____ y _____3_____.
3. Las llamas producen _____4_____.
4. La lana de las llamas es muy _____5_____.

Differentiated Instruction

DEVELOPING LEARNERS

- Have students read the dialogue in small groups. Ask them to stop after each line to summarize what they just read in Spanish and then say the meaning of the sentence in English, if necessary. Once students have finished, ask them to write a paragraph to summarize the entire dialogue in Spanish.

EXPANDING LEARNERS

- Have students write a "bulletin board post" to summarize what they read and saw in the *fotonovela*. Then have them get into small groups. Each group member will pass his or her post to another group member, who will in turn reply to the post. Tell students to keep passing their post until everyone in the group has responded. Once everyone has responded, ask students to pass the papers back to the original owner for him or her to read the replies.

24 ¿Comprendes?

▶ **Responde** a estas preguntas.

1. ¿De qué es la carrera en la que participan Tess y Patricia?
2. ¿Qué son las llamas?
3. ¿Dónde viven las llamas?
4. ¿Qué tienen que hacer Tess y Patricia en este desafío?
5. Al principio, Tess confunde (*confuses*) dos palabras. ¿Cuáles son?

25 Querido diario...

▶ **Lee** el diario de Tess y busca tres datos falsos. Después, escribe el diario con los datos correctos.

> Huancavelica, 17 de octubre
>
> Querido diario:
>
> Estoy con mi mamá en Huancavelica, una pequeña ciudad en las montañas de Argentina. Tenemos que participar en una carrera. ¡Una carrera de quince kilómetros!
>
> Al principio entendí «carrera de lamas» y pensé: ¡Qué raro! Pero luego mamá me lo explicó. Un lama es un monje del Tíbet que lleva ropa de color anaranjado. Y una llama es un animal de esta zona, de color blanco y negro. ¡Qué vergüenza!

 **CULTURA**

Huancavelica

Huancavelica es una pequeña ciudad situada en la parte central de Perú. Está en los Andes, al lado del río Ichu. Es una ciudad de origen colonial que conserva la típica Plaza de Armas y algunos edificios antiguos.

En la ciudad hay ocho iglesias de estilo colonial. También hay importantes ruinas arqueológicas en la zona.

Iglesia de San Juan Bautista.

26 Piensa y explica. ¿Fueron los Estados Unidos una colonia? ¿De quién? ¿Conoces ejemplos de la influencia colonial en los Estados Unidos?

 **TU DESAFÍO** | Visita la página web para aprender más sobre Huancavelica.

ciento cuarenta y siete **147**

HERITAGE LANGUAGE LEARNERS

• Ask students to imagine that Tess and Patricia were going to run a *lama* race instead of a *llama* race. Have students rewrite the dialogue to reflect a *lama* race. Students must include a description of the setting, what the participants would wear, and what they would look like. Have volunteers share their new dialogue with the class.

CRITICAL THINKING

• There are words that are spelled similarly in Spanish but have a very different meaning. The example from the *fotonovela* (*lama* and *llama*) is a prime example of how a misspelling or mispronunciation could change the entire meaning of a word. Ask students to discuss the importance of spelling and pronunciation, especially in a second language. As an example, consider the verb *sentir* (to feel). If conjugated or spelled incorrectly, it could be *sentar* (to sit).

Activities

24. Have students use the answers from the questions in this activity to write a paragraph to summarize the *fotonovela*.

25. Read the paragraph to students. Pause after each sentence. Tell students to raise their hands if the sentence has a false statement. They will nod if the entire sentence is true.

26. Discuss with students that downtown Richmond, Virginia, has original cobblestone streets from colonial times and Pensacola Village in Florida has preserved original architecture from colonial times.

 CULTURA

Huancavelica

Huancavelica is a small Peruvian city of about 40,000 people, most of whom are Quechua-speaking and practice subsistence farming and shepherding. The original name of Huancavelica was Villa Rica de Oropesa, given by its Spanish founders in 1572. The town was an important mercury-mining center during most of the colonial period.

Answer Key

23. 1. anaranjado   4. lana
2. blanco   5. suave
3. café

24. 1. Es una carrera de llamas.
2. Son animales de color blanco y café.
3. En los Andes.
4. Tienen que correr tres kilómetros detrás de los animales.
5. *Lama* y *llama.*

25. montañas de Argentina → de Perú
una carrera de 15 km → 3 km
blanco y negro → blanco y café

26. Answers will vary.

Additional Resources

Fans Online activities

147

DESAFÍO 2

Vocabulario – Describir la ropa

Presentation

- In this section, students will learn:
  - Words for colors, materials, and patterns of clothing.
  - To describe the look and fit of clothing.

Activities	Standards	Resources
Vocabulario	1.2	
27.	1.2	Audio
28.	1.2, 1.3	Audio
29.	1.1	
30.	1.1, 1.3, 5.1	
31. Conexiones	1.1, 1.2, 2.2, 3.1, 3.2, 4.2, 5.1	

Teaching Suggestions

Warm-Up / Independent Starter

- Ask students to look at the vocabulary presentation and note the pattern(s) that they like. Then have students write what the pattern(s) is / are similar to. For example: *Las rayas se parecen mucho a las rayas del sofá de mi sala.* This kind of association will help students remember their patterns.

Preparation

- Go over the vocabulary presentation with students. Draw their attention to the dialogue between Tess and Patricia. Ask students if shopping vocabulary is the same in English and in Spanish. Is this what students usually say when shopping with a friend or family member?

- Once you have finished going over the vocabulary presentation, ask students to go back to the vocabulary presentation from *Desafío 1*. Have them describe each article of clothing and each accessory using the new vocabulary they have just learned in this section.

Activities

27. Before you play the audio recording, ask students to describe each picture in words. Once they have finished, play the recording and then go over the answers with students. Did they get all the answers right?

148

DESAFÍO 2

Vocabulario

Describir la ropa

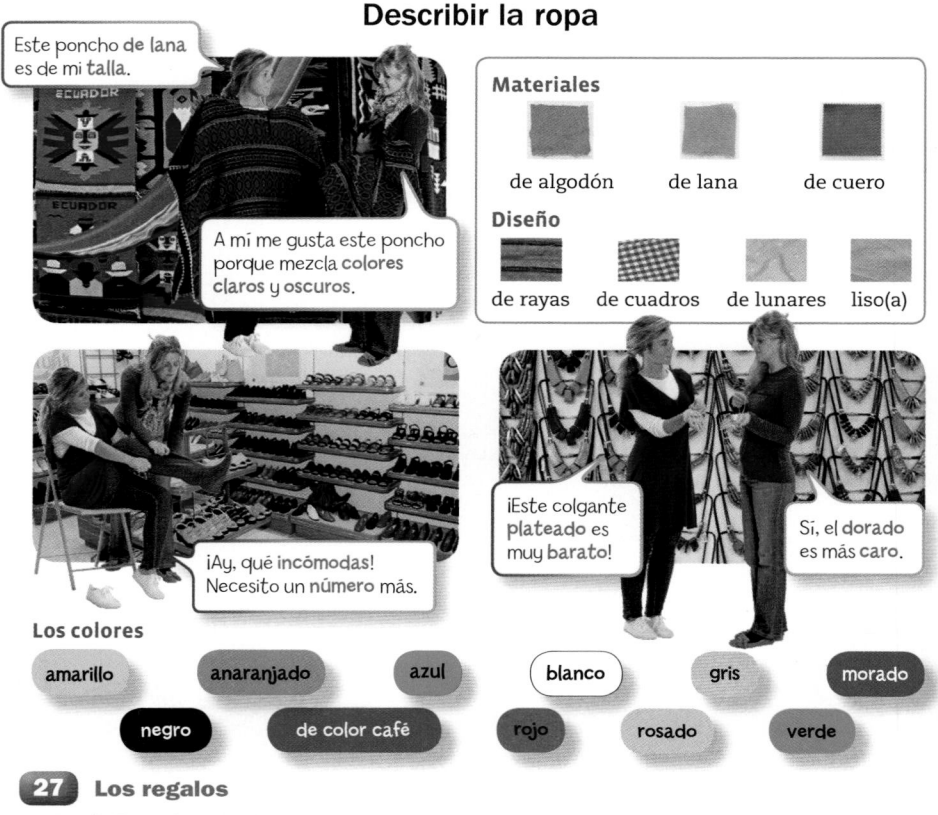

Este poncho de lana es de mi talla.

A mí me gusta este poncho porque mezcla colores claros y oscuros.

Materiales

de algodón · de lana · de cuero

Diseño

de rayas · de cuadros · de lunares · liso(a)

¡Ay, qué incómodas! Necesito un número más.

¡Este colgante plateado es muy barato!

Sí, el dorado es más caro.

Los colores

amarillo · anaranjado · azul · blanco · gris · morado

negro · de color café · rojo · rosado · verde

27 Los regalos

▶ **Escucha** a Patricia y relaciona cada regalo con la persona apropiada.

1. su mamá
2. su mejor amiga
3. su compañera de trabajo
4. su esposo
5. Tess

 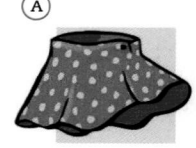  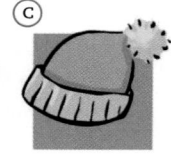 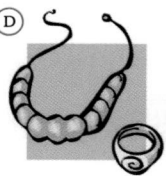 

(A) (B) (C) (D) (E)

148 ciento cuarenta y ocho

Differentiated Instruction

DEVELOPING LEARNERS

- Ask students to divide a sheet of white paper into four squares. Have them label each square with the name of one of the four seasons (i.e., *la primavera, el verano, el otoño,* and *el invierno*). Have students list in each square the colors, patterns, and materials they normally wear in each season. Once students have finished, have them share their answers with a classmate.

EXPANDING LEARNERS

- Have students get into pairs. Ask them to use the clothing items from activity 27 to say whether they would wear that particular item or not. For example:
  - A. *¿Te gusta esta falda de lunares?*
  - B. *No, no me gusta la ropa de lunares. ¿Y a ti?*
  - A. *A mí me gusta. Me parece muy alegre.*

28 Las compras

▶ **Escucha** y completa estas oraciones.

1. A Patricia le gustan unas botas azules _____.
2. Las botas de Tess no son _____.
3. A Tess le queda bien el suéter _____.
4. A Patricia le quedan mal los pantalones negros _____.
5. Tess va a comprar una falda gris _____.

29 Un desfile

▶ **Habla** con tu compañero(a). ¿Qué ropa llevan estos modelos?

Modelo *El chico lleva un pantalón...*

30 ¿Quién es?

▶ **Escribe** la ropa que lleva un(a) compañero(a) sin decir su nombre.

▶ **Habla.** Lee tu descripción a otro(a) compañero(a). Él/Ella tiene que adivinar a quién corresponde la descripción.

> Lleva unos jeans anchos muy modernos y una camiseta de rayas.

> ¿Es Sonia?

CONEXIONES: CIENCIAS

Los camélidos andinos

La llama y la alpaca son dos tipos de camélidos muy comunes en los Andes. La lana de estos animales se utiliza para hacer ropa tradicional y moderna, como ponchos, gorros, suéteres, etc. La lana de la alpaca es más cara que la lana de la llama, porque es muy suave *(soft)* y cálida *(warm)*.

31 **Piensa y explica.** ¿De qué material es la ropa que llevas habitualmente? ¿De dónde viene ese material?

Vocabulario – Describir la ropa

29. Make sure that students complete this activity with interactive conversation. Interactive conversation begins with a question and continues with an answer. For example:
A. *¿Qué lleva el chico?*
B. *El chico lleva pantalones...*

31. Seasons usually dictate the material we wear. Have students make a chart with the four seasons and the materials they wear in each season. Once students have finished, ask them to get into small groups and discuss the similarities and differences in their charts.

 AUDIO SCRIPT
See page 131I.

 CONEXIONES: CIENCIAS

Los camélidos andinos

Llamas are the largest of the South American camelids, which include the alpaca, guanaco, and vicuña. Llamas and alpacas are different animals. Alpacas are shorter and are not hard laborers. They are specifically bred for their expensive, warm wool. Llamas are used as pack animals for carrying heavy loads and are usually sheared every two years to make clothing. Both the llama and the alpaca are domestic animals. The guanaco and the vicuña are their wild counterparts.

Answer Key

27. 1. C   2. E   3. D   4. B   5. A
28. 1. incómodas   3. de rayas   5. de lana
         2. de su número 4. de cuero
29. Answers will vary.
30. Answers will vary.
         ▶ Answers will vary.
31. Answers will vary.

Additional Resources

Fans Online activities
Practice Workbook

HERITAGE LANGUAGE LEARNERS

- Ask students to imagine that they have a time portal that will take them to the year 3000. Have students describe the clothes, shoes, and accessories they see the people wearing. Tell students they must include the colors, patterns, and materials they see. Then have students compare the clothing we wear today to that of the people in the year 3000.

COOPERATIVE LEARNING

- Have students draw pictures on note cards to represent the colors and patterns in the vocabulary presentation. Then ask them to write the vocabulary words on the back of the note cards. In small groups, have students quiz each other on the flashcards. Students will have one minute to go through as many of the flashcards as possible. If the student guesses incorrectly, then the person holding the flashcards may correct him or her, but only after the person guesses incorrectly.

Gramática – Verbos regulares en *-er* y en *-ir*. Pretérito

Presentation

- In this section, students will learn:
  - Regular *-er* and *-ir* verbs in the preterite.
  - Time expressions to talk about the past.

Activities	Standards	Resources
Gramática	3.1	
32.	1.1, 4.1	
33.	1.3	
34.	1.2	Audio
35.	1.3	

Teaching Suggestions

Warm-Up / Independent Starter

- Ask students to look through a Spanish-language magazine to find words to describe what they are wearing today. Have students draw the clothing they are wearing today in their notebooks, then cut and paste the words from a magazine next to the drawing in their notebooks.

Preparation

- Read over the grammar presentation with students.
- Play a game as a class. Have students sit in a circle and choose one student to start the game. This student will say something he or she did yesterday (*ayer*). The next student will tell something he or she did the day before yesterday (*anteayer*), without repeating what the first student did. The third student will say something he did three days ago (*hace tres días*), but he or she must do so without repeating activities. Encourage students to mention the people involved as well.

Activities

32. Ask students to flip back to the grammar presentation in *Desafío 1*: regular *-ar* verbs in the preterite. Have them look at the *nosotros/nosotras* form to see if it follows the same pattern as the *nosotros* form of the regular *-er* and *-ir* verbs in the preterite.

Gramática

Verbos regulares en *-er* y en *-ir*. Pretérito

- Regular -er and -ir verbs have the same endings in the preterite tense.

VERBO COMER. PRETÉRITO

Singular		Plural	
yo	comí	nosotros nosotras	comimos
tú	comiste	vosotros vosotras	comisteis
usted él ella	comió	ustedes ellos ellas	comieron

VERBO ESCRIBIR. PRETÉRITO

Singular		Plural	
yo	escribí	nosotros nosotras	escribimos
tú	escribiste	vosotros vosotras	escribisteis
usted él ella	escribió	ustedes ellos ellas	escribieron

Marcadores temporales de pasado

- You can use these expressions to refer to the past tense:

el año pasado — la semana pasada — ayer — hoy
el mes pasado — anteayer — anoche

- You can also use the word *hace* to express the amount of time elapsed since an action was completed.

> Hace + time expression + que + verb in the preterite tense

Hace una semana que Tess y Patricia llegaron a los Andes.

> Verb in the preterite tense + hace + time expression

Tess y Patricia llegaron a los Andes **hace una semana**.

32 **Piensa.** En los verbos en -ar la forma nosotros es igual en el pasado y en el presente. ¿Sucede lo mismo en los verbos en -er y en -ir?

33 **¿Cuándo?**

▶ **Escribe** oraciones. ¿Cuándo hiciste estas actividades por última vez?

Modelo *Comí fruta por última vez ayer.*

1. comer fruta
2. escribir un mensaje de correo
3. correr
4. ver una película
5. beber un refresco
6. salir con tus amigos

Differentiated Instruction

DEVELOPING LEARNERS

- Have students create a two-column table. In the first column, students will write seven events that took place in the past using preterite *-er* and *-ir* verbs. In the second column, they will write how long ago these events took place. Then have students use this chart to write sentences. For example, if in the first column the event is *comí*, and in the second column the phrase is *hace una hora*, then the sentence would read, *Yo comí el almuerzo hace una hora.*

EXPANDING LEARNERS

- In groups of four, have students create a story. Ask them to elect one person to write. Taking turns within the group, each person has to add a line to the story. Begin with *Hace un año*, and keep adding lines until everyone in the group has added three lines. Ask volunteers to read the stories aloud to the class.

**34** **Final del día**

▶ **Escucha** a Patricia y decide si las oraciones se refieren al presente o al pasado.

1. a. presente   b. pasado
2. a. presente   b. pasado
3. a. presente   b. pasado

4. a. presente   b. pasado
5. a. presente   b. pasado
6. a. presente   b. pasado

▶ **Escucha** otra vez y escribe los cuatro marcadores temporales de pasado que utiliza Patricia.

35 **¿Qué más hicieron?**

▶ **Escribe.** ¿Qué más hicieron Tess y Patricia en Huancavelica?

Modelo *Tess y Patricia comieron en…*

▶ **Habla** con tu compañero(a). Imagina qué más cosas hicieron Tess y Patricia. Usa estos verbos.

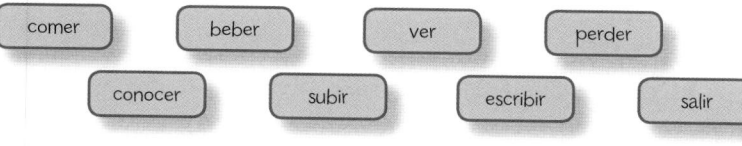

comer   beber   ver   perder

conocer   subir   escribir   salir

DESAFÍO 2
Gramática – Verbos regulares en *-er* y en *-ir*. Pretérito

33. To extend this activity, have students add the following activities to the list: *leer una revista, sacudir el polvo,* and *barrer la casa.*

35. To complete the second part of this activity, have students refer back to the *Cultura* box on the *fotonovela* page of this *Desafío.* Remind students that Huancavelica is a small and relatively poor city in Peru, so they must be inventive with their answers because technology may not always be an option.

AUDIO SCRIPT
See page 131I.

Answer Key

32. La forma *nosotros* es igual en el pretérito y en el presente de los verbos en *-ir: -imos.* En los verbos en *-er* es diferente: *-emos* (presente), *-imos* (pretérito).

33. Answers will vary. Sample answers:
1. Comí fruta por última vez esta mañana.
2. Escribí un correo por última vez anoche.
3. Corrí por última vez la semana pasada.
4. Vi una película por última vez el domingo pasado.
5. Bebí un refresco por última vez hace una hora.
6. Salí con mis amigos por última vez anteayer.

34. 1. a   2. b   3. b   4. b   5. a   6. b
▶ Anoche, la semana pasada, ayer, el mes pasado.

35. Answers will vary. Sample answers:
A. Ellas comieron en un restaurante.
B. Tess visitó una iglesia colonial.
C. Patricia subió a una montaña.
D. Tess y Patricia conocieron a alguien.
▶ Answers will vary.

Additional Resources

Fans Online activities
Practice Workbook

HERITAGE LANGUAGE LEARNERS

• Ask students to chronicle the fans' adventures through the different regions of the Spanish-speaking world. Have students begin with the *desafíos* in Central America, continue through the Antilles Islands, and end with what they have seen so far in the Andes region. The only rule is that they cannot use the verb *ir* in the past tense.

SPECIAL-NEEDS LEARNERS

• For students with auditory difficulties or auditory processing disorders, hand out copies of audio scripts so that they can read along while you play the audio recording. Also, some students may prefer to write a script instead of talking to a partner for the speaking portion of certain activities. They can still use the verbs on the page for inspiration.

Comunicación

Presentation

- In this section, students will integrate the vocabulary and grammar from *Desafío 2* in order to describe the colors, materials, patterns, and the look and fit of clothing. They will also use regular *-er* and *-ir* verbs in the preterite, and time expressions to talk about the past.

Activities	Standards	Resources
36.	1.2, 1.3	Audio
37.	1.1	
38.	1.3, 5.2	
39. Final del desafío	1.2, 1.3, 2.1	
Tu desafío	1.2, 1.3	

Teaching Suggestions

Warm-Up / Independent Starter

- Ask students to answer the following questions:
  1. *¿Qué hicieron tú y tus amigos el fin de semana pasado?*
  2. *¿Qué ropa llevaste ayer?*
  3. *¿Qué nota sacaste en el examen de Español hace un mes?*

Preparation

- Take 10 minutes to review the vocabulary and grammar themes from *Desafío 2*.
- Refer students back to the *fotonovela* for *Desafío 2*. Have them find all of the colors, materials, and patterns of clothing, the look and fit of clothing, regular *-er* and *-ir* verbs in the preterite, and time expressions to talk about the past within the dialogue. Do students understand the dialogue better now that they have gone through the vocabulary and grammar from the *Desafío*?
- Ask students to complete the *Comunicación* activities individually. Have them take note of any of the activities that they need help or more practice with. Once students have finished the *Comunicación* activities, group them by the activities with which they had trouble or needed more practice. Within the group, have students work together to help each other learn the theme.

Comunicación

  36 ¿Qué pasó?

▶ **Escucha** a Manuel, un amigo de Tess y de Patricia, y ordena las ilustraciones.

▶ **Escribe** un texto explicando lo que le pasó a Manuel. Utiliza las palabras del cuadro.

perder las llaves	volver a casa	tocar a la puerta	no responder nadie
llamar por teléfono	escribir un mensaje	abrir la puerta	salir corriendo

  37 Tus vacaciones

▶ **Habla** con tu compañero(a) de tus últimas vacaciones. ¿Adónde viajaste? ¿Qué viste? ¿Qué comiste? ¿Qué bebiste?

Modelo

> En mis últimas vacaciones viajé a Perú.

> ¿Y qué viste?

Differentiated Instruction

DEVELOPING LEARNERS

- To reinforce the vocabulary from this *Desafío*, have students make a visual guide to the terms. On a small poster board, they should write the words using visual cues to trigger the meaning, such as writing the colors and patterns using the corresponding color or pattern, or decorating the letters of the word to suggest the meaning. These posters can be used at home or at school.

EXPANDING LEARNERS

- Have students ask a partner the following questions. Then have them write a paragraph to summarize their partner's answers.
  1. *¿Hace cuánto tiempo escribiste un mensaje?*
  2. *¿Hace cuánto tiempo comiste?*
  3. *¿Hace cuánto tiempo corriste?*
  4. *¿Hace cuánto tiempo bebiste agua?*
  5. *¿Hace cuánto tiempo seguiste una receta para hacer un pastel?*

38 Un disfraz

▶ **Escribe.** Tim va a una fiesta de disfraces *(costumes)*. Dibuja un disfraz de payaso *(clown)* para él y escribe un texto describiéndolo con detalle.

Modelo

Para la fiesta, Tim necesita una camisa ancha, de lunares rojos. También...

Final del desafío

La Gaceta de Huancavelica

Carrera de llamas de Huancavelica
Sorprendente victoria de dos estadounidenses
Por GERMÁN VILLEGAS

Las estadounidenses Patricia y Tess Williams ___1___ (vencer) ayer en la Carrera de Llamas de Huancavelica, por delante de Ismael Sánchez y Casimiro Luján.

Los periodistas les preguntaron y las dos mujeres estadounidenses ___2___ (responder) así:

«Nosotras solo ___3___ (correr) detrás de los animales.

Las llamas ___4___ (decidir) colaborar. Ellas son las verdaderas campeonas.»

Patricia y Tess Williams.

39 ¡Tess y Patricia campeonas!

▶ **Lee** el artículo del periódico local y complétalo con las formas correspondientes del pretérito.

 **TU DESAFÍO** — Visita la página web. Escucha las preguntas de tu *Minientrevista Desafío 2* y escribe las respuestas.

HERITAGE LANGUAGE LEARNERS

• Have students visit a world news website and take notes on what happened yesterday around the world. They can look at weather, sports, current events, politics, etc. Based on what they read, have students write their own world news report. Their report must include at least three Spanish-speaking countries and at least ten events. Have students record their reports to play for the class.

MULTIPLE INTELLIGENCES:
Intrapersonal Intelligence

• Ask students to write a description of what they wore yesterday. They must include clothes, shoes, accessories, colors, patterns, and materials in their descriptions. Tell students to talk to their classmates and group themselves by what they wore yesterday. Do they dress similarly to their classmates or do they have their own particular style?

Activities

36. Before you play the audio, ask students to guess the order in which they believe the story progressed. Then have them write a short story about what they believe happened to Manuel. Have volunteers share their stories with the class. Play the audio. Afterwards, see which students' stories came the closest to what actually happened to Manuel.

37. Instead of talking to a partner, have students write a script. Tell them their scripts need an introduction, a question and answer dialogue, and a conclusion in order to be a complete skit.

38. Ask students to think about the costume they wore last Halloween and draw a picture of Tim wearing that costume. Have students share their pictures with the class.

 AUDIO SCRIPT
See page 131I.

Answer Key

36. B, E, D, A, C
▶ Answers will vary. Sample answer: Manuel perdió las llaves. Volvió a su casa y llamó a su esposa por teléfono, pero ella no contestó. Entonces le escribió un mensaje a su hija y ella le abrió la puerta. Después él salió corriendo para encontrarse con Patricia y Tess.

37. Answers will vary.

38. Answers will vary.

39. 1. vencieron   3. corrimos
      2. respondieron 4. decidieron

Additional Resources

Fans Online activities
Practice Workbook

153

DESAFÍO 3

Hablar de lugares en la comunidad

Presentation

- In *Desafío 3*, Diana and Rita are in Oruro, Bolivia. There they must wear a costume and participate in the most famous carnival in the Andes.

- In this section, students will preview:
  - Words for stores and public establishments.
  - The verbs *ser, ir, decir, tener, estar* and *hacer* in the preterite tense.

Activities	Standards	Resources
Fotonovela	1.2, 2.1	Vis. Pres.
40.	1.2, 1.3	
41.	1.2	
42.	1.2	Audio
43. Cultura	1.1, 1.2, 2.1, 3.2, 4.2, 5.1	Video
Tu desafío	2.1, 5.2	

Teaching Suggestions

Warm-Up / Independent Starter

- Ask students to answer the following questions in complete sentences:
  1. *¿Cuándo fue la última vez que llevaste una camisa de rayas?*
  2. *¿Hace cuánto tiempo llevaste un suéter de lana?*
  3. *¿Hace cuánto tiempo llevaste ropa incómoda?*

Preparation

- Have a volunteer read the introduction to the *fotonovela*. Ask students what the difference between a carnival and a parade is. (A carnival is a week's worth of festivities that include parades, but a parade is a single event.) Do you have a *carnaval* or special parades in your city or town? Discuss the event(s) in your community.

 ### La fotonovela

Before Viewing

- Ask volunteers to read the parts of Diana and Rita. Tell students to pay close attention to the pictures as the volunteers read their parts.

After Viewing

- Ask students why they think Diana and Rita had to find all of those places to prepare for the *carnaval*.

154

El carnaval de Oruro

Diana and Rita have just arrived in Oruro, a former mining town in Bolivia that holds the most famous carnival in the Andean region. They must don traditional costumes and parade through the streets of Oruro with all the dancers.

Continuará…

40 **Detective de palabras**

▶ **Completa** estas oraciones.

1. Rita va a una _____1_____ de disfraces.
2. Diana quiere comprar _____2_____ en la tienda de _____3_____.
3. Los disfraces a cuadros se venden en las tiendas de _____4_____.
4. Rita quiere ir a una _____5_____.
5. Hay una peluquería en el _____6_____.

Differentiated Instruction

DEVELOPING LEARNERS

- Ask students to imagine that they are going with Diana and Rita to the carnival in Oruro. Before they can go, students must research traditional carnival costumes. Have them write a detailed description of these costumes, including color, material, patterns, and design. Then have students work with a partner to write a dialogue similar to the one in the *fotonovela*. Ask volunteers to read their dialogues aloud.

EXPANDING LEARNERS

- Ask students to go through the *fotonovela* and classify all the verbs by their meaning, use, and conjugation. For example, the first sentence of the first scene says, *¡Ay, tía, mira qué bonitas!* The verb *mira* is in the affirmative *tú* command form. Diana used it to urge her aunt Rita to look at the costumes. Have students go through each scene and classify the verbs.

41 Tiendas y establecimientos

▶ **Relaciona** cada palabra con la fotografía correspondiente.

una peluquería

un centro comercial

una tienda de bisutería

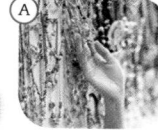 A 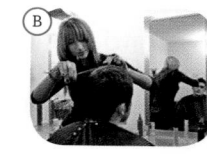 B  C

42 ¿Estuviste en el carnaval?

 ▶ **Escucha** la conversación de Rita y la dependienta de la tienda de disfraces y decide a quién corresponden estos hechos.

1. Es la primera vez que está en el carnaval de Oruro.
2. Fue al desfile del carnaval con un disfraz.
3. Hizo muchas fotos en el desfile.
4. Hoy no fue al desfile.
5. Dijo que Diana compró unos complementos.

RITA

DEPENDIENTA

 **CULTURA**

El carnaval de Oruro

La ciudad de Oruro está en Bolivia, a 3.706 metros de altitud (12.159 pies). Allí se celebra el carnaval de Oruro, la fiesta tradicional más famosa de Bolivia. En el carnaval mezclan las tradiciones indígenas y españolas, y los hechos históricos de Bolivia. En 2001 la UNESCO declaró esta celebración Obra Maestra del Patrimonio Oral e Intangible de la Humanidad.

Durante los diez días que dura la fiesta, varios grupos folclóricos recorren la ciudad y la gente baila con disfraces y máscaras de muchos colores. Las danzas más famosas son la diablada y la morenada.

43 Compara. ¿En qué fiestas o celebraciones se utilizan disfraces? Compara el carnaval de Oruro con otras fiestas similares.

▶→ **TU DESAFÍO** Visita la página web para aprender más sobre el carnaval de Oruro.

HERITAGE LANGUAGE LEARNERS

• The carnival celebrations are an important part of the culture of Latin America. Ask students to share the traditions surrounding the carnivals in their country of origin. Then have them draw their own carnival costumes. These costumes must represent the history and culture of their country, and must be accompanied by a description of each element of the costume.

CRITICAL THINKING

• Ask students to discuss the similarities and differences between a carnival and a parade. One similarity is that they both attract thousands of spectators, but what are the fundamental differences between the two? Discuss this in small groups or as a class. Then have students who have attended a carnival share their experiences with the rest of the class. Encourage students to describe the carnival with their five senses.

Hablar de lugares en la comunidad

Activities

41. Before students begin this activity, ask them to compare the pictures in this activity to the pictures and words associated with them from the *fotonovela*.

42. Have students rewrite the sentences to include the person's name. For example: *Es la primera vez que Rita está en el carnaval de Oruro.*

 AUDIO SCRIPT
See page 131l.

 CULTURA

El carnaval de Oruro

The Oruro Carnival has been an annual event since the late 1700s, but its origins go back much further. This carnival is based on the festivals that the pre-Columbian inhabitants of this region, the Uro people, used to have. The elaborate masks dancers wear represent animals, devils, and Inca rulers and gods. Some of these masks and costumes are exhibited at the *Museo de la Diablada*, in Oruro.

Answer Key

40. 1. tienda   4. artesanía
2. complementos   5. peluquería
3. bisutería   6. centro comercial

41. A. Una tienda de bisutería
B. Una peluquería
C. Un centro comercial

42. Rita: 1, 3, 5
Dependienta: 2, 4

43. Answers will vary.

Additional Resources

Fans Online activities

Unit 3
DESAFÍO 3

Vocabulario – Tiendas y establecimientos

Presentation

- In this section, students will learn vocabulary for stores and public establishments.

Activities	Standards	Resources
Vocabulario	1.2	
44.	1.2, 1.3	
45.	1.2, 1.3	Audio
46.	1.1, 5.1	
47. Comparaciones	1.1, 1.2, 2.2, 3.2, 4.2, 5.1	

Teaching Suggestions

Warm-Up / Independent Starter

- Ask students to decide if they would like to go to the carnival in Oruro, Bolivia. Have them write a paragraph to say why they would or wouldn't like to go. They may do more research on the Internet about the carnival or the city of Oruro if necessary.

Preparation

- Go over the vocabulary presentation with students. Have them write the names of their favorite stores to go with the vocabulary. This way, students can associate the vocabulary with places in their everyday lives.
- Remind students that the suffix -ería represents a store that specializes in one thing. For example, the peluquería specializes in pelo, or hair.

Activities

45. Before you play the audio recording, have students write where they would go to buy each item. Then ask them to take notes as they listen to the recording. Finally, have them write a short paragraph about what Diana and Rita purchased and where they purchased it.

46. Have students organize their conversation before they begin. Ask them to list all of the family members and friends they would buy gifts for, and what each person would like. Then have students decide where they would buy each gift. This will help the conversation flow smoothly.

156

DESAFÍO 3

Vocabulario

Tiendas y establecimientos

Primero fui a una tienda de disfraces, compré una revista en el quiosco y al final fui a hacer la compra a un supermercado.

Yo compré unos aretes en la tienda de bisutería y luego fui a la peluquería y a una librería.

44 ¿Adónde fueron?

▶ **Completa** estas oraciones.

1. Rita fue a una _____ para comprarse unos aretes.
2. Rita fue a la _____ para comprar un libro sobre el carnaval de Oruro.
3. Diana y Rita fueron a una _____ para comprar recuerdos de Bolivia.
4. Diana fue al _____ para comprar unos periódicos y unas revistas.
5. Diana y Rita fueron a la _____ para comprar un CD.

156 ciento cincuenta y seis

Differentiated Instruction

DEVELOPING LEARNERS

- Have students get into small groups to play a guessing game. One student will say an item that someone could buy at one of the stores from the vocabulary presentation. The rest of the group guesses the store where the item can be found. The student who guesses correctly will take the next turn. For example, student A says, *camisa de rayas* and the rest of the group will try to guess *la tienda de ropa*.

EXPANDING LEARNERS

- Ask students to design and draw their own shopping malls. Their mall must have two levels, and they should name and clearly label each store. Have students use large pieces of construction paper to draw and design their malls. Once students have finished, have them get into groups of three to explain the stores in their malls to each other. Students may also combine their malls to make a mega shopping center to present to the class.

45 **Las compras de Rita y Diana**

 ▶ **Escucha** y decide. ¿Qué cosas compraron Diana y Rita en Oruro?

 (A)    (B)    (C)   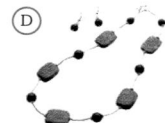 (D)

 (E)    (F)    (G)    (H)

▶ **Escribe**. ¿Qué compraron y adónde fueron Rita y Diana?

46 **Los recuerdos**

 ▶ **Habla** con tu compañero(a). ¿Cuándo compraste regalos para tu familia o para tus amigos(as)? ¿Qué compraste? ¿Dónde?

Modelo   A. *¿Qué compraste?*
B. *A mi mamá le compré una pulsera porque le gustan mucho las joyas.*
A. *¿Dónde la compraste?*
B. *En una joyería.*

 **COMPARACIONES**

El aguayo, un textil tradicional

El aguayo es un textil tradicional de las zonas andinas de Perú y Bolivia. Es un cuadrado de lana o de algodón tejido con figuras y motivos simbólicos. En estas regiones, cada mujer tiene un aguayo.

Los aguayos tienen múltiples usos. Se usan como prenda de vestir, para llevar a los niños pequeños, para sentarse, para llevar mercancías (*merchandise*), para poner alimentos encima… Pero principalmente son una muestra de identidad y de la cultura de cada región.

47 **Piensa y explica.** ¿Conoces alguna prenda similar al aguayo? ¿De qué país es? Descríbela y explica para qué sirve.

ciento cincuenta y siete 157

Vocabulario – Tiendas y establecimientos

47. Encourage students to research garments such as the *rebozo* and *sarape* (from Mexico), and the *huipil* (from Guatemala).

 AUDIO SCRIPT
See page 131I.

 COMPARACIONES

El aguayo, un textil tradicional

Weaving has been an important part of the Andean way of life for thousands of years. In small towns and rural areas, girls learn to weave at a young age. Before the arrival of the Europeans, llama and alpaca wool was used almost exclusively, but today sheep wool and cotton are also used. One of the most common Andean garments is the *aguayo*, which is a square shawl made of two hand-woven strips joined edge to edge. Patterns, colors, weaving style, and motifs vary from region to region.

Answer Key

44. 1. tienda de bisutería   4. quiosco
2. librería   5. tienda de música
3. tienda de artesanía

45. B, D, A, G

▶ Answers will vary. Sample answer: Rita y Diana fueron a un quiosco a comprar unas revistas. Después fueron a una tienda de bisutería y compraron unos aretes y un collar. Luego compraron una máscara en una tienda de artesanía. Al final fueron a un supermercado para comprar fruta.

46. Answers will vary.

47. Answers will vary.

Additional Resources

Fans Online activities
Practice Workbook

HERITAGE LANGUAGE LEARNERS

• Ask students to list some other specialty stores not mentioned in the vocabulary presentation. Then have them get into pairs and talk about the specialty stores. One student will say a specialty store and his or her partner will describe it. For example:
A. *La mueblería.*
B. *Es un lugar donde se venden muebles.*

SPECIAL-NEEDS LEARNERS

For students with vision impairments, pair the visually impaired student with another student. The students without vision impairments will describe the vocabulary in the presentation in words to their partners. For example: *la zapatería. Se venden zapatos en este lugar. Los zapatos son la especialidad de este tipo de tienda. La zapatería.* This is also an excellent exercise for all students, regardless of physical impairment.

DESAFÍO 3

Gramática – Verbos irregulares en el pretérito. *Ser, ir, decir, tener, estar* y *hacer*

Presentation

- In this section, students will learn to conjugate the irregular verbs *ser, ir, hacer, estar, tener,* and *decir* in the preterite tense.

Activities	Standards	Resources
Gramática	3.1	
48.	1.2, 1.3	
49.	1.2, 1.3	
50.	1.3	
51.	1.2	Audio
52.	1.1, 1.3	
53. Conexiones	1.1, 1.2, 3.1, 5.1	

Teaching Suggestions

Warm-Up / Independent Starter

- Have students list the places they have visited in the last two weeks, and describe what they purchased at each location. For example: *La tienda de bisutería → unos aretes azules y un collar plateado.*

Preparation

- Go over the grammar presentation with students. Have them note that the verbs *ir* and *ser* have the same conjugation.
- Let students know that they can use the acronym "dish" to remember some of the irregular preterite verbs. Write the words **D**ecir, **I**r, **S**er, and **H**acer on the board, one under the other, so the first letters spell out the word *dish*. Encourage students to come up with their own acronyms to help them remember these irregular verbs.

Activities

49. Remind students that verbs are conjugated based on the subject of the sentence. Sometimes the pronoun is not used, so students need to determine which word(s) is / (are) used in place of the pronoun. For instance, if the subject is *Silvia y yo,* the verb should be conjugated in the *nosotros* form.

158

Gramática

Verbos irregulares en el pretérito. *Ser, ir, decir, tener, estar* y *hacer*

- These are some common irregular verbs in the preterite:

VERBOS SER E IR. PRETÉRITO

Singular		Plural	
yo	fui	nosotros nosotras	fuimos
tú	fuiste	vosotros vosotras	fuisteis
usted él ella	fue	ustedes ellos ellas	fueron

VERBO DECIR. PRETÉRITO

Singular		Plural	
yo	dije	nosotros nosotras	dijimos
tú	dijiste	vosotros vosotras	dijisteis
usted él ella	dijo	ustedes ellos ellas	dijeron

VERBO TENER. PRETÉRITO

Singular		Plural	
yo	tuve	nosotros nosotras	tuvimos
tú	tuviste	vosotros vosotras	tuvisteis
usted él ella	tuvo	ustedes ellos ellas	tuvieron

VERBO ESTAR. PRETÉRITO

Singular		Plural	
yo	estuve	nosotros nosotras	estuvimos
tú	estuviste	vosotros vosotras	estuvisteis
usted él ella	estuvo	ustedes ellos ellas	estuvieron

VERBO HACER. PRETÉRITO

Singular		Plural	
yo	hice	nosotros nosotras	hicimos
tú	hiciste	vosotros vosotras	hicisteis
usted él ella	hizo	ustedes ellos ellas	hicieron

48 **Compara.** ¿En inglés también hay verbos irregulares en el pasado? Pon algunos ejemplos.

49 **La fiesta de Oruro**

▶ **Completa** estas oraciones.

1. Yo _____ en el carnaval de Oruro. *(estar)*
2. Rita _____ a la joyería. *(ir)*
3. ¿Tú _____ tiempo para ir de compras? *(tener)*
4. La fiesta de disfraces _____ ayer. *(ser)*

Differentiated Instruction

DEVELOPING LEARNERS

- Ask students to write sentences using all of the conjugations of each verb. Over-practice each theme, so that students will not forget how to conjugate these irregular verbs in the preterite tense. Tell students to pay close attention to the *vosotros/vosotras* conjugation form, as it is not practiced as frequently as the other forms. Have volunteers share their sentences with the class.

EXPANDING LEARNERS

- Ask students to create a story using all of the irregular verbs presented in the grammar presentation. They may use one of the following themes: *Mi familia*, *Mi ropa*, or *Mi comunidad*. Their stories must be at least ten sentences long and have an introduction, a body, and a resolution. Ask volunteers to read their stories aloud and have the rest of the class vote for the student that made the best use of all of the verbs in the grammar presentation.

50 Un día divertido

▶ **Escribe.** ¿Qué hicieron Rita y Diana ayer?

Modelo estar → *Rita y Diana estuvieron en Oruro para asistir al carnaval.*

① hacer ② estar ③ ir

51 ¿Recuerdas?

▶ **Escucha** y une las dos columnas. ¿Quién hizo estas cosas?

Ⓐ

1. ir a cenar a un restaurante
2. tener una fiesta
3. estar enferma
4. ir a comprar ropa de abrigo
5. ser voluntarias en una asociación
6. hacer fotos con su cámara nueva

Ⓑ

a. Andy
b. Mack
c. Diana y Rita
d. Patricia y Tess
e. Janet
f. Tim

52 ¿Qué hicieron ustedes?

▶ **Habla** con tres compañeros(as). Pregúntales qué hicieron la semana pasada. ¿Tienen alguna coincidencia?

Modelo A. ¿Qué hicieron la semana pasada?
   B. Yo fui a ver un partido de béisbol.

CONEXIONES: CIENCIAS

El mal de altura

Bolivia es un país muy elevado. Su altitud media es de 3.658 metros (12.000 pies). En algunas zonas altas, los visitantes pueden sufrir el llamado «mal de altura» o «mal de montaña»: les duele la cabeza, se sienten cansados o mareados *(dizzy)*, no pueden respirar *(breathe)* o tienen náuseas.

Los expertos recomiendan subir gradualmente para acostumbrarse *(get used to)* a la altitud.

53 Explica. ¿Por qué crees que la altitud puede producir esos síntomas?

ciento cincuenta y nueve 159

Gramática – Verbos irregulares en el pretérito. *Ser, ir, decir, tener, estar y hacer*

51. Before playing the audio, have students write in their notebook the third person singular and plural forms of each of the verbs in items 1–6. Then play the recording.

AUDIO SCRIPT
See page 131J.

CONEXIONES: CIENCIAS

El mal de altura

At higher altitudes, air pressure is reduced and there are lower amounts of breathable oxygen available. These two conditions may cause mild reactions in some people, including shortness of breath, headaches, and nausea. These symptoms usually dissipate as the body gradually adapts to the altitude. Doctors recommend sleeping at a lower altitude than the highest you reach during the day, and ascending gradually.

Answer Key

48. Sí, por ejemplo: *to be, to go, to do, to have y to say.*

49. 1. estuve   3. tuviste
   2. fue   4. fue

50. 1. Diana hizo fotos.
   2. Diana estuvo en la peluquería.
   3. Rita fue a una tienda de disfraces.

51. 1. b   2. f   3. e   4. a   5. c   6. d

52. Answers will vary.

53. Answers will vary.

Additional Resources

Fans Online activities
Practice Workbook

HERITAGE LANGUAGE LEARNERS

• Ask students to look for fairy tales or fables in Spanish that frequently use the verbs mentioned in the grammar presentation. Have them read the fairy tale or fable to the class. If the story is similar to one in another culture, have students discuss the similarities and differences between the two.

TOTAL PHYSICAL RESPONSE (TPR)

• Read the following story to students. Have them pat their head if they hear a form of the preterite of the verb *ser* and to raise both hands if they hear the preterite of the verb *ir*. *Ayer, cuando fui a casa de mis abuelos, vi un cuadro nuevo en la pared. Mi abuelo me dijo que él fue a un mercadillo la semana pasada y lo compró. Para mí fue toda una sorpresa porque a mi abuelo no le gusta la pintura. Pasé una tarde divertida y durante unas horas fuimos una familia unida por el arte.*

159

Unit 3
DESAFÍO 3

Comunicación

Presentation

- In this section, students will integrate the vocabulary and grammar from *Desafío 3* in order to talk about stores and public establishments. They will also use the verbs *ser*, *ir*, *decir*, *tener*, and *hacer* in the preterite tense.

Activities	Standards	Resources
54.	1.2, 1.3	
55.	1.3	
56.	1.2, 1.3	Audio
57. Final del desafío	1.2, 1.3, 5.1	

Teaching Suggestions

Warm-Up / Independent Starter

- Ask students what kind of store they would own if they could. Have them describe the inside and outside of the store, and include a description of the inventory. Then have students illustrate their written descriptions.

Preparation

- Have volunteers share their descriptions and illustrations with the class. While students work on the *Comunicación* activities, collect all of the illustrations and create a shopping mall. Paste each illustration to cardboard or poster board cut out in the shape of a mall plan. Once students have finished the *Comunicación* activities, show the class the mall. You can name it after your school as a personal touch.
- Take 10 minutes to review the vocabulary and grammar themes from *Desafío 3*.
- Refer students back to the *fotonovela* for *Desafío 3*. Have them find all of the stores and public establishments and the verbs *ser*, *ir*, *hacer*, *estar*, *tener*, and *decir* in the preterite tense within the dialogue. Do students understand the dialogue better now that they have gone through the vocabulary and grammar from the *Desafío*?
- Go over the *Comunicación* activities as a class as the review for the *Desafío* quiz. Encourage students to ask questions about the topics they do not fully understand.

160

Comunicación

54 **¿Comprendes?**

▶ **Lee** el mensaje de correo de Diana y decide si las oraciones son ciertas o falsas. Después, corrige las oraciones falsas.

> Hola, Pablo. ¿Cómo estás? Yo estoy con mi tía en Oruro, una ciudad boliviana. Ayer salimos a la calle para ver las celebraciones del carnaval. Vimos un desfile con mucha gente disfrazada y bandas tocando música típica. ¡Qué espectáculo!
> Más tarde, mi tía fue a una tienda de disfraces porque decidió vestirse como los participantes del desfile. Compró un disfraz y una máscara. Yo fui a una tienda de bisutería y me compré unos aretes y un collar. Mañana vamos a un mercado de artesanía.
> Un beso de tu amiga,
> Diana

1. Diana y su tía hicieron un viaje a una ciudad mexicana.
2. Ayer ellas se quedaron en casa.
3. En el desfile participó poca gente.
4. Diana fue a un quiosco a comprar unos aretes y un collar.
5. Diana y Rita fueron ayer a comprar comida al mercado.

55 **El diario de Rita**

▶ **Escribe** una página del diario de Rita. ¿Qué hicieron ayer Diana y ella en Oruro?

Por la mañana	Por la tarde	Por la noche
 IR	 COMPRAR	 CENAR
 ESTAR	 VER	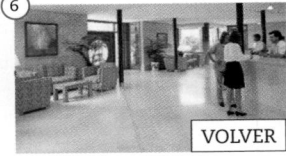 VOLVER

160 ciento sesenta

Differentiated Instruction

DEVELOPING LEARNERS

- Have students describe a typical shopping day at the mall. They must include the stores they went to, what they purchased at each store, and how much time they spent in each store. Their descriptions should use the preterite tense and should be in a paragraph of at least ten sentences. Once students have finished, have them compare their shopping day with that of a classmate.

EXPANDING LEARNERS

- Have students hypothesize about the preterite tense conjugations of the following verbs. Since they are all related to the verbs in this *Desafío*, students should associate them to the core verb and use them to expand their language skills.
  – *mantener* (to maintain)
  – *contener* (to contain)
  – *predecir* (to predict)
  – *contradecir* (to contradict)
  – *deshacer* (to undo)
  – *rehacer* (to redo)

56 **Los lugares de la comunidad**

 ▶ **Escucha** y une las tres columnas. ¿Qué compró cada persona? ¿Dónde?

Ⓐ	Ⓑ	Ⓒ
Diana	un libro	centro comercial
Rita	unos aretes y un collar	quiosco
Mack	una revista y unos periódicos	librería
Tim	un suéter de lana y un abrigo azul	tienda de artesanía
Andy	unas gafas de sol	tienda de complementos
Janet	regalos para su familia	joyería

▶ **Escribe** oraciones con la información anterior.

Modelo   *Andy compró una revista y unos periódicos en un quiosco.*

Final del desafío

Hola. Estoy buscando a mi tía. Estuvo aquí hace media hora.

¡Huy! Aquí entra y sale mucha gente.

Es una señora morena. Hoy salió de casa con un vestido morado.

¡Ah, sí! ¡La señora americana! Se fue a la peluquería, en el centro comercial.

Compró un disfraz de rayas y una máscara como esta.

Lo siento, yo no soy tu tía Rita.

57 **¿Quién es Rita?**

▶ **Escribe.** Diana tiene problemas. Su tía está disfrazada y ella no puede encontrarla. Dibuja y escribe el final de la historia.

ciento sesenta y uno   161

HERITAGE LANGUAGE LEARNERS

• Ask students to reply to Diana's e-mail. Have them imagine they are going to participate in a carnival in their country of origin and they will need to go to different specialty stores to pick up their costumes and accessories. Tell students to reply to Diana with what they did and where they went to get ready for the carnival, and then describe what they purchased from each store. They must include any other preparations they had to do to completely dress in costume.

COOPERATIVE LEARNING

• Ask students to get into groups of four. Tell them that your class planned last year's Halloween experience in the mall for children aged 2–10. Instead of candy, the mall gave away specialty items from each store. One student in the group will decide what each store gave away, another student will decide and describe the theme of the Halloween costumes, another student will decide which stores the children visited, and the last student will record all of the information on paper. Each group member must add his or her part to complete the story.

Activities

54. Start at one end of the classroom and ask each student to read one sentence from Diana's e-mail to Pablo. Encourage the class to pay attention, so they don't lose the flow of the e-mail. Once students have finished reading, you can read each item aloud, and allow students to call out *cierto* or *falso*.

56. Have students guess what they think each person purchased and where they purchased each item. Then play the audio recording twice and ask students whether they were mostly right or wrong.

57. Tell students to imagine they were in Diana's shoes. What would they do to find their aunt? Have students put their scene in the preterite tense as if this is what they did to find Aunt Rita.

 AUDIO SCRIPT
See page 131J.

Answer Key

54. 1. Falso. Viajaron a una ciudad boliviana.
2. Falso. Ayer ellas salieron a la calle.
3. Falso. En el desfile participó mucha gente.
4. Falso. Fue a una tienda de bisutería.
5. Falso. Fueron a ver el carnaval.

55. Answers will vary.

56. Diana compró unos aretes y un collar en una joyería.
Rita compró un libro en una librería.
Mack compró regalos para su familia en una tienda de artesanía.
Tim compró unas gafas de sol en una tienda de complementos.
Janet compró un suéter de lana y un abrigo azul en un centro comercial.

57. Answers will vary.

Additional Resources

Fans Online activities
Practice Workbook

161

Unit 3
DESAFÍO 4
Hablar sobre compras en pasado

Presentation

- In *Desafío 4*, Tim and Mack are in Potosí, Bolivia. There they must use the coat of arms in the Bolivian flag to decipher an enigma in order to find a valuable coin.
- In this section, students will preview:
  - The different steps in the shopping process.
  - Ways to pay for purchases.
  - Stem-changing *-ir* verbs in the preterite tense.

Activities	Standards	Resources
Fotonovela	1.2, 3.1, 3.2	Vis. Pres.
58.	1.2, 1.3	
59.	1.2, 1.3	
60.	1.2, 1.3	Audio
61. Cultura	1.1, 1.3, 2.2, 3.1, 3.2, 4.2, 5.1	

Teaching Suggestions

Warm-Up / Independent Starter

- Have students read the introduction to the *fotonovela* silently. Then display a U.S. quarter and ask students to decipher the front and back of the coin.

Preparation

- Ask volunteers to share with the class their decoding of the U.S. quarter. Discuss, as a class, the different symbols pictured on a quarter and their meaning. Invite students to think of other places where some of these symbols and mottos are also present (e.g., the U.S. coat of arms, the Seal of the President, etc.).

La fotonovela

Before Viewing

- Have students get into pairs to read the dialogue. Tell students to choose the part of either Tim or Mack, and alternate reading the dialogue.

After Viewing

- Tim and Mack are standing in front of Cerro Rico Mountain. Ask students why they think this mountain is depicted in the Bolivian coat of arms. Have this discussion with students.

La montaña de plata

Tim and Mack are in the Bolivian town of Potosí, where the Spanish colonists mined the largest silver deposit in the world in the 16th century. The *Casa de la Moneda* in Potosí minted large amounts of coins. Using the coat of arms of the Bolivian flag, Mack and Tim must solve a riddle that will lead them to a valuable coin.

58 Detective de palabras

Continuará...

▶ **Completa** estas oraciones.

A
1. ¿Cómo la _____?
2. La _____ en una tienda.
3. ¿Nos _____, abuelo?
4. No, nos _____ la verdad.
5. ¿_____ esa montaña?

B
1. _____ una moneda de plata, ¿verdad?
2. Solo _____ este escudo como pista.
3. _____ muchos descuentos.
4. Solo _____ una montaña y un pájaro.
5. Allí _____ una importante mina de plata.

▶ **Responde.** ¿En qué tiempo están los verbos de la columna A: en presente o en pretérito? ¿Y los de la columna B?

Differentiated Instruction

DEVELOPING LEARNERS

- Ask students to make up a story to precede the *fotonovela*. Tell students to imagine that Tim and Mack have just come from the mall in Potosí. Based on Tim and Mack's clothing, write a description of where they went, what they purchased, and any other preparations they made. Ask volunteers to share their stories with the class.

EXPANDING LEARNERS

- Ask students to read the dialogue silently. Then have them write all of the questions from the dialogue on a separate sheet of paper. Ask students to respond to each question to create a new *fotonovela*. Tell students they can be as creative as they want. Ask volunteers to read their new *fotonovelas* aloud, then take a vote for the most creative new *fotonovela*.

Left Page

59 **¿Comprendes?**

▶ **Responde** a estas preguntas.

1. ¿Dónde están Tim y Mack?
2. ¿Qué están buscando?
3. ¿Qué consiguió Mack? ¿Dónde lo consiguió?
4. ¿Qué información importante vio Mack en el escudo?

60 **¿De qué están hablando?**

 ▶ **Escucha** y decide. ¿De qué fotografía están hablando Tim y Mack?

 ▶ **Escucha** otra vez y escribe las palabras que mencionan.

| montaña | mapa | bandera | plata | escudo | moneda | pájaro |

▶ **Escribe** una oración para describir cada fotografía.

 **CULTURA**

Potosí

Potosí es una ciudad de Bolivia famosa por sus antiguas minas de plata. Está situada al sur, a más de 4.000 metros (13.000 pies) sobre el nivel del mar; se considera la tercera ciudad más alta del mundo.

En Potosí hay una montaña que se conoce como Cerro Rico por la cantidad de plata que se encontró en ella. Desafortunadamente (*unfortunately*), en las minas hay muy poca plata.

61 **Investiga.** ¿Qué minerales se explotan en los Estados Unidos? ¿Cuáles son las zonas mineras más importantes?

HERITAGE LANGUAGE LEARNERS

• Tim and Mack are following the clues that are embedded in the Bolivian coat of arms in order to find the valuable coin. Have students research the Bolivian flag, paying close attention to the coat of arms, and write more clues for Tim and Mack to follow. They can use any part of the flag, including the colors, to write their clues. See if students can come up with at least three clues on their own and at least five as a class.

MULTIPLE INTELLIGENCES:
Visual-Spatial Intelligence

• Ask students to cover up the pictures as they read the *fotonovela*. Have them draw or use scenic pictures from a magazine to represent Tim and Mack's surroundings, what they describe in each scene, and their situation in this *Desafío*. Display students' scenes around the classroom.

Right Page

Hablar sobre compras en pasado

Activities

59. Tell students to cover up the dialogue, and answer these questions by memory.

60. For the second part of this activity, have students raise their hands when they hear one of the words mentioned.

61. There was a "rush" for one precious metal in the United States. Ask students what this "rush" was for. (gold)

AUDIO SCRIPT
See page 131 J.

CULTURA

Potosí

Tons upon tons of silver were mined in the Cerro Rico Mountain during the colonial period, making it one of the most important cities in the Spanish empire. Now Potosí plays host to the National Mint of Bolivia, formerly the Spanish Colonial Mint.

Answer Key

58. A: 1. conseguiste; 2. pedí; 3. mintieron; 4. dijeron; 5. Viste

B: 1. Buscamos; 2. tenemos; 3. Tienen; 4. veo; 5. hay

▶ A: pretérito.   B: presente.

59. 1. Están en Potosí, Bolivia.
2. Están buscando una moneda de plata.
3. Mack consiguió una postal en una tienda.
4. Vio una montaña como el Cerro Rico.

60. Fotografía 2.
▶ escudo, montaña, pájaro, bandera
▶ Answers will vary.

61. Answers will vary.

Additional Resources

Fans Online activities

DESAFÍO 4

Vocabulario – Las compras

Presentation

- In this section, students will learn:
  - The different steps in the shopping process.
  - Ways to pay for a purchase.

Activities	Standards	Resources
Vocabulario	1.2	
62.	1.2, 1.3	
63.	1.2	Audio
64.	1.1, 1.2, 1.3	
65. Comunidades	1.1, 1.2, 2.1, 3.2, 4.2, 5.1	

Teaching Suggestions

Warm-Up / Independent Starter

- Ask students to imagine that they go shopping in Potosí. Have them describe the clothing they would buy, the stores they would visit to buy these clothing items, and how they would pay for the items. Remind students that some places do not accept U.S. currency or credit cards, so they should consider other payment options.

Preparation

- Go over the vocabulary presentation with students. Ask them to think about their last shopping experience. Have students use the vocabulary to list the steps they took in the purchasing process.
- Ask students to imagine they have gone shopping, but nothing they've tried on has fit well. Have them get into small groups and discuss what happens when they go shopping and find things they like, but nothing fits well. Do students keep trying on different sizes or do they give up and go to another store or mall?

Activities

64. Once students have finished answering the questions, have them write a paragraph to describe their last shopping experience. Ask them to read their paragraphs to their partner. In pairs, have students write another paragraph to compare their shopping experiences.

Vocabulario

Las compras

El dinero
- el billete
- la moneda
- la tarjeta de crédito

El precio
- $20 — es barato
- $1400 — es caro

- CAJA
- la fila
- ¿Es usted la última?
- el probador
- la caja
- probarse ropa
- la etiqueta
- el cajero
- ¿Puedo ayudarlo?
- Sí. Mi amigo me pidió un recuerdo de Bolivia. ¿Este gorro tiene descuento?
- el dependiente
- el cliente

| pagar en efectivo | pagar con tarjeta | estar de moda | estar en oferta | quedar bien/mal | quedar pequeño/grande |

62 De compras

▶ **Completa** estas oraciones.

1. Inés se prueba una camisa en el _____.
2. La tienda bajó los precios. Por eso compramos la ropa con _____.
3. La señora Gómez tiene que esperar porque hay una _____ para pagar.
4. Martín mira la _____ porque quiere saber el precio de los zapatos.
5. Si la tienda no acepta tarjetas de crédito, tienes que pagar en _____.
6. Mi padre no se compra el traje porque no le _____ bien.

164 ciento sesenta y cuatro

Differentiated Instruction

DEVELOPING LEARNERS

- Ask students to use the vocabulary they have learned so far in this unit to act out the roles of a client (*cliente*) and a salesperson (*vendedor*). Have students create a ten-line dialogue to perform for the class. Let students know that they cannot use their notes during their performance, so they should take the time to memorize their scripts.

EXPANDING LEARNERS

- Have students work in small groups to come up with sale signs to hang up in the windows of *la zapatería*, *la tienda de ropa*, *la tienda de bisutería*, and *la tienda de deportes*. Students will need one sign for each store. Tell them to be sure to include the store name, the items for sale, the discount, and accepted forms of payment. Once students have finished, display the signs for each store side-by-side. Ask the rest of the class to line up in front of the store where they would like to shop. Which store has the longest line?

63 **¿Qué pasa en la tienda?**

 ▶ **Escucha** y decide si las oraciones sobre estas fotos son ciertas (C) o falsas (F). Después, corrige las oraciones falsas.

64 **Tu día de compras**

▶ **Responde** a estas preguntas sobre tu último día de compras.

1. ¿Adónde fuiste?
2. ¿Qué compraste?
3. ¿Te probaste algo?
4. ¿Compraste algo con descuento?
5. ¿Cómo pagaste?
6. ¿Tuviste que esperar en una fila?

 ▶ **Habla** con tu compañero(a) sobre las experiencias de compras de ustedes dos. ¿Cuál fue más divertida?

COMUNIDADES

LOS MERCADILLOS

En muchos países se puede comprar ropa, zapatos, complementos y otros productos en los mercadillos. Los mercadillos son mercados al aire libre que se suelen instalar un día determinado de la semana.

Los precios generalmente son más bajos en los mercadillos que en las tiendas. En algunos se puede regatear *(bargain)*. También hay puestos *(stalls)* donde venden ropa y productos de segunda mano *(second-hand)*.

65 **Compara.** ¿Qué diferencias hay entre los mercadillos del mundo hispano y los mercados de pulga o las tiendas *outlet* de los Estados Unidos?

ciento sesenta y cinco **165**

HERITAGE LANGUAGE LEARNERS

- Bargaining is a major part of making purchases in many Spanish-speaking countries. Ask students to name the places where they can bargain for the best prices in their country of origin. For example, could families bargain for the price of a hotel room? Then ask students which form of payment people would offer to get the best prices. With the example of the hotel, which form of payment should the family offer to get the best price if the innkeeper is willing to bargain?

CRITICAL THINKING

- Some areas that have many U.S. visitors allow travelers to pay in either local currency or in U.S. dollars. Ask students if knowing the currency conversion of the country you are visiting makes a difference in getting the best price for an item. For example, if students were in Mexico City and the price tag on a pair of jeans said 200 pesos or $20, would students want to pay in Mexican pesos or U.S. dollars? Why? (In this example, you may want to look up the current currency exchange rate for Mexican pesos before class.)

DESAFÍO 4

Vocabulario – Las compras

65. If students are not familiar with *mercadillos,* refer them back to the Chichicastenango Market from Unit 3 in Level 1. Students may also research the topic on the Internet.

 AUDIO SCRIPT
See page 131J.

 COMUNIDADES

Los mercadillos

Farmer's markets, flea markets, open-air markets, street fairs, and swap shops are also common in many American cities and towns. Vendors come to sell their goods and bargaining is an accepted practice. These markets are usually reserved for certain days of the week and are placed in a central, easily accessible location.

Answer Key

62.
1. probador
2. descuento
3. fila
4. etiqueta
5. efectivo
6. queda

63.
1. Falso. Luz va a pagar con tarjeta de crédito.
2. Falso. En esta tienda hay descuentos.
3. Cierto.
4. Falso. Está en la caja porque quiere pagar.

64. Answers will vary. Sample answers:
1. Fui a un centro comercial.
2. Compré ropa y zapatos.
3. Me probé tres pantalones distintos.
4. Compré unos zapatos con descuento.
5. Pagué en efectivo.
6. No tuve que esperar en una fila.
▶ Answers will vary.

65. Answers will vary.

Additional Resources

Fans Online activities
Practice Workbook

Unit 3

DESAFÍO 4

Gramática – Verbos en *-ir* con raíz irregular en el pretérito

Presentation

- In this section, students will learn irregular, stem changing *-ir* verbs in the preterite tense.

Activities	Standards	Resources
Gramática	3.1	
66.	1.2, 1.3, 4.1	
67.	1.3	
68.	1.2, 1.3	Audio
69.	1.1	
70. Conexiones	1.1, 1.2, 2.2, 3.2, 4.1, 5.1	

Teaching Suggestions

Warm-Up / Independent Starter

- Ask students to think of the last time they went shopping for clothes or accessories and have them summarize what they did. Remind them to use the preterite tense.

Preparation

- Ask volunteers to share their paragraphs from the Independent Starter with the class.
- Go over the grammar presentation with students. Remind them that they can identify the root of the verb by taking off the *-ar, -er,* or *-ir* ending from the infinitive form of a verb.

Activities

66. Ask students to conjugate the following verbs in English, both in the present and preterite tenses: to follow, to get, to choose.

69. Ask students to imagine that all of these things happened to them during a Saturday. Have students write a sequential story, using the same verbs from the activity.

70. Make a list of your own with phrases you heard your parents or grandparents say on a piece of paper. Then list on the board the expressions that students have come up with. Is your list different? Many sayings are generational. Share your list with students.

166

Gramática

Verbos en *-ir* con raíz irregular en el pretérito

- In Spanish, *-ir* verbs that are e > i stem-changing in the present tense (pedir > pido) have the same change in the third person of the preterite tense.

  e > i → pedir: él pide (presente), él pidió (pretérito)

- The verbs dormir and morir are also irregular in the third person of the preterite tense. In this case, the o of the stem changes to u.

  o > u → dormir: él durmió

VERBO PEDIR. PRETÉRITO

Singular		Plural	
yo	pedí	nosotros nosotras	pedimos
tú	pediste	vosotros vosotras	pedisteis
usted él ella	pidió	ustedes ellos ellas	pidieron

VERBO DORMIR. PRETÉRITO

Singular		Plural	
yo	dormí	nosotros nosotras	dormimos
tú	dormiste	vosotros vosotras	dormisteis
usted él ella	durmió	ustedes ellos ellas	durmieron

- Other verbs conjugated like pedir in the preterite are:

  elegir *(to choose)*   medir *(to measure)*   competir *(to compete)*
  vestirse *(to get dressed)*   repetir *(to repeat)*   corregir *(to correct)*
  preferir *(to prefer)*   servir *(to serve)*   convertir *(to turn into)*
  sentirse *(to feel)*   despedirse *(to say goodbye)*   mentir *(to lie)*
  seguir *(to follow)*   conseguir *(to get)*

66 **Piensa.** ¿En inglés los verbos también tienen raíz y terminación? ¿Hay verbos con la raíz irregular, como en español?

67 **¿Qué hicieron ayer?**

 Escribe oraciones en pasado con estos elementos.

Modelo 1. *Ayer yo elegí unos zapatos muy baratos.*

1. ayer - yo - elegir - unos zapatos - muy baratos
2. anoche - tú - dormir - en casa de una amiga
3. hace dos días - mi planta - morirse
4. esta mañana - Tim - pedir - al dependiente - una chaqueta
5. ayer - yo - ir - a la librería - y conseguir - una novela de aventuras

166 ciento sesenta y seis

Differentiated Instruction

DEVELOPING LEARNERS

- Ask students to conjugate the verbs listed under "Other verbs conjugated like *pedir*" in the present tense in a column on the left side of their paper. Then have them conjugate the same verbs in the preterite tense in a column on the right side of the paper. Have students use a highlighter to highlight the similarities in the verb conjugations and a different color highlighter to note the differences between the two. Students should visually note that the highlighter will be the same color in the same places for each verb.

EXPANDING LEARNERS

- Have students number a sheet of paper 1–16. Then have them choose a topic and write 16 sentences in the preterite tense—one for each of the verbs given in the grammar presentation. Once students have finished, write the numbers 1–16 in random order on the board. Ask students to rewrite their sentences in the order you specified on the board. Have students read their paragraphs aloud. Did anyone create an interesting story?

68 La fiesta sorpresa

▶ **Escucha.** Tim y Mack organizaron una fiesta para su guía boliviano. Une los personajes con las acciones apropiadas. Después, escribe oraciones completas.

A

1. Tim
2. Tess y Patricia
3. Rita
4. Mack
5. Andy y Janet
6. Diana

B

a. vestirse con ropa típica de Bolivia
b. conseguir los refrescos
c. elegir un regalo
d. pedir ayuda para preparar la comida
e. servir los postres
f. despedirse de los invitados

Modelo 1. *Tim sirvió los postres.*

69 Al final del día

▶ **Habla** con un compañero(a). ¿Qué hicieron los personajes ayer?

① vestirse

② dormirse

③ elegir

④

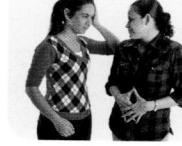
⑤ servir

⑥ sentirse mal

despedirse

CONEXIONES: LENGUA

Vale un potosí

En español, la expresión «valer un potosí» significa que algo es muy valioso (*valuable*). Esta expresión procede de la ciudad boliviana de Potosí, donde existió la mina de plata más grande del mundo durante el imperio español.

70 **Compara.** ¿Qué expresiones hay en inglés para indicar que algo es muy valioso?

Unit 3

DESAFÍO 4

Gramática – Verbos en *-ir* con raíz irregular en el pretérito

 AUDIO SCRIPT
See page 131J.

CONEXIONES: LENGUA

Vale un potosí

The phrase *vale un potosí* means that something "is worth its weight in gold." Place names are sometimes used in this manner. For example, if someone says a place is like Fort Knox, then it's hard to get into. If a place is like Timbuktu, it is a place that's far away from civilization. If a place is the new Silicon Valley, then it is technologically advanced. Ask students what metaphor your city or town could represent.

Answer Key

66. Sí, por ejemplo: *work → worked*. También hay verbos con cambios en la raíz, por ejemplo: *awake → awoke, sing → sang.*

67. 2. Anoche tú dormiste en casa de una amiga.
3. Hace dos días mi planta se murió.
4. Esta mañana Tim le pidió al dependiente una chaqueta.
5. Ayer yo fui a la librería y conseguí una novela de aventuras.

68. 2. Tess y Patricia se vistieron con ropa típica de Bolivia. (a)
3. Rita pidió ayuda para preparar la comida. (d)
4. Mack consiguió los refrescos. (b)
5. Andy y Janet eligieron un regalo. (c)
6. Diana se despidió de los invitados. (f)

69. Answers will vary. Sample answer:
1. Tim se vistió con ropa para el frío.

70. Answers will vary.

Additional Resources

Fans Online activities
Practice Workbook

167

HERITAGE LANGUAGE LEARNERS

• Ask students to look at the verbs in the grammar presentation. None of the verbs have similar meanings. Ask students to get into small groups and come up with tips to help the class remember which verbs are stem-changing verbs. Have students list their tips on a poster and display it for the class. Each group must be able to thoroughly explain their tips or mnemonic devices.

MULTIPLE INTELLIGENCES:
Intrapersonal Intelligence

• Have students write a reflection that expresses what they were thinking when they got dressed this morning. Students may choose to think back to the time when they went shopping for the clothes they were putting on. Once students have finished, have them fold their reflection and place it in an envelope with their name on it. Keep their letters until the end of the school year, when you will return the letters to the students to look back upon.

Unit 3
DESAFÍO 4
Comunicación

Presentation

- In this section, students will integrate the vocabulary and grammar from *Desafío 4* to talk about the different steps in the shopping process and ways to pay for purchases. They will also use irregular, stem-changing *-ir* verbs in the preterite.

Activities	Standards	Resources
71.	1.1, 1.2	
72.	1.2, 1.3	Audio
73.	1.1, 1.3	
74. Final del desafío	1.3, 2.2, 5.1	
Tu desafío	1.2, 1.3	

Teaching Suggestions

Warm-Up / Independent Starter

- Ask students to come up with five ways to simplify the shopping process at a store. For example: *abrir más cajas, marcar los descuentos en la etiqueta con letras más grandes*, etc.

Preparation

- Have students share their ideas to simplify the shopping process. Then ask them if they know of any stores that do some of these things and at what time of year.
- Take 10 minutes to review the vocabulary and grammar themes from *Desafío 4*.
- Refer students back to the *fotonovela* for *Desafío 4*. Have them find all of the words associated with the different steps in the shopping process, ways to pay for purchases, and irregular, stem-changing *-ir* verbs in the preterite tense within the dialogue. Do students understand the dialogue better now that they have gone through the vocabulary and grammar from the *Desafío*?
- Split the class into four groups. Have each group complete one of the *Comunicación* activities, including the *Final del desafío* activity. This is a Cooperative Learning assignment, so each person in the group needs to assume a role such as recorder, speaker, etc. Once students have finished, have the speaker from each group go over the activity with the rest of the class.

168

DESAFÍO 4

Comunicación

71 Las compras de Tim

▶ **Lee** la conversación entre Tim y Janet y decide si estas oraciones son ciertas o falsas.

> TIM: ¿Te gustó la camisa a rayas que compré ayer?
>
> JANET: ¿La camisa roja que te pusiste esta tarde? No mucho… Es que no me gustó el color. Y creo que te queda grande.
>
> TIM: El color no me importa. Es muy cómoda y conseguí un buen descuento.
>
> JANET: ¿Quieres ir conmigo de compras mañana?
>
> TIM: De acuerdo.
>
> JANET: Esta mañana vi una camisa amarilla de cuadros perfecta para ti.
>
> TIM: Bueno, pero no me gusta mucho el color amarillo. No soy un experto, pero…
>
> JANET: Yo sí, Tim. Creo que el amarillo te queda muy bien. Y además está de moda este año.
>
> TIM: De acuerdo, me la pruebo mañana. Pero… si me queda bien, tú me regalas la camisa, ¿ok?
>
> JANET: ¡Jajajaja!

1. Tim y Janet fueron juntos a una tienda de ropa.
2. Tim se compró una camisa amarilla.
3. A Janet no le gustó la camisa de Tim.
4. Janet vio una camisa de rayas para Tim.
5. Tim piensa que el color amarillo le queda bien.
6. Tim decidió probarse la camisa que eligió Janet.

▶ **Escribe** una conversación con tu compañero(a). Imagina que están en un chat y hablan de las compras que hicieron.

72 Un mensaje en el contestador

▶ **Escucha.** Tim dejó un mensaje para su mamá. Toma notas de lo que dice. Después, escribe un resumen.

El mes pasado	La semana pasada	Anteayer	Ayer	Hoy
				llamó por teléfono

Differentiated Instruction

DEVELOPING LEARNERS

- For students who are still having trouble with the stem-changing verbs in the third person of the preterite tense, write the verb *conseguir* on the board. Then draw a large X over the letter e and write the letter *i* over the top of the X. For the verb *preferir* draw an X over the second e and write the letter *i* over the top of the X. Continue with all of the verbs on page 166, so students can see which letter is the focal point of each word.

EXPANDING LEARNERS

- Have students research the shopping proccess in a medium-sized clothing store in the United States and one other Spanish-speaking country. Are they similar or different? Ask students to discuss the similarities and differences between the shopping process in the United States and the Spanish-speaking country they researched.

73 ¿Qué compraron?

▶ **Habla** con tres compañeros(as) sobre sus últimas compras. Toma notas.

Nombre	¿Qué compró?	¿Dónde?	¿Cuánto costó?	¿Cómo pagó?
William	una camiseta roja	una tienda de ropa	barata	en efectivo

▶ **Escribe** un párrafo con la información de la tabla.

Final del desafío

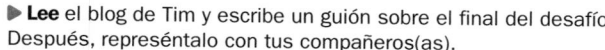

Queremos comprar una moneda de plata.

Tienen que ir a la Real Casa de la Moneda.

9 de noviembre
Potosí, Bolivia

Finalmente conseguimos resolver el desafío. Vimos muchas monedas de plata en la Casa de la Moneda. Pero, ¿comprar una? ¡Qué va! La Casa de la Moneda es un museo. ¡Y además esas monedas valen miles de dólares! Eso sí, en la tienda del museo compré una postal con una moneda de plata. Y una camiseta para mi abuelo. Pero elegí una camiseta un poco pequeña, no le queda bien. Luego volví a la tienda y le compré otra. No me la cambiaron porque quité la etiqueta, pero bueno. Por suerte la camiseta no me costó un potosí. ☺

74 ¿Qué pasó?

▶ **Lee** el blog de Tim y escribe un guión sobre el final del desafío. Después, represéntalo con tus compañeros(as).

→ TU DESAFÍO | Visita la página web. Escucha las preguntas de tu *Minientrevista Desafío 4* y escribe las respuestas.

ciento sesenta y nueve 169

Activities

71. Have students correct the false statements.

72. Give the group that was assigned this activity a copy of the audio script so you do not have to play the audio recording. Also give them a transparency to recreate the chart on the page to fill in and display for the rest of the class.

73. Have students write the paragraph on poster board, large enough for someone sitting across the room to see.

74. Have students memorize their script before they perform it.

 AUDIO SCRIPT
See page 131J.

Answer Key

71. 1. F   2. F   3. C   4. F   5. F   6. C
▶ Answers will vary.

72. El mes pasado: llegaron a Bolivia
La semana pasada: eligió un poncho de lana
Anteayer: buscaron la moneda
Ayer: consiguieron su desafío
El mes pasado Tim y Mack llegaron a Bolivia. La semana pasada Tim eligió un poncho de lana para su mamá. Anteayer Tim y Mack buscaron la moneda, pero no la encontraron. ¡Ayer consiguieron su desafío! Tim llamó hoy por teléfono a su mamá.

73. Answers will vary.
▶ Answers will vary. Sample answer:
William compró una camiseta roja en una tienda de ropa. La camiseta le costó barata y pagó en efectivo.

74. Answers will vary.

Additional Resources

Fans Online activities
Practice Workbook

HERITAGE LANGUAGE LEARNERS

• Ask students to talk about the currency from their country of origin. Who or what appears on each side of the bills and coins? What is the significance of each image? How often does the money change in physical appearance? What aspects are altered when there is a change? Have students bring in some bills or coins from their country of origin to pass around.

CRITICAL THINKING

• Ask students to think how stores price their goods. This process begins with a concept that eventually makes it to a store with a price tag. Ask students to think about this process and discuss it in small groups. Then have them think about being a storeowner. What type of store would they own and how would they price their goods? Have them consider the differences in this process between a small rural store and a busy urban location.

Unit 3
TODO JUNTO

Presentation

- In this section, students will review the unit objectives and put them into practice.

Activities	Standards	Resources
75.	1.2	Audio
76.	1.1, 1.2	
77.	1.1, 1.2, 1.3, 2.2, 3.1, 4.2, 5.1, 5.2	

Teaching Suggestions

Warm-Up / Independent Starter

- Ask students to go back to the vocabulary and grammar presentations in this unit. Have them create a quick reference guide to the information in these presentations on the front and back of several note cards. This will serve as a study guide. Be sure students add this study guide to the study guides from Units 1 and 2.

Preparation

- Today you will have a Spanish class garage sale. Have students fold a blank piece of paper in half. First they draw a picture of the item they want to sell on one half of the paper. Then they write a description of what they are selling on the other half of the paper. The description must include where they originally purchased the item and a detailed physical description. This will serve as the sales pitch. Don't forget the price tag! Once students have finished, display all of their garage sale items on the board.

- Now you must organize your garage sale. Go over the *Todo junto* activities as a class. You will ask each question and call on a volunteer to answer it. If the student answers correctly, then he or she may browse the board and "purchase" an item in the garage sale. If time allows, you may play the role of the cashier and bargain.

Activities

75. Play the audio recording twice and then read each statement aloud. After each statement, call on a volunteer. Try not to call on the same volunteer, as you want different students to have the opportunity to browse the sale items.

170

TODO JUNTO

ESCUCHAR

75 **¡Rebajas!**

 ▶ **Escucha** un anuncio de un centro comercial y decide si estas afirmaciones son ciertas o falsas.

1. Hay descuentos en las secciones de ropa y zapatería.
2. Tienen pantalones para hombre de todas las tallas.
3. Hay faldas de muchos colores.
4. No hay descuentos en ropa para niños.
5. Hay aretes y collares muy baratos.

LEER Y HABLAR

76 **Un cuestionario**

▶ **Completa** este cuestionario sobre tus gustos.

Las compras y tú

1. ¿Dónde prefieres comprar ropa?
   - ☐ En centros comerciales.
   - ☐ En tiendas de ropa.
   - ☐ En mercados y mercadillos.

2. ¿Qué prendas llevas normalmente?
   - ☐ Jeans y camisetas anchas, cómodas.
   - ☐ Pantalones y camisas o blusas.
   - ☐ Vestidos o trajes.

3. ¿Qué calzado prefieres?
   - ☐ Zapatos.
   - ☐ Tenis.
   - ☐ Botas.

4. ¿Usas complementos? ¿Cuáles?
   - ☐ Gafas de sol.
   - ☐ Sombrero.
   - ☐ Reloj.

5. ¿Cuál de estas prendas no llevas nunca?
   - ☐ Pantalón corto.
   - ☐ Gorra.
   - ☐ Sandalias.

6. ¿Qué diseño prefieres?
   - ☐ Las rayas o los cuadros.
   - ☐ Los lunares.
   - ☐ Los colores lisos.

7. ¿Cuál es tu color favorito?
   - ☐ El rojo.
   - ☐ El negro.
   - ☐ El azul.

8. ¿Qué miras cuando vas a comprar ropa?
   - ☐ Si está en oferta.
   - ☐ Si me queda bien.
   - ☐ Si está de moda.

 ▶ **Compara** tus respuestas con las de tu compañero(a). ¿Tienen gustos similares?

170 ciento setenta

Differentiated Instruction

DEVELOPING LEARNERS

- Have students turn back to the introduction page for this unit to see the objectives. Ask them to use each of these objectives as a heading and to divide their paper into sections according to the headings. In each section, have students write sentences to show that they have grasped the concept of each objective and are ready to be formally assessed.

EXPANDING LEARNERS

- Ask students to imagine that their Bolivian friends are going to go shopping for them in a mall before they come to visit in the United States. Have students use the answers to the questionnaire to write a letter to their friends about the things they like to wear and what they would like to receive from Bolivia. Tell students to be sure to include a greeting, a body, and an appropriate closing to their letters.

LEER Y ESCRIBIR

77 **Ropa tradicional**

▶ **Lee** este texto y complétalo.

sombrero   prendas   falda   rojos   complementos

algodón   colores   modernos   fiestas   prenda

La ropa tradicional andina

La industria textil en los Andes es muy importante. Los tejidos son apreciados en todo el mundo por la variedad de _____1_____ y diseños. Estas son algunas _____2_____ tradicionales típicas de la zona andina:

Pollera

Es una _____3_____ de lana. Las mujeres llevan muchas veces tres o cuatro polleras a la vez, y pueden llevar hasta quince para _____4_____ especiales.

Poncho

Es una _____5_____ de abrigo. Los ponchos son de lana y normalmente son _____6_____ y están decorados con rayas y otros diseños. Algunos los llevan habitualmente, pero muchas personas se visten con ponchos en los festivales y días especiales.

Montera

Es un _____7_____ de lana o de _____8_____ con colores brillantes y diseños muy variados. Muchas veces se puede identificar la comunidad de origen de una persona por el tipo de montera que lleva.

Actualmente también se fabrica ropa y _____9_____ basados en las prendas tradicionales andinas, pero con diseños más _____10_____ y sofisticados.

 ▶ **Habla** con tu compañero(a). ¿Te gustan estas prendas? ¿Cómo es la ropa tradicional de tu comunidad?

▶ **Escribe.** Busca más información sobre prendas tradicionales de los Andes y escribe un texto describiéndolas. Incluye fotos o dibujos.

---

76. Since this activity does not have a right or a wrong answer, have students answer the questions to the survey in complete sentences. For example:

1. *¿Dónde prefieres comprar ropa?*
   Prefiero comprar ropa en centros comerciales.

77. Read each sentence aloud. When you get to a blank, pause and call on a volunteer to fill in the blank. Since this is the last activity, have the students who have not "purchased" an item from the garage sale talk to you to complete the *Habla* part of this activity. If a student would prefer, he or she can take their turn in the garage sale by completing the *Escribe* part of this activity.

 AUDIO SCRIPT
See page 131J.

Answer Key

75.
1. Falso	4. Falso
2. Cierto	5. Cierto
3. Cierto	

76. Answers will vary.
▶ Answers will vary.

77.
1. colores	6. rojos
2. prendas	7. sombrero
3. falda	8. algodón
4. fiestas	9. complementos
5. prenda	10. modernos

▶ Answers will vary.
▶ Answers will vary.

Additional Resources

Fans Online activities
Practice Workbook

HERITAGE LANGUAGE LEARNERS

• Ask students to find pictures on the Internet or in a magazine of different Andean garments and use eight of the words from activity 77 in order to describe the garments. Then have students repeat this process with garments from Guatemala. Have students compare and contrast these two styles, still using the words from the activity.

SPECIAL-NEEDS LEARNERS

• Sometimes physical disabilities or space considerations limit the ability to move freely around the classroom, inhibiting the possibility of speaking to a variety of classmates. Have students organize a systematic way of "milling around" for speaking activities, so that some students may stay in their seats and allow their classmates to come to them. This way, students get sufficient practice with the speaking activities and no student feels left out.

Unit 3
El encuentro

Presentation

- The four pairs meet in the *avenida Olmedo* in Guayaquil, Ecuador. There they must read their diary entry to prove the completion of their challenge.

- Students will vote for the winner of the *Desafíos* in the central Andes.

Activities	Standards	Resources
Fotonovela	1.2, 2.1, 2.2	
78.	1.3, 5.1	Audio
79.	1.2, 1.3, 5.1	

Teaching Suggestions

Warm-Up / Independent Starter

- Ask students to close their textbooks and write a summary of each pair's challenge in the Andes. Have them use the unit vocabulary and grammar to explain the *desafío* in each description.

Preparation

- Remind students that in *Desafío 1*, Andy and Janet traveled to Riobamba, Ecuador, where they had to climb one of the glaciers on Mount Chimborazo to collect some snow and make an iced drink. In *Desafío 2*, Tess and Patricia traveled to Huancavelica, Peru, where they met the mayor, Héctor Gonzáles, and participated in the annual llama race. In *Desafío 3*, Diana and Rita traveled to Oruro, Bolivia, where they had to wear a traditional mask and costume and participate in the most famous carnival in the Andes. In *Desafío 4*, Tim and Mack traveled to Potosí, Bolivia, where they had to decode the coat of arms on the Bolivian flag to be able to find the location of a valuable coin.

La fotonovela

- Ask a volunteer to read the introduction to *El encuentro* aloud.

- Have students look at the pictures. Ask them to describe what each pair is wearing, the item(s) they are holding in their hands, and their facial expressions and body language.

172

El encuentro

En la avenida Olmedo de Guayaquil

The pairs gather in the *avenida Olmedo* in Guayaquil. Now, each pair must tell whether they succeeded or not.

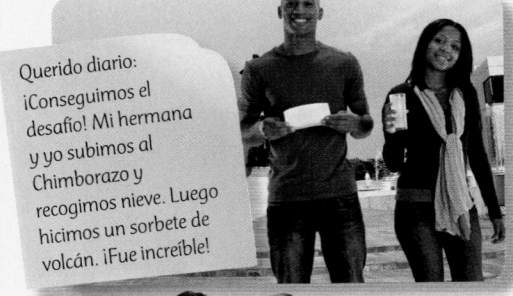

Querido diario:
¡Conseguimos el desafío! Mi hermana y yo subimos al Chimborazo y recogimos nieve. Luego hicimos un sorbete de volcán. ¡Fue increíble!

10 de noviembre
Nosotras corrimos en una carrera de llamas. Y fuimos las primeras en llegar.

11 de noviembre
Mi tía y yo estuvimos en el carnaval de Oruro. ¡Fue una experiencia muy interesante! Ella se vistió con un disfraz y una máscara. Yo la encontré… ¡pero fue difícil!

Al final resolvimos el enigma de la bandera boliviana. Fuimos a la Real Casa de la Moneda y vimos las monedas de plata. Pero tuvimos que comprar una moneda un poco más barata…

172 ciento setenta y dos

Differentiated Instruction

DEVELOPING LEARNERS

- Ask students to copy each diary entry of *El encuentro* in their notebook. Then ask them to underline each verb and say if it is regular or irregular, say what person it is conjugated in, and why it was used. For example, in the first sentence of Andy's diary, he uses the verb *logramos*. *Logramos* is a regular *-ar* verb in the preterite tense, it is conjugated in the first person plural (*nosotros*) form, and it is used to say that Andy and Janet achieved their goal.

EXPANDING LEARNERS

- Ask students to imagine that they were part of each *desafío* and have just accomplished their challenge in the Andes. Have them write what they would say in their diary if they were the participants. Then have students describe in their diary what they wore during their challenges to help them accomplish their task, where they purchased it, how much it cost, and how much they paid.

El encuentro

78 **Recuerdos de Ecuador**

 ▶ **Escucha** y completa este diálogo.

> JANET: Yo compré unas botas negras muy ___1___. Mira.
>
> TESS: ¡Qué bonitas!
>
> JANET: ¿Y tú?
>
> TESS: Yo compré un ___2___ y una bufanda de ___3___ de muchos colores.
>
> JANET: ¿Y encontraste regalos originales?
>
> TESS: Sí, miré muchas cosas y al final elegí una muñeca vestida con ropa ___4___ andina.
>
> JANET: ¡Yo también! ¿Dónde compraste todo eso?
>
> TESS: El gorro y la bufanda en un ___5___. Y la muñeca en una ___6___. ¿Y tú?
>
> JANET: Yo compré las botas en una ___7___ del centro de Guayaquil. Y la muñeca en un ___8___.
>
> TESS: ¿Cuánto te costó?
>
> JANET: Tres dólares.

▶ **Escribe** un diálogo similar con tu compañero(a). Después, represéntenlo. Incluyan:

– La ropa que compraron.
– Los recuerdos y los regalos que compraron.
– Las tiendas y lugares donde compraron.
– El precio que pagaron.

Un diario incluye experiencias personales y anécdotas. Puedes escribirlo en primera persona y en pasado.

79 **Las votaciones**

▶ **Lee** los diarios de los personajes de la página 172. ¿Cuál te gusta más? ¿Por qué?

▶ **Escribe** un diario. Estas preguntas te pueden ayudar.

1. ¿Qué hiciste la semana pasada? ¿Compraste algo?
2. ¿Adónde fuiste? ¿Con quién?
3. ¿Fue divertido?

ciento setenta y tres **173**

■ Ask for different volunteers to read each pair's diary entry. Ask students if they would feel comfortable reading their diary entries aloud or publishing them in a book. People mostly regard a diary as private, but ask students to discuss other uses for a diary. One possible answer is to keep a record of the day's events to eventually share with other people. For example, the President could have written a diary entry every day to document his campaign. Then after he won the presidency, when people asked him how he was feeling, he could share his diary.

Activities

78. For the *Escribe* part of this activity, remind students that this dialogue will be in the preterite tense. Refer them back to the grammar presentations in this unit if they have any questions about how to form the preterite tense. Have students take notice of the fact that the conversation is interactive. That means that someone must ask questions in order to continue the conversation. Ask volunteers to read or perform their conversations in front of the class.

AUDIO SCRIPT
See page 131J.

Answer Key

78. 1. cómodas   5. centro comercial
2. gorro   6. tienda de artesanía
3. lana   7. zapatería
4. tradicional   8. mercado
▶ Answers will vary.

79. Answers will vary.
▶ Answers will vary.

HERITAGE LANGUAGE LEARNERS

• Ask students to imagine that they were part of each *desafío*, but they did *not* accomplish their challenge in the Andes. Have them write what they would say in their diary entry if they were the participants. Then have students describe in their diary what they did wrong that caused them to fail each task. Invite them to also mention in their diaries what they should have done differently.

COOPERATIVE LEARNING

• Pair developing learners with heritage language learners. Have the developing learners read *El encuentro* to the heritage language learners. As they read, the heritage language learner will help them with pronunciation and reading proficiency. Once students have finished reading, ask the developing learners to summarize what they have just read.

MAPA CULTURAL

Andes centrales

Presentation

- This section presents the central Andes region by using scenes from Ecuador, Peru, and Bolivia. The map of the region serves as a reference point for additional cultural readings and activities.

Activities	Standards	Resources
Mapa cultural	1.2, 2.1, 3.1, 3.2	Video
80.	1.2, 3.1	
81.	1.1, 2.1, 2.2, 3.1, 3.2, 4.2	

Cultural Topics

- **Quechuas y aymaras.** British railroad workers introduced the derby, or bowler, hat (also known in Spanish as *bombín*) in Bolivia. Indigenous women began to wear it and it has become part of the Aymara women's dress. Fashion has also traveled in the opposite direction—from the Andes to the world. Men in the highlands of the Andes have worn *chullo* hats since pre-Hispanic times, and today this woolen cap with earflaps is also fashionable in North America and Europe.

- **Los equecos.** The *equeco* doll is a symbol of good luck in the Andes. One of several legends associated with the *equecos* has it that a farmer worked around the clock and made a lot of money. He purchased many fancy items with his money, which he carried around in a sack. The dolls were made in his likeness to represent wealth and success. Today, many people in the Andean region have an *equeco* doll to bring them success, but the *equeco* has to be a gift from somebody else.

- **Las islas Galápagos.** The Galapagos Islands are made up of thirteen major islands and six smaller islands. These islands have stirred scientific interest since Charles Darwin visited them in the 1800s. Tourism has increased dramatically ever since, as has the human population, which has grown tenfold in the past 30 years.

  There are thousands of species endemic to the Galapagos Islands. Some examples include plants that reproduce without pollination, the only penguin species in the northern hemisphere, the only known marine iguana, and the Galapagos giant turtle. Human population growth, pollution, and the introduction of non-native plants and animals are some of the environmental threats affecting the Galapagos. Efforts are being made to protect the unique natural treasure of these islands.

MAPA CULTURAL

Andes centrales

La cordillera de los Andes atraviesa tres países con rasgos culturales comunes: Ecuador, Perú y Bolivia. En esta área se desarrollaron importantes culturas indígenas, en especial la cultura inca.

– Ecuador debe su nombre a su situación: por su territorio pasa la línea ecuatorial terrestre. Su capital es Quito.

– Perú es la cuna de la civilización inca. Su capital es Lima.

– Bolivia es el único país de esta zona que no tiene salida al mar. Su capital, Sucre, está a 9.153 pies de altura. La Paz es la sede del gobierno y está a 11.492 pies.

Nacionalidades
Ecuador → ecuatoriano(a)
Perú → peruano(a)
Bolivia → boliviano(a)

¿Sabes que la moneda de Ecuador es el dólar?

80 Tres países andinos

▶ **Observa** el mapa e identifica a qué país de los Andes centrales se refieren estas oraciones.

1. No tiene playa.
2. Tiene territorio en el hemisferio norte y en el hemisferio sur.
3. Es un país más grande que los otros dos.

Differentiated Instruction

DEVELOPING LEARNERS

- To enhance comprehension, ask students to work with a classmate to read and analyze together the information presented in the *Mapa cultural*. Ask them to draw, on chart paper, the map of the central Andes region from page 174. Have students label the different countries and their capital cities. Then ask them to draw, in the appropriate places on the map, icons representative of the information presented in the *Mapa cultural* (e.g., a derby hat, an *equeco* doll, an animal species unique to the Galapagos, etc.).

EXPANDING LEARNERS

- Ask students to pick one of the three topics from page 175 and have them create a mini-encyclopedia entry about the topic. They must include a picture, two paragraphs of pertinent information, and a personal opinion on the topic.

- Remind students to use reliable sources and to cite their sources properly. You may want to require them to include a bibliography with their entry.

1. Quechuas y aymaras

En la región andina gran parte de la población es indígena (quechua y aymara) o mestiza. Los indígenas conservan sus tradiciones y van incorporando otras de origen europeo. Un ejemplo lo vemos en el sombrero hongo (derby) de las mujeres bolivianas. Se trata de un sombrero pequeño y duro que llevaron a Bolivia los británicos en la década de 1920.

(1) Mujeres bolivianas con sombrero hongo.

2. Los equecos

Los equecos son muñecos (dolls) tradicionales de la cultura andina, en particular, de la cultura aymara. Están hechos de barro y pueden llevar distintas cosas, como dinero o comida, que representan aquello que queremos conseguir.

(2) Equecos.

3. Las islas Galápagos

Las islas Galápagos pertenecen a Ecuador y se encuentran a 603 millas de su costa. La situación alejada de este archipiélago las convierte en una reserva excepcional y un «museo vivo» de especies únicas estudiado por los biólogos desde el siglo XIX.

(3) Tortugas de las islas Galápagos.

 **81** **La vida en altura**

▶ **Imagina** y explica. ¿Cómo influye la altura en el modo de vida de los habitantes de la región andina?

- Ropa
- Bebida
- Comida
- Otras cosas

«Para vivir en altura: andar despacito y comer poquito.»

Teaching Suggestions

Warm-Up / Independent Starter

- Ask students to list two pieces of information about each of the countries in the central Andes region (i.e., Ecuador, Peru, and Bolivia).

Preparation

- Explain that the Andes Mountain Range is the dominant geographical feature in this region of South America. It is the longest continental mountain range in the world and the second highest, after the Himalayas. Peru, with a total area of 496,218 square miles and a population of 29,907,000 (2010 est.), is the largest of the three countries that comprise the central Andes region. Bolivia, with a population of 9,947,418 (2010 est.), is the least populated of the three. It also has the highest percentage of indigenous population. Ecuador is the smallest of the three countries in area, but it is a land of contrasts, from the coastal plains to the high elevations of the Andes.

Activities

80. Once students have answered all three items, ask a volunteer to read the clue aloud and ask another volunteer to say the answer. Point to each country on the map as students correctly answer the clues.

81. Ask students to find a picture of a person from the Andes to serve as inspiration for their assessment of daily life in the Andes.

Answer Key

80. 1. Bolivia   2. Ecuador   3. Perú
81. Answers will vary.

Additional Resources

Fans Online activities
Practice Workbook

HERITAGE LANGUAGE LEARNERS

- The speech bubble on page 174 represents an interesting fact about Ecuador. Ask students to create one speech bubble for each of the three countries covered in the *Mapa cultural*. Encourage students to research the information so that the facts they mention are new information not included in the *Mapa cultural*. Emphasize the importance of using reliable sources of information.

COOPERATIVE LEARNING

- Pair a developing learner with an expanding or heritage learner. Ask the developing learner to read the left page of the *Mapa cultural* aloud. As he or she reads, the expanding or heritage learner will point to the locations on the map and use his or her fingers to demonstrate the meaning of the words. For example, as the developing learner reads "[…] *atraviesa tres países con rasgos culturales comunes: Ecuador, Perú y Bolivia,*" the expanding or heritage learner will point to the three countries on the map as they are mentioned.

LECTURA

Textiles andinos bolivianos

Presentation

- In this section, students will increase their understanding of Andean culture by reading about traditional Bolivian textiles. In addition, students will focus on making inferences when reading in order to understand the deeper meaning of a text.

Activities	Standards	Resources
Lectura	1.2, 2.2, 3.1, 3.2	
82.	1.2, 1.3, 2.1, 2.2	
83.	1.3, 2.2	
84.	1.2, 1.3, 3.1	
Tu desafío	1.2, 3.1, 3.2, 5.2	

Teaching Suggestions

Warm-Up / Independent Starter

- Ask students to write a short paragraph summarizing what they know about traditional clothing and textiles from the Andes.

Preparation

- Before reading the text, ask students what the reading strategies were in the previous two units. (Identify the global idea of a text; identify the main idea and the most important details.) Then ask a volunteer to read the Reading Strategy aloud.

- Explain to students that when they make inferences from a reading, they become aware of the text's deeper meaning. Tell students these are some things they can do to hone their skills at making inferences: use context clues to figure out the meaning of unknown words, provide details about the setting, provide an explanation for the events and information presented in the text, recognize and understand the author's view, relate the text to their own knowledge of the world, provide conclusions from facts and information presented in the text.

- To enhance students' reading comprehension, ask them to familiarize themselves with the textiles described in the text by observing the pictures on this page and visiting the following web pages:
  - *Museo del Arte Textil Andino Boliviano:* http://www.linxs.com.bo/museotextil/.
  - "Sala de Textiles" at the *Museo Nacional de Etnografía y Folklore*: http://www.musef.org.bo/.

LECTURA

Fiesta popular boliviana.

Textiles andinos bolivianos

La cultura tradicional andina conserva en el presente su riqueza. Un reflejo de esta cultura milenaria es la elaboración de tejidos[1], una tradición muy arraigada[2] en la cultura andina, llamada «la civilización del tejido».

En Bolivia, más de 400 comunidades elaboran sus propias vestimentas[3] típicas con tejidos que hablan de la historia y la cultura de la comunidad. Cada comunidad tiene su tejido, con sus colores, sus figuras y su estilo. Los artesanos elaboran sus tejidos con lana de alpaca, vicuña, llama u oveja, o con fibra vegetal de algodón.

Se pueden visitar las exposiciones de tejidos y de piezas de la vestimenta andina en el Museo Nacional de Etnografía y Folklore y en el Museo del Arte Textil Andino Boliviano de La Paz, y admirar el colorido y la belleza de *uncus, chullos* y *aguayos*.

El *uncu* es una prenda utilizada antiguamente por los hombres en fiestas rituales o como vestimenta matrimonial.

El *chullo* es el tradicional gorro de lana con orejeras. Es una prenda masculina. Su tejido es grueso[4] y multicolor.

El *aguayo* es una pieza cuadrada de lana. Lo usan las mujeres para llevar a los bebés y niños a la espalda o para transportar productos.

---

1. *textiles* 2. *deeply rooted* 3. *clothing* 4. *thick*

176 ciento setenta y seis

Differentiated Instruction

DEVELOPING LEARNERS

- Graphic organizers help students draw inferences. Have students use the graphic organizer from activity 84 and ask them to add a third column with their thoughts about what they read. For example:

What the reading says	What I think	What I infer
Un reflejo de esta cultura milenaria es la elaboración de tejidos.	Thousands of years are a lot of years! This reminds me of the Egyptians.	La cultura andina es muy antigua.

EXPANDING LEARNERS

- Students may not know or not be aware of the rich textile traditions of the Native-American peoples of the Southwest (e.g., Pueblo and Navajo textiles). Have students research the weaving traditions of these American peoples and compare them with what they have learned about the Andean textile traditions.

- Encourage students to organize their findings in a Venn diagram. Ask them to compare and contrast the colors, designs, fibers used, weaving techniques, type of items manufactured, etc. Then, invite students to present their findings to the class.

COMPRENSIÓN

82 **Sobre los textiles andinos**

▶ **Completa** estas oraciones de acuerdo con el texto.

a. La cultura andina conserva…
b. La elaboración de tejidos es…
c. En Bolivia, muchas comunidades…
d. El tejido de cada comunidad tiene…

83 **Características de los textiles**

▶ **Escribe** el nombre de las prendas tradicionales de las fotografías. Después, descríbelas y di para qué sirven.

ESTRATEGIA Hacer inferencias

84 **También lo dice el texto**

▶ **Escribe** las palabras del texto que sustentan (support) estas inferencias.

	→	1. La cultura andina es muy antigua.
	→	2. Los indígenas dan mucha importancia a la ropa tradicional.
	→	3. Los tejidos tradicionales son una manifestación artística de las culturas indígenas.
	→	4. Los tejidos tienen un valor simbólico en las comunidades andinas.
	→	5. En las montañas de los Andes hace frío.

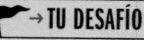 **TU DESAFÍO** Visita la página web para aprender más sobre el arte textil de Taquile.

LECTURA

Textiles andinos bolivianos

Activities

83. Once students have finished this activity, have them think of a clothing item or accessory that represents their own culture (e.g., jeans, a certain type of jewelry, etc.) and ask them to imagine that they have to describe it to someone who has never seen such an item. Have students write a paragraph describing the item in detail, explaining how it is worn, who wears it, the material it is made of, and what the purpose the item is.

Answer Key

82. Answers will vary. Sample answers:
   a. … en el presente su riqueza.
   b. … una tradición muy arraigada en la cultura andina.
   c. … elaboran sus propias vestimentas típicas.
   d. … sus colores, sus figuras y su estilo.

83. Answers will vary. Sample answers:
   1. *Chullo.* Es un gorro con orejeras. Es de lana de muchos colores. Sirve para protegerse del frío.
   2. *Aguayo.* Es de lana de colores. Sirve para llevar a los niños a la espalda o para transportar cosas.

84. Answers will vary. Sample answers:
   1. Un reflejo de esta cultura milenaria es la elaboración de tejidos.
   2. La elaboración de tejidos es una tradición muy arraigada en la cultura andina, llamada "la civilización del tejido".
   3. En Bolivia, más de 400 comunidades elaboran sus propias vestimentas con tejidos que hablan de la historia y la cultura de la comunidad.
   4. Cada comunidad tiene su tejido, con sus colores, sus figuras y su estilo.
   5. Los artesanos elaboran sus tejidos con lana de alpaca, vicuña, llama u oveja.

Additional Resources

Fans Online activities

HERITAGE LANGUAGE LEARNERS

• Discuss with students that even in our modern and globalized world we can sometimes tell where someone is from by the clothes or accessories he or she wears. Some designs, fashions, dress codes, and materials tend to be culture-specific.

• Have students create a poster for a specific clothing item or accessory from their country of origin. It can be a traditional item or something more current. They may ask their families or research on the Internet if they are not sure. Students should include a picture and a brief description and history of the item.

SPECIAL-NEEDS LEARNERS

• This may be a challenging text for visually impaired learners or those who have some form of color blindness. Pair these students with a learner who has advanced verbal skills and can describe in detail the different textiles and clothing items mentioned in the reading. Focus students' attention on the "feel" of these textiles by emphasizing the materials they are made of. If you or some students in the class have samples of these or similar textiles, bring them to class and allow visually impaired students to examine these clothing items.

Unit 3
REPASO

Vocabulario

Presentation

- In this section, students will review all key vocabulary from the unit, organized by themes, to prepare for an assessment. Students will complete practice activities for each of the four *Desafíos*.

Activities	Standards	Resources
1.	1.2	
2.	1.2, 1.3	
3.	1.2	
4.	1.2	

Teaching Suggestions

Warm-Up / Independent Starter

- Ask students to create a three-column chart and write down, as quickly as they can, a list of all the words for clothing items, shoes, and accessories they remember from this unit. Give students two minutes to complete their lists.

Preparation

- Ask students to review the vocabulary on page 178 for a couple of minutes and if neccessary, correct their list from the Independent Starter. Have students associate each item in their list with the type of store where it is sold and add two words to describe the item.

- Then have students sit in a circle to play a vocabulary game. Have a student start the game by calling out one of the items on his or her list from the Independent Starter. The student to the right of the caller says something about the item. Then the next student to the right adds something else, and so on. The words used must be from the vocabulary list. For example: *zapatos → de cuero → caros → negros → zapatería*. If a student doesn't have anything more to say about the item and the student to his or her right does, the student who didn't have anything to say loses a turn. Once there are no more vocabulary words to describe the item, the student whose turn it is calls out a new word.

- Review, as a class, any words and categories students had difficulties with when they were playing the vocabulary game.

178

REPASO Vocabulario

La ropa y los complementos

		Complementos	
el abrigo	coat	el anillo	ring
la bata	robe	los aretes	earrings
la corbata	tie	el bolso	purse
el impermeable	raincoat	el collar	necklace
el pijama	pajamas	las gafas de sol	sunglasses
la sudadera	sweatshirt	la gorra	cap
el traje	suit	la pulsera	bracelet
el traje de baño	swimsuit	el reloj	watch

Calzado
las zapatillas	slippers

Describir la ropa

		Colores	
el número	shoe size	amarillo(a)	yellow
la talla	size	anaranjado(a)	orange
		azul	blue
Características		blanco(a)	white
cómodo(a)	comfortable	de color café	brown
incómodo(a)	uncomfortable	dorado(a)	gold
		gris	gray
Diseños		morado(a)	purple
de cuadros	plaid	negro(a)	black
de lunares	polka dot	plateado(a)	silver
de rayas	striped	rojo(a)	red
liso(a)	plain	rosado(a)	pink
		verde	green
Materiales			
de algodón	cotton	colores claros	light colors
de cuero	leather	colores oscuros	dark colors
de lana	wool		

Tiendas y establecimientos

el centro comercial	shopping mall
la farmacia	drugstore
la joyería	jewelry store
la librería	bookstore
la papelería	stationery store
la peluquería	hair salon
la perfumería	perfume store
el quiosco	kiosk
el supermercado	supermarket
la zapatería	shoe store
la tienda de artesanía	handicrafts store
la tienda de bisutería	costume jewelry store
la tienda de deportes	sports store
la tienda de disfraces	costume shop
la tienda de música	music store
la tienda de regalos	gift shop
la tienda de ropa	clothing store
el ascensor	elevator
las escaleras mecánicas	escalator

Las compras

		El dinero		**Expresiones**	
la caja	cash register	el billete	bill	estar de moda	to be in style
el/la cajero(a)	cashier	la moneda	coin	estar en oferta	to be on sale
el/la cliente(a)	customer	la tarjeta			
el/la dependiente(a)	salesclerk	de crédito	credit card	pagar con tarjeta	to pay by credit card
el descuento	discount			pagar en efectivo	to pay in cash
la etiqueta	tag, label	**El precio**			
la fila	line	ser barato(a)	to be cheap,	probarse ropa	to try clothes on
el probador	fitting room		inexpensive	quedar bien	to fit well
		ser caro(a)	to be expensive	quedar mal	to fit badly
				quedar grande	to be too big
				quedar pequeño	to be too small

178 ciento setenta y ocho

Differentiated Instruction

DEVELOPING LEARNERS

- As students review the vocabulary, ask them to try to get the most senses involved in the learning process. For the clothing items they could create flashcards with a picture or drawing on one side and the word on the other. For the stores and public establishments, they could pronounce the words out loud, paying attention to patterns in sounds (e.g., the ending *-ería*, the repetition of the word *tienda*). For the materials they can try to imagine the smell (e.g., the smell of leather). For the colors they could think of a food associated with each color.

EXPANDING LEARNERS

- Ask students to write five true (C) and five false (F) statements based on the unit vocabulary. For example:
  – *Los aretes son de lana.* (F)
  – *Usas monedas y billetes para pagar en efectivo.* (C)

- Once students have finished their ten statements, ask them to proofread them. Then have students exchange papers with a classmate and take each other's quiz. Once they finish the quiz, they should give the paper back to the person who wrote it for correction. How did they do on the quiz?

DESAFÍO 1

1 **La ropa adecuada.** Lee estas oraciones
y elige la ropa adecuada para cada situación.

1. Ernesto estuvo en un cámping en la montaña.
2. Julieta fue al cumpleaños de su prima Eva.
3. Antonio se durmió temprano.
4. María fue a la playa con sus amigos.
5. Luis fue a la boda de su amigo Pedro.

vestido	pijama
collar	sudadera
botas	traje de baño
corbata	zapatillas
traje	pantalones cortos

DESAFÍO 2

2 **Los gustos de Celia.** Completa las oraciones con la palabra correcta.

Me gusta este poncho de _____ (lana/talla) porque es muy _____ (cómodo/incómodo).
Tiene _____ (colores/sabores) claros y oscuros. También me gustan esas botas
de _____ (caro/cuero) y aquella falda de _____ (lunares/collares).

DESAFÍO 3

3 **Lugares.** Relaciona cada oración con la imagen adecuada.

1. Compraron estos
cuadernos en
la papelería.

2. Carlos estuvo en dos
mercados esta mañana.

3. ¿Fuiste a la peluquería
ayer por la tarde?

DESAFÍO 4

4 **Problemas en la tienda.** Completa el texto.

fila	etiqueta	bien	tarjeta	probador

Problemas en la tienda

Quiero comprar este impermeable, pero no tiene ___1___ y no sé el precio. Además,

no hay ___2___ en la tienda para saber si me queda ___3___ o mal. La ___4___ para pagar

es muy larga y creo que no puedo pagar con ___5___. ¡Me voy a otra tienda!

Unit 3

REPASO

Vocabulario

Activities

1. To extend this activity, ask students to include information about the materials these items are made of and their patterns. For example: 1. *una sudadera de rayas y unas botas de cuero.*

3. Call students' attention to the ending *-ería* in the words *papelería* and *peluquería*. Explain that the suffix *-ería* is used in this case to turn a noun (*papel*) into the name for the store that sells such an item. Have students work with a partner to come up with a list of names not included in the vocabulary for other types of stores that also end in *-ería* such as, *ferretería* (hardware store), *heladería* (ice cream parlor), *panadería* (bakery), etc. Have partners share their lists with the rest of the class, and have the class try to guess which items are sold in each type of store.

4. Have students add two sentences to this paragraph to change the ending. They should use two expressions or words from the vocabulary in *Desafío 4* that were not used in this activity.

Answer Key

1. Answers will vary. Sample answers:
1. una sudadera, unas botas
2. un vestido, un collar
3. un pijama, unas zapatillas
4. un traje de baño, unos pantalones cortos
5. un traje, una corbata

2. lana; cómodo; colores; cuero; lunares

3. 1. B   2. C   3. A

4. 1. etiqueta   4. fila
2. probador   5. tarjeta
3. bien

Additional Resources

Fans Online activities
Practice Workbook

REPASO

Gramática

Presentation

- Students will review grammatical structures presented in the unit. Each grammar point is cross-referenced to the corresponding page on which it was introduced. The activities here provide systematic practice by *Desafío*.

Activities	Standards	Resources
5.	1.3	
6.	1.2, 1.3	
7.	1.2	
8.	1.3	
9. Cultura	1.3, 2.1, 2.2, 5.2	

Teaching Suggestions

Warm-Up / Independent Starter

- Write the following phrases on the board:
  1. *comprar algo caro*, 2. *comer en un restaurante*, 3. *ir a una fiesta*. Ask students to write a sentence saying something about the last time they did each one of these things. For example: *La semana pasada compré un reloj caro para mi padre.*

Preparation

- Have students interview two classmates about the last time they did the three things mentioned in the Independent Starter. The classmate responds with the sentences he or she wrote. For example:
  A. *¿Cuándo fue la última vez que compraste algo caro y qué pasó?*
  B. *La semana pasada compré un reloj...*
  Invite volunteer pairs to report their partner's answers. Remind them to use the third person singular form of the verbs.
- Write the different verb forms students use on the board. As you go over the *Repaso* presentation, use the verbs you wrote on the board as examples of the grammar being reviewed.

Activities

6. Ask students to personalize three of these questions and use them to interview a classmate. For example:
   A. *¿Comiste en un restaurante latino el fin de semana pasado?*
   B. *No, comí en un restaurante italiano.*

REPASO Gramática

Verbos regulares. Pretérito (págs. 142 y 150)

	COMPRAR	COMER	ESCRIBIR
yo	compré	comí	escribí
tú	compraste	comiste	escribiste
usted, él, ella	compró	comió	escribió
nosotros(as)	compramos	comimos	escribimos
vosotros(as)	comprasteis	comisteis	escribisteis
ustedes, ellos(as)	compraron	comieron	escribieron

Verbos con cambios ortográficos

Verbs ending in -car, -gar, or -zar change spelling in the yo form:

buscar → yo busqué
llegar → yo llegué
empezar → yo empecé

Marcadores temporales de pasado (pág. 150)

el año pasado	last year
el mes pasado	last month
la semana pasada	last week
anteayer	the day before yesterday
anoche	last night
ayer	yesterday

Hace + time expression + que + verb in the preterite tense

Verb in the preterite tense + hace + time expression

Verbos irregulares. Pretérito (pág. 158)

	SER e IR	DECIR	TENER	ESTAR	HACER
yo	fui	dije	tuve	estuve	hice
tú	fuiste	dijiste	tuviste	estuviste	hiciste
usted, él, ella	fue	dijo	tuvo	estuvo	hizo
nosotros(as)	fuimos	dijimos	tuvimos	estuvimos	hicimos
vosotros(as)	fuisteis	dijisteis	tuvisteis	estuvisteis	hicisteis
ustedes, ellos(as)	fueron	dijeron	tuvieron	estuvieron	hicieron

Verbos en -ir con raíz irregular. Pretérito (pág. 166)

	PEDIR	DORMIR
yo	pedí	dormí
tú	pediste	dormiste
usted, él, ella	pidió	durmió
nosotros(as)	pedimos	dormimos
vosotros(as)	pedisteis	dormisteis
ustedes, ellos(as)	pidieron	durmieron

Differentiated Instruction

DEVELOPING LEARNERS

- Ask students to look at the verbs listed on page 180 and write down one thing they associate with each verb. For example: *escribir → mensaje; buscar → las llaves, etc.* Then have students come up with a sentence in the preterite about themselves or someone else in which they use these verbs and the word they associated with each verb. For example:
  – *Esta mañana yo escribí un mensaje telefónico.*
  – *Ayer mi madre buscó las llaves del carro por toda la casa.*

EXPANDING LEARNERS

- Have students work in small groups of three. Ask them to create a short dialogue for a group of three friends who haven't seen each other in a few months. They get together and talk about some of the things they did during the previous months.
- Students should agree on a plot. Then they should write down their dialogue and check it for grammar accuracy. Allow for time to rehearse and then invite groups to act out their scene in front of the class. After each performance, ask the class comprehension questions about the role-play.

DESAFÍO 1

5 **Actividades.** Escribe una oración sobre lo que hicieron estas personas ayer.

Modelo Patricia y yo - almorzar juntas → *Ayer Patricia y yo almorzamos juntas.*

1. Gloria - comprar una sudadera y un reloj
2. Marieta y Vero - practicar deporte
3. Yo - empezar las clases de guitarra
4. Luisa y yo - hablar por teléfono

 DESAFÍO 2

6 **En el pasado.** Responde a las preguntas con una oración completa.

1. ¿Pablo y Ángel corrieron el maratón?
2. ¿Aprendiste a nadar el verano pasado?
3. ¿Ustedes salieron ayer por la tarde?
4. ¿Comiste en un restaurante peruano?

 DESAFÍO 3

7 **De vacaciones.** Elige la forma verbal correcta y completa el texto.

CECILIA: Ana me ___1___ que ___2___ de vacaciones a Perú.
          dijeron/dijo   fue/fuiste

BRUNO: Sí, el verano pasado ___3___ a Perú con mi familia.
                            fue/fui

CECILIA: ¡Qué bien! ¿Dónde ___4___?
                          estuvo/estuvieron

BRUNO: ___5___ en Lima y en los Andes peruanos. ___6___
       Estuvimos/estuvisteis   Hicimos/Hicieron
muchas cosas, pero quiero regresar a Perú el próximo año. ¡Es un país muy especial!

 **DESAFÍO 4**

8 **¿Qué hicieron?** Escribe oraciones en pasado con estos elementos.

1. ayer - ella - pedir - un postre delicioso
2. anoche - nosotros - servir la cena - en el jardín
3. la semana pasada - mis primos - dormir - en mi casa
4. hace dos días - mi padre - sentirse - mal del estómago

CULTURA

9 **Conoce la región andina.** Responde a las siguientes preguntas.

1. ¿Por qué países pasa la cordillera de los Andes?
2. ¿Qué es El Chimborazo?
3. ¿Qué sabes del carnaval de Oruro?
4. ¿Cómo es la ropa tradicional andina?

ciento ochenta y uno 181

---

7. Have pairs of students act out the dialogue. They may add one or two lines.

8. Have students choose one of these sentences and add two more sentences to make it a brief story. For example: *Hace dos días mi padre se sintió mal del estómago. Comió pescado y le sentó mal. Tuvo que ir al médico.*

Answer Key

5. 1. Gloria compró una sudadera y un reloj.
   2. Marieta y Vero practicaron deporte.
   3. Yo empecé las clases de guitarra.
   4. Luisa y yo hablamos por teléfono.

6. 1. Sí, Pablo y Ángel corrieron el maratón.
   2. Sí, aprendí a nadar el verano pasado.
   3. Sí, nosotros salimos ayer por la tarde.
   4. Sí, comí en un restaurante peruano.

7. 1. dijo   3. fui   5. Estuvimos
   2. fuiste   4. estuvieron   6. Hicimos

8. 1. Ayer ella pidió un postre delicioso.
   2. Anoche nosotros servimos la cena en el jardín.
   3. La semana pasada mis primos durmieron en mi casa.
   4. Hace dos días mi padre se sintió mal del estómago.

9. Answers will vary. Sample answers:
   1. La cordillera de los Andes pasa por Venezuela, Colombia, Ecuador, Perú, Bolivia, Chile y Argentina.
   2. El Chimborazo es el volcán más alto de Ecuador.
   3. El carnaval de Oruro es una de las celebraciones más importantes de Bolivia. Es una mezcla de las tradiciones indígenas y españolas. Son diez días de fiesta. La gente baila y se disfraza.
   4. La ropa tradicional andina tiene diseños muy variados. Los hombres llevan a veces ponchos de lana. Las mujeres llevan unas faldas llamadas polleras. También usan un sombrero llamado montera.

Additional Resources

Fans Online activities
Practice Workbook

HERITAGE LANGUAGE LEARNERS

- Remind students that the verbs that end in *-zar* change to *-cé* in the *yo* form of the preterite tense. These verbs pose spelling difficulties to Spanish speakers.

- Ask students to come up with sentences using the *yo* form in the preterite for the following *verbs*.
  – *abrazar*
  – *comenzar*
  – *analizar*
  – *localizar*

TOTAL PHYSICAL RESPONSE (TPR)

- Have students play a game of charades in groups of four. Make sure there is a mix of students of different skills and language levels in each group. Each group divides into two teams. Each team pantomimes a phrase in the preterite using one of the verbs studied. They cannot make any sound or speak. The other team attempts to guess the verb and then the phrase. If time allows, you may want to have winning teams play against each other for a final match and in order to have a class champion team.

181

Unit 3
PROYECTO
Moda andina

Presentation

■ In this section, students will apply the vocabulary, grammar, and cultural information they have learned in this unit to write a description of six outfits for a fashion magazine. Students will follow step-by-step Instructions.

Activities	Standards	Resources
Paso 1	1.2, 1.3, 2.2, 3.1, 5.2	
Paso 2	1.2, 3.1	
Paso 3	1.3	
Paso 4	3.1	
Paso 5	1.1, 1.2, 1.3	

Teaching Suggestions

Warm-Up / Independent Starter

■ Ask students to think for a few moments about the type of outfits they like to wear in different situations (e.g., to school, to a party, to do sports, etc.). Have them also consider the accessories they would wear with each of these outfits.

Preparation

■ Have students get together in small groups and ask them to read the introduction to the project and all the tasks involved. Have them discuss their ideas about fashion and what they know about fashion journalism. You may want to bring fashion magazines to class or ask students to bring them. They can also look at some online magazines, such as http://www.vogue.es/, http://www.glamour.es/, and http://www.elle.es/ to get ideas.

Step-by-Step Instructions

Paso 1

■ Encourage students to create an index card for each outfit. Have them record on it information specific to each outfit, including season, color, material, target customers, sizes available, appropriate accessories, price (see *Paso 2*), etc.

■ For images, in addition to Peru Moda (http://www.perumoda.com), students can visit the websites of Andean designers such as the Bolivian designer Liliana Castellanos (http://www.lilianacastellanos.com/). Remind students to record all of the sources they are using on their index cards.

Una revista sobre
moda andina

Imagine that you are the editor of an international fashion magazine and have to write a section about clothing in the Andes region of South America. You will write about six outfits for this magazine. Each outfit must be in color, priced, and have a short description.

PASO 1 Decide la ropa de tu colección

● Answer the following questions to decide what clothing you will put together for your six outfits.
 – ¿Es ropa para hombres o para mujeres? ¿Es ropa para gente joven, para personas mayores o para niños?
 – ¿Es ropa de invierno o ropa de verano?
 – ¿Es ropa de vestir, ropa informal o ropa deportiva?
 – ¿Qué complementos necesita?

● Select the clothing you will include in your magazine article. You can draw your clothing items or cut them out of a magazine. Also, you can find images on the Internet about fashion events in Andean countries, such as PerúModa.

● When you have all the pieces, place your outfits side by side to ensure they are all complete, including shoes and accessories.

PASO 2 Pon el precio

● Decide how much your outfits will cost and create a price list.
 – Vestido: 40 dólares
 – Botas: 30 dólares
 You can use the Internet again to investigate about prices. Think about these questions to set a price for each piece.
 – ¿Los precios son adecuados al material (lana, algodón…)?
 – ¿Y al tipo de ropa (elegante, informal…)?

182 ciento ochenta y dos

Rubric for Evaluation

	Content	Organization	Presentation
1 point	Limited relevance. Information is incomplete or not based on research. Little Spanish is used.	Inefficient use of class time. Information is disorganized or unclear. Images and pages are not well designed and organized.	Communication is unclear. Delivery is not fluent. Many errors in vocabulary and grammar.
3 points	Basic information is correct. Relevant information but lacks significance. Spanish is used most of the time.	Class time is used well. Information and content are mostly organized but lack some clarity. Images and pages are mostly well designed and organized.	Good communication. Fluent delivery. Mostly correct vocabulary and grammar.

PASO 3 Escribe el texto

- Write a description of each outfit using two or more complete sentences. Include the name of each piece, the color, the material, how much it costs, and where one can find it.

El vestido verde es de algodón y cuesta 80 dólares. Lo puedes encontrar en la tienda Moda Total, en el centro comercial Miraflores.

El collar y el bolso son...

PASO 4 Prepara las páginas de la sección

- Take one large piece of paper and fold it in half. Design the cover or the first page of your magazine section: give a name to your section and select a photo or a drawing for the first page.

- Spread your collection across each of the remaining blank pages. Do not put anything in the crease of the page. Put the texts with the correct images and be sure your pages are neatly designed and organized.

PASO 5 Presenta tu trabajo

- Once you have finished, share your magazine article with your classmates. Select the clothing you would most like to buy from the other magazines and talk to your classmates.

Modelo Me gusta esta pulsera de cuero.
Es bonita, barata y...

Unidad 3

Autoevaluación

¿Qué has aprendido en esta unidad?

Do the following activities to evaluate how well you understood this unit's concepts.

Evaluate your skills. For each item, say Very well, Well, or I need more practice.

a. Can you talk about clothing?
- ▶ Describe what you are wearing to a classmate.
- ▶ Ask a classmate where he or she purchased each article of clothing he or she is wearing.

b. Can you describe clothes?
- ▶ Look through the textbook and describe the clothing items you see to a classmate.
- ▶ Tell your classmate how long ago you wore the same items as the ones you see in the textbook.

c. Can you talk about places in the community?
- ▶ Tell a classmate the names of the different stores in your community.
- ▶ Tell a classmate about the last time you went to the stores in your community.

d. Can you talk about past shopping experiences?
- ▶ Walk a classmate through your last clothes-shopping experience.

PROYECTO

Moda andina

Paso 2

- Discuss with students the criteria commonly used to price a product. Ask them to consider the materials their outfits are made of and the cost of these materials, labor costs (Was the product handmade or machine made?), target customers, the perceived value of the product (Will customers perceive the product as a high-quality luxury item, a short-lived fashion trend or something casual to be worn often?), competitors' prices for similar products, etc.

Paso 3

- Ask students to use the index cards they created to write the description of each outfit.

Paso 4

- Emphasize the importance of making their magazine visually appealing. Encourage students to be organized as well as creative in their page design.

Paso 5

- Have students ask their classmates for the reasons for their clothing selections. What appealed to them most? What was the deciding factor?

Evaluation

- Distribute copies of the rubric to students. Discuss the evaluation criteria and explain how this project will be graded. Encourage students to refer to the rubric as they prepare their projects. It may be helpful to correlate the points with the traditional grade scale and indicate how much each project counts towards the final grade.

Content

- Emphasize the importance of including thorough and vivid descriptions. Tell students to also keep in mind their intended audience and tailor their description accordingly.

Organization

- Students should consider carefully what information to include. They should strike a balance between making their descriptions sufficiently detailed, yet succinct.

Presentation

- Students should use as much Spanish as possible. Encourage creativity and a presentation style that will hold their classmates' attention.

	Content	Organization	Presentation
5 points	Relevant, interesting information. Many details and significance are highlighted. Spanish is used exclusively.	Class time is used wisely. Information and content are clearly organized visually and logically. Images and pages are very well designed and organized.	Clear communication. Correct and complete vocabulary and grammar. Very motivating upbeat delivery.

Unit 4 Norteamérica

Objectives

- To talk about food.
- To give shopping-related commands.
- To give commands related to cooking.
- To communicate in common dining-related situations.
- To talk about grocery shopping.
- To talk about utensils and food preparation.
- To talk about a restaurant experience.

- To use expressions to order food in a restaurant, expressions to ask a waiter for something, and expressions to ask for something on the table.
- To explore cultural aspects of North America.
- To acquire facts about the geography and history of the countries in North America.

Contents

Vocabulary
- Food.
- Food packaging and actions in the grocery store.
- Utensils, condiments, and food preparation.
- Place settings.
- Food preparation and flavors.
- Expressions used to order food in a restaurant.
- Expressions used to ask a waiter for something.
- Expressions used to ask for something on the table.

Grammar
- To express quantity: Indefinites.
- Singular affirmative commands.
- Plural affirmative commands.
- Negative commands.

Culture
- *El Día de Muertos.*
- Traditional dishes: two different *tortillas.*
- *¿Fruta o fruto?*
- Cacao and chocolate: origin, history, and products.
- The history of *El Álamo.*
- *El chile.*
- Cultural aspects of meal times.
- *El mole.*
- *Los restaurantes tex-mex.*
- The use of *tú* and *usted.*
- North America.

Evaluation Criteria

- Order food in a restaurant.
- Ask a waiter to bring something to the table.
- Ask a table mate to pass something on the table.
- List food items.
- Simulate a grocery shopping experience.
- List types of food packaging.
- Simulate preparing a dish.

- List kitchen utensils, condiments, and food preparation processes.
- Simulate a restaurant dining scene.
- List items in a place setting.
- Describe a meal.
- Recognize and use indefinite adjectives of quantity.
- Recognize and use singular commands.
- Recognize and use plural commands.

- Recognize and use negative commands.
- Express understanding of selected North American customs, geographical aspects, and historical facts.
- Express understanding of the use of *tú* and *usted.*
- Develop an original recipe using American ingredients and put together a class cookbook.

Unit Plan _____

La llegada

Estimated time: 1 session.

Dialogue: *En Santa Fe.*

Functions & forms:
- Expressions for ordering food in a restaurant.
- Expressions for asking a waiter for something.
- Expressions for asking for something on the table.

Culture:
- Santa Fe, New Mexico.

⚑DESAFÍO 1

Estimated time: 4 sessions.

Dialogue: *¿Un pan de muerto?*

Functions & forms:
- Foods.
- To express quantity: Indefinites.

Culture:
- *El Día de Muertos.*
- *La tortilla.*
- *¿Fruta o fruto?*

⚑DESAFÍO 2

Estimated time: 4 sessions.

Dialogue: *La moneda más antigua de América.*

Functions & forms:
- Grocery shopping.
- Singular affirmative commands.

Culture:
- *La ruta del cacao.*
- *El chocolate.*
- *Los nombres científicos.*

⚑DESAFÍO 3

Estimated time: 4 sessions.

Dialogue: *Un concurso de chile en San Antonio.*

Functions & forms:
- Cooking utensils, condiments, and cooking instructions.
- Plural affirmative commands.

Culture:
- *El Álamo.*
- *El chile.*
- *Los horarios.*

⚑DESAFÍO 4

Estimated time: 4 sessions.

Dialogue: *El ingrediente secreto de Cholula.*

Functions & forms:
- Place settings, food preparation, and flavors.
- Negative commands.

Culture:
- *El mole.*
- *Los restaurantes tex-mex.*
- *¿Vosotros o ustedes ?*

TODO JUNTO/El encuentro

Estimated time: 1 session.

Dialogue: *En el Camino Real de Tierra Adentro.*

Functions & forms:
- Review of *Desafíos 1–4.*

Culture:
- The *Camino Real de Tierra Adentro* Heritage Center, Santa Fe, New Mexico.

MAPA CULTURAL/LECTURA

Estimated time: 1 session.

Mapa cultural: *Norteamérica.*

Reading: *La receta del guacamole.*

PROYECTO/EVALUACIÓN

Estimated time: 2 sessions.

Project: *Un menú con ingredientes americanos.*

Self-evaluation: *Autoevaluación.*

Standards for Learning Spanish

COMMUNICATION

1.1. Interpersonal mode

- Discuss the challenge for each team in the selected regions of North America.
- Speculate on which pair will win the challenge.
- Discuss traditional foods in different regions of North America.
- Interview a classmate.
- With a classmate, plan a dialogue between people in a photograph.
- Survey the class on a question.

1.2. Interpretive mode

- Give advice to a problem raised in an oral conversation.
- Read a cultural text.
- Summarize information in a written text.
- Research cultural topics.
- Read about the Alamo on the Internet.
- Read a blog.

1.3. Presentational mode

- Write a slogan for a food advertisement.
- Write a summary of an oral text.
- Write captions for photographs.
- Make a grocery list.
- Present survey results to the class.
- Write a balanced menu for a given meal.
- Develop interview questions.

CULTURE

2.1. Practices and perspectives

- Discuss meal times in different regions and countries.
- Discuss the use of *vosotros* and *ustedes*.
- Discuss the manifestations of a fusion of cultures.
- Read about the role of the tortilla in Mexican cuisine.
- Read about the *Día de Muertos*.

2.2. Products and perspectives

- Read about the historical role of the cacao and its products.
- Research typical Mexican dishes.
- Read about the historical significance of the Alamo.

CONNECTIONS

3.1. Interdisciplinary connections

- Acquire knowledge of the history of the Alamo.
- Research the etymology of certain words.
- Research the history of money.
- Read about types of fruits and fruit trees.
- Discuss commands in English and Spanish.
- Understand the characteristics of instructional texts.

3.2. Viewpoints through language/culture

- Read a *fotonovela* in Spanish.
- Read a cultural text in Spanish.
- Read about Spanish-speaking areas in North America on the Internet.
- Read an instructional text.
- Read a recipe.

COMPARISONS

4.1. Compare languages

- Compare indefinites in English and in Spanish.
- Compare command forms in English and in Spanish.

4.2. Compare cultures

- Discuss *Día de Muertos* celebrations in the community.
- Compare traditional foods in the United States and in other countries.
- Discuss spicy foods in the community.
- Compare traditional meal times.
- Reflect about the influence of different cultures on a country's food and eating habits.

COMMUNITIES

5.1. Spanish within and beyond the school setting

- Write a balanced meal menu.
- Discuss products derived from cacao.
- Advise someone who is planning a trip to Mexico.

5.2. Spanish for lifelong learning

- Write a slogan for a food advertisement.
- Compile a collection of recipes.
- Share travel experiences.

Communicative Skills

Interpersonal Mode

		Activities
Speaking	• Engage in conversation with a classmate. • Compare information with a classmate. • Talk to a partner about your food likes. • Talk to a partner about food preparation. • Give instructions or advice to a partner.	• 9, 13, 19, 22, 28, 32, 41, 57, 87 • 14, 24, 42, 58 • 22, 40, 52, 70, 83, 84, 85 • 52, 87 • 55, 57, 75, 79
Writing	• Create a menu based on preference. • Make a list.	• 14, 80, *Proyecto* • 32, 84
Listening	• Understand verbal questions and respond appropriately.	• *Minientrevistas*
Reading	• Understand the components and instructions in a recipe. • Understand simple texts that describe food and healthy living.	• *Lectura* • 25

Interpretive Mode

		Activities
Listening	• Obtain basic information from a conversation. • Understand statements or texts related to food likes and habits. • Understand the instructions in a recipe. • Listen and identify ideas or photos. • Interpret audio and video about culture.	• 12, 31, 61, 65, 77, 82 • 17, 22 • 47, 82 • 42, 47, 50, 69 • *Tu desafío*, videos
Reading	• Understand brief written exchanges. • Understand the instructions in a recipe. • Infer meanings based on a cultural text. • Reflect on and explain cultural elements related to personal experience.	• 1, 7, 25, 27, 44, 45, 46, 62, 64 • 6, 7, 51, 59, 86, 87 • 10, 15, 20, 29, 33, 48, 53, 58, 67, 71, 76 • 10, 15, 29, 53, 58, 67, 71, 76

Presentational Mode

		Activities
Speaking	• Act out a short skit aloud. • Present an original creation or representation to the class.	• 62 • 55, 80, 87, *Proyecto*
Writing	• Write a descriptive food list. • Display the results of a survey.	• 21, 24, 40 • 19, 80

Cross-Curricular Standards

Subject	Standard	Activities
Language Arts	• Read about the etymology of words. • Compare expressions used in social situations in English and in Spanish. • Compare elements of English grammar with Spanish equivalents.	• 39 • 76 • 16, 34, 54, 72
History	• Read about the Alamo.	• 48
Science	• Read about types of fruits and fruit-bearing trees. • Research foods of North American origin.	• 20 • *Proyecto*

Lesson Plans (50-Minute Classes)

Day	Objectives	Sessions	Activities	Time	Standards	Resources / Homework
1	To introduce North America and to discuss the pairs' challenges	**Norteamérica / La llegada** (184–189) • Warm-Up: Region orientation • *Norteamérica* • Images and functions • Presentation: *En Santa Fe* • *Expresiones útiles* and *¿Quién ganará?*	 1 2–5	5 m. 5 m. 10 m. 10 m. 20 m.	1.1, 1.2, 1.3, 2.1, 2.2, 4.1, 5.1	Visual Presentation Audio Video Practice Workbook
2	To talk about food	**Desafío 1 – ¿Un pan de muerto?** (190–191) • Warm-Up: Independent Starter • *Fotonovela: ¿Un pan de muerto?* • *Comunidades: El Día de Muertos*	 6–9 10	 5 m. 35 m. 10 m.	1.1, 1.2, 1.3, 2.1, 3.2, 4.2, 5.2	Visual Presentation Audio Video *Tu desafío*
3	To talk about food	**Desafío 1 – Vocabulario** (192–193) • Warm-Up: Independent Starter • Vocabulary: *Los alimentos* • *Comparaciones: La tortilla*	 11–14 15	 5 m. 35 m. 10 m.	1.1, 1.2, 1.3, 2.2, 3.2, 4.2, 5.1, 5.2	Audio Practice Workbook *Tu desafío*
4	To learn and use indefinites	**Desafío 1 – Gramática** (194–195) • Warm-Up: Independent Starter • Grammar: *Expresar cantidad. Los indefinidos* • *Conexiones: ¿Fruta o fruto?*	 16–19 20	 5 m. 35 m. 10 m.	1.1, 1.2, 1.3, 3.1, 3.2, 4.1	Audio Practice Workbook
5	To integrate vocabulary and grammar and to assess student proficiency	**Desafío 1 – Comunicación / Evaluación** (196–197) • Warm-Up: Independent Starter • *Comunicación:* Review • *Final del desafío* • Quiz on *Desafío 1*	 21–24 25	 5 m. 20 m. 10 m. 15 m.	1.1, 1.2, 1.3, 2.2, 3.1	Audio Practice Workbook
6	To give commands related to grocery shopping	**Desafío 2 – La moneda más antigua de América** (198–199) • Warm-Up: Independent Starter • *Fotonovela: La moneda más antigua de América* • *Cultura: La ruta del cacao*	 26–28 29	 5 m. 35 m. 10 m.	1.1, 1.2, 1.3, 2.1, 2.2, 3.1, 3.2, 5.2	Visual Presentation *Tu desafío*
7	To talk about food packaging, weights, and grocery shopping	**Desafío 2 – Vocabulario** (200–201) • Warm-Up: Independent Starter • Vocabulary: *Comprar comida* • *Cultura: El chocolate*	 30–32 33	 5 m. 35 m. 10 m.	1.1, 1.2, 1.3, 2.2, 3.1, 3.2, 5.1	Audio Practice Workbook
8	To learn and use singular affirmative commands	**Desafío 2 – Gramática** (202–203) • Warm-Up: Independent Starter • Grammar: *El imperativo afirmativo singular* • *Conexiones: Los nombres científicos*	 34–38 39	 5 m. 35 m. 10 m.	1.1, 1.2, 1.3, 3.1, 3.2, 4.1, 5.1	Audio Practice Workbook
9	To integrate vocabulary and grammar and to assess student proficiency	**Desafío 2 – Comunicación / Evaluación** (204–205) • Warm-Up: Independent Starter • *Comunicación:* Review • *Final del desafío* • Quiz on *Desafío 2*	 40–43 44	 5 m. 20 m. 10 m. 15 m.	1.1, 1.2, 1.3, 2.1, 2.2, 5.1	Audio Practice Workbook *Tu desafío*
10	To give instructions related to food preparation	**Desafío 3 – Un concurso de chile en San Antonio** (206–207) • Warm-Up: Independent Starter • *Fotonovela: Un concurso de chile en San Antonio* • *Conexiones: El Álamo*	 45–47 48	 5 m. 35 m. 10 m.	1.1, 1.2, 1.3, 2.2, 3.1, 3.2, 5.2	Visual Presentation Audio Video *Tu desafío*

Day	Objectives	Sessions	Activities	Time	Standards	Resources / Homework
11	To talk about utensils, condiments, and food preparation	**Desafío 3 – Vocabulario** (208–209) • Warm-Up: Independent Starter • Vocabulary: *En la cocina* • *Cultura: El chile*	49–52 53	5 m. 35 m. 10 m.	1.1, 1.2, 1.3, 2.1, 2.2, 3.2, 4.2, 5.2	Audio Practice Workbook *Tu desafío*
12	To learn and use plural affirmative commands	**Desafío 3 – Gramática** (210–211) • Warm-Up: Independent Starter • Grammar: *El imperativo afirmativo plural* • *Comunidades: Los horarios*	54–57 58	5 m. 35 m. 10 m.	1.1, 1.2, 1.3, 2.1, 3.1, 3.2, 4.1, 4.2, 5.1, 5.2	Practice Workbook
13	To integrate vocabulary and grammar and to assess student proficiency	**Desafío 3 – Comunicación / Evaluación** (212–213) • Warm-Up: Independent Starter • *Comunicación:* Review • *Final del desafío* • Quiz on *Desafío 3*	59–61 62	5 m. 20 m. 10 m. 15 m.	1.2, 1.3, 2.2	Audio Practice Workbook
14	To communicate in a restaurant setting	**Desafío 4 – El ingrediente secreto de Cholula** (214–215) • Warm-Up: Independent Starter • *Fotonovela: El ingrediente secreto de Cholula* • *Cultura: El mole*	63–66 67	5 m. 35 m. 10 m.	1.1, 1.2, 1.3, 2.2, 3.2, 4.2, 5.2	Visual Presentation Audio *Tu desafío*
15	To order a meal in a restaurant, list items in a place setting, and describe a dish	**Desafío 4 – Vocabulario** (216–217) • Warm-Up: Independent Starter • Vocabulary: *En el restaurante* • *Cultura: Los restaurantes tex–mex*	68–70 71	5 m. 35 m. 10 m.	1.1, 1.2, 2.2, 3.2, 4.2, 5.2	Audio Practice Workbook
16	To learn and use negative commands	**Desafío 4 – Gramática** (218–219) • Warm-Up: Independent Starter • Grammar: *El imperativo negativo* • *Comunidades: ¿Vosotros o ustedes?*	72–75 76	5 m. 35 m. 10 m.	1.1, 1.2, 1.3, 2.1, 3.2, 4.1, 4.2, 5.2	Audio Practice Workbook
17	To integrate vocabulary and grammar and to assess student proficiency	**Desafío 4 – Comunicación / Evaluación** (220–221) • Warm-Up: Independent Starter • *Comunicación:* Review • *Final del desafío* • Quiz on *Desafío 4*	77–80 81	5 m. 20 m. 10 m. 15 m.	1.1, 1.2, 1.3, 2.2	Audio Practice Workbook
18	To integrate language in context	**Todo junto / El encuentro** (222–225) • Warm-Up: Independent Starter • *Todo junto* • *El encuentro: En el Camino Real de Tierra Adentro*	82–85 86–87	5 m. 20 m. 25 m.	1.1, 1.2, 1.3, 2.1, 2.2, 3.2, 5.2	Audio Practice Workbook
19	To learn about customs and traditions in North America	**Mapa cultural / Lectura** (226–229) • Warm-Up: Independent Starter • *Mapa cultural: Norteamérica* • *Lectura: La receta del guacamole*	88–89 90–92	5 m. 20 m. 25 m.	1.2, 1.3, 2.1, 2.2, 3.1, 3.2	Video Practice Workbook *Tu desafío* Project work
20	To create a dish using indigenous American ingredients and to compose a cookbook	**Proyecto** (234–235) • Warm-Up: Prepare project presentations • Project presentations		10 m. 40 m.	1.1, 1.2, 1.3, 2.2, 3.1, 5.2	Practice Workbook **Repaso – Vocabulario** (230–231) **Repaso – Gramática** (232–233)
21	To assess student proficiency	**Assessment** • *Autoevaluación* (235) • Test		10 m. 40 m.	1.2, 1.3	

Lesson Plans (90-Minute Classes)

Day	Objectives	Sessions	Activities	Time	Standards	Resources / Homework
1	To introduce North America and to discuss the pairs' challenges	***Norteamérica / La llegada*** (184–189) • Warm-Up: Region orientation • *Norteamérica/*Images and functions • Presentation: *En Santa Fe* • *Expresiones útiles* and *¿Quién ganará?*	 1 2–5	 10 m. 15 m. 30 m. 35 m.	1.1, 1.2, 1.3, 2.1, 2.2, 4.1, 5.1	Visual Presentation Audio Video Practice Workbook
2	To talk about food	***Desafío 1 – ¿Un pan de muerto? / Vocabulario*** (190–193) • Warm-Up: Independent Starter • *Fotonovela: ¿Un pan de muerto?* • *Comunidades: El día de Muertos* • Vocabulary: *Los alimentos* • *Comparaciones: La tortilla*	 6–9 10 11–14 15	 5 m. 30 m. 10 m. 35 m. 10 m.	1.1, 1.2, 1.3, 2.1, 2.2, 3.2, 4.2, 5.1, 5.2	Visual Presentation Audio Video Practice Workbook *Tu desafío*
3	To learn and use indefinites, to integrate vocabulary and grammar, and to assess student proficiency	***Desafío 1 – Gramática / Comunicación / Evaluación*** (194–197) • Warm-Up: Independent Starter • Grammar: *Expresar cantidad. Los indefinidos* • *Conexiones: ¿Fruta o fruto?* • *Comunicación:* Review • *Final del desafío* • Quiz on *Desafío 1*	 16–19 20 21–24 25	 5 m. 25 m. 10 m. 25 m. 10 m. 15 m.	1.1, 1.2, 1.3, 2.2, 3.1, 3.2, 4.1	Audio Practice Workbook
4	To give commands related to grocery shopping and to talk about food packaging, weights, and grocery shopping	***Desafío 2 – La moneda más antigua de América / Vocabulario*** (198–201) • Warm-Up: Independent Starter • *Fotonovela: La moneda más antigua de América* • *Cultura: La ruta del cacao* • Vocabulary: *Comprar comida* • *Cultura: El chocolate*	 26–28 29 30–32 33	 5 m. 30 m. 10 m. 35 m. 10 m.	1.1, 1.2, 1.3, 2.1, 2.2, 3.1, 3.2, 5.1, 5.2	Visual Presentation Audio *Tu desafío* Practice Workbook
5	To learn and use singular affirmative commands, to integrate vocabulary and grammar, and to assess student proficiency	***Desafío 2 – Gramática / Comunicación / Evaluación*** (202–205) • Warm-Up: Independent Starter • Grammar: *El imperativo afirmativo singular* • *Conexiones: Los nombres científicos* • *Comunicación:* Review • *Final del desafío* • Quiz on *Desafío 2*	 34–38 39 40–43 44	 5 m. 25 m. 10 m. 25 m. 10 m. 15 m.	1.1, 1.2, 1.3, 2.1, 2.2, 3.1, 3.2, 4.1, 5.1	Audio Practice Workbook *Tu desafío*
6	To give instructions related to food preparation and to talk about utensils, condiments, and food preparation	***Desafío 3 – Un concurso de chile en San Antonio / Vocabulario*** (206–209) • Warm-Up: Independent Starter • *Fotonovela: Un concurso de chile en San Antonio* • *Conexiones: El Álamo* • Vocabulary: *En la cocina* • *Cultura: El chile*	 45–47 48 49–52 53	 5 m. 35 m. 10 m. 30 m. 10 m.	1.1, 1.2, 1.3, 2.1, 2.2, 3.1, 3.2, 4.2, 5.2	Visual Presentation Audio Video *Tu desafío*

Day	Objectives	Sessions	Activities	Time	Standards	Resources / Homework
7	To learn and use plural affirmative commands, to integrate vocabulary and grammar, and to assess student proficiency	**Desafío 3 – Gramática / Comunicación / Evaluación** (210–213) • Warm-Up: Independent Starter • Grammar: *El imperativo afirmativo plural* • *Comunidades: Los horarios* • *Comunicación:* Review • *Final del desafío* • Quiz on *Desafío 3*	 54–57 58 59–61 62	5 m. 25 m. 10 m. 25 m. 10 m. 15 m.	1.1, 1.2, 1.3, 2.1, 2.2, 3.1, 3.2, 4.1, 4.2, 5.1, 5.2	Audio Practice Workbook
8	To communicate in a restaurant setting, to order a meal in a restaurant, to list items in a place setting, and to describe a dish	**Desafío 4 – El ingrediente secreto de Cholula / Vocabulario** (214–217) • Warm-Up: Independent Starter • *Fotonovela: El ingrediente secreto de Cholula* • *Cultura: El mole* • Vocabulary: *En el restaurante* • *Cultura: Los restaurantes tex–mex*	 63–66 67 68–70 71	 5 m. 35 m. 10 m. 30 m. 10 m.	1.1, 1.2, 1.3, 2.2, 3.2, 4.2, 5.2	Visual Presentation Audio Practice Workbook *Tu desafío*
9	To learn and use negative commands, to integrate vocabulary and grammar, and to assess student proficiency	**Desafío 4 –Gramática / Comunicación / Evaluación / Todo junto** (218–223) • Warm-Up: Independent Starter • Grammar: *El imperativo negativo* • *Comunidades: ¿Vosotros o ustedes?* • *Comunicación:* Review • *Final del desafío* • Quiz on *Desafío 4* • *Todo junto*	 72–75 76 77–80 81 82–85	5 m. 20 m. 5 m. 20 m. 5 m. 15 m. 20 m.	1.1, 1.2, 1.3, 2.1, 2.2, 3.2, 4.1, 4.2, 5.2	Audio Practice Workbook
10	To integrate language in context and to learn about customs and traditions in North America	**El encuentro / Mapa cultural / Lectura** (224–229) • Warm-Up: Independent Starter • *El encuentro: En el Camino Real de Tierra Adentro* • *Mapa cultural: Norteamérica* • *Lectura: La receta del guacamole*	 86–87 88–89 90–92	 5 m. 30 m. 25 m. 30 m.	1.1, 1.2, 1.3, 2.1, 2.2, 3.1, 3.2, 5.2	Video Practice Workbook *Tu desafío* **Repaso – Vocabulario** (230–231) **Repaso – Gramática** (232–223) Project work
11	To create a dish using indigenous American ingredients, to compose a cookbook, and to assess student proficiency	**Proyecto / Assessment** (234–235) • Warm-Up: Prepare project presentations • Project presentations • *Autoevaluación* • Test		10 m. 40 m. 10 m. 30 m.	1.1, 1.2, 1.3, 2.2, 3.1, 5.2	

Unit 4 Norteamérica

2 Expresiones

1. ¿Qué van a comer de postre?
2. ¿Puede traerme otro tenedor, por favor?
3. Arturo, ¿puedes pasarme la sal?

9 Día de Muertos

¡Bienvenidos a Oaxaca! La celebración del Día de Muertos les va a
encantar. Es una fiesta para recordar a los parientes muertos. Ese día
mucha gente va al cementerio para llevar ofrendas de alimentos. Por
ejemplo, yo llevo fruta y dulces. Y lo más importante: pan de muerto.

12 El restaurante recomendado

–Hola, Pedro. ¿Qué tal?
–Bien, ¿y tú? ¿Qué tal te lo estás pasando?
–Muy bien. Oye, ayer fuimos al restaurante de Oaxaca que nos
  recomendaste.
–¿Les gustó?
–Sí, sí, es buenísimo. Las verduras son muy frescas.
–¿Qué comieron?
–Mi abuelo pidió una ensalada deliciosa, con lechuga, tomate
  y zanahoria. Yo comí unos tacos de carne de res bastante buenos,
  ¡pero muy picantes!
–¿Te gusta la comida picante?
–Sí, me encanta.

17 ¿Cuánta fruta?

1. A mí no me gusta mucho la fruta. A veces como una naranja para
   desayunar, pero en general como muy poca fruta.
2. Yo como poca fruta. Como una pieza todos los días. Sobre todo
   entre las comidas.
3. Yo como mucha fruta. Antes de comer, después de comer, entre las
   comidas… ¡A todas horas! La fruta es muy sana.
4. Yo como fruta casi todos los días. Sí… como bastante fruta.

22 ¿Qué le gusta más?

A mí me gusta todo… Bueno, todo no. Hay una fruta que no me gusta
nada. Es la piña. Pero las otras frutas sí me gustan. Las verduras me
gustan bastante, pero las espinacas me gustan poco, la verdad.
Lo que más me gusta es el pescado. El salmón, por ejemplo,
me gusta muchísimo. Y la carne también me gusta bastante, sobre
todo el pollo.

31 ¿Qué hay en la lista?

–Toma estas latas, Janet. A mí me encanta el atún y hoy está de oferta.
–De acuerdo. ¿Qué más? Ah, aquí está la leche. ¿Cuánta llevamos?
  ¿Un litro?
–Lleva dos. También tenemos que comprar una caja de galletas.
–Y arroz. ¡Me encanta el arroz!

37 ¿En casa o en el supermercado?

1. Prepara la cena.
2. Escribe una lista de la compra.
3. Dile al dependiente que quieres un kilo de carne.

4. Ve a la cocina a buscar un refresco.
5. Compra un melón.
6. Selecciona los productos que están en oferta.
7. Ve a pagar a la caja.
8. Prepara unos huevos para desayunar.

42 Consejos apropiados

1. Tengo que ir al supermercado para hacer la compra, pero no quiero
   gastarme mucho dinero. ¿Qué me recomiendas?
2. Quiero preparar una cena para mis amigos, pero no sé cocinar muy
   bien. ¿Qué me recomiendas?
3. Tengo que ir a una fiesta y no sé qué llevar. ¿Qué me recomiendas?
4. Tengo que preparar un postre para el cumpleaños de Janet.
   ¿Qué me recomiendas?

47 Paso a paso

Ya tenemos todos los ingredientes y utensilios que necesitamos para
preparar chile con carne. Primero cortamos la cebolla y el ajo. Después
echamos la carne en la cazuela. Luego añadimos la cebolla, el ajo
y la salsa de tomate, y mezclamos todo muy bien. Por último, el toque
final: añadimos unos chiles de diferentes tipos a la carne. Hum. ¡Qué
bien huele!

50 Adivina, adivinanza

1. Usamos este objeto para llevar la comida a la mesa.
2. Usamos este condimento en las hamburguesas, por ejemplo.
   Es de color amarillo.
3. Usamos este objeto para servir agua, refrescos…
4. Usamos este condimento en la pizza, los espaguetis, el arroz…

61 La mesera nueva

1. –¿En qué puedo servirles?
   –No nos gusta mucho el picante. ¿Nos recomienda probar el chile?
   –¡Sí! ¡Pruébenlo! Es delicioso.
2. –¿Están listas para pedir?
   –Sí, pero quiero hacerle una pregunta. Mi tía y yo queremos un plato
     saludable. ¿Debemos pedir el pollo frito?
   –No. Pidan el pollo asado con arroz.
3. –¡Ay! La sopa está muy caliente.
   –Sí, tengan cuidado.
4. –¿Cómo está la comida?
   –El pescado está muy salado.
   –Pongan más sal. Les va a gustar más.

65 La iglesia y la pirámide

–¡Mamá, estoy nerviosa por el desafío!
–¿Por qué?
–No entiendo qué tenemos que hacer.
–Pues tenemos que encontrar el ingrediente secreto del mole.
–Sí, pero ¿vamos a la iglesia o a la pirámide?
–El secreto está en los túneles de la pirámide. Y la pirámide está debajo
  de la iglesia.
–¡Qué extraño! ¿Por qué está debajo de la iglesia?
–Cuando los españoles conquistaron Cholula, construyeron la iglesia

encima de la pirámide. Y muchos años después unos científicos descubrieron un sistema de túneles en la pirámide.

–¡Increíble! ¡Quiero ver la pirámide, pero no quiero entrar!

–¿Por qué?

–Porque los túneles están muy oscuros.

–Pero tenemos que entrar en la pirámide para encontrar el ingrediente secreto.

–Está bien, vamos.

69 ¿Qué se dice?

1. –¿Me pasas el agua, por favor?
   –Claro, toma.

2. –Mesero, por favor, ¿nos trae la cuenta?

3. –¿Saben ya lo que van a comer?
   –Sí. De primero, yo quiero espaguetis.
   –Y yo, una ensalada.

4. –Por favor, ¿me puede traer un poco de sal?
   –Claro, señor.

74 El buen chef

Queridos amigos, hoy dedico el minuto de consejos a algunas recomendaciones que todo buen chef debe saber:

1. No tengan muchos productos en lata en la cocina. Los productos frescos son más sabrosos y más sanos.

2. No usen muchas veces el mismo aceite. No es saludable. Deben usar aceite limpio.

3. No pongan mucha sal en las comidas. La sal no es buena para la salud.

4. No cocinen las comidas mucho tiempo. Cocinen sus platos solo el tiempo necesario. Así no pierden sabor ni vitaminas.

5. No guarden el pescado en el refrigerador muchos días. Deben consumirlo muy fresco.

77 La cena sorpresa

–Tía Rita, ¿voy al supermercado esta tarde?

–No. No vayas, Diana. Voy yo.

–De acuerdo. Oye, tía, para el postre quiero hacer una torta de chocolate.

–No, no hagas una torta para el postre. Pon fruta, que es más sano.

–Está bien. También quiero poner unos huevos con mayonesa.

–No, no pongas huevos con mayonesa. Mejor prepara unos huevos fritos.

–Y voy a cocinar una sopa con chiles.

–Excelente idea, me encantan los chiles.

–Tía, voy a decirles a nuestros amigos que estamos preparando una cena para todos.

–No les digas nada, es mejor darles una sorpresa.

–Sí, tienes razón. Bueno, pues voy a empezar. Voy a lavar los platos y los vasos.

–Sí, muy bien. Yo te ayudo, Diana.

82 Los chiles rellenos

–¿Sí?

–¿Cómo estás, hermana?

–¡Hola, Rita! Muy bien. ¿Cómo está Diana?

–Tu hija está muy bien. Nos encanta San Antonio. Aquí hay una comida excelente.

–¿Ah, sí? Dime, ¿cuál es tu plato favorito?

–Los chiles, me encantan los chiles. Sobre todo los chiles rellenos.

–Hum. Yo quiero aprender a prepararlos. ¿Qué llevan?

–Pues llevan medio kilo de chiles frescos, medio kilo de queso, cuatro huevos y un poco de aceite.

–¿Y cómo los preparo?

–Primero cortas los chiles y los lavas. Luego pones el queso dentro de los chiles.

–¿Y después los frío?

–No. Tienes que batir los huevos en un bol.

–¿Y qué más?

–Echas los chiles en el bol con los huevos batidos y los fríes en una sartén con aceite.

–¡Qué rico!

–¡Sí! Es un plato un poco picante, pero es delicioso.

–Gracias, Rita.

–De nada. Hasta luego.

83 Un restaurante auténtico

1. Si quieren un primer plato auténtico, pidan la ensalada de aguacate. Está deliciosa.

2. Mi plato favorito es el mole. Es una salsa con chiles y muchas especias. Si les gusta el picante, prueben el mole poblano con pollo.

3. Si prefieren comer pescado, elijan los tacos. Llevan una salsa muy rica y no es un plato picante.

4. De postre les recomiendo la tarta de chocolate. Es nuestra especialidad.

Unit 4
Norteamérica

The Unit

- The theme for Unit 4 is food in the context of North America. The pairs meet in Santa Fe, New Mexico, at a Tex-Mex restaurant to try the spiciest dishes on the menu and to receive their tasks in North America.
  - *Desafío* 1. Tim and Mack travel to Oaxaca, Mexico, where they must make *pan de muerto* for a Oaxacan baker.
  - *Desafío* 2. Andy and Janet travel to Tabasco, Mexico, where they visit Hacienda La Luz, and look for the oldest currency in the Americas.
  - *Desafío* 3. Diana and Rita travel to San Antonio, Texas, where they must prepare a recipe for an outdoor *chile con carne* cooking contest.
  - *Desafío* 4. Tess and Patricia travel to San Pedro de Cholula, Mexico, where they must taste a famous *mole poblano* recipe and find the secret ingredient inside the Great Pyramid of Cholula.

Activities	Standards	Resources
Norteamérica	1.2, 2.1, 2.2	Video

Teaching Suggestions

Warm-Up / Independent Starter

- Ask students to look at a map of mainland North America and write down, in Spanish, the names of the countries and their capital cities. Then ask students to take note of the countries and places to which the four pairs will travel.

North America

- North America is the world's third-largest continent. It occupies the northern portion of the landmass known as the Americas, and is comprised of 23 independent countries and more than 20 dependent territories between the Arctic Ocean and the Caribbean Sea, most notably Canada, the United States, Mexico, all of Central America, the Bahamas, Bermuda, the Greater and Lesser Antilles, and Greenland. Over half a billion people populate North America.

184

UNIDAD 4
Norteamérica
La herencia hispana

DESAFÍO 1

▶ **To talk about food**

Vocabulario
Los alimentos

Gramática
Expresar cantidad.
Los indefinidos

Pan de muerto

Fruto del cacao

DESAFÍO 2

▶ **To give commands related to shopping**

Vocabulario
Comprar comida

Gramática
El imperativo afirmativo singular

184 ciento ochenta y cuatro

The Challenge

DESAFÍO 1

Pan de muerto

The *pan de muerto,* or "bread of the dead," is made in Mexico and in Mexican communities around the world to celebrate the *Día de Muertos* on November 2nd. It is usually made with typical bread ingredients, such as flour, butter, milk, eggs, yeast, sugar, and salt. But some added ingredients include orange juice, orange zest, and anise seed. The bread is sometimes decorated with a skull and crossbones, and is taken to the cemetery to leave at the gravesite of a family member.

DESAFÍO 2

Fruto del cacao

The scientific name for the cacao tree is *Theobroma cacao,* which means "food of the gods." This tree yields from 20 to 70 elongated fruits, or pods, annually. Each pod has between 20 to 60 seeds, or beans, which are fermented, dried, roasted, and ground up to release the cocoa butter that is used to make chocolate. Even though this tree originated in the rainforests of the Americas, the world's largest producers are now Ivory Coast and Ghana, in West Africa.

To give commands related to cooking

Vocabulario
En la cocina

Gramática
El imperativo afirmativo plural

DESAFÍO 3

To communicate in common dining-related situations

Vocabulario
En el restaurante

Gramática
El imperativo negativo

DESAFÍO 4

Chiles

Mole poblano

ciento ochenta y cinco 185

DESAFÍO 3

Chiles

The hotness of a chile pepper is measured on the Scoville scale. It ranges from 0 units (a bell pepper) to 16,000,000 units (pure capsaicin). To give the units some perspective, the jalapeño pepper is between 2,500 and 8,000 units. So for those who believe a jalapeño is hot, they should know that there are chile peppers that range from 855,000 to 1,359,000 units on the Scoville scale.

DESAFÍO 4

Mole poblano

The origin of *mole poblano* has been up for discussion for centuries. Some people say that the nuns from Santa Rosa Convent in Puebla invented it as they were trying to put together a meal for a visiting archbishop. Other people say it was created by accident when the wind knocked a variety of spices into a pot where a turkey was cooking. There is, however, a consensus that it was invented in Mexico during the colonial period. Mole sauces are a mix of Mesoamerican, European, and Asian ingredients.

- Explain to students that in Latin America, Spain, and Portugal, North and South America are viewed as a single continent called *América*. Have students look at a map of the Americas and ask them which one of the two geographical divisions they think is more appropriate and why.

Picture Discussion

- Have students look at the pictures. Has anyone ever tried any of the dishes pictured? Encourage students to share when and where they tried the dish.

Pan de muerto

- Have students close their eyes and read the caption aloud. Ask them if they would be tempted to try this bread just judging by its name. Have students open their eyes and observe the picture. Does this bread look tasty? Invite students to try to guess the ingredients.

Fruto del cacao

- Working in small groups, have students discuss what they know about cacao, including its origin, countries where it is grown, how it is processed, etc. Ask groups to summarize the information in a bulleted paragraph and present it to the class. If they are not sure about some of the information, encourage them to research the topic.

Chiles

- Ask students whether they think the peppers depicted in this picture are hot or sweet. Why? Have students work with a partner to list all of the different chile pepper varieties they know and classify them in a three-column chart by degree of spiciness: mild, medium, hot. Invite volunteer pairs to present their chart to the class.

Mole poblano

- Ask students what kinds of sauces they know and how they are usually served. Examples include ketchup, steak sauce, and Tabasco sauce. Based on the picture, ask students what kind of sauce they think *mole poblano* is.

Objectives

- By the end of Unit 4, students will be able to
  - Talk about food and cooking utensils.
  - Communicate in common dining-related situations.
  - Give recommendations and commands related to shopping and cooking.
  - Share a recipe and give preparation instructions.
  - Talk about different cultural aspects of North America.

185

Presentation

- This section presents the pairs' arrival in North America. They meet in Santa Fe, New Mexico, at a Mexican restaurant. There, the participants must try all of the spicy dishes on the menu before they can receive their challenges for this unit.

- Students will see vocabulary in context, with pictures and illustrations. Presenting new words in this manner helps students develop their Spanish vocabulary with background knowledge while engaging them with the context.

Activities	Standards	Resources
Fotonovela	1.2, 2.2	Vis. Pres.
1.	1.2	

Teaching Suggestions

Warm-Up / Independent Starter

- Have students read the introduction to the *fotonovela* silently. Ask them to find the word that recurs the most within the dialogue (*picante*). Then have students count the number of times it occurs in the dialogue (four). Finally, have them decide what this word means (spicy).

Preparation

- Review the answers to the Independent Starter with students. Ask them if they can handle spiciness in a dish. Then ask students how they would feel if they had to try all of the spiciest dishes on a menu in one sitting.

- Read the *fotonovela* to students, changing your voice for each character. Pay special attention to the dialogue between Tess and the waitress. The waitress suggests that Tess eat slowly and drink milk in order to remedy the burning sensation in her mouth. Ask students for some other suggestions for getting rid of the burn (e.g., bread, honey, sugar).

La fotonovela

Before Viewing

- Ask students to get into pairs and read the dialogue together. Tell students to read through it twice so each person can read each speech bubble.

La llegada

En Santa Fe

The pairs are at a Mexican restaurant in Santa Fe, the capital of New Mexico. Before they depart, they must taste the spiciest dishes on the menu.

Differentiated Instruction

DEVELOPING LEARNERS

- The words *poco* and *pequeño* often confuse students because they both mean "little" in English. However, *poco* and *un poco de* both refer to quantity, whereas *pequeño* is used to describe size. Have students choose the correct option.
  1. *El restaurante es muy poco / pequeño.* (pequeño)
  2. *¿Comes pequeño / poco o mucho?* (poco)
  3. *Quiero pequeño / un poco de pollo.* (un poco de)
  4. *Estos vasos son pocos / pequeños. Los necesito más grandes.* (pequeños)

EXPANDING LEARNERS

- Have students work in small groups and assign a role from the *fotonovela* to each one. Ask them to add several new lines for each scene. Give students time to practice their roles and explain that they should pantomime as much of the action as they can and even add music and special effects. After rehearsing, have them present their newly revised *fotonovela* to the class. The class will vote for the best new *fotonovela*, based on correct language use, best acting, best sound effects or music, and most original script.

La llegada

¿Este pescado frito es muy picante?

No, no mucho. Solo tiene un poco de ajo.

¿Tiene algún remedio para el picante?

Tomen leche en vez de agua. Y no coman muy rápido.

Abuelo, ¿me pasas el bote de salsa picante, por favor?

Claro, toma. ¡A mí también me encanta el picante!

¡Achís!

¡Perdona! Eché mucha pimienta a mis frijoles.

Ah, y todos tienen que traer una receta típica de las zonas de sus desafíos.

1 ¿Comprendes?

▶ **Elige** en cada caso la información correcta y escribe las oraciones.

1. Janet quiere pollo con papas **de primero/de segundo**.
2. Para quitar el picante deben tomar **agua/leche**.
3. A Mack **le encanta/no le gusta** el picante.
4. Janet pide **un taco picante/pescado frito**.
5. Tim pide **un bote/una caja** de salsa picante.
6. Los frijoles de Patricia **son picantes/no son picantes**.

ciento ochenta y siete **187**

After Viewing

- Now that all the pairs have tried the spicy dishes, they are informed that they must bring a recipe for a typical dish from the region they are traveling to. Do students think the pairs' experience at a Mexican restaurant was a good introduction to their task? Why or why not?

Activities

1. Have students work in pairs to complete this activity. Have one student read the statement, including the two answer choices, and his or her partner will answer it. Ask students to be sure to alternate the person reading and answering the statements.

Answer Key

1. 1. de segundo
2. leche
3. le encanta
4. pescado frito
5. un bote
6. son picantes

Additional Resources

Fans Online activities
Practice Workbook

HERITAGE LANGUAGE LEARNERS

- The characters are asked to bring back a typical recipe from the places they are visiting. Ask students what a typical recipe from their community or from their family's heritage would be. Ask them to research the history of this particular dish and explain its origins to the other students. Have students display the recipe to the class and, if possible, bring in pictures to share with their classmates.

CRITICAL THINKING

- Ask students which pairs they think have had the most challenging *desafíos* up to now. Also ask students which pairs always seem to have the most fun completing their tasks, and if they think they will continue to enjoy them. Students need to explain and justify their opinions.

Unit 4

La llegada

Presentation

- In this section, students will learn useful expressions for ordering food in a restaurant, asking the waiter for something, and for asking for something on the table.

Activities	Standards	Resources
Expresiones útiles	1.2, 1.3, 4.1	
2.	1.2	Audio
3.	1.3	
4.	1.1, 5.1	
5.	1.1, 5.1	

Teaching Suggestions

Warm-Up/Independent Starter

- Have students look at the themes for the *Expresiones útiles* section. Then ask them to list all the places in your community where they can go to practice this vocabulary. Tell students to be specific with the names and locations of the places.

Preparation

- Ask students to share their Independent Starter with the class. Create a class list of these places to display in the room. Tell students to try to go to some of these places to practice their vocabulary during this unit. As students go to the places, cross them off the list.

- Go over the *expresiones útiles* with the class. To practice these expressions, have one student place a variety of items on his or her desk and have a classmate ask him or her for one of the items. If there is an item the student wants but is not on the table, have the student ask for it.

Activities

2. Once students have completed this activity, have them use each incorrect answer to create three scenarios in which those answers can be used. Ask students to scramble the scenarios. Then have them exchange papers with a classmate and write the answer to each other's scenarios.

EXPRESIONES ÚTILES

> ¿Me pasas la sal, por favor?

To order food in a restaurant:
–¿Qué van a comer?
–De primero.../segundo.../postre...

–¿Y para beber?
–**Para mí**, agua mineral.

To ask the waiter for something:
¿Nos trae otra servilleta, por favor?
¿Nos puede traer un poco más de agua, por favor?

To ask for something on the table:
¿Me das/Me pasas la salsa?
¿Puedes darme/pasarme la salsa?
Dame/Pásame la salsa, por favor.

2 **Expresiones**

 ▶ **Escucha** y elige la respuesta adecuada.

1. a. De primero, una sopa.
   b. Para mí, fruta.

2. a. Sí, señora.
   b. ¿Qué van a tomar?

3. a. Sí, toma.
   b. De segundo, carne con papas.

3 **Diálogos incompletos**

▶ **Completa** los bocadillos.

①

> ¿Me puede ___1___ un tenedor, por favor?

②

> ¿Qué van a comer?

> Para mí, de ___2___, una ensalada. Y de ___3___, salmón.

③

> ¿Me ___4___ el agua?

> Sí, claro.

188 ciento ochenta y ocho

Differentiated Instruction

DEVELOPING LEARNERS

- Give students more practice with the *expresiones útiles* by having them choose the correct phrase that completes each statement or question.
  1. *¿Me pasas/Me echas la salsa, por favor?* (Me pasas)
  2. *¿Qué van a comer? Para ti/Para mí, el pollo.* (Para mí)
  3. *¿Puede traernos/Puede echarnos un tenedor, por favor?* (Puede traernos)
  4. *De primero/De postre, una ensalada.* (De primero)
  5. *Pásame/De segundo la sal, por favor.* (Pásame)

EXPANDING LEARNERS

- Tell students that they are going to practice the *expresiones útiles* by working with a partner and imagining that they are at a restaurant. They will create short dialogues with the new terms, and then role-play the parts and present their skits to the class. For example:
  A. *¿Qué vas a pedir?*
  B. *De primero, voy a tomar la sopa.*
  A. *¿Y de segundo?*
  B. *De segundo, el pollo, por favor.*

188

¿Quién ganará?

4 **Los desafíos**

▶ **Habla.** ¿Cuál será el desafío para cada pareja? Piénsalo y coméntalo con tus compañeros(as).

DESAFÍO ①

¿Un pan de muerto?

Tim y Mack

DESAFÍO ②

La moneda más antigua de América

Andy y Janet

DESAFÍO ③

Un concurso de chile en San Antonio

Diana y Rita

DESAFÍO ④

El ingrediente secreto de Cholula

Tess y Patricia

▶ **Habla.** Las parejas viajan a los Estados Unidos y a México. ¿Qué sabes de México? ¿Hay zonas de herencia hispana en los Estados Unidos? Coméntalo con tus compañeros(as).

5 **La tarea final**

▶ **Decide.** ¿Qué tarea tienen que hacer los personajes al final? ¿Qué pareja crees que ganará?

LA TAREA
Una receta

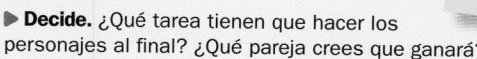

3. Ask students to cover up the speech bubbles and write the *expresión útil* that would fit each picture. Then have students uncover the speech bubbles to see if they guessed correctly.

¿Quién ganará?

4. Have students get into small groups and discuss the pairs' challenges. Ask groups to look at the pictures, read the captions, and write a brief paragraph about what they believe the pairs will do in their challenges. They must also include any information they know about the items pictured.

5. Students have been provided a clue as to what the pairs will have to do to win their *desafío* in North America. The clue is *una receta*. As a class, have students discuss different kinds of recipes they think the pairs will need to find or make in order to win their *desafío* in North America.

 AUDIO SCRIPT
See page 183I.

Answer Key

2. 1. b   2. a   3. a
3. 1. traer
   2. primero
   3. segundo
   4. das / pasas
4. Answers will vary.
   ▶ Answers will vary
5. Answers will vary.

Additional Resources

Fans Online activities
Practice Workbook

HERITAGE LANGUAGE LEARNERS

• Have students brainstorm different ways of expressing "please" and "you're welcome" in Spanish. Students might include such expressions as *Tenga / Ten la bondad de...; Haga / Haz el favor de...; ¿Pudiera / Pudieras pasarme...?; ¿No le / te importa / importaría...?; De nada; No hay de que; No faltaba más; Un placer.* Then ask students to prepare a short dialogue using some of these expressions and present it to the class.

SPECIAL-NEEDS LEARNERS

• Students with auditory processing disorders can benefit from reading the directions to all of the activities and repeating the directions back to you. Doing this will reinforce their comprehension of the tasks they are expected to complete. Whenever there is an audio component to the activities, provide students with the audio script to enhance comprehension. If possible, have students record their voices for speaking portions in order to compare their delivery with that of the narrators.

189

DESAFÍO 1

Hablar sobre comida

Presentation

- In *Desafío* 1, Tim and Mack are in Oaxaca, Mexico, where they must make *pan de muerto*.
- In this section, students will preview:
  - Vocabulary for foods.
  - The indefinites.

Activities	Standards	Resources
Fotonovela	1.2, 2.1, 3.2	Vis. Pres.
6.	1.2	
7.	1.2, 1.3, 3.1	
8.	1.3	
9.	1.1, 1.2, 1.3	Audio
10. Comunidades	1.1, 1.2, 2.1, 3.2, 4.2	Video
Tu desafío	1.2, 2.1, 3.2, 5.2	

Teaching Suggestions

Warm-Up / Independent Starter

- Have students read only the introduction to the *fotonovela*. Ask them to write a paragraph about what they think are the differences and similarities between regular bread and *pan de muerto*.

Preparation

- Ask students to direct their attention to the *pan de muerto* recipe. Then display a recipe for white bread on the overhead projector. Ask volunteers to share how close they were to the actual similarities and differences between the two.
- Ask a volunteer to read the *pan de muerto* recipe and have the class raise their hands each time they hear a food they recognize.

 La fotonovela

Before Viewing

- Ask students if they have ever made bread or any baked goods. Encourage them to share both their good and bad baking experiences.

After Viewing

- Tell students that baking is like doing a chemistry experiment. Discuss what would happen if Tim and Mack did not follow the exact recipe.

190

¿Un pan de muerto?

 What is your favorite type of bread? How about "bread of the dead"? That's right. Tim and Mack have to make *pan de muerto*. The name of the recipe alludes to *Día de Muertos*. Adela, a baker from Oaxaca de Juárez, México, will judge their results.

6 Detective de palabras

▶ **Completa** estas oraciones.

1. Los mexicanos recuerdan a _____ sus parientes muertos.

2. Les ofrecen _____ frutas, dulces y otros alimentos.

3. ¿Tiene _____ recomendación especial para hacer el pan de muerto?

4. No, _____. Es muy fácil.

5. ¿Lleva _____ ingredientes?

Differentiated Instruction

DEVELOPING LEARNERS

- To check students' comprehension of the *fotonovela*, have them choose the correct answer for each question.
  1. ¿Dónde están Mack y Tim?
     a. en casa   b. en Oaxaca (b)
  2. ¿Qué tienen que hacer?
     a. pan de muerto   b. postre (a)
  3. ¿Cómo es la receta?
     a. difícil   b. fácil (b)
  4. ¿A quién recuerdan los mexicanos el Día de Muertos?
     a. a sus vecinos   b. a sus parientes (b)
  5. ¿Qué les llevan al cementerio?
     a. alimentos   b. ropa (a)

EXPANDING LEARNERS

- Ask students to think of their favorite family or holiday celebration and a food associated with it. Then have them write two or more paragraphs that describe the celebration and explain why it is their favorite and what role food plays in it. They should include some other information that addresses the food served at this celebration, including a brief history of the food, a recipe, or an interesting anecdote surrounding it. Call on volunteers to read their paragraphs aloud.

7 Pan de muerto

▶ **Lee** la receta del pan de muerto y ayuda a Tim y a Mack a clasificar los ingredientes.

Ingredientes líquidos	Ingredientes sólidos
	la harina

8 Los alimentos

▶ **Escribe** el nombre de estos alimentos.

 ①
 ②
 ③
 ④

9 Día de Muertos

▶ **Escucha** a Adela. ¿Qué ingredientes menciona?

1. leche 2. pollo 3. fruta 4. sal 5. dulces 6. pan

▶ **Habla** con tu compañero(a). Preparen preguntas para Adela sobre el Día de Muertos.

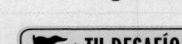 COMUNIDADES

EL DÍA DE MUERTOS

Una de las celebraciones más importantes de México es el Día de Muertos. Se celebra el 2 de noviembre. La gente va ese día al cementerio a llevar flores, pero en México es una fiesta muy alegre. Los familiares preparan altares con una fotografía de la persona difunta y los llenan con flores, velas y comida (dulces, fruta, pan de muerto...). En Oaxaca, además, adornan las calles principales con grandes alfombras de flores.

10 **Piensa y explica.** ¿Por qué piensas que el Día de Muertos es una fiesta alegre en México? ¿Cómo se celebra en tu comunidad?

▶ **TU DESAFÍO** Visita la página web para aprender más sobre el Día de Muertos en México.

HERITAGE LANGUAGE LEARNERS

• Hold a show-and-tell for those students who have celebrated, observed, or have familiarity with *Día de Muertos*. Ask them to bring in photos of this celebration or typical gifts and treats that are prepared and left in the cemeteries. Then have students set up an imaginary "tombstone" in the classroom for a historical figure or celebrity who is deceased, and decorate it as they would if they were in Oaxaca de Juárez. Ask students to explain the significance of the objects they have placed on the "grave."

MULTIPLE INTELLIGENCES:
Logical-Mathematical Intelligence

• Explain that cooks in Spanish-speaking countries typically use the metric system. Dry ingredients are shown in grams, or kilos for larger quantities. Cooks measure liquids in liters, or units thereof. In the United States, cooks measure both dry and liquid ingredients by the cup and use tablespoons and teaspoons to measure small amounts. Ask students to research the metric system, and a recipe that shows metric measurements, and have them rewrite the recipe in cups and tablespoons.

Activities

6. Pair up students to complete this activity. One student will read the dialogue from the beginning. The other student will fill in the sentences.

8. If students are having trouble identifying the foods in this activity, refer them to *Unidad preliminar*, pp. 8–9, for a quick review.

10. Have students look up the origin of Halloween and compare it to the traditions of *Día de Muertos*.

AUDIO SCRIPT
See page 183I.

 COMUNIDADES

El Día de Muertos

This Mexican holiday is a gathering of family and friends to remember those family members who have passed away. Most people visit their loved ones at the cemetery, make and eat the favorite foods of their loved ones, and bake sugar skulls, or *calaveritas*, to leave at the gravesites. The Mexican traditions of *Día de Muertos* have pre-Columbian roots.

Answer Key

6. 1. todos   4. ninguna
    2. algunas   5. muchos
    3. alguna

7. Ingredientes líquidos: el agua, el té. Ingredientes sólidos: la harina, el azúcar, la mantequilla, los huevos, la levadura, la sal, la cáscara de naranja.

8. 1. fruta   2. pan   3. huevos   4. mantequilla

9. fruta, dulces, pan de muerto
    ▶ Answers will vary.

10. Answers will vary.

Additional Resources

Fans Online activities

191

DESAFÍO 1

Vocabulario – Los alimentos

Presentation

- In this section, students will learn vocabulary for foods and food groups.

Activities	Standards	Resources
Vocabulario	1.2	
11.	1.3	
12.	1.2	Audio
13.	1.1, 1.3	
14.	1.1, 1.3, 5.1	
15. Comparaciones	1.1, 1.2, 2.2, 3.2, 4.2, 5.1	
Tu desafío	1.2, 2.2, 3.2, 5.2	

Teaching Suggestions

Warm-Up / Independent Starter

- Have students list the ingredients for the *pan de muerto* recipe without looking at the previous page.

Preparation

- Go over the vocabulary presentation with students. Have them write the vocabulary words in their notebook for additional practice with spelling. Then have them mark with a check mark the foods they like, an X the foods they don't like, and a dash the foods they somewhat like.

- Go over the vocabulary presentation a second time. If students put a check mark next to the food, have them give it a thumbs up. If they put an X, have them give it a thumbs down. If they put a dash, tell them to keep their hands by their sides. Have students look around the room to see who agrees with them and who disagrees.

Activities

11. Have students use their lists from the Preparation section and categorize the foods they liked by *desayuno, almuerzo,* and *cena.*

12. Play the audio script three times. The first time, students will simply listen to the dialogue. The second time, students will answer if the statements are true or false. The third time, students will correct the false statements.

Vocabulario

Los alimentos

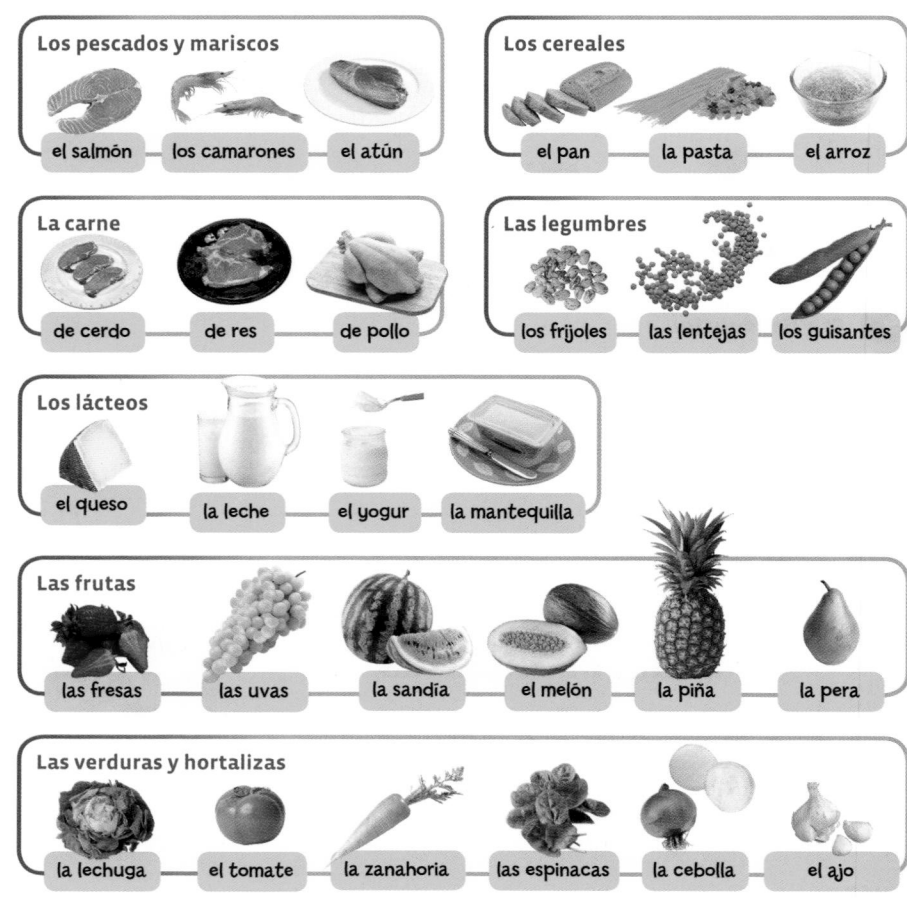

Los pescados y mariscos: el salmón, los camarones, el atún

Los cereales: el pan, la pasta, el arroz

La carne: de cerdo, de res, de pollo

Las legumbres: los frijoles, las lentejas, los guisantes

Los lácteos: el queso, la leche, el yogur, la mantequilla

Las frutas: las fresas, las uvas, la sandía, el melón, la piña, la pera

Las verduras y hortalizas: la lechuga, el tomate, la zanahoria, las espinacas, la cebolla, el ajo

11 Las comidas

▶ **Escribe.** ¿Qué alimentos tomas normalmente en el desayuno, el almuerzo y la cena?

1. Desayuno: yogur...
2. Almuerzo: _____
3. Cena: _____

192 ciento noventa y dos

Differentiated Instruction

DEVELOPING LEARNERS

- Ask students to find or draw images of the foods pictured on the page and place them on an index card. They should write the name of the food on the back of the card, including its corresponding food group (e.g., *el queso: los lácteos*). Then have them work with a partner to test their vocabulary skills by taking turns showing the flashcards to their partner, who must identify both the food pictured and its food group.

EXPANDING LEARNERS

- Ask students to make a food pyramid poster. They should include all the foods listed on this page in the corresponding categories (they will find additional information at: http://www.mypyramid.gov). Then ask students to include two or more foods in each category that they can either name or look up in a bilingual dictionary. Display their work in the classroom.

12 El restaurante recomendado

 ▶ **Escucha** a Tim y decide si estas afirmaciones son ciertas o falsas.

1. El restaurante está en México D. F.
2. Las verduras son muy frescas (*fresh*).
3. Mack comió una ensalada deliciosa.
4. La ensalada tiene espinacas.
5. Tim pidió tacos.
6. A Tim le encanta el picante.

13 Alimentos preferidos

▶ **Habla** con tu compañero(a). ¿Qué alimentos comen estas personas?

1. Luisa es vegetariana.
2. Javier come muchas proteínas.
3. A Carmen y a Manuel les gusta todo (*everything*).
4. A Alicia le encantan las verduras.

Modelo 1. *Luisa come lechuga, espinacas, naranjas…*

▶ **Escribe.** ¿Qué te gusta comer a ti?

14 Una dieta equilibrada

 ▶ **Escribe** un menú equilibrado para el desayuno, el almuerzo y la cena.

 ▶ **Compara** tu menú con el menú de tu compañero(a) y contesta. ¿Qué menú es más saludable?

COMPARACIONES

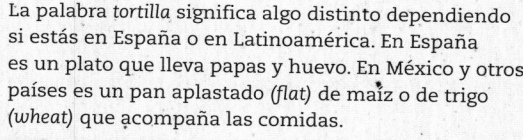
La tortilla

La palabra *tortilla* significa algo distinto dependiendo si estás en España o en Latinoamérica. En España es un plato que lleva papas y huevo. En México y otros países es un pan aplastado (*flat*) de maíz o de trigo (*wheat*) que acompaña las comidas.

15 **Compara.** ¿Qué alimentos sirven normalmente en tu país para acompañar las comidas? ¿Y en otros países?

 → **TU DESAFÍO** Visita la página web para aprender más sobre alimentos de México.

HERITAGE LANGUAGE LEARNERS

• Many Spanish speakers use other words for some of the foods pictured on these pages. Have students create a list of the different names they know or might research for the food items presented in this lesson, including the country or regions where these words are used. Students might mention *el puerco* or *el chancho* for *el cerdo*, *las arvejas* or *los chícharos* for *los guisantes*, etc. Encourage them to also include alternative words for other foods (e.g., an apricot might be called *el albaricoque, el chabacano,* or *el damasco*).

TOTAL PHYSICAL RESPONSE (TPR)

• Play a version of "Simón dice" with students. Give commands such as, *Simón dice: "Coman una manzana."* Students should pantomime that they are eating an apple. However, when you give nonsense commands such as, *Simón dice: "Coman un vaso de agua,"* or *Simón dice: "Beban un salmón,"* students should remain seated. Players are eliminated when they either stand or sit incorrectly for the command, or they pantomime the wrong action.

---

13. Remind students to keep in mind, when they discuss what Luisa would eat, that there are different types of vegetarians (e.g. vegan, macrobiotic, lacto-ovo, etc.).

 AUDIO SCRIPT
See page 183I.

 COMPARACIONES

La tortilla

In Mexico, tortillas are served with almost every meal. In the United States, one can find tortillas at various mealtimes as well. The breakfast burrito is a popular staple at fast-food chains. *Taquitos* (tortillas filled with meat, rolled, and fried) are a quick snack for lunch, and *enchiladas* are on every authentic Mexican dinner menu; and for dessert, there are *sopapillas* (puffed tortillas drizzled with honey).

Answer Key

11. Answers will vary.

12. 1. F   2. C   3. C   4. F   5. C   6. C

13. Answers will vary. Sample answers:
   2. Javier: carne de res y de cerdo, pollo y también legumbres.
   3. Carmen y Manuel: pescados y mariscos, carne, cereales, legumbres, verduras y hortalizas, productos lácteos y frutas.
   4. Alicia: zanahorias, tomates, espinacas, pimientos, lechuga, etc.
   ▶ Answers will vary.

14. Answers will vary.
   ▶ Answers will vary.

15. Answers will vary.

Additional Resources

Fans Online activities
Practice Workbook

193

Unit 4
DESAFÍO 1

Gramática – Expresar cantidad. Los indefinidos

Presentation

- In this section, students will learn to express quantity by using indefinites.

Activities	Standards	Resources
Gramática	3.1	
16.	1.2, 1.3, 4.1	
17.	1.2, 1.3	Audio
18.	1.3	
19.	1.1, 1.3	
20. Conexiones	1.1, 1.2, 3.1, 3.2	

Teaching Suggestions

Warm-Up / Independent Starter

- Ask students to think of dishes that contain the following ingredients: *camarones, arroz, carne de res, guisantes, piña, zanahoria.*

Preparation

- Go over the grammar presentation with students. Then ask for a volunteer to mimic the indefinites. Ask the volunteer to start off with his or her hands clasped together in front of his or her chest to represent *ningún*. As you say the indefinites in order, the volunteer will separate his or her hands little by little to represent each word. Then say the indefinites in reverse order until the student's hands are clasped together again.
- Call on volunteers to use the foods from the Independent Starter in complete sentences, using indefinites.

Activities

17. The United States government recommends eating about two cups of fruit per day. Knowing this, have students write sentences based on the amount of fruit each person eats. For example: *María come muy poca fruta.*

18. Ask students to read the entire dialogue. Then have them read each sentence entirely before filing in the blank. Many times students get the gender or number of their answer wrong because they don't read the word after the blank.

194

Gramática

Expresar cantidad. Los indefinidos

- To express quantity, you can refer to nouns using specific numbers or non-specific terms of number. These are called *indefinites*.

  Hay **tres** fresas en el plato.   Hay **algunos** tomates allí.

- These are the most common indefinites:

PRINCIPALES INDEFINIDOS

| ningún ninguno(a) | algún alguno(a) algunos(as) | poco(a) pocos(as) | mucho(a) muchos(as) | todo(a) todos(as) | demasiado(a) demasiados(as) |

Uso de los indefinidos

- Before a masculine singular noun, use algún or ningún instead of alguno and ninguno.

  –¿Hay **algún** huevo?
  –Sí, hay **alguno**.

- When ningún, ninguno, and ninguna go after the verb, use no or tampoco at the beginning of the sentence.

  No hay **ningún** yogur en el refrigerador.

- When the forms poco, mucho, and demasiado go before an adjective or an adverb, there is no variation of gender or number, because they are adverbs.

  Las papas están **demasiado** saladas.

16 **Compara.** ¿Qué semejanzas y diferencias hay entre los indefinidos en inglés y en español?

17 **¿Cuánta fruta?**

 ▶ **Escucha** a las siguientes personas y escribe cuánta fruta comen cada día.

1. María   2. Pedro   3. Elena   4. Luis

194 ciento noventa y cuatro

Differentiated Instruction

DEVELOPING LEARNERS

- Remind students that most indefinites agree in number and gender with the noun they are modifying. Have them choose the correct word to complete these sentences.

1. *¿Hay fresas? No, no hay ningún/ninguna. (ninguna)*
2. *Tengo demasiado/demasiada comida en el refrigerador. (demasiada)*
3. *¿Compraste mucho/muchos pescado? (mucho)*
4. *¿Hay algún/alguno melón en el refrigerador? (algún)*
5. *Carlos se comió todo/todas las galletas. (todas)*

EXPANDING LEARNERS

- Have students work with a partner to write a dialogue. Ask them to imagine that they are preparing a meal for Mack and Tim, but discover that they are out of key ingredients or find out that their guests don't like certain foods. For example:

A. *Quiero preparar una ensalada. ¿Tenemos lechuga y tomates?*
B. *Tenemos pocos tomates y no hay ninguna lechuga en el refrigerador.*
A. *¿Hay camarones?*
B. *Sí, hay bastantes, pero a Tim no le gustan.*
A. *Hum… ¿Tenemos algún pedazo de carne o un poco de pollo?*

18 **¿Qué hacemos para cenar?**

▶ **Completa** el diálogo entre Tim y Mack.

algún	poca	demasiado	todos	mucha	poco

Tim: ¿Qué tenemos para cenar, abuelo? Tengo __1__ hambre.
Mack: No sé, vamos a la cocina. Mira, hay arroz. Y a ti te encanta.
Tim: Sí, pero hay muy __2__.
Mack: No importa. Yo puedo comer otra cosa.
Tim: ¿Quieres __3__ huevo? Hay tres.
Mack: No, gracias. Puedes comerte tú __4__ los huevos.
Tim: ¡No! ¡Es __5__! Solo quiero dos.
Mack: Mañana hacemos la compra. Hay muy __6__ comida en el refrigerador.

19 **Una encuesta**

▶ **Habla** con tres compañeros(as). ¿Qué comen cada semana? Toma notas y presenta los resultados a la clase. ¿Quién tiene mejores hábitos alimenticios?

Modelo   A. ¿Ustedes comen mucha fruta cada semana?
         B. No. Solo como fruta dos o tres veces por semana.

	Sally	Jane	Matt
	poca		

CONEXIONES: CIENCIAS

¿Fruta o fruto?

La palabra *fruta* se aplica a los frutos comestibles. El fruto es la parte de la planta que protege a las semillas (*seeds*).
Hay dos tipos de frutos: los frutos secos, como la almendra (*almond*), la avellana (*hazelnut*) y la nuez (*walnut*), y los carnosos, como el durazno (*peach*), la manzana y las uvas.

20 **Piensa y explica.** ¿Qué fruta abunda más en los climas fríos? ¿Y en los climas cálidos?

ciento noventa y cinco   195

HERITAGE LANGUAGE LEARNERS

• Ask students to write a few paragraphs that describe their likes and dislikes of some foods. They should include as many indefinites as they can and mention the foods shown in the food groups on page 192. Encourage students to also include foods that have not been mentioned in this unit. Invite them to read their work to the class and explain any unfamiliar words.

COOPERATIVE LEARNING

• Ask students to work in groups of four and think of other things they can describe with the words used in the chart for activity 19. For example, they might want to describe the clothes they have in their closet or classes they have at school. Ask them to write at least five questions about this topic and interview each other. Then ask them to make a chart like the one on page 195 to list the results of their interviews. Next, have them compile the outcome in paragraph form and present it to the class.

Gramática – Expresar cantidad. Los indefinidos

19. Have students use the data they collected to write a paragraph to summarize the group's eating habits. One person from the group will read the paragraph to the class. Then have the class decide which group is the healthiest.

20. Have students think of fruits and vegetables that could grow in your community, as well as those that would not grow there.

 AUDIO SCRIPT
See page 183I.

 CONEXIONES: CIENCIAS

¿Fruta o fruto?

We think of apples and oranges when we think about *fruta*. *Fruto*, on the other hand, is the word used in botany to refer to the fertilized and developed ovary of a flower. Besides protecting the seed, the *fruto* is the means plants use to disseminate their seeds.

Answer Key

16. Los indefinidos tienen las mismas funciones en ambos idiomas, pero en inglés no cambian de número o género.

17. 1. María: muy poca fruta
     2. Pedro: poca fruta
     3. Elena: mucha fruta
     4. Luis: bastante fruta

18. 1. mucha   4. todos
     2. poco   5. demasiado
     3. algún   6. poca

19. Answers will vary.

20. Answers will vary.

Additional Resources

Fans Online activities
Practice Workbook

195

DESAFÍO 1

Comunicación

Presentation

- In this section, students will integrate the vocabulary and grammar from *Desafío 1* in order to talk about food and indefinite quantities.

Activities	Standards	Resources
21.	1.1, 1.3	
22.	1.1, 1.2, 1.3	Audio
23.	1.2, 1.3, 3.1	
24.	1.1, 1.3	
25. Final del desafío	1.2, 2.2	

Teaching Suggestions

Warm-Up / Independent Starter

- Ask students to draw and label all of the foods from the vocabulary presentation, grouped by their colors. Then have them write sentences about the foods they grouped together, using indefinites. For example: *Hay pocos alimentos amarillos.*

Preparation

- Take 10 minutes to review the vocabulary and grammar themes from *Desafío 1*.
- Refer students back to the *fotonovela* for *Desafío 1*. Have them find all of the foods and indefinites within the dialogue. Do students understand the dialogue better now that they have gone through the vocabulary and grammar from the *Desafío*?
- Ask students to copy all of the food vocabulary and the indefinites into their notebook. Have them mark off each word that they see as they go through the *Comunicación* spread. If there are any words left on the paper afterwards, have students use them in a sentence to practice on their own.

Activities

22. Do the *Habla* part of this activity as a class. Put a chart with the indefinities on the board. Say: *el salmón.* Then ask students to raise their hands as you read off the indefinites in the chart. Write down the number of students for each indefinite and repeat for pineapple, spinach, and chicken. Once you have taken your class poll, have students write sentences to summarize the findings.

196

Comunicación

21 **Las diferencias**

▶ **Compara** las fotografías y escribe una lista de diferencias. Utiliza los indefinidos.

Modelo *En la foto 1 hay muchos tomates y en la foto 2 hay pocos.*

22 **¿Qué le gusta más?**

▶ **Escucha** a Tim y escribe. ¿Cuánto le gustan estos alimentos?

▶ **Habla** con tus compañeros(as). ¿Cuánto les gustan esos alimentos?

Modelo A. *¿A ti te gusta el salmón?*
B. *Sí, me gusta mucho.*

23 **La mejor dieta**

▶ **Escribe.** El médico recomienda una dieta sana a Mack. Busca cinco errores en esta lista y corrígela.

¿Una dieta sana?

1. Come pocas verduras.
2. Come muchas frutas, como fresas, piña y salmón.
3. Come algo de carne durante la semana. Puedes comer carne de res, pollo o camarones.
4. Come pescado. Es bueno porque ningún pescado tiene proteínas.
5. Cocina con mucha mantequilla y mucho aceite.

Differentiated Instruction

DEVELOPING LEARNERS

- Ask students to make a chart with the following headings: *Me gusta(n), Me gusta(n) mucho, No me gusta(n) nada.* They should include each of the foods mentioned in this unit under the corresponding heading. Next, have them work with a partner to compare their likes and dislikes. Finally, ask pairs to write several sentences that show these comparisons. For example:
A. *A mí me gusta mucho la piña, pero a [B] no le gusta nada.*
B. *A los dos nos gustan las zanahorias, y nos gusta la lechuga también.*

EXPANDING LEARNERS

- Have students make their own list of tips for staying healthy. You might want to start them out with some of the following suggestions: *Bebe mucha agua todos los días, come poca carne, duerme bastante, participa en muchas actividades deportivas.* Encourage students to add any other tips they can think of, including those that promote good mental health (e.g., *Ríete con frecuencia, piensa en cosas agradables,* etc.).

24 **¿Qué comemos?**

▶ **Escribe** una lista de los alimentos que prefieres en cada una de las siguientes situaciones. Depués, compara la lista con la de tu compañero(a).

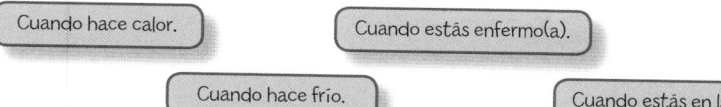

Cuando hace calor.

Cuando estás enfermo(a).

Cuando hace frío.

Cuando estás en la escuela.

Final del desafío

Ya tenemos todos los ingredientes, abuelo. ¡Vamos a hacer el pan!

¿Esto es un poco de mantequilla?

Hay que medirlos bien.

¡Huy, Tim! ¡Ten cuidado! Eso es mucha mantequilla...

Yo puse dos tazas de ___1___, una taza de azúcar y tres ___2___.

¡Yo puse ___3___ harina, ___4___ azúcar y ___5___ huevos!

El blog de Tim

Oaxaca, 8 de diciembre

Al principio pensé, ¡qué fácil! Pero no medí los ingredientes. En vez de poner dos tazas de harina puse mucha harina. En lugar de poner una taza de azúcar puse demasiada azúcar. Y en lugar de poner tres huevos puse pocos huevos. Creo que usar palabras como *poco*, *mucho* o *demasiado* no es una buena forma de cocinar...

COMENTARIOS (0) ENVIAR UN COMENTARIO

25 **¿Cuánta harina es *mucha harina*?**

▶ **Lee y escribe.** Tim y Mack terminaron su pan de muerto, con resultados distintos. Lee el diálogo y el blog, y completa los bocadillos.

ciento noventa y siete **197**

---

23. Ask students to go to the "Food and Nutrition" section of the USDA's website to see facts about nutrition. Have students rewrite the sentences to include the corrected information.

24. Ask students to include the ingredients for the foods they mention for each category. For example, if they say chicken soup for the foods they eat when they are sick, they must list the ingredients that are typically found in the soup.

25. Have students read Tim's blog before they begin the *Final del desafío*. This will give them some clues as to how this challenge went for Tim and Mack. Then refer students back to the "After Viewing" discussion from the *fotonovela* page.

 AUDIO SCRIPT
See page 183l.

Answer Key

21. Answers will vary.

22. 1. A Tim no le gusta nada la piña.
2. A Tim le gustan poco las espinacas.
3. A Tim le gusta mucho el salmón.
4. A Tim le gusta bastante el pollo.
▶ Answers will vary.

23. Answers will vary. Sample answers:
1. pocas → muchas   4. ningún → todo
2. salmón → sandía   5. mucha → poca;
3. camarones → cerdo   mucho → poco

24. Answers will vary. Sample answers:
Hace calor: ensaladas, sándwiches fríos.
Hace frío: cocido de garbanzos, sopa de lentejas.
Estás enfermo: sopa de pollo, consomé de carne.
Estás en la escuela: hamburguesas, pollo, pasta.

25. 1. harina   3. mucha   5. pocos
2. huevos   4. demasiada

Additional Resources

Fans Online activities
Practice Workbook

197

DESAFÍO 2

Dar órdenes relacionadas con la compra

Presentation

- In *Desafío 2*, Andy and Janet are at the Hacienda La Luz in Tabasco, Mexico. They must find the oldest currency in the Americas.
- In this section, students will preview:
  - Food shopping and packaging vocabulary.
  - Regular and irregular affirmative *tú* and *usted* command forms.

Activities	Standards	Resources
Fotonovela	1.2, 2.1, 2.2	Vis. Pres.
26.	1.2	
27.	1.3	
28.	1.1, 1.3	
29. Cultura	1.1, 1.2, 2.2, 3.1, 3.2	
Tu desafío	1.2, 2.2, 3.1, 3.2, 5.2	

Teaching Suggestions

Warm-Up / Independent Starter

- Ask students to think about the items in their kitchens at home. Using indefinites, have students write sentences about how much of each of the following items they currently have: *atún, pollo, tomate, pan, queso, sandía.*

Preparation

- Chocolate is used in many dishes. Ask students to create a five-column chart and label the columns *Desayuno, Almuerzo, Cena, Postre,* and *Bebidas.* In small groups, have students fill in the columns with dishes made with chocolate, even if it is not the main ingredient. Have them share their chocolate dishes and drinks with the class.
- Ask a volunteer to read the introduction to the *fotonovela* aloud. Point out the state of Tabasco on a map.

La fotonovela

Before Viewing

- Ask students to discuss why they believe Tabasco would be the site of the oldest currency in the Americas.

La moneda más antigua de América

Andy and Janet are at Hacienda La Luz, a farm and cacao museum in the Mexican state of Tabasco. Their task is to find the oldest currency in the Americas. Amalia shares with them the many secrets of chocolate. But there are no coins to be found!

Hola, muchachos. Bienvenidos a la Hacienda La Luz.

¡Qué verduras más frescas!

Sí, las cultivamos aquí. Solo compramos la carne y las botellas de leche en el supermercado.

Hola. Estamos buscando la moneda más antigua de América. ¿Sabes dónde está?

Claro. Acompáñenme.

Aquí cultivamos cacao. Producimos miles de kilos cada año.

Toma, Andy. Abre el fruto con el cuchillo. ¡Pero ten cuidado!

¿Qué son estos granos?

¿Y la moneda?

Espera un poco, Janet.

Son las semillas del cacao. Con ellas hacemos el chocolate. Pruébalas.

¡¡¡Están muy amargas!!!

Continuará…

26 **Detective de palabras**

▶ **Completa** estas oraciones.

1. _____ cuidado.
2. _____ un poco.
3. _____ el fruto.
4. _____, Andy.
5. _____ las.

Differentiated Instruction

DEVELOPING LEARNERS

- Ask students to rewrite the following false statements to make them true:
  1. *En la Hacienda La Luz cultivan verduras y chocolate.* (*En la Hacienda La Luz cultivan verduras* y cacao.)
  2. *En la hacienda venden carne y leche.* (*Compran la carne y la leche en el supermercado.*)
  3. *Andy pregunta por la moneda.* (*Janet pregunta por la moneda.*)
  4. *Janet abre el fruto de cacao.* (*Andy abre el fruto de cacao.*)
  5. *Las semillas de cacao son muy dulces.* (*Las semillas de cacao son muy* amargas.)

EXPANDING LEARNERS

- Ask students to work in groups of three and research how chocolate is made from cacao. Two students will role-play friends who are visiting a cacao farm in Mexico. A third student will join them and role-play the manager of the farm, who will take them on a tour and explain how chocolate is made. The visitors must ask pertinent questions on their tour, showing that they have some knowledge of the process. Allow groups time to rehearse their dialogue and then call on them to present their skits in front of the class.

27 ¿Comprendes?

▶ **Escribe** la respuesta a estas preguntas.

1. ¿Dónde están Janet y Andy?
2. ¿Qué buscan Janet y Andy en la Hacienda La Luz?
3. ¿Por qué están tan frescas las verduras?
4. ¿Qué usa Andy para abrir el fruto de cacao?
5. Según Janet, ¿cómo están las semillas del cacao?

28 ¿Qué dicen?

▶ **Habla** con tu compañero(a). Escriban un diálogo para cada una de estas fotos.

Modelo JANET: *¿Qué cultivan aquí?*
AMALIA: *Verduras.*

①  ②  ③  ④

CULTURA
La ruta del cacao

El estado de Tabasco, al sureste de México, está muy relacionado con la historia del cacao. Allí se produce el 75 % del chocolate del país.

En Tabasco se puede seguir la ruta del cacao y visitar alguna hacienda cacaotera para aprender cómo se siembra *(plant)* y se cosecha *(harvest)* el cacao, y cómo se hace el excelente chocolate de la zona.

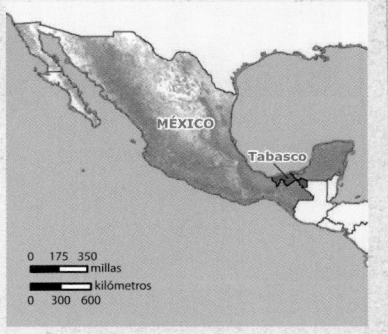

MÉXICO

Tabasco

0 175 350 millas
0 300 600 kilómetros

Mapa del estado de Tabasco.

29 Piensa y explica. ¿Cuántos productos derivados del cacao tienes en casa?

 → TU DESAFÍO Visita la página web para aprender más cosas sobre la ruta del cacao.

HERITAGE LANGUAGE LEARNERS

- In the *fotonovela*, Janet describes the cacao beans as *muy amargas*. Explain that other foods could be categorized as *dulce, amargo, agrio,* or *salado.* Ask students to make a four-column chart and label the columns, *Dulce, Amargo, Agrio,* and *Salado.* Then ask them to list as many foods as they can name under the corresponding heading. Next, ask them to think of their favorite foods and name the category under which most of these foods fall.

MULTIPLE INTELLIGENCES:
Intrapersonal Intelligence

- Tell students that the Chilean poet Pablo Neruda won the Nobel Prize for Literature in 1971. Among his many works are several odes (i.e., poems that are characterized by admiration and praise of the subject matter) to various foods, among them *el tomate, la cebolla,* and *las papas fritas.* Ask students to think of a food worthy of an ode and have them write an ode to it. Explain that odes may have varying line lengths and have no special rhyming pattern.

Dar órdenes relacionadas con la compra

After Viewing

▪ Do students have an idea of the kind of currency Andy and Janet are looking for? Have students guess what the answer might be, without telling them that the answer is cacao beans.

Activities

27. Ask students to answer the questions in complete sentences. Make sure they make a mental note that they must work backwards to answer the questions in complete sentences. In the response, the subject of the sentence comes first, the verb comes second, and the answer to the question comes third.

CULTURA

La ruta del cacao

In the Mexican state of Tabasco, tourists can take a tour of the cacao plantations, see a chocolate-making demonstration, and sample the famous local chocolate on what is known as the Cacao Route. The following haciendas are open to the public: Hacienda La Luz, Hacienda Jesús María, Hacienda La Chonita, and Hacienda Cholula.

Answer Key

26. 1. Ten   4. Toma
      2. Espera   5. Pruébalas
      3. Abre

27. Answers will vary. Sample answers:
   1. Están en la Hacienda La Luz en Tabasco.
   2. Buscan la moneda más antigua de América.
   3. Porque las cultivan en la hacienda.
   4. Usa un cuchillo.
   5. Janet dice que están muy amargas.

28. Answers will vary.

29. Answers will vary.

Additional Resources

Fans Online activities

199

DESAFÍO 2

Vocabulario – Comprar comida

Presentation

- In this section, students will learn:
  - Food shopping and packaging vocabulary.
  - Packaging measurements.

Activities	Standards	Resources
Vocabulario	1.2	
30.	1.2	
31.	1.2	Audio
32.	1.1, 1.2, 1.3	
33. Cultura	1.2, 1.3, 2.2, 3.1, 3.2, 5.1	

Teaching Suggestions

Warm-Up / Independent Starter

- Have students write a paragraph to describe the importance of the cacao plant in Tabasco, Mexico, without looking in the textbook or on the Internet.

Preparation

- Go over the vocabulary presentation with students. Draw their attention to the dialogue between Andy and Janet. They use the words *kilo* and *litro*. Ask students which system of measurement Andy and Janet are using (International System of Units). Then ask them which system we usually see in the grocery stores in the United States (United States Customary System).

- Have students look at the different types of packaging in this vocabulary presentation. Then have them write how each of the foods presented in *Desafío 1* is typically packaged.

Activities

30. Tell students that some of these items may have more than one packaging option. Have them list all of the possible packaging options for each item.

31. Once students have listened to the audio recording, have them list, using complete sentences, the items that Andy and Janet purchased. Encourage students to use other verbs in place of *comprar* (e.g., *elegir, llevar*).

200

Vocabulario

Comprar comida

Los envases

un tarro de mermelada

una lata de atún

un bote de tomate

una caja de galletas

una bolsa de papas fritas

una botella de agua mineral

un paquete de cereales

¿Tienes la lista de la compra, Janet?

Sí, necesitamos un kilo de frijoles y un litro de leche.

¿Qué precio tienen los frijoles?

Dos dólares.

Acciones

comprar / hacer la compra
vender
costar
pedir
pesar
hacer cola / fila

30 Las compras

▶ **Une** las dos columnas.

Ⓐ
1. una botella de _____.
2. dos cajas de _____.
3. un bote de _____.
4. una bolsa de _____.
5. dos latas de _____.
6. un paquete de _____.

Ⓑ
a. papas
b. galletas
c. atún
d. salsa picante
e. leche
f. azúcar

200 doscientos

Differentiated Instruction

DEVELOPING LEARNERS

- Review stem-changing verbs with students. You might write the conjugations of *costar* (o > ue) and *pedir* (e > i) on the board and have students identify the changes. Then ask them to write the conjugations of *probar* and *servir* in their notebooks. After you check their work, ask students to say or write a sentence for each of these four verbs.

EXPANDING LEARNERS

- Ask students to work with a partner and write a dialogue that uses each of the verbs listed under *Acciones*. Also encourage students to use as much of the new vocabulary included in *Los envases* as they can in the dialogue. Give students time to practice their dialogues and then ask them to present their conversation to the class. Take a class vote on the most original dialogue, the one that used the most vocabulary words, as well as the best performance.

31 **¿Qué hay en la lista?**

▶ **Escucha** la conversación entre Andy y Janet en el supermercado. ¿Qué productos compran?

① ② ③ ④
⑥
⑤ ⑦

32 **Una ensalada de fruta**

▶ **Lee** la lista de Janet y clasifica los alimentos en la tabla. ¿Cuáles sirven para hacer una ensalada de fruta?

sirven	no sirven
una sandía	

▶ **Habla** con tu compañero(a). ¿Qué más frutas sirven para hacer una ensalada? Haz una lista de la compra.

Lista de la compra

Una sandía
Dos tarros de guisantes
Un kilo de peras
Un bote de salsa de tomate
Medio kilo de uvas
Una botella de leche
Una lata de atún
Una piña

CULTURA

El chocolate

El chocolate se obtiene de las semillas del cacao, un alimento que procede de América. Los mayas cultivaban *(grew)* el árbol del cacao hace 2.500 años.

Para los mayas y los aztecas, el cacao era *(was)* un regalo de los dioses y lo utilizaban *(used)* como moneda. El emperador azteca Moctezuma dio una taza de chocolate al conquistador Hernán Cortés y los españoles descubrieron el poder energético del chocolate y su valor económico.

Indígena mexicana preparando chocolate. Museo de América (Madrid).

33 **Investiga.** ¿Qué otras cosas curiosas se usaron como moneda en el pasado?

DESAFÍO 2

Vocabulario – Comprar comida

32. Have students get into pairs and create a menu with dishes that only contain the items from the shopping list (e.g., a fruit salad, a pear milkshake, a tuna casserole). Then have the class vote for the most creative menu.

33. Paper currency is a recent phenomenon. Ask students to think about how currency will be handled in the future. How will you pay for food and clothing? How will you pay for sporting events or other forms of entertainment?

AUDIO SCRIPT
See page 183I.

CULTURA

El chocolate

The cacao tree is indigenous to the tropical regions of the Americas. It is believed that the Olmecs were the first pre-Columbian civilization to cultivate it about 3,000 years ago. The Mayas and Aztecs turned the cacao beans into a drink by adding water and spices. This drink was too bitter for European taste and they sweetened it with sugar. Today, the most common forms of chocolate in the United States are cocoa powder, which is ground cacao, and chocolate bars.

Answer Key

30. 1. e 2. b 3. d 4. a 5. c 6. f
31. 1, 2, 3, 6
32. Sirven: una sandía, un kilo de peras, medio kilo de uvas y una piña.
No sirven: dos tarros de guisantes, un bote de salsa de tomate, una botella de leche, y una lata de atún.
▶ Answers will vary.
33. Answers will vary.

Additional Resources

Fans Online activities
Practice Workbook

HERITAGE LANGUAGE LEARNERS

• Students may confuse the letters *b* and *v* when writing, since they have the same sound in Spanish. Ask students to close their books and conduct the following dictation:

1. *Bienvenidos a la fábrica de mi abuelo Benito Vélez.*
2. *Volvimos a la tienda para comprar un tarro de mermelada de uva, una bolsa de avellanas y una botella de vinagre.*
3. *La palabra verdura viene del color verde.*
4. *¿Qué venden en la tienda de ropa: vasos, velas o blusas?*
5. *Por favor, prueba el bacalao. ¡Está muy sabroso!*

SPECIAL-NEEDS LEARNERS

• Whenever possible, use real objects that sight impaired students can touch and feel while introducing vocabulary. For this lesson, bring in samples of boxes, bottles, cans, bags, packages, tablets, and jars of food so students can hold them while they say the corresponding word for each one. Always seat these students where they can hear well, since they depend more on their hearing than others, both for learning and participation.

DESAFÍO 2

Gramática – El imperativo afirmativo singular

Presentation

- In this section, students will learn regular and irregular affirmative *tú* and *usted* command forms.

Activities	Standards	Resources
Gramática	3.1	
34.	1.3, 4.1	
35.	1.2	
36.	1.3	
37.	1.2	Audio
38.	1.1, 1.3	
39. Conexiones	1.2, 1.3, 3.1, 3.2, 5.1	

Teaching Suggestions

Warm-Up / Independent Starter

- Ask students to complete these sentences with the actions that are needed to resolve the situations. If needed, students should also add the corresponding direct object pronoun.
  1. *El precio de las papas es por kilo. Hay que...* (pesarlas)
  2. *Hay mucha gente esperando para pagar. Hay que...* (hacer fila)
  3. *No veo atún en lata. Hay que...* (pedirlo)

Preparation

- Read over the grammar presentation with students. Then have them get into pairs to play a game to practice these commands. One student will give a command and his or her partner models the action. Be sure students switch roles.

Activities

35. Once students have selected the correct command form, have them write a command using the verb. For example: 1. *Viaja en tren.*

36. You may extend this activity by asking students to add a second command to each sentence. For example: *Haz la lista de la compra y ve al supermercado.*

202

Gramática

El imperativo afirmativo singular

- To tell one person to do something, use an informal or a formal command.

  Camina más rápido, por favor.   Come tu almuerzo.   Escribe la receta.

EL IMPERATIVO REGULAR. FORMAS DEL SINGULAR

Caminar	Comer	Escribir	
camina	come	escribe	tú
camine	coma	escriba	usted

Note: Commands are generally used without a subject pronoun, or with the pronoun after the verb.

Come pollo con arroz. Está delicioso.

Coma usted pollo con arroz. Está delicioso.

- Tú commands are based on the tú form of the present tense without the final -s. Therefore, if the tú form is irregular, the tú command is also irregular.

tú caminas → camina	tú comes → come	tú escribes → escribe
tú pides → pide	tú cierras → cierra	tú pruebas → prueba

- Usted commands are based on the yo form of the present tense, substituting the -o for these endings:
  1. -e for -ar verbs: yo camino → camine
  2. -a for -er, -ir verbs: yo como → coma; yo escribo → escriba

  Therefore, if the yo form is irregular, the usted command is also irregular.

  yo cierro → cierre   yo pruebo → pruebe   yo pido → pida   yo salgo → salga

Irregularidades especiales

- These verbs have special irregularities:

IMPERATIVOS CON IRREGULARIDADES ESPECIALES

Tener	Hacer	Poner	Venir	Salir	
ten	haz	pon	ven	sal	tú
tenga	haga	ponga	venga	salga	usted

Ser	Decir	Ir	Dar	
sé	di	ve	da	tú
sea	diga	vaya	dé	usted

34 **Piensa.** ¿Cómo se forma el imperativo en inglés? ¿Hay formas diferentes para el imperativo formal e informal?

35 **La forma correcta**

▶ **Decide** cuál es la forma de imperativo para la persona tú.

1. viajas - viaja
2. prueba - pruebo
3. venden - vende
4. subimos - sube
5. hace - haz
6. pongo - pon
7. sirve - servir
8. duermes - duerme
9. salgo - sal

Differentiated Instruction

DEVELOPING LEARNERS

- Give students more practice with the irregular commands by asking them to choose the correct verb to complete the following sentences.
  1. *Pon / Pone el bote en la bolsa. (Pon)*
  2. *¡Sal / Sale de aquí! (Sal)*
  3. *Hácelo / Hazlo ahora. (Hazlo)*
  4. *Ve / Vaya usted al mercado, por favor. (Vaya)*
  5. *¡Tiene / Ten cuidado! (Ten)*
  6. *Viene / Ven con nosotros al cine. (Ven)*

EXPANDING LEARNERS

- Have students come up with a list of rules for their school, classroom, home, or social relationships. They should first write the rules using informal command forms and then rewrite them using formal commands. Have students read one of their lists to the class and afterwards engage them in a discussion about the effectiveness of their rules.

- You may want to post a list of rules for the Spanish classroom based on students' suggestions.

36 Instrucciones de viaje

▶ **Lee** la lista de las cosas que hay que hacer.
Escribe las instrucciones que Janet le da a Andy.

Modelo Preparar la mochila. → *Prepara la mochila.*

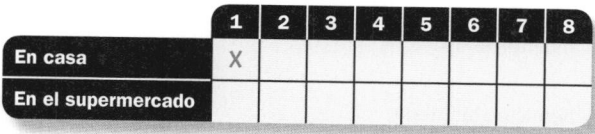

> **Instrucciones para Andy**
> 1. Hacer la lista de la compra.
> 2. Comprar pan.
> 3. Preparar unos sándwiches.
> 4. Llenar una botella de agua.
> 5. Poner una bolsa de papas en la mochila.
> 6. Meter las latas de atún en la mochila.

37 ¿En casa o en el supermercado?

▶ **Escucha** y decide. ¿Dónde se hace cada actividad?

	1	2	3	4	5	6	7	8
En casa	X							
En el supermercado								

38 Sugerencias

▶ **Habla** con tu compañero(a). La mamá de Janet va a México de visita. ¿Qué sugerencias pueden hacerle?

1. ¿Debo salir por la mañana o por la tarde? → *Salga por la mañana. Hace menos calor.*
2. ¿Debo comer pescado o unos sándwiches?
3. ¿Debo bañarme en la playa o en la piscina del hotel?
4. ¿Debo ir a la ruta del cacao o a la ruta de los tesoros coloniales?

CONEXIONES: LENGUA

Los nombres científicos

El árbol del cacao es el cacaotero (*cacao tree*). Y el nombre científico del cacaotero es *Theobroma cacao. Theobroma* es una palabra griega que significa *alimento de los dioses.*

39 Piensa y explica.
La palabra *cacao* viene del náhuatl *cacáhuatl.* Las palabras *chilli, tomatl* y *ahuacatl* también son del náhuatl. ¿Qué crees que significan esas palabras en español?

DESAFÍO 2

Gramática – El imperativo afirmativo singular

39. Explain to students that the English words, *chili, tomato,* and *avocado* come from the Spanish words *chile, tomate,* and *aguacate.* Spanish took these words from Nahuatl.

🎧 **AUDIO SCRIPT**
See page 183I.

CONEXIONES: LENGUA

Los nombres científicos

Spanish is a Romance language because it comes from Latin, whereas Nahuatl is not associated with any other language outside of Mesoamerica. How is it possible then for Spanish and Nahuatl to have cognate words? As the Spaniards were introduced to the plants, animals, and foods of Mesoamerica they adapted the Nahuatl words to fit the Spanish language.

Answer Key

34. En inglés no hay una conjugación especial para el imperativo ni hay diferencias entre el formal y el informal (e.g., *You jump.* → *Jump!*).

35.
1. viaja	4. sube	7. sirve
2. prueba	5. haz	8. duerme
3. vende	6. pon	9. sal

36.
1. Haz la lista de la compra.
2. Compra pan.
3. Prepara unos sándwiches.
4. Llena una botella de agua.
5. Pon una bolsa de papas en la mochila.
6. Mete las latas de atún en la mochila.

37. En casa: 1, 2, 4, 8.
En el supermercado: 3, 5, 6, 7.

38. Answers will vary.

39. Chile, tomate y aguacate.

Additional Resources

Fans Online activities
Practice Workbook

HERITAGE LANGUAGE LEARNERS

- Students have read about the origin of the word *cacao.* Now ask them to research the origin of some other words related to food and drinks in Spanish (e.g., *barbacoa, pozole, maíz, tamal, papa*). You might suggest that they look into the history surrounding the word, and the fables and legends associated whit the food that the word names. Ask students to write a brief report based on their findings, and accompany it with images, if possible. Display their work in the classroom for others to read.

TOTAL PHYSICAL RESPONSE (TPR)

- Ask students to count off by 2s: the 1s will be the *tú* group, and the 2s, the *usted* group. Give the *tú* group a sheet of white paper, and give the *usted* group a sheet of colored paper. You will give students a variety of affirmative commands, some informal and some formal. Be sure to give students practice with both regular and irregular verbs. When you give an informal command, the *tú* group should raise their white papers. When you give a formal command, the *usted* group should raise their colored papers.

DESAFÍO 2

Comunicación

Presentation

- In this section, students will integrate the vocabulary and grammar from *Desafío 2* in order to practice food shopping and packaging vocabulary, packaging measurements, and regular and irregular affirmative *tú* and *usted* commands.

Activities	Standards	Resources
40.	1.2, 1.3	
41.	1.1, 1.3	
42.	1.1, 1.2, 1.3, 5.1	Audio
43.	1.3	
44. Final del desafío	1.2, 2.1, 2.2	
Tu desafío	1.2, 1.3	

Teaching Suggestions

Warm-Up / Independent Starter

- Ask students to create a dialogue between a father and his son as he gives instructions for things to buy for dinner. The father is making shrimp pasta with peppers, onions and spinach. He wants bread and butter to accompany the meal, and a fruit salad for dessert. Since this is the son's first time going to the grocery store alone, the father must explain how each food is packaged and how to purchase it.

Preparation

- Allow students sufficient time to finish their dialogues. Then have them get into pairs to decide which dialogue from the Independent Starter is the best written and the most entertaining. Once partners have reached a decision, have them practice reading the lines together. Then ask for volunteers to role-play their dialogues to the class. Take a class vote for the pair with the best performance.
- Take 10 minutes to review the vocabulary and grammar themes from *Desafío 2*.
- Refer students back to the *fotonovela* and have them find all of the food shopping and packaging vocabulary, and regular and irregular affirmative *tú* and *usted* commands within the dialogue. Do students understand the *fotonovela* better now?

DESAFÍO 2

Comunicación

40 **Los ingredientes necesarios**

▶ **Escribe** la lista de la compra con los ingredientes necesarios para preparar tu plato favorito. Usa estas palabras.

paquete   kilo   caja   bolsa   lata   bote

 ▶ **Lee** la lista de la compra de tu compañero(a). ¿Cuál crees que es su plato favorito?

41 **Órdenes**

 ▶ **Imagina** que estás en estos lugares. Dile a tu compañero(a) qué tiene que hacer. Usa el imperativo.

1. una tienda de bisutería
2. la clase de Español
3. un museo
4. la cocina
5. el supermercado
6. una tienda de ropa

Compra una pulsera.

42 **Consejos apropiados**

▶ **Escucha** y escribe qué problemas tienen Andy y Janet. Las fotografías pueden ayudarte.

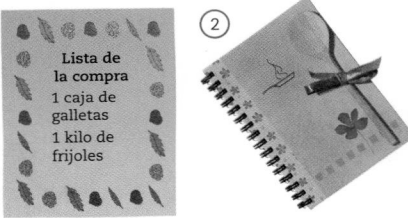  

Lista de la compra
1 caja de galletas
1 kilo de frijoles

▶ **Escribe** un consejo apropiado para cada problema.

Modelo 1. *Haz la lista de la compra antes de ir al supermercado.*

 ▶ **Compara** tus consejos con los de tu compañero(a). ¿Son similares?

204 doscientos cuatro

Differentiated Instruction

DEVELOPING LEARNERS

- Have students make a six-column chart and label the columns *Paquete, Caja, Lata, Bote, Bolsa,* and *Botella*. Then have them think of the foods or drinks they know or have learned in this unit and how they are generally packaged. Have them list these items under the corresponding heading. Ask them what the most common packaging is for the foods and drinks they selected.

EXPANDING LEARNERS

- Have students make their own lists of five or six places, following the model for activity 41. Ask them to write appropriate commands for someone at each place. Remind them to vary between informal and formal commands, and explain why they chose the form they did. Were they asking a stranger who was an adult? Were they talking to a friend or family member? Have them share their lists and commands with the rest of the class.

43 Un anuncio

▶ **Escribe** un eslogan para el anuncio de uno de estos alimentos.

Modelo tortillas ⟶ *Come tortillas. Descubre el sabor de México.*

Final del desafío

Este método tiene más de mil años.

¡Qué interesante! ¡Janet, __2__ una foto!

__1__, usamos las millas para preparar chocolate, pero no ¸ comemos!

Pero __3__, ¿dónde está la moneda más antigua de América?

__4__, Janet. Esta es la moneda más antigua de América.

44 ¿Una moneda de chocolate?

▶ **Completa.** Andy y Janet descubren que la moneda más antigua de América fue el cacao. Lee su diálogo y complétalo con las formas correctas de imperativo.

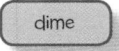 dime   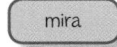 mira   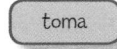 toma   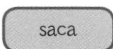 saca

 **TU DESAFÍO**   Visita la página web. Escucha las preguntas de tu *Minientrevista Desafío 2* y escribe las respuestas.

doscientos cinco 205

HERITAGE LANGUAGE LEARNERS

- Students will create a radio ad for a food. First, they need to think of a food and how it appeals to all their senses: *la vista, el oído, el olfato, el gusto, el tacto.* The ad, therefore, must describe what the food looks like, what it sounds like when people are eating or cooking it, what it smells like, tastes like, and feels like when people touch it. Have students read or play their ads to the rest of the class.

MULTIPLE INTELLIGENCES:
Visual-Spatial Intelligence

- Students will create an ad for the world's best chocolate bar! They will need to find a name for their product and draw a logo or special character that represents it. Ads should include the ingredients and the health benefits or other advantages associated with the product. Creativity is key. Students might try writing a slogan, a song, or even *una oda* to extol the virtues of their product. Display their work in the classroom and hold a class vote for the best ad.

- Ask students to complete the *Comunicación* activities individually. Have them take note of any of the activities that they need help or more practice with. Once students have finished, group them by the activities with which they needed more practice. Within the group, have students work together to help each other learn the theme.

Activities

41. Ask students to speak to their partners as friends, and then to speak to each other formally.

43. Make this activity a class competition. Divide the class into four groups and ask students to come up with the four slogans. Call one representative from each group to present their slogans, and hold a class vote for the best.

AUDIO SCRIPT
See page 183I.

Answer Key

40. Answers will vary.
  ▶ Answers will vary.

41. Answers will vary.

42. Answers will vary. Sample answers:
  1. Janet no quiere gastar mucho dinero en el supermercado.
  2. Andy no sabe cocinar muy bien.
  3. Janet no sabe qué llevar de comida a una fiesta.
  4. Andy no sabe qué postre preparar.
  ▶ Answers will vary. Sample answers:
  1. Haz una lista de compra.
  2. Busca recetas en un libro de cocina.
  3. Lleva sándwiches.
  4. Prepara un pastel de cumpleaños.
  ▶ Answers will vary.

43. Answers will vary.

44. 1. Mira   2. saca   3. dime   4. Toma

Additional Resources

Fans Online activities
Practice Workbook

205

DESAFÍO 3

Dar instrucciones relacionadas con la cocina

Presentation

- In *Desafío 3*, Diana and Rita are in San Antonio, Texas. There they must prepare a recipe for a *chile con carne* contest.

- In this section, students will preview:
  – Condiments and cooking utensils vocabulary.
  – Actions in the kitchen.
  – Regular and irregular affirmative plural command forms.

Activities	Standards	Resources
Fotonovela	1.2, 2.1, 3.2	Vis. Pres.
45.	1.2	
46.	1.3	
47.	1.2, 1.3	Audio
48. Conexiones	1.1, 1.2, 2.2, 3.1, 3.2	Video
Tu desafío	1.2, 3.1, 3.2, 5.2	

Teaching Suggestions

Warm-Up / Independent Starter

- Ask students to answer the following question in four complete sentences: *¿Cómo afectan los envases de plástico al medio ambiente?*

Preparation

- Read the introduction to the *fotonovela* to students. Ask them if they have ever been to a baking, cooking, or eating contest. Have students write some of the rules for these types of contests.

 **La fotonovela**

Before Viewing

- Have students close their books and ask them to simply watch and listen to the visual presentation.

After Viewing

- Have students open their books and follow along as you play the visual presentation one more time. Once it has finished playing, ask students which method was more helpful in understanding the dialogue.

Un concurso de chile en San Antonio

Diana and Rita have bought an assortment of chilies in a local market in San Antonio, Texas, and must prepare a recipe for an outdoor *chile con carne* contest. María, one of their fellow contestants, gives them advice.

45 **Detective de palabras**   Continuará…

▶ **Completa** estas oraciones.

1. Primero, tienen que _____ la cebolla.
2. Luego, hay que _____ la cebolla en trozos pequeños.
3. Después, tienen que _____ la salsa de tomate.
4. A continuación, hay que _____ de picar los ingredientes.
5. Luego, hay que _____ los ingredientes en la olla.
6. Finalmente, hay que pelar y _____ los chiles.

> poner
> añadir
> terminar
> freír
> pelar
> cortar

Differentiated Instruction

DEVELOPING LEARNERS

- María uses several commands as she tells Diana and Rita how to make *chile con carne*. Ask students to write a list of these commands (*pelen, córtenla, añadan, terminen, pónganlos, fríanlos*) and the command Diana gives to Rita (*corta*). Then have students write their own sentences using three of these commands.

EXPANDING LEARNERS

- Have students imagine that they are making *chile con carne* for a contest. Ask them to write a letter to a friend explaining the steps they need to follow in order to make this dish. They should also describe how they feel about participating in this competition and mention something about the other contestants.

46 **Chile con carne**

▶ **Elige.** ¿Qué ingredientes necesitan Rita y Diana para cocinar chile con carne?

leche	salsa de tomate	papas	chile
carne	lechuga	ajo	cebolla

 **47** **Paso a paso**

▶ **Escucha** a Rita y ordena las fotografías.

Ⓐ   Ⓑ   Ⓒ   Ⓓ

▶ **Escribe** una oración para describir cada fotografía en el orden correcto.

CONEXIONES: HISTORIA

El Álamo

La famosa fortaleza de El Álamo está situada en la ciudad de San Antonio (Texas). La construcción de la fortaleza empezó en 1724. Originalmente fue una misión: la Misión de San Antonio de Valero. Fue la fortaleza más importante en la Revolución de Texas, cuando Davy Crockett y algunos texanos lucharon contra los mexicanos. Hoy en día es un museo.

 **48** **Piensa y explica.** ¿Qué sabes sobre El Álamo? ¿Qué ocurrió allí?

⚑→ **TU DESAFÍO** Visita la página web para aprender más sobre El Álamo.

 doscientos siete 207

HERITAGE LANGUAGE LEARNERS

• *Chile con carne* is a typical dish of the American Southwest. Ask students to describe some typical dishes from their family's country of origin, or from a Spanish-speaking country they have visited or know about. If there are students with backgrounds from, or knowledge of, several different Spanish-speaking countries, encourage them to compare and contrast the cuisines of these places. Have them address how the geography, climate, and proximity to the sea, lakes, or rivers influence the food of a nation or region.

CRITICAL THINKING

• The Alamo is the symbol of the struggle for Texas independence. Discuss with students what other buildings or monuments symbolize the struggle for freedom, and whether they think it is important to maintain these symbols. Can they identify such a building or monument in their community or state? What does it symbolize? If they were to erect a monument tomorrow in their community, what would it symbolize? Where would they place it? Why? Be sure all students participate in the discussion.

 Unit 4

DESAFÍO 3

Dar instrucciones relacionadas con la cocina

Activities

45. After students have finished, ask them to use every word in the word bank to fill in the blanks in each sentence. Do students find that most words complete the sentences correctly?

46. Ask students to look up three *chile con carne* recipes on the Internet. What are the common ingredients in all three recipes?

 AUDIO SCRIPT
See page 183I.

 CONEXIONES: HISTORIA

El Álamo

The Alamo was a Franciscan mission, but in 1793, the Spanish authorities secularized it. The first hospital in Texas was established at the Alamo in the early 1800s. During Mexico's War of Independence, the Alamo was used by both sides of the conflict. In 1836, the Tejano revolutionaries garrisoned themselves in the Alamo and defended it. After a fierce struggle, the Mexican army was able to capture the fortress. However, the Mexicans were eventually defeated in the Battle of San Jacinto and Texas gained its independence.

Answer Key

45. 1. pelar   4. terminar
2. cortar   5. poner
3. añadir   6. freír

46. cebolla, ajo, chiles, carne, salsa de tomate

47. B, A, D, C.
▶ Answers will vary.

48. Answers will vary.

Additional Resources

Fans Online activities

DESAFÍO 3

Vocabulario – En la cocina

Presentation

- In this section, students will learn:
  - Condiments and cooking utensils vocabulary.
  - Actions in the kitchen.

Activities	Standards	Resources
Vocabulario	1.2	
49.	1.2, 1.3	
50.	1.2	Audio
51.	1.2, 1.3	
52.	1.1	
53. Cultura	1.1, 1.2, 2.1, 3.2, 4.2	
Tu desafío	1.2, 2.1, 2.2, 3.2, 5.2	

Teaching Suggestions

Warm-Up / Independent Starter

- Have students look at the vocabulary presentation and determine how each *utensilio* and *condimento* comes packaged from the store. Ask students to write their conclusions in complete sentences.

Preparation

- Go over the vocabulary presentation with students. Ask them to write the list of *condimentos* in their notebook, and then write their favorite name brand next to each condiment. This will help students associate what they use on a regular basis with the vocabulary.

- Then have students look at the *acciones* list. Ask them to write a list of all the cooking utensils that they will need to perform all of these actions in the kitchen.

Activities

49. Ask students to add a second sentence to each item to give it a storyline. For example: *Voy a hervir la pasta en una cazuela. Luego la pongo en un bol.*

52. Have partners give each other step-by-step instructions on how to prepare their favorite dish.

Vocabulario

En la cocina

Utensilios

Condimentos

la sartén
la olla
la cazuela
el bol
la bandeja
la jarra

el aceite
el vinagre
la sal
la pimienta
el azúcar

la salsa de tomate
la mayonesa
la mostaza

Acciones

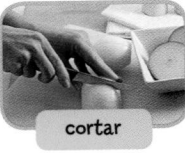

pelar
cortar
mezclar
echar

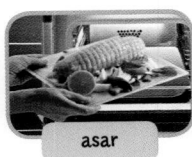

batir
cocer/hervir
freir
asar

49 Utensilios y condimentos

▶ **Completa** estas oraciones.

| azúcar | cazuela | sartén | vinagre | bol | jarra |

1. Voy a hervir la pasta en una _____.
2. La carne la frío en la _____.
3. ¿Quieres _____ para el café?
4. Lleva la _____ de agua a la mesa, por favor.
5. Echa los ingredientes en un _____.
6. Me gustan las ensaladas con aceite y _____.

Differentiated Instruction

DEVELOPING LEARNERS

- Have students choose the correct word to complete each sentence.
  1. *Voy a freír los huevos en una jarra/sartén.* (sartén)
  2. *Primero hay que pelar/batir la cebolla.* (pelar)
  3. *Me sirven la comida en una bandeja/jarra.* (bandeja)
  4. *El agua está hirviendo en el bol/la olla.* (la olla)
  5. *Aso/Mezclo los ingredientes en el bol.* (Mezclo)
  6. *Bato/Corto los huevos y frío el azúcar/la carne. (Bato; la carne)*

EXPANDING LEARNERS

- Ask students to indicate which word does not belong.
  1. aceite — vinagre — bol *(bol)*
  2. vaso — bandeja — jarra *(bandeja)*
  3. asar — pelar — cortar *(asar)*
  4. freír — mezclar — asar *(mezclar)*
  5. olla — cazuela — sartén *(sartén)*
  6. hervir — salsa de tomate — agua *(salsa de tomate)*
  7. echar — mezclar — asar *(asar)*

50 Adivina, adivinanza

 ▶ **Escucha** las definiciones. ¿A qué fotografía se refiere cada una?

 Ⓐ Ⓑ  Ⓒ  Ⓓ

51 ¡A cocinar!

▶ **Lee** esta receta y ordena los pasos que faltan.

Frijoles al estilo Zacatecas

1. Hervir los frijoles en una olla.
2.
3. Freírlos en una sartén con medio vaso de aceite.
4. Echar los frijoles en un bol.
5.
6.
7. Añadir sal y pimienta.
8.

| Mezclar todo bien. |

| Añadir el tomate, la cebolla y el ajo al bol de los frijoles. |

| Servir muy caliente. |

| Cortar tomates, cebolla y ajo. |

▶ **Escribe** la receta usando la forma *tú* del imperativo.

Modelo *Hierve los frijoles.*

52 Tu plato favorito

▶ **Habla** con tu compañero(a). ¿Cuál es tu plato favorito? ¿Qué ingredientes y utensilios necesitas para prepararlo?

  **CULTURA**

El chile

Los chiles son originarios de las Américas y son un ingrediente fundamental en la cocina mexicana. Se comen crudos (*raw*), cocidos (*boiled*) o fritos (*fried*). Hay muchas variedades de chiles dulces y picantes, con formas y colores distintos.

53 Piensa y explica. ¿Alguna vez probaste los chiles? ¿Dónde? ¿En tu comunidad es habitual la comida picante?

▶ **TU DESAFÍO** Visita la página web para aprender más cosas sobre el chile.

---

53. Ask students what they believe is the hottest part of a chile (the veins). Ask them if they have ever tried or made a dish with chile peppers. Discuss, as a class, the different cuisines they know that use chiles.

 AUDIO SCRIPT
See page 183I.

 CULTURA

El chile

Remains of this vegetable have been found in pre-Columbian settlements all over North and South America. The Spanish conquistadors carried the pepper seeds with them to Europe and from there, peppers spread rapidly throughout the world. Hot chile peppers contain a substance called capsaicin, which gives them their pungency.

Answer Key

49. 1. cazuela   3. azúcar   5. bol
      2. sartén   4. jarra   6. vinagre

50. 1. C   2. D   3. A   4. B

51. 2. Cortar tomates, cebolla y ajo.
      5. Añadir el tomate, la cebolla y el ajo.
      6. Mezclar todo bien.
      8. Servir muy caliente.
   ▶ 2. Corta tomates, cebolla y ajo.
      3. Fríelos en una sartén con aceite.
      4. Echa los frijoles en un bol.
      5. Añade el tomate, la cebolla y el ajo.
      6. Mezcla todo bien.
      7. Añade sal y pimienta.
      8. Sírvelo muy caliente.

52. Answers will vary.

53. Answers will vary.

Additional Resources

Fans Online activities
Practice Workbook

209

HERITAGE LANGUAGE LEARNERS

• Ask students to describe other condiments that are commonly found in the cuisine of some Spanish-speaking countries and name some dishes that are made with them. Have students identify other alternative cooking methods, as well as some food-specific cooking utensils, such as the pan used to make paella, commonly referred to as *una paellera*, or the pan used to heat the tortillas: *el comal*. If they can, ask students to bring in some of these condiments and cooking utensils and explain their uses to the class.

MULTIPLE INTELLIGENCES:
Musical-Rhythmic Intelligence

• Because chiles are such an important ingredient in many of the dishes from the American Southwest, as well as from many parts of the Spanish-speaking world, they are worthy of a song! Ask students to create a catchy tune with some clever lyrics that will be part of an ad campaign to promote *los chiles*. Students should praise the healthful qualities of chiles and address their appearance too. Encourage those students who play a musical instrument to accompany themselves, if possible.

Unit 4
DESAFÍO 3

Gramática – El imperativo afirmativo plural

Presentation

- In this section, students will learn regular and irregular affirmative plural command forms.

Activities	Standards	Resources
Gramática	3.1	
54.	1.3, 4.1	
55.	1.3	
56.	1.2, 1.3	
57.	1.1, 5.2	
58. Comunidades	1.1, 1.2, 2.1, 3.2, 4.2, 5.1	

Teaching Suggestions

Warm-Up / Independent Starter

- Ask students to think about the most exotic dish they have ever eaten. Have them list the ingredients and describe how the dish was cooked. Ask students to also include in their description the cooking utensils that were used to cook this dish.

Preparation

- Have volunteers share their Independent Starter with the class. Then go over the grammar presentation with students. Let them know that the *vosotros* command forms are only used in Spain. They are useful when speaking to people from Spain, but of the 21 Spanish-speaking countries around the world, Spain is the only one that uses the *vosotros* commands.

Activities

55. Before students get into groups, have them write their five instructions individually. Walk around the room to ensure students have captured the concept of the affirmative plural commands. Once they have finished, group students in fours to complete this activity.

56. There is more than one answer possible for each item, but there is only one correct answer. Have students read over each item before they begin to match and write the commands.

210

DESAFÍO 3

Gramática

El imperativo afirmativo plural

- To tell more than one person what to do, use plural commands.

  Señores, **prueben** el chile.

EL IMPERATIVO REGULAR. FORMAS DEL PLURAL

Caminar	Comer	Escribir	
caminad	**com**ed	**escrib**id	vosotros(as)
caminen	**com**an	**escrib**an	ustedes

Note: Like in other cases, the vosotros form is used in Spain to give informal plural commands. In the Americas, the ustedes form is used in formal and informal plural commands.

- Vosotros(as) commands are always regular. They are formed by changing the -r of the infinitive to a -d.

  caminar $\longrightarrow$ caminad   comer $\longrightarrow$ comed   escribir $\longrightarrow$ escribid

- Ustedes commands are formed by adding an -n to the usted command form.
  1. -ar verbs: usted camine $\longrightarrow$ caminen
  2. -er and -ir verbs: usted coma $\longrightarrow$ coman; usted escriba $\longrightarrow$ escriban

  If the usted command is irregular, the ustedes command is also irregular.

  cierre (usted) $\longrightarrow$ cierren   vuelva (usted) $\longrightarrow$ vuelvan   pida (usted) $\longrightarrow$ pidan

Irregularidades especiales

- As in usted commands, these verbs have irregular ustedes command forms:

Tener	Hacer	Poner	Venir	Salir	Ser	Decir	Ir	Dar
tengan	hagan	pongan	vengan	salgan	sean	digan	vayan	den

El imperativo con pronombres

- Attach object pronouns to the end of affirmative singular and plural commands:

  Pruebe el pollo. $\longrightarrow$ Pruébelo.   Pidan la ensalada. $\longrightarrow$ Pídanla.

54 **Piensa.** En español se usa una forma verbal para dar órdenes a un grupo de personas. ¿Qué se usa en inglés?

55 **Simón dice**

 ▶ **Habla.** Da cinco instrucciones a tus compañeros(as). Usa la forma *ustedes* del imperativo. Ellos(as) tienen que representar lo que les pides.

Modelo *Escriban su nombre en la pizarra.*

210 doscientos diez

Differentiated Instruction

DEVELOPING LEARNERS

- Give students practice with object pronouns and commands by having them answer the following questions with an affirmative *ustedes* command.
  1. ¿Podemos cortar la cebolla? (Sí, córtenla.)
  2. ¿Podemos pelar las papas? (Sí, pélenlas.)
  3. ¿Podemos batir los huevos? (Sí, bátanlos.)
  4. ¿Podemos hervir el agua? (Sí, hiérvanla.)
  5. ¿Podemos mezclar los ingredientes? (Sí, mézclenlos.)
  6. ¿Podemos probar el chile con carne? (Sí, pruébenlo.)

EXPANDING LEARNERS

- Have students work with a partner and take turns giving orders with affirmative plural commands, using both *vosotros* and *ustedes*. The other student will explain that the task has already been carried out. For example:
  A. *Vayan al supermercado.*
  B. *Pero ya fuimos al supermercado.*
  A. *Pelad las papas.*
  B. *Ya pelamos las papas.*

56 **Recomendaciones**

▶ **Une** las dos columnas. Después, escribe las recomendaciones correspondientes.

(A)

1. Tenemos hambre.
2. Nos encanta la comida picante.
3. Estamos listas para pedir.
4. La comida está sosa.
5. Tenemos sed.
6. Queremos un postre dulce.

(B)

a. probar el chile con carne
b. pedir una bebida
c. ir a un restaurante
d. pedir sal
e. comer un pastel de chocolate
f. llamar al mesero

Modelo Tenemos sed. → *Pidan una bebida.*

 57 **Una visita sorpresa**

▶ **Habla** con tu compañero(a). Imagina que Diana y Rita visitan tu ciudad. ¿Qué recomendaciones pueden hacerles?

Modelo

Vengan a San Francisco en primavera. El tiempo es muy bueno.

Y vayan a comer al restaurante italiano de la calle principal. La comida es buenísima.

 **COMUNIDADES**

LOS HORARIOS

Los horarios de las comidas no son los mismos en todos los países. Por ejemplo, en México el desayuno es entre las ocho y las nueve de la mañana; el almuerzo es entre la una y las tres de la tarde; y la cena suele ser a partir de las ocho de la noche.

58 **Compara y explica.** Compara estos horarios con los tuyos. ¿Son diferentes? ¿Por qué crees que hay diferencias?

Gramática – El imperativo afirmativo plural

57. Ask students who show a good grasp of the affirmative commands to add some places Diana and Rita should not go to. For example: *No vayan al centro comercial Springfield porque es muy caro ir de compras allí.*

 COMUNIDADES

Los horarios

It is not uncommon to see "out to lunch" signs on storefront windows in Mexico, especially in the smaller cities. Businesses usually close during a two-hour period so that employees can go home to eat. Families usually get together for lunch, which is the biggest meal of the day, between one and three o'clock in the afternoon. After lunch, people return to work to complete their day.

Answer Key

54. En inglés se usa la forma básica del verbo y no hay diferencia entre singular o plural. Por ejemplo: *Come here, please.*

55. Answers will vary.

56. 1. Vayan a un restaurante. (c)
2. Prueben el chile con carne. (a)
3. Llamen al mesero. (f)
4. Pidan sal. (d)
5. Pidan una bebida. (b)
6. Coman un pastel de chocolate. (e)

57. Answers will vary.

58. Answers will vary.

Additional Resources

Fans Online activities
Practice Workbook

HERITAGE LANGUAGE LEARNERS

• Remind students that adjectives may change their meaning depending on whether they are used with the verb *ser* or *estar*. For instance, *la comida está sosa* means that the food is bland or lacking salt, but *Marta es sosa* means that Marta is dull. *Miguel es listo* means that Miguel is smart or clever, but *Miguel está listo* means that Miguel is ready or prepared. Have students brainstorm other adjectives that change meaning when used with *ser* and *estar*. Ask them to write a sentence with each verb and explain the difference in meaning.

TOTAL PHYSICAL RESPONSE (TPR)

• Have students work in small groups. One student in the group will give his or her group partners plural commands, and students will pantomime the actions. Have students switch the caller. For example:
A. *Pelen una papa.*
   (Group members pantomime peeling a potato.)
B. *Batan los huevos.*
   (Group members pantomime beating eggs.)
C. *Beban un vaso de agua.*
   (Group members pantomime drinking a glass of water.)

DESAFÍO 3

Comunicación

Presentation

■ In this section, students will integrate the vocabulary and grammar from *Desafío 3* in order to talk about actions in the kitchen, as well as condiments and cooking utensils. Students will also use regular and irregular affirmative plural commands.

Activities	Standards	Resources
59.	1.2, 1.3, 2.2	
60.	1.3	
61.	1.2	Audio
62. Final del desafío	1.3, 2.2	

Teaching Suggestions

Warm-Up / Independent Starter

■ Have students read the following sentences and rewrite each of them using an affirmative *ustedes* command.
1. *Poner aceite en la sartén para freír el pollo.* (*Pongan…*)
2. *Mezclar la mayonesa y la salsa de tomate.* (*Mezclen…*)
3. *Batir los huevos para el pastel.* (*Batan…*)
4. *Echar azúcar en el té.* (*Echen…*)

Preparation

■ Ask students to imagine that they are busy hot dog vendors in New York City, and they just hired several apprentices to help with the lunch crowd. Have students get into small groups and role-play the vendor and the apprentices. The vendor must tell the apprentices how to cook and dress the hot dogs in his or her own special way. You may want to invite volunteer groups to act out their skit in front of the class.

■ Take 10 minutes to review the main vocabulary and grammar themes from *Desafío 3*.

■ Refer students back to the *fotonovela* for *Desafío 3*. Have them find all of the actions in the kitchen, condiments and cooking utensils, and regular and irregular affirmative plural command forms within the dialogue. Do students understand the dialogue better now that they have gone through the vocabulary and grammar from the *Desafío*?

Comunicación

59 **Un postre delicioso**

▶ **Completa** esta receta de cocina.

mezclar	batir	echar	pelar	freír

Dulce de plátano

Ingredientes:
3 plátanos
200 gramos de azúcar
1 taza de crema
5 gramos de vainilla
50 gramos de mantequilla

Preparación:
_____1_____ los plátanos y cortarlos.
Poner mantequilla en una sartén y _____2_____ los plátanos. Colocarlos en un plato.
_____3_____ la vainilla y 100 gramos de azúcar en un bol. _____4_____ la mezcla por encima del plátano.
Poner la crema en un bol, añadir el resto del azúcar y _____5_____ bien. Echar la crema por encima del plátano.

▶ **Escribe** la receta usando la forma *ustedes* del imperativo.

60 **La escuela de cocina**

▶ **Escribe** órdenes para los alumnos de esta escuela de cocina. Usa el imperativo.
Modelo 1. *Pelen las papas.*

Differentiated Instruction

DEVELOPING LEARNERS

• Read or write the following commands on the board. Explain that each one has at least one error. Ask students to correct them.
1. *Lávense los pies antes de preparar la comida.* (las manos)
2. *Primero corten las papas y luego pélenlas.* (pelen; córtenlas)
3. *Batan los huevos después de freírlos.* (Frían; batirlos)
4. *Preparen la olla con lechuga y tomate.* (ensalada)
5. *Al final de la comida, sirvan la sopa.* (el postre)
6. *Sirvan el café con crema y sal.* (azúcar)

EXPANDING LEARNERS

• Have students review the steps to making *chile con carne*. Then have them play a chain word game. The first student begins by telling the next student the first step in the process. The second student repeats the first step and describes the second step of the recipe to the third student. The third student repeats the first two steps and adds the third step of the recipe to the next student, and so on. Players who fail to repeat the previously mentioned steps, or add an incorrect one, are out of the game.

61 La mesera nueva

▶ **Escucha.** Diana y Rita están en un restaurante. Decide si las recomendaciones de la mesera son lógicas o ilógicas.

	Lógico	Ilógico
1		
2		
3		
4		

Final del desafío

Midan bien los ingredientes.

Pica bien los chiles, Diana.

Sí. Hay que poner dos chiles y medio, tía.

Tiene buena pinta. Pruébenlo.

No, ustedes primero. Díganme si está bien.

Chile con carne

- 1/2 kilo de carne picada
- 200 gramos de cebollas
- 1 diente de ajo (garlic clove)
- 3 tomates
- 3 cucharadas de aceite
- 2 1/2 cucharaditas de chile
- 1 cucharadita de pimienta
- Sal

¡No hay tiempo!

CONCURSO ANUAL DE CHILE CON CARNE

62 ¿Qué les pasa a Diana y a Rita?

▶ **Escribe.** ¿Qué problema hay con el plato de Diana y Rita? ¿Por qué? ¿Qué pasa después? Escribe el final del desafío. Después, represéntalo con tus compañeros(as).

Activities

59. To extend this activity, ask students to write two additional versions of this recipe, using the affirmative *tú* and *usted* command forms.

60. To extend this activity, ask students to write a description of everything they see in the image. This includes the foods, how the foods are packaged, cooking utensils, and any other vocabulary students have seen so far in this unit.

61. If the statement is illogical, have students write a logical statement to replace it.

62. Ask students to get into small groups and discuss what they think will happen once the judge tastes Diana and Rita's *chile con carne*. Based on their discussion, have students answer the *Final del desafío*.

 AUDIO SCRIPT
See page 183I.

Answer Key

59. 1. Pelar 4. Echar
2. freír 5. batir
3. Mezclar

▶ Pelen los plátanos y córtenlos. Pongan mantequilla en una sartén y frían los plátanos. Colóquenlos en un plato. Mezclen la vainilla y 100 gramos de azúcar en un bol. Echen la mezcla por encima del plátano. Pongan la crema en un bol, añadan el resto del azúcar y batan bien. Echen la crema por encima del plátano.

60. Answers will vary. Sample answers:
2. Cocinen los espaguetis.
3. Frían la carne.
4. Laven las sartenes.

61. Lógico: 2, 3. Ilógico: 1, 4.

62. Answers will vary.

Additional Resources

Fans Online activities
Practice Workbook

HERITAGE LANGUAGE LEARNERS

- María says that the *chile con carne tiene buena pinta*. Ask students in what other ways they can express that something or someone looks good. Encourage them to include one-word expressions like *genial, sensacional, bárbaro, estupendo,* and *excelente*, and phrases such as *¡qué padre!, ¡qué chulada!,* and *¡está bacano!* Ask them to make a master list of these expressions and post it on the bulletin board for all to see and refer to the next time they want to describe that something or someone looks good.

CRITICAL THINKING

- Ask students what kind of food contest they would like to celebrate in their community. Ask them to explain how the food is tied to the community: Are most of the ingredients grown locally? Is there a historical or cultural connection between the food and the community? Why do students think that food contests are so popular? Ask if they would rather be the participants or the judges in these contests and have them explain their answers.

213

Unit 4
DESAFÍO 4
Comunicarse en el restaurante

Presentation

- In *Desafío 4*, Tess and Patricia are in San Pedro de Cholula, Mexico, where they must enter a pyramid to find a secret ingredient.
- In this section, students will preview:
  - Vocabulary for place settings.
  - Food descriptors and ways to prepare food.
  - Regular and irregular negative commands.
  - Negative commands with pronouns.

Activities	Standards	Resources
Fotonovela	1.2, 2.2, 3.2	Vis. Pres.
63.	1.2	
64.	1.2, 1.3	
65.	1.2	Audio
66.	1.1	
67. Cultura	1.1, 1.2, 2.2, 3.2, 4.2	
Tu desafío	1.2, 2.2, 3.2, 5.2	

Teaching Suggestions

Warm-Up / Independent Starter

- Ask students to list the questions from the *fotonovela* in their notebooks. Then have them write a command for each question. For example: *¿Qué van a comer?* → *Coman la carne de res.*

Preparation

- Read the introduction to the *fotonovela* to students. Ask them to get into groups and gather facts about Cholula and the Great Pyramid on the Internet. Once they have finished, have volunteers read some of their facts to the class.

 La fotonovela

Before Viewing

- Ask students to cover up the dialogue in the *fotonovela* and just look at the pictures. Have them guess what Tess and Patricia are saying in each scene, based on the pictures.

After Viewing

- Ask students if they correctly predicted the conversations. If not, have them add their dialogue to the *fotonovela* and act it out for the class.

214

El ingrediente secreto de Cholula

 Tess and Patricia are in San Pedro de Cholula, México, one of the oldest cities in the Americas. They will have to taste the famous *mole poblano*, and a new recipe cooked with an ancient ingredient. What is it? The answer lies within the innermost part of the Great Pyramid of Cholula.

Buenos días. ¿Qué van a comer?

De primer plato, yo quiero sopa de tortilla. Se ve deliciosa.

Y yo, unas quesadillas.

¿Qué lleva el mole poblano?

El mole es una salsa típica de esta zona. Se sirve con pollo asado.

¿Es un plato picante?

El mío tiene un sabor delicioso... ¿Qué ingrediente es?

No preguntes, Tess, tienes que descubrirlo tú sola.

El secreto está en la Gran Pirámide de Cholula.

¿Es allí arriba? ¡Vamos!

No corras, Tess. Aquello es una iglesia. La pirámide está debajo.

Continuará...

63 Detective de palabras

▶ **Completa** estas oraciones.

1. ¿Qué van a _____?
2. ¿Qué _____ el mole poblano?
3. El mole se sirve con pollo _____.
4. ¿Es un plato _____?

214 doscientos catorce

Differentiated Instruction

DEVELOPING LEARNERS

- Ask students to say whether the following sentences are true (*cierto*) or false (*falso*). Have them correct the false statements.
  1. *Tess y Patricia están en una iglesia.* (falso; están en un restaurante)
  2. *El mole es un postre.* (falso; es una salsa)
  3. *El mole poblano se sirve con pollo.* (cierto)
  4. *Tess dice que el mole es muy amargo.* (falso; tiene un sabor delicioso)
  5. *La mesera les dice dónde está el ingrediente secreto.* (cierto)

EXPANDING LEARNERS

- Ask students to paraphrase what is happening in the *fotonovela*. Then ask them:
  1. *¿Por qué crees que la pirámide es el lugar ideal para guardar el "secreto"?* (Students should see the relation in finding an ancient ingredient of pre-Columbian origin in a pre-Columbian structure such as the pyramid.)
  2. *¿Has probado mole alguna vez? ¿Te gustó? ¿Por qué? Si nunca lo has probado, ¿te gustaría probarlo? ¿Por qué?*

64 **¿Comprendes?**

▶ **Responde** a estas preguntas.

1. ¿Dónde están Tess y Patricia?
2. ¿Qué pide Tess de primer plato?
3. ¿Qué plato típico prueban?
4. ¿Dónde está la respuesta sobre el ingrediente secreto?
5. ¿Dónde está la pirámide?

65 **La iglesia y la pirámide**

▶ **Escucha** y decide si estas oraciones son ciertas o falsas.

1. Tess está nerviosa.
2. El ingrediente secreto del mole está en la iglesia.
3. La pirámide está encima de la iglesia.
4. En la pirámide hay muchos túneles.
5. A Tess no le gustan los túneles porque están muy oscuros.

66 **Tus experiencias**

▶ **Pregunta** a tu compañero(a).

1. ¿Conoces la cocina mexicana?
2. ¿Te gusta probar platos nuevos?
3. ¿Te gusta la comida picante?
4. ¿Alguna vez probaste el mole?

 **CULTURA**

El mole

Es una salsa típica de la cocina mexicana que se prepara con distintos tipos de chiles y muchas especias. Se sirve con pollo o pavo. Hay muchas variedades de mole. El más famoso es el mole poblano. Contiene más de veinte ingredientes, además del chile y el chocolate.

La palabra *mole* viene del náhuatl y significa *salsa*. Hay muchas teorías sobre el origen de este plato. Empezó a prepararse en época prehispánica y durante el periodo colonial se le añadieron ingredientes procedentes de Asia y de Europa.

67 **Piensa y explica.** ¿Qué platos conoces que combinan ingredientes de varias partes del mundo?

⚑→ **TU DESAFÍO** Visita la página web para aprender más sobre el mole poblano.

HERITAGE LANGUAGE LEARNERS

• Explain that the *Gran Pirámide de Cholula* is the largest structure built by a pre-Columbian civilization of Mesoamerica. The pyramid is 177 feet high and is the world's largest pyramid by volume. Have students research other interesting facts about this pyramid and other pyramids in Mexico. You might suggest Chichén Itzá, Teotihuacán, and the site at Comalcalco in the state of Tabasco. Ask students to prepare either a written or an oral report with images, if possible, and share their information with the class.

COOPERATIVE LEARNING

• Have students work in small groups and imagine that they are traveling with Patricia and Tess, and are trying to discover the secret ingredient in the *mole*. Ask them to work together and write a sequel to the *fotonovela* detailing their entry into the pyramid, and their possible adventures or mishaps in the miles of tunnels that lie below. Ask them to rehearse their lines and then give a performance for the rest of the class.

Comunicarse en el restaurante

Activities

66. Have students add the questions *¿cómo?* and *¿por qué?* as follow-up questions. Ask students to try to have one fluid conversation with all four questions and follow-up questions.

67. Ask students to think of ingredients that are common in the American diet, but that are not originally from the United States (e.g., mozzarella cheese from Italy, curry powder from India).

 AUDIO SCRIPT
See page 183I.

 CULTURA

El mole

The word *mole* comes from the Nahuatl word *chilmolli*, which means "chile pepper sauce." A good mole sauce should be subtle and flavors should blend smoothly so that they don't overpower the chicken or turkey with which the mole is served. There is an annual mole festival in San Pedro Atocpan, one of the boroughs of Mexico City.

Answer Key

63. 1. comer   2. lleva   3. asado   4. picante

64. Answers will vary. Sample answers:
   1. Están en un restaurante en San Pedro de Cholula, México.
   2. Tess pide unas quesadillas.
   3. Ellas prueban el mole poblano.
   4. Está en la Gran Pirámide de Cholula.
   5. La pirámide está debajo de una iglesia.

65. 1. C   2. F   3. F   4. C   5. C

66. Answers will vary.

67. Answers will vary.

Additional Resources

Fans Online activities

215

Unit 4
DESAFÍO 4

Vocabulario – En el restaurante

Presentation

- In this section, students will learn:
  - Vocabulary for place settings.
  - Food descriptors and ways to prepare food.

Activities	Standards	Resources
Vocabulario	1.2	
68.	1.2	
69.	1.2	Audio
70.	1.1	
71. Cultura	1.1, 1.2, 2.2, 3.2, 4.2, 5.2	

Teaching Suggestions

Warm-Up / Independent Starter

- Ask students to look up a recipe for *mole poblano* in English on the Internet. Then have them write a list of ingredients, how the ingredients are packaged, and how they are cooked in Spanish.

Preparation

- Go over the vocabulary presentation with students. Then draw a giant circle on the board and call on volunteers to help you set the table. As students name the different place settings, draw or have students draw them in the circle.

- Ask students to get into pairs. Have one student make a face or perform an action to represent one of the food descriptors. The other student will guess what their classmate is acting out.

- Have students write a food they associate with each food preparation method. For example: *asado → pollo*. Then invite students to share their associations with the class and tally the results on the board.

Activities

68. Complete this activity as a class. Have different volunteers read each item aloud. When they get to the blank, have the students say the word "blank" and continue to read the sentence. Once the volunteer has finished reading the sentence, ask the rest of the class to call out the answer, not just the letter.

216

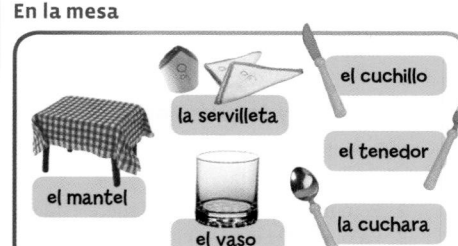

DESAFÍO 4

Vocabulario

En el restaurante

¿Van a pedir el menú del día?

Sí. Yo de primero quiero sopa de verduras. Y de segundo, carne empanada.

En la mesa

- el cuchillo
- la servilleta
- el tenedor
- el mantel
- el vaso
- la cuchara

¿Cómo está?

agrio(a)	bueno(a)
dulce	malo(a)
picante	delicioso(a)
salado(a)	caliente
soso(a)	frío(a)
amargo(a)	fresco(a)

Tráigame la cuenta, por favor.

¿Le damos una propina al mesero?

Preparación de los alimentos

frito(a)

asado(a)

a la plancha

cocido(a)/hervido(a)

empanado(a)

68 En el restaurante

▶ **Elige** la opción correcta.

1. Esta sopa está muy _____, no sabe a nada. a. sosa b. salada
2. De segundo, yo quiero carne _____. a. mala b. a la plancha
3. Pues yo voy a comer pollo _____. a. asado b. soso
4. Estas verduras son muy _____, están deliciosas. a. frías b. frescas
5. No me gusta el café, está muy _____. a. empanado b. amargo

216 doscientos dieciséis

Differentiated Instruction

DEVELOPING LEARNERS

- Ask students to choose the correct word to complete the following sentences.
  1. *Necesito un mantel / una cuchara para tomar la sopa.* (una cuchara)
  2. *Dale una servilleta / una propina al mesero.* (una propina)
  3. *Me gustan las papas empanadas / fritas.* (fritas)
  4. *Los chiles son muy agrios / picantes.* (picantes)
  5. *¡Cuidado! La sopa está muy caliente / deliciosa.* (caliente)
  6. *El café está muy empanado / dulce.* (dulce)

EXPANDING LEARNERS

- Have students complete the following word associations.
  1. *chile: picante | pan de muerto: agrio / dulce* (dulce)
  2. *sal: pimienta | cuchillo: cortar / tenedor* (tenedor)
  3. *hervir: cocido | freír: a la plancha / frito* (frito)
  4. *sal: soso | azúcar: fresco / amargo* (amargo)
  5. *pastel: dulce | limón: agrio / amargo* (agrio)
  6. *frío: caliente | soso: empanado / salado* (salado)

69 **¿Qué se dice?**

▶ **Escucha** y relaciona cada diálogo con la fotografía correspondiente.

Ⓐ

Ⓑ

Ⓒ

Ⓓ

70 **¿Cómo se prepara?**

▶ **Habla** con tu compañero(a). Nombra una comida y digan cómo se prepara.

Modelo

El arroz.

Se prepara hervido.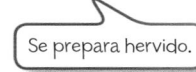

¡...o frito!

CULTURA

Los restaurantes tex-mex

La comida tex-mex representa el contacto entre la cultura estadounidense y la mexicana. Algunos ingredientes populares son los chiles, el queso, la carne, los frijoles, las tortillas y las especias.

La comida tex-mex es muy popular en el suroeste de los Estados Unidos pero hay restaurantes que la sirven en muchas partes del mundo.

71 **Piensa y habla.** ¿Es popular la comida tex-mex donde vives? ¿Te gusta? ¿Hay otros restaurantes en tu ciudad que representan una fusión de culturas?

doscientos diecisiete **217**

Unit 4

DESAFÍO 4

Vocabulario – En el restaurante

69. Once students have finished the activity, ask them to put the scenes in order. Then have them role-play the story in groups of three students.

70. Ask students to create a list of ten foods and drinks that they can mention to a classmate. Then have students get into pairs and talk about the foods they listed.

 AUDIO SCRIPT
See page 183J.

 CULTURA

Los restaurantes tex-mex

It is said that the term *Tex-Mex* comes from the abbreviation listed in the newspapers for the Texas-American Railway. Tex-Mex cuisine first surfaced in the late 19th century with the Tejanos, or Texans of Hispanic descent, but the first printed reference to Tex-Mex food didn't take place until 1945. An original dish and a staple in Tex-Mex cuisine is tortilla chips with salsa. Fajitas, chile con carne, and nachos are also Tex-Mex creations. Today, it is possible to dine in a Tex-Mex restaurant in cities such as New York, London, and Paris.

Answer Key

68. 1. a   2. b   3. a   4. b   5. b
69. 1. D   2. C   3. A   4. B
70. Answers will vary.
71. Answers will vary.

Additional Resources

Fans Online activities
Practice Workbook

HERITAGE LANGUAGE LEARNERS

• Spanish speakers have many ways of expressing that they really like something or can't stand something. For example, some might say, *¡Me encantan las espinacas!*, if they love spinach. On the other hand, if they hate spinach, they might say, *¡Detesto las espinacas!* Ask students to tell the class some other ways to communicate their likes and dislikes. For example: *¡Chévere!, ¡padrísimo!, ¡qué guay!; no tolero / soporto / aguanto…, odio / detesto / aborrezco…*

MULTIPLE INTELLIGENCES:
Verbal-Linguistic Intelligence

• Explain to students that *el menú del día* is an economic way to enjoy a first and second course, plus dessert and something to drink in many restaurants. Have students create a restaurant menu that offers several choices on its *menú del día*. Be sure students list two courses, desserts, and drinks. Have them establish the country where their restaurant is located, and include prices in the corresponding currency. They should also think of an original name for the restaurant and draw or use computer software to make an attractive menu.

217

DESAFÍO 4

Gramática – El imperativo negativo

Presentation

- In this section, students will learn:
  – Regular and irregular negative commands.
  – Negative commands with pronouns.

Activities	Standards	Resources
Gramática	3.1	
72.	1.3, 4.1	
73.	1.3	
74.	1.2, 1.3	Audio
75.	1.1	
76. Comunidades	1.1, 1.2, 2.1, 3.2, 4.2, 5.2	

Teaching Suggestions

Warm-Up / Independent Starter

- Ask students to create a five-column chart with these headings: *frito, asado, a la plancha, cocido, empanado*. Then have them list five foods under each heading that can be cooked in that manner.

Preparation

- Go over the grammar presentation with students. Clarify that not all stem-chaging verbs change in the *vosotros* negative command form. For example: *No cierres la puerta (tú). No cierre la puerta (usted). No cierren la puerta (ustedes). No cerréis la puerta (vosotros).*

- Ask students to create negative commands with the following prompts.
  Model: *comer / guisantes → Si no te gustan los guisantes, no los comas.*
  1. *Probar / carne asada*
  2. *Beber / jugo de piña*
  3. *Hervir / huevos*
  4. *Servir / frijoles*

Activities

73. Before students begin this activity, have them use the affirmative *tú* command forms to make recommendations for Diana to stay in shape.

76. Ask students to think about the people with whom they communicate. With whom are they on a first-name basis? Would this be roughly equivalent to the use of *tú* in Spanish?

Gramática

El imperativo negativo

- Use negative commands when telling someone what not to do.

  Nico, **no bebas** refrescos.   Chicos, **no coman** dulces.

IMPERATIVO NEGATIVO. VERBOS REGULARES

Caminar	Comer	Escribir	
no camin**es**	no com**as**	no escrib**as**	tú
no camin**e**	no com**a**	no escrib**a**	usted
no camin**éis**	no com**áis**	no escrib**áis**	vosotros(as)
no camin**en**	no com**an**	no escrib**an**	ustedes

Note: The usted and ustedes negative commands are the same as in the affirmative, with the word no.

Abra la puerta, por favor.
→ **No abra** la puerta.

- Some verbs have irregular negative command form:

VERBOS IRREGULARES EN EL IMPERATIVO NEGATIVO

Dar	Estar	Ir	Ser	
no des	no estés	no vayas	no seas	tú
no dé	no esté	no vaya	no sea	usted
no deis	no estéis	no vayáis	no seáis	vosotros(as)
no den	no estén	no vayan	no sean	ustedes

- Verbs that are irregular in the first person of the present tense have the same change in the negative tú, usted and ustedes command forms and, sometimes, in the vosotros(as) form.

  yo cierro → no cierres   yo digo → no digas   yo hago → no hagas
  yo vuelvo → no vuelvas   yo pido → no pidas   yo salgo → no salgas

El imperativo negativo con pronombres

- With negative commands, place object and reflexive pronouns between no and the command:

  No **lo** cocinen.   No **nos** llame.   No **te** levantes.

72 **Piensa.** En español hay formas distintas de mandatos dependiendo del grado de formalidad. ¿Hay formas distintas en inglés?

73 **Buenos hábitos**

▶ **Escribe.** ¿Qué no debe hacer Diana si quiere mantenerse en forma?
Modelo *No comas muchas papas fritas.*

Differentiated Instruction

DEVELOPING LEARNERS

- Have students play "Concentración" with negative singular and plural commands. Write commands (two of each) on small index cards and place them face-down on a desk. Have students take turns trying to match each pair as they read the command aloud. If they make a match, they get to keep their cards, but only if they say a sentence using the command. If no match is made, or if the sentence is not correct, players must return the cards. The winner is the player with the most cards when you call time.

EXPANDING LEARNERS

- Have students work with a partner and make a list of things they should *not* do in order to improve safety at their school and their classroom performance. Ask them to entitle their lists *Reglas para evitar accidentes en la escuela* and *Reglas para ser mejores estudiantes*. For example: *No corran en los pasillos. No hablen en la clase cuando la profesora habla.* Then have them get together with three other pairs of students and make a composite list. Finally, have the groups read their lists aloud to compare and contrast their rules.

74 El buen chef

▶ **Escucha** y decide si estas afirmaciones son ciertas o falsas.

1. Hay que usar siempre productos en lata.
2. No deben usar el mismo aceite muchas veces. No es saludable.
3. Es importante poner mucha sal para dar sabor a los platos.
4. Hay que cocinar los alimentos mucho tiempo.
5. Pueden guardar el pescado muchos días en el refrigerador.

▶ **Escribe** órdenes negativas a partir de las oraciones anteriores.
Usa la forma *ustedes*.

Modelo *No usen siempre productos en lata. Usen productos frescos.*

75 Consejos

▶ **Habla** con tu compañero(a). ¿Qué puedes decir a estas personas? Usa imperativos afirmativos y negativos en forma *tú* o *usted*.

Modelo una persona que tiene frío → *No comas helado. Bebe un té caliente.*

1. un(a) amigo(a) que tiene calor
2. un(a) compañero(a) de clase que va a un restaurante mexicano
3. un(a) profesor(a) que bebe mucho café
4. un(a) niño(a) que come muy poco
5. un(a) amigo(a) con dolor de estómago
6. una persona que tiene que perder peso

COMUNIDADES

¿VOSOTROS O USTEDES?

La forma *usted* se emplea para dirigirse a alguien en una situación formal. Sin embargo, con el plural *ustedes* hay algunas diferencias de uso entre los países hispanohablantes.

En las Américas y en parte de España *ustedes* se emplea tanto en situaciones formales como informales. Pero en muchas zonas de España se usa la forma *vosotros* en situaciones informales.

76 Piensa y explica. ¿Hay formas de expresar el respeto en tu idioma? ¿Cómo te diriges a alguien en una situación formal?

HERITAGE LANGUAGE LEARNERS

- Ask students to make a list of things they hear every day that tell them what not to do, and another list that the students often tell their siblings or friends not to do. Have them compare and contrast both lists. Then have them discuss what they believe is more effective: telling people what to do or telling them what *not* to do. Students should justify their opinions with concrete examples.

TOTAL PHYSICAL RESPONSE (TPR)

- Have students count off from 1 to 4 and assign each number the following categories of negative commands: 1s → *tú*, 2s → *usted*, 3s → *vosotros(as)*, 4s → *ustedes*. Then say a verb in the infinitive form and call out a number from 1 to 4. Be sure to include verbs that have irregular forms. The first student to stand up and give the corresponding command is the winner of that round and is awarded 1 point. Keep a tally of students' scores and continue playing until you call time.

DESAFÍO 4

Gramática – El imperativo negativo

 AUDIO SCRIPT
See page 183J.

 COMUNIDADES

¿Vosotros o ustedes?

Students may be familiar with *tú* and *usted*, but they may not be familiar with the word *vos* used in many parts of Latin America. *Vos* is used like *tú* when talking to a single person you know; this is called *voseo*. Several countries in the Spanish-speaking world (e.g., Argentina, Uruguay, Paraguay, most of Central America, etc.) use *vos* instead of *tú*. However, they do not use *vosotros* when talking to several people they know; they use *ustedes*.

Answer Key

72. No hay formas verbales distintas en inglés, pero la formalidad se expresa con palabras como *please, would, could,* etc.

73. Answers will vary. Sample answer:
No pases el día sentada frente al televisor.
No vayas siempre en carro.
No bebas refrescos.

74. 1. F   2. C   3. F   4. F   5. F
▶ Answers will vary.

75. Answers will vary. Sample answers:
1. No tomes un chocolate caliente, bebe una limonada.
2. No pidas una hamburguesa, pide unas enchiladas.
3. No beba tanto café, beba té.
4. No comas tan poco, come más.
5. No comas picante, bebe leche.
6. No vaya siempre en carro, camine.

76. Answers will vary.

Additional Resources

Fans Online activities
Practice Workbook

Unit 4

DESAFÍO 4

Comunicación

Presentation

- In this section, students will integrate the vocabulary and grammar from *Desafío 4* to talk about place settings, food descriptors, and different ways to prepare food. They will also use regular and irregular negative commands, and negative commands with pronouns.

Activities	Standards	Resources
77.	1.2, 1.3	Audio
78.	1.2	
79.	1.1, 1.3	
80.	1.3	
81. Final del desafío	1.2, 1.3, 2.2	
Tu desafío	1.1	

Teaching Suggestions

Warm-Up / Independent Starter

- Ask students to come up with classroom rules in Spanish. Their rules should consist of five things students should not do in Spanish class and five things students should do in Spanish class.

Preparation

- Ask students to get into small groups. Have each group use their Independent Starters to create a poster with the rules. Have groups decorate their posters to display in the classroom.

- Take 10 minutes to review the main vocabulary and grammar themes from *Desafío 4*.

- Refer students back to the *fotonovela* for *Desafío 4*. Have them find all of the words associated with place settings, food descriptors, different ways to prepare food, regular and irregular negative commands, and negative commands with pronouns within the dialogue. Do students understand the dialogue better now that they have gone through the vocabulary and grammar?

- Split the class into five groups. Have each group complete one of the *Comunicación* activities, including the *Final del desafío*. Each person in the group needs to assume a role such as recorder, speaker, etc. Once students have finished, have the speaker from each group go over the activity with the rest of the class.

220

Comunicación

77 La cena sorpresa

▶ **Escucha** a Diana. ¿Qué le sugiere Rita?

1. _____ al supermercado.
   Ve/No vayas

2. _____ una torta de chocolate.
   Haz/No hagas

3. _____ huevos con mayonesa.
   Pon/No pongas

4. _____ sopa con chiles.
   Cocina/No cocines

5. _____ a tus amigos nada sobre la cena.
   Diles/No les digas

6. _____ los platos y los vasos.
   Lava/No laves

78 ¡Mi receta va a ganar!

▶ **Completa** el diálogo con las formas *usted* de imperativo.

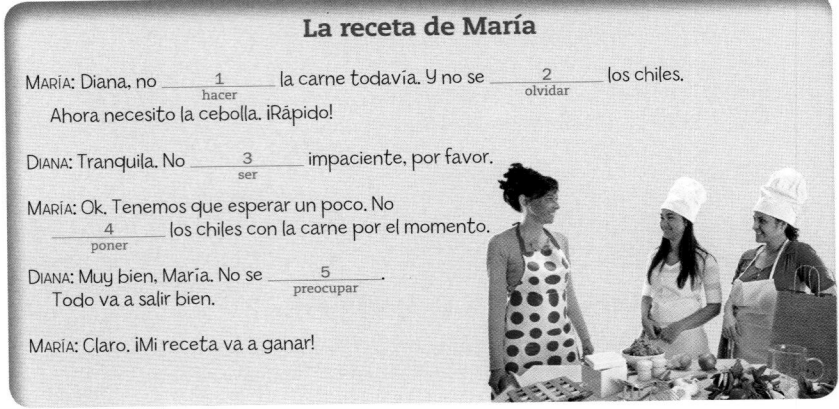

La receta de María

MARÍA: Diana, no ___1___ la carne todavía. Y no se ___2___ los chiles.
        hacer   olvidar
Ahora necesito la cebolla. ¡Rápido!

DIANA: Tranquila. No ___3___ impaciente, por favor.
                      ser

MARÍA: Ok. Tenemos que esperar un poco. No
___4___ los chiles con la carne por el momento.
poner

DIANA: Muy bien, María. No se ___5___.
                              preocupar
Todo va a salir bien.

MARÍA: Claro. ¡Mi receta va a ganar!

79 Consejos para vivir mejor

 ▶ **Habla** con tus compañeros(as). Piensen cinco problemas y escriban dos consejos para cada uno usando el imperativo negativo.

Modelo Tenemos mucha tarea cada día.
        → *Empiecen a hacer la tarea en clase.*
        → *No esperen mucho tiempo para hacer la tarea después de clase.*

Differentiated Instruction

DEVELOPING LEARNERS

- Have students read the following affirmative commands and change them to negative commands. If there are direct object pronouns, remind students where to place them.

1. *Pide más agua. (No pidas más agua.)*
2. *Ve al mercado. (No vayas al mercado.)*
3. *Haz el postre. (No hagas el postre.)*
4. *Pruébenlo. (No lo prueben.)*
5. *Diles la receta. (No les digas la receta.)*
6. *Ponla en la mesa. (No la pongas en la mesa.)*

EXPANDING LEARNERS

- Ask students to write the steps in a process. The process could be a recipe, a crafts project, a scientific experiment, or even something as simple as making a bed. Students should include both affirmative and negative commands, and decide if they will use formal or informal forms, and singular or plural forms.

- After students have completed their writing, invite some of them to read their directions aloud to the class.

80 **Mi menú**

▶ **Escribe** un menú con varios platos y descríbelos: ingredientes, forma de preparación, sabor…

▶ **Presenta** tu menú a la clase y haz recomendaciones a tus compañeros(as). Puedes usar estos verbos.

| comer | beber | elegir | pedir | probar |

Final del desafío

— 1
—i, mamá!

¡Vamos, Tess! No ___2___ tan nerviosa.

Creo que en esta cueva hay animales.

¡No me ___3___ eso!

¡Mira, mamá! ¡Ahí está la respuesta!

¿El ingrediente secreto es una bebida de los antiguos indígenas?

¡Exacto! El mole blanco lleva el jugo de una planta que se llama maguey.

¡Muchas gracias!

Gracias a ustedes. Pero, por favor, no se ___4___ sin pagar la cuenta.

81 **Un restaurante inolvidable**

▶ **Completa**. Tess y Patricia tuvieron un desafío difícil… ¡pero delicioso! Completa su diálogo con los imperativos de estos verbos.

| entrar (tú) | decir (tú) | ir (ustedes) | estar (tú) |

 **TU DESAFÍO** Visita la página web. Escuha las preguntas de tu *Minientrevista Desafío 4* y escribe las respuestas.

Activities

78. Ask students to add two more lines for Diana and two more lines for María at the end of the conversation for a classmate to fill in. Each sentence must include the infinitive form of the verb students wish to be the answer and a blank for their classmates to fill in.

80. Ask students to think about how different cultures eat food. For instance, in India many dishes are eaten with the hands. Also, in Italy people don't use a spoon to help them wrap the pasta, they use only a fork. Have students create an ethnic menu and instructions on how to eat the food.

 AUDIO SCRIPT
See page 183J.

Answer Key

77. 1. No vayas   4. Cocina
2. No hagas   5. No les digas
3. No pongas   6. Lava

78. 1. hagas   4. pongas
2. olvide   5. preocupe
3. sea

79. Answers will vary.

80. Answers will vary.
▶ Answers will vary.

81. 1. entres   3. digas
2. estés   4. vayan

Additional Resources

Fans Online activities
Practice Workbook

HERITAGE LANGUAGE LEARNERS

• Students sometimes confuse the letters *g* and *j* when writing Spanish because *g* sounds like /j/ when it is followed by *e* or *i*. Conduct the following dictation:

1. *Jorge va a hacer una gira con su conjunto musical por Argentina.*
2. *Escoge esos jitomates. ¡Son gigantes!*
3. *En general, la gente va al gimnasio para hacer ejercicio con mucha energía.*
4. *A Gerardo le gusta la geografía y la geometría, pero Jimena prefiere la ecología y la biología.*
5. *Todos los jinetes han elegido el mismo jersey.*

MULTIPLE INTELLIGENCES:
Naturalist Intelligence

• Tell students that the maguey plant, the "secret ingredient" of the *mole blanco* that Patricia and Tess were searching for, is also known as *agave* and *the century plant*, and is considered to be a "wonder" plant due to its many uses. Have students research the maguey and prepare a report that details its characteristics, where it grows, its many uses, and something about its long history, since it had been used centuries before the Europeans arrived in the Americas.

TODO JUNTO

Presentation

- In this section, students will review the unit objectives and put them into practice.

Activities	Standards	Resources
82.	1.2	Audio
83.	1.1, 1.2, 1.3, 2.2	Audio
84.	1.1, 1.3	
85.	1.1, 1.2, 1.3, 3.2	

Teaching Suggestions

Warm-Up / Independent Starter

- Ask students to turn back to the vocabulary and grammar presentations in this unit. Have them create a quick reference guide to the information in these presentations on the front and back of several note cards. This will serve as a study guide for the unit test, midterm exam, and final exam. Be sure students add this study guide to the ones from Units 1–3.

Preparation

- Ask students to imagine that they are helping to plan the reception for a cousin's wedding, but their cousin decided to fly in a caterer from Mexico to cater the reception. In small groups, have students create a dialogue and role-play the parts of the cousin and the caterer. They will need to tell the caterer what dishes are desired, where to go for the ingredients, how they are packaged, how the food will be seasoned and cooked, and they must design the place settings for the tables. Remind students to use the indefinites and affirmative and negative command forms in their conversations.
- Once students have finished, ask volunteers to reenact their roles in front of the class.

Activities

83. Ask students to choose a *primer plato*, *segundo plato*, or *postre*, and to write the ingredients and flavors in each dish. Then have them decide if this is a menu they would like. If not, then have students replace each item they do not like with an item they do like.

222

ESCUCHAR

 82 **Los chiles rellenos**

▶ **Escucha** la conversación de Rita y su hermana y decide si estas afirmaciones son ciertas o falsas.

1. A Rita no le gustan los chiles.
2. La hermana de Rita quiere la receta de los chiles rellenos.
3. Para preparar los chiles rellenos necesitan tres kilos de chiles.
4. Primero se cortan los chiles y después se pone dentro el queso.
5. Hay que freír los chiles en una sartén con mantequilla.
6. Los chiles rellenos son un plato dulce y delicioso.

 ▶ **Escucha** otra vez y corrige las afirmaciones falsas.

ESCUCHAR Y HABLAR

83 **Un restaurante auténtico**

▶ **Lee** el menú y responde a estas preguntas.

MENÚ DEL CHEF

1 primer plato + 1 segundo plato + 1 postre o café = $ 11,99

Primer plato	Segundo plato	Postre
Ensalada de aguacate	Mole poblano con pollo	Torta de chocolate
Sopa de pollo	Carne asada de res con papas	Helado
Frijoles con arroz	Tacos de pescado	Fruta
	Camarones con salsa	

1. ¿Cuántos platos comes si pides el menú del chef?
2. ¿Hay alguna sopa en el menú?
3. ¿Qué platos contienen carne?
4. ¿Hay algún plato con pescado o marisco?

 ▶ **Escucha** y escribe. ¿Qué platos del menú recomienda el mesero?

 ▶ **Habla** con tu compañero(a). ¿Qué platos le recomiendas? ¿Por qué?

222 doscientos veintidós

Differentiated Instruction

DEVELOPING LEARNERS

- Ask students to name as many foods as they can that they associate with the following:

1. *picante*	5. *dulce*
2. *soso*	6. *frío*
3. *agrio*	7. *amargo*
4. *caliente*	8. *salado*

- Then ask them to name foods that are usually packaged in the following:

1. *botella*	4. *bote*
2. *bolsa*	5. *caja*
3. *lata*	6. *paquete*

EXPANDING LEARNERS

- Ask students to write a review of a restaurant. They should consider not only the quality of the food, but the service, the décor, and the general ambiance. They will also need to mention something about the prices and information concerning the hours of operation. Encourage them to add other anecdotal information; for example, they might mention entertainment or special meals for celebrations.

HABLAR Y ESCRIBIR

 84 **¡Vamos al supermercado!**

 ▶ **Habla** con tu compañero(a). ¿Cuál es su plato favorito?
¿Qué ingredientes lleva? ¿Cómo se prepara?
Hagan una lista de la compra con todo lo necesario.

> ¿Qué lleva la
> ensalada César?

> Lleva lechuga,
> pollo, queso...

La lista de la compra
1 lechuga
150 gramos de pollo
40 gramos de queso
...

LEER, ESCRIBIR Y HABLAR

 85 **¡Vengan al restaurante Tepoztlán!**

▶ **Lee** el anuncio de un nuevo
restaurante mexicano y complétalo
con las formas de imperativo
usted de estos verbos.

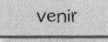

tener	venir
probar	pedir
escuchar	beber

▶ **Escribe** un anuncio similar
con tu compañero(a).

 ▶ **Habla** con tus compañeros(as).
En grupos, elijan un restaurante
para visitar y decidan
qué van a comer y a beber.

Restaurante Tepoztlán

Un restaurante para disfrutar

El restaurante Tepoztlán abre sus
puertas el próximo sábado. Disfrute
de un auténtico ambiente mexicano.

____1____ nuestros platos típicos.
____2____ o los tacos al pastor, son
nuestra especialidad. ____3____
nuestros deliciosos jugos de fruta
fresca y pida alguno de nuestros
postres típicos.

____4____ a nuestros mariachis
mientras disfruta de una auténtica
comida mexicana.

Y no ____5____ miedo al picante,
preparamos los platos a su gusto.

¡____6____ pronto! y... ¡dígaselo
a sus amigos!

doscientos veintitrés 223

HERITAGE LANGUAGE LEARNERS

- Ask students to bring in a recipe that reflects
either the cuisine of their family's country of
origin or that of a country or region with which
they are familiar. Ask them to supplement
the list of ingredients and directions with
some background information about the
dish—perhaps something about the role this
food or one of the ingredients has played in
the gastronomic history of the place, or how
this dish has been adapted to other world
cuisines.

COOPERATIVE LEARNING

- Have students work in small groups to create
an ad for a new restaurant. One student will
decide what kind of cuisine they will serve.
Another student must come up with a name
and a location. Another student will decide
which meals they will serve and the hours
of operation. Together, they should all include
some of the dishes in the ad, and some
copy that uses commands and illustrations
or photos to convince readers to try out this
new restaurant. Display their work in the
classroom.

TODO JUNTO

85. To extend this activity, have students write the
verbs in the *ustedes* command forms to make
the advertisement plural. Invite volunteers to
read the ad aloud using the *ustedes* command
forms. Ask the class which of the two command
forms they think is more effective for this type
of advertisement. Have pairs reach a decision
regarding the command form they will use (i.e.,
usted, tú, ustedes, or *vosotros*) before they start
writing their own ad. You may want to guide the
discussion by asking them to consider their
prospective customers.

 AUDIO SCRIPT
See page 183J.

Answer Key

82. 1. F   2. C   3. F   4. C   5. F   6. F
   ▶ 1. A Rita le encantan los chiles.
   3. Para preparar los chiles rellenos
      necesitan medio kilo de chiles.
   5. Hay que freír los chile en una sartén
      con aceite.
   6. Los chiles rellenos son un poco
      picantes.

83. Answers will vary. Sample answers:
   1. El menú del chef incluye dos platos
      (primer plato y segundo plato)
      y postre o café.
   2. Sí, hay una sopa de pollo.
   3. La carne asada de res con papas.
   4. Sí, los tacos de pescado y los camarones.
   ▶ 1. la ensalada de aguacate
      2. el mole poblano con pollo
      3. los tacos de pescado
      4. la tarta de chocolate
   ▶ Answers will vary.

84. Answers will vary.

85. 1. Pruebe   4. Escuche
   2. Pida   5. tenga
   3. Beba   6. Venga
   ▶ Answers will vary.
   ▶ Answers will vary.

Additional Resources

Fans Online activities
Practice Workbook

El encuentro

Presentation

- The four pairs meet in front of the *Camino Real de Tierra Adentro* Heritage Center in Santa Fe, New Mexico. There they must bring their recipes to prove the completion of their challenges.

- Students will vote for the winner of the *Desafíos* in North America.

Activities	Standards	Resources
Fotonovela	1.2, 2.1, 2.2	
86.	1.2, 1.3, 2.2	
87.	1.1, 1.2, 1.3, 5.2	

Teaching Suggestions

Warm-Up / Independent Starter

- Ask students to close their textbooks and write a summary of each pair's challenge in North America. Then have students use the vocabulary and grammar studied in this unit to talk about the *desafío* in each description.

Preparation

- Remind students that in *Desafío 1*, Tim and Mack traveled to Oaxaca, Mexico, where they had to make *pan de muerto*. In *Desafío 2*, Andy and Janet traveled to Tabasco, Mexico, where they met Amalia at the Hacienda La Luz, and looked for the oldest currency in the Americas. In *Desafío 3*, Diana and Rita traveled to San Antonio, Texas, where they prepared a *chile con carne* and entered a cook-off. In *Desafío 4*, Tess and Patricia traveled to San Pedro de Cholula, in the state of Puebla, Mexico, where they had to taste the famous *mole poblano* and find a secret ingredient inside the pyramid in Cholula.

La fotonovela

- Ask a volunteer to read the introduction to *El encuentro* aloud.

- Have students observe the pictures before they read the dialogues. Ask them to describe what each pair is doing, the food or dishes they are holding in their hands, and their facial expressions and body language. Then have students read each pair's speech bubbles silently.

El encuentro

En el Camino Real de Tierra Adentro

The pairs gather in Santa Fe, in front of the *Camino Real de Tierra Adentro* Heritage Center. The four pairs have all completed their tasks, and they have written typical Mex recipes.

224 doscientos veinticuatro

Differentiated Instruction

DEVELOPING LEARNERS

- Have students explain in their own words what each of the four pairs of participants did for their *desafío*. Encourage them to add as many details as they can. Remind them that they will use the narrative form in the third person to describe what each pair did.

EXPANDING LEARNERS

- Ask students to work in small groups to expand the participants' conversations. Then they will incorporate the new lines and role-play the new dialogues. You may call on some groups to make a presentation in front of the class.

86 Las recetas

▶ **Lee.** Las cuatro parejas llevaron sus recetas. ¿Cuál crees que corresponde a cada plato?

1. Enchiladas de pollo al mole. (Tim y Mack)
2. Pollo en salsa de chocolate. (Andy y Janet)
3. Sopa de manzana. (Diana y Rita)
4. Frijoles cocidos. (Tess y Patricia)

(A)
... lávelas, pélelas y córtelas en trozos. Échelas en un bol. Añada mantequilla sin sal, crema agria y un poco de sal y pimienta. Bata todos los ingredientes con un poco de caldo de pollo. Cocínelo diez minutos en una sartén y añada sal a la sopa.

(B)
... lávenlos y pónganlos 12 horas en un bol con agua. Échenlos en una cazuela con las especias. Cuézanlos dos horas. Después, añadan la cebolla y...

(C)
Calienta el aceite y la mantequilla en una sartén. Pon los trozos de pollo y fríelos. Corta las cebollas y échalas en la sartén. Añade el cacao y la salsa de tomate...

(D)
Coloque las tortillas en una fuente y ponga el pollo encima. Corte cebolla y añádala. Después, eche el mole y cocine todo en el horno...

▶ **Lee** otra vez las recetas. ¿En qué forma del imperativo está escrita cada una: *tú*, *usted* o *ustedes*?

Una receta de cocina tiene que incluir todos los ingredientes necesarios, las cantidades exactas y las instrucciones. Puedes escribirla en imperativo.

87 Las votaciones

▶ **Decide.** ¿Qué receta de las parejas te gusta más? ¿Por qué?

▶ **Escribe** la receta de tu plato favorito.

 ▶ **Habla** con tu compañero(a). Explícale cómo se prepara tu plato favorito y pregúntale por el suyo.

doscientos veinticinco 225

El encuentro

■ Have students look at Tim and Mack's finished product. It appears that Tim didn't complete his part of the task, but Mack saved the day. Ask students how they would feel if they were the only ones who did not complete the *desafío* and were disqualified. Ask students where Tim went wrong (when he used indefinites instead of measuring his ingredients).

■ Ask students to write a reflection letter about the importance of chocolate in the pre-Columbian times that they learned in this unit.

Activities

86. Before students match the recipes with the corresponding pair of participants, have them answer the questions below.
1. What verb form is being used in each recipe?
2. What ingredients are being used in each recipe?
3. What cooking utensils are needed to prepare each dish?
4. What is the final product of each recipe?

87. Take a class vote for the pair that completed the best recipe. Have students look over the description they wrote in their Independent Starter before they vote. If time allows, invite volunteer students to explain why they chose their winning pair.

Answer Key

86. 1. D   2. C   3. A   4. B
   ▶ A. usted   C. tú
     B. ustedes   D. usted

87. Answers will vary.
   ▶ Answers will vary.
   ▶ Answers will vary.

HERITAGE LANGUAGE LEARNERS

• Ask students to create an alternative *desafío* for one of the pairs. First, they will need to research the history of a food that originated in the Americas, or one that was brought to the New World by European explorers, and the role this food has had on the culture of a country or region. Students should also show how this food is used in typical dishes. Or, they might explore celebrations associated with this food, much like *el pan de muerto* is associated with *el Día de Muertos*.

CRITICAL THINKING

• Ask students to think of the *desafíos* the characters have completed in this unit. Then ask them which one they would best be suited to complete if they were handed these challenges. Which one would they be least likely to complete well? They will need to examine their strengths and weaknesses to answer these questions, and they will have to justify their answers.

225

MAPA CULTURAL

Norteamérica

Presentation

- This section presents Mexico and the Hispanic heritage of the United States. The map of North America serves as a reference point for additional cultural readings and activities.

Activities	Standards	Resources
Mapa cultural	1.2, 2.1, 3.1, 3.2	Video
88.	1.2, 1.3, 3.1	
89.	3.1	

Cultural Topics

- **El Camino Real de Tierra Adentro.** This route was used for about 300 years, from the mid-16th to the 19th centuries. Although its objectives were commercial—to transport silver extracted from Mexican mines and mercury imported from Europe—it also promoted an active cultural and social exchange among the Spaniards, indigenous peoples, and American colonists. Towns, forts, missions, and hacienda estates sprouted up along the Camino, facilitating the emergence of a distinctive culture along the route.

- **Los chicanos.** The Chicano movement developed over a long period of time, but it gained national recognition during the 1960s and 1970s. The movement worked to combat discrimination against Chicanos in public and private institutions, as well as to create an awareness of the distinctive cultural identity of Chicanos in the United States. The movement also fostered a renaissance in the arts. Novels such as *Bless Me, Ultima* (1972) by Rudolfo Anaya and *House on Mango Street* (1984) by Sandra Cisneros, as well as the mural *Great Wall of Los Angeles* by Judy Baca, are some well-known examples.

Teaching Suggestions

Warm-Up / Independent Starter

- Have students complete the following sentences with information they know about Mexico and the United States.
  - … es un plato de la comida tex-mex.
  - En el estado mexicano de… se produce mucho cacao.
  - El Álamo se encuentra en…
  - … es una celebracón mexicana.

MAPA CULTURAL

Nacionalidades
Estados Unidos → estadounidense
México → mexicano(a)

México, la Florida y el suroeste de los Estados Unidos pertenecieron a la corona española desde el siglo XVI hasta el siglo XIX. Por eso, California, Arizona, Nevada, Utah, Colorado, Nuevo México, Texas y Florida comparten con México las raíces hispanas. Los nombres de algunos lugares muestran ese origen hispano.

México, con 112 millones de habitantes, es hoy el país con más hablantes de español del mundo. Le siguen los Estados Unidos con 50,5 millones de hispanos, la mayoría de origen mexicano, según datos de la Oficina del Censo del año 2010. De ellos, unos 40 millones hablan normalmente español.

¿Sabías que el nombre oficial de México es *Estados Unidos Mexicanos*?

88 **Lugares con nombre hispano**

▶ **Escribe** el nombre de varios lugares de los Estados Unidos con nombre hispano.

Modelo *Florida, Colorado…*

Differentiated Instruction

DEVELOPING LEARNERS

- Have students identify on a map of North America two countries mentioned in the *Mapa cultural*. Then ask students to identify and label the following states: California, Arizona, Nevada, Colorado, New Mexico, Texas, and Florida. Ask them to create a profile of each of these states with both the total population of the state and the Hispanic population. A good reference source is the U.S. Census Bureau (http://www.census.gov/). Ask students to also include their own state if it is not one of the states above. Then have students present their findings to the class.

EXPANDING LEARNERS

- Divide students into small groups and assign each group one of the following Mexican-American personalities. Ask them to research their assigned person and write a brief report to present to the class.
  - César Chávez (civil rights activist)
  - Gloria Anzaldúa (author)
  - Carlos Santana (musician)
  - Gilbert "Magú" Luján (artist)
  - Lorna Dee Cervantes (poet)
  - José M. Hernández (astronaut)
  - "Cheech" Marin (comedian)
  - Romualdo Pacheco (politician)

1. El Camino Real de Tierra Adentro

Durante la época colonial, los españoles crearon
o ampliaron caminos en el territorio que hoy
ocupan México, la Florida y los estados del
suroeste de los Estados Unidos. El más
importante es el Camino Real de Tierra
Adentro, que une Santa Fe con Ciudad de
México. Este camino fue una vía de intercambio
económico y cultural.

Mapa del virreinato de Nueva España (1767)

Día del Parque Chicano (San Diego).

2. Los chicanos

La palabra *chicano* proviene de *mexicano*.
Los chicanos son ciudadanos de los Estados
Unidos descendientes de mexicanos.
La cultura chicana es una mezcla
de las culturas estadounidense
y mexicana con características propias.

89 **El Camino Real**

▶ **Copia** la ruta del Camino
Real y sitúa en ella estas
ciudades.

- Alburquerque
- Santa Fe
- Aguascalientes
- Ciudad de México
- El Paso

Preparation

- Explain that trade, movement of people, and
cultural exchanges between the United States and
Mexico have existed since pre-Hispanic times.
They continued during Mexico's colonial period
and into today. In fact, recognizing the great level
of economic interdependence and large volume
of trade that exists between Mexico, the United
States, and Canada, the North American Free
Trade Agreement (NAFTA) was implemented in
1994. As an example of the importance of this
trade, it is worth noting that Mexico is the second-
largest supplier of oil to the United States, after
Canada. Mexico is also the second-largest export
market for the United States (the first is Canada).

- The U.S.-Mexico border is one of the most dynamic
borders in the world. Nearly one million people and
one billion dollars' worth of commerce cross this
border each day. Four states on the American side
and six on the Mexican side share 1,950 miles of
the border, or *La Línea*, as it is known in Mexico.
From the Gulf Coast to El Paso, TX, the border
follows the Rio Grande (*río Bravo* in Mexico).

Activities

88. Have students work in seven small groups.
Assign one of the states listed in the *Mapa
cultural* (California, Arizona, Nevada, Colorado,
New Mexico, Texas, and Florida) to each group.
Then ask students to look at a detailed map
of their assigned state and list the names of
towns and geographical features that they find
in Spanish. Which group has the longest list?

Answer Key

88. Answers will vary. Sample answers:
Florida, Nevada, El Álamo, San Francisco,
Santa Bárbara, Las Vegas
▶ Answers will vary.

89. Santa Fe, Albuquerque, El Paso,
Aguascalientes, Ciudad de México

Additional Resources

Fans Online activities
Practice Workbook

HERITAGE LANGUAGE LEARNERS

- Have students research a famous person
(e.g., an artist, writer, singer, sport personality,
politician, etc.) from their country of origin
who has excelled in the United States.
Ask students to focus on this person's
contributions to American society, as well
as his or her role in bridging the Latino and
Anglo communities.

- Ask students to create a report about this
person. They should include a picture, some
biographical information, and a list of works
or accomplishments for which this person is
best known.

MULTIPLE INTELLIGENCES:
Verbal-Linguistic Intelligence

- Ask pairs of students to expand on activity 88.
Have them research a list of 20 Spanish place
names in the United States. They should
include names of cities and towns, as well as
geographical features. Once pairs have their
list, ask them to look up the meaning of words
they don't understand. Then have them classify
the place names in a graphic organizer in a way
that makes sense to them. Possible categories
include, plant and animal names, names of
saints, descriptive words, place names in
Spanish-speaking countries, etc.

LECTURA

La receta del guacamole

Presentation

- In this section, students will increase their understanding of Mexican culture by reading a recipe for a typical Mexican dip. In addition, students will focus on recognizing the structure and language of instructional texts.

Activities	Standards	Resources
Lectura	1.2, 2.1, 2.2, 3.1, 3.2	
90.	1.2, 2.1, 2.2	
91.	1.3, 2.1, 2.2	
92.	1.3, 3.1	
Tu desafío	1.2, 1.3	

Teaching Suggestions

Warm-Up / Independent Starter

- Ask students to look at the text features (title, image, caption, headings, and subheadings) of the reading. Have them take an educated guess about the information they will encounter in this reading.

Preparation

- Ask students what the reading strategies were in the previous units. (Identify the global idea; identify the main idea and the most important details; make inferences.) Then point out the Reading Strategy box and ask a volunteer to read it aloud.

- Ask students what they think is the objective of this text. (To explain how to make guacamole.) Have them note the format used to achieve this objective: ingredients are listed first, imperative verb forms are used for the preparation instructions, advice and additional information are offered at the end.

- To introduce the reading, you may want to give students some background information. Explain that guacamole has existed since pre-Hispanic times. In fact, the term comes from Nahuatl *ahuacamolli* (i.e., *ahuacatl* = avocado + *molli* = sauce). There are several varieties of avocados but Hass, which in North America is produced in Mexico and California, is considered the best variety for guacamole. The lime juice helps preserve the color of the avocado. However, the guacamole should be eaten right away. In Mexico, the guacamole is usually prepared in a *molcajete*, a traditional Mexican mortar made of lava stone.

LECTURA

Plato e ingredientes del guacamole.

La receta del guacamole

Read instructional texts

Instructional texts are those that contain rules or instructions to do something.

Recognizing the structure and characteristic language of instructional texts can help you understand them better.

The main characteristics of instructional texts are:

- They main have a practical objective. For example, to prepare a meal or to turn on electrical appliances.

- In order to achieve that objective, they outline a clear, concise sequence of actions.

- These actions are normally listed as commands or using the forms *tener que*, or *hay que*, or the infinitive.

Puebla, 28 de octubre de 2011

Querido nieto:

¿Cómo estás? ¿De verdad vas a preparar guacamole para la fiesta de la escuela? ¡Qué bien! El guacamole es una salsa mexicana muy popular y muy fácil de preparar. ¡Con los tacos y con la carne está delicioso! Aquí tienes la receta:

Guacamole

Ingredientes:

2 aguacates[1] maduros
1 chile serrano
80 gramos de tomates
40 gramos de cebolla

1 diente de ajo
Unas hojas de cilantro fresco
Sal
El jugo de medio limón

Preparación:

1.° Corta los tomates en cubos pequeños, pica la cebolla, el ajo y el cilantro. Pon cada cosa en un bol.
2.° Pela los aguacates y aplástalos[2] con un tenedor.
3.° Muele[3] el chile y añade la sal.
4.° Mezcla el aguacate con el chile molido y con el tomate.
5.° Añade a la mezcla la cebolla, el ajo, el cilantro y el jugo de limón.

Recuerda que si lo quieres más picante, tienes que poner más chiles.

¡Mucha suerte con la receta y disfruta!

Muchos besos.

Tu abuela

_____
1. avocados   2. mash them   3. Crush

Differentiated Instruction

DEVELOPING LEARNERS

- Conduct a guided reading of the text. Have different volunteers read the text sentence by sentence. As they pause between sentences, ask them yes / no questions to check their comprehension. For example:
  - ¿La abuela va a preparar el guacamole? (no)
  - ¿El guacamole es de México? (sí)
  If students get an answer wrong, have them read the sentence again. If students don't yet understand the sentence, restate it in Spanish using simpler language. Do not translate the sentence into English, but rather continue to explain it in Spanish.

EXPANDING LEARNERS

- Have students work with a partner to role-play this recipe. Ask them to imagine that they are two celebrity chefs who have a TV show where they cook live (e.g., *Mexico: One Plate at a Time* with Rick Bayless). If students have access to video recording equipment, you may want to ask them to video tape their performance as if it were a live TV show. Have pairs of students perform for the class, or ask them to play the video they recorded.

90 Sobre el guacamole

▶ **Decide** si estas afirmaciones son ciertas o falsas.

1. Los mexicanos no comen los tacos con guacamole.
2. El guacamole combina bien con la carne.
3. El ingrediente principal del guacamole es el aguacate.
4. El guacamole es picante porque lleva chiles.

91 Para hacer guacamole

▶ **Escribe** la acción correspondiente a cada imagen en infinitivo. Después, ordena las imágenes de acuerdo con la receta del guacamole.

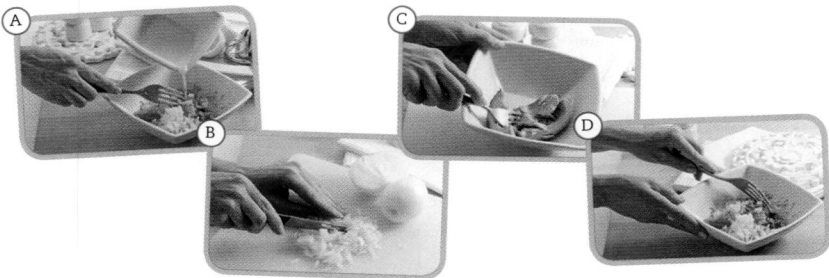

ESTRATEGIA **Leer textos prescriptivos**

92 La receta

▶ **Completa** un esquema como este con los pasos de la receta. Puedes utilizar las formas *hay que*, *tener que*, o el imperativo.

- Primero, tienes que cortar los tomates, la cebolla, el ajo y el cilantro.
- Después,
- A continuación,
- Luego,
- Por último,

→ TU DESAFÍO | Visita la página web para aprender otra receta mexicana.

doscientos veintinueve **229**

HERITAGE LANGUAGE LEARNERS

• Have students create their own instructional text with a recipe from their country of origin. First, ask them to research, on the Internet or by talking with family members, several dishes from their heritage culture. Then have them choose one dish to write the instructional text about. Have students consider the ease of preparation and of finding the ingredients in local supermarkets when they make their choice. They should also include some background information about the origin of the dish. Invite students to share their recipe with the class.

CRITICAL THINKING

• Explain that avocados originated in Mexico. They were cultivated and eaten by different pre-Hispanic groups thousands of years before the arrival of the Europeans. Today, this fruit is grown in practically every tropical and subtropical region of the world.

• Have students look at a world map and ask them to trace the route they imagine the spread of avocados took. Where do they think the avocado was taken first? Why? Where did it spread to next? Etc. Once students have traced their avocado route, ask them to research the topic. How accurate was their route?

LECTURA
La receta del guacamole

Activities

91. Once students have listed the instructions in the infinitive verb form and have put them in order, have them rewrite the instructions in the *ustedes* imperative form.

92. Have students read the beginning of the letter again, where the grandmother explains why she is sharing this recipe with her grandson. Then ask students to add four instructions to tell what to do next, once the guacamole has been prepared. Have students use the imperative *tú* form, both in the affirmative and negative forms. For example:

– No le pongas más chiles y así todos pueden comerlo.
– Sírvelo con totopos (tortilla chips).

Answer Key

90. 1. Falso 3. Cierto
2. Cierto 4. Cierto

91. A. Añadir el jugo de limón.
B. Picar la cebolla.
C. Aplastar los aguacates.
D. Mezclar los ingredientes.
Orden: B, C, D, A.

92. Answers will vary. Sample answers:
Primero, tienes que cortar los tomates y picar la cebolla y el cilantro.
Después, hay que pelar y aplastar los aguacates.
A continuación, tienes que moler el chile y añadir la sal.
Luego, hay que mezclar el aguacate con el chile molido y con el tomate.
Por último, añade a la mezcla la cebolla, el ajo, el cilantro y el jugo de limón.

Additional Resources

Fans Online activities

REPASO

Vocabulario

Presentation

- In this section, students will review all key vocabulary from the unit, organized by themes, to prepare for an assessment. Students will complete practice activities for each of the four *Desafíos*.

Activities	Standards	Resources
1.	1.2, 3.1	
2.	1.2	
3.	1.3	
4.	1.2, 1.3	

Teaching Suggestions

Warm-Up / Independent Starter

- Ask students to list the foods they eat in a typical week for breakfast, lunch, and dinner in a table like the one below.

Desayuno	Almuerzo	Cena
cereal con leche	hamburguesa	espaguetis con queso

Preparation

- Ask students to classify the foods they recorded in the Independent Starter into the following categories: *Lácteos, Cereales y legumbres, Pescados y mariscos, Carnes, Frutas y verduras, Otros*.

- Then have students work with a classmate to discuss their eating habits. Have each student imagine that he or she is a nutritionist who is analyzing his or her partner's eating habits. Are they eating a well-balanced diet? If not, what foods should they eat more of? What foods or beverages should they eat less of? Does the partner agree with the assessment?

- Ask students to switch partners and have them take turns calling out a food. The other partner should say where, on a menu, they would find this food and describe the most salient characteristic of this food. For example:
  A. *el melón*
  B. *postre; es dulce*

- As a class, go over the *Vocabulario* review. You may want to conduct an echo reading to practice the pronunciation of the words.

230

REPASO Vocabulario

Los alimentos

Los pescados y mariscos
el atún	tuna
los camarones	shrimp
el salmón	salmon

Los cereales
el arroz	rice
el pan	bread
la pasta	pasta

La carne
de cerdo	pork
de pollo	chicken
de res	beef

Las legumbres
los frijoles	beans
los guisantes	peas
las lentejas	lentils

Los lácteos
la leche	milk
la mantequilla	butter
el queso	cheese
el yogur	yogurt

Las frutas
las fresas	strawberries
el melón	melon
la pera	pear
la piña	pineapple
la sandía	watermelon
las uvas	grapes

Las verduras y hortalizas
el ajo	garlic
la cebolla	onion
las espinacas	spinach
la lechuga	lettuce
el tomate	tomato
la zanahoria	carrot

Comprar comida

la lista de la compra	shopping list	**Acciones**	
el litro	liter	comprar	to buy
el kilo	kilogram	costar	to cost
el precio	price	hacer cola/fila	to stand in li
		hacer la compra	to shop
Los envases		pedir	to ask for
la bolsa	bag	pesar	to weigh
el bote	can	vender	to sell
la botella	bottle		
la caja	box		
la lata	can		
el paquete	package		
el tarro	jar		

En la cocina

Utensilios		**Acciones**			
la bandeja	tray	asar	to roast	hervir	to b
el bol	bowl	batir	to beat	mezclar	to m
la cazuela	casserole dish	cocer	to boil	pelar	to pe
la jarra	pitcher	cortar	to cut		
la olla	pressure cooker	echar	to put		
la sartén	frying pan	freír	to fry		

Condimentos
el aceite	oil	la pimienta	pepper
el azúcar	sugar	la sal	salt
la mayonesa	mayonnaise	la salsa de tomate	tomato sauce
la mostaza	mustard	el vinagre	vinegar

En el restaurante

		Preparación de los alimentos	
la cuenta	check	a la plancha	grilled
el menú del día	specials	asado(a)	roasted
el primer plato	appetizer	cocido(a)/hervido(a)	boiled
el segundo plato	entrée	empanado(a)	breaded
el postre	dessert	frito(a)	fried
la propina	tip		

¿Cómo está?				**En la mesa**	
agrio(a)	sour	fresco(a)	fresh	la cuchara	spoon
amargo(a)	bitter	frío(a)	cold	el cuchillo	knife
bueno(a)	good	malo(a)	bad	el mantel	tableclo
caliente	hot	picante	hot (spicy)	la servilleta	napkin
delicioso(a)	delicious	salado(a)	salty	el tenedor	fork
dulce	sweet	soso(a)	tasteless	el vaso	glass

230 doscientos treinta

Differentiated Instruction

DEVELOPING LEARNERS

- Have students create word webs with the vocabulary. They can organize the words following a similar criterion to the one used in this section or they can organize them in a way that makes sense to them. For example, they could organize the foods by how they are usually packed (e. g., *bote, lata, caja*), or by the mealtimes when they are usually consumed (*desayuno, almuerzo...*), etc.

- Once students have finished, ask them to swap word webs with a classmate. Can they tell which criterion their partner used to organize the vocabulary?

EXPANDING LEARNERS

- Have students analyze the vocabulary list to see where they can add more words. For example: *el acompañante* (side dish) under "En el restaurante," *la cucharilla* (teaspoon) under "En la mesa," *libra* (pound) under "Comprar comida," *revolver* (to stir) under "Acciones," etc.

- Then have students work with a partner to see which words each of them have added to the *Vocabulario*. Ask them to quiz each other verbally. For example:
  – *La usamos para revolver el café.*
  – *La cucharilla.*

DESAFÍO 1

1 **Un almuerzo especial.** Clasifica estos ingredientes.

entrantes 	platos principales 	postres 
ensalada		

salmón   fresas
espinacas   ensalada
carne de res   helado
sopa   atún
yogur   pollo

DESAFÍO 2

2 **Envases.** Relaciona cada envase con la fotografía correspondiente.

1. un tarro
2. una caja
3. una botella
4. una lata

(A)   (B)   (C)   (D)

DESAFÍO 3

3 **¡Vamos a cocinar!** Completa estas oraciones.

pelar
vinagre
hervir
sartén
azúcar

1. A esta ensalada le falta un poco de ___1___.
2. Primero tienes que ___2___ las papas y luego freírlas.
3. Vamos a ___3___ la pasta en esta cazuela.
4. Este postre no tiene mucho ___4___, no está muy dulce.
5. Echa el huevo en la ___5___.

DESAFÍO 4

4 **¿Frito o empanado?** Responde a las siguientes preguntas.

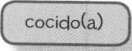 cocido(a)   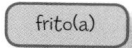 frito(a)   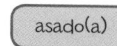 asado(a)   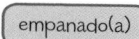 empanado(a)

Modelo ¿Cómo preparas las verduras? → *Las preparo cocidas.*

1. ¿Cómo preparas el pollo?
2. ¿Cómo preparas los huevos?
3. ¿Cómo preparas la pasta?

Activities

1. Ask students to specify which utensil(s) they would need to eat each of these foods. If they don't need any specific utensil, as in the case of a fruit, have them explain how they would eat it (i.e., *se come con la mano*).

3. Once students have finished this activity, ask them to get together with a partner. Have partners take turns calling out a food; the other partner should mention an action associated with the food. For example:
   A. *la sandía*
   B. *cortar*

4. Ask students to think of something they eat that is fried, something that is broiled, something that is boiled, and something that is eaten raw (*crudo*). Have them write a sentence where they explain this. For example: *Como los huevos fritos, la carne a la plancha, las verduras hervidas y la fruta cruda.*

Answer Key

1. Entrantes: ensalada, espinacas, sopa.
   Platos principales: salmón, carne de res, atún, pollo.
   Postres: yogur, fresas, helado.

2. 1. A   2. C   3. D   4. B

3. 1. vinagre   4. azúcar
   2. pelar   5. sartén
   3. hervir

4. Answers will vary. Sample answers:
   1. Lo preparo empanado.
   2. Los preparo fritos.
   3. La preparo cocida.

Additional Resources

Fans Online activities
Practice Workbook

HERITAGE LANGUAGE LEARNERS

• This might be a good opportunity to have students from different cultural backgrounds—not just Spanish speakers—think of some food traditions associated with their heritage culture. Ask them to think of the food, the utensils used to cook the food and to eat it, the spices added to the food, how the food is prepared, the flavors and textures of this food, etc.

• Then have students do a brief presentation (in Spanish) for the rest of the class. If time allows, hold a question and answer session at the end of each presentation.

MULTIPLE INTELLIGENCES:
Intrapersonal Intelligence

• Have students analyze their Independent Starter and the classification they did for the Preparation activity. What can they do to improve what they eat and the way they eat it?

• Ask students to come up with a realistic plan to introduce positive changes in their eating habits. They should list the things they think that they can realistically change and give themselves a time frame. Then have students date their list and keep it for future reference and progress follow-up.

REPASO

Gramática

Presentation

- Students will review grammatical structures presented in the unit. Each grammar point is cross-referenced to the corresponding page on which it was introduced. The activities provide systematic practice by *Desafío*.

Activities	Standards	Resources
5.	1.3	
6.	1.3	
7.	1.3	
8.	1.3	
9. Cultura	1.2, 1.3, 2.1, 2.2	

Teaching Suggestions

Warm-Up / Independent Starter

- Have students write down five recommendations for fostering the learning of Spanish in their Spanish classroom. Ask them to include three affirmative and two negative recommendations, using the *ustedes* form of the verb.

Preparation

- Divide the class into small groups and have them discuss their suggestions from the Independent Starter. Then have each group choose the four recommendations they find most useful and create a group list on chart paper. Have groups present their lists to the class.

- Divide the class into four groups and assign a grammar theme to each group. As you go over the *Repaso* presentation, ask each group for two examples that illustrate their grammar theme.

Activities

8. Ask students to work with a partner to come up with a list of etiquette rules for a classmate who is attending a very formal dinner. Ask them to use the *tú* form of the verbs as well as affirmative and negative commands. For example:
   – *Lleva saco y corbata.*
   – *No pongas los codos en la mesa.*
   Ask pairs to share some of their suggestions with the class. Does the class agree or do they think some of these rules are excessive?

REPASO Gramática

Expresar cantidad. Los indefinidos (pág. 194)

ningún, ninguno(a)	no, (not) any, none	mucho(a), muchos(as)	many, a lot of
algún, alguno(a),		todo(a), todos(as)	all, every, throughout
algunos(as)	a few, any, one, some	demasiado(a),	
poco(a), pocos(as)	some, few	demasiados(as)	too much, too many

El imperativo afirmativo (pág. 202 y 210)

IMPERATIVO REGULAR

CAMINAR	COMER	ESCRIBIR	
camina	come	escribe	tú
camine	coma	escriba	usted
caminad	comed	escribid	vosotros(as)
caminen	coman	escriban	ustedes

IRREGULARIDADES ESPECIALES

TENER	HACER	PONER	VENIR	SALIR	SER	DECIR	IR	DAR	
ten	haz	pon	ven	sal	sé	di	ve	da	tú
tenga	haga	ponga	venga	salga	sea	diga	vaya	dé	usted
tened	haced	poned	venid	salid	sed	decid	id	dad	vosotros(as)
tengan	hagan	pongan	vengan	salgan	sean	digan	vayan	den	ustedes

El imperativo negativo (pág. 218)

IMPERATIVO NEGATIVO REGULAR

CAMINAR	COMER	ESCRIBIR	
no camines	no comas	no escribas	tú
no camine	no coma	no escriba	usted
no caminéis	no comáis	no escribáis	vosotros(as)
no caminen	no coman	no escriban	ustedes

IRREGULARIDADES ESPECIALES

DAR	ESTAR	IR	SER	
no des	no estés	no vayas	no seas	tú
no dé	no esté	no vaya	no sea	usted
no deis	no estéis	no vayáis	no seáis	vosotros(as)
no den	no estén	no vayan	no sean	ustedes

Differentiated Instruction

DEVELOPING LEARNERS

- For further practice with the irregular formal and informal imperative forms, ask students to complete the following sentences.
  1. [*Hacer – tú*, affirmative] *las tareas todos los días.* (*Haz*)
  2. [*Ir – usted*, negative] *a ese restaurante, no es bueno.* (*No vaya*)
  3. [*Tener – tú*, affirmative] *paciencia con tus amigos.* (*Ten*)
  4. [*Poner – ustedes*, negative] *tanta sal en la comida.* (*No pongan*)

EXPANDING LEARNERS

- Have students get together with a partner. Ask them to imagine that they are in the school cafeteria during lunchtime, and have students exchange recommendations regarding food. Remind students to use direct and indirect object pronouns when necessary. For example:
  A. *No me gustan las cosas muy dulces.*
  B. *Come fruta de postre.*
  B. *¡Puaj! Estas papas están sosas.*
  A. *Ponles un poco de sal.*

DESAFÍO 1

5 **¿Cuántos hay?** Mira los dibujos y escribe oraciones con indefinidos.

Modelo 1. *Hay muchas manzanas.*

 ① 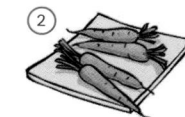 ②  ③  ④

 DESAFÍO 2

6 **Instrucciones.** Escribe las instrucciones que una madre da a su hijo.

Modelo Comer el pollo. → *Come el pollo. Cómelo.*

1. Beber el jugo de naranja.
2. Poner los sándwiches en la mesa.
3. Preparar la mochila.
4. Decir la verdad.

 DESAFÍO 3

7 **Sugerencias.** Une las dos columnas y escribe recomendaciones con la forma *ustedes*.

Modelo Nos gusta el pescado. → *Pidan el salmón con papas.*

1. Tenemos sed.
2. Queremos un postre ligero.
3. Nos gusta mucho la pasta.

a. probar el helado de melón
b. comer los espaguetis con salsa de tomate
c. beber té frío con limón

 DESAFÍO 4

8 **Consejos.** Usa el imperativo negativo y escribe oraciones con lo que no deben hacer estas personas.

Modelo Tus hermanos están corriendo por el pasillo. → *No corran por el pasillo.*

1. Hace calor y tus padres están cerrando las ventanas.
2. Tu hermano pone dos cuadernos encima de tu cama.
3. Tu prima quiere alimentarse bien y está comiendo helado de chocolate.

 **CULTURA**

9 **En Norteamérica.** Responde a las siguientes preguntas.

1. ¿Cómo se celebra el Día de Muertos en México?
2. ¿Qué alimento utilizaron los mayas como moneda?
3. ¿Qué sabes sobre El Álamo?
4. ¿Qué es el mole?

doscientos treinta y tres **233**

Gramática

9. Answer these questions as a class. Encourage different students to add different pieces of information to each answer. If there are students who know more about one of the topics, invite them to share what they know with the class.

Answer Key

5. 2. Hay algunas zanahorias.
3. Hay pocos tomates.
4. Hay algunos huevos.

6. 1. Bebe el jugo de naranja. Bébelo.
2. Pon los sándwiches en la mesa. Ponlos.
3. Prepara la mochila. Prepárala.
4. Di la verdad. Dila.

7. 1. c – Beban té frío con limón.
2. a – Prueben el helado de melón.
3. b – Coman los espaguetis con salsa de tomate.

8. 1. No cierren las ventanas.
2. No pongas los cuadernos encima de la cama.
3. No comas helado de chocolate.

9. Answers will vary. Sample answers:
1. La gente va al cementerio a llevar flores. Además, los familiares preparan altares con una fotografía de la persona difunta y los llenan de flores, velas y comida.
2. La semillas del cacao.
3. El Álamo está en San Antonio, Texas. Originalmente fue una misión y luego una fortaleza. Fue la fortaleza más importante en la Revolución de Texas. Hoy es un museo.
4. Es una salsa típica mexicana que se prepara con distintos tipos de chiles y muchas especias. El más famoso es el mole poblano que tiene más de veinte ingredientes.

Additional Resources

Fans Online activities
Practice Workbook

HERITAGE LANGUAGE LEARNERS

• Ask students to prepare a presentation about the usage of *tú* and *usted* to help their classmates determine when to use the *tú* and *usted* imperative forms. Remind students that there are differences among different Spanish-speaking countries, but as a general rule, they can use the informal forms under roughly the same circumstances they would use a person's first name in English.

• Invite students to share their information with the class and to include examples of *tú* and *usted* imperative forms in different situations.

TOTAL PHYSICAL RESPONSE (TPR)

• Have students play "Simon Says" ("Simón dice") with the negative and affirmative *ustedes* imperative forms. You may want to divide the class into an even number of groups. Be sure there are students of different skills and levels in each group, and have each group act as a team to play against another group. Stress the importance of speaking clearly and pronouncing the words carefully.

• You may want to allow students to use flashcards for the verb forms in the first couple of rounds. Then, as the game progresses, they should do without the cards.

PROYECTO

Ingredientes americanos

Presentation

- In this section, students will apply the vocabulary, grammar, and cultural information they have learned in this unit to create a dish made with indigenous American ingredients. Students will follow step-by-step instructions.

Activities	Standards	Resources
Paso 1	1.2, 2.2, 3.1	
Paso 2	1.3, 2.2, 3.1, 5.2	
Paso 3	1.1, 1.3, 5.2	
Paso 4	1.1, 1.3, 2.2, 5.2	

Teaching Suggestions

Warm-Up / Independent Starter

- Ask students to think of typical Thanksgiving fare (e.g., turkey, squash, sweet potatoes, cranberries, corn on the cob, pumpkin pie, etc.), and have them list the ingredients for the different dishes.

Preparation

- Have students exchange their list from the Independent Starter with a classmate. Do they have similar foods? Ask partners to determine which of the products they listed are indigenous to the Americas. If they are not sure, ask them to research the food on the Internet.
- Ask students to start a list of indigenous American foods with the information from the previous activity. This is a partial list: corn, tomatoes, peppers, potatoes, sweet potatoes, cassava, beans, pumpkins, squash, avocados, jicama (yam bean), cacao, papaya, pineapple, guava, blueberries, cranberries, cherimoya, passion fruit, prickly pear, pecans, peanuts, vanilla, maple syrup, sunflower, turkey.

Step-by-Step Instructions

Paso 1

- Have students add to the list they started in the Preparation section. They will find an interesting essay and program about indigenous American foods at: http://www.pbs.org/kcet/when-worlds-collide/essays/the-journey-of-new-world-foods.html. You may assign this step as homework the day before the activity is scheduled.
- Encourage students to use ingredients that are relatively easy to find in local supermarkets.

234

Un menú con

ingredientes americanos

In this project you will create a dish made with an indigenous American ingredient in the recipe. After you create the dish individually, you will come together as a group to share your dishes and to create a menu. *¡Buen provecho!*

PASO 1 **Decide qué plato vas a hacer**

- Research native American foods and ingredients in order to decide which dish you will prepare. Use these questions to guide you:
  - –¿Qué alimentos de origen americano conoces?
  - –¿Cuáles prefieres?
  - –¿Cómo se llaman esos alimentos en español?
  - –¿Qué vas a preparar: un primer plato, un plato principal, un postre?
  - –¿Qué plato vas a cocinar?

PASO 2 **Busca la receta**

- Research recipes for the type of dish you have selected. You need to know the ingredients, the measurements, and how to prepare your dish. In order to organize the information about your recipe, make a card like this one:

Ensalada de maíz

Ingredientes
3 tazas de maíz
2 tazas de tomates
½ taza de pimientos verdes
½ taza de aguacates
1 cucharada de aceite y vinagre

Preparación
–Colocar los ingredientes en un bol.
–Mezclar.
–Echar aceite, vinagre y sal.
–Cubrir.
–Llevar al refrigerador.

- Find photos to illustrate your recipe. You can get photos in magazines or on the Internet, or you can draw them yourself.

Rubric for Evaluation

	Content	Organization	Presentation
1 point	Limited relevance. Information is incomplete or not based on research. Little Spanish is used.	Inefficient use of class time. Information is disorganized. Images and menu are not well designed and organized.	Communication is unclear. Delivery is not fluent. Many errors in vocabulary and grammar.
3 points	Basic information is correct. Relevant information but lacks significance. Spanish is used most of the time.	Class time is used well. Content is mostly organized but lacks some clarity. Images and menus are mostly well designed and organized.	Good communication. Fluent delivery. Mostly correct vocabulary and grammar.

PASO 3 Escribe la receta

- Write the recipe with the information that you have obtained. It must be very detailed so that anyone can follow the steps to make your dish. Add a picture to illustrate your dish.

Ensalada de maíz

Ingredientes:
3 tazas de maíz fresco
2 tazas de tomates
½ taza de pimientos
...

Preparación:
Mezcla el maíz, los tomates...

- Combine your recipe with your classmates' recipes to make a cookbook. Organize your recipes by appetizers, entrées, and desserts.

PASO 4 Prepara tu menú favorito

- Choose two dishes that complement the recipe that you have prepared. They might be an appetizer and a dessert or an appetizer and an entrée, for example.
- Write an attractive menu with the dishes that you have chosen. Include some information in Spanish about each dish.

Primer plato
- **Ensalada de maíz**
  Este plato lleva maíz, tomates, pimientos verdes, aguacate, aceite y vinagre.

Segundo plato
- **Pollo con mole**
  Este plato lleva pollo, mole, limón, cilantro, sal y pimienta.

Postre
- **Torta de chocolate**
  Este plato lleva chocolate negro, harina, azúcar, huevos y extracto de vainilla.

- Present your menu to the class.
  Choose the best menu with your classmates.

Unidad 4

Autoevaluación

¿Qué has aprendido en esta unidad?

Do these activities to evaluate how well you can manage in Spanish.

> Evaluate your skills.
> For each item, say
> Very well, Well, or
> I need more practice.

a. Can you talk about food?
  ▶ Describe your favorite foods to a classmate.
  ▶ Describe your least favorite foods to a classmate.

b. Can you express shopping–related commands?
  ▶ Tell your classmate in what container he or she should buy the following products.
  pan   atún   refrescos   galletas   uvas

c. Can you talk about and give commands related to cooking?
  ▶ Tell your classmate your favorite condiments and on what food you use them.
  ▶ Tell your classmate how you cook the foods on which you put the condiments.

d. Can you communicate in common dining–related situations?
  ▶ In groups, role–play a scene in a restaurant. Be sure to ask how each person wants his or her food prepared and what flavors he or she wants incorporated in the meal.

	Content	Organization	Presentation
5 points	Relevant, interesting information. Many details and significance are highlighted. Spanish is used exclusively.	Class time is used wisely. Information and content are clearly organized visually and logically. Images and menus are very well designed and organized.	Clear communication. Correct and complete vocabulary and grammar. Very motivating upbeat delivery.

PROYECTO

Ingredientes americanos

Paso 2

- Encourage students to look for recipes from the country of origin of the food(s) they are using. A good source, which also includes videos of how the different dishes are prepared, is the Mexican TV program *La ruta del sabor*, located at: http://oncetv-ipn.net/rutadelsabor/.
- If students have found the recipe in a Spanish-speaking source, the measurements are probably in the metric system. They can use an online converter to convert the measurements into the American system.
- Ask students to record the links and other pertinent information of all the sources they use. Require them to include a general list of references at the end of their recipe.

Paso 3

- Ask students to avoid terms in their instructions with which their classmates might not be familiar. If they had to look up the word in a bilingual dictionary, it is likely that their classmates will not know its meaning.

Paso 4

- Students may also include information about how the food in the dish is prepared (e.g., *asado*, *a la plancha*, *frito*, etc.).

Evaluation

- Distribute copies of the rubric to students. Discuss the evaluation criteria and explain how this project will be graded. Encourage students to refer to the rubric as they prepare their projects.

Content

- Explain the importance of proofreading their work before presenting it. Have students check their recipes for correct usage of the imperative verb forms.

Organization

- The recipe instructions should be clear, well organized, and easy to follow. The descriptions of each dish in students' menus should include the ingredients in the order of importance (i.e. main ingredients first, condiments last).

Presentation

- Students should use as much Spanish as possible. Encourage creativity and a presentation style that will hold their classmates' attention.

Unit 5 Española

Objectives

- To describe body parts.
- To talk about personal hygiene habits.
- To talk about illness and healthcare.
- To recommend healthy habits.
- To use expressions to get someone's attention, to talk about people or places, to ask for help, and to ask about feelings.
- To talk about medical personnel.
- To explore certain cultural aspects of Spain.
- To acquire knowledge about the geography and history of Spain.

Contents

Vocabulary

- Body parts.
- Personal hygiene.
- Common ailments and basic remedies.
- Healthcare professionals.
- Healthy habits.
- Expressions used to get someone's attention.
- Expressions used to ask for help.
- Expressions used to ask someone how he or she feels.

Grammar

- The past participle.
- Adverbs ending in *-mente*.
- *Por* and *para*.
- To make recommendations and to express obligation using the structures *hay que / tener que / deber / necesitar / poder* + infinitive.

Culture

- A universal artist: Pablo Picasso.
- Cultural aspects of greetings in the Hispanic world.
- The Catalan language.
- *La Universidad de Salamanca.*
- Student housing: the *colegios mayores.*
- *La siesta.*
- *Los sanfermines.*
- The Spanish healthcare system and Spaniards' health.
- *El gazpacho andaluz.*
- *La dieta mediterránea.*
- *Un cuadro de Velázquez: Las Meninas.*
- Spain and the Mediterranean.
- *Figura en una ventana* by Salvador Dalí.

Evaluation Criteria

- Use expressions that ask for help.
- Use expressions that get someone's attention.
- Use expressions that ask someone how he or she feels.
- Describe common routines of personal hygiene.
- List parts of the body and face.
- Describe products used for personal hygiene.

- Discuss common ailments and basic remedies.
- Talk about healthy habits and exercise.
- List healthcare professionals.
- Recognize and use participles.
- Recognize and use adverb forms ending in *-mente*.
- Understand the uses of *por* and *para*.
- Make recommendations using *hay que* and *tener que*.

- Recognize and use *deber, necesitar,* and *poder* + infinitive to make suggestions.
- Express understanding of selected Spanish customs, geographical aspects, and historical facts.
- Recognize descriptive devices in a text.
- Develop a poster that illustrates the similarities and differences between the Mediterranean and U.S. diets.

Unit Plan

La llegada

Estimated time: 1 session.

Dialogue: *En Sevilla.*

Functions & forms:
- Expressions to get someone's attention.
- Express familiarity with a person or place.
- Expressions to ask for help.
- Expressions to ask someone how he or she feels.

Culture:
- *Plaza de España*, Sevilla.
- Palos de la Frontera, Huelva.

DESAFÍO 1

Estimated time: 4 sessions.

Dialogue: *Una margarita cubista.*

Functions & forms:
- Body parts.
- The past participle.

Culture:
- *Pablo Picasso.*
- *Los saludos y las despedidas.*
- *El catalán.*

DESAFÍO 2

Estimated time: 4 sessions.

Dialogue: *La rana de la suerte.*

Functions & forms:
- Personal hygiene.
- Adverbs ending in *-mente.*

Culture:
- *La Universidad de Salamanca.*
- *Los colegios mayores.*
- *La siesta.*

DESAFÍO 3

Estimated time: 4 sessions.

Dialogue: *Los encierros de Pamplona.*

Functions & forms:
- Common ailments and basic remedies.
- Healthcare professionals.
- *Por* and *para.*

Culture:
- *Los sanfermines.*
- *La Seguridad Social.*
- *Los medicamentos.*

DESAFÍO 4

Estimated time: 4 sessions.

Dialogue: *Gazpacho para todos.*

Functions & forms:
- Healthy habits.
- To make recommendations and to express obligation using the structures *hay que/tener que/ deber/necesitar/poder* + infinitive.

Culture:
- *El gazpacho andaluz.*
- *La salud de los españoles.*
- *La dieta mediterránea.*

TODO JUNTO/El encuentro

Estimated time: 1 session.

Dialogue: *En el Monasterio de la Rábida.*

Functions & forms:
- Review of *Desafíos 1–4.*

Culture:
- *Un cuadro de Velázquez.*
- The *Monasterio de la Rábida*, Palos de la Frontera, Huelva.

MAPA CULTURAL/LECTURA

Estimated time: 1 session.

Mapa cultural: *España y el Mediterráneo.*

Reading: *Figura en una ventana.*

PROYECTO

Estimated time: 1 session.

Project: *Una presentación sobre hábitos de alimentación.*

Standards for Learning Spanish

COMMUNICATION

1.1. Interpersonal mode
- Discuss the challenge for each team in Spain.
- Discuss what students know about Spain.
- Speculate on which pair will win the challenge.
- Discuss the importance of a healthy diet and exercise.
- Interview a classmate.
- Play a guessing game.
- Survey the class on a question.

1.2. Interpretive mode
- Take notes from an oral text.
- Read a cultural text.
- Summarize information in a written text.
- Research cultural topics.
- Read about cubism on the Internet.

1.3. Presentational mode
- Describe a sketch in the cubist style.
- Write a summary of an oral text.
- Write a description of a person in a photograph.
- Write a description of *Las Meninas*.
- Describe a typical day at school.
- Act out a conversation with a waiter.
- Write an ad for a personal hygiene product and present it to the class.
- Make a list of personal hygiene products to take on a trip.

CULTURE

2.1. Practices and perspectives
- Recognize and distinguish gestures related to saying hello and good-bye.
- Read about the function of the *colegios mayores*.
- Read about the siesta and the extent of the practice.

2.2. Products and perspectives
- Read about the *sanfermines*.
- Read about the Spanish healthcare system.

- Read about the acquisition of prescription medications in Spain.
- Read about *gazpacho andaluz* as an example of a dish appropriate to the climate where it was first developed.
- Read about statistics related to the health of Spaniards.
- Read about the Mediterranean diet.
- Read about Velázquez and *Las Meninas*.

CONNECTIONS

3.1. Interdisciplinary connections
- Learn about Spanish geography and history.
- Learn about two renowned Spanish painters.
- Learn about Spain's second official language.
- Read about Spain's oldest university still in operation.

3.2. Viewpoints through language / culture
- Discover aspects of Spanish history and culture.

COMPARISONS

4.1. Compare languages
- Compare the formation of past participles in English and in Spanish.
- Compare adverb endings in English and in Spanish.
- Compare the prepositions *por* and *para* in Spanish to their equivalents in English.
- Compare demands and suggestions in English and in Spanish.

4.2. Compare cultures
- Compare health statistics in Spain and in the United States.
- Compare the prescription drug processes in Spain and in the United States.
- Compare healthcare systems in Spain and in the United States.
- Compare student housing in Spain and in the United States.

COMMUNITIES

5.1. Spanish within and beyond the school setting
- Create an ad for a personal hygiene product.
- Describe people in the community.

5.2. Spanish for lifelong learning
- Compare a painting by Velázquez and Picasso's version of the same subject.
- Research the healthcare system in the United States.
- Do a presentation on the nutritional food plans used in the United States and in Spain.

Communicative Skills

Interpersonal Mode

Mode		Activities
Speaking	• Engage in conversation with a classmate. • Role-play with a partner. • Describe people in a visual display to a partner. • Gain information about a classmate by asking guided questions.	• 4, 63, 70 • 13, 28 • 9, 18, 81 • 34
Writing	• Write a passage with personal information and/or recommendations. • Create a graphic design to compare a partner's answers.	• 29, 39, 57 • 29, 36, *Proyecto*
Listening	• Interpret a classmate's answers. • Obtain information from an oral exchange.	• 9, 65, 70 • 25, 60, 73, 80
Reading	• Understand simple texts that describe people or places. • Understand an online article on a particular topic.	• 13, 20, 39, 54, 74 • *Tu desafío*

Interpretive Mode

Mode		Activities
Listening	• Identify and extract key concepts from a listening passage. • Demonstrate understanding of an audio recording. • Interpret audio and video about culture.	• 2, 8, 13, 21, 25, 45, 60, 80 • 17, 29, 33, 36, 42, 44, 45, 68, 73, 75 • *Tu desafío, videos*
Reading	• Extract the main ideas from a passage. • Identify the key concepts of a picture story. • Understand cultural texts using knowledge of descriptive texts as a reading strategy. • Relate the theme of a reading passage to your own life or experiences. • Demonstrate understanding of a reading passage.	• 20, 50, 54, 74, *Lectura* • 1, 7, 24, 59 • *Lectura* • 10, 14, 26, 35, 43, 47, 53, 66 • 19, 30, 62, 71, 78, 81, *Lectura*

Presentational Mode

Mode		Activities
Speaking	• Act out a dialogue for the class. • Design and present an original creation.	• 28, 55 • 38, 70, *Proyecto*
Writing	• Select a photograph and write a description of the person depicted. • Write a dialogue to present to the class. • Write recommendations for the characters or a classmate. • Create a poster comparing a cultural element in the United States and in Spain.	• 38, 39, 48, 76 • 61, 70 • 56, 68, 69, 72, 74, 76, 78 • *Proyecto*

Cross-Curricular Standards

Subject	Standard	Activities
Language Arts	• Compare the form of the past participle in English and in Spanish. • Read a descriptive text.	• 15 • 86
Art	• Draw a sketch of a classmate in the cubist style. • Prepare a poster comparing the food plans used in the United States and in Spain.	• 9 • *Proyecto*
Math	• Graph the frequency of common physical hygiene routines. • Do a Venn diagram to show commonalities in the routines of two people.	• 34 • 36

Unit 5 España

Lesson Plans (50-Minute Classes)

Day	Objectives	Sessions	Activities	Time	Standards	Resources/Homework
1	To introduce Spain and to discuss the pairs' challenges	**España / La llegada** (236–241) • Warm-Up: Country orientation • *España* • Images and functions • Presentation: *En Sevilla* • *Expresiones útiles* and *¿Quién ganará?*	 1 2–5	5 m. 5 m. 10 m. 10 m. 20 m.	1.1, 1.2, 1.3, 2.1, 2.2, 5.1	Visual Presentation Audio Video Practice Workbook
2	To describe parts of the body and face	**Desafío 1 – Una margarita cubista** (242–243) • Warm-Up: Independent Starter • *Fotonovela: Una margarita cubista* • *Cultura: Pablo Picasso*	 6–9 10	5 m. 35 m. 10 m.	1.1, 1.2, 1.3, 2.2, 3.2, 5.1	Visual Presentation Audio *Tu desafío*
3	To identify parts of the body and face	**Desafío 1 – Vocabulario** (244–245) • Warm-Up: Independent Starter • Vocabulary: *Partes del cuerpo* • *Comparaciones: Los saludos y las despedidas*	 11–13 14	5 m. 35 m. 10 m.	1.1, 1.2, 1.3, 2.1, 3.2, 4.2, 5.1	Audio Practice Workbook *Tu desafío*
4	To learn and use present and past participles	**Desafío 1 – Gramática** (246–247) • Warm-Up: Independent Starter • Grammar: *El participio* • *Conexiones: El catalán*	 15–18 19	5 m. 35 m. 10 m.	1.1, 1.2, 1.3, 2.1, 3.1, 3.2, 4.1, 5.1	Audio Practice Workbook *Tu desafío*
5	To integrate vocabulary and grammar and to assess student proficiency	**Desafío 1 – Comunicación / Evaluación** (248–249) • Warm-Up: Independent Starter • *Comunicación:* Review • *Final del desafío* • Quiz on *Desafío 1*	 20–21 22	5 m. 20 m. 10 m. 15 m.	1.1, 1.2, 1.3, 2.2, 3.1, 5.1	Audio Practice Workbook
6	To talk about personal hygiene practices	**Desafío 2 – La rana de la suerte** (250–251) • Warm-Up: Independent Starter • *Fotonovela: La rana de la suerte* • *Cultura: La Universidad de Salamanca*	 23–25 26	5 m. 35 m. 10 m.	1.1, 1.2, 1.3, 2.2, 3.1, 3.2, 4.2, 5.1	Visual Presentation Audio Video *Tu desafío*
7	To talk about personal hygiene practices	**Desafío 2 – Vocabulario** (252–253) • Warm-Up: Independent Starter • Vocabulary: *La higiene personal* • *Cultura: Los colegios mayores*	 27–29 30	5 m. 35 m. 10 m.	1.1, 1.2, 1.3, 2.1, 3.2, 4.2	Audio Practice Workbook
8	To learn and use adverbs	**Desafío 2 – Gramática** (254–255) • Warm-Up: Independent Starter • Grammar: *Los adverbios en '-mente'* • *Cultura: La siesta*	 31–34 35	5 m. 35 m. 10 m.	1.1, 1.2, 1.3, 2.1, 3.2, 4.1, 4.2, 5.1	Audio Practice Workbook
9	To integrate vocabulary and grammar and to assess student proficiency	**Desafío 2 – Comunicación / Evaluación** (256–257) • Warm-Up: Independent Starter • *Comunicación:* Review • *Final del desafío* • Quiz on *Desafío 2*	 36–38 39	5 m. 20 m. 10 m. 15 m.	1.1, 1.2, 1.3, 2.2, 4.2, 5.1, 5.2	Audio Practice Workbook *Tu desafío*
10	To talk about health and illnesses	**Desafío 3 – Los encierros de Pamplona** (258–259) • Warm-Up: Independent Starter • *Fotonovela: Los encierros de Pamplona* • *Cultura: Los sanfermines*	 40–42 43	5 m. 35 m. 10 m.	1.1, 1.2, 1.3, 2.1, 3.2, 4.2, 5.1, 5.2	Visual Presentation Audio Video *Tu desafío*

Day	Objectives	Sessions	Activities	Time	Standards	Resources/Homework
11	To talk about health and illnesses	**Desafío 3 – Vocabulario** (260–261) • Warm-Up: Independent Starter • Vocabulary: *La salud: síntomas y enfermedades* • Comparaciones: *La Seguridad Social*	44–46 47	5 m. 35 m. 10 m.	1.1, 1.2, 1.3, 2.2, 3.2, 4.2, 5.2	Audio Practice Workbook
12	To use *por* and *para*	**Desafío 3 – Gramática** (262–263) • Warm-Up: Independent Starter • Grammar: *'Por' y 'para'* • Comparaciones: *Los medicamentos*	48–52 53	5 m. 35 m. 10 m.	1.1, 1.2, 1.3, 2.1, 3.1, 3.2, 4.1, 4.2, 5.1	Audio Practice Workbook
13	To integrate vocabulary and grammar and to assess student proficiency	**Desafío 3 – Comunicación / Evaluación** (264–265) • Warm-Up: Independent Starter • *Comunicación:* Review • *Final del desafío* • Quiz on *Desafío 3*	54–56 57	5 m. 20 m. 10 m. 15 m.	1.1, 1.2, 1.3, 2.1, 5.1	Audio Practice Workbook *Tu desafío*
14	To recommend healthy habits	**Desafío 4 – Gazpacho para todos** (266–267) • Warm-Up: Independent Starter • *Fotonovela: Gazpacho para todos* • *Cultura: El gazpacho andaluz*	58–61 62	5 m. 35 m. 10 m.	1.1, 1.2, 1.3, 2.2, 3.1, 3.2, 4.2, 5.2	Visual Presentation Audio *Tu desafío*
15	To talk about healthy habits	**Desafío 4 – Vocabulario** (268–269) • Warm-Up: Independent Starter • Vocabulary: *Hábitos saludables* • Comunidades: *La salud de los españoles*	63–65 66	5 m. 35 m. 10 m.	1.1, 1.2, 1.3, 2.1, 3.2, 4.2, 5.2	Audio Practice Workbook
16	To recommend healthy habits	**Desafío 4 – Gramática** (270–271) • Warm-Up: Independent Starter • Grammar: *Hacer recomendaciones* • Conexiones: *La dieta mediterránea*	67–70 71	5 m. 35 m. 10 m.	1.1, 1.2, 1.3, 2.1, 3.1, 3.2. 4.1, 5.1, 5.2	Audio Practice Workbook *Tu desafío*
17	To integrate vocabulary and grammar and to assess student proficiency	**Desafío 4 – Comunicación / Evaluación** (272–273) • Warm-Up: Independent Starter • *Comunicación:* Review • *Final del desafío* • Quiz on *Desafío 4*	72–75 76	5 m. 20 m. 10 m. 15 m.	1.1, 1.2, 1.3, 2.2, 5.2	Audio Practice Workbook
18	To integrate language in context	**Todo junto / El encuentro** (274–277) • Warm-Up: Independent Starter • *Todo junto* • Conexiones: *Un cuadro de Velázquez* • *El encuentro: En el Monasterio de la Rábida*	77–80 81 82–83	5 m. 20 m. 5 m. 20 m.	1.1, 1.2, 1.3, 2.1, 2.2, 3.1, 3.2, 5.1	Audio Practice Workbook
19	To learn about Spanish culture and traditions and to learn about Spanish history	**Mapa cultural / Lectura** (278–281) • Warm-Up: Read the *Mapa cultural* • *Mapa cultural: España y el Mediterráneo* • *Lectura: Figura en una ventana* • Read project outline (286-287)	84–85 86–89	5 m. 20 m. 20 m. 5 m.	1.2, 1.3, 2.1, 2.2, 3.1, 3.2, 5.2	Practice Workbook *Tu desafío* Project work
20	To present healthy eating habits	**Proyecto** (286–287) • Warm-Up: Prepare project presentations • Project presentations		5 m. 45 m.	1.1, 1.2, 1.3, 2.1, 3.1, 4.2, 5.2	Practice Workbook **Repaso – Vocabulario** (282–283) **Repaso – Gramática** (284–285) **Autoevaluación** (287)

Lesson Plans (90-Minute Classes)

Day	Objectives	Sessions	Activities	Time	Standards	Resources/Homework
1	To introduce Spain and to discuss the pairs' challenges	**España / La llegada** (236–241) • Warm-Up: Country orientation • España / Images and functions • Presentation: *En Sevilla* • *Expresiones útiles* and *¿Quién ganará?*	 1 2–5	 10 m. 20 m. 25 m. 35 m.	1.1, 1.2, 1.3, 2.1, 2.2, 5.1	Visual Presentation Audio Video Practice Workbook
2	To identify and describe parts of the body and face	**Desafío 1 – Una margarita cubista / Vocabulario** (242–245) • Warm-Up: Independent Starter • *Fotonovela: Una margarita cubista* • *Cultura: Pablo Picasso* • Vocabulary: *Partes del cuerpo* • *Comparaciones: Los saludos y las despedidas*	 6–9 10 11–13 14	 5 m. 35 m. 5 m. 35 m. 10 m.	1.1, 1.2, 1.3, 2.1, 2.2, 3.1, 3.2, 4.2, 5.1	Visual Presentation Audio Practice Workbook *Tu desafío*
3	To learn and use the present and past participles, to integrate vocabulary and grammar, and to assess student proficiency	**Desafío 1 – Gramática / Comunicación / Evaluación** (246–249) • Warm-Up: Independent Starter • Grammar: *El participio* • *Conexiones: El catalán* • *Comunicación:* Review • *Final del desafío* • Quiz on *Desafío 1*	 15–18 19 20–21 22	 5 m. 25 m. 10 m. 25 m. 10 m. 15 m.	1.1, 1.2, 1.3, 2.1, 2.2, 3.1, 3.2, 4.1, 5.1	Audio Practice Workbook *Tu desafío*
4	To talk about personal hygiene practices	**Desafío 2 – La rana de la suerte / Vocabulario** (250–253) • Warm-Up: Independent Starter • *Fotonovela: La rana de la suerte* • *Cultura: La Universidad de Salamanca* • Vocabulary: *La higiene personal* • *Cultura: Los colegios mayores*	 23–25 26 27–29 30	 5 m. 25 m. 15 m. 35 m. 10 m.	1.1, 1.2, 1.3, 2.1, 2.2, 3.1, 3.2, 4.2, 5.1	Visual Presentation Audio Video *Tu desafío*
5	To learn and use adverbs, to integrate vocabulary and grammar, and to assess student proficiency	**Desafío 2 – Gramática / Comunicación / Evaluación** (254–257) • Warm-Up: Independent Starter • Grammar: *Los adverbios en '-mente'* • *Cultura: La siesta* • *Comunicación:* Review • *Final del desafío* • Quiz on *Desafío 2*	 31–34 35 36–38 39	 5 m. 25 m. 10 m. 25 m. 10 m. 15 m.	1.1, 1.2, 1.3, 2.1, 2.2, 3.2, 4.1, 4.2, 5.1, 5.2	Audio Practice Workbook *Tu desafío*
6	To talk about health and illnesses	**Desafío 3 – Los encierros de Pamplona / Vocabulario** (258–261) • Warm-Up: Independent Starter • *Fotonovela: Los encierros de Pamplona* • *Cultura: Los sanfermines* • Vocabulary: *La salud: síntomas y enfermedades* • *Comparaciones: La Seguridad Social*	 40–42 43 44–46 47	 5 m. 30 m. 10 m. 35 m. 10 m.	1.1, 1.2, 1.3, 2.1, 2.2, 3.2, 4.2, 5.1, 5.2	Visual Presentation Audio Video Practice Workbook *Tu desafío*

Day	Objectives	Sessions	Activities	Time	Standards	Resources/Homework
7	To use *por* and *para*, to integrate vocabulary and grammar, and to assess student proficiency	***Desafío 3 – Gramática / Comunicación / Evaluación*** (262–265) • Warm-Up: Independent Starter • Grammar: *Por y para* • *Comparaciones: Los medicamentos* • Comunicación: Review • *Final del desafío* • Quiz on *Desafío 3*	48–52 53 54–56 57	5 m. 30 m. 5 m. 25 m. 10 m. 15 m.	1.1, 1.2, 1.3, 2.1, 3.1, 3.2, 4.1, 4.2, 5.1	Audio Practice Workbook *Tu desafío*
8	To recommend healthy habits	***Desafío 4 – Gazpacho para todos / Vocabulario*** (266–269) • Warm-Up: Independent Starter • *Fotonovela: Gazpacho para todos* • *Cultura: El gazpacho andaluz* • Vocabulary: *Hábitos saludables* • *Comunidades: La salud de los españoles*	58–61 62 63–65 66	5 m. 30 m. 10 m. 35 m. 10 m.	1.1, 1.2, 1.3, 2.1, 2.2, 3.1, 3.2, 4.2, 5.2	Visual Presentation Audio Practice Workbook *Tu desafío*
9	To recommend healthy habits, to integrate vocabulary and grammar, and to assess student proficiency	***Desafío 4 – Gramática / Comunicación / Evaluación / Todo junto*** (270–275) • Warm-Up: Independent Starter • Grammar: *Hacer recomendaciones* • *Conexiones: La dieta mediterránea* • Comunicación: Review • *Final del desafío* • Quiz on *Desafío 4* • *Todo junto* • *Cultura: Un cuadro de Velázquez*	67–70 71 72–75 76 77–80 81	5 m. 15 m. 5 m. 15 m. 10 m. 20 m. 15 m. 5 m.	1.1, 1.2, 1.3, 2.1, 2.2, 3.1, 3.2, 4.1, 5.1, 5.2	Audio Practice Workbook *Tu desafío*
10	To integrate language in context and to learn about Spanish culture and traditions	***El encuentro / Mapa cultural / Lectura*** (276–281) • Warm-Up: Independent Starter • *El encuentro: En el Monasterio de la Rábida* • *Mapa cultural: España y el Mediterráneo* • *Lectura: Figura en una ventana*	82–83 84–85 86–89	5 m. 30 m. 25 m. 30 m.	1.2, 1.3, 2.1, 2.2, 3.1, 3.2, 5.1, 5.2	Video Practice Workbook *Tu desafío* ***Repaso – Vocabulario*** (282–283) ***Repaso – Gramática*** (284–285) Project work
11	To present healthy eating habits and to assess student proficiency	***Proyecto / Assessment*** (286–287) • Warm-Up: Prepare project presentations • Project presentations • *Autoevaluación* • Test		10 m. 40 m. 10 m. 30 m.	1.1, 1.2, 1.3, 2.1, 3.1, 4.2, 5.2	

2 **Expresiones**

1. Disculpe, ¿sabe dónde está la Plaza Mayor, por favor?
2. María, por favor, ¿puedes ayudarme?
3. ¿Cómo te encuentras hoy, Marisa?

8 **¿Qué ves tú?**

1. Esta chica es morena y lleva un vestido y un sombrero rojo. Tiene los labios y los ojos pintados. Y tiene los codos apoyados en la mesa.
2. Hay una chica rubia con un vestido muy elegante. Tiene las manos pequeñas.
3. Esta chica tiene la cara de color azul y verde. ¡Qué raro! Lleva un vestido amarillo.

13 **¿Cómo es?**

Es moreno y tiene el pelo corto. Tiene barba y la nariz un poco grande. Tiene los ojos azules, muy bonitos.

17 **En el salón de clase**

1. Hay un chico sentado en el suelo.
2. Todos los libros están abiertos.
3. La puerta no está abierta, está cerrada.
4. Hay muchas chicas con los labios pintados.
5. Hay una chica dormida.
6. En la pizarra hay verbos escritos en español.

21 **Adivinanzas**

1. Esta parte del cuerpo forma parte de las manos. Hay diez. Nos ayudan a escribir y a pintar. ¿Qué son?
2. Esta parte del cuerpo está en la cara. Hay dos y están encima de los ojos. ¿Qué son?
3. Esta parte del cuerpo está en las piernas. Tenemos dos. Las necesitamos para caminar y para sentarnos. ¿Qué son?
4. Esta parte del cuerpo está en los brazos. Tenemos dos. Están entre las muñecas y los hombros. ¿Qué son?
5. Esta parte de la cara está en la boca. A veces las mujeres los llevan pintados. ¿Qué son?

25 **La vida estudiantil**

1. –¿Qué hacen tú y tus amigos por las tardes?
   –Por las tardes, a mis amigos y a mí nos gusta dar un paseo por la Plaza Mayor.
2. –¿A qué hora te levantas?
   –Temprano. Me levanto a las siete de la mañana.
3. –¿Qué haces normalmente de lunes a viernes?
   –Voy a clase y estudio.
4. –¿A qué hora almuerzas?
   –A las dos. Normalmente voy al comedor de la universidad.

5. –¿Qué haces por las tardes?
   –Voy a la biblioteca a estudiar.

29 **El horario de Diana**

De lunes a viernes me despierto temprano. Primero me ducho. Después de ducharme, desayuno y me visto. Ah, antes de vestirme me pongo desodorante, claro. Luego me peino y me lavo los dientes. ¡Soy muy rápida!

Los fines de semana me despierto más tarde. Primero desayuno y me baño. Luego me lavo el pelo. Después me pongo desodorante, me lavo los dientes y me visto.

33 **¿Encontraron la rana?**

Rita se levantó temprano, se duchó y se arregló tranquilamente. Diana se despertó más tarde. Se duchó y se lavó el pelo. Normalmente ella se seca el pelo con el secador, pero ese día no lo hizo. Se peinó y se vistió rápidamente y las dos bajaron a desayunar al comedor del hotel. Después de desayunar fueron a la universidad. Buscaron la rana de la fachada cuidadosamente, pero no pudieron encontrarla. La rana no se ve fácilmente porque es muy pequeña. Un niño fue a ayudarlas amablemente.

36 **¡Mi horario cambió!**

–¿Sí?

–Hola, mamá. Soy yo, Diana. ¿Qué tal?

–Hola, cariño. ¡Qué sorpresa! Oye, ¿qué hora es allí, en España? ¿No es muy tarde?

–Sí. Son las doce de la noche, pero es que el horario en España es muy diferente al horario de los Estados Unidos.

–¿No te levantas temprano?

–Sí, pero no tanto como allí. En casa generalmente me levanto a las seis y media y desayuno a las siete, pero aquí en España me levanto a las ocho y desayuno entre las nueve y las diez.

–¿Y a qué hora almuerzas?

–A las dos.

–¡Qué tarde! Aquí almuerzas a la una.

–Sí. Y después del almuerzo dormimos una siesta, desde las tres hasta las tres y media, aproximadamente.

–Claro, por eso ahora no tienes sueño. En casa no duermes por la tarde y normalmente te acuestas a las nueve.

–Sí. Te llamo mañana, mamá. Ahora voy a acostarme, que ya son las doce. Dale un beso a papá.

–Sí, Diana. Hasta mañana. Un beso.

42 **¡No es justo!**

Hola, Tess. Soy Tim. Estamos en la ciudad de Pamplona y no puedo creer el desafío que tenemos mi abuelo y yo. ¡Tenemos que correr delante de unos toros por la calle! ¡No es justo! ¡Es un desafío peligroso! Creo que voy a terminar en un hospital con una pierna rota o con un brazo roto... ¡o algo peor! Y no me gustan los hospitales. Lo peor es que el abuelo está contento... ¿o está loco? Sí, yo creo que está loco. Adiós, Tess, mañana hablamos.

44 ¿Qué enfermedad es?

1. Anoche comí paella de pescado y ahora tengo la cara muy roja. Y me pica todo el cuerpo.
2. Ayer estuve toda la tarde en el parque y pasé mucho frío. Estuve toda la noche tosiendo y me duele el pecho.
3. Me siento muy mal. Me duelen la cabeza y el estómago, y tengo fiebre.

45 Enfermedades y más enfermedades

1. Tengo que ir al dentista, me duelen las muelas.
2. Yo tengo gripe. Toso y me duele mucho la garganta.
3. Me pican los brazos y las piernas porque tengo alergia.
4. Tengo catarro. Estornudo mucho y me pica la nariz.

60 ¿De qué hablan?

1. –Mira esa torre. ¡Qué alta!
   –Es la Giralda, hombre. Es la torre de la catedral.
   –Es muy bonita.
2. La especialidad de la casa es el gazpacho. Se lo recomiendo. Es una sopa fría con tomate, pimiento y cebolla.
3. Señores viajeros, próxima parada: Sevilla. No olviden recoger todos sus objetos personales. Gracias por viajar con nosotros.

68 Recomendaciones

1. Tim, tú puedes correr por las mañanas. Es un buen ejercicio.
2. Diana, tú debes comer de forma más saludable.
3. Mack, necesitas comer menos y hacer más ejercicio.
4. Janet, debes caminar una hora todos los días para estar en forma.
5. Andy, tú tienes que nadar. Es un ejercicio excelente.

6. Rita, tú puedes hacer yoga o practicar algún deporte para estar en forma.

73 Janet está enferma

–Hola, doctor.
–Buenos días. Dígame, ¿qué le pasa?
–Pues que últimamente me siento muy cansada y me duele la cabeza.
–¿Tiene fiebre?
–No.
–¿Y está muy nerviosa o preocupada?
–No, tampoco.
–Entonces no le voy a recetar ningún medicamento. Debe cuidar más su alimentación: coma alimentos variados y saludables: fruta, verdura... Y también debe descansar más.
–De acuerdo.
–Si no se siente mejor en unos días, vuelva a verme.
–Gracias, doctor.

75 ¿Qué me recomiendas?

1. Me gusta hacer algo de ejercicio, pero en la ciudad donde vivo hace mucho calor y no puedo hacer deporte en la calle.
2. Yo estoy siempre muy nervioso. No sé qué hacer para relajarme.
3. A mí no me gusta practicar deporte. Solo quiero hacer algún ejercicio para mantenerme en forma.
4. A mí me encanta la montaña y estar al aire libre. Me gusta disfrutar del campo, del paisaje, del aire puro...

80 Encuentra las diferencias

1. Esa chica está haciendo ejercicio. Está patinando.
2. Hay un chico sentado en un banco. Creo que está dormido, porque tiene los ojos cerrados.
3. Veo a una mujer caminando. Va despacio porque tiene una pierna rota. ¡Pobrecita!

España

The Unit

- The themes for Unit 5 are body parts, personal hygiene, and health in the context of a trip to Spain.
- The pairs gather at the *Plaza de España*, in Seville. They will travel to Palos de la Frontera, where they must solve a riddle.
  - *Desafío 1*. Tess and Patricia must visit a museum in Barcelona and find a Picasso painting that depicts Margarita, a proper name that is also the Spanish word for daisy.
  - *Desafío 2*. Diana and Rita go to Salamanca, where they will have to find a frog that brings good luck to the university students.
  - *Desafío 3*. Tim and Mack will travel to Pamplona in order to participate in the running of the bulls during the *sanfermines*.
  - *Desafío 4*. Andy and Janet travel to Seville on a high-speed train. In Seville they must buy enough gazpacho for all their friends.

Activities	Standards	Resources
España	1.2, 2.1, 2.2	Video

Teaching Suggestions

Warm-Up / Independent Starter

- Ask students to observe the four locations and answer the following questions:
  1. Which cities are the pairs visiting in Spain?
  2. Which of these places seem more interesting? Why?

Spain

- Spain is located on the Iberian Peninsula, which lies between the Atlantic Ocean and the Mediterranean Sea. This peninsula includes the countries of Spain, Portugal, Andorra, and the British overseas territory of Gibraltar.
- Focus students' attention on the map on this page and point to the area where Palos de la Frontera is located. Explain that Christopher Columbus sailed from this port to cross the Atlantic. Remind students of the three ships that he used: *Pinta*, *Niña*, and *Santa María*.

UNIDAD 5
España
Entre el Atlántico y el Mediterráneo

DESAFÍO 1

▶ **To describe body parts**

Vocabulario
Partes del cuerpo

Gramática
El participio

Museo Picasso (Barcelona)

DESAFÍO 2

Universidad de Salamanca

▶ **To talk about personal hygiene habits**

Vocabulario
La higiene personal

Gramática
Los adverbios en *-mente*

The Challenge

DESAFÍO 1

Museo Picasso
Barcelona is the city where the well-known Spanish painter Pablo Picasso spent part of his youth, between 1895 and 1904. After he moved to Paris, he still returned to Barcelona regularly and kept his strong ties with the city, where there is a museum in his honor. The Picasso Museum houses an important collection of his cubist paintings, including several versions of *Las Meninas*, a famous 17th century painting by Diego Velázquez. The painting depicts the daughter of the Spanish king Philip IV, Margarita, surrounded by her handmaidens.

DESAFÍO 2

Universidad de Salamanca
The University of Salamanca, founded in 1218, is the oldest existing Spanish university. During the 15th and 16th centuries the University of Salamanca grew in number of students and prestige, and some well-known scholars, such as Antonio de Nebrija and Fray Luis de León, taught there. The main façade is a masterpiece of the plateresque style, a highly ornamented style that emulates in stone the work of a silversmith. Among its many ornaments, there is a small frog on a skull. It is said that finding the frog without help will give you luck.

► **To talk about illness and health care**

Vocabulario
La salud: síntomas y enfermedades

Gramática
Por y para

DESAFÍO 3

DESAFÍO 4

Gazpacho

Los sanfermines (Pamplona)

► **To recommend healthy habits**

Vocabulario
Hábitos saludables

Gramática
Hacer recomendaciones

doscientos treinta y siete **237**

Picture Discussion

- Ask students to look at the pictures. Has anyone in the class ever been to any of the places mentioned or participated in any of the activities? Encourage students to share their experiences.

Museo Picasso (Barcelona)

- Invite students to talk about their favorite artistic styles (e.g., realism, impressionism, surrealism, etc.) and their favorite artists. Do students in the class have similar preferences? Then ask them if they are familiar with Pablo Picasso. Invite students to share with the class what they know about Picasso and his work.

Universidad de Salamanca

- Have students work in small groups to list all the universities they know in the United States. Then ask groups to add what they know about each of the universities they listed (e.g., location, whether it is private or public, degrees it is most famous for, sport teams, etc.). Once they have finished, invite groups to share their list with the rest of the class.

Los sanfermines (Pamplona)

- Ask students to observe the picture for one minute. Then invite them to share with the class their thoughts and feelings. Discuss, as a class, some of the students' opinions and impressions about what they see in this picture. Do they have a strong opinion—either in favor of or against— these types of events?

Gazpacho

- Recycle some of the vocabulary from Unit 4 and ask students to identify the ingredients they see in this picture. Then have them look at the finished dish (i.e., the gazpacho) and explain that this soup is eaten cold, as if it were a salad. Have any students in the class tried it before? Did they like it? Poll the rest of the class to see how many students would like to try it.

Objectives

- By the end of Unit 5, students will be able to
  - Describe body parts.
  - Talk about personal hygiene habits.
  - Talk about illness and healthcare.
  - Recommend healthy habits.
  - Talk about different cultural aspects of the Mediterranean region.

⚑ **DESAFÍO 3**

Los sanfermines

The festival of San Fermín, or *sanfermines,* in the city of Pamplona, in northern Spain, is deeply rooted in tradition and attracts more than one million visitors every year. This week-long fiesta is set off by the burning of a fireworks rocket, called *chupinazo*, at noon on July 6. The main event is the *encierro*, or the running of the bulls. Every morning, hundreds of young people run ahead of a pack of bulls as they make their way to the bullfight ring through the city streets. In the afternoon, there is a bullfight where the six bulls that ran in the morning are fought.

⚑ **DESAFÍO 4**

Gazpacho

Gazpacho is one of Andalusia's best-known dishes. It is a cold soup made with raw tomatoes, which is widely enjoyed throughout Spain, especially in the summer. In addition to tomatoes, gazpacho may also have cucumbers, green peppers, garlic, olive oil and vinegar, and may be accompanied with small pieces of bread, a hardboiled egg, and a diced onion. There are many different recipes and regional variations of gazpacho. Some recipes, for instance, may include almonds and grapes.

237

La llegada

Presentation

- This section presents the pairs' arrival in Seville. They meet at the *Plaza de España*, in Maria Luisa Park, the site of a world exhibit in 1929. The participants must travel to Palos de la Frontera, in the province of Huelva, which is a one-hour drive from Seville. There they will solve a riddle before they can receive the challenges for this unit.

- Students will see vocabulary in context, with pictures and illustrations. Presenting new words in this manner helps students develop their Spanish vocabulary with background knowledge while engaging them with the context.

Activities	Standards	Resources
Fotonovela	1.2, 2.1, 2.2	Vis. Pres.
1.	1.2	

Teaching Suggestions

Warm-Up / Independent Starter

- Ask students to make a list of facts they know about Christopher Columbus. They may include who he was, where he was from, what he is best known for, etc. They should write as many facts as possible in about two minutes.

Preparation

- Ask students to share their Independent Starter. Write some of your students' facts on the board. You may want to remind students of some information about Columbus and his first voyage to the Americas, if it was not mentioned in their Independent Starters.

- Columbus was from Genoa, Italy, but he made his voyages under the sponsorship of Fernando and Isabel, the Spanish monarchs. The three caravels, or sailing ships, he took with him on his first voyage were fitted out at Palos de la Frontera, on the banks of the Tinto River. Columbus departed from Palos on August 3rd, 1492. He sailed southward to the Canary Islands, where he and his crew stayed for about a month. On September 6, Columbus and his small fleet set out from the Canary Islands in an attempt to find a new route to the Far East. He made landfall in the Caribbean on October 12, 1492.

238

En Sevilla

 The pairs gather at the *Plaza de España* in Seville. They travel from Seville to Palos de la Frontera, in Huelva, the town where Christopher Columbus sailed out from in 1492. There, our friends must solve a riddle: *¿Cuál es la niña más famosa de Palos?*

Hace mucho calor y no hay niños en la calle. ¿Preguntamos en aquella farmacia?

Olvídalo, mamá. A estas horas todas las tiendas están cerradas.

Disculpe, ¿sabe dónde está la niña?

¿Qué niña?

Vamos, Janet. Hay que encontrar a la niña.

Perdone, ¿puede ayudarnos? ¿Conoce a la niña más famosa de Palos?

¿La niña más famosa de Palos? Vayan al puerto.

238 doscientos treinta y ocho

Differentiated Instruction

DEVELOPING LEARNERS

- Ask students to go through the dialogue and make a list in their notebooks of any words they don't know. Have them look up these terms in a bilingual dictionary and write the definitions in their list. Ask students if this helps their reading comprehension. Also ask them to identify all the command forms they can find (*olvídalo, disculpe, perdone, vayan*), and explain if they are formal or familiar, plural or singular.

EXPANDING LEARNERS

- Tell students that the 50 or so miles that separate Seville from Palos de la Frontera will give the participants plenty of time to talk to one another during the trip, speculating on what lies ahead for them. Have students imagine they are among the participants and write a dialogue that takes place during this excursion and then role-play it for the class. You might want to have students work in groups of at least four and decide among themselves which roles they will play.

¿Qué tal te encuentras, Janet? ¿Te sientes mejor?

Hace mucho calor. Y estoy muy cansada.

Entonces, los desafíos están escondidos en la Niña...

...aro... Ahí está. Esa ...la Niña, uno de los ...es barcos de Colón.

Aquí dice que tenemos que traer un reportaje fotográfico de nuestros desafíos y escribir pies de foto.

¡Qué bien! ¡Vamos al barco para recoger los desafíos!

1 **¿Comprendes?**

▶ **Une** cada pregunta con la respuesta adecuada.

1. ¿En qué ciudad se reúnen los personajes?
2. ¿A qué pueblo van a buscar los desafíos?
3. ¿Qué es la Niña?
4. ¿Dónde está la Niña?
5. ¿Dónde están escondidos los desafíos?
6. ¿Cómo están las tiendas?

a. En el puerto.
b. Cerradas.
c. En el barco.
d. En Sevilla.
e. Un barco.
f. A Palos de la Frontera.

La llegada

■ Have students read the *fotonovela* silently. Remind them of some reading and listening strategies, such as recognizing prefixes and suffixes, checking the dictionary for unknown words, paraphrasing, and asking questions. Students can also use the reading strategies from previous units in this level.

La fotonovela

Before Viewing

■ Now that the students have read the dialogues, check the board to see if anyone knew the names of the sailing boats used by Columbus on his first voyage. Write down the names: *Santa María, Pinta, Niña.* Ask students if they remember the meaning of the word *niña,* and if they can explain the misunderstanding portrayed in the *fotonovela.*

After Viewing

■ Ask students questions about what happens in the *fotonovela* and how some of the characters are feeling: *¿Qué tiempo hace? ¿Por qué están cerradas las tiendas? ¿Cómo se siente Janet?*

Activities

1. Have students work in pairs to complete this activity. One student asks a question and his or her partner answers it. Tell students to be sure to alternate the person asking and the person answering the questions.

Answer Key

1. 1. d   4. a
     2. f   5. c
     3. e   6. b

Additional Resources

Fans Online activities
Practice Workbook

HERITAGE LANGUAGE LEARNERS

• Students sometimes confuse the verbs *saber* and *conocer.* Have them complete the following sentences with the correct forms of *saber* and *conocer.*

1. *Yo ... España muy bien. (conozco)*
2. *¿... (tú) la diferencia entre ser y estar? (Sabes)*
3. *Nosotros no ... a Cristóbal Colón, pero ... quién es. (conocemos; sabemos)*
4. *Yo ... que tú ... la respuesta a la pregunta. (sé, sabes)*
5. *¿... ustedes la ciudad de Sevilla? (Conocen)*
6. *A mí me gusta la geografía, por eso yo ... dónde está Sevilla. (sé)*

MULTIPLE INTELLIGENCES:
Intrapersonal Intelligence

• Ask students to imagine that they are sailors on one of Columbus's three ships during that historic first crossing from Spain to the Americas and have them keep a diary. Columbus calculated that the trip would take four weeks from their September 6 departure date from the Canary Islands, but as of October 10, no land had been sighted. The crew was losing patience and demanded that they return to Spain. On October 12, land was sighted from the *Pinta* and history was changed.

239

La llegada

Presentation

- In this section, students will learn useful expressions to get someone's attention, to ask about and to express that you are familiar with a person or place, to ask for help, and to ask someone how he or she feels.

Activities	Standards	Resources
Expresiones útiles	1.2, 4.1	
2.	1.2	Audio
3.	1.2, 1.3	
4.	1.1, 5.1	
5.	1.1	

Teaching Suggestions

Warm-Up / Independent Starter

- Ask students to close their textbooks and write down all of the words and expressions they can remember from the *fotonovela*.

Preparation

- Invite volunteer students to share their Independent Starter with the class. Write down some of the expressions and words students mention.
- Go over the *Expresiones útiles* section with students. Then refer them to the board. Did they remember any of the *expresiones útiles* that were used in the *fotonovela*?
- Have students get into pairs to write an impromptu dialogue using as many of the *expresiones útiles* as possible. Have them practice their dialogues and then ask them to role-play the dialogues in front of the class without using their notes.
- Ask the class to vote for the most creative dialogue.

Activities

2. Have students listen to the audio once and ask them to write down the number of the sentence that matches each picture. Play the audio a second time to make sure that everybody understands.

240

EXPRESIONES ÚTILES

¿Cómo te sientes?

To get someone's attention:
Perdón / Perdona… Perdone…
Disculpa… Disculpe…

To ask about and to express that you are familiar with a person or place:
–¿Conoces a mi profesor? –¿Conoces mi país?
–Sí, lo conozco. –No, no lo conozco.

To ask for help:
¿Me ayudas? ¿Me ayuda?
¿Puedes ayudarme? ¿Puede ayudarme?

To ask someone how he/she feels:
¿Qué tal te encuentras? ¿Qué tal se encuentra?
¿Cómo te sientes? ¿Cómo se siente?
¿Cómo estás? ¿Cómo está?

2 Expresiones

▶ **Escucha** y relaciona. ¿A qué fotografía corresponde cada oración?

 A 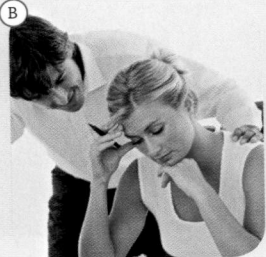 B  C

3 Conversaciones

▶ **Completa** estos diálogos con las expresiones útiles.

1. – ___1___, ¿sabe usted dónde está el barco?
   –No, lo siento. No lo sé.

2. – ___2___, ¿hay alguna farmacia cerca?
   –Lo siento, no ___3___ esta ciudad.

3. –Mamá, pareces cansada. ¿ ___4___ ?
   –Me encuentro un poco enferma.

4. – Necesito encontrar el puerto. ___5___
   –Sí, claro. Está al final de esta calle.

240 doscientos cuarenta

Differentiated Instruction

DEVELOPING LEARNERS

- Ask students to choose the appropriate word or expression to use with the following people or situations:
  1. *Hablas con tu profesora de Español:* ¿Cómo estás? / ¿Cómo está? (¿Cómo está?)
  2. *Llevas un paquete enorme:* ¿Qué tal te encuentras? / ¿Me ayuda? (¿Me ayuda?)
  3. *Hablas con tu primo:* ¿Qué tal se encuentra? / ¿Qué tal te encuentras? (¿Qué tal te encuentras?)
  4. *Necesitas información:* Perdón… / ¿Qué tal te encuentras? (Perdón…)
  5. *Tu médico te pregunta:* ¿Me ayudas? / ¿Cómo te sientes? (¿Cómo te sientes?)

EXPANDING LEARNERS

- Give students more practice with the *expresiones útiles* by asking them to work with a partner and develop several short dialogues. In their conversations, they should imagine they are asking someone for help in finding something on the street, at school, or in another location. Then they should inquire about someone's health or well-being. Be sure that partners take turns asking and answering the questions.

¿Quién ganará?

 4 **Los desafíos**

▶ **Habla.** ¿Cuál será el desafío para cada pareja? Piénsalo y coméntalo con tus compañeros(as).

DESAFÍO 1

Una margarita cubista

Tess y Patricia

DESAFÍO 2

La rana de la suerte

Diana y Rita

DESAFÍO 3

Los encierros de Pamplona

Tim y Mack

DESAFÍO 4

Gazpacho para todos

Andy y Janet

 ▶ **Habla.** ¿En qué país son los desafíos? ¿Qué sabes de ese país? Coméntalo con tus compañeros(as).

 5 **La tarea final**

▶ **Decide.** ¿Qué tarea tienen que hacer los personajes al final? ¿Qué pareja crees que ganará?

LA TAREA
Un reportaje fotográfico

doscientos cuarenta y uno **241**

---

3. Ask students to complete the activity individually. Then pair them up to read the dialogues. Make sure they take turns in initiating the dialogue.

¿Quién ganará?

4. Have students get into small groups and discuss the pairs' challenges. Ask groups to look at the pictures, read the captions, and write a brief paragraph about what they believe the pairs will do in their challenges. They must also include any information they know about Spain in the paragraph. Also, refer students to the unit about Spain from Level 1.

5. Students have been provided a clue as to what the pairs will have to do to win their *desafío* in Spain. The task is *un reportaje fotográfico*. Discuss, as a class, what constitutes a good photo report and what kind of photos and captions the pairs will need in order to win their *desafío* in Spain.

 AUDIO SCRIPT
See page 235l.

Answer Key

2. 1. A   2. C   3. B

3. 1. Perdone / Disculpe
2. Perdone / Disculpe
3. conozco
4. ¿Qué tal te encuentras?
5. ¿Me ayuda? / ¿Puede ayudarme?

4. Answers will vary.
▶ Answers will vary.

5. Answers will vary.

Additional Resources

Fans Online activities
Practice Workbook

HERITAGE LANGUAGE LEARNERS

- There are many other ways of getting someone's attention, asking for help, and asking people how they feel. Have students brainstorm some more of these expressions and list them in a three-column chart under the corresponding category. They should be prepared to say in which countries these expressions are popular. Have them use these new terms in short dialogues and present them to the class.

CRITICAL THINKING

- After completing activity 4, and without looking ahead in their textbooks, ask students who they think will be the most successful at completing their *desafío*. Ask them if they think one of the participant pairs might fail their challenge. Students will need to justify their answers, keeping in mind the strengths and weaknesses of the characters, as well as their past performances.

241

Unit 5

DESAFÍO 1

Describir partes del cuerpo

Presentation

- In this *Desafío*, Tess and Patricia are in Barcelona, where they must find a cubist painting that depicts Margarita.

- In this section, students will preview:
  - Vocabulary to describe body parts.
  - The past participle used as an adjective.

Activities	Standards	Resources
Fotonovela	1.2, 2.2, 3.1	Vis. Pres.
6.	1.2	
7.	1.2, 1.3, 2.2	
8.	1.2	Audio
9.	1.1, 3.1	
10. Cultura	1.1, 1.2, 2.2, 3.1, 3.2	
Tu desafío	1.2, 2.2, 3.1, 3.2, 5.1	

Teaching Suggestions

Warm-Up / Independent Starter

- Have students read the title of this *Desafío*. Ask them to think about possible meanings of the title. Have them write four sentences that reflect their brainstorming.

Preparation

- Ask students to share their Independent Starter with a partner. Then read the introduction to the *fotonovela* and ask students to think of any other words in Spanish that have more than one meaning. What confusion can this cause?

👁 La fotonovela

Before Viewing

- Ask students to look at the pictures and answer the following questions: *¿Dónde están Tess y Patricia? ¿Qué hacen? ¿Qué cuadros son de Picasso? ¿Cuál es de Velázquez? ¿Cuál de los cuadros es cubista?*

After Viewing

- Tess and Patricia are confused about the meaning of the word *Margarita*. Using the command forms, ask students to give advice to Tess and Patricia so that they will successfully meet this challenge.

242

Una margarita cubista

👁 Tess and Patricia's task in Barcelona is an unusual and tricky one. They must find a cubist painting that depicts Margarita, a proper noun which is also the Spanish word for *daisy*. Their misinterpretation sets them on the wrong foot from the beginning.

Este cuadro es muy raro, mamá. La niña tiene la cabeza muy grande y el cuerpo muy pequeño.

Es un cuadro de Picasso basado en esta pintura de Velázquez.

¡Es verdad! Aquí se ven todos los detalles. Mira sus caras.

Claro. Es un cuadro cubista. Pero en ese cuadro no hay una flor.

Este cuadro también es de Picasso.

Vamos, hija. Tenemos que buscar la famosa margarita.

Me encanta la posición de la mujer con los codos apoyados en la mesa.

A mí me gustan los labios pintados de rojo.

Pero aquí no hay flores. ¡Este desafío es muy difícil!

Continuará...

6 **Detective de palabras**

▶ **Completa** estas oraciones.

1. La niña tiene la ___1___ muy grande y el ___2___ muy pequeño.
2. En el cuadro de Velázquez, se ven los detalles en las ___3___ de las chicas.
3. A Tess le encanta la posición de la mujer con los ___4___ apoyados en la mesa.
4. A Patricia le gustan los ___5___ pintados de rojo.

242 doscientos cuarenta y dos

Differentiated Instruction

DEVELOPING LEARNERS

- To assist students in comprehending the *fotonovela*, help them identify the cognates in the dialogue: *mamá, cubista, basado, pintura, detalles, posición, pintados,* and *famosa.* Be sure to point out that *raro* is a false cognate; it does not mean *rare*. Ask students what they think it means. (strange) Then ask students to role-play the dialogue with a partner. Remind them to read with proper intonation and reflect the interest that Patricia and Tess exhibit at the museum.

EXPANDING LEARNERS

- Ask students to work with a partner and say what they have observed in each of the paintings shown in the *fotonovela* and what they like, or do not like, about each one. Then have then write their observations and opinions in a revised dialogue, as if they were two other visitors in the museum and also on a quest to find *la famosa margarita*.

7 **¿Comprendes?**

▶ **Responde** a estas preguntas.

1. ¿Dónde están Tess y Patricia?
2. ¿Qué están buscando?
3. ¿Cómo es la niña del primer cuadro? ¿Quién lo pintó?
4. ¿Quién es Velázquez?
5. ¿Cómo tiene los labios la mujer del segundo cuadro de Picasso?

 8 **¿Qué ves tú?**

 ▶ **Escucha** y relaciona cada descripción con la fotografía correspondiente.

Ⓐ 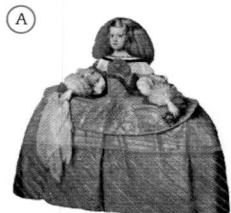   Ⓑ 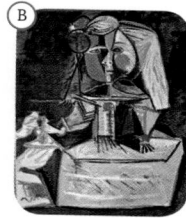   Ⓒ

 9 **Tu cuadro**

▶ **Dibuja** a tu compañero(a) o a otra persona que conozcas. Imita el estilo cubista de Picasso.

 ▶ **Describe** tu cuadro a tu compañero(a) y pregúntale por el suyo.

Modelo A. ¿Esto es la cabeza?
         B. No, es una pierna.

CULTURA

Pablo Picasso

Pablo Ruiz Picasso es uno de los pintores españoles más importantes del siglo XX. Nació en Málaga en 1881 y murió en Francia en 1973. Pintó más de dos mil cuadros y cultivó diversos estilos, entre ellos, el cubismo.

Muchas de sus obras están en el Museo Picasso de Barcelona y en el Museo Picasso de Málaga, pero hay cuadros de este autor en museos de todo el mundo. Una de sus obras más conocidas, *Guernica*, está en el Museo Reina Sofía de Madrid.

10 **Piensa y explica.** ¿Te gusta el estilo cubista? ¿Por qué?

▶ **TU DESAFÍO** Visita la página web para aprender más sobre el cubismo.

HERITAGE LANGUAGE LEARNERS

• Ask students to research the life and works of Diego Velázquez after they have visited the web page for Picasso. Then ask them to compare and contrast the lives and paintings of these two great Spanish artists. Have students select one painting by each of these men and describe the subject, the colors, the style, and what they find interesting and attractive about the work they have chosen.

MULTIPLE INTELLIGENCES:
Interpersonal Intelligence

• Ask students to set the clock back about 100 years: Picasso has just exhibited a collection of cubist paintings and is the new sensation in the art world! Students will work with a partner: one will role-play Picasso and the other will be a journalist eager to interview the artist. Both students will need to familiarize themselves with Picasso's life and cubism so the interview is more realistic. Have students present their interviews before the class.

Describir partes del cuerpo

Activities

8. After listening to the audio, assign students to groups of three where they will role-play a conversation between the people in these paintings. Students may only write down three to five key words. They will then present to the class.

9. To extend this activity, have students write a description of their partner's picture on a card. Then post students' drawings around the room. Collect the cards and redistribute them randomly. Students should look for the picture that matches the description on their card.

 AUDIO SCRIPT
See page 235I.

 CULTURA

Pablo Picasso

Picasso had a long and fruitful career as a painter, ceramist, sculptor, and printmaker. He and Georges Braque developed the cubist art movement. Soon cubism and Picasso's work would become extremely influential on the art of the 20th century.

Answer Key

6. 1. cabeza   3. caras   5. labios
    2. cuerpo   4. codos

7. 1. Están en el Museo Picasso.
    2. Buscan un cuadro cubista de Margarita.
    3. Tiene la cabeza muy grande y el cuerpo muy pequeño. Lo pintó Picasso.
    4. Es un pintor español del siglo XVII.
    5. Los tiene pintados de rojo.

8. 1. C   2. A   3. B

9. Answers will vary.
    ▶ Answers will vary.

10. Answers will vary.

Additional Resources

Fans Online activities

243

Unit 5
DESAFÍO 1

Vocabulario – Partes del cuerpo

Presentation

- In this section, students will learn vocabulary pertaining to parts of the body.

Activities	Standards	Resources
Vocabulario	1.2	
11.	1.2	
12.	1.3	
13.	1.1, 1.2, 1.3	Audio
14. Comparaciones	1.1, 1.2, 2.1, 3.2, 4.2	
Tu desafío	1.2, 2.1, 3.2, 5.1	

Teaching Suggestions

Warm-Up / Independent Starter

- Ask students to list all of the body parts they remember in a chart like the one below. Use gestures to pantomime the words *cabeza* (head), *tronco* (trunk / torso), and *extremidades* (limbs).

La cabeza	El tronco	Las extremidades

Preparation

- Have students share their Independent Starter with the class. Then ask them what body parts they use to: *oír, respirar, hablar, ver, cantar, comer, pensar, escribir, correr, caminar,* etc.

Activities

13. Before playing the audio recording, ask students to use descriptive adjectives and clothing vocabulary to describe the different people seen in these pictures. For example: *La chica rubia tiene el pelo largo y usa gafas. Lleva una chaqueta verde de cuadros.*

14. Brainstorm greetings and goodbyes in Spanish. Then assign roles to pairs of students (e.g., two high school girlfriends meet at café in Barcelona, a male student meets a female student on the first day of school, etc). Ask pairs to act out their assigned meetings using different greetings and culturally appropriate gestures.

244

Vocabulario

Partes del cuerpo

la cabeza · los dedos · la muñeca · el brazo · el cuello · el pecho · la rodilla · el pie · el hombro · el codo · la espalda · la mano · la cintura · la pierna · el tobillo

La cara

las cejas · las pestañas · las orejas · la boca · los dientes · los labios · la frente · los ojos · la nariz · las mejillas · la barbilla

11 ¿Dónde están?

▶ **Clasifica** estas partes del cuerpo.

la cabeza	el cuello
los hombros	las piernas
los pies	los tobillos
la espalda	el pecho
las manos	las rodillas

Encima de la cintura	Debajo de la cintura
la cabeza	

244 doscientos cuarenta y cuatro

Differentiated Instruction

DEVELOPING LEARNERS

- Ask students to close their books and draw a large stick figure on one sheet of paper and a face on another. Then have them label the body and the face with as many body parts as they can. Pair students with heritage language learners who will listen and correct them as they read the labels for the body parts they have drawn while pointing to them. If some labels are missing, ask the heritage language learners to name these body parts and guide their partners in labeling them.

EXPANDING LEARNERS

- Ask students to imagine that their town has been visited by an extraterrestrial. Have them work with a partner and draw a figure based on their partners' descriptions of this creature. For example: *tiene tres cabezas, cejas verdes, ocho dedos en la mano derecha.* Taking turns, partners will read their description while their partner draws it. When you call time, students exchange drawings and verify that their partners have followed their descriptions.

12 Actividades físicas

▶ **Escribe.** ¿Qué partes del cuerpo utilizas para realizar estas actividades?

Modelo tocar la guitarra → *Toco la guitarra con los dedos.*

1. jugar al fútbol   2. hablar   3. cepillarte los dientes   4. pintar   5. bailar

13 ¿Cómo es?

▶ **Escucha** y decide. ¿A qué fotografía corresponde la descripción?

▶ **Escribe.** Elige una fotografía y escribe una descripción de esa persona.

Modelo *Tiene la nariz grande y los ojos oscuros…*

▶ **Lee** el texto de tu compañero(a). ¿A qué persona corresponde su descripción?

COMPARACIONES

Los saludos y las despedidas

En cada cultura hay distintos gestos para saludar y despedirse. En España, como en otros países, es habitual estrechar la mano (*shake hands*), especialmente entre los hombres. Entre las mujeres es habitual saludarse y despedirse con dos besos en las mejillas. Y entre un hombre y una mujer, el saludo varía dependiendo del grado de formalidad. En otros países hispanos, es más común dar un solo beso.

14 **Piensa.** ¿En tu cultura es habitual saludarse con un beso? ¿Conoces otros gestos de otras culturas?

▶ **TU DESAFÍO** Visita la página web para aprender más sobre los saludos y las despedidas.

HERITAGE LANGUAGE LEARNERS

- Ask students to imagine that they have witnessed a crime, and are the only ones who can describe the culprit. Have them bring in a headshot of a person and, without showing it to their partners, have them explain what this person looks like. The partners are sketch artists for the police and will try to make a likeness of that individual. As they draw, their partners will suggest changes or modifications so the sketch resembles the criminal. After you call time, students compare the sketch with the original image. See which pairs have produced the most authentic likeness.

SPECIAL-NEEDS LEARNERS

- Help visually impaired students learn the vocabulary for parts of the body by saying each word and tapping that part of your body as they repeat the words. Then say each word, and ask them to repeat the word and touch that corresponding body part on themselves.

 AUDIO SCRIPT
See page 235I.

 COMPARACIONES

Los saludos y las despedidas

Introductions and leave-taking in business contexts in Spain may seem rather formal to many Americans. Men almost always shake hands upon greeting one another. However, in casual settings, men and women will generally kiss on both cheeks, left to right, as do women. It is also common for male friends to embrace or pat one another on the back. Generally speaking, Spaniards do not require as much "personal space" as people from the United States seem to need.

Answer Key

11. Encima de la cintura: la cabeza, los hombros, la espalda, las manos, el cuello, el pecho
Debajo de la cintura: los pies, las piernas, los tobillos, las rodillas

12. Answers will vary. Sample answers:
1. Juego al fútbol con los pies.
2. Hablo con la boca.
3. Me cepillo los dientes con la mano.
4. Pinto con las manos.
5. Bailo con los pies.

13. Fotografía 4.
▶ Answers will vary.
▶ Answers will vary.

14. Answers will vary.

Additional Resources

Fans Online activities
Practice Workbook

DESAFÍO 1

Gramática – El participio

Presentation

- In this section, students will learn to form the past participle and to use it as an adjective.

Activities	Standards	Resources
Gramática	3.1	
15.	1.1, 4.1	
16.	1.2	
17.	1.2, 1.3	Audio
18.	1.3	
19. Conexiones	1.1, 1.2, 2,1, 3.1, 3.2	
Tu desafío	1.2, 2.1, 3.1, 3.2, 5.1	

Teaching Suggestions

Warm-Up / Independent Starter

- Write on the board the following sentences for students to translate.
  1. *Los estudiantes están <u>sentados</u> en el suelo.*
  2. *Ella tiene las uñas <u>pintadas</u> de rojo.*
  3. *Todas las ventanas están <u>abiertas</u>.*

Preparation

- Go over the grammar presentation with students. Emphasize that regular past participles are formed by using the infinitive; therefore, there are no spelling and stem changes. Practice verbs such as *conocer, dirigir, escoger, empezar, perder, dormir, repetir.*

- Emphasize that past participles used as adjectives must agree in number and gender with the noun described. For example: *El museo está cerrado. La tienda está cerrada.*

Activities

15. Have students practice the difference between the preterite and the past participle in Spanish. Find pictures of the following and show them to cue possible infinitives: wrist *(romperse);* chair *(sentarse);* pen *(escribir);* fingernails *(pintar).* Students should write sentences using the preterite of these verbs (e.g., *Me rompí la muñeca).* Then have them rewrite the sentences using the past participle as adjective (e.g., *La muñeca está rota).* Compare with English.

Gramática

El participio

- In Spanish, verbs have a form that is sometimes used as an adjective: the participle.

  María se maquilló. → María está **maquillada.**

- The past participle (participio) of a verb can be used as an adjective to describe a noun. Like other Spanish adjectives, the past participle must agree in number and gender with the noun described.

  María está **maquillada.** Lleva los labios **pintados.**

Formación del participio pasado

- The past participle is formed this way:

-ar verbs	Add the ending -ado.	pintar → pintado
-er and -ir verbs	Add the ending -ido.	vestir → vestido

- The following verbs have irregular past participles:

abrir	abierto	morir	muerto
decir	dicho	poner	puesto
descubrir	descubierto	romper	roto
escribir	escrito	ver	visto
hacer	hecho	volver	vuelto

- The past participle oído and the past participles ending in -aído and -eído have an accent.

  caer → **caído**   traer → **traído**   leer → **leído**   creer → **creído**

15 **Compara.** ¿Cómo se forma el participio pasado en inglés? ¿Hay formas irregulares?

16 **¿Cómo se forma?**

▶ **Completa** estas oraciones con los participios correspondientes.

1. ¡Cuidado! Los niños están _____ . (dormir)
2. No entiendo este mensaje porque está _____ en alemán. (escribir)
3. Entra, la puerta está _____ . (abrir)
4. Me gusta el cuadro de la mujer _____ en la silla. (sentar)
5. ¡Terminé! Todas las tareas están _____ . (hacer)

Differentiated Instruction

DEVELOPING LEARNERS

- Ask students to say or rewrite the sentences in activity 16 so that the singular participles are plural, and the plural participles, singular. Remind them to make any other necessary changes. For example: *No entiendo estos mensajes porque están escritos en alemán.*

EXPANDING LEARNERS

- Ask students to complete the following sentences with the correct form of the past participle of the verb in parentheses:
  1. *¡Qué lástima! Las jarras están … (romper).* (rotas)
  2. *Esa carta está mal … (escribir).* (escrita)
  3. *¿Cuáles son los libros más … (leer) de la clase?* (leídos)
  4. *La mesa está … (poner).* (puesta)
  5. *Esto está muy bien … (decir) y … (hacer).* (dicho; hecho)
  6. *Las islas … (descubrir) por Colón están en el Caribe.* (descubiertas)
  7. *Está mal … (ver) no dar las gracias.* (visto)

17 En el salón de clase

▶ **Escucha** y completa estas oraciones.

1. Hay un chico _____ en el suelo.
2. Todos los libros están _____.
3. La puerta no está abierta, está _____.
4. Hay muchas chicas con los labios _____.
5. Hay una chica _____.
6. En la pizarra hay verbos _____ en español.

▶ **Escribe.** Mira a las personas y los objetos en tu salón de clase y decide si las oraciones anteriores son ciertas (C) o falsas (F). Si son falsas, corrígelas.

Modelo *En mi salón de clase no hay ningún chico sentado en el suelo.*

18 ¿Qué pasa?

▶ **Habla.** Describe estas fotografías. Usa participios pasados.

Modelo 1. *La chica está sorprendida. Tiene la boca abierta.*

①  ②  ③  ④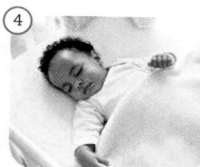

CONEXIONES: LENGUA

El catalán

En la fotografía puedes ver una reproducción de la página web del Museo Picasso de Barcelona. La página está escrita en catalán y tiene versiones en inglés y en castellano.

El catalán y el castellano son las lenguas oficiales de Cataluña, Baleares y la Comunidad Valenciana, regiones situadas en el este de España.

19 Investiga. ¿Sabes cuántas lenguas oficiales hay en España?

▶ **TU DESAFÍO** Visita la página web para aprender más sobre las lenguas oficiales de España.

HERITAGE LANGUAGE LEARNERS

• Explain that the past participle is also used with the perfect tenses, as in the following sentences in the present perfect: *He leído esta historia. Hemos vuelto de nuestro viaje a Palos de la Frontera.* Ask students to write at least ten sentences using the past participle either as an adjective or as part of the present perfect tense. Encourage them to use as many of the verbs with an irregular past participle as they can.

CRITICAL THINKING

• Explain that in several regions of Spain, it is common for people to speak their regional language (*catalán, gallego, valenciano,* or *euskera*) in addition to Spanish. Many people feel that a region's culture and history is best preserved this way, yet others feel there should be only one official language for the entire nation. Explore what students think. Have them debate this issue, selecting several teams of debaters and having some be in favor of official bilingualism and others opposed.

---

17. Once students have completed this activity, review noun / adjective agreement by forming questions: *¿Hay algún chico sentado?*

 AUDIO SCRIPT
See page 235I.

 CONEXIONES: LENGUA

El catalán

The Constitution of Spain states that the official language of Spain is Castilian (i.e., Spanish) and it recognizes the right of each autonomous community to determine its own co-official language. The following languages are co-official, along with Spanish: Catalan in Catalonia and the Balearic Islands; Euskera, or Basque, in the Basque Country and in some Euskera-speaking areas of Navarre; Valencian in Valencia; Galician in Galicia.

Answer Key

15. En los verbos regulares se forma añadiendo -*d* o -*ed.* Hay muchas formas irregulares, por ejemplo: *broken, chosen, gone, sent,* etc.

16.
1. dormidos
2. escrito
3. abierta
4. sentada
5. hechas

17.
1. sentado
2. abiertos
3. cerrada
4. pintados
5. dormida
6. escritos
▶ Answers will vary.

18. Answers will vary. Sample answers:
2. El chico tiene la pierna rota.
3. La mujer tiene los labios pintados.
4. El niño está dormido.

19. Answers will vary.

Additional Resources

Fans Online activities
Practice Workbook

247

Unit 5

DESAFÍO 1

Comunicación

Presentation

- In this section, students will integrate the vocabulary and grammar from *Desafío 1* in order to talk about body parts and to use the past participle as an adjective.

Activities	Standards	Resources
20.	1.1, 1.2, 1.3, 2.2, 3.1, 5.1	
21.	1.2	Audio
22. Final del desafío	1.3, 2.2	

Teaching Suggestions

Warm-Up / Independent Starter

- Have students correct these illogical sentences:
  1. *Las chicas están sentadas con las orejas cruzadas.*
  2. *Los estudiantes no pueden ver porque las luces están encendidas.*
  3. *Las modelos llevan los codos pintados.*
  4. *No se puede caminar con los brazos rotos.*
  5. *Para leer hay que cerrar el libro abierto.*

Preparation

- Invite volunteers to write on the board their corrected sentences from the Independent Starter. Ask the rest of the class to check theirs.
- Take 10 minutes to review the vocabulary and grammar themes of the *Desafío*. Use the sentences on the board to illustrate the different vocabulary and grammar points.
- Refer students back to the *fotonovela*. Have them identify the vocabulary for parts of the body and past participles used as adjectives. Do students understand the dialogue better now that they have gone through the vocabulary and grammar from the *Desafío?*
- Show students Fernando Botero's version of Margarita: *Menina* (1978). You will find a picture of this painting at http://www.all-art.org/art_20th_century/botero1.html. Ask students to work with a partner to compare and contrast this painting with those of Picasso and Velázquez. Encourage students to use the vocabulary they learned in this *Desafío*.

248

Comunicación

20 **¿Quién es quién?**

▶ **Lee** las descripciones que hacen tres estudiantes sobre estos cuadros de Picasso. ¿A qué fotografía corresponde cada una?

Marie Thérèse. Pablo Picasso.

Los tres músicos. Pablo Picasso.

Jacqueline agachada. Pablo Picasso.

1. Hay tres personas sentadas, se pueden ver las piernas y los pies. No se ven sus caras con claridad, pero se ven los ojos y la boca. También se ven las manos de dos personas. Están tocando instrumentos musicales.

2. Hay una mujer sentada en una silla. Tiene los ojos grandes y muy separados. Su nariz también es grande. Tiene los labios pintados de color amarillo. Tiene el pelo largo y lleva un sombrero.

3. Hay una mujer sentada. Probablemente está sentada en el suelo. Está muy seria. En su cara se pueden ver con claridad los ojos, las cejas, la nariz y los labios. Tiene el cuello muy largo y sus manos y sus pies son bastante grandes. Lleva un sombrero y un traje de rayas amarillas.

▶ **Escribe** una descripción de uno de los cuadros de este desafío. Léesela a tu compañero(a). Él/Ella tiene que adivinar a qué cuadro corresponde.

248 doscientos cuarenta y ocho

Differentiated Instruction

DEVELOPING LEARNERS

- Ask students to make a three-column list and label the columns *Solo uno(a), Dos, Más de dos*. Have them review the names for the parts of the body and face and write each one under the corresponding heading; for example, *cabeza* would go in the first column, *manos* would be included in the second, and *dedos* would go in the third column.

EXPANDING LEARNERS

- Ask students to create a riddle that describes a body part, or uses parts of the body as clues, read it aloud to the class, and see who will be the first person to guess the word. Give them one or two examples to get them started: *Somos dos. Unimos el muslo con la pierna. Te ayudamos muchísimo cuando juegas al fútbol. Nos necesitas para sentarte y levantarte. ¿Quiénes somos? (Las rodillas).*

21 Adivinanzas

▶ **Escucha** estas adivinanzas sobre partes del cuerpo. ¿A qué fotografía corresponde cada una?

Ⓐ 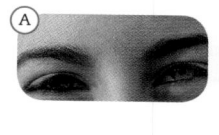 Ⓑ 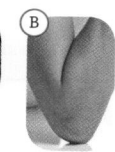 Ⓒ  Ⓓ 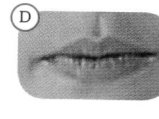 Ⓔ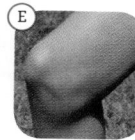

Final del desafío

Tiene que haber un cuadro con una margarita pintada.

Quizás estamos en el museo equivocado.

Mamá, quiero comprar un cartel de ese cuadro.

Retrato de la madre del artista. Pablo Picasso.

Bien, pero ¿cómo se llama? ¿Te acuerdas?

¿Margarita de Austria? ¿Margarita es un nombre?

Esta es Margarita de Austria, la hija del rey Felipe IV.

¡Claro! ¡Esta niña es nuestra Margarita!

22 Un recuerdo del museo

▶ **Escribe.** Tess y Patricia deciden ir a la tienda del museo a comprar un cartel, pero no recuerdan el título. Escribe una descripción del cuadro para ayudarlas.

doscientos cuarenta y nueve **249**

Activities

20. Ask students to write five questions for the people in Picasso's paintings. Ask them to imagine that these people come from very different backgrounds and that they meet at a party. Have students work with a partner to role-play the different characters and take turns asking and answering each other's questions.

21. Before playing the audio recording, have students identify each of the body parts depicted in this activity. Then play the audio and ask students to complete the activity.

22. Have students work with two partners to act out the scene in the museum's gift shop. Student A is the gift shop employee; Student B, Tess; Student C, Patricia. In order to avoid reading from a script, tell students they may write only a list of five important words. Have them present their scene to the class.

AUDIO SCRIPT
See page 235I.

Answer Key

20. 1. B   2. A   3. C
   ▶ Answers will vary

21. 1. C   4. B
   2. A   5. D
   3. E

22. Answers will vary.

Additional Resources

Fans Online activities
Practice Workbook

HERITAGE LANGUAGE LEARNERS

• Ask students to come up with a list of idiomatic expressions and sayings that mention parts of the body and explain them to the class. For instance, *cuesta un ojo de la cara* indicates that something is very expensive (i.e., it costs an arm and a leg). You might include some of the following to get students started, but have them brainstorm their lists: *tomarle el pelo a alguien* (to pull someone's leg); *no pegar ojo* (to not get any sleep); *más vale pájaro en mano que cien volando* (a bird in the hand is worth two in the bush).

MULTIPLE INTELLIGENCES:
Verbal-Linguistic Intelligence

• Divide the class into teams and have one player from each team come to the board and write a word you tell them that names a part of the body (e.g., *cabeza*). Students must write the word vertically, writing one letter per line. Then, without looking at their opponents' list, they must write a word that starts with each of the letters from the first word (e.g., *codo, arte, brazo, enero, zapato, amigo*). Players who complete the words correctly, and within a given time, earn 1 point. Repeat the process with other players.

Unit 5
DESAFÍO 2

Hablar de hábitos de higiene personal

Presentation

- In this *Desafío*, Diana and Rita are in Salamanca, Spain, where they must find an elusive frog.
- In this section, students will preview:
  - Beauty products and personal hygiene verbs.
  - Adverbs ending in *-mente*.

Activities	Standards	Resources
Fotonovela	1.2, 2.1, 3.1, 3.2	Vis. Pres.
23.	1.2, 1.3	
24.	1.2, 1.3	
25.	1.1, 1.2	Audio
26. Cultura	1.1, 1.2, 2.2, 3.1, 4.2, 5.1	Video
Tu desafío	1.2, 3.2, 5.1	

Teaching Suggestions

Warm-Up / Independent Starter

- Have students read the introduction to the *fotonovela* silently. Ask them to write whether they think there is some truth to the frog legend.

Preparation

- Ask students to share their response from the Independent Starter. Do they know of any other legend related to student life?

La fotonovela

Before Viewing

- Have students read the *fotonovela*. Ask them how they think Rita and Diana are feeling based on the pictures and dialogue.

After Viewing

- Ask students to hypothesize where the frog might be located.

Activities

23. As an extension of this activity, have students close their books and read one of Rita's or Diana's speech bubbles. See if students are able to identify the speaker. Ask them to raise their right hand to symbolize Rita and their left hand to symbolize Diana.

La rana de la suerte

Diana and Rita are in Salamanca, the city that is home to one of the oldest universities in the world. Together, they must find an elusive frog that, according to legend, all students at the university must see at least once if they don't want to fail their exams.

> ¿Hasta qué hora podemos desayunar? Antes de ir, tengo que ducharme, lavarme el pelo, peinarme...

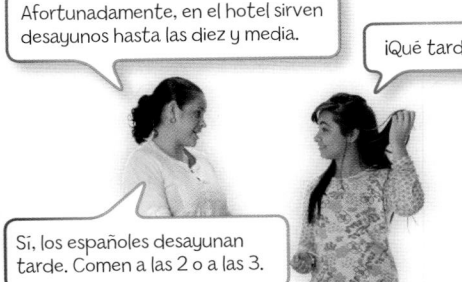

> Afortunadamente, en el hotel sirven desayunos hasta las diez y media.

> ¡Qué tarde!

> Sí, los españoles desayunan tarde. Comen a las 2 o a las 3.

> Toma, Diana, date crema solar. ¿No te vas a secar el pelo?

> No, hace mucho calor. Estoy sudando.

> Creo que está cerrada.

> ¡Claro, es que hoy es domingo! ¿Cómo vamos a encontrar la rana?

> ¿Saben dónde está la rana?

> ¡No! Y la estamos buscando cuidadosamente...

Continuará...

23 **Detective de palabras**

▶ **Completa** estas oraciones.

1. _____, en el hotel sirven desayunos hasta las diez y media.

2. Diana y Rita buscan la rana _____.

▶ **Responde** a estas preguntas.

1. ¿Qué tiene que hacer Diana antes de ir a desayunar?

2. ¿Qué haces tú antes de desayunar?

Differentiated Instruction

DEVELOPING LEARNERS

- Ask students the following questions to test their comprehension of their daily routine:
  1. *¿Qué haces primero: ducharte o levantarte? (levantarte)*
  2. *¿Qué haces por la mañana: cenar o desayunar? (desayunar)*
  3. *Si estás sudando, ¿te duchas o te peinas? (te duchas)*
  4. *¿Qué te das cuando vas a la playa: crema solar o jabón? (crema solar)*
  5. *¿Qué haces después de acostarte: dormirte o levantarte? (dormirte)*
  6. *¿Usas jabón para lavarte o para desayunar? (lavarte)*

EXPANDING LEARNERS

- Ask students to identify all the verbs in the *fotonovela* that have to do with one's daily routine: *desayunar, ducharme, lavarme (el pelo), peinarme, date crema solar, secar el pelo.* Then ask students to write a sentence with each of these verbs, explaining when they carry out these actions or under what circumstances. For example: *Desayuno a las siete todos los días. Me doy crema solar si salgo a hacer ejercicio.* Ask them to read their sentences aloud.

24 **¿Comprendes?**

▶ **Responde** a estas preguntas.

1. ¿Quién se levantó primero, Diana o Rita?
2. ¿A qué hora comen habitualmente los españoles?
3. ¿Por qué no se seca el pelo Diana?
4. ¿Por qué está cerrada la puerta de la universidad?
5. ¿Qué tienen que buscar Rita y Diana?

25 **La vida estudiantil**

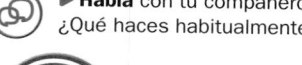 ▶ **Escucha** a unos estudiantes de la Universidad de Salamanca y relaciona cada diálogo con la fotografía correspondiente.

 ▶ **Habla** con tu compañero(a). ¿Cómo es para ti un día en la escuela? ¿Qué haces habitualmente?

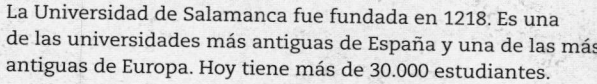 **CULTURA**

La Universidad de Salamanca

La Universidad de Salamanca fue fundada en 1218. Es una de las universidades más antiguas de España y una de las más antiguas de Europa. Hoy tiene más de 30.000 estudiantes.

La fachada de la universidad es de piedra tallada *(sculpted)*. En ella hay una pequeña rana de piedra sobre un cráneo *(skull)*. La leyenda dice que los estudiantes que consiguen ver la rana tienen buena suerte en los exámenes.

 26 **Piensa y habla.** ¿Cuál es la universidad más importante cerca de donde vives? ¿Conoces algún símbolo o leyenda relacionado con ella?

 **→ TU DESAFÍO** | Visita la página web para aprender más sobre la Universidad de Salamanca.

doscientos cincuenta y uno 251

HERITAGE LANGUAGE LEARNERS

• Ask students to address the different times people have their meals in the Spanish-speaking cultures they know. You might want them to make a chart or graph that shows their typical schedule for breakfast, lunch, and dinner, as well as when they have a "formal" snack, or what would be called *la merienda* in Spain and *las once* in other countries. Ask them to address their preferences in schedules and explain why.

SPECIAL-NEEDS LEARNERS

• Give students with auditory impairments a copy of the audio script for activity 25, and for all other activities of this type. Have them listen to the audio as many times as needed, and follow along on the printed page. Be sure these students are seated in a quiet area of the classroom, away from doors, windows, and other distractions.

Hablar de hábitos de higiene personal

25. After completing the speaking activity, ask students to compare their typical school day with the information presented by the speakers during the listening activity.

 AUDIO SCRIPT
See page 235l.

CULTURA

La Universidad de Salamanca

The University of Salamanca is one of the top universities in Spain, attracting students from all regions pursuing undergraduate, graduate, and doctorate degrees. It also has a program for international students looking to study Spanish. The university's facade is one of Salamanca's tourist attractions. It is divided into three parts: the medallion of Fernando and Isabel, the coat of arms of Carlos V, and a scene of Pope Benedict XIII. The frog is located on the third level to the right, atop a skull.

Answer Key

23. 1. Afortunadamente
2. cuidadosamente
▶ 1. Tiene que ducharse, lavarse el pelo y peinarse.
2. Answers will vary.

24. 1. Rita se levantó primero.
2. Comen a las 2 o a las 3.
3. Porque hace mucho calor.
4. Porque es domingo.
5. Tienen que buscar una rana.

25. 1. E 2. C 3. A 4. D 5. B
▶ Answers will vary.

26. Answers will vary.

Additional Resources

Fans Online activities

DESAFÍO 2

Vocabulario – La higiene personal

Presentation

- In this section, students will learn:
  - Vocabulary for beauty products.
  - Personal hygiene verbs.

Activities	Standards	Resources
Vocabulario	1.2	
27.	1.2	
28.	1.3, 5.1	
29.	1.2, 1.3	Audio
30. Cultura	1.1, 1.2, 2.1, 3.2, 4.2	

Teaching Suggestions

Warm-Up / Independent Starter

- Have students write a list of what they might use to get ready in the bathroom, using vocabulary they have learned in the past.

Preparation

- Ask students to share their list from the Independent Starter. Record their responses on the board to verify the spelling for students.

- Go over the vocabulary presentation with students. Ask for one female and one male student to read the speech bubbles.

- Use gestures to act out the list of verbs. Have students stand and repeat the words while mimicking your gestures. Ask for a student volunteer to play the role of the teacher demonstrating the gestures after you have introduced the words.

- Bring in a bag of realia or photos of personal care products. Have students close their books. As you pull the objects out of the bag, have students identify them.

Activities

27. To challenge more advanced learners, ask students to provide the response in a complete sentence and indicate when the action is usually done. For example: *Se lava las manos con el jabón antes de comer.*

28. When students guess the action correctly, ask them to mention some products that would be used to complete the action.

Vocabulario

La higiene personal

A mí me gusta arreglarme. Todos los días, después de ponerme crema, me maquillo.

¡Estoy sudando! Voy a ducharme y a ponerme desodorante.

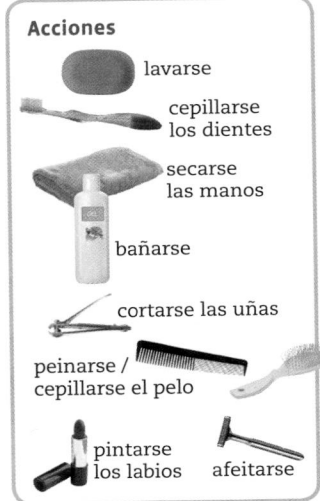

Acciones

- lavarse
- cepillarse los dientes
- secarse las manos
- bañarse
- cortarse las uñas
- peinarse / cepillarse el pelo
- pintarse los labios
- afeitarse

 el secador

 la crema

 el maquillaje

 el esmalte de uñas

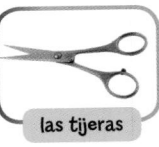 las tijeras

27 Parejas lógicas

▶ **Une.** ¿Con qué objeto se relaciona cada acción?

A
1. lavarse las manos
2. cepillarse el pelo
3. secarse el pelo
4. ducharse
5. lavarse el pelo
6. secarse las manos
7. lavarse los dientes

B
a. el champú
b. la pasta de dientes
c. la toalla
d. el gel
e. el cepillo
f. el jabón
g. el secador

Differentiated Instruction

DEVELOPING LEARNERS

- To reinforce vocabulary, ask students the following questions about personal hygiene:
  1. *¿Qué se pone una mujer en la cara: maquillaje o esmalte? (maquillaje)*
  2. *¿Cómo te secas la cara: con un secador o con una toalla? (con una toalla)*
  3. *¿Con qué se pinta una chica las uñas: con esmalte o con tijeras? (con esmalte)*
  4. *¿Qué usas para lavarte las manos: toallas o jabón? (jabón)*
  5. *¿Con qué te cortas las uñas: con tijeras o con esmalte? (con tijeras)*
  6. *¿Qué usas si estás sudando: maquillaje o desodorante? (desodorante)*

EXPANDING LEARNERS

- Have students complete the following word associations:
  1. *el champú: el pelo | el jabón: el cuerpo / las uñas (el cuerpo)*
  2. *bañarse: agua | peinarse: cepillo / champú (cepillo)*
  3. *afeitarse: la cara | pintarse: el maquillaje / las uñas (las uñas)*
  4. *pintarse: los labios | maquillarse: el pelo / la cara (la cara)*
  5. *secarse: toalla | peinarse: crema / cepillo (cepillo)*
  6. *arreglarse: el pelo | afeitarse: la barba / las tijeras (la barba)*

¿Qué hago?

▶ **Representa** una acción relacionada con la higiene personal. Tus compañeros(as) tienen que adivinar cuál es.

Modelo ¡Te peinas!

 El horario de Diana

▶ **Escucha** y completa la tabla. ¿Qué hace Diana?

De lunes a viernes	Los fines de semana
Se despierta temprano.	
	Desayuna.
Desayuna.	Se baña.
Se viste.	Se pone desodorante.
Se peina.	
	Se viste.

▶ **Escribe** un texto comparando tu rutina y la rutina de Diana.

Modelo De lunes a viernes Diana se despierta temprano, se ducha y desayuna.
Yo también me despierto temprano, pero desayuno antes de ducharme.

 CULTURA

Los colegios mayores

Los colegios mayores son residencias para los estudiantes universitarios. Muchos dependen de la universidad, pero otros son autónomos (independent).

En las residencias suele haber dormitorios individuales y dobles. Normalmente tienen baño propio, pero a veces el cuarto de baño es compartido. Por lo general, ofrecen servicio de limpieza de las habitaciones y zonas comunes: cafetería, comedor, salas de estudio, gimnasio o piscina, etc.

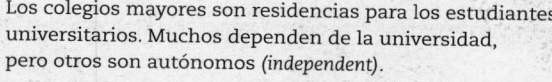

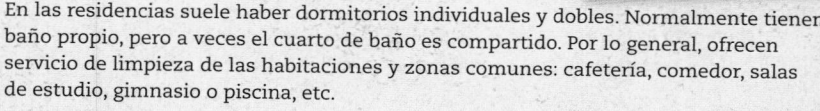

Compara. ¿Dónde suelen alojarse los estudiantes universitarios en los Estados Unidos? ¿Cómo son los dormitorios y los baños: individuales o compartidos?

HERITAGE LANGUAGE LEARNERS

- Ask students to think of some additional actions they commonly perform to maintain good hygiene or to look good (e.g., *usar el hilo dental por lo menos una vez al día; hacerse la manicura / pedicura*). Also ask them to think of some alternative terms for the words presented (e.g., *el dentífrico* or *la pasta dentífrica* for *la pasta de dientes*). Have students find magazine cutouts or draw pictures of these new verbs or nouns, label them with the new or alternative terms, and present them to the class.

CRITICAL THINKING

- Remind students that many of them will be going to college soon. Even though many schools in the United States require freshmen to live on campus, students may have several options when they are older; among them would be living off-campus alone or with one or more roommates. Of course, many students study close to home, so they continue to live with their families. Have students discuss the pros and cons of these various living arrangements, including living in a *colegio mayor*.

Vocabulario – La higiene personal

29. Play the audio recording twice and review students' responses before continuing to the second part of the activity. As a prewriting activity, have students organize their thoughts by creating a Venn diagram comparing their schedule with Diana's.

30. If students are unable to draw comparisons with university residence halls, you can also ask about other experiences of living among students, such as at a summer camp.

 AUDIO SCRIPT
See page 235I.

 CULTURA

Los colegios mayores

Today, in Spain, *colegios mayores* are residence halls that promote forming the whole student. Some are associated with the university and others are completely independent. In Salamanca, many have traditions that date hundreds of years and are considered prestigious. In the past, the *colegios mayores* were university colleges, where classes were held.

Answer Key

27.
1. f	3. g	5. a	7. b
2. e	4. d	6. c	

28. Answers will vary.

29. De lunes a viernes: Se ducha. Se pone desodorante. Se lava los dientes.
Los fines de semana: Se despierta más tarde. Se lava el pelo. Se lava los dientes.
▶ Answers will vary.

30. Answers will vary.

Additional Resources

Fans Online activities
Practice Workbook

253

Unit 5
DESAFÍO 2

Gramática – Los adverbios en -mente

Presentation

- In this section, students will learn adverbs ending in -mente.

Activities	Standards	Resources
Gramática	3.1	
31.	1.1, 4.1	
32.	1.2, 1.3	
33.	1.2, 1.3	Audio
34.	1.1, 1.3	
35. Cultura	1.1, 1.2, 2.1, 3.2, 4.2, 5.1	

Teaching Suggestions

Warm-Up / Independent Starter

- Write the following adjectives on the board and ask students to write down their feminine form if they have a different one from the masculine: *rápido, lento, fácil, tranquilo, normal, general.*

Preparation

- Review the responses to the Independent Starter. Ask students how these words are used in a sentence. Ask probing questions to elicit that these words are adjectives which are used to describe nouns. Then ask students if they know any words to describe the action of a sentence and if they know what these words are called.

- Read the grammar presentation to the class. Pay close attention to changing the adjective into the feminine form prior to forming the adverb. Then provide additional examples of how to sequence two or more adverbs: *Rita se arregla tranquila, lenta y cuidadosamente.*

Activities

32. Prior to completing the sentences, ask students to form the adverbial form of the adjectives provided in the box.

33. After completing this activity, ask for three volunteers to present the paragraph to the class. One student will be the narrator, and the other two will be Rita and Diana, acting out the paragraph.

254

Gramática

Los adverbios en -mente

- Adverbs are words that express several circumstances:

  Place: aquí   Manner: bien   Quantity: mucho   Time: ayer   Frequency: nunca

  Siempre me cepillo los dientes después de comer.

- Words that express negation (no), affirmation (sí), or doubt (quizás) are also adverbs.

  Mi padre **no** se afeita todos los días.

Adverbios en –mente

- In Spanish, many adverbs are formed from adjectives by adding the suffix -mente to the feminine singular form.

Adjectives ending in -o.	Change -o to -a and add -mente.	lento ⟶ lentamente
Adjectives ending in -e or in a consonant.	Add -mente.	frecuente ⟶ frecuentemente habitual ⟶ habitualmente

- In many cases, the ending -mente means how one does an action (cuidadosamente, rápidamente, alegremente...). There are also some adverbs of frequency ending in -mente (habitualmente, generalmente, normalmente...).

- Some adjectives do not allow the formation of an adverb with -mente, like those that tell origin (español, peruano...) or those that describe physical or material qualities (rojo, caro...).

- When using a sequence of two or more adverbs, only add the ending -mente to the last one.

  Paco se afeita **lenta** y **cuidadosamente.**

31 **Compara.** ¿En inglés hay adverbios derivados de adjetivos, como los adverbios en -mente?

32 **¡Ayuda!**

▶ **Completa** estas oraciones con las formas correctas de los adverbios en –mente.

| cuidadoso |
| fácil |
| lento |
| alegre |
| rápido |
| habitual |

1. Me gusta este maquillaje porque se aplica ___fácilmente___.
2. Tess no suele hacer la tarea en casa. _____ va a la biblioteca.
3. Tim se arregla despacio, sin prisa. Él se viste _____.
4. Andy es muy deportista. Él corre _____.
5. Patricia tiene cuidado con el esmalte de uñas. Ella se pinta las uñas _____.
6. Mack se siente feliz por las mañanas. Se levanta _____.

254 doscientos cincuenta y cuatro

Differentiated Instruction

DEVELOPING LEARNERS

- Ask students to choose the adverb or expression that describes how or how often they do the following things:
1. *Hablo español rápidamente / lentamente.*
2. *Hago mi tarea alegremente / habitualmente.*
3. *Escucho a los profesores distraídamente / atentamente.*
4. *Me corto las uñas frecuentemente / cuidadosamente.*
5. *Me río fácilmente / difícilmente.*
6. *Me lavo el pelo cuidadosamente / frecuentemente.*
7. *Camino rápidamente / tranquilamente.*

EXPANDING LEARNERS

- Ask students to write a sentence using an adverb ending in -mente to explain how or how frequently they do the following things:
1. *estudiar*
2. *hacer la tarea*
3. *escuchar a la profesora de español*
4. *dormir la siesta*
5. *salir con tus amigos*
6. *darte crema solar*
7. *ir al centro comercial*
8. *vestirte con ropa elegante*

33 **¿Encontraron la rana?**

▶ **Completa** este texto con las formas correctas de los adverbios en –*mente*. Puede haber varias posibilidades.

| fácil | cuidadoso | rápido | amable | tranquilo | normal |

Un día en Salamanca

Rita se levantó temprano, se duchó y se arregló _____. Diana se despertó más tarde. Se duchó y se lavó el pelo. _____ ella se seca el pelo con el secador, pero ese día no lo hizo. Se peinó y se vistió _____ y las dos bajaron a desayunar al comedor del hotel.

Después de desayunar fueron a la universidad. Buscaron la rana de la fachada _____, pero no pudieron encontrarla. La rana no se ve _____ porque es muy pequeña. Un niño fue a ayudarlas _____. ¿Crees que encontraron la rana?

 ▶ **Escucha** y comprueba los resultados.

34 **¿Con qué frecuencia?**

 ▶ **Habla** con tu compañero(a). ¿Qué cosas hace habitualmente? ¿Con qué frecuencia?

Modelo A. *¿Con qué frecuencia te lavas el pelo?*
B. *Normalmente me lavo el pelo los fines de semana.*

1. lavarse el pelo   3. maquillarse o afeitarse   5. cepillarse los dientes
2. bañarse   4. cortarse las uñas   6. vestirse con ropa elegante

▶ **Organiza** los resultados en un gráfico. Indica la frecuencia de los hábitos de tu compañero(a).

 **CULTURA**

La siesta

En muchos países latinos existe la costumbre de dormir la siesta, es decir, dormir unos minutos después de comer. Algunos relacionan esta costumbre con el clima y otros con la cantidad de comida que se come en el almuerzo.

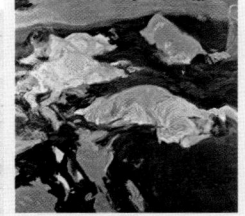

Joaquín Sorolla. *La siesta.*

La siesta no es una costumbre generalizada porque pocas personas almuerzan en casa, especialmente en las grandes ciudades.

35 **Explica.** ¿Crees que es una buena idea dormir la siesta? ¿Tienes algún momento de descanso durante el día?

HERITAGE LANGUAGE LEARNERS

• Have students work with a partner to write a dialogue using the adverbs from this unit as well as any others they know, including those that do not end in -*mente* (e.g., *nunca, siempre, a menudo, jamás*). The conversation will be between two friends who see and do things differently. For instance, if one friend likes to walk *rápidamente*, the other will counter with *a mí me gusta caminar lentamente*. See how many pairs of adverbs that are antonyms the students can use. Have them present their dialogues to the class.

CRITICAL THINKING

• Discuss the custom of the siesta with students. See how many think that it is a practical and healthful habit that should be practiced at your school and at home. How many think that it is a waste of time? For this last group, you might mention that even if students rested only 15 minutes a day, this totals an hour and 45 minutes a week, or 91 hours a year. Ask students to think about what they could be doing with this extra time instead of taking a nap and discuss.

DESAFÍO 2

Gramática – Los adverbios en -*mente*

34. You may choose to have students interview two classmates. Students can then use the results to write a paragraph comparing the routines of the two classmates they interviewed and themselves.

 AUDIO SCRIPT
See page 235l.

 CULTURA

La siesta

In Spain, people typically have lunch at 2:00 p. m. In smaller cities and towns, stores and businesses close at lunchtime. Some people return home to eat, while others choose to go to restaurants. Businesses reopen around 5:00 p. m. In larger cities, the siesta is not practiced as frequently and many businesses remain open. Most stores and businesses are closed on Sundays, even in major cities, because it is considered a day of rest.

Answer Key

31. Sí. Por ejemplo: *slowly, quickly, beautifully,* etc.

32. 2. Habitualmente   5. cuidadosamente
3. lentamente   6. alegremente
4. rápidamente

33. Answers will vary.
▶ 1. tranquilamente   4. cuidadosamente
2. Normalmente   5. fácilmente
3. rápidamente   6. amablemente

34. Answers will vary.
▶ Answers will vary.

35. Answers will vary.

Additional Resources

Fans Online activities
Practice Workbook

255

DESAFÍO 2

Comunicación

Presentation

- In this section, students will integrate the vocabulary and grammar from *Desafío 2* in order talk about personal hygiene and describe actions using adverbs ending in *-mente*.

Activities	Standards	Resources
36.	1.2, 1.3, 4.2	Audio
37.	1.1, 1.3	
38.	1.3, 5.2	
39. Final del desafío	1.2, 1.3, 2.2, 5.1	
Tu desafío	1.2, 1.3	

Teaching Suggestions

Warm-Up / Independent Starter

- Have students rewrite the following list of verbs in the order in which they complete these actions during the day. Also ask them to indicate the time when they complete the action.
  - *acostarse*
  - *vestirse*
  - *despertarse*
  - *almorzar*
  - *desayunar*
  - *hacer la tarea*

Preparation

- Ask students to share their responses from the Independent Starter. Based on students' answers, have the class make generalizations about the typical schedule in the United States.
- Take 10 minutes to review the vocabulary and grammar themes of the *Desafío*.
- Refer students back to the *fotonovela* in *Desafío 2*. Have them identify the words associated with the daily routine and the adverbs ending in *-mente*. Do students understand the dialogue better now that they have gone through the vocabulary and grammar from the *Desafío*?
- Have students compare their daily routine with the information provided by Rita and Diana in the *fotonovela* dialogue. Do they have to put on sun block every morning? Do they wash their hair daily? Do they blowdry their hair?

256

DESAFÍO 2

Comunicación

36 **¡Mi horario cambió!**

 ▶ **Escucha** y completa una tabla como esta. ¿A qué hora hace estas actividades Diana en España? ¿Y en los Estados Unidos?

	En España	En los Estados Unidos
1. levantarse	A las ocho.	
2. desayunar		
3. almorzar		
4. dormir la siesta		
5. acostarse		

▶ **Escribe** un texto con la información anterior.

Modelo *En España Diana se despierta a las ocho. Pero en los Estados Unidos ella se despierta a las…*

 ▶ **Compara** el horario de Diana en España con el tuyo. Usa un gráfico para organizar tu trabajo y después coméntalo con tu compañero(a).

 mi horario    el horario de Diana en España

37 **Tu neceser**

▶ **Escribe.** ¿Qué productos de higiene llevas normalmente cuando viajas? Haz una lista.

Modelo

Gel
Crema solar
...

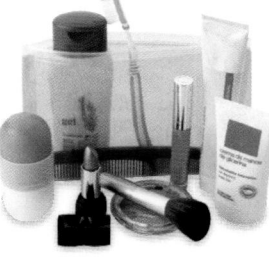

 ▶ **Habla** con tu compañero(a). ¿Llevan las mismas cosas? ¿Quién lleva más productos?

Differentiated Instruction

DEVELOPING LEARNERS

- Have students go back to the chart they completed for activity 36, but ask them to say at what time they do the activities shown on the weekend. Then have them say a sentence comparing what time they do these activities during the week and what time they do them on weekends. For example: *Durante la semana me levanto a las ocho, pero los fines de semana me levanto a las diez.*

EXPANDING LEARNERS

- Ask students which word does not belong.
1. *pintarse*   *peinarse*   *cepillarse*
   (*pintarse*)
2. *maquillarse*   *secarse*   *afeitarse*
   (*secarse*)
3. *nunca*   *normalmente*   *generalmente*
   (*nunca*)
4. *gel*   *esmalte*   *champú*
   (*esmalte*)
5. *rápidamente*   *velozmente*   *amablemente*
   (*amablemente*)
6. *tijeras*   *toalla*   *secador*
   (*tijeras*)

38 ¡Cómpraselo!

▶ **Escribe** con tu compañero(a) un anuncio para un producto de higiene personal. Después, preséntalo a la clase.

Modelo El jabón «La rana verde» es el mejor para su familia. Es tan suave que puede usarlo diariamente.

Final del desafío

Es muy pequeña. Pero si la buscan pacientemente, la pueden encontrar. Aquí siempre hay muchos turistas buscándola.

¿Pero es una rana de verdad?

No. Es de piedra. Primero, busquen los cráneos. Luego fíjense ciudadosamente, uno por uno.

¡Sí, ya la veo!

¡Yo también! ¡Está justamente encima de un cráneo!

39 La rana

▶ **Escribe.** ¿Finalmente encontraron la rana? Lee el diálogo y escribe el correo electrónico que le envió Diana a su mamá explicándole la experiencia en Salamanca.

 **→ TU DESAFÍO** Visita la página web. Escucha las preguntas de tu *Minientrevista Desafío 2* y escribe las respuestas.

HERITAGE LANGUAGE LEARNERS

- Ask students to make a chart similar to the one in activity 36, but with more activities in the first column and the name of a Spanish-speaking country they know as the head of the second column. Encourage them to include activities that are only practiced in that country, and not in the United States (e.g., *cantarle una serenata a alguien*). They should also include activities they practice only in the United States.

COOPERATIVE LEARNING

- Have students work in small groups to create a legend for your school that is centered around an animal, plant, or a nonliving object. First, students should select the subject of the legend and draw it. Next, they will create a legend related to the school and the object selected. Then they will write the legend, including an appropriate title, and attach their drawing to it. Finally, they will read their legend to the class.

DESAFÍO 2
Comunicación

Activities

37. After students have completed this activity, ask them to share their partner's responses with the class. You can also turn this into a memory game. Have the class form a circle. You start the game by saying, *Vamos de vacaciones y yo llevo el esmalte de uñas.* The student to your right then says, *Vamos de vacaciones y yo llevo el champú, y la profesora lleva el esmalte de uñas.* As you continue to go around the circle, each student needs to state what he or she will bring and repeat what the others have said. See if the last students can remember what everyone is bringing on the trip!

38. Turn the presentations into a contest. As students present, their classmates should write down a score of 1–10, based on whether or not they would buy the product after watching the commercial. After all groups have presented, have students vote for the product they would be most likely to buy.

 AUDIO SCRIPT
See page 235I.

Answer Key

36. 1. A las ocho. A las seis y media.
2. Entre las nueve y las diez. A las siete.
3. A las dos. A la una.
4. De las tres a las tres y media. No duerme siesta.
5. A las doce. A las nueve.
▶ Answers will vary.
▶ Answers will vary.
37. Answers will vary.
▶ Answers will vary.
38. Answers will vary.
39. Answers will vary.

Additional Resources

Fans Online activities
Practice Workbook

Unit 5
DESAFÍO 3
Hablar de salud y enfermedades

Presentation

- In this *Desafío*, Tim and Mack are in Pamplona, Spain. There they have to run in front of a herd of bulls during the *sanfermines*.
- In this section, students will preview:
  - Words to talk about health and injuries.
  - Uses of *por* and *para*.

Activities	Standards	Resources
Fotonovela	1.2, 2.1, 3.2	Vis. Pres.
40.	1.2, 1.3	
41.	1.2, 2.1	
42.	1.2	Audio
43. Cultura	1.1, 1.2, 2.1, 3.2, 4.2, 5.2	Video
Tu desafío	1.2, 2.1, 2.1, 3.2, 5.1	

Teaching Suggestions

Warm-Up / Independent Starter

- Ask students to list all the words and phrases they remember in Spanish to talk about common illnesses and injuries.

Preparation

- Read the introduction to the *fotonovela* to the class. Ask students why people would like to run in front of the bulls, when there is a possibility of serious injury. Ask them if they know other sports or events in which there is a high incidence of injuries. Discuss, as a class, what might prompt people to participate in these kinds of events.

La fotonovela

Before Viewing

- Have students look at the pictures and ask them what they find surprising and interesting. Is it crowded? How are people dressed? Why?

After Viewing

- Ask students about what they think happened to Tim. Is his leg / foot injured? Ask them if this injury will affect the outcome of Tim and Mack's *desafío*. If so, ask students to think ways to help Tim and Mack to be ready for the *desafío*.

258

Los encierros de Pamplona

Tim and Mack always suspected they were given the most difficult challenges. This time is no different. Our friends will have to show their bravery by running in front of a herd of angry bulls along the streets of Pamplona during the *sanfermines*.

Continuará...

40 Detective de palabras

▶ **Completa** estas oraciones.

1. ¿_____ qué estamos en los sanfermines?
2. ¿_____ qué siempre tenemos los desafíos más difíciles?
3. _____ ti, el desafío va a ser fácil.
4. Tim está listo _____ correr.
5. ¿_____ dónde salen los toros?
6. Los toros salen _____ esa calle a las ocho.

258 doscientos cincuenta y ocho

Differentiated Instruction

DEVELOPING LEARNERS

- Read the following false statements to students and ask them to make them true, according to the *fotonovela*:
  1. *Mack dice que están en Pamplona para correr un maratón. (para correr un encierro)*
  2. *Mack y Tim van a correr detrás de los toros. (delante de los toros)*
  3. *Los toros salen a las ocho de la tarde. (ocho de la mañana)*
  4. *Los toros salen por una ventana. (por una calle)*
  5. *Tim no quiere acabar con una pierna rota. (un brazo roto)*
  6. *Mack se va a caer. (Tim)*

EXPANDING LEARNERS

- Ask students if the spectacle of *los encierros* appeals to them or not, and why. Encourage them to discuss why they think people take part in this celebration. Is it because they like the "rush" and excitement of being so close to danger? Do they do it simply to join their friends who are running with the bulls? Is it the ultimate *desafío* to see if they can actually outrun a bull?

41 **¡Que vienen los toros!**

▶ **Decide** si estas oraciones son ciertas o falsas. Si son falsas, corrígelas.

1. Tim y su abuelo tienen que grabar la fiesta de los sanfermines.
2. Tim piensa que es un desafío fácil.
3. Tim no quiere correr delante de los toros.
4. Los toros salen a las nueve de la mañana.
5. En los sanfermines, los toros corren por la calle.
6. Tim tiene un pequeño accidente.

42 **¡No es justo!**

▶ **Escucha** el mensaje de Tim y elige la respuesta más apropiada.

1. Tim está en la ciudad de…
   a. Barcelona b. Pamplona c. Sevilla

2. Tim piensa que su desafío es…
   a. fácil b. divertido c. peligroso

3. Tim cree que con este desafío puede terminar en…
   a. una calle b. un hospital c. un café

4. Tim opina que su abuelo está…
   a. enfermo b. aburrido c. loco

 **CULTURA**

Los sanfermines

Los sanfermines es el nombre popular de las fiestas de San Fermín que se celebran del 6 al 14 de julio en Pamplona, la capital de la Comunidad Foral de Navarra, al norte de España.

La actividad más famosa de estas fiestas son los encierros. Cada día, a las ocho de la mañana, cientos de personas corren delante de seis toros por las calles de Pamplona hasta llegar a la plaza de toros. Es una actividad muy peligrosa y a veces hay accidentes muy graves.

Un encierro en Pamplona.

43 **Piensa y explica.** ¿Sabes algo más sobre los sanfermines? ¿Qué opinas de los encierros? ¿Hay alguna celebración similar en los Estados Unidos?

 → TU DESAFÍO Visita la página web para aprender más sobre los sanfermines.

HERITAGE LANGUAGE LEARNERS

- At this point, students have come to know the participants through their interactions with each other. Keeping in mind what they know about Tim and Mack, ask students if they think that both of them are really going to participate in the running of the bulls in Pamplona. Have them justify their answers with reflections on the participants' athletic ability, their enthusiasm to tackle these challenges, and their familiarity with this *desafío*.

CRITICAL THINKING

- In the *fotonovela*, Tim tells his grandfather that they always have the most difficult *desafíos*. Ask students if they agree with him. Then ask those who agree to explain why this is so. Ask those who do not agree to explain which pair of participants they think usually have the most difficult tasks. Be sure they justify their opinions with concrete examples from the *Desafíos*.

DESAFÍO 3

Hablar de salud y enfermedades

Activities

41. Ask students to take Tim's role and imagine that he is sending an e-mail to his Spanish best friend in the United States, letting him know what is going on. Students should use true information only.

42. Before playing the recording, have students read each sentence and make logical guesses.

 AUDIO SCRIPT
See page 235I.

 CULTURA

Los sanfermines

The festival of San Fermín was a local festivity, little known in the English-speaking world, until it was made famous by Ernest Hemingway in his novel *The Sun Also Rises* (1926). Today, it is one of Spain's most famous festivities. In addition to the running of the bulls, the festival features a *comparsa*, or parade, of large puppets. The festivities end on July 14 with the people gathering to sing "Pobre de mí" ("Poor Me").

Answer Key

40. 1. Para 3. Para 5. Por
       2. Por   4. para 6. por

41. 1. Falso. Tienen que correr delante de los toros.
       2. Falso. Tim piensa que es difícil.
       3. Cierto.
       4. Falso. Salen a las ocho.
       5. Cierto.
       6. Cierto.

42. 1. b 2. c 3. b 4. c

43. Answers will vary.

Additional Resources

Fans Online activities

DESAFÍO 3

Vocabulario – La salud: síntomas y enfermedades

Presentation

- In this section, students will learn:
  - Words to describe symptoms of common illnesses and remedies.
  - Words to name medical professions.

Activities	Standards	Resources
Vocabulario	1.2	
44.	1.2	Audio
45.	1.2, 1.3	Audio
46.	1.1	
47. Comparaciones	1.1, 1.2, 2.2, 3.2, 4.2, 5.2	

Teaching Suggestions

Warm-Up / Independent Starter

- Have students answer the following questions in writing about Tim and Mack:
  1. ¿Dónde están ahora Tim y Mack? ¿Qué tienen que hacer?
  2. ¿Qué piensa Tim de su desafío?
  3. ¿Qué le pasa a Tim cuando pasea con su abuelo por la calle?

Preparation

- You may want to create a short story incorporating target vocabulary. Act out words that can be represented physically and bring realia to enhance your acting (e.g., cough syrup, band-aids, aspirin, etc.). Elicit choral repetition for pronunciation practice. For example: *Hola. Hoy me encuentro mal. Me pica el brazo porque tengo alergia* (act out *pica* and *alergia*; students repeat actions and words). *Además toso mucho y tengo dolor de garganta* (act out *toso* and *garganta*; students repeat actions and words). *Tengo fiebre. ¿Creen ustedes que es gripe?* (Touch your forehead.) *El médico me recomienda jarabe y aspirina…*

- Make students aware that many health-related words are cognates (e.g., *hospital, clínica, paciente, dentista, alergia, fiebre*). Explain that although some words are not cognates, they can be easily related to English health words: *médico* (→ medical), *enfermero* (→ infirmary).

Vocabulario

La salud: síntomas y enfermedades

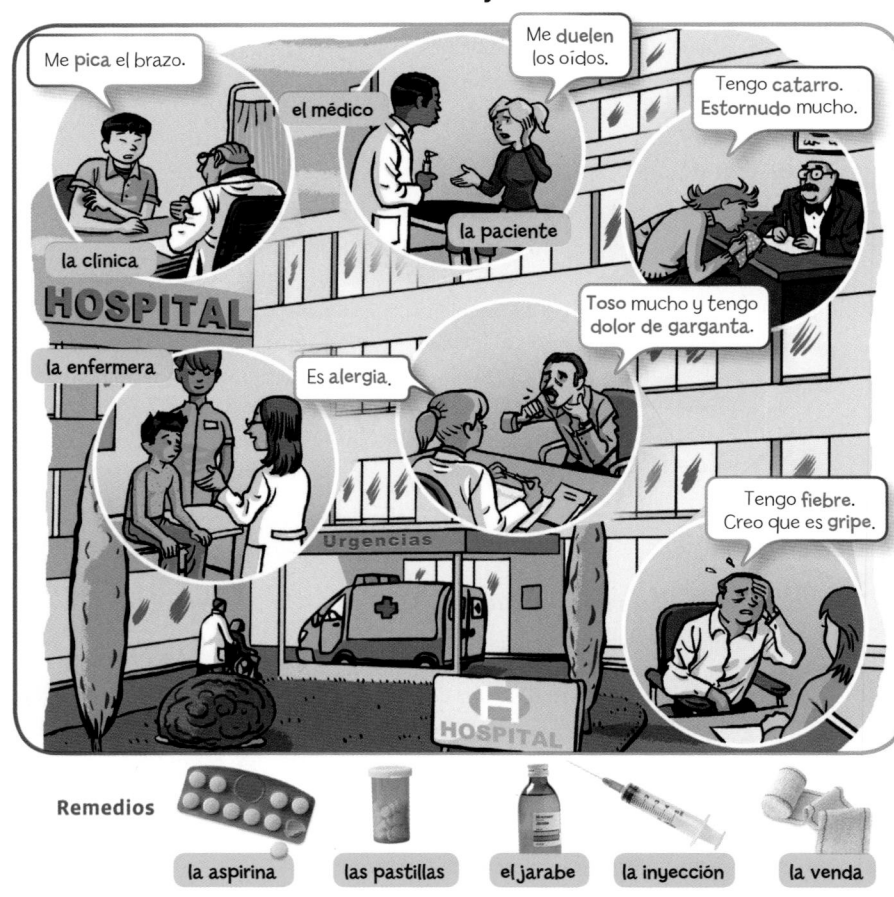

Remedios: la aspirina — las pastillas — el jarabe — la inyección — la venda

44 ¿Qué enfermedad es?

▶ **Escucha** a tres pacientes. ¿Qué enfermedad tiene cada uno?

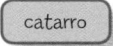 catarro   gripe   alergia

Differentiated Instruction

DEVELOPING LEARNERS

- Give students more practice with the verbs *doler* and *picar* by asking them to complete the following sentences:
  1. Me … (picar) las manos y la espalda. (pican)
  2. ¿Te … (doler) el codo? (duele)
  3. A los pacientes les … (picar) los ojos. (pican)
  4. Me … (doler) los pies. (duelen)
  5. A Miguel le … (doler) la cabeza y a mí me … (doler) las muelas. (duele; duelen)
  6. No me … (doler) nada. (duele)
  7. A la enfermera le … (doler) la garganta. (duele)

EXPANDING LEARNERS

- Have students imagine that they are visiting a hospital or clinic and come upon a scene where many patients are complaining about their many ailments. Ask them to write a dialogue using as much of the vocabulary on these pages as they can, explaining what ails those who are sick or in pain, and the recommendation of the health professionals. Have them role-play and present their dialogue to the class.

45 Enfermedades y más enfermedades

 ▶ **Escucha** y relaciona cada oración con el dibujo correspondiente.

(A)  (B)  (C)  (D)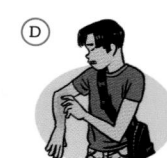

 ▶ **Completa** estas oraciones. Después, escucha otra vez y comprueba los resultados.

1. Tengo que ir al dentista (*dentist*), me _____ las muelas.
   _{duele/duelen}

2. Yo tengo gripe. Toso y me _____ mucho la garganta.
   _{duele/duelen}

3. Me _____ los brazos y las piernas porque tengo alergia.
   _{pica/pican}

4. Tengo catarro. Estornudo mucho y me _____ la nariz.
   _{pica/pican}

46 ¡Ay... doctor!

 ▶ **Habla** con tu compañero(a). Tú eres médico(a) y tu compañero(a) es un(a) paciente. Decide qué remedio es mejor para cada enfermedad.

Modelo

Problemas
dolor de cabeza
tos
dolor de garganta
gripe
dolor de tobillo
catarro
dolor de oídos

Remedios
tomar una aspirina
tomar un jarabe
tomar unas pastillas
poner una inyección
poner una venda

> Doctora, me duele mucho la cabeza.

> Tome estas pastillas.

COMPARACIONES

La Seguridad Social

En España hay hospitales y clínicas privados, pero también hay un sistema público que garantiza la atención sanitaria (*health care*) de todos los ciudadanos.

Los pacientes pueden acudir a un centro de salud o, si es necesario, al servicio de urgencias (*emergency*) de los hospitales.

47 **Compara.** ¿Cómo funciona el sistema sanitario en tu país?

Vocabulario – La salud: síntomas y enfermedades

Activities

44. Divide the class in pairs. Give each pair a set of cards with the name of an illness or symptom on each card. Taking turns, one student represents the disease or symptom and his or her partner tries to guess it.

45. For extra practice, make a list of body parts and ask students to decide which verb to use and which verb form is needed.

 AUDIO SCRIPT
See page 235J.

 COMPARACIONES

La Seguridad Social

Spain has a universal healthcare system, funded through payroll taxes. Coverage is free of charge for people paying social security taxes and their dependents, and for retirees. This plan allows patients to choose their primary care doctor, through whom they access the rest of the system. The Spanish healthcare system covers everything from routine visits to emergencies and major surgeries, and offers a heavily subsidized medicine program. It does not cover dental and eye care.

Answer Key

44. 1. alergia   2. catarro   3. gripe
45. 1. C   2. B   3. D   4. A
  ▶ 1. duelen   3. pican
    2. duele   4. pica
46. Answers will vary.
47. Answers will vary.

Additional Resources

Fans Online activities
Practice Workbook

HERITAGE LANGUAGE LEARNERS

- Ask students to describe health care in a Spanish-speaking country that they or their families know, and compare it to health care in their community. Encourage them to talk about any alternative medical practices or natural cures in Hispanic cultures, and whether they think these practices are as effective as traditional medicine. Ask them to give some examples. Have students also describe the more prominent role pharmacists play in dispensing medications and offering medical advice in the Spanish-speaking world.

COOPERATIVE LEARNING

- Divide the class in small groups. Be sure groups have a mix of students with different language levels and skills. Have groups research a hospital or clinic in their community or state. They should make a floor plan of the hospital and label, in Spanish, the different areas, as well as state the different medical professionals who work in the hospital. Then ask students to write a paragraph describing the kind of illnesses that are treated in this hospital and the symptoms some of the patients may exhibit.

DESAFÍO 3

Gramática – *Por y para*

Presentation

- In this section, students will learn different uses of *por* and *para*.

Activities	Standards	Resources
Gramática	3.1	
48.	1.1, 4.1	
49.	1.2, 1.3	
50.	1.2, 1.3	
51.	1.3,	
52.	1.1	
53. Comparaciones	1.1, 1.2, 2.1, 3.2, 4.2, 5.1	

Teaching Suggestions

Warm-Up / Independent Starter

- Have students choose the correct preposition to complete the following sentences:
  1. *Los sábados por la mañana voy a / de / en la biblioteca. (a)*
  2. *Este jarabe es a / de / en mi abuela. (de)*
  3. *Estamos a / de / en Pamplona. (en)*
  4. *Tess visita a / de / en Tim a / de / en el hospital. (a; en)*

Preparation

- Go over the grammar presentation with students. Explain that many uses of *por* and *para* are idiomatic and should be practiced thoroughly to be mastered.

Activities

49. To extend the activity, ask students questions based on the sentences. For example:
  1. *Tienes que tomar estas pastillas por la noche.* → *¿Cuándo tienes que tomar estas pastillas? ¿Puedes tomarlas por la mañana?*

51. Ask students to interview at least three classmates using the questions. They should write the information and present it to the class. Once they have completed the activity, have students write a paragraph using the information from the interview and comparing it to their own responses to these questions.

Gramática

Por y para

- *Por* and *para* can usually be translated as *for* in English, but they also have other meanings in Spanish.

Usos de *por*

- *Por* may be used to express the following:

cause or reason	No me puedo concentrar **por** el dolor de cabeza.
time periods during the day	Tomo este jarabe **por** las mañanas.
approximate time	Siempre tengo exámenes **por** Navidad.
approximate place	¿Hay una farmacia **por** aquí?
movement within an area	Los toros pasan **por** esa calle.

Usos de *para*

- *Para* may be used to express the following:

purpose	Este medicamento es **para** curar su enfermedad.
recipient of an action	La inyección es **para** Tim.
opinion	**Para** mí, este médico es muy bueno.
movement toward a place	Mack y Tim van **para** la clínica.
deadline	La cita es **para** mañana.

48 **Compara.** ¿A qué preposiciones equivalen *por* y *para* en inglés?

49 **¿Por o para?**

▶ **Completa** estas oraciones.

1. Tienes que tomar estas pastillas _____ la noche.
2. La tarea de Ciencias es _____ mañana.
3. Me gusta pasear _____ el centro de la ciudad.
4. Las aspirinas son _____ el dolor de cabeza.
5. Mañana salgo _____ Madrid.
6. Este regalo es _____ mi hermano.
7. Hay un hospital _____ el centro de la ciudad.
8. No entiendo _____ qué te da miedo ir al médico.

Differentiated Instruction

DEVELOPING LEARNERS

- Ask students to answer the questions in the first column with an appropriate response from the second column.

  1. ¿Dónde hay una biblioteca? (d)
  2. ¿Por dónde pasa el autobús? (e)
  3. ¿Por qué no bailaste? (c)
  4. ¿Para quién es el jarabe? (a)
  5. ¿Para qué son las aspirinas? (b)

  a. Es para mí.
  b. Son para el dolor de cabeza.
  c. No lo hice por el dolor de piernas
  d. Por aquella calle hay una.
  e. Pasa por la calle Mayor.

EXPANDING LEARNERS

- Ask students to complete the following sentences with either *por* or *para*:
  1. *El médico siempre va al hospital … las mañanas. (por)*
  2. *Necesito el jarabe … esta tarde. (para)*
  3. *No puedo cantar … el dolor de garganta. (por)*
  4. *La enfermera iba … la clínica cuando empezó a llover. (para)*
  5. *¿… qué sirve este medicamento? (Para)*
  6. *¿Está la clínica … esa calle? (por)*
  7. *… mí, la medicina es una profesión muy necesaria. (Para)*

50 **Instrucciones**

▶ **Completa** las instrucciones de este medicamento con *por* o *para*.

> Lea estas instrucciones antes de tomar el medicamento.
>
> **ALERGÍN**
>
> **Indicaciones:** Alergín es un medicamento ___1___ aliviar los problemas causados ___2___ la alergia.
>
> **Uso:** Tome este medicamento dos veces al día: una ___3___ la mañana y otra ___4___ la noche antes de acostarse. Puede tomarlo después de las comidas ___5___ evitar posibles dolores de estómago.
>
> **Advertencias:** Alergín no está indicado ___6___ mujeres embarazadas (*pregnant*). No tome este medicamento más de dos semanas. Si los síntomas continúan, consulte con su médico.

51 **Tus experiencias**

▶ **Responde** a estas preguntas. Usa *por* y *para*.

1. ¿Caminas mucho? ¿Por dónde paseas?
2. Para ti, ¿cuál es el mejor deporte?
3. ¿En qué momento del día prefieres practicar deporte?
4. ¿Tomas medicamentos alguna vez? ¿Para qué?

52 **Para sentirse mejor**

 ▶ **Habla** con tu compañero(a). ¿Qué cosas haces para sentirte bien? ¿Por qué?

Modelo A. ¿Comes muchas frutas y verduras?

B. *Claro que sí. Para sentirse bien es importante comer frutas y verduras.*

COMPARACIONES

Los medicamentos

En España los medicamentos se venden exclusivamente en las farmacias. Es fácil identificarlas porque normalmente tienen una cruz (*cross*) de color verde en la puerta.

Muchos medicamentos se pueden comprar directamente, pero otros solo se venden con una receta (*prescription*) del médico. Los medicamentos se venden envasados. Normalmente hay que comprar el envase (*pack*) completo; no se puede comprar solo la dosis justa, como en otros países.

53 **Compara.** ¿Dónde se venden los medicamentos en tu país? ¿Se puede comprar la dosis justa? ¿Siempre es necesario llevar una receta del médico?

doscientos sesenta y tres 263

---

52. You may provide a list of questions to prepare for the activity or for extra practice. For example: *¿Qué comes para tener buena salud? ¿Haces ejercicio con frecuencia para estar en forma?*

53. Lead a discussion about the advantages and disadvantages of the Spanish system when buying medicines. Do students think it is a good idea to sell over-the-counter medicines only at pharmacies?

COMPARACIONES

Los medicamentos

In Spain you can buy prescription medicines at any pharmacy, whereas in the United States you usually have a preferred pharmacy and orders are sometimes handled by your doctor's office. However, non-prescription medicines in Spain are only available in pharmacies and can't be obtained at supermarkets or other outlets as in the United States. Pharmacies in Spain are locally owned and must be authorized by the government. There are no pharmacy chains. Medicines tend to cost significantly less than in other countries due to government-imposed price restrictions.

Answer Key

48. Según el caso, equivalen a *because of, to, for, by.*

49.
1. por	4. para	7. por
2. para	5. para	8. por
3. por	6. para	

50.
1. para	4. por
2. por	5. para
3. por	6. para

51. Answers will vary.

52. Answers will vary.

53. Answers will vary.

Additional Resources

Fans Online activities
Practice Workbook

HERITAGE LANGUAGE LEARNERS

• Ask students to make a list of some other uses of *por* and *para*. Have them include some idiomatic expressions. Examples with *para* might include: *Habla muy bien para su edad* (standard). Examples with *por* include: *lo hizo por mí* (on my behalf); *pagué $20 por la camiseta* (exchange); *hablé con él por teléfono* (means); *cantó por María* (in substitution of). Have students read their lists to the class and explain their uses and meanings.

TOTAL PHYSICAL RESPONSE (TPR)

• Prepare at least twenty sentences that are missing either *por* or *para*. Then tell students that you are going to read a series of incomplete sentences, and they must decide which preposition—*por* or *para*—is correct. Give each student two sheets of paper, one white and the other colored. Explain that they should hold up the white sheet if they think *por* best completes the sentence, and hold up the colored sheet if they think *para* is the right choice.

Unit 5
DESAFÍO 3
Comunicación

Presentation

- In this section, students will integrate the vocabulary and grammar from *Desafío 3* in order to talk about health, common illnesses and symptoms, and medical professionals, as well as to practice different uses of *por* and *para*.

Activities	Standards	Resources
54.	1.2, 1.3	
55.	1.1, 1.3	
56.	1.3	
57. Final del desafío	1.2, 1.3, 2.1, 5.1	
Tu desafío	1.2, 1.3	

Teaching Suggestions

Warm-Up / Independent Starter

- Have students write a brief paragraph in Spanish about the last time they were sick: what they felt (symptoms), where they went for help, which medical professional assisted them, what this person prescribed or recommended, and what medicine they took.

Preparation

- Take 10 minutes to review the vocabulary and grammar themes of the *Desafío*.
- Refer students back to the *fotonovela* for *Desafío 3*. Have them find all the *por* and *para* examples, as well as words to talk about health. Make sure that students understand the use of each example of *por* and *para*. Do students understand the dialogue better now that they have gone through the vocabulary and grammar from the *Desafío*?

Activities

54. Have students work in pairs to write the e-mail that Tim's mom is sending back to him with some medical advice. Ask pairs to create five true / false statements based on their e-mail to quiz their classmates. Then ask pairs to read their e-mail to the class. Have the class take notes and then ask the presenters to read their true / false statements for the class to answer.

264

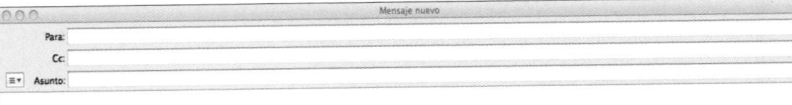
Comunicación

54 **¡Qué noche!**

▶ **Lee** el mensaje de Tim y responde a estas preguntas.

> Mensaje nuevo
>
> Para:
> Cc:
> Asunto:
>
> Querida mamá:
>
> Pamplona es fascinante. Esta semana celebran los sanfermines, una fiesta popular muy famosa en todo el mundo. Pero no todo son buenas noticias...
>
> Anoche el abuelo y yo fuimos a un restaurante. ¡La cena fue deliciosa! Pero después de cenar los dos nos pusimos enfermos. Fuimos a una clínica y la médica nos dijo que tuvimos una alergia al pescado. Nos puso una inyección y nos dio un jarabe y unas pastillas para el abuelo. Hoy estamos mejor.
>
> Mañana te escribo y te cuento más cosas. Te quiero mucho. Un beso.
>
> Tim

1. ¿Cuándo se pusieron enfermos Tim y su abuelo?
2. ¿Fueron a ver a un médico?
3. ¿Por qué se sintieron mal?
4. ¿Qué le dio el doctor a Tim para sentirse mejor? ¿Y a Mack?
5. ¿Cómo se sienten ahora?

55 **¿Por qué?**

▶ **Representa.** Mack quiere hacer muchas cosas en Pamplona, pero Tim le da excusas para no hacerlas. Con tu compañero(a), representa un diálogo entre Mack y Tim.

Ideas de Mack	Excusas de Tim
correr delante de los toros	dolor de rodillas
probar una comida típica	tener alergia a una comida
salir de fiesta	dolor de espalda
ir a bailar	tener gripe
ir a un concierto	dolor de oídos

Modelo

> Tim, quiero correr delante de los toros.

> Lo siento abuelo, yo no puedo correr. Me duele una rodilla.

Differentiated Instruction

DEVELOPING LEARNERS

- Have students work with a partner and make a list similar to the one in activity 55, but with different activities and excuses. Based on the list, ask students to write a dialogue in which one student shows interest in doing one of the activities mentioned, but the other always has a ready excuse. For example:

Idea: jugar al tenis;
Excusa: dolor de piernas.
A. *¿Quieres jugar al tenis?*
B. *Lo siento, pero me duelen las piernas.*

EXPANDING LEARNERS

- Have students imagine that they are Tim's mother and write an answer to his e-mail. The letter or note should comment positively on Tim's learning experience in Pamplona, but also show concern for his and his grandfather's health. Students should include a health tip for the food allergy and a suggestion for what Tim and Mack should eat, or what they should not eat, the next time they go out for dinner. Encourage students to give additional advice and perhaps an update about what is going on at home.

56 **¿Qué me recomiendas?**

▶ **Escribe** un problema de salud y una recomendación relacionada con cada fotografía.

Modelo *Toso mucho y me pica la garganta.* → *Tómate estas pastillas.*

①  ②  ③ 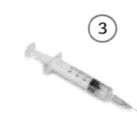 ④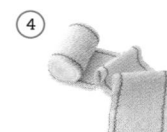

Final del desafío

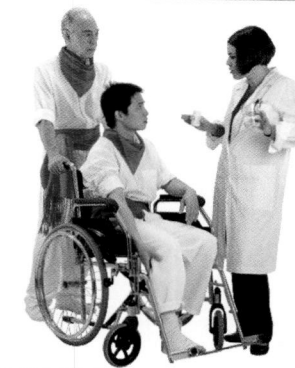

MÉDICA: Toma aspirinas _____ el dolor. Tienes que

tomar una _____ la mañana, otra _____

la tarde y otra _____ la noche.

TIM: ¡Pero mañana tengo que correr en el encierro

con mi abuelo!

MÉDICA: Olvídalo. _____ mañana no vas a estar curado.

MACK: Tranquilo, Tim. Corro yo solo.

57  **Tim está preocupado**

▶ **Completa** la conversación con *por* o *para*. Después, escribe el mensaje de correo que le manda Mack a su esposa para explicarle lo que pasó con el desafío.

🏁→ **TU DESAFÍO** Visita la página web. Escucha las preguntas de tu *Minientrevista Desafío 3* y escribe las respuestas.

HERITAGE LANGUAGE LEARNERS

• Students will play the role of journalists who are covering the running of the bulls for a local paper. They need to describe the *encierros* for readers who know nothing about this event, so students should be prepared to offer some insight into the history and reason for the *sanfermines*, as well as a description of some of the participants and their emotional state before and after the run. After they write their articles, ask students to read them to the class.

CRITICAL THINKING

• Every year, people question whether spectacles such as Pamplona's famous *encierros* should be banned. They argue that there are too many injuries, and in some years, even deaths. Organize students into teams and have them debate this issue. Some teams will be in favor of keeping *los encierros* as they are, others will want to abolish this celebration or modify it drastically. Give the first team member a minute to present his or her initial argument, then two minutes for rebuttal, and finally another minute to summarize.

---

55. Make sure students know all the vocabulary under *Ideas de Tim* and *Excusas de Mack*. You may write on the board some useful oral expressions to enhance the dialogues. For example: *¡Ay! ¡Qué pena! ¡Lo siento mucho! ¡Qué dolor!*

57. Have students explain the uses of *por* and *para* for each of the blanks in the conversation. Then ask them to get together in groups of three students to add three lines to the dialogue, one for each character. Allow students time to rehearse and then ask groups to role-play their dialogue in front of the class. Invite the class to vote for the most original dialogue.

Answer Key

54. 1. Se sintieron mal después de cenar.
2. Sí, fueron a una clínica.
3. Se sintieron mal por una alergia al pescado.
4. A Tim y a Mack les puso una inyección y les dio un jarabe. A Mack le dio unas pastillas.
5. Ahora están mejor.

55. Answers will vary.

56. Answers will vary. Sample answers:
2. Tengo gripe. → Toma este jarabe.
3. Tuve una reacción alérgica. → Voy a ponerte esta inyección.
4. Me caí y me duele el tobillo. → Ponte esta venda.

57. 1. para   4. por
2. por   5. Para
3. por

Additional Resources

Fans Online activities
Practice Workbook

Unit 5
DESAFÍO 4
Recomendar hábitos saludables

Presentation

- In this *Desafío*, Andy and Janet travel to Seville, where they must buy enough gazpacho for all their friends.
- In this section, students will preview:
  - Vocabulary for healthy habits.
  - Making recommendations for healthy habits.

Activities	Standards	Resources
Fotonovela	1.2, 2.2, 3.2	Vis. Pres.
58.	1.2, 1.3	
59.	1.2, 1.3	
60.	1.2	Audio
61.	1.3	
62. Cultura	1.1, 1.2, 2.2, 3.1, 3.2, 4.2, 5.2	
Tu desafío	1.2, 2.2, 3.2, 5.2	

Teaching Suggestions

Warm-Up / Independent Starter

- Ask students to create a three-column chart about eating habits in Spain. The chart should have the following headings: *Lo que sé; Lo que quiero saber; Lo que aprendí.* Ask students to fill in the first two columns. They will continue to fill in the third column during this *Desafío.*

Preparation

- Before reading, have students scan the *fotonovela* for cognates and vocabulary that they can identify. Write the words on the board.
- Read the introduction to the *fotonovela* aloud to the class. Ask students: *En tu opinión, ¿cómo van Andy y Janet a encontrar el gazpacho?*

👁 La fotonovela

Before Viewing

- Ask for two volunteers to read the parts of Andy and Janet in the *fotonovela.*

After Viewing

- Have students write a paragraph to summarize what happened in the *fotonovela* based on what they heard from their peers and saw in the visual presentation.

266

Gazpacho para todos

👁 Andy and Janet went to Madrid for a quick visit. Now they are flying low in the AVE, a bullet train, on their way to Seville, where they must buy enough *gazpacho* for all their friends.

¿Esta es la famosa dieta mediterránea?

Sí, queremos ofrecer una dieta deliciosa y equilibrada a nuestros viajeros.

¡Y rica en vitaminas!

Perdone, necesitamos localizar el mejor gazpacho de Sevilla. ¿Puede ayudarnos?

Cerca de la plaza de toros hay un sitio muy bueno. Tienen que ir por allí.

¿Descansamos un rato?

Podemos subir a esa torre para buscar la plaza. Y así nos mantenemos en forma.

No, Andy. Hay que cumplir la misión. ¡Mira, allí está la plaza!

DON GAZPACHO

Continuará...

58 Detective de palabras

▶ **Completa** estas oraciones con un verbo.

1. _____ ofrecer una dieta equilibrada a nuestros viajeros.
2. _____ localizar el mejor gazpacho de Sevilla.
3. _____ que ir por allí.
4. _____ subir a esa torre.
5. _____ que cumplir la misión.

266 doscientos sesenta y seis

Differentiated Instruction

DEVELOPING LEARNERS

- Have students work in groups of four to read the dialogue aloud and role-play the parts of Janet, Andy, the train attendant, and the passerby. Remind them to use correct intonation when reading the questions and exclamations, and to demonstrate Janet's enthusiasm and Andy's tiredness. If necessary, model some sentences.

EXPANDING LEARNERS

- Have students work in groups of three: two students will role-play Andy and Janet, and the third will be a journalist who is interviewing them about their trip to Seville and their *desafío.* The interview might address the Mediterranean diet, high-speed trains, typical foods and sights such as *gazpacho*, the Giralda, and the bull ring in Seville, as well as the emotions and feelings of the participants. Invite some groups to present their interview to the class.

59 ¿Comprendes?

▶ **Responde** a estas preguntas con oraciones completas.

1. ¿Cómo es el tipo de comida que ofrecen en el AVE?
2. ¿Qué tienen que hacer Andy y Janet en Sevilla?
3. ¿Qué ven Andy y Janet desde la torre?

▶ **Lee** la ficha de Cultura y explica:

1. ¿Qué es el gazpacho?
2. ¿Conoces algún alimento similar al gazpacho?

60 ¿De qué hablan?

▶ **Escucha** las conversaciones y relaciónalas con estas fotos.

El AVE.

Restaurante en Sevilla.

La Giralda.

61 ¡Vamos a comer!

▶ **Escribe.** Andy y Janet entran en un restaurante para comprar gazpacho. Escribe con dos compañeros(as) su diálogo con el mesero. Después, represéntenlo para la clase.

Modelo
A. *Buenos días. ¿Qué desean?*
B. *Hola. Queremos comprar gazpacho para nuestros amigos.*

CULTURA

El gazpacho andaluz

El gazpacho es una sopa fría que se prepara con tomates frescos, pan, cebolla, pepino, pimiento, ajo, aceite de oliva, vinagre y sal. Es un plato típico de Andalucía, pero se come en toda España, especialmente en verano.

62 Piensa. ¿Cómo influye el clima en la dieta? ¿Puedes poner algunos ejemplos?

 **→ TU DESAFÍO** Visita la página web para aprender cómo se hace el gazpacho.

HERITAGE LANGUAGE LEARNERS

• Encourage students to enrich their vocabulary by naming or looking up alternative words or expressions for those in the *fotonovela*. For example, they might say *el régimen* for *la dieta*. Ask them to find other synonyms or related words or expressions for the following: *famosa, querer ofrecer, deliciosa, equilibrada, tener que, ayudar, sitio, bueno, mantenerse en forma*. Ask students to share these words with the other students, who may choose to write them in their notebooks.

COOPERATIVE LEARNING

• Ask students to work in small groups and create a travel brochure for Seville. Have each student research a landmark in the city. The landmark could be the famous *Giralda, La Maestranza (plaza de toros), la Torre del Oro, la Catedral, la Plaza de España*, or something else that interests the students. Each member of the group will prepare one or two paragraphs, describing the landmark and its influence on the city. Suggest that they include images. Then the group will combine their reports into a brochure to promote tourism.

Recomendar hábitos saludables

Activities

60. Before playing the audio recording, ask students to look at the photos and decide on alternative captions that logically describe each picture.

62. Ask students to research other typical Spanish foods and write down their favorite recipes. Form pairs and ask them to engage in a question / answer session regarding a partner's recipe. Compile recipes to create a class cookbook.

 AUDIO SCRIPT
See page 235J.

 CULTURA

El gazpacho andaluz

The oldest version of gazpacho was probably nothing more than bread, garlic, olive oil, vinegar, and water. Later, shepherds and farmers added vegetables to make it heartier. Tomatoes and bell peppers were added after the arrival of these products from the Americas. Since then, the main ingredients have not changed radically.

Answer Key

58.
1. Queremos
2. Necesitamos
3. Tienen
4. Podemos
5. Hay

59. Answers will vary. Sample answers:
1. Es una dieta deliciosa y equilibrada.
2. Tienen que localizar el mejor gazpacho.
3. Ven la plaza.
▶ Answers will vary.

60. 1. C   2. B   3. A

61. Answers will vary.

62. Answers will vary.

Additional Resources

Fans Online activities

267

DESAFÍO 4

Vocabulario – Hábitos saludables

Presentation

- In this section, students will learn words to describe healthy habits.

Activities	Standards	Resources
Vocabulario	1.2	
63.	1.1	
64.	1.1, 1.3	
65.	1.1, 1.2, 1.3	
66. Comunidades	1.1, 1.2, 2.1, 3.2, 4.2, 5.2	

Teaching Suggestions

Warm-Up / Independent Starter

- Ask students to write down a list of at least four things they do to keep healthy.

Preparation

- Do a brainstorming activity to reactivate previously learned vocabulary related to sports and food. Ask students what sports they practice and what food they eat. Write down vocabulary on the board.
- Ask for volunteers to read the speech bubbles and captions. Act out the words *sano(a)* and *enfermo(a)*. Show students the difference between *enfermo(a)*, and *enfermar*. On the board, write down *Para no enfermar* as a heading, and make a list of the verbs that appear in the vocabulary presentation: *practicar yoga, tomar vitaminas, patinar,* etc. Invite students to add activities not listed on the vocabulary presentation which also promote healthy living.

Activities

63. To expand this activity, divide the class in two groups. One group will give examples of bad habits, and the other group of healthy habits. You may turn the activity into a contest by awarding points to each group based on their responses.

64. Have students share their lists with the rest of the class. Discuss, as a class, some of the activities mentioned by students, and poll the class to select the top five activities in terms of usefulness.

Vocabulario

Hábitos saludables

Yo sigo una dieta equilibrada para estar sano.

Yo tomo vitaminas y mucha fruta para no enfermar.

Ellos patinan y montan en bicicleta regularmente para estar en forma.

A él le gusta meditar y practicar yoga para mantenerse sano.

| beber agua | comer bien | cuidarse | descansar | hacer deporte / hacer ejercicio |

63 ¿Bueno o malo?

 ▶ **Habla** con tu compañero(a). ¿Estos hábitos son saludables o son malos hábitos?

1. Beber dos litros de refresco al día.
2. Hacer ejercicio una vez al año.
3. Practicar un deporte regularmente.
4. Seguir una dieta equilibrada.
5. Caminar o correr todos los días.

64 Para estar en forma

▶ **Escribe** una lista de todo lo que haces para estar en forma.

Modelo *Juego al tenis los fines de semana...*

 ▶ **Habla** con tus compañeros(as). ¿Tienen listas similares?

268 doscientos sesenta y ocho

Differentiated Instruction

DEVELOPING LEARNERS

- Write or read the following list of habits to students and ask them to categorize them under the headings *Hábitos saludables* or *Hábitos no saludables*. When they finish, ask them to say which of these habits they follow.

1. *Comer mucha carne y pocas verduras.*
2. *Hacer ejercicio todos los días.*
3. *No beber agua.*
4. *Ir al dentista regularmente.*
5. *Beber muchos refrescos.*
6. *Pasar muchas horas mirando la televisión.*
7. *Descansar bien.*

EXPANDING LEARNERS

- Ask students to make a list of at least six things that they do every day to stay healthy and explain why doing these things helps them. They might include some of the following actions. The reasons for doing them will vary.

  – *Duermo las horas necesarias.*
  – *Como muchas frutas y verduras.*
  – *Hago ejercicio.*
  – *Bebo bastante agua.*
  – *Me lavo las manos a menudo.*
  – *Me lavo los dientes por la mañana y por la noche.*
  – *No bebo muchos refrescos.*

65 Un cuestionario

▶ **Lee** este cuestionario y elige el título más apropiado.

¿Llevas una vida sana?   **El deporte y tú**   **¿Eres un buen cocinero?**

1. ¿Practicas algún deporte?
☐ Sí, todos los días.
☐ Sí, frecuentemente.
☐ Sí, a veces.
☐ No, nunca.

2. ¿Caminas todos los días una hora?
☐ Sí.
☐ No.

3. ¿Comes frutas y verduras cada día?
☐ Sí.
☐ No.

4. ¿Bebes, al menos, un litro de agua al día?
☐ Sí.
☐ No.

5. ¿Comes dulces?
☐ Sí, todos los días.
☐ Sí, frecuentemente.
☐ Sí, a veces.
☐ No, nunca.

6. ¿Duermes las horas necesarias?
☐ Sí.
☐ No.

7. ¿Vas al médico regularmente?
☐ Sí.
☐ No.

8. ¿Te pones enfermo(a) a menudo?
☐ Sí.
☐ No.

▶ **Escribe** dos preguntas más para el cuestionario. Después, complétalo.

▶ **Habla** con tu compañero(a). Hazle el cuestionario y toma nota de sus respuestas. ¿Crees que lleva una vida saludable? ¿Por qué?

Modelo *Pienso que llevas una vida muy saludable porque haces ejercicio y...*

 **COMUNIDADES**

LA SALUD DE LOS ESPAÑOLES

Según datos del Instituto Nacional de Estadística del año 2009, el 71,6 % de la población adulta come verduras y el 62,8 % come frutas al menos una vez al día.

Respecto al ejercicio físico, el 62,3 % de la población realiza alguna actividad física intensa o moderada a la semana.

66 **Explica.** Según los datos de la encuesta, ¿crees que los españoles llevan una vida saludable? ¿Piensas que las cifras son similares o muy distintas en tu país?

Vocabulario – Hábitos saludables

65. If you prefer, you may ask students to walk around the class and ask at least three different classmates to answer the questions. Have students pose and answer the questions orally. Then, you may have them tally the answers and explain their findings.

66. Ask students to guess which fruits and vegetables Spaniards most commonly eat. Write down their answers on the board.

 COMUNIDADES

La salud de los españoles

According to the 2009 European Health Interview Survey carried out in Spain, seven out of ten Spaniards consider their health as good or very good. In terms of preventive care, a similar proportion of people (i.e., seven out of ten) have had their blood pressure, blood sugar, and cholesterol levels checked by a medical professional in the last year. In the United States, the Centers for Disease Control and Prevention publishes the results of the National Health Interview Survey conducted in the U.S., as well as other health-related information about the U.S. population. This information is available online at: http://www.cdc.gov/nchs/fastats/Default.htm.

Answer Key

63.
1. mal hábito
2. mal hábito
3. hábito saludable
4. hábito saludable
5. hábito saludable

64. Answers will vary.
▶ Answers will vary.

65. ¿Llevas una vida sana?
▶ Answers will vary.
▶ Answers will vary.

66. Answers will vary.

Additional Resources

Fans Online activities
Practice Workbook

HERITAGE LANGUAGE LEARNERS

• Ask students to research the health-related habits of people in the United States and in the country of their family's origin (or one with which they are familiar). Have them compile the statistics they find and compare the habits of both groups. Then have them compare the results with those of the Spaniards in the article on page 269. Have them draw conclusions about which group seems to have the healthiest lifestyle. Encourage them to share their information with the rest of the class.

MULTIPLE INTELLIGENCES:
Visual-Spatial Intelligence

• Have students make a poster that promotes healthier habits among their classmates. Students should list both good habits that students should follow as well as bad habits to avoid, and include suggestions for making them a part of their everyday routine. Ask students to include images on their poster. Then take a class vote to see which poster offers the soundest advice, which one offers the most unique advice, and which one has the best visuals.

DESAFÍO 4

Gramática – Hacer recomendaciones

Presentation

- In this section, students will learn to recommend healthy habits using *hay que, tener que, deber, necesitar*, and *poder* in the present tense.

Activities	Standards	Resources
Gramática	3.1	
67.	1.1, 4.1	
68.	1.2, 1.3	Audio
69.	1.3	
70.	1.1, 1.3	
71. Conexiones	1.1, 1.2, 2.1, 3.2, 5.2	
Tu desafío	1.2, 2.1, 3.2, 5.2	

Teaching Suggestions

Warm-Up / Independent Starter

- Ask students to write a list of five actions a doctor would recommend they do to remain healthy. Tell students to write the verbs in the infinitive form.

Preparation

- Go over the grammar presentation with students. Remind them that *hay que* is a general recommendation, but the other recommendations require the verb to agree with the subject.

- Have students take their list from the Independent Starter and use each of the expressions from the grammar presentation to make recommendations to their classmates.

- Ask students how using these recommendations differ from the commands they learned in previous units. Remind students that these expressions are suggestions and can be a more courteous way of making a request.

Activities

68. For additional practice, you may choose to have students write an additional recommendation for each character.

69. Call on students to read one of the statements they wrote. The class needs to guess for whom their classmates wrote the recommendations.

Gramática

Hacer recomendaciones

Hay que y tener que

- To make recommendations and to express obligation, use these structures:

  hay que + infinitivo   tener que + infinitivo

- Hay que is used in impersonal expressions and does not change form.

  Hay que tomar vitaminas.

- Tener que is used to say that someone in particular must do something. In this expression, you must conjugate the verb tener to make it agree with the subject.

  Javier **tiene que** comer más.   Yo **tengo que** cuidarme.

Otras estructuras

- The following expressions are also used to express obligation and to make recommendations. The verbs must agree with their subjects:

  deber + infinitivo   No **debes** beber muchos refrescos.

  necesitar + infinitivo   **Necesitas** hacer más ejercicio.

  poder + infinitivo   **Puedes** hacer yoga para relajarte.

67 **Compara.** Algunas estructuras sirven para expresar obligación y para hacer recomendaciones. ¿Cómo distingues entre una orden y una recomendación en español? ¿Y en inglés?

68 **Recomendaciones**

 ▶ **Escucha** y completa estas recomendaciones de un médico.

1. Tim, tú _____ correr por las mañanas. Es un buen ejercicio.
2. Diana, tú _____ comer de forma más saludable.
3. Mack, _____ comer menos y hacer más ejercicio.
4. Janet, _____ caminar una hora todos los días para estar en forma.
5. Andy, tú _____ nadar. Es un ejercicio excelente.
6. Rita, tú _____ hacer yoga o practicar algún deporte para estar en forma.

▶ **Escribe** las recomendaciones anteriores usando otras estructuras.

Modelo 1. *Tim, tú tienes que correr por las mañanas. Es un buen ejercicio.*

Differentiated Instruction

DEVELOPING LEARNERS

- Ask students to complete the following sentences with the correct form of the verb in parentheses.
  1. *Yo … (deber) hacer más ejercicio. (debo)*
  2. *Nosotros … (tener que) practicar algún deporte. (tenemos que)*
  3. *Nuestros vecinos … (poder) hacer yoga para relajarse. (pueden)*
  4. *Ustedes … (tener que) comer más verduras. (tienen que)*
  5. *… (hay que) caminar todos los días. (Hay que)*
  6. *¿Cuántas horas … (necesitar) dormir los niños? (necesitan)*

EXPANDING LEARNERS

- Tell students that their best friend's advice is usually welcome, but sometimes the friend is a bit overbearing. Ask students to write a note from their best friend's point of view, telling them what to do and what not to do in order to stay healthy. Be sure students include plenty of tips and use a variety of verbs to express recommendations. Encourage creativity.

69 Buenos consejos

▶ **Escribe** recomendaciones para estas personas.

Modelo 1. *Mary puede tomar vitaminas, fruta y jugos naturales.*

1

2

3

4

Mary está muy cansada.

Peter está nervioso.

Tom quiere estar más fuerte.

Anne no sabe qué deporte practicar.

70 Para estar en forma

▶ **Escribe** cuatro preguntas sobre hábitos saludables. Después, entrevista a tus compañeros(as) y toma nota de sus respuestas.

Modelo William, ¿tú haces ejercicio?

▶ **Presenta.** Prepara una lista de recomendaciones para tus compañeros(as) y preséntala a la clase.

Modelo William debe practicar algún deporte.

CONEXIONES: SALUD

La dieta mediterránea

La dieta mediterránea es propia de los países del Mediterráneo: España, Italia, Grecia... Su origen es muy antiguo y está muy relacionada con la forma de vida de estos pueblos.

Es una dieta equilibrada y muy variada. Se basa en el consumo de aceite de oliva y de productos frescos y de temporada (principalmente, alimentos vegetales), y en un consumo menor de pescado y marisco, carne, huevos y productos lácteos. Además, la dieta se complementa con ejercicio moderado.

71 **Piensa y explica.** ¿Por qué crees que la dieta mediterránea se considera tan saludable?

 **→ TU DESAFÍO** Visita la página web para aprender más sobre la dieta mediterránea.

HERITAGE LANGUAGE LEARNERS

• Have students research more data about the Mediterranean diet and how it has influenced eating habits in the United States. Also ask students to compare it to the typical diet of a Hispanic country they know. Have them point out the major differences, and why they think the diets differ as they do. They may make their comparisons in a written report or with illustrations and charts, including the food pyramid, along with some text.

MULTIPLE INTELLIGENCES:
Interpersonal Intelligence

• Tell half of the students that they are journalists and are going to interview the oldest person in Seville: doña Penélope Pérez. The other half of the class will role-play doña Penélope, who is about to celebrate her 102nd birthday! In their interview, students need to find out this lady's secret for her longevity. Doña Penélope must reveal what she has been doing all her life and what she has been avoiding to reach this remarkable age.

71. Have students make connections between the culture, the geography, and the typical diet where they live.

 AUDIO SCRIPT
See page 235J.

 CONEXIONES: SALUD

La dieta mediterránea
UNESCO has recently identified this diet as being part of the cultural heritage of Spain, Greece, Italy, and Morocco. Fruits, vegetables, unrefined carbohydrates, and legumes are important components of this diet. Although the diet is based on the use of olive oil, this oil contains monounsaturated fat, which is a healthier type of fat.

Answer Key

67. En español se usan el imperativo para dar órdenes y expresiones como *hay que, deber,* etc. para hacer recomendaciones. En inglés se usan el presente para dar órdenes y expresiones como *you should, you need to,* etc. para hacer recomendaciones.

68. 1. puedes   4. debes
2. debes   5. tienes que
3. necesitas   6. puedes
▶ Answers will vary.

69. Answers will vary. Sample answers:
2. Peter necesita hacer yoga.
3. Tom debe levantar pesas.
4. Anne puede jugar al tenis.

70. Answers will vary.
▶ Answers will vary.

71. Answers will vary.

Additional Resources

Fans Online activities
Practice Workbook

Unit 5
DESAFÍO 4
Comunicación

Presentation

- In this section, students will integrate the vocabulary and grammar from *Desafío 4* in order to talk about healthy habits and make recommendations.

Activities	Standards	Resources
72.	1.1, 1.3	
73.	1.2	Audio
74.	1.2, 1.3	
75.	1.2, 1.3	Audio
76. Final del desafío	1.3, 2.2, 5.2	

Teaching Suggestions

Warm-Up / Independent Starter

- Have students list what they usually eat for breakfast, lunch, and dinner, and snacks that they have during the day. Ask them to also list the approximate number of glasses of water they drink daily.
- Then have them complete a table like the one below for their lifestyle and health habits.

Deporte o ejercicio	Frecuencia de ejercicio o deporte	Horas de sueño cada noche	Visitas al médico anualmente
caminar	4 veces a la semana		

Preparation

- Take 10 minutes to review the vocabulary and grammar themes of the *Desafío*.
- Refer students back to the *fotonovela* for *Desafío 4*. Have them find all the words about healthy habits and verbs that express recommendations. Do students understand the dialogue better now that they have gone through the vocabulary and grammar from the *Desafío*?
- Have pairs of students exchange their Independent Starters. Ask them to analyze their partner's eating habits and health routines and offer their assessment. Does the partner have a healthy lifestyle or is there room for improvement? What could be improved?

DESAFÍO 4

Comunicación

72 **A cada uno, su dieta**

▶ **Escribe** y habla. Mira esta tabla y elabora una dieta ideal para tu compañero(a). Después, hazle las recomendaciones necesarias.

Modelo *Por la mañana debes desayunar cereales con leche y una manzana.*

Alimentos	Frecuencia
Papas, cereales, pan, pasta, arroz.	Todos los días (de 4 a 6 raciones)
Fruta y verdura.	Todos los días (de 3 a 4 raciones)
Leche, queso, yogur.	Todos los días (de 2 a 3 raciones)
Pescado, carne, pollo, huevos.	3 o 4 veces por semana
Refrescos, dulces, postres.	Ocasionalmente

73 **Janet está enferma**

▶ **Escucha** y decide. ¿Qué recomendaciones le hace el médico a Janet?

1. Hacer ejercicio.
2. Beber mucha agua.
3. Descansar.
4. Comer bien.
5. Tomar medicamentos.

74 **La mala vida**

▶ **Lee** el mensaje de correo de Andy y respóndele. ¿Qué recomendaciones puedes darle?

> Para:
> Cc:
> Asunto:
>
> Mi amigo Peter tiene muchos problemas. Siempre está cansado porque se acuesta muy tarde y no saca buenas notas porque no estudia, no hace la tarea y siempre está pensando en otras cosas durante la clase. Creo que Peter no se encuentra bien porque no sigue una dieta equilibrada y tampoco hace ejercicio. Su hermano dice que tiene una bicicleta en casa, pero no la usa. ¿Puedes darme algunas recomendaciones para él? Gracias.
> Andy

Modelo *Querido Andy, tu amigo Peter tiene que escuchar al profesor y estudiar más...*

Differentiated Instruction

DEVELOPING LEARNERS

- Have students choose the correct word to complete these sentences.
  1. *El gazpacho es una sopa picante / fría.* (fría)
  2. *Janet y Andy aprenden a comer / preparar el gazpacho.* (preparar)
  3. *El gazpacho es un plato típico de Madrid / la dieta mediterránea.* (la dieta mediterránea)
  4. *El gazpacho tiene / no tiene muchas vitaminas.* (tiene)
  5. *Los dos hermanos prueban / no prueban el gazpacho.* (prueban)

EXPANDING LEARNERS

- Have students write a suitable dialogue for the last scene of the *fotonovela*. How do they think Janet will react when Andy trips? How do they think Andy will feel after he spills the gazpacho? Have them write the lines accordingly. Then ask them to explain what they think will happen next. Will Janet and Andy fail their *desafío* or will they find a solution? Ask students to explain their answers.

75 **¿Qué me recomiendas?**

 ▶ **Escucha** a varias personas y recomiéndales la actividad más apropiada para sus necesidades.

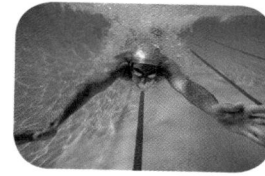

Modelo *Tienes que nadar…*

Final del desafío

> Necesitamos preparar gazpacho para ocho personas. ¿Nos puede enseñar cómo se hace?

> Hay que poner tomate, pepino, cebolla, pimiento y un poco de aceite de oliva.

> ¿Y luego hay que batirlo mucho?

> A mí me gusta líquido, pero puedes hacerlo a tu gusto. ¡Pruébenlo!

> Humm. Está muy rico.

> Claro, es un plato típico de la dieta mediterránea.

> Sí, y tiene muchas vitaminas. Nos lo llevamos hecho.

> ¡Oh, no!

76 **Un desastre de última hora**

▶ **Escribe.** Andy tiene un accidente… ¡y el restaurante Don Gazpacho está cerrado! Escribe recomendaciones para ayudar a Andy y a Janet a preparar un buen gazpacho para sus amigos.

doscientos setenta y tres 273

HERITAGE LANGUAGE LEARNERS

• Have students imagine that they are copywriters for a health spa. Ask them to make a before and after illustration on poster board that shows the positive results of having a healthy lifestyle. The illustrations should be accompanied by text and creative advertising to convince people to come to the spa.

CRITICAL THINKING

• Guide students in a discussion about why the process of searching for a solution for something is usually more rewarding, challenging, interesting, and entertaining than simply being handed the solution. Have students address the skills involved in the solution to the challenges in this unit: working cooperatively with another student or with a group, developing imagination and resourcefulness, and asking pertinent questions. Also address the problem-solving skills involved in each *desafío*.

Activities

72. Once students have offered their dietary recommendations to their partners, ask the partners to comment on the recommendations. Do they agree or are there some recommendations that would not be practical in their case?

74. Before doing this activity, ask students to get together in small groups and brainstorm a list of the most common bad health habits among students their age. For example: *ver mucho la televisión, beber muchos refrescos, comer comida rápida, dormir poco, pasar muchas horas en Internet,* etc. Once they have completed the list, ask groups to come up with recommendations to modify this incorrect behavior. Remind students that their recommendations should be age appropriate and practical.

76. As a follow-up, ask students to write down in pairs two situations in which there was an accident that ruined a meal, party, etc. Then ask them to explain the experience to the class.

AUDIO SCRIPT
See page 235J.

Answer Key

72. Answers will vary.

73. 3, 4

74. Answers will vary.

75. Answers will vary. Sample answers:
1. Tienes que ir a un gimnasio.
2. Puedes hacer yoga.
3. Necesitas caminar o pasear.
4. Debes hacer senderismo.

76. Answers will vary.

Additional Resources

Fans Online activities
Practice Workbook

273

Unit 5
TODO JUNTO

Presentation

- In this section, students will review the unit objectives and put them into practice.
- Students will use the vocabulary for body parts. They will also practice how to talk about personal hygiene and health, and will make recommendations regarding healthy habits.

Activities	Standards	Resources
77.	1.3	
78.	1.1, 1.2, 1.3, 3.1	
79.	1.1, 1.3	
80.	1.2, 1.3	Audio
81. Conexiones	1.1, 1.2, 1.3, 2.2, 3.1, 3.2	

Teaching Suggestions

Warm-Up / Independent Starter

- Have students go back in the unit and review all the vocabulary listed on the vocabulary presentation pages.

Preparation

- Draw a three-column table on the board with the following headings: *Partes del cuerpo*, *Problemas de salud o de higiene*, and *Recomendaciones*. Ask students to come up to the board and fill in these columns with expressions they have learned throughout the unit.

Partes del cuerpo	Problemas de salud o de higiene	Recomendaciones
uñas	muy largas	cortárselas

- Then ask students to write down five sentences drawing ideas from the three columns and making the necessary adjustments. For example: *uñas / muy largas / cortarse → Pedro tiene que cortarse las uñas porque las tiene muy largas.*

Activities

78. You may turn this activity into a contest by asking pairs of students to design their own *Guía saludable* with at least three recommendations for each category. They can then vote for the best *guía*.

79. Have students share their ideas with the rest of the class. You may list their ideas on the board.

274

ESCRIBIR

 Unos apuntes errados

▶ **Escribe.** Tim lee unos apuntes que tomó en clase, ¡pero hay errores! Decide si estas oraciones son ciertas o falsas. Después, corrige las oraciones falsas.

1. El codo, las pestañas y las cejas son partes de la cara.
2. Necesitas cortarte las uñas cada día.
3. Para cuidar el pelo hay que usar un buen desodorante.
4. Puedes usar crema para la cara y para el cuerpo.
5. Hay que lavarse los dientes todos los días.

LEER, ESCRIBIR Y HABLAR

78 **Buenas recomendaciones**

▶ **Lee** estas recomendaciones para una página web. ¿A qué categoría corresponde cada una?

1. Hay que visitar al médico una vez al año.
2. Debes cepillarte los dientes frecuentemente.
3. Necesitas beber al menos un litro de agua al día.

vidasaludable.com

Ayúdanos a elaborar una guía saludable. Envíanos sugerencias sobre estos temas:

HIGIENE PERSONAL   SALUD   DIETA

Participa y entra en el sorteo de un fin de semana en un balneario. ¡Anímate!

 ▶ **Escribe** otras recomendaciones para cada categoría.

▶ **Habla** con tus compañeros(as). Elijan las diez mejores recomendaciones.

274   doscientos setenta y cuatro

Differentiated Instruction

DEVELOPING LEARNERS

- Ask students if the following statements are true (*cierto*) or false (*falso*):
  1. *Tengo dos manos, dos pies y dos dedos.* (falso)
  2. *Te pones esmalte si sudas.* (falso)
  3. *Hay que maquillarse las orejas.* (falso)
  4. *Hay que hacer ejercicio con frecuencia.* (cierto)
  5. *El tobillo y la rodilla son parte de la cara.* (falso)
  6. *El jarabe es una sopa fría.* (falso)
  7. *A veces las inyecciones te duelen.* (cierto)

EXPANDING LEARNERS

- Ask students which word does not belong and to explain why it doesn't belong.

1.	piernas	ojos	boca	(piernas)
2.	cejas	mejillas	pestañas	(mejillas)
3.	gripe	aspirina	catarro	(aspirina)
4.	dedos	muñecas	orejas	(orejas)
5.	fiebre	pastilla	dolor	(pastilla)
6.	pie	barbilla	tobillo	(barbilla)
7.	hombro	frente	nariz	(hombro)
8.	pecho	venda	jarabe	(pecho)

HABLAR Y ESCRIBIR

 79 **Un día normal**

 ▶ **Representa** con tu compañero(a) una entrevista. ¿Qué recomendaciones de salud pueden hacer estas personas?

1. una médica   2. una dentista   3. un enfermero

ESCUCHAR Y ESCRIBIR

80 **Encuentra las diferencias**

 ▶ **Escucha.** Andy y Janet hablan mientras caminan por Sevilla. Escúchalos y escribe las diferencias entre lo que dicen y estas ilustraciones.

Modelo   1. *Andy dice que hay una chica patinando, pero en el dibujo está corriendo.*

CONEXIONES: ARTE

Un cuadro de Velázquez

Diego Velázquez es uno de los pintores españoles más importantes. Nació en Sevilla en 1599. Vivió en Madrid y fue pintor del rey Felipe IV. *Las Meninas* es probablemente su obra más famosa. En este cuadro aparecen la infanta Margarita, sus damas de compañía y Velázquez (el personaje que está pintando). También se ve a los reyes reflejados en el espejo *(mirror)*.

Velázquez. *Las Meninas.*
Museo del Prado (Madrid).

81 **Describe** a los personajes del cuadro con tu compañero(a). Después, elige uno y escribe un párrafo con una descripción detallada.

doscientos setenta y cinco **275**

---

80. Before playing the audio recording, have students describe the pictures. You may help them do so using guiding questions: ¿*Dónde está esta chica? ¿Qué está haciendo?*, etc.

 AUDIO SCRIPT
See page 235J.

 CONEXIONES: ARTE

Un cuadro de Velázquez

Diego Velázquez painted *Las Meninas* in 1656. It is an imposing wall-sized picture. Princess Margarita—the daughter of the Spanish king—is the central figure. Velázquez uses multiple planes and it is difficult to ascertain what is real and what is a reflection in a mirror or an illusion.

Answer Key

77. Answers will vary. Sample answers:
1. Falso. Los ojos, las pestañas y las cejas forman parte de la cara.
2. Falso. Necesitas cortarte las uñas cada semana.
3. Falso. Hay que usar un buen champú.
4. Cierto.
5. Cierto.

78. 1. Salud
2. Higiene personal
3. Dieta
▶ Answers will vary.
▶ Answers will vary.

79. Answers will vary.

80. 2. Janet dice que hay un chico dormido en un banco, pero en el dibujo está leyendo.
3. Andy dice que ve una mujer con una pierna rota, pero tiene un brazo roto.

81. Answers will vary.

Additional Resources

Fans Online activities
Practice Workbook

275

El encuentro

Presentation

- The four pairs gather in front of the *Monasterio de la Rábida*, in southern Spain. There they must provide their photos with captions to prove the completion of their challenge.
- Students will vote for the winner of the *Desafíos* in Spain.

Activities	Standards	Resources
Fotonovela	1.2, 2.1, 2.2	
82.	1.3	
83.	1.2, 1.3, 5.1	

Teaching Suggestions

Warm-Up / Independent Starter

- Ask students to close their textbooks and write a summary of each pair's challenge in Spain.

Preparation

- Have students exchange their summaries from the Independent Starter with a classmate. Then ask them to help you write down a complete summary on the board.
- Remind students that in *Desafío 1*, Tess and Patricia traveled to Barcelona where they visited the Picasso Museum. There, they had to find Margarita. In *Desafío 2*, Diana and Rita visited the University of Salamanca, in western Spain, where they had to find a frog. In *Desafío 3*, Tim and Mack traveled to Pamplona, in northern Spain, where they had to run in front of the bulls during the *sanfermines*. In *Desafío 4*, Andy and Janet traveled to Seville, in southern Spain, on a bullet train. There, they had to get gazpacho for all their friends.

La fotonovela

- Ask a volunteer to read the introduction to *El encuentro* aloud.
- Have students look at the pictures. Ask them to explain what each pair is holding in their hands, and describe their surroundings in the pictures. Then have students read each pair's speech bubble silently.

En el Monasterio de la Rábida

The pairs gather in front of the *Monasterio de la Rábida*, where Christopher Columbus stayed before persuading the Spanish King and Queen to back his expedition. Did all the pairs succeed in their assignments?

Aquí está la famosa rana de la Universidad de Salamanca. Qué trabajo para encontrarla... ¡pero al final apareció!

Fuimos al Museo Picasso de Barcelona para buscar una flor... y encontramos la cara de otra Margarita.

Yo corrí un encierro... ¡pero detrás de los toros!

Tuvimos que aprender a preparar gazpacho, ¡y nos salió muy bien!

276 doscientos setenta y seis

Differentiated Instruction

DEVELOPING LEARNERS

- Ask students to decide if the following statements are true or false:
  1. *La rana estaba en un restaurante de Salamanca. (falso)*
  2. *Patricia y Tess encontraron un cuadro de Picasso. (cierto)*
  3. *Patricia y Tess fueron a Barcelona. (cierto)*
  4. *Mack y Tim corrieron en los encierros. (falso)*
  5. *Mack se vistió con ropa especial para correr en el encierro. (cierto)*
  6. *El gazpacho les salió bien a Janet y Andy. (cierto)*
  7. *El gazpacho es un plato caliente. (falso)*

EXPANDING LEARNERS

- Ask students to describe what they learned about Spain after studying this unit. Have them include as much information as they can on the cities and landmarks mentioned in the *Desafíos*. Encourage them to do more research on these places. Ask students to also explain in their description which city they would like to visit and which landmark holds the most interest for them and why.

82 Las fotografías de los personajes

▶ **Completa** los pies de foto con *por* o *para*.

①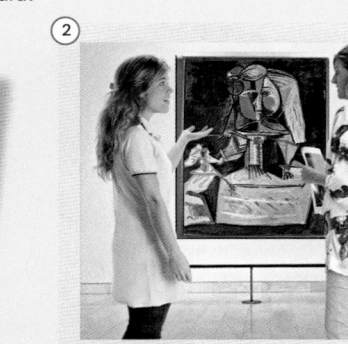

Buscamos la rana _____ toda la fachada de la universidad.

②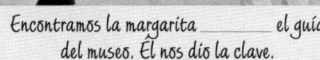

Encontramos la margarita _____ el guía del museo. Él nos dio la clave.

③

Mi abuelo y yo preparados _____ correr el encierro.

④

Aquí estamos preparando un gazpacho _____ nuestros amigos.

83 Las votaciones

▶ **Lee** los pies de foto que escribieron los personajes. ¿Cuál crees que es mejor? ¿Por qué?

▶ **Elige** tres fotografías de esta unidad y escribe un pie de foto para cada una.

▶ **Lee** los pies de foto a tu compañero(a). Él/Ella tiene que adivinar a qué fotografías corresponden.

Un pie de foto debe ser breve. Tiene que explicar el contenido de la imagen.

doscientos setenta y siete **277**

■ Call students' attention to Mack's statement: *Yo corrí un encierro... ¡pero detrás de los toros!* Ask students to describe Mack and Tim's challenge. (To run in front of the bulls during the *encierro*.) Ask students why they think Mack ran behind the bulls instead of in front of them. And what about Tim? What did he do?

■ Then assign the scenes to different pairs of students to act out for the class. For each scene, have the partners divide the dialogue between both characters so that each student participates equally. Students may add appropriate expressions to their dialogue.

Activities

82. Before completing the task, you may want to ask students to check the uses of *por* and *para* on page 262.

83. On the board, write the names of the participants and tally the results of the class vote for the best photo caption. Invite students to share with the class their reasons for voting as they did.

Answer Key

82. 1. por   3. para
      2. por   4. para

83. Answers will vary.
      ▶ Answers will vary.
      ▶ Answers will vary.

HERITAGE LANGUAGE LEARNERS

• At the end of their *desafíos*, the participants gather at the *Monasterio de la Rábida*, in Palos de la Frontera. Ask students to research this monastery as well as the difficulties Columbus faced in convincing the monarchs to finance his trip to the New World. Then have them write a letter in which Columbus briefly describes the monastery and makes his final argument to Isabel and Fernando.

COOPERATIVE LEARNING

• Have students work in small groups and assign them one of the *desafíos*, but explain that they must rewrite it from beginning to end. Students will need to get together and discuss their strategy, then work as a team to put together an original plot and dialogue. Encourage them to add as many details as they can about the place where the *desafío* takes place. After they complete the writing, give them time to rehearse their lines and present the new *desafío* to the class.

MAPA CULTURAL

España y el Mediterráneo

Presentation

- This section presents Spain through facts and physical features so learners can see the country from other perspectives.

Activities	Standards	Resources
Mapa cultural	1.2, 3.1, 3.2	Video
84.	1.3, 3.1	
85.	2.1, 3.1, 5.2	

Cultural Topics

- **Paisaje mediterráneo.** The Mediterranean landscape is, in large part, the result of the weather and human action. The Mediterranean climate is made up of long, hot summers with little rainfall and mild, rainy winters. The Mediterranean region has long been settled, and humans have impacted the environment through farming and livestock grazing. Figs, grapes, citrus, almonds, walnuts, and olives are some of the fruits that thrive in this region.

- **La Noche de San Juan.** Midsummer celebrations are common throughout Europe on the night of June 21st, which marks the summer solstice and is the shortest night of the year. In Spain, midsummer celebrations take place on June 24, in honor of St. John. In Alicante, large and elaborate figures are erected in the different city districts on June 20. This is called *la plantà*, or the set up. Then, at midnight on June 24, there is an impressive display of fireworks, followed by *la cremà*, or burning of the figures that were set up before.

- **Las lenguas romances.** Vulgar Latin—an amalgam of nonstandard, or colloquial, forms of Latin—was the language spoken by most of the Roman population, including the soldiers that conquered the territories that would become part of the Roman Empire. This language, mixed with vernacular elements of the pre-Roman languages spoken in the different provinces of the Roman Empire, gave rise to the Romance languages we know today.

Teaching Suggestions

Warm-Up / Independent Starter

- Have students glance quickly through the *Mapa cultural*.

MAPA CULTURAL

España y el Mediterráneo

Nacionalidades
España → español(a)

España está situada al suroeste de Europa, entre el océano Atlántico y el mar Mediterráneo. Su territorio comprende la mayor parte de la península Ibérica, las islas Baleares, las islas Canarias y las ciudades de Ceuta y Melilla, situadas en el norte de África. La capital de España es Madrid.

España es un país mediterráneo y comparte muchos rasgos culturales con otros países mediterráneos de origen latino, como Francia o Italia.

84 **Conoce España**

▶ **Escribe.** Observa el mapa y relaciona las ciudades según su situación.

Modelo *Madrid está al norte de Toledo.*

1. Salamanca – Santiago de Compostela
2. Barcelona – Valencia
3. Bilbao – Santander
4. Toledo – Granada
5. Melilla – Ceuta

La cultura española tiene base latina. Y también fue importante la contribución de los árabes.

278 doscientos setenta y ocho

Differentiated Instruction

DEVELOPING LEARNERS

- Have students identify Spain on a map of Western Europe. Then ask them to draw the map of Spain and label the following: two bodies of water surrounding Spain, two countries bordering Spain, one of the two groups of islands that belong to Spain, Spain's capital city, and a physical feature.

- Then ask students to draw a map of the United States and label the same items. When they have finished the maps, have them write a paragraph comparing both countries. For example: *La capital de los Estados Unidos es Washington DC y la de España es Madrid…*

EXPANDING LEARNERS

- Explain that there are some areas around the world that also have a Mediterranean-like climate. For instance, the coast of California, in the United States, has a similar climate and produces some of the same fruits and vegetables as those grown in Spain and other Mediterranean countries.

- Have students research the weather, landscape, and farming in coastal California and compare these elements with those of the Mediterranean coast of Spain. Ask students to summarize their findings in a Venn diagram and share it with the class.

1. Paisaje mediterráneo

El este de la península Ibérica es un área de clima mediterráneo, con temperaturas suaves y plantaciones de naranjas, limones, palmeras y olivos. La flor del naranjo se llama *azahar* y su perfume es típico en las calles de ciudades como Valencia.

(1) Flor de azahar.

2. La Noche de San Juan

En muchos lugares de la costa mediterránea se celebra la Noche de San Juan. Esta fiesta tiene lugar el 24 de junio y coincide con la llegada del verano. Esa noche se encienden hogueras *(bonfires)* y algunas personas saltan por encima de las brasas *(embers)*.

Existe la creencia de que la Noche de San Juan es mágica y se hacen algunos ritos para pedir deseos.

(2) Noche de San Juan (Alicante).

3. Las lenguas romances

España es la cuna del español. El español es una lengua de origen latino, como el portugués, el francés, el italiano o el rumano. El latín era la lengua que hablaban los antiguos romanos.

El español se habla en toda España. Pero en España se hablan también otras lenguas: el gallego en Galicia, el vasco en el País Vasco y el catalán en la zona del Mediterráneo (Cataluña, Baleares y Valencia).

SOPA DE LETRAS

C	A	T	A	L	Á	N	D	O	E
A	S	R	A	U	A	L	I	R	S
Ó	G	I	O	F	E	N	T	E	P
V	F	Y	G	I	Ó	N	A	A	A
R	R	Y	E	O	É	Y	L	U	Ñ
S	A	O	L	N	A	M	I	N	O
A	N	Y	L	A	R	Y	A	L	L
É	C	Y	A	M	S	Y	N	A	F
S	É	U	G	U	T	R	O	P	E
A	S	Y	U	R	E	S	D	A	S

 85 **Sopa de letras**

▶ **Encuentra** en la sopa de letras el nombre de siete lenguas romances.

doscientos setenta y nueve 279

MAPA CULTURAL
España y el Mediterráneo

Preparation

- Invite students to talk about what caught their attention from their quick glance of the *Mapa cultural* and have them explain why.

- Explain that Spain occupies 195,364 square miles and has a population of 46,152,925. (2011 est.). The highest peak in Spain is Pico del Teide (12,198 ft.), located on the island of Tenerife. Spain has 17 autonomous communities, including the Balearic Islands in the Mediterranean Sea and the Canary Islands in the Atlantic Ocean.

- Spain's strategic location and mild climate have made it attractive to humans for millennia. In fact, some of Europe's most well-known Paleolithic sites are located in Spain. A succession of peoples (e.g., Iberians, Celts, Phoenicians, Carthaginians, Romans, Visigoths, and Arabs) have settled Spain at different points in history.

Activities

84. Ask students to draw a compass rose on chart paper. Then have them label the following eight cardinal points in Spanish: *Norte, Noreste, Este, Sureste, Sur, Suroeste, Oeste, Noroeste.* Ask students to use their compass rose to complete this activity.

Answer Key

84. 1. Salamanca está al sureste de Santiago de Compostela.
 2. Barcelona está al noreste de Valencia.
 3. Bilbao está al este de Santander.
 4. Toledo está al norte de Granada.
 5. Melilla está al sureste de Ceuta.

85. catalán, español, portugués, francés, italiano, rumano, gallego

Additional Resources

Fans Online activities
Practice Workbook

HERITAGE LANGUAGE LEARNERS

- Discuss with students the important contribution that the indigenous languages of the Americas, as well as the native languages spoken by the African slaves, made to the Spanish language. Words such as *canoa, barbacoa,* and *maíz,* from the Taino language, were some of the first words incorporated into the Spanish language.

- Ask students to research and compile a list of Spanish words that come from American and African languages. Have them include the Spanish word, the language it comes from, and the original word. For example: *tomate – náhuatl – tomatl.*

CRITICAL THINKING

- Discuss with students that humanity's transformation from small hunting and gathering clans into agrarian societies, organized in villages, had its most successful beginnings in the Fertile Crescent, along the Eastern Mediterranean (Levant) coast. Ask students what role they think the Mediterranean climate and varied topography played in the development of agriculture, animal domestication, and the subsequent rise of the Mesopotamian and Egyptian civilizations.

LECTURA

Figura en una ventana

Presentation

- In this section, students will practice and extend their reading skills by reading a descriptive text. In addition, students will increase their understanding of Spanish culture and art by analyzing a painting by Salvador Dalí.

Activities	Standards	Resources
Lectura	1.2, 2.2, 3.1, 3.2	
86.	1.3, 2.2, 3.1	
87.	1.2, 1.3, 3.1	
88.	1.2, 1.3, 3.1	
89.	1.3, 2.2, 3.1, 5.2	
Tu desafío	1.2, 3.1, 3.2, 5.2	

Teaching Suggestions

Warm-Up / Independent Starter

- Ask students to look briefly at the painting, then close their books and write two sentences describing what they remember about the painting.

Preparation

- Have students meet in small groups to share their Independent Starter. Do they have similar impressions or did each of them remember something different about the painting?

- Before reading the passage, ask for a volunteer to read the Reading Strategy box. Explain that the main objective of descriptive texts is to show details. The vocabulary in a descriptive text is chosen carefully, since its aim is to create an image in the mind of the reader. Discuss with students similes and metaphors. Clarify that a simile is a figure of speech in which two unlike things are explicitly compared, whereas a metaphor suggests, or implies, a comparison between two unlike things.

- To introduce the reading, explain that Salvador Dalí was one of the most-recognized Spanish painters of the 20th century. He is best known as a surrealist painter. Surrealism was an art and cultural movement that developed in Europe in the 1920s, and which produced art that went against reason. One of Dalí's best-known surrealist paintings is *The Persistence of Memory* (1931).

Salvador Dalí. *Figura en una ventana.* 1925. Museo Nacional Centro de Arte Reina Sofía. Madrid.

READING STRATEGY
Read descriptive texts

Descriptive texts present the characteristics of people, objects, or places, so that the reader can form a clear mental image of them.

The description can be **objective** (an accurate reflection of reality) or **subjective** (from the point of view of the writer). When the description is of a person, it is called a **portrait** *(retrato).*

The main language tools used in descriptive texts are **adjectives** —to express the qualities of what is described—and stylistic devices such as **comparisons** and **metaphors**.

Figura en una ventana,
de Salvador Dalí

Uno de los cuadros más famosos de Salvador Dalí (1904-1989) es *Figura en una ventana.* Esta obra representa a una mujer de espaldas mirando el paisaje por la ventana. La joven es la hermana del pintor, Ana María. Está en la casa familiar de veraneo y el paisaje visto desde la ventana es la bahía de Cadaqués, en la costa mediterránea.

La muchacha tiene el pelo largo, recogido en la nuca, y está apoyada en la ventana. Como una escultura clásica, la joven contempla pensativa el mar y el horizonte. Su vestido, claro y ligero, dibuja su cuerpo. Las cortinas, azules y onduladas[1], enmarcan[2] la figura de la muchacha. No vemos su rostro, pero podemos imaginar su mirada tranquila y melancólica. Un cielo triste y un mar en calma entran por la ventana como una suave brisa.

Figura en una ventana es una pintura realista. A través de la muchacha, la ventana se abre al espectador; la joven nos introduce en el paisaje y nos invita a mirar más allá.

---

1. *wavy*   2. *frame*

Differentiated Instruction

DEVELOPING LEARNERS

- Figures of speech may be difficult to understand, especially in a foreign language. The second paragraph might cause students some difficulties. Ask them to work with a partner and have them break the paragraph into sentences and take turns reading each sentence out loud. As one of the partners reads a sentence, his or her partner should point to the item(s) that is / are being described. For example, for the first sentence (*La muchacha tiene el pelo largo, recogido en la nuca*), students should point to the girl's hair and neck.

EXPANDING LEARNERS

- Have students read the text silently one more time and observe the painting for a couple of minutes. Then ask them to write one more paragraph to add to the reading about something else from the painting. They could, for instance, focus on the pale hues and uniformity in color Dalí used in this painting. Or they could focus on the bareness of the room.

- Ask students to include both objective and subjective descriptions in their paragraph, as well as figures of speech. Invite volunteers to share their paragraphs with the rest of the class.

COMPRENSIÓN

86 **¿Qué sabes del cuadro?**

▶ **Responde** a las siguientes preguntas.

1. ¿Quién pintó *Figura en una ventana*?
2. ¿Qué representa el cuadro?
3. ¿Quién es la mujer del cuadro?
4. ¿Dónde está la playa del cuadro?
5. ¿De qué estilo es esta pintura?

Salvador Dalí.

ESTRATEGIA **Leer textos descriptivos**

87 **Tipos de descripción**

▶ **Lee** otra vez el texto y escribe tres ejemplos de descripción objetiva y tres de descripción subjetiva.

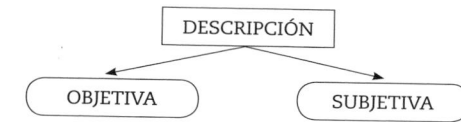

DESCRIPCIÓN

OBJETIVA → SUBJETIVA

88 **Recursos para describir**

▶ **Escribe** algunos recursos utilizados en el texto para describir el cuadro de Dalí.

Adjetivos calificativos	Comparaciones y metáforas

89 **Tu texto descriptivo**

▶ **Escribe** una descripción de este cuadro de Dalí. Se titula *Muchacha de espaldas*. ¿Reconoces a la modelo del pintor?

 **TU DESAFÍO** Visita la página web para aprender más sobre la obra de Dalí.

Salvador Dalí. *Muchacha de espaldas.*
1925. Museo Nacional Centro
de Arte Reina Sofía. Madrid.

Activities

87. Clarify that in an objective description, words convey information, but they don't produce positive or negative reactions about the subject they are describing. In a subjective description, words convey feelings, positive or negative connotations, mood, perspectives, etc.

89. Explain to students that Dalí was an admirer of the French painter Jean Auguste Ingres. Have students look at Ingres's *La Grande Odalisque*, located at: http://mini-site.louvre.fr/ingres/ 1.4.2.1_en.html. Do they see some common elements between Ingres's and Dalí's paintings?

Answer Key

86. 1. Salvador Dalí
2. A una joven mirando por la ventana.
3. Es la hermana del pintor, Anna María.
4. En la bahía de Cadaqués, en la costa mediterránea.
5. Es una pintura realista.

87. Answers will vary. Sample answers:
Objetiva: la obra representa a una mujer de espaldas; la muchacha tiene el pelo largo, recogido en la nuca; es una pintura realista
Subjetiva: como una escultura clásica; su mirada tranquila y melancólica; un cielo triste

88. Answers will vary. Sample answers:
Adjetivos calificativos: famoso, largo, pensativa, blanco, ligero, azules, onduladas, tranquila, melancólica, triste, suave, realista
Comparaciones y metáforas: como una escultura clásica; su vestido dibuja su cuerpo; las cortinas enmarcan la figura de la muchacha; un cielo triste y un mar en calma entran por la ventana como una suave brisa; la ventana se abre al espectador; la joven nos introduce en el paisaje

89. Answers will vary.

Additional Resources

Fans Online activities

HERITAGE LANGUAGE LEARNERS

• Have students research a painter from their country of origin, or from their heritage culture. Ask them to look at several of this artist's paintings and choose the piece that impacts them most. Then have students write a three-paragraph descriptive text to present the painting to the rest of the class. As an introduction to the presentation, have them include a brief biography of the artist and a picture of the painting.

COOPERATIVE LEARNING

• Place students in mixed-level groups of three. Then have them create a Venn diagram comparing and contrasting *Figura en una ventana* and *Muchacha de espaldas*. One of the students in the group can focus on what is different about *Figura en una ventana*, another student can do the same with *Muchacha de espaldas*, and the third student can focus on the common elements in these two pictures. Then have students discuss their opinions before they complete the diagram.

REPASO

Vocabulario

Presentation

- In this section, students will review all key vocabulary from the unit, organized by themes, to prepare for an assessment. Students will complete practice activities for each of the four *Desafíos*.

Activities	Standards	Resources
1.	1.2	
2.	1.2, 3.1	
3.	1.3	
4.	1.2	

Teaching Suggestions

Warm-Up / Independent Starter

- Ask students to think of their daily morning routine, the body part(s) involved, and the object(s) they use. Then have them record this information in a table like the one below.

Acción	Parte(s) del cuerpo	Objeto(s)
ducharse	el cuerpo	el jabón y el champú
cepillarse	los dientes	el cepillo de dientes y la pasta

Preparation

- Have students work with a classmate to come up with a narrative based on their daily routines. Ask them to look at each other's tables from the Independent Starter and write a paragraph combining their routines. But ask students to mix up the actions, body parts, and objects to come up with an absurd, but funny, narrative. For example: *Janice se ducha los dientes con champú. Yo me cepillo el cuerpo con pasta de dientes. Después, las dos nos maquillamos los pies con el gel…*

- Have pairs get together with another pair and take turns reading their narratives. One of the partners reads the paragraph and the other pantomimes the actions. At the end of the presentation, the other group offers their corrections, explaining what they think really happened. For example: *Janice se lava el pelo con champú. Tú te cepillas los dientes con pasta de dientes. Después…*

REPASO Vocabulario

Partes del cuerpo

el brazo	arm
la cabeza	head
la cintura	waist
el codo	elbow
el cuello	neck
los dedos	fingers, toes
la espalda	back
el hombro	shoulder
la mano	hand
la muñeca	wrist
el pecho	chest
el pie	foot
la pierna	leg
la rodilla	knee
el tobillo	ankle

La cara

la barbilla	chin
la boca	mouth
las cejas	eyebrows
los dientes	teeth
la frente	forehead
los labios	lips
las mejillas	cheeks
la nariz	nose
los ojos	eyes
las orejas	ears
las pestañas	eyelashes

La higiene personal

el cepillo	hairbrush
el champú	shampoo
la crema	moisturizing cream
el esmalte de uñas	nail polish
el gel	gel
el jabón	soap
el maquillaje	makeup
la pasta de dientes	toothpaste
el secador	hair dryer
las tijeras	scissors
la toalla	towel

Acciones

afeitarse	to shave
arreglarse	to get ready
bañarse	to take a bath
cepillarse	to brush (one's hair, teeth)
cortarse las uñas	to cut one's nails
ducharse	to take a shower
lavarse	to wash (up)
maquillarse	to put makeup on
peinarse	to comb (one's hair)
pintarse	to put makeup on
pintarse los labios	to put lipstick on
ponerse desodorante	to put deodorant on
secarse	to dry (one's hands, face, hair)
sudar	to sweat

La salud: síntomas y enfermedades

la alergia	allergy	**Remedios**	
el catarro	cold	la aspirina	aspirin
el dolor	pain	la inyección	injection, shot
la fiebre	fever	el jarabe	cough syrup
la gripe	flu	la pastilla	pill
		la venda	bandage
doler	to hurt		
Me duele(n)…	I have a … ache.		
estornudar	to sneeze	el / la enfermero(a)	nurse
picar	to itch	el / la médico(a)	doctor
toser	to cough	el / la paciente	patient
la clínica	clinic		
el hospital	hospital		

Hábitos saludables

beber agua	to drink water
comer bien	to eat well
cuidarse	to take care of oneself
descansar	to rest
estar en forma	to be in shape
estar / mantenerse sano(a)	to be / stay healthy
hacer deporte	to play sports
hacer ejercicio	to exercise
meditar	to meditate
montar en bicicleta	to ride a bicycle
patinar	to skate
practicar yoga	to do yoga
seguir una dieta equilibrada	to have a balanced diet
tomar vitaminas	to take vitamins

Differentiated Instruction

DEVELOPING LEARNERS

- Have students work with a partner to reorganize the vocabulary for body parts in the order in which the different parts are located on our body, from our head to our feet. For example: *la cabeza, la frente, las cejas, los ojos, las pestañas, … los pies.*

- Then have partners take turns calling out an action. His or her partner completes the phrase with an appropriate body part. Allow them to consult their vocabulary lists and textbooks when in doubt. For example:

  A. *Lavarse…*
  B. *las manos.*

EXPANDING LEARNERS

- Have students think of a Spanish definition for each vocabulary word. Then ask them to team up with a classmate to play a vocabulary game with another two-student team. A team calls out a vocabulary word; the other team has one minute to come up with a definition and a sentence. For example:

  A. *Las cejas.*
  B. *Pelo que está encima de los ojos. Tengo dos cejas.*

  Each team earns a point for a correct definition and sentence. If a team is unable to complete the task, it loses a turn. The first team to earn 10 points wins.

DESAFÍO 1

1 **Partes del cuerpo.** Une cada acción con una parte del cuerpo.

1. hablar
2. dibujar
3. caminar
4. ver

a. las manos y los dedos
b. la boca
c. los ojos
d. las piernas y los pies

DESAFÍO 2

2 **Una lista.** Clasifica estos hábitos de higiene.

cepillarse los dientes
cortarse las uñas
maquillarse
  o afeitarse
ducharse
secarse el pelo
ponerse crema
bañarse
peinarse
ponerse desodorante

Una vez al mes	Una vez por semana	Todos los días
		cepillarse los dientes

DESAFÍO 3

3 **¿Cuál es la solución?** Escribe. ¿Qué remedio les da el médico a estas personas?

Modelo Tengo tos. → *Tome un jarabe.*

1. Me duele el tobillo.
2. Tengo gripe.
3. Me duele la cabeza.
4. Tengo dolor de garganta.

DESAFÍO 4

4 **¡Tienes que cuidarte!** Decide qué hábito saludable es mejor para estas personas.

practicar yoga

descansar

montar en bicicleta

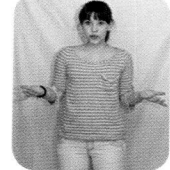

1. Pedro está muy cansado.
2. A Ana no le gusta ir al gimnasio.
3. A Silvia le gusta meditar.

doscientos ochenta y tres **283**

Activities

1. To extend this activity, ask students to think of four actions related to personal hygiene to add to the left column (e.g., *pintarse, peinarse*, etc.) and four body parts related to these actions to add to the right column. Have students exchange papers with a classmate and have them complete each other's matching activity.

3. Ask students to think of what might have caused these people's aliments. Ask them to write a brief story explaining what they think happened. For example: *Jugó un partido de fútbol y le dieron un golpe, por eso le duele el tobillo.* Invite different volunteers to share their stories with the class. Are their explanations plausible?

4. Have students think of the four healthy habits that they believe would benefit them most (e.g., *comer bien, hacer ejercicio*, etc.). Are they incorporating all of these habits into their daily routines? If not, what is preventing them from doing so?

Answer Key

1. 1. b   2. a   3. d   4. c
2. Answers will vary. Sample answers:
   Una vez al mes: bañarse.
   Una vez por semana: cortarse las uñas.
   Todos los días: cepillarse los dientes, maquillarse o afeitarse, secarse el pelo, ponerse crema, ducharse, peinarse, ponerse desodorante.
3. Answers will vary. Sample answers:
   1. Descanse.
   2. Descanse y beba agua.
   3. Tome una aspirina.
   4. Tome unas pastillas.
4. 1. descansar
   2. montar en bicicleta
   3. practicar yoga

Additional Resources

Fans Online activities
Practice Workbook

HERITAGE LANGUAGE LEARNERS

- Have heritage learners work in groups of three with other students in the class. Explain that there is a pressing need for medical interpreters in many cities across the United States and that, for this activity, they will play the role of a medical interpreter. Have one of the students play the role of the doctor, another plays the patient, and the heritage learner plays the interpreter.

- Have the groups create a scene based on the unit vocabulary. Allow each group rehearsal time and then invite them to perform their sketch in front of the class.

MULTIPLE INTELLIGENCES:
Visual-Spatial Intelligence

- Ask students to draw the human body on chart paper or look for a diagram on the Internet and print it out. Have them also draw or find a diagram of a human head. Then ask students to label the different parts. Next to some of the body parts, have students list a symptom associated with the body part (e.g., *la boca → estornudar*).

- Then have students exchange papers with a classmate and have them give their diagnosis and a recommendation for each problem (e.g., *la boca → estornudar → gripe → tomar un remedio*).

REPASO

Gramática

Presentation

- Students will review grammatical structures presented in the unit. Each grammar point is cross-referenced to the corresponding page in which it was introduced. The activities here provide systematic practice by *Desafío*.

Activities	Standards	Resources
5.	1.3	
6.	1.3	
7.	1.2, 1.3	
8.	1.3	
9. Cultura	1.3, 2.1, 2.2	

Teaching Suggestions

Warm-Up / Independent Starter

- Have students answer the following questions in writing and with complete sentences:
  1. *Cuando estás en tu dormitorio, ¿dejas la puerta abierta o cerrada?*
  2. *¿Te arreglas para ir a la escuela rápidamente o lentamente?*
  3. *¿Por dónde vas para llegar al gimnasio?*
  4. *¿Qué debes hacer cuando tienes gripe?*

Preparation

- Have students discuss their answers from the Independent Starter in small groups. Do they have similar answers? Then invite different volunteers to share their answers with the class.
- Write on the board some of the students' answers. As you go over the *Repaso* presentation, use the grammatical structures from the sentences you wrote on the board as examples of the grammar being reviewed.

Activities

5. Have students look around them and describe the state of some of their classmates, teacher, and objects in the room. For example: *Leslie tiene el libro de Español cerrado. Mark está entretenido. Tiene el libro abierto y lee algo. La profesora está sentada.* Invite volunteers to share their descriptions with the class. Were the people who were described aware of these states?

REPASO Gramática

El participio (pág. 246)

PARTICIPIOS REGULARES

-ar **verbs**	Add the ending -ado.	pintar ⟶ pintado
-er **and** -ir **verbs**	Add the ending -ido.	vestir ⟶ vestido

PARTICIPIOS IRREGULARES

abrir	abierto	morir	muerto
decir	dicho	poner	puesto
descubrir	descubierto	romper	roto
escribir	escrito	ver	visto
hacer	hecho	volver	vuelto

Los adverbios en -*mente* (pág. 254)

Adjectives ending in -o	Change -o to -a and add -mente.	lento ⟶ lentamente
Adjectives ending in -e or in a consonant	Add -mente.	frecuente ⟶ frecuentemente / habitual ⟶ habitualmente

Por y *para* (pág. 262)

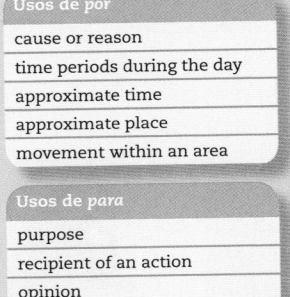

Usos de por

- cause or reason
- time periods during the day
- approximate time
- approximate place
- movement within an area

Usos de para

- purpose
- recipient of an action
- opinion
- movement toward a place
- deadline

Hacer recomendaciones (pág. 270)

Hay que + infinitivo
  Hay que **beber** más agua.

Tener que + infinitivo
  Tienes que **cuidarte.**

Deber + infinitivo
  Debes **hacer** ejercicio.

Necesitar + infinitivo
  Necesitas **comer** bien.

Poder + infinitivo
  Puedes **tomar** vitaminas.

Differentiated Instruction

DEVELOPING LEARNERS

- Before they work on activity 7, ask students to analyze the following sentences and determine which usage of *por* and *para* is taking place in each sentence.
  1. *No sé por qué él hizo eso.* (reason)
  2. *¿Para qué son estas pastillas?* (purpose)
  3. *Ella busca las tijeras por toda la casa.* (movement within an area)
  4. *Tenemos dos proyectos para este viernes.* (deadline)
  5. *Por la mañana me levanto temprano.* (time period)
  6. *El regalo es para ti.* (recipient of an action)

EXPANDING LEARNERS

- Have students create a context for the following phrases. Ask them to analyze the phrase and think about the situation when it would be used, the person who would say it, and to whom would the phrase be directed. Have students create a short dialogue to illustrate each phrase.
  - *Tienes que cuidarte.*
  - *Hay que cuidarse.*
  - *¡Cuídate!*
  - *Debe cuidarse.*

DESAFÍO 1

5 **¡Todo terminado!** Responde a estas preguntas.

Modelo ¿Dónde está Miguel? (dormir en la sala)
→ *Miguel está dormido en la sala.*

1. ¿Dónde están sus tíos? (sentar en la cocina)
2. ¿En qué idioma está ese libro? (escribir en chino)
3. ¿Cómo están las tareas de la escuela? (hacer desde ayer)
4. ¿Cómo están los niños? (emocionar con la noticia)

 DESAFÍO 2

6 **¿Cómo lo haces?** Completa estas oraciones.

| fácil |
| habitual |
| cuidadoso |

1. _____ me corto las uñas cada semana.
2. Este maquillaje es muy bueno, se aplica _____.
3. Mi madre se pinta las uñas tranquila y _____.

 DESAFÍO 3

7 **¿Por qué? ¿Para qué?** Une las tres columnas y escribe oraciones completas.

1. Fui a la farmacia
2. La tarea de Ciencias es
3. El autobús no pasa
4. Fueron al hospital

por
para

a. la calle Colombia.
b. comprar medicamentos.
c. ver al médico.
d. mañana.

 DESAFÍO 4

8 **Buenas recomendaciones.** Escribe oraciones completas usando estructuras para hacer recomendaciones. Usa los verbos *deber, poder, tener* y *necesitar*.

Modelo tú - deber beber dos litros de agua. → *Debes beber dos litros de agua.*

1. Sus padres – hacer deporte con frecuencia.
2. Nosotros – seguir una dieta equilibrada.
3. Tú – descansar más.
4. Berta – comer más fruta.

 **CULTURA**

9 **De viaje por España.** Responde a las siguientes preguntas.

1. ¿Qué sabes de Pablo Picasso?
2. ¿Dónde se celebran los sanfermines?
3. ¿Qué alimentos incluye la dieta mediterránea?

HERITAGE LANGUAGE LEARNERS

- Explain to students that there are a few cases in which a verb has two participles, a regular one and an irregular one. Give students the following two verbs and ask them to write down the participle form that first comes to their minds for each verb: *freír, imprimir.*

- Then ask students to research the two participles for each of these verbs and when each one is used. Have students write four sentences to illustrate each of these uses. Be sure students use the participles *frito* and *impreso* as adjectives, and *freído* and *imprimido* as verbs.

CRITICAL THINKING

- Have students work with a partner to analyze the following pairs of questions and explain the difference in meaning between each question. Then have them answer the questions with information about themselves.

  – *¿Para qué estudias Español? / ¿Por qué estudias Español?*
  – *¿Para dónde vas por las mañanas? / ¿Por dónde vas por las mañanas?*
  – *¿Para quién fue escrito tu libro de Español? / ¿Por quién fue escrito tu libro de Español?*

---

7. Have students work with a partner to come up with a brief dialogue between a doctor and a patient in which they use *por* and *para*. Then have partners act out the dialogue. For example:
A. *Doctor, me duele la espalda por la mañana.*
B. *Para sentirte mejor, es importante descansar.*

Answer Key

5. 1. Están sentados en la cocina.
2. Está escrito en chino.
3. Están hechas desde ayer.
4. Están emocionados con la noticia.

6. 1. Habitualmente
2. fácilmente
3. cuidadosamente

7. 1. b. Fui a la farmacia para comprar medicamentos.
2. d. La tarea de Ciencias es para mañana.
3. a. El autobús no pasa por la calle Colombia.
4. c. Fueron al hospital para ver al médico.

8. 1. Pueden hacer deporte con frecuencia.
2. Tenemos que seguir una dieta equilibrada.
3. Necesitas descansar más.
4. Debe comer más fruta.

9. 1. Answers will vary. Sample answer: Picasso es uno de los pintores españoles más importantes del siglo XX. Cultivó diversos estilos, entre ellos, el cubismo. Una de sus obras más conocidas es el *Guernica*.
2. Se celebran en Pamplona, capital de Navarra, en el norte de España.
3. Incluye el aceite de oliva y productos frescos y de temporada, principalmente verduras y frutas.

Additional Resources

Fans Online activities
Practice Workbook

PROYECTO

Hábitos de alimentación

Presentation

- In this section, students will apply the vocabulary, grammar, and cultural information they have learned in this unit to compare and contrast the nutritional guide of the United States with that of the Mediterranean countries. Students will follow step-by-step instructions.

Activities	Standards	Resources
Paso 1	1.2, 3.1	
Paso 2	1.2, 2.1, 3.1	
Paso 3	1.3, 2.1, 3.1, 4.2, 5.2	
Paso 4	1.1, 1.3, 2.1, 5.2	

Teaching Suggestions

Warm-Up / Independent Starter

- Without looking anywhere, have students draw a food guide and complete it with the information they remember.

Preparation

- Have students check their Independent Starter against the food plan of the United States in their textbook. Is their guide mostly correct or incorrect? Did they remember all the food groups?

- Discuss with students that several factors, such as genetics, access to health care, and disease impact life expectancy, and that nutrition and lifestyle choices are among the most significant factors.

Step-by-Step Instructions

Paso 1

- Have each group assign different questions to different students in the group to research. They will find the nutritional guide of the United States at: http://www.choosemyplate.gov.

- To make comparisons between the two nutritional guides easier, suggest to students that they write the answers to the questions in a two-column table. The first column is for the U.S. plan and the second for the Mediterranean pyramid.

PROYECTO

Una presentación sobre

hábitos de alimentación

In the Mediterranean, people have a high life expectancy, exceeded only by Japan. This may be attributed to dietary and personal hygiene habits.

In this project you will analyze the food guide of the United States and the food guide of Mediterranean countries in order to prepare a comparison between them. You will present the results of your report in a poster.

PASO 1 Analiza los hábitos de alimentación en los Estados Unidos

- In a small group, analyze the food guide of the United States. Look at the picture and answer the questions.
  - ¿Cuántos grupos componen el plato?
  - ¿Qué productos se deben comer con más frecuencia? ¿Y con menos frecuencia?
  - ¿Qué cantidad de proteínas hay que comer?
  - ¿Cuál es la proporción de lácteos adecuada?

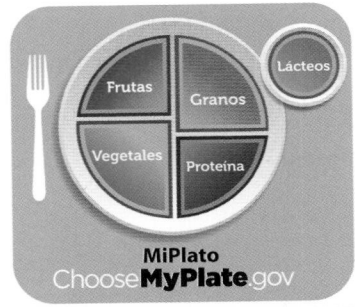

VEGETALES	FRUTAS	GRANOS	LÁCTEOS	PROTEÍNAS
Consuma 2 ¹/₂ tazas al día	Consuma 2 tazas al día	Consuma 6 onzas al día	Consuma 3 tazas al día	Consuma 5 ¹/₂ onzas al día

PASO 2 Analiza los hábitos de alimentación en España y en el Mediterráneo

Fuente: Ministerio de Sanidad y Consumo (España).

- Look at the picture and answer the questions in order to analyze the food guide pyramid of the Mediterranean countries.
  - ¿En cuántos grupos se divide la pirámide?
  - ¿Qué productos hay que comer con más frecuencia? ¿Y con menos frecuencia?
  - ¿Cuántas porciones de carne se deben comer?
  - ¿Cuál es la proporción de lácteos adecuada?

Rubric for Evaluation

	Content	Organization	Presentation
1 point	Limited relevance. Information is incomplete or not based on research. Little Spanish is used.	Inefficient use of class time. Information is disorganized or unclear. Chart is not well designed and organized.	Communication is unclear. Delivery is not fluent. Many errors in vocabulary and grammar.
3 points	Basic information is correct. Relevant information but lacks significance. Spanish is used most of the time.	Class time is used well. Information and content are mostly organized but lack some clarity. Chart is mostly well designed and organized.	Good communication. Fluent delivery. Mostly correct vocabulary and grammar.

PASO 3 Compara los hábitos y escribe tu presentación

- Based on your research and using your answers, compare the two food guides. Prepare a chart with the results of your comparison, including the similarities and differences.

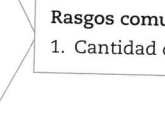

Rasgos diferenciales
1. Cantidad de...
2. ...

Rasgos comunes
1. Cantidad de...

Rasgos diferenciales
1. Cantidad de...

- Paste the chart with the comparison on a large piece of paper to display the results.

Modelo

En la dieta mediterránea y en la dieta de los Estados Unidos hay rasgos comunes. Por ejemplo, las dos recomiendan comer muchos vegetales y frutas. También...

PASO 4 Presenta tu trabajo

- Create a poster to present your work to the class. Explain the results of your comparison.
- During each group's presentation, take notes about the things that you find most interesting and important, and talk to your classmates.

5 points	Content	Organization	Presentation
	Relevant, interesting information. Many details and significance are highlighted. Spanish is used exclusively.	Class time is used wisely. Information and content are clearly organized visually and logically. Chart is very well designed and organized.	Clear communication. Correct and complete vocabulary and grammar. Very motivating upbeat delivery.

Unidad 5

Autoevaluación

¿Qué has aprendido en esta unidad?

Do these activities to evaluate how well you can manage in Spanish.

Evaluate your skills. For each item, say Very well, Well, or I need more practice.

a. Can you describe body parts?
  ▶ Tell a classmate what body parts you use when you swim, play baseball, and play chess.
  ▶ Describe how you perform each part of your hygiene routines.

b. Can you talk about personal hygiene habits?
  ▶ Tell a classmate your morning and evening hygiene routines.

c. Can you talk about illness and health care?
  ▶ Describe your health and how you feel during each season of the year. Then, describe why you feel that way in each season.

d. Can you recommend healthy habits?
  ▶ Tell a classmate what you do to live a healthy lifestyle.
  ▶ Tell your classmate what he or she should do to live a healthy lifestyle.

PROYECTO

Hábitos de alimentación

Paso 2

- Before students look at the picture, have them discuss in their groups what foods they associate with the Mediterranean diet (e.g., olive oil, legumes, vegetables, fruits, fish, grains, moderate amounts of dairy products, and small amounts of meat and sugar).
- Students will find additional food pyramids for the Mediterranean diet at: http://www.alimentacion.es/es/conoce_lo_que_comes/dietamediterranea/default.aspx. Have students complete the two-column table they started for *Paso 1*.

Paso 3

- Ask students to use the information in their two-column table to create a comparison chart. They can use a chart like the one in their textbook or a Venn diagram.

Paso 4

- Encourage students to include a brief statement at the end of the comparison expressing their opinion regarding these two diets. Invite the class to indicate whether they agree or not with the presenter's opinions.

Evaluation

- Distribute copies of the rubric to students. Discuss the evaluation criteria and explain how this project will be graded. Encourage students to refer to the rubric as they prepare their projects.

Content

- Have students proofread their work carefully, and ask them to check the accuracy of the information in their comparison chart.

Organization

- Encourage students to follow a clear order in their comparisons. For instance, they can focus on the common elements first, then on the U.S. diet, and then on the Mediterranean diet. Switching back and forth between the diets might confuse their audience.

Presentation

- Students should use as much Spanish as possible. Encourage creativity and a presentation style that will hold their classmates' attention.

287

Unit 6 Caribe continental

Objectives

- To describe past habits.
- To talk about past actions.
- To talk about events in the past.
- To tell an anecdote in the past.
- To use expressions to make, accept, and reject suggestions.
- To talk about travel.
- To list items necessary for a trip.
- To talk about modes of transportation.
- To list parts of trains and airplanes and the people who work in them.

- To list parts of an automobile and describe actions related to driving.
- To use expressions for checking into a hotel and bank transactions.
- To list items in a hotel and items used in a bank, and the people who work at these places.
- To explore certain cultural aspects of Colombia and Venezuela.
- To acquire facts about the geography and history of Colombia and Venezuela.

Contents

Vocabulary

- Expressions used to make, accept, and reject suggestions.
- Travel and excursions.
- Travel by bus.
- Luggage.
- Actions related to travel.
- Travel by train and airplane.
- Parts of an automobile.
- Actions related to driving.
- Elements of a hotel.
- Transactions at a bank.

Grammar

- The imperfect tense.
- Irregular verbs in the preterite tense: *Dar, poder, poner, querer, saber,* and *venir.*
- To narrate past actions: The preterite tense or the imperfect tense.
- To narrate and describe in the past: The preterite tense and the imperfect tense.
- To determine the meaning of a phrase based on the verb tense used.

Culture

- The legend of El Dorado.
- *El aeropuerto internacional El Dorado.*
- *El Museo del Oro de Bogotá.*
- *El salto Ángel.*
- The transportation system in Venezuela.
- *El transporte público: el autobús.*
- *¿Litros o galones?*
- The use of synonyms in Spanish-speaking countries.
- The production and export of coffee in Colombia.
- The Colombian economy.
- *El Río de la Plata.*

Evaluation Criteria

- Use an expression to make a suggestion.
- Use an expression to accept a suggestion.
- Use an expression to reject a suggestion.
- Describe the steps for planning a trip by plane.
- List parts of an automobile.
- List parts of a train station.

- List parts of an airport.
- Talk about planning a trip.
- Talk about a train or bus trip.
- Recognize and use forms of the preterite.
- Recognize and use forms of the imperfect.
- Narrate a story using the preterite and the imperfect.

- Recognize and use preterite forms of *dar, poder, poner, querer, saber,* and *venir.*
- Express understanding of selected South American customs, geographical aspects, and historical facts.
- Recognize informative devices in a text.
- Develop a travel brochure for Lake Guatavita.

Unit Plan

La llegada

Estimated time: 1 session.

Dialogue: *En Cartagena de Indias.*

Functions & forms:
- Expressions used to make suggestions.
- Expressions used to accept suggestions.
- Expressions used to reject suggestions.

Culture:
- The *Torre del Reloj*, Cartagena de Indias, Colombia.

DESAFÍO 1

Estimated time: 4 sessions.

Dialogue: *El tesoro más valioso de Colombia.*

Functions & forms:
- Travel and excursions.
- Travel by bus.
- Luggage.
- The imperfect tense.

Culture:
- *La leyenda de El Dorado.*
- *El aeropuerto internacional El Dorado.*
- *El Museo del Oro de Bogotá.*

DESAFÍO 2

Estimated time: 4 sessions.

Dialogue: *El salto Ángel.*

Functions & forms:
- Travel by train and airplane.
- Irregular verbs in the preterite tense: *Dar*, *poder*, *poner*, *querer*, *saber*, and *venir*.

Culture:
- *El salto Ángel.*
- *La red de transportes en Venezuela.*

DESAFÍO 3

Estimated time: 4 sessions.

Dialogue: *Un paseo en bus.*

Functions & forms:
- Parts of an automobile.
- Actions related to driving.
- To narrate past actions: The preterite tense and the imperfect tense.

Culture:
- *El transporte público: el autobús.*
- *¿Litros o galones?*
- *Los nombres de las cosas.*

DESAFÍO 4

Estimated time: 4 sessions.

Dialogue: *El mejor café del mundo.*

Functions & forms:
- Elements of a hotel.
- Transactions at a bank.
- To narrate and describe past actions: The preterite tense and the imperfect tense.
- To determine the meaning of a phrase based on the verb tense used.

Culture:
- *El eje cafetero.*
- *La economía de Colombia.*

TODO JUNTO/El encuentro

Estimated time: 1 session.

Dialogue: *En el castillo de San Felipe de Barajas.*

Functions & forms:
- Review of *Desafíos 1–4.*

Culture:
- San Felipe de Barajas Castle, Cartagena de Indias, Colombia.

MAPA CULTURAL/LECTURA

Estimated time: 1 session.

Mapa cultural: *Caribe continental.*

Reading: *El Dorado, ecos de una leyenda.*

PROYECTO/EVALUACIÓN

Estimated time: 2 sessions.

Project: *Un folleto sobre la laguna de Guatavita.*

Self-evaluation: *Autoevaluación.*

Standards for Learning Spanish

 COMMUNICATION

1.1. Interpersonal mode

- Discuss the challenge for each team in the selected South American countries.
- Discuss what students know about Colombia and Venezuela.
- Speculate on which pair will win the challenge.
- Discuss legends similar to El Dorado.
- Plan a trip with a classmate.
- Discuss how airports are named in the United States.
- Comment on a classmate's blog.
- Interview classmates.

1.2. Interpretive mode

- Take notes from an oral text.
- Read a cultural text.
- Read an e-mail.
- Research cultural topics.
- Read about the coffee industry on the Internet.

1.3. Presentational mode

- Write a caption for a photograph.
- Write a newspaper article.
- Write a description of a photograph.
- Write a paragraph based on recollections from childhood.
- Post a blog.
- Write a dialogue between a tourist and a hotel reception clerk.
- Write an ad for a hotel and present it to the class.
- Make a list of things to do in preparation for taking a trip.

 COMPARISONS

4.1. Compare languages

- Compare the expression of past habitual actions in English and in Spanish.
- Compare the use of time expressions when forming past tenses in English and in Spanish.
- Compare the expression of past completed actions in English and in Spanish.

4.2. Compare cultures

- Compare regional vocabulary differences in Spanish and in English.
- Compare rural tourism in South America and in the United States.
- Compare coffee production in South America and in the United States.

 CULTURE

2.1. Practices and perspectives

- Recognize and distinguish mass transit practices in South America.
- Read about a famous South American legend.
- Read about the role of gold in El Dorado.
- Read about dialectal vocabulary differences.
- Understand the system of measurement used for pumping gas in South America.

2.2. Products and perspectives

- Read about public transportation in Venezuela.
- Read about the coffee plantations.
- Read about the products that Colombia exports.
- Read information on the Internet about Lake Guatavita and the legend of El Dorado.
- Research South American foods and influences.

 COMMUNITIES

5.1. Spanish within and beyond the school setting

- Create an ad for a hotel.
- Describe a photograph.

5.2. Spanish for lifelong learning

- Draw a comic strip to illustrate a statement.
- Research coffee production in Colombia.
- Make a travel brochure on Lake Guatavita.

CONNECTIONS

3.1. Interdisciplinary connections

- Learn about South American geography and history.
- Learn about the largest airport in Latin America.
- Learn about Angel Falls.
- Read about the most popular form of mass transit in Caracas.

3.2. Viewpoints through language / culture

- Discover aspects of South American history and culture.
- Read the anecdotes by the pairs during their visit to South America.

Communicative Skills

Interpersonal Mode

		Activities
Speaking	• Engage in conversation with a classmate. • Compare information with a classmate. • Role-play with a partner. • Discuss the pairs' challenges.	• 3,4,12,21, 40, 54, 76 • 12, 21, 58, 81 • 22, 62, 66 • 4, 5, 81
Writing	• Write a dialogue. • Write a personal reflection.	• 22, 53, 62, 66 • 21, 79
Listening	• Understand verbal questions and respond appropriately. • Determine the legitimacy of an oral text. • Display understanding of an oral text.	• 8, 11, 29 • 19, 37 • 25, 34, 44, 47, 73
Reading	• Read the participants' personal reflections. • Read a conversation. • Extract the main ideas from a passage.	• 20, 35, 38, 56, 70, 72, 80 • 78 • 7, 20, 43, 61, 65, 82

Interpretive Mode

		Activities
Listening	• Obtain information from a conversation. • Understand oral descriptions. • Obtain cultural information from audio and video.	• 51, 62, 66, 73, 78 • 77 • *Tu desafío, videos*
Reading	• Understand brief written exchanges. • Determine the legitimacy of a written text. • Understand an extended informative text.	• 10, 20, 23, 38, 56, 59, 65, 70, 72 • 28, 84 • *Lectura*

Presentational Mode

		Activities
Speaking	• Act out a short skit aloud. • Participate in a guided conversation. • Present an original creation or representation to the class. • Explain a thought or rationale to classmates.	• 7, 59 • 9 • *Proyecto* • 13, 31, 36
Writing	• Describe the actions denoted in a photograph. • Write a guided dialogue. • Develop a travel brochure.	• 16, 69, 71 • 22, 53 • *Proyecto*

Cross-Curricular Standards

Subject	Standard	Activities
Language Arts	• Read an informative text. • Compare the past tense forms in English and Spanish. • Compare use of varieties of regional vocabulary in Latin America and in the United States. • Outline an informative text.	• *Mapa Cultural, Lectura* • 14, 32, 50, 68 • 55 • 86
Geography	• Read about the fourth largest airport in Latin America. • Read about the tallest waterfall in the world. • Read about the products that Colombia exports.	• 13 • 27 • 67
Math	• Convert liters to gallons.	• 49

Lesson Plans (50-Minute Classes)

Day	Objectives	Sessions	Activities	Time	Standards	Resources/ Homework
1	To introduce selected South American countries and to discuss the pairs' challenges	**Caribe continental / La llegada** (288–293) • Warm-up: Region orientation • *Caribe continental* • Images and functions • Presentation: *En Cartagena de Indias* • *Expresiones útiles* and *¿Quién ganará?*	 1 2–5	 5 m. 5 m. 10 m. 10 m. 20 m.	1.1, 1.2, 1.3, 2.1, 2.2, 5.1	Visual Presentation Audio Video Practice Workbook
2	To describe past habitual actions	**Desafío 1 – El tesoro más valioso de Colombia** (294–295) • Warm-up: Independent Starter • *Fotonovela: El tesoro más valioso de Colombia* • *Cultura: La leyenda de El Dorado*	 6–8 9	 5 m. 35 m. 10 m.	1.1, 1.2, 1.3, 2.1, 2.2, 3.2, 4.2, 5.1	Visual Presentation Audio *Tu desafío*
3	To talk about planning and taking a trip	**Desafío 1 – Vocabulario** (296–297) • Warm-up: Independent Starter • Vocabulary: *Viajes y excursiones* • *Conexiones: El aeropuerto internacional El Dorado*	 10–12 13	 5 m. 35 m. 10 m.	1.1, 1.2, 1.3, 3.1, 3.2, 4.2	Audio Practice Workbook
4	To learn and use the present imperfect tense	**Desafío 1 – Gramática** (298–299) • Warm-up: Independent Starter • Grammar: *El imperfecto* • *Cultura: El Museo del Oro de Bogotá*	 14–17 18	 5 m. 35 m. 10 m.	1.1, 1.2, 1.3, 2.2, 3.1, 3.2, 4.1, 5.1	Audio Practice Workbook *Tu desafío*
5	To integrate vocabulary and grammar and to assess student proficiency	**Desafío 1 – Comunicación / Evaluación** (300–301) • Warm-up: Independent Starter • *Comunicación:* Review • *Final del desafío* • Quiz on *Desafío 1*	 19–21 22	 5 m. 20 m. 10 m. 15 m.	1.1, 1.2, 1.3, 2.2, 3.1, 5.2	Audio Practice Workbook *Tu desafío*
6	To talk about past actions	**Desafío 2 – El salto Ángel** (302–303) • Warm-up: Independent Starter • *Fotonovela: El salto Ángel* • *Conexiones: El salto Ángel*	 23–26 27	 5 m. 35 m. 10 m.	1.1, 1.2, 1.3, 3.1, 3.2, 5.1	Visual Presentation Audio Video *Tu desafío*
7	To talk about trips by air and by train	**Desafío 2 – Vocabulario** (304–305) • Warm-up: Independent Starter • Vocabulary: *El tren y el avión* • *Cultura: La red de transportes en Venezuela*	 28–30 31	 5 m. 35 m. 10 m.	1.1, 1.2, 1.3, 2.2, 3.2, 4.2	Audio Practice Workbook
8	To learn and use certain irregular verbs in the preterite	**Desafío 2 – Gramática** (306–307) • Warm-up: Independent Starter • Grammar: *Verbos irregulares en el pretérito. 'Dar', 'poder', 'poner', 'querer', 'saber' y 'venir'*	 32–36	 5 m. 45 m.	1.1, 1.2, 1.3, 3.1	Audio Practice Workbook
9	To integrate vocabulary and grammar and to assess student proficiency	**Desafío 2 – Comunicación / Evaluación** (308–309) • Warm-up: Independent Starter • *Comunicación:* Review • *Final del desafío* • Quiz on *Desafío 2*	 37–40 41	 5 m. 20 m. 10 m. 15 m.	1.2, 1.3, 3.1	Audio Practice Workbook
10	To talk about past actions	**Desafío 3 – Un paseo en bus** (310–311) • Warm-up: Independent Starter • *Fotonovela: Un paseo en bus* • *Conexiones: El transporte público: el autobús*	 42–44 45	 5 m. 35 m. 10 m.	1.1, 1.2, 1.3, 2.1, 3.1, 3.2, 4.2, 5.1	Visual Presentation Audio *Tu desafío*

Day	Objectives	Sessions	Activities	Time	Standards	Resources/Homework
11	To talk about parts of an automobile and driving	**Desafío 3 – Vocabulario** (312–313) • Warm-up: Independent Starter • Vocabulary: *El coche* • *Conexiones: ¿Litros o galones?*	46–48 49	5 m. 35 m. 10 m.	1.1, 1.2, 1.3, 2.1, 3.1, 3.2, 5.1	Audio Practice Workbook
12	To learn and use the imperfect and preterite tenses	**Desafío 3 – Gramática** (314–315) • Warm-up: Independent Starter • Grammar: *Narrar hechos pasados. El pretérito y el imperfecto* • *Conexiones: Los nombres de las cosas*	50–54 55	5 m. 35 m. 10 m.	1.1, 1.2, 1.3, 2.1, 3.1, 3.2, 4.1, 4.2, 5.2	Audio Practice Workbook
13	To integrate vocabulary and grammar and to assess student proficiency	**Desafío 3 – Comunicación / Evaluación** (316–317) • Warm-up: Independent Starter • *Comunicación:* Review • *Final del desafío* • Quiz on *Desafío 3*	56–58 59	5 m. 20 m. 10 m. 15 m.	1.2, 1.3, 2.1	Practice Workbook *Tu desafío*
14	To tell an anecdote that happened in the past	**Desafío 4 – El mejor café del mundo** (318–319) • Warm-up: Independent Starter • *Fotonovela: El mejor café del mundo* • *Cultura: El eje cafetero*	60–62 63	5 m. 35 m. 10 m.	1.1, 1.2, 1.3, 2.2, 3.2, 4.2, 5.1, 5.2	Visual Presentation Audio Video *Tu desafío*
15	To talk about checking into a hotel and bank transactions	**Desafío 4 – Vocabulario** (320–321) • Warm-up: Independent Starter • Vocabulary: *El hotel. El banco* • *Conexiones: La economía de Colombia*	64–66 67	5 m. 35 m. 10 m.	1.1, 1.2, 1.3, 2.1, 2.2, 3.1, 3.2, 5.2	Audio Practice Workbook
16	To narrate past events	**Desafío 4 - Gramática** (322–323) • Warm-up: Independent Starter • Grammar: *Narrar y describir en pasado. El pretérito y el imperfecto*	68–71	5 m. 45 m.	1.1, 1.2, 1.3, 3.1, 4.1	Practice Workbook
17	To integrate vocabulary and grammar and to assess student proficiency	**Desafío 4 – Comunicación / Evaluación** (324–325) • Warm-up: Independent Starter • *Comunicación:* Review • *Final del desafío* • Quiz on *Desafío 4*	72–74 75	5 m. 20 m. 10 m. 15 m.	1.1, 1.2, 1.3, 2.2, 5.2	Audio Practice Workbook
18	To integrate language in context	**Todo junto / El encuentro** (326–329) • Warm-up: Independent Starter • *Todo junto* • *El encuentro: En el castillo de San Felipe de Barajas*	76–79 80–81	5 m. 20 m. 25 m.	1.1, 1.2, 1.3, 2.1, 2.2, 3.1, 3.2, 5.2	Audio Practice Workbook
19	To learn about South American culture and traditions and to read an informative text	**Mapa cultural / Lectura** (330–333) • Warm-up: Read the *Mapa cultural* • *Mapa cultural: Caribe continental* • *Lectura: El Dorado, ecos de una leyenda* • Read project outline (338–339)	82–83 84–86	5 m. 20 m. 20 m. 5 m.	1.1, 1.2, 1.3, 2.1, 2.2, 3.1, 3.2, 5.1	Practice Workbook *Tu desafío* Project work
20	To develop a travel brochure for Lake Guatavita	**Proyecto** (338–339) • Warm-up: Prepare project presentations • Project presentations		5 m. 45 m.	1.1, 1.2, 1.3, 2.2, 3.1, 3.2, 5.1, 5.2	Practice Workbook **Repaso – Vocabulario** (334–335) **Repaso – Gramática** (336–337)
21	To assess student proficiency	**Assessment** • *Autoevaluación* (339) • Test		10 m. 40 m.	1.2, 1.3	

Lesson Plans (90-Minute Classes)

Day	Objectives	Sessions	Activities	Time	Standards	Resources/ Homework
1	To introduce selected South American countries and to discuss the pairs' challenges	**Caribe continental / La llegada** (288–293) • Warm-up: Region orientation • *Caribe continental* / Images and functions • Presentation: *En Cartagena de Indias* • *Expresiones útiles* and *¿Quién ganará?*	 1 2–5	 10 m. 20 m. 25 m. 35 m.	1.1, 1.2, 1.3, 2.1, 2.2, 5.1	Visual Presentation Audio Video Practice Workbook
2	To describe past habitual actions, to talk about planning and taking a trip, and to learn and use the imperfect tense	**Desafío 1 – El tesoro más valioso de Colombia / Vocabulario** (294–297) • Warm-up: Independent Starter • *Fotonovela: El tesoro más valioso de Colombia* • *Cultura: La leyenda de El Dorado* • Vocabulary: *Viajes y excursiones* • *Conexiones: El aeropuerto internacional El Dorado*	 6–8 9 10–12 13	 5 m. 35 m. 10 m. 35 m. 5 m.	1.1, 1.2, 1.3, 2.1, 2.2, 3.1, 3.2, 4.2, 5.1	Visual Presentation Audio Practice Workbook *Tu desafío*
3	To integrate vocabulary and grammar and to assess student proficiency	**Desafío 1 – Gramática / Comunicación / Evaluación** (298–301) • Warm-up: Independent Starter • Grammar: *El imperfecto* • *Cultura: El Museo del Oro de Bogotá* • *Comunicación:* Review • *Final del desafío* • Quiz on *Desafío 1*	 14–17 18 19–21 22	 5 m. 30 m. 5 m. 25 m. 10 m. 15 m.	1.1, 1.2, 1.3, 2.2, 3.1, 3.2, 4.1, 5.1, 5.2	Audio Practice Workbook *Tu desafío*
4	To talk about past actions and to talk about trips by air and by train	**Desafío 2 – El salto Ángel / Vocabulario** (302–305) • Warm-up: Independent Starter • *Fotonovela: El salto Ángel* • *Conexiones: El salto Ángel* • Vocabulary: *El tren y el avión* • *Cultura: La red de transportes en Venezuela*	 23–26 27 28–30 31	 5 m. 25 m. 15 m. 35 m. 10 m.	1.1, 1.2, 1.3, 2.2, 3.1, 3.2, 4.2, 5.1	Visual Presentation Audio Video *Tu desafío*
5	To learn and use certain irregular verbs in the preterite, to integrate vocabulary and grammar, and to assess student proficiency	**Desafío 2 – Gramática / Comunicación / Evaluación** (306–309) • Warm-up: Independent Starter • Grammar: *Verbos irregulares en el pretérito. 'Dar', 'poder', 'poner', 'querer', 'saber' y 'venir'* • *Comunicación:* Review • *Final del desafío* • Quiz on *Desafío 2*	 32–36 37–40 41	 5 m. 35 m. 25 m. 10 m. 15 m.	1.1, 1.2, 1.3, 3.1	Visual Presentation Audio
6	To talk about past actions and to talk about parts of an automobile and driving	**Desafío 3 – Un paseo en bus / Vocabulario** (310–313) • Warm-up: Independent Starter • *Fotonovela: Un paseo en bus* • *Conexiones: El transporte público: el autobús* • Vocabulary: *El coche* • *Conexiones: ¿Litros o galones?*	 42–44 45 46–48 49	 5 m. 30 m. 10 m. 35 m. 10 m.	1.1, 1.2, 1.3, 2.1, 3.1, 3.2, 4.2, 5.1	Visual Presentation Audio Practice Workbook *Tu desafío*

Day	Objectives	Sessions	Activities	Time	Standards	Resources/Homework
7	To learn and use the imperfect and preterite tenses, to integrate vocabulary and grammar, and to assess student proficiency	***Desafío 3 – Gramática / Comunicación / Evaluación*** (314–317) • Warm-up: Independent Starter • *Grammar: Narrar hechos pasados. El pretérito y el imperfecto* • *Conexiones: Los nombres de las cosas* • *Comunicación*: Review • *Final del desafío* • Quiz on *Desafío 3*	50–54 55 56–58 59	5 m. 30 m. 5 m. 25 m. 10 m. 15 m.	1.1, 1.2, 1.3, 2.1, 3.1, 3.2, 4.1, 4.2, 5.2	Audio Practice Workbook *Tu desafío*
8	To tell an anecdote that happened in the past and to talk about checking into a hotel and bank transactions	***Desafío 4 – El mejor café del mundo / Vocabulario*** (318–321) • Warm-up: Independent Starter • *Fotonovela: El mejor café del mundo* • *Cultura: El eje cafetero* • Vocabulary: *El hotel. El banco* • *Conexiones: La economía de Colombia*	 60–62 63 64–66 67	 5 m. 30 m. 10 m. 35 m. 10 m.	1.1, 1.2, 1.3, 2.1, 2.2, 3.1, 3.2, 4.2, 5.1, 5.2	Visual Presentation Audio Video Practice Workbook *Tu desafío*
9	To narrate past events, to integrate vocabulary and grammar, and to assess student proficiency	***Desafío 4 – Gramática / Comunicación / Evaluación / Todo junto*** (322–327) • Warm-up: Independent Starter • *Grammar: Narrar y describir en pasado. El pretérito y el imperfecto* • *Comunicación*: Review • *Final del desafío* • Quiz on *Desafío 4* • *Todo junto*	 68–71 72–74 75 76–79	 5 m. 20 m. 20 m. 10 m. 15 m. 20 m.	1.1, 1.2, 1.3, 2.2, 3.1, 4.1, 5.2	Audio Practice Workbook
10	To integrate language in context and to learn about selected South American cultures and traditions	***El encuentro / Mapa cultural / Lectura*** (328–333) • Warm-up: Independent Starter • *El encuentro: En el castillo de San Felipe de Barajas* • *Mapa cultural: Caribe continental* • *Lectura: El Dorado, ecos de una leyenda* • Read project outline (338–339)	80–81 82–83 84–86	5 m. 30 m. 25 m. 25 m. 5 m.	1.1, 1.2, 1.3, 2.1, 2.2, 3.1, 3.2, 5.1, 5.2	Video Practice Workbook *Tu desafío* **Repaso – Vocabulario** (334–335) **Repaso – Gramática** (336–337) Project work
11	To develop a travel brochure for Lake Guatavita and to assess student proficiency	***Proyecto / Assessment*** (338–339) • Warm-up: Prepare project presentations • Project presentations • *Autoevaluación* • Test		10 m. 40 m. 10 m. 30 m.	1.1, 1.2, 1.3, 2.2, 3.1, 3.2, 5.1, 5.2	

2 Expresiones

1. –¿Qué tal si viajamos en tren?
   –Es que prefiero viajar en coche.
2. –¿Nos alojamos en un hotel del centro?
   –Sí, de acuerdo.
3. –¿Por qué no vamos a la oficina de turismo?
   –No sé... Podemos preguntar en el hotel.
4. –¿Reservo los boletos por Internet?
   –Perfecto.

8 El viaje a Guatavita

–Tess, te va a gustar este viaje.

–Espero que sí. ¿Cuánto tiempo vamos a estar en el autobús?

–No es un viaje largo. En solo 90 minutos llegamos a Guatavita.

–¿Y qué sabes de Guatavita?

–El folleto dice que es el nombre de un pueblo y también de una laguna.

–¿La laguna es bonita?

–Sí, mira esta foto.

–Ah, sí, es muy bonita. Mamá, ¿por qué no damos un paseo en barca por la laguna?

–Sí, buena idea. Pero también quiero pasear por el pueblo.

–De acuerdo. Oye, mamá, ¿regresamos a Bogotá esta noche?

–No sé... Podemos quedarnos en Guatavita o volver a Bogotá.

–¡Pero dejamos las maletas en el aeropuerto!

–Tienes razón. Entonces debemos regresar a Bogotá.

11 El itinerario

Buenos días, Patricia. Soy Antonio Guzmán, el agente de viajes. Quiero confirmar la reserva para usted y su hija. Viajan de Bogotá a Guatavita el día veintiuno. El autobús sale a las doce y media. Repito: viajan de Bogotá a Guatavita el día veintiuno, y el autobús sale a las doce y media. Ah, y cada boleto cuesta veinte dólares. Si tienen alguna duda, llámenme, por favor. ¡Buen viaje!

15 Las costumbres de Tess

Hoy Tess no es igual que antes, sus costumbres no son las mismas. Cuando era niña, siempre hablaba por teléfono con sus amigas, pero ahora prefiere comunicarse con ellas por Internet.
Generalmente veía comedias en la televisión, pero ahora prefiere las películas de acción.
Ahora viaja mucho conmigo, pero cuando era pequeña no viajábamos tanto.
Hace tiempo que no va al parque con sus amigas, pero antes iba mucho.
Antes jugaba al fútbol frecuentemente, pero ahora no hace mucho deporte.
De pequeña no le interesaba nada ir de compras, pero ahora quiere ir al centro comercial todas las semanas. ¡Le encanta comprar!

19 Consejos de una agente

1. Hay que reservar el viaje con tiempo.
2. No pidan información sobre las tarifas del viaje, no es importante.
3. Lean bien la información sobre las excursiones en los folletos.
4. Comprueben los horarios de salida del autobús en la estación.
5. Paguen los boletos en la agencia después de volver de su viaje.

25 ¿Quién es?

1. Vinieron tarde al aeropuerto.
2. Está mareado porque el avión dio muchas vueltas.
3. Nunca se puso un chaleco salvavidas.
4. Siempre quiso ver el salto Ángel.
5. No pudieron acercarse más a la catarata.

29 Fotos de viajes

1. Aquí tiene su pasaporte y la tarjeta de embarque.
2. Yo prefiero llevar equipaje de mano, así no tengo que facturar.
3. Señores pasajeros, bienvenidos al vuelo con destino Caracas. El avión va a despegar en unos minutos.
4. ¿Puedo ver su boleto, por favor? Muchas gracias.
5. El avión sale con retraso, vamos a llegar tarde.

34 ¡Nos encanta viajar!

1. Andy y yo vamos al aeropuerto para tomar un avión.
2. Andy y yo vinimos tarde al aeropuerto.
3. Andy no factura nunca el equipaje.
4. El avión dio muchas vueltas.
5. Andy nunca supo ponerse un chaleco salvavidas.
6. Yo siempre quise venir a este lugar.
7. El piloto no pudo acercarse mucho a la catarata.
8. Andy se pone muy nervioso.

37 En el avión

–El avión está dando muchas vueltas, Janet. ¡Me siento enfermo! ¡Estoy mareado!

–¿No te gusta nuestra aventura? Vinimos a Venezuela a ver su naturaleza fabulosa: los saltos de agua, los ríos, las montañas... ¿Ves el paisaje? Es precioso.

–No, Janet, no veo nada porque no quiero mirar. Tengo miedo.

–No tienes que tener miedo, Andy. El piloto es muy bueno. Mira, yo quiero bañarme en ese río. ¿Y tú?

–¡No, Janet! ¿Estás loca?

–¡Ay, Andy! No tienes que tener tanto miedo.

–De acuerdo, pero... ¡la próxima vez viajamos en tren!

44 ¡Al autobús!

1. Mientras el abuelo hablaba con el conductor, yo llené el tanque de gasolina.
2. El abuelo estaba sorprendido porque el autobús tenía tres pedales en lugar de dos.
3. Yo no pude ayudar al abuelo porque no tengo licencia de conducir.
4. El abuelo puso la marcha atrás y casi tuvimos un accidente. ¡Qué susto!

47 Aprendiendo a manejar

Manejar en Venezuela puede ser un poco difícil si usted no sabe manejar un coche con marchas. Vamos a recordarle los pasos más importantes que tiene que seguir:

Primero, hay que ponerse el cinturón de seguridad, por su seguridad y para evitar multas.

Después, ponga la llave en el contacto para arrancar el motor.

A continuación, tiene que pisar el embrague. Esta es una gran diferencia con los coches automáticos. Pise el embrague, mueva la palanca de marchas, acelere y empiece a manejar.

Finalmente, respete siempre las señales de tráfico. Es muy importante.

51 Tim pasea por Caracas

—Abuelo, ¿sabes lo que me pasó esta mañana?

—No, ¿qué?

—Pues que estaba paseando tranquilamente por las calles de Caracas cuando alguien me llamó.

—¿Quién era?

—Era el guía del hotel. Y mientras hablaba con él, un autobús tuvo un pequeño accidente con un coche.

—¿Y qué hicieron?

—Fuimos a ayudar. Mientras el guía y yo nos acercábamos, el conductor bajó del autobús. Entonces empezó a discutir con el conductor del coche. Cuando llegó la policía, los dos estaban muy enojados y gritaban.

—¿Y qué pasó?

—Pues que, al final, el policía les puso una multa a los dos.

62 La reserva

—Buenos días. Habla Nela.

—Buenos días. Llamo para reservar una habitación.

—¡Cómo no! ¿Para cuándo la quiere?

—Para los días 19 y 20 de noviembre.

—Déjeme ver… ¿Desea una habitación individual?

—No, por favor, una habitación doble con dos camas. ¿Todas las habitaciones tienen baño?

—Sí, todas nuestras habitaciones tienen baño. ¿Prefieren vistas al jardín o a la plantación de café?

—A la plantación de café. Queremos aprender cómo se cultiva el grano y cómo se prepara el café.

—Ah, pues yo les puedo explicar todo el proceso. Es muy intereresante.

—Qué bien, muchas gracias.

—Ahora le voy a pedir algunos datos. ¿Su nombre, por favor?

66 En el banco

—Hola, buenos días. Necesito cambiar dinero.

—Sí, señor. ¿Cuánto necesita?

—Necesito cambiar cien dólares a pesos colombianos.

—¿Quiere monedas o solo billetes?

—Necesito billetes, pero deme también algunas monedas, por favor.

—Bien, aquí tiene.

—¿Puede darme una factura?

—Lo siento, señor, pero tenemos un problema. No puedo darle una factura porque no funciona la computadora.

—No importa, gracias.

—A usted.

73 ¿Cómo era la hacienda?

—Diana, ¿te acuerdas de la hacienda donde nos alojamos en Colombia?

—Sí, ¡qué maravilla! Era muy grande y muy bonita. Y la recepcionista era muy simpática.

—¿Cuántas habitaciones tenía: cinco o seis?

—No, tenía más. Yo vi cinco habitaciones dobles y otras cinco habitaciones sencillas.

—¿Todas tenían baño?

—No, algunas habitaciones no tenían baño. Pero todas tenían unas vistas espectaculares a los campos de café.

—¿Recuerdas los desayunos? Eran buenísimos.

—Sí, claro.

77 ¡Qué mala suerte!

1. Subí al avión y me senté en mi asiento. Me puse el cinturón de seguridad. Entonces vino una auxiliar de vuelo y me llevó a un asiento en primera clase. ¡Qué suerte!

2. Cuando llegué al hotel, fui a la recepción. Pedí la llave y subí a la habitación. Entonces llamé a una amiga. Mientras hablaba por teléfono, llamaron a la puerta. Abrí y… ¡qué sorpresa! Un empleado del hotel trajo una cesta con frutas. Era un regalo del hotel.

3. Necesitaba pesos colombianos. Fui a un banco a cambiar dinero, pero no tenía el pasaporte. Entonces volví al hotel a buscarlo. Y cuando iba a entrar al banco, cerraron la caja. ¡Qué mala suerte!

Unit 6
Caribe continental

The Unit

- The themes for Unit 6 are traveling and modes of transportation in the context of the continental Caribbean region.
- The pairs gather in Cartagena de Indias, a walled city in Colombia located on the Caribbean Sea, where they will receive their tasks.
  - *Desafío 1.* Tess and Patricia have to find El Dorado and take a picture of a golden raft.
  - *Desafío 2.* Andy and Janet's task is to fly over the Venezuelan rainforest and take an aerial photo of the tallest waterfall in the world.
  - *Desafío 3.* Tim and Mack have to drive a city bus through the busy streets of Caracas.
  - *Desafío 4.* Diana and Rita must harvest, roast, and grind enough coffee beans to make themselves a delicious cup of Colombian coffee.

Activities	Standards	Resources
Caribe continental	1.2, 2.1, 2.2	Video

Teaching Suggestions

Warm-Up / Independent Starter

- Ask students to look at a map and list all of the countries that comprise the Caribbean region and their capital cities. Then have them classify these countries in two lists:
  1. Countries that are islands or part of them.
  2. Countries that are in the continental area.

The Continental Caribbean Region

- The Caribbean Sea is located in the western Atlantic Ocean, south of the Gulf of Mexico. The term "Caribbean" comes from the word *Carib*, which was what the indigenous inhabitants of the southern Caribbean region called themselves. Christopher Columbus was the first European to explore the Caribbean Sea in 1492. Following the colonization of the region, the Caribbean became an important European base for trade and transportation. Today, it is an important tourist destination.

Caribe continental

En busca de El Dorado

DESAFÍO 1

▶ **To describe past habits**

Vocabulario
Viajes y excursiones

Gramática
El imperfecto

El salto Ángel (Venezuela)

DESAFÍO 2

Laguna de Guatavita (Colombia)

▶ **To talk about past actions**

Vocabulario
El tren y el avión

Gramática
Verbos irregulares en el pretérito. *Dar, poder, poner, querer, saber* y *venir.*

The Challenge

DESAFÍO 1

Laguna de Guatavita

Lake Guatavita is located on a high plateau about 37 miles from Bogotá, the capital city of Colombia. The lake is part of a protected forest of 1,515 acres known as *Reserva Forestal Laguna del Cacique Guatavita y Cuchilla de Peñas Blancas.* Tourists have the choice of taking one of several guided walking tours. These tours allow visitors to climb to the lake, admire the local flora and fauna, and familiarize themselves with the rich history of the place, including the legend of El Dorado which is believed to have originated in this lake.

DESAFÍO 2

El salto Ángel

This waterfall is located in Bolivar state, southeastern Venezuela, and is part of the Canaima National Park. One of the unique geological features of this area is the table mountain formations, or *tepuis,* that cover about 65% of the park. There are numerous waterfalls in the park, but Angel Falls, with a free drop of 3,212 feet, is the highest. This spectacular landscape was registered as a UNESCO World Heritage Site in 1994. A dense tropical rainforest surrounds the waterfalls, which makes access to the area very difficult. For this reason, Angel Falls is best seen from the air.

Plantación de café
(Colombia)

Caracas
(Venezuela)

DESAFÍO 3

▶ **To talk about events in the past**

Vocabulario
El coche

Gramática
Narrar hechos pasados.
El pretérito
y el imperfecto

▶ **To tell an anecdote in the past**

DESAFÍO 4

Vocabulario
El hotel
El banco

Gramática
Narrar y describir
en pasado. El pretérito
y el imperfecto

doscientos ochenta y nueve 289

■ Check students' lists from the Independent Starter. You may ask them to identify the major languages spoken in the region. Clarify that many indigenous and creole languages are spoken, but in most countries Spanish is the official language, with the exception of the old French and English colonies.

Picture Discussion

■ Ask students to describe the pictures. Has anyone in the class ever been to any of these places? Encourage students to share their experiences.

Laguna de Guatavita (Colombia)

■ Ask students to observe the picture and compare Lake Guatavita with Lake Atitlán (from Unit 1). Have them think of geographical similarities and differences, as well as legends associated with these lakes. Do students know of similar lakes in the United States? (e.g., Crater Lake in Oregon).

El salto Ángel (Venezuela)

■ Are students familiar with Niagara or Iguazu Falls? Ask them to look at this picture and think of what is different about Angel Falls. They may, for instance, comment on the volume of water. Students may also comment on the altitude of Angel Falls in relation to other waterfalls.

Caracas (Venezuela)

■ Explain that Caracas is located in a narrow valley. Have students observe the picture and note the building density and type of constructions. Discuss, as a class, how the terrain and the availability—or lack—of land influence the architecture of a city. Invite students to draw a parallel with American cities (e.g., New York City).

Plantación de café (Colombia)

■ Have students work in small groups to discuss what they know about coffee (e.g., its origin, where it grows, processing, roasting, brewing, etc.). Ask groups to designate a student to take notes on the information shared in the group. Then invite groups to share their information with the class.

Objectives

■ By the end of Unit 6, students will be able to
  – Describe past habits.
  – Talk about past actions.
  – Talk about events in the past.
  – Tell anecdotes in the past.
  – Talk about different cultural aspects of the continental Caribbean region.

DESAFÍO 3

Caracas

Caracas, the capital city of Venezuela, is part of the Metropolitan District of Caracas, which includes four other neighboring municipalities besides the capital itself. It was founded in 1567 and given the name of Santiago de León de Caracas. The location of the city, next to the Coastal Mountain Range, offers wonderful views of the surrounding peaks, such as the Cerro Ávila, which is connected to the city via a cable car used by many tourists. Besides being one of the largest cities in South America, Caracas is also a very important center for both commerce and finance.

DESAFÍO 4

Plantación de café

In the minds of many Colombians, coffee production is associated with two traditional images. The first such image is that of the *recolector de café*, or coffee picker—a man or a woman wearing a traditional small poncho called a *mulera* and a basket tied around his or her waist to collect the coffee beans. This image was developed into the iconic Juan Valdez that everyone knows. The other image associated with coffee production is that of the Willys, the all-terrain vehicle used during and shortly after World War II, and still used in Colombia for cargo and transportation.

Unit 6
La llegada

Presentation

- This section presents the pairs' arrival in Colombia. They meet in Cartagena de Indias, a city on the northern coast of Colombia and a major economic enclave of the Caribbean region. The challenges are hidden in the city's fortress, San Felipe de Barajas.

- Students will see vocabulary in context, with pictures and illustrations. Presenting new words in this manner helps students develop their Spanish vocabulary with background knowledge while engaging them with the context.

Activities	Standards	Resources
Fotonovela	1.2, 2.1, 2.2	Vis. Pres.
1.	1.2	

Teaching Suggestions

Warm-Up / Independent Starter

- Ask students to read the introduction to the *fotonovela*. Next have them look at the location of Cartagena de Indias on a map of Colombia and observe the pictures on this page. Then ask students to write a short paragraph describing the city of Cartagena de Indias as they imagine it. Give them ideas on what to write about (e.g., the size, the weather, the places to visit, the architecture, the people, etc.).

Preparation

- Ask volunteer students to share their Independent Starter with the rest of the class. Write some of your students' ideas on the board. Ask the class to add others. Then discuss, as a class, the similarities between Cartagena de Indias and other Caribbean cities with which students are familiar (e.g., Santo Domingo in the Dominican Republic, San Juan in Puerto Rico).

- Have students read the *fotonovela* silently. Remind them of some of the reading and listening strategies from Level 1, such as looking for cognates, checking the dictionary for unknown words, paraphrasing, and asking questions. Students can also use the reading strategies from previous units in this level, such as identifying the main idea and the details, making inferences, etc.

La llegada

En Cartagena de Indias

The pairs gather at the plaza overlooking the *Torre del Reloj*, one of the entryways of Cartagena de Indias, a walled city in Colombia located on the Caribbean Sea. Our friends' tasks are kept in the mightiest military bastion ever built.

Differentiated Instruction

DEVELOPING LEARNERS

- Help students identify the cognates in the *fotonovela* in order to facilitate their comprehension. Remind students that some words are not cognates, even though they may look like cognates. For instance, *revista* means "magazine," not "review." There are other cases in which the context determines whether a word is a cognate or not. For instance, in this reading, *varias* means "several," not "various."

EXPANDING LEARNERS

- Ask students to rewrite the dialogue in narrative form to explain what the participants are doing and where they have to go, as well as to describe the places they visit or see along the way. Even though students are using the narrative form, explain that they may choose to write it from the first-person perspective, or from the neutral third-person point of view.

La llegada

Esa fortaleza es el Castillo de San Felipe de Barajas. Los ingleses intentaron tomarla en el siglo dieciocho.

¡Mack, eres una enciclopedia!

¡Qué va! Lo leyó en una revista cuando veníamos en el avión.

Aquí dice que tenemos que escribir una anécdota de nuestros viajes. ¡Qué divertido!

¡Hasta pronto!

---

1 **¿Comprendes?**

▶ **Une** las palabras con sus correspondientes definiciones.

 (A)   (B)

1. maleta	a. Persona que trabaja en un hotel.
2. recepcionista	b. Lugar donde organizan y venden viajes.
3. oficina de turismo	c. Medio de transporte aéreo.
4. avión	d. Lugar donde informan a turistas y visitantes.
5. agencia de viajes	e. Objeto para llevar la ropa en un viaje.

doscientos noventa y uno 291

La fotonovela

Before Viewing

- Now that students have read the dialogues, write some of the cognates on the board: *fortaleza, famosa, agencia, información, recepcionista, hotel, oficina de turismo, castillo, enciclopedia, anécdota*. Do all students know what these words mean? Then ask students for words in the *fotonovela* that they did not understand and write them on the board. Use gestures to make sure they understand the meaning of these words.

After Viewing

- Ask students if they understand what the pairs need to do at the end of their adventures. Underline the word *anécdota* on the board and if possible give students an example from your own travel experience. Ask them to think of anecdotes of their own. At this point, students will not be prepared to tell their anecdotes in Spanish, but having some in mind will be helpful for later.

Activities

1. Ask students to identify the expressions in column A that refer to *personas*, *lugares*, and *objetos*. This will facilitate the task of identifying their meaning in column B.

Answer Key

1.
1. e   4. c
2. a   5. b
3. d

Additional Resources

Fans Online activities
Practice Workbook

HERITAGE LANGUAGE LEARNERS

- Explain that metaphors (*metáforas*) and similes (*símiles*) are used to make comparisons. Ask students to identify the *metáfora* in the *fotonovela* (*¡Mack, eres una enciclopedia!*). Then ask them to write or say a *metáfora* or a *símil* to describe each of the participants, now that students know them well. Remind students that when comparing with a *símil* they need to use the word *como* (e.g., *¡Mack, eres* como *una enciclopedia!*). Have students share their comparisons with the rest of the class without identifying the participant, and see if the others can identify the person through the comparison made.

SPECIAL-NEEDS LEARNERS

- Help students with visual impairment by giving them verbal descriptions of the images on the page. Assist them in identifying the characters who are talking, and with recognizing who is asking questions and who is answering these questions in each scene. Help them to pinpoint the sentences that are exclamations by expressing surprise or amazement when reading them.

291

Unit 6
La llegada

Presentation

- In this section, students will learn useful expressions to make suggestions, to accept suggestions, and to reject them.

Activities	Standards	Resources
Expresiones útiles	1.2, 1.3, 4.1	
2.	1.2, 1.3	Audio
3.	1.1	
4.	1.1, 5.1	
5.	1.1	

Teaching Suggestions

Warm-Up / Independent Starter

- Ask students to write a list of the things they think people may be able to do in a city like Cartagena de Indias. You may give them some examples: *ir a la playa, comer comida colombiana, visitar monumentos históricos,* etc.

Preparation

- Ask students to share their Independent Starter with the class. Write some of your students' ideas on the board. Then have the class analyze the suggestions and decide which are the most useful and which would not be appropriate. Ask them to offer a brief explanation for their acceptance and rejection of the different suggestions their classmates made. Create two lists on the board: one for the accepted suggestions and one for the rejected suggestions.

- Go over the *Expresiones útiles* section with students. Then have them get into pairs and write four brief dialogues using the list of accepted suggestions on the board and the *expresiones útiles.* You may want to use the following dialogue as an example:
  A. *¿Qué tal si vamos a la Torre del Reloj?*
  B. *Estupendo, ¿por qué no vamos por la tarde?*
  A. *Es que probablemente está cerrado.*
  B. *¿Qué tal si vamos mañana por la mañana?*
  A. *De acuerdo.*

- Have pairs of students read their dialogues to the class. Alternatively, you may ask students to role-play their dialogue. Tell the class to vote for the most interesting dialogue.

292

EXPRESIONES ÚTILES

¿Por qué no vamos al cine?

¡Estupendo!

To make suggestions:
  ¿Vamos por los desafíos? (suggestion in question form)
  ¿Por qué no...?
  ¿Qué tal si...?

To accept suggestions:
  De acuerdo.   Fenomenal.
  Perfecto.   Estupendo.

To reject suggestions:
  No sé...
  Es que...

2 Expresiones

 ▶ **Escucha** y completa una tabla como esta.

	¿Qué sugieren?	¿Acepta la sugerencia?
1	Viajar en tren.	No. Prefiere viajar en coche.
2		
3		
4		

3 ¿Qué tal si...?

 ▶ **Habla** con tu compañero(a). Hazle sugerencias y responde a las suyas.

Modelo A. *¿Por qué no nos alojamos en un cámping?*
        B. *No sé... Yo prefiero ir a un hotel. Es más cómodo.*

① viajar en coche   ② comprar boletos de ida y vuelta   ③ pedir un plano en la oficina de turismo   ④ cenar en el hotel

292 doscientos noventa y dos

Differentiated Instruction

DEVELOPING LEARNERS

- Ask students to draw or use magazine cutouts to illustrate each of the *expresiones útiles.* To illustrate making suggestions or rejecting them, students should show images that propose an activity they can easily identify and use both the new expression and the activity in a question and statement. For example:
  A. *¿Por qué no montamos en bicicleta?*
  B. *Es que no tengo bicicleta.*

EXPANDING LEARNERS

- Ask students to work in groups of three and create a dialogue using as many of the *expresiones útiles* as they can. Explain that the first student should propose several activities, and while the second student will always be in favor of doing the suggested activity, the third member of the group will not be interested and should express this, then propose an alternative action. For example:
  A. *¿Qué tal si entramos en la fortaleza?*
  B. *¡Fenomenal!*
  C. *No sé... ¿Por qué no vamos a la playa?*

¿Quién ganará?

4 Los desafíos

 ▶ **Habla.** ¿Cuál será el desafío de cada pareja? Piénsalo y coméntalo con tus compañeros(as).

DESAFÍO ①

El tesoro más valioso de Colombia

Tess y Patricia

DESAFÍO ②

El salto Ángel

Andy y Janet

DESAFÍO ③

Un paseo en bus

Tim y Mack

DESAFÍO ④

El mejor café del mundo

Diana y Rita

 ▶ **Habla.** Los países de los desafíos son Colombia y Venezuela. ¿Qué sabes de esos lugares? Coméntalo con tus compañeros(as).

5 La tarea final

▶ **Decide.** ¿Qué tarea tienen que hacer los personajes al final? ¿Qué pareja crees que ganará?

LA TAREA
Una anécdota

doscientos noventa y tres **293**

Activities

2. Ask students to give different answers to the ones they hear, either accepting or rejecting the suggestions. You can turn it into a pair activity by asking them to create their own dialogues.

3. Expand the activity by asking students to add three to four questions and answers.

¿Quién ganará?

4. Have students get into small groups and discuss the pairs' challenges. Ask groups to look at the pictures, read the captions, and write a brief paragraph about what they believe the pairs will do in their challenges. They must also include in the paragraph any information they know about the places the pairs will visit.

5. Students have been provided a clue as to what the pairs will have to do to win their *desafíos* in the continental Caribbean region. They need to write an anecdote. As a class, have students discuss what kind of anecdotes the pairs might bring from their adventures.

 AUDIO SCRIPT
See page 287 l.

Answer Key

2. 2. Alojarse en un hotel del centro; Sí, acepta.
   3. Ir a la oficina de turismo; No. Prefiere preguntar en el hotel.
   4. Reservar los billetes por Internet; Sí, acepta.

3. Answers will vary.

4. Answers will vary.
   ▶ Answers will vary.

5. Answers will vary.

Additional Resources

Fans Online activities
Practice Workbook

HERITAGE LANGUAGE LEARNERS

• In addition to the expressions on the page, ask students to come up with other ways to make suggestions or to show interest or disinterest in doing something and make a chart with their expressions under the appropriate heading. After they complete their charts, have them write or say several sample sentences with the new expressions, read them to the class, and explain what they mean. Examples might include the following for making suggestions: *¿Te apetece…? ¿Te gustaría…?* For accepting suggestions: *Vale.* And for rejecting suggestions: *No, no tengo ganas de… ¡Ni hablar, porque…!*

MULTIPLE INTELLIGENCES:
Visual-Spatial Intelligence

• Explain that when the Spanish king Carlos III realized how much money had been spent on building the castle fortresses of Havana and Cartagena de Indias, he remarked from Spain: "This is an outrage! For this price those castles should be visible from here!" Keeping this anecdote in mind, ask students to illustrate the king's remark in a format they choose. This format could range from a fine art style to a cartoon and anything in between. Display their work in the classroom.

DESAFÍO 1

Describir hábitos del pasado

Presentation

- In *Desafío 1*, Tess and Patricia are in Colombia. They must find El Dorado and take a picture of a golden raft.

- In this section, students will preview:
  - Vocabulary related to travel and excursions.
  - Regular and irregular conjugations in the imperfect.

Activities	Standards	Resources
Fotonovela	1.2, 2.2, 3.2	Vis. Pres.
6.	1.2, 1.3	
7.	1.2, 1.3, 2.2	
8.	1.2, 1.3	Audio
9. Cultura	1.1, 1.2, 2.1, 2.2, 3.2, 4.2	
Tu desafío	1.2, 2.2, 3.2, 5.1	

Teaching Suggestions

Warm-Up / Independent Starter

- Have students read the introduction to the *fotonovela* and the dialogues silently. Ask them to identify the statements in which Tess and Patricia refer to the past and those in which they refer to the present.

Preparation

- Review students' responses from the Independent Starter. Ask them how they determined the verb tenses. If students struggle, point out how the words *antes* and *siglo dieciséis* indicate the past.

- Ask students if they have ever heard any references to the myth of El Dorado in stories or movies.

👁 La fotonovela

Before Viewing

- Read the *fotonovela* aloud to your students, changing your voice for each character. Ask students why Tess and Patricia are confused. Then have them read aloud.

After Viewing

- Tess and Patricia do not see any gold when they reach Laguna de Guatavita. Have students guess where they will find it. You may choose to have students work in groups. Ask them to share their ideas with the class.

El tesoro más valioso de Colombia

👁 Tess and Patricia travel to Bogotá. They have to find El Dorado and take a picture of a golden raft. Will they find it?

Yo antes siempre llevaba el equipaje en la mano. Así no tenía que esperar.

Tenemos que encontrar El Dorado y fotografiar una balsa de oro.

Tienes razón, mamá.

Pero El Dorado es este aeropuerto.

El Dorado es un lugar lleno de oro. Muchos exploradores lo buscaron desde el siglo dieciséis.

¡Qué interesante! ¿Y dónde está?

Dos boletos de ida y vuelta a Guatavita, por favor.

En la laguna de Guatavita. Tenemos que tomar un autobús en Bogotá.

Ahí está la laguna. Pero yo no veo oro...

6 Detective de palabras

▶ **Completa** estas oraciones.

1. Antes siempre llevaba el _____ en la mano.
2. Patricia y Tess están en el _____ de El Dorado, en Bogotá.
3. Para ir a Guatavita hay que tomar un _____.
4. Patricia pide dos boletos de _____.

Continuará...

Differentiated Instruction

DEVELOPING LEARNERS

- Have students choose the correct answer to each question.

1. ¿Qué llevaba antes Patricia en la mano?
   a. *el boleto*   b. *el equipaje* (b)
2. ¿Qué tienen que encontrar?
   a. *El Dorado*   b. *el aeropuerto* (a)
3. ¿Qué tienen que fotografiar?
   a. *una balsa*   b. *El Dorado* (a)
4. ¿Qué es El Dorado?
   a. *un lugar*   b. *un explorador* (a)
5. ¿Dónde está El Dorado?
   a. *en Bogotá*   b. *en una laguna* (b)
6. ¿Qué compran?
   a. *dos billetes* b. *oro* (a)

EXPANDING LEARNERS

- At the end of this *Desafío*, the participants must write an anecdote. First, ask students to define the word *anecdote*, and talk about how anecdotes add interest to someone's writing. Then ask students to write one or more paragraphs about a trip they took or a day at school that includes an interesting, amusing, or biographical anecdote. Their descriptions could address a positive experience or one they would not wish to repeat. Call on students to read their narratives aloud.

7 ¿Comprendes?

▶ **Responde** a estas preguntas.

1. ¿Cómo se llama el aeropuerto de Bogotá?
2. ¿Qué tienen que hacer Tess y Patricia en este desafío?
3. ¿Qué es El Dorado?
4. ¿Adónde viajan Tess y Patricia desde Bogotá?
5. ¿Cómo van hasta ese lugar?

8 El viaje a Guatavita

 ▶ **Escucha** y elige la opción correcta.

1. El viaje a Guatavita dura _____.
   a. una hora　　　b. una hora y media　　　c. tres horas
2. En Guatavita Tess y Patricia van a ver _____.
   a. una laguna　　　b. una montaña　　　c. un río
3. Tess quiere _____ en la laguna.
   a. pasear en barca　　b. nadar　　　c. tomar fotos
4. Patricia quiere _____ por el pueblo.
   a. ir de compras　　b. montar a caballo　　c. dar un paseo
5. Tess y Patricia van a dormir _____.
   a. en Guatavita　　b. en Bogotá　　c. cerca de la laguna

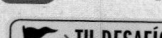 **CULTURA**

La leyenda de El Dorado

El Dorado es un lugar mítico lleno de oro (*gold*). Durante muchos años, varias expediciones buscaron este lugar por la selva amazónica.

Símbolo del jaguar.
Museo del Oro (Bogotá).

La leyenda de El Dorado tiene su origen en las ceremonias que los indígenas celebraban en la laguna de Guatavita, en los Andes colombianos. Los indígenas cubrían con oro el cuerpo del cacique, entraban en la laguna en una balsa (*raft*) y arrojaban (*threw*) piezas de oro y esmeraldas como ofrenda (*offering*) para los dioses.

En la laguna de Guatavita se encontraron varias piezas de oro que hoy están en el Museo del Oro de Bogotá.

9 Piensa y explica. ¿Conoces otras leyendas similares? ¿Crees en ellas? ¿Por qué?

▶ **TU DESAFÍO** Visita la página web para aprender más sobre esta leyenda.

HERITAGE LANGUAGE LEARNERS

• Ask students to write a story having to do with the legend of El Dorado. Explain that they should write from the perspective of an explorer or one of the indigenous Muiscas. Suggest that they use the information on page 295 as well as researching in the library or online. Ask students to read their stories to the class and explain any unfamiliar words.

CRITICAL THINKING

• Lead students in a discussion about the qualities they believe are essential for an explorer and what motivates these individuals to go beyond the known. Enable a discussion on the explorers of previous centuries, when there was scant knowledge of the Earth's geography and then ask students who the explorers of the twenty-first century are. While they may cite astronauts and those who explore our oceans, encourage students to go beyond and include those who explore the human body, those who seek solutions to economic and political problems, as well as those who look for new forms in art.

DESAFÍO 1
Describir hábitos del pasado

Activities

7. As an extension to question 1, ask students why they think the airport is also called El Dorado.

8. Have students read the statements and potential responses. Then play the recording two times. After students have completed the activity, play the recording a third time and ask them to write three questions related to the conversation.

9. Ask students to research other legends about gold and riches. Discuss when and how these stories originated.

 AUDIO SCRIPT
See page 287l.

 CULTURA

La leyenda de El Dorado
During their explorations in South America, the Spanish conquistadors heard of El Dorado, a distant land full of riches. In 1538, several expeditions converged on the highlands close to Bogotá in search of El Dorado. They didn't find it, but they found Lake Guatavita and tried to drain it in 1545. They were able to lower the water level, but they were never able to recover the presumed riches that rested on the bottom of the lake.

Answer Key

6. 1. equipaje　　　3. autobús
   2. aeropuerto　　4. ida y vuelta

7. 1. Se llama El Dorado.
   2. Tienen que encontrar El Dorado y fotografiar una balsa de oro.
   3. Es un lugar lleno de oro.
   4. Van a la laguna de Guatavita.
   5. Van en autobús.

8. 1. b　　2. a　　3. a　　4. c　　5. b

9. Answers will vary.

Additional Resources

Fans Online activities

DESAFÍO 1

Vocabulario – Viajes y excursiones

Presentation

- In this section, students will learn:
  - Vocabulary related to travel and excursions.
  - Verbs related to travel.

Activities	Standards	Resources
Vocabulario	1.2	
10.	1.2	
11.	1.2, 1.3	Audio
12.	1.1, 1.3	
13. Conexiones	1.1, 1.2, 3.1, 3.2, 4.2	

Teaching Suggestions

Warm-Up / Independent Starter

- Ask students to draw a suitcase and the objects that they would put in it to take a trip to Lake Guatavita. See if students are able to label all of the objects they would want to bring.

Preparation

- Ask students to share with the class what they have put in their suitcase. Have them help each other finish labeling what they would pack.
- Review the vocabulary presentation with students. Ask for one female and one male student to read the speech bubbles.
- Ask students to create definitions for the vocabulary using words they already know. For example: *El agente de viajes planea viajes…*
- Ask students which verbs would be used with the nouns provided, such as *hablar con el agente de viajes, mirar el horario*, etc. Then have students think of the nouns that would be used with the verbs provided. For example: *visitar un museo, llegar a la estación de autobuses*, etc. For additional practice, ask students to use the associations they just created in sentences. They may use the present tense or the preterite. For example: *Visito / Visité el Museo del Oro de Bogotá.*

Activities

10. After students have put the sentences in the proper order, ask for volunteers to act out the situation. You will need three students: Tess, Patricia, and a travel agent.

296

Vocabulario

Viajes y excursiones

¿Cuánto cuesta el viaje?

En este folleto vienen las **tarifas**.

el agente de viajes

la agencia de viajes

¿Hiciste el **equipaje**?

Sí. Recuerda llevar el **mapa**.

la maleta

la bolsa

la puerta

Mira, ahí están los **horarios**.

SALIDAS

LLEGADAS

Señores **viajeros**, la **salida** para Guatavita es a las doce y media.

¡Vamos! No quiero **perder** el autobús.

la estación de autobuses

la parada de autobús

Acciones

| salir | llegar | viajar | visitar | ir | volver |

10 Planeando un viaje

▶ **Ordena** los pasos que siguen Tess y Patricia para preparar su viaje.

a. Patricia hace las maletas.
b. Tess y Patricia hablan con un agente de viajes.
c. Tess y Patricia llegan a la estación de autobuses.
d. Tess y Patricia consultan las tarifas del viaje en un folleto.
e. Patricia paga los boletos.

Differentiated Instruction

DEVELOPING LEARNERS

- Review the verbs listed on the page. Ask students to categorize the verbs that have stem changes and specify what these changes are (*costar, recordar, volver: o > ue; venir, querer: e > ie*). Then have students categorize the verbs in the dialogue by verb tense: present tense (*cuesta, vienen, es, están, vamos, quiero*), commands (*recuerda, mira*), and preterite (*hiciste*). Ask students how the verbs *venir* and *salir* are irregular in the present tense (in the first person: *vengo, salgo*). Also review the preterite of the irregular verbs *ir* and *hacer* by having students write the conjugations in their notebook.

EXPANDING LEARNERS

- Ask students to match each word in the first column with its definition in the second column.

1. *la agencia de viajes*	a. *personas que viajan*	(e)
2. *las tarifas*	b. *preparar las maletas*	(d)
3. *el folleto*	c. *lo contrario de "llegada"*	(f)
4. *el mapa*	d. *los precios*	(g)
5. *los viajeros*	e. *lugar que ayuda a planear viajes*	(a)
6. *la salida*	f. *librito con información sobre algo*	(c)
7. *hacer el equipaje*	g. *Indica dónde están los lugares*	(b)

11 El itinerario

▶ **Escucha** el mensaje del celular de Patricia y toma nota. Después, responde a estas preguntas.

1. ¿Quién es Antonio Guzmán?
2. ¿De qué ciudad salen Patricia y Tess?
3. ¿A qué lugar viajan?
4. ¿Qué día viajan?
5. ¿A qué hora sale el autobús?
6. ¿Cuál es la tarifa de los boletos?

12 Un viaje imaginario

▶ **Habla** y escribe. Tu compañero(a) y tú van a hacer un viaje. Toma notas de todos los detalles: ¿adónde van?, ¿cómo van?, ¿qué van a visitar?...

Modelo A. ¿Adónde vamos?
        B. Podemos ir a Cartagena de Indias.
        A. De acuerdo. ¿Vamos en avión o en autobús?

▶ **Pregunta** a otros(as) compañeros(as) por su viaje y responde a sus preguntas.

Modelo

¿Adónde van a viajar ustedes?

Vamos a ir a Bogotá.

¿Y qué van a visitar allí?

CONEXIONES: CIENCIAS SOCIALES

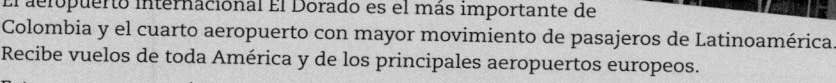

El aeropuerto internacional El Dorado

El aeropuerto internacional El Dorado es el más importante de Colombia y el cuarto aeropuerto con mayor movimiento de pasajeros de Latinoamérica. Recibe vuelos de toda América y de los principales aeropuertos europeos.

Este aeropuerto está situado a 15 kilómetros de Bogotá. Se inauguró en 1959 y recibió su nombre por la famosa leyenda de El Dorado.

13 **Piensa y explica.** ¿Conoces el nombre de algún aeropuerto de tu país? ¿Sabes por qué se llama así?

doscientos noventa y siete 297

Vocabulario – Viajes y excursiones

11. Prior to listening to the audio recording, review the questions with your students. Play the recording twice. You may choose to have students answer the questions orally or in writing. Check that students remember to use the prepositions in their answers 2, 3, and 5.

13. You may ask students to research the names of other airports in the Caribbean region and explain the origin of the names or their meaning.

AUDIO SCRIPT
See page 287 I.

CONEXIONES: CIENCIAS SOCIALES

El aeropuerto internacional El Dorado
El Dorado International Airport is Colombia's largest and most important airport. It is located about 9 miles from Bogotá. El Dorado was inaugurated in 1959, but an extensive renovation and capacity enlargement project began in 2007. El Dorado Airport is essential to the economy of Colombia, since it is the largest cargo airport in all of Latin America. It is also important for passenger travel because due to Colombia's mountainous geography, a large proportion of the population travels by air.

Answer Key

10. b, d, a, c, e

11. 1. El agente de viajes.
2. Salen de Bogotá.
3. Viajan a Guatavita.
4. El veintiuno.
5. A las 12:30 p. m.
6. Cuesta 20 dólares cada uno.

12. Answers will vary.
   ▶ Answers will vary.

13. Answers will vary.

Additional Resources

Fans Online activities
Practice Workbook

DESAFÍO 1

Gramática – El imperfecto

Presentation

- In this section, students will learn:
  - Regular and irregular conjugations in the imperfect.
  - Expressions that are used with the imperfect.

Activities	Standards	Resources
Gramática	3.1	
14.	1.1, 3.1, 4.1	
15.	1.2	Audio
16.	1.3	
17.	1.3	
18. Cultura	1.2, 2.2, 3.1, 3.2, 5.1	
Tu desafío	1.2, 2.2, 3.2, 5.1	

Teaching Suggestions

Warm-Up / Independent Starter

- Have students conjugate these verbs in the present and preterite tenses: *viajar, salir, ir,* and *ver.*

Preparation

- Go over the grammar presentation with students. Note the placement of accents. Clarify that there are no stem changes in the imperfect.
- Ask students to think of other expressions that indicate frequency and the verb tenses with which they are associated. Point out how some frequency expressions, such as *todos los días,* indicate habitual actions, either in the present or in the past. The verb conjugation communicates the tense.

Activities

15. Before playing the audio recording, have students conjugate each verb in the present tense and the preterite *yo* form, and remind them to listen to the endings of the verbs, which will indicate the tense.

16. After completing this activity, have other realia or clip art prepared. Show the item or picture to the class. In groups, students will write as many sentences using the imperfect as they can think of relating to the item. Each sentence should contain a different verb. See which groups are able to use the imperfect most accurately.

Gramática

El imperfecto

- We use the imperfect tense to talk about habitual actions or actions that happened repeatedly in the past.

  Cuando **tenía** un examen, Tess **estudiaba** mucho.

- There are only three irregular verbs in the imperfect tense: ser, ir, and ver. The other verbs are regular.

IMPERFECTO. VERBOS REGULARES

	Viajar	Volver	Salir
yo	via**j**aba	vol**v**ía	sal**í**a
tú	via**j**abas	vol**v**ías	sal**í**as
usted, él, ella	via**j**aba	vol**v**ía	sal**í**a
nosotros, nosotras	via**j**ábamos	vol**v**íamos	sal**í**amos
vosotros, vosotras	via**j**abais	vol**v**íais	sal**í**ais
ustedes, ellos, ellas	via**j**aban	vol**v**ían	sal**í**an

VERBOS IRREGULARES EN EL IMPERFECTO

	Ser	Ir	Ver
yo	era	iba	veía
tú	eras	ibas	veías
usted, él, ella	era	iba	veía
nosotros, nosotras	éramos	íbamos	veíamos
vosotros, vosotras	erais	ibais	veíais
ustedes, ellos, ellas	eran	iban	veían

Expresiones temporales que se usan con el imperfecto

- Some expressions that indicate frequency, like siempre, muchas veces, a menudo, or generalmente, can be used with the imperfect. You can also use these other expressions with the imperfect to express that an action was habitual:

antes	de pequeño(a)	cuando era pequeño(a)
entonces	de niño(a)	cuando era joven

  Cuando era pequeña, yo **vivía** en Nueva York.

14 **Compara.** ¿Cómo se expresa en inglés la idea de acción habitual en el pasado?

15 **Las costumbres de Tess**

 ▶ **Escucha** y decide. ¿Estas acciones de Tess corresponden al presente o al pasado?

1. hablar por teléfono con sus amigas
2. ver películas de acción
3. viajar mucho con Patricia
4. ir al parque con sus amigas
5. jugar al fútbol
6. ir de compras

298 doscientos noventa y ocho

Differentiated Instruction

DEVELOPING LEARNERS

- Give students practice with the imperfect, including the irregular forms. Prepare a cube with the different subject pronouns on each side (i.e., *yo, tú, él / ella / usted, nosotros / nosotras, vosotros / vosotras, ellos / ellas / ustedes*). Then say any verb in the infinitive and have a student roll the cube. Students will repeat the infinitive and say the pronoun that is indicated on the cube, then they will conjugate the verb in the imperfect for the pronoun they got. Repeat with other students and be sure all have several chances to roll the cube to practice the imperfect.

EXPANDING LEARNERS

- Ask students to write at least two paragraphs describing what they used to do when they were children. Suggest that they include topics as diverse as where they lived, what games they played, what they liked to eat, what they liked to study at school, and how they got along with their siblings. Be sure to remind them to use the imperfect tense in their descriptions and to use some of the following expressions: *de pequeño(a), de niño(a), siempre, a menudo, muchas veces, frecuentemente, generalmente.*

16 Cuando eran pequeños

▶ **Escribe.** ¿Qué hacían los personajes durante sus vacaciones cuando eran niños(as)?

Modelo *Mack jugaba con coches.*

 leer   montar   ver   jugar ir

1. Diana

2. Tim

3. Andy

4. Tess

5. Rita

17 Unas vacaciones típicas

▶ **Escribe.** ¿Qué hacías en vacaciones cuando eras niño(a)?

1. ¿Adónde ibas?
2. ¿Con quién ibas?
3. ¿Qué llevabas?
4. ¿Qué hacías?
5. ¿A qué jugabas?

CULTURA

El Museo del Oro de Bogotá

El Museo del Oro de Bogotá tiene la mayor colección de orfebrería *(gold/silversmithing)* prehispánica del mundo. Allí se pueden ver objetos de oro, cerámica, piedra y textiles.

Una de las piezas más importantes del museo es una balsa de la cultura muisca que representa la ceremonia de El Dorado. Esta pieza apareció en 1969 en una cueva en Pasca junto a otros objetos de oro.

Balsa de oro.
Museo del Oro (Bogotá).

18 Investiga. ¿Qué tipo de objetos hay en el Museo del Oro de Bogotá?

 → TU DESAFÍO Visita la página web para aprender más sobre este museo.

Gramática – El imperfecto

17. Ask students to draw or bring in a picture that is representative of their usual summer vacations as children. Remind them that they are communicating habitual actions during vacations in the past, not just one summer vacation.

AUDIO SCRIPT
See page 287I.

CULTURA

El Museo del Oro de Bogotá
Bogotá's Gold Museum has gold pieces from all the archaeological regions of Colombia. The Bank of Colombia owns the Museum, and its holdings provide part of the gold reserves that back the Colombian currency. A raft from the Muisca culture is one of the most valuable artifacts that the museum holds. The Muisca people—also known as Chibcha—lived on the high valleys that surround present-day Bogotá.

Answer Key

14. Con la expresión *used to*, el verbo *would* y expresiones de tiempo como *every day/ week,* etc.

15.
1. pasado
2. presente
3. presente
4. pasado
5. pasado
6. presente

16. Answers will vary. Sample answers:
1. Diana iba a la playa.
2. Tim jugaba al baloncesto.
3. Andy montaba en bicicleta.
4. Tess veía la televisión.
5. Rita leía cuentos.

17. Answers will vary.

18. Answers will vary.

Additional Resources

Fans Online activities
Practice Workbook

HERITAGE LANGUAGE LEARNERS

• Ask students to write a few paragraphs explaining what they or a family member used to do in their country of origin or in another country where they lived, and compare this to what they do now in the United States. Topics might include what and how they studied at school, what their daily schedules were like, how they used to travel, how they spent their free time, and what foods they would eat.

MULTIPLE INTELLIGENCES:
Intrapersonal Intelligence

• Ask students to imagine that they are treasure hunters and, after many years of searching, have finally come across some fantastic pre-Columbian gold relics. Ask them to describe how they happened to discover this treasure and the hardships and dangers they had to face along the way, where they found it, what artifacts were found, and how they felt after making this amazing discovery.

299

Unit 6

DESAFÍO 1

Comunicación

Presentation

- In this section, students will integrate the vocabulary and grammar from *Desafío 1* in order to talk about travel and the past using the imperfect tense.

Activities	Standards	Resources
19.	1.2, 1.3	Audio
20.	1.2, 1.3, 2.2	
21.	1.1, 1.3, 5.2	
22. Final del desafío	1.3, 2.2, 3.1	
Tu desafío	1.2, 1.3	

Teaching Suggestions

Warm-Up / Independent Starter

- Ask students to think about the trips they used to take as children. (They may also think about excursions or field trips they used to take.) Then have them write a list of the steps they used to take in order to prepare for the trip. Students should also include in their list the items they used to bring on the trip.

Preparation

- Invite students to share their Independent Starter with the class. Did students follow similar steps or are there marked differences between students? Discuss, as a class, what might account for the differences (e.g., the type of trip, the destination, the duration of the trip).
- Take 10 minutes to review the vocabulary and grammar themes of *Desafío 1*.
- Refer students back to the *fotonovela*. Have them identify travel-related vocabulary, the verb in the imperfect, and the expression that indicates a habitual action. Do students understand the dialogue better now that they have gone through the vocabulary and grammar from the *Desafío*?

Activities

19. Have students copy the chart onto a piece of paper. Tell them to skip lines as they are completing the activity, so that they will have room to go back and correct the sentences that are illogical.

Comunicación

19 **Consejos de una agente**

 ▶ **Escucha** y escribe los consejos que da una agente de viajes a Tess y Patricia. ¿Son lógicos o ilógicos?

Consejos	Lógico	Ilógico
1. Hay que reservar el viaje con tiempo.	X	

▶ **Corrige** los consejos ilógicos.

20 **Dificultades con el desafío**

▶ **Lee** el mensaje de correo de Tess y complétalo. Usa el imperfecto.

▶ **Responde** a estas preguntas.

1. ¿Dónde está Tess?
2. ¿Quiénes vivían en ese territorio en el pasado?
3. ¿Qué hacían durante sus ceremonias religiosas?
4. ¿Qué tienen que hacer Tess y Patricia en este desafío?

Mensaje nuevo

Para:
Cc:
Asunto:

Hola, Ana. ¿Cómo estás?

Te escribo desde Guatavita (Colombia). Mi mamá y yo vinimos aquí para fotografiar una balsa de oro de la cultura muisca, pero no sabemos dónde está. Este desafío es un poco difícil...

Hasta ahora, mi mamá y yo no ___1___ (saber) mucho de la cultura muisca. Ellos ___2___ (vivir) en estas tierras antes de la llegada de los españoles. ___3___ (Tener) una economía basada en el cobre (*copper*), el carbón (*coal*) y el oro. También ___4___ (cultivar) maíz, papas y otros productos. Pero lo más interesante ___5___ (ser) sus ceremonias religiosas: los muiscas ___6___ (elegir) a un cacique y ___7___ (ofrecer) oro a sus dioses en la laguna.

¿Crees que la balsa de oro está en Guatavita? Tenemos que conseguir más información y completar nuestro desafío.

¡Hasta pronto!

Tess

Differentiated Instruction

DEVELOPING LEARNERS

- Ask students to complete the following sentences with the imperfect tense of the verb in parentheses:
1. *De niña tú … (ver) esas películas, pero ya no te gustan. (veías)*
2. *Cuando éramos jóvenes, … (ir) a las montañas en verano. (íbamos)*
3. *Nosotros no … (saber) dónde … (estar) Guatavita. (sabíamos, estaba)*
4. *Ellos siempre … (viajar) en primera clase. (viajaban)*
5. *De pequeño Miguel … (ir) al colegio en bicicleta. (iba)*
6. *De joven, mi abuela … (ser) muy bonita. (era)*

EXPANDING LEARNERS

- Ask students to write a postcard, letter, or e-mail to a friend explaining what they learned from a recent vacation or day trip. This trip could be real or imaginary, but should include concrete facts or lessons that the students learned from the experience. Remind students to use as many verbs in the imperfect tense as they can to indicate actions that happened repeatedly during their trip or to describe aspects of their experience. Students may use the e-mail from activity 20 as a model.

21 Recuerdos

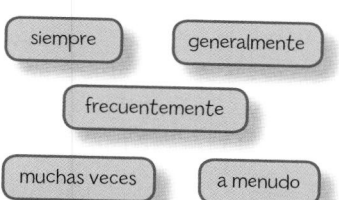

▶ **Escribe** un párrafo sobre recuerdos de tu infancia. Usa estas expresiones.

siempre   generalmente

frecuentemente

muchas veces   a menudo

Modelo

De pequeña vivía en el campo. Mi hermano y yo jugábamos siempre al fútbol con otros niños. Muchas veces nadábamos en el río.

▶ **Habla** con tu compañero(a). ¿Hacían cosas similares?

Modelo   *De pequeño, yo jugaba al fútbol, pero mi compañero prefería jugar al baloncesto.*

Final del desafío

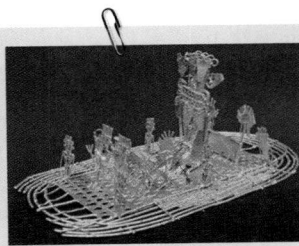

Al final no había oro en Guatavita. Hace muchos años intentaron secar la laguna y se llevaron el oro que había en el fondo. El Dorado era una leyenda. ¡Qué desilusión!

Pero el viaje fue muy interesante y aprendimos muchas cosas. Una mujer nos contó que en la laguna había objetos de oro porque en Guatavita celebraban la ceremonia de El Dorado. Y luego nos habló del Museo del Oro. Fuimos a Bogotá y... ¡¡¡allí estaba la balsa!!! Esta es la foto. Somos las mejores fans del español.

22 ¿Dónde está la balsa de oro?

▶ **Escribe.** ¿Qué pasó en Guatavita? Escribe el diálogo entre Tess, Patricia y la mujer. Después, represéntalo con dos compañeros(as).

 **→ TU DESAFÍO**   Visita la página web. Escucha las preguntas de tu *Minientrevista Desafío 1* y escribe las respuestas.

HERITAGE LANGUAGE LEARNERS

• Ask students to summarize what Tess and Patricia had to do for their *desafío* and what they learned about Colombian culture and history. If there are students with knowledge of Colombia, invite them to share what else they know about the country with the rest of the class.

COOPERATIVE LEARNING

• Ask students to work in groups of three and write a dialogue for the conclusion of Tess and Patricia's *desafío*. Each student will role-play one of the participants as well as the person who tells them about *la laguna* and *la balsa*. Ask them to rehearse their lines and then present their skits in front of the class.

---

20. As students are completing the verbs in the e-mail, check their accuracy with the endings and accents. Ask students to think of the reason for the use of the imperfect tense in each case. For additional practice, have students create additional questions related to the text.

21. Prior to writing, have students brainstorm a list of verbs that they can use to write the paragraph. Write this list on the board and ask students to use at least five of these verbs in their paragraphs.

22. Ask students to use props to support their dialogue. They can even make replicas of the golden raft!

 AUDIO SCRIPT
See page 287I.

Answer Key

19. Lógico: 1, 3, 4
Ilógico: 2, 5
   ▶ 2. Pidan información sobre las tarifas del viaje.
   5. Paguen los boletos antes de salir de viaje.

20. 1. sabíamos   5. eran
2. vivían   6. elegían
3. Tenían   7. ofrecían
4. cultivaban
   ▶ 1. Está en Guatavita, Colombia.
   2. La cultura muisca vivía en ese territorio.
   3. Elegían un cacique y ofrecían oro a los dioses.
   4. Tienen que fotografiar una balsa de oro de la cultura muisca.

21. Answers will vary.
   ▶ Answers will vary.

22. Answers will vary.

Additional Resources

Fans Online activities
Practice Workbook

Unit 6

DESAFÍO 2

Hablar de acciones pasadas

Presentation

- In *Desafío 2*, Andy and Janet's task is to fly over the Venezuelan rainforest and take an aerial photo of the tallest waterfall in the world.
- In this section, students will preview:
  - Vocabulary to describe train and air travel.
  - Irregular verbs in the preterite tense.

Activities	Standards	Resources
Fotonovela	1.2, 3.1, 3.2	Vis. Pres.
23.	1.2, 1.3	
24.	1.2	
25.	1.2, 1.3	Audio
26.	1.1, 1.3	
27. Conexiones	1.1, 1.2, 3.1, 3.2	Video
Tu desafío	1.2, 3.1, 3.2, 5.1	

Teaching Suggestions

Warm-Up / Independent Starter

- Write these statements on the board: *Tengo miedo de volar en avión. Me encanta volar en avión.* Ask students to react in writing.

Preparation

- Have students read the introduction to the *fotonovela*. Ask them to locate Venezuela on a map of South America. Then have students brainstorm possible obstacles that Janet and Andy may face while attempting to take an aerial photo of Angel Falls.

La fotonovela

Before Viewing

- Ask students to look at the pictures and list previously learned vocabulary and cognates that they recognize. Then ask students to combine this vocabulary to create three to five original sentences in which they predict the outcomes of *Desafío 2*.

After Viewing

- Ask students to form pairs and to note the differences in the reactions of Janet and Andy. Have students explain to one another if they can relate more to Andy's fear or Janet's boldness.

El salto Ángel

After witnessing the majestic power of Iguazú Falls in Argentina, Andy and Janet must now investigate another natural wonder of the South American continent. Their task is to fly over the Venezuelan rainforest and take an aerial photo of the tallest waterfall in the world.

¡Qué avión tan viejo! No hay primera clase.

Vinimos muy tarde, Andy. No hay otro avión.

¿Pudiste sacar la tarjeta de embarque?

No es necesario. Y tampoco se factura el equipaje. ¡Vámonos!

Los chalecos salvavidas están debajo de los asientos.

¡Yo nunca me puse un chaleco! ¡No sé hacerlo!

Tenemos que hacer una foto de la catarata. ¿Podemos acercarnos más?

¡Es espectacular! Siempre quise venir a este lugar.

Sí, pero no sé por qué vinimos. Dimos muchas vueltas... ¡Estoy mareado!

¿Crees que es necesario, Janet?

23   **Detective de palabras**

▶ **Completa** estas oraciones.

1. _____ muy tarde.
2. ¿_____ sacar la tarjeta de embarque?
3. ¡Yo nunca me _____ un chaleco!
4. Siempre _____ venir a este lugar.
5. _____ muchas vueltas.

▶ **Responde.** ¿Sabes a qué infinitivos corresponden esos verbos? ¿En qué tiempo verbal están?

Continuará...

Differentiated Instruction

DEVELOPING LEARNERS

- Ask students to say whether the following statements are true (*cierto*) or false (*falso*), according to the *fotonovela*:
1. *Janet y Andy sacaron la tarjeta de embarque.* (falso)
2. *No era necesario facturar el equipaje.* (cierto)
3. *Los chalecos salvavidas están debajo de los asientos.* (cierto)
4. *Andy sabe ponerse el chaleco salvavidas.* (falso)
5. *Janet siempre quiso ir al salto Ángel.* (cierto)
6. *Andy está mareado.* (cierto)
7. *Andy hace una foto.* (falso)

EXPANDING LEARNERS

- Have students work in groups of three and prepare an interview with Janet and Andy when they return from Angel Falls. One student will role-play the reporter; the other two will be the participants. The reporter should ask them why they went to the falls, how they traveled there, what their reaction was to seeing the falls the first time, how they liked flying in a small plane, and if they would like to repeat the experience and why. Encourage students to add other questions.

24 **¿Qué hicieron?**

▶ **Ordena** estas oraciones según la fotonovela.

a. El piloto se acercó a la catarata *(waterfall)* y Janet hizo una foto.
b. Andy y Janet llegaron tarde al aeropuerto.
c. Andy se mareó porque el avión dio muchas vueltas.
d. Andy y Janet se sentaron en sus asientos.
e. Andy y Janet subieron al avión.

25 **¿Quién es?**

▶ **Escucha** y decide. ¿A quién se refiere cada oración?

	A Andy	A Janet	A los dos
1			
2			
3			
4			
5			

26 **¡Más información, por favor!**

▶ **Escribe** cinco preguntas para entrevistar a Andy y a Janet.

▶ **Habla.** Por turnos, haz las preguntas a dos compañeros(as) y responde a las suyas.

Modelo A. *Janet, ¿no te dan miedo los aviones?*
B. *No, yo soy una chica atrevida.*

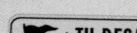
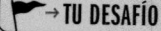

CONEXIONES: CIENCIAS

El salto Ángel

El salto Ángel es una famosa catarata del Parque Nacional de Canaima, en la selva venezolana. Tiene más de 3.000 pies de altura y es la caída libre de agua más alta del mundo.

Es mejor visitarlo durante la temporada de lluvia (de mayo a noviembre) porque las cascadas y los saltos de agua aumentan su volumen.

27 **Explica.** ¿Alguna vez viste cataratas? ¿Cómo se llaman? ¿Dónde están?

▶ TU DESAFÍO Visita la página web para aprender más sobre el Parque Nacional de Canaima y el salto Ángel.

HERITAGE LANGUAGE LEARNERS

• In the *fotonovela*, Janet says: *Siempre quise venir a este lugar.* Ask students to think about a place they have always wanted to visit and have not been able to, or a place they had always wanted to visit and finally had the opportunity to see. Ask them to write one or more paragraphs describing the place, why they have or had wanted to visit it, and how they felt after seeing it, or how they feel about not having been able to visit.

MULTIPLE INTELLIGENCES:
Intrapersonal Intelligence

• Explain that Jimmie Angel, an American aviator, is credited with being the first person to fly over the falls in 1933. Ask students to research his adventures and to write several journal entries from his point of view. Suggest that students reflect on his reaction to seeing the waterfall for the first time, his difficulty in landing his plane on his second trip, his dangerous trip by foot from atop the waterfall to reach civilization, and any other anecdotes they would like to include.

Activities

25. Before playing the audio recording, ask students questions to stimulate vocabulary that they may hear in the listening selection. Make sure to use the preterite tense in your questions: *¿Dónde estuvieron? ¿Qué hicieron?*

26. Before forming the groups, ask the class to generate a list of eight to ten important vocabulary words / verbs used in the *fotonovela*. Ask all the groups to include these words in their dialogues.

 AUDIO SCRIPT
See page 287I.

 CONEXIONES: CIENCIAS

El salto Ángel
Angel Falls is named after an American pilot from Missouri, Jimmie Angel, who was searching for gold and instead "discovered" the falls. Angel Falls are located in Canaima National Park. From Canaima, visitors have the option of taking a small plane for an aerial view of the falls, or traveling by river to the base of the falls.

Answer Key

23. 1. Vinimos 4. quise
2. Pudiste 5. Dimos
3. puse

▶ 1. venir; 2. poder; 3. poner; 4. querer; 5. dar. Los verbos están en el pretérito.

24. b, e, d, a, c

25. A Andy: 2, 3 A los dos: 1, 5
A Janet: 4

26. Answers will vary.
▶ Answers will vary.

27. Answers will vary.

Additional Resources

Fans Online activities

Vocabulario – El tren y el avión

Presentation

- In this section, students will learn vocabulary pertaining to air and train travel.

Activities	Standards	Resources
Vocabulario	1.2	
28.	1.2, 1.3	
29.	1.2	Audio
30.	1.1	
31. Cultura	1.1, 1.2, 2.2, 3.2, 5.2	

Teaching Suggestions

Warm-Up / Independent Starter

- Ask students to create a three-column chart like the one below. Have them look at the photos and list vocabulary that pertains to each category. Next to each vocabulary word, have students write other word(s) associated with it. For example: *los pasajeros → viajar; el andén → esperar*, etc.

En la estación de tren	En el aeropuerto	En el avión

Preparation

- Have students share their associations from the Independent Starter with the rest of the class. Then ask them to use the associations to write definitions in Spanish for the vocabulary. For example, *los pasajeros: las personas que viajan; el andén: lugar donde los pasajeros esperan la llegada del tren.*

- Have students work with a partner to "polish" their definitions. Then ask several different pairs to present their definitions to the class. The class will match the vocabulary to the corresponding definition.

Activities

29. After completing this listening activity, ask students to play "Charades" with the vocabulary. Class members will guess the word being dramatized.

30. Before completing this activity, remind students that an infinitive must be used after a preposition. You may want to list some common Spanish prepositions on the board: *a, de, con, por, para…*

Vocabulario

El tren y el avión

En la estación de tren

los pasajeros · el vagón · el andén · la vía

En el aeropuerto

10 la tarjeta de embarque

El avión sale con **retraso**. No despega hasta las cinco.

Este es un **vuelo directo**, sin escalas. Aterrizamos en Houston.

facturar el equipaje

En el avión

el equipaje de mano · el chaleco salvavidas · el asiento · el auxiliar de vuelo · el pasillo

boleto sencillo · boleto de ida y vuelta

primera clase · clase turista

 28 **¿Lógico o ilógico?**

▶ **Decide** si cada oración es lógica o ilógica. Corrige las oraciones ilógicas.

Modelo El tren circula por el andén → *Ilógica. El tren circula por la vía.*

1. El auxiliar de vuelo trabaja en un tren.
2. Un vuelo directo hace varias escalas.
3. Los viajeros facturan el equipaje de mano.
4. Normalmente es más caro viajar en primera clase que en clase turista.
5. Después de subir al avión, hay que mostrar la tarjeta de embarque.
6. Los viajeros esperan la llegada del tren en el vagón.

304   trescientos cuatro

Differentiated Instruction

DEVELOPING LEARNERS

- Have students practice the new vocabulary by drawing or attaching magazine cutouts to one side of an index card and writing the corresponding word on a different card. Then have them play a game with a partner by placing both sets of cards facedown on a desk and trying to match images and words. As students select cards, they should say the words aloud. If students make a match they can keep the cards. If not, they must place the cards where they were. The winner is the player with the most cards.

EXPANDING LEARNERS

- Ask students to write at least two paragraphs comparing air travel to traveling by train. Students will need to include both the advantages and the disadvantages of each mode of transportation, and explain which one of the two they prefer, and why.

29 Fotos de viajes

 ▶ **Escucha.** ¿A qué fotografía corresponde cada oración?

 Ⓐ

 Ⓑ

 Ⓒ

 Ⓓ

 Ⓔ

30 Preguntas sobre viajes

 ▶ **Habla.** Por turnos, haz preguntas a tu compañero(a). Usa estas palabras.

Modelo A. *¿Cuándo es necesario mostrar la tarjeta de embarque?*
B. *Antes de subir al avión.*

¿qué?	¿por qué?
¿cómo?	¿adónde?
¿quién?	¿cuándo?

primera clase	el andén
el pasaporte	el avión
el tren	el boleto
el auxiliar de vuelo	el equipaje
la tarjeta de embarque	el retraso

 **CULTURA**

La red de transportes en Venezuela

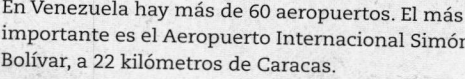

PUENTE INTERNACIONAL SIMON BOLIVAR

En Venezuela hay más de 60 aeropuertos. El más importante es el Aeropuerto Internacional Simón Bolívar, a 22 kilómetros de Caracas.

Por sus características geográficas, Venezuela tiene puertos *(ports)* muy importantes, que reciben barcos procedentes de todo el mundo.

Para viajar por el interior, Venezuela cuenta con una importante red de autopistas *(expressways)* y carreteras *(highways)*. El sistema ferroviario *(rail system)* está en construcción y gran parte de las líneas férreas se destinan al transporte de hierro y carbón.

31 Explica. ¿Qué medios de transporte se utilizan más en tu país? ¿Por qué?

HERITAGE LANGUAGE LEARNERS

• Ask students to make a list of some alternative words for those presented on the page, or for other terms related to travel. For example, some students might use *valija* or *petaca* for *maleta*, and *azafata* or *sobrecargo* instead of *auxiliar de vuelo*. Encourage students to introduce other words related to travel by train or air, such as: *furgón, furgón de cola, tripulación, piloto, navegante,* and *ingeniero.* Ask them to share their lists with the class.

SPECIAL-NEEDS LEARNERS

• For students with visual impairments, write each of the new words on large index cards so students can easily see and identify them. Then say each word, and as you say each one, ask students to point to the corresponding item or pick up the correct index card and repeat the word after you.

Vocabulario – El tren y el avión

31. To extend this activity ask students to write a paragraph explaining which means of transportation they prefer and why.

 AUDIO SCRIPT
See page 287 I.

 CULTURA

La red de transportes en Venezuela

Venezuela has an extensive network of transportation possibilities. The international airport near Caracas is busy with traffic from all over the world. In addition, small planes are used to serve even the remote spots of the Amazon region. Another travel option is the ferry. There are ferry connections that link the mainland with Venezuela's biggest island, Margarita. For the more adventurous travelers, Venezuela's main rivers can be explored aboard indigenous dugout canoes called *curiaras*. Finally, there is land transportation, which is popular with Venezuelans due to the very cheap gas and the broad network of paved roads the country has.

Answer Key

28. 1. Ilógica. Trabaja en un avión.
2. Ilógica. Un vuelo directo no hace escalas.
3. Ilógica. Los viajeros no facturan el equipaje de mano.
4. Lógica.
5. Ilógica. Hay que mostrar la tarjeta de embarque antes de subir al avión.
6. Ilógica. Los viajeros esperan la llegada del tren en el andén.

29. 1. C   2. A   3. E   4. D   5. B

30. Answers will vary.

31. Answers will vary.

Additional Resources

Fans Online activities
Practice Workbook

Unit 6
DESAFÍO 2

Gramática – Verbos irregulares en el pretérito. *Dar, poder, poner, querer, saber* y *venir*

Presentation

- In this section, students will learn to form and use the irregular preterite of the verbs *dar, poder, poner, querer, saber,* and *venir*.

Activities	Standards	Resources
Gramática	3.1	
32.	1.1, 3.1	
33.	1.2, 1.3	
34.	1.2, 1.3	Audio
35.	1.2, 1.3	
36.	1.1	

Teaching Suggestions

Warm-Up / Independent Starter

- Ask students to look at the sentences presented in the grammar chart. Ask them to identify the infinitive of each of the verbs and to then write the sentences in the present tense.

Preparation

- Ask six students to write the conjugations of the regular present tense of the verbs on the board (*dar, poder, poner, querer, saber, venir*).

- Ask students to write down two or three uses of the preterite. Have them list key words that might indicate completed action in the past (e.g., *ayer*). Then ask students to share their list. Discuss students' lists as a class.

- Ask students to note any similarities observed in these irregular conjugations. For example: There are no accent marks on any of these irregular verb forms; all but *dar* use the same endings; *dar* uses the -er/-ir endings; etc.

Activities

33. Ask students to identify clues they might use to match the subject with the remainder of the sentence. Then have them identify the infinitives of each conjugated verb used in the exercise and then ask them to create three to five additional sentences. Invite volunteers to share their sentences with the class.

306

Gramática

Verbos irregulares en el pretérito.
Dar, poder, poner, querer, saber y *venir*

- Remember: we use the preterite tense to talk about completed actions in the past.

  Teresa **viajó** a Caracas la semana pasada.

- These are some common irregular verbs in the preterite:

VERBOS IRREGULARES EN EL PRETÉRITO

	Dar	Poder	Poner	Querer	Saber	Venir
yo	di	pude	puse	quise	supe	vine
tú	diste	pudiste	pusiste	quisiste	supiste	viniste
usted, él, ella	dio	pudo	puso	quiso	supo	vino
nosotros, nosotras	dimos	pudimos	pusimos	quisimos	supimos	vinimos
vosotros, vosotras	disteis	pudisteis	pusisteis	quisisteis	supisteis	vinisteis
ustedes, ellos, ellas	dieron	pudieron	pusieron	quisieron	supieron	vinieron

El agente de viajes nos **dio** un folleto.   Juan no **quiso** visitar el museo.
No **pude** comprar los boletos antes.   ¿**Supiste** hacer la reserva por Internet?
Yo nunca me **puse** un chaleco salvavidas.   Ayer **vinimos** a esta agencia de viajes.

32 **Piensa.** Compara estas formas del pretérito. ¿Qué diferencia ortográfica hay entre ellas?

volvió - quiso
salió - vino
comió - pudo

33 **Hay que incluir a todos**

▶ **Une** las dos columnas.

   (A)   (B)

1. Andy   a. pudieron viajar a Venezuela.
2. Yo   b. viniste conmigo al aeropuerto.
3. Andy y Janet   c. supe encontrar el hotel sin mirar el mapa.
4. Tú   d. no quiso acercarse a la catarata.
5. Janet y yo   e. pusimos las maletas debajo de los asientos.

▶ **Escribe** seis oraciones. Usa el pretérito de los verbos de la ficha de gramática.

Modelo *Ayer di un paseo por el parque.*

306   trescientos seis

Differentiated Instruction

DEVELOPING LEARNERS

- Prepare cards to practice the preterite tense of the verbs on this page and to review the irregular preterite of verbs that have previously been introduced (*ir, ser, decir, hacer, estar,* and *tener*). Write a subject pronoun and one of these verbs in the infinitive form on one side of the card, and the corresponding preterite conjugation on the other side. Place cards in a pile with the infinitive side up. Have pairs of students take turns picking a card and giving its conjugation. Partners will check the accuracy by looking at the other side of the card.

EXPANDING LEARNERS

- Ask students to write a paragraph using each of these verbs in the preterite. Students may choose to explain what they or others did in the past. Then tell them that *saber* changes its meaning in the preterite (i.e., *supe* = I found out). Other verbs change their meaning when they are negative in the preterite (e.g., *no quise* = I refused). Ask students to write a sentence with each of these two verbs that reflect their meaning in the preterite and in the negative, or incorporate them into their paragraph.

34 **¡Nos encanta viajar!**

▶ **Escucha** y clasifica las formas verbales de las oraciones en una tabla como esta.

	Presente	Pretérito
1	vamos	
2		
3		
4		
5		
6		
7		
8		

▶ **Completa** la tabla con las formas verbales que faltan.

Modelo 1. *vamos ⟶ fuimos*

35 **Una turista atrevida**

▶ **Completa** el diario de Andy con las formas apropiadas del pretérito.

25 de abril

Janet y yo ___1___ tarde al aeropuerto y ___2___ que viajar en un avión muy pequeño.
            venir   tener

___3___ y nos ___4___ rápidamente. Cuando el avión ___5___, yo ___6___ mucho
Subir   sentar   despegar   sentir
miedo.

Cuando ___7___ mirar por la ventana del avión, ___8___ la catarata. ¡El paisaje
         poder   ver
era impresionante!

Janet le ___9___ al piloto: «¿Podemos acercarnos más para hacer una foto?»
         decir

Afortunadamente, él no ___10___. ¡Creo que mi hermana está loca!
                        querer

36 **¿Qué hicieron Janet y Andy en Canaima?**

▶ **Habla.** Explica lo que hicieron Andy y Janet cuando llegaron a Canaima. Usa estos verbos y expresiones.

Verbos	
tener	llegar
volar	visitar
hacer	poder
ver	querer
ir	volver

Expresiones	
Primero	A continuación
Luego	Más tarde
Después	Finalmente

Unit 6

DESAFÍO 2

Gramática – Verbos irregulares en el pretérito. *Dar, poder, poner, querer, saber* y *venir*

35. Before beginning this activity, review with students the conjugation of *-gar, -car,* and *-zar* verbs in the preterite. It may also be necessary to review the conjugation of stem-changing verbs. Ask volunteers to come to the board and conjugate an example of each of these verbs.

36. Using the verbs and expressions in this exercise, have students act out Janet and Andy's adventure in Canaima. Ask them to include a "twist" and how they meet their challenge. Then hold a class vote for the most original dialogue and for the best acting.

AUDIO SCRIPT
See page 287I.

Answer Key

32. Los verbos *querer, venir* y *poder* tienen un cambio en la raíz y no llevan acento en el pretérito.

33. 1. d   2. c   3. a   4. b   5. e
▶ Answers will vary.

34. Presente: 1. vamos, 3. factura, 8. se pone
Pretérito: 2. vinimos, 4. dio, 5. supo, 6. quise, 7. pudo
▶ 2. vinimos → venimos
   3. factura → facturó
   4. dio → da
   5. supo → sabe
   6. quise → quiero
   7. pudo → puede
   8. se pone → se puso

35. 1. vinimos   6. sentí
       2. tuvimos   7. pude
       3. Subimos   8. vi
       4. sentamos   9. dijo
       5. despegó   10. quiso

36. Answers will vary.

Additional Resources

Fans Online activities
Practice Workbook

HERITAGE LANGUAGE LEARNERS

• Ask students to research Francisco de Orellana's expedition to the Amazon rainforest in 1542. Then have them imagine they took part in this expedition and ask them to write a diary entry describing what happened on the day they entered the Amazon River basin for the first time.

• Invite volunteer students to share their diary entry with the class. Tell students to be prepared to answer their classmates' questions regarding unfamiliar vocabulary.

CRITICAL THINKING

• Ask students to imagine that they have been put in charge of airport security. What rules and regulations would they impose on both employees and travelers? Have them make a list of these rules, read them to the class, and be prepared to explain why they are important for everyone's safety.

• Then have students think of what would happen if some of these rules were not followed. Ask them to write a paragraph explaining what happened one day at the airport when several of the rules were not followed.

Unit 6
DESAFÍO 2
Comunicación

Presentation

- In this section, students will integrate the vocabulary and grammar from *Desafío 2* in order to talk about air and train travel. They will use the verbs *dar, venir, poder, poner, querer, saber,* and *venir* in the preterite.

Activities	Standards	Resources
37.	1.2	Audio
38.	1.1, 1.3, 2.2	
39.	1.3	
40.	1.1	
41. Final del desafío	1.2, 1.3, 3.1	

Teaching Suggestions

Warm-Up / Independent Starter

- Ask students to complete the paragraph that begins with the following crazy travel experience: *Yo puse a mi gato en la maleta y viajamos juntos a Venezuela.*

Preparation

- Have students share their Independent Starter paragraph with a partner.
- Take 10 minutes to review the vocabulary and grammar themes of the *Desafío*. In order to assess students' command of these themes, show them pictures that reflect the titles of *El salto Ángel* and *El tren y el avión.* Ask students to write sentences in the preterite that reflect the activities depicted in the photos.
- Refer students back to the *fotonovela* for *Desafío 2.* Have them provide synonyms and antonyms for the vocabulary used, identify the infinitive form of the verbs used, as well as role-play an interview of Janet and Andy for the local newspaper where they talk about their adventure. Students will take on the roles of a reporter, Janet, and Andy.

Activities

37. Before listening to the audio recording, ask students to read the six sentences so that they understand their purpose for listening. Have them note infinitives of conjugated verbs. After listening, ask students to correct those sentences determined to be false.

DESAFÍO 2

Comunicación

37 **En el avión**

 ▶ **Escucha** y decide si estas oraciones son ciertas o falsas.

1. Andy y Janet tuvieron que viajar en avión para llegar al salto Ángel.
2. Andy se sintió mal porque el avión dio muchas vueltas.
3. Andy miró el paisaje desde el avión.
4. Andy quiere bañarse en el río.
5. Janet es una viajera muy atrevida.
6. Andy prefiere viajar en barco.

38 **El viaje de Andy y Janet**

▶ **Completa** el blog de Janet con el pretérito de estos verbos.

ponerse
aterrizar
subir
ver
querer
llegar
volar
despegar
sentarse
hacer

Un día extraordinario

___1___ al aeropuerto a las seis de la mañana y ___2___ al avión. Andy ___3___ en su asiento. ___4___ un poco nervioso porque no le gustan los aviones. Por fin el avión ___5___. El piloto ___6___ muy cerca del salto Ángel y yo ___7___ una foto muy buena. Al final, el avión ___8___ en el pequeño pueblo indígena de Kavac. Después de llegar, Andy ___9___ explorar la montaña Auyantepuy. Allí nosotros ___10___ un paisaje magnífico.

39 **¿Qué ves?**

▶ **Escribe** un pie de foto para cada imagen. Usa el pretérito.

Modelo 1. *Unos viajeros miraron los horarios antes de subir al avión.*

308 trescientos ocho

Differentiated Instruction

DEVELOPING LEARNERS

- Give students more practice with the preterite, including the irregular forms, by giving them a verb in the infinitive, plus a pronoun, and calling on individual students to say the corresponding conjugated preterite form with that pronoun. Then ask the same student to say or write a sentence on the board with that form.

EXPANDING LEARNERS

- Ask students to summarize what happened in this *Desafío* either verbally or in writing. Explain that they should assume their audience is made up of listeners or readers who have no prior knowledge of this Spanish program, the participants, the reason for giving the participants *desafíos* to confront, or the country where the challenge takes place. Students must provide this information in addition to explaining what occurred during the *Desafío.*

40 **Mi aventura**

▶ **Habla** con tu compañero(a) sobre algún viaje que hiciste en el pasado. Usa estas preguntas.

1. ¿Cuándo saliste?
2. ¿Adónde fuiste?
3. ¿Cómo fuiste?
4. ¿Qué viste?
5. ¿Qué compraste?
6. ¿Tuviste problemas durante el viaje?

Modelo *El verano pasado, mi familia y yo salimos para....*

Final del desafío

_____1_____ ver el salto Ángel a más de cuarenta kilómetros de distancia.

Janet se _____2_____ muy contenta. Siempre _____3_____ ver este lugar.

Yo me asusté y le _____4_____ la cámara a Janet. Ella _____5_____ una foto fantástica.

41 **¡No tan cerca!**

▶ **Completa** los pies de foto con la forma correcta del pretérito de estos verbos.

 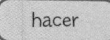 hacer 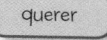 querer   poner 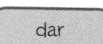 dar   poder

trescientos nueve 309

38. Using the information given in Janet's blog, ask students to create questions. For example: *¿A qué hora llegaron Janet y Andy al aeropuerto? ¿Dónde aterrizaron ellos? ¿Qué hizo Andy después de llegar?* Etc. Then have students exchange their questions with a partner and answers each other's questions.

39. After students have completed the activity, have them work with a partner to come up with a dialogue for one of the pictures. Then ask pairs to role-play their dialogue for the class. In order to avoid students reading the dialogue, tell them they may only write five important words. After each pair acts out their dialogue, the class will guess which picture is being dramatized.

40. Turn this activity into a writing exercise. Ask students to write their partner's "travel adventure" in the form of a postcard. Collect these writing samples and then redistribute them to random students. Ask students to prepare a written response.

 AUDIO SCRIPT
See page 287I.

Answer Key

37. 1. C 2. C 3. F 4. F 5. C 6. F

38.
1. Llegamos
2. subimos
3. se sentó
4. Se puso
5. despegó
6. voló
7. hice
8. aterrizó
9. quiso
10. vimos

39. Answers will vary.

40. Answers will vary.

41.
1. Pudimos
2. puso
3. quiso
4. di
5. hizo

Additional Resources

Fans Online activities
Practice Workbook

HERITAGE LANGUAGE LEARNERS

• Share these quotes about travel with students and ask them which one they identify with most and why. Ask them to give examples of a trip they took and to explain their answer in at least one paragraph.

– *He descubierto que no hay forma más segura de saber si amas u odias a alguien que hacer un viaje con él.* (Mark Twain)

– *Cuando se viaja en avión solamente existen dos clases de emociones: el aburrimiento y el terror.* (Orson Welles)

MULTIPLE INTELLIGENCES:
Intrapersonal Intelligence

• Some people might say that Janet and Andy had an adventurous trip by flying as close as they did to *salto Ángel*. Ask students to reflect on some daring, crazy thing they did (or thought about doing) while on a vacation. Ask them to describe this act and its consequences. If students had thought about taking an adventure tour, but chose not to do it, ask them to describe what persuaded them to change their mind.

Unit 6
DESAFÍO 3

Hablar de acciones en pasado

Presentation

- In *Desafío 3*, Mack and Tim are in Caracas, Venezuela, where they must drive a city bus.
- In this section, students will preview:
  - Words to describe car parts and driving.
  - Narration of past events.

Activities	Standards	Resources
Fotonovela	1.2, 2.1, 3.2	Vis. Pres.
42.	1.2	
43.	1.2, 1.3	
44.	1.2	Audio
45. Conexiones	1.1, 1.2, 2.1, 3.1, 3.2, 4.2	
Tu desafío	1.2, 2.1, 3.2, 5.1	

Teaching Suggestions

Warm-Up / Independent Starter

- Have students answer these questions individually:
  1. ¿Sabes manejar? ¿Quién te enseñó/te va a enseñar?
  2. ¿Cuál es tu modelo de coche favorito? ¿Por qué?

Preparation

- Start a group conversation going over the Independent Starter questions.
- Read the introduction to the *fotonovela* to the class. Ask students if they think that driving a bus is more difficult than driving a car and have them explain why.

La fotonovela

Before Viewing

- Have students look at the pictures and ask them if there is something they find surprising.
- Have students go over the text of the *fotonovela* and write a list of words related to cars and driving. Practice the vocabulary list with students to emphasize pronunciation.

After Viewing

- Divide the class into small groups. Ask students to imagine and describe two more scenes for the *fotonovela*, guessing what will happen next.
- Have two students from each group act out what they created and have the class decide which scenes they like best.

310

Un paseo en bus

Are you ready for a bumpy ride? Tim and Mack have to drive a city bus through the busy streets of Caracas. Mack will be at the wheel. Will they make it?

¿Podemos salir?

Sí. Mientras tú hablabas con el conductor, yo llené el tanque de gasolina.

¡Este autobús tiene tres pedales!

Claro, aquí se maneja con marchas, como en mi videojuego. ¿Me dejas manejar a mí?

No, tú no tienes licencia de conducir.

¡Cuidado! ¡Pusiste la marcha atrás! Tienes que pisar el embrague. ¿Seguro que sabes manejar con marchas?

No, pero no hay tanta diferencia. Mientras volábamos a Caracas, leí un manual.

¡Cambia de marcha, abuelo! ¡Vas a romper el motor!

Continuará...

42 Detective de palabras

▶ **Completa** estas oraciones.

1. Mientras Mack hablaba con el ___1___ del autobús, Tim llenó el ___2___ de ___3___.
2. Mack está sorprendido porque el autobús tiene tres ___4___.
3. Tim no tiene ___5___ de conducir.
4. Mack no sabe manejar con ___6___.
5. Tim piensa que Mack va a romper el ___7___.

310 trescientos diez

Differentiated Instruction

DEVELOPING LEARNERS

- Help students identify the cognates in the *fotonovela* (tanque, gasolina, autobús, pedales, licencia, diferencia, manual, motor) to enhance their comprehension. Be sure to point out the false cognates: *conductor* and *marchas*. Ask students what these words mean and elicit "driver" (not "conductor") and "gears" (not "marches"). Also ask students to identify any commands in the dialogues (*cambia*), as well as the tense of the verbs (present: *podemos, tiene, se maneja, dejas, tienes, sabes, hay, vas*; preterite: *llené, pusiste, leí*; imperfect: *hablabas, volábamos*).

EXPANDING LEARNERS

- Ask students to think about how this *desafío* might end and to write a paragraph explaining their reasoning. They need to keep in mind these participants' resourcefulness as well as their character, plus consider how they would answer the following questions: Do they think that Mack will let Tim drive? Why or why not? Mack says that he read a manual. Do students think that anyone can learn to drive a stick shift vehicle after simply reading a manual? What do students think will happen to the bus? Call on students to read their paragraphs aloud.

43 ¿Comprendes?

▶ **Responde** a estas preguntas.

1. ¿Qué hizo Tim mientras Mack hablaba con el conductor?
2. ¿Por qué se sorprende Mack cuando sube al autobús?
3. ¿Por qué no puede manejar Tim?
4. ¿Por qué Mack no maneja bien el autobús?
5. ¿Qué va a ocurrir si Mack no cambia de marcha?

44 ¡Al autobús!

▶ **Escucha** y relaciona cada oración con la fotografía correspondiente.

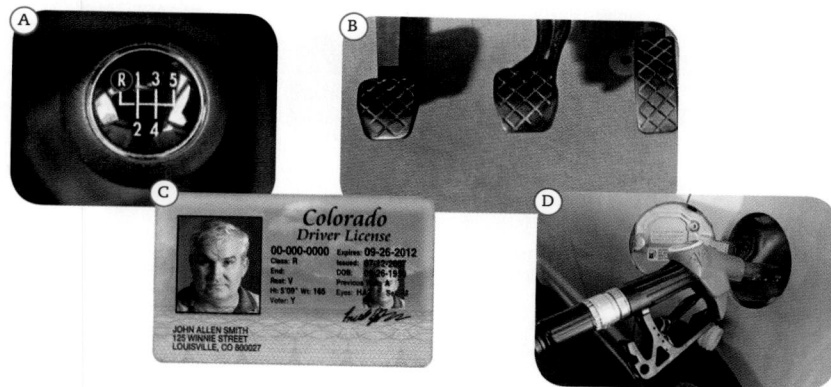

A

B

C

Colorado Driver License

D

CONEXIONES: CIENCIAS SOCIALES

El transporte público: el autobús

En Caracas, como en muchas ciudades en Latinoamérica, los autobuses son un medio de transporte común y barato. Pero funcionan de forma distinta a los autobuses en los Estados Unidos. No hay paradas establecidas y tienes que hacer una señal al conductor si quieres subir o bajar del bus.

45 **Compara.** ¿Qué tipo de transporte público hay en tu ciudad? ¿Funciona bien? ¿Cuál es el medio de transporte público más utilizado?

➡ TU DESAFÍO | Visita la página web para aprender más sobre el transporte público en Venezuela.

trescientos once **311**

Unit 6

DESAFÍO 3

Hablar de acciones en pasado

Activities

42. As a follow-up, ask students to close their books. Divide the class into teams and have students play a guessing game (e.g., "Pictionary") with the vocabulary words from this activity.

43. Turn this activity into a game. Prepare 3 x 5 cards with the answers to the five questions. Divide the class into five teams. Give one card to each team. Have each group act out their assigned answer and ask the other groups to guess the question. Give points to the group that answers more quickly and accurately.

45. Lead a discussion in class about the benefits of public transportation.

AUDIO SCRIPT
See page 287I.

CONEXIONES: CIENCIAS SOCIALES

El transporte público: el autobús
The bus system is complemented in Caracas by an efficient subway system. Construction started in 1977 and it opened for operation in 1983. It is still expanding today. Most of the system is built underground and it is well known for its safety and cleanness.

Answer Key

42. 1. conductor   5. licencia
    2. tanque   6. marchas
    3. gasolina   7. motor
    4. pedales

43. 1. Llenó el tanque de gasolina.
    2. Porque el autobús tiene tres pedales.
    3. Porque no tiene licencia de conducir.
    4. Porque no sabe manejar con marchas.
    5. Va a romper el motor.

44. 1. D   2. B   3. C   4. A

45. Answers will vary.

Additional Resources

Fans Online activities

311

HERITAGE LANGUAGE LEARNERS

• Invite students to talk about modes of transportation in their family's country of origin or in a Hispanic country they know. Ask them to address the following: Are there modes of transportation in that country that are not commonly used where they now live? Do people usually drive or take public transportation to go to school, shop, and run errands? Do people tend to walk more to go from place to place than in their present community? To what do students attribute this? Encourage discussion and then sharing their ideas with other students.

MULTIPLE INTELLIGENCES:
Visual-Spatial Intelligence

• Your community is trying to reduce its carbon footprint, and one way to do this is to reduce the number of cars on the road. Ask students to work in small groups and come up with a campaign, complete with a slogan or song, to encourage residents to walk, ride with others, and use public transportation to get around. The campaign could be a TV or radio spot, a print ad or flyer, or even a web page from the city council. Have groups make their presentations and then take a class vote to see whose campaign is the most convincing.

Unit 6
DESAFÍO 3

Vocabulario – El coche

Presentation

- In this section, students will learn:
  - Words to describe different car parts.
  - Words to talk about driving.

Activities	Standards	Resources
Vocabulario	1.2	
46.	1.2	
47.	1.2	Audio
48.	1.2, 1.3	
49. Conexiones	1.1, 1.2, 2.1, 3.1, 3.2, 5.1	

Teaching Suggestions

Warm-Up / Independent Starter

- Have students draw a car (or give students a picture of a car) and have them name the parts they already know.

Preparation

- Draw or post a picture of a car on the board. Ask different students to go to the board and write the name of the car parts they thought of in the Independent Starter.
- Act out, involving your students, a narration similar to the following, which includes the new vocabulary words: *Cada mañana abro la puerta de mi coche, me siento, me pongo el cinturón de seguridad, pongo la llave en el contacto, bajo la ventanilla —si hace calor— y arranco. Después piso el embrague y el freno, y muevo la palanca de marchas a primera. En ese momento quito el pie del freno, piso el acelerador y quito lentamente el pie del embrague. ¡Ya estoy manejando! Soy un(a) conductor(a) muy prudente porque no me gustan nada las multas. Llego a la escuela y estaciono.*

Activities

46. As a follow-up you can ask students what is more common at gas stations in the United States: full service or self-service. Lead a discussion about advantages and disadvantages of both services.

47. Before listening to the recording, have students describe the pictures. After listening, ask them to write a complete sentence for each picture.

312

DESAFÍO 3

Vocabulario

El coche

el volante • la ventanilla • el freno frenar • el acelerador acelerar • el cinturón de seguridad • el embrague

Muy bien. En poco tiempo vas a tener tu licencia de conducir.
la instructora • el conductor • la autoescuela

el empleado • el tanque de gasolina • la gasolinera

el motor • el faro • la rueda

 arrancar

 manejar

 estacionar

 poner una multa

46 ¿Quién lo hace?

▶ **Completa** estas oraciones.

1. El _____ estaciona el coche.
2. El _____ pone una multa.
3. El _____ de la autoescuela enseña a manejar.
4. El _____ de la gasolinera echa gasolina.

 policía   empleado

instructor   conductor

Differentiated Instruction

DEVELOPING LEARNERS

- Ask students to choose the word that best relates to each item.

1. el policía
   a. arrancar   b. poner una multa (b)
2. llenar de gasolina
   a. el tanque   b. el faro (a)
3. el conductor
   a. conducir   b. volar (a)
4. hay cuatro
   a. licencias   b. ruedas (b)
5. el empleado
   a. el trabajador   b. el motor (a)
6. la licencia
   a. de arrancar   b. de conducir (b)

EXPANDING LEARNERS

- Ask students to work with a partner and create a crossword puzzle (*crucigrama*) with the vocabulary items on the page. Students will write clues for the words and draw the grid for the puzzle, or use computer software to generate the grid. Encourage students to use as many of the new words as they can. Possible clues might include: *persona que pone multas (policía); persona que maneja (conductor); los coches tienen cuatro (ruedas)*. Review students' work and then have them exchange puzzles with another pair to see if they can solve the other pair's crossword puzzle.

47 Aprendiendo a manejar

▶ **Escucha** las instrucciones y ordena estas fotografías.

(A)

(B)

(C)

(D)

48 Un conductor cívico

▶ **Completa** estos consejos del manual de una autoescuela.

Manual del buen conductor

Sé un conductor prudente y respetuoso:

1. Maneja con las dos manos sobre el _____.
2. No _____ el coche en una zona prohibida.
3. No tires papeles por la _____.
4. Recuerda ponerte siempre el _____.
5. _____ las señales de tráfico.
6. No olvides llenar el tanque de _____.

respetar
cinturón de seguridad
gasolina
estacionar
volante
ventanilla

CONEXIONES: MATEMÁTICAS

¿Litros o galones?

En Latinoamérica y en muchos otros países usan el sistema métrico. Por eso, los líquidos se miden en litros, no en galones, como en los Estados Unidos. Un galón equivale a 3,8 litros.

$ **34.00** Sale
22.987 Gallons

$ Price Per Gallon (Including Tax)

UNLEADED   **14.79**   **EXTRA**   **PREMIUM**

49 **Calcula.** ¿A cuántos galones equivalen 20 litros de gasolina?

HERITAGE LANGUAGE LEARNERS

• Ask students to explain how drivers obtain a driver's license in their family's country of origin or in a Spanish-speaking country they know well. Have them compare the steps applicants must take with the process in their state. You might want to have them create a Venn diagram to compare and contrast similarities and differences. Ask them to present this information to the class. Be sure that heritage language learners explain any unfamiliar vocabulary. Ask the other students what was the most surprising difference between the two procedures.

COOPERATIVE LEARNING

• After students complete activity 48, ask them to work in small groups and write additional rules for safe driving or for keeping a car in top shape. Each member of the group must come up with at least two ideas, discuss them with other members of the group, and then write them on poster board. Encourage students to decorate their work. Some suggestions might include: *No uses el teléfono celular mientras manejas. Hay que parar cuando se acerca una ambulancia. Debes cambiar el aceite periódicamente.*

DESAFÍO 3

Vocabulario – El coche

48. Have students write other sentences that include these words. Then ask them to share some of their sentences with the class, as you write them on the board. You may also ask them to come up to the board and write them individually while the rest of the class suggests the necessary corrections.

49. Prepare a list of a variety of different metric measurements. Divide the class into small groups. Organize a game in which students should give approximate U.S. equivalents.

 AUDIO SCRIPT
See page 287J.

 CONEXIONES: MATEMÁTICAS

¿Litros o galones?
The United States is still one of the few countries in the world that does not use the metric system to measure volume, mass, and dimension. Some of the most common units in the metric system are liters (for liquids), kilos (for solids), meters (for length), and kilometers (for distances). Some equivalents to American measurement units are: 1 gallon equals 3.78 liters, 1 pound equals 0.453 kilos, 1 foot equals 0.305 meters, 1 mile equals 1.6 kilometers.

Answer Key

46. 1. conductor   3. instructor
      2. policía   4. empleado

47. B, D, C, A

48. 1. volante   4. cinturón de seguridad
      2. estaciones   5. Respeta
      3. ventanilla   6. gasolina

49. Equivalen a 5.3 galones.

Additional Resources

Fans Online activities
Practice Workbook

313

DESAFÍO 3

Gramática – Narrar hechos pasados. El pretérito y el imperfecto

Presentation

- In this section, students will learn to talk about past actions using the preterite and the imperfect.

Activities	Standards	Resources
Gramática	3.1	
50.	1.2, 4.1	
51.	1.2	Audio
52.	1.3	
53.	1.1, 1.2, 1.3, 5.2	
54.	1.1	
55. Conexiones	1.1, 1.2, 2.1, 3.1, 3.2, 4.2, 5.2	

Teaching Suggestions

Warm-Up / Independent Starter

- Ask students to write the appropriate preterite and imperfect verb forms for the following verbs:
  1. *Dar (yo)*
  2. *Ir (tú)*
  3. *Poder (ella)*
  4. *Ver (nosotros)*
  5. *Saber (vosotros)*
  6. *Manejar (ellos)*

Preparation

- Review the responses to the Independent Starter. Provide more examples to ensure students remember how to conjugate both tenses. Then go over the grammar presentation with the class.

- Provide more examples to make clear the difference between a past action that is presented as completed, and a past action that lasts a certain time, without mentioning the end. For example: *Mack manejó un autobús ayer* vs. *Mack trabajaba como conductor.*

- Act out some sentences to review the contrast between preterite and imperfect used in the same sentence to talk about past actions that coincide in time (e.g., *Me duchaba cuando sonó el teléfono*).

Activities

50. Provide more examples to be translated: *Cuando estábamos en Caracas, perdimos el pasaporte. Cuando Tim y Mack estacionaban el autobús, llegó la policía. Mientras Mack hablaba con la policía, Tim llamó a su mamá por teléfono.*

Gramática

Narrar hechos pasados. El pretérito y el imperfecto

- The preterite and the imperfect are past tenses:
  - In general, use the **preterite** to talk about past actions or events that are presented as completed actions.

    Tim y Mack **llegaron** ayer a Venezuela.

  - On the other hand, use the **imperfect** to talk about ongoing actions or events in the past, without mentioning the end.

    Mack **manejaba** muy mal el autobús.

- The preterite and the imperfect are used frequently in the same sentence to talk about past actions that coincided in time:

  Cuando <u>llegaste</u>, <u>yo hablaba por teléfono</u>. (I was talking on the phone and,
  Acción terminada   Acción en desarrollo   at that moment, you arrived.)

  In these cases, you can also use the past progressive:

  Cuando llegaste, yo **estaba hablando** por teléfono.

- To relate two past actions you can use the conjunctions cuando and mientras:

  Cuando salí a la calle, empezó a llover.
  Mientras caminaba, pasó un taxi.

Usos del pretérito y el imperfecto

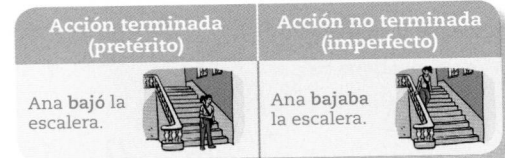

Acción terminada (pretérito)	Acción no terminada (imperfecto)
Ana **bajó** la escalera.	Ana **bajaba** la escalera.

50 **Piensa.** ¿Cómo se dice en inglés Cuando íbamos al cine, empezó a llover?

51 **Tim pasea por Caracas**

 ▶ **Escucha.** Tim le cuenta a su abuelo lo que le ocurrió mientras paseaba por las calles de Caracas. Escribe si estas acciones se expresan en pretérito o en imperfecto.

1. estar paseando por la calle
2. llamar alguien a Tim
3. hablar con el guía
4. tener un accidente un autobús
5. acercarse Tim y el guía
6. bajar el conductor del autobús
7. llegar la policía
8. estar enojados y gritar

Differentiated Instruction

DEVELOPING LEARNERS

- Have students work with a partner and take turns completing sentences to indicate past actions that either interrupted something (preterite) or were ongoing (imperfect). Give them some examples to get them started.

  A. *Yo estaba leyendo cuando…*
  B. *… María llamó por teléfono.*
  B. *Llené el tanque mientras…*
  A. *… tú hablabas con el conductor.*

- You might want to omit the verb tense (i.e., use the infinitive) in the second part of the sample sentences so students can come up with it.

EXPANDING LEARNERS

- Ask students to name five things that they were doing earlier today or yesterday when something or someone interrupted them. For example: *Estaba estudiando anoche cuando mi hermano empezó a tocar la guitarra eléctrica.* Monitor their correct use of the preterite and the imperfect.

52 **¿Qué pasó mientras…?**

▶ **Escribe** oraciones con estos elementos. Usa la conjunción *mientras*.

Modelo 1. *Mientras subía al coche, oí un ruido.*

1. subir al coche (yo) - oír un ruido (yo)
2. estacionar el coche (tú) - llegar (un policía)
3. ponerse el cinturón (nosotros) - arrancar el coche (el conductor)
4. manejar (ella) - llamar por teléfono (yo)
5. echar gasolina (usted) - comprar un mapa (yo)

53 **Las aventuras de Tim y Mack**

▶ **Completa** estas oraciones. ¿Qué crees que les pasó a Tim y a Mack en Caracas?

1. Mack manejaba el autobús cuando…
2. Tim estaba durmiendo cuando…
3. Mientras Tim echaba gasolina en el autobús…
4. Tim y Mack estaban buscando un restaurante en Caracas cuando…
5. Tim estaba hablando por teléfono con su mamá cuando…
6. Mientras Mack y Tim iban para el hotel…

▶ **Dibuja.** Lee las oraciones de tu compañero(a) y elige una. Dibuja una tira cómica (*comic strip*) para ilustrarla y escribe un diálogo.

54 **Mientras dormía…**

 ▶ **Habla.** ¿Qué cosas inesperadas (*unforeseen*) pasaron ayer en tu casa? Cuéntaselas a tu compañero(a).

Modelo A. *Ayer todos estábamos durmiendo cuando, de repente, oímos la alarma del coche.*
B. *¿Y qué pasó?*

CONEXIONES: LENGUA

Los nombres de las cosas

En español, hay palabras que se dicen de forma distinta según los países. Por ejemplo, en Venezuela, el autobús se llama también *buseta* o simplemente *bus*; en México, *camión*; en Argentina, *colectivo*; y en las Antillas, *guagua*.

55 **Piensa y explica.** ¿En inglés hay también palabras que se dicen de forma distinta según la zona o los países? ¿Puedes poner algún ejemplo?

trescientos quince **315**

HERITAGE LANGUAGE LEARNERS

• Ask students to write a narrative that makes good use of verbs in both the preterite and the imperfect. Tell students that they might write about things they or others used to do, describe what people were like, mention actions that were interrupted, or address actions that had a definite beginning and end.

MULTIPLE INTELLIGENCES:
Logical-Mathematical Intelligence

• Give students the names of several cities that range in distance from your community, some by a few miles and others by hundreds or thousands of miles. Then ask students to research the distance these cities are from your town (or the closest large city), decide which mode of transportation would be the most logical or the most interesting for them to use to get to those cities, and explain their reasons for choosing it.

Unit 6

DESAFÍO 3

Gramática – Narrar hechos pasados. El pretérito y el imperfecto

51. Turn this activity into a writing activity. Have students write a text message that Tim sends to a friend telling him/her what happened.

52. Have students write two more examples using their own experience.

 AUDIO SCRIPT
See page 287J.

 CONEXIONES: LENGUA

Los nombres de las cosas
There are also different ways to name trains and subways. While the word most used to refer to the subway is *metro*, in Argentina you call it the *subte*. In general, if a train is elevated or runs on the surface it is not considered a *metro*, but rather a *tren* or *tren ligero*.

Answer Key

50. *When we were on our way to the movies, it started to rain.*

51.
1. imperfecto	5. imperfecto
2. pretérito	6. pretérito
3. imperfecto	7. pretérito
4. pretérito	8. imperfecto

52. 2. Mientras estacionabas el coche, llegó un policía.
3. Mientras nos poníamos el cinturón, arrancó el coche.
4. Mientras manejaba, llamé por teléfono.
5. Mientras echaba gasolina, compré un mapa.

53. Answers will vary.
▶ Answers will vary.

54. Answers will vary.

55. Answers will vary.

Additional Resources

Fans Online activities
Practice Workbook

315

Unit 6
DESAFÍO 3
Comunicación

Presentation

- In this section, students will integrate the vocabulary and grammar from *Desafío 3* in order to talk about car parts, driving, and actions in the past.

Activities	Standards	Resources
56.	1.2, 1.3, 2.1	
57.	1.3	
58.	1.2, 1.3	
59. Final del desafío	1.2, 1.3	
Tu desafío	1.2, 1.3	

Teaching Suggestions

Warm-Up / Independent Starter

- Ask students to write a list of all the car parts and verbs related to driving that they can remember. Allow them two minutes and then ask them to stop writing. They should not consult their textbooks for this activity.
- Then have students write the following sentences in the most logical order:
  1. *Mack pisó el acelerador.*
  2. *Mack se puso el cinturón de seguridad.*
  3. *Mack metió la primera marcha mientras pisaba el embrague.*
  4. *Mack arrancó el coche.*
  5. *Mack puso la llave en el contacto.*

Preparation

- Ask students to share their responses from the Independent Starter.
- Take 10 minutes to review the vocabulary and grammar themes of *Desafío 3*.
- Refer students back to the *fotonovela* for *Desafío 3*. Have them find all the words that describe different car parts and driving, as well as verbs in the preterite and imperfect tenses that are used to talk about past actions. Do students understand the dialogue better now that they have gone through the vocabulary and grammar from the *Desafío?*
- Have students write a dialogue in which one of them is teaching the other how to drive a stick shift car. Have students act out the dialogue in front of the class.

316

Comunicación

56 El blog de Tim

▶ **Completa** el blog de Tim.

estacionó
licencia
motor
pedales
gasolina
manejar
hablaba

En autobús por Caracas

14 de marzo

Ayer fue un día terrible. Mi abuelo tenía que ___1___ un autobús por las calles de Caracas. ¡Qué desafío tan difícil!

Mientras mi abuelo ___2___ con el conductor del autobús, yo eché ___3___. Después, los dos subimos al autobús. Cuando el abuelo estaba arrancando, se sorprendió, «¡Tiene tres ___4___!» Entonces empezó a manejar. ¡Pero puso la marcha atrás! Yo quise ayudarlo, pero no tengo ___5___ de conducir.

De pronto, el ___6___ empezó a hacer un sonido extraño.

Por fin, el abuelo ___7___ el autobús. ¡Manejar en Caracas no es igual que manejar en San Francisco!

57 Reporteros

▶ **Escribe.** Mira el dibujo y escribe el nombre de estos objetos y personajes.

Modelo 1. *un gato*

▶ **Escribe** una noticia para explicar cómo ocurrió el accidente, por qué chocaron (crashed) los coches y qué daños (damages) tienen.

Modelo *Un hombre iba manejando por una calle. Llegó al semáforo y paró. Entonces…*

Differentiated Instruction

DEVELOPING LEARNERS

- Ask students to work with a partner and write questions asking the partner what he or she was doing when something else happened or someone interrupted the action. Then have them start a sentence using the preterite to describe what happened, plus *cuando* or *mientras* to encourage their partners to complete the sentence with the imperfect. Give them the following examples:
  A. *¿Qué hacías cuando llegaron tus padres del trabajo?*
  B. *Yo hablaba por teléfono.*
  A. *Hice la tarea mientras…*
  B. *… yo hablaba por teléfono.*

EXPANDING LEARNERS

- Ask students to imagine that they had the good luck or misfortune of being on the bus Mack was driving. Have them think about what they would say or ask Mack, and then write a dialogue that reflects this conversation. Some students might treat Mack as if he were another bus driver and not be worried about his driving. Others might want to get off at the nearest stop because they do not feel safe. Encourage creativity! Ask students to read or act out their dialogues in front of the class.

58 **¿Qué pasó?**

▶ **Escribe.** Completa estas oraciones. Luego, compáralas con las de tu compañero(a).

1. Un día, mientras mi papá manejaba...
2. ... cuando mi mamá me llamó por teléfono.
3. Mientras yo echaba gasolina...
4. ... cuando, de pronto, el motor del coche se rompió.
5. Mientras mi mamá estacionaba el coche...

Final del desafío

Abuelo, ¿por qué no ___1___ otra marcha?
poner

Cuando ___2___ cambiando de marcha, el autobús se ___3___.
estar / parar

Claro, ¡es que no pisaste el embrague! ¡Y ___4___ el motor!
romper

Yo ___5___ enseñarte, abuelo, pero no tengo licencia de conducir.
querer

¡Abuelo, nos ___6___ mientras ___7___!
perder / caminar

¿Estás seguro? Bueno, vamos a tomar un taxi.

59 **¡Qué desastre!**

▶ **Completa** el diálogo poniendo los verbos en pretérito o en imperfecto.

 **→ TU DESAFÍO**   Visita la página web. Escucha las preguntas de tu *Minientrevista Desafío 3* y escribe las respuestas.

Activities

56. Turn this activity into a speaking activity. Have students talk in pairs or small groups about a bad driving experience they may have had or they may have known about. Have each pair or group share these experiences with the class.

57. You can turn this activity into a game. Divide the class into groups and provide each group with a set of 3 × 5 cards to practice car parts and driving words. Write a different word on each card. In turns, one member of each group should pick up a card and provide a definition for his or her group. Each group should start the definition at the same time.

As an alternative to writing the news about the accident, have students pretend they are policemen and they must write a report on the accident.

58. Ask students to explain their choice of verb tense for each of the sentences in this activity.

59. Have student improvise a conversation between Tim and Mack and the cab driver.

Answer Key

56.
1. manejar   5. licencia
2. hablaba   6. motor
3. gasolina   7. estacionó
4. pedales

57.
2. un coche   5. la rueda
3. la ventanilla   6. el paso de cebra
4. el faro   7. el semáforo
▶ Answers will vary.

58. Answers will vary.

59.
1. pusiste   5. quise
2. estaba   6. perdimos
3. paró   7. caminábamos
4. rompiste

Additional Resources

Fans Online activities
Practice Workbook

HERITAGE LANGUAGE LEARNERS

• Have students summarize in writing what happened during this challenge. Then ask them to conclude their summary with an appropriate *moraleja* (moral). Remind students that a moral is the lesson to be learned from a story. Ask students to read aloud their summaries as well as *las moralejas*. Discuss the different lessons to be learned from this *desafío*.

TOTAL PHYSICAL RESPONSE (TPR)

• Divide the class into teams and appoint one student from each team to be the "word keeper." Explain that now that they know words and expressions related to cars and driving, they will play a game in which each team member says one word or expression (e.g., *el cinturón de seguridad*). Each of the other team members must, in turn, say another word related to cars and driving without repeating any along the way. Team members who repeat or cannot come up with any words are out. The winner is the last student standing, or the team with the most players still standing.

317

Unit 6
DESAFÍO 4

Contar una anécdota en pasado

Presentation

- In *Desafío 4*, Diana and Rita must harvest, roast, and grind enough coffee beans to make themselves a delicious cup of Colombian coffee.

- In this section, students will preview:
  - Vocabulary used in banks and hotels.
  - Using the preterite and the imperfect tenses to narrate events in the past.

Activities	Standards	Resources
Fotonovela	1.2, 2.2, 3.2	Vis. Pres.
60.	1.2, 2.2	
61.	1.2, 1.3, 2.1	
62.	1.2, 1.3	Audio
63. Cultura	1.1, 1.2, 2.2, 3.2, 4.2, 5.2	Video
Tu desafío	1.2, 2.2, 3.2, 5.1	

Teaching Suggestions

Warm-Up / Independent Starter

- Have students read the introduction and look at the pictures of this *fotonovela*. Ask them to write four to five questions about the photos.

Preparation

- Have students work in pairs to answer each other's questions from the Independent Starter.

 La fotonovela

Before Viewing

- In the same pairs, have students ask and answer the following questions: *¿Tomas café normalmente? ¿Sabes prepararlo? ¿En qué lugares se vende?*

After Viewing

- Divide the class into small groups to brainstorm vocabulary related to coffee cultivation, processing, and drinking. Then have groups write a poem about coffee. (It doesn't need to rhyme.) Compile the poems and share them with the entire class.

Activities

60. Have pairs of students reread the *fotonovela* and generate a list of words that they don't recognize. Have them share these lists with another pair to see if they can help each other identify the meaning.

El mejor café del mundo

Coffee is the most well-known Colombian export. But do we really know how coffee beans become a tasty cup of coffee? Diana and Rita must harvest, roast, and grind enough coffee beans to make themselves a delicious cup of Colombian coffee.

> ¡Nela, esta hacienda es impresionante!

> Gracias. Mi padre venía mucho a esta zona. Un día vio la casa, se enamoró de ella y la compró.

> Mi padre dirigía la hacienda, pero el año pasado ocupé su lugar.

> ¿Tienes muchos huéspedes?

> Sí. Antes solo trabajábamos en el café, pero ahora también nos dedicamos al turismo.

> ¿Reservaron dos habitaciones sencillas?

> No, pedimos una habitación doble.

> Ah, sí, aquí está. Una habitación doble con dos camas y baño completo.

> ¿Cómo se recoge el grano?

> A mano. Una vez trajeron máquinas, pero rompían las plantas. Después les enseño cómo se prepara el café.

Continuará...

60 Detective de palabras

 Une cada palabra con su definición.

(A)
1. hacienda cafetera
2. recepción
3. habitación doble
4. habitación sencilla
5. huésped

(B)
a. Lugar donde se recibe a los clientes en un hotel.
b. Persona que se aloja en un hotel.
c. Dormitorio para una persona.
d. Plantación de café.
e. Dormitorio para dos personas.

Differentiated Instruction

DEVELOPING LEARNERS

- To see how well students understood the *fotonovela*, ask them to say whether the following statements are true (*cierto*) or false (*falso*):
  1. *Antes, el padre de Nela venía mucho a la zona.* (cierto)
  2. *Rita y Diana reservaron dos habitaciones sencillas.* (falso)
  3. *Antes, el padre de Nela dirigía la hacienda.* (cierto)
  4. *Ahora Nela dirige la hacienda.* (cierto)
  5. *Se recoge el café a mano.* (cierto)
  6. *Las máquinas rompían el café.* (cierto)

EXPANDING LEARNERS

- Ask students to work in groups of four and memorize the dialogue. Then ask them to come in front of the class and role-play the scenes as if they were making a documentary about travel to a coffee plantation. The fourth student will be the narrator and will need to prepare a short introduction, explaining where the characters are, and the purpose of the documentary. The roles of Nela, Rita, and Diana can be easily accommodated for male students.

61 **¿Comprendes?**

▶ **Responde** a estas preguntas.

1. ¿Dónde están Rita y Diana?
2. ¿Quién dirigía antes la hacienda? ¿Y ahora?
3. ¿Qué tipo de habitación reservaron Rita y Diana?
4. ¿De dónde provienen los ingresos de la hacienda?
5. ¿Cómo se recogen los granos de café?

62 **La reserva**

▶ **Escucha** la conversación entre Nela y Rita y completa estas oraciones.

1. Rita llama por teléfono para ___1___ una habitación.
2. Necesita una habitación para los días 19 y 20 de ___2___.
3. Rita no quiere una habitación sencilla, sino una habitación ___3___ con ___4___ camas.
4. Todas las habitaciones tienen ___5___.
5. Rita prefiere una ___6___ con vistas a la plantación de café.

▶ **Escribe** un diálogo con tu compañero(a) entre el/la recepcionista de un hotel y un(a) turista que reserva una habitación. Después, represéntenlo.

Modelo   A. *Buenos días. Quiero reservar una habitación sencilla, por favor.*
         B. *¿Para cuándo la quiere?*

 **CULTURA**

El eje cafetero

En Colombia hay una zona llamada *eje cafetero* que es el principal centro productor y exportador de café del país. En esta zona hay muchas haciendas cafeteras que funcionan también como hoteles rurales y organizan actividades para conocer sus tradiciones y disfrutar del paisaje.

Las haciendas cafeteras tienen una arquitectura muy característica. Son de madera, tienen grandes balcones y están pintadas de muchos colores.

63 **Explica.** ¿Hay alguna zona en tu país famosa por el turismo rural? ¿Qué tipo de actividades ofrecen allí los hoteles?

▶→ TU DESAFÍO Visita la página web para aprender más sobre las haciendas cafeteras.

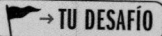

trescientos diecinueve **319**

HERITAGE LANGUAGE LEARNERS

• Have students write a travel blog entry about a trip they took either to their family's country of origin or to another Spanish-speaking country. In addition to describing the place(s) they visited, ask them to comment on what they learned from this trip. If students have not had the opportunity to travel abroad, ask them to explain why they would like to visit a particular country or city, and what they hope to learn from their visit.

COOPERATIVE LEARNING

• Assign students to work in groups of four and explain that they need to create an advertising campaign to promote tourism in their community or state. They should research places of interest, available modes of transportation, accommodations, and recreational activities. Each member of the group should contribute ideas and information, and all will work together to create an effective campaign to convince tourists to visit.

Contar una anécdota en pasado

62. After completing the first part of this activity, have pairs of students reenact the conversation between Rita and Nela.

63. Ask students to explore the web page in order to learn more about *las haciendas cafeteras*. Then have them write a short essay entitled *El mejor café del mundo*. Require that they include an introduction, the body, and a conclusion.

 AUDIO SCRIPT
See page 287J.

 CULTURA

El eje cafetero

Colombia is the third country in coffee production in the world, after Brazil and Vietnam. The fact that Colombia has ports on both the Atlantic and Pacific Oceans has been extremely important in shipping this export to countries all over the world. There are more than 500,000 families dedicated to growing coffee in Colombia's well-drained, rich volcanic soils. The combination of high altitude and moist climate makes for an especially high-quality coffee.

Answer Key

60. 1. d   2. a   3. e   4. c   5. b

61. 1. Están en una hacienda cafetera.
2. El padre de Nela dirigía antes la hacienda, pero ahora Nela la dirige.
3. Reservaron una habitación doble.
4. Del cultivo de café y del turismo.
5. Se recogen a mano.

62. 1. reservar   4. dos
2. noviembre   5. baño
3. doble   6. habitación
▶ Answers will vary.

63. Answers will vary.

Additional Resources

Fans Online activities

319

Unit 6
DESAFÍO 4

Vocabulario – El hotel. El banco

Presentation

- In this section, students will learn vocabulary related to hotel stays and banking.

Activities	Standards	Resources
Vocabulario	1.2	
64.	1.2	
65.	1.2, 1.3, 2.1	
66.	1.1, 1.2, 1.3	Audio
67. Conexiones	1.1, 1.2, 2.2, 3.1, 3.2, 5.2	

Teaching Suggestions

Warm-Up / Independent Starter

- Ask students to go back to the *fotonovela* and read it silently again. Then have them brainstorm a list of items that Diana and Rita might find in their room at the *hacienda*.

Preparation

- Have students share their responses from the Independent Starter. Ask volunteer students to compare different hotels where they have stayed.

- Review the vocabulary presentation with students. Point out the difference between *habitación doble* and *habitación sencilla*. Ask students to look back at the *fotonovela* to see these two words in another contextual sentence.

- Then have students explain the purpose of the items listed. For example: *La llave es para entrar en la habitación.*

Activities

64. To challenge advanced learners, ask them to form a question using each statement. For example: *¿Quiénes se alojan en el hotel? ¿Cuál es el total de la factura?*

65. To help developing students, write the following words, which are necessary to complete the paragraph, on the board: *monedas, cheque, banco, cambiar, habitación.*

66. Review the questions with students prior to listening to the audio recording. Before partners write their dialogues, brainstorm words that will be helpful to students.

Vocabulario

El hotel

Aquí tienen su factura. Una habitación doble para dos personas y una habitación sencilla. Son 50.000 pesos.

los huéspedes

la recepcionista

la recepción

la llave

la percha

la toalla

la almohada

El banco

Necesito cambiar dinero.

Yo voy a sacar dinero.

el cheque

el cajero automático

64 De viaje

▶ **Completa** estas oraciones con la opción correcta.

1. Los _____ se alojan en el hotel.
2. Aquí tienen la _____. Son 20.000 pesos.
3. Necesito una habitación _____.
4. En el hotel cambian las _____ todos los días.
5. Esta es la _____ para entrar en la habitación.
6. Voy al cajero a _____ dinero.
7. Aquí no aceptan _____.

	a. huéspedes	b. recepcionistas
a. moneda	b. factura
a. sencilla	b. reserva
a. toallas	b. llaves
a. percha	b. llave
a. pagar	b. sacar
a. cheques	b. monedas

320 trescientos veinte

Differentiated Instruction

DEVELOPING LEARNERS

- Tell students that the following words in each group are related to either *el hotel* or *el banco*. Ask them to say which word does not belong.

1. *la recepcionista   el cajero   el huésped*
   (*el cajero*)
2. *el cheque   el banco   la percha*
   (*la percha*)
3. *la reserva   la recepción   el cheque*
   (*el cheque*)
4. *cambiar dinero   la toalla   la llave*
   (*cambiar dinero*)
5. *la factura   el huésped   las monedas*
   (*las monedas*)

EXPANDING LEARNERS

- Ask students to describe the steps that they usually take at home when they are preparing for a trip. Then have them describe the steps that they or their families take when they arrive at a hotel. Ask them to use these steps to create a dialogue between a hotel guest and the hotel receptionist.

65 Dólares y pesos

▶ **Completa** el mensaje de correo de Diana a sus padres.

Para:
Cc:
Asunto:

¡Hola!

¿Qué tal están? En Colombia todo va bien. Ayer, la tía Rita y yo tuvimos que ir al 1 a 2 dinero. Por un dólar te dan más o menos 1.800 pesos colombianos. ¿Se imaginan?

Necesitábamos dinero para pagar el hotel porque no aceptan ___3___. La ___4___ cuesta 40.800 pesos por noche. Después de pagar la factura de dos noches y la comida, nos quedaron unos billetes y unas ___5___ y las dejamos de propina.

▶ **Responde** a estas preguntas.

1. ¿Cuántos pesos colombianos recibieron Diana y Rita por un dólar?
2. ¿Cuántas noches se quedaron Diana y Rita en el hotel?
3. ¿Cuánto dinero pagaron en el hotel?

66 En el banco

 ▶ **Escucha** la conversación entre una empleada y un cliente en el banco y responde a estas preguntas.

1. ¿Qué necesita el cliente?
2. ¿Necesita monedas o solo billetes?
3. ¿Qué pide el cliente después?
4. ¿Qué problema tienen en el banco?

▶ **Escribe.** Con tu compañero(a), escribe un diálogo entre un(a) empleado(a) de banco y alguien que necesita cambiar dinero. Después, represéntenlo.

 CONEXIONES: ECONOMÍA

La economía de Colombia

La producción de café es muy importante en la economía colombiana. Colombia exporta café a todo el mundo y también exporta otros productos agrícolas, como plátanos, arroz, cacao o maíz.

Además de los recursos agrícolas, Colombia es un país muy rico en recursos minerales: oro, esmeraldas, petróleo, etc.

Colombia *Supremo*

67 Piensa. ¿Hay producción de café en tu país? ¿De dónde viene el café que conoces?

trescientos veintiuno **321**

Vocabulario – El hotel. El banco

67. You may want to bring in a variety of coffee containers and have students observe the ways in which coffee is marketed. You can also find images of different coffees that show the fair trade logo and discuss what that means.

 AUDIO SCRIPT
See page 287J.

 CONEXIONES: ECONOMÍA

La economía de Colombia
Colombia's main industries are agriculture and mining, with coffee, textiles, and oil being its major export products. Colombian coffee commands premium prices in the world market due to its high quality. Cotton, sugarcane, fruit, grains, flowers, and beef are all products that make up important sectors of Colombia's economy. The United States is its main trading partner.

Answer Key

64. 1. a   3. a   5. b   7. a
   2. b   4. a   6. b

65. 1. banco   4. habitación
   2. cambiar   5. monedas
   3. cheques
   ▶ 1. Recibieron 1.800 pesos.
   2. Se quedaron una noche
   3. Pagaron 40.800 pesos.

66. 1. Necesita cambiar cien dólares.
   2. Necesita billetes y también algunas monedas.
   3. Pide una factura.
   4. No les funciona la computadora.
   ▶ Answers will vary.

67. Answers will vary.

Additional Resources

Fans Online activities
Practice Workbook

HERITAGE LANGUAGE LEARNERS

• Ask students to come up with a list of other terms related to banking. You might want to ask them to say the names in Spanish for the following terms and share them with the other students: credit card, checking account, savings account, deposit, withdrawal, balance, cashier. Ask those students who have familiarity with using ATMs in a Spanish-speaking country to walk the other students through the process, and explain the terms along the way.

MULTIPLE INTELLIGENCES:

Logical-Mathematical Intelligence

• The price quoted for the room (50,000 pesos) might seem very high, until students realize it is approximately U.S. $28. Explain that travelers need to be familiar with the currency exchange rates for the countries they are visiting. These rates can be found in many newspapers or online. Ask students to research the current exchange rates for the currencies throughout the Spanish-speaking world. Then give them some amounts in U.S. dollars and other amounts in the foreign currency and ask them to make the conversions.

Unit 6
DESAFÍO 4

Gramática – Narrar y describir en pasado. El pretérito y el imperfecto

Presentation

- In this section, students will learn to narrate events of the past using the preterite and imperfect tenses.

Activities	Standards	Resources
Gramática	1.2, 3.1	
68.	1.1, 4.1	
69.	1.3	
70.	1.2, 1.3	
71.	1.3	

Warm-Up / Independent Starter

- Have students write two paragraphs in English. In the first one they will answer the following question: What did you do your first day at school? In the second paragraph they will answer the following question: What was going on at school on the first day?

Preparation

- Review the students' Independent Starters. Explain to them that in Spanish the preterite is used to tell "what happened" during a fixed period of time. The imperfect is used to tell "how things used to be" or "what was going on" during a period of time.

- Ask students to conjugate the following verbs in the preterite and the imperfect: *conocer, poder, querer,* and *saber.* Explain the different meanings of these verbs by giving extra examples: *Conocíamos las obras del escritor colombiano pero ayer lo conocimos a él. Sabíamos que era muy bueno, pero ayer supimos que recibió el premio Nobel.*

Activities

69. Before students begin this activity, ask them to do a brainstorming session of other things that could have been happening in the *hacienda* when Diana and Rita arrived. Encourage them to use their imagination. For example: *un cliente tomaba café, unos amigos comían en el restaurante, un gato dormía en el sofá,* etc.

Gramática

Narrar y describir en pasado. El pretérito y el imperfecto

El pretérito y el imperfecto en la narración

- When telling a story in the past, we use both the preterite and the imperfect tenses:
  - Use the **preterite** to talk about past actions or events that happened in the story.
  - Use the **imperfect** to describe characters and setting, and, in general, to explain the circumstances surrounding an event.

  El tiempo en Colombia **era** bueno, pero a veces **llovía**. Entonces nos **íbamos** a la hacienda y **preparábamos** café. Un día **llovió** tanto que no **pudimos** volver y nos **quedamos** en casa de unos amigos.

Narración de acciones o eventos (pretérito)	Descripción y explicación (imperfecto)
Ana llamó por teléfono.	Ana era morena.

Verbos con distintos significados

- Some verbs express a different meaning if they are used in the preterite or in the imperfect.

Imperfect	Preterite
Yo conocía a Nela. (*I knew Nela.*)	Yo conocí a Nela. (*I met Nela.*)
Tú podías ir a casa. (*You could go home.*)	Tú pudiste ir a casa. (*You managed to go home.*)
Ella quería llamar. (*She wanted to call.*)	Ella quiso llamar. (*She tried to call.*)
Tú sabías la verdad. (*You knew the truth.*)	Tú supiste la verdad. (*You found out the truth.*)

68 **Compara.** ¿Cómo se usan en inglés los tiempos del pasado en la narración?

69 **¿Qué hacían?**

▶ **Escribe.** ¿Qué estaban haciendo estas personas cuando Diana y Rita volvieron a la hacienda?

DEVELOPING LEARNERS

- Ask students to complete the following sentences with either the preterite or the imperfect of the verbs in parentheses.
  1. … (llover) mucho ayer. (Llovió)
  2. Por fin … (yo – conocer) a la profesora. (conocí)
  3. Cuando Miguel … (ser) niño, él … (vivir) en Texas. (era; vivía)
  4. Yo … (ver) esa película anteayer. (vi)
  5. De joven, mi padre … (jugar) al fútbol. (jugaba)
  6. Anoche, nosotros … (ir) al teatro. (fuimos)
  7. Yo … (ir) a estudiar, pero Miguel me … (invitar) al cine. (iba; invitó)

EXPANDING LEARNERS

- Ask students to bring in postcards from friends' or family members' past vacations or trips. Based on the images on the cards and their imagination, ask them to write a narrative about these trips, using both the preterite and the imperfect. Alternatively, you may ask them to use e-mails, postings to their wall, blog entries, etc. from their friends or family members as sources of information (and inspiration) for their narrative.

70 **Un día de lluvia**

▶ **Lee** el mensaje de correo de Diana y clasifica los verbos en pasado en una tabla como esta.

Pretérito	Imperfecto
pasó	

¡Hola, Tess!
¿Sabes lo que nos **pasó** ayer? A las cinco de la tarde **salimos** de la hacienda para dar un paseo por el pueblo. Mi tía Rita **llevaba** unas sandalias y yo, unas botas. El tiempo **era** bueno y **hacía** calor. Pero de pronto **comenzó** a llover mucho. Las calles **estaban** llenas de agua y no **podíamos** caminar. Por suerte, **pasó** un autobús y nos **llevó** a la hacienda.

71 **De viaje por Colombia**

▶ **Escribe.** ¿Qué hicieron Diana y Rita en Colombia? Usa el pretérito.

Modelo 1. *Diana y Rita fueron a visitar el Museo del Oro de Bogotá.*

① Museo del Oro (Bogotá).

② Tienda de artesanía.

③ Puesto de fruta en un mercado.

④ Catedral de Bogotá.

⑤ Plato de sancocho.

⑥ Plaza de la Aduana (Cartagena de Indias).

▶ **Escribe** descripciones y circunstancias relacionadas con las acciones anteriores. Usa el imperfecto.

Modelo 1. *Diana y Rita fueron a visitar el Museo del Oro de Bogotá. Cuando llegaron, no había mucha gente.*

Gramática – Narrar y describir en pasado. El pretérito y el imperfecto

70. To expand this activity ask students to determine which sentences are describing something and which ones refer to actions. You may ask them to add two descriptive sentences and two more actions to the message.

71. Start this activity as an oral exercise. Divide the class in two groups and have pairs work together in each group. The students in Group 1 will talk about the actions that Diana and Rita did in Colombia. Students in Group 2 will describe the places that Diana and Rita went to and the food that they ate. Then ask students to share their sentences as you write them on the board. Ask students to combine the sentences of both groups in order to create texts that are richer and more complex.

Answer Key

68. En inglés se usa el pasado para narrar algo que ocurrió en el pasado. En ciertos casos en los que en español se usa el imperfecto, en inglés se usan verbos y expresiones como *would, used to,* etc.

69. A. Hablaban por teléfono.
B. Leían.
C. Cocinaba.

70. Pretérito: pasó, salimos, comenzó, pasó, llevó
Imperfecto: llevaba, era, hacía, estaban, podíamos

71. Answers will vary. Sample answers:
2. Compraron un recuerdo en una tienda de artesanía.
3. Compraron fruta en un mercado.
4. Tomaron una foto de la Catedral de Bogotá.
5. Comieron sancocho.
6. Visitaron Cartagena de Indias.
▶ Answers will vary.

Additional Resources

Fans Online activities
Practice Workbook

HERITAGE LANGUAGE LEARNERS

• Ask students to recommend places of interest to visit in their family's country of origin. Students should accompany each place they mention with a short description, a visual if possible, and an anecdote from their personal experience or their family's experience with the place. If there are students in the classroom who are familiar with Colombia, invite them to elaborate on the places mentioned on this page.

CRITICAL THINKING

• Ask students to discuss the most important factor for them and their families when choosing a travel destination. You might get them started by suggesting the following: scenery and natural wonders; availability of activities such as sports, amusement or theme parks; cultural places of interest such as museums or monuments; cultural events such as concerts or art exhibits; tours to historical sites; rest and relaxation with a pool, a golf course, or tennis courts nearby; good restaurants, and places to go shopping or dancing. Prompt a discussion and be sure all students participate and explain their choices.

Unit 6
DESAFÍO 4
Comunicación

Presentation

- In this section, students will integrate the vocabulary and grammar from *Desafío 4* in order to talk about lodging. They will also use the preterite and imperfect tenses to tell a story in the past.

Activities	Standards	Resources
72.	1.2, 2.2	
73.	1.2, 1.3, 2.2	Audio
74.	1.1, 1.3, 5.2	
75. Final del desafío	1.2	

Teaching Suggestions

Warm-Up / Independent Starter

- Ask students to imagine that they need to make hotel reservations. Have them write the questions they need to ask before calling the hotel.

Preparation

- Have students bring pictures of landscapes. Ask them to work in pairs and describe the pictures in the past using the imperfect. Then, have them create a list of activities that can be done in each specific landscape. Finally, ask them to imagine that they were there on vacation and they have to create a story in the past combining the descriptions with the list of actions they wrote.
- Take 10 minutes to review the vocabulary and grammar themes of the *Desafío*.
- Refer students back to the *fotonovela* for *Desafío 4*. Have them find all the words about lodging and banks, as well as verbs in the preterite and imperfect tenses. Do students understand the dialogue better now that they have gone through the vocabulary and grammar from the *Desafío*?

Activities

72. As a follow-up, ask students to imagine the conversation between Rita and Pablo. Have students write a second letter sent by Rita to Luisa telling her what Pablo told Rita. You may write down some questions on the board to guide students: *¿Qué hacía Pablo en el Parque del Café? ¿En qué hotel se alojaba?*

Comunicación

72 **Una anécdota**

▶ **Lee** la carta que escribe Rita a su amiga Luisa y elige la forma correcta de estos verbos.

> Luisa, ¿cómo estás? Yo estoy muy contenta. Me lo estoy pasando muy bien en este viaje. Estoy en una hacienda maravillosa de la zona cafetera de Colombia.
>
> Ayer mi sobrina y yo ___1___ (ibamos/fuimos) de excursión al Parque del Café. ___2___ (Había/Hubo) muchas palmeras y muchas plantas de café. Diana y yo nos ___3___ (sentábamos/sentamos) a descansar en una terraza y yo tomé el mejor café del mundo. Cuando ___4___ (estuvimos/estábamos) en la terraza, se ___5___ (acercó/acercaba) un turista que ___6___ (llevó/llevaba) un sombrero colombiano. ¿Sabes quién era? ¡Tu primo Pablo! ¡Qué casualidad!
>
> Escríbeme pronto. Un beso.
>
> Rita

73 **¿Cómo era la hacienda?**

▶ **Escucha** la descripción de Diana y Rita. ¿En qué hacienda se alojaron?

Hacienda El Cobre

Antigua hacienda cafetera. Habitaciones dobles grandes y confortables. Todas con baño completo.

Hacienda La Argelia

Vistas fantásticas. Habitaciones dobles (con baño completo) y sencillas (baño opcional). Desayuno incluido.

Hacienda Colibrí

El hotel más barato del eje cafetero.

Posibilidad de hacer cámping. Habitaciones sencillas, dobles y triples.

▶ **Escribe.** Imagina que eres el/la director(a) de un nuevo hotel en el eje cafetero de Colombia. Escribe un anuncio y preséntalo.

Differentiated Instruction

DEVELOPING LEARNERS

- Ask students to put the following events in order, according to the *fotonovela*.
  1. *Mientras Diana molía el café, Rita puso agua en la cafetera.* (5)
  2. *Diana y Rita recogieron los granos de café.* (1)
  3. *Los granos de café se tostaban lentamente.* (4)
  4. *Salió el sol y Diana y Rita secaron los granos de café.* (3)
  5. *Rita y Nela tomaron el café.* (7)
  6. *Empezó a llover.* (2)
  7. *Diana fue a buscar a Nela mientras Rita preparaba el café.* (6)

EXPANDING LEARNERS

- Ask students to write a summary of this *Desafío*, starting from the moment Rita and Diana are given their challenge in Cartagena de Indias, their arrival at the hacienda, to their preparing coffee, and Rita having a cup with Nela. Call on students to read their summaries in front of the class.

324

74 Cuenta un viaje

▶ **Escribe.** Piensa en un viaje que hiciste y haz una lista de acciones (en pretérito) y de descripciones y circunstancias (imperfecto).

Acciones	Descripciones
Fui de cámping a la montaña.	Era verano. Llovía mucho.

▶ **Habla.** Usa tu lista para contar tu viaje a tu compañero(a).

Final del desafío

① Diana y Rita __1__ estar recogiendo los granos de café cuando, de pronto, __2__ empezar a llover.

② Cuando Diana y su tía __3__ volver a la hacienda, salió el sol. Entonces ellas __4__ secar los granos de café.

③ Vieron cómo los granos de café se tostaban lentamente. El olor __5__ ser delicioso.

④ Mientras Diana __6__ moler el café, Rita puso agua en la cafetera.

⑤ Luego, mientras Rita __7__ preparar el café, Diana __8__ ir a buscar a Nela.

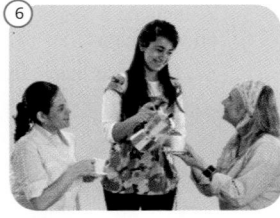
⑥ Al final, Rita y Nela __9__ tomar una taza del café más rico del mundo.

 75 ¡Lo conseguimos!

▶ **Completa.** ¡Por fin lograron hacer las tazas de café! Lee los pies de foto y complétalos con las formas correctas del pretérito o del imperfecto.

trescientos veinticinco **325**

HERITAGE LANGUAGE LEARNERS

• Students have learned something about the process of making coffee in this *Desafío*. Now ask them to describe another process. It could be a description of how some food from their family's country of origin is grown, harvested, and then processed. It could be a product that is manufactured, or some original art, or even a service that is provided to the community. Whatever the product or service is, ask students to write as many details as they can that explain how it comes to be.

MULTIPLE INTELLIGENCES:
Verbal-Linguistic Intelligence

• Many of the e-mails and postcards sent from vacationers to friends and family are often overly cheerful and focus on the positive. Explain that students must now write a card or e-mail to someone back home and describe a vacation that was a total disaster. They should include situations that would make the average traveler try to catch the first plane or train home. Encourage them to be creatively negative and unenthusiastic about their experience.

---

73. Before they begin this activity, have students read the information in the ads and make sure they understand the vocabulary. After they have finished the activity, have students work in pairs or groups and imagine they are looking for a *hacienda* to stay in. Ask them to choose one of the three and explain why they chose it.

74. To expand this activity, have students write a message to their teacher explaining in detail the trip they took.

75. After students have finished the activity, you can start a group conversation about coffee. These are some questions to get students started: *¿Bebes té o café, o ninguno de los dos? ¿Cuántos cafés tomas al día / a la semana? En tu casa, ¿se compra el café molido o sin moler? Después de leer este Desafío, ¿qué sabes sobre el café?*

AUDIO SCRIPT
See page 287J.

Answer Key

72.
1. fuimos
2. Había
3. sentamos
4. estábamos
5. acercó
6. llevaba

73. Se alojaron en la hacienda La Argelia.
▶ Answers will vary.

74. Answers will vary.
▶ Answers will vary.

75.
1. estaban
2. empezó
3. volvían
4. secaron
5. era
6. molía
7. preparaba
8. fue
9. tomaron

Additional Resources

Fans Online activities
Practice Workbook

Unit 6

TODO JUNTO

Presentation

- In this section, students will review the unit objectives and put them into practice.

Activities	Standards	Resources
76.	1.1	
77.	1.2, 1.3	Audio
78.	1.2, 1.3	
79	1.2, 1.3, 5.2	

Teaching Suggestions

Warm-Up / Independent Starter

- Ask students to go back to the vocabulary and grammar presentations in this unit. Have them write a paragraph describing what each of the pairs did and what the places they visited were like.

Preparation

- Have students work in pairs to check their Independent Starter paragraph. Have them exchange the information and together write a more detailed paragraph. Ask students to proofread their paragraph, paying special attention to the use of the preterite and the imperfect verb tenses.

- Ask for volunteers to write their paragraphs on the board, and check with the rest of the class that they have properly used the preterite and the imperfect tenses.

Activities

76. Before doing this activity, do a brainstorming session with students about memories that they have from their childhood. You may divide the board in two columns: *Recuerdos de la escuela* and *Recuerdos de las vacaciones.* To initiate the discussion you may model the activity by sharing with students some of your own memories.

77. As a follow-up to this activity, ask students to write an anecdote. To give students some ideas for writing, you may ask them to share some anecdotes they may have heard of related to a plane, a hotel, or a bank. Model the activity with an anecdote of your own. Remind students to pay special attention to the use of the preterite and imperfect tenses.

326

HABLAR

 76 **De niño...**

 ▶ **Habla** con tu compañero(a). ¿Qué hacías de pequeño(a) en la escuela? ¿Y durante las vacaciones?

Modelo A. *De niño, me gustaba mucho ir a la escuela porque siempre estábamos jugando.*
B. *A mí también me gustaba. Nosotros jugábamos al fútbol.*

ESCUCHAR Y ESCRIBIR

 77 **¡Qué mala suerte!**

 ▶ **Escucha** a Tess. ¿Qué le pasó en Colombia? Escribe dos cosas que pasaron en cada lugar.

Modelo *En el avión, Tess se sentó en su asiento. Después...*

1. En el avión... 2. En el hotel... 3. En el banco...

326 trescientos veintiséis

Differentiated Instruction

DEVELOPING LEARNERS

- Ask students to identify the word that does not belong in each group.

1. *el andén el vagón la factura*
(la factura)
2. *las maletas la vía el equipaje*
(la vía)
3. *el equipaje la bolsa la tarifa*
(la tarifa)
4. *aterrizar estacionar despegar*
(estacionar)
5. *la llave el pasillo la habitación*
(el pasillo)
6. *conducir estacionar reservar*
(reservar)

EXPANDING LEARNERS

- Ask students to work with a partner and to interview each other about their childhoods. They should find out what their partners were like and what they used to do. Tell them to take brief notes from the interview. Then ask students to write a narrative that describes what their partners were like as children, and what they liked to do. Call on students to read their narratives aloud.

LEER

 78 El viaje de Sandra

▶ **Completa** esta conversación poniendo los verbos en pretérito o en imperfecto.

SANDRA: ¡Hola, Louise!

LOUISE: ¡Hola, Sandra! ¿Cuándo ___1___ de tu viaje?
_{volver}

SANDRA: Ayer por la noche.

LOUISE: ¿Y qué hiciste? Cuéntame cosas.

SANDRA: El lunes nosotros ___2___ a Bogotá. Yo ___3___
_{llegar}   _{estar}
un poco cansada porque el avión salió con retraso y llegamos
muy tarde. Mis amigos y yo ___4___ un taxi y fuimos al hotel.
_{tomar}

LOUISE: ¿Cómo era el hotel?

SANDRA: ___5___ muy grande y estaba muy bien situado, en el centro
_{Ser}
de la ciudad.

LOUISE: ¿Y qué hiciste en Bogotá?

SANDRA: Caminé por el centro histórico y tomé muchas fotos. Luego almorcé
en un restaurante fantástico. La comida ___6___ buenísima.
_{estar}

LOUISE: ¿Fuiste a algún sitio famoso?

SANDRA: Sí, claro. Yo ___7___ el Museo del Oro. También vi la catedral
_{visitar}
y di un paseo por el Parque de la Independencia.

LOUISE: ¿Y compraste muchas cosas?

SANDRA: No. Un día ___8___ en un mercado de artesanía, pero no ___9___ mucho
_{estar}   _{tener}
dinero. Solo ___10___ algunos regalos. Y a ti te ___11___ un recuerdo.
_{comprar}   _{traer}

LOUISE: ¡Qué bien! Muchas gracias, Sandra. ¿Nos vemos mañana?

SANDRA: Claro, llámame. Hasta mañana.

ESCRIBIR Y LEER

79 El mejor viaje

▶ **Escribe.** Imagina que ayer volviste de un viaje a otro país. Escribe un *post*
en un blog de viajes sobre tus vacaciones. Puedes incluir esta información:

a. ¿Adónde fuiste? ¿Cuándo fuiste?

b. ¿Cómo era ese lugar?

c. ¿Qué medios de transporte utilizaste?

d. ¿Cómo eran los hoteles en los que te alojaste? ¿Y la gente?

e. ¿Qué hiciste allí? ¿Te pasó algo divertido?

▶ **Lee** el blog de tu compañero(a) y escribe un comentario.

trescientos veintisiete 327

---

78. You may use this activity as an assessment to make sure students have understood the use of the preterite and the imperfect. Before they begin this activity, ask them to organize the information in the letter by identifying the actions (what people did), and the descriptions of people, things, or places (where they were, how they were feeling, what they were like).

79. You may turn this activity into an oral activity by having pairs of students interview each other. Make sure they take turns asking and answering questions. Then you may ask them to role-play the activity in front of the class.

AUDIO SCRIPT
See page 287J.

Answer Key

76. Answers will vary.

77. Answers will vary. Sample answers:
   1. En el avión, Tess se sentó en su asiento. Después una auxiliar de vuelo la llevó a primera clase.
   2. En el hotel, Tess pidió la llave, subió a la habitación y llamó a una amiga.
   3. En el banco, le pidieron el pasaporte para cambiar dinero, así que volvió al hotel a buscarlo.

78.
1. volviste	7. visité
2. llegamos	8. estuve
3. estaba	9. tenía
4. tomamos	10. compré
5. Era	11. traje
6. estaba	

79. Answers will vary.
   ▶ Answers will vary.

Additional Resources

Fans Online activities
Practice Workbook

HERITAGE LANGUAGE LEARNERS

• Invite students to bring in brochures (or show a travel webpage) from their family's country of origin or another Hispanic country that promote tourism to the United States. Ask them to address the tours that are available, the monuments and landmarks that seem to be the most popular, the cost of these trips, where and how payment can be made, and what documents these travelers need. Then ask students to compare and contrast this information with what they think American citizens are interested in seeing and what documents they need if they were to visit the aforementioned country.

COOPERATIVE LEARNING

• Have students work in groups of three and tell them to imagine that they have been given $100,000 to spend on a dream vacation around the world. First, they should decide from which city in the United States they will depart. Then they need to name countries and cities they would like to visit and the reasons for visiting them, and name the mode of transportation they will take to get there. They can name other traveling companions if they wish, and should describe the accommodations they hope to find. Ask students to describe their plans to the class.

Unit 6
El encuentro

Presentation

- The four pairs gather in a plaza near San Felipe de Barajas Castle, in Cartagena de Indias. There they must share their anecdotes to prove the completion of their challenge.

- Students will vote for the winner of the *Desafíos* in the continental Caribbean region.

Activities	Standards	Resources
Fotonovela	1.2, 2.2, 3.1	
80.	1.2, 2.1, 2.2, 3.2	
81.	1.1, 1.2, 1.3, 5.2	

Teaching Suggestions

Warm-Up / Independent Starter

- Ask students to close their textbooks and write a summary of each pair's challenge in the continental Caribbean region. Have them use the vocabulary and grammar presented in this unit to represent the *desafío* in each description.

Preparation

- Have students exchange their summaries from the Independent Starter with a classmate. Then ask them to help you write down a complete summary on the board.

- Remind students that in *Desafío 1*, Tess and Patricia traveled to Bogotá, Colombia, where they took a bus to Lake Guatavita. They had to find El Dorado and take a picture of a golden raft. In *Desafío 2*, Andy and Janet traveled to Venezuela, where they had to fly over the rainforest and take an aerial photo of the tallest waterfall in the world. In *Desafío 3*, Tim and Mack went to Caracas, the capital city of Venezuela. There, they had to drive a bus through the busy streets of the city. In *Desafío 4*, Diana and Rita traveled to the coffee-growing region of Colombia. There, they stayed in a hacienda where they had to harvest, roast, and grind enough coffee beans to brew a delicious cup of Colombian coffee.

- Brainstorm with students the kinds of anecdotes that the pairs might be likely to bring back from their adventures. You may want to suggest that students go back to the *fotonovela* for each of the *Desafíos*. Have them look at the pictures and note the participants' facial expressions and body language.

328

El encuentro

En el castillo de San Felipe de Barajas

The pairs gather in Cartagena de Indias, in a plaza near the San Felipe de Barajas Castle, presided by a statue of the heroic Blas de Lezo.

Salimos de Bogotá para encontrar la balsa de oro.

El salto Ángel es una catarata espectacular.

Hicimos una foto, pero no pudimos acercarnos mucho... porque Andy se asustó.

¡Y tuvimos que regresar a Bogotá para encontrarla!

Nos alojamos en una hacienda cafetera y aprendimos a hacer café.

Manejamos un autobús en Caracas.

Sí, pero... ¡el abuelo rompió el motor porque no sabía manejar con marchas!

Yo trabajé muy duro... ¡pero no probé el café más rico del mundo porque no me gusta el café!

328 trescientos veintiocho

Differentiated Instruction

DEVELOPING LEARNERS

- Have students imagine that they are with the participants when they return from their *desafíos*. Ask them to write one question for each pair that has to do with their challenge. For example, they might ask Tess and Patricia: *¿Dónde encontraron la balsa de oro?* And ask Andy: *¿Por qué estabas asustado?*

EXPANDING LEARNERS

- Ask students to explain which of these *desafíos* they would have liked to participate in, and why. Also prompt a discussion about the participants' ability to carry out their assigned *desafío*. Ask students if they were taken aback by how some of the participants reacted. For example, were they surprised by Andy's dizzy spell, or Mack's inability to drive a stick shift? Who do students think did the best job? Be sure students explain why they think so.

80 Las anécdotas de los personajes

▶ **Completa** las anécdotas de los personajes. ¿A qué anécdota corresponde cada oración?

a. El olor era delicioso.

b. Las vistas eran increíbles.

c. Estaba muy nervioso.

d. Era muy bonita, pero allí no había nada.

1

Nuestro desafío parecía fácil: teníamos que fotografiar una balsa de oro muisca.

En un folleto leímos que la balsa estaba en Guatavita. Allí los antiguos muiscas ofrecían oro a los dioses. Entonces tomamos un autobús y fuimos de Bogotá a Guatavita. Llegamos a la laguna. ___1___. Preguntamos a una mujer y nos dijo que la balsa de oro estaba en el Museo del Oro de Bogotá. ¡Y tuvimos que volver a Bogotá!

2

Andy y yo fuimos al salto Ángel en un pequeño avión. Yo estaba muy emocionada, pero mientras volábamos, Andy se mareó.

Llegamos a la catarata y miré por la ventanilla. ___2___. Mientras yo hablaba con el piloto, Andy intentó hacer una fotografía, pero no pudo porque tenía miedo. Al final, tuve que hacerla yo.

3

El abuelo y yo teníamos que manejar un autobús en Caracas. Cuando se sentó, estaba muy sorprendido. Mientras yo le explicaba que en Venezuela se maneja con marchas, él pisó el embrague... ¡pero se equivocó de marcha! ___3___. Al final, el motor se rompió y tuvimos que volver andando al hotel. ¡Pero nos perdimos!

4

La tía Rita y yo fuimos a una hacienda cafetera. La propietaria era muy simpática.

Ella nos enseñó todo sobre el café: recogimos los granos, los secamos, los tostamos y al final preparamos un café auténtico de Colombia. ___4___. Y mientras Rita y Nela se bebían el café, yo me fui a dar un paseo... porque no me gusta el café.

Una anécdota es una historia real sobre algo divertido o curioso. Tiene que ser entretenida. Puedes escribirla usando el pretérito y el imperfecto.

81 Las votaciones

▶ **Lee** las anécdotas de los personajes. ¿Cuál te gusta más? ¿Por qué?

▶ **Escribe** una anécdota real que recuerdes.

▶ **Lee** la anécdota de tu compañero(a). Después, hazle preguntas para conocer más detalles.

Modelo A. ¿Había mucha gente?

B. No, estaba yo sola.

trescientos veintinueve 329

El encuentro

■ Then ask students to work with a partner. Tell them to imagine they are reporters and they must make up questions to ask one of the pairs about their challenge, their experiences during their trip, their difficulties in carrying out the task they were assigned, and their feelings while they were carrying it out. Have pairs write down a list of questions. Then ask them to get together with another pair to interview each other.

La fotonovela

■ Ask for eight volunteers to read aloud what each character says in the *fotonovela*.

■ Have students identify the verbs in the dialogue and give their infinitives. Then ask them to identify the tense of each of these verbs.

Activities

80. Ask students to read each anecdote individually. Then have them choose one of the anecdotes and retell the story to a partner. When retelling the anecdote they should have the books closed.

81. Brainstorm with students the types of anecdotes that they may write about. To initiate the discussion, ask them if something interesting ever happened to them when they were on vacation, or at school. Model the activity by telling them about something interesting that happened to you. Make sure to use descriptions and actions.

Answer Key

80. 1. d   2. b   3. c   4. a

81. Answers will vary.

▶ Answers will vary.

▶ Answers will vary.

HERITAGE LANGUAGE LEARNERS

• Angel Falls is one of the natural wonders of the Hispanic world. Ask students to research another natural wonder in a Spanish-speaking country with which they are familiar and write a brief report describing the site and offering a glimpse at its history and any legends surrounding it. You may want to have them share this information with their classmates. Ask them to read their reports aloud very clearly, and to be prepared to explain any unfamiliar words and to answer questions.

CRITICAL THINKING

• Prompt a discussion about the reasons people have for traveling abroad. Discuss the advantage of knowing another culture and learning another language. Does this outweigh the downside of foreign travel (e.g., long waits at airports, crowded planes and trains, strange surroundings, being taken out of one's comfort zone)? You may also want to talk about changes students would propose to improve the situation of travelers.

MAPA CULTURAL

Caribe continental

Presentation

- This section presents Colombia and Venezuela through facts and physical features so learners can see these countries from other perspectives. The map serves as a reference point for additional cultural readings and activities that expand on the skills students learned in this unit.

Activities	Standards	Resources
Mapa cultural	1.2, 2.1, 2.2, 3.1, 3.2	Video
82.	1.2, 1.3, 3.1	
83.	1.1, 1.2, 2.1, 2.2, 3.1	

Cultural Topics

- **Símbolos nacionales.** Colombia and Venezuela have a common history that goes back several centuries. Both were part of the Viceroyalty of New Granada during the colonial period. When this region gained its independence from Spain, the modern-day countries of Colombia, Venezuela, Ecuador, and Panama formed an independent republic called Gran Colombia from 1819 to 1830.

- **El mestizaje y los bailes.** Colombia and Venezuela also share similar cultural backgrounds, especially along their Caribbean coasts. Indigenous populations, Europeans, and descendants from the slaves the Europeans brought from Africa intermarried and make up today's population. As is also the case with the music from the Antilles, Colombian and Venezuelan rhythms reflect this tri-cultural mix.

- **Cocina del Caribe: color y sabor.** *Arepas* are to Venezuelans and Colombians what tortillas are to Mexicans: a key element of their diet, served with practically every meal. The most common recipe for *arepas* calls for mixing pre-cooked corn flour with water, salt, and butter, and shaping it into a patty that is then grilled, fried, or baked. *Arepas* can be filled with all sort of ingredients (e.g., meat, cheese, beans, ham, etc.) or eaten plain.

Teaching Suggestions

Warm-Up / Independent Starter

- Have students look at the map on this page and choose two places—one in each country—that they would like to visit.

Caribe continental

Mar Caribe — Barranquilla — Cartagena de Indias — Lago Maracaibo — Caracas — TRINIDAD Y TOBAGO — PANAMÁ — VENEZUELA — OCÉANO PACÍFICO — COLOMBIA — Río Orinoco — GUYANA — Bogotá — BRASIL — ECUADOR — PERÚ

Nacionalidades
Colombia → colombiano(a)
Venezuela → venezolano(a)

Colombia y Venezuela están en Suramérica, en la costa del mar Caribe. Los dos países tienen una cultura y una historia común y por eso tienen costumbres y tradiciones muy similares.

– Colombia debe su nombre a Cristóbal Colón. Su capital es Bogotá, donde se conserva un barrio colonial: La Candelaria. Las ciudades más importantes de la región caribeña son Santa Marta, Barranquilla y Cartagena de Indias, una de las ciudades coloniales más destacadas de América.

– Venezuela significa «pequeña Venecia». El nombre se debe a las casas de los indígenas sobre el lago Maracaibo, similares a las de Venecia en Italia. Su capital es Caracas. Tiene islas en el Caribe muy turísticas, como la isla Margarita.

82 **¿Venezuela o Colombia?**

▶ **Lee** las descripciones y clasifícalas en un diagrama como este según correspondan a Venezuela, a Colombia o a ambos países.

1. Tiene costa en el océano Pacífico.
2. Su capital está en la costa.
3. El río Orinoco pasa por su territorio.
4. Tiene un lago muy grande.
5. Limita con Panamá.

Venezuela   Colombia

330 trescientos treinta

Differentiated Instruction

DEVELOPING LEARNERS

- Before students do activity 82, ask them to trace the maps of Colombia and Venezuela from their book onto a blank sheet of paper. Have them shade the countries in different colors. Then ask them to close their textbooks and draw and label the following places on the map they traced:
  – The capital city of each country.
  – The Pacific Ocean and Caribbean Sea.
  – The Orinoco River.
  – The Andes Mountain Range.
Then ask students to open their books and check their answers. Next have them do activity 82.

EXPANDING LEARNERS

- Ask students to use the information they exchanged with their classmates for activity 83 and what they already know to compare in greater detail the Spanish-speaking countries that are part of the Caribbean Basin. Have students consider the music, food, architecture, traditions, ethnic background, and history of the people who live along the Caribbean coast of Central America, and the people from the Antilles, Colombia, and Venezuela. What are the common elements? What are the differences? Do students think there are more similarities than differences?

1. Símbolos nacionales

Colombia y Venezuela comparten los colores de la bandera: amarillo, azul y rojo. Y los dos países consideran la orquídea flor nacional.

(1) Orquídea.

2. El mestizaje y los bailes

Igual que en las Antillas, el mestizaje es una característica cultural en Colombia y Venezuela. Los ritmos africanos unidos a la tradición indígena y española dan lugar a una música con mucho ritmo.

En Colombia los bailes más conocidos son la *cumbia*, en la que suenan tambores, y el *vallenato*, característico de la costa caribeña y con sonido de acordeón. En Venezuela el baile nacional es el *joropo*, que se baila por parejas y es similar al vals. Para tocar su música se utiliza el arpa, el cuatro y las maracas.

(2) Niños bailando joropo.

3. Cocina del Caribe: color y sabor

Un elemento fundamental en la cocina de Colombia y de Venezuela es la *arepa*. Se trata de una torta de maíz que se puede comer sola o con carne y otros ingredientes.

Un plato muy extendido en estos países es el *sancocho*. El sancocho es una sopa hecha con muchos ingredientes: papa, yuca, plátano verde, frijoles y carne.

(3) Arepas.

83 **Recuerda**

▶ **Consulta** los mapas culturales de las unidades 1 (págs. 70-71) y 2 (págs. 122-123) y escribe tres características de Colombia y Venezuela comunes a la cultura caribeña.

▶ **Lee** a tu compañero(a) las características que has escrito. ¿Coinciden?

HERITAGE LANGUAGE LEARNERS

• Ask students to choose one cultural element from the three presented on page 331 and thoroughly research the topic. Suggest that they organize the information on chart paper to do a class presentation. Encourage students to include visuals. If they chose the topic about music and dance, they may include a brief recording or video containing a sampling of the music and dances mentioned in their presentation.

• If time allows, you may want to hold a question and answer session at the end of each presentation.

MULTIPLE INTELLIGENCES:
Musical Intelligence

• Ask students to listen to three songs that exemplify each of the three musical styles mentioned in the cultural topics (i.e., *cumbia*, *vallenato*, and *joropo*). Have students look for the following songs on the Internet and listen to them: "La pollera colorá" (*cumbia*), "La gota fría" (*vallenato*), "Alma llanera" (*joropo*).

• Then ask students to get together in small groups to compare the rhythms, instruments, styles, beat, etc. of these three musical styles. Invite groups to share their opinions and comparisons with the rest of the class. Does the class agree or are there different opinions?

MAPA CULTURAL
Caribe continental

Preparation

■ Invite students to talk about their choices from the Independent Starter and explain why they would like to visit those places. What places received the most interest? Why?

■ Explain that Colombia, with 439,736 square miles, is slightly less than twice the size of Texas. It has a population of 44,725,543 (July 2011 est.)—the third largest population of Spanish speakers, after Mexico and Spain. The highest point in Colombia is Pico Cristóbal Colón (18,947 ft.). Colombia is the only country in South America with coastlines on both the Caribbean Sea and the Pacific Ocean.

■ Venezuela is smaller than Colombia (352,144 sq. mi.) and it also has a smaller population: 27,635,743 (July 2011 est.). It has a long Caribbean Coast (1,740 mi.) and an important inland waterway, the Orinoco River. The highest point in Venezuela is Pico Bolívar (16,427 ft.). Venezuela has large deposits of oil and is one of the world's top exporters of this product.

Activities

83. Before students begin this activity, ask them to create a three-column chart and label the columns *Centroamérica*, *Las Antillas*, and *Caribe continental*. Have them read the cultural topics of each *Mapa cultural* and list, in the appropriate column, the most relevant information from each cultural topic. Then have students circle the common elements to all three regions.

Answer Key

82. Venezuela: 2, 4.   Ambos: 3.
Colombia: 1, 5.

83. Answers will vary. Sample answer:
   – El mestizaje racial y cultural.
   – La música y el baile con influencias africanas, indígenas y europeas.
   – La arquitectura colonial de varias ciudades.
   ▶ Answers will vary.

Additional Resources

Fans Online activities
Practice Workbook

331

LECTURA

El Dorado, ecos de una leyenda

Presentation

- In this section, students will practice and extend their reading skills by reading an informative text about the legend of El Dorado and Lake Guatavita in Colombia. In addition, students will increase their knowledge and understanding of the history of this region of South America.

Activities	Standards	Resources
Lectura	1.2, 2.1, 3.1, 3.2	
84.	1.2, 2.1, 3.1	
85.	1.2, 1.3, 2.1, 3.1	
86.	1.2, 1.3, 2.1, 3.1	
Tu desafío	1.2, 2.1, 3.1, 3.2, 5.1	

Teaching Suggestions

Warm-Up / Independent Starter

- Ask students to read silently the title and headings of the reading. Have them think for a couple of minutes about what they know about El Dorado —both what they have learned in this unit and any other information they might have from previous readings, movies, or popular culture.

Preparation

- Have students meet in small groups to discuss what they know about El Dorado. Invite them to think about, and discuss in their groups, how much of the information we have about El Dorado is myth and how much is based on reality.

- Before reading the passage, point to the Reading Strategy box and ask a volunteer to read it aloud. Explain that the main objective of informative texts is to convey unbiased information about a certain topic. Examples of informative texts include textbooks, news articles, research papers, and encyclopedias.

- To introduce the reading, discuss with students that legends like El Dorado have caused much misery, but that they have also brought about unintended discoveries and fostered artistic creativity. You may want to assign this reading as homework: http://www.pbs.org/conquistadors/orellana/orellana_b00.html.

332

LECTURA

Laguna de Guatavita.

READING STRATEGY
Read informative texts

Informative texts are used to present or **explain** cultural, scientific, or technological information.

Informative texts usually consist of three fundamental parts:

- **Introduction:** the presentation of the topic.
- **Body:** the main section which explains the topic.
- **Conclusion:** the final part which summarizes the information.

The language of informative texts is **objective**, **clear**, **organized**, and **precise**.

El Dorado, ecos de una leyenda

En el siglo XVI los conquistadores españoles creyeron que en América había un lugar lleno de oro y lo llamaron El Dorado. Y durante siglos, aventureros e investigadores intentaron encontrar ese lugar.

La obsesión por El Dorado fue causa de saqueos[1] y destrucción. Muchas personas murieron buscando El Dorado y ahora forman parte de la leyenda.

Los orígenes de la leyenda

La leyenda de El Dorado tiene su origen en un hecho real. Los indígenas de la cultura muisca celebraban un rito en la laguna de Guatavita (Colombia): los nuevos caciques cubrían[2] su cuerpo con polvo de oro y ofrecían regalos a la diosa del agua.

Las grandes expediciones

En el siglo XVI varias expediciones cruzaron tierras desconocidas para buscar El Dorado. La más importante fue la expedición de Francisco de Orellana en 1541. Orellana no encontró El Dorado, pero descubrió el río Amazonas.

El interés por encontrar El Dorado continuó durante siglos. En 1912 unos investigadores vaciaron la laguna de Guatavita, pero encontraron poco oro.

La leyenda continúa

Actualmente, la leyenda de El Dorado forma parte de la cultura popular y es el tema de libros, películas y videojuegos. Igual que hace cinco siglos, El Dorado es hoy un mito envuelto en misterio y aventura.

---

1. *lootings*   2. *used to cover*

332 trescientos treinta y dos

Differentiated Instruction

DEVELOPING LEARNERS

- Informative texts can be intimidating due to the amount of text and data they contain. It may therefore be a good idea to divide the reading process into stages. Ask students to begin by reading the headings and skimming the text. Next, assist them in identifying the topic sentences, which will give them an idea of each paragraph's content. When students encounter unknown words, ask them to resist the temptation to refer to a dictionary. Instead, encourage them to use the context clues to guess the meaning. As they read, have students pause frequently to recap what they have just read.

EXPANDING LEARNERS

- Explain to students that there have been positive and negative consequences to the legend of El Dorado. Ask them to reread the passage with this in mind. Then have them create a two-column chart and label the left column *Consecuencias positivas* and the right column *Consecuencias negativas*. Ask students to list, in the appropriate columns, what they perceive as the positive and negative outcomes of El Dorado.

- Once students have finished their chart, ask them to get together with a classmate and exchange charts. Are there differences in their perception of some events?

COMPRENSIÓN

 84 **El Dorado**

▶ **Decide** si estas afirmaciones son ciertas o falsas.

1. Según la leyenda, El Dorado estaba en Colombia.
2. Según la leyenda, El Dorado era un rey cubierto de oro.
3. La búsqueda de El Dorado originó grandes expediciones.
4. Las expediciones en busca de El Dorado eran muy peligrosas.
5. En el siglo XX encontraron oro en la laguna de Guatavita.

ESTRATEGIA Leer textos informativos

 85 **Orden y claridad**

▶ **Relaciona** cada imagen con un apartado del texto.

  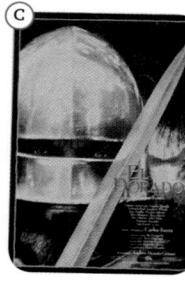

▶ **Resume** en una oración la idea principal de cada apartado del texto.

 86 **Datos, información, ideas**

▶ **Completa** este esquema con las ideas principales y secundarias del texto.

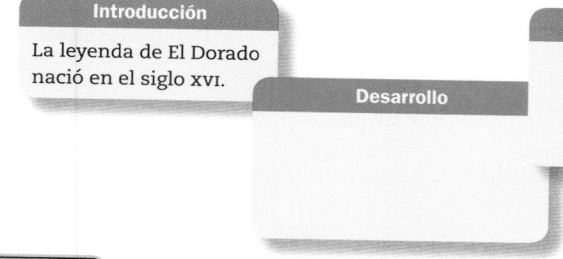

Introducción
La leyenda de El Dorado nació en el siglo XVI.

Conclusión

Desarrollo

 Visita la página web para aprender más sobre El Dorado hoy en día.

HERITAGE LANGUAGE LEARNERS

- Ask students to research a legend from their country of origin. This legend could be associated with a geographic feature (e.g., a mountain, lake, river), an indigenous group, or an episode in the country's history. Have students write a brief informative text to present and explain this legend. They may also include pictures or images to illustrate their text.

- Invite volunteer students to share their informative text with the class. You may want to hold a class vote for the best informative text.

CRITICAL THINKING

- Ask students to consider and discuss the reasons for humans' fascination with legendary places like El Dorado. Why might the prospect of instant riches make people embark on all sorts of risky and improbable ventures?

- Invite students to consider and compare what happened with the search for El Dorado to the California Gold Rush. Could we say that California was a sort of El Dorado? Does our modern society have an "El Dorado"?

LECTURA

El Dorado, ecos de una leyenda

Activities

85. Ask students to read the three sections again and choose an idea that they find interesting. Then have them make a drawing to illustrate that idea. Once students have their images, ask them to get together in small groups and exchange images. Can they associate their classmates' images with a section of the text?

86. Have students work in pairs to help each other identify the main and secondary ideas. Ask partners to alternate reading aloud each paragraph. As one of the partners reads, the other takes notes of what he or she thinks are the main and secondary ideas of the paragraph.

Answer Key

84. 1. C   2. C   3. C   4. C   5. C

85. A. Las grandes expediciones.
B. Los orígenes de la leyenda.
C. La leyenda continúa.

▶ Answers will vary. Sample answers:
Los orígenes de la leyenda: Un rito de los indígenas muiscas de Colombia dio origen a la leyenda de El Dorado.
Las grandes expediciones: En el siglo XVI se realizaron importantes expediciones en busca de El Dorado.
La leyenda continúa: La leyenda de El Dorado forma parte de nuestra cultura popular en la actualidad.

86. Answers will vary. Sample answers:
Introducción: La búsqueda de El Dorado se convirtió en una obsesión.
Desarrollo:
– Un hecho real dio origen a la leyenda de El Dorado.
– Se hicieron muchas expediciones e investigaciones durante siglos.
– No se encontró El Dorado, pero se descubrieron otros lugares.
Conclusión: El mito de El Dorado es parte de nuestra cultura popular actual.

Additional Resources

Fans Online activities

333

Unit 6
REPASO

Vocabulario

Presentation

- In this section, students will review all key vocabulary from the unit, organized by themes, to prepare for an assessment. Students will complete practice activities for each of the four *Desafíos*.

Activities	Standards	Resources
1.	1.3	
2.	1.2	
3.	1.2	
4.	1.2	

Teaching Suggestions

Warm-Up / Independent Starter

- Ask students to imagine that they are going on a vacation trip to Colombia. Have them list ten of the steps involved in planning and taking the trip. For example: 1. *Leer un folleto informativo.* 2. *Comprar el boleto.* 3. *Hacer la maleta.* 4. *Facturar el equipaje en el aeropuerto.* Etc.

Preparation

- Have students work with a partner to compare their lists from the Independent Starter. Ask them to make a new list on chart paper combining their lists. Then have partners think about what would happen once the plane lands and they arrive at their destination. Invite them to think about the hotel(s) where they will stay, the modes of transportation they will use to move around Colombia, how they will pay for things there, etc. Ask students to add more actions to their list to describe, in order, what would happen during their trip.

- Go over the vocabulary with the class. Ask pairs to check their list from the previous activity as you all review the vocabulary. Allow them time to correct any mistakes they find. Then have pairs present their lists to the class. Ask the class to offer their comments and suggestions on each presentation.

- Ask pairs to incorporate into their lists those suggestions that they find most useful and to create a brief *folleto*, or brochure, about how to prepare, what to see, how to move around, etc. on a vacation trip to Colombia. Circulate the brochures around the class and have students choose their favorite vacation plan.

334

REPASO Vocabulario

Viajes y excursiones

la agencia de viajes	travel agency
el/la agente de viajes	travel agent
la bolsa	bag
la estación de autobuses	bus station
el folleto	brochure
el horario	schedule
la llegada	arrival
la maleta	suitcase
el mapa	map
la parada de autobús	bus stop
la puerta	gate
la salida	departure
la tarifa	price
el/la viajero(a)	traveler
ir	to go
volver	to come back
salir	to leave
llegar	to arrive
hacer el equipaje	to pack
perder el autobús	to miss the bus
viajar	to travel
visitar	to visit

El coche

el acelerador/acelerar	gas pedal/to accelerate
el cinturón de seguridad	seat belt
el embrague	clutch
el faro	headlight
el freno/frenar	brake/to brake
el motor	engine
la rueda	wheel
el tanque de gasolina	gas tank
la ventanilla	window
el volante	steering wheel
la autoescuela	driving school
el/la conductor(a)	driver
el/la empleado(a)	employee
la gasolinera	gas station
el/la instructor(a)	instructor
la licencia de conducir	driver's license
arrancar	to start (a car)
estacionar	to park
manejar	to drive
poner una multa	to give a ticket

El tren y el avión

En la estación de tren

el andén	train platform
el/la pasajero(a)	passenger
el vagón	train car
la vía	train track

En el aeropuerto

la tarjeta de embarque	boarding pass
el retraso	delay
el vuelo directo	direct flight
aterrizar	to land
despegar	to take off (plane)
facturar el equipaje	to check luggage
hacer escala	to stop over

En el avión

el asiento	seat
el/la auxiliar de vuelo	flight attendant
el chaleco salvavidas	life jacket
el equipaje de mano	carry–on luggage
el pasillo	aisle
la primera clase	first class
la clase turista	coach class
el boleto sencillo	one–way ticket
el boleto de ida y vuelta	round–trip ticket

El hotel

la almohada	pillow
la factura	bill
la habitación doble	double room
la habitación sencilla	single room
el/la huésped	guest
la llave	key
la percha	hanger
la recepción	reception
el/la recepcionista	receptionist
la toalla	towel

El banco

el cajero automático	ATM
el cheque	check
cambiar dinero	to change money
sacar dinero	to take out money

334 trescientos treinta y cuatro

Differentiated Instruction

DEVELOPING LEARNERS

- Have students go over the vocabulary list, but ask them to cover the English translations with a piece of paper. Ask them to read each Spanish word and think of its meaning. Have students mark with an X all the words for which they don't know the meaning, and ask them to create flashcards for those words. They can use cut outs from magazines and their own drawings for the image side of the cards.

- Then have students get together with a classmate to quiz each other on the vocabulary using the flashcards they created.

EXPANDING LEARNERS

- Have students write a travelogue entry about a trip they have taken. If they can't think of a particular trip they took, ask them to write about a trip they would like to take. Encourage students to use as much of the vocabulary taught in this unit as they can in their entry.

- Once students have finished, have them exchange their travelogue entry with a classmate for peer review. Ask students to offer commentary on their peers' work.

DESAFÍO 1

1 **Un viaje.** ¿Qué ves en estas fotografías? Escríbelo.

 ①  ②  ③  ④

 # DESAFÍO 2

2 **Nos vamos a Venezuela.** Ordena estos pasos de un viaje en avión.

a. facturar el equipaje

b. aterrizar

c. sentarse en el asiento

d. comprar el boleto de ida y vuelta

e. escuchar las instrucciones del auxiliar de vuelo

 # DESAFÍO 3

3 **En la autoescuela.** Completa el mensaje de María.

> Para:
> Cc:
> Asunto:
>
> Mensaje nuevo
>
> Querido papá:
> ¿Qué tal estás? Yo estoy muy contenta. Ahora estoy aprendiendo a ___1___ en la autoescuela Juanita. El ___2___ de la autoescuela es muy bueno. Me enseñó a pisar el ___3___ para llegar a la velocidad apropiada y a usar bien el ___4___ para no tener un ___5___. No te preocupes, papá, siempre llevo el ___6___ para estar segura y sé que hay que respetar la ley para no recibir una ___7___.
> Te quiero mucho, papá, te cuento más mañana.
> Un beso.
> María

 # DESAFÍO 4

4 **En el hotel.** Une las dos columnas.

Ⓐ
1. Llave
2. Percha
3. Recepcionista
4. Huésped

Ⓑ
a. Persona que se aloja en un hotel.
b. Objeto para colgar la ropa en el armario.
c. La necesitas para entrar en la habitación.
d. Persona que trabaja en un hotel.

trescientos treinta y cinco 335

Unit 6

REPASO

Vocabulario

Activities

1. You may bring more pictures to display on the board, and have students identify them. Alternatively, you may ask students to look for images in magazines and books. Then, have them show these images to the class for identification.

2. Once students have finished this activity, ask them to get together with a classmate. Have them draw a plane cabin or look for an image of one on the Internet or in a magazine. Then ask them to label as many things in the cabin as they remember (they should not look in the textbook). Once they have finished, have them look at the vocabulary list on page 334. Did they get most of the words?

4. Before students begin this activity, ask them to work with a partner. Have pairs copy the activity on a blank sheet of paper and add five more words and their definitions from the word box titled *El hotel* on page 334. Then ask pairs to exchange papers with another pair and complete each other's activity.

Answer Key

1. 1. el mapa   3. las maletas
2. el folleto   4. la agencia de viajes

2. d, a, c, e, b

3. 1. conducir   5. accidente
2. instructor   6. cinturón de seguridad
3. acelerador   7. multa
4. freno

4. 1. c   2. b   3. d   4. a

Additional Resources

Fans Online activities
Practice Workbook

HERITAGE LANGUAGE LEARNERS

• Have students look at the official website for the main airport of their country of origin. For instance, if they—or their families—are from Mexico, they should look at the website of Aeropuerto Internacional Benito Juárez (http://www.aicm.com.mx). Ask students to look at the different areas of the airport, the signs, modes of transportation to and from the airport, recommendations for travelers, etc. Do students see words from this unit's vocabulary? Are there any lexical variations? For instance, in Mexico they say *documentar el equipaje* instead of *facturar*. Ask students to report on things that caught their attention.

MULTIPLE INTELLIGENCES:

Verbal-Linguistic Intelligence

• Ask students to look for rhyming words in each of the four vocabulary themes, and have them list the words they find. For instance, in the vocabulary for *El coche*, the words *motor, conductor, instructor,* and *acelerador* rhyme. Once students have their lists of rhyming words, have them get together with a partner to write a rhyme. For example: *Soy el hábil conductor / de un coche con gran motor. / Piso el acelerador, / y no me ve el instructor*. Have pairs recite their rhyme in front of the class. Hold a class vote for the most original rhyme.

335

Unit 6
REPASO
Gramática

Presentation

- Students will review grammatical structures presented in the unit. Each grammar point is cross-referenced to the corresponding page on which it was introduced. The activities here provide systematic practice by *Desafío*.

Activities	Standards	Resources
5.	1.2	
6.	1.2, 1.3	
7.	1.2	
8.	1.2, 1.3	
9. Cultura	1.2, 1.3, 2.1, 2.2	

Teaching Suggestions

Warm-Up / Independent Starter

- Have students use the following prompts to write five sentences.
  1. *Cuando yo era niño(a)...*
  2. *En las últimas vacaciones que tomé...*
  3. *Mi primer día de clases en esta escuela...*
  4. *Mientras los pasajeros subían al avión...*
  5. *No me gustó el hotel porque...*

Preparation

- Invite volunteers to share their sentences from the Independent Starter with the class. Ask students to justify their choice of verb tense (preterite or imperfect) for each of their sentences. As students read their sentences, write on the board some of the sentences that best exemplify the different uses of the preterite and imperfect tenses.
- As you go over the *Repaso* presentation, use the grammatical structures from the sentences you wrote on the board as examples of the grammar being reviewed.

Activities

5. Once students have finished the activity, ask them to complete the three sentences with true information about themselves and about the bus station in their city. Then ask students to compare, for each of the sentences, the situation in the past with the situation now. For example: *Cuando era niño, viajaba con frecuencia en avión. Ahora rara vez viajo en avión.*

336

El imperfecto (pág. 298)

VERBOS REGULARES			VERBOS IRREGULARES		
VIAJAR	VOLVER	SALIR	SER	IR	VER
viajaba	volvía	salía	era	iba	veía
viajabas	volvías	salías	eras	ibas	veías
viajaba	volvía	salía	era	iba	veía
viajábamos	volvíamos	salíamos	éramos	íbamos	veíamos
viajabais	volvíais	salíais	erais	ibais	veíais
viajaban	volvían	salían	eran	iban	veían

Verbos irregulares en el pretérito. *Dar, poder, poner, querer, saber y venir* (pág. 306)

DAR	PODER	PONER	QUERER	SABER	VENIR
di	pude	puse	quise	supe	vine
diste	pudiste	pusiste	quisiste	supiste	viniste
dio	pudo	puso	quiso	supo	vino
dimos	pudimos	pusimos	quisimos	supimos	vinimos
disteis	pudisteis	pusisteis	quisisteis	supisteis	vinisteis
dieron	pudieron	pusieron	quisieron	supieron	vinieron

Narrar hechos pasados.
El pretérito y el imperfecto (pág. 314)

Pretérito	Acción terminada. Ana bajó la escalera.
Imperfecto	Acción no terminada. Ana bajaba la escalera.

Narrar y describir en pasado.
El pretérito y el imperfecto (pág. 322)

Pretérito	Narración de acciones o eventos. Ana llamó por teléfono.	
Imperfecto	Descripción y explicación. Ana era morena.	

336 trescientos treinta y seis

Differentiated Instruction

DEVELOPING LEARNERS

- Ask students to choose the correct form of the verb to complete these sentences.
  1. *El domingo pasado llovía / llovió mucho y no salí.* (llovió)
  2. *El primer día de clase conocí / conocía a muchos compañeros.* (conocí)
  3. *En las vacaciones, me levanté / levantaba tarde todos los días.* (levantaba)
  4. *¿Te pusiste / ponías el cinturón de seguridad la última vez que viajaste en coche?* (pusiste)
  5. *Cuando mi novio llamó por teléfono, yo veía / vi la tele.* (veía)

EXPANDING LEARNERS

- Have students use one of the prompts from the Independent Starter to write a two-paragraph anecdote. They can use as inspiration something that happened to them, a family member, or a friend. Or they can just make up a story.
- Ask students to focus on the plot first as they develop their story. Then ask them to proofread their work and analyze the usage of the preterite and imperfect tenses. Once students have corrected any mistakes they discovered, invite volunteers to share their anecdote with the class.

DESAFÍO 1

5 **Acciones.** Elige la opción correcta.

1. Cuando era niña, nunca _____ en avión.
   viajaba/viajo

2. Antes, la estación de autobuses _____ muy pequeña.
   fue/era

3. De pequeña, yo _____ todos los días con mi perro.
   jugaba/juego

 DESAFÍO 2

6 **En pasado.** Completa estas oraciones con la forma correcta del pretérito.

dar
saber
venir
poder

1. Anoche mis tíos no _____ cenar con nosotros.
2. Ángel solo _____ a la fiesta para ver a sus primos.
3. ¿Tú _____ contestar a todas las preguntas del examen?
4. Mi amiga _____ un paseo por el parque.

 DESAFÍO 3

7 **Interrupciones.** Une las dos columnas.

A

1. Mientras tú echabas gasolina, yo
2. Él iba manejando cuando, de pronto,
3. El policía me puso una multa
4. El teléfono sonó

B

a. porque manejaba muy deprisa.
b. fui a comprar un mapa.
c. mientras estaba estacionando.
d. el coche se paró.

DESAFÍO 4

8 **Mi mascota.** Completa la historia poniendo los verbos en la forma correcta del pretérito o del imperfecto.

Un día, cuando yo ___1___ doce años, ___2___ corriendo por el parque cuando, de pronto,
                        tener   estar
___3___ a un gato solo. Pensé que su dueño ___4___ a venir pronto, así que lo ___5___
 ver   ir   dejar
allí y me ___6___ a casa. De vez en cuando, lo ___7___ en el parque. Un día lo llevé
            ir   ver
a mi casa. ___8___ un gato muy bonito.
              Ser

 **CULTURA**

9 **Por Colombia y Venezuela.** Responde a las siguientes preguntas.

1. ¿Cómo se llama la ciudad de oro que buscaban los exploradores por la selva amazónica?
2. ¿En qué país está el salto Ángel?
3. ¿Qué es el eje cafetero?

---

6. Have students come up with two additional sentences in the preterite using the verbs *poner* and *querer*. For example: *Antes de arrancar el coche nos pusimos el cinturón de seguridad.*

8. Ask students to work with a partner to add five sentences to this story. Encourage them to think about what might have happened with the cat. Did it adapt to living at home or did it try to escape? Once pairs have finished, ask them to read their new story to the class. Invite the class to vote for the most original story.

Answer Key

5. 1. viajaba   3. jugaba
     2. era

6. 1. pudieron   3. supiste
     2. vino   4. dio

7. 1. b   2. d   3. a   4. c

8. 1. tenía   5. dejé
     2. estaba   6. fui
     3. vi   7. veía
     4. iba   8. Era

9. 1. Se llama El Dorado.
     2. Están en Venezuela.
     3. Answers will vary. Sample answer: Es una zona de Colombia con muchas haciendas cafeteras que funcionan también como hoteles rurales. Es el principal centro productor y exportador de café de Colombia.

Additional Resources

Fans Online activities
Practice Workbook

HERITAGE LANGUAGE LEARNERS

• Ask students to leaf through a Spanish-language newspaper (it could be an online paper) and focus on a piece of news that catches their attention. Then have them read it to try to get the gist. What is the news about? What happened? Next, ask students to focus on the verbs used in the text, and identify with a "P" those verbs that are in the preterite and with an "I" those that are in the imperfect. Can students explain why the writer used the preterite or the imperfect in each case?

TOTAL PHYSICAL RESPONSE (TPR)

• Assign to one half of the class the preterite and to the other half the imperfect. Explain that you will say some sentences. When students hear their assigned verb tense, they should stand up and pantomime the action. For sentences that have both tenses, each group should pantomime their corresponding verb.

1. *El año pasado viajé por avión al Caribe.* (preterite)
2. *Esta mañana hacía mucho calor.* (imperfect)
3. *Cuando mi madre entró en la habitación, yo dormía.* (preterite; imperfect)
4. *Mientras esperaba el autobús comenzó a llover.* (imperfect; preterite)

Unit 6

PROYECTO

La laguna de Guatavita

Presentation

- In this section, students will apply the vocabulary, grammar, and cultural information they have learned in this unit to create a travel brochure about Lake Guatavita, in Colombia, and the legend of El Dorado, which is associated with this lake. Students will follow step-by-step instructions.

Activities	Standards	Resources
Paso 1	1.2, 2.2, 3.1, 3.2, 5.1	
Paso 2	1.3, 3.1, 5.2	
Paso 3	1.3, 5.2	
Paso 4	1.1, 3.1, 5.2	
Paso 5	1.3, 5.2	

Teaching Suggestions

Warm-Up / Independent Starter

- Have students read the introduction to the project and all the tasks involved. Then have them think of sources they could use to research the topic. Ask students to list these sources in their notebook.

Preparation

- Discuss, as a class, possible reasons for the endurance of the legend of El Dorado. Why does El Dorado still inspire us today? Why have humans kept seeking El Dorado? Encourage students to keep this discussion in mind when they create their brochure. They should aim to convince people to visit Lake Guatavita, and understanding what fascinates humans about seeking El Dorado is a good way to motivate people to visit this place.

Step-by-Step Instructions

Paso 1

- Ask students to take out their list from the Independent Starter and analyze the usefulness of each source. Have students concentrate on the most useful ones to save time. Remind them that they should list their sources.

- If you wish to expedite the research process, suggest these links. http://science.nationalgeographic.com/science/archaeology/el-dorado/ and http://www.car.gov.co/?idcategoria=3863.

338

Un folleto sobre

la laguna de Guatavita

Lake Guatavita is the presumed site for El Dorado, the "Lost City of Gold."

You will create a travel brochure to advertise a trip to Lake Guatavita. You must include information about the lake and El Dorado, and some advice for travelers.

PASO 1 Investiga sobre el destino

- Do research on the Internet to find the geographic information and legends surrounding Lake Guatavita and El Dorado. Answer the following questions to guide your research:
  - ¿Dónde está la laguna? ¿A qué distancia está de Bogotá?
  - ¿Cómo es la laguna?
  - ¿Cuál es la historia de la laguna?

- Gather images to illustrate your brochure:
  - Fotos de la laguna de Guatavita y relacionadas con El Dorado.
  - Un mapa de la localización de la laguna dentro del país.

PASO 2 Escribe un texto informativo

- Write an informative text about the lake and the legend.

  Organize your text in three parts: introduction, body, and conclusion. Try to make it interesting for someone who is going to travel there.

La laguna de Guatavita y El Dorado

La laguna de Guatavita es una laguna circular. Está a 63 kilómetros de Bogotá, a 3.000 metros sobre el nivel del mar y...

La laguna era un lugar sagrado para...

Rubric for Evaluation

	Content	Organization	Presentation
1 point	Limited relevance. Information is incomplete or not based on research. Little Spanish is used.	Inefficient use of class time. Information is disorganized or unclear. Brochure is not well designed and organized.	Communication is unclear. Delivery is not fluent. Many errors in vocabulary and grammar.
3 points	Basic information is correct. Relevant information but lacks significance. Spanish is used most of the time.	Class time is used well. Information and content are mostly organized but lack some clarity. Brochure is mostly well designed and organized.	Good communication. Fluent delivery. Mostly correct vocabulary and grammar.

PASO 3 Prepara una sección con consejos para el viajero

- Think about basic tips for travelers. These questions can help you.

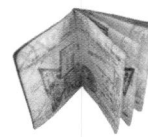

- ¿Es necesario visado?
- ¿Qué ropa debes llevar?
- ¿Hay que vacunarse?

- Write these tips in a short section.

Información práctica
– Visado:
– Ropa y calzado:
– Vacunas:

PASO 4 Haz el folleto

- Fold a piece of paper to make a travel brochure and complete it using this layout:

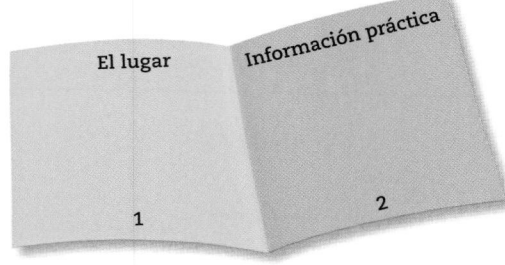

El lugar

Información práctica

1

2

- **Sección 1** → El lugar: la historia de la laguna de Guatavita y sus leyendas.

- **Sección 2** → Información práctica: consejos para viajeros.

- Add the pictures to illustrate your brochure, and compare it to that of a classmate. Take notes on the things you would add or eliminate from yours.

PASO 5 Presenta tu folleto

- Once you have finished, present your final travel brochure to the class.

Unidad 6

Autoevaluación

¿Qué has aprendido en esta unidad?

Do these activities to evaluate how well you can manage in Spanish.

Evaluate your skills. For each item, say Very well, Well, or I need more practice.

a. Can you describe past habits?
▶ Tell a classmate what you need to travel with your friends.
▶ Describe what your vacations were like when you were a child.

b. Can you talk about past actions?
▶ Tell a classmate about your last trip and what you did.
▶ Listen to your classmate's story and ask him or her questions about it.

c. Can you talk about events in the past?
▶ Imagine that last weekend unexpected things happened in your house. Tell two classmates what happened.

d. Can you tell an anecdote in the past?
▶ Think about a funny story that you experienced. Tell your story to a classmate.

	Content	Organization	Presentation
5 points	Relevant, interesting information. Many details and significance are highlighted. Spanish is used exclusively.	Class time is used wisely. Information and content are clearly organized visually and logically. Brochure is very well designed and organized.	Clear communication. Correct and complete vocabulary and grammar. Very motivating upbeat delivery.

PROYECTO

La laguna de Guatavita

Paso 2

- Remind students that the main purpose of informative texts is to convey information about the natural or social world. An informative text in this case would describe the attributes and characteristics of Lake Guatavita. Encourage students to strive to address the travelers' interests and questions about this area of Colombia.

Paso 3

- Explain to students that a good source of information for American travelers is the U.S. Department of State Consular Information Sheet. Students will find information specific to Colombia at: http://travel.state.gov/travel/cis_pa_tw/cis/cis_1090.html.

Paso 4

- If access to computers with brochure creation software is available to all of the students, you may want to ask them to use this software for the brochure layout. This will give their brochures a more professional look.

Paso 5

- Encourage students to interact with their audience as they present their brochures. Emphasize the importance of having eye contact with their listeners as a way of keeping them all interested.

Evaluation

- Distribute copies of the rubric to students. Discuss the evaluation criteria and explain how this project will be graded. Encourage students to refer to the rubric as they prepare their projects.

Content

- There isn't much space in a brochure for extensive explanations; therefore, students should select information that is relevant and interesting. Ask students to include a list of sources.

Organization

- Ask students to pay attention to the instructions on how to organize their informative text given in *Paso 2*. Remind them to keep in mind the importance of headings and captions when organizing the different sections and images of their brochure.

Presentation

- Students should use as much Spanish as possible. Have them remember to speak slowly and clearly, and encourage them to use a presentation style that will hold their classmates' attention.

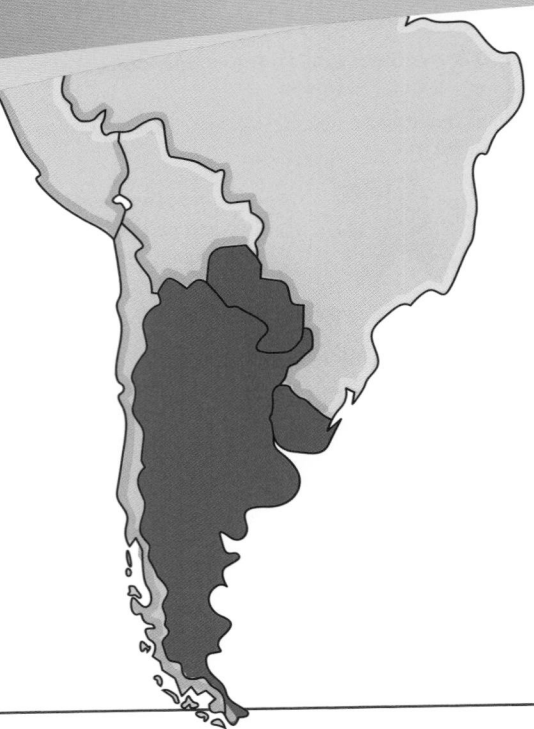

Objectives

- To identify people and things.
- To express wishes.
- To express feelings and emotions.
- To make value statements.
- To express opinion.
- To express agreement or disagreement.
- To talk about school.
- To identify existence of people and things.

- To discuss various professions.
- To talk about free-time activities.
- To talk about sports and actions related to sports.
- To express value and doubt.
- To explore cultural aspects of the region surrounding the Río de la Plata.

Contents

Vocabulary

- Parts of the school.
- Subjects in school.
- Actions associated with learning.
- Professions.
- Free-time activities and hobbies.
- Board games.
- Sports and actions related to sports.
- Words to express opinion.
- Words to express agreement and disagreement.

Grammar

- To express existence: Indefinites.
- To express wishes: The subjunctive mood.
- To express feelings using regular and irregular verbs in the subjunctive mood.
- To express doubt in the subjunctive mood.
- To make value statements in the subjunctive mood.

Culture

- The Guaraní language.
- The University of Asunción.
- *Requisitos: hablar guaraní.*
- *La Ciudad Vieja de Montevideo.*
- Jorge Drexler.
- The Uruguayan monetary system.
- The tango dance.
- The popularity of soap operas in Latin America.
- *El barrio de La Boca.*
- *El Aconcagua.*
- The importance of soccer in Argentina.
- Buenos Aires.
- The Río de la Plata region.
- Mario Benedetti.

Evaluation Criteria

- Use expressions to state an opinion.
- Use expressions to show agreement.
- Use expressions to show disagreement.
- Identify parts of the school.
- Discuss class schedules and identify classes.
- Demonstrate understanding of the actions associated with learning.
- Use indefinites to express the existence of people and things.

- Talk about professions and future aspirations.
- Express wishes in a straightforward way.
- Identify free-time activities and the places where they are performed.
- Express feelings, emotions, or opinions using regular and irregular verbs in the subjunctive mood.
- Talk about sports and actions associated with sports.

- Express doubt using the subjunctive mood.
- Make value statements using the subjunctive mood.
- Express understanding of cultural aspects of the region surrounding the Río de la Plata.
- Read a narrative text, understanding its characteristics as a reading strategy.
- Create the script to a *telenovela*.

Unit Plan

La llegada

Estimated time: 1 session.

Dialogue: *En Córdoba.*

Functions & forms:
- Expressions of opinion.
- Expressions of agreement and disagreement.

Culture:
- Plaza San Martín, Córdoba, Argentina.

DESAFÍO 1

Estimated time: 4 sessions.

Dialogue: *¿Un idioma imposible?*

Functions & forms:
- Parts of the school.
- Subjects in school.
- Actions associated with learning.
- To express existence: Indefinites.

Culture:
- *El guaraní.*
- *La Universidad de Asunción.*
- *Requisitos: hablar guaraní.*

DESAFÍO 2

Estimated time: 4 sessions.

Dialogue: *¡Ojalá encontremos a Bruno!*

Functions & forms:
- Professions.
- To express wishes: The subjunctive mood.

Culture:
- *La Ciudad Vieja de Montevideo.*
- *Jorge Drexler.*
- *La moneda de Uruguay.*

DESAFÍO 3

Estimated time: 4 sessions.

Dialogue: *Estrellas de telenovela.*

Functions & forms:
- Free-time activities and hobbies.
- Board games.
- To express feelings using regular and irregular verbs in the subjunctive mood.

Culture:
- *El tango.*
- *Las telenovelas.*
- *El barrio de La Boca.*

DESAFÍO 4

Estimated time: 4 sessions.

Dialogue: *El clásico y el Aconcagua.*

Functions & forms:
- Sports and actions related to sports.
- To express doubt in the subjunctive mood.
- To assign value in the subjunctive mood.

Culture:
- *El Aconcagua.*
- *El fútbol argentino.*

TODO JUNTO / El encuentro

Estimated time: 1 session.

Dialogue: *En la Manzana Jesuítica de Córdoba.*

Functions & forms:
- Review of *Desafíos 1–4.*

Culture:
- *Buenos Aires.*
- The Manzana Jesuítica, Córdoba, Argentina.

MAPA CULTURAL / LECTURA

Estimated time: 1 session.

Mapa cultural: *Río de la Plata.*

Reading: *Un cuento de Benedetti.*

PROYECTO

Estimated time: 1 session.

Project: *Un guión para una telenovela.*

Unit 7 Río de la Plata

Standards for Learning Spanish

COMMUNICATION

1.1. Interpersonal mode
- Discuss the challenge for each team in the selected South American countries.
- Discuss what students know about Paraguay, Uruguay, and Argentina.
- Speculate on which pair will win the challenge.
- Discuss class schedules and the school environment with classmates.
- Plan a sporting event.
- Discuss how official languages are chosen in different countries.
- Reply to an e-mail with personal opinions and knowledge.
- Interview classmates.

1.2. Interpretive mode
- Take notes from an oral text.
- Read a cultural text.
- Read an e-mail.
- Research cultural topics.
- Associate oral descriptions with pictures.
- Understand written exchanges between friends.
- Draw conclusions from a classmate's answers to an interview question.

1.3. Presentational mode
- Present opinions to the class.
- Use a chart to display the results of a survey.
- Write a description of a photograph.
- Write a paragraph about what you like to do on vacation.
- Write interview questions.
- Write an e-mail to a friend about your classmates.
- Read an original essay aloud.

CULTURE

2.1. Practices and perspectives
- Investigate the origins of a popular dance.
- Understand about the popularity of soap operas in Latin America.
- View photographic depictions of historical sites.
- Understand the value of speaking a second or native language.

2.2. Products and perspectives
- Read about a special neighborhood in Buenos Aires.
- Understand the national sport of Argentina.
- Learn about the singer Jorge Drexler.
- Discover new facts about the University of Asunción.
- Analyze the touristic features of Montevideo.

CONNECTIONS

3.1. Interdisciplinary connections
- Explore South American geography and its history.
- Learn about the largest city in Latin America.
- Discover more information about the Guaraní language.
- Investigate the characteristics that are needed to work in certain professions.
- Determine the difference between the subjunctive in English and in Spanish.

3.2. Viewpoints through language / culture
- Discover aspects of South American history and culture.
- Learn about why countries have more than one official language.
- Explore the cultural benefits of knowing a second language.
- Understand the influence of foreign nationals on a country.

COMPARISONS

4.1. Compare languages
- Compare indefinites in English and in Spanish.
- Compare expressions that make a value statement or express doubt in English and in Spanish.
- Compare the percentages of a population that speak English and Spanish.
- Compare the subjunctive in English and in Spanish.

4.2. Compare cultures
- Compare regional vocabulary differences in Spanish and in English.
- Compare faces and symbols on money in South America and in the United States.
- Compare neighborhoods in South America and in the United States.
- Compare the popularity of soccer in Argentina and in the United States.

COMMUNITIES

5.1. Spanish within and beyond the school setting
- Describe the places in your community where someone could do schoolwork or research.
- Investigate the Guaraní language.
- Research and develop a script for a *telenovela*.

5.2. Spanish for lifelong learning
- Develop a relationship with a pen pal.
- Understand the importance of learning a second language for use in a future profession.

Communicative Skills

Interpersonal Mode

		Activities
Speaking	• Engage in conversation with a classmate. • Compare information with a classmate. • Talk with a classmate about opinions and preferences. • Interview a classmate.	• 10, 31, 35, 63, 64, 68, 78, 80, 81 • 13, 75 • 9, 73, 78, 80, 81 • 18, 47
Writing	• Write a passage to express a personal opinion or knowledge on a subject. • Write passage to compare personal knowledge with acquired knowledge. • Write an e-mail.	• 3, 14, 15, 27, 32, 45, 49, 50, 79 • 36, 54, 69 • 21
Listening	• Understand verbal questions and respond appropriately. • Understand someone's personal opinion.	• 9, 18, 47 *Minientrevistas* • 2, 34, 46, 52, 56, 76
Reading	• Understand the information in a letter or an e-mail. • Understand a narrated story.	• 21, 57, 59, 79 • 23, 81, 86, *Lectura*

Interpretive Mode

		Activities
Listening	• Understand someone's personal opinion. • Obtain information from an oral exchange. • Obtain cultural information from audio and video. • Understand oral descriptions. • Interpret a classmate's answers and draw conclusions.	• 34, 46, 52, 56, 76 • 2, 72, 80 • *Tu desafío, videos* • 8, 12, 13, 28, 34, 37, 46, 52, 55, 67 • 18, 47, 48
Reading	• Understand brief written exchanges. • Demonstrate an understanding of written dialogues. • Draw comparisons or conclusions from a cultural text. • Resolve a classmate's mystery message. • Draw conclusions from written descriptions or a narrative text.	• *Fotonovelas*, 17, 59 • 1, 7, 41, 43, 61, 89 • 10, 14, 19, 27, 36, 49, 54, 64, 69, 81 • 23 • 31, 38, 57, 86, *Lectura*

Presentational Mode

		Activities
Speaking	• Present the results of an interview. • Read an original passage to classmates. • Describe the actions pictured in a photograph.	• 18, 53 • 21, 23, 48, 86 • 22, 25, 44, 47, 58, 62, 76, 78
Writing	• Chart the results of a questionnaire to display understanding. • Write a dialogue to be presented to the class. • Write an original passage. • Write interview questions.	• 2, 12, 38, 46, 55, 65 • 41, *Proyecto* • 48, 57, 79, 85, 86, 90 • 53

Cross-Curricular Standards

Subject	Standard	Activities
Language Arts	• Read a narrative text. • Compare use of the subjunctive mood in English and Spanish. • Write an original passage.	• *Mapa cultural, Lectura* • 33 • 48, 57, 79, 85, 86, 90
Social Studies	• Learn about dances from different cultures. • Learn about the culture in a neighborhood from another country.	• 45 • 54
Geography	• Read about the the highest mountain in the Southern Hemisphere.	• 64
Math	• Convert meters to feet.	• 66

Lesson Plans (50-Minute Classes)

Day	Objectives	Sessions	Activities	Time	Standards	Resources/Homework
1	To introduce selected South American countries and to discuss the pairs' challenges	**Río de la Plata / La llegada** (340–345) • Warm-Up: Countries orientation • *Río de la Plata* • Images and functions • Presentation: *En Córdoba* • *Expresiones útiles* and *¿Quién ganará?*	1 2–5	5 m. 5 m. 10 m. 10 m. 20 m.	1.1, 1.2, 1.3, 2.2, 4.1, 5.1, 5.2	Visual Presentation Audio Video Practice Workbook
2	To identify a person or object	**Desafío 1 – ¿Un idioma imposible?** (346–347) • Warm-Up: Independent Starter • *Fotonovela: ¿Un idioma imposible?* • *Cultura: El guaraní*	6–9 10	5 m. 35 m. 10 m.	1.1, 1.2, 1.3, 2.1, 2.2, 3.1, 3.2, 5.1	Visual Presentation Audio *Tu desafío*
3	To talk about school	**Desafío 1 – Vocabulario** (348–349) • Warm-Up: Independent Starter • Vocabulary: *La escuela* • *Cultura: La Universidad de Asunción*	11–13 14	5 m. 35 m. 10 m.	1.1, 1.2, 1.3, 2.2, 3.1, 5.1	Audio Practice Workbook *Tu desafío*
4	To express existence of people and things	**Desafío 1 – Gramática** (350–351) • Warm-Up: Independent Starter • Grammar: *Expresar existencia. Los indefinidos* • *Cultura: Requisitos: hablar guaraní*	15–18 19	5 m. 35 m. 10 m.	1.1, 1.2, 1.3, 2.1, 3.1, 4.1, 5.2	Audio Practice Workbook
5	To integrate vocabulary and grammar and to assess student proficiency	**Desafío 1 – Comunicación / Evaluación** (352–353) • Warm-Up: Independent Starter • *Comunicación:* Review • *Final del desafío* • Quiz on *Desafío 1*	20–22 23	5 m. 20 m. 10 m. 15 m.	1.1, 1.2, 1.3, 2.1, 5.1	Audio Practice Workbook *Tu desafío*
6	To express wishes	**Desafío 2 – ¡Ojalá encontremos a Bruno!** (354–355) • Warm-Up: Independent Starter • *Fotonovela: ¡Ojalá encontremos a Bruno!* • *Cultura: La Ciudad Vieja de Montevideo*	24–26 27	5 m. 35 m. 10 m.	1.1, 1.2, 1.3, 2.1, 2.2, 5.2	Visual Presentation Audio Video *Tu desafío*
7	To discuss professions	**Desafío 2 – Vocabulario** (356–357) • Warm-Up: Independent Starter • Vocabulary: *Profesiones* • *Conexiones: Jorge Drexler*	28–31 32	5 m. 35 m. 10 m.	1.1, 1.2, 1.3, 2.2, 3.1, 3.2, 5.2	Audio Practice Workbook
8	To express wishes	**Desafío 2 – Gramática** (358–359) • Warm-Up: Independent Starter • Grammar: *Expresar deseo. El modo subjuntivo* • *Cultura: La moneda de Uruguay*	33–35 36	5 m. 35 m. 10 m.	1.1, 1.2, 1.3, 2.2, 3.1, 3.2, 4.1, 4.2, 5.2	Audio Practice Workbook
9	To integrate vocabulary and grammar and to assess student proficiency	**Desafío 2 – Comunicación / Evaluación** (360–361) • Warm-Up: Independent Starter • *Comunicación:* Review • *Final del desafío* • Quiz on *Desafío 2*	37–40 41	5 m. 20 m. 10 m. 15 m.	1.1, 1.2, 1.3, 5.1	Audio Practice Workbook
10	To express feelings and emotions	**Desafío 3 – Estrellas de telenovela** (362–363) • Warm-Up: Independent Starter • *Fotonovela: Estrellas de telenovela* • *Cultura: El tango*	42–44 45	5 m. 35 m. 10 m.	1.1, 1.2, 1.3, 2.2, 3.1, 3.2, 5.1	Visual Presentation *Tu desafío*

Day	Objectives	Sessions	Activities	Time	Standards	Resources/ Homework
11	To talk about free-time activities and hobbies	**Desafío 3 – Vocabulario** (364–365) • Warm-Up: Independent Starter • Vocabulary: *Aficiones, actividades y espectáculos* • *Cultura: Las telenovelas*	46–48 49	5 m. 35 m. 10 m.	1.1, 1.2, 1.3, 2.2, 3.2, 4.2, 5.1	Audio Practice Workbook *Tu desafío*
12	To express feelings	**Desafío 3 – Gramática** (366–367) • Warm-Up: Independent Starter • Grammar: *Expresar sentimientos* • *Comparaciones: El barrio de La Boca*	50–53 54	5 m. 35 m. 10 m.	1.1, 1.2, 1.3, 2.1, 2.2, 3.2, 4.2, 5.1	Audio Practice Workbook *Tu desafío*
13	To integrate vocabulary and grammar and to assess student proficiency	**Desafío 3 – Comunicación / Evaluación** (368–369) • Warm-Up: Independent Starter • *Comunicación:* Review • *Final del desafío* • Quiz on *Desafío 3*	55–58 59	5 m. 20 m. 10 m. 15 m.	1.2, 1.3, 2.2, 5.1	Audio Practice Workbook *Tu desafío*
14	To express doubt or to make value statements	**Desafío 4 – El clásico y el Aconcagua** (370–371) • Warm-Up: Independent Starter • *Fotonovela: El clásico y el Aconcagua* • *Conexiones: El Aconcagua*	60–63 64	5 m. 35 m. 10 m.	1.1, 1.2, 1.3, 2.1, 2.2, 3.1, 3.2	Visual Presentation
15	To talk about sports	**Desafío 4 – Vocabulario** (372–373) • Warm-Up: Independent Starter • Vocabulary: *Deportes* • *Cultura: El fútbol argentino*	65–68 69	5 m. 35 m. 10 m.	1.1, 1.2, 1.3, 2.2, 3.1, 3.2, 4.2, 5.1, 5.2	Audio Video Practice Workbook *Tu desafío*
16	To express doubt or to make value statements	**Desafío 4 - Gramática** (374–375) • Warm-Up: Independent Starter • Grammar: *Expresar duda y hacer valoraciones*	70–73	5 m. 45 m.	1.1, 1.2, 1.3, 3.1, 4.1	Audio Practice Workbook
17	To integrate vocabulary and grammar and to assess student proficiency	**Desafío 4 – Comunicación / Evaluación** (376–377) • Warm-Up: Independent Starter • *Comunicación:* Review • *Final del desafío* • Quiz on *Desafío 4*	74–76 77	5 m. 20 m. 10 m. 15 m.	1.1, 1.2, 1.3, 2.1, 2.2	Audio Practice Workbook
18	To integrate language in context	**Todo junto / El encuentro** (378–381) • Warm-Up: Independent Starter • *Todo junto* • *Cultura: Buenos Aires* • *El encuentro: En la Manzana Jesuítica de Córdoba*	78–81 82 83–84	5 m. 20 m. 5 m. 20 m.	1.1, 1.2, 1.3, 2.1, 2.2, 3.1, 3.2, 5.1, 5.2	Audio Practice Workbook
19	To learn about selected South American countries and to read a narrative story	**Mapa cultural / Lectura** (382–385) • Warm-Up: Read the *Mapa cultural* • *Mapa cultural: Río de la Plata* • *Lectura: Un cuento de Benedetti* • Read project outline (390–391)	85–86 87–88	5 m. 20 m. 20 m. 5 m.	1.2, 1.3, 2.1, 2.2, 3.1, 3.2, 5.1	Video Practice Workbook *Tu desafío* Project work
20	To write a script for a soap opera	**Proyecto** (390–391) • Warm-Up: Prepare project presentations • Project presentations		5 m. 45 m.	1.2, 1.3, 2.2, 3.1, 5.2	Practice Workbook **Repaso – Vocabulario** (386–387) **Repaso – Gramática** (388–389) **Autoevaluación** (391)

Lesson Plans (90-Minute Classes)

Day	Objectives	Sessions	Activities	Time	Standards	Resources/ Homework
1	To introduce selected South American countries and to discuss the pairs' challenges	***Río de la Plata / La llegada*** (340–345) • Warm-Up: Region orientation • *Río de la Plata* / Images and functions • Presentation: *En Córdoba* • *Expresiones útiles* and *¿Quién ganará?*	 1 2–5	 10 m. 20 m. 25 m. 35 m.	1.1, 1.2, 1.3, 2.2, 4.1, 5.1, 5.2	Visual Presentation Audio Video Practice Workbook
2	To identify a person or object and to talk about school	***Desafío 1 – ¿Un idioma imposible? / Vocabulario*** (346–349) • Warm-Up: Independent Starter • *Fotonovela: ¿Un idioma imposible?* • *Cultura: El guaraní* • Vocabulary: *La escuela* • *Cultura: La Universidad de Asunción*	 6–9 10 11–13 14	 5 m. 30 m. 10 m. 35 m. 10 m.	1.1, 1.2, 1.3, 2.1, 2.2, 3.1, 3.2, 5.1	Visual Presentation Audio Practice Workbook *Tu desafío*
3	To express existence of people and things, to integrate vocabulary and grammar, and to assess student proficiency	***Desafío 1 – Gramática / Comunicación / Evaluación*** (350–353) • Warm-Up: Independent Starter • Grammar: *Expresar existencia. Los indefinidos* • *Cultura: Requisitos: hablar guaraní* • *Comunicación:* Review • *Final del desafío* • Quiz on *Desafío 1*	 15–18 19 20–22 23	 5 m. 25 m. 10 m. 25 m. 10 m. 15 m.	1.1, 1.2, 1.3, 2.1, 3.1, 4.1, 5.1, 5.2	Audio Practice Workbook *Tu desafío*
4	To express wishes and to discuss professions	***Desafío 2 – ¡Ojalá encontremos a Bruno! / Vocabulario*** (354–357) • Warm-Up: Independent Starter • *Fotonovela: ¡Ojalá encontremos a Bruno!* • *Cultura: La Ciudad Vieja de Montevideo* • Vocabulary: *Profesiones* • *Conexiones: Jorge Drexler*	 24–26 27 28–31 32	 5 m. 25 m. 15 m. 35 m. 10 m.	1.1, 1.2, 1.3, 2.1, 2.2, 3.1, 3.2, 5.2	Visual Presentation Audio Video Practice Workbook *Tu desafío*
5	To express wishes, to integrate vocabulary and grammar, and to assess student proficiency	***Desafío 2 – Gramática / Comunicación / Evaluación*** (358–361) • Warm-Up: Independent Starter Grammar: *Expresar deseo. El modo subjuntivo* • *Cultura: La moneda de Uruguay* • *Comunicación:* Review • *Final del desafío* • Quiz on *Desafío 2*	 33–35 36 37–40 41	 5 m. 25 m. 10 m. 25 m. 10 m. 15 m.	1.1, 1.2, 1.3, 2.2, 3.1, 3.2, 4.1, 4.2, 5.1, 5.2	Audio Practice Workbook
6	To express feelings and emotions and to talk about free-time activities and hobbies	***Desafío 3 – Estrellas de telenovela / Vocabulario*** (362–365) • Warm-Up: Independent Starter • *Fotonovela: Estrellas de telenovela* • *Cultura: El tango* • Vocabulary: *Aficiones, actividades y espectáculos* • *Cultura: Las telenovelas*	 42–44 45 46–48 49	 5 m. 30 m. 10 m. 35 m. 10 m.	1.1, 1.2, 1.3, 2.2, 3.1, 3.2, 4.2, 5.1	Visual Presentation Audio Practice Workbook *Tu desafío*
7	To express feelings, to integrate vocabulary and grammar, and to assess student proficiency	***Desafío 3 – Gramática / Comunicación / Evaluación*** (366–369) • Warm-Up: Independent Starter • Grammar: *Expresar sentimientos* • *Comparaciones: El barrio de La Boca* • *Comunicación:* Review • *Final del desafío* • Quiz on *Desafío 3*	 50–53 54 55–58 59	 5 m. 25 m. 10 m. 25 m. 10 m. 15 m.	1.1, 1.2, 1.3, 2.1, 2.2, 3.2, 4.2, 5.1	Audio Practice Workbook *Tu desafío*

Day	Objectives	Sessions	Activities	Time	Standards	Resources/ Homework
8	To express doubt or to make value statements and to talk about sports	**Desafío 4 – El clásico y el Aconcagua / Vocabulario** (370–373) • Warm-Up: Independent Starter • *Fotonovela: El clásico y el Aconcagua* • *Conexiones: El Aconcagua* • *Vocabulary: Deportes* • *Cultura: El fútbol argentino*	 60–63 64 65–68 69	 5 m. 30 m. 10 m. 35 m. 10 m.	1.1, 1.2, 1.3, 2.1, 2.2, 3.1, 3.2, 4.2, 5.1, 5.2	Visual Presentation Audio Video Practice Workbook *Tu desafío*
9	To express doubt or to make value statements, to integrate vocabulary and grammar, and to assess student proficiency	**Desafío 4 – Gramática / Comunicación / Evaluación / Todo junto** (374–379) • Warm-Up: Independent Starter • Grammar: *Expresar duda y hacer valoraciones* • *Comunicación:* Review • *Final del desafío* • Quiz on *Desafío 4* • *Todo junto*	 70–73 74–76 77 78–82	 5 m. 20 m. 20 m. 10 m. 15 m. 20 m.	1.1, 1.2, 1.3, 2.1, 2.2, 3.1, 3.2, 4.1, 5.1	Audio Practice Workbook
10	To integrate language in context, to learn about selected South American countries, and to read a narrative story	**El encuentro / Mapa cultural / Lectura** (380–385) • Warm-Up: Independent Starter • *El encuentro: En la Manzana Jesuítica de Córdoba* • *Mapa cultural: Río de la Plata* • *Lectura: Un cuento de Benedetti* • Read project outline (390–391)	 83–84 85–86 87–88	 5 m. 30 m. 25 m. 25 m. 5 m.	1.2, 1.3, 2.1, 2.2, 3.1, 3.2, 5.1, 5.2	Video Practice Workbook *Tu desafío* **Repaso – Vocabulario** (386–387) **Repaso – Gramática** (388–389) Project work
11	To write a script for a soap opera and to assess student proficiency	**Proyecto / Assessment** (390–391) • Project presentations • *Autoevaluación* • Test		40 m. 10 m. 40 m.	1.2, 1.3, 2.2, 3.1, 5.2	

Unit 7 Río de la Plata

 2 ¿Están de acuerdo?

1. –Para mí, el español es una lengua muy bonita.
   –Sí, tienes razón.
2. –En mi opinión, aprender idiomas es muy aburrido.
   –No, no es verdad. Es muy interesante.
3. –Creo que la escuela de nuestros hijos es muy buena.
   –Por supuesto. Es buenísima.
4. –Pienso que para hablar bien español hay que practicar mucho.
   –Sí, claro. Leer, hablar con nativos...
5. –Yo creo que hacer la tarea todos los días no es importante.
   –¡Qué va! Es muy importante.

 8 En la universidad

1. Cuando no entiendo una palabra, uso un diccionario.
2. Yo siempre estudio en la biblioteca.
3. Me pongo muy nervioso cuando hago un examen.
4. En clase siempre tomo apuntes. Los utilizo para estudiar.

 12 El horario de Panambi

Hola, ¿qué tal? Me llamo Panambi. Este es mi horario de clases.
Los lunes, miércoles y jueves tengo clase de Historia a las nueve.
A las diez, tengo clase de Matemáticas. Y a las once, de Biología.
Después del almuerzo, a primera hora tengo Literatura y después
Geografía.
Los martes tengo clase de Química de nueve a once, y después
tengo clase de Literatura. Por la tarde, tengo Física y después
Matemáticas.
Los viernes tengo clase de Física a las nueve, Geografía a las diez
y Química a las once. Por la tarde no tengo clase. Normalmente
voy a la biblioteca o a la sala de computación a hacer la tarea.

 13 La agenda de Pedro

Hola, ¿qué tal? Hoy tengo un día muy complicado. A primera hora
tengo examen de Física. ¡Qué horror! Después tengo clase de Biología
en el aula 3. Y a las once, tengo clase de Química. Tengo que pedir
los apuntes a mi amiga Cristina. A las doce voy a estudiar con Sofía
en la sala de computación. Y después voy a ir a almorzar al comedor
con mi amigo Juan. Por la tarde tengo clase de Historia. Al final de la
clase tengo que hablar con el profesor porque no hice mi tarea.

 16 Las fotos de Andy

1. Hay alguien en ese despacho.
2. No hay nadie en la biblioteca.
3. Hay algunos estudiantes en el comedor.

 20 Una conversación telefónica

–¿Diga?
–Hola, mamá.
–¿Qué tal, mamá?

–Hola, hijos. Yo bien. ¿Y ustedes?
–Muy bien, pero nuestro desafío es difícil.
–¿Qué tienen que hacer?
–Tenemos que descubrir el significado de un mensaje muy raro.
–¿Muy raro? ¿Por qué?
–Porque está en una lengua que no conocemos. Al principio Andy
 y yo pensamos que el mensaje estaba escrito en guaraní porque
 en Paraguay mucha gente habla esa lengua. Por eso fuimos
 a la Universidad de Asunción a buscar ayuda.
–¿Y qué pasó?
–Primero fuimos a un aula con algunos estudiantes, pero no pudimos
 hablar con ellos porque estaban tomando apuntes.
–Luego fuimos a la biblioteca y miramos algunos diccionarios. Pero
 no encontramos nada.
–¿Preguntaron a alguien?
–Sí. Hablamos con una estudiante de guaraní, pero ella tampoco
 entendió ninguna palabra. Nos dijo que el mensaje no está escrito
 en guaraní.
–¡Qué extraño! ¿Y no hablaron con ningún profesor?
–No, pero es una buena idea.
–Claro, Andy, ya te lo dije.
–Gracias, mamá. Un beso.
–¡Chao, mamá!
–Adiós.

 26 Ojalá...

1. Espero que un día Tess trabaje como veterinaria.
2. Prefiero que tú preguntes a la gente.
3. Quiero que veamos pronto a Bruno.
4. Ojalá alguien nos ayude.

28 La familia de Patricia

1. Mi papá es muy bueno con las computadoras.
2. Mi mamá diseña casas y edificios.
3. Mi tío Ricardo prepara unos platos deliciosos.
4. Mi hermana canta muy bien, tiene una voz excelente.
5. Mi hermano puede arreglar cualquier problema en un coche.

34 Deseos para el futuro

1. Ojalá trabaje como dentista.
2. Ojalá viva en un país hispano y trabaje con hispanos.
3. Ojalá estudie Leyes, quiero ser abogado.
4. Ojalá trabaje en una biblioteca.

 37 Se necesita

1. Necesitamos un secretario o una secretaria para nuestra oficina.
   Queremos que esta persona hable inglés y francés.
2. Nuestra escuela necesita un bibliotecario o una bibliotecaria.
   Esperamos que esta persona use bien las computadoras.
3. Nuestra empresa necesita un telefonista. Preferimos que esta
   persona trabaje de lunes a sábado.

4. Necesitamos un socorrista para la piscina municipal. Preferimos que esta persona trabaje bien con niños.

 Mis aficiones

Yo tengo muchas aficiones. Por ejemplo, me gusta mucho coleccionar monedas y sellos. Ese es mi pasatiempo favorito. También tengo otras aficiones, claro. Me gusta ir al teatro y al cine. Y también me gusta pasear y hacer deporte. Lo que no me gusta es estar en casa viendo la televisión; prefiero salir. Y tampoco me gusta nada jugar al ajedrez ni jugar a los naipes; es muy aburrido.

 Las impresiones de Rita

1. Me alegra mucho que podamos ir al Teatro Colón.
2. Siento que no tengamos clases de tango. ¡Es tan divertido...!
3. Me preocupa que Diana solo quiera comer carne.
4. Me encanta que nos sirvan pasta con el almuerzo.

 Las aficiones de Roberto

Hola, soy Roberto. Les voy a contar cuáles son mis aficiones.
A mí me gusta mucho hacer deporte. Por eso, todos los días, después de la escuela, practico deporte durante una hora. Generalmente, los lunes, miércoles y viernes monto en bicicleta. Y los martes y los jueves voy a montar a caballo.
Además de practicar deporte, también me gusta hacer otras actividades en mi tiempo libre. Los lunes tengo clase de piano y los viernes juego al ajedrez en el club de la escuela. Los fines de semana leo libros y veo la televisión. Y a veces voy al cine con mis amigos.

56 **Diana y Andrea**

1. Andrea es mi mejor amiga. Ella es muy simpática y nos llevamos muy bien. A las dos nos encanta la música. Me gusta que siempre quiera ir a conciertos conmigo.
2. A Andrea y a mí nos gusta mucho la naturaleza, pasear, etc. Pero a mí me gusta montar a caballo y a ella no. Me da pena que no pueda montar a caballo conmigo.
3. Andrea dibuja muy bien. No me sorprende que siempre quiera ir a ver exposiciones.
4. Quiero que Andrea y yo estudiemos en la misma universidad y me da miedo que ella prefiera ir a una universidad diferente de la mía.

 Deportistas

1. A mí me gustan los deportes de equipo; por eso me gusta el fútbol. Y mi equipo siempre gana.
2. A mí me encanta la nieve. Esquiar es un deporte muy emocionante.
3. A mí me gusta mucho el golf. Juego todas las semanas.

4. Mi deporte favorito es el béisbol. Desde pequeño me gusta mucho este deporte.
5. Mi deporte favorito es el alpinismo. Es una experiencia única.
6. Yo voy con frecuencia al gimnasio. Me gusta cuidarme.

72 **¡Qué emocionante!**

–Oye, Miguel, ¿piensas que vamos a poder ver el partido entre el Boca y el River?
–Es posible, Tim. Pero es necesario que caminemos muy rápido si queremos llegar a tiempo.
–No creo que Mack pueda caminar más rápido.
–¿Sabes, Tim? Mack tiene razón. Es cierto que esto no es una competición.
–¿A qué hora empieza el partido?
–A las dos.
–¿Cuál es tu equipo favorito?
–El Boca. Soy un fan del Boca Junior desde que era pequeño.
–¿Piensas que el Boca puede ganar hoy?
–Claro, estoy seguro de que mi equipo va a ganar hoy.
–¿Por qué?
–Porque es imposible que el River gane, ja, ja.
–¿Siempre ves los partidos en la televisión?
–Sí, pero algún día espero ver un partido en el estadio.

76 **Las opiniones de una experta**

1. Estas chicas juegan al baloncesto. Es importante que entrenen mucho para jugar bien.
2. Estos jóvenes practican senderismo. Es necesario que sigan las señales o que usen un mapa.
3. Este chico está levantando pesas. Es bueno que tenga un entrenador para ayudarlo.

80 **Pasatiempos en Argentina**

1. Hola, me llamo Ángela. ¡Me encanta coleccionar monedas! Tengo monedas de otros países y muchas monedas antiguas.
2. Hola, soy Ernesto. A mí me gusta hacer senderismo. Vivo en un pueblo muy bonito en el norte de Argentina y hay muchos bosques para explorar. El año que viene voy a intentar hacer alpinismo por primera vez. ¡El Aconcagua está tan cerca!
3. Buenas tardes. Soy Adán. Mi espectáculo favorito es el teatro. Quiero ser actor o cantante famoso. ¡Ojalá que algún día pueda actuar en el Teatro Colón de Buenos Aires!
4. Hola, me llamo Catalina. Durante el verano me gusta mucho montar en bici. ¡Lo hago todos los días! Además, en invierno nieva mucho en mi ciudad, así que voy a esquiar a la montaña los fines de semana. ¡Es bueno para estar en forma!

Unit 7
Río de la Plata

The Unit

- The themes for Unit 7 are school, work, and free-time activities in the context of the Río de la Plata region in South America.
- The pairs gather at San Martín Plaza in Córdoba, Argentina. There they meet Ricardo, a police officer, who will give them their tasks.
  - *Desafío 1.* Andy and Janet must decipher a mysterious message at the University of Asunción in Paraguay.
  - *Desafío 2.* Tess and Patricia have to find a missing dog called Bruno in Montevideo, the capital of Uruguay.
  - *Desafío 3.* Diana and Rita go to Buenos Aires to participate in a *telenovela*.
  - *Desafío 4.* Tim and Mack must hike up Aconcagua in the Argentine Andes.

Activities	Standards	Resources
Río de la Plata	1.2, 2.1, 2.2	Video

Teaching Suggestions

Warm-Up / Independent Starter

- Have students look at a map of the Río de la Plata region and ask them to locate the cities of Buenos Aires, Montevideo, Asunción, and Córdoba in the province of Mendoza, and Mount Aconcagua.

The Río de la Plata Region

- Explain that the river known as *Río de la Plata* forms a gulf, or estuary, at its mouth on the Atlantic Ocean. La Plata River is formed by the confluence of the Uruguay and Paraná rivers, and is part of the border between Uruguay and Argentina. In fact, the capital cities of these two countries are located on either side of the estuary, and the areas alongside are the most densely populated in both countries. The city of Córdoba, the center of a major business district in Argentina, lies approximately 450 miles northwest of Buenos Aires. Further west, on the Andean border with Chile, in the province of Mendoza, lies Aconcagua, the highest mountain peak in the Southern and Western hemispheres.

340

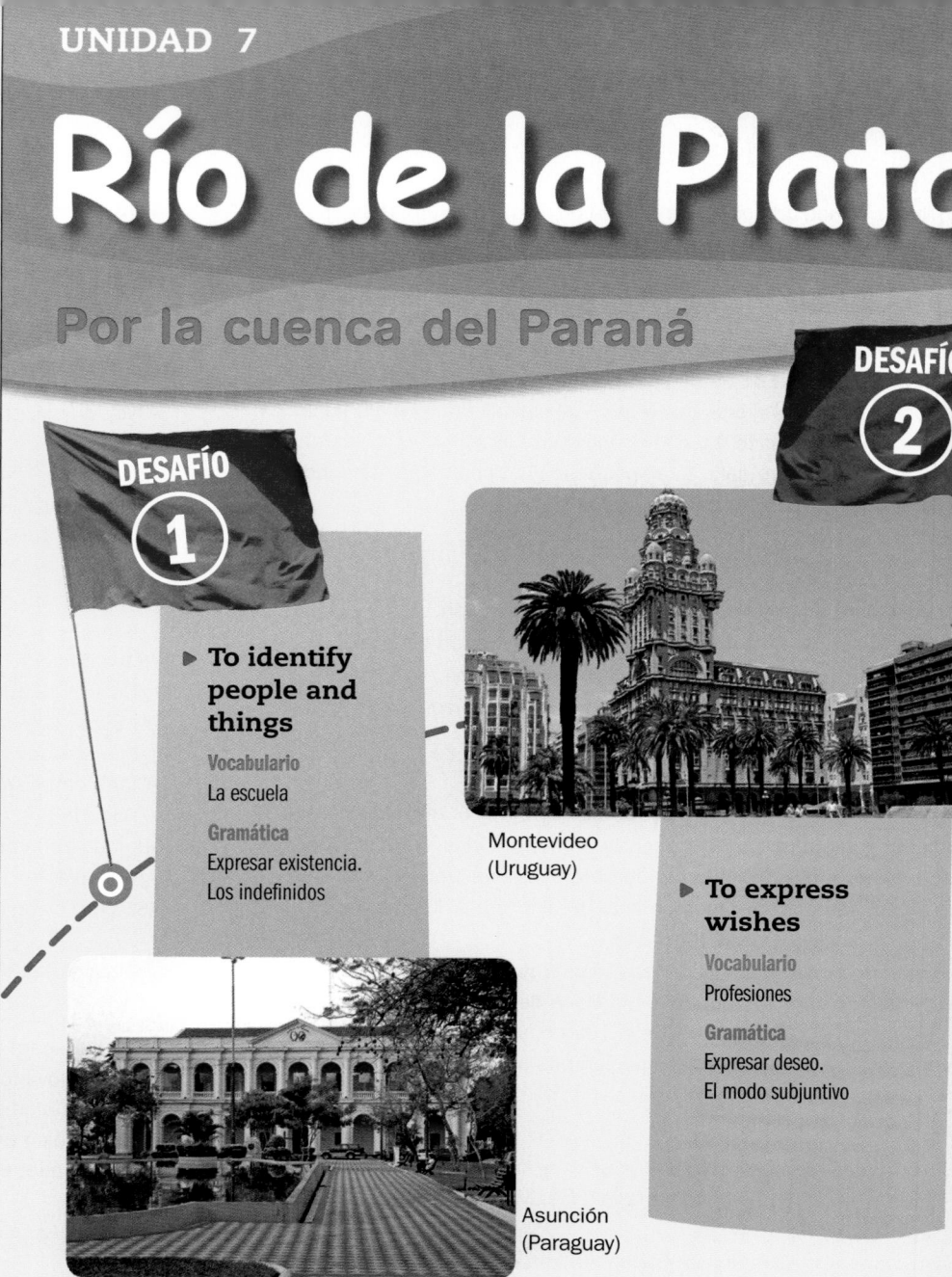

UNIDAD 7

Río de la Plata

Por la cuenca del Paraná

DESAFÍO 1

▶ **To identify people and things**

Vocabulario
La escuela

Gramática
Expresar existencia.
Los indefinidos

Montevideo (Uruguay)

DESAFÍO 2

▶ **To express wishes**

Vocabulario
Profesiones

Gramática
Expresar deseo.
El modo subjuntivo

Asunción (Paraguay)

340 trescientos cuarenta

The Challenge

DESAFÍO 1
Asunción

Asunción, the capital city of Paraguay, developed along the Paraguay River near its confluence with the Pilcomayo River. The city was founded on the Feast of the Assumption (i.e., La Asunción) on August 15, 1537. Asunción was an important administrative center during the Spanish colony, due to its strategic position at the head of the Río de la Plata Basin—the river system linking Uruguay, Argentina, and Brazil. Today, about two million people live in the metropolitan area of Asunción.

DESAFÍO 2
Montevideo

Situated on the northeastern bank of the Río de la Plata, Montevideo is the capital of Uruguay. This vibrant city has one of the largest natural harbors in the Southern Cone. In the early 20th century, many Europeans established themselves in Montevideo and the city expanded quickly into multiple neighborhoods around the Bay. An important site along the coastline for leisure and recreation is the Rambla, a long avenue where people go to stroll, jog, or rollerskate.

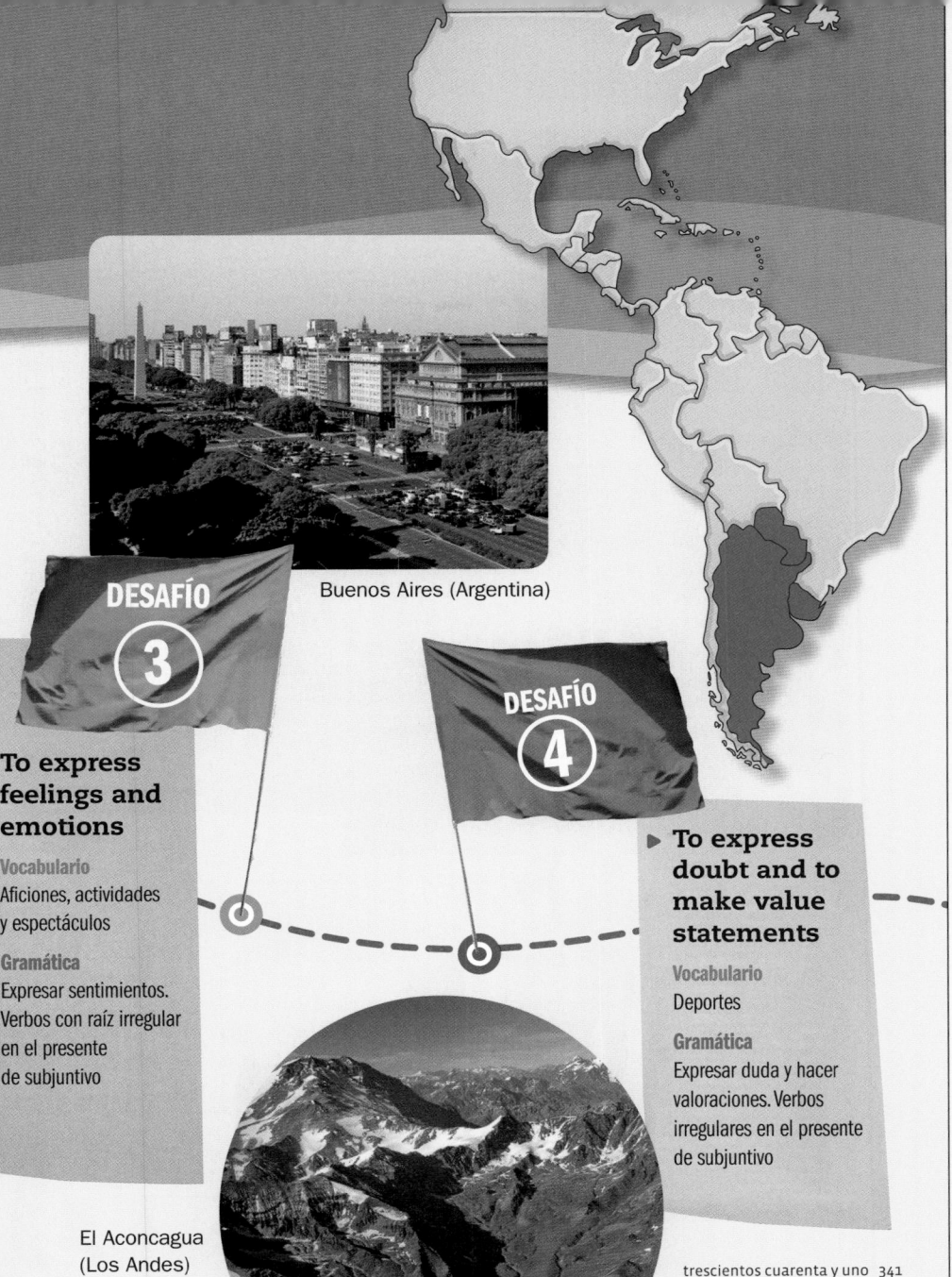

Buenos Aires (Argentina)

DESAFÍO 3

To express feelings and emotions

Vocabulario
Aficiones, actividades y espectáculos

Gramática
Expresar sentimientos. Verbos con raíz irregular en el presente de subjuntivo

El Aconcagua (Los Andes)

DESAFÍO 4

To express doubt and to make value statements

Vocabulario
Deportes

Gramática
Expresar duda y hacer valoraciones. Verbos irregulares en el presente de subjuntivo

trescientos cuarenta y uno 341

Picture Discussion

- Ask students to look at the pictures. Has anyone in the class ever been to any of the places pictured? Encourage students to share their experiences.

Asunción (Paraguay)

- Ask students what type of building they think this picture shows (e.g., a theater, government offices, the President's residence, etc.). List students' ideas on the board. Then explain that this building is the Cabildo Museum. It used to be the Senate, but now is a museum and cultural center. Did any of the students guess correctly?

Montevideo (Uruguay)

- Tell students that this picture shows the Salvo Palace, in downtown Montevideo. Explain that this building was inaugurated in 1928 and for several years, it was the tallest building in South America. Which architectural features of this building catch students' attention? Encourage them to research the Tribune Tower in Chicago, and compare these two buildings. Both have gothic elements and they were both criticized at the time of their construction.

Buenos Aires (Argentina)

- Focus students' attention on the avenue depicted on this picture. Have they seen or been on a similar city thoroughfare? Is there a similar avenue in their own community? Explain that this is Avenida del Libertador, one of the most important avenues in Buenos Aires, and a city landmark. Discuss, as a class, the importance of these types of thoroughfares for a city.

El Aconcagua (Los Andes)

- Ask students to work with a partner to compare Aconcagua with Chimborazo, a volcano in Ecuador which students learned about in Unit 3. Have pairs list common elements (e.g., both are located in the Andes, volcanic origins) as well as differences (e.g., located in different countries, difference in altitude). Invite volunteer pairs to share their comparisons with the class.

Objectives

- By the end of Unit 7, students will be able to
  - Identify people and things.
  - Express wishes.
  - Express feelings and emotions.
  - Express doubt and make value statements.
  - Talk about different cultural aspects of the Río de la Plata region.

DESAFÍO 3
Buenos Aires

Buenos Aires is the second-largest city in the Southern Hemisphere after Sao Paulo, Brazil. It is located on the western shore of the Río de la Plata estuary, about 150 miles from the Atlantic Ocean. People from Buenos Aires are referred to as *porteños*. The city has always had an active cultural life, with many theaters, music halls, art galleries, and museums. Buenos Aires is a city of distinctive neighborhoods, each with its own particular character and architectural landmarks.

DESAFÍO 4
El Aconcagua

Mount Aconcagua, which lies in the Southern Andes, is considered one of the Seven Summits (i.e., the highest peaks in each of the seven continents). The peak itself is located in the Mendoza Province in Argentina, whereas the western flanks are located in Chile. Aconcagua is an obvious attraction for mountaineers and climbers, although some claim that it is not one of the most difficult to conquer! The first person to ascend to the summit was Mathias Zurbriggen, a Swiss alpinist, in 1897.

341

Unit 7
La llegada

Presentation

- This section presents the pairs' arrival in the Río de la Plata region in South America. They meet in Córdoba, Argentina, at the Plaza San Martín. There, the participants meet Ricardo, a police officer, who gives them their challenges for this unit and wishes them luck.

- Students will see vocabulary in context, with pictures and illustrations. Presenting new words in this manner helps students develop their Spanish vocabulary with background knowledge while engaging them with the context.

Activities	Standards	Resources
Fotonovela	1.2, 2.1, 2.2	Vis. Pres.
1.	1.2	

Teaching Suggestions

Warm-Up / Independent Starter

- Ask student to write three sentences explaining what they have to do for the day. You may want to give them a model. For example: *Tengo que visitar a mis abuelos. También tengo que hacer la tarea de la escuela.*

Preparation

- Review the Independent Starter while emphasizing the expression *tener que* + infinitive. Ask some students to express the same meaning of obligation with the expression *deber* + infinitive.

- Ask the students to share their obligations for the day. Use some expressions with *ojalá*, or wish them luck with their tasks. You may write these expressions on the board: *Ojalá tengas tiempo de hacer todo. Espero que estudies mucho para el examen. ¡Que tengas suerte!*

- Focus students' attention on the *fotonovela* and ask them to read the introduction silently. Then have them observe the pictures.

La fotonovela

Before Viewing

- Divide the class into small groups and ask them to read the dialogue of the *fotonovela* silently. Then have students in each group identify the sentences that express obligation.

La llegada

En Córdoba

In Córdoba, Argentina, the pairs gather at the Plaza San Martín, where they are welcomed by Ricardo, a local guide.

> Bienvenidos a Argentina, amigos. Presten atención.

> Ustedes tienen que descifrar un mensaje misterioso.

> ¡Estupendo! Creo que es un desafío muy interesante.

Differentiated Instruction

DEVELOPING LEARNERS

- Remind students how cognates help them to decipher new words in Spanish while enriching their vocabulary in English. Ask students to identify the cognates in the dialogues and say what their English-language equivalents are: *atención* (attention), *descifrar* (decipher), *mensaje* (message), *misterioso* (mysterious), *estupendo* (stupendous), *interesante* (interesting), *animales* (animals), *series* (series), *televisión* (television), *practicar* (practice), *presentación* (presentation). You may want to point out that *original* means both "original" and "unique" in English. Ask students which meaning is meant here ("unique").

EXPANDING LEARNERS

- After students read the dialogues, ask them to identify those words or expressions in the dialogues that indicate interest (*¡Estupendo!*), agreement (*¡Sí, claro! ¡Qué bien!*), and offer clues as to the person's opinion about something (*Creo que... muy interesante. Para mí, este es el mejor...*). Then ask students to use each of these expressions in oral or written sentences.

Ojalá les gusten los animales.

Espero que a ustedes les gusten las series de televisión.

¡Sí, claro! ¡Soy adicta a las telenovelas!

¿Por qué lo dice?

Porque tienen que trabajar en un oficio muy original en Montevideo.

Entonces les espera un buen trabajo en Argentina.

Ustedes tienen que practicar senderismo en los Andes.

Además deben hacer una presentación de sus desafíos. ¡Que tengan suerte!

¡Qué bien! Abuelo, para mí, este es el mejor desafío.

1 **¿Comprendes?**

▶ **Une** las dos columnas. ¿Qué tienen que hacer los personajes?

(A)

1. Andy y Janet
2. Tess y Patricia
3. Diana y Rita
4. Tim y Mack
5. Las cuatro parejas

(B)

a. tienen que practicar senderismo.
b. deben hacer una presentación.
c. tienen que trabajar en un oficio muy original.
d. tienen que participar en una serie de televisión.
e. necesitan entender un mensaje.

- Once groups have finished, ask them to share their findings with the rest of the class. You may challenge the students further by then asking them to point out the sentences that, according to them, express wishes. This is only an activity of recognition, and they should not yet be expected to produce these expressions.

After Viewing

- Make sure students understand the dialogues by asking comprehension questions such as *¿Dónde están las parejas? ¿Qué desafío tienen Andy y Janet? ¿Qué es un mensaje?* Explain words like *mensaje, misterioso,* and *descifrar* by using gestures and mimicking the actions.

- Make connections with students' experiences by asking them related questions: *¿Te gustan los animales? ¿Te gustan las telenovelas? ¿Practican senderismo?* Etc.

Activities

1. To make the activity a bit more challenging, ask students to rewrite the answers using a different expression of obligation. For example: *Andy y Janet necesitan entender un mensaje.* → *Andy y Janet tienen que entender un mensaje.* Invite volunteer students to read some of their sentences to the rest of the class.

Answer Key

1. 1. e   4. a
   2. c   5. b
   3. d

Additional Resources

Fans Online activities
Practice Workbook

HERITAGE LANGUAGE LEARNERS

- Point out the subjunctive mood used in the dialogues (*gusten, tengan*) and ask students to identify the words that triggered its use (*ojalá, espero, que*) on these pages. Then ask students to write two sentences using each of these words that require the use of the subjunctive.

SPECIAL-NEEDS LEARNERS

- Ask those students with an auditory processing disorder to read the directions to the activities and repeat these directions to you. Doing this will reinforce students' comprehension of what they are expected to do. For any audio or video components of the activities, provide students with the script to improve their comprehension. Have students record their voices for audio portions so that they may be able to compare their pronunciation and intonation with those of the narrators.

Unit 7

La llegada

Presentation

- In this section, students will learn useful expressions to express opinion, as well as to express agreement and disagreement.

Activities	Standards	Resources
Expresiones útiles	1.2, 1.3, 4.1	
2.	1.2, 1.3	Audio
3.	1.1, 1.2, 1.3	
4.	1.1, 2.1, 2.2, 5.2	
5.	1.1, 5.1	

Teaching Suggestions

Warm-Up / Independent Starter

- Have students choose an answer for each of the following statements:

1. *Es importante aprender una lengua extranjera.*
   a. *Estoy de acuerdo.*   b. *No estoy de acuerdo.*
2. *Hacer deporte es bueno para la salud.*
   a. *Es cierto.*   b. *No es cierto.*
3. *Tener una computadora es mejor que tener un teléfono celular.*
   a. *Creo que sí.*   b. *Pienso que no.*

Preparation

- Review the Independent Starter orally. Then go over the *Expresiones útiles* section with the class.
- Have students work in groups to create statements in which other groups will have to express their opinion. Have them exchange the statements and express their opinions using the *expresiones útiles*.

Activities

2. Before playing the audio recording, say each *expresión útil* and have students repeat. After completing the activity, play the audio a third time and have students write their own opinion about the given statements.

3. To expand this activity, ask students to give one argument starting with *porque* (reason) or *para* (purpose) to support their opinion (e.g., *Yo creo que aprender idiomas es importante porque puedes hablar con amigos de otros países*).

344

EXPRESIONES ÚTILES

> Para mí, el español es una lengua muy interesante.

> Desde luego.

To express opinion:
Creo que...	Para mí...
Pienso que...	En mi opinión...

To express agreement:
Es verdad. / Es cierto.	Sí, claro.
Tienes razón.	Por supuesto.
Estoy de acuerdo.	Desde luego.

To express disagreement:
No es verdad / No es cierto.	No, no.
No llevas razón.	¡Qué va!
No estoy de acuerdo.	En absoluto.

2 **¿Están de acuerdo?**

▶ **Escucha** los diálogos y completa una tabla como esta.

	Están de acuerdo	No están de acuerdo
1		
2		
3		
4		
5		

 ▶ **Escucha** otra vez y escribe. ¿Qué expresiones utilizan para expresar acuerdo y desacuerdo?

Modelo 1. *Tienes razón.*

3 **¿Qué opinas?**

▶ **Escribe** tres oraciones con tu opinión sobre algunos de estos temas.

[las telenovelas] [hacer la tarea] [tu escuela] [aprender idiomas] [el fútbol]

 ▶ **Lee** tus opiniones a tu compañero(a). ¿Está de acuerdo?

Modelo A. *Yo creo que hacer la tarea todos los días es muy importante.*
B. *Sí, estoy de acuerdo.*

344 trescientos cuarenta y cuatro

Differentiated Instruction

DEVELOPING LEARNERS

- Tell students a series of statements, some of which should be outrageous, and ask them to use the *expresiones útiles* in order to express their agreement or disagreement with you. Help them to form some opinions of their own by giving them more topics on which to state their opinion. Additional topics might include: *el equipo de fútbol / béisbol / baloncesto local, las películas que ponen en el cine local, su clase de..., la música de un(a) cantante o grupo popular, la comida en la cafetería de la escuela.*

EXPANDING LEARNERS

- Have students work in groups of three and create a dialogue in which one student expresses several opinions with which the second student always agrees, and the third consistently disagrees. Ask groups to practice their lines so they can reenact them without looking at their scripts, and call on groups to come before the class and present their skits.

¿Quién ganará?

4 Los desafíos

▶ **Habla.** ¿Cuál será el desafío de cada pareja? Piénsalo y coméntalo con tus compañeros(as).

DESAFÍO ① ¿Un idioma imposible?

AGURANGE LINAU

Andy y Janet

DESAFÍO ② ¡Ojalá encontremos a Bruno!

Tess y Patricia

DESAFÍO ③ Estrellas de telenovela

Diana y Rita

DESAFÍO ④ El clásico y el Aconcagua

Tim y Mack

▶ **Habla.** Las parejas viajan a Paraguay, Uruguay y Argentina. ¿Qué sabes de esos países? Coméntalo con tus compañeros(as).

5 La tarea final

▶ **Decide.** ¿Qué tarea tienen que hacer los personajes al final? ¿Qué pareja crees que ganará?

LA TAREA
Una presentación

¿Quién ganará?

4. Have students get into small groups and discuss the pairs' challenges. Ask groups to look at the pictures and make inferences about what the challenges will be like for each pair.

5. Explain to students that at the end of this unit, they will decide and vote on which pair gives the best presentation of their challenge. Let students discuss their opinions and then help them to reach an agreement.

 AUDIO SCRIPT
See page 339I.

Answer Key

2. Están de acuerdo: 1, 3, 4
   No están de acuerdo: 2, 5
   ▶ 2. No es verdad.
   3. Por supuesto.
   4. Sí, claro.
   5. ¡Qué va!

3. Answers will vary.
   ▶ Answers will vary.

4. Answers will vary.
   ▶ Answers will vary.

5. Answers will vary.

Additional Resources

Fans Online activities
Practice Workbook

HERITAGE LANGUAGE LEARNERS

• Have students brainstorm other popular expressions that express opinion (e.g., *Me parece que..., A mi parecer..., A mi juicio...*), agreement (e.g., *Vale. Bueno. Vaya pues.*), and disagreement (e.g., *De ninguna manera. ¡Ni hablar!*). You may want to ask them to share these new expressions with the class and also to prepare a short dialogue to highlight these new phrases.

COOPERATIVE LEARNING

• Students will work in groups of four or five and imagine that they are running for office and competing against each other. They might be seeking a national, state, or local office, or running for student government. They will need to name one student as moderator and then hold a debate on pertinent issues. Encourage them to interject as many of the new *expresiones útiles* as they can into their remarks.

Unit 7
DESAFÍO 1
Identificar a personas y objetos

Presentation

- In *Desafío 1*, Andy and Janet are at the University of Asunción in Paraguay. They have to decipher a strange phrase.
- In this section, students will preview:
  - Vocabulary related to school.
  - Expressing existence with indefinite words.

Activities	Standards	Resources
Fotonovela	1.2, 2.1, 2.2	Vis. Pres.
6.	1.2, 1.3	.
7.	1.2, 1.3	
8.	1.2	Audio
9.	1.1, 1.2, 1.3	
10. Cultura	1.1, 1.2, 2.1, 3.1, 3.2, 5.1	
Tu desafío	1.2, 3.1, 3.2, 5.1	

Teaching Suggestions

Warm-Up / Independent Starter

- Have students brainstorm three things that they can do to figure out a word or sentence they do not understand.

Preparation

- Ask for a student volunteer to read aloud the introduction to Andy and Janet's challenge. Have students ever heard of Guaraní?

La fotonovela

Before Viewing

- Ask students to take a quick look at the pictures and hypothesize what Andy and Janet are doing to complete their task.

After Viewing

- Ask students if they have any additional ideas about how Andy and Janet might decipher the message. See if they can try to form any Spanish words with the letters provided.

Activities

8. Before listening, have students brainstorm vocabulary that describes what the pictured students are doing and where they are.

346

¿Un idioma imposible?

Andy and Janet are about to explore Paraguay, a country where people speak Spanish and a native language called Guaraní. Their task is to decipher a strange phrase at the University of Asunción.

AGURANGE LINAU

- ¿Entiendes algo, Janet?
- No, no entiendo nada. ¿Vamos a preguntar a alguien?
- ¿Están haciendo un examen?
- No, están tomando apuntes. Aquí no puede ayudarnos nadie. Vamos a la biblioteca.
- La primera palabra no está en el diccionario.
- Esto no es guaraní.
- ¿Estás segura?
- ¿Y si preguntamos a algún profesor?
- ¡Pues la segunda tampoco! Necesitamos ayuda.

Continuará…

6 Detective de palabras

▶ **Completa** estas oraciones.

1. ¿Entiendes ___1___ ?
2. No entiendo ___2___ . ¿Vamos a preguntar a ___3___ ?
3. Aquí no puede ayudarnos ___4___ .
4. ¿Preguntamos a ___5___ profesor?

Differentiated Instruction

DEVELOPING LEARNERS

- Review the letters of the alphabet by having students say each of the letters that appear in the first scene. Then spell out some words for students to give them practice in identifying more letters, especially the vowels *a*, *e*, and *i*, and the consonants *g*, *h*, *j*, and *z*. After students have spelled each word, ask them to pronounce it.

EXPANDING LEARNERS

- Janet and Andy need to decipher a phrase. Ask students if they have ever written or had to decipher a secret message. Explain that some messages use a code of numbers that signify letters, or even letters that represent other letters. Ask students to create a secret code and then write a message in Spanish with it that warrants a reply. Ask them to exchange messages with a partner, who must first try to solve it and, once the code is cracked, respond to it using the same code.

¿Comprendes?

▶ **Responde** a estas preguntas.

1. ¿Qué tienen que hacer Andy y Janet? ¿Qué problema tienen?
2. ¿Qué hacen para resolver el problema? ¿A quién piden ayuda?
3. ¿Qué sugiere Janet al final?

 En la universidad

 ▶ **Escucha** y decide. ¿A qué estudiante se refiere cada oración?

 Mis estudios

▶ **Responde** a estas preguntas.

1. ¿Dónde prefieres estudiar? ¿Por qué?
2. ¿Haces la tarea solo(a) o con tus compañeros(as)? ¿Por qué?
3. ¿Qué haces cuando no entiendes una palabra en la clase de Español?
4. ¿Por qué es importante tomar apuntes en clase?

 ▶ **Pregunta** a tu compañero(a) qué opina. ¿Está de acuerdo contigo?

 CULTURA

El guaraní

El guaraní es una lengua indígena hablada en regiones de Paraguay, Argentina, Bolivia y Brasil.

En Paraguay aproximadamente el 90% de la población habla guaraní. Desde la Constitución de 1992, el guaraní es lengua oficial junto con el español. También es lengua oficial en Bolivia y en la provincia argentina de Corrientes.

Cartel en guaraní.

10 **Piensa y habla.** ¿Conoces otros países con dos o más idiomas oficiales? En tu opinión, ¿qué porcentaje de la población de un país tiene que hablar una lengua para que se considere lengua oficial?

 **TU DESAFÍO** Visita la página web para aprender más sobre el guaraní.

trescientos cuarenta y siete 347

---

9. Compile the results of the questions and create pie charts to represent the students' responses. Divide the class into groups and have each group create one chart.

10. Have students find a Guaraní-Spanish online dictionary to search for some basic words in the language.

 AUDIO SCRIPT
See page 339I.

CULTURA

El guaraní

The Guaraní language is part of the Tupian linguistic group. The Tupians lived in the vast territory south of the Amazon. The word *guaraní* comes from *guarini*, which means "war." The Guaraní language stands apart from other native languages of the Americas because a large number of non-indigenous people speak it. Some words in both Spanish and English are influenced by Guaraní, such as *jaguar* (*jaguara*) and *piranha* (*pirá* + *sanha*). *Paraguay* is also a Guaraní word.

Answer Key

6. 1. algo 4. nadie
2. nada 5. algún
3. alguien

7. 1. Tienen que descifrar una frase. No entienden nada.
2. Buscan en el diccionario. Después le preguntan a una estudiante.
3. Sugiere preguntarle a algún profesor.

8. 1. D 2. A 3. B 4. C

9. Answers will vary.
▶ Answers will vary.

10. Answers will vary.

Additional Resources

Fans Online activities

HERITAGE LANGUAGE LEARNERS

• Ask students to research some of the other indigenous languages that are spoken in Paraguay, Argentina, and Bolivia and make a brief presentation to the class. Ask students if they are familiar with any of these languages, or have ever heard anyone speak them. If students know some words or phrases, invite them to share these with the class. If they know someone who is fluent in one of these languages, encourage them to invite the person to class to share their linguistic and cultural knowledge with students.

MULTIPLE INTELLIGENCES:

Interpersonal Intelligence

• Working with a partner, have students survey other students in the class to see how, where, and with whom they like to study, as well as how many hours each day they study. Ask them to make a chart or graph that shows students' preferred study styles: *con música, en silencio, en casa, en la biblioteca, en otro lugar (¿cuál?), solo(a), con alguien,* etc. Also have them include in the chart the average number of hours a day students spend studying.

Unit 7

DESAFÍO 1

Vocabulario – La escuela

Presentation

- In this section, students will learn words related to student activities and academic subjects.

Activities	Standards	Resources
Vocabulario	1.2	
11.	1.3	
12.	1.2, 1.3	Audio
13.	1.1, 1.2, 1.3, 5.1	Audio
14. Cultura	1.1, 1.2, 2.2, 3.1, 5.1	
Tu desafío	1.2, 2.2, 3.1, 5.1	

Teaching Suggestions

Warm-Up / Independent Starter

- Ask students to write out their daily school schedule including their classes and where they take place.

Preparation

- Have students share their favorite subjects with the class and an action that they do in the class (e.g., *En la clase de Inglés, leemos novelas*).
- Ask students to come up with a school schedule for someone in the same grade in Paraguay. Elicit from students that Paraguayan students might take Spanish, Guaraní, and English classes, therefore becoming multilingual.

Activities

11. As an alternative to this activity, have each student write five to six logical and illogical sentences about activities that they would do during the school day, and where they would do them. Have students exchange the sentences with a partner and say whether they think they are logical or not. For example: *Leo libros en el laboratorio.*

13. Prior to playing the audio, have students see if they can identify any activities that do not make sense. For the second part of the activity, suggest to students that they create a Venn diagram to organize their comparison.

348

DESAFÍO 1

Vocabulario

La escuela

Lugares en la escuela

la biblioteca

el laboratorio

la sala de computación

Asignaturas

el gimnasio

la cafetería / el comedor

los aseos

Acciones

Perdona, ¿sabes dónde está la oficina del director?

Sí, está al final de este pasillo, al lado del aula de Ciencias.

prestar atención

levantar la mano

tomar apuntes

hacer un examen

11   Lugares en tu escuela

▶ **Escribe.** ¿En qué lugares de la escuela puedes hacer estas actividades?

Modelo estudiar ⟶ *Puedo estudiar en la biblioteca o en un aula.*

1. hablar con un(a) profesor(a)
2. hacer la tarea
3. comer un sándwich
4. lavarte las manos
5. hacer un examen
6. hacer deporte

348   trescientos cuarenta y ocho

Differentiated Instruction

DEVELOPING LEARNERS

- Ask students to use the schedule in activity 12 as a guide to making their own schedule of classes for the week. They should label the days at the top and the time classes begin along the left side. Help them with the names of any classes that might not be part of their known vocabulary; for example, *Informática* would be used to describe a computer class. Encourage students to form sentences that describe what day and at what time they have their classes.

EXPANDING LEARNERS

- Ask students to create their ideal class schedule, including any new subjects they would like to study. They might even prefer to start their day early and come to school for breakfast and finish before 2:00 p. m., or they might prefer night classes so they could have the day free. After students finish their schedules, they should be prepared to explain why they want these changes and how said changes would improve their school day and year.

12 **El horario de Panambi**

▶ **Escucha** y completa el horario de esta estudiante.

	Lunes	Martes	Miércoles	Jueves	Viernes
9:00 a. m.	Historia		Historia	Historia	
10:00 a. m.	Matemáticas		Matemáticas	Matemáticas	Geografía
11:00 a. m.		Literatura			
	ALMUERZO				
12:30 p. m.	Literatura		Literatura	Literatura	
1:30 p. m.		Matemáticas	Geografía	Geografía	

13 **La agenda de Pedro**

▶ **Escucha** y corrige los errores de la agenda de Pedro.

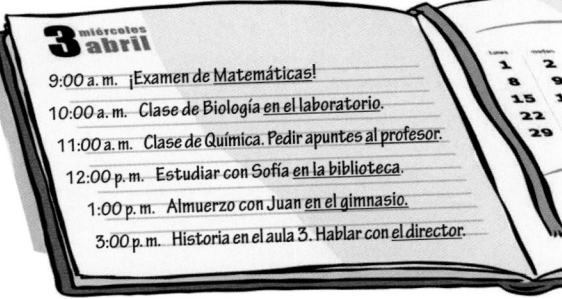

3 miércoles **abril**

9:00 a. m. ¡Examen de Matemáticas!
10:00 a. m. Clase de Biología en el laboratorio.
11:00 a. m. Clase de Química. Pedir apuntes al profesor.
12:00 p. m. Estudiar con Sofía en la biblioteca.
1:00 p. m. Almuerzo con Juan en el gimnasio.
3:00 p. m. Historia en el aula 3. Hablar con el director.

▶ **Escribe** tu agenda para hoy. Después, compárala con la de tu compañero(a).

Modelo   A. *A las doce voy a estudiar en la sala de computación con mi amigo Pedro.*
         B. *Yo también.*

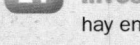 

CULTURA

La Universidad de Asunción

La Universidad Nacional de Asunción es la más antigua de Paraguay. En ella se pueden estudiar 74 carreras universitarias *(degree programs)*. Actualmente hay unos 40.000 alumnos matriculados *(registered)* y se imparten cursos de Lengua y Literatura guaraní.

14 **Investiga.** ¿Te parece grande la Universidad de Asunción? ¿Cuántos estudiantes hay en las universidades de tu región?

→ TU DESAFÍO   Visita la página web para aprender más sobre esta universidad.

trescientos cuarenta y nueve   349

AUDIO SCRIPT
See page 339I.

CULTURA

La Universidad de Asunción

The University of Asunción was founded in 1889, making it the oldest university in the country. It also has the largest student body. The classes are taught in Spanish, but students can also study Guaraní as their major. There are both undergraduate and graduate programs. The University slogan is *Vitan Impendere Vero*, and it promises to seek the truth through knowledge.

Answer Key

11. Answers will vary. Sample answers:
1. Puedo hablar con un profesor en el aula.
2. Puedo hacer la tarea en la biblioteca.
3. Puedo comer un sándwich en la cafetería.
4. Puedo lavarme las manos en los aseos.
5. Puedo hacer un examen en el aula.
6. Puedo hacer deporte en el gimnasio.

12. 11:00 a. m.; lunes, miércoles y jueves: Biología.
1:30 p. m., lunes: Geografía.
De 9:00 a 11:00 a. m., martes: Química.
12:30 p. m., martes: Física.
9:00 a. m., viernes: Física.
11:00 a. m., viernes: Química.

13. Examen de Física a primera hora; clase de Biología en el aula 3; pedir apuntes a Cristina; estudiar en la sala de computación; almuerzo en el comedor; hablar con el profesor.
▶ Answers will vary.

14. Answers will vary.

Additional Resources

Fans Online activities
Practice Workbook

HERITAGE LANGUAGE LEARNERS

• Invite students to describe differences in the number and variety of subjects studied and class schedules in your school and in one in their family's country of origin or in any Hispanic country they know well. Students may also include differences in the grading systems, clothes, or uniforms students must wear to school, opportunities for extra-curricular activities or sports, and length of the school year. Ask them to explain these differences to the rest of the class.

CRITICAL THINKING

• Ask students to discuss their favorite classes (including Spanish!) and then explain why these are their favorites. Ask them to say whether they plan to continue their studies in this field and if these classes will lead to a career, and if so, what career path they will choose. Even if a career is not their ultimate goal with these studies, encourage them to talk about what they plan to do with the knowledge they have received from these classes.

Unit 7
DESAFÍO 1
Gramática – Expresar existencia. Los indefinidos

Presentation

- In this section, students will learn to use indefinites to refer to an identifiable but not specified person or thing.

Activities	Standards	Resources
Gramática	3.1	
15.	1.1, 4.1	
16.	1.2	Audio
17.	1.2	
18.	1.1, 1.3	
19. Cultura	1.2, 2.1, 5.2	

Teaching Suggestions

Warm-Up / Independent Starter

- Show students a photograph of a classroom. Have them identify at least ten things in the picture.

Preparation

- Ask students to share their responses from the Independent Starter. When they provide responses, you can ask follow-up questions to identify if there are a lot or a few of the people or object. You can also repeat the response, adding in indefinites that they have already studied (e.g., *Sí, hay algunos libros encima del pupitre. Sí, hay muchos lápices.*).

- After going over the grammar presentation, students can take another look at the picture used during the Independent Starter and write practice sentences, applying *alguien, nadie, algo,* and *nada* according to the picture.

Activities

15. You may want to discuss the use of the double negative in Spanish, which is not grammatically correct in English. For example: *Nadie sabe nada*. Ask students to try to translate this phrase into English. (<u>Nobody</u> knows <u>anything</u>.)

16. Prior to playing the audio recording, ask students to make a statement about what is shown in each picture (e.g., *En la fotografía B, hay algunas sillas*).

350

DESAFÍO 1

Gramática

Expresar existencia. Los indefinidos

- Remember: We use indefinites (ninguno, alguno, poco, mucho, todo, demasiado) to refer to nouns using nonspecific terms of number.

  Tengo **algunos** libros en la mochila.

- You can use these indefinite pronouns to refer to an identifiable but not specified person or thing.

  1. To refer to people:

  ALGUIEN

  Hay **alguien** en el aula.

  NADIE

  No hay **nadie** en el aula.

  2. To refer to things:

  ALGO

  En la mesa hay **algo** para escribir.

  NADA

  En la mesa no hay **nada**.

Uso de los indefinidos

- Affirmative indefinites usually go with verbs in the affirmative form. Negative indefinites usually go after verbs in the negative form.

  –¿Ayer vino algún estudiante a clase?
  –No. Y no vino tampoco ningún profesor.

15 **Piensa.** ¿Cuáles son los equivalentes a alguien, nadie, algo y nada en inglés?

16 **Las fotos de Andy**

 ▶ **Escucha** y decide. ¿A qué fotografía se refiere cada oración?

Differentiated Instruction

DEVELOPING LEARNERS

- Prepare some magazine cutouts that show scenes in which there are several people or no one, and other scenes that show several objects or no object. Show these images to students and ask them questions such as: *¿Hay algunos [persons / objects] en [name of place]?* or *¿Ves algo en [object or place]?* to solicit an answer using one of the indefinites.

EXPANDING LEARNERS

- Give students more practice with indefinites by having them choose the correct word to complete each sentence.

  1. *No veo a nadie / alguien en el laboratorio.* (nadie)
  2. *Tampoco veo a ningún / algún profesor.* (ningún)
  3. *¿Hay ningunos / algunos libros en la biblioteca?* (algunos)
  4. *¿Está alguien / nadie en el comedor?* (alguien)
  5. *No hay ninguna / alguna computadora en esta sala.* (ninguna)
  6. *¿Hay algo / nada en el gimnasio? No, no hay algo / nada.* (algo; nada)

350

17 **¿Alguien puede ayudarnos?**

▶ **Completa** esta conversación entre Andy y Janet.

ANDY: ¡Qué mensaje tan extraño! ¿Tú entiendes ___1___ ?
<u>algo / nada</u>

JANET: No, yo tampoco entiendo ___2___ . Vamos a buscar ayuda.
<u>nada / alguno</u>

ANDY: ¿Vamos al comedor? Seguramente allí hay ___3___ estudiantes.
<u>alguien / algunos</u>

JANET: Es muy temprano para el almuerzo. ¿Por qué no vamos a la biblioteca?

ANDY: Sí, tienes razón. Vamos. Oh, no hay ___4___ en la biblioteca, Janet.
<u>nadie / alguien</u>
¿Qué hacemos?

JANET: Vamos a preguntar a ___5___ dónde está el departamento de Lengua
<u>algún / alguien</u>
guaraní.

ANDY: Sí, quizás podamos encontrar a ___6___ profesor de guaraní.
<u>alguien / algún</u>

 18 **Preguntas sobre la escuela**

 ▶ **Entrevista** a dos compañeros(as) y toma notas de sus respuestas.

Modelo A. *¿Tienes algún cuaderno en tu mochila?*
B. *No, no tengo ningún cuaderno en mi mochila.*

1. ¿Tienes alguna tarea de Matemáticas para mañana?
2. ¿Hay algún diccionario en el aula?
3. ¿Piensas que hay alguien en el comedor ahora?
4. ¿Conoces a algunos(as) profesores(as) simpáticos(as)?
5. ¿Conoces a algún estudiante responsable?

▶ **Presenta** las respuestas de tus compañeros(as) a la clase.

Modelo *Paco no tiene nada en su mochila, pero Lola tiene algunas carpetas.*

 **CULTURA**

SE BUSCAN
vendedores
Importante empresa
de moda busca
vendedores en Asunción.
Requisitos: experiencia
demostrable y dominio
del español y el guaraní.

Requisitos: hablar guaraní

Hablar guaraní puede ser un requisito *(requirement)* o una ventaja
para encontrar trabajo en Paraguay. Algunas ofertas de empleo
incluyen como requisito hablar perfectamente español y guaraní.

19 **Explica.** ¿Es una ventaja en tu país hablar otras lenguas? ¿En qué profesiones?

HERITAGE LANGUAGE LEARNERS

• In Paraguay, many jobs require applicants
to be bilingual in Spanish and Guaraní. Ask
students if workers in their family's country
of origin need to be bilingual or multilingual
and, if so, what languages they are required
to speak and write fluently. Then ask
students to brainstorm jobs or professions
in their family's country of origin that require
knowledge of a second or third language
and what these languages are. Ask them
to compare these jobs and language
requirements with those in the United
States.

CRITICAL THINKING

• Have students imagine that they live in a
bilingual community, in which one of the
languages has a long-standing cultural
tradition. Although both languages enjoy
an official status, some lawmakers want to
abolish the bilingual concept and impose
English only. Have students debate this
issue, some taking the side of the "English
only" supporters, and others the side of
those who want to preserve the bilingualism
of the community.

Gramática – Expresar existencia. Los indefinidos

18. After students present their findings to the
class, ask them to form additional comparisons
using the information that was presented.

19. Have students look at the jobs section of a
local or regional newspaper to see if there are
positions for which knowing another language is
a requirement or an advantage.

 AUDIO SCRIPT
See page 339I.

 CULTURA

Requisitos: hablar guaraní

In 1994, Paraguay's Bilingual Education Plan
introduced Guaraní as the language of
instruction—alongside Spanish—beginning
with first grade. The Plan has progressively
added one grade each year up to secondary
school. In addition, many schools and
academies offer language courses in Guaraní
so that those who are not familiar with the
language have the opportunity to learn it.

Answer Key

15. Son: *somebody / someone, nobody / no one,*
something, nothing.

16. 1. C   2. B   3. A

17. 1. algo   4. nadie
2. nada   5. alguien
3. algunos   6. algún

18. Answers will vary.
▶ Answers will vary.

19. Answers will vary.

Additional Resources

Fans Online activities
Practice Workbook

351

Presentation

■ In this section, students will integrate the vocabulary and grammar from *Desafío 1* in order to identify people and things related to school using indefinites.

Activities	Standards	Resources
20.	1.2, 1.3	Audio
21.	1.1, 1.2, 1.3, 5.1	
22.	1.1	
23. Final del desafío	1.1, 1.2, 1.3, 2.1, 5.1	
Tu desafío	1.2, 1.3	

Teaching Suggestions

Warm-Up / Independent Starter

■ Ask students to write five questions about the existence of people or objects in the classroom. For example: *¿Hay algún libro de Química? ¿Hay muchos libros de Español?*

Preparation

■ Break students into pairs. Students will ask each other the questions they wrote during the Independent Starter. For example:
A. *¿Hay algún libro de Química?*
B. *No, no hay ningún libro de Química.*
Then have each pair present a question and response to the class.

■ Take 10 minutes to review the vocabulary and grammar themes of *Desafío 1*.

■ Refer students back to the *fotonovela* for *Desafío 1*. Have them identify vocabulary related to school, as well as the indefinites used in the conversation. Do students understand the dialogue better now that they have gone through the vocabulary and grammar from the *Desafío?*

Activities

20. Prior to completing the activity, ask students to recall Andy and Janet's challenge. After completing the activity, ask students if they think the pair is closer to deciphering the message.

352

Comunicación

20 Una conversación telefónica

 ▶ **Escucha** y decide si estas oraciones son ciertas o falsas. Después, corrige las oraciones falsas.

1. Andy y Janet fueron a un aula, pero no había nadie.
2. Después fueron a la biblioteca y miraron algunos diccionarios.
3. Encontraron información útil en un diccionario.
4. A continuación, pidieron ayuda a una estudiante de guaraní.
5. La estudiante entendió algunas palabras del mensaje.
6. Andy y Janet hablaron con algunos profesores.

21 Un mensaje de correo desde Atlanta

▶ **Lee** y completa el mensaje de correo de Teresa, una amiga de Andy.

algo	alguien	algunos	nada	nadie	algún

De:
Para:
Asunto:

¡Hola, Andy! ¿Qué tal estás?

Aquí, en Atlanta, todo está igual. No hay ___1___ nuevo. Esta semana tenemos ___2___ exámenes: de Física, de Geografía, de Matemáticas… En Física tengo ___3___ problema: ¡necesito ayuda de ___4___ ! A la hora del almuerzo fui a la biblioteca para estudiar, pero no había ___5___ para ayudarme. ¿Tú sabes ___6___ de Física?

¡Escríbeme pronto!

Teresa

▶ **Escribe** un mensaje de correo a un(a) amigo(a). Cuéntale algo sobre tus clases y tus compañeros(as). Usa los indefinidos.

Differentiated Instruction

DEVELOPING LEARNERS

• Ask sudents to decipher the following scrambled words. You may give students clues to help them. For example: *CIETABILBO → Aquí encuentras muchos libros. (biblioteca)*
1. NOMIGSAI → *Aquí haces ejercicio. (gimnasio)*
2. TELANARV AL AMON → *Haces esto si quieres preguntar algo. (levantar la mano)*
3. ATOAOROIRLB → *Aquí estudias Ciencias. (laboratorio)*
4. ROMAT ETUNPAS → *Hacer esto te ayuda a estudiar. (tomar apuntes)*
5. TÍRAFEACE → *Comes aquí. (cafetería)*
6. SOASE → *Aquí te lavas las manos. (aseos)*

EXPANDING LEARNERS

• Have students write a reply from Andy to Teresa's e-mail. Encourage them to answer her question and to explain, from Andy's point of view, what he and Janet have been doing in Paraguay. Students should describe the steps they had to take in order to successfully complete the *desafío*, as well as any other interesting details they would like to add.

22 ¿En qué se diferencian?

 ▶ **Habla** con tu compañero(a). Compara estas fotografías.

Modelo *En la fotografía 1 hay algunos estudiantes hablando. Están haciendo una presentación. Y en la fotografía 2 están todos escuchando al profesor.*

Final del desafío

Necesitamos entender el significado de este mensaje misterioso. ¿Puede ayudarnos?

¿No es guaraní?

Ustedes no necesitan ningún profesor de guaraní. Esto no es guaraní.

No. Tomen las letras y jueguen con ellas.

23 El mensaje descifrado

▶ **Escribe** tres mensajes misteriosos sobre el desafío. Usa los cuadros de cultura, vocabulario y gramática.

▶ **Lee** los mensajes de tu compañero(a) y resuélvelos.

⚑→ **TU DESAFÍO** Visita la página web. Escucha las preguntas de tu *Minientrevista Desafío 1* y escribe las respuestas.

trescientos cincuenta y tres 353

---

21. Once students have finished the second part of this activity, ask them to exchange papers and write a response to their partner's e-mail.

22. After students have had time to compare the two photographs, ask them to close their books. Have them share a statement about the pictures and see who can remember to which classroom the statement applies.

23. Provide each student with two blank sheets of paper and have them write two of their secret messages in a colored marker, large enough for others to read. Post the messages on a wall or bulletin board and see how many each student can decipher.

AUDIO SCRIPT
See page 339I.

Answer Key

20. 1. Falso. Había algunos estudiantes.
2. Cierto.
3. Falso. No encontraron nada.
4. Cierto.
5. Falso. No entendió ninguna palabra.
6. Falso. No hablaron con ningún profesor.

21. 1. nada   4. alguien
2. algunos   5. nadie
3. algún   6. algo
▶ Answers will vary.

22. Answers will vary.

23. Answers will vary.
▶ Answers will vary.

Additional Resources

Fans Online activities
Practice Workbook

HERITAGE LANGUAGE LEARNERS

• Ask students to brainstorm phrases and expressions with "nothing" in English and give their counterparts in Spanish. Suggest some of the following, but have students come up with more:
1. To do something for nothing: *hacer algo gratis*.
2. To him / her, I'm nothing: *para él / ella soy un cero a la izquierda*.
3. There's nothing to it: *es muy fácil*.
4. It was all for nothing: *todo fue en vano*.
Ask students to share these expressions with the class and have all students use them aloud.

TOTAL PHYSICAL RESPONSE (TPR)

• Divide the class into two teams: one will be the "positives" and the other, the "negatives." Say several incomplete sentences that may be completed with an indefinite. If the *indefinido* that completes the sentence is *algo, alguien,* or a form of *alguno*, the positives must stand and say the word. However, if the sentence requires *nada, nadie,* or a form of *ninguno*, the negatives must stand and say the word.

353

Unit 7
DESAFÍO 2
Expresar deseos

Presentation

- In *Desafío 2*, Tess and Patricia are in Montevideo, Uruguay, where they must walk a dozen dogs. They will have the extra challenge of finding Bruno, a former police dog that has escaped.

- In this section, students will preview:
  – Words to talk about different professions.
  – How to express wishes and preferences.

Activities	Standards	Resources
Fotonovela	1.2, 2.1	Vis. Pres.
24.	1.2, 1.3	
25.	1.2, 1.3	
26.	1.2	Audio
27. Cultura	1.1, 1.2, 2.1, 2.2, 5.2	Video
Tu desafío	1.2, 2.1, 2.2, 5.1	

Teaching Suggestions

Warm-Up / Independent Starter

- Write *¿Qué debes hacer?* on the board. Have students write three sentences in which they describe what they would do if they lost their dog or their neighbor's dog.

Preparation

- Have students share their Independent Starters.
- Read the introduction to the *fotonovela* to the class. Ask students if they have walked dogs in their city or if they have seen somebody do it. Have students discuss if they consider walking dogs to be a good job and why or why not.

La fotonovela

Before Viewing

- Have students go over the *fotonovela* and look for words that express wishes and emotions.

After Viewing

- Divide the class in small groups. Ask students to talk about where Bruno could be, and how Tess and Patricia will find him. Then have students from each pair or group share their ideas with the class. Do students think Tess and Patricia will do some of the things they have suggested to find Bruno?

354

¡Ojalá encontremos a Bruno!

Tess and Patricia are in Montevideo, the capital of Uruguay. Fortunately, both are animal lovers, because they must walk a dozen dogs through the streets of the city. Will they be able to handle the task?

> ¿Saben? Bruno fue un perro policía.
> ¿De verdad?
> ¡Me encantan los perros! Ojalá trabaje con perros algún día.
> Si te gustan los animales, puedes ser bióloga.
> Sí, pero tengan cuidado porque se escapa fácilmente.
> ¡O veterinaria! ¡Sí! ¡Ojalá pueda trabajar como veterinaria!
> Uno, dos, tres, cuatro... ¡Oh, no! ¡Bruno se escapó!
> ¿Quieres que miremos por la plaza?
> Prefiero que preguntes a la gente. Yo voy a buscarlo por toda esta zona.
> ¡Espero que esté cerca! ¡Corre!
> Buena idea. Espero que alguien nos ayude.

Continuará...

24 Detective de palabras

▶ **Completa** estas oraciones.

1. _____ trabaje con perros algún día.
2. _____ pueda trabajar como veterinaria.
3. _____ Bruno esté cerca.
4. ¿_____ miremos por la plaza?
5. _____ preguntes a la gente.
6. _____ alguien nos ayude.

Differentiated Instruction

DEVELOPING LEARNERS

- To verify students' comprehension, have them put the following events in order.
  1. *Bruno se escapa.* (5)
  2. *Tess y Patricia van a la casa de Bruno.* (1)
  3. *Patricia va a buscar a Bruno por toda la zona.* (7)
  4. *Tess dice que espera que Bruno esté cerca.* (6)
  5. *Patricia le dice a Tess que puede ser bióloga.* (4)
  6. *La dueña de Bruno dice que él se escapa fácilmente.* (2)
  7. *Tess dice que algún día quiere trabajar con perros.* (3)

EXPANDING LEARNERS

- Ask students to write a new script for the *fotonovela* or write a short story, but from Bruno's perspective. Students should keep in mind what Bruno might be thinking when Patricia and Tess arrive at his house. You might mention some of the following possibilities, while encouraging students to come up with their own ideas: Does he run away because he is afraid? Does he escape because he is looking for an adventure? Does he have a secret plan that might involve his other dog friends? Or is he on a secret mission for the Montevideo Police Department?

25 Profesiones

▶ **Relaciona** estas profesiones con la fotografía correspondiente.

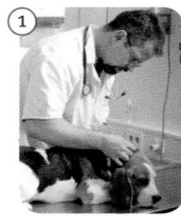

> policía
> veterinario(a)
> biólogo(a)

▶ **Explica.** ¿Qué hacen esas personas en su trabajo?

26 Ojalá...

▶ **Escucha** y une las dos columnas.

A	B
1. Espero que	a. veamos pronto a Bruno.
2. Prefiero que	b. alguien nos ayude.
3. Quiero que	c. un día Tess trabaje como veterinaria.
4. Ojalá	d. tú preguntes a la gente.

Catedral de Montevideo.

CULTURA

La Ciudad Vieja de Montevideo

El barrio histórico de Montevideo, también conocido como Ciudad Vieja, es una de las zonas más visitadas de la ciudad y un punto de encuentro habitual para los habitantes de la ciudad y los turistas. En el centro del barrio histórico está la Plaza Matriz o Plaza Constitución, donde se pueden ver importantes edificios, como la Catedral Metropolitana. En los alrededores de la Plaza Matriz hay numerosos comercios y restaurantes.

27 **Explica.** ¿Cómo es el punto de encuentro habitual o el más visitado de tu ciudad? ¿Por qué crees que se reúne allí la gente?

▶ **TU DESAFÍO** Visita la página web para aprender más sobre Montevideo.

Activities

25. Ask students to think about their interactions with some of these professionals. Then have them share with the rest of the class some of their experiences. You may want to ask questions to guide students. For example: *¿Alguna vez fuiste al veterinario con tu mascota? ¿Qué pasó? ¿Qué hizo y dijo el veterinario?*

26. Ask students to work in pairs to come up with a response to each of these wishes. For example: *Quiero que veamos pronto a Bruno.* → *¡Por supuesto! Yo también lo deseo.*

AUDIO SCRIPT
See page 339 l.

CULTURA

La Ciudad Vieja de Montevideo

The Plaza Matriz is also known as *Plaza de la Constitución* because it was the place where the first Uruguayan constitution was signed in 1830. The most notable features are the Cathedral, the Town Council, and a circular public fountain in the middle. The Cathedral was built in 1804 using a previous colonial church located on the same site. There is an open-air market every Saturday morning at the Plaza Matriz.

Answer Key

24.
1. Ojalá	4. Quieres que
2. Ojalá	5. Prefiero que
3. Espero que	6. Espero que

25. 1. veterinario   2. policía   3. biólogo
▶ Answers will vary.

26. 1. c   2. d   3. a   4. b

27. Answers will vary.

Additional Resources

Fans Online activities

HERITAGE LANGUAGE LEARNERS

- Invite students to talk about the historical district of a city or town in their family's country of origin or in another Hispanic country they know well. Ask them to describe what attracts visitors to this district or zone, what historical or cultural importance it has for the area, and why they would recommend that others visit. If students have photos, brochures, or other images of these areas, ask them to bring them to class in order to share with other students.

MULTIPLE INTELLIGENCES:
Verbal-Linguistic Intelligence

- Students will create a web page or a brochure announcing their services as a professional dog walker. The text should capture potential customers' attention, so creativity is key. The text may include the student's experience with walking dogs, any training they might have had in this business, any unique aspect of his or her services, the student's love of animals, and the fees and contact information. Students should also include an original name for their dog-walking business. Display their work in the classroom and have students vote on the most original one.

Unit 7
DESAFÍO 2
Vocabulario – Profesiones

Presentation

- In this section, students will learn words related to professions.

Activities	Standards	Resources
Vocabulario	1.2	
28.	1.2, 1.3	Audio
29.	1.2, 1.3	
30.	1.1, 1.2, 1.3	
31. Conexiones	1.1, 1.2, 2.2, 3.1, 3.2, 5.2	

Teaching Suggestions

Warm-Up / Independent Starter

- Have students draw a picture of their dream profession.

Preparation

- Before students open their book, write this question on the board: *¿Qué quieres ser de mayor?* Then invite students to share their Independent Starters to answer this question.
- Hand students cards with pictures of some professions. Have them act out the professions in front of the class. Let the class guess the profession. Be sure to practice pronunciation and gender agreement.

Activities

28. Have students work in pairs. Ask them to think of someone they know. They should alternate asking yes / no questions to guess the profession of that person. For example: *¿Trabaja en una escuela? ¿En un restaurante?*

29. To extend this activity, ask students to write a sentence providing additional information related to each profession. For example: *El arquitecto estudia Arquitectura. Diseña planos y trabaja en un estudio o en una oficina.*

30. To extend the oral activity, ask students to specify which professions they should <u>not</u> have, according to their qualities. For example:
    A. *Me gusta ayudar a la gente. Y soy muy atrevida.*
    B. *No debes ser veterinaria.*
    C. *Ni bibliotecaria.*

Vocabulario

Profesiones

Nosotros somos artistas. Juan es pintor, Ana es cantante y yo soy actriz.

Nosotros trabajamos en un hospital. Yo soy cirujano y ella es dentista.

Nosotros trabajamos en una oficina. Eva es arquitecta, Sonia es telefonista y yo soy técnico informático.

Nosotros ayudamos a la gente. Pepe es policía, Ana es bombera y yo soy socorrista.

el agricultor   la mecánica   la bibliotecaria   el cocinero

Nombres de profesiones. Terminaciones frecuentes:

-tor(a)	pintor(a)
-dor(a)	entrenador(a)
-sor(a)	profesor(a)
-ero(a)	bombero(a)
-ario(a)	bibliotecario(a)
-ante	el/la cantante
-ista	el/la dentista

28 La familia de Patricia

 ▶ **Escucha** y escribe las profesiones de la familia de Patricia.

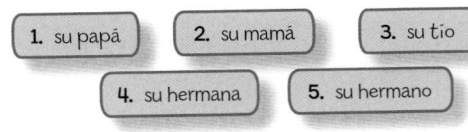

1. su papá   2. su mamá   3. su tío

4. su hermana   5. su hermano

356 trescientos cincuenta y seis

Differentiated Instruction

DEVELOPING LEARNERS

- In order to reinforce the vocabulary on this page ask students the following questions:
  1. *¿Quién trabaja en un hospital: un cirujano o un policía? (un cirujano)*
  2. *¿Qué hace una telefonista: canta o contesta el teléfono? (contesta el teléfono)*
  3. *¿Qué deben estudiar los abogados: Leyes o Bellas Artes? (Leyes)*
  4. *¿Quién es artista: el socorrista o el cantante? (el cantante)*
  5. *¿Quién estudia Interpretación: un arquitecto o un actor? (un actor)*
  6. *¿Quién rescata a las personas: un socorrista o un pintor? (un socorrista)*

EXPANDING LEARNERS

- Ask students to write at least one paragraph that describes jobs or professions their family members have, or ask them to make up a family and describe what each person does for a living. Encourage students to include what motivated these people to look for these particular jobs, what qualifications they have, including their education and past experience, what some of their responsibilities are, and how long have they been at the job. Students might also include any advice from these workers to people who are looking for similar jobs.

29 ¿Qué tengo que estudiar?

▶ **Une** las dos columnas y escribe oraciones.

Ⓐ

1. arquitecto
2. pintor
3. cirujano
4. actor
5. técnico informático
6. abogado

Ⓑ

a. Medicina
b. Interpretación
c. Leyes
d. Arquitectura
e. Informática
f. Arte

Modelo *Para ser arquitecto, estudia Arquitectura.*

30 ¿Qué pueden ser?

▶ **Escribe** una profesión adecuada para cada personaje según sus cualidades.

Modelo A Mack le encanta manejar. → *Mack puede ser conductor.*

1. Tim es muy ordenado. Le gusta tener todos sus libros organizados.
2. A Tess le encantan los animales.
3. A Andy le gustan mucho los coches y las motos.
4. Patricia tiene una voz muy bonita.
5. El hermano de Tess dibuja muy bien.

▶ **Habla** con dos compañeros(as) sobre sus cualidades. Da recomendaciones profesionales para cada uno(a).

Modelo A. *A mí me gusta ayudar a la gente. Y soy muy atrevida.*
B. *Pues puedes ser policía.*
C. *O bombera.*

CONEXIONES: MÚSICA

Jorge Drexler

Jorge Drexler es un famoso cantante uruguayo nacido en Montevideo en 1964. En el año 2005 ganó un Oscar con su canción *Al otro lado del río*, incluida en la película *Diarios de motocicleta*.

Jorge Drexler estudió Medicina y trabajó como médico, pero pronto decidió cambiar su profesión para dedicarse a la música.

31 Explica. ¿Cuál es tu profesión favorita? ¿Qué necesitas hacer para tener esa profesión?

HERITAGE LANGUAGE LEARNERS

• Ask students to name some professions that might be more common in their family's country of origin than in the United States, or that might be unique to that culture. Ask them if there are some professions that are held in higher esteem in one country than in others, and why they think this might be so. Conversely, ask if there are some professions or jobs that are not highly regarded in some cultures or communities, and to what they attribute this.

MULTIPLE INTELLIGENCES:

Interpersonal Intelligence

• Ask students to work with a partner and create a Help Wanted section in their local newspaper. They should work together to list several different types of jobs and the qualifications for each one. There should be a mix of opportunities for those who are just starting their professional lives, as well as job offers for seasoned professionals. The ads should look authentic, and include a brief description of the company or organization looking for employees.

AUDIO SCRIPT
See page 339I.

CONEXIONES: MÚSICA

Jorge Drexler

Jorge Drexler is a popular singer in Spain and Latin America. He became known in the United States after he won the Oscar for Best Original Song in 2005. The Academy asked two celebrities, Antonio Banderas and Carlos Santana, to sing Drexler's song, "Al otro lado del río," at the awards ceremony. When awarded the prize, Jorge Drexler protested by singing his own song instead of giving an acceptance speech.

Answer Key

28. 1. técnico informático   4. cantante
2. arquitecta   5. mecánico
3. cocinero

29. 2. f. Para ser pintor, estudia Arte.
3. a. Para ser cirujano, estudia Medicina.
4. b. Para ser actor, estudia Interpretación.
5. e. Para ser técnico informático, estudia Informática.
6. c. Para ser abogado, estudia Leyes.

30. Answers will vary. Sample answers:
1. Tim puede ser bibliotecario.
2. Tess puede ser veterinaria.
3. Andy puede ser mecánico.
4. Patricia puede ser cantante.
5. Puede ser artista.
▶ Answers will vary.

31. Answers will vary.

Additional Resources

Fans Online activities
Practice Workbook

DESAFÍO 2

Gramática – Expresar deseo. El modo subjuntivo

Presentation

- In this section, students will learn to express wishes and preferences using the subjunctive mood.

Activities	Standards	Resources
Gramática	3.1	
32.	1.1, 3.1, 4.1	
33.	1.3	
34.	1.2, 1.3	Audio
35.	1.1	
36. Cultura	1.1, 1.2, 2.2, 3.1, 3.2, 4.2, 5.2	

Teaching Suggestions

Warm-Up / Independent Starter

- To recycle the conjugations of stem-changing verbs, have students conjugate the verbs *querer* and *preferir* in the present indicative.

Preparation

- Have students fill in a two-column chart with the following verbs in the *yo* form of the present indicative in the first column and the formal negative command (*usted* form) in the second column: *trabajar, aprender, escribir*. After students complete the activity, use the chart to introduce the present subjunctive forms.

- After learning how to express wishes and preferences, ask students to write an activity they want to do in their free time. Then, have them write one activity they want their parents or best friend to do in their free time.

Activities

32. Have students translate the following sentences into Spanish:

 a. I want you to speak Spanish. (*Quiero que hables español.*)

 b. My parents want me to study architecture. (*Mis padres quieren que yo estudie Arquitectura.*)

 Have students point out the differences between the English and Spanish structures.

Gramática

Expresar deseo. El modo subjuntivo

- To express wishes in a straightforward way, use ojalá (optionally followed by que) followed by a verb in the subjunctive mood.

 Me encantan los perros. Ojalá **pueda** trabajar como veterinaria.

PRESENTE DE SUBJUNTIVO. VERBOS REGULARES

	Cantar	Comer	Vivir
yo	cante	coma	viva
tú	cantes	comas	vivas
usted, él, ella	cante	coma	viva
nosotros, nosotras	cantemos	comamos	vivamos
vosotros, vosotras	cantéis	comáis	viváis
ustedes, ellos, ellas	canten	coman	vivan

- To express wishes, you can also use verbs like querer, esperar, desear, and preferir followed by a dependent clause with the verb in the infinitive or in the subjunctive:

 – Use the infinitive when the main clause verb and the dependent clause verb have the same subject.

 Querer / Esperar / Desear / Preferir + infinitivo

 Quiero **estudiar** Medicina.
 (yo)   (yo)

 – Use the subjunctive when the main clause verb and the dependent clause verb have different subjects.

 Querer / Esperar / Desear / Preferir + que + subjuntivo

 Quiero que **estudies** Medicina.
 (yo)   (tú)

 Piensa. ¿Cómo expresas deseo en inglés? ¿Existe en inglés el modo subjuntivo?

 Actividades para Tess y Patricia

▶ **Escribe** oraciones expresando tus deseos para Tess y Patricia.

Modelo 1. *Espero que Tess y Patricia visiten sitios interesantes en Uruguay.*

1. visitar sitios interesantes
2. aprender mucho
3. hablar con gente simpática
4. tomar muchas fotografías
5. divertirse mucho
6. completar su desafío

Differentiated Instruction

DEVELOPING LEARNERS

- Ask students to complete the following sentences with the correct form of the present subjunctive:
 1. *Patricia prefiere que Tess … (preguntar) a la gente. (pregunte)*
 2. *¡Ojalá que ellas … (trabajar) como veterinarias! (trabajen)*
 3. *Yo quiero que ustedes … (comer) en la cafetería. (coman)*
 4. *Tú esperas que yo … (estudiar) contigo. (estudie)*
 5. *Ellos desean que nosotros … (vivir) en Montevideo. (vivamos)*

EXPANDING LEARNERS

- Ask students to write at least one paragraph using the present subjunctive to express wishes by using *esperar, desear, querer, preferir,* and *ojalá*. They may choose to focus on writing about a profession that they would like to have in the future, or a summer job they are interested in having. If there is another topic of interest to them, they can write about it as long as they express their wishes with the subjunctive. Remind students to include a title for their work.

34 Deseos para el futuro

 ▶ **Escucha** los deseos de varias personas para el futuro y escribe oraciones. Usa *ojalá* y el subjuntivo.

Modelo 1. *Ojalá trabaje como dentista.*

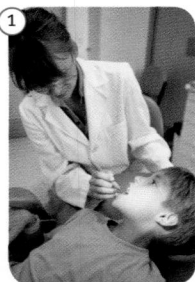   

35 Un viaje a Uruguay

 ▶ **Imagina** que vas de viaje a Uruguay con tu familia. Habla con tu compañero(a) sobre lo que tú y tu familia esperan que pase en el viaje. Usa estos verbos.

Modelo *Mi mamá quiere que mi hermana aprenda español.*

aprender	visitar	hablar
comprar	ver	trabajar
estudiar	vivir	leer
cantar	bailar	tomar

 CULTURA

La moneda de Uruguay

La moneda de Uruguay es el peso uruguayo. Hay monedas de 1 y 2 pesos, y billetes con valor entre 5 y 2.000 pesos.

En la fotografía puedes ver un billete de 1.000 pesos. El billete lleva la cara de Juana de Ibarbourou, una poeta uruguaya del siglo xx muy famosa.

36 Compara. ¿Qué personajes aparecen en las monedas y los billetes estadounidenses? ¿Hay alguna mujer? ¿A qué personaje femenino escogerías *(would you choose)*? ¿Por qué?

HERITAGE LANGUAGE LEARNERS

- Ask students to research the life and work of Juana de Ibarbourou, also known as "Juana de América." Much of her work deals with nature and love. Enable a discussion about the relationship between these two seemingly unrelated topics. You may help students choose some of her poems that exemplify these themes and have students read them aloud to the class, explaining any unfamiliar words or difficult passages to the other students.

MULTIPLE INTELLIGENCES:
Visual-Spatial Intelligence

- Tell students that they have been selected to design a new look for the *peso uruguayo*! They will need to research significant people, events, and objects from the arts, history, and nature of Uruguay and decide which ones deserve to have their images on the new currency. To finish the project, students must draw the new *peso* and include the value. Remind students to draw both a front and back for the bill, and a heads (*cara*) and tails (*cruz*) for the coins. Students should be prepared to explain the significance of the images they chose.

Gramática – Expresar deseo. El modo subjuntivo

34. Ask students to talk about their wishes for the future using the same structures.

35. After students have completed the activity, ask them to write a paragraph about what they would like to do with their family in Uruguay.

 AUDIO SCRIPT
See page 339 I.

 CULTURA

La moneda de Uruguay

In addition to Juana de Ibarbourou, Uruguayan banknotes bear images of noted Uruguayans like the poet Juan Zorrilla de San Martín; Pedro Figari, a painter, lawyer, and writer; and Dámaso Antonio Larrañaga, a politician, botanist, and naturalist.

Answer Key

32. En inglés se usan expresiones como *I wish, I want* y *I hope* para expresar deseo. En algunos casos se usa el modo subjuntivo. Por ejemplo: *If I <u>were</u> you, I'd study law.*

33. Answers will vary. Sample answers:
  2. Ojalá aprendan mucho en su viaje.
  3. Deseo que hablen con gente simpática.
  4. Quiero que tomen muchas fotografías.
  5. Deseo que se diviertan mucho.
  6. Ojalá completen su desafío.

34. Answers will vary. Sample answers:
  2. Ojalá trabaje con hispanos.
  3. Ojalá trabaje como abogado.
  4. Ojalá trabaje en una biblioteca.

35. Answers will vary.

36. Answers will vary.

Additional Resources

Fans Online activities
Practice Workbook

359

Unit 7

DESAFÍO 2

Comunicación

Presentation

- In this section, students will integrate the vocabulary and grammar from *Desafío 2* in order to talk about professions and to express wishes and preferences.

Activities	Standards	Resources
37.	1.2, 1.3	Audio
38.	1.2, 1.3, 5.1	
39.	1.1	
40.	1.1	
41. Final del desafío	1.2, 1.3, 5.1	

Teaching Suggestions

Warm-Up / Independent Starter

- Before coming to class, have students find photos (from magazines, newspapers, Internet, clip art, etc.) of people that portray different professions. As a warm-up ask them to write a description of their photos, what the person does, what he or she is wearing, and if they see any object related to the profession. Alternatively, you may provide the pictures.

Preparation

- Have students work in pairs and share their Independent Starters. Ask them to write captions for their pictures.
- Take 10 minutes to review the vocabulary and grammar themes of the *Desafío*.
- Refer students back to the *fotonovela* for *Desafío 2*. Have them identify vocabulary related to professions, as well as verb forms that express wishes. Do students understand the dialogue better now that they have gone through the vocabulary and grammar from the *Desafío*?

Activities

38. Have students work in pairs. Ask them to choose one of the given professions and write a job interview between the employer and a candidate. Ask for volunteer pairs to act out the interview, and have the class decide if the candidate got the job.

360

DESAFÍO 2

Comunicación

37 **Se necesita**

 ▶ **Escucha** varias ofertas de trabajo y une las dos columnas.

(A)	(B)
1. secretario(a)	a. trabajar de lunes a sábado
2. bibliotecario(a)	b. trabajar bien con niños
3. telefonista	c. hablar inglés y francés
4. socorrista	d. usar bien las computadoras

▶ **Escribe** oraciones con la información anterior.

Modelo 1. *Queremos que el secretario hable inglés y francés.*

38 **Tu futuro profesional**

▶ **Clasifica** estas profesiones. ¿En cuáles te gustaría *(would you like)* trabajar en el futuro? ¿Y en cuáles no? ¿Por qué?

Modelo *Ojalá no trabaje como cantante porque soy muy tímido y no me gusta cantar.*

cantante	telefonista
policía	actor / actriz
abogado(a)	agricultor(a)
cocinero(a)	arquitecto(a)
dentista	socorrista

39 **Un mundo ideal**

 ▶ **Habla** con tu compañero(a). Combina elementos de las tres columnas para expresar deseos y completa las oraciones.

Modelo *Deseo que el director de la escuela prohíba los exámenes.*

(A)	(B)	(C)
Ojalá (que) Espero que Deseo que Prefiero que	el/la director(a) de la escuela el/la profesor(a) de... mis compañeros(as) de clase mis amigos(as) mis padres	prohibir estudiar trabajar decidir llevar

---

Differentiated Instruction

DEVELOPING LEARNERS

- Ask students to use the results from activity 38 and make a chart that shows the most and least popular professions that students would like to have in the future. Ask students to review the reasons for the professions' popularity or lack thereof, and indicate the top two reasons next to each profession. Invite students to explain the results to the rest of the class.

EXPANDING LEARNERS

- Have students work with a partner to expand on activity 37. Ask pairs to choose one of the four job offers and write a script for an interview between a candidate and the employer. Then invite volunteer pairs to role-play their dialogues in front of the class. For example:

  A. *Queremos un secretario que hable inglés y francés.*

  B. *Yo hablo muy bien inglés y estoy estudiando francés.*

  A. *Esperamos que el secretario domine bien el francés. ¿Qué nivel de francés tienes?*

  B. *Nivel intermedio.*

40 **Deseos**

▶ **Habla** con tu compañero(a). Por turnos, expresa un deseo para tu futuro.
Él / Ella debe responder siguiendo el modelo.

| vivir | estudiar | viajar |
| hablar | ver | trabajar |

Modelo
A. *Ojalá viva en Argentina para aprender más español.*
B. *Prefiero que vivas en México porque está más cerca.*

Final del desafío

te es el contestador de la
ciedad Protectora de
imales. Deje un mensaje
spués de la señal.

¿Puedo hablar con...?

Espero que
encontremos a
Bruno, mamá.

Sí, ojalá llamen de la
Sociedad Protectora
de Animales.

¡Estás aquí! ¡Te buscamos
por todas partes!

¡Qué susto, Bruno!
¡Eres un perro muy malo!

¿Qué tal todo?

41 **La próxima vez**

▶ **Escribe.** Finalmente, Tess y Patricia encontraron a Bruno.
¿Qué crees que pasó después? Elige un final y escribe el diálogo.

1. Prefiero que Tess y Patricia hablen con la mujer sobre lo que pasó. Deben ser sinceras.
2. Espero que no hablen con la señora de que Bruno se escapó. No fue culpa suya.

---

39. Turn this activity into a class discussion, and give students the opportunity to express their wishes for their school. Create a list and write it on the board. Have students rank their choices.

40. In order to prepare students for this activity, ask them to imagine how their lives will be when they are 25 years old. Have them use the following verbs: *vivir, estudiar, viajar, aprender, hablar, ver, trabajar,* and *comprar*. For example: *Voy a vivir en Nueva York. Quiero ser técnico informático…* Then have students get together with a partner and work on the activity.

41. To extend this activity, break the class into small groups. Ask students to share what they would do in the same situation. Have them write at least one pro and one con about telling the truth to Bruno's owner. Have a final discussion with the class as a group.

AUDIO SCRIPT
See page 339I.

Answer Key

37. 1. c   2. d   3. a   4. b
▶ Answers will vary. Sample answers:
2. Esperamos que el bibliotecario use bien las computadoras.
3. Preferimos un telefonista que trabaje de lunes a sábado.
4. Preferimos un socorrista que trabaje bien con los niños.

38. Answers will vary.
39. Answers will vary.
40. Answers will vary.
41. Answers will vary.

Additional Resources

Fans Online activities
Practice Workbook

HERITAGE LANGUAGE LEARNERS

• Ask students to think about what could have transpired between the time Bruno escaped and the time he returned home. Then ask students to write a few paragraphs explaining these events. Tell them that they can write from Tess and Patricia's point of view, or write a first-person account from Bruno's perspective, or write a narrative in the third person. Students might even write an additional dialogue that would explain what happened.

SPECIAL-NEEDS LEARNERS

• Help students see the difference between the indicative and subjunctive moods by color-coding the verbs. For the activities on these pages, assign one color to the verbs in the indicative and another for those in the subjunctive, and ask students to write their sentences in a notebook using these colors. Ask students to use the same colors and write additional sentences with new subjects in the main clause. Guide them as they write their sentences.

361

Unit 7
DESAFÍO 3

Expresar sentimientos y emociones

Presentation

- In *Desafío 3*, Diana and Rita are at Platavisión Studios in Buenos Aires. Their task is to play a small part in a *telenovela*.
- In this section, students will preview:
  - Vocabulary for pastimes and hobbies.
  - Subjunctive after expressions of feelings, emotions, and opinions.

Activities	Standards	Resources
Fotonovela	1.2, 2.2, 3.1, 3.2	Vis. Pres.
42.	1.2	
43.	1.2, 1.3	
44.	1.1	
45. Cultura	1.1, 1.2, 2.2, 3.1, 3.2, 5.1	
Tu desafío	1.2, 2.2, 3.1, 5.1	

Teaching Suggestions

Warm-Up / Independent Starter

- Write the following statements on the board and ask students to react in writing.
  - *Ver la televisión es una pérdida de tiempo.*
  - *Me encanta ver la televisión.*
  - *Me gustan bastante las telenovelas.*

Preparation

- Lead a class discussion about the reactions described in the Independent Starter.
- If possible, play a one to two minute excerpt of a *telenovela* from a Spanish-speaking country. (Be sure to preview it before showing it to students.) Although students may not understand every word, ask them to comment on the emotions that they think are portrayed in the scene.

La fotonovela

Before Viewing

- Ask students to predict how Diana and Rita will meet their acting challenge.

After Viewing

- Ask students to identify the following: a) *qué le preocupa a Rita;* b) *qué quiere hacer Arturo;* c) *qué no quiere Marcela que haga Arturo.*

362

DESAFÍO 3   Expresar sentimientos y emociones

Estrellas de telenovela

Diana and Rita are at Platavisión Studios in Buenos Aires. Their task is to play a small part for the Argentinean *telenovela Marcela*.

42 Detective de palabras

▶ **Une** las dos columnas.

(A)	(B)
1. Me preocupa	a. que cuente chistes.
2. ¿Te molesta	b. que nos visites.
3. No soporto	c. que vuelvas.
4. Me encanta	d. que no quiera a Arturo?
5. No quiero	e. que no pienses tu decisión.

▶ **Escribe.** ¿En qué tiempo verbal están los verbos de la columna A? ¿Y los de la columna B?

362 trescientos sesenta y dos

Differentiated Instruction

DEVELOPING LEARNERS

- Read or write the following statements and ask students to identify the person from the *telenovela* that each one describes.
  1. *Quiere dar un paseo. (Arturo)*
  2. *Le gusta el tango. (Marcela)*
  3. *Quiere ir a la ciudad. (Marcela)*
  4. *No le gustan los chistes que cuenta. (Marcela)*
  5. *Pregunta si puede volver mañana. (Arturo)*
  6. *Dice que Arturo es joven, rico y divertido. (la madre de Marcela)*
  7. *No ama a Arturo. (Marcela)*
  8. *Quiere jugar al ajedrez. (Arturo)*

EXPANDING LEARNERS

- Ask students to identify the present subjunctive forms in the *fotonovela* (*pienses, quiera, cuente, visites, venga, vuelvas*). Ask them if they can extrapolate the rules for this use of the subjunctive (the main verb expresses feelings, emotions, or opinions). Then ask students to write original sentences about themselves using the verbs in column A (activity 42). They will need to change *te molesta* to the first person form (i.e., *me molesta*). Ask students to read their sentences aloud.

43 **¿Comprendes?**

▶ **Decide** si estas oraciones son ciertas o falsas. Si son falsas, corrígelas.

1. En la telenovela, Diana es la hija de Rita.
2. Marcela quiere marcharse a vivir en la ciudad.
3. La mamá de Marcela no se lleva bien con Arturo.
4. Marcela piensa que Arturo es muy divertido.
5. Arturo ama a Marcela.
6. Marcela ama a Arturo.

44 **¿Qué ves?**

▶ **Habla** con tu compañero(a). ¿Qué están haciendo estas personas?

Modelo A. *¿Qué está haciendo esa chica?*

B. *Está dando un paseo.*

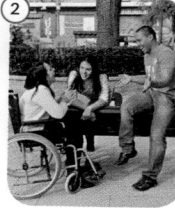

CULTURA

El tango

De todos los productos culturales de Argentina, el tango es posiblemente el más famoso. La UNESCO lo declaró Patrimonio Cultural Inmaterial de la Humanidad en 2009.

El tango nació en los barrios populares de Argentina y Uruguay como resultado de la fusión de distintos estilos musicales y bailes.

45 **Explica.** ¿Qué otros bailes de salón (*ballroom dances*) conoces, además del tango?

→ TU DESAFÍO Visita la página web para aprender más sobre el tango.

HERITAGE LANGUAGE LEARNERS

• Invite students to talk about Spanish-language *telenovelas* they, or members of their family, are familiar with. Ask them to talk about the plots, the actors, the settings, and the length of these soap operas, since *telenovelas* from Spanish-speaking countries play out over a designated period of time, and do not go on for many years as they do in the United States. If students have any magazines that deal with this TV genre, ask them to bring some copies to share with the class.

MULTIPLE INTELLIGENCES:
Bodily-Kinesthetic Intelligence

• Convert your classroom into a ballroom! Bring in some recordings of tango music and/or songs. Teach students how to tango, or ask if they or someone from their family knows how to dance. After a brief explanation and a demonstration, have students choose a partner and experiment with their tango moves. In place of personal instruction, you may find a video that demonstrates the tango step-by-step. You may want to consider a dance contest: affix numbers to the contestants' backs and, by a process of elimination, choose the top three pairs.

Expresar sentimientos y emociones

Activities

42. Remind students of the uses of the subjunctive learned in *Desafío 2*. Ask them what they will need to consider in making their matches.

44. Before completing this exercise, review the formation of the present progressive with students.

45. Play excerpts of tango music. Ask students to brainstorm verbs, nouns, and adjectives that come to mind as they listen. Have them work with a partner to compare and contrast their reactions to the music.

CULTURA

El tango

The tango is one of the most recognizable art forms of the Spanish-speaking world. It is believed to have its origins in the Río de la Plata region of Uruguay and Argentina at the end of the 19th century. It symbolizes the joy and pain of love, as well as the struggle to survive in a new culture. The instrument most closely associated with tango music is the *bandoneón*, an instrument related to the accordion.

Answer Key

42. 1. e   2. d   3. a   4. b   5. c
▶ Los verbos de la columna A están en el presente de indicativo y los de la columna B en el presente del subjuntivo.

43. 1. Cierto.
2. Cierto.
3. Falso. La mamá se lleva bien con Arturo.
4. Falso. Marcela no soporta sus chistes.
5. Cierto.
6. Falso. Marcela no lo ama.

44. Answers will vary.

45. Answers will vary.

Additional Resources

Fans Online activities

DESAFÍO 3

Vocabulario – Aficiones, actividades y espectáculos

Presentation

- In this section, students will learn vocabulary for hobbies and free-time activities.

Activities	Standards	Resources
Vocabulario	1.2	
46.	1.2, 1.3	Audio
47.	1.1, 1.2, 1.3	
48.	1.1, 1.3, 5.1	
49. Cultura	1.1, 1.2, 2.2, 3.2, 4.2, 5.1	
Tu desafío	1.2, 2.2, 5.1	

Teaching Suggestions

Warm-Up / Independent Starter

- Ask students to write down a list of things that they like to do in their free time.

Preparation

- Have students share their Independent Starters in pairs. Ask volunteers to describe to the class what their partners like to do in their free time.
- Write students' answers on the board and ask them to come up and sign their names under the activities that they like. Count the signatures and circle the most popular activity.

Activities

46. Ask students to draw a similar chart expressing their likes and dislikes about the activities on the board from the Preparation section.

47. Before doing the interview, brainstorm with the class a list of possible questions in which they include the vocabulary presented.

48. To expand the activity prepare three batches of index cards. In one batch include cards where you write *querer que, esperar que,* and *desear que.* On a second batch include cards with the vocabulary words. Include these infinitives on the third batch: *jugar, coleccionar, ir.* Have small groups pick the same number of cards from each batch and build sentences by matching their cards. The group with the largest number of accurate sentences wins.

364

Vocabulario

Aficiones, actividades y espectáculos

46 Mis aficiones

▶ **Escucha** a Rita hablar de sus aficiones y clasifícalas en una tabla como esta.

Le gusta mucho	Le gusta	No le gusta	No le gusta nada

Differentiated Instruction

DEVELOPING LEARNERS

- Have students find images of the activities pictured in the vocabulary and attach each one to a large index card. Then have them write the name of each activity on separate, smaller cards. Pair students with heritage speakers who will display the images and ask the developing learners to identify each one by matching the written word to the image and saying the word aloud.

EXPANDING LEARNERS

- Ask students to choose four of their favorite activities mentioned in this spread and have them complete a chart like the one below.

Actividad	¿Por qué?	¿Cuándo?	¿Dónde?	¿Con quién?
jugar al ajedrez	me hace pensar	por la noche	en casa	con mi padre

Then ask students to write sentences that pull together the information from their charts: *Me gusta jugar al ajedrez porque me hace pensar. Juego por la noche en casa. Juego con mi padre.*

47 ¿Qué les gusta?

▶ **Completa** estas oraciones.

Mi afición preferida es ___4___.

A mí me encanta jugar a las ___1___.

A nosotros lo que más nos gusta es ir al ___2___.

A mí me gusta mucho ___3___.

 ▶ **Habla.** Prepara una entrevista y pregunta a cuatro compañeros(as) por sus aficiones. Después, presenta la información a la clase.

Modelo *A mis compañeros(as) les gusta ir al cine. También...*

48 ¿Qué quieres que hagan?

▶ **Escribe** un párrafo sobre las actividades que quieres hacer durante las vacaciones.

Modelo *Yo quiero hacer deporte por las mañanas: patinar o montar en bici.*

 ▶ **Habla** con tu compañero(a). ¿Qué actividades quieres que hagan tus amigos(as) y familiares en sus vacaciones?

Modelo A *¿Qué quieres que haga tu hermano en sus vacaciones?*
B. *Ojalá monte en bici conmigo todas las mañanas.*

CULTURA

Las telenovelas

Las telenovelas (*soap operas*) son programas de televisión que cuentan una historia de tipo sentimental en muchos capítulos (*episodes*).

Las telenovelas tienen gran importancia económica en países como México, Argentina, Venezuela o Colombia. Cuentan con grandes presupuestos (*budgets*) y se exportan a países de todo el mundo.

Protagonistas de *Pasión de Gavilanes*.

49 **Explica.** ¿Te gustan las telenovelas? ¿Por qué crees que tienen tanto éxito en todo el mundo?

 ▶**TU DESAFÍO** Visita la página web para aprender más sobre las telenovelas.

 AUDIO SCRIPT
See page 339J.

 CULTURA

Las telenovelas

Telenovelas in Latin America have their roots in pre-TV radio dramas. They have become a very important business and cultural product, and some of these productions become international successes. *Yo soy Betty la fea*, for example, was originally produced in Colombia before it was successfully remade for an American audience as *Ugly Betty*. Argentina has produced several popular *telenovelas*, such as *Hombre de mar*, a romantic melodrama involving two half-brothers who love the same woman.

Answer Key

46. Le gusta mucho: coleccionar monedas y sellos.
Le gusta: ir al teatro y al cine, pasear y hacer deporte.
No le gusta: estar en casa viendo la televisión.
No le gusta nada: jugar al ajedrez y a los naipes.

47. 1. las damas   3. montar a caballo
2. teatro   4. patinar
▶ Answers will vary.

48. Answers will vary.
▶ Answers will vary.

49. Answers will vary.

Additional Resources

Fans Online activities
Practice Workbook

HERITAGE LANGUAGE LEARNERS

- Invite students to explain the Spanish-language names of the pieces in chess and the terms used in this game. Also ask students if they are familiar with these additional words to describe stamp and coin collecting: *la filatelia* (stamp collecting), *el/la filatelista* (stamp collector), *colección filatélica* (stamp collection), *la numismática* (coin collecting), *el/la numismático(a)* (coin collector). Encourage all students to write these words in their notebooks for vocabulary enrichment in both Spanish and English.

MULTIPLE INTELLIGENCES:
Verbal-Linguistic Intelligence

- Have students imagine that they are members of an extra-curricular club at their school and that they need to promote their club to attract new members. Students will need to design a public relations campaign that includes an oral presentation explaining the purpose of the club, as well as posters or handouts with details such as the club's name, meeting days and times, along with the names of its officers, and how to get in touch with current members. Students should also include the advantages of joining this club and how being a member will enhance their lives.

DESAFÍO 3

Gramática – Expresar sentimientos

Presentation

- In this section, students will learn:
  - Subjunctive with statements of emotion.
  - Present subjunctive stem-changing verbs.

Activities	Standards	Resources
Gramática	3.1	
50.	1.1, 3.1	
51.	1.3	
52.	1.2, 2.1, 2.2	Audio
53.	1.1, 1.3, 5.1	
54. Comparaciones	1.1, 1.2, 2.2, 3.2, 4.2, 5.1	
Tu desafío	1.2, 2.2, 3.2, 5.1	

Teaching Suggestions

Warm-Up / Independent Starter

- Write the following sentence starters on the board and ask students to complete each statement logically, using the subjunctive or infinitive.
  - Hoy espero que…
  - Los fans de las telenovelas quieren…
  - Mi madre prefiere que…
  - Mis amigos desean…

Preparation

- Have students share their responses from the Independent Starter section. Ask them how to determine if a sentence requires the use of the subjunctive.
- Review how to conjugate regular verbs in the present subjunctive. Then go over the grammar presentation with the class.

Activities

51. Have students write additional sentences using the verbs from the grammar presentation.

52. Ask students to make statements about how someone might react when coming to their community for the first time.

Gramática

Expresar sentimientos

- To express feelings, emotions, or opinions, you can use verbs like *alegrar* or *encantar* followed by a dependent clause with the verb in infinitive or in subjunctive.

  Use the infinitive when the main clause and the dependent clause have the same subject.

  Me alegra **volver** a casa.

  Use the subjunctive if they have different subjects.

  Me alegra que Pedro **vuelva** a casa.

Verbos útiles	
alegrar	to be glad
encantar	to love
molestar	to dislike
preocupar	to worry
sentir	to be sorry
sorprender	to be surprised
dar pena	to be sorry
dar miedo	to fear

Note: These verbs are used with indirect object pronouns, like *gustar*.

- In general, the present subjunctive is formed from the *yo* form of the present indicative. Therefore, irregular verbs in the indicative *yo* form are also irregular in the subjunctive.

  yo hago (verbo *hacer*) → haga, hagas, haga, hagamos, hagáis, hagan
  yo tengo (verbo *tener*) → tenga, tengas, tenga, tengamos, tengáis, tengan

- Stem-changing -ar and -er verbs follow the same pattern as they do in the present indicative. Stem-changing -ir verbs have an additional change in the *nosotros(as)* and *vosotros(as)* forms.

VERBOS CON RAÍZ IRREGULAR EN EL PRESENTE DE SUBJUNTIVO

	Pensar	Jugar	Volver	Pedir	Dormir
yo	piense	juegue	vuelva	pida	duerma
tú	pienses	juegues	vuelvas	pidas	duermas
usted, él, ella	piense	juegue	vuelva	pida	duerma
nosotros, nosotras	pensemos	juguemos	volvamos	pidamos	durmamos
vosotros, vosotras	penséis	juguéis	volváis	pidáis	durmáis
ustedes, ellos, ellas	piensen	jueguen	vuelvan	pidan	duerman

50 **Piensa.** ¿Puedes poner otros ejemplos de verbos con la raíz irregular?

51 **Emociones**

▶ **Escribe** estas oraciones con la forma correcta del presente de subjuntivo.

1. Me alegra que Rosa _____ (hacer) deporte.
2. Siento mucho que tú no _____ (querer) ir al teatro conmigo.
3. Me encanta que los niños _____ (jugar) en el parque.

Differentiated Instruction

DEVELOPING LEARNERS

- Before introducing the present subjunctive of stem-changing verbs to students, review these verbs in the present indicative with them. Then help students prepare conjugation charts to show the present subjunctive for the verbs listed that have an irregular *yo* form in the present tense of the indicative. Ask students to write these conjugations in their notebooks and refer to them when working on the activities.

EXPANDING LEARNERS

- Ask students to complete the following sentences with the present subjunctive of the verbs in parentheses:
  1. Temo que el tren … (salir) tarde. (salga)
  2. Me preocupa que tú no … (poder) terminar el trabajo. (puedas)
  3. A mi padre le molesta que nosotros … (volver) tarde. (volvamos)
  4. Siento que él no … (jugar) al ajedrez. (juegue)
  5. Me encanta que tú … (conducir) tan bien. (conduzcas)
  6. Nuestros padres no quieren que nosotros … (dormir) tanto. (durmamos)

52 **Las impresiones de Rita**

 ▶**Escucha** las impresiones de Rita sobre su viaje a Buenos Aires. ¿A qué fotografía se refiere cada oración?

Ⓐ  Ⓑ  Ⓒ Ⓓ

 53 **¿Qué sientes?**

▶**Escribe** las respuestas a estas preguntas.

1. ¿Qué te gusta que hagan tus profesores(as)?
   → *Me gusta que hagan clases interesantes.*
2. ¿Qué te sorprende que digan tus compañeros(as)?
3. ¿Qué te preocupa que piensen tus amigos(as)?
4. ¿Qué te encanta que haga tu comunidad?
5. ¿Qué te molesta que haga tu comunidad?

▶**Habla** con tus compañeros(as). ¿Tienen respuestas similares?

COMPARACIONES
El barrio de La Boca

La Boca es un barrio muy turístico de Buenos Aires. En este barrio vivían los inmigrantes europeos –sobre todo, italianos– a finales del siglo XIX y principios del XX. Ellos pintaban sus casas con los restos de pintura que les daban los marineros del puerto, por lo que el barrio adquirió un aspecto muy colorido.

Calle Caminito.

En la actualidad hay muchos artistas callejeros, pintores y artesanos que venden sus productos a los visitantes. También es habitual ver a músicos y bailarines de tango.

54 **Compara.** ¿Hay en tu ciudad algún barrio similar a La Boca?

▶**TU DESAFÍO** Visita la página web para aprender más sobre La Boca.

HERITAGE LANGUAGE LEARNERS

• Ask students to describe a neighborhood in their family's country of origin that attracts tourism. Students should explain something about the history of this *barrio*, describe several places of interest, address any celebrations or festivals that take place there, and make recommendations of when and what to visit. If possible, have them bring in images of the neighborhood. They may make their reports orally or in writing.

SPECIAL-NEEDS LEARNERS

• Help students who have either reading difficulties or visual impairments to comprehend the verbs shown on the page, including those with an irregular *yo* form in the present tense of the indicative, by recording your voice for the conjugations of these verbs in the present subjunctive. Have students listen to the recording and pronounce the verbs after you. Monitor their pronunciation and the accuracy of their conjugations.

---

53. Have students use their notes from talking with their partners and from the class presentations to write a letter to a local official, stating likes and dislikes about their community. They can also give suggestions on how to improve the community using the expressions learned in *Desafío 2*.

 AUDIO SCRIPT
See page 339J.

 COMPARACIONES

El barrio de La Boca

La Boca is located in southeastern Buenos Aires, near the mouth of the Riachuelo River, hence its name (*boca* means "mouth"). La Boca's main street, *calle Caminito*, is always filled with action that attracts tourists, such as people selling art, playing the guitar, and dancing the famous tango. *El Club Atlético Boca Juniors* is a famous soccer team that was started by five residents of La Boca in 1905, and attending one of the games is another great way to get an authentic Argentine experience.

Answer Key

50. poder → pueda, querer → quiera, servir → sirva

51. 1. haga 2. quieras 3. jueguen

52. 1. A 2. D 3. C 4. B

53. Answers will vary.
   ▶ Answers will vary.

54. Answers will vary.

Additional Resources

Fans Online activities
Practice Workbook

Unit 7

DESAFÍO 3

Comunicación

Presentation

- In this section, students will integrate the vocabulary and grammar from *Desafío 3* in order to talk about hobbies and free-time activities, and to express feelings.

Activities	Standards	Resources
55.	1.2, 1.3	Audio
56.	1.2	Audio
57	1.2, 1.3, 5.1	
58.	1.3	
59. Final del desafío	1.2, 1.3, 2.2, 5.1	
Tu desafío	1.2, 1.3	

Teaching Suggestions

Warm-Up / Independent Starter

- Have students write a list of after-school activities they have to do next week.

Preparation

- Divide the class into small groups and have them share their Independent Starters and decide who has the most exciting week.

Activities

56. You may extend this activity by playing "Family Feud," providing similar statements to the ones in this listening activity. For example:

A los estudiantes les molesta que...
a. *... los profesores manden tarea.*
b. *... los exámenes sean difíciles.*
c. *... las clases no sean divertidas.*

57. Provide groups of students with a situation from Rita's e-mail, and ask them to act it out in front of the class. The rest of the class should try to guess the situation and come up with a complete sentence to express likes or dislikes. You may want to act out the following model:

A. Student eating a lot of meat.
B. Student shaking his or her head in disapproval.
Class. *A (Student B) le molesta que/no le gusta que (Student A) coma mucha carne.*

Comunicación

55 **Las aficiones de Roberto**

▶ **Escucha** a Roberto y escribe. ¿Qué actividades hace cada día?

lunes	martes	miércoles	jueves	viernes	sábado	domingo

56 **Diana y Andrea**

▶ **Escucha** a Diana y elige la opción correcta.

1. a. A Diana le gusta que Andrea quiera ir a conciertos con ella.
   b. A Diana le molesta que Andrea no quiera ir a conciertos con ella.
2. a. A Diana le da pena que Andrea no pueda montar a caballo.
   b. A Diana le preocupa que Andrea monte a caballo.
3. a. A Diana no le gusta que Andrea quiera ir a ver exposiciones.
   b. A Diana no le sorprende que Andrea quiera ir a ver exposiciones.
4. a. A Diana le da miedo que Andrea estudie en una universidad diferente de la suya.
   b. A Diana le alegra que Andrea piense ir a la misma universidad que ella.

57 **¿Qué piensa Rita?**

▶ **Lee** el mensaje de correo de Rita y escribe. ¿Qué cosas le gusta que haga Diana? ¿Y qué cosas no le gusta que haga?

Modelo *A Rita le gusta que Diana se divierta.*

▶ **Escribe.** ¿Qué actividades te gusta que hagan tus amigos(as) o tus familiares? ¿Qué no te gusta que hagan?

Modelo

Me alegra que mi hermana pequeña aprenda a nadar porque en junio vamos a ir a la playa.

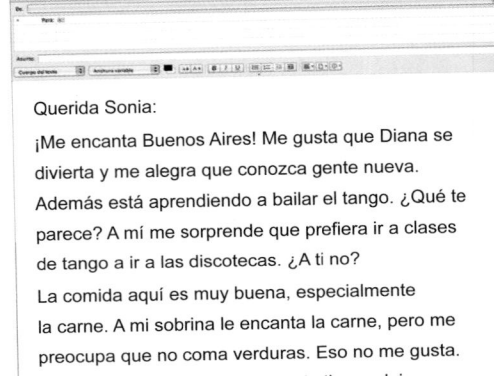

Querida Sonia:

¡Me encanta Buenos Aires! Me gusta que Diana se divierta y me alegra que conozca gente nueva. Además está aprendiendo a bailar el tango. ¿Qué te parece? A mí me sorprende que prefiera ir a clases de tango a ir a las discotecas. ¿A ti no?

La comida aquí es muy buena, especialmente la carne. A mi sobrina le encanta la carne, pero me preocupa que no coma verduras. Eso no me gusta. Me da pena que Diana pase tanto tiempo lejos de casa, pero esta es una buena experiencia.

¡Hasta pronto!
Rita

368 trescientos sesenta y ocho

Differentiated Instruction

DEVELOPING LEARNERS

- To reinforce students' comprehension of the subjunctive with verbs that express emotions, feelings, and opinions, ask them to complete each of the following sentences with something that describes how they feel.

  – *Me gusta que...*   – *Me molesta que...*
  – *Me alegra que...*   – *No soporto que...*
  – *Me sorprende que...* – *Temo que...*
  – *Me preocupa que...* – *Siento que...*

EXPANDING LEARNERS

- Using Rita's letter to Sonia as an example, ask students to write a letter to a friend or family member, describing their feelings and opinions about what another friend or family member does. Encourage them to use verbs that express feelings, emotions, and opinions throughout their letters. Call on students to read their letters aloud.

58 Tus sentimientos

▶ **Escribe** oraciones. ¿Qué sentimientos te producen estas acciones?

Modelo *No me gusta nada que la gente llegue tarde al cine.*

| me sorprende | no me gusta nada | me encanta |
| me preocupa | me gusta | me da miedo |

llegar tarde al cine   hacer deporte   manejar deprisa

Final del desafío

Me preocupa que no actuemos bien.

No, no. Lo están haciendo muy bien. Y me encanta que quieran trabajar con nosotros.

Queridas amigas:

¡Felicidades! Estoy muy contento con su trabajo. Tienen mucho talento. Me encanta que ___1___ en esta serie.

Me da pena que no ___2___ más tiempo en nuestro país y que no ___3___ terminar la telenovela. Solo tiene 200 capítulos...

Un saludo.

Claudio

59 La nueva promesa de la televisión

▶ **Completa.** Al director de la telenovela le gustó mucho trabajar con Diana y Rita. Lee su nota y complétala con la forma correcta de estos verbos.

 poder   pasar   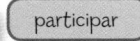 participar

 **→ TU DESAFÍO**   Visita la página web. Escucha las preguntas de tu *Minientrevista Desafío 3* y escribe las respuestas.

---

58. Have groups think about things they like and do not like in their community. Ask them to create a poster or flyer that includes pictures, drawings, and clip art. Then, have them post it in their classroom. For example: *Nos preocupa que la gente tire papeles al suelo.*

59. Have groups write a scene for a *telenovela* and encourage them to use vocabulary and grammar learned in this *Desafío*. If possible, ask them to act the scene out and record it. Play the recordings in class and have the class vote for the best scene.

🎧 **AUDIO SCRIPT**
See page 339J.

Answer Key

55. lunes: monta en bicicleta, tiene clases de piano; martes: monta a caballo; miércoles: monta en bicicleta; jueves: monta a caballo; viernes: monta en bicicleta, juega al ajedrez; sábado y domingo: lee libros, ve la tele, va al cine con sus amigos

56. 1. a   2. a   3. b   4. a

57. Answers will vary. Sample answer:
A Rita le gusta que Diana se divierta y que conozca a gente nueva. También le gusta que Diana vaya a clases de tango. A Rita no le gusta que Diana no coma verduras. Tampoco le gusta que Diana pase tanto tiempo lejos de casa.
▶ Answers will vary.

58. Answers will vary.

59. 1. participen   2. pasen   3. puedan

Additional Resources

Fans Online activities
Practice Workbook

HERITAGE LANGUAGE LEARNERS

• Ask students to imagine that they are visiting their family's country of origin. Have them write a letter to a friend in the United States, explaining what they have been doing. They need to cite some actual places of historical or cultural interest in their letters, and should address other topics such as pastimes and activities they have been enjoying. Students should use a variety of verbs that express emotions, feelings, and opinions and use the subjunctive correctly.

MULTIPLE INTELLIGENCES:
Intrapersonal Intelligence

• Ask students to think about their answers to the following questions:
  – ¿Qué te preocupa?
  – ¿Qué no soportas?
  – ¿Qué temes?/¿De qué tienes miedo?
  – ¿Qué te alegra?
  – ¿Qué te da pena?

• Ask them to write at least two paragraphs elaborating their answers to these questions. Encourage them to use the subjunctive as much as possible.

DESAFÍO 4

Expresar duda y hacer valoraciones

Presentation

- In *Desafío 4*, Tim and Mack must hike up to the *Mirador del Aconcagua* to get a glimpse of the highest mountain in the Western Hemisphere.

- In this section, students will preview:
  - Vocabulary related to sports.
  - Subjunctive after expressions of doubt, uncertainty, and value judgments.
  - Irregular verbs in the subjunctive.

Activities	Standards	Resources
Fotonovela	1.2, 2.1, 2.2, 3.1	Vis. Pres.
60.	1.2, 1.3	
61.	1.2, 1.3	
62.	1.3	
63.	1.1, 1.2, 2.2	
64. Conexiones	1.1, 1.2, 3.1, 3.2	

Teaching Suggestions

Warm-Up / Independent Starter

- Write the following questions on the board and ask students to answer in complete sentences.
  1. *¿Qué deportes te gustan?*
  2. *¿Eres fan de algún equipo?*
  3. *¿Fuiste a algún partido en el pasado?*

Preparation

- Have students form pairs and share the information from their Independent Starters.

- Then ask pairs to note the title of this *Desafío* and to brainstorm the possible connection between "el clásico" and "el Aconcagua." Ask four or five pairs to share their ideas with the class.

 La fotonovela

Before Viewing

- Begin a discussion with students: *Si tienes que elegir entre subir una montaña o ver un partido de fútbol entre tu equipo favorito y su rival, ¿qué prefieres hacer?*

After Viewing

- Have students write as many sentences as they can about what they have learned in this *fotonovela* about Tim, Mack, and Miguel.

El clásico y el Aconcagua

Tim and Mack have to walk all the way up to the *Mirador del Aconcagua* in the Andes. Unfortunately, the climb coincides with the day of the biggest soccer match of the season, and their guide wants to be back in time to see it on TV.

Continuará…

60 **Detective de palabras**

▶ **Completa** estas oraciones.

1. _____ que empecemos pronto.
2. ¿_____ que subamos tan deprisa?
3. _____ lleguemos a tiempo.
4. _____ que lleguemos.

▶ **Escribe.** ¿Qué oraciones expresan duda? ¿Y cuáles expresan una opinión?

Differentiated Instruction

DEVELOPING LEARNERS

- Ask students if the following statements about the *fotonovela* are true (*cierto*) or false (*falso*):
  1. *Mack y Tim van a subir al Aconcagua en bicicleta. (falso)*
  2. *El guía dice que le gusta montar a caballo. (falso)*
  3. *La pasión del guía es el fútbol. (cierto)*
  4. *El Boca Juniors es un equipo muy famoso de Córdoba. (falso)*
  5. *El guía se llama Miguel. (cierto)*
  6. *El clásico empieza a las dos. (cierto)*
  7. *Mack duda que lleguen a tiempo. (cierto)*

EXPANDING LEARNERS

- Ask students to read the dialogues in the *fotonovela* silently and then close their books. Next, ask them to write a few paragraphs to explain in their own words what is going on in the *fotonovela*. Students should also include a vivid description of what they believe the characters are thinking as they hike up the mountain. Encourage students to add more dialogues, too. Call on individuals to read their paragraphs aloud.

61 **¿Comprendes?**

► **Responde** a estas preguntas.

1. ¿Qué deportes le gustan a Miguel?
2. ¿Qué es el Boca Juniors?
3. ¿Por qué Miguel quiere subir deprisa al mirador?
4. ¿A qué hora empieza el partido?

62 **Deportes**

► **Escribe** el nombre de estos deportes. Busca información en la fotonovela.

①  ②  ③

63 **¡Hay que ser lógico!**

► **Habla** con tu compañero(a). ¿Qué palabra no pertenece a cada grupo?

1. El Aconcagua
   a. los Andes
   b. el Boca Juniors
   c. la montaña

2. El mirador del Aconcagua
   a. el esquí
   b. el senderismo
   c. el fútbol

3. El Boca Juniors
   a. el senderismo
   b. el fútbol
   c. el equipo

4. El clásico
   a. el equipo
   b. el partido
   c. el esquí

CONEXIONES: GEOGRAFÍA

El Aconcagua

El Aconcagua es una montaña de 6.962 metros situada en la cordillera de los Andes. Es el pico más alto del hemisferio sur.

Miles de senderistas y alpinistas de todo el mundo van a esta montaña cada año. Entre diciembre y marzo la visitan de 6.000 a 7.000 montañeros.

64 **Piensa y explica.** ¿Por qué crees que los alpinistas eligen los meses de diciembre a marzo para subir al Aconcagua?

HERITAGE LANGUAGE LEARNERS

• Invite students to talk about *fútbol* in their family's country of origin. Encourage them to share what they know about teams, players, and trainers, including the rivalry between certain teams. Students might also address the World Cup that is played every four years to see which national team is the best. If possible, have students bring to class any realia associated with the sport (e.g., ticket stubs, programs, and team memorabilia). If students know any cheers or team songs, ask them to teach these to the rest of the class.

MULTIPLE INTELLIGENCES:

Naturalist Intelligence

• Recall that Mack and Tim are going to go hiking in the Andes. In addition to being an excellent exercise, hiking offers individuals a chance to get in touch with nature. Where would students recommend visitors go in order to enjoy nature in their community? Have them research some local nature trails, scenic walks, or even forest preserves or national parks. Then ask students to plan a walk or hike for visitors to one of these places, and point out places of interest or flora and fauna they can expect to see along the way.

DESAFÍO 4

Expresar duda y hacer valoraciones

Activities

61. Expand this activity by asking students to use the "wishing" and "wanting" expressions learned in *Desafío 3* to write additional sentences. For example: *Quiero que Miguel tenga la oportunidad de ver el partido.*

62. Ask students to work with a partner to identify not only the name, but the equipment necessary to participate in each of the sports depicted.

63. Ask students to explain the relationship that exists between those words that belong together and why the other word in the group does not belong.

CONEXIONES: GEOGRAFÍA

El Aconcagua

Mount Aconcagua is located on the Argentine-Chilean border. At about 22,834 feet, this mountain is the highest peak in the Western Hemisphere. There are two possible origins for the word *Aconcagua*: from the Arauca words *aconca hue*, meaning "from the other side," or from the Quechua words *ackon cahuak*, meaning "stone sentinel."

Answer Key

60. 1. Es importante   3. Y quizás
2. Es necesario   4. Dudo
► Duda: 3 y 4. Opinión: 1 y 2.

61. 1. Le gustan el senderismo, el esquí y el fútbol.
2. Es un equipo de fútbol de Buenos Aires.
3. Porque quiere ver el partido entre el Boca Juniors y el River.
4. Empieza a las dos.

62. 1. fútbol   2. esquí   3. senderismo

63. 1. b   2. c   3. a   4. c

64. Answers will vary.

Additional Resources

Fans Online activities

371

Unit 7
DESAFÍO 4
Vocabulario – Deportes

Presentation

- In this section, students will learn vocabulary for sports.

Activities	Standards	Resources
Vocabulario	1.2, 3.1	
65.	1.2, 1.3	
66.	1.2	
67.	1.2	Audio
68.	1.1, 5.1	
69. Cultura	1.1, 1.2, 2.2, 3.1, 3.2, 4.2, 5.2	Video
Tu desafío	1.2, 2.2, 3.1, 5.1	

Teaching Suggestions

Warm-Up / Independent Starter

- Ask students to look at the vocabulary and make a list of cognates and words that they recognize. In addition, have students identify any previously learned words.

Preparation

- Ask students to work together to review their Independent Starters. Have them give you examples of teams or players that won (*ganaron*) or lost (*perdieron*) a competition.

Activities

65. Divide the class into the three groups listed in the exercise according to the students' preferences. Ask them to talk with one another regarding why they practice, watch, or don't like the sports listed.

67. Form groups to brainstorm a list of vocabulary related to each of the sports that students will hear about. Before listening to the audio, have groups share their lists.

68. Ask students to prepare three additional questions to use to interview their classmates. After the activity is completed, ask students to write a paragraph describing their partner's interests. Then collect their paragraphs. Read them aloud without giving names and ask the class to guess who is being described.

372

Vocabulario

Deportes

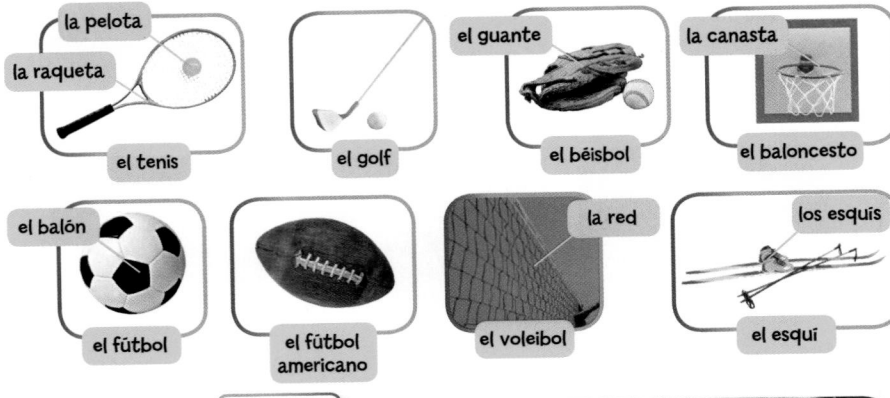

la pelota
la raqueta
el tenis

el golf

el guante
el béisbol

la canasta
el baloncesto

el balón
el fútbol

el fútbol americano

la red
el voleibol

los esquís
el esquí

¿Tú haces alpinismo?

No, es muy duro. Prefiero hacer senderismo.

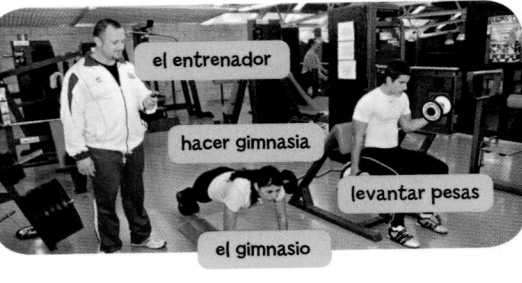

el entrenador

hacer gimnasia

levantar pesas

el gimnasio

Acciones

competir

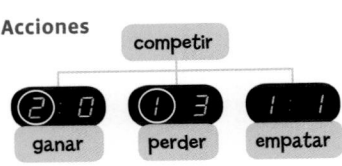

ganar   perder   empatar

65 Tus preferencias

▶ **Clasifica** los deportes anteriores según tus preferencias.

Deportes que practico	Deportes que veo en la televisión	Deportes que no me gustan

Differentiated Instruction

DEVELOPING LEARNERS

- Distribute index cards to students and ask them to make flashcards for the vocabulary on this page. Have students write the Spanish word on one side and the English word on the opposite side. Then have them work with a partner and quiz one another with the cards. Point out the cognates among the new words (*gimnasio, tenis, golf, béisbol, fútbol, voleibol, esquí*) and monitor students' pronunciation so that they are not influenced by the words' pronunciation in English.

EXPANDING LEARNERS

- Ask students to write a newspaper article describing an important game between two archrival teams in a sport they are familiar with. First, they need to choose the sport and two actual teams or make them up. They also need to provide some background information on the teams' rivalry and the players. Then they should provide a general description of the game, with details of key plays or scores. Encourage students to add an interesting anecdote about the place where the game is being played, a player, or the history of the team rivalry. Ask volunteers to read their articles aloud.

66 ¡Estoy confundido!

▶ **Decide** si estas oraciones son ciertas (C) o falsas (F). Después, corrige las oraciones falsas.

1. Los alpinistas practicamos el alpinismo en la piscina.

2. Yo levanto pesas en el gimnasio.

Estoy muy emocionado porque mi equipo perdió la competición.

3.

4. Aquí hago gimnasia.

5. Este deporte es muy fácil. Solo necesitas un balón.

67 Deportistas

▶ **Escucha** a varias personas. ¿Qué deporte practica cada una?

a. alpinismo　　**b.** fútbol　　**c.** béisbol　　**d.** esquí　　**e.** gimnasia　　**f.** golf

68 Nuestro deporte favorito

▶ **Habla** con cuatro compañeros(as). ¿Qué deportes practican?

CULTURA
El fútbol argentino

El fútbol es el deporte más popular en Argentina. Algunos de los jugadores más famosos de todos los tiempos son argentinos: Di Stefano, Maradona, Messi...

Boca Juniors y River Plate son los equipos más populares. Hay una rivalidad intensa entre ellos y sus fans son famosos por su pasión durante los partidos.

Lionel Messi.

69 Compara. ¿Cuál es el deporte más popular en tu país? ¿Existe una rivalidad similar a la del Boca y el River entre dos equipos?

▶ TU DESAFÍO　Visita la página web para aprender más sobre el fútbol argentino.

trescientos setenta y tres　**373**

---

69. As an extension of this activity, ask students to research other famous Argentine sports figures and to write a short biography. As a follow-up, you may ask students to dramatize a party that all of these athletes attend. Each student must stay "in character" as they chat about their accomplishments.

AUDIO SCRIPT
See page 339J.

CULTURA
El fútbol argentino

Argentina has won the World Cup—the trophy that symbolizes the world championship—twice: in 1978 and 1986. The Argentine football (soccer) team has also won two Olympic Gold medals: in 2004 and 2008. The traditional rivalry between the two leading soccer teams in Argentina, Boca Juniors and River Plate, is well known. The match that they play against each other, in one of the national competitions, is known as *el clásico*.

Answer Key

65. Answers will vary.

66. 1. Falso. Los alpinistas practicamos el alpinismo en las montañas.
2. Cierto.
3. Falso. Estoy muy emocionado porque mi equipo ganó la competición.
4. Cierto.
5. Falso. Solo necesitas una pelota y una raqueta.

67. 1. b　　2. d　　3. f　　4. c　　5. a　　6. e

68. Answers will vary.

69. Answers will vary.

Additional Resources

Fans Online activities
Practice Workbook

HERITAGE LANGUAGE LEARNERS

- Point out that ball games have been popular on the American continents for centuries. Invite students to research some of these *juegos de pelota*. Students should describe some of the following: where and how these games were played, how the playing field was organized, who the players were and how they were selected, and why these games were played. They might also like to research what the consequences were for being the winner or the loser. Students might prepare a written report or make an oral presentation to the rest of the class, explaining any unfamiliar terms.

TOTAL PHYSICAL RESPONSE (TPR)

- Divide the class into two or more teams and give each team member one of the vocabulary words on a piece of paper. Without revealing their word to anyone, team members take turns pantomiming their word for the team, and the team must guess what it is in a predetermined period of time. Teams get one point for each correct answer. You may want to include words for hobbies and free-time activities from *Desafío 3*.

DESAFÍO 4

Gramática – Expresar duda y hacer valoraciones

Presentation

- In this section, students will learn:
  - Subjunctive after expressions of doubt, uncertainty, and value judgments.
  - Irregular verbs in the subjunctive.

Activities	Standards	Resources
Gramática	3.1	
70.	1.1, 4.1	
71.	1.2, 1.3	
72.	1.2, 1.3	Audio
73.	1.1	

Teaching Suggestions

Warm-Up / Independent Starter

- Ask students to analyze the sentences in each of the following groups and to write an explanation for the use of the subjunctive (A), indicative (B), and infinitive (C).

  A. *Dudo que Tomás juegue al baloncesto.*
  Es horrible que los beisbolistas no estén preparados para jugar.

  B. *No dudo que Tomás juega al baloncesto.*
  Es cierto que los jugadores de béisbol no están preparados para jugar.

  C. *Es importante jugar al baloncesto.*
  Es horrible no estar preparado para jugar.

Preparation

- Have students share their explanations from their Independent Starters. Be sure they understand that the sentences in Group A use the subjunctive to express doubt and value judgment. The sentences in Group B use the indicative to express certainty. The sentences in Group C do not need to use the subjunctive because two different subjects are not involved.

- Now that your students have been introduced to the use of the subjunctive after expressions of doubt and value judgment, go over the grammar presentation. Provide additional examples, if necessary.

374

Gramática

Expresar duda y hacer valoraciones

El subjuntivo para expresar duda

- There are many expressions to show doubt, and they are normally paired with clauses that have the verb in the subjunctive. There are also expressions that indicate certainty and are therefore followed by the verb in the indicative.

Expresiones con subjuntivo
Es posible / probable / imposible que
Quizás
Dudo que

Expresiones con indicativo
Es verdad / cierto / evidente que
Estoy seguro(a) de que / Sé que
No dudo que

Dudo que Pedro **esté** en casa. Sé que Pedro **está** en casa.

El subjuntivo para hacer valoraciones

- The subjunctive is used in expressions that show value judgments.

  Adjetivos útiles
  bueno
  malo
  importante
  necesario
  increíble
  horrible

Es + adjective + que + subjunctive

  Es importante que ustedes **practiquen** deporte.

- The following verbs are irregular in the present subjunctive forms:

VERBOS IRREGULARES EN EL PRESENTE DE SUBJUNTIVO

	Dar	Estar	Saber	Ser	Ir
yo	dé	esté	sepa	sea	vaya
tú	des	estés	sepas	seas	vayas
usted, él, ella	dé	esté	sepa	sea	vaya
nosotros, nosotras	demos	estemos	sepamos	seamos	vayamos
vosotros, vosotras	deis	estéis	sepáis	seáis	vayáis
ustedes, ellos, ellas	den	estén	sepan	sean	vayan

- Verbs ending in -car, -gar, -zar, -ger, -gir, and -guir have spelling changes.

  -car sacar → saque, saques…   -ger, -gir dirigir → dirija, dirijas…
  -gar llegar → llegue, llegues…   -guir seguir → siga, sigas…
  -zar abrazar → abrace, abraces…

70 **Piensa.** ¿Cómo se expresa una valoración o una duda en inglés?

Differentiated Instruction

DEVELOPING LEARNERS

- Give students practice with the present subjunctive of irregular verbs. Prepare a cube with the different subject pronouns on each side. Then say the infinitive of one of the verbs featured on the page, including those with spelling changes, and have a student roll the cube. The student will repeat the verb you said and say the pronoun that is indicated on the cube, along with the correct form of the present subjunctive. Repeat with other students and be sure all have several chances to roll the cube to practice the subjunctive.

EXPANDING LEARNERS

- Have students complete these sentences with the present tense of either the indicative or the subjunctive.
  1. *Estoy segura de que tú … (saber) conjugar todos estos verbos. (sabes)*
  2. *Es importante que tú … (estar) en el estadio antes de las dos. (estés)*
  3. *Es necesario que su equipo … (empatar). (empate)*
  4. *Es posible que ellos … (saber) jugar al tenis. (sepan)*
  5. *Dudo que los exámenes … (ser) difíciles. (sean)*
  6. *Quizás nosotros … (ir) a Argentina este verano. (vayamos)*

71 Todos tienen una opinión diferente

▶ **Escribe** si estas oraciones expresan duda, certeza o una valoración. Después, complétalas poniendo el verbo en la forma correcta.

Modelo Es necesario que nosotros _____ en el gimnasio a las nueve.
      _{estar}
    → *Valoración. Es necesario que nosotros estemos en el gimnasio a las nueve.*

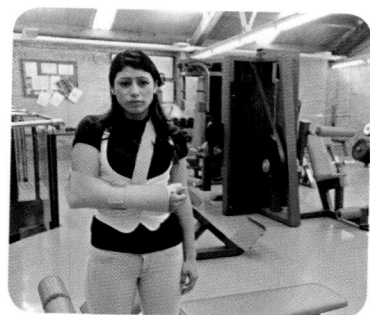

1. Es imposible que ella _____ levantando pesas con el brazo roto. _{seguir}

2. Estoy segura de que Miguel _____ esquiar. _{saber}

3. No dudo que mi equipo _____ el mejor. _{ser}

4. Quizás yo _____ mañana a nadar a la piscina. _{ir}

5. Dudo que ella _____ alpinismo, es un deporte muy duro. _{practicar}

▶ **Escribe** tres oraciones que expresen duda y tres oraciones que expresen una valoración. Después, intercámbialas con tu compañero(a). ¿Son correctas?

72 ¡Qué emocionante!

▶ **Escucha** la conversación entre Tim y Miguel y responde a estas preguntas.

1. Para ver el clásico, ¿qué es necesario que hagan los tres?
2. ¿Qué duda Tim?
3. Según Miguel, ¿qué es cierto?
4. ¿De qué está seguro Miguel?
5. Según Miguel, ¿qué es imposible?
6. ¿Qué espera ver Miguel algún día?

73 ¡Te toca a ti!

▶ **Habla** con tu compañero(a). Expresa tu opinión.

1. ¿El guía es un buen profesional?
2. ¿Tim y Mack están en forma?
3. ¿Mack puede caminar más rápido?
4. ¿Tim, Mack y el guía van a subir hasta el mirador?
5. ¿Al final, llegan todos a tiempo para ver el partido?

> Estoy segura de que el guía es un buen profesional. ¿Y tú?

HERITAGE LANGUAGE LEARNERS

• Ask students to work together and design a crossword puzzle for the new vocabulary presented in this *Desafío*, as well as some of the verb forms in the present subjunctive. Students will write the clues and use computer software to create the crossword grid, or design one on graph paper. After they verify that the clues and solutions are correct, have them make copies of the puzzle, and distribute them to the rest of the students, who will work with partners and try to solve the puzzle.

MULTIPLE INTELLIGENCES:
Intrapersonal Intelligence

• Ask students to imagine that it is the eve of a championship game or match and that they are one of the players. Ask them to write an entry in their diary or journal describing how they feel, and what they hope the outcome will be. Encourage them to use expressions of doubt and uncertainty as well as those that express value judgments so they can incorporate the present subjunctive into their entries.

Activities

72. Ask students to read the questions and predict the answers. After students listen to the audio selection, ask six volunteers to write their responses on the board. Ask other students to read the sentences written on the board, identify any grammatical errors that they find, and judge whether they are factually correct.

73. Have students include information that supports their answers (e.g., *Estoy seguro de que el guía es un buen profesional porque hace cinco años que trabaja en el Aconcagua*).

AUDIO SCRIPT
See page 339J.

Answer Key

70. En inglés se usa la fórmula *It is + adjective + that + indicative* para hacer valoraciones. Para expresar duda se usan frases como *Perhaps, I don't think that, It's possible,* etc.

71. 1. Duda. Es imposible que ella siga...
   2. Certeza. Estoy segura de que Miguel sabe...
   3. Certeza. No dudo que mi equipo es...
   4. Duda. Quizás yo vaya...
   5. Duda. Dudo que ella practique...
   ▶ Answers will vary.

72. 1. Es necesario que caminen muy rápido.
   2. Duda que Mack pueda caminar más rápido.
   3. Es cierto que no están en una competición.
   4. Está seguro de que su equipo va a ganar.
   5. Es imposible que el River gane.
   6. Espera ver un partido en el estadio.

73. Answers will vary.

Additional Resources

Fans Online activities
Practice Workbook

Unit 7

DESAFÍO 4

Comunicación

Presentation

- In this section, students will integrate the vocabulary and grammar from *Desafío 4* in order to use the vocabulary for sports and to use the subjunctive after expressions of doubt, uncertainty, and value judgments.

Activities	Standards	Resources
74.	1.2, 1.3, 2.1	
75.	1.1, 1.3	
76.	1.2, 1.3	Audio
77. Final del desafío	1.3, 2.1, 2.2	

Teaching Suggestions

Warm-Up / Independent Starter

- In order to determine if students understand the dialogue better now that they have gone through the vocabulary and grammar practices, have them turn to the *fotonovela* for *Desafío 4*. Ask students to make a list of the sports vocabulary used, explain how the subjunctive is used, and identify the infinitive form of the verbs used.

Preparation

- Ask students to use the vocabulary and verb list generated in the Independent Starter activity to write an interview between a news reporter and Tim and Mack.

Activities

74. Based on the content of the article, ask students to identify the following: *el deporte, los dos equipos, el entrenador de uno de los equipos, cuándo se jugó el partido, el jugador que marcó el gol, cuándo lo marcó, el resultado del partido, el equipo que ganó,* and *el equipo que perdió.* As a further extension of this activity, assign students to groups of two. Tell them that they will have eight to ten minutes to prepare a role-play scene between two people who are at the game. Ask them to incorporate the vocabulary of the *Desafío.* They are to express their doubts, their preferences, their wishes, and their emotions about the game that they are watching.

Comunicación

74 Sobre el clásico

▶ **Lee** este artículo de prensa y complétalo.

aficionados	entrenador	equipo	fútbol
gol	Boca	partido	ganó

El River Plate vence al Juniors

El encuentro supone la séptima derrota en catorce jornadas del equipo del ___2___ Claudio Borghi

EFE - Buenos Aires - 17/11/2010

El River Plate ___3___ este martes al Boca Juniors por 1-0 en el ___4___ clásico del ___5___ argentino y le dejó sin objetivos en las cinco jornadas del torneo Apertura que quedan por delante. Un ___6___ del defensa Jonathan Maidana, exjugador boquense, con un remate de cabeza a los 53 minutos, provocó la primera gran alegría de la temporada a los ___7___ del River Plate y aportó tres puntos vitales al ___8___ que lucha por mantenerse en la categoría.

Diario *El País* (España).

75 ¿Estás seguro(a)?

▶ **Escribe** sobre estas afirmaciones. Usa expresiones de certeza si estás seguro(a) o expresiones de duda si no lo estás.

Modelo *Sé que la profesora de Español practica deporte porque la vi en el gimnasio.*

1. Tu profesor(a) de Español practica deporte.
2. Un(a) estudiante de tu clase juega al tenis.
3. Ningún(a) estudiante de tu clase sabe esquiar.
4. El baloncesto se empezó a jugar en los Estados Unidos.
5. El béisbol es el deporte nacional en Venezuela.
6. En el fútbol juegan dos equipos de once jugadores.

 ▶ **Habla** con tu compañero(a). ¿Saben las mismas cosas?

Modelo A. *Sé que la profesora de Español practica deporte porque la vi en el gimnasio.*
B. *Ah, no lo sabía.*

Differentiated Instruction

DEVELOPING LEARNERS

- Before beginning the activities in this spread, review the present subjunctive of irregular verbs, including those with stem changes. Also review the phrases expressing doubt and value judgments that require the use of the subjunctive. Contrast phrases of doubt with those that express certainty and give students several examples of each so they can recognize when to use the indicative or the subjunctive. Then give students some sentences to complete. For example:
  – *Ella está segura de que tú ... (llegar) a tiempo. (llegas)*
  – *Dudo que ellos ... (saber) jugar. (sepan)*

EXPANDING LEARNERS

- Have students rewrite the *Final del desafío,* but choose a different genre. You may suggest that they write a simple narrative in the first- or third-person, an essay, a newspaper account, or even a poem. Students are free to change the ending to the story, but should follow the overall plot and keep the same characters and setting.

76 Las opiniones de una experta

 ▶ **Escucha** las opiniones de una entrenadora. ¿A qué deportistas se refiere en cada caso?

 ▶ **Escucha** otra vez. ¿Qué opina la entrenadora?

Modelo *Es importante que entrenen mucho para jugar bien.*

Final del desafío

¡Hoy toda la Argentina va a ver el clásico en la televisión!

Pero tenemos que cumplir nuestro desafío.

Sí, claro. Vinimos a ver el Aconcagua. ¡Adelante!

¡Un momento! Quizás podamos ver el partido.

¡¡GOOOOOOOOOOL!!

¡Al final subimos al mirador! Y vimos el Aconcagua.

¡Es espectacular! Quizás tú ____1____ venir un día.

Para subir al Aconcagua es importante que ____2____ porque el camino es largo. También es necesario que ____3____ ropa adecuada. Es bueno que ____4____ mucha agua. Y es mejor que lo ____5____ en verano porque no hace tanto frío.

77 ¡Misión cumplida!

▶ **Completa** el mensaje de correo de Tim con la forma correcta de estos verbos.

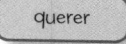 querer

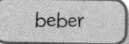 beber

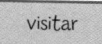 visitar

 llevar

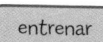 entrenar

trescientos setenta y siete 377

---

75. Before beginning this activity, ask students what they will need to consider as they create their sentences and choose between the use of the indicative and the subjunctive.

76. Before listening, ask students to talk with one another about what they observe about the activities of the people depicted.

77. Ask students to form groups of three. Give them five minutes to create an "event map" in which they will answer questions about one of the three parts of this *Desafío*. After five minutes, reorganize groups so that there is a "1," "2," and "3" in each group. Ask students to review each part of the *Desafío* with their new partners.

 AUDIO SCRIPT
See page 339J.

Answer Key

74. 1. Boca
  2. entrenador
  3. ganó
  4. partido
  5. fútbol
  6. gol
  7. aficionados
  8. equipo

75. Answers will vary.
  ▶ Answers will vary.

76. 1. B   2. A   3. C
  ▶ 2. Es necesario que sigan las señales o que usen un mapa.
  3. Es bueno que tenga un entrenador para ayudarlo.

77. 1. quieras
  2. entrenes
  3. lleves
  4. bebas
  5. visites

Additional Resources

Fans Online activities
Practice Workbook

277

HERITAGE LANGUAGE LEARNERS

• Ask students to describe an important championship of any sport in their family's country of origin. They should include the name of the sport, the teams and / or players involved and some anecdotal information about them, when and where the championship takes place, and if their family's hometown has ever won this championship. If a member of their family has witnessed or participated in this contest, ask students to interview him or her about his or her experiences.

CRITICAL THINKING

• Point out that ever since the first human being climbed to the top of a mountain, people have been asking those who do it why they do it. Have students imagine that they are mountain climbers and have been asked to write an essay for an outdoor magazine explaining their love of this sport. They need to describe how they feel when they are reaching the summit, including any doubts they may have along the way. Of course, they must also answer that age-old question: Why climb a mountain?

Unit 7
TODO JUNTO

Presentation

- In this section, students will review the unit objectives and put them into practice.

Activities	Standards	Resources
78.	1.1, 1.3	
79.	1.2, 1.3	
80.	1.1, 1.2	Audio
81.	1.1, 1.2, 2.1, 2.2	
82. Cultura	1.2, 2.1, 2.2, 3.1, 3.2, 5.1	

Teaching Suggestions

Warm-up / Independent Starter

- Have students list three things associated with each of the professions listed in this unit. Give a model: *plano, lápiz, casa → arquitecto.*

Preparation

- Ask students to share their lists from the Independent Starter (they should not mention the profession) and have others guess the professions. Keep a tally of the answers.

Activities

78. Brainstorm with students what is important or necessary to be good at a profession (e.g., *Es importante que un ingeniero sepa matemáticas.*). You may want to use the list of professions from the Independent Starter.

79. After completing the activity, have students read their letters aloud. Have them vote on the most interesting profession.

80. Before beginning the second part of this activity, have students write a list of ten guesses about their partner's hobbies and free-time activities. For example: *Es probable que William coleccione monedas. Dudo que William juegue al ajedrez.* After partners complete the activity, ask them to assess how accurate they were in their guesses.

82. Have pairs of students work on a flyer where they advertise the leisure activities in their community. Ask them to include sections on culture, sports, and one on other activities and hobbies. Encourage creativity.

378

HABLAR

78 **¿Qué necesitan?**

▶ **Escribe.** ¿Con qué profesión relacionas cada fotografía?

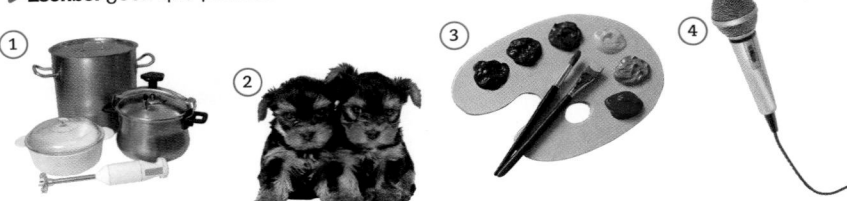

① ② ③ ④

▶ **Habla** con tu compañero(a). ¿Qué cualidades debe tener cada profesional?

Modelo A. *Es necesario que un cocinero sepa cocinar muy bien.*
B. *Claro. Y también es bueno que no sea una persona muy nerviosa porque en los restaurantes se trabaja muy deprisa.*

LEER Y ESCRIBIR

79 **¿A qué te dedicas?**

▶ **Lee** la carta de Tess y responde a estas preguntas.

1. ¿A qué se dedica Lilián Pérez?
2. ¿Dónde trabaja Lilián?
3. ¿En qué trabaja Armando?
4. ¿Tess conoció a algún ingeniero?

▶ **Escribe** una carta a Tess sobre personas con profesiones interesantes. Usa estructuras para hacer valoraciones.

> Es bueno
> Es malo
> Es importante
> Es necesario   que...
> Es increíble
> Es horrible

Querido papá:

¿Qué tal estás? Hoy conocí a varias personas interesantes en Uruguay. Primero conocí a Lilián Pérez. Es socorrista en una piscina municipal de Montevideo. Es joven y atlética, y entrena todos los días. Es importante que nade mucho para estar en forma.

Luego conocí a Armando. Es veterinario. Cuida a los animales enfermos. Normalmente trabaja con mascotas, pero a veces cuida a los animales del zoológico. Es bueno que sepa cuidar a todo tipo de animales, ¿no crees? Mucha gente sabe cuidar a los perros y a los gatos... ¡pero quizás sean más interesantes los leones!

Un abrazo.

Tess

378 trescientos setenta y ocho

Differentiated Instruction

DEVELOPING LEARNERS

- Guide students as you have them write ten sentences about classes, professions, activities, and sports. Give them some sentence starters such as *Ojalá, Quiero que, A mis padres les molesta que, Mi profesora duda que, Me encanta que, Es importante que.* Help students complete each one with an appropriate verb in the present subjunctive. Examples might include: *Ojalá sea biólogo algún día. Quiero que mis amigos estudien conmigo. A mis padres les molesta que yo no estudie Matemáticas. Mi profesora duda que yo preste atención.*

EXPANDING LEARNERS

- Ask students to imagine that they are looking for a part-time job after school or for the summer. Explain that potential employers will ask about their grades, hobbies, and the extracurricular activities they have participated in. Students must first state the job they are hoping to find, and then write at least one paragraph explaining how their interests and extracurricular activities or sports will be an asset to their new job. Encourage them to include the present subjunctive in their paragraphs by using verbs or phrases that express wishes, feelings, emotions, opinions, doubt, and value judgments.

ESCUCHAR Y HABLAR

80 Pasatiempos en Argentina

 ▶ **Escucha** a unos(as) amigos(as) de Diana en Argentina hablando de sus pasatiempos favoritos. Decide si estas oraciones son lógicas o no.

1. Es probable que Ángela tenga unas monedas muy valiosas (*valuable*).
2. Ojalá Ernesto aprenda a tocar un instrumento.
3. Es evidente que Adán va mucho al teatro.
4. Espero que Catalina juegue bien al ajedrez.

 ▶ **Habla** con tu compañero(a) sobre tus pasatiempos y deportes favoritos.

Modelo A. *A mí me gusta mucho ir al cine.*
  B. *A mí también. Pero no me gusta ir al teatro.*

LEER Y HABLAR

81 Buenos Aires

 ▶ **Lee** este fragmento de una guía turística sobre Buenos Aires. Después, habla con tu compañero(a) de lo que te gusta o no te gusta de esa ciudad.

Modelo *Me gusta que Buenos Aires sea una ciudad grande.*

CULTURA
Buenos Aires

Buenos Aires, la capital de Argentina, es una de las ciudades más grandes de Latinoamérica. Es una ciudad que recibe inmigrantes de todo el mundo. Uno de los barrios más interesantes es La Boca, donde viven muchos argentinos de origen italiano.

Teatro Colón.

La vida cultural de Buenos Aires es muy activa. Cada año se celebran numerosos eventos culturales y festivales de arte, música, cine, teatro, artesanía, etc. El Teatro Colón es uno de los escenarios de ópera y teatro más importantes del mundo.

82 **Investiga.** Busca más información sobre la vida cultural de Buenos Aires. ¿A qué espectáculo te gustaría (*would you like*) asistir?

AUDIO SCRIPT
See page 339J.

CULTURA
Buenos Aires

Nuestra Señora Santa María del Buen Aire (Our Lady Saint Mary of the Good Air), known today as Buenos Aires, was founded by Pedro de Mendoza in 1536. In the centuries since its settlement, Buenos Aires has grown exponentially, but it is still a city of neighborhoods, whose residents maintain loyalty to their neighborhood's political candidates, coffee houses, and local sports teams. The arts have always been important to the people of Buenos Aires, and the Colón Theater (1908) is a major venue for opera stars. It also houses the national symphony and ballet.

Answer Key

78. 1. cocinero(a)   3. pintor(a)
   2. veterinario(a)   4. cantante
   ▶ Answers will vary.

79. 1. Es socorrista.
   2. Trabaja en una piscina municipal de Montevideo.
   3. Es veterinario.
   4. No, Tess no conoció a ningún ingeniero.
   ▶ Answers will vary.

80. 1. Lógica.   3. Lógica.
   2. Ilógica.   4. Ilógica.
   ▶ Answers will vary.

81. Answers will vary.

82. Answers will vary.

Additional Resources

Fans Online activities
Practice Workbook

HERITAGE LANGUAGE LEARNERS

• Ask students to work with a partner. One will write a letter to an advice columnist, describing an imaginary problem he or she is having at school or home. Students will give their letter to their partners, who will play the role of the advice columnist, and will write back to them with some good or humorous advice. Encourage students to incorporate the present subjunctive in their letters by using verbs and phrases that trigger its use. Call on pairs to read their letters aloud.

COOPERATIVE LEARNING

• Have students work in small groups and assign an aspect of Argentina to each group in order to make a report. You may want to assign some of the following topics: history, geography, current political situation, population demographics, holidays and festivals, monuments and historical buildings, contributions to literature, the role of the *gaucho*, the tango, food, and a closer look at one or more of its major cities. Each member of the group will contribute to either doing the research, writing a draft, editing and making a final copy, providing visuals, or presenting a summary before the rest of the class.

Unit 7
El encuentro

Presentation

- The four pairs meet at the Manzana Jesuítica in Córdoba. There they must demonstrate that they have successfully completed their challenge.
- Students will vote for the winner of the *Desafíos* in the Río de la Plata region.

Activities	Standards	Resources
Fotonovela	1.2, 2.1, 2.2, 3.1, 3.2	
83.	1.3, 2.1, 2.2	
84.	1.2, 1.3, 5.1, 5.2	

Teaching Suggestions

Warm-up / Independent Starter

- Ask students to close their textbooks and write a summary of each pair's challenge in the Río de la Plata region. Have them use the vocabulary and grammar presented in this unit to represent the *desafío* in each description.

Preparation

- Have students exchange their summaries from the Independent Starter with a classmate. Then ask them to help you write down a complete summary on the board.
- Remind students that in *Desafío 1*, Andy and Janet visited the University of Asunción, in Paraguay, where they had to decipher a message. In *Desafío 2*, Tess and Patricia had to find a dog called Bruno, who disappeared while they walked a group of dogs through the streets of Montevideo. In *Desafío 3*, Diana and Rita traveled to Buenos Aires to participate in a *telenovela*. In *Desafío 4*, Tim and Mack had to hike up Aconcagua, in the Argentine Andes.
- Brainstorm with students the various kinds of presentations that the pairs may make detailing their adventures.

La fotonovela

- Have students read the speech bubbles independently and ask a partner if there is anything that they do not understand. If their partner does not know the answer, they should ask another student.

El encuentro

En la Manzana Jesuítica de Córdoba

In Córdoba, the pairs gather in front of the Manzana Jesuítica, an architectural landmark of Argentina. Did all the pairs succeed in their assignments?

Nosotros tuvimos que descubrir el significado de unas palabras misteriosas.

Y resolvimos el enigma.

Nosotras tuvimos que pasear a doce perros por Montevideo.

¡Se nos escapó un perro! ¡Por fortuna, regresó solo a su casa!

Nosotras actuamos en una telenovela argentina.

Nosotros subimos hasta el Mirador del Aconcagua.

Y lo hicimos muy bien. El director nos felicitó.

¡Y vimos el clásico del fútbol argentino en los Andes!

Differentiated Instruction

DEVELOPING LEARNERS

- Ask students to look at the images of the participants on page 380. Then have them write a sentence with one of the verbs or phrases that triggers the use of the present subjunctive. Each sentence must be related to the *desafío*. For example: *¡Ojalá que Janet y Andy resuelvan el enigma! Patricia y Tess esperan que no se les escape ningún perro. El director quiere que Rita y Diana trabajen en otra telenovela. Es importante que Mack y Tim suban hasta el Mirador del Aconcagua.*

EXPANDING LEARNERS

- Ask students which *desafío* they would have liked to participate in and why. They should also explain why they believe they might have been more successful or less successful at completing each of the challenges than our characters. They will need to describe their special talents and interests (or the lack of such talents or interests) that make them either the ideal, or the imperfect, candidates for these *desafíos*.

83 Las presentaciones

▶ **Escribe.** Cada una de las parejas hizo una presentación de su desafío. Elige una diapositiva *(slide)* y haz un resumen del desafío.

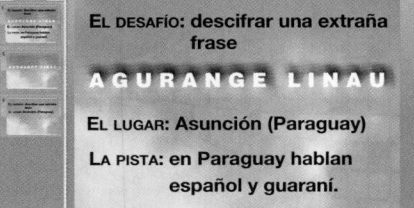

EL DESAFÍO: descifrar una extraña frase

AGURANGE LINAU

EL LUGAR: Asunción (Paraguay)

LA PISTA: en Paraguay hablan español y guaraní.

Andy y Janet

¿CUÁL CREEN QUE FUE NUESTRO DESAFÍO?

Tess y Patricia

Título:	Marcela
Director:	Claudio Nocioni
Capítulo:	120

Diana y Rita

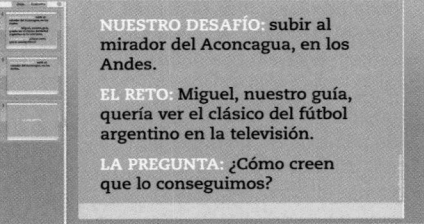

NUESTRO DESAFÍO: subir al mirador del Aconcagua, en los Andes.

EL RETO: Miguel, nuestro guía, quería ver el clásico del fútbol argentino en la televisión.

LA PREGUNTA: ¿Cómo creen que lo conseguimos?

Tim y Mack

> Una presentación tiene que ser atractiva. La información se escribe en forma de esquema. Y debes incluir fotografías, dibujos o gráficos.

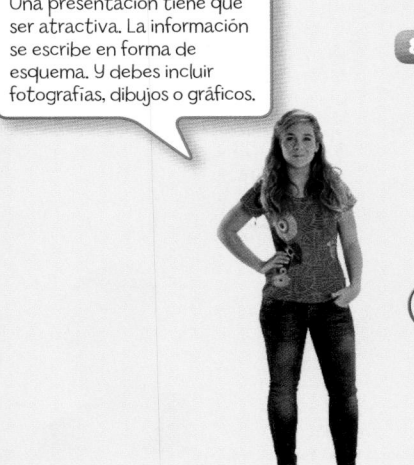

84 Las votaciones

▶ **Lee** las diapositivas de los personajes. ¿Cuál te gusta más? ¿Por qué?

Modelo   A. *Yo creo que la diapositiva de Andy y Janet es muy buena.*

B. *Sí, pero no tiene fotos.*

▶ **Prepara** una presentación sobre tu deporte o tu actividad de tiempo libre preferida.

▶ **Lee** la presentación de tu compañero(a). ¿Qué es lo que más te gusta? ¿Piensas que puede mejorar? Coméntaselo.

Modelo   *Creo que debes incluir más fotografías. Es importante que la presentación sea atractiva.*

trescientos ochenta y uno **381**

■ Ask for four different volunteer pairs to read aloud by impersonating the characters. Encourage good pronunciation and intonation.

■ Have students share their opinions about what the characters have achieved.

Activities

83. Ask for volunteers to write their summaries on the board. Have other students suggest revisions.

84. Have students work with a partner to create a challenge for their teacher or for another classmate in the Río de la Plata region. They should include two wishes in their challenge. For example: *Queremos que el/la maestro(a) baile tango en Buenos Aires. Ojalá que baile bien.* Invite pairs to present their challenge to the class.

Answer Key

83. Answers will vary.

84. Answers will vary.
   ▶ Answers will vary.
   ▶ Answers will vary.

HERITAGE LANGUAGE LEARNERS

• The participants have gathered at the *Manzana Jesuítica*, an architectural landmark in Córdoba, Argentina. Ask students to describe a famous landmark in their family's country of origin or in a Spanish-speaking country they know well. Have them write a brief report detailing where the landmark is located, its history and cultural significance, and what activities are centered around it. Encourage students to bring in visuals of the landmark and share them with the class.

COOPERATIVE LEARNING

• Have students work in groups of three or four and ask them to evaluate the *desafíos* of this unit as well as the presentation each of the pairs made of their challenge. Students need to discuss the difficulty, creativity, and satisfactory completion of each *desafío* and presentation, and assign a grade to each category. They should also write a short paragraph explaining the criteria they followed in order to come to this decision. After each group makes its presentation to the class, determine which *desafío* and *presentación* received the highest marks.

MAPA CULTURAL

Río de la Plata

Presentation

- This section presents the Río de la Plata region through facts and physical features so learners can see this region from other perspectives. The map serves as a reference point for additional cultural readings and activities that expand on the skills students learned in this unit.

Activities	Standards	Resources
Mapa cultural	1.2, 2.1, 2.2, 3.1, 3.2	Video
85.	1.2, 1.3, 3.1	
86.	1.2, 2.1, 2.2, 3.1, 3.2, 5.1	

Cultural Topics

- **Influencia italiana.** Nearly half of the European immigrants who arrived in Argentina in the late 19th century and the first half of the 20th century were Italian. This large influx left an imprint on the culture, language, and ethnicity of Argentines. In fact, it is still possible to hear Italian spoken in some areas of Buenos Aires. Some of these immigrants settled across the La Plata River, in Uruguay, and this has contributed to many of the common elements in the cultures of Argentina and Uruguay.

- **Cultura rioplatense.** Argentina and Uruguay share a similar historical and cultural background, which accounts for the *Rioplatense* Spanish, a variety of Spanish that is spoken in both countries. But tango music is perhaps the most famous product of this region. This music developed in the immigrant and working-class neighborhoods of Buenos Aires and Montevideo.

- **El chipá.** This bread, which is common in Paraguay, Argentina, Bolivia, and Brazil, is usually made with corn or cassava flour, cheese, eggs, and milk. In Paraguay, it is popular at breakfast, as a snack, and during Holy Week. *Chipá* is sold by street vendors, called *chiperos*. It is also found in small stores, and in *chiperías*.

Teaching Suggestions

Warm-Up / Independent Starter

- Ask students to imagine that they have been offered the opportunity of spending a semester in one of the countries featured on this page. Have them decide where they would like to go.

Río de la Plata

El Río de la Plata, formado por la unión del río Paraná y el río Uruguay, está situado en Suramérica, sobre la costa atlántica. En esa región hay dos países: Uruguay y Argentina. Al norte de Argentina, en el corazón de Suramérica, está Paraguay.

– Argentina es el segundo país más extenso de Suramérica. Su capital, Buenos Aires, está situada junto al Río de la Plata.

– Uruguay es, en cambio, el segundo país más pequeño de Suramérica. Su capital, Montevideo, está también situada junto al Río de la Plata.

– Paraguay está situado en el interior, pero tiene salida al Río de la Plata y al océano Atlántico por los ríos Paraguay y Paraná. Su capital es Asunción. La mayor parte de la población paraguaya es de origen guaraní.

Nacionalidades
Argentina → argentino(
Uruguay → uruguayo(a)
Paraguay → paraguayo(a

85 Frontera

▶ **Une** las dos columnas. ¿A qué país corresponde cada descripción?

1. Limita con dos países.
2. Limita con cinco países.
3. Limita con tres países.

a. Argentina
b. Uruguay
c. Paraguay

▶ **Responde** a estas preguntas.

1. ¿Qué río pasa entre Paraguay y Argentina?
2. ¿Qué países divide el río Uruguay?
3. ¿Qué cordillera separa Chile y Argentina?

Entre Paraguay y Brasil se encuentra la central hidroeléctrica de Itaipú. Es la central más grande del mundo.

Differentiated Instruction

DEVELOPING LEARNERS

- Ask students to observe the map of the Río de la Plata region. Then have them do activity 85 with a partner. Once they have finished, ask partners to answer the following questions regarding the geography of this region:
  – *Menciona dos diferencias entre Argentina y Uruguay.*
  – *Menciona dos similitudes entre Uruguay y Paraguay.*
  – *¿Qué tienen en común estos tres países?*
  – *Menciona tres diferencias y tres similitudes entre la región del Río de la Plata y la región de los Andes centrales.*

EXPANDING LEARNERS

- Explain to students that close to 90% of the population in Paraguay speaks Guaraní. Paraguay is the only country in the Americas in which the majority of the population is bilingual in a European language (Spanish) and an indigenous language (Guaraní).

- Ask students to research the history of the Guaraní language in Paraguay. Encourage them to look at the factors that have contributed to the preservation and widespread usage of this language in Paraguay. Have students summarize their findings in a brief essay entitled *El idioma guaraní en Paraguay*.

1. Influencia italiana

Muchos argentinos descienden de emigrantes italianos. Por eso en Argentina son muy frecuentes los apellidos italianos.

Los emigrantes italianos dejaron huella en la cultura argentina, por ejemplo, en la cocina: entre las comidas típicas de Buenos Aires están la pizza y la pasta.

(1) Pizzería de Buenos Aires.

(2) Cartel de una película argentina.

2. Cultura rioplatense

La sociedad uruguaya comparte muchas tradiciones con la argentina. Igual que los argentinos, los uruguayos beben mate, bailan tango y son fans del fútbol, y los gauchos son también un símbolo de su identidad.

Además, uruguayos y argentinos comparten la misma variedad del español: usan el pronombre *vos* en lugar de *tú* y dicen *¿Vos querés cantar?* en lugar de *¿Tú quieres cantar?*

3. El chipá

El chipá es un pequeño pan de maíz y queso. Es típico de Paraguay, pero también se hace en Argentina.

En otros países de Suramérica hay panes parecidos, por ejemplo, el *cuñapé* de Bolivia o el *pan de yuca* de Colombia.

(3) Chipá paraguayo.

86 **Queremos saber más**

▶ **Investiga** sobre una de las siguientes cuestiones. Después, pon la información en común con tus compañeros(as).

– Otras comidas típicas argentinas.
– Las particularidades del español de Argentina y Uruguay.
– La receta del chipá paraguayo.

Preparation

- Invite students to talk about their choices from the Independent Starter and explain why they would like to study there.

- Explain to students that Argentina, with a total area of 1,073,518 sq. mi. and a population of 41.7 million (2011 est.), is the largest of the three countries that comprise the Río de la Plata region. It also has the largest city, Buenos Aires, with a population of almost 13 million. Argentina boasts the tallest mountain in the Western Hemisphere (Cerro Aconcagua at 22,831 feet above sea level), as well as the lowest point (Laguna del Carbón at 345 feet below sea level).

- Uruguay, with a total area of 68,037 sq. mi. and a population of 3.3 million (2011 est.) is the smallest and least populated of the three. Almost half of Uruguay's population lives in the metropolitan area of Montevideo.

- Paraguay is about the size of California (157,047 sq. mi.), but it is sparsely populated, with just 6,459,058 million inhabitants (2011 est.). Rivers are very important for the economy of Paraguay. Agricultural products and hydropower are Paraguay's two main exports, both of which depend on the rivers that cut through Paraguay.

Activities

85. Have students work with a partner to complete this activity. One partner will read aloud the question and the other will look at the map of the Río de la Plata region and answer the question. Ask partners to alternate the person reading the question and the person looking at the map.

Answer Key

85. 1. b   2. a   3. c
   ▶ 1. El río Paraná.
      2. Argentina y Uruguay.
      3. La cordillera de Los Andes.
86. Answers will vary.

Additional Resources

Fans Online activities
Practice Workbook

HERITAGE LANGUAGE LEARNERS

- Ask students to compare the influence immigrants have had on the culture of Argentina and Uruguay with the influence that immigrants to the United States have had on the culture of this country. Students may narrow the scope of their research by focusing on just one group of immigrants to the United States (e.g., Mexicans, Puerto Ricans, Chinese, Irish, etc.). Have students explain in a brief essay the main contributions of this particular group of immigrants to the cuisine, language, ethnicity, and traditions of the United States, especially in those cities and states where they have settled.

CRITICAL THINKING

- Explain that the Río de la Plata region is an important supplier of agricultural and beef products to the world. The development of agriculture was greatly responsible for the advancement of Argentina, Uruguay, and Paraguay after the mid-19th century.

- Ask students to discuss how vital they think the geography of this region—especially the river system consisting of the Paraguay, Paraná, and Uruguay Rivers—has been to its economic development. Invite students to consider the importance of rivers, both as a source of water to be used in agriculture and as a means of transportation and trade.

Unit 7

LECTURA

Un cuento de Benedetti

Presentation

- In this section, students will practice and extend their reading skills by reading an excerpt from a short story by Mario Benedetti, a Uruguayan writer. In addition, students will focus on recognizing the structure and elements of narrative texts.

Activities	Standards	Resources
Lectura	1.2, 2.2, 3.1, 3.2	
87.	1.2, 1.3	
88.	1.3, 3.1, 5.1	
Tu desafío	1.2, 2.2, 3.1, 3.2, 5.1	

Teaching Suggestions

Warm-Up / Independent Starter

- Ask students to read silently the first sentence of the reading: *Al principio no quiso creerlo.* Then ask them to close their textbooks and jot down their ideas about what will happen next in the story. What might this thing that the main character didn't want to believe be?

Preparation

- Have students report their ideas from the Independent Starter to the class. Write them on the board, and come back to this list once students have read the story to see if any of them guessed what would happen next in the story.

- Before reading the passage, point to the Reading Strategy box and ask for two volunteers to read it aloud. Clarify that narrative texts need not be factual. Explain to students that the story in narrative texts is usually told from one of the following points of view: 1. first person → the story is told through the eyes of the narrator (e.g., I heard some strange noises); 2. second person → the narrator talks to the reader directly (e.g., You heard some strange noises); 3. third person → the narrator is "outside" the story and knows everything that happens in the story (e.g., She heard some strange noises). The third person point of view is the most common narrative form; it gives the writer freedom to show the story through the eyes of the different characters.

384

LECTURA

READING STRATEGY

Read narrative texts

Narrative texts tell events that happen to characters in a certain time and place. Narrative texts have three common components:

- **Setting** *(marco)*—the time and place in which the events of the story occur *(where and when)*.
- **Characters** *(personajes)*—the people or sometimes the animals in the story *(who)*.
- **Plot** *(argumento)*— the sequence of events *(what)*.

In the plot it is possible to identify three parts:

- The **initial event** that begins the story.
- The **body**. The series of events that make up the focus or the conflict of the story.
- The **ending**. The conclusion or resolution of the story.

Un cuento de Benedetti

Al principio no quiso creerlo. Después se convenció, pero lo tomó a broma[1]. El extraño ruidito[2] no podía ser otra cosa: alguien escuchaba sus conversaciones por teléfono. Armando no sabía el motivo, pero estaba seguro. No le divertía especialmente ni le daba miedo tampoco: sencillamente le parecía una tontería[3]. Siempre había creído[4] que la palabra espionaje, con su significado importante, oscuro, peligroso, no tenía lugar[5] en un país tan pequeñito como el suyo. […] Sin embargo era cierto, alguien escuchaba sus conversaciones telefónicas.

MARIO BENEDETTI, «Ganas de embromar» (texto adaptado).

---

1. *he took it as a joke*   2. *slight noise*   3. *silly thing*   4. *he had thought*   5. *took plac*

Mario Benedetti (1920-2009) es un escritor uruguayo muy conocido por sus poemas y sus cuentos. Escribió muchos libros, más de ochenta. Algunos de ellos están traducidos a más de veinte idiomas.

384 trescientos ochenta y cuatro

Differentiated Instruction

DEVELOPING LEARNERS

- Writing a short story in a foreign language can be a disquieting activity for some learners. They will probably have good ideas for their story plot and characters, but they may lack the language knowledge to express what they want to say in Spanish.

- Assist students in breaking down the writing process. Ask them to write a sentence for each event in the story and another one for the end. Then, have them join this string of sentences into a narrative by using connectors. Then assist them with fleshing out the narrative by adding some descriptions.

EXPANDING LEARNERS

- Ask students to analyze the use of the preterite and the imperfect in each of the sentences of the narrative on page 384. Have them write each sentence on a separate line in their notebook and underline the verbs. Then ask them to identify the verb tense for each verb and explain the uses of the preterite and the imperfect in each case. This will help students understand the uses of the past tenses in a narrative.

COMPRENSIÓN

 87 ¿Qué pasó?

▶ **Completa** estas oraciones.

1. Armando oyó…
2. Armando descubrió que…
3. Armando estaba seguro, pero…
4. Armando vivía en…
5. Armando se lo tomó…

ESTRATEGIA Leer textos narrativos

88 Un cuento de espías

▶ **Escribe** un cuento a partir del texto de Mario Benedetti.

1.º Completa este esquema sobre el marco y los personajes. Toma los datos del texto e inventa los demás: ¡es tu cuento! Puedes inventar también otros personajes.

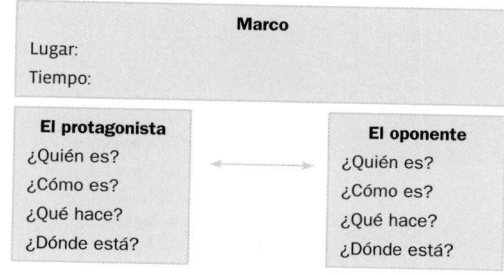

2.º Piensa en el argumento. Completa el cuadro sobre el acontecimiento inicial del cuento e inventa una secuencia de eventos.

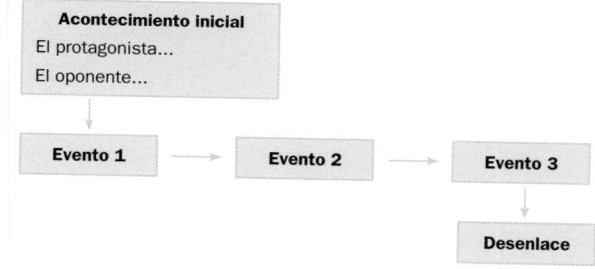

3.º Ahora escribe el cuento utilizando tiempos de pasado. No olvides ponerle un título.

 **→ TU DESAFÍO**   Visita la página web para aprender más sobre Mario Benedetti y otros escritores argentinos y uruguayos.

■ To introduce the reading, explain to students that Mario Benedetti (1920–2009) was a well-known Uruguayan author whose literary production includes novels, short stories, poetry, plays, and essays. Benedetti was the son of Italian immigrants who belonged to the growing Uruguayan middle class in the first half of the 20th century. Benedetti was forced into exile after the 1973 military coup in Uruguay, and could not return until 12 years later. His writing career spanned more than 60 years, during which he wrote more than 80 books. The short story presented here was published in the book *La muerte y otras sorpresas* (1968), a collection of 19 short stories. "Ganas de embromar" is a political short story in which reality and fiction intermix. The story alludes to the political situation in Uruguay at the time, and it tells the story of a politically active fictional character, Armando, who finds out that his phone has been wiretapped.

Activities

88. This is a guided writing activity. Circulate around the room to assist students in completing the graphic organizers. These organizers will serve as the basis for the development of the short story. Encourage students to be creative. As a follow-up listening activity, have students read their stories aloud to the class.

Answer Key

87. 1. Armando oyó un ruidito extraño.
2. Armando descubrió que alguien escuchaba sus conversaciones por teléfono.
3. Armando estaba seguro, pero no sabía el motivo.
4. Armando vivía en un país pequeñito.
5. Armando se lo tomó a broma.

88. Answers will vary.

Additional Resources

Fans Online activities

HERITAGE LANGUAGE LEARNERS

- Ask students to read this sentence from the story: *Siempre había creído que la palabra espionaje, con su significado importante, oscuro, peligroso, no tenía lugar en un país tan pequeñito como el suyo.* Then have students research the political situation in Uruguay between 1966 and 1973. Who might be doing the wiretapping? Who might be the person being spied on and why? Have students write a paragraph with their theories and share it with the class. What does the class think?

MULTIPLE INTELLIGENCES:
Visual-Spatial Intelligence

- Explain that illustrations often play an important role in texts. They are a complement to writing and serve to clarify the meaning of the content.

- Ask students to illustrate the story they create for activity 88. Remind them that the illustrations should be relevant and should contribute to the understanding of the story. After students have finished, you may want to hold a class exhibit of their illustrations.

Unit 7
REPASO
Vocabulario

Presentation

- In this section, students will review all key vocabulary from the unit, organized by themes, to prepare for an assessment. Students will complete practice activities for each of the four *Desafíos*.

Activities	Standards	Resources
1.	1.3	
2.	1.3	
3.	1.2, 1.3	
4.	1.2, 1.3	

Teaching Suggestions

Warm-Up / Independent Starter

- Ask students to think of an ideal weekend in which they will be able to do all the things they like, practice their favorite sports, and go to their preferred places. Then ask them to write a paragraph summarizing their weekend.

Preparation

- Invite students to read their paragraphs from the Independent Starter and record the information on the board, in a table like the one below.

Actividades	Aficiones	Espectáculos	Deportes
montar en bicicleta	ilustrar un cómic	ir a un concierto	jugar al baloncesto

- Are there some activities and hobbies that are clear favorites in your class? Discuss what might account for these preferences. Then go over the vocabulary under *Aficiones, actividades y espectáculos* and *Deportes*. Are there activities no one mentioned? Why do students think these activities are not popular among the class?

- Review the vocabulary under *La escuela* and *Profesiones*. Ask students to think about possible favorite subjects at school for each of the professionals listed under *Profesiones*. Then divide the class into small groups and say a profession. The first student representing his or her group who comes up with the correct answer wins a point for the group. For example: You say, *la cirujana*, and a student says, *Biología*. Groups should alternate the student representing them.

La escuela

los aseos	restrooms
el aula	classroom
la biblioteca	library
la cafetería	cafeteria
el comedor	cafeteria
el gimnasio	gym
el laboratorio	lab
la oficina del director	principal's office
el pasillo	hallway
la sala de computación	computer lab
Biología	biology
Física	physics
Geografía	geography
Historia	history
Literatura	literature
Matemáticas	math
Química	chemistry
hacer un examen	to take an exam
levantar la mano	to raise your hand
prestar atención	to pay attention
tomar apuntes	to take notes

Aficiones, actividades y espectáculos

coleccionar monedas	to collect coins
coleccionar sellos	to collect stamps
dibujar	to draw
hacer crucigramas	to do crossword puzzles
hacer picnic	to have a picnic
ir al cine	to go to the movies
ir al teatro	to go to the theater
ir a un concierto	to go to a concert
ir a una exposición	to go to an exhibit
jugar al ajedrez	to play chess
jugar a las damas	to play checkers
jugar a los naipes	to play cards
montar a caballo	to ride a horse
montar en bici	to ride a bicycle
montar en monopatín	to ride a skateboard
pasear	to go for a walk
patinar	to skate
tocar la guitarra	to play the guitar
tomar el sol	to sunbathe

Profesiones

el actor, la actriz	actor, actress
el/la agricultor(a)	farmer
el/la arquitecto(a)	architect
el/la artista	artist
el/la bibliotecario(a)	librarian
el/la bombero(a)	firefighter
el/la cantante	singer
el/la cirujano(a)	surgeon
el/la cocinero(a)	cook
el/la dentista	dentist
el/la mecánico(a)	mechanic
el/la pintor(a)	painter
el/la policía	policeman / policewoman
el/la socorrista	lifeguard
el/la técnico informático	computer technician
el/la telefonista	operator

Deportes

el/la entrenador(a)	coach
el gimnasio	gym
el alpinismo	mountain climbing
el baloncesto	basketball
el béisbol	baseball
el esquí	ski
el fútbol	soccer
el fútbol americano	football
el golf	golf
el senderismo	hiking
el tenis	tennis
el voleibol	volleyball
el balón	ball
la canasta	basket
los esquís	skis
el guante	glove
la pelota	ball
la raqueta	racket
la red	net
competir	to compete
empatar	to tie
ganar	to win
hacer gimnasia	to work out
levantar pesas	to lift weights
perder	to lose

Differentiated Instruction

DEVELOPING LEARNERS

- Ask students to classify the vocabulary on page 386 into categories that make sense to them. Have students create word webs or charts to list the words using the new categories they have created. Some examples of categories and subcategories include: *Deportes* → *al aire libre* (outdoors), *bajo techo* (indoors), *equipamiento* (equipment). *Aficiones* → *juegos de mesa* (board games), *actividades artísticas* (art-related activities), *actividades físicas* (physical activities), *otras* (other).

- Invite students to share their reclassifications. Encourage them to explain their reasoning for classifying the words as they did.

EXPANDING LEARNERS

- Allow students a few minutes to study the vocabulary on page 386. Then ask them to close their books and get together with a classmate to play a guessing game. For example:

  A. *Es una actividad que se realiza con un animal. Se puede hacer en las montañas o en el campo.*

  B. *El alpinismo.*

  A. *No. Recuerda que se hace con un animal.*

  B. *Montar a caballo.*

  A. *¡Sí!*

DESAFÍO 1

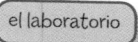

1 **¿Qué puedo hacer?** Escribe qué puedes hacer en estos lugares de la escuela.

[el laboratorio]   [el gimnasio]   [el comedor]   [la sala de computación]

Modelo *En el laboratorio puedo aprender Química.*

DESAFÍO 2

2 **Profesiones.** ¿A qué se dedican estas personas? Escríbelo.

DESAFÍO 3

3 **Yo prefiero...** Completa las palabras de Alfonso.

> Mis hermanos y yo tenemos distintas aficiones. A mi
> hermana le gusta ___1___ la guitarra y ___2___ al ajedrez.
> A mi hermano le encanta coleccionar cosas. Tiene una
> colección de ___3___ antiguos y otra de monedas.
> Yo prefiero hacer deporte. Me gusta mucho ___4___
> a caballo. Y también me encanta la música. Hoy voy a
> un ___5___ de mi grupo favorito. Y a ti, ¿qué te gusta?

DESAFÍO 4

4 **¿Qué necesito?** Relaciona las dos columnas.

Ⓐ

1. Voleibol
2. Baloncesto
3. Tenis
4. Fútbol

Ⓑ

a. Una raqueta y una pelota.
b. Un balón.
c. Una pelota y una red.
d. Un balón y una canasta.

trescientos ochenta y siete **387**

Unit 7

REPASO
Vocabulario

Activities

1. Have students get together with a classmate to compare their answers. Then ask them to think of two things they could do in each of the following school places: *el aula, el pasillo,* and *la biblioteca.*

3. Once students have finished, ask them to interview two classmates about their hobbies and favorite free-time activities. Then have students summarize their findings in a paragraph similar to the one in this activity. They should explain what their classmates like doing, as well as what they do. Invite students to share their paragraphs with the class.

4. To extend this activity, ask students to add two more items (i.e., two additional sports and the equipment needed to play them) to this matching activity. Then have them exchange papers with a classmate and answer each other's activity.

Answer Key

1. Answers will vary. Sample answers:
   En el gimnasio puedo hacer ejercicio.
   En el comedor puedo almorzar.
   En la sala de computación puedo hacer la tarea.

2. Answers will vary. Sample answers:
   1. La cantante canta en festivales.
   2. La cirujana opera a los pacientes.
   3. El bombero apaga los incendios.
   4. La pintora pinta cuadros.

3. 1. tocar   4. montar
   2. jugar   5. concierto
   3. sellos

4. 1. c   2. d   3. a   4. b

Additional Resources

Fans Online activities
Practice Workbook

HERITAGE LANGUAGE LEARNERS

- Have students research the school system of their heritage country. What are the core subjects in high school? Which subjects are elective? How many years do students need to attend school before they can access the university? What are the university entrance requirements? Are there other higher learning institutions in addition to universities (e.g., vocational schools, technical colleges)?

- Ask students to organize the information on chart paper. Encourage them to find images of schools and colleges from the country they are researching. Then have them present their information to the class.

TOTAL PHYSICAL RESPONSE (TPR)

- Play a word association game with this vocabulary. Ask students to sit in a circle. Begin the game by pantomiming a word and then saying it aloud. Have the student to your right pantomime and then say a word that relates to the word you just said. The next student to this student's right will pantomime and say a word that relates to the word, and so on. For example: *laboratorio → Biología → aula.* If a student repeats a word, hesitates for too long, or performs an incorrect pantomime, he or she is out.

387

Unit 7
REPASO
Gramática

Presentation

- Students will review grammatical structures presented in the unit. Each grammar point is cross-referenced to the corresponding page on which it was introduced. The activities here provide systematic practice by *Desafío*.

Activities	Standards	Resources
5.	1.2, 1.3	
6.	1.2	
7.	1.2, 1.3	
8.	1.2, 1.3	
9. Cultura	1.2, 1.3, 2.1, 2.2, 3.1	

Teaching Suggestions

Warm-Up / Independent Starter

- Write the following sentence starters on the board. Then ask students to copy them in their notebooks and complete each sentence with information about themselves.

  1. *Ojalá...*
  2. *Me preocupa que...*
  3. *Me alegra...*
  4. *Dudo que...*
  5. *Quiero...*

Preparation

- Ask students to get together with a classmate and exchange their sentences from the Independent Starter for peer review. Have students circle—but not correct—any mistakes they think their classmate made and then return the paper to its owner.
- Go over the *Repaso* presentation with the class. Then ask students to check their sentences from the Independent Starter. Did they make any mistakes? Did their partner mark the mistakes? Finally, have students correct their mistakes, if they had any. Do they understand now what they did wrong?

Activities

6. Once students have finished the activity, ask them to complete the first sentence about themselves and their parents and the last sentence about their Spanish class. Then invite volunteer students to share their answers with the class.

388

Expresar existencia. Los indefinidos (pág. 350)

▶ Alguien and nadie refer to people.
Hay alguien en el aula.
No hay nadie en el aula.

▶ Algo and nada refer to things.
En la mesa hay algo para escribir.
En la mesa no hay nada.

Expresar deseo. El modo subjuntivo (pág. 358)

Ojalá pueda ser veterinaria.
Quiero que estudies Medicina.

VERBOS REGULARES

CANTAR	COMER	VIVIR
cante	coma	viva
cantes	comas	vivas
cante	coma	viva
cantemos	comamos	vivamos
cantéis	comáis	viváis
canten	coman	vivan

Expresar sentimientos (pág. 366)

Me molesta llegar tarde al cine.
Me molesta que la gente llegue tarde al cine.

VERBOS CON RAÍZ IRREGULAR EN EL PRESENTE DE SUBJUNTIVO

PENSAR	JUGAR	VOLVER	PEDIR	DORMIR
piense	juegue	vuelva	pida	duerma
pienses	juegues	vuelvas	pidas	duermas
piense	juegue	vuelva	pida	duerma
pensemos	juguemos	volvamos	pidamos	durmamos
penséis	juguéis	volváis	pidáis	durmáis
piensen	jueguen	vuelvan	pidan	duerman

Expresar duda y hacer valoraciones (pág. 374)

Dudo que Pedro esté en casa.
Es necesario que hagas deporte.

VERBOS IRREGULARES EN EL PRESENTE DE SUBJUNTIVO

DAR	ESTAR	SABER	SER	IR
dé	esté	sepa	sea	vaya
des	estés	sepas	seas	vayas
dé	esté	sepa	sea	vaya
demos	estemos	sepamos	seamos	vayamos
deis	estéis	sepáis	seáis	vayáis
den	estén	sepan	sean	vayan

Differentiated Instruction

DEVELOPING LEARNERS

- For additional practice with the subjunctive and the infinitive, ask students to choose the correct form of the verb to complete these sentences.

  1. *Quiero hablar / hable español bien. (hablar)*
  2. *Me alegra que mi equipo de fútbol ganar / gane. (gane)*
  3. *Me molesta no poder / pueda dormir ocho horas. (poder)*
  4. *Dudo que tener / tengamos dinero para viajar estas vacaciones. (tengamos)*
  5. *Me encanta hacer / haga ejercicio. (hacer)*
  6. *Ojalá que comenzar / comience pronto el buen tiempo. (comience)*

EXPANDING LEARNERS

- Ask students to think of the following:
  – Two things that they love about their school.
  – One thing that they want to accomplish by the end of high school.
  – One thing that they want to change at school but that they doubt would change.
  – One thing that worries them about their school.

- Have students write their answers to each of these items using complete sentences. Then ask them to get together in small groups to discuss their answers. Do students in each group have similar opinions?

DESAFÍO 1

5 **Mi cumpleaños.** Completa este texto.

todos
nadie
algo
nada
alguien

Hoy es mi cumpleaños; pero no hay ___1___ en casa. Tampoco hay ___2___ preparado para cenar. Veo ___3___ en la mesa; pero no sé qué es. Qué raro, ___4___ me llama por teléfono. ¡Ya sé! Es una fiesta sorpresa, ¡están ___5___ en el jardín!

DESAFÍO 2

6 **¡Ojalá!** Relaciona las dos columnas.

1. Quiero que mis padres
2. Deseo que Álvaro
3. Espero que tú
4. Prefiero que nosotros

a. trabajes como abogado.
b. vayan de vacaciones a la playa.
c. aprobemos los exámenes.
d. pueda ser actor.

DESAFÍO 3

7 **Cuéntame de ti.** Responde a estas preguntas. Usa el subjuntivo.

1. ¿Qué te gusta de tus profesores(as)?
2. ¿Qué te molesta de tus compañeros(as)?
3. ¿Qué te encanta de tu familia?
4. ¿Qué te sorprende de tus amigos(as)?

DESAFÍO 4

8 **¿Qué opinas?** Elige la opción correcta.

1. Dudo que Amelia _____ el concierto de piano esta noche.
   a. dé   b. demos   c. da
2. Es posible que Julio y Gloria _____ a la playa a tomar el sol.
   a. vayamos   b. van   c. vayan
3. No dudo que tú _____ cuál es la respuesta correcta.
   a. sepas   b. sepa   c. sabes
4. Es importante que tú y yo _____ buenos jugadores de baloncesto.
   a. sea   b. seamos   c. somos

CULTURA

9 **En Suramérica.** Responde a las siguientes preguntas.

1. ¿Cuáles son las dos lenguas oficiales de Paraguay?
2. ¿En qué ciudad argentina está el barrio de La Boca?
3. ¿Cuál es la montaña más alta de la cordillera de Los Andes?

---

7. Create a four-column chart on the board with the following headings: *Me gusta de mis profesores que...*, *Me molesta de mis compañeros que...*, *Me encanta de mi familia que...*, *Me sorprende de mis amigos que...* Tally students' responses to the four questions in this chart. Once you have completed the chart, ask students to analyze it. Do they have similar opinions or were the class's responses to these questions quite varied?

8. Go over the responses to this activity as a class. Then, together with students, choose a topic that lends itself to a debate. Possible topics include: the list of required high school subjects, funds allocated to sports in high school, whether more funds should be allocated to scientific and engineering professions than to the arts and humanities. Divide the class into two groups that will hold opposite views. Allow each group a few minutes to prepare their arguments. Write the following phrases on the board and remind students to use them as they express their opinions: *Quizás...*, *Es posible / probable / imposible que...*, *Dudo que...*, *Es necesario que...*

Answer Key

5. 1. nadie   4. alguien
       2. nada   5. todos
       3. algo

6. 1. b   2. d   3. a   4. c

7. Answers will vary. Sample answers:
   1. Me gusta que mis profesores sean pacientes.
   2. Me molesta que mis compañeros hablen en clase.
   3. Me encanta que mi familia esté tan unida.
   4. Me sorprende que mis amigos(as) no quieran ir al cine.

8. 1. a   2. c   3. c   4. b

9. 1. El castellano y el guaraní.
       2. En Buenos Aires.
       3. El Aconcagua.

Additional Resources

Fans Online activities
Practice Workbook

389

HERITAGE LANGUAGE LEARNERS

- Heritage language students probably know more expressions to convey feelings and to express doubt and value judgments. Ask them to work with a partner to compile a list. You may get them started with the following:
  – *Expresar sentimientos: me entristece que..., me emociona que...*
  – *Expresar duda: es difícil que..., es poco probable que...*
  – *Hacer valoraciones: es bueno que..., es aconsejable que...*
- Have partners include a sample sentence for each expression. You may want to check their lists and point out any errors.

MULTIPLE INTELLIGENCES:
Intrapersonal Intelligence

- Ask students to think about the end of the school year. What do they want to have accomplished? Is there something that worries them? What do they think their grades will be? Have them write a two-paragraph personal statement expressing their thoughts, desires, fears, opinions, etc. Provide an example: *Ojalá que tenga buenas calificaciones en todas las clases. Me da pena que tenga que despedirme de mis compañeros...* Ask students to keep this statement until the end of the school year to compare it with what actually happens.

Unit 7

PROYECTO

Una telenovela

Presentation

- In this section, students will apply the vocabulary, grammar, and cultural information they have learned in this unit to write the script for a *telenovela* and represent a scene with their classmates. Students will follow step-by-step instructions.

Activities	Standards	Resources
Paso 1	1.3, 3.1	
Paso 2	1.2, 1.3, 2.2, 3.1, 5.2	
Paso 3	1.3, 3.1, 5.2	
Paso 4	3.1, 5.2	
Paso 5	1.3, 3.1, 5.2	

Teaching Suggestions

Warm-Up / Independent Starter

- Have students write, in a bulleted list, what they know about Latin American *telenovelas*.

Preparation

- Explain that a *telenovela* is a type of television drama which is aired five nights a week for about six to twelve months. This genre was pioneered in Latin America, where *telenovelas* are not just a form of entertainment; they also provide a way to express the social and political problems affecting the country. In the United States, *telenovelas* serve as a link between Spanish-speaking communities and their countries of origin and play an important role in the preservation of the Spanish language.

- Latin American *telenovelas* are popular in a large number of countries and regions throughout the world. Mexico and Brazil are the main producers of *telenovelas* in Latin America, but Colombia, Argentina, and Venezuela are also important producers.

Step-by-Step Instructions

Paso 1

- Discuss with students that the characters in *telenovelas* are well defined. There must be a villain and a hero or heroine. It is also common for two of the characters to be rivals for the love of a third character.

390

Un guión para

una telenovela

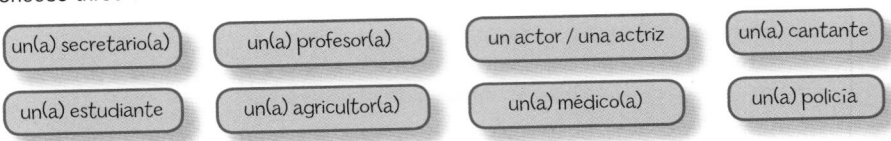

Acting is a skill. Each actor or actress in a scene must know his or her lines and often do research to become more like the character. In this project you will write the script for a *telenovela* and act out a scene with your classmates.

PASO 1 Elige a los personajes

- Choose three characters. Here are some suggestions:

  un(a) secretario(a)   un(a) profesor(a)   un actor / una actriz   un(a) cantante

  un(a) estudiante   un(a) agricultor(a)   un(a) médico(a)   un(a) policía

- Decide the relationships between the characters.
  - ¿Son familiares?
  - ¿Son amigos(as)?
  - ¿Trabajan juntos(as)?
  - ¿Se llevan bien?

PASO 2 Decide el argumento

- Decide where and when the action takes place.
  - ¿En qué país se desarrolla la historia?
  - ¿La telenovela transcurre en el campo o en la ciudad?
  - ¿En qué época ocurre: en el siglo XXI o antes?

- Write an outline for two scenes:
  - ¿Dónde están los personajes?
  - ¿Qué sucede en las escenas?
  - ¿Qué sienten los personajes?

Rubric for Evaluation

	Content	Organization	Presentation
1 point	Lacks interest. Poor characterization. Little Spanish is used.	Inefficient use of time. Plot is disorganized or unclear. Story is difficult to follow.	Unclear communication. Lines were not memorized. Many errors in vocabulary and grammar.
3 points	Holds audience's interest. Good characterization. Spanish is used most of the time.	Time is used well. Plot is mostly organized but lacks some clarity. Story is relatively easy to follow.	Clear communication. Most lines were memorized. Mostly correct vocabulary and grammar.

PASO 3 Escribe el guión

- Write the script for each scene:
  - Each scene should have at least 10 lines of dialogue and a captivating storyline.
  - This being a *telenovela*, there should be emotion and drama in each scene.
  - Include notes about each character's movements. Props and wardrobe are also encouraged.

En el interior de la hacienda. Rodrigo y su hija Teresa están discutiendo en el salón. Rodrigo está sentado en el sofá y su hija Teresa está de pie, bastante enfadada. Él lleva un traje oscuro y una corbata. Teresa lleva un vestido blanco.

- TERESA: Papá, mañana por la noche es la fiesta. Puedo ir, ¿verdad?
- RODRIGO: No, Teresa, prefiero que no asistas a esa fiesta.
- TERESA: ¿Por qué?
- RODRIGO: Porque eres demasiado joven, hija.
- TERESA: Pero papá, yo quiero ir. Todas mis amigas van a estar allí.
- RODRIGO: Lo siento, pero no quiero que vayas.
- TERESA: ¿Qué? ¡No me lo puedo creer!

María, la madre de Teresa, los escucha discutir desde el piso de arriba y baja por las escaleras un poco asustada.

- MARÍA: Hija, ¿qué sucede?

PASO 4 Elige una escena y ensaya

- In a group, choose a scene and assign the roles for each actor or actress. One of you will introduce the characters and the scene.
  Each person in the group will be responsible for memorizing his or her lines.
- Practice the scene.

PASO 5 Representa la telenovela

- Act out the scene of your *telenovela*.
- While you are watching the other groups, take notes to make value statements. Give constructive criticism on the group's performance.

Autoevaluación

¿Qué has aprendido en esta unidad?

Do these activities to evaluate how well you can manage in Spanish.

Evaluate your skills. For each item, say Very well, Well, or I need more practice.

a. Can you identify people and things?

▶ Look at your classroom and describe it: what objects and people there are, and what they are doing. Use words like *alguien, nadie, nada…*

b. Can you express wishes?

▶ Tell a classmate what you want to do in the future and why.

c. Can you express feelings and emotions?

▶ Play a guessing game. Mime leisure activities. Your classmate guesses what you are acting out.

▶ Describe the things you like and don't like about your school. Use these verbs:

gustar	molestar
encantar	alegrar
preocupar	sorprender

d. Can you make value statements?

▶ Write three sentences expressing certainty and three sentences expressing doubt.

▶ Discuss with your partner what you should do to improve your Spanish. Use the structure *es + adjetivo + que + subjuntivo*.

Paso 2

- Students may draw ideas by reading about some successful *telenovelas*, such as *Yo soy Betty, la fea* (1999, Colombia), *Rubí* (2005, Mexico), *Terra nostra* (1999, Brazil). They will find information about these *telenovelas* on the Internet. Tell students that *telenovelas* deal with issues the viewers confront in their own lives. Ask them to keep their characters real and their plot simple and linear.

Paso 3

- Explain that music is also a very important element in *telenovelas*. Ask students to consider providing their *telenovela* with a theme song/music.

Paso 4

- Suggest that the student in charge of introducing the characters also take on the role of director during rehearsal.

Paso 5

- Explain that *telenovelas* are reactive to viewers' tastes. It is common for plots to be changed, new characters added and old characters killed off in response to the audience's reactions. Ask students to write their reaction to their classmates' *telenovela* as if they were the audience.

Evaluation

- Distribute copies of the rubric to students. Discuss the evaluation criteria and explain how this project will be graded. Encourage students to refer to the rubric as they prepare their projects.

Content

- Remind students that in most *telenovelas* the hero or heroine must overcome the obstacles in his or her way. The ending is always happy. Emotion, love, suspense, and a clear-cut plot are some of the expected components. Encourage students to strive to attain this in their script.

Organization

- *Telenovelas* consist of a beginning, a middle, and an end. Tell students that their scene must mirror this organization.

Presentation

- Remind students that they must memorize their lines. They should speak clearly and loud enough for students in the back of the room to hear them.

	Content	Organization	Presentation
5 points	Riveting. Excellent characterization. Spanish is used exclusively.	Time is used wisely. Plot is clearly organized. Story is easy to follow and clear.	Clear communication. Lines were memorized. Correct and complete vocabulary and grammar.

Unit 8 La Panamericana

Objectives

- To identify, compare, and describe places.
- To talk about future plans.
- To talk about future events.
- To make impersonal statements.
- To express cause, consequence, contrast, or restriction.
- To talk about geography.
- To use superlatives to describe nouns.

- To identify places on a map.
- To talk about weather conditions.
- To describe animals and their habitat.
- To speak in general terms.
- To explore different cultural aspects of the Pan-American Highway.
- To report the weather from different regions of the world.

Contents

Vocabulary

- Geography: The oceans, continents, and landscapes.
- Countries and cardinal directions.
- Weather.
- Natural disasters.
- Wild and domestic animals.
- Environmental issues.
- Words to express cause and consequence.
- Words to express contrast and restriction.

Grammar

- The relative superlatives.
- To express plans and intentions.
- To talk about the future.
- To hide the subject: The pronoun se.

Culture

- The history of the Panama Canal.
- El casco viejo de Panamá.
- Mi Pueblito.
- The location and influence of the equator.
- La capital de Ecuador.
- Las islas Galápagos.
- Parque Nacional Volcán Isluga.
- The active volcanoes in the Pacific Ring of Fire.
- El Parque Nacional Tortuguero.
- ¡Pura vida!
- Las onomatopeyas.
- The route along the Pan-American Highway.

Evaluation Criteria

- Use expressions to express cause and consequence.
- Use expressions to express contrast and restriction.
- Identify continents and countries on a map.
- Use cardinal directions to find places on a map.

- Use superlatives to describe a noun.
- Talk about the weather.
- Describe the conditions leading up to and surrounding natural disasters.
- Express plans and intentions.
- Label and differentiate wild and domestic animals.
- Discuss environmental issues.

- Talk about future plans.
- Express understanding of cultural aspects of the Pan-American Highway.
- Read an argumentative text, understanding its characteristics as a reading strategy.
- Create a seven-day weather report for the news.

Unit Plan

La llegada

Estimated time: 1 session.

Dialogue: *En Santiago de Chile.*

Functions & forms:
- Expressions of cause and consequence.
- Expressions of contrast and restriction.

Culture:
- The *Mercado Central,* Santiago de Chile.

DESAFÍO 1

Estimated time: 4 sessions.

Dialogue: *Una obra de gigantes.*

Functions & forms:
- Geography: the continents and landscapes.
- The relative superlative.

Culture:
- *El canal de Panamá.*
- *El casco viejo de Panamá.*
- *Mi Pueblito.*

DESAFÍO 2

Estimated time: 4 sessions.

Dialogue: *La mitad del mundo.*

Functions & forms:
- Countries and cardinal directions.
- To express plans and intentions.

Culture:
- *La línea del ecuador.*
- *La capital de Ecuador.*
- *Las islas Galápagos.*

DESAFÍO 3

Estimated time: 4 sessions.

Dialogue: *Aire frío y agua caliente.*

Functions & forms:
- Weather.
- Natural disasters.
- To express future plans.

Culture:
- *El Parque Nacional Volcán Isluga.*
- *El Cinturón de Fuego del Pacífico.*

DESAFÍO 4

Estimated time: 4 sessions.

Dialogue: *El paraíso de las tortugas.*

Functions & forms:
- Wild and domestic animals.
- Environmental issues.
- To hide the subject: The pronoun *se.*

Culture:
- *El Parque Nacional Tortuguero.*
- *¡Pura vida!*
- *Las onomatopeyas.*

TODO JUNTO/**El encuentro**

Estimated time: 1 session.

Dialogue: *En Denver, Colorado.*

Functions & forms:
- Review of *Desafíos 1–4.*

Culture:
- Denver, Colorado.

MAPA CULTURAL/LECTURA

Estimated time: 1 session.

Mapa cultural: *La ruta Panamericana.*

Reading: *El Tapón de Darién: un corte en la Panamericana.*

PROYECTO/EVALUACIÓN

Estimated time: 2 sessions.

Project: *Un boletín sobre la predicción meteorológica.*

Self-evaluation: *Autoevaluación.*

Standards for Learning Spanish

 COMMUNICATION

1.1. Interpersonal mode
- Discuss the challenge for each team in the selected places along the Pan-American Highway.
- Speculate on which pair will win the challenge.
- Discuss what students know about the Panama Canal and the Pan-American Highway.
- Play a guessing game with a classmate.
- Write about personal experiences in a national park or reserve.
- Write what one would do in an imaginary situation.
- Reply to an e-mail with personal opinions and knowledge.
- Interview classmates.
- Understand someone's personal opinion.
- Read opposing points of view.

1.2. Interpretive mode
- Take notes from an oral text.
- Read a cultural text.
- Read an e-mail.
- Research cultural topics.
- Associate oral descriptions with pictures.
- Understand written exchanges between friends.
- Draw conclusions from a classmate's answers to an interview question.
- Demonstrate understanding of a person's opinion.
- Read a map and identify different aspects.

1.3. Presentational mode
- Present opinions to the class.
- Use a chart to display the results of a questionnaire.
- Write a description of a photograph.
- Create a list of the things one could do to protect the environment.
- Write interview questions.
- Present a list of descriptions to classmates.

COMPARISONS

4.1. Compare languages
- Compare the formulation of the relative superlative in English and in Spanish.
- Compare the ways to express future plans in English and in Spanish.
- Compare impersonal expressions in English and in Spanish.
- Compare onomatopoeia in English and in Spanish.

4.2. Compare cultures
- Compare the influence of the mixture of cultures in Panama City and in the student's city.
- Compare the significance of historical tourist attractions in Panama City and in the student's city.

CULTURE

2.1. Practices and perspectives
- Discuss the popularity of certain cities around the world.
- Read about how the mix of cultures in the past has influenced current culture.
- Understand how the phrase *¡Pura vida!* is more like a way of life instead of a motto.

2.2. Products and perspectives
- Read about the origins of popular tourist attractions in Panama City.
- Discuss the geographical features of a National Park.
- Explore the variation in onomatopoeia in different languages.

COMMUNITIES

5.1. Spanish within and beyond the school setting
- Visit the website to further explore cultural aspects along the Pan-American Highway.
- Discuss previous knowledge or experiences in famous cities around the world.
- Read a tourist guide.
- Research the Pan-American highway.

5.2. Spanish for lifelong learning
- Explore the history of the architecture in Panama City and in your community.
- Compare the significance of historical tourist attractions in Panama City and your city.
- Describe your ideal trip and what you would do during it.

CONNECTIONS

3.1. Interdisciplinary connections
- Explore the geography along the Pan-American Highway and its history.
- Learn about the largest volcano in a Chilean National Park.
- Discover more information about onomatopoeia.
- Read about the collective effort that went into the construction of the Panama Canal.
- Understand the similarities and differences between superlatives in English and in Spanish.
- Discuss the influence of seismic activity on a people.

3.2. Viewpoints through language / culture
- Discover aspects of the Pan-American Highway's history and culture.
- Read about how the mix of cultures in the past has influenced current culture.
- Read travel brochures about various Spanish-speaking countries.

Communicative Skills

Interpersonal Mode

		Activities
Speaking	• Engage in conversation with a classmate. • Talk with a classmate about opinions and preferences. • Interview a classmate.	• 4, 25, 27, 34, 37, 47, 70, 76 • 17, 54, 56, 85 • 63
Writing	• Write a passage to express a personal opinion or knowledge on a subject. • Write a passage to compare personal knowledge and acquired knowledge. • Write a personal reflection.	• 9, 13, 18, 29, 30, 35, 47, 52, 54, 61 • 14, 43, 48, 65, 66 • 56, 77
Listening	• Understand verbal questions and respond appropriately. • Understand someone's personal opinion.	• 16, 34, 76, *Minientrevistas* • 17, 20, 85
Reading	• Understand a personal reflection. • Understand an informational or a narrated story.	• 36, 59, 78 • 72, *Lectura*

Interpretive Mode

		Activities
Listening	• Understand someone's personal opinion. • Obtain information from an oral exchange. • Obtain cultural information from audio and video. • Understand oral descriptions. • Interpret a classmate's answers and draw conclusions.	• 20, 28 • 25, 37, 46, 55, 67, 72 • *Tu desafío, videos* • 15, 25, 32, 42, 49, 51, 62, 63, 75 • 12, 85
Reading	• Understand brief written exchanges. • Demonstrate an understanding of written dialogues. • Draw comparisons or conclusions from a cultural text. • Draw conclusions from written descriptions or a narrative text.	• *Fotonovelas*, 39, 57, 74 • 1, 7, 24, 41, 22 • 9, 13, 18, 30, 35, 43, 52, 65 • 19, 36, 53, 59, 72, 74, 77, 79, *Lectura*

Presentational Mode

		Activities
Speaking	• Act out a short skit aloud. • Present a list of descriptions to classmates.	• 3, 75 • 21, 29
Writing	• Chart results to display understanding. • Write a dialogue to be presented to the class. • Write a description based on the actions or scenery shown in a picture. • Write questions to be used in an interview or a game. • Create a poster to present results. • Create a list of the things one could do to protect the environment.	• 12, 38, 51, 82, 85 • 3 • 6, 11, 39, 57, 60, 73, 79 • 16, 45, 56 • 76, 80 • 64

Cross-Curricular Standards

Subject	Standard	Activities
Language Arts	• Use superlatives to describe nouns. • Compare the use of the subjunctive mood in English and in Spanish. • Write a personal reflection.	• 14 • 33 • 56, 77
Geography	• Learn about the continents and oceans. • Read about the Pan-American Highway. • Read about the tallest volcano in a Chilean National Park.	• 15 • *Mapa cultural* • 43
Science	• Read about the Panama Canal. • Learn about weather and natural disasters.	• 9 • 45, 47

Lesson Plans (50-Minute Classes)

Day	Objectives	Sessions	Activities	Time	Standards	Resources / Homework
1	To introduce the Pan-American Highway and to discuss the pairs' challenges	**La Panamericana / La llegada** (392–397) • Warm-Up: Countries orientation • *La Panamericana* • Images and functions • Presentation: *En Santiago de Chile* • *Expresiones útiles* and *¿Quién ganará?*	 1 2–5	 5 m. 5 m. 10 m. 10 m. 20 m.	1.1, 1.2, 1.3, 2.1, 2.2, 3.1, 4.1, 5.1	Visual Presentation Video Practice Workbook
2	To identify, describe, and compare places	**Desafío 1 – Una obra de gigantes** (398–399) • Warm-Up: Independent Starter • *Fotonovela: Una obra de gigantes* • *Conexiones: El canal de Panamá*	 6–8 9	 5 m. 35 m. 10 m.	1.1, 1.2, 1.3, 2.2, 3.1, 3.2, 5.1, 5.2	Visual Presentation Audio Video *Tu desafío*
3	To talk about geography and landscapes	**Desafío 1 – Vocabulario** (400–401) • Warm-Up: Independent Starter • Vocabulary: *Geografía* • *Cultura: El casco viejo de Panamá*	 10–12 13	 5 m. 35 m. 10 m.	1.1, 1.2, 1.3, 2.1, 2.2, 3.1, 3.2, 4.2, 5.1, 5.2	Audio Practice Workbook *Tu desafío*
4	To express the extreme degree of an adjective	**Desafío 1 – Gramática** (402–403) • Warm-Up: Independent Starter • Grammar: *El superlativo relativo* • *Cultura: Mi Pueblito*	 14–17 18	 5 m. 35 m. 10 m.	1.1, 1.2, 1.3, 2.2, 3.1, 4.1, 4.2, 5.1, 5.2	Audio Practice Workbook
5	To integrate vocabulary and grammar and to assess student proficiency	**Desafío 1 – Comunicación / Evaluación** (404–405) • Warm-Up: Independent Starter • *Comunicación:* Review • *Final del desafío* • Quiz on *Desafío 1*	 19–21 22	 5 m. 20 m. 10 m. 15 m.	1.1, 1.2, 1.3, 2.1, 2.2, 3.1	Audio Practice Workbook
6	To talk about future plans	**Desafío 2 – La mitad del mundo** (406–407) • Warm-Up: Independent Starter • *Fotonovela: La mitad del mundo* • *Conexiones: La línea del ecuador*	 23–25 26	 5 m. 35 m. 10 m.	1.1, 1.2, 1.3, 2.2, 2.2, 3.1	Visual Presentation Audio *Tu desafío*
7	To talk about countries	**Desafío 2 – Vocabulario** (408–409) • Warm-Up: Independent Starter • Vocabulary: *Países* • *Cultura: La capital de Ecuador*	 27–29 30	 5 m. 35 m. 10 m.	1.1, 1.2, 1.3, 2.1, 3.1, 3.2, 4.2, 5.1	Audio Practice Workbook *Tu desafío*
8	To express plans and intentions	**Desafío 2 – Gramática** (410–411) • Warm-Up: Independent Starter • Grammar: *Expresar planes e intenciones* • *Conexiones: Las islas Galápagos*	 31–34 35	 5 m. 35 m. 10 m.	1.1, 1.2, 1.3, 3.1, 3.2, 5.1, 5.2	Audio Practice Workbook *Tu desafío*
9	To integrate vocabulary and grammar and to assess student proficiency	**Desafío 2 – Comunicación / Evaluación** (412–413) • Warm-Up: Independent Starter • *Comunicación:* Review • *Final del desafío* • Quiz on *Desafío 2*	 36–38 39	 5 m. 20 m. 10 m. 15 m.	1.1, 1.2, 1.3, 2.2, 3.1, 3.2, 5.2	Audio Practice Workbook *Tu desafío*
10	To talk about future actions	**Desafío 3 – Aire frío y agua caliente** (414–415) • Warm-Up: Independent Starter • *Fotonovela: Aire frío y agua caliente* • *Conexiones: El Parque Nacional Volcán Isluga*	 40–42 43	 5 m. 35 m. 10 m.	1.1, 1.2, 1.3, 2.1, 3.1, 3.2, 4.2, 5.1	Visual Presentation Audio *Tu desafío*
11	To talk about weather and natural disasters	**Desafío 3 – Vocabulario** (416–417) • Warm-Up: Independent Starter • Vocabulary: *El clima*	 44–47	 5 m. 45 m.	1.1, 1.2, 1.3, 3.1, 5.2	Audio Practice Workbook

Day	Objectives	Sessions	Activities	Time	Standards	Resources / Homework
12	To talk about the future	**Desafío 3 – Gramática** (418–419) • Warm-Up: Independent Starter • Grammar: *El futuro* • Conexiones: *El Cinturón de Fuego del Pacífico*	48–51 52	5 m. 35 m. 10 m.	1.1, 1.2, 1.3, 3.1, 3.2, 4.1, 5.1	Audio Practice Workbook *Tu desafío*
13	To integrate vocabulary and grammar and to assess student proficiency	**Desafío 3 – Comunicación / Evaluación** (420–421) • Warm-Up: Independent Starter • *Comunicación:* Review • *Final del desafío* • Quiz on *Desafío 3*	53–56 57	5 m. 20 m. 10 m. 15 m.	1.1, 1.2, 1.3, 5.1	Audio Practice Workbook *Tu desafío*
14	To make impersonal affirmations	**Desafío 4 – El paraíso de las tortugas** (422–423) • Warm-Up: Independent Starter • *Fotonovela: El paraíso de las tortugas* • Conexiones: *El Parque Nacional Tortuguero*	58–60 61	5 m. 35 m. 10 m.	1.1, 1.2, 1.3, 2.2, 3.1, 3.2, 5.1	Visual Presentation *Tu desafío*
15	To describe nature and the environment	**Desafío 4 – Vocabulario** (424–425) • Warm-Up: Independent Starter • Vocabulary: *La naturaleza y el medio ambiente* • Comunidades: *¡Pura vida!*	62–64 65	5 m. 35 m. 10 m.	1.1, 1.2, 1.3, 2.1, 3.2, 4.2, 5.1, 5.2	Audio Video Practice Workbook *Tu desafío*
16	To speak in impersonal terms	**Desafío 4 – Gramática** (426–427) • Warm-Up: Independent Starter • Grammar: *Ocultar el sujeto. El pronombre 'se'* • Conexiones: *Las onomatopeyas*	66–70 71	5 m. 35 m. 10 m.	1.1, 1.2, 1.3, 2.1, 3.1, 4.1, 5.1	Audio Practice Workbook
17	To integrate vocabulary and grammar and to assess student proficiency	**Desafío 4 – Comunicación / Evaluación** (428–429) • Warm-Up: Independent Starter • *Comunicación:* Review • *Final del desafío* • Quiz on *Desafío 4*	72–73 74	5 m. 20 m. 10 m. 15 m.	1.1, 1.2, 1.3, 2.2, 3.1, 5.1	Audio Practice Workbook
18	To integrate language in context	**Todo junto / El encuentro** (430–433) • Warm-Up: Independent Starter • *Todo junto* • *El encuentro: En Denver, Colorado*	75–78 79–80	5 m. 20 m. 25 m.	1.1, 1.2, 1.3, 3.1, 3.2, 5.1, 5.2	Audio Practice Workbook
19	To learn about the Pan-American Highway and to read an argumentative text	**Mapa cultural / Lectura** (434–437) • Warm-Up: Read the *Mapa cultural* • *Mapa cultural: La ruta Panamericana* • *Lectura: El Tapón de Darién: un corte en la Panamericana.* • Read project outline (442–443)	81–83 84–86	5 m. 20 m. 20 m. 5 m.	1.1, 1.2, 1.3, 2,1, 2.2, 3.1, 3.2, 5.1, 5.2	Video Practice Workbook *Tu desafío* Project work
20	To create a seven-day weather forecast	**Proyecto** (442–443) • Warm-Up: Prepare project presentations • Project presentations		5 m. 45 m.	1.1, 1.2, 1.3, 3.1, 5.2	Practice Workbook **Repaso – Vocabulario** (438–439) **Repaso – Gramática** (440–441)
21	To assess student proficiency	**Assessment** • *Autoevaluación* (443) • Test		10 m. 40 m.	1.2, 1.3	

Unit 8 La Panamericana

Lesson Plans (90-Minute Classes)

Day	Objectives	Sessions	Activities	Time	Standards	Resources / Homework
1	To introduce the Pan-American Highway and to discuss the pairs' challenges	**La Panamericana / La llegada** (392–397) • Warm-Up: Countries orientation • *La Panamericana /* Images and functions • Presentation: *En Santiago de Chile* • *Expresiones útiles* and *¿Quién ganará?*	 1 2–5	5 m. 15 m. 10 m. 20 m.	1.1, 1.2, 1.3, 2.1, 2.2, 3.1, 4.1, 5.1	Visual Presentation Video Practice Workbook
2	To identify, describe, and compare places and to talk about geography and landscapes	**Desafío 1 – Una obra de gigantes / Vocabulario** (398–401) • Warm-Up: Independent Starter • *Fotonovela: Una obra de gigantes* • *Conexiones: El canal de Panamá* • Vocabulary: *Geografía* • *Cultura: El casco viejo de Panamá*	 6–8 9 10–12 13	 5 m. 30 m. 10 m. 35 m. 10 m.	1.1, 1.2, 1.3, 2.1, 2.2, 3.1, 3.2, 4.2, 5.1, 5.2	Visual Presentation Audio Video Practice Workbook *Tu desafío*
3	To express the extreme degree of an adjective, to integrate vocabulary and grammar, and to assess student proficiency	**Desafío 1 – Gramática / Comunicación / Evaluación** (402–405) • Warm-Up: Independent Starter • Grammar: *El superlativo relativo* • *Cultura: Mi Pueblito* • *Comunicación:* Review • *Final del desafío* • Quiz on *Desafío 1*	 14–17 18 19–21 22	 5 m. 25 m. 10 m. 25 m. 10 m. 15 m.	1.1, 1.2, 1.3, 2.1, 2.2, 3.1, 4.1, 4.2, 5.1, 5.2	Audio Practice Workbook
4	To talk about future plans and to talk about countries	**Desafío 2 – La mitad del mundo / Vocabulario** (406–409) • Warm-Up: Independent Starter • *Fotonovela: La mitad del mundo* • *Conexiones: La línea del ecuador* • Vocabulary: *Países* • *Cultura: La capital de Ecuador*	 23–25 26 27–29 30	 5 m. 25 m. 15 m. 35 m. 10 m.	1.1, 1.2, 1.3, 2.1, 3.1, 3.2, 4.2, 5.1	Visual Presentation Audio Practice Workbook *Tu desafío*
5	To express plans and intentions, to integrate vocabulary and grammar, and to assess student proficiency	**Desafío 2 – Gramática / Comunicación / Evaluación** (410–413) • Warm-Up: Independent Starter • Grammar: *Expresar planes e intenciones* • *Conexiones: Las islas Galápagos* • *Comunicación:* Review • *Final del desafío* • Quiz on *Desafío 2*	 31–34 35 36–38 39	 5 m. 25 m. 10 m. 25 m. 10 m. 15 m.	1.1, 1.2, 1.3, 2.2, 3.1, 3.2, 5.1, 5.2	Audio Practice Workbook *Tu desafío*
6	To talk about future actions and to talk about weather and natural disasters	**Desafío 3 – Aire frío y agua caliente / Vocabulario** (414–417) • Warm-Up: Independent Starter • *Fotonovela: Aire frío y agua caliente* • *Conexiones: Parque Nacional Volcán Isluga* • Vocabulary: *El clima*	 40–42 43 44–47	 5 m. 35 m. 10 m. 40 m.	1.1, 1.2, 1.3, 2.1, 3.1, 3.2, 4.2, 5.1, 5.2	Visual Presentation Audio Practice Workbook *Tu desafío*
7	To talk about the future, to integrate vocabulary and grammar, and to assess student proficiency	**Desafío 3 – Gramática / Comunicación / Evaluación** (418–421) • Warm-Up: Independent Starter • Grammar: *El futuro* • *Conexiones: El Cinturón de Fuego del Pacífico* • *Comunicación:* Review • *Final del desafío* • Quiz on *Desafío 3*	 48–51 52 53–56 57	 5 m. 25 m. 10 m. 25 m. 10 m. 15 m.	1.1, 1.2, 1.3, 3.1, 3.2, 4.1, 5.1	Audio Practice Workbook *Tu desafío*

Day	Objectives	Sessions	Activities	Time	Standards	Resources / Homework
8	To make impersonal affirmations and to describe nature and the environment	**Desafío 4 – El paraíso de las tortugas / Vocabulario** (422–425) • Warm-Up: Independent Starter • *Fotonovela: El paraíso de las tortugas* • *Conexiones: El Parque Nacional Tortuguero* • *Vocabulary: La naturaleza y el medio ambiente* • *Comunidades: ¡Pura vida!*	 58–60 61 62–64 65	 5 m. 30 m. 10 m. 35 m. 10 m.	1.1, 1.2, 1.3, 2.1, 2.2, 3.1, 3.2, 4.2, 5.1, 5.2	Visual Presentation Audio Video Practice Workbook *Tu desafío*
9	To speak in impersonal terms, to integrate vocabulary and grammar, and to assess student proficiency	**Desafío 4 – Gramática / Comunicación / Evaluación / Todo junto** (426–431) • Warm-Up: Independent Starter • *Grammar: Ocultar el sujeto. El pronombre 'se'* • *Conexiones: Las onomatopeyas* • *Comunicación: Review* • *Final del desafío* • Quiz on *Desafío 4* • *Todo junto*	 66–70 71 72–73 74 75–78	 5 m. 20 m. 5 m. 20 m. 5 m. 15 m. 20 m.	1.1, 1.2, 1.3, 2.1, 2.2, 3.1, 3.2, 4.1, 5.1, 5.2	Audio Practice Workbook
10	To integrate language in context, to learn about the Pan-American Highway and to read an argumentative text	**El encuentro / Mapa cultural / Lectura** (432–437) • Warm-Up: Independent Starter • *El encuentro: En Denver, Colorado* • *Mapa cultural: La ruta Panamericana* • *Lectura: El Tapón de Darién: un corte en la Panamericana* • Read project outline (442–443)	 79–80 81–83 84–86 	 5 m. 30 m. 25 m. 25 m. 5 m.	1.1, 1.2, 1.3, 2.1, 2.2, 3.1, 3.2, 5.1, 5.2	Video Practice Workbook *Tu desafío* **Repaso – Vocabulario** (438–439) **Repaso – Gramática** (440–441) Project work
11	To create a seven-day weather forecast and to assess student proficiency	**Proyecto / Assessment** (442–443) • Project presentations • *Autoevaluación* • Test	 40 m. 10 m. 40 m.		1.1, 1.2, 1.3, 3.1, 5.2	

Unit 8 La Panamericana

8 Una conversación en el kayak

–¡Qué grande es este lago!

–Sí, el lago Gatún es enorme. ¡Y muy importante! Ayuda a los barcos a pasar por el canal durante unos kilómetros.

–¿Y cuántos kilómetros tenemos que remar nosotros?

–Aproximadamente 32, es decir, 20 millas.

–¡Pero eso es mucho!

–Ánimo, Janet. Podemos hacerlo.

–Si tú lo dices… ¡Mira, Andy! ¿Qué es eso?

–Es la isla Barro Colorado. Ahí viven miles de especies de plantas y animales en peligro de extinción.

–Aquí el paisaje es hermosísimo, ¿verdad? ¡Cuántas plantas tropicales y animales exóticos!

–Estoy de acuerdo. Para mí, Panamá es el país más bonito de Centroamérica.

12 ¿Cuánto sabes?

–Vamos a ver cuánto saben de geografía. Tres preguntas para cada uno, ¿de acuerdo?

–Venga.

–Empiezo yo. Pregúntame.

–A ver… primera pregunta para Ana: ¿Cuál es el continente más grande?

–Creo que es Asia.

–Sí, muy bien. Ahora Juan, a ver si sabes la respuesta. ¿Qué desierto está en el sur de los Estados Unidos?

–No lo sé… ¿Cuál es?

–Es el desierto de Chihuahua.

–¡Qué difícil!

–Ana, ahora tú. Segunda pregunta. ¿Cómo se llama el océano que está entre América y Asia?

–Océano Pacífico.

–Muy bien. Juan, te toca. Segunda pregunta para ti: ¿Cuál es el río más largo de América del Sur?

–Esta sí la sé. Es el Amazonas.

–Correcto. Última pregunta para Ana: ¿Cuál es el lago más grande de África?

–No estoy segura… ¿El lago Victoria?

–Muy bien, Ana. ¡Ganaste!

15 Los lugares que conozco

1. La ciudad más famosa de mi país es Nueva York.
2. España es el país más turístico que conozco.
3. El salto Ángel es la catarata más alta del mundo. ¡Es impresionante!
4. El lago de Atitlán es el lugar más misterioso que visité en Guatemala.
5. Suramérica me gustó mucho. Es el continente más fascinante que conozco.
6. En nuestros viajes vimos muchas cosas extrañas, pero Vieques tiene la bahía más extraña del mundo. ¡Hay luz en el agua!

20 Opiniones

1. Mack cree que Buenos Aires es la ciudad más grande de Latinoamérica.
2. A Janet le parece que Venezuela tiene el mejor clima de Latinoamérica.
3. Para Tim, Costa Rica tiene los paisajes más bonitos del mundo.
4. Andy piensa que el desierto de Atacama es el más impresionante del mundo.
5. Para Patricia, el glaciar Perito Moreno es el lugar más espectacular de Argentina.

25 ¡Cuántos viajes!

–¿Y adónde vas?

–Hoy voy a Lisboa. Allí preparan un pescado delicioso. Pero no me voy a quedar mucho tiempo.

–Ah, ¿no?

–No, solo voy a estar un día. Mañana voy a Berlín. Estamos en primavera y hay muchas flores. Voy a sacar muchas fotos de la ciudad.

–¡Qué divertido! ¿Y después?

–Pasado mañana voy a Roma. Quiero comer una pizza auténtica antes de volver a los Estados Unidos.

–¿Cuándo vuelves a casa?

–La semana que viene. Tengo entradas para un musical en Broadway.

–¡Qué suerte! ¿Y qué vas a hacer después? ¿Vas a quedarte en casa?

–No. En dos semanas viajo a Brasil. Voy a hacer un curso intensivo de samba. Y el próximo mes vuelvo a Europa. Mi esposa y yo queremos ir a París para celebrar nuestro aniversario. Vamos a visitar la torre Eiffel.

–Oye, ¿y por qué viajas tanto? ¿Eres millonario?

–¿Yo? ¡Qué va! Soy escritor. Mi trabajo es escribir guías de viaje.

28 Recomendaciones

1. Me encanta bailar. La samba es mi baile favorito.
2. Yo quiero ver a los actores y actrices más famosos del mundo.
3. A mí me gusta visitar sitios antiguos. Me interesa la cultura clásica.
4. La comida asiática es mi favorita. Me encanta el sushi.
5. Yo quiero aprender a cocinar platos típicos de la cocina mediterránea. Sobre todo, paella y gazpacho. ¡Me encantan!
6. Yo voy mucho al teatro y me encantan los musicales.

32 Los planes de José

¡Hola, Tess! Soy José, tu primo favorito. Espero que todo te vaya bien en Ecuador. Tengo muy buenas noticias. ¡Voy a trabajar en una agencia de viajes! Empiezo a trabajar la semana que viene y voy a viajar mucho. En tres semanas voy a ir a Japón y a China. Cuando esté en Asia, voy a probar la comida típica de todos los países. Me encanta la cocina oriental. Cuando regrese de ese viaje, tengo que ir a Nueva York. Quiero ir a la Estatua de la Libertad y visitar los museos de arte más importantes. También voy a visitar Francia, el Reino Unido, España y Portugal cuando esté en Europa. Bueno, Tess, luego te llamo. Un beso.

37 Vamos de vacaciones

–Hola, cariño. ¿Qué tal?

–Muy bien. ¿Y ustedes?

–Muy bien, pero ya tenemos ganas de volver a casa. Dime, ¿conseguiste información para nuestras próximas vacaciones?

–Sí, busqué información en Internet y también hablé con nuestra agente de viajes. Ya tengo planeado el viaje perfecto.

–Cuéntame. ¿Qué quieres hacer?

–Vamos a ir a Nueva York. Allí hay muchas cosas interesantes que ver: los museos, Central Park, la estatua de la Libertad, la Quinta Avenida… ¿Qué te parece?

–Yo prefiero ir a Francia.

–¡A Francia! Está un poco lejos… ¿A qué parte de Francia quieres ir?

–Al norte. Quiero conocer la región de Normandía. Y también la capital. Es una ciudad maravillosa.

–De acuerdo. Entonces, vamos a Francia.

–¡Genial! Cuando estemos en París, vamos a visitar el Museo del Louvre, Notre Dâme, la Torre Eiffel…

—También podemos ir en avión a Londres y pasar unos días allí.

—Ah, perfecto. Londres es una ciudad muy interesante. Cuando puedas, llama a la agencia de viajes y pide los precios, ¿de acuerdo?

—Muy bien. Mañana hablamos. Un beso, mi amor.

42 ¿Qué foto es?

1. Este volcán no es peligroso porque no es un volcán activo.
2. Mañana bajarán las temperaturas en todo el país.
3. Mañana hará sol y buen tiempo, y subirán las temperaturas.
4. El volcán Villarrica entró en erupción en 1971.

46 El tiempo nos influye mucho

—Hace un día perfecto para hacer deporte, ¿no?

—Sí, la temperatura es buena, pero yo prefiero que haga sol.

—Yo no. Prefiero caminar cuando está nublado porque no hace tanto calor.

49 ¿En el pasado o en el futuro?

1. Cuando empiece a llover, Tim se pondrá el impermeable.
2. Cuando vaya a la playa, Tim se bañará.
3. Cuando se marche de Chile, Tim irá a Denver.
4. Cuando subió al volcán, Tim sacó una fotografía.
5. Cuando miró el termómetro, Tim se puso el abrigo y la bufanda.
6. Cuando nieve, Tim irá a esquiar a Bariloche.
7. Cuando empezó a nevar, Tim volvió al hotel.
8. Cuando vuelva a casa, Tim llamará a sus amigos.

51 ¿Qué tiempo hará?

—Y ahora pasamos a la previsión meteorológica para los próximos días en Santiago de Chile.

—Hoy lunes estará nublado, pero mañana y pasado mañana tendremos sol y subirán las temperaturas. El jueves habrá nubes. Para el viernes y el fin de semana tendremos lluvias y bajarán las temperaturas.

55 Un viaje, dos ciudades

—¿Ya te vas al aeropuerto, mamá?

—Sí, hijo. Hoy veré a tus tíos en Valparaíso, estoy muy contenta.

—Pero llevas poca ropa en la maleta.

—Cuando llegue, compraré algo más. Ya sabes, me gusta ir de compras. Además, nunca se sabe cómo será el tiempo en Valparaíso. En Internet vi que por las mañanas hará frío, y la semana que viene lloverá mucho.

—Ten cuidado, mamá.

—No te preocupes. Me quedo en Valparaíso solo tres días. Luego viajaré a Santiago. Hubo un terremoto hace algunos meses y voy a visitar una escuela para ayudarlos.

—¡Qué bien, mamá! Podrás ayudar a muchos niños.

62 Mascotas

1. Margarita tiene un gato blanco.
2. Ángel tiene un perro muy bonito.
3. Eva tiene un pájaro que canta muy bien.
4. Julio tiene un acuario con muchos peces tropicales.
5. Mercedes tiene una tortuga.

63 Los animales que me gustan

1. —Hola, ¿cómo te llamas?
   —Me llamo Mario.

—Mario, ¿cuáles son los animales que más te gustan?

—Me encantan las tortugas. Pero también me gusta mucho observar insectos. Son muy interesantes.

2. —¿Y tú cómo te llamas?
   —Sofía. A mí los animales que más me gustan son los animales domésticos. En casa tengo dos perros y muchos gatos.

3. —Yo soy Rodrigo.
   —Hola, Rodrigo. ¿Y a ti qué animales te gustan?
   —A mí me gustan todos los animales, pero prefiero los animales salvajes, como los elefantes.

4. —¿Y tú?
   —Yo soy Irene. No tengo un solo animal favorito. Me gustan todos los animales. Pero sobre todo me gustan los peces. Especialmente, los peces tropicales.

67 Rita quiere saber más…

—¿Puedo hacerte una pregunta? ¿Por qué se llama así este parque?

—El parque se llama Tortuguero porque está en una zona que las tortugas visitan cada año.

—Ah, claro. Y además de las tortugas y las aves, ¿qué más se puede ver en el parque?

—Aquí hay muchísimas plantas y animales de todas las especies. Los más divertidos son los monos. [...] ¿Oyes? ¡Ahí hay uno!

—¡Ah, sí, ya lo veo! Oye, aquí vienen muchos turistas, ¿verdad?

—Sí, viene gente de todo el mundo.

—¿Y tú crees que es posible proteger la naturaleza en un lugar tan turístico?

—Sí, claro. Si se respetan las normas y todo el mundo se preocupa por cuidar la naturaleza, nuestros hijos y nuestros nietos podrán disfrutar del parque en el futuro.

72 Un viaje a Costa Rica

—Hola, Carmen, ¿cómo estás?

—¡Hola, Diana! ¡Qué sorpresa! ¿Qué tal en Costa Rica?

—Muy bien, es un país fantástico. Hay muchos parques naturales, muchísimas playas y un paisaje maravilloso.

—¿Qué se puede hacer allí?

—Pues, por ejemplo, se puede subir a un volcán.

—¿En serio? ¿No es peligroso?

—No, yo subí al volcán Irazú. Fue increíble.

—Creo que en las playas se puede hacer mucho surf, ¿no?

—Sí, y también buceo, senderismo… Todo tipo de deportes acuáticos.

—Qué divertido. ¿Y qué más?

—También se puede hacer turismo cultural. Hay museos y galerías de arte muy interesantes en San José. Ah, y se come muy bien, sobre todo arroz, frijoles, verduras, frutas tropicales… y mucho marisco.

—¡Qué rico! Tendré que ir a visitarte, Diana.

75 El tiempo en Latinoamérica

El tiempo en el continente americano será muy variado. En diciembre, empieza el invierno en el hemisferio norte. Lloverá en la península de Yucatán. El clima más frío lo tendrán en Baja California, donde habrá temperaturas muy bajas. En Centroamérica, continuarán las lluvias. En el hemisferio Sur, donde entra el verano, las temperaturas serán muy altas en la zona del Río de la Plata. Nevará en los Andes. Y en la ciudad de Concepción, Chile, habrá bastantes lluvias y tormentas.

La Panamericana

The Unit

- The themes of Unit 8 are geography, climate, and nature in the context of some outstanding geographic features that are found along the Pan-American Highway.

- The pairs meet in Santiago de Chile to figure out how to get to Denver, Colorado, which will be their final destination.

  – *Desafío 1.* Andy and Janet must paddle a 20-mile stretch of the Panama Canal.

  – *Desafío 2.* Patricia and Tess travel to Quito, Ecuador, to find the Earth's equator and step in the Northern and Southern hemispheres simultaneously at noon.

  – *Desafío 3.* Tim and Mack must swim in a hot spring at 12,000 feet above sea level in the Chilean Andes.

  – *Desafío 4.* Diana and Rita's task is to rescue as many baby sea turtles as possible in Tortuguero, a national park and turtle sanctuary in Costa Rica.

Activities	Standards	Resources
La Panamericana	1.2, 2.1, 2.2	Video

Teaching Suggestions

Warm-Up / Independent Starter

- Ask students to take note of the places where the four pairs will travel. Then have them complete the following sentence:

  El lugar más interesante es… porque…

The Pan-American Highway

- The Pan-American Highway is a system of roads and highways that connects the mainland nations of the Americas. It is made up of close to 30,000 miles of roads, from Southern Chile and Argentina to Alaska. This network was originally conceived as a single route, but it was later decided to adapt some existing roads in participating countries and complete the necessary connections. There is a break, called the Darién Gap, of about 57 miles in southern Panama and northern Colombia, due to inaccessible rainforest.

UNIDAD 8

La Panamericana

De vuelta a casa

DESAFÍO 1

▶ **To identify, describe, and compare places**

Vocabulario
Geografía

Gramática
El superlativo relativo

DESAFÍO 2

Mitad del Mundo (Ecuador)

▶ **To talk about future plans**

Vocabulario
Países

Gramática
Expresar planes e intenciones

Canal de Panamá

The Challenge

DESAFÍO 1

Canal de Panamá

The Panama Canal is a ship canal that connects the Atlantic and Pacific Oceans. Its length, from shoreline to shoreline, is about 51 miles. Construction of the Canal was started by the French developer Ferdinand de Lesseps, who had successfully directed the construction of the Suez Canal. However, his company went bankrupt and the rights to build the Canal were sold to the United States. Construction was restarted by the Americans in 1904, and the Panama Canal opened in 1914. Complete ownership and control of the Canal were returned to the government of Panama in 1999.

DESAFÍO 2

Mitad del Mundo

The equator is an imaginary circle around the Earth that is located at the same distance from the two poles and divides the planet into the Northern and Southern hemispheres. Mitad del Mundo is a town that is located at about 10 miles from Quito, the capital city of Ecuador. A monument marks the equator, although more recent and accurate measurements have determined that the location of the monument is off by about 788 feet. This has not deterred tourists who flock to the place to get their picture taken at the middle of the world, however.

Volcán Isluga
(Chile)

La Panamericana

DESAFÍO 3

▶ **To hide the agent**

Vocabulario
La naturaleza y el medio ambiente

Gramática
Ocultar el agente.
El pronombre *se*

talk about
ure events

cabulario
iempo meteorológico

mática
uturo

DESAFÍO 4

Tortugas
marinas

■ Show students a map of the Pan-American Highway and review the countries that it crosses and their capitals. You may ask students questions about the climate they think they would find along the road. *¿Qué clima hay probablemente en Ushuaia, Argentina? ¿Y en Ecuador?*

Picture Discussion

■ Ask students to look at the pictures. Has anyone in the class ever been to any of the places mentioned? If they haven't, would they like to visit any of these places?

Canal de Panamá

■ Have students work in small groups to compile a list of what they know about the Canal (e.g., location, oceans it connects, year it was built and by whom, etc.). Then have groups report their information to the class. Did students come up with similar data? Discuss, as a class, the importance of the Panama Canal for worldwide trade.

Mitad del Mundo (Ecuador)

■ Ask students to observe the picture. What tells them that this picture shows the equator? (the yellow line and the letter E) Invite a volunteer to explain what the equator is (an imaginary line around the Earth that is at equal distance from the North and South poles).

Volcán Isluga (Chile)

■ Ask students to use what they already know about the geography of South America to describe the mountains shown in this picture. They should be able to identify these mountains as being part of the Andes Mountain Range. Students may also be able to identify the region as northern Chile.

Tortugas marinas

■ Ask students to share with the class what they know about sea turtles. Explain that six of the seven species of sea turtles are listed as endangered or critically endangered. Discuss, as a class, reasons for this grim outlook (e.g., illegal trade, poaching, habitat loss).

Objectives

■ By the end of Unit 8, students will be able to
 – Identify, compare, and describe places.
 – Talk about future plans.
 – Express future events.
 – Make impersonal statements.
 – Talk about different cultural aspects of several geographic regions in Latin America.

DESAFÍO 3
Volcán Isluga
The Isluga volcano has the typical conical shape of stratovolcanoes, also known as composite volcanoes. These volcanoes are built by successive lava-flow eruptions. Located near the border between Chile and Bolivia, the Isluga volcano is part of a series of volcanoes, including the Cabaray and the Tata Sabaya. The last known eruption took place in 1913. The Isluga National Park houses the geothermic field of Puchuldiza, which has geysers and hot springs where the water reaches temperatures approaching 200 °F.

DESAFÍO 4
Tortugas marinas
Although the Tortuguero National Park is one of the most biologically diverse regions of the world, containing 11 different habitats, it is best known as a nesting site for leatherback turtles from March through May, and green sea turtles from July through October. It is one of the most-visited natural parks in the world. Tourists can canoe through the park's extensive network of rivers, canals, and lagoons to enjoy the amazing wild nature of these wetlands.

Unit 8
La llegada

Presentation

- This section presents the pairs at their final meeting point before returning to Denver, in the United States. They are in front of the *Mercado Central* in Santiago de Chile, where they must find Augusto, who has their final challenges. They must also decide how to return to Denver.

- Students will see vocabulary in context, with pictures and illustrations. Presenting new words in this manner helps students develop their Spanish vocabulary with background knowledge while engaging them with the context.

Activities	Standards	Resources
Fotonovela	1.2, 2.1, 2.2, 3.1	Vis. Pres.
1.	1.2, 1.3	

Teaching Suggestions

Warm-Up / Independent Starter

- Ask students to read the introduction to the *fotonovela* and to write a paragraph explaining their guess on how the pairs will go back to Denver, and what countries they will visit along the way. You may help students by initiating the first sentence on the board:
Creo que Andy y Janet van a tomar un autobús y van a…

Preparation

- Ask students to share their Independent Starters. Write some of their predictions on the board and keep a tally of the most popular predictions.

- Have students read the *fotonovela* silently. Remind them of some reading strategies, such as looking for cognates, recognizing prefixes and suffixes, checking the dictionary for unknown words, paraphrasing, and asking questions. Ask students to identify the overall theme of the text and to note the main ideas.

 ## La fotonovela

Before Viewing

- Ask students to read the dialogue silently, and have them list the different ways of returning home to the United States that the pairs mention.

La llegada

En Santiago de Chile

 Our friends gather in front of the *Mercado Central,* in Santiago de Chile. This will be their final mission before reuniting in Denver, CO. But how will they get there? They consider driving several thousand miles up the Pan-American Highway.

Differentiated Instruction

DEVELOPING LEARNERS

- To help students build their vocabulary and reinforce comprehension of the *fotonovela,* ask them to match the words in the first column with their antonyms in the second column.

1. *última*
2. *muchos*
3. *más de*
4. *algunas*
5. *buena*
6. *encontrar*

a. *menos de* (c)
b. *perder* (d)
c. *primera* (a)
d. *pocos* (f)
e. *mala* (e)
f. *ninguna* (b)

EXPANDING LEARNERS

- Ask students to write a narrative that describes what has happened in the *fotonovela.* They may choose to write from the point of view of one of the participants, or as a neutral third person. Have students add more details, especially with regard to finding Augusto. Encourage them to add a twist to the plot.

394

La llegada

¡Cuántas cosas! Aquí se vende todo tipo de pescado.

Sí, pero tenemos que encontrar nuestros desafíos. Los tiene Augusto.

¿Augusto? ¿Y quién es Augusto?

Aquí hay miles de personas. ¿Tenemos que preguntarles su nombre una por una?

Aquí tienen sus desafíos. Y recuerden: tienen que traer un anuncio de turismo sobre los destinos de sus desafíos. ¡Que tengan buen viaje!

¡Miren! ¡Allí está! Ese restaurante se llama Casa Augusto.

1 ¿Comprendes?

▶ **Responde** a estas preguntas.

1. ¿Cómo van a volver las parejas a Denver?
2. ¿Qué distancia hay entre Santiago de Chile y Denver?
3. ¿Qué venden en el Mercado Central?
4. ¿Quién es Augusto?
5. ¿Qué les desea Augusto?

After Viewing

■ Assess students' comprehension through questions, and make sure they understand what the pairs have to do after completing their challenges: *¿Dónde están las parejas? ¿Quién es Augusto? ¿Qué tienen que hacer después del desafío?*

Activities

1. Have students work in pairs to complete this activity. Have one student ask the question and the other student answer it. Tell students to be sure to alternate the person asking and the person answering the question.

Answer Key

1. 1. Van a hacer parte del viaje en autobús y otra parte en tren o en avión.
   2. Hay miles de millas de distancia.
   3. Se vende todo tipo de pescado.
   4. Augusto es el dueño de un restaurante del mercado. Él tiene los desafíos.
   5. Les desea que tengan buen viaje.

Additional Resources

Fans Online activities
Practice Workbook

HERITAGE LANGUAGE LEARNERS

Tim asks Janet: *¿Estás loca?* Have students brainstorm other ways to describe someone who has gone crazy. Examples might include: *estar mal del coco, estar chiflado, estar como una cabra.* Ask students to share these and other expressions they know with the rest of the class.

SPECIAL-NEEDS LEARNERS

• Initiate a fragmented reading and repetition to benefit students with listening disabilities. Read the dialogues aloud and pause after each word and ask students to repeat each one after you. Then elongate the sentences, phrase by phrase, until students can link together the meaning of the words.

Unit 8
La llegada

Presentation

- In this section students will learn useful expressions to express cause and consequence. They will also learn to express contrast or restriction.

Activities	Standards	Resources
Expresiones útiles	1.2, 4.1	
2.	1.2, 1.3	
3.	1.2, 1.3	
4.	1.1, 5.1	
5.	1.1, 5.1	

Teaching Suggestions

Warm-Up / Independent Starter

- Ask students to list three reasons why they think learning Spanish is useful or important. You may want to initiate the sentence on the board. For example: *Estudiar español es importante porque…* As an alternative, ask students to list three reasons why they think that traveling is necessary.

Preparation

- Go over the *Expresiones útiles* section with students. Then have them get into groups of four to write a paragraph, using the *expresiones útiles*, about the importance of learning Spanish and/or traveling. They should use their ideas from the Independent Starter and add new ones.

- Have groups share their paragraphs with the rest of the class. Tell students to vote for the most interesting rationale.

Activities

2. Ask students to compare their answers with a classmate. Are there sentences for which more than one of the *expresiones útiles* is possible? To extend this activity, have students write a sentence with each one of the new expressions.

3. Have students learn their dialogues after they have written them. Allow partners a few minutes to rehearse their dialogues and then have them perform in front of the class. Ask the class to vote for the best use of vocabulary in a dialogue.

396

EXPRESIONES ÚTILES

> Estoy muy contenta porque volvemos a casa.

To express cause:
  Podemos alquilar un coche **porque** es barato.
  Como es barato, podemos alquilar un coche.

To express consequence:
  El viaje terminó, **así que** volvemos a casa.
  Los participantes quieren ver el paisaje y **por eso** van en autobús.

To express contrast or restriction:
  El camino es largo, **pero** vamos a ir en coche.

2 Diálogos

▶ **Completa** estas oraciones con una de las expresiones útiles.

1. _____ está lloviendo, no vamos al parque.
2. Quiero ir a Quito _____ ahora hace buen tiempo allí.
3. No hice mi tarea anoche, _____ hoy no puedo salir con mis amigos.
4. No puedo manejar _____ no tengo licencia.
5. Hoy estoy muy cansada y _____ me voy a acostar pronto.
6. Me da miedo volar, _____ voy a viajar en avión.

3 Usa las expresiones

▶ **Escribe** un diálogo utilizando expresiones útiles. Después, represéntalo con tu compañero(a).

> Como el viaje es largo, podemos ir en avión.

> Pero el tren es más barato.

Differentiated Instruction

DEVELOPING LEARNERS

- Before students read the *Expresiones útiles* section on the page, help them understand the terms *cause*, *consequence*, and *contrast* or *restriction*. Then ask them to identify expressions in English that exemplify these terms. Examples include *because* and *since* for cause; *so, for that reason,* and *that's why* for consequence; and *but, nevertheless,* and *however* for contrast or restriction. You may want to translate the examples shown on the page so that students can see how these expressions help to link the parts of the sentence.

EXPANDING LEARNERS

- Ask students to make statements based on the places shown on the page and what they think the *desafíos* might be. In their statements, they should include one of the *expresiones útiles* to express cause, consequence, or contrast or restriction. For example: *Como me interesa la ecología, me parece interesante trabajar con las tortugas marinas. Voy a estar en Ecuador este verano, así que puedo visitar Mitad del Mundo. Quiero pasar por el canal de Panamá, pero no va a ser posible.*

¿Quién ganará?

4 Los desafíos

 ▶ **Habla.** ¿Cuál va a ser el desafío para cada pareja? Piénsalo y coméntalo con tus compañeros(as).

DESAFÍO ①

Una obra de gigantes

Andy y Janet

DESAFÍO ②

La mitad del mundo

Tess y Patricia

DESAFÍO ③

Aire frío y agua caliente

Tim y Mack

DESAFÍO ④

El paraíso de las tortugas

Diana y Rita

▶ **Decide.** ¿Cuál crees que va a ser tu desafío favorito? ¿Por qué?

▶ **Habla.** Los personajes van a viajar a Panamá, Ecuador, Chile y Costa Rica. ¿Qué sabes de esos países? Coméntalo con tus compañeros(as).

5 La tarea final

▶ **Decide.** ¿Qué tarea tienen que hacer los personajes al final? ¿Qué pareja crees que ganará?

LA TAREA

Un anuncio de turismo

Unit 8
La llegada

¿Quién ganará?

4. Divide the class into small groups and ask them to research the four countries to which the participants will travel (i.e., Panama, Ecuador, Chile, and Costa Rica). To narrow the scope of their research, have students look for information related to the places pictured (the Panama Canal, the equator, Isluga National Park, and sea turtles on Costa Rica's Caribbean coast). Have groups prepare an oral presentation to present their findings to the class. Then, as a class, discuss what they think will be the challenges the participants will face in each of these places.

5. As a class, have students discuss what kind of advertisement the pairs will need in order to win their *desafío*. Brainstorm with them the type of information they should include in their ads. Explain to students that, at the end of this unit, they will decide and vote on which pair created the best tourism advertisement. Let students discuss their opinions and then help them to reach an agreement.

Answer Key

2.
1. Como	4. porque
2. porque	5. por eso
3. así que	6. pero

3. Answers will vary.

4. Answers will vary.
  ▶ Answers will vary.
  ▶ Answers will vary.

5. Answers will vary.

Additional Resources

Fans Online activities
Practice Workbook

HERITAGE LANGUAGE LEARNERS

Ask students to imagine that they are among the participants in this last unit. Ask them what they would like their challenge to be, based on the photos on the page. Invite them to do some research on the places or the animals shown and create a challenging and original *desafío* for themselves and a partner. Ask students to describe their *desafío* either orally or in writing.

CRITICAL THINKING

• Enable a discussion about the advantages and disadvantages of different modes of transportation. Find out what students think of Janet's suggestion of renting a car and driving along the Pan-American Highway. Ask them if this is something they might do one day. Have them talk about other ways the participants could travel from Chile to Denver. Encourage students to be creative, and suggest that, if time and money were not a concern, they might even travel by ship around Cape Horn and proceed along the Atlantic coast of South America.

DESAFÍO 1

Identificar, describir y comparar lugares

Presentation

- In *Desafío 1*, Andy and Janet have to paddle a 20-mile stretch of the Panama Canal.
- In this section, students will preview:
  - Vocabulary related to geographic features.
  - The relative superlative.

Activities	Standards	Resources
Fotonovela	1.2, 2.2, 3.1	Vis. Pres.
6.	1.2, 1.3	
7.	1.2, 1.3	
8.	1.2, 1.3	Audio
9. Conexiones	1.1, 1.2, 3.1, 3.2, 5.2	Video
Tu desafío	1.2, 3.1, 3.2, 5.1	

Teaching Suggestions

Warm-Up / Independent Starter

- Display pictures of a beach, a city, and a mountain. Ask students to write one or two activities they like to do in those places.

Preparation

- Have students skim the *fotonovela* and write a list of words related to geographical places. Review their lists as a class and emphasize pronunciation.
- Ask a volunteer to read the introduction to Andy and Janet's *desafío*. Ask students if they have ever paddled in a river. If they have done it, ask students to share their experience with the class.

La fotonovela

Before Viewing

- Have students form pairs and discuss the meaning of the title of this *Desafío*.
- Ask students whether they think this is a difficult *desafío* for Andy and Janet and explain why.

After Viewing

- Lead a class discussion to brainstorm ideas about what Andy and Janet would do next to finish their *desafío*.

Una obra de gigantes

The Panama Canal is one of the largest engineering projects ever achieved. It connects the Atlantic and Pacific oceans. Andy and Janet must paddle a 20-mile stretch of the canal, from Lake Gatún out to the Pacific Ocean.

Tenemos que remar veinte millas desde aquí.

¡Qué emoción, Andy! Vamos a cruzar el canal más famoso del mundo.

¡Cuánta vegetación! Esto parece una selva.

¿Seguro que esto es un canal? A mí me parece un lago.

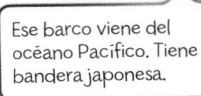
¡Mira, Janet!

Hola, aquí Andy y Janet Douglas. ¿Podemos pasar?

Claro. Son 45.000 dólares.

Ese barco viene del océano Pacífico. Tiene bandera japonesa.

¿45.000 dólares? ¡No puede ser!

Continuará...

6 Detective de palabras

▶ **Relaciona.** ¿Qué palabra de la fotonovela corresponde a cada fotografía?

1

2

3

▶ **Escribe** una oración con cada una de esas palabras.

Differentiated Instruction

DEVELOPING LEARNERS

- Ask students to work in groups of three and reenact the *fotonovela*. They should add as many gestures as they can to make the actions seem realistic; for example, they might pantomime that they are rowing a canoe, looking through binoculars, and talking by means of walkie-talkies. After they read the dialogue a few times among themselves, have them present their skits in front of the class.

EXPANDING LEARNERS

- Explain to students that long before the Panama Canal was completed, ships had to pass around South America through the dangerous waters of Cape Horn and the Strait of Magellan, at the southernmost part of South America. Ask students to imagine what a trip like this must have been like for travelers going from the east coast of the United States, for example, to California. Ask them to write a brief narrative describing this experience.

7 **¿Comprendes?**

▶ **Responde** a estas preguntas.

1. ¿Dónde están Andy y Janet?
2. ¿Cuántas millas tienen que remar (row)?
3. ¿De dónde viene el barco que ve Janet?
4. ¿De qué país es la bandera del barco?

8 **Una conversación en el kayak**

▶ **Escucha** la conversación entre Janet y Andy, y elige la opción correcta.

1. Andy y Janet están en el _____.
   a. lago Alajuela   **b.** lago Miraflores   **c.** lago Gatún

2. Andy y Janet tienen que remar aproximadamente _____.
   a. diez kilómetros   **b.** dieciséis kilómetros   **c.** treinta kilómetros

3. Barro Colorado es una _____.
   a. selva   **b.** isla   **c.** montaña

4. A Janet le encanta _____.
   a. el paisaje   **b.** el canal   **c.** el lago

5. Andy opina que Panamá es el país más _____ de Centroamérica.
   a. interesante   **b.** importante   **c.** bonito

CONEXIONES: CIENCIAS SOCIALES

El canal de Panamá

El canal de Panamá es una de las obras civiles más importantes de todos los tiempos. Mide 50 millas y une el océano Atlántico y el océano Pacífico a través del istmo (isthmus) de Panamá.

Francia empezó el proyecto, pero lo terminaron los Estados Unidos. El canal se inauguró en 1914.

9 **Piensa y explica.** ¿Conoces otras obras con mucho impacto en la historia de la humanidad?

→ TU DESAFÍO Visita la página web para aprender más sobre el canal de Panamá.

ERITAGE LANGUAGE LEARNERS

Ask students to imagine they are working on the original construction of the Panama Canal. They might be one of the engineers who came up with the idea or devised a plan to complete it, or one of the workers who has to endure difficult working conditions and possible death from malaria or yellow fever. Ask students to write a few brief journal entries or letters home describing the conditions and their hopes for the successful completion of the project.

COOPERATIVE LEARNING

• Ask students to work in small groups and research the history of the Panama Canal, either the original construction or the present expansion. Be sure that each member of the group focuses on one specific aspect to research, such as its inception, the engineering feat, the politics involved, the health and welfare of the workers, the heterogeneous composition of the workers and planners, the fees ships must pay, or the process of passing through the locks. After students assemble the different facets, display their work or ask them to make an oral presentation to the class.

DESAFÍO 1

Identificar, describir y comparar lugares

Activities

7. Have students prepare a short news report about Andy and Janet's *desafío* using the answers from the questions.

8. Have students find information about the places mentioned in this activity: *lago Alajuela*, *lago Miraflores*, *lago Gatún*, and *Barro Colorado*. Ask them to make a brief presentation about their findings.

9. Ask students to bring in a picture of a major civil engineering project and explain why it is important. If they have been there, ask them to share their experience.

 AUDIO SCRIPT
See page 391I.

 CONEXIONES: CIENCIAS SOCIALES

El canal de Panamá

An expansion project that will double the capacity of the Panama Canal was approved in 2006. The most important part of this project consists of the construction of two new sets of locks (*esclusas*): one on the Pacific side of the Canal and one on the Atlantic side. This project also includes the improvement of existing navigational channels in Gatún Lake. It is expected to be completed by 2014.

Answer Key

6. 1. canal   2. lago   3. selva
   ▶ Answers will vary.

7. 1. Están en el canal de Panamá.
   2. Tienen que remar veinte millas.
   3. Viene del océano Pacífico.
   4. Es de Japón.

8. 1. c   2. c   3. b   4. a   5. c

9. Answers will vary.

Additional Resources

Fans Online activities

Unit 8
DESAFÍO 1

Vocabulario – Geografía

Presentation

■ In this section, students will learn words to name geographic features.

Activities	Standards	Resources
Vocabulario	1.2	
10.	1.3, 3.1	
11.	1.3, 3.1	
12.	1.2, 1.3, 3.1	Audio
13. Cultura	1.1, 1.2, 2.1, 2.2, 3.1, 3.2, 4.2, 5.2	
Tu desafío	1.2, 2.2, 3.2, 5.1	

Teaching Suggestions

Warm-Up / Independent Starter

■ Ask students to answer the following questions:
 – *¿Qué deportes y actividades practicas al aire libre (outdoors)?*
 – *¿En qué lugares los practicas?*

Preparation

■ Have students share their answers from the Independent Starter and create a list on the board with the outdoor places they mention.

■ Divide the class into groups of three and ask them not to open their books. Provide students with a world map with no names on it and the list of words under *Los continentes* on the vocabulary section. Have students label the map.

Activities

10. Turn this activity into "Jeopardy." Create a chart similar to the one below. Then prepare 3 x 5 cards with a number on the front side and a question on the back. For example:
   1. *¿En qué continente está el río Amazonas?*

ríos	montañas	selvas	océanos
1	2	3	4
5	6	7	8
9	10	11	12

12. Have students work in groups of three or four and prepare two additional questions. Have groups compete against each other.

400

Vocabulario

Geografía

Océanos y continentes

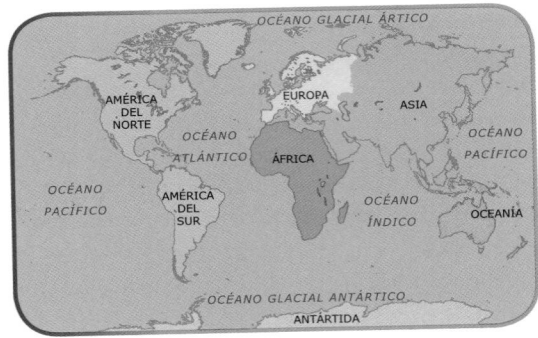

El paisaje

10 **Lugares famosos**

▶**Escribe** con tu compañero(a) ejemplos de estos lugares.

1. una montaña → *el Aconcagua*
2. una bahía
3. una cascada
4. un cañón
5. un río
6. una selva
7. un volcán
8. un océano
9. una isla

400 cuatrocientos

Differentiated Instruction

DEVELOPING LEARNERS

• Display a map of the world and guide students as they identify and say the names of the continents and some of the geographical features mentioned on the page. For those features not easily identifiable on the map (*la colina, la pradera, el puerto, la cascada / catarata, el cañón, el bosque, el valle*), ask students to find images of each one, attach the image to an index card, and write the name on the back. Students can exchange these cards with a partner and test each other's knowledge of the terms.

EXPANDING LEARNERS

• Tell students that they will play a game to test their knowledge of geographical features. Students will name two geographical features, plus a proper noun that fits one of the features (e.g., *¿Río o valle? el Orinoco*). The next student must say what *el Orinoco* is (i.e., *El Orinoco es un río*). Explain that they may use names for geographical features from around the world. If students fail to categorize the features correctly, or if they fail to name one, they are out of the game. Crown the last student remaining *el campeón / la campeona de geografía!*

11 Un poco de geografía panameña

▶ **Investiga y escribe.** Janet y Andy quieren visitar en Panamá algunos lugares destacados. ¿Qué son esos lugares? ¿Qué características tienen?

Modelo Baru → *Es un volcán. Es el volcán más alto de Panamá.*

Sambú

Pelícano

San Ramón

12 ¿Cuánto sabes?

▶ **Responde** a estas preguntas con tu compañero(a).

1. ¿Cuál es el continente más grande?
2. ¿Qué desierto está en el sur de los Estados Unidos?
3. ¿Cómo se llama el océano que está entre América y Asia?
4. ¿Cuál es el río más largo de América del Sur?
5. ¿Cuál es el lago más grande de África?

 ▶ **Escucha** y toma nota de las respuestas. ¿Qué pareja de la clase tiene más respuestas correctas?

CULTURA
El casco viejo de Panamá

El casco viejo de la ciudad de Panamá es la segunda atracción turística después del canal de Panamá. En esta zona predomina el estilo colonial, pero se aprecia una mezcla de estilos arquitectónicos: caribeño, francés, modernista...

Algunos de los monumentos más famosos del casco viejo son la Catedral Metropolitana y el Teatro Nacional de Panamá.

Catedral Metropolitana de Panamá.

13 **Explica.** ¿En tu ciudad hay zonas con mezcla de distintos estilos artísticos? ¿Cuáles son los monumentos más visitados? ¿Cómo son?

→ TU DESAFÍO Visita la página web para ver más imágenes del casco viejo de Panamá.

ERITAGE LANGUAGE LEARNERS

Ask students to identify and describe some of the geographical features mentioned on the page in their family's country of origin. Ask them to give as much additional information as they can, either from their own knowledge or their family's, or after doing some research. For example, they may know or research a legend surrounding a lake or river, describe how tall a certain mountain is or how deep a canyon might be, or how any of these geographical features have been impacted by the environment.

MULTIPLE INTELLIGENCES:
Visual-Spatial Intelligence

- The cultural feature addresses different architectural styles: *caribeño, francés,* and *modernista*. Do students know what characterizes these styles? Ask them to research these three styles; that is, how each one is described, what are some examples of each, and which one is each student's preferred architectural style. Also ask students to bring in images of each style if they can.

Unit 8
DESAFÍO 1
Vocabulario – Geografía

13. Have students work in pairs. Ask them to discuss what kind of monument they would like to have in their city and why.

 AUDIO SCRIPT
See page 391I.

CULTURA
El casco viejo de Panamá

The historic district of Panama City was designated a UNESCO World Heritage Site in 1997. The original town, which had been the oldest European settlement on the Pacific coast of the Americas, was destroyed by the privateer Henry Morgan and abandoned in 1671. The town was moved to its present location in 1673.

Answer Key

10. Answers will vary. Sample answers:

2. bahía de Vieques	6. Amazonas
3. El salto Ángel	7. Chimborazo
4. Colorado	8. océano Pacífico
5. Orinoco	9. Puerto Rico

11. Answers will vary. Sample answers:
   A. Sambú → Es un río. Cruza un bosque donde viven animales fascinantes.
   B. Pelícano → Es una isla. Tiene playas maravillosas.
   C. San Ramón → Es una cascada. Está en la falda de un volcán.

12. 1. Es Asia.
   2. El desierto de Chihuahua.
   3. El océano Pacífico.
   4. El río Amazonas.
   5. El lago Victoria.
   ▶ Answers will vary.

13. Answers will vary.

Additional Resources

Fans Online activities
Practice Workbook

DESAFÍO 1

Gramática – El superlativo relativo

Presentation

- In this section, students will learn how to describe a noun in comparison to a larger group.

Activities	Standards	Resources
Gramática	3.1	
14.	1.1, 3.1, 4.1	
15.	1.2, 1.3, 2.2	Audio
16.	1.2, 1.3	
17.	1.1, 3.1, 5.1	
18. Cultura	1.1, 1.2, 2.2, 4.2, 5.2	

Teaching Suggestions

Warm-Up / Independent Starter

- Have students pick two of the eight participants from the book and compare them. You may want to provide a short questionnaire in which students answer questions comparing the two participants they picked. For example: *¿Quién es más alto, Andy o Tim? ¿Quién es mayor, Mack o Patricia? ¿Quién es más simpática, Diana o Janet?*

Preparation

- Ask for volunteers to write some of their comparisons from the Independent Starter on the board. Use these sentences to review comparative structures in Spanish.

- As you go over the grammar section, use visuals to reinforce the explanation and to provide students with more examples.

- Using the sentences from the Independent Starter, ask students to add information about the characters using a relative superlative (e.g., *Andy es el más alto de todos*).

Activities

15. After completing the activity, have students work in pairs and give their own opinions about each of these places. Are their ideas similar to or different from Andy's?

16. You may turn this activity into a game. Divide the class in two groups and ask each group to write five questions using the relative superlative. Before starting the game, make sure the groups have different questions.

Gramática

El superlativo relativo

- Remember that superlatives are used to express an extreme degree of an adjective.

  Asia es un continente grandísimo.

- The relative superlative is used to describe a noun in comparison with a larger group.

  El Everest es la montaña más alta del mundo.

- To form the relative superlative in Spanish, use the following structures:

el / la / los / las + nombre +	más / menos	+ adjetivo +	de… / que…

  El Amazonas es el río más largo del mundo.
  Este es el país más bonito que conozco.

- Remember to use the irregular forms mejor(es), peor(es) when talking about the *best*, or *worst*.

  Los mejores monumentos de Ciudad de Panamá están en el casco viejo.
  Hoy es el peor día para viajar porque llueve mucho.

14 **Compara.** ¿Qué palabras se usan en inglés para formar el superlativo relativo?

15 **Los lugares que conozco**

 ▶ **Escucha** a Andy y une cada lugar con la característica correspondiente.

(A)
1. Nueva York
2. España
3. El salto Ángel
4. El lago de Atitlán
5. Suramérica
6. La bahía de Vieques

(B)
a. fascinante
b. alto
c. misterioso
d. extraño
e. turístico
f. famoso

▶ **Escribe** tres oraciones similares. Después, léeselas a tu compañero(a). ¿Está de acuerdo contigo?

Modelo A. *Hawái tiene las mejores playas del mundo.*
B. *Sí, tienes razón. Son espectaculares.*

Differentiated Instruction

DEVELOPING LEARNERS

- Ask students to choose the appropriate word to complete these sentences.
  1. *Mi perro tiene mucha gracia. Es el perro (más / menos) gracioso del mundo. (más)*
  2. *Miguel nunca juega deportes. Es el chico (menos / más) atlético de la escuela. (menos)*
  3. *Es un libro muy bueno. Es el (mejor / peor) de la biblioteca. (mejor)*
  4. *Nunca haces nada. Eres el estudiante (más / menos) perezoso de la clase. (más)*
  5. *¡Qué horrible es este programa! Es el (peor / mejor) de todos. (peor)*

EXPANDING LEARNERS

- Ask students to work with a partner and take turns creating more sentences with the relative superlative. They should use the adjectives on the page, as well as others they know, to describe a person, place, or thing to one another. Partners will try to guess who or what the other is describing within an established period of time.

► **Escribe** la respuesta a estas preguntas.

1. ¿Quién es el jugador más alto de la NBA?
2. ¿Cuál es la ciudad más poblada de los Estados Unidos?
3. ¿Dónde está el edificio más alto del mundo?

► **Escribe** tres preguntas similares y házselas a tu compañero(a). Usa el superlativo relativo.

17 **¡Tienes razón!**

► **Habla** con tu compañero(a) para dar tu opinión sobre estos lugares famosos. ¿Está de acuerdo contigo?

Modelo   Nueva York ⟶ A. *Yo pienso que Nueva York es la ciudad más importante del mundo.*
   B. *Sí, puede ser. Todo el mundo la conoce.*

Río Amazonas

Monte Everest

Ciudad de México

Cataratas del Niágara

CULTURA

Mi Pueblito

Mi Pueblito es un complejo turístico situado en la ciudad de Panamá. Allí se pueden ver réplicas de construcciones de tres culturas distintas:

– Mi Pueblito Afroantillano muestra la cultura de la población de las Antillas que llegó a este país cuando se construyó el canal de Panamá.
– Mi Pueblito Campesino es una réplica de un pueblo del interior del país, con casas, un museo, un aula escolar, una plaza…
– Mi Pueblito Indígena representa una aldea (*village*) típica.

18 **Piensa y explica.** ¿Conoces alguna atracción turística de tu país que represente formas de vida del pasado? En tu opinión, ¿son interesantes este tipo de atracciones? ¿Por qué?

ERITAGE LANGUAGE LEARNERS

Share with students that there are many other adjectives to describe someone who s lazy. Ask students to come up with other words for *perezoso*. Examples might nclude *vago, flojo, holgazán,* and *gandul,* but encourage students to include others, as well as expressions that describe a person's degree of laziness. You may also ask students to mention synonyms for *rabajador: diligente, laborioso, aplicado, empeñoso.* Have students share these words with their classmates, who may want to write them in their notebooks.

CRITICAL THINKING

• Ask students to name an engineering feat or some advanced technology that would benefit their community, state, or the nation. Suggest that they think about projects such as a bridge to an isolated location, a tunnel under a body of water, or a high-speed train that could drastically reduce commuting or travel time. Have students describe their proposed projects in a brief report and read it aloud to their classmates.

Gramática – El superlativo relativo

17. After finishing the activity, divide the class into four groups and assign one place to each group. Ask students to write a paragraph about their place using the relative superlative. Students should try to convince the rest of the class that theirs is the best place to go on vacation.

AUDIO SCRIPT
See page 391I.

 CULTURA

Mi Pueblito

The Panamanian village at *Mi Pueblito* is a replica of a small town at the turn of the 19th century. It is a complex built around a cobblestone plaza and includes government offices, shops, a school, and a tiny church. In addition, there is a museum devoted to Panama's national dress, *la pollera.* The visitor will also find replicas of the villages of Panama's other major ethnic groups: Afro-Antilleans and indigenous peoples.

Answer Key

14. Se usa el artículo *the* y el adjetivo con la terminación *-est.* Por ejemplo: *the tallest, the biggest.*

15. 1. f   2. e   3. b   4. c   5. a   6. d
► Answers will vary

16. 1. Yao Ming (mide 7'6").
2. Nueva York.
3. En Dubai.
► Answers will vary.

17. Answers will vary.

18. Answers will vary.

Additional Resources

Fans Online activities
Practice Workbook

Unit 8
DESAFÍO 1
Comunicación

Presentation

■ In this section, student will integrate the vocabulary and grammar from *Desafío 1* in order to talk about geographic features. They will also describe a noun in comparison with a larger group.

Activities	Standards	Resources
19.	1.2, 1.3, 2.1, 2.2	
20	1.1, 1.2, 1.3, 2.2	Audio
21.	1.1, 1.2, 1.3, 3.1	
22. Final del desafío	1.2, 1.3, 3.1	

Teaching Suggestions

Warm-Up / Independent Starter

■ Bring in pictures of famous people, important cities, fruits, or objects, and ask students: *¿Qué/ A quién prefieres? ¿Por qué?* Ask students to use a relative superlative in their answers.

Preparation

■ Take 10 minutes to review the vocabulary and grammar themes of *Desafío 1*.

■ Have students share their Independent Starters. Then use students' examples to review how to express the idea of extremity of an adjective.

■ Refer students back to the *fotonovela* for *Desafío 1*. Have them identify vocabulary related to geographic features, as well as the relative superlative. Do students understand the dialogue better now that they have gone through the vocabulary and grammar from the *Desafío*?

Activities

19. Have students write a reaction entry to Janet's blog. Janet is sad because she has to leave those beautiful places, so ask students to include in their entry similar places in the United States to make her feel better.

20. Before the listening part, you may want to review with the class where the places mentioned in this activity are located. You may ask extra questions to recycle vocabulary learned in the *Desafío*.

404

Comunicación

19 **Las maravillas de Panamá**

▶ **Lee** el blog de Janet sobre su experiencia en Panamá y complétalo.

mejor	maravillosas	peor
bonitos	limpia	grande

Mi experiencia en Panamá
6 de mayo

Panamá es fascinante. Ayer fuimos al archipiélago Bocas del Toro. En sus islas están las playas más ___1___ del Caribe. Allí puedes tomar el sol, relajarte, nadar y hacer surf. La isla Colón es la más ___2___ del archipiélago: tiene 10.000 habitantes, aproximadamente. ¡Y es tan bonita! Allí puedes bucear o hacer *snorkel*. ¡Es el agua más ___3___ y más azul del mundo! En estas islas tienen los paisajes marinos más ___4___ que vi en toda mi vida. Para mí, esta es la ___5___ zona turística de Panamá: hay muchos hoteles y restaurantes, y el paisaje es maravilloso.

Desgraciadamente, mañana nos vamos. ¡Qué lástima! ¡Es el ___6___ día de mi vida!

20 **Opiniones**

 ▶ **Escucha** y completa estas oraciones con las opiniones de los personajes sobre sus viajes y desafíos.

1. Mack cree que Buenos Aires es...
2. A Janet le parece que Venezuela tiene...
3. Para Tim, Costa Rica tiene...
4. Andy piensa que el desierto de Atacama es...
5. Patricia opina que el glaciar Perito Moreno es...

 ▶ **Habla** con tu compañero(a). ¿Están de acuerdo con las opiniones de los personajes?

Differentiated Instruction

DEVELOPING LEARNERS

• Help students who have difficulty in completing activity 19 by going through a logical process of elimination for the word choices. For example, show students that both *grande* and *limpia* work for the second blank because both could describe *isla*. However, help them see that the answer must be *grande* because a reference to population size immediately follows.

EXPANDING LEARNERS

• Ask students to write a letter to a friend describing a place they visited recently (it can be real or imaginary) and include the relative superlative in as many of their descriptions as they can. They should focus their descriptions on the geographical features of the place, so they also practice the vocabulary from this *Desafío*.

21 Un juego

▶ **Escribe.** Selecciona un lugar famoso (país, río, montaña, valle, etc.) de cada categoría y escribe una descripción.

1. Un lugar en Latinoamérica.
2. Un lugar en los Estados Unidos.
3. Un lugar en otra parte del mundo.

▶ **Presenta** tus descripciones a la clase. Tus compañeros(as) tienen que adivinar de qué lugares se trata.

Modelo A. *Este lugar está en los Estados Unidos. Es uno de los sitios más turísticos del país. Son unas montañas con caras de personas muy famosas.*
B. *Es el monte Rushmore.*
A. *¡Sí!*

Final del desafío

¡Por favor, déjenos pasar! ___1___

Sí. Le podemos dar esta gorra. ___2___

___3___

Y al oeste se ve el océano Pacífico. ___4___

22 La experiencia más memorable

▶ **Ordena** estas palabras para formar oraciones y completa los bocadillos.

1. especial - el viaje - Este - de nuestras vidas. - es - más
2. del mejor - Es - equipo - la gorra - del mundo.
3. de la capital. - tenemos - más - Desde aquí - la vista - espectacular
4. extenso - el océano - más - del mundo. - Es

cuatrocientos cinco 405

RITAGE LANGUAGE LEARNERS

Most of the units have focused on traveling o Spanish-speaking countries. However, ourism is a healthy industry in the United tates. Ask students to write a letter to a iend in their family's country of origin escribing a trip they took within the United tates. Ask them to identify the place they sited and describe several *accidentes* eográficos they observed either there or long the way. Encourage students to use e relative superlative with *más* or *menos* us an appropriate adjective.

SPECIAL-NEEDS LEARNERS

• Allow students with auditory processing difficulties to read the audio script for activity 20 while others are listening to the recording. Do this for all audio portions of this unit. Doing so will enable students to complete all such activities with a marked degree of success.

---

21. You may want to keep track of students' answers to see which student has the highest number of right answers.

22. Ask students to remember the *fotonovela* at the beginning of Janet and Andy's *desafío*. What was the *desafío*? And now, why are they offering the lock (*esclusa*) operator a Yankees cap? Have students write a dialogue between Andy, Janet, and the *esclusa* operator in which they convince him to accept the Yankees cap. Ask students to act out their dialogues.

AUDIO SCRIPT
See page 391I.

Answer Key

19. 1. maravillosas
2. grande
3. limpia
4. bonitos
5. mejor
6. peor

20. 1. ... la ciudad más grande de Latinoamérica.
2. ... el mejor clima de Latinoamérica.
3. ... los paisajes más bonitos del mundo.
4. ... el más impresionante del mundo.
5. ... el lugar más espectacular de Argentina.
▶ Answers will vary.

21. Answers will vary.
▶ Answers will vary.

22. 1. Este es el viaje más especial de nuestras vidas.
2. Es la gorra del mejor equipo del mundo.
3. Desde aquí tenemos la vista más espectacular de la capital.
4. Es el océano más extenso del mundo.

Additional Resources

Fans Online activities
Practice Workbook

Unit 8
DESAFÍO 2
Hablar de planes de futuro

Presentation

- In *Desafío 2*, Tess and Patricia have to find the Earth's equator and step in the Northern and Southern hemispheres simultaneously exactly at noon.
- In this section, students will preview:
  - Vocabulary related to countries.
  - Expressing plans and intentions for the future.

Activities	Standards	Resources
Fotonovela	1.2, 3.1, 3.2	Vis. Pres.
23.	1.1, 1.2, 1.3	
24.	1.2, 1.3	
25.	1.1, 1.2, 1.3, 5.1	Audio
26. Conexiones	1.2, 1.3, 3.1, 3.2, 5.1	
Tu desafío	1.2, 3.1, 3.2, 5.1	

Teaching Suggestions

Warm-Up / Independent Starter

- Ask students to brainstorm a list of things that they know about Ecuador (the country). Tell them to think about location, geographical features, and culture.

Preparation

- Ask students to share their responses from the Independent Starter. If necessary, ask further questions so that students identify the capital, Quito, and the relationship between the country's name and the location of the equator.

La fotonovela

Before Viewing

- Introduce the title by drawing a circle on the board and drawing a horizontal line though the middle. Use the drawing to help students understand the word *mitad*.
- Ask a student to read the introduction aloud.

After Viewing

- Ask students if they think this is a difficult challenge. Have them predict what could affect whether or not Tess and Patricia are able to arrive on time.

La mitad del mundo

Patricia and Tess have just arrived in Quito. Their task is to find the Earth's equator and step simultaneously on the Northern and Southern Hemispheres at noon.

¡Bienvenidas a Quito! Me llamo Emilio y voy a enseñarles la ciudad.

Hola, Emilio. Tenemos que estar en el ecuador antes de las doce.

¡Pero ya están en el Ecuador!

No, no. Me refiero a la línea del ecuador.

Ah, ustedes quieren ir a Mitad del Mundo. Eso está fuera de la ciudad. Pero les voy a hacer un precio especial.

¿Está lejos la catedral?

No, cuando pasemos por allí, las aviso.

Mamá, tengo hambre. ¿Cuándo vamos a comer?

Cuando lleguemos, Tess. Tenemos que estar en el ecuador a las doce.

Hummm, no sé si vamos a llegar a tiempo.

Continuará...

23 Detective de palabras

▶ **Completa** estas oraciones.

1. Voy a _____ la ciudad.
2. Les voy a _____ un precio especial.
3. Cuando _____ por allí, las aviso.
4. Vamos a comer cuando _____.
5. No sé si vamos a _____ a tiempo.

▶ **Responde.** ¿Las oraciones anteriores se refieren al presente, al pasado o al futuro?

Differentiated Instruction

DEVELOPING LEARNERS

- Review the use of *ir a* + verb with students to show future plans or intentions. Remind them that this is like saying "going to do something" in English. Help students find examples of this construction in the *fotonovela* and ask them to write each of these expressions in their notebooks. Follow up by asking them to write or say one sentence with each of these expressions.

EXPANDING LEARNERS

- Ask students to write a "to do" list of the chores and activities they have to do in the next few months. They should write these activities in the order in which they are going to do them. For each activity, they will need to specify a time period. For example: *Hoy voy a tocar el piano. Mañana voy a estudiar en la biblioteca. Pasado mañana...* You may want to turn this into a game to see who can come up with the longest (and most accurate) list within a given period of time.

406

24 ¿Comprendes?

▶ **Escribe** la respuesta a las siguientes preguntas.

1. ¿En qué ciudad están Tess y Patricia? ¿Y en qué país?
2. ¿Dónde tienen que estar antes de las doce?
3. ¿Qué es Mitad del Mundo?
4. ¿Cómo van a llegar allí?

25 ¡Cuántos viajes!

 ▶ **Escucha** la conversación entre Tess y un viajero en el aeropuerto. ¿Qué planes tiene él? Une las dos columnas.

Ⓐ	Ⓑ
1. Hoy	a. ir a la Torre Eiffel en París.
2. Mañana	b. comer pescado en Lisboa.
3. Pasado mañana	c. aprender a bailar samba en Brasilia.
4. La semana que viene	d. sacar fotos en Berlín.
5. En dos semanas	e. comer una pizza en Roma.
6. El próximo mes	f. ver un musical en Broadway.

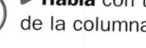 ▶ **Habla** con tu compañero(a) sobre sus planes. Usa las expresiones de tiempo de la columna A.

Modelo   A. *¿Qué vas a hacer hoy?*
B. *Primero voy a hacer la tarea y luego voy a ver una película con mi hermana.*

 ## CONEXIONES: GEOGRAFÍA

La línea del ecuador

El ecuador es una línea imaginaria que divide la superficie de la Tierra en dos hemisferios: el hemisferio Norte y el hemisferio Sur.

Durante muchos años se pensó que el ecuador pasaba por San Antonio de Pichincha, al norte de Quito. Allí se construyó un monumento y una línea para marcar el ecuador en un terreno conocido como Mitad del Mundo. Pero hoy sabemos que el ecuador pasa unos metros más al sur. Esta nueva «mitad del mundo» está representada por un gran reloj de sol situado en el centro turístico-cultural Quitsato.

Monumento de Mitad del Mundo.

26 Explica. En Mitad del Mundo se realizan experimentos de física muy curiosos, como, por ejemplo, observar el sentido de rotación del agua. Investiga sobre este fenómeno y explica en qué consiste.

▶ **TU DESAFÍO** Visita la página web para aprender más sobre Mitad del Mundo.

Activities

24. Create true/false statements about the *fotonovela*. Read them to students and have them show thumbs up or thumbs down according to whether the statement is true or false.

25. Prior to playing the recording, use a calendar to review the time expressions in column A. After students are done speaking with each other, ask them to share one thing that their partner will be doing in the future.

26. Ask students to research other experiments that have been performed at the equator and the findings of these studies.

 AUDIO SCRIPT
See page 391I.

 ### CONEXIONES: GEOGRAFÍA

La línea del ecuador

Ecuador is the country with the highest elevation through which the imaginary equatorial line crosses. The exact location of the equator has been readjusted in recent years due to the use of the Global Positioning System, and the Quitsato Center is now considered to mark the real equator.

Answer Key

23. 1. enseñarles   4. lleguemos
2. hacer   5. llegar
3. pasemos
▶ Se refieren al futuro.

24. 1. Están en Quito, Ecuador.
2. Tienen que estar en el ecuador.
3. El lugar por donde pasa el ecuador.
4. En taxi.
▶ Answers will vary.

25. 1. b   2. d   3. e   4. f   5. c   6. a
26. Answers will vary.

Additional Resources

Fans Online activities

DESAFÍO 2

Vocabulario – Países

Presentation

- In this section, students will learn vocabulary related to countries and geographical location.

Activities	Standards	Resources
Vocabulario	1.2, 3.1	
27.	1.1, 1.3, 3.1	
28.	1.2, 1.3, 2.1, 3.1	Audio
29.	1.1, 1.3, 3.1	
30. Cultura	1.1, 1.2, 2.1, 3.1, 3.2, 4.2	
Tu desafío	1.2, 2.1, 3.1, 3.2, 5.1	

Teaching Suggestions

Warm-Up / Independent Starter

- Write the following countries on the board and ask students to identify the capitals: *Estados Unidos, México, Canadá, España, Ecuador, Chile, Panamá, Argentina.*
- Then have students sketch a map of the world and mark the approximate locations of the countries and their capitals.

Preparation

- Provide a visual display of the world and highlight or point out the countries and capitals from the Independent Starter activity.
- Have students add the additional countries listed on the vocabulary presentation to their maps. Then have them form sentences using the direction words and the countries (e.g., *Francia está al noreste de España*).

Activities

28. Prior to playing the recording, review the construction of *gustar* using the model. Remind students that the personal *a* is required before the character's name. Before writing the recommendations, use the model to review the subjunctive in statements of recommendation.

29. As an extension of this activity, have students use a map of their city or state and identify the location of other cities and states using the directional words. You may provide the map or have students find one of their own.

Vocabulario

Países

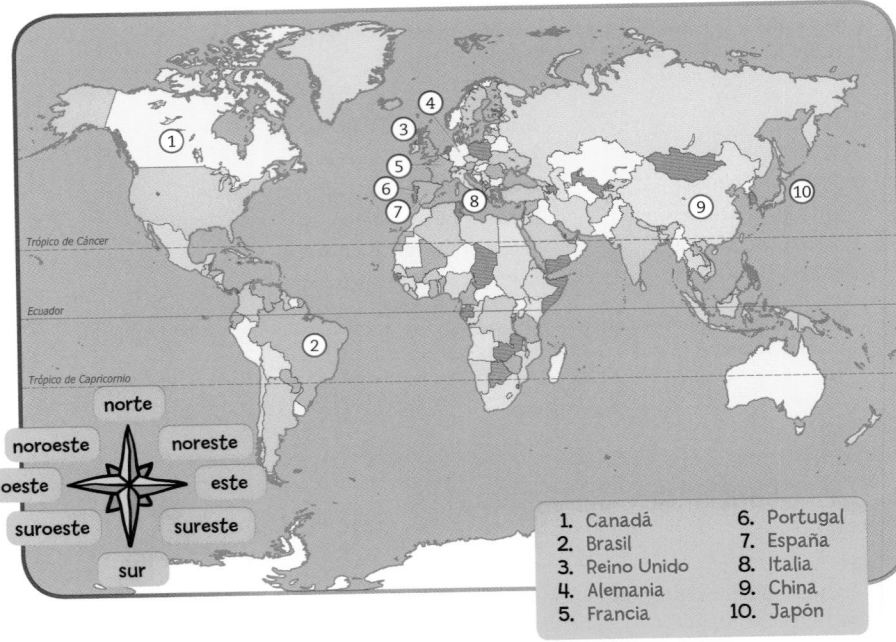

1. Canadá
2. Brasil
3. Reino Unido
4. Alemania
5. Francia
6. Portugal
7. España
8. Italia
9. China
10. Japón

27 **Países y capitales**

 ▶ **Habla** con tu compañero(a). ¿A qué países corresponden estas capitales?

Modelo A. *Berlín es la capital de Alemania, ¿no?*
         B. *Sí.*

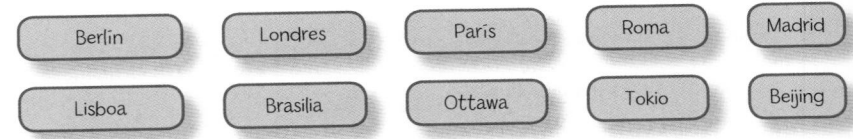

Berlín   Londres   París   Roma   Madrid

Lisboa   Brasilia   Ottawa   Tokio   Beijing

▶ **Escribe** con tu compañero(a) el nombre de otras ciudades famosas de esos países.

Differentiated Instruction

DEVELOPING LEARNERS

- Have students make their own compass rose. Then have them partner with a more proficient student and give them a map of the Americas with major cities shown. The more proficient student will point to a city on the map, say its name and that of the country. Then he or she will say the name of another city, in the same or neighboring country, and the partner must find it and determine in which direction that city is located with respect to the first one mentioned. For example:
A. *Buenos Aires, Argentina; Rosario.*
B. *Rosario está al noroeste de Buenos Aires.*

EXPANDING LEARNERS

- Have students work with a world map and trace the imaginary lines of the equator, the Tropic of Cancer, Tropic of Capricorn, and those that measure longitude and latitude. Then have them work with a partner to determine the latitude and longitude of several world cities. They will give the information for one city at a time to another pair, but without revealing the city. The other pair must locate and name the city. Then pairs exchange roles. Be sure to introduce the terms *longitud, latitud,* and *grados.*

28 Recomendaciones

 ▶ **Escucha** y escribe las preferencias de cada personaje.

Modelo 1. *A Diana le gusta bailar samba.*

1. Diana   2. Andy   3. Janet   4. Rita   5. Tim   6. Patricia

▶ **Escribe.** ¿Qué ciudad del mundo le recomiendas visitar a cada persona?

Modelo *Diana puede ir a Brasilia o a Río de Janeiro para bailar samba.*

29 ¿Dónde está Guayaquil?

▶ **Escribe.** Patricia quiere ir a Guayaquil, pero no sabe dónde está. Escríbele un correo electrónico explicando su ubicación (location).

Modelo *¿Qué tal, Patricia? Guayaquil está al suroeste de Quito…*

 ▶ **Habla.** Describe la ubicación de otra ciudad en Ecuador a tu compañero(a) sin decir el nombre. Él/Ella tiene que adivinar la ciudad.

Modelo A. *Está al sureste de Manta.*
B. *¡Portoviejo!*

CULTURA

La capital de Ecuador

Quito es la capital de Ecuador desde 1563. Está en el norte del país y es una ciudad de gran riqueza histórica y cultural.

En Quito se puede ver la influencia indígena mezclada con el mundo moderno en el arte y la cultura.

30 Piensa y explica. ¿Conoces otras ciudades donde se puede ver el contacto entre culturas?

 **→ TU DESAFÍO** Visita la página web para aprender más sobre Quito.

cuatrocientos nueve 409

RITAGE LANGUAGE LEARNERS

sk students what they know about the ndigenous cultures of their family's country f origin, or of any other Hispanic ountry. Ask them to bring in any related ems they may have at home, such as ooks and photos that describe customs, lothes, and festivals, as well as the history f the native people. Family members ight be able to help them compile this formation, or students may research on eir own. Have them share these data with e rest of the class.

TOTAL PHYSICAL RESPONSE (TPR)

• Instead of a "spelling bee," give students a chance to take part in a "capital bee." Students will play a game to see who can name more capital cities throughout the world. Have students line up in the classroom and say the name of a country. The first student must name that country's capital. You might start out with the Spanish-speaking nations since students should be familiar with the capitals. If students answer incorrectly, or cannot answer within an established period of time, they are out. The winner is the last student standing.

 AUDIO SCRIPT
See page 391I.

 CULTURA

La capital de Ecuador

Situated on the slopes of the Pichincha volcano, in the north of Ecuador, Quito is one of the highest capital cities in the world. Like other capitals, it is a cultural and political center. Even though today Quito is a very modern city, it is the oldest of all South American capitals, and it has a well-preserved old town, which was designated a UNESCO World Heritage Site in 1978. Guayaquil is actually the largest city in Ecuador.

Answer Key

27. Lisboa → Portugal; Londres → Reino Unido; Brasilia → Brasil; París → Francia; Ottawa → Canadá; Roma → Italia; Tokio → Japón; Madrid → España; Beijing → China

▶ Answers will vary. Sample answers: Portugal → Oporto; Reino Unido → Edimburgo; Brasil → Río de Janeiro; Francia → Marsella; Canadá → Toronto; Italia → Milán; Japón → Osaka; España → Barcelona; China → Shangai

28. 2. A Andy le gusta ver a los actores y actrices.

3. A Janet le gusta visitar sitios antiguos.

4. A Rita le encanta la comida asiática.

5. A Tim le encanta la cocina mediterránea.

6. A Patricia le encantan los musicales.

▶ Answers will vary.

29. Answers will vary.

▶ Answers will vary.

30. Answers will vary.

Additional Resources

Fans Online activities
Practice Workbook

Unit 8
DESAFÍO 2

Gramática – Expresar planes e intenciones

Presentation

■ In this section, students will learn:
  – To express plans and intention in the future.
  – Future time expressions.
  – The use of subjunctive after *cuando*.

Activities	Standards	Resources
Gramática	3.1	
31.	1.2, 3.1	
32.	1.2, 1.3	Audio
33.	1.3	
34.	1.1, 1.3	
35. Conexiones	1.1, 1.2, 3.1, 3.2, 5.2	
Tu desafío	1.2, 3.1, 3.2, 5.1	

Teaching Suggestions

Warm-Up / Independent Starter

■ Have students answer the following questions in writing:
  – *¿Cuáles son tus planes para después de clase hoy?*
  – *¿Qué vas a hacer mañana?*
  – *¿Qué quieres hacer este fin de semana?*

Preparation

■ Ask students what part of a sentence or question communicates when an action is taking place.

■ Have students brainstorm other future time expressions that they remember and create a time line of the words, starting with *hoy*.

Activities

31. Remind students that the subjunctive implies doubt, and is therefore needed after *cuando* when talking about the future, since the action may not happen. Ask students to use the sentences as models and write three original sentences talking about the past, a habitual action in the present, and an intention for the future.

34. You can also ask students to use the information provided to create statements with *cuando* (e.g., *Cuando Patricia esté en el barrio La Mariscal, va a almorzar*).

Gramática

Expresar planes e intenciones

● You can use the present tense to talk about the future when you refer to timetables, pre–arranged events, and when you want to present the information as a fact.

| presente | La semana que viene **viajamos** a Nueva York. |

● You can use ir a + *infinitive* to express intention or future plans.

| ir a + infinitivo | El próximo año **vamos a ir** a Canadá. |

Expresiones temporales de futuro

● You can use adverbs and other expressions to refer to the future.

hoy	mañana	pasado mañana

ahora   luego / después

esta mañana   por la mañana
esta tarde   por la tarde
esta noche   por la noche

en un rato
en media hora

| el | lunes mes año | que viene |

| el próximo | lunes mes año |

Cuando + presente de subjuntivo

● Use cuando + *present subjunctive* to refer to events that have not yet occurred.

Cuando estemos en Ecuador, vamos a conocer Mitad del Mundo.

31 **Piensa.** ¿Estas oraciones se refieren al presente, al pasado o al futuro?

Cuando **estuve** de vacaciones, hice muchas fotos.
Cuando **estoy** de vacaciones, hago muchas fotos.
Cuando **esté** de vacaciones, voy a hacer muchas fotos.

32 **Los planes de José**

 ▶ **Escucha** el mensaje que José le dejó a Tess y responde a estas preguntas.

1. ¿Cuándo empieza José su trabajo?
2. ¿Cuándo va a viajar a Asia?
3. ¿Qué va a hacer cuando esté en Asia?
4. ¿Cuándo va a ir a Nueva York?
5. ¿Qué quiere hacer José en Nueva York?
6. ¿Qué lugares quiere visitar en Europa?

Differentiated Instruction

DEVELOPING LEARNERS

● Write the following sentences on the board and ask students to copy and complete them with the correct form of *ir*. Then have students underline the infinitive in each sentence.
1. *Esta noche yo … a bailar. (voy)*
2. *Mañana tú … a visitar el museo. (vas)*
3. *El año que viene nosotros … a viajar a Ecuador. (vamos)*
4. *Mañana ustedes … a tomar el sol. (van)*
5. *Luego ella … a buscar un taxi. (va)*

EXPANDING LEARNERS

● Ask students to write a short letter to a friend explaining their future plans for one of the following topics: their next summer vacation, a new after-school job, the next school year, a self-improvement plan, or a topic of their own choosing. Explain to students that they should express the future by using *ir a* + verb or *cuando* and the present subjunctive. Ask students to read their letters aloud.

33 **Vacaciones en Europa**

▶ **Escribe** oraciones. ¿Qué va a hacer cada persona en sus vacaciones?
Usa las palabras y expresiones de las columnas.

Modelo *Cuando Patricia y yo vayamos a Barcelona, vamos a visitar un museo.*

1. Patricia y yo
2. Mack
3. Diana
4. Tim
5. Rita
6. Andy y Janet

ir a
viajar a
estar en

Londres
Lisboa
París
Barcelona
Río de Janeiro
Venecia

comprar recuerdos
probar la comida típica
visitar un museo
visitar un palacio
ir a la playa
ver un partido de fútbol

▶ **Escribe** cuatro oraciones sobre tus planes para las próximas vacaciones.

34 **La semana que viene**

▶ **Habla** con tu compañero(a) sobre los planes de Patricia para la semana que viene.
Pregunta y responde sobre su agenda. Imagina que hoy es domingo día 7.

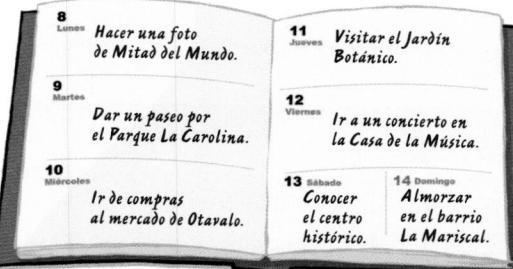

8 Lunes Hacer una foto de Mitad del Mundo.

9 Martes Dar un paseo por el Parque La Carolina.

10 Miércoles Ir de compras al mercado de Otavalo.

11 Jueves Visitar el Jardín Botánico.

12 Viernes Ir a un concierto en la Casa de la Música.

13 Sábado Conocer el centro histórico.

14 Domingo Almorzar en el barrio La Mariscal.

Modelo
A. ¿Cuándo va a ir de compras al mercado de Otavalo?
B. El próximo miércoles.

CONEXIONES: CIENCIAS

Las islas Galápagos

El archipiélago de Galápagos está situado al oeste de Ecuador, en el océano Pacífico. Es un lugar de gran interés científico por la flora y la fauna autóctonas *(native)*. El 97% de la superficie total de las islas es parte del Parque Nacional Galápagos.

Galápago gigante.

35 **Piensa y habla.** ¿Crees que el turismo en las islas Galápagos afecta a la flora y la fauna? ¿Qué hay que hacer para preservar las especies únicas?

▶ **TU DESAFÍO** Visita la página web para aprender más sobre las islas Galápagos.

 AUDIO SCRIPT
See page 391I.

 CONEXIONES: CIENCIAS

Las islas Galápagos

These islands are the only habitat for certain species of iguanas, tortoises, sea lions, and birds. In recent years, the islands have been listed as World Heritage in Danger because of external threats, such as tourism, fishing, and the introduction of nonnative species to the islands.

Answer Key

31. pasado; presente; futuro

32. 1. Empieza la semana que viene.
2. En tres semanas.
3. Va a probar comida típica.
4. Cuando regrese de Asia.
5. Quiere ir a la Estatua de la Libertad y visitar museos de arte.
6. Va a visitar Francia, el Reino Unido, España y Portugal.

33. Answers will vary. Sample answers:
2. Cuando Mack esté en Río de Janeiro, va a ir a la playa.
3. Cuando Diana viaje a París, va a comprar recuerdos.
4. Cuando Tim vaya a Londres, va a ver un partido de fútbol.
5. Cuando Rita viaje a Lisboa, va a probar la comida típica.
6. Cuando Andy y Janet estén en Venecia, van a visitar un palacio.
▶ Answers will vary.

34. Answers will vary.

35. Answers will vary.

Additional Resources

Fans Online activities
Practice Workbook

HERITAGE LANGUAGE LEARNERS

Ask students to research some animal and plant species that are native to their family's country of origin and compare and contrast them with those that are found in their community in the United States. Have them list the species' characteristics, where they are found, and whether they are in danger of extinction. If they are in danger of extinction, ask students to describe what steps are being taken to protect these plants or animals.

MULTIPLE INTELLIGENCES:

Naturalist Intelligence

• Have students work in small groups and research one or more of the unique species of animals found on the Galapagos Islands. Be sure each group addresses a different animal. After the groups gather their information, they will prepare a report, complete with images of the selected animals. They need to include any relevant information regarding the animal's status as an endangered species and what is being done, if anything, to protect it.

DESAFÍO 2

Comunicación

Presentation

- In this section, student will integrate the vocabulary and grammar from *Desafío 2* in order to express plans and intentions for the future.

Activities	Standards	Resources
36.	1.2, 1.3, 2.2, 3.2	
37.	1.1, 1.2, 1.3	Audio
38.	1.3, 3.1, 5.2	
39. Final del desafío	1.3, 3.1	
Tu desafío	1.2, 1.3, 3.1	

Teaching Suggestions

Warm-Up / Independent Starter

- Write the following sentence starters on the board and ask students to complete them with the present tense, the formula *ir a* + infinitive, or the present subjunctive as appropriate.
  - *Pasado mañana, yo...*
  - *La semana que viene mi familia y yo...*
  - *Cuando cumpla 20 años...*

Preparation

- Ask students to write a short paragraph about what they now know about Ecuador, and ask them to share it with the class.
- Take 10 minutes to review the vocabulary and grammar themes of the *Desafío*.
- Refer students back to the *fotonovela* for *Desafío 2*. Have them identify vocabulary related to countries and geographical locations, as well as verb forms that express plans and intention for the future. Do students understand the dialogue better now that they have gone through the vocabulary and grammar from the *Desafío*?

Activities

36. To extend this activity, have students write an e-mail to a friend about a trip that they are planning to take. Ask them to use Tess's blog entry as a model. Then invite volunteers to share their plans with the class by reading their e-mail aloud.

Comunicación

36 **El blog de Tess**

▶ **Lee** el blog de Tess sobre sus planes para el viaje a Ecuador y responde a las preguntas.

> **Próximo viaje: Ecuador**
> 1 de junio
>
> Mañana mi mamá y yo vamos a Ecuador. Estoy muy emocionada. Nuestro vuelo llega a Quito, la capital del país. Desde allí vamos a tomar un taxi hacia el norte para ir a Mitad del Mundo. Cuando lleguemos, nos vamos a hacer una foto con un pie en cada hemisferio. ¡Qué divertido! Por la noche vamos a explorar un poco la ciudad.
> Pasado mañana mi mamá quiere visitar museos, pero yo prefiero ir de compras a algún mercado tradicional.
> Cuando vuelva a San Antonio la semana que viene, voy a poner la foto de nuestro desafío. ¡Hasta pronto!

1. ¿Qué va a hacer Tess cuando llegue a Quito?
2. ¿En qué dirección tienen que ir Tess y Patricia para ir de Quito a Mitad del Mundo?
3. ¿Qué quieren hacer cuando lleguen a Mitad del Mundo?
4. ¿Qué van a hacer al día siguiente por la noche?
5. ¿Qué planes tiene Tess para pasado mañana?
6. ¿Qué va a hacer Tess cuando vuelva a casa?

37 **Vamos de vacaciones**

▶ **Escucha** los planes de Patricia y su esposo y decide si estas oraciones son ciertas o falsas. Si son falsas, corrígelas.

1. El esposo de Patricia quiere ir a Nueva York.
2. Patricia prefiere ir a Asia.
3. Patricia y su esposo van a conocer el norte de Francia y la capital.
4. Cuando estén allí, van a visitar museos y monumentos famosos.
5. Después van a viajar al Reino Unido.
6. El esposo de Patricia va a pedir precios para ir a Asia.

▶ **Habla** con tu compañero(a). Imagina que van a hacer el mismo viaje que Patricia y su esposo. ¿Qué planes tienen?

Modelo A. *¿Qué vamos a hacer en París?*
         B. *Vamos a cenar en un restaurante de nouvelle cuisine.*

Differentiated Instruction

DEVELOPING LEARNERS

- Give students more practice with the present subjunctive after *cuando* when referring to future events by having them complete the following sentences:
  1. *Cuando ... (venir) tu padre, vamos al restaurante. (venga)*
  2. *Cuando yo ... (llegar) al hotel, te llamo. (llegue)*
  3. *Cuando ... (sonar) el teléfono, contesta, por favor. (suene)*
  4. *Cuando tu abuela ... (ir) al mercado, acompáñala. (vaya)*
  5. *Cuando tú ... (ser) mayor, lo vas a entender. (seas)*

EXPANDING LEARNERS

- Ask students to think about where they like to go or what they like to do when they visit a new place. Then have students imagine that they are going on a trip and ask them to write a blog entry describing the trip and what they are planning to do. Ask them to use expressions with *ir a* + infinitive, as well as *cuando* with the present subjunctive to describe what may happen in the future. They may use Tess's blog as a model, but the content must be original!

38 **Un viaje alrededor del mundo**

▶ **Escribe.** Tus padres van a hacer un viaje alrededor del mundo. Escribe un itinerario por diez ciudades y algo para hacer en cada lugar.

Modelo *Primero van a ir en avión a Londres.*
Allí van a visitar...

▶ **Presenta** tu itinerario a tus compañeros(as).
¿Cuál es el más divertido?

Final del desafío

Estamos muy cerca, pero me parece que no vamos a llegar a Mitad del Mundo a las doce.

¡No puede ser!

 **39** **¿Llegaron a tiempo?**

▶ **Escribe** el final del desafío. ¿Crees que Tess y Patricia llegaron a Mitad del Mundo a tiempo? ¿Qué pasó después?

Modelo *Yo creo que Tess y Patricia llegaron a tiempo.*

→TU DESAFÍO Visita la página web. Escucha las preguntas de tu *Minientrevista Desafío 2* y escribe las respuestas.

38. You may choose to have students focus on a particular region of the world, assigning a certain number of students to each continent. Ask students to research famous destinations in the region. To challenge more advanced learners, encourage them to use the subjunctive, rather than *ir a + infinitivo.*

39. Ask students to recycle other expressions, such as *Pienso que..., Es posible que..., Quizás..., Dudo que...*

 AUDIO SCRIPT
See page 391I.

Answer Key

36. 1. Va a tomar un taxi para ir a Mitad del Mundo.
2. Tienen que ir en dirección norte.
3. Quieren hacerse una foto con un pie en cada hemisferio.
4. Van a explorar un poco la ciudad.
5. Quiere ir de compras a algún mercado tradicional.
6. Va a poner la foto de su desafío en su blog.

37. 1. Cierto.
2. Falso. Patricia prefiere ir a Francia.
3. Cierto.
4. Cierto.
5. Cierto.
6. Falso. Va a pedir precios para ir a Francia y al Reino Unido, a Londres.
▶ Answers will vary.

38. Answers will vary.
▶ Answers will vary.

39. Answers will vary.

Additional Resources

Fans Online activities
Practice Workbook

RITAGE LANGUAGE LEARNERS

sk students to write a blog entry about a uture trip, but one that describes what hey think tourists would like to see and do hile they are visiting a city in their family's ountry of origin. They should point out ome cultural activities as well as sports r physical activities that can be enjoyed utdoors, and include tips on restaurants nd musical events or other spectacles.

MULTIPLE INTELLIGENCES:
Interpersonal Intelligence

• The taxi takes Tess and Patricia along a stretch of *la Panamericana.* Have students work in small groups and research the history of the Pan-American Highway, how the idea of its creation came to be, how the construction was started, how it was funded, what problems arose along the way, and how its completion helped countries along the route. Then ask students to trace this route, or network of roads, on a map of the Americas and to name the countries and major cities it passes through.

Unit 8
DESAFÍO 3
Hablar de acciones futuras

Presentation

■ In *Desafío 3*, Tim and Mack visit Isluga Volcano National Park in Chile. While there, they must swim in a hot spring at 12,000 feet above sea level.

■ In this section, students will preview:
  – Vocabulary related to weather and climate.
  – The future tense.

Activities	Standards	Resources
Fotonovela	1.2, 2.1, 3.1, 3.2	Vis. Pres.
40.	1.2, 1.3	
41.	1.2, 1.3	
42.	1.2	Audio
43. Conexiones	1.1, 1.2, 2.1, 3.1, 3.2, 4.2	
Tu desafío	1.2, 3.1, 3.2, 5.1	

Teaching Suggestions

Warm-Up / Independent Starter

■ Ask students to study the pictures of the *fotonovela* for a couple of minutes and then close their books. Give them three minutes to write as many sentences as they can that describe the events of the *fotonovela*.

Preparation

■ Ask students to form pairs and share their Independent Starters. Invite one volunteer per group to go to the board and write one of the group's sentences. Review together as a class.

■ Display photos of the hot springs at Isluga Volcano National Park in Chile and those at Yellowstone National Park in Wyoming. Have students write their observations of each.

La fotonovela

Before Viewing

■ Ask for a volunteer to read the introduction to the *fotonovela*. Discuss, as a class, how they think Tim and Mack will accomplish their task.

After Viewing

■ Ask students whether they think Tim will end up swimming in the spring or not. You may want to poll the class.

Aire frío y agua caliente

 Tim and Mack are back in the Andes. They are in the Isluga Volcano National Park, in Chile. Tim and his grandpa must don their swimsuits in sub-zero temperatures, and swim in a hot spring at 12,000 feet above sea level!

¿Sabías que la Panamericana pasa muy cerca de muchos volcanes?

¡Qué miedo!

¿Miedo? ¡Qué va!

Este volcán se llama Isluga y es un volcán activo.

¿Se sabe cuándo entrará en erupción?

Tranquilo, Tim. Eso no pasará ni hoy ni mañana.

¡Ah, mira qué sol! Hace un día estupendo para darse un baño.

¡Pero si estamos a tres grados bajo cero! Si nos bañamos hoy, mañana estaremos enfermos.

¡Venga, Tim! Mañana no hará sol y bajarán las temperaturas. Hoy es un día perfecto para bañarnos.

¿Se bañará Tim?

Continuará...

40 **Detective de palabras**

▶ **Completa** estas oraciones.

1. ¿Se sabe cuándo ___1___ en erupción?
2. Tranquilo, Tim. Eso no ___2___ ni hoy ni mañana.
3. Si nos bañamos hoy, mañana ___3___ enfermos.
4. Mañana no ___4___ sol y ___5___ las temperaturas.
5. ¿Se ___6___ Tim?

▶ **Escribe.** ¿A qué infinitivos corresponden esos verbos?

Differentiated Instruction

DEVELOPING LEARNERS

• Ask students to work with a partner and read aloud the speech bubbles in the *fotonovela*. As they read, have them pay special attention to their intonation for questions and exclamations to make the reading sound more natural. Also encourage them to use gestures while they are reading. After they practice a few times with their partner, ask pairs to come to the front of the class and act out the dialogue.

EXPANDING LEARNERS

• Have students work in groups of three. Two students will play the roles of Mack and Tim; the other will be a reporter from the local news, who is going to interview them about their experience of taking a swim in the thermal waters of the Isluga Volcano National Park. The reporter may ask them questions such as what they were doing in Chile, why they took the plunge, and how they felt before going in and coming out. Give students time to prepare questions and answers, and rehearse their lines before presenting their interview in front of the class.

41 **¿Comprendes?**

▶ **Decide** si estas oraciones son ciertas o falsas. Si son falsas, corrígelas.

1. Tim y Mack están en un parque nacional.
2. El volcán Isluga no está activo.
3. Mack quiere bañarse porque hace mucho calor.
4. Tim no quiere bañarse porque hace frío.
5. Mack piensa que es imposible que Tim se bañe.

42 **¿Qué foto es?**

▶ **Escucha** y relaciona cada oración con la imagen correspondiente.

 (A)
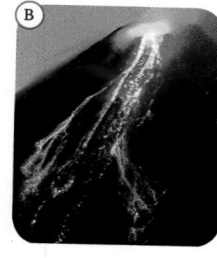 (B)
 (C)
 (D)

 CONEXIONES: CIENCIAS

El Parque Nacional Volcán Isluga

El Parque Nacional Volcán Isluga está en Chile. Se llama así por el volcán Isluga, la montaña más alta del parque.

La altitud de este parque nacional va desde los 2.100 metros hasta más de 5.000 metros sobre el nivel del mar. La temperatura media anual está entre los −5 °C y los 10 °C (23-50 °F).

Uno de los principales atractivos del parque son las termas naturales de Enquelga. Están a 3.700 metros de altitud, pero el agua alcanza una temperatura de unos 30 °C (86 °F).

43 **Compara.** ¿Conoces algún parque nacional en tu país? ¿Cuáles son sus características geográficas?

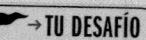 **TU DESAFÍO** Visita la página web para aprender más sobre el volcán Isluga.

RITAGE LANGUAGE LEARNERS

There are many legends from the Americas that explain the origins of things. Ask students to investigate legends surrounding the origin of volcanoes or other natural phenomena from their family's country of origin or another Hispanic country; for example, the volcanoes Popocatépetl ("Popo") and Iztaccíhuatl ("Izta") near Mexico City. Students may ask family members about these legends, or they could look for information in the library or on the Internet and share their findings with the class. Encourage students to read portions of a legend to their classmates.

MULTIPLE INTELLIGENCES:
Verbal-Linguistic Intelligence

• Ask students to write their own legend explaining the origin of a phenomenon of nature. They may write about how the sun, moon, or stars came to be, or what caused the first rainfall or bolt of lighting, or why a particular mountaintop is always covered with snow. Encourage creativity! Students may develop their legends with a first- or third-person narrative, a play, a poem, or even a song. Call on individuals to read, or sing, their work to the rest of the class.

Unit 8
DESAFÍO 3
Hablar de acciones futuras

Activities

41. Place students in pairs. Ask them to re-enact Tim and Mack's adventure in their own words. Have students include their own ideas about how Tim and Mack will meet their challenge.

42. Before listening, ask students to orally create complete sentences that describe the weather or event depicted in each photo.

AUDIO SCRIPT
See page 391J.

CONEXIONES: CIENCIAS

El Parque Nacional Volcán Isluga

One of the most remarkable features of this park are the fumaroles. Fumaroles are openings in the Earth's crust from which steam and gases are released. As the extremely hot water emerges from beneath the ground, the pressure drops and it turns to steam. During the coldest months of the year, these spurts of boiling water form incredible blocks of ice.

Answer Key

40. 1. entrará   3. estaremos   5. bajarán
2. pasará   4. hará   6. bañará
▶ 1. entrar   3. estar   5. bajar
2. pasar   4. hacer   6. bañar

41. 1. Cierto.
2. Falso. El volcán Isluga está activo.
3. Falso. Mack quiere bañarse porque hace sol.
4. Cierto.
5. Falso. Mack piensa que es posible que Tim se bañe.

42. 1. D   2. A   3. C   4. B

43. Answers will vary.

Additional Resources
Fans Online activities

DESAFÍO 3

Vocabulario – El tiempo meteorológico

Presentation

■ In this section, students will learn vocabulary relating to weather.

Activities	Standards	Resources
Vocabulario	1.2	
44.	1.2, 1.3	
45.	1.1, 1.3, 5.2	
46.	1.2	Audio
47.	1.1, 1.3, 3.1	

Teaching Suggestions

Warm-Up / Independent Starter

■ Ask students to answer the following questions:
  – ¿Cuál es tu estación favorita?
  – ¿Por qué te gusta tanto?
  – Describe el tiempo y las actividades en que participas durante esta estación.

Preparation

■ Ask students to share their answers from the Independent Starter. Create a chart on the board to track the responses of the class.

■ Go over the vocabulary presentation and model pronunciation. Then ask students to think of the weather in their community during the different seasons. What is wintertime like? And summer? Are some of the natural disasters presented in the vocabulary common in your area?

Activities

44. Convert this activity into a speaking exercise by having students work with a partner to ask and answer questions based on the sentences formed. For example:

A. ¿Qué te gusta hacer cuando el termómetro marca -4 °C?

B. Me gusta patinar sobre hielo.

45. After students have completed the activity, write the following words on the board: volcánico, lluvioso, soleado, la llovizna, nevada, enfriar, calentar, helar. Ask students to identify the parts of speech of these words. Have them write sentences with the vocabulary.

Vocabulario

El tiempo meteorológico

Los desastres naturales

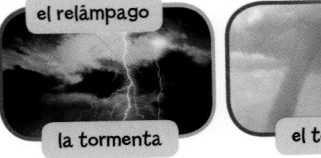  

44 **La madre naturaleza**

▶ **Completa** estas oraciones.

1. El termómetro marca −4 °C, hace mucho _____.
2. Hoy hace muy mal tiempo: llueve y hace _____.
3. En mi país hay muchos _____.
4. El volcán entró en _____.
5. Maneja con cuidado, hay _____ en la carretera.
6. En mi país _____ mucho en invierno.

tornados
viento
hielo
frío
nieva
erupción

Differentiated Instruction

DEVELOPING LEARNERS

• Visual learners will benefit from creating images of the new vocabulary. Have them find and cut out illustrations for the weather conditions and natural disasters pictured on the page. Ask them to attach these images to a large index card. Then have them write the corresponding words for each image on a smaller card. Working with a partner, students will test one another on their vocabulary comprehension by matching each word to the corresponding picture.

EXPANDING LEARNERS

• Students will create a radio ad to attract tourism to an area or city of a country of their choice. The focus of the ad should be on the area's excellent weather and the availability of weather-related activities, so students will need to research typical temperatures, weather conditions, and absence of natural disasters. Ask students to write their script and then read it with enthusiasm, proper pronunciation, and intonation, as if they were recording at a studio. Music and sound effects would be a plus.

45 Asociaciones

▶ **Habla** con tu compañero(a). ¿Qué palabra no corresponde a cada grupo?

1
frío
nieve
calor
invierno

2
erupción
tornado
terremoto
temperatura

3
temperatura
viento
grados
termómetro

4
sol
lluvia
tormenta
relámpago

▶ **Escribe** otras series similares con tu compañero(a) e intercámbienlas con las de otra pareja. Ellos(as) tienen que adivinar qué palabra no corresponde.

46 El tiempo nos influye mucho

▶ **Escucha** el diálogo. ¿A cuál de estas fotografías corresponde?

1

2

3

4

47 Lo bueno y lo malo

▶ **Escribe** qué cosas te gustan más y menos de estos lugares.

Modelo *En Hawái hace sol y hace calor, pero hay volcanes que pueden entrar en erupción.*

1. Los Ángeles, CA
2. Chicago, IL
3. Phoenix, AZ
4. Omaha, NE
5. Miami, FL
6. Nueva York, NY

▶ **Habla** con tu compañero(a). ¿Cómo es el tiempo en tu ciudad o en tu pueblo en cada estación? ¿Qué cosas te gustan más y menos?

Modelo A. *Lo que más me gusta del tiempo de esta ciudad es que en verano no hace demasiado calor.*
B. *Sí, a mí también. Y lo que menos me gusta es que nunca nieva porque me encanta esquiar.*

cuatrocientos diecisiete 417

Unit 8
DESAFÍO 3
Vocabulario – El tiempo meteorológico

46. Before playing the audio selection, ask students to identify the activities and weather conditions depicted in each image. After listening, divide the class into four groups and assign each group one of the pictures. Ask each group to come up with a dialogue between the characters depicted in their assigned picture (in the case of picture 2, ask students to imagine that this person is part of a group of cross-country skiers). Allow the groups rehearsal time and then ask them to role-play their dialogues in front of the class.

47. Before completing this exercise, divide the class into six groups and assign one city to each group. For homework, ask them to use the Internet to investigate tomorrow's weather forecast for each town. The next day, students in each group can share their answers with the class. Extend the activity by showing students the weather forecast for Santiago, Chile and Isluga National Park.

AUDIO SCRIPT
See page 391 J.

Answer Key

44.
1. frío
2. viento
3. tornados
4. erupción
5. hielo
6. nieva

45.
1. calor
2. temperatura
3. viento
4. sol
▶ Answers will vary.

46. Fotografía 4.

47. Answers will vary.
▶ Answers will vary.

Additional Resources

Fans Online activities
Practice Workbook

Unit 8
DESAFÍO 3
Gramática – El futuro

Presentation

- In this section, students will learn regular and irregular forms of the future tense.

Activities	Standards	Resources
Gramática	3.1	
48.	1.1, 3.1, 4.1	
49.	1.2, 1.3	Audio
50.	1.2, 1.3	
51.	1.2, 1.3, 5.1	Audio
52. Conexiones	1.1, 1.2, 3.1, 3.2	
Tu desafío	1.2, 3.1, 3.2, 5.1	

Teaching Suggestions

Warm-Up / Independent Starter

- Have students answer these questions in writing.
  - ¿Qué quieres hacer después de graduarte en la escuela secundaria?
  - ¿Dónde vas a vivir?

Preparation

- Remind students of the formula *ir a* + infinitive to express future actions. Use the verbs in the chart as examples (e.g., *Yo voy a entrar en la tienda porque está lloviendo*).

- Go over the grammar presentation. Then ask students to conjugate the following verbs in the future tense: *nieva, llueve, sigue.* Point out that it is key that they identify the infinitive before forming the future tense.

Activities

50. Have students create a list of future time expressions: *mañana, pasado mañana, la semana que viene, el próximo mes,* etc. Have them use these expressions with weather vocabulary and the future tense to write more sentences.

51. As students listen to the audio, ask them to represent the weather by drawing what they hear, rather than by writing responses. Then have them share their drawings with a partner and ask and answer each other's questions about the weather each day of the week.

418

DESAFÍO 3

Gramática

El futuro

- To talk about the future, you can use *ir a + infinitive* or the future tense.

  La semana que viene **voy a ir** de excursión a la montaña.
  La semana que viene **iré** de excursión a la montaña.

Futuro. Verbos regulares

- Add the following endings to the infinitive to form the future tense. Note that all -ar, -er, and -ir verbs use the same endings.

FUTURO. VERBOS REGULARES

	Entrar	Comer	Seguir
yo	entraré	comeré	seguiré
tú	entrarás	comerás	seguirás
usted, él, ella	entrará	comerá	seguirá
nosotros, nosotras	entraremos	comeremos	seguiremos
vosotros, vosotras	entraréis	comeréis	seguiréis
ustedes, ellos, ellas	entrarán	comerán	seguirán

Verbos irregulares en el futuro

- These verbs have stem changes:

VERBOS IRREGULARES EN EL FUTURO

| poder → podr- |
| poner → pondr- |
| salir → saldr- |
| tener → tendr- |
| venir → vendr- |

| decir → dir- |
| hacer → har- |
| querer → querr- |
| saber → sabr- |

Mañana no **podré** salir.
Saldré el domingo.

El domingo **hará** calor.
Podremos ir de excursión.

48 **Compara.** ¿Cómo se expresa el futuro en inglés?

49 **¿En el pasado o en el futuro?**

▶ **Escucha** a Mack y decide si Tim hizo estas actividades en el pasado o si las hará en el futuro.

1. ponerse el impermeable
2. bañarse
3. ir a Denver
4. sacar una fotografía
5. ponerse el abrigo y la bufanda
6. ir a esquiar a Bariloche
7. volver al hotel
8. llamar a sus amigos

418 cuatrocientos dieciocho

Differentiated Instruction

DEVELOPING LEARNERS

- Give students more practice with the future tense of *poder* by having them write the correct form to complete the following sentences.
  1. *Yo … salir a las dos. (podré)*
  2. *Tú … comprar ese coche. (podrás)*
  3. *Él … cantar en la ópera. (podrá)*
  4. *Nosotros … visitar a la abuela. (podremos)*
  5. *Vosotros … viajar a España. (podréis)*
  6. *Ellos … aprender italiano. (podrán)*

EXPANDING LEARNERS

- Have students talk with a partner about what they will do in the future. Challenge them to use as many of both the regular and the irregular verbs in the future as they can, and as many words that express plans and intentions as they can. As they express their plans to one another, both students will take notes and then tell the rest of the class what their partners will do.

50 **Hay que prepararse**

▶ **Escribe** lo que harán estas personas si ocurren estos fenómenos naturales. Usa el futuro.

1. Si hay un tornado, nosotros _____ al sótano.
   (bajar)

2. Mack _____ con mucho cuidado si hay hielo en la carretera.
   (manejar)

3. Ellos no _____ subir a la montaña si hay una tormenta.
   (poder)

4. Si hace mucho frío, Tim y Mack _____ a la calle con ropa de abrigo.
   (salir)

5. Ana no _____ ir a la playa si está nublado porque le encanta tomar el sol.
   (querer)

6. Si bajan las temperaturas, ustedes se _____ ropa de abrigo.
   (poner)

51 **¿Qué tiempo hará?**

▶ **Escucha** la previsión meteorológica para Santiago de Chile y completa una tabla como esta.

Lunes	Martes	Miércoles	Jueves	Viernes
Estará nublado.				

▶ **Escribe** con tu compañero(a) un pronóstico del tiempo para la próxima semana en tu ciudad o en tu pueblo.

CONEXIONES: CIENCIAS

El Cinturón de Fuego del Pacífico

Aproximadamente el 75% de los volcanes del mundo se sitúa alrededor de la cuenca del océano Pacífico. Por eso, a esta zona se la llama el Cinturón de Fuego del Pacífico.

El Cinturón de Fuego del Pacífico es también una zona de gran actividad sísmica. El 90% de los terremotos del mundo se produce en esta área, que incluye países de Suramérica, Centroamérica, Norteamérica, Asia y Oceanía.

Volcán en Chile.

52 **Piensa y explica.** ¿Cómo piensas que afecta la actividad sísmica al estilo de vida de los habitantes de esta zona?

→ TU DESAFÍO Visita la página web para aprender más sobre el Cinturón de Fuego del Pacífico.

ERITAGE LANGUAGE LEARNERS

Ask students to think about what their lives might be like fifty years from now. Then have them write a few paragraphs describing what they predict for their future: what they will be doing, where they will live, what they will look like, whether they will be married, how many children/grandchildren they will have, what job they will have—or if they will be retired, where they will travel, and what other languages they will speak fluently. Ask another student to read their paragraphs aloud, and see if the class can guess who wrote them.

MULTIPLE INTELLIGENCES:
Visual-Spatial Intelligence

• Ask students to research active volcanoes throughout the Spanish-speaking world. Then have them indicate the location of these volcanoes on a map of the Americas and Spain, label them with their names, and indicate their altitude in meters. From their research, they should also indicate the most recent eruptions of these volcanoes.

 AUDIO SCRIPT
See page 391J.

 CONEXIONES: CIENCIAS

El Cinturón de Fuego del Pacífico

The Ring of Fire, also known as the Circum-Pacific Belt, is an area of frequent earthquakes and volcanic eruptions that encircles the Pacific Ocean. It is situated at the edge of the Pacific plate and other major tectonic plates. These plates resemble giant rafts that move; they may slide next to, collide with, and move underneath other plates. There is a tremendous amount of energy created by the violent movements of these plates, causing rock to melt into magma, which rises to the surface as lava and forms volcanoes.

Answer Key

48. Se usa el verbo auxiliar *will* y el presente del verbo principal.

49.
1. futuro	5. pasado
2. futuro	6. futuro
3. futuro	7. pasado
4. pasado	8. futuro

50.
1. bajaremos	4. saldrán
2. manejará	5. querrá
3. podrán	6. pondrán

51. Martes y miércoles: Hará sol y subirán las temperaturas.
Jueves: Habrá nubes.
Viernes: Lloverá y bajarán las temperaturas.
▶ Answers will vary.

52. Answers will vary.

Additional Resources

Fans Online activities
Practice Workbook

Unit 8
DESAFÍO 3

Comunicación

Presentation

- In this section, students will integrate the vocabulary and grammar from *Desafío 3* in order to use the future tense to describe the weather and other phenomena of nature.

Activities	Standards	Resources
53.	1.1, 1.2, 1.3	
54.	1.1, 1.3	
55.	1.1, 1.2, 1.3, 5.1	Audio
56.	1.1, 1.3	
57. Final del desafío	1.2, 1.3, 5.1	
Tu desafío	1.2, 1.3	

Teaching Suggestions

Warm-Up / Independent Starter

- Have students write a summary of this *Desafío* entitled *Aire frío y agua caliente*.

Preparation

- Using the students' summaries, take 10 minutes to review the main themes of the *Desafío*.
- Refer students back to the *fotonovela*. Ask them to identify the verbs that are used in the future and the vocabulary for weather conditions and natural disasters. Do students understand the dialogue better now that they have gone through the vocabulary and grammar from the *Desafío*?
- Have students provide additional examples of the future tense in order to communicate actions that will happen in the future (e.g., *Tim se bañará en las aguas termales aunque hace mucho frío*).

Activities

54. Convert this speaking activity into a writing exercise. For homework, ask students to write a short story based on how the weather will impact Tim and Mack's adventure. In class, have students exchange papers with one another for peer review. Students should ask questions that they have after reading the first draft of this short story. They should then revise their story, including the answers to the questions asked by their partners.

420

DESAFÍO 3

Comunicación

53 **¿Qué tiempo hará mañana?**

▶ **Escribe** la predicción del tiempo para mañana en tu país. Haz un mapa y coloca símbolos para ilustrarlo.

▶ **Lee** tu predicción a tu compañero(a). Él/Ella debe colocar los símbolos correctos en un mapa en blanco.

Modelo A. *Mañana lloverá en la costa este.*
  B. *¿En toda la costa?*
  A. *Sí.*

54 **¿Qué pasará?**

▶ **Escribe.** ¿Qué harás mañana si hace este tiempo?

Si hay una tormenta…

Si hace calor…

Si nieva…

Si hace mucho viento…

▶ **Habla** con tu compañero(a). ¿Qué crees que harán Tim y Mack en esas situaciones?

Modelo *Si hay una tormenta, Tim y Mack no saldrán a la calle. Se quedarán en el hotel y…*

420 cuatrocientos veinte

Differentiated Instruction

DEVELOPING LEARNERS

- Help students come up with three or four suggestions for improving their schoolwork. Elicit the future tense for all suggestions. You may start them off with the following examples: *Escucharé a la profesora. Durante la clase, no hablaré con mis amigos. Haré mis tareas todos los días. Siempre llevaré mis libros y cuadernos a clase.* Encourage students to write other suggestions, and assist them with ideas. Then ask students to illustrate their suggestions and display their work in the classroom.

EXPANDING LEARNERS

- Ask students what they will do in the following situations. Remind them to use the future tense.
  1. *Hay muchísima nieve delante de la puerta de tu casa. (Limpiaré…)*
  2. *Un policía te hace una pregunta. (Diré la verdad. / Contestaré…)*
  3. *Tu madre quiere que hagas tu tarea. (Haré…)*
  4. *Hace muchísimo calor y no tienes aire acondicionado. (Compraré…)*
  5. *El termómetro marca 10 °F y acabas de comprar un abrigo. (Me pondré…)*
  6. *Estás solo y aburrido en casa. (Saldré…)*

55 **Un viaje, dos ciudades**

 ▶ **Escucha** la conversación y responde a estas preguntas.

1. ¿Qué hará la mujer en Valparaíso?
2. ¿Por qué no lleva mucha ropa?
3. ¿Qué tiempo hará en Valparaíso?
4. ¿Para qué irá de viaje a Santiago?

▶ **Escribe** tres cosas que tú y tus compañeros(as) podrán hacer por una escuela afectada por un desastre natural.

 ▶ **Compara** tu lista con tres compañeros(as). Entre todos(as), elijan las cinco mejores cosas y hagan un cartel.

56 **Te toca a ti**

▶ **Escribe.** ¿Cómo imaginas tu vida dentro de diez años? Puedes usar estas preguntas.

– ¿Dónde vivirás?
– ¿Cuál será tu profesión?
– ¿Estarás casado(a)? ¿Tendrás hijos(as)?
– ¿Dónde pasarás tus vacaciones?
– ¿Qué harás en tu tiempo libre?

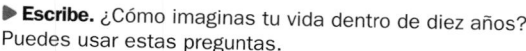 Cuando tenga 25 años, viviré en...

 ▶ **Habla** con tu compañero(a) sobre tu vida futura y hazle preguntas sobre la suya.

Final del desafío

No hace tiempo para bañarse, abuelo...

¡Venga, anímate! El agua está deliciosa. Y si no te bañas, se lo diré a todo el mundo.

 57 **¿Qué hará Tim?**

▶ **Escribe** el final del desafío. ¿Crees que Tim se bañará? Usa el futuro.

 **→ TU DESAFÍO** Visita la página web. Escucha las preguntas de tu *Minientrevista* *Desafío 3* y escribe las respuestas.

HERITAGE LANGUAGE LEARNERS

Have students imagine that they are going to take part in a *desafío* in a Hispanic country where the atmospheric conditions are not optimal. Explain that they might be in an area of an active volcano that is about to erupt, in the path of a tornado, or in the midst of a severe thunderstorm or even a hurricane! In a first-person narrative or a monologue, ask students to describe the challenge they must perform, the weather conditions where they are located, and what they will do to protect themselves from danger.

MULTIPLE INTELLIGENCES:
Verbal-Linguistic Intelligence

• Write words or phrases related to the weather on small index cards, put them in a bag, and have each student pick a card. The student will then write the word vertically on the board, and within a given time limit write words related to the weather, using each letter of the original word as the initial letter for a word. For example:
Nublado
Erupción
Viento
Alerta
Relámpago

Unit 8
DESAFÍO 3
Comunicación

55. Before listening to the audio selection, use a map of Chile to show the location of Valparaíso and Santiago. Lead a discussion of the geographical features of the two cities. Then, as a class, predict what types of weather one would expect to encounter in each city.

57. Have students work in pairs to imagine how this *Desafío* will end. Have each pair make a list of five to seven key words that they will use during a "dramatic presentation" in front of the class. Invite students to vote for best actor, best ending, best comedic role, best use of vocabulary, etc.

 AUDIO SCRIPT
See page 391J.

Answer Key

53. Answers will vary.
   ▶ Answers will vary.
54. Answers will vary.
   ▶ Answers will vary.
55. Answers will vary. Sample answers:
   1. Verá a sus hermanos.
   2. Porque le gusta ir de compras y porque no sabe qué tiempo hará en Valparaíso.
   3. Por las mañanas hará frío y la semana siguiente lloverá mucho.
   4. Para visitar una escuela. Hubo un terremoto allí y va a ayudarlos.
   ▶ Answers will vary.
   ▶ Answers will vary.
56. Answers will vary.
   ▶ Answers will vary.
57. Answers will vary.

Additional Resources

Fans Online activities
Practice Workbook

DESAFÍO 4
Ocultar el agente

Presentation

- In *Desafío 4* Diana and Rita are visiting Tortuguero National Park in Costa Rica. There they must rescue as many sea turtles as possible and deliver them safely to the ocean.
- In this section, students will preview:
  – Vocabulary related to nature and the environment.
  – The use of the impersonal *se*.

Activities	Standards	Resources
Fotonovela	1.2, 2.2, 3.1, 3.2	Vis. Pres.
58.	1.2	
59.	1.2, 1.3, 2.2	
60.	1.1	
61. Conexiones	1.1, 1.2, 2.2, 3.1, 3.2	
Tu desafío	1.2, 2.2, 3.1, 3.2, 5.1	

Teaching Suggestions

Warm-Up / Independent Starter

- Ask students to create a list of five ways in which they might be able to help save the planet.

Preparation

- Form pairs to share the information brainstormed in the Independent Starter.
- To emphasize multidisciplinary studies, you may invite a science teacher to come in to discuss the plight of the sea turtles. Ask students to make a list of five questions that they would like the science teacher to answer.

La fotonovela

Before Viewing

- Ask for a volunteer to read the introduction to the *fotonovela*. Then have students look at the pictures and tell what they find surprising or interesting.

After Viewing

- Discuss with students the data and information provided in the dialogue. You may want to initiate the discussion by asking students questions (e.g., *¿Cuántas tortugas se calcula que mueren cada año?*).

El paraíso de las tortugas

Diana and Rita are in Tortuguero, one of the largest sea turtle sanctuaries in the world. After they hatch, the baby turtles run to sea, but some get lost. Diana and Rita's task is to rescue as many baby sea turtles as possible and take them to the ocean.

> ¿Sabías que las tortugas marinas están en peligro de extinción? Se calcula que cada año mueren cerca de un millón de tortugas.

> Según se dice, es posible que en cien años no existan tortugas marinas.

> ¿Y no se puede hacer nada para evitarlo?

> ¡Cuánto sabes! Se nota que te gusta la naturaleza.

> ¿Tienes el repelente de mosquitos? Con tantos insectos se recomienda llevarlo a todas horas.

> ¿Cuánto se tarda en llegar a la playa?

> ¡Una araña! ¡Mátala!

> ¿Estás loca? Las arañas forman parte del ecosistema.

> Creo que ya llegamos.

Continuará...

58 **Detective de palabras**

▶ **Une** las dos columnas.

A
1. Se calcula
2. ¿No se puede
3. Según se dice,
4. Se nota
5. Se recomienda
6. ¿Cuánto se tarda

B
a. llevar repelente de mosquitos a todas horas.
b. en llegar a la playa?
c. hacer nada para evitarlo?
d. es posible que en cien años no existan tortugas marinas.
e. que te gusta la naturaleza.
f. que cada año mueren cerca de un millón de tortugas.

Differentiated Instruction

DEVELOPING LEARNERS

- Ask students if the following statements are true (*cierto*) or false (*falso*).
  1. *Las tortugas marinas no están en peligro de extinción.* (falso)
  2. *Cada año mueren casi un millón de tortugas.* (cierto)
  3. *Se dice que quizás en diez años no existan tortugas marinas.* (falso)
  4. *A Diana le gusta la naturaleza.* (cierto)
  5. *Rita y Diana tienen repelente de mosquitos.* (cierto)
  6. *Diana quiere matar la araña.* (falso)

EXPANDING LEARNERS

- Have students imagine that they are producing a documentary on the life of a sea turtle at the Tortuguero National Park in Costa Rica. They have the actors and the turtles, but they need a script. Students will work with a partner to write this script. Then they will rehearse with the actors portraying two ecologically concerned citizens. Finally, they will present their "documentary" to the rest of the class.

59 Un mensaje desde Tortuguero

▶ **Completa** el mensaje que le manda Diana a su familia desde Tortuguero.

parque
playa
cocodrilos
plantas
tortugas

De
    Para:
Asunto:

Cuerpo del texto | Anchura variable | B / U

Hola a todos. ¿Qué tal están? La tía Rita y yo estamos en el Parque
Nacional Tortuguero, en Costa Rica. Este lugar es famoso porque de julio
a octubre las ___1___ van a la ___2___ a dejar sus huevos. Esta noche
vamos a hacer una excursión para verlas. La mejor forma de ver
este ___3___ es en lancha. Así se puede disfrutar del paisaje y ver todas
las ___4___ y animales. ¿Saben que hay ___5___? ¡Qué miedo!
Diana

60 La naturaleza

▶ **Describe** las fotografías que tomó Diana en Tortuguero con tu compañero(a).

CONEXIONES: CIENCIAS

El Parque Nacional Tortuguero

El Parque Nacional Tortuguero está situado en la costa norte
de Costa Rica. Allí podemos encontrar más de 400 tipos de árboles
y más de 2.000 especies de plantas. También hay una gran
diversidad de fauna: aves, reptiles, insectos, peces, anfibios
y animales en peligro de extinción, como el jaguar.

Dentro del parque se encuentra el pueblo de Tortuguero. Miles
de tortugas verdes van a sus playas cada año para dejar sus huevos.

61 **Explica.** ¿Conoces alguna reserva natural de animales?

→ **TU DESAFÍO** | Visita la página web para aprender más sobre Tortuguero.

Activities

59. Ask students to work in pairs to talk about what
will happen during this challenge using the
future tense (e.g., *Rita y Diana irán al Parque
Tortuguero en Costa Rica...*).

60. After partners have described the pictures, ask
them to choose one of the places and come up
with a brief narrative describing what is
happening there.

61. Have students research endangered species in
the Americas. In pairs, they should choose one
animal, and then create a children's story about
this animal. They should also include ways in
which the children may help save these at-risk
animals. Look for ways in which students can
share these stories with the Spanish-speaking
population in your area or with younger students
who are also studying Spanish.

CONEXIONES: CIENCIAS

El Parque Nacional Tortuguero

Tortuguero was declared a national park in
1970 in order to help save the Caribbean
green turtle from extinction. Tortuguero beach
is the most important nesting site of this turtle
in the Western Hemisphere. The Park takes
every measure to protect the turtles' mating
and nesting period, known as *arribadas*.
Consequently, in order to witness this event,
it is necessary to be accompanied by an
authorized guide.

Answer Key

58. 1. f 2. c 3. d 4. e 5. a 6. b

59. 1. tortugas 4. plantas
  2. playa 5. cocodrilos
  3. parque

60. Answers will vary.

61. Answers will vary.

Additional Resources

Fans Online activities

HERITAGE LANGUAGE LEARNERS

Ask students to describe an ecological
preserve in their family's country of origin.
In their description, they should use the
impersonal *se* with as many verbs as they
can. Encourage them to describe the
geographical features of this preserve or
park, and include a description of activities
and animal and plant sightings that they
consider to be of interest. If they know
something about the history of the park,
they should include that too.

COOPERATIVE LEARNING

• Have students work in small groups and
assign an animal that is in danger of
extinction to each group. Each student in
the group should have a specific task to do,
which may include research, compiling the
research, writing the final draft, proofreading,
or supplying visuals to enhance the project's
presentation. Students may describe the
animal's characteristics, its habitat, and the
problems it is facing from the environment
or from predators.

DESAFÍO 4

Vocabulario – La naturaleza y el medio ambiente

Presentation

- In this section, students will learn:
  – Words to name some domestic and wild animals.
  – Words to talk about environmental issues.

Activities	Standards	Resources
Vocabulario	1.2	
62.	1.2, 1.3	Audio
63.	1.1, 1.2, 1.3	Audio
64.	1.3, 5.2	
65. Comunidades	1.1, 1.2, 2.1, 3.2, 4.2, 5.2	Video
Tu desafío	1.2, 2.1, 3.2, 5.1	

Teaching Suggestions

Warm-Up / Independent Starter

- Have students draw a picture of their favorite animal for each of these categories: *animal doméstico, animal salvaje, mascota.*

Preparation

- Ask for volunteers to show the pictures to the class. The rest of the class tries to guess the name of the animal.
- Go over the vocabulary presentation with the class. To add some humor, have students perform animals by imitating their sounds. You can point out that in Spanish, animal sounds are expressed differently than in English.
- To review vocabulary on environmental issues, bring visuals that deal with pollution (city smog), fires (forest fires), and animals in danger of extinction.

Activities

62. Ask students to write a brief paragraph describing their favorite pet without identifying what animal it is. Have them read the descriptions while the rest of the class guesses the animal.

63. Ask students to take notes while interviewing their classmates to present the information to the class.

Vocabulario

La naturaleza y el medio ambiente

Animales domésticos

el caballo   la vaca   el cerdo   la oveja   el gallo   la gallina

Animales salvajes

el lobo   el águila   el mono   el cocodrilo   el oso   el elefante

Problemas medioambientales

la contaminación

la sequía

los incendios forestales

Voy a plantar un árbol. Debemos cuidar el medio ambiente.

Hay que proteger a las especies en peligro de extinción, conservar los recursos naturales y ahorrar energía.

62 Mascotas

▶ **Escucha** y escribe. ¿Qué animal tiene cada persona como mascota (*pet*)?
1. Margarita   2. Ángel   3. Eva   4. Julio   5. Mercedes

Differentiated Instruction

DEVELOPING LEARNERS

- Ask students to attach images of the new words from the lesson on large index cards. The images can be from magazines, computer-generated, or their own drawings. Then have them write the name for each image on a smaller card and have them practice identifying each one by matching the word to the image with a partner. Then help students categorize each of the animals according to where it is usually found: *en la casa, en la granja,* or *en la selva / en el bosque.*

EXPANDING LEARNERS

- Ask students to think of other ways we can help protect our environment. In addition to the suggestions presented on the page, ask them to write more ideas for saving the planet. Students should express their ideas with a form of *deber, tener que, hay que,* or the impersonal *se* plus a verb. Have them present their ideas to the class and have the class vote on the best suggestions.

63 Los animales que me gustan

 Escucha y relaciona cada diálogo con la foto correspondiente.

 A
 B
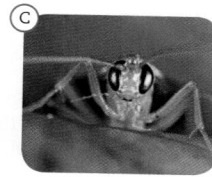 C
 D

 Escucha de nuevo y escribe. ¿Qué animales le gustan a cada uno?

Modelo *A Mario le gustan...*

1. Mario   2. Sofía   3. Rodrigo   4. Irene

Habla. Entrevista a cuatro compañeros(as) sobre sus animales favoritos.

1. ¿Tienen alguna mascota en casa? ¿Cuál?
2. ¿Cuáles son sus animales favoritos? ¿Por qué?
3. ¿Pueden contar alguna anécdota relacionada con un animal?

64 Cuidar el medio ambiente

Escribe. Haz una lista de tres cosas que puedes hacer para cuidar el medio ambiente.

Modelo *Para proteger el medio ambiente se puede usar el transporte público.*

 COMUNIDADES

¡PURA VIDA!

En Costa Rica se oye mucho la expresión *¡Pura vida!*: para saludar, para despedirse, para dar las gracias, para decir que algo está bien, etc. Al saludo «¿Cómo estás?» se responde casi siempre con la expresión «¡Pura vida!».

Esta expresión refleja la esencia de la cultura y la vida cotidiana de los habitantes de Costa Rica: tranquilidad *(peace)*, respeto por la naturaleza y amabilidad *(kindness)*.

65 **Compara.** ¿Tu cultura tiene un lema similar? ¿Cuál sería *(would be)* el lema para tu cultura o para describir la actitud de tu comunidad frente a la vida diaria?

→ TU DESAFÍO Visita la página web para aprender más sobre Costa Rica.

HERITAGE LANGUAGE LEARNERS

There are many colorful and amusing expressions and proverbs in Spanish that include animals. Have students brainstorm some of these and share them with the class. Students may have to translate some of these expressions for their classmates. After presenting these expressions, you may want to ask for their English-language equivalents and discuss their meaning. For example: *Gato escaldado del agua fría huye* (once bitten, twice shy); *cuando el gato duerme, bailan los ratones* (when the cat's away, the mice will play); *perro ladrador, poco mordedor* (his bark is worse than his bite).

TOTAL PHYSICAL RESPONSE (TPR)

• Divide the class into teams and tell them that they will need to pantomime an animal for their teammates to guess. Write the names of the animals on page 424, and any others students know, on slips of paper and place them in a bag. Have each student pick one. Establish a time limit for teams to guess the animal's identity. For each correct answer, the team scores one point.

Vocabulario – La naturaleza y el medio ambiente

64. Have students create a poster presentation or flyer with a list of environmental issues that affect their own community.

65. Have students make a slogan similar to *¡pura vida!* that captures the spirit of their community. Encourage students to combine visuals and text to make their slogan more appealing.

 AUDIO SCRIPT
See page 391J.

 COMUNIDADES

¡Pura vida!

¡Pura vida! is a Costa Rican expression that expresses the idea of something being *cool*. In the Spanish-speaking world, each country has its own set of expressions to express this idea. Some examples include, *¡qué padre!* in Mexico, *¡qué guay!* in Spain, *¡bárbaro!* in Argentina, *¡qué bacán!* in Colombia, and *¡chévere!* in Venezuela.

Answer Key

62. 1. un gato   4. peces tropicales
2. un perro   5. una tortuga
3. un pájaro

63. 1. C   2. A   3. D   4. B
▶ 1. Le gustan las tortugas y los insectos.
2. Le gustan los animales domésticos.
3. Le gustan los animales salvajes.
4. Le gustan los peces tropicales.
▶ Answers will vary.

64. Answers will vary.

65. Answers will vary.

Additional Resources

Fans Online activities
Practice Workbook

DESAFÍO 4

Gramática – Ocultar el agente. El pronombre *se*

Presentation

- In this section, students will learn to express impersonal statements using the pronoun *se*.

Activities	Standards	Resources
Gramática	3.1	
66.	1.1, 3.1, 4.1	
67.	1.2, 1.3, 3.1	Audio
68.	1.3	
69.	1.2	
70.	1.1, 5.1	
71. Conexiones	1.2, 2.1, 3.1, 4.1	

Teaching Suggestions

Warm-Up / Independent Starter

- Have students respond to the following question: *¿Qué se puede hacer para proteger el medio ambiente?*

Preparation

- Have students share their responses from the Independent Starter with the rest of the class.
- Ask students who is doing the activities to protect the environment. If they respond *nosotros*, remind them that the question and responses do not have a verb in the *nosotros* form. Point out how *se* is used for impersonal actions.

Activities

68. Ask students to come up with additional expressions that would be found on signs in the rainforest.

69. For further practice, have students write sentences about what they do in school. Ask them to write two sentences for each action: one sentence with an explicit subject and the other sentence with the impersonal *se*. For example: *Nosotros almorzamos en la cafetería.* → *Se almuerza en la cafetería.*

70. Ask students to summarize their conversations by creating a travel brochure for their community. Have them present their brochures to the class.

Gramática

Ocultar el agente. El pronombre *se*

- In English, we use indefinite subjects, such as *they, you, one,* and *people,* or the passive voice when we want to present the information without telling who does the action. In Spanish, use this formula:

> se + verbo en tercera persona

Se prohíbe dar de comer a los animales.
Se permite hacer fotos.
Se habla español.
Se dice que las tortugas están en peligro de extinción.
Se cuenta que en Costa Rica cuidan mucho a los animales.
Se vive muy bien en este país.
Se trabaja mucho en este parque natural.

66 **Compara.** ¿Cómo se dice en inglés Se prohíbe hacer fotos?

67 **Rita quiere saber más...**

 ▶ **Escucha** la conversación de Rita y el guía. Responde a estas preguntas con ayuda de las fotos.

1. ¿Por qué se llama así el Parque Nacional Tortuguero?
2. ¿Qué más se puede ver en el parque?
3. ¿Qué se puede hacer para proteger la naturaleza?

426 cuatrocientos veintiséis

Differentiated Instruction

DEVELOPING LEARNERS

- Ask students to answer the following questions in complete sentences to practice the impersonal *se*.
  1. ¿Se habla español en Chile?
  2. ¿A qué hora se puede almorzar en tu escuela?
  3. ¿Se debe estudiar antes de los exámenes?
  4. ¿Se trabaja mucho en la clase de Español?
  5. ¿Se prohíbe usar teléfonos celulares en la escuela?
  6. ¿Se puede usar la computadora del director de la escuela?

EXPANDING LEARNERS

- Ask students to make a list of at least five things that they have observed about their home, their school, and their community. For example: *En casa no se puede ver la televisión si no se terminan antes las tareas. En la clase de Español se prohíbe hablar inglés. En nuestra comunidad se debe reciclar la basura.*

68 Carteles

▶ **Completa** estos carteles que vieron Diana y Rita en el parque. Utiliza formas verbales con *se*.

1.
_____ **INGLÉS**
hablar

2. **NO** _____ **TOMAR FOTOS**
permitir

3. _____ **CORTAR LAS PLANTAS**
prohibir

4. **NO** _____ **DAR COMIDA A LOS ANIMALES**
poder

69 Las notas de Rita

▶ **Transforma** estas oraciones. Usa formas verbales con *se*.

Modelo   Los turistas no pueden tomar fotos de las tortugas.
→ *Se prohíbe tomar fotos de las tortugas.*

1. Los turistas pueden hacer fotos de las plantas.
2. Los turistas pueden contratar un guía.
3. Los turistas pueden visitar el parque en lancha.
4. Los turistas no pueden cortar flores en el parque.
5. Los encargados del parque prohíben bañarse en los canales.
6. Los encargados del parque no permiten tocar a los animales.

70 Una guía turística

▶ **Habla** con tu compañero(a). ¿Qué lugares famosos hay en tu ciudad? Escribe una lista de cosas que se puede o no se puede hacer en esos lugares.

Modelo   A. *En nuestra ciudad se puede visitar el zoológico. Allí se permite tomar fotos de los animales.*
B. *Sí, pero no se puede dar comida a los animales.*

CONEXIONES: LENGUA

Las onomatopeyas

Las onomatopeyas son palabras que imitan el sonido de algo. Por ejemplo, los sonidos de los animales. Estas son algunas onomatopeyas del español:

Perro: *guau*   Pájaro: *pío*
Gato: *miau*   Gallo: *quiquiriquí*

71 **Investiga.** Busca las onomatopeyas en español de tres animales. ¿Son similares en inglés?

ERITAGE LANGUAGE LEARNERS

Have students describe how communities in their family's country of origin deal with recycling. If students don't have first-hand knowledge of how this is done, they may ask family members to describe the process. Then have them compare this method with how recycling is handled in their community in the United States. Ask them which method they think is more effective and why.

TOTAL PHYSICAL RESPONSE (TPR)

• Display a map of the world and have two students stand by it. The first student will ask the second one to point to a country where a specific language is spoken by saying: *Señala un país donde se habla* [name of language]. The second student must point to a country where this language is spoken and say, for example, *En Colombia se habla español.* If answered incorrectly, the student is out, but if answered correctly, he or she will exchange places with the first student and the game continues. Before starting, review the words for languages with students.

Gramática – Ocultar el agente. El pronombre se

 AUDIO SCRIPT
See page 391J.

CONEXIONES: LENGUA

Las onomatopeyas

Because of the phonetic differences between languages, onomatopoeia often varies from one language to another. Some additional onomatopoeia in Spanish is: *mu* (cow), *cri-cri* (cricket), *be* (sheep and goat), *jiii* (horse), *¡cataplúm!* (explosion or sudden noise), *¡achís!* (sneeze), *tictac* (clock), *talán, talán* (bell), and *gluglú* (water).

Answer Key

66. *It is forbidden to take pictures.*

67. 1. Se llama Tortuguero porque está en una zona que las tortugas visitan cada año.
2. Hay plantas, aves y muchos animales como, por ejemplo, los monos.
3. Se deben respetar las normas y cuidar la naturaleza.

68. 1. Se habla   3. Se prohíbe
2. se permite   4. se puede

69. Answers will vary. Sample answers:
1. Se permite hacer fotos de las plantas.
2. Se puede contratar a un guía.
3. Se permite visitar el parque en lancha.
4. Se prohíbe cortar flores en el parque.
5. Se prohíbe bañarse en los canales.
6. No se permite tocar a los animales.

70. Answers will vary.

71. Answers will vary.

Additional Resources

Fans Online activities
Practice Workbook

DESAFÍO 4

Comunicación

Presentation

- In this section, students will integrate the vocabulary and grammar from *Desafío 4* in order to talk about nature and the environment. They will also use impersonal statements with *se* to talk about protecting the environment.

Activities	Standards	Resources
72.	1.1, 1.2, 1.3, 2.2, 3.1	Audio
73.	1.2, 1.3, 3.1, 5.1	
74. Final del desafío	1.2, 1.3, 3.1, 5.1	

Teaching Suggestions

Warm-Up / Independent Starter

- Ask students to make a list of five things that are done in their school or in their town to protect the environment. For example: *En mi ciudad se reciclan los plásticos.*

Preparation

- Take 10 minutes to review the main vocabulary and grammar themes of the *Desafío*.
- Refer students back to the *fotonovela* for this *Desafío*. Ask them to identify the vocabulary related to nature and the environment. Then have students look for sentences in the dialogue in which the characters use the impersonal *se*. Do students understand the dialogue better now?
- Have students share their Independent Starters with the class. Then, in pairs, have them work on an educational brochure in which they inform others of the measures taken in an ideal town to protect the environment and to encourage energy conservation. If time allows, students may research what is being done in some environmentally-friendly towns around the world. They may include photos or drawings as well as impersonal statements that explain the measures that are being taken in this ideal town. Encourage them to be creative. For example: *Se apagan los televisores a las 10:00 p. m. Se comparte el automóvil para ir de compras.* Once students have finished their brochures, collect them and pass them around for the rest of the class to see and read.

Comunicación

72 **Un viaje a Costa Rica**

▶ **Lee** esta información sobre Costa Rica y complétala.

> playas   parques   senderismo   medio ambiente
>
> fauna   costa   capital   geografía

EL TURISMO EN COSTA RICA

Costa Rica es un país de ___1___ única. Posee una gran superficie de ___2___ nacionales y áreas protegidas con una rica variedad de flora y ___3___. En este país cuidan mucho la naturaleza y protegen el ___4___.

Costa Rica tiene numerosas ___5___ tanto en la ___6___ este (mar Caribe) como en la oeste (océano Pacífico).

Por eso es el destino perfecto para los amantes del ___7___, el buceo o el surf. San José, la ___8___, es una ciudad muy animada. En esta ciudad se encuentran los monumentos y sitios históricos más importantes del país. También hay museos y galerías de arte, como el Museo de Arte Costarricense o el Museo del Jade.

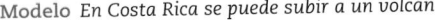

▶ **Escucha** la conversación entre Diana y una amiga. ¿Qué cosas se pueden hacer en Costa Rica? Escríbelo.

Modelo *En Costa Rica se puede subir a un volcán.*

▶ **Habla** con tu compañero(a). ¿Qué más cosas piensas que se pueden hacer en Costa Rica?

Modelo *Se dice que Costa Rica es un buen destino para hacer surf.*

Differentiated Instruction

DEVELOPING LEARNERS

- To review the vocabulary and grammar of this *Desafío*, begin by asking students to name three things, using the infinitive form of the verb, that people can do in their community (e.g., *practicar el senderismo*). Then have students use the impersonal *se* with this verb: *Se puede practicar el senderismo.* Next, have students complete the idea by saying where people can do this activity: *Se puede practicar el senderismo en el bosque.*

EXPANDING LEARNERS

- Have students think about things that people should do in your community to help protect the environment and things that they should not do. Then have them write five suggestions for each category in two separate lists, using the impersonal *se*. Select a group of students to review these suggestions and compile a master list that reflects the most practical and effective ideas. You may want to promote students' ideas in the community by sending their suggestions to a local Spanish-language newspaper.

73 Animales en peligro de extinción

▶ **Escribe.** Estos animales están en peligro de extinción. Investiga sobre uno de ellos y responde a estas preguntas.

La mariposa monarca.

El cóndor.

El caimán.

1. ¿Dónde vive este animal?
2. ¿Cómo es?
3. ¿Qué se puede hacer para protegerlo?

Final del desafío

Se espera que las primeras tortugas salgan de sus nidos esta noche.

¡Ahí están! ¡Cuántas tortugas!

Venga, vamos a llevarlas al mar.

Sí. Se cree que van hacia el reflejo de la luna en el agua.

74 Conciencia medioambiental

▶ **Completa** la entrada de Diana para la página web de su escuela. Utiliza formas verbales con *se*.

¡Salvemos a las tortugas!

___1___ que cada año mueren más de un millón de tortugas
calcular
marinas. En Costa Rica ___2___ a las tortugas, pero muchas
proteger
caen en las redes *(nets)* de los pescadores. También ___3___
saber
que muchas tortuguitas mueren porque confunden las luces
artificiales con el reflejo de la luna. Si no ___4___ algo, las
hacer
tortugas se extinguirán en pocos años.

HERITAGE LANGUAGE LEARNERS

Ask students to reflect on the dilemma of the baby sea turtles. Then ask them to compose a poem or a song to focus people's attention on their plight and to persuade listeners to come to the turtles' aid. Suggest that students add visuals to their poem and, if possible, that they accompany themselves on a musical instrument if they choose to sing a song. If their song has a chorus, encourage the entire class to sing along.

CRITICAL THINKING

• Have students imagine that they are observing the Earth 10,000 years from now. There is a species that is in danger of extinction: the human being. Enable a discussion about this dilemma: how it may have developed, what might be done to save the species or, better yet, what could have been done to prevent its demise. Encourage all students to contribute their ideas and opinions and participate in the discussion.

Activities

72. Before doing this activity, brainstorm with students what they know about Costa Rica. You may want to ask questions pertaining to the location of this country, some of its geographic features, capital city, economic resources, tourist destinations, etc. Write the students' answers to your questions on the board.

73. To extend this activity, ask students to make a list of other animals they know which are also in danger of extinction. If they don't know the names in Spanish they should look them up in a dictionary. Then ask students to answer the three questions in this activity for the animals in their list. Invite volunteers to share their answers with the class.

 AUDIO SCRIPT
See page 391J.

Answer Key

72. 1. geografía   5. playas
2. parques   6. costa
3. fauna   7. senderismo
4. medio ambiente   8. capital
▶ Answers will vary. Sample answer: En Costa Rica se puede subir a un volcán. En las playas se puede hacer surf, senderismo, buceo y todo tipo de deportes acuáticos. También se puede hacer turismo cultural. Se puede comer arroz, frijoles, verduras, frutas tropicales y mucho marisco.
▶ Answers will vary.

73. Answers will vary.

74. 1. Se calcula   3. se sabe
2. se protege   4. se hace

Additional Resources

Fans Online activities
Practice Workbook

Unit 8
TODO JUNTO

Presentation

- In this section, students will review the unit objectives and put them into practice.

Activities	Standards	Resources
75.	1.2, 1.3, 3.1	Audio
76.	1.1, 1.3, 3.1	
77.	1.2, 1.3, 5.1	
78.	1.1, 1.2, 3.1	

Teaching Suggestions

Warm-Up / Independent Starter

- Ask students to write ten questions for an imaginary interview with the mayor of their community. They should include questions about the measures taken to protect the environment, preparedness for natural disasters that may affect your community (e.g., tornadoes, earthquakes, storms, etc.), and conservation and tourism promotion of local geographic features (e.g., rivers, lakes, forests, etc.).

Preparation

- Have students work with a partner to use their questions from the Independent Starter to interview each other, as if they were interviewing the mayor. Monitor their use of Spanish in their conversations.

- Invite volunteer pairs to role-play their interviews in front of the class. Encourage the class to participate in a question and answer session after each presentation in which they bring forward to the "mayor" their concerns about different issues that affect their community.

Activities

75. After students have finished the second part of this activity, have pairs write a weather report for your community as if it were to be published in a local Spanish-language newspaper. You may show them examples from online papers in Spanish.

76. Before doing this activity, review the conjugation of the future tense with your students.

430

ESCUCHAR Y HABLAR

75 **El tiempo en Latinoamérica**

 ▶ **Escucha** y elige la opción correcta.

1. El tiempo en el continente será _____.
   a. poco variado   b. muy variado   c. muy bueno

2. Lloverá en _____.
   a. Baja California   b. Cancún   c. la península de Yucatán

3. En Centroamérica _____.
   a. hará mucho frío   b. lloverá   c. hará calor

4. En la zona del Río de la Plata las temperaturas serán _____.
   a. altas   b. bajas   c. muy altas

5. En los Andes habrá bastante _____.
   a. lluvia   b. viento   c. nieve

6. En la ciudad de Concepción _____.
   a. nevará mucho   b. lloverá mucho   c. hará mucho calor

 ▶ **Escribe** con tu compañero(a) un pronóstico del tiempo para dos países de Latinoamérica. Usen un mapa y presenten la información a la clase.

HABLAR Y ESCRIBIR

76 **¡De viaje!**

 ▶ **Habla.** En grupos pequeños, seleccionen un lugar del mundo para ir de vacaciones. Decidan adónde irán, qué países o ciudades visitarán, qué elementos geográficos verán y qué actividades harán.

Modelo

> Yo creo que podemos ir a las islas Galápagos.

> Yo prefiero ir a un lugar menos turístico.

▶ **Haz** un póster con tus compañeros(as) sobre el viaje. Después, preséntenlo a la clase.

 ▶ **Pregunta** a los demás grupos por su viaje.

430 cuatrocientos treinta

Differentiated Instruction

DEVELOPING LEARNERS

- Ask students to make predictions about the weather in their community for any six months on the calendar. First, review the vocabulary for weather and natural disasters on page 416. Then guide them in using the correct form of *hacer* as well as the future tense of other verbs that have to do with weather: *nevará, lloverá, estará, habrá,* etc. Students' predictions do not need to be detailed, but should only give a general overview for the month. For example:
  En agosto hará mucho calor y no lloverá.
  En enero hará frío y nevará mucho.
  Students may illustrate their predictions.

EXPANDING LEARNERS

- Ask students to work with a partner and discuss what they think some world leaders and other newsmakers (from the arts, sports, politics, and business world) will do in the future. Partners will discuss the same individuals, but one student must play the role of a pessimist in this discussion; the other will be the optimist. After they make their predictions, have students write them down and read them to the class. Take a vote to see if more students agree with the pessimist or the optimist.

LEER Y ESCRIBIR

77 El blog de Tim

▶ **Lee** el blog de Tim y decide si estas afirmaciones son ciertas o falsas. Si son falsas, corrígelas.

> **Una visita al Parque Nacional Volcán Isluga**
>
> Mi abuelo y yo visitamos ayer el Parque Nacional Volcán Isluga. Hacía sol, pero las temperaturas eran muy bajas. Llevábamos gorras de lana y anoraks. Cuando vi el volcán, me asusté. ¿Y si entra en erupción? Pero el abuelo me dijo que no era peligroso. Cuando llegamos a los baños termales, mi abuelo se quitó el anorak y se metió en el agua. El guía nos dijo que la temperatura de los baños podía alcanzar treinta grados centígrados, pero fuera el termómetro marcaba tres grados bajo cero. ¡Creo que mi abuelo está loco!

1. Cuando Tim y Mack llegaron al parque nacional, hacía bastante calor.
2. Tim y Mack llevaban ropa de invierno.
3. Tim no tenía miedo del volcán porque no es activo.
4. Mack se bañó en las aguas termales.
5. Tim no se bañó porque el agua estaba fría.

▶ **Imagina** que vas a visitar el Parque Nacional Volcán Isluga. ¿Cuándo irás? ¿Qué ropa llevarás? ¿Te bañarás? Escribe tu propio blog.

Modelo *Yo visitaré el Parque Nacional Volcán Isluga con mis amigos. Iremos en verano porque...*

LEER Y HABLAR

78 Pronósticos

▶ **Lee** estas opiniones sobre el futuro del planeta. Habla con tu compañero(a): ¿con qué opinión estás de acuerdo?; ¿por qué?

> Yo creo que en los próximos años habrá un calentamiento global *(global warming)* y los glaciares desaparecerán. Esto hará que suba el nivel del agua de los océanos y habrá inundaciones *(floods)* en muchos lugares. También habrá más enfermedades.
>
> Un pesimista

> Yo opino que entre todos encontraremos una solución al calentamiento global. En el futuro usaremos nuevas fuentes de energía y dejaremos de contaminar la atmósfera. Además, usaremos sistemas de reciclaje que protegerán la naturaleza.
>
> Un optimista

cuatrocientos treinta y uno **431**

Unit 8

TODO JUNTO

77. Have students write two extra true or false statements based on the reading. Then have them exchange them with a partner and answer each other's exercise.

78. Have students write four future predictions on a piece of paper about a classmate but without indicating the classmate's name (e.g., *será abogado/a, se casará a los 28 años, vivirá en Houston, tendrá tres hijos*). Then mix all the predictions in a bag and have each student pick one and read it aloud. Invite the class to try to guess who the person might be. Then ask the person to whom the predictions refer to share his or her reaction. Does he or she think the predictions have a good chance of being true?

AUDIO SCRIPT
See page 391J.

Answer Key

75. 1. b   2. c   3. b   4. c   5. c   6. b
   ▶ Answers will vary.
76. Answers will vary.
   ▶ Answers will vary.
   ▶ Answers will vary.
77. 1. Falso. Hacía frío (las temperaturas eran bajas).
   2. Cierto.
   3. Falso. Tim se asustó cuando vio el volcán.
   4. Cierto.
   5. Cierto.
   ▶ Answers will vary.
78. Answers will vary.

Additional Resources

Fans Online activities
Practice Workbook

ERITAGE LANGUAGE LEARNERS

Students will write a blog entry about a national park they have visited in their family's country of origin (or write about an imaginary trip to one). They should describe what people can do at the park, but they should include some activities that cannot be practiced there or some statements that are false. Have them exchange their papers with a classmate, who must determine which activities don't belong or which statements in the blog are false and correct them. To do this, the classmate may have to do some research.

CRITICAL THINKING

• Have students imagine that they live in a community that is divided over saving a rare bird that is in great danger of becoming extinct because its only nesting place is in certain trees that grow in an area where city planners hope to build a community hospital. Have students debate this issue, some taking the side of protecting the birds, and others the side of those who want to build the hospital. Encourage debaters to come up with other solutions: a new site for the hospital, perhaps, or moving trees and birds to a new location.

El encuentro

Presentation

- The four pairs meet in Denver, Colorado. There they bring brochures from the places they have visited to prove the completion of their challenge.
- Students will vote for the winner of the *Desafíos* along the Pan-American Highway.

Activities	Standards	Resources
Fotonovela	1.2, 2.1, 2.2, 3.1, 3.2	
79.	1.2, 1.3, 2.1, 2.2, 3.1, 3.2	
80.	1.2, 1.3, 3.1, 5.2	

Teaching Suggestions

Warm-Up / Independent Starter

- Have students answer the following questions about our pair**s' last *desafíos*:**
  - *¿Quién estuvo en la línea del ecuador?*
  - *¿Qué hicieron Diana y Rita en Costa Rica?*
  - *¿En qué lugar de Chile estuvieron Tim y Mack?*
  - *¿Quién visitó el canal de Panamá?*

Preparation

- Ask students to share their responses for the Independent Starter with the rest of the class.
- Remind students that in *Desafío 1*, Andy and Janet had to paddle a 20-mile stretch of the Panama Canal, from Lake Gatún out to the Pacific Ocean. In *Desafío 2*, **Tess and Patricia had to travel to Quito, Ecuador, to find the Earth's equator and step in the Northern and Southern hemispheres simultaneously at noon.** In *Desafío 3*, **Tim and Mack** traveled to Chile to swim in a hot spring at 12,000 feet above sea level in the Chilean Andes. In *Desafío 4*, Diana and Rita **had to** rescue some baby sea turtles in Tortuguero, a national park and turtle sanctuary in Costa Rica.
- Have students rank the *desafíos* according to difficulty, danger, and interest. These rankings will help students justify their votes at the end of the spread.

La fotonovela

- Have students read the *fotonovela* individually. Then ask them to share their opinions with the class. Which *desafío* do they find most interesting? Why? Which one was the most difficult?

El encuentro

En Denver, Colorado

The pairs gather in a park near The Colorado State Capitol Building. Each pair brings along the advertisements they wrote about the place they visited.

> Pues nosotras fuimos a Quito y estuvimos en la línea del ecuador.

> Nosotros fuimos en barca al canal de Panamá.

> ¡Y logramos cruzarlo!

> Pusimos un pie en el hemisferio norte y otro en el sur.

> Nosotros estuvimos en Chile. Yo me bañé en aguas termales.

> ¡Pero a tres grados bajo cero!

> Nosotras fuimos a Tortuguero. Y ayudamos a las tortugas a llegar al mar.

> Fue la mejor experiencia de mi vida.

432 cuatrocientos treinta y dos

Differentiated Instruction

DEVELOPING LEARNERS

- Have students read the dialogue in the *fotonovela*, paying special attention to the verbs in the preterite (i.e., *fuimos, logramos, estuvimos, pusimos, me bañé, ayudamos, fue*). Have them imagine that the participants have not yet completed their *desafío*, and are talking about what they will do. Then ask students to read the dialogue aloud, but this time changing all the verbs to the future tense.

EXPANDING LEARNERS

- Have students work with a partner and, taking turns, develop a dialogue in which one asks the other if he or she did something, and the other replies with *no*, but that he or she will do it. For example:
  A. *¿Me preparaste el anuncio de turismo?*
  B. *No, pero te lo prepararé ahora mismo.*
  Encourage students to use direct and indirect object pronouns, as in the example, whenever possible.

79 Los anuncios

▶ **Lee** los anuncios de turismo que hicieron los personajes. Elige uno y escribe un resumen del desafío.

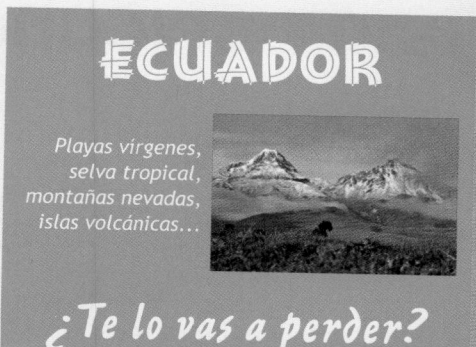

ECUADOR

Playas vírgenes,
selva tropical,
montañas nevadas,
islas volcánicas...

¿Te lo vas a perder?

PANAMÁ
El mejor lugar para conocer

Disfruta de los paisajes más bellos
del mundo rodeado de ríos, playas
y montañas que no olvidarás.

CHILE

Un país lleno de contrastes

El desierto de Atacama, Viña
del Mar, la Región de los Lagos,
la isla de Pascua... Descúbrelos.

COSTA RICA, ¡PURA VIDA!

Verás la naturaleza
más increíble, podrás
practicar tus deportes
favoritos, te olvidarás
del mundo en nuestras
maravillosas playas
y harás nuevos amigos.

> Un anuncio tiene que ser
> atractivo para captar la atención.
> Y debe incluir un eslogan.

80 Las votaciones

▶ **Decide.** ¿Qué anuncio de las parejas te gusta más? ¿Por qué?

▶ **Escribe.** Elige un destino de todos los países que visitaron las parejas y busca información para hacer un anuncio.

▶ **Presenta** tu anuncio a tus compañeros(as).

Unit 8
El encuentro

■ Put students in pairs to read the dialogues aloud. Then invite volunteer pairs to role-play the dialogues in front of the class.

■ Have students make predictions about the characters and what they will likely do in the future. Write down their answers while correcting their use of the future tense.

Activities

79. Have students read the ads and express their opinions. What country are they most likely to visit based on the ads? Ask students to identify the slogans in the ads and to write an alternative slogan for each one. Have them share their slogans with the rest of the class, and ask the class to vote for the best one.

80. As an alternative, have students work on a tourist brochure for their own town. They should include an ad with a slogan. Have students vote for the two best ones and post them on the wall.

Answer Key

79. Answers will vary.

80. Answers will vary.
   ▶ Answers will vary.
   ▶ Answers will vary.

HERITAGE LANGUAGE LEARNERS

Ask students to make a tourism ad for their family's country of origin, complete with a catchy slogan. They may model their ads on those the participants prepared, but the content must be original! They may, for example, focus on ecotourism, cultural events in major cities, indigenous festivals in towns, a program for learning Spanish and the local culture, or simply rest and relaxation on beaches or mountains, in forests or jungles. Display their ads in the classroom.

COOPERATIVE LEARNING

• Have students work in small groups and create a tourism campaign for your community. Each member of the group will concentrate on one aspect of the campaign. It may be creating a spot on TV, an announcement over the radio, a print ad, a website, or a catchy slogan that will appear in all media. After students complete their portion, they will get together and make a joint presentation of their work. Have the class vote on the best campaign.

Unit 8
MAPA CULTURAL
La ruta Panamericana

Presentation

- This section presents different facts about the regions traversed by the Pan-American Highway. The map serves as a reference point for additional readings and activities that expand on the skills students learned in this unit.

Activities	Standards	Resources
Mapa cultural	1.2, 2.1, 3.1, 3.2	Video
81.	1.2, 1.3, 3.1	
82.	1.2, 1.3, 3.1	
83.	1.2, 1.3, 2.2, 3.1, 3.2, 5.1	

Cultural Topics

- **Variedad geográfica.** The Pan-American Highway traverses North and South America, which are connected by the Isthmus of Panama. North America is north of the equator and most of South America is south of it. For this reason, the seasons are reversed. Notwithstanding the variety of landscapes and climates along the Pan-American Highway, there are some common geographical features. Both the Pacific Ocean and mountain chains border the western parts of the countries along this highway. This region is also part of the Pacific Ring of Fire, so seismic activity is high.

- **El mundo hispano: unidad y diversidad.** Some of the differences as well as some common elements in the Americas had their origins long before the arrival of Europeans. The differences in climate gave rise to the domestication of different food crops (e.g., corn in Mesoamerica and potatoes in the Andes). However, trade routes were established in pre-Hispanic times and most food crops became widespread throughout both North and South America. In this sense, a sort of "Pan-American Highway" has been in existence for centuries.

Teaching Suggestions

Warm-Up / Independent Starter

- Have students observe the map of the Pan-American Highway. Allow them two minutes to jot down what they remember about the geography of the regions along this highway.

La ruta Panamericana

América está atravesada por una gran carretera que va desde Alaska hasta el extremo sur de Argentina: la Panamericana. En total son 26.000 kilómetros que cruzan catorce países, con extensiones a varios países más.

La parte de la Panamericana comprendida entre Laredo (Texas) y la ciudad de Panamá se conoce también como carretera Interamericana.

La carretera Panamericana permite conocer la diversidad geográfica, cultural y humana de las Américas utilizando como lengua el español.

Ruta oficial
Extensiones

81 **Los países de la ruta Panamericana**

▶ **Juega.** Mira el mapa de la Panamericana durante un minuto. Después, tápalo y escribe:

1. ¿Cuáles son los países por los que pasa la ruta?
2. ¿Cuáles son las capitales de esos países?

434 cuatrocientos treinta y cuatro

Differentiated Instruction

DEVELOPING LEARNERS

- Ask students to expand on their Independent Starters. Have them go back to each *Mapa cultural* for all eight units and compile a list of the most salient geographical features and cultural characteristics of the different regions studied. Encourage students to use a graphic organizer to organize the information.

- Then have students get together with a classmate to exchange their lists. Finally, ask pairs to use their lists to create a more comprehensive list in which they describe the landscapes, geography, and cultures of the Spanish-speaking world.

EXPANDING LEARNERS

- Explain to students that the Northern and Southern hemispheres are, in some respects, mirror images of each other. Have students research this topic. To narrow the scope of their research, focus their attention on a particular region of North America and have students compare it with a particular region of South America (e.g., northern California and the Pacific Northwest compared with central and southern Chile). Ask students to look at the weather, seasons, plants, marine life, and geography of these two regions. Then have them summarize their findings and share them with the class.

434

1. Variedad geográfica

Un viaje en coche por la Panamericana nos permite pasar en unos días de los climas cálidos y húmedos de Centroamérica a los fríos y secos de la Patagonia chilena y argentina.

De la misma manera, la Panamericana nos permite ver todo tipo de paisajes: los desiertos de México o de Chile, las selvas tropicales de Centroamérica, las grandes montañas de los Andes, las extensas llanuras de la Pampa o las tierras heladas de la Patagonia. Y cada paisaje tiene su flora y su fauna características.

La variedad geográfica es un rasgo propio del mundo hispano.

(1) Carretera Panamericana a su paso por el desierto de Atacama (Chile).

2. El mundo hispano: unidad y diversidad

La carretera Panamericana une la mayor parte de los países que hablan español. Viajando por ella se puede observar la unidad y la diversidad cultural del mundo hispano.

– La herencia española actúa como un factor de unidad presente en la lengua, la religión, la arquitectura, las costumbres…

– La herencia indígena actúa como un factor de diversidad presente en la ropa, las tradiciones y las formas de vida fuera de las ciudades.

El mestizaje es la clave para comprender la riqueza cultural de los países hispanos.

(2) Mercado tradicional (Perú).

82 Visión global

▶ **Completa** una tabla como esta con la información más importante de los textos.

Variedad de paisajes	Unidad y diversidad cultural

83 Lugares emblemáticos

▶ **Investiga.** Busca información acerca de los lugares emblemáticos que pueden visitarse a través de la ruta Panamericana.

HERITAGE LANGUAGE LEARNERS

• Ask students to work with a partner to research the variants of the Spanish language spoken in the different regions traversed by the Pan-American Highway. Have pairs compile a list of the distinguishing characteristics of these dialectal variants. Ask students to include examples of lexical, pronunciation, and grammatical variations. Encourage them to include audio samples of some of the regional variants they have researched. When they have finished, ask pairs to present their findings to the class.

MULTIPLE INTELLIGENCES: Visual-Spatial Intelligence

• Have students work in small groups. Ask them to use what they have learned in all of the units of this book as well as the information they already knew about the different regions of the Americas to create an illustrated map of the Pan-American Highway. Students will copy the map of North and South America onto chart paper and then draw and color icons and other illustrations that represent the different landscapes and cultures of each country or region traversed by the highway. Exhibit students' work in the classroom.

Unit 8

MAPA CULTURAL
La ruta Panamericana

Preparation

■ Discuss, as a class, some of the geographical features from students' Independent Starters.

■ Explain that the idea of having a highway uniting the Americas was originally conceived in 1923, but construction did not begin until the end of the 1930s and it has not yet been completed. Clarify that the Pan-American Highway is not centrally administered; each country has jurisdiction over its part. The outcome is a network that is not uniform, since some countries have more resources than others.

Activities

81. Have students work with a partner to prepare a ten-question quiz based on the information in this activity. Then ask students to administer their quiz to another pair.

Answer Key

81. 1. Estados Unidos, Canadá, México, Guatemala, El Salvador, Honduras, Nicaragua, Costa Rica, Panamá, Colombia, Ecuador, Perú, Chile y Argentina.

2. Washington DC, Ottawa, Ciudad de México, Ciudad de Guatemala, San Salvador, Tegucigalpa, Managua, San José, Ciudad de Panamá, Bogotá, Quito, Lima, Santiago y Buenos Aires.

82. Answers will vary. Sample answers:
Variedad de paisajes: los desiertos de México o de Chile, las selvas tropicales de Centroamérica, las montañas de los Andes, las llanuras de la Pampa, las tierras heladas de la Patagonia
Unidad y diversidad cultural: La herencia española es factor de unidad. La herencia indígena es factor de diversidad.
El mestizaje es esencial para entender la riqueza cultural de los países hispanos.

83. Answers will vary.

Additional Resources

Fans Online activities
Practice Workbook

LECTURA

El Tapón de Darién: un corte en la ruta Panamericana

Presentation

- In this section, students will practice and extend their reading skills by reading an article about the Darien Gap. In addition, students will focus on recognizing the structure and elements of argumentative texts.

Activities	Standards	Resources
Lectura	1.2, 2.1, 3.1, 3.2, 5.2	
84.	1.2, 1.3, 2.1, 3.1	
85.	1.1, 1.2, 1.3, 2.1, 3.1	
86.	1.3, 3.1, 5.2	
Tu desafío	1.2, 3.1, 3.2, 5.1	

Teaching Suggestions

Warm-Up / Independent Starter

- Ask students to locate on a map the Isthmus of Panama and the Darien region, also in Panama.

Preparation

- Before reading the passage, ask for a volunteer to read the Reading Strategy box aloud. Then discuss, as a class, who would use this type of text, when it is most frequently used, and where we usually find examples of it. If time allows, you may want to show students examples of argumentative texts in Spanish-speaking newspapers and magazines (e.g., letters to the editor, environmental articles, editorials, etc.).

- Refer students back to the Independent Starter and ask a volunteer to point to the Isthmus of Panama. Explain that scientists believe that the Panamanian Peninsula joined with South America about 4 million years ago. The formation of this isthmus, or land bridge, between the two continents was an important geologic event with vast consequences on Earth's climate. Since water could no longer flow freely between the Atlantic and Pacific oceans, the Atlantic currents formed a new current pattern: the Gulf Stream. This isthmus also opened the way for animals and plants to move between the continents, contributing to the biodiversity we see today.

El Tapón de Darién: un corte en la ruta Panamericana

READING STRATEGY
Read argumentative texts

Argumentative texts are written in order to defend an idea or an opinion with supporting reasons.

Argumentative texts have two fundamental parts: the thesis and the arguments.

- The **thesis** is the idea that is going to be defended.
- The **arguments** are the reasons that support the thesis.

Argumentative texts use cause-and-effect transition words and phrases, especially the conjunction *porque*.

La carretera Panamericana se planeó entre 1923 y 1939 como un sistema para unir los diferentes países de las Américas. Hoy solo faltan por construir 87 kilómetros en una zona conocida como el Tapón de Darién, entre Colombia y Panamá.

El Tapón de Darién es un obstáculo geográfico natural formado por cordilleras, manglares[1] y selvas tropicales. Y es una zona de extraordinario valor ecológico habitada por indígenas y declarada Reserva de la Biosfera y Patrimonio de la Humanidad por la UNESCO.

La construcción de la carretera en la zona de Darién tiene partidarios[2] y detractores:

- Los partidarios de la construcción defienden que la carretera es un impulso[3] económico para la zona y beneficia a toda América porque facilita el paso de personas y mercancías.

- Los detractores de la construcción piensan que la carretera pone en peligro el equilibrio ecológico de la zona y a las comunidades de indígenas que allí viven. Y argumentan que Darién es una barrera natural para evitar el paso de las enfermedades entre Centroamérica y Suramérica.

Hoy hay un proyecto para construir en Colombia un tramo hasta la frontera con Panamá, pero la polémica[4] sigue abierta.

---

1. *mangrove swamps*   2. *supporters*   3. *boost*   4. *controversy*

Differentiated Instruction

DEVELOPING LEARNERS

- To help students understand how argumentative texts are organized, ask them to put the following sentences in order to create a paragraph.
  - *La construcción de la carretera en esta zona beneficiará el comercio y creará riqueza.* (2)
  - *Aún no hay un acuerdo sobre la construcción de la Panamericana en el Tapón de Darién.* (4)
  - *Sin embargo, muchos piensan que esta carretera dañará la ecología de la zona.* (3)
  - *La carretera Panamericana se corta en el Tapón de Darién y hay una propuesta para continuarla.* (1)

EXPANDING LEARNERS

- Explain that debates stimulate a person's argumentative thinking and help him or her reflect on a topic from several perspectives. Ask students to read the passage about the Darien Gap again and consult their notes on the subject. Then divide students into two groups. Assign each group one of the arguments presented in the reading and allow them several minutes to prepare their opening statements and arguments. Act as the moderator and hold the debate.

- After this debate, students should be better prepared to work on their argumentative text for activity 86.

COMPRENSIÓN

84 **El Tapón de Darién**

▶ **Responde** a estas preguntas.

1. ¿Cuántos kilómetros faltan para completar la Panamericana?
2. ¿Dónde está el Tapón de Darién?
3. ¿Qué accidentes geográficos (*geographical features*) forman el Tapón de Darién?
4. ¿Por qué hay gente que piensa que la construcción de la carretera en Darién es buena para toda América?
5. ¿Por qué otros piensan que la construcción de la carretera es perjudicial (*damaging*) para la zona?

ESTRATEGIA Leer textos argumentativos

85 **Opiniones y razones**

▶ **Copia** este esquema del texto y complétalo.

Tema	

Tesis 1	Tesis 2
PARTIDARIOS	DETRACTORES
La construcción de la carretera es buena.	
Argumentos	**Argumentos**
A FAVOR	EN CONTRA

 ▶ **Habla.** ¿Qué opinas tú? Da argumentos y contrasta tu opinión con la de tus compañeros(as).

86 **Tus argumentos**

▶ **Escribe** un texto argumentativo sobre el tema «¿Naturaleza o progreso?». Primero haz un esquema con tu tesis y dos argumentos.

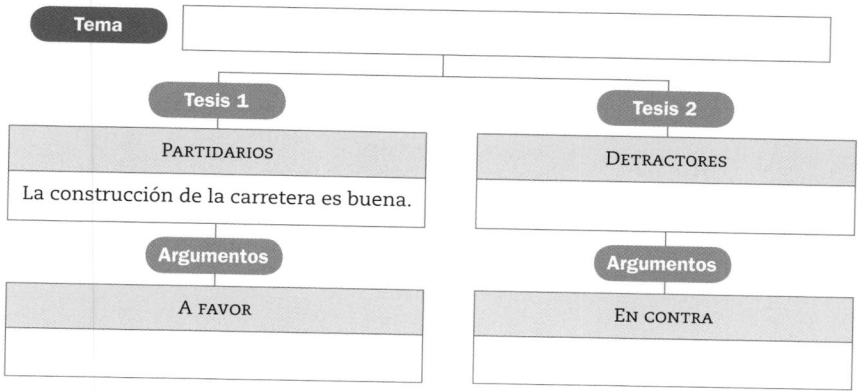

TU DESAFÍO 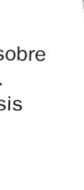 Visita la página web para aprender más sobre la zona de Darién.

cuatrocientos treinta y siete 437

El Tapón de Darién: un corte en la ruta Panamericana

Activities

84. Have students work with a partner to answer these questions. Ask partners to attempt to answer the questions without referring back to the text. Then have them verify their answers.

86. You may want to write some transition words and phrases on the board so that students use them in their texts. For example: *por lo tanto* (therefore), *así que* (so), *sin embargo* (however), *por otra parte* (on the other hand), *aunque* (although), *a pesar de* (in spite of).

Answer Key

84. 1. Faltan 87 km.
2. Está entre Panamá y Colombia.
3. En esta zona hay cordilleras, manglares y selvas tropicales.
4. Porque facilita el paso de personas y mercancías, y eso crea un impulso económico para la zona.
5. Porque pone en peligro la ecología del lugar y a las comunidades indígenas de la región. La carretera también facilita el paso de las enfermedades de un continente a otro.

85. Answers will vary. Sample answers:
Tema: La construcción de la Panamericana en la zona del Tapón de Darién.
Tesis 1: La construcción de la carretera es buena.
Argumentos a favor: Supone un impulso económico para la zona. Facilita el paso de personas y mercancías. Beneficia a toda América.
Tesis 2: La construcción de la carretera es perjudicial.
Argumentos en contra: Pone en peligro el equilibrio ecológico. Afecta a las comunidades indígenas. Facilita el paso de enfermedades.
▶ Answers will vary.

86. Answers will vary.

Additional Resources

Fans Online activities

ERITAGE LANGUAGE LEARNERS

Ask students to research one of these three indigenous peoples who inhabit the Darien Gap: Embera, Wounaan, Kuna. Have students gather information regarding the group's history, culture, lifestyle, and the areas where they live. Ask students to include pictures, graphic organizers, and any other audiovisual materials they think would enhance their presentation.

Then have students do a class presentation. If time allows, encourage a question and answer session at the end of each presentation.

CRITICAL THINKING

• Explain that people describe the Darien region as *despoblada* (uninhabited), *vacía* (empty), *salvaje* (wild), *inhóspita* (inhospitable). But these lands are not empty. The Embera, Wounaan, and Kuna call this region home, and some argue that by declaring these lands "empty," the indigenous communities are deprived of their voice.

• Ask students to think about the construction of the Pan-American Highway from the point of view of the peoples who inhabit this region. Discuss, as a class, what the feelings and opinions of these communities might be towards the construction of this road.

Unit 8

REPASO

Vocabulario

Presentation

- In this section, students will review all key vocabulary from the unit, organized by themes, to prepare for an assessment. Students will complete practice activities for each of the four *Desafíos*.

Activities	Standards	Resources
1.	1.2, 3.1	
2.	1.2, 3.1	
3.	1.3	
4.	1.2, 1.3, 5.2	

Teaching Suggestions

Warm-Up / Independent Starter

- Give students two minutes to list all of the geographical features (e.g., rivers, mountains, lakes, oceans), weather conditions, and flora and fauna they remember from the United States.

Preparation

- Go over the *Repaso* presentation with the class. You may want to model pronunciation for words that cause students difficulty. Then ask them to share their Independent Starters with the class. How much do students know about the geography, weather, and nature of the United States?

- Divide the class into five groups and assign each group one of these regions: 1. Northeast (ME, NH, VT, MA, RI, CT, NY, PA, NJ, DE); 2. Midwest (WI, MI, IL, IN, OH, MO, ND, SD, NE, KS, MN, IA); 3. South (MD, VA, WV, NC, SC, GA, FL, KY, TN, MS, AL, OK, TX, AR, LA); 4. Mountain (ID, MT, WY, NV, UT, CO, AZ, NM); 5. West (CA, OR, WA, AK, HI). Ask groups to research salient geographical features, weather patterns, and flora and fauna of their region, as well as two of the most pressing environmental issues in their region.

- Ask groups to organize their information on chart paper. Encourage them to look for pictures of some of the places featured in their report. Then have groups present their findings to the class. After each presentation, have volunteers from the class locate, on a map of the United States, the region and some of the geographical features mentioned in the presentation.

438

REPASO Vocabulario

Geografía

África	Africa	la bahía	bay
América del Norte/Norteamérica	North America	el bosque	forest
América del Sur/Suramérica	South America	el cañón	canyon
Antártida	Antarctica	la cascada/la catarata	waterfall
Asia	Asia	la colina	hill
Europa	Europe	el mar	sea
Oceanía	Oceania	la montaña	mountain
Océano Atlántico	Atlantic Ocean	la pradera	prairie
Océano Glacial Ártico	Arctic Ocean	el puerto	port
Océano Glacial Antártico	Southern Ocean	el río	river
Océano Índico	Indian Ocean	la selva	jungle
Océano Pacífico	Pacific Ocean	el valle	valley

Países

Alemania	Germany	norte	north
Brasil	Brazil	sur	south
Canadá	Canada	este	east
China	China	oeste	west
España	Spain	noreste	northeast
Francia	France	noroeste	northwest
Italia	Italy	sureste	southeast
Japón	Japan	suroeste	southwest
Portugal	Portugal		
Reino Unido	United Kingdom		
ecuador		equator	
Trópico de Cáncer		Tropic of Cancer	
Trópico de Capricornio		Tropic of Capricorn	

El tiempo meteorológico

Está nublado.	It's cloudy.
Hace calor.	It's hot.
Hace frío.	It's cold.
Hace sol.	It's sunny.
Hace viento.	It's windy.
bajo cero	below zero
los grados	degrees
la temperatura	temperature
el termómetro	thermometer
la erupción	eruption
la lluvia/llover	rain/to rain
la nieve/nevar	snow/to snow
el relámpago	lightning
el terremoto	earthquake
la tormenta	storm
el tornado	tornado

La naturaleza y el medio ambiente

el caballo	horse	ahorrar energía	to save energy
el cerdo	pig	conservar	to conserve
la gallina	hen	la contaminación	pollution
el gallo	rooster	cuidar	to take care of
la oveja	sheep	las especies	
la vaca	cow	en peligro de extinción	endangered species
el águila	eagle	los incendios forestales	forest fires
el cocodrilo	crocodile	el medio ambiente	environment
el elefante	elephant	plantar un árbol	to plant a tree
el lobo	wolf	proteger	to protect
el mono	monkey	los recursos naturales	natural resources
el oso	bear	la sequía	drought

438 cuatrocientos treinta y ocho

Differentiated Instruction

DEVELOPING LEARNERS

- Ask students to create a vocabulary booklet with the four categories studied in this unit (i.e., *geografía*, *el clima*, *países*, *la naturaleza y el medio ambiente*). The booklet will consist of four spreads (i.e., eight pages), one for each category. Allow students to organize the vocabulary in each category as they see fit. Encourage them to illustrate their spreads. They may use images from magazines or the Internet.

- Tell students they should use this booklet as a study tool. They may also use it to work on the four vocabulary activities from this *Repaso*.

EXPANDING LEARNERS

- Ask students to create a true/false activity to quiz their classmates on the vocabulary. The activity should consist of ten statements, some false (*falso*) and some true (*cierto*), about the physical features, weather, location, and nature of your community. For example: *En* [name of community] *nieva en invierno.* [Name of community] *está al noreste de la capital del estado.*

- Have students proofread their quiz before they administer it to a classmate. Then have them take each other's quizzes. How did they do? Do they know their community well?

DESAFÍO 1

1 **Geografía.** Une las dos columnas.

Ⓐ
1. África
2. El Everest
3. El Yunque
4. El Mississippi
5. El Atlántico

Ⓑ
a. un río
b. un bosque tropical
c. un continente
d. un océano
e. una montaña

DESAFÍO 2

2 **¿Cierto o falso?** Decide si estas afirmaciones son ciertas o falsas.

1. Beijing es la capital de Guatemala.
2. Arizona está al suroeste de Colorado.
3. España está en el continente europeo.
4. Maine está al sureste de los Estados Unidos.

DESAFÍO 3

3 **¿Qué tiempo hace?** Mira las fotografías y escribe qué tiempo hace.

DESAFÍO 4

4 **¡Cuántas cosas!** Responde a estas preguntas.

1. ¿Cómo protegen el medio ambiente en tu escuela?
2. ¿Qué hace tu familia para ahorrar energía?
3. ¿Qué puedes hacer tú para proteger a los animales en peligro de extinción?

Unit 8
REPASO
Vocabulario

Activities

1. To extend this activity, have students work with a partner to add *un cañón* (e.g., Colorado), *un lago* (e.g., Superior), *una catarata* (e.g., Niagara), *una bahía* (e.g., Chesapeake), and *un puerto* (e.g., Houston, TX). Then have pairs exchange their extended activity with another pair and complete each other's activity.

3. Ask students to work in small groups and look for pictures on the Internet or in magazines that depict different weather conditions. Have them write a caption for each picture describing the weather depicted.

4. After students have finished this activity, discuss, as a class, their answer to question 3. You may want to list on the board some of your students' ideas. Then, hold a class vote to see which are the three most effective ideas according to students.

Answer Key

1. 1. c   2. e   3. b   4. a   5. d
2. 1. Falso   3. Cierto
   2. Cierto   4. Falso
3. Answers will vary. Sample answers:
   1. Está nublado. Parece que hace frío.
   2. Está nublado y llueve.
   3. Hace viento, llueve y está nublado.
   4. Hace sol y calor.
4. Answers will vary.

Additional Resources

Fans Online activities
Practice Workbook

HERITAGE LANGUAGE LEARNERS

Have students research the geography of a region, state, or province of their heritage country. Ask them to list the following:
- Location of the region in relation to the capital city of the country.
- Main geographical features.
- Weather conditions throughout the year.
- Typical flora and fauna.
- Environmental issues.

Ask students to organize their data in a logical and visually attractive manner to do a class presentation.

COOPERATIVE LEARNING

- Have students work in small groups to create a campaign to save energy and protect the environment in your school. Be sure there is a mix of language levels and learning styles in each group. Ask groups to assign specific tasks to each group member and encourage the use of audiovisual aids to support their presentations.

- Allocate 10-minute time slots to each group and have them present their campaign to the class. Then hold a class vote for the most convincing, most appealing, and most informative campaigns.

REPASO

Gramática

Presentation

- Students will review grammatical structures presented in the unit. Each grammar point is cross-referenced to the corresponding page on which it was introduced. The activities here provide systematic practice by *Desafío*.

Activities	Standards	Resources
5.	1.2, 1.3, 3.1	
6.	1.2, 1.3	
7.	1.2, 1.3	
8.	1.3	
9. Cultura	1.3, 2.1, 2.2, 3.1	

Teaching Suggestions

Warm-Up / Independent Starter

- Ask students to answer the following questions in writing:
  1. *¿Quién es, para ti, el mejor cantante? ¿Y la mejor actriz?*
  2. *¿Qué vas a hacer este verano?*
  3. *¿Qué tiempo hará mañana en tu comunidad?*
  4. *¿Qué se puede hacer para ahorrar energía en tu escuela?*

Preparation

- Ask students to use the questions in the Independent Starter to interview at least three classmates. Do they have similar answers?
- Go over the *Repaso* presentation with the class. Then ask students to check their answers from the Independent Starter and identify the different grammar structures being reviewed in this *Repaso*.

Activities

6. Once students have finished, have them interview a partner using the following question: *¿Qué vas a hacer pasado mañana después de salir de la escuela?* Then ask partners to report their answers to the class. Keep a tally of their responses on the board. Then ask students the following question regarding the results posted on the board: *¿Cuál es la actividad más popular de la clase pasado mañana?*

440

El superlativo relativo (pág. 402)

el la los las	+ nombre +	más menos	+ adjetivo +	de… que…

El Amazonas es el río más largo del **mundo**.
Este es el país más bonito que **conozco**.

El futuro (pág. 418)

VERBOS REGULARES

ENTRAR	COMER	SEGUIR
entraré	comeré	seguiré
entrarás	comerás	seguirás
entrará	comerá	seguirá
entraremos	comeremos	seguiremos
entraréis	comeréis	seguiréis
entrarán	comerán	seguirán

VERBOS IRREGULARES

poder → podr-
poner → pondr-
salir → saldr-
tener → tendr-
venir → vendr-

decir → dir-
hacer → har-

querer → querr-
saber → sabr-

Expresar planes e intenciones (pág. 410)

presente

La semana que viene viajamos a Chile.

ir a + infinitivo

El próximo año vamos a ir a Canadá.

cuando + presente de subjuntivo

Cuando estemos en Ecuador, vamos a ir a Mitad del Mundo.

Expresiones temporales de futuro

ahora	now
luego/después	later
en un rato	in a while
en media hora	in half an hour
hoy	today
esta mañana	this morning
esta tarde	this afternoon
esta noche	tonight
mañana	tomorrow
pasado mañana	the day after tomorrow
el lunes que viene / el próximo lunes	next Monday
el mes que viene / el próximo mes	next month
el año que viene / el próximo año	next year

Ocultar el agente. El pronombre se (pág. 426)

Se prohíbe dar de comer a los animales.
Se permite hacer fotos.
Se habla español.
Se dice que las tortugas están en peligro de extinción.

Se cuenta que en Costa Rica cuidan mucho a los animales.
Se vive muy bien en este país.
Se trabaja mucho en este parque natural.

Differentiated Instruction

DEVELOPING LEARNERS

- Ask students to write two versions for each of the following sentences: one using the future tense of the verb in parentheses and the other using the formula *ir a* + infinitive.
  1. *La próxima semana … (llover). (lloverá / va a llover)*
  2. *Cuando esté en la universidad, yo … (pasar) un semestre en Costa Rica. (pasaré / voy a pasar)*
  3. *Este verano Tom y yo … (trabajar) en un restaurante. (trabajaremos / vamos a trabajar)*
  4. *El equipo de baloncesto de la escuela … (ganar) el campeonato. (ganará / va a ganar)*

EXPANDING LEARNERS

- Ask students to interview two classmates about their plans after they graduate from high school. Give students two to three minutes to write down their questions. Remind them to use both the future tense and the formula *ir a* + infinitive to ask and answer questions about future plans.
- Once students have their questionnaire, ask them to interview two classmates and to write down their answers. Then have students write a two-paragraph summary of their interviews. They should compare in their paragraphs their classmates' plans with their own plans.

DESAFÍO 1

5 **Tus conocimientos.** Une los elementos de las tres columnas y escribe oraciones.

1. Asia	es el continente	más pequeño del mundo.
2. El Everest	es la montaña	más largo de América.
3. El Amazonas	es el río	más poblado del mundo.
4. China	es el país	más alta del mundo.
5. Oceanía	es el continente	más grande del mundo.

DESAFÍO 2

6 **¿Hacemos planes?** Decide cuáles de estas oraciones se refieren a planes futuros.

1. El próximo verano vamos de vacaciones a Japón.
2. Pasado mañana voy a ir a una fiesta.
3. Estoy buscando a mi gato hace una semana.
4. Cuando visite a mi abuela, voy a escribirte un correo.

DESAFÍO 3

7 **En el futuro.** Completa estas oraciones. Usa el futuro.

1. El próximo verano mi hermano _____ a la universidad.
   _{ir}
2. Mis padres _____ de compras pasado mañana.
   _{salir}
3. Alejandro y yo _____ un examen el viernes que viene.
   _{tener}
4. Tú _____ la tarea de Biología mañana.
   _{hacer}

DESAFÍO 4

8 **¿Se puede saber...?** Responde a estas preguntas con oraciones completas.

1. ¿Cómo se llama tu mejor amigo(a)?
2. ¿Qué se dice cuando llega un(a) chico(a) nuevo(a) al aula?
3. ¿Qué se puede hacer en tu clase de Español?
4. ¿Qué idiomas se hablan en tu escuela?

CULTURA

9 **Por la Panamericana.** Responde a las siguientes preguntas.

1. ¿Qué océanos une el canal de Panamá?
2. ¿Dónde están las islas Galápagos?
3. ¿Qué es el Cinturón de Fuego del Pacífico?
4. ¿Qué significa la expresión «¡Pura vida!»?

HERITAGE LANGUAGE LEARNERS

Explain to students that in addition to expressing something that will happen in the future, the future tense also has these uses: 1. To express a probability or a supposition (e.g., *Serán las 12:00 p. m. No sé por qué no vino hoy a clase, estará enferma.*). 2. To indicate an intense demand (e.g., *¡Lo harás porque lo digo yo!*).

Ask students to think of three more examples for each of these two uses of the future tense in Spanish. Then have students discuss their examples with the class and explain these uses of the future tense.

MULTIPLE INTELLIGENCES:
Verbal-Linguistic Intelligence

• Explain to students that Spanish commonly uses the present tense for actions that will occur in the near future (e.g. *Te llamo esta noche.* – I will call you tonight.). Also we use the verb *querer* to express a willingness to do something (e.g., *¿Quieres llamar a Carlos?* – Will you call Carlos?).

• Have pairs of students translate these sentences into Spanish.
   1. Will you go to the supermarket? (*¿Quieres ir al supermercado?*)
   2. I'll answer your message in a few minutes. (*Te contesto el mensaje en unos minutos.*)

REPASO

Gramática

8. Once students have finished, discuss their answers to question 3. You may want to list their answers on the board. Then ask: *¿Qué no se puede hacer en la clase de Español?* Give students a couple of minutes to answer this question and add their answers to your list on the board.

9. Ask students to complete this activity without referring back to their textbooks. Then have them compare answers with a partner.

Answer Key

5. 1. Asia es el continente más grande del mundo.
2. El Everest es la montaña más alta del mundo.
3. El Amazonas es el río más largo de América.
4. China es el país más poblado del mundo.
5. Oceanía es el continente más pequeño del mundo.

6. Planes futuros: 1, 2, 4.

7. 1. irá   3. tendremos
2. saldrán   4. harás

8. Answers will vary. Sample answers:
1. Se llama…
2. Se dice: "¡Bienvenido!"
3. Se puede hablar español.
4. Se habla inglés y un poco de español.

9. Answers will vary. Sample answers:
1. El océano Atlántico y el Pacífico.
2. Están al oeste de Ecuador, en el océano Pacífico.
3. Es una zona con muchos volcanes y gran actividad sísmica. Está alrededor de la cuenca del océano Pacífico.
4. Esta expresión se utiliza mucho en Costa Rica para saludar, despedirse, dar las gracias, decir que algo está bien, etc. Significa tranquilidad, respeto por la naturaleza y amabilidad.

Additional Resources

Fans Online activities
Practice Workbook

Unit 8
PROYECTO
La predicción meteorológica

Presentation

- In this section, students will apply the vocabulary, grammar, and cultural information they have learned in this unit to write a script and then present a seven-day weather forecast for South America.

Activities	Standards	Resources
Paso 1	1.2, 3.1	
Paso 2	1.2, 3.1	
Paso 3	1.2, 1.3, 3.1	
Paso 4	3.1	
Paso 5	1.3, 3.1, 5.2	
Paso 6	1.1, 1.3, 3.1	
Paso 7	1.1, 1.3, 3.1, 5.2	

Teaching Suggestions

Warm-Up / Independent Starter

- Have students use what they know about the geography of South America to make an informed guess about the different climate conditions of that continent.

Preparation

- Explain that South America encompasses a great variety of climates, but over half of the continent lies in the equatorial zone, making tropical and subtropical conditions prevalent in most regions. The Andes Mountain Range is another important factor in the climate of the western coast.

- Ask students to watch a weather report on a Spanish-language channel beforehand. Alternatively, you may record one of these programs and play it for the class. Discuss, as a class, some of the characteristics of these reports.

Step-by-Step Instructions

Paso 1

- Ask students to trace the map of South America on chart paper. Have them label each country and shade the countries in different colors. Students should also label the capital city for each country, major geographical features, and the continent's climatic regions. Students will use this map for their presentation and as a reference for themselves when doing research.

442

Un boletín sobre
la predicción meteorológica

Today you are an honorary weather reporter for the local news. They have asked you to do a seven–day forecast for South America.

PASO 1 Busca información sobre las zonas climáticas

- Find information about climatic zones in South America and take notes. Is the climate arid, tropical, temperate…?

PASO 2 Busca información sobre qué tiempo hace ahora

- Find information about the current weather conditions in each place and take notes. You can use the Internet, newspapers, etc.

PASO 3 Decide qué tiempo hará los próximos días

- Take notes about the weather conditions in each place for the next week. You can use these questions:
  - –¿Subirán o bajarán las temperaturas?
  - –¿Lloverá?
  - –¿Nevará?
  - –¿Hará viento?
  - –¿Hará sol o estará nublado?

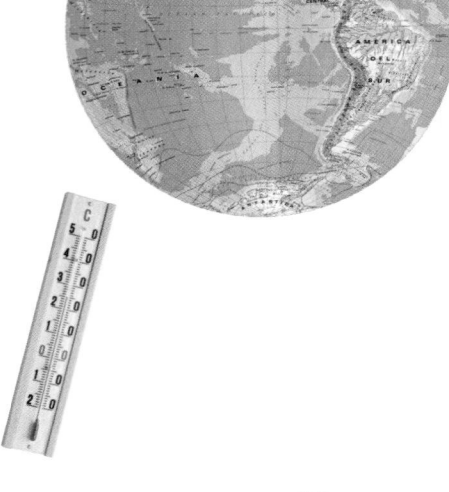

PASO 4 Prepara el material gráfico

- Since you are presenting the weather, you will need a map as your background.
- Clearly mark your map with the places and weather conditions you selected in previous steps. Design symbols to illustrate your map.

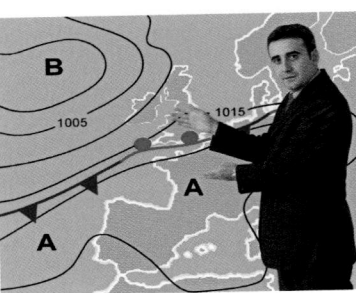

442 cuatrocientos cuarenta y dos

Rubric for Evaluation

	Content	Organization	Presentation
1 point	Limited relevance. Information is incomplete or not based on research. Little Spanish is used.	Inefficient use of time. Report is disorganized, unclear, and difficult to follow.	Unclear communication, not fluent. Many errors in vocabulary and grammar.
3 points	Basic information is correct. Relevant information but lacks significance. Spanish is used most of the time.	Time is used well. Report is mostly organized but lacks some clarity. It is relatively easy to follow.	Clear communication, mostly fluent. Mostly correct vocabulary and grammar.

PASO 5 Escribe el boletín

- Write the script for your weather report.
  - Organize your weather report from west to east or north to south, so look at your map as you write the script.
  - Keep in mind you will be doing a seven–day report, so be as clear and concise as possible.
  - Remember to focus on clear communication, but you can add humor and props to your weather report.

PASO 6 Ensaya

- Ask a classmate to look over your script to check for grammatical and spelling errors.
- Practice your weather report before presenting it to the class.

Mañana habrá mucha lluvia en la costa oeste.

PASO 7 Haz tu presentación

- Present your weather report to the class.
- Allow your classmates to ask you questions about your weather report.

	Content	Organization	Presentation
points	Relevant, interesting information. Many details and significance are highlighted. Spanish is used exclusively.	Time is used wisely. Report is well organized, concise, and clear. It is very easy to follow.	Clear communication. Fluent delivery. Correct and complete vocabulary and grammar.

Unidad 8

Autoevaluación

¿Qué has aprendido en esta unidad?

Do these activities to evaluate how well you can manage in Spanish.

Evaluate your skills. For each item, say Very well, Well, or I need more practice.

a. Can you identify, compare, and describe places?

▶ Describe three geographical features in the world. Your classmate guesses which ones you are talking about.

b. Can you talk about future plans?

▶ Ask three classmates about their plans for next week.

▶ Role–play with a classmate. Pretend to plan a trip to somewhere in the world and talk about your plans.

c. Can you express future events?

▶ Tell your partner five things you will probably do when you get older.

d. Can you make impersonal statements?

▶ Ask three classmates what they do to protect the environment.

▶ Tell five things that are allowed and three things that are prohibited in your Spanish class. Use the structure *(No) Se puede.*

PROYECTO

La predicción meteorológica

Paso 2

- To narrow the scope of the search, have students research the weather conditions in South America's climatic regions rather than in each individual country. Suggest that they use a note card for each region.

Paso 3

- Ask students to use the same note cards from *Paso 2* to add this *Paso's* information.

Paso 4

- Ask students to research and use the symbols weather forecasters use.

Paso 5

- Have students label their map with the cardinal directions in Spanish.

Paso 6

- If students have access to audio recording equipment, encourage them to record their weather report and use the recording to improve their pronunciation and polish their delivery.

Paso 7

- Remind students to keep eye contact with their audience. They should not look at their weather map or at their notes for more than a few seconds at a time.

Evaluation

- Distribute copies of the rubric to students. Discuss the evaluation criteria and explain how this project will be graded. Encourage students to refer to the rubric as they prepare their projects.

Content

- Ask students to check their script against their map to make sure that the information matches. Remind them to check both their map and script for accuracy and relevance. Have students pay special attention to the use of the future tense in their statements.

Organization

- An efficient use of time is of the utmost importance in any newscast. Ask students to time themselves during their rehearsal and adjust their script accordingly.

Presentation

- Encourage creativity and a presentation style that will hold their classmates' attention.

RESUMEN DE GRAMÁTICA

Nouns

Nouns are words for people, animals, places, and things. Spanish nouns have a masculine and a feminine form. Most nouns that end in -o are masculine, and most nouns that end in -a are feminine. Nouns that end in -e or in a **consonant** can be either masculine or feminine.

Masculine form	Feminine form	Examples
Ends in -o.	Changes -o to -a.	el niño → la niña
Ends in a consonant.	Adds -a.	el profesor → la profesora

Nouns can be singular (one person or thing) or plural (more than one person or thing).

Singular form	Plural form	Examples
Ends in a vowel.	Adds -s.	el edificio → los edificios
Ends in a consonant.	Adds -es.	el ascensor → los ascensores

Articles

Articles agree in gender and number with the noun they accompany. That is, they show the same gender and number as the noun.

Definite articles refer to a specific noun. In English, the definite article has only one form: *the*. In Spanish, there are four forms: el, la, los, and las.

Indefinite articles refer to a nonspecific noun. In Spanish, the indefinite article has four forms: un, una (*a* or *an*) and unos, unas (*some* or *a few*).

DEFINITE ARTICLES

	Masculine	Feminine
Singular	el	la
Plural	los	las

INDEFINITE ARTICLES

	Masculine	Feminine
Singular	un	una
Plural	unos	unas

Contractions

The combination of the preposition a and de with the definite article el results in a contraction.

a + el → al	de + el → del

Adjectives

Adjectives describe nouns and in Spanish usually follow the noun:
el músico **calvo**, la cantante **morena**.

Spanish adjectives can be masculine or feminine, singular or plural.
They must agree with the noun both in gender and in number.

End in -o: 4 forms	el chico simpático la chica simpática	los chicos simpáticos las chicas simpáticas
End in -e: 2 forms	el niño inteligente la niña inteligente	los niños inteligentes las niñas inteligentes
End in a consonant: usually, 2 forms	el señor débil la señora débil	los señores débiles las señoras débiles

Adjectives of Nationality

Adjectives that express nationality also have variation of gender and number.

End in -o or in a consonant: 4 forms	el niño español la niña española	los niños españoles las niñas españolas
End in -e: 2 forms	el señor canadiense la señora canadiense	los señores canadienses las señoras canadienses

Demonstrative adjectives and pronouns

To indicate where something or someone is located in relation
to the person speaking, use demonstratives. Demonstrative adjectives
and pronouns show gender and number.

Demonstrative pronouns can be used to point or to avoid repetition.
They mean *this one / that one* or *these / those*.

Distance from speaker	Singular		Plural	
	Masculine	Feminine	Masculine	Feminine
Near	este	esta	estos	estas
At a distance	ese	esa	esos	esas
Far away	aquel	aquella	aquellos	aquellas

Neutral forms esto, eso, and aquello are always pronouns. They are used
to refer to situations or facts, and to present or to refer to unknown objects.

Possessive adjectives and pronouns

Possessive adjectives and pronouns express ownership. Possessive adjectives agree with the noun they accompany. They agree with the thing (or person) possessed, not with the owner. They can be placed before or after the noun they accompany.

Possessive pronouns are used instead of a noun. The forms are the same as those of the possessive adjectives after the noun. When the possessive pronoun is used to identify, it is preceded by an article.

	Before the noun (*mi tío*)				After the noun (*un tío mío*)			
	Singular		Plural		Singular		Plural	
	Masculine	Feminine	Masculine	Feminine	Masculine	Feminine	Masculine	Feminine
my	mi		mis		mío	mía	míos	mías
your (inf.)	tu		tus		tuyo	tuya	tuyos	tuyas
his, her, your	su		sus		suyo	suya	suyos	suyas
our	nuestro	nuestra	nuestros	nuestras	nuestro	nuestra	nuestros	nuestras
your (inf.)	vuestro	vuestra	vuestros	vuestras	vuestro	vuestra	vuestros	vuestras
their, your	su		sus		suyo	suya	suyos	suyas

Indefinites

To indicate existence or quantity in an imprecise way or to indicate absence, use indefinites.

ningún, ninguno(a)	*no, (not) any, none*	alguien	*someone*
algún, alguno(a)(os)(as)	*a few, any, one, some*	algo	*something*
poco(a)(os)(as)	*some, few*	nadie	*nobody*
mucho(a)(os)(as)	*many, a lot of*	nada	*nothing*
todo(a)(os)(as)	*all, every, throughout*		
demasiado(a)(os)(as)	*too much, too many*		

Before a masculine singular noun, use algún or ningún instead of alguno and ninguno.

Alguien and nadie refer to people.

Algo and nada refer to things.

Comparatives and superlatives

Comparisons of equality and inequality

To express equality, use:

tan + adjective + como	*as … as*
verb + tanto como	*… as much as …*

To express inequality, use:

más / menos + adjective + que	*more / less … than*
verb + más / menos que	*… more / less than*

Comparative adjectives

Mejor and **peor** are used just like the English words *better* and *worse*.

bueno → mejor, mejores	malo → peor, peores
good *better*	*bad* *worse*

Superlatives

The superlative is used to express an extreme degree of an adjective.
You can also use adverbs like muy before the adjective to express
the same idea.

Adjectives ending in a consonant	Add -ísimo, -ísima, -ísimos, -ísimas. popular + ísimo → popularísimo
Adjectives ending in a vowel	Drop the vowel and add the superlative ending. triste + ísimo → tristísimo

The relative superlative is used to describe a noun in comparison to
a larger group.

el / la / los / las + noun + más / menos + adjective + de… / que…

Remember to use the irregular forms **mejor(es)** and **peor(es)** when talking
about *the best* or *the worst*.

Pronouns

Subject pronouns

Subject pronouns identify the person who is performing an action.

	Singular			Plural
yo	I		nosotros nosotras	we
tú	you (informal)		vosotros vosotras	you (informal)
usted él ella	you (formal) he she		ustedes ellos ellas	you they they

Direct object pronouns

To avoid repeating words that have already been mentioned, you can replace the direct object with a pronoun.

	Singular		Plural
me	me	nos	us
te	you (informal)	os	you (informal)
lo la	you (formal), him, it you (formal), her, it	los las	you, them you, them

Indirect object pronouns

To avoid repeating words that have already been mentioned, you can replace the indirect object with a pronoun.

	Singular		Plural
me	to / for me	nos	to / for us
te	to / for you (informal)	os	to / for you (informal)
le	to / for you (formal), him, her	les	to / for you, them

Position of pronouns

Direct and indirect object pronouns are placed before the conjugated verb, or attached to the infinitive, the present participle, or the command.

Direct and indirect object pronouns may be used in the same sentence. In this case, the indirect object pronoun goes before the direct object pronoun. Le and les become se when placed in front of a direct object pronoun.

The pronoun *se*

To present the information without telling who does the action, use this formula:

> se + verb in the third person

Adverbs

Adverbs of frequency

These adverbs and adverbial phrases express how often something is done.

nunca	*never*	muchas veces	*many times, often*
casi nunca	*almost never*	casi siempre	*usually, normally*
rara vez	*seldom, rarely*	siempre	*always*
a veces	*sometimes*	todos los días	*every day*

Adverbs of quantity

Some verbs and adjectives can be modified by a word that expresses quantity.

nada	poco	bastante	mucho	demasiado
not at all	*little, not much*	*quite, enough*	*a lot, much*	*too, too much*

Adverbs and phrases about the future

When you express intention or future plans you can use these adverbs or expressions.

ahora	*now*	mañana	*tomorrow*
luego, después	*later*	pasado mañana	*the day after tomorrow*
en un rato	*in a while*	mañana por la mañana	*tomorrow morning*
en media hora	*in half an hour*	mañana por la tarde	*tomorrow afternoon / evening*
		mañana por la noche	*tomorrow night*
hoy	*today*	el lunes que viene / el próximo lunes	*next Monday*
esta mañana	*this morning*	el mes que viene / el próximo mes	*next month*
esta tarde	*this afternoon*		
esta noche	*tonight*	el año que viene / el próximo año	*next year*

Adverbs and phrases about the past

These adverbs and time expressions refer to the past tense.

antes	*before*	la semana pasada	*last week*
anoche	*last night*	el mes pasado	*last month*
ayer	*yesterday*	el año pasado	*last year*
anteayer	*the day before yesterday*		

Use the word hace to express the amount of time elapsed since an action was completed.

hace + time expression + que + verb in the preterite tense

verb in the preterite tense + hace + time expression

Adverbs and phrases of location

Many words and phrases are used to show location.

aquí	*here*	encima de	*on, on top of*
ahí	*there*	debajo de	*under*
allí	*over there*	delante de	*in front of*
al lado de	*next to*	detrás de	*behind*
a la derecha de	*to the right of*	cerca de	*near, close to*
a la izquierda de	*to the left of*	lejos de	*far from*

Adverbs ending in -*mente*

Many adverbs are formed from adjectives by adding the suffix -mente to the feminine singular form.

Adjectives ending in -o	Change -o to -a and add -mente	lento → lentamente
Adjectives ending in -e or in a consonant	Add -mente	frecuente → frecuentemente habitual → habitualmente

Prepositions

Prepositions of place

en	*at, in, on, inside* (to express location)	de	*from* (to express origin)
a	*to* (after the verb *ir* indicating destination)	desde... hasta de... a	*from ... to* (to express direction or destination)

Prepositions *por* and *para*

Por and para can usually be translated as *for* in English.

Por may be used to express:	Para may be used to express:
approximate time	deadline
approximate place	purpose
time periods during the day	opinion
cause or reason	movement toward a place
movement within an area	recipient of an action

Interrogatives

Interrogative words

Interrogatives are words that are used to ask questions. Normally, interrogatives go at the beginning of a sentence.

¿Qué? *What?*	¿Cuál(es)? *Which?*	¿Quién(es)? *Who?*
¿Cuándo? *When?*	¿Cómo? *How?*	¿Por qué? *Why?*
¿Cuánto(a)? *How much?*	¿Cuántos(as)? *How many?*	¿Para qué? *What for?*
¿Dónde? *Where?*	¿Adónde? *Where to?*	¿De dónde? *Where from?*

Verbs

Verbs are words that express actions and events, and place them in time (past, present, and future). Spanish verbs fall into three conjugations: -**ar** (*hablar, estudiar…*), -**er** (*aprender, comer…*), and -**ir** (*vivir, subir…*).

The infinitive

1st conjugation: -ar	comprar, hablar, estudiar…
2nd conjugation: -er	comer, tener, vender…
3rd conjugation: -ir	abrir, pedir, escribir…

The present participle

Regular present participle forms

The present participle (gerundio) is formed by adding the following endings to the verb stem.

-ando for -ar verbs	lavar → lavando
-iendo for -er, -ir verbs	hacer → haciendo escribir → escribiendo

Irregular present participle forms

e > i		o > u
decir → diciendo	servir → sirviendo	dormir → durmiendo
medir → midiendo	vestir → vistiendo	morir → muriendo
pedir → pidiendo		poder → pudiendo

The past participle

The past participle (participio) of a verb can be used as an adjective to describe a noun.

Regular past participle forms

The past participle is formed by adding the following endings to the verb stem.

-ar verbs	Add the ending -ado.	pintar → pintado
-er and -ir verbs	Add the ending -ido.	vestir → vestido

Irregular past participle forms

abrir → abierto	morir → muerto
decir → dicho	poner → puesto
descubrir → descubierto	romper → roto
escribir → escrito	ver → visto
hacer → hecho	volver → vuelto

The present tense

Use the present tense to speak about the present and to talk about the future when you refer to timetables, pre-arranged events, and when you want to present the information as a fact.

Regular verbs (-ar, -er, -ir)

		Comprar (to buy)	Vender (to sell)	Abrir (to open)
Singular	yo	compro	vendo	abro
	tú	compras	vendes	abres
	usted él, ella	compra	vende	abre
Plural	nosotros(as)	compramos	vendemos	abrimos
	vosotros(as)	compráis	vendéis	abrís
	ustedes ellos(as)	compran	venden	abren

Stem-changing verbs

		Cerrar (e > ie) (to close)	Poder (o > ue) (be able to)	Pedir (e > i) (to ask)
Singular	yo	cierro	puedo	pido
	tú	cierras	puedes	pides
	usted él, ella	cierra	puede	pide
Plural	nosotros(as)	cerramos	podemos	pedimos
	vosotros(as)	cerráis	podéis	pedís
	ustedes ellos(as)	cierran	pueden	piden

Verbs with irregular yo forms

		Hacer (to make, to do)	Poner (to put)	Traer (to bring)	Salir (to leave)
Singular	yo	hago	pongo	traigo	salgo
	tú	haces	pones	traes	sales
	usted él, ella	hace	pone	trae	sale
Plural	nosotros(as)	hacemos	ponemos	traemos	salimos
	vosotros(as)	hacéis	ponéis	traéis	salís
	ustedes ellos(as)	hacen	ponen	traen	salen

Verbs *ser* and *estar*

Ser *(to be)*			
Singular		**Plural**	
yo	soy	nosotros(as)	somos
tú	eres	vosotros(as)	sois
usted él, ella	es	ustedes ellos(as)	son

Estar *(to be)*			
Singular		**Plural**	
yo	estoy	nosotros(as)	estamos
tú	estás	vosotros(as)	estáis
usted él, ella	está	ustedes ellos(as)	están

The verb **ser** is used mainly to identify people, places, and things, and to describe physical characteristics and personality traits: La señora Flores **es** mi profesora de Español. Ella **es** joven y muy inteligente.

The verb **estar** is used to express feelings and conditions: Ellos **están** tristes porque **están** enfermos.

The verb *ir*

Ir *(to go)*			
Singular		**Plural**	
yo	voy	nosotros(as)	vamos
tú	vas	vosotros(as)	vais
usted él, ella	va	ustedes ellos(as)	van

- To say where someone is going, use this structure: ir a + place.
- To express intention or future plans, use this structure: ir a + infinitive.

The verb *haber*

To say that someone or something exists or to ask about the existence of something, use the form **hay** (*there is, there are*).

Hay que and *tener que*

To make recommendations and to express obligation, you can use these structures:

> hay que + infinitive (is used in impersonal expressions and does not change form)
>
> tener que + infinitive

The verb *gustar*

To express likes or dislikes, use the verb *gustar*.

Gustar *(to like)*		
	Singular	Plural
(A mí)	me **gust**a	me **gust**an
(A ti)	te **gust**a	te **gust**an
(A usted) (A él/a ella)	le **gust**a	le **gust**an
(A nosotros/as)	nos **gust**a	nos **gust**an
(A vosotros/as)	os **gust**a	os **gust**an
(A ustedes) (A ellos/a ellas)	les **gust**a	les **gust**an

Reflexive verbs

Peinarse *(to comb one's hair)*			
Singular		Plural	
yo	me **pein**o	nosotros(as)	nos **pein**amos
tú	te **pein**as	vosotros(as)	os **pein**áis
usted él, ella	se **pein**a	ustedes ellos(as)	se **pein**an

Other reflexive verbs are: acostarse (ue) (*to go to bed*), despertarse (ie) (*to wake up*), dormirse (ue) (*to fall asleep*), levantarse (*to get up*)…

The present progressive

In Spanish we use the present progressive (presente continuo) to talk about actions that are happening at the moment of speaking. The present progressive is formed with estar + gerundio (present participle).

Lavar *(to wash)*			
Singular		Plural	
yo	estoy lavando	nosotros(as)	estamos lavando
tú	estás lavando	vosotros(as)	estáis lavando
usted él, ella	está lavando	ustedes ellos(as)	están lavando

The preterite tense

We use the preterite tense to talk about actions completed in the past, without mentioning the duration.

Regular verbs (-ar, -er, -ir)

		Comprar (to buy)	Comer (to eat)	Escribir (to write)
Singular	yo	compré	comí	escribí
	tú	compraste	comiste	escribiste
	usted él, ella	compró	comió	escribió
Plural	nosotros(as)	compramos	comimos	escribimos
	vosotros(as)	comprasteis	comisteis	escribisteis
	ustedes ellos(as)	compraron	comieron	escribieron

Verbs ending in -car, -gar, and -zar require a spelling change in the yo form of the preterite tense.

-car → -qué: buscar → yo busqué
-gar → -gué: llegar → yo llegué
-zar → -cé: empezar → yo empecé

Irregular verbs: *ser, ir, decir, tener, estar,* and *hacer*

		Ser (to be), ir (to go)	Decir (to say)	Tener (to have)	Estar (to be)	Hacer (to make, to do)
Singular	yo	fui	dije	tuve	estuve	hice
	tú	fuiste	dijiste	tuviste	estuviste	hiciste
	usted él, ella	fue	dijo	tuvo	estuvo	hizo
Plural	nosotros(as)	fuimos	dijimos	tuvimos	estuvimos	hicimos
	vosotros(as)	fuisteis	dijisteis	tuvisteis	estuvisteis	hicisteis
	ustedes ellos(as)	fueron	dijeron	tuvieron	estuvieron	hicieron

Irregular verbs: *pedir* and *dormir*

In Spanish, -ir verbs that are e > i stem-changing in the present tense (pedir > pido) have the same change in the third person of the preterite tense.

The verbs dormir and morir are also irregular in the third person (o > u).

		Pedir (to ask)	Dormir (to sleep)
Singular	yo	pedí	dormí
	tú	pediste	dormiste
	usted él, ella	pidió	durmió
Plural	nosotros(as)	pedimos	dormimos
	vosotros(as)	pedisteis	dormisteis
	ustedes ellos(as)	pidieron	durmieron

Irregular verbs: *dar, poder, poner, querer, saber,* and *venir*

		Dar (to give)	Poder (to be able)	Poner (to put)	Querer (to want)	Saber (to know)	Venir (to come)
Singular	yo	di	pude	puse	quise	supe	vine
	tú	diste	pudiste	pusiste	quisiste	supiste	viniste
	usted él, ella	dio	pudo	puso	quiso	supo	vino
Plural	nosotros(as)	dimos	pudimos	pusimos	quisimos	supimos	vinimos
	vosotros(as)	disteis	pudisteis	pusisteis	quisisteis	supisteis	vinisteis
	ustedes ellos(as)	dieron	pudieron	pusieron	quisieron	supieron	vinieron

The imperfect tense

Use the imperfect tense to talk about habitual actions or actions that happened repeatedly in the past.

Regular verbs (-*ar*, -*er*, -*ir*)

		Viajar (to travel)	Volver (to return)	Salir (to leave)
Singular	yo	viajaba	volvía	salía
	tú	viajabas	volvías	salías
	usted él, ella	viajaba	volvía	salía
Plural	nosotros(as)	viajábamos	volvíamos	salíamos
	vosotros(as)	viajabais	volvíais	salíais
	ustedes ellos(as)	viajaban	volvían	salían

Irregular verbs

		Ser (to be)	Ir (to go)	Ver (to see)
Singular	yo	era	iba	veía
	tú	eras	ibas	veías
	usted él, ella	era	iba	veía
Plural	nosotros(as)	éramos	íbamos	veíamos
	vosotros(as)	erais	ibais	veíais
	ustedes ellos(as)	eran	iban	veían

Differences between the past tenses

The imperfect and the preterite

- The preterite and the imperfect are used frequently in the same sentence to talk about past actions that coincide in time.

- When telling a story in the past, we use both the preterite and the imperfect tenses:
  - Use the preterite to talk about past actions or events that happened in the story.
  - Use the imperfect to describe characters and environment, and, in general, to explain the circumstances surrounding an event.

The future

You can use the future tense to talk about things that will happen in the future.

Regular verbs (*-ar, -er, -ir*)

		Entrar (to come in)	Comer (to eat)	Seguir (to follow)
Singular	yo	entraré	comeré	seguiré
	tú	entrarás	comerás	seguirás
	usted él, ella	entrará	comerá	seguirá
Plural	nosotros(as)	entraremos	comeremos	seguiremos
	vosotros(as)	entraréis	comeréis	seguiréis
	ustedes ellos(as)	entrarán	comerán	seguirán

Irregular verbs

poder → podr-	decir → dir-
poner → pondr-	hacer → har-
salir → saldr-	querer → querr-
tener → tendr-	saber → sabr-
venir → vendr-	

The present subjunctive

We use the subjunctive to express wishes, feelings, emotions, or opinions, to express doubt or uncertainty, and to express value judgments.

Regular verbs (-*ar*, -*er*, -*ir*)

		Cantar *(to sing)*	Comer *(to eat)*	Vivir *(to live)*
Singular	yo	cante	coma	viva
	tú	cantes	comas	vivas
	usted él, ella	cante	coma	viva
Plural	nosotros(as)	cantemos	comamos	vivamos
	vosotros(as)	cantéis	comáis	viváis
	ustedes ellos(as)	canten	coman	vivan

Verbs ending in -car, -gar, -zar, -ger, -gir, and -guir have spelling changes.

-car → -que: sacar → saque, saques...	-ger, -gir → -ja: dirigir → dirija, dirijas...
-gar → -gue: llegar → llegue, llegues...	-guir → -ga: seguir → siga, sigas...
-zar → -ce: abrazar → abrace, abraces...	

Irregular verbs

In general, the present subjunctive is formed from the yo form of the present indicative. Therefore, irregular verbs in the yo form of the indicative are also irregular in the subjunctive.

yo hago → haga, hagas, haga, hagamos, hagáis, hagan
yo tengo → tenga, tengas, tenga, tengamos, tengáis, tengan

Stem-changing verbs

		Pensar *(to think)*	Jugar *(to play)*	Volver *(to return)*	Pedir *(to ask)*	Dormir *(to sleep)*
Singular	yo	piense	juegue	vuelva	pida	duerma
Singular	tú	pienses	juegues	vuelvas	pidas	duermas
Singular	usted él, ella	piense	juegue	vuelva	pida	duerma
Plural	nosotros(as)	pensemos	juguemos	volvamos	pidamos	durmamos
Plural	vosotros(as)	penséis	juguéis	volváis	pidáis	durmáis
Plural	ustedes ellos(as)	piensen	jueguen	vuelvan	pidan	duerman

Irregular verbs: *dar, estar, saber, ser,* and *ir*

		Dar *(to give)*	Estar *(to be)*	Saber *(to know)*	Ser *(to be)*	Ir *(to go)*
Singular	yo	dé	esté	sepa	sea	vaya
Singular	tú	des	estés	sepas	seas	vayas
Singular	usted él, ella	dé	esté	sepa	sea	vaya
Plural	nosotros(as)	demos	estemos	sepamos	seamos	vayamos
Plural	vosotros(as)	deis	estéis	sepáis	seáis	vayáis
Plural	ustedes ellos(as)	den	estén	sepan	sean	vayan

Affirmative commands

To tell one person or more than one person to do something, you can use an informal or a formal command.

Regular verbs (*-ar, -er, -ir*)

	Caminar *(to walk)*	Comer *(to eat)*	Escribir *(to write)*
Singular	camina (tú)	come (tú)	escribe (tú)
Singular	camine (usted)	coma (usted)	escriba (usted)
Plural	caminad (vosotros(as))	comed (vosotros(as))	escribid (vosotros(as))
Plural	caminen (ustedes)	coman (ustedes)	escriban (ustedes)

Irregular verbs: *tener*, *hacer*, *poner*, *venir*, and *salir*

	Tener (to have)	Hacer (to do, to make)	Poner (to put)	Venir (to come)	Salir (to leave)	
Singular	ten	haz	pon	ven	sal	tú
Singular	tenga	haga	ponga	venga	salga	usted
Plural	tened	haced	poned	venid	salid	vosotros(as)
Plural	tengan	hagan	pongan	vengan	salgan	ustedes

Irregular verbs: *ser*, *decir*, *ir*, and *dar*

	Ser (to be)	Decir (to say)	Ir (to go)	Dar (to give)	
Singular	sé	di	ve	da	tú
Singular	sea	diga	vaya	dé	usted
Plural	sed	decid	id	dad	vosotros(as)
Plural	sean	digan	vayan	den	ustedes

Negative commands

Use negative commands when telling someone what not to do.

Regular verbs (*-ar*, *-er*, *-ir*)

	Caminar (to walk)	Comer (to eat)	Escribir (to write)
Singular	no camines (tú)	no comas (tú)	no escribas (tú)
Singular	no camine (usted)	no coma (usted)	no escriba (usted)
Plural	no caminéis (vosotros(as))	no comáis (vosotros(as))	no escribáis (vosotros(as))
Plural	no caminen (ustedes)	no coman (ustedes)	no escriban (ustedes)

Irregular verbs: *dar*, *estar*, *ir*, and *ser*

	Dar (to give)	Estar (to be)	Ir (to go)	Ser (to be)	
Singular	no des	no estés	no vayas	no seas	tú
Singular	no dé	no esté	no vaya	no sea	usted
Plural	no déis	no estéis	no vayáis	no seáis	vosotros(as)
Plural	no den	no estén	no vayan	no sean	ustedes

GLOSARIO ESPAÑOL-INGLÉS

A

a to 21
a causa de because of 71
a continuación next 206
a cuadros plaid, checkered 154
a la derecha to the right 22
a la izquierda to the left 22
a la plancha grilled 216
a menudo often 301
a partir de from 95 based on 219
¿A qué te dedicas? What do you do for a living? 378
a través de through 280
abierto opened 246
el/la **abogado(a)** attorney, lawyer 357
abrazar to hug 374
el **abrigo** coat 140
abril April 307
abrir (irreg.) to open 12
el/la **abuelo(a)** grandfather/ grandmother 36
los **abuelos** grandparents 37
abundante abundant 124
abundar to abound 71
aburrido(a) boring 13 bored 52
aburrirse to be/to get bored 14
acabar to end up 258
los **accesorios** accessories 96
el **accidente** accident 259
la **acción** action 1
el **aceite** oil 208
el **aceite de oliva** olive oil 267
el **acelerador** gas pedal 312
acelerar to accelerate 312
aceptar to accept 164
la **acera** sidewalk 112
acerca de about 435
acercarse to move closer 302
acompañar to go with 51 to be served with 193
el **acontecimiento** event 385
el **acordeón** accordion 71
acostarse (irreg. **ue**) to go to bed 16
acostumbrarse a to get used to 159
la **actitud** attitude 425
la **actividad** activity 1
activo(a) active 15
el **actor** actor 357

la **actriz** actress 356
la **actuación** performance 111
actual present 60
actualmente nowadays 171
actuar to act 37 to appear (in a TV show) 380
acudir to go 261
adecuado(a) correct 83
¡Adelante! Let's go! 377
además also 47
adicto(a) addicted 343
la **adivinanza** riddle 209
adivinar to guess 49
el **adjetivo** adjective 1
administrativo(a) administrative 113
admirar to admire 59
adónde where 20
adornar to decorate 191
el **adorno** ornament 95
adquirir (irreg. **ie**) to gain 367
la **aduana** customs 323
adulto(a) adult 269
el **adverbio** adverb 1
la **advertencia** warning 263
aéreo(a) air (adjective) 291
el **aeropuerto** airport 20
afectado(a) affected 421
afectar to affect 55
afeitarse to shave 252
la **afición** hobby 364
el/la **aficionado(a)** fan, supporter 376
la **afirmación** statement 67
afirmativo(a) affirmative 64
africano(a) African 43
afroantillano(a) Afro-Caribbean 403
las **afueras** outskirts 112
la **agencia de viajes** travel agency 296
la **agenda** appointment book 349
el/la **agente de viajes** travel agent 296
el/la **agente inmobiliario(a)** realtor 92
agosto August 77
agrícola agricultural 321
el/la **agricultor(a)** farmer 356
agrio(a) sour 216
el **agua** water 14
el **agua mineral** mineral water 188
el **aguacate** avocado 222
las **aguas termales** hot springs 59

el **aguayo** traditional multicolored blanket from Peru and Bolivia 157
el **águila** eagle 424
ahí there 22
ahora now 60
ahorrar energía to save energy 424
el **aire** air 20
el **aire acondicionado** air conditioning 104
el **aire puro** fresh air 20
el **ajo** garlic 192
al to the 8
al aire libre open-air 165
al final in the end 136
al lado de beside, next to 22
al menos at least 269
al principio at first 147
el **álamo** poplar 206
la **alarma** alarm 315
el **álbum** album 119
alcanzar to reach 415
el **alcázar** fortress 82
la **aldea** small village 403
alegrar to be glad 366
alegre lively 42
alegremente happily 254
la **alegría** joy 124
alejado(a) distant 175
el **alemán** German (language) 246
el/la **alemán(a)** German (nationality) 46
la **alergia** allergy 260
la **alfombra** rug 96
algo something 8
el **algodón** cotton 148
alguien someone 321
algún, alguno(a)(os)(as) a few, any, one, some 194
el **alimento** food 192
aliviar to relieve 263
allí there 20
la **almendra** almond 195
la **almohada** pillow 320
almorzar (irreg. **ue**) to have lunch 142
el **almuerzo** lunch 8
alojarse to stay (at a hotel, etc.) 253
la **alpaca** alpaca 141
el **alpinismo** mountain climbing 372
el/la **alpinista** mountain climber 371

alquilar   to rent 394
alrededor   around 23
el **altar**   altar 191
la **altitud**   altitude 139
alto(a)   tall 44
la **altura**   height 45
el/la **alumno(a)**   student 212
la **amabilidad**   kindness 425
amable   kind 72
amado(a)   loved 103
el/la **amante**   lover 428
amar   to love 102
amargo(a)   bitter 216
amarillo(a)   yellow 148
amazónico(a)   Amazonian 295
el **ámbar**   amber 94
ambos(as)   both 330
americano(a)   American 161
el/la **amigo(a)**   friend 3
el **amor**   love 55
ampliar   to extend 227
analizar   to analyze 286
anaranjado(a)   orange (in color) 148
ancho(a)   wide 112 loose-fitting 149
andaluz(a)   Andalusian 267
andar (irreg.)   to walk 175
el **andén**   train platform 304
andino(a)   Andean 141
la **anécdota**   anecdote 173
el **anfibio**   amphibian 423
el **anillo**   ring 140
animado(a)   lively 428
el **animal**   animal 59
¡Anímate!   Go on! 274
el **anís**   anise 190
anoche   last night 150
el **anorak**   parka, anorak 431
antártico(a)   Antarctic 400
anteayer   the day before yesterday 150
anterior   previous 107
antes de   before 38
antiguamente   in the past 176
antiguo(a)   old 35
antipático(a)   unpleasant 4
anual   annual 50
anunciar   to advertise 144
el **anuncio**   advertisement 92
añadir   to add 206
el **año**   year 3
el **año que viene**   next year 410
años de antigüedad   years old 95

el **aparato**   machine 27
aparecer (irreg.)   to appear 275
el **apartado**   paragraph 333
el **apartamento**   apartment 100
el **apellido**   last name, surname 60
la **apertura**   opening 376
aplastado(a)   flat, crushed 193
aplastar   to crush 228
aplicar   to apply 195
aportar   to contribute 376
apoyado(a)   leaning 242
apreciado(a)   valued 171
apreciar   to see, to notice 401
aprender   to learn 35
aprobar (irreg. **ue**)   to pass 389
apropiado(a)   appropriate 32
aproximadamente   approximately 347
aquel, aquella   that 2 that one 114
aquello   that 114
aquellos, aquellas   those 38
aquí   here 9
árabe   Arab 278
la **araña**   spider 422
el **árbol**   tree 20
arbóreo(a)   arboreal 33
el **archipiélago**   archipelago 175
el **área**   area 139
la **arepa**   pancake made of corn flour 331
el **arete**   earring 140
argentino(a)   Argentinean 373
argumentar   to argue 436
argumentativo(a)   discursive 437
el **argumento**   plot 385 argument 437
el **armario**   wardrobe, closet 8
el **arpa**   harp 331
arqueológico(a)   archaeological 147
el/la **arquitecto(a)**   architect 356
arquitectónico(a)   architectural 401
la **arquitectura**   architecture 119
arraigado(a)   deeply rooted 176
arrancar   to start (a car) 312
arreglar   to fix 109
arreglarse   to get ready 252
arriba   up 214 upstairs 391
arrojar   to throw 295
el **arroz**   rice 192
arrugado(a)   wrinkled 89
el **arte**   art 116
la **artesanía**   handicrafts 154

el/la **artesano(a)**   craftsman/craftswoman 176
ártico(a)   Arctic 400
el **artículo**   article 1
artificial   artificial 429
el/la **artista**   artist 356
artístico(a)   artistic 177
asado(a)   roasted 216
asar   to roast 208
el **ascensor**   elevator 156
los **aseos**   restrooms 348
así   this way 89
así que   so 20
el **asiento**   seat 304
la **asignatura**   (school) subject 348
asistir   to attend 159
la **asociación**   association 159
asociado(a)   associated 122
el **aspecto**   (physical) appearance 74 aspect 111
el **aspecto físico**   appearance 69
la **aspiradora**   vacuum (cleaner) 91
la **aspirina**   aspirin 260
asustado(a)   frightened 391
asustarse   to be frightened 309
atacar   to attack 93
atareado(a)   busy 90
la **atención sanitaria**   health care 261
Atentamente.   Sincerely/Truly yours. 19
aterrizar   to land 304
el **Atlántico**   Atlantic 70
atlético(a)   athletic 5
la **atmósfera**   atmosphere 431
la **atracción**   attraction 111
atractivo(a)   attractive 381
atravesado(a)   crossed 71
atravesar (irreg. **ie**)   to go through 139
atrevido(a)   daring 68
el **atún**   tuna 192
el **aula**   classroom 348
aumentar   to increase 303
ausente por enfermedad   out sick 14
auténtico(a)   genuine 145
el **autobús**   bus 21
autóctono(a)   indigenous 411
la **autoescuela**   driving school 312
la **autoevaluación**   self-assessment 79
el **automóvil**   automobile 316
autónomo(a)   independent 253
la **autopista**   expressway 305

auxiliar   *auxiliary* 62

el/la **auxiliar de vuelo**   *flight attendant* 304

avanzar   *to move forward* 131

el **AVE**   *high-speed train* 266

el **ave**   *bird* 423

la **avellana**   *hazelnut* 195

la **avenida**   *avenue* 112

la **aventura**   *adventure* 83

el/la **aventurero(a)**   *adventurer* 332

el **avión**   *airplane* 20

ayer   *yesterday* 41

ayer por la noche   *last night* 327

aymara   *Aymara* 175

la **ayuda**   *help* 97

ayudar   *to help* 69

el **azahar**   *orange blossom* 190

azteca   *Aztec* 201

el **azúcar**   *sugar* 208

azul   *blue* 148

el **azulejo**   *tile* 91

la **bachata**   *bachata (lively Caribbean dance)* 123

la **bahía**   *bay* 400

el/la **bailador(a)**   *dancer* 154

bailar   *to dance* 15

el/la **bailarín(a)**   *dancer* 123

el **baile**   *dance* 43

bajar   *to go/come down* 127 *to get off* 311

bajo(a)   *short* 5

bajo cero   *below zero* 416

la **balada**   *ballad* 103

la **balanza**   *scales* 85

el **balcón**   *balcony* 88

el **balneario**   *spa* 274

el **balón**   *ball* 372

el **baloncesto**   *basketball* 372

la **balsa**   *raft* 294

el **banco**   *bench* 112 *bank* 112

la **banda**   *band* 160

la **bandeja**   *tray* 208

la **bandera**   *flag* 2

la **bandurria**   *small 12-stringed guitar* 105

bañarse   *to take a bath* 252 *to go for a swim* 308

la **bañera**   *bathtub* 96

el **baño**   *bathroom* 8

los **baños termales**   *hot springs* 431

barato(a)   *cheap* 164

la **barba**   *beard* 44

la **barbilla**   *chin* 244

la **barca**   *dinghy* 295

el **barco**   *ship, boat* 20

el **bardo**   *bard* 105

barrer   *to sweep* 13

la **barrera**   *barrier* 436

el **barrio**   *neighborhood* 112

el **barro**   *mud* 53

basado(a) en   *based on* 171

basarse en   *to be based on* 271

la **base**   *base* 71

básico(a)   *basic* 121

bastante   *quite, enough* 10

la **basura**   *garbage* 93

la **bata**   *robe* 140

batir   *to beat* 208

el **bautizo**   *baptism, christening* 37

el/la **bebé**   *baby* 36

beber   *to drink* 14

la **bebida**   *drink* 1

el **béisbol**   *baseball* 372

beliceño(a)   *Belizean* 70

la **belleza**   *beauty* 176

bello(a)   *beautiful* 433

beneficiar   *to benefit* 436

el **beso**   *kiss* 57

la **biblioteca**   *library* 112

el/la **bibliotecario(a)**   *librarian* 356

la **bicicleta**   *bicycle* 15

bien   *well* 8

bienvenido(a)   *welcome* 2

el **bigote**   *moustache* 42

el **billete**   *bill* 164

la **Biología**   *biology (subject)* 348

el/la **biólogo(a)**   *biologist* 175

la **biosfera**   *biosphere* 71

blanco(a)   *white* 148

la **blusa**   *blouse* 89

la **boca**   *mouth* 244

el **bocadillo**   *speech bubble* 41

la **boda**   *wedding* 179

el **bol**   *bowl* 208

el **boletín**   *report* 442

el **boleto**   *ticket* 20

el **boleto de ida y vuelta**   *round-trip ticket* 304

el **boleto sencillo**   *one-way ticket* 304

el **bolígrafo**   *ballpoint pen* 26

boliviano(a)   *Bolivian* 160

la **bolsa**   *bag* 20

el **bolso**   *purse* 140

el/la **bombero(a)**   *firefighter* 356

bonito(a)   *pretty* 4 *nice* 84

boquense   *from Boca Juniors (a Buenos Aires soccer team)* 376

el **borrador**   *draft* 6

el **bosque**   *forest* 400

la **bota**   *boot* 138

botánico(a)   *botanic* 411

el **bote**   *can* 200

la **botella**   *bottle* 200

la **brasa**   *ember* 279

el **brazo**   *arm* 244

breve   *brief* 277

brillante   *bright* 171

la **brisa**   *breeze* 280

británico(a)   *British* 70

la **broma**   *joke* 384

bucear   *to dive* 404

el **buceo**   *diving* 428

buen   *good* 48

¡Buen provecho!   *Enjoy your meal!* 234

¡Buena suerte!   *Good luck!* 136

bueno(a)   *good* 216

buenos días   *good morning* 2

la **bufanda**   *scarf* 140

buscar   *to look for* 31

la **buseta**   *bus* 315

el **caballo**   *horse* 424

la **cabeza**   *head* 14

cabezón(a)   *giant-headed* 51

el **cacao**   *cacao* 198

el **cacaotero**   *cacao tree* 203

cacaotero(a)   *cacao-growing* 199

el **cacique**   *chief* 295

cada   *each* 32

caer (irreg.)   *to fall* 246

el **café**   *coffee* 10 *café* 112

la **cafetera**   *coffee maker/pot* 325

la **cafetería**   *cafeteria* 348

cafetero(a)   *coffee-producing* 318

el **caimán**   *alligator* 429

la **caja**   *cash register* 164 *box* 200

el/la **cajero(a)**   *cashier* 164

el **cajero automático**   *ATM* 320

el **calcetín**   *sock* 138

calcular   *to estimate* 429

la **caldera de calefacción**   *furnace* 104

el **caldo (de pollo)**   *chicken stock* 225

el **calentamiento global**   *global warming* 139

el **desarrollo** *development* 86
el **desastre** *disaster* 138
desayunar *to have breakfast* 10
el **desayuno** *breakfast* 250
descansar *to rest* 14
el **descanso** *rest* 255
descargar el lavaplatos *to unload the dishwasher* 88
descender de (irreg. **ie**) *to be descended from* 43
descendiente *descendant* 47
descifrar *to decipher* 342
desconocido(a) *unknown* 332
describir (irreg.) *to describe* 1
la **descripción** *description* 65
descriptivo(a) *descriptive* 281
descubrir (irreg.) *to find out* 246
el **descuento** *discount* 164
desde *since* 47 *from* 65
Desde luego. *Of course.* 344
desear *to wish* 358
el **desenlace** *ending* 385
el **deseo** *wish* 279
el **desfile** *parade* 149
desgraciadamente *unfortunately* 404
el **deshielo** *melting* 139
el **desierto** *desert* 401
la **desilusión** *disappointment* 301
desordenado(a) *untidy* 89
despacio *slowly* 254
la **despedida** *goodbye, farewell* 2
despedirse (irreg. **i, i**) *to say goodbye* 166
despegar *to take off* 304
la **despensa** *pantry* 88
el **despertador** *alarm clock* 104
despertarse (irreg. **ie**) *to wake up* 16
después *after* 14 *then* 14 *later* 53
después de *after* 8
destinar a *to use for* 305
el **destino** *destination* 21
la **destrucción** *destruction* 332
el **desván** *attic* 88
la **desventaja** *disadvantage* 59
detallado(a) *detailed* 275
el **detalle** *detail* 59
el/la **detective** *detective* 34
determinado(a) *specific* 165
el/la **detractor(a)** *detractor* 436
detrás de *behind* 22
el **día** *day* 14
la **diablada** *Bolivian carnival dance* 155

el **diagrama** *diagram* 45
el **diálogo** *dialogue* 41
la **diapositiva** *slide* 381
diariamente *every day* 257
el **diario** *diary* 135 *newspaper* 376
diario(a) *daily* 16
dibujar *to draw* 283
el **dibujo** *drawing* 91
el **diccionario** *dictionary* 108
diciembre *December* 197
el **diente** *tooth* 244
la **diferencia** *difference* 38
diferencial *distinguishing* 287
diferenciarse *to be different* 353
diferente *different* 5
difícil *hard* 5 *difficult* 64
la **dificultad** *problem, difficulty* 300
difunto(a) *deceased* 191
el **dinero** *money* 164
el/la **dios(a)** *god/goddess* 53
la **dirección** *address* 67 *direction* 412
directamente *directly* 263
directo(a) *direct* 98
el/la **director(a)** *principal* 2 *manager* 324 *director* 369
dirigir *to lead* 87 *to run* 318
dirigirse *to address* 219
el **disco** *record, CD* 106
la **discoteca** *nightclub, disco* 368
Disculpa./Disculpe. *Excuse me.* 240
discutir *to argue* 36
el **diseño** *design* 148
el **disfraz** *costume* 153
disfrazarse *to dress up* 154
disfrutar (de) *to enjoy* 121
la **distancia** *distance* 65
distinguir *to distinguish* 270
distinto(a) *different* 10
la **diversidad** *diversity* 47
diverso(a) *diverse* 124
diversos(as) *several* 243
divertido(a) *funny, fun* 32
divertirse (irreg. **ie, i**) *to enjoy oneself* 358
dividir *to divide* 382
dividirse en *to be made up of* 113
doblar a la derecha/a la izquierda *to turn right/left* 20
el/la **doctor(a)** *doctor* 261
el **dólar** *dollar* 169
doler (irreg. **ue**) *to hurt* 260

el **dolor** *pain, ache* 260
doméstico(a) *domestic* 89
el **domicilio** *address* 59
el **domicilio actual** *current address* 60
el **domingo** *Sunday* 13
dominicano(a) *Dominican* 80
el **dominó** *dominoes* 124
don *title of respect before a man's first name* 82
donde *where* 35
dónde *where* 20
dorado(a) *gold, golden* 148
dormido(a) *asleep* 285
dormir (irreg. **ue, u**) *to sleep* 25
dormirse (irreg. **ue, u**) *to fall asleep* 16
el **dormitorio** *bedroom* 8
la **dosis** *dose* 263
ducharse *to take a shower* 252
la **duda** *doubt* 370
dudar *to doubt* 370
el/la **dueño(a)** *owner* 121
dulce *sweet* 216
los **dulces** *candy* 127
durante *during* 111 *for* 119
durar *to last* 155
el **durazno** *peach* 195
duro(a) *hard* 175

echar *to put* 208
echar gasolina *to put some gas in* 315
el **eco** *echo* 332
ecológico(a) *ecological* 436
la **economía** *economy* 300
económico(a) *economic* 201
el **ecosistema** *ecosystem* 422
el **ecoturismo** *ecotourism* 59
la **edad** *age* 58
la **Edad Media** *Middle Ages* 105
el **edificio** *building* 89
el **ejemplo** *example* 61
el **ejercicio** *exercise* 270
el **ejercicio físico** *physical exercise* 269
el *the* 2
él *he* 4
la **elaboración** *manufacture* 176
elaborar *to make* 176 *to prepare* 274
eléctrico(a) *electrical* 105

la **fiebre** *fever* 14
la **fiesta** *festivity* 51 *party* 84
la **figura** *figure, shape* 157
fijarse en *to pay attention to, to notice* 86
el **filtro solar** *sunblock* 25
el **fin de semana** *weekend* 17
el **final** *end* 33
finalmente *finally* 70
la **Física** *physics (subject)* 348
físicamente *physically* 44
la **flauta** *flute* 71
la **flor** *flower* 22
la **flora** *flora* 71
el **florero** *vase* 96
el **folclore** *folklore* 51
folclórico(a) *folk (adjective)* 155
el **folleto** *brochure* 296
el **fondo** *bottom* 301
la **forma** *way* 21 *form* 63
la **formación** *formation* 246
formal *formal* 202
la **formalidad** *formality* 218
formar *to form* 402
la **fortaleza** *fortress* 120
el **fósil** *fossil* 94
fosilizado(a) *fossilized* 95
la **foto** *photo* 7
la **fotografía** *photography, photo* 48
fotografiar *to take a photo of* 35
fotográfico(a) *photographic* 122
la **fotonovela** *photonovel* 49
el **fragmento** *excerpt* 379
el **francés** *French (language)* 122
francés(a) *French* 401
la **frase** *sentence* 79
la **frecuencia** *frequency* 1
frecuente *frequent* 254
frecuentemente *frequently* 254
freír (irreg.) *to fry* 208
frenar *to brake* 312
el **freno** *brake* 312
la **frente** *forehead* 244
frente a *in front of* 127
la **fresa** *strawberry* 192
fresco(a) *fresh* 216
frijol *bean* 192
el **frío** *cold* 3
frío(a) *cold* 216
frito(a) *fried* 216
la **frontera** *border* 382
frustrado(a) *frustrated* 52
la **fruta** *fruit* 10
el **fruto** *fruit* 195
los **frutos secos** *nuts* 195

el **fuego** *fire* 419
la **fuente** *fountain* 91 *dish* 225
la **fuente de energía** *energy source* 431
fuera (de) *outside* 88
fuerte *strong* 44
la **función** *function* 15
funcionar *to work* 261
fundado(a) *founded* 82
fundamental *fundamental, basic* 209
furioso(a) *furious* 52
la **fusión** *fusion, mixture* 71
el **fútbol** *soccer* 372
el **fútbol americano** *football* 372
el/la **futbolista** *soccer player* 45
el **futuro** *future* 359

la **gaceta** *newspaper* 153
las **gafas** *glasses* 44
las **gafas de sol** *sunglasses* 140
la **galería de arte** *art gallery* 428
el **gallego** *Galician (language)* 279
la **galleta** *cookie* 200
la **gallina** *hen* 424
el **gallo** *rooster* 424
el **galón** *gallon* 313
ganador(a) *winning* 117
ganar *to win* 372
el **garaje** *garage* 13
garantizar *to ensure* 261
la **garganta** *throat* 260
garífuna *from an ethnic group of Central America and the Caribbean* 31
la **gasolina** *gas* 312
la **gasolinera** *gas station* 312
el **gato** *cat* 52
el **gaucho** *gaucho* 383
el **gazpacho** *Andalusian vegetable soup, served chilled* 266
el **gel** *gel* 252
generalizado(a) *widespread* 255
generalmente *generally* 46
el **género** *type* 123
generoso(a) *generous* 44
la **gente** *people* 25
la **Geografía** *geography (subject)* 348
geográfico(a) *geographic* 434
el **gerundio** *present participle* 90
el **gesto** *gesture* 245

el **gigante** *giant* 30
el **gimnasio** *gym* 372
el **glaciar** *glacier* 139
global *global* 73
el **gobierno** *government* 174
el **golf** *golf* 372
gordo(a) *fat* 44
la **gorra** *cap* 140
el **gorro** *cap* 141
grabar *to record* 27
gracias *thank you* 39
gracioso(a) *funny* 44
el **grado** *degree* 416
gradualmente *gradually* 159
el **gráfico** *chart* 73
la **gramática** *grammar* 1
el **gramo** *gram* 190
gran *big* 20 *great* 59
grande *big* 7
los **grandes almacenes** *department store* 144
el **grano** *seed* 198
el **grano de café** *coffee bean* 319
griego(a) *Greek* 203
la **gripe** *flu* 260
gris *gray* 148
gritar *to shout* 314
grueso(a) *thick* 176
el **grupo** *group* 43
el **guacamole** *guacamole* 228
la **guagua** *bus* 315
el **guante** *glove* 372
el **guaraní** *Guarani* 346
guardar *to put away* 97 *to keep* 219
guatemalteco(a) *Guatemalan* 70
¡guau! *woof!* 427
el/la **guía** *guide* 139
la **guía turística** *tourist guide book* 20
el **guión** *script* 169
los **guisantes** *peas* 192
gustar *to like* 1
los **gustos** *likes* 1

la **habitación** *room* 27
la **habitación doble** *double room* 320
la **habitación sencilla** *single room* 320
habitado(a) *inhabited* 436

el/la **habitante** *inhabitant* 47

el **hábito** *habit* 1

los **hábitos alimenticios** *eating habits* 195

los **hábitos de alimentación** *eating habits* 286

habitual *habitual* 1

habitualmente *usually* 104

el/la **hablante** *speaker* 226

hablar *to speak* 13

Hace calor. *It's hot.* 416

Hace frío. *It's cold.* 416

Hace sol. *It's sunny.* 416

hace una semana/dos días/... *one week/two days/... ago* 150

Hace viento. *It's windy.* 416

hacer (irreg.) *to do, to make* 14

hacer cámping *to go camping* 25

hacer cola/fila *to stand in line* 200

hacer daño *to hurt* 138

hacer deporte *to play sports* 268

hacer ejercicio *to exercise* 19

hacer el equipaje *to pack* 296

hacer gimnasia *to work out* 372

hacer la compra *to shop* 200

hacer picnic *to have a picnic* 364

hacer un crucigrama *to do a crossword puzzle* 364

hacer un examen *to take an exam* 348

hacia *towards* 412

la **hacienda** *country estate* 198

el **hambre** *hunger* 3

la **harina** *flour* 190

Hasta la vista. *See you.* 2

Hasta luego. *See you later.* 2

Hasta mañana. *See you tomorrow.* 2

Hasta pronto. *See you soon.* 2

hay *there is/there are* 22

el **helado** *ice cream* 10

helado(a) *frozen* 435

el **hemisferio** *hemisphere* 174

la **herencia** *legacy* 184

el/la **hermano(a)** *brother/sister* 36

los **hermanos** *siblings* 36

hermoso(a) *beautiful* 123

el **héroe** *hero* 87

hervido(a) *boiled* 216

hervir (irreg. **ie, i**) *to boil* 208

el **hielo** *ice* 416

el **hierro** *iron* 305

la **higiene** *hygiene* 252

el/la **hijo(a)** *son/daughter* 36

los **hijos** *children (offspring)* 34

hispano(a) *Hispanic* 61

hispanoamericano(a) *Spanish American* 105

hispanohablante *Spanish-speaking* 219

la **Historia** *history (subject)* 348

la **historia** *story* 35

histórico(a) *historic* 118

la **hoguera** *bonfire* 279

la **hoja** *leaf* 20

la **hoja de inscripción** *registration form* 60

el **hombre** *man* 7

el **hombro** *shoulder* 244

hondureño(a) *Honduran* 70

la **hora** *time* 15 *hour* 161

el **horario** *schedule* 296

el **horizonte** *horizon* 280

el **horno** *oven* 104

horrible *horrible* 374

las **hortalizas** *garden vegetables* 192

el **hospital** *hospital* 258

hospitalario(a) *hospitable* 124

el **hotel** *hotel* 320

el **hotel rural** *country hotel* 319

hoy *today* 5

el/la **huésped** *guest* 320

el **huevo** *egg* 8

humano(a) *human* 14

húmedo(a) *humid* 435

la **idea** *idea* 73

ideal *ideal* 19

identificar *to identify* 1

el **idioma** *language* 219

la **iglesia** *church* 112

igual *same* 150

igual que *like* 106

ilógico(a) *illogical* 213

la **ilusión** *hope* 55

la **ilustración** *illustration* 66

ilustrar *to illustrate* 315

la **imagen** *image* 102

imaginar *to imagine* 39

imaginario(a) *fictional* 41 *imaginary* 407

imitar *to sound like* 243

impaciente *impatient* 44

el **impacto** *impact* 399

impartir *to give* 349

el **imperativo** *imperative* 202

el **imperfecto** *imperfect* 298

el **imperio** *empire* 167

el **impermeable** *raincoat* 140

impersonal *impersonal* 270

la **importancia** *importance* 177

importante *important* 37

importar *to matter* 168

imposible *impossible* 34

la **impresión** *impression* 7

impresionante *impressive* 307

el **impulso económico** *economic boost* 436

inaugurar *to open* 297

inca *Inca* 174

el **incendio forestal** *forest fire* 424

incluir (irreg.) *to include* 225

incómodo(a) *uncomfortable* 148

incompleto(a) *incomplete* 188

incorporar *to incorporate* 175

increíble *incredible* 20

los **indefinidos** *indefinites* 194

la **independencia** *independence* 135

las **indicaciones** *uses (of medicine)* 263

indicar *to indicate* 167

indígena *indigenous* 43

el/la **indígena** *native* 51

indirecto(a) *indirect* 106

la **industria** *industry* 171

inesperado(a) *unforeseen* 315

la **infancia** *childhood* 301

la **infanta** *infanta, princess* 275

la **inferencia** *inference* 177

el **infinitivo** *infinitive* 229

la **influencia** *influence* 71

influir (irreg.) *to influence* 175

la **información** *information* 20

informal *casual* 182 *informal* 202

informar *to inform* 291

la **informática** *computer science* 357

informativo(a) *informative* 333

el/la **ingeniero(a)** *engineer* 378

el **inglés** *English (language)* 38

inglés(a) *English* 87

el **ingrediente** *ingredient* 189

los **ingresos** *revenue* 319

inicial *initial* 385

inmaterial *immaterial, intangible* 363

el/la **inmigrante** *immigrant* 367

el **inodoro** *toilet* 9

inolvidable *unforgettable* 221

inscribirse (irreg.) *to register, to enter* 58

melancólico(a) *melancholic* 125

mellizo(a) *twin* 47

el melón *melon* 192

memorable *memorable* 405

la memoria *memory* 122

mencionar *to mention* 116

menor *less* 271

menos *less* 54

el mensaje *message* 66

el mensaje de correo *e-mail message* 57

mentir (irreg. **ie, i**) *to lie* 90

el menú del día *specials (on a menu)* 216

el mercadillo *street market* 165

el mercado *market* 139

el mercado de pulga *flea market* 165

las mercancías *merchandise* 157

el merengue *merengue* 123

la mermelada *jam* 200

el mes que viene *next month* 410

la mesa *table* 8

el/la mesero(a) *waiter/waitress* 216

la mesita de noche *nightstand* 96

el mestizaje *mixed race group* 71

mestizo(a) *of mixed ancestry* 47

la metáfora *metaphor* 281

meteorológico(a) *weather (adjective)* 416

meter *to put in* 203

el método *method* 205

métrico(a) *metric* 45

el metro *subway* 21 *meter* 45

metropolitano(a) *metropolitan* 355

mexicano(a) *Mexican* 226

la mezcla *mixture* 71

mezclar *to mix* 208

mi, mis *my* 2

¡miau! *meow!* 427

el microondas *microwave* 104

el miedo *fear* 3

mientras *while* 223

el miércoles *Wednesday* 349

milenario(a) *ancient* 176

la milla *mile* 45

el millón *million* 47

la mina *mine* 162

el mineral *mineral* 163

minero(a) *mining* 163

el minuto *minute* 102

mío(a)(os)(as) *mine* 38

la mirada *gaze* 280

el mirador *viewpoint* 370

mirar *to look* 135 *to look at* 306

la misión *mission* 31

mismo(a) *same* 150

los misquitos *Miskitos* 71

el misterio *mystery* 332

misterioso(a) *mysterious* 342

la mitad *half* 406

mítico(a) *mythical* 295

el mito *myth* 332

la mochila *backpack* 2

el modelo *model (example)* 3

el/la modelo *model (person)* 281

moderado(a) *moderate* 269

el Modernismo *modernism* 55

modernista *modernist* 55 *Art Nouveau* 401

moderno(a) *modern* 149

el modo *way* 175 *mood (in grammar)* 358

el mole *typical Mexican chili sauce* 214

moler (irreg. **ue**) *to crush* 228 *to grind* 325

molestar *to bother, to upset* 362

el momento *moment* 255

el monasterio *monastery* 276

la moneda *coin* 164

el monje *monk* 147

el mono *monkey* 424

la montaña *mountain* 400

el/la montañero(a) *mountain climber* 371

montañoso(a) *mountainous* 70

montar *to ride* 58

montar a caballo *to ride a horse* 364

montar en bici *to ride a bicycle* 364

montar en monopatín *to ride a skateboard* 364

el monte *mount* 403

la montera *typical Andean hat* 171

el monumento *monument* 91

morado(a) *purple* 148

la morenada *Bolivian carnival dance* 155

moreno(a) *brunet/brunette* 2

morir (irreg.) *to die* 90

morirse (irreg.) *to die* 166

el mosquito *mosquito* 83

la mostaza *mustard* 208

el mostrador de información *information desk* 20

mostrar (irreg. **ue**) *to show* 101

el motivo *motif* 157 *reason* 384

la moto *bike* 357

la motocicleta *motorcycle* 357

el motor *engine* 312

el movimiento *movement* 24 *transit* 297

la muchacha *girl* 280

muchachos *guys (form of address)* 198

muchas veces *many times* 16

mucho *a lot, much* 10

mucho(a) *a lot of* 194

Mucho gusto. *Pleased to meet you.* 2

muchos(as) *many* 194

los muebles *furniture* 96

la muela *tooth (molar)* 261

muerto(a) *dead* 134

la muestra *sign* 157

la mujer *woman* 2

multicolor *multicolored* 176

múltiple *multiple* 157

el mundo *world* 45

municipal *municipal, public* 378

la muñeca *wrist* 244

el/la muñeco(a) *doll* 51

el museo *museum* 20

la música *music* 14

musical *musical* 111

el musical *musical* 407

el/la músico(a) *musician* 31

muy *very* 2

nacer (irreg.) *to be born* 135

nacional *national* 29

la nacionalidad *nationality* 46

nada *not at all* 10 *nothing* 34 *anything (in questions)* 422

nadar *to swim* 15

nadie *nobody* 25

náhuatl *Nahuatl* 71

la naranja *orange* 190

el naranjo *orange tree* 279

la nariz *nose* 244

la narración *story* 322

narrar *to tell* 314

narrativo(a) *narrative* 385

nativo(a) *native* 47

natural *natural* 59

la naturaleza *nature* 20

el/la navegante *navigator* 87

la Navidad *Christmas* 262

necesario(a) *necessary* 20

el **neceser** *toiletries bag* 256

la **necesidad** *need* 273

necesitar *to need* 27

negativo(a) *negative* 63

negro(a) *black* 148

nervioso(a) *nervous* 52

neutro(a) *neuter* 128

nevar (irreg. **ie**) *to snow* 416

nicaragüense *Nicaraguan* 51

el **nido** *nest* 429

el/la **nieto(a)** *grandson/ granddaughter* 36

la **nieve** *snow* 416

ningún, ninguno(a) *no, (not) any, none* 194

el/la **niño(a)** *child* 4

el **nivel** *level* 163

no *no* 8

… ¿no? *… isn't it?/doesn't it?/ etc.* 84

No es cierto. *That's not true.* 344

No es verdad. *That's not true.* 344

No estoy de acuerdo. *I disagree.* 344

No llevas razón. *You're wrong.* 344

No sé… *I don't know …* 292

la **noche** *evening* 211 *night* 279

el **nombre** *noun* 1 *name* 19

el **noreste** *northeast* 408

normal *normal* 131

normalmente *normally* 27

el **noroeste** *northwest* 408

el **norte** *north* 408

nos *ourselves* 16 *(to) us* 106

nosotros(as) *we* 4

la **nota** *note* 56 *grade* 272

la **noticia** *news* 264

la **novela de aventuras** *adventure novel* 166

noviembre *November* 169

el/la **novio(a)** *boyfriend/girlfriend* 57

la **nuca** *nape (of the neck)* 280

nuestro(a) *our* 38

el/la **nuestro(a)** *ours* 38

nuevo(a) *new* 5

la **nuez** *walnut* 195

el **número** *number* 37

el **número de identidad** *ID number* 60

el **número de pasaporte** *passport number* 60

numerosos(as) *many* 355

nunca *never* 16

o *or* 49

el **objetivo** *goal, objective* 376

objetivo(a) *objective* 281

el **objeto** *object* 1

la **obligación** *obligation* 270

la **obra** *work* 243

la **obra de teatro** *play* 116

la **obra maestra** *masterpiece* 155

observar *to watch* 407

la **obsesión** *obsession* 332

el **obstáculo** *obstacle* 436

obtener (irreg.) *to gather* 61

ocasionalmente *occasionally* 272

el **océano** *ocean* 400

el **océano Glacial Antártico** *Southern Ocean* 400

el **océano Glacial Ártico** *Arctic Ocean* 400

el **ocio** *leisure* 1

octubre *October* 144

ocultar *to hide* 426

ocupado(a) *busy* 109

ocupar *to occupy* 87 *to take up* 122

ocurrir *to happen* 43

el **oeste** *west* 408

la **oferta de empleo** *job offer* 351

oficial *official* 226

la **oficina** *office* 58

la **oficina de correos** *post office* 112

la **oficina del director** *principal's office* 348

el/la **oficinista** *office worker* 59

el **oficio** *job, profession* 343

ofrecer (irreg.) *to offer* 190

la **ofrenda** *offering* 295

el **oído** *ear* 14

oír (irreg.) *to hear* 90

Ojalá… *I hope …* 343

el **ojo** *eye* 244

oler (irreg.) *to smell* 15

el **olivo** *olive tree* 279

la **olla** *pressure cooker* 208

el **olor** *smell* 325

olvidar *to forget* 220

ondulado(a) *wavy* 280

la **onomatopeya** *onomatopoeia* 427

la **onza** *ounce* 286

la **opción** *option* 21

la **ópera** *opera* 379

opinar *to think* 84

el/la **oponente** *opponent* 385

la **oportunidad** *opportunity* 92

optimista *optimistic* 44

la **oración** *sentence* 43

oral *oral* 155

el **orden** *order (arrangement)* 77

la **orden** *order (command)* 270

ordenado(a) *tidy* 357

ordenar *to tidy up* 13 *to put in order* 17 *to order* 109

la **oreja** *ear* 244

las **orejeras** *earflaps* 176

la **orfebrería** *gold/silversmithing* 299

organizado(a) *organized* 77

organizar *to organize* 64

el **oriente** *east* 55

el **origen** *origin* 35

original *original* 154

originalmente *originally* 207

originar *to cause* 333

originario(a) de *native to* 209

el **oro** *gold* 87

la **orquídea** *orchid* 331

la **ortografía** *spelling* 79

os *(to) you (plural, informal)* 106 *yourselves (informal)* 16

oscuro(a) *dark* 127

el **oso** *bear* 424

el **otoño** *fall, autumn* 20

otro(a) *other* 35 *another* 51

la **oveja** *sheep* 424

paciente *patient* 44

el/la **paciente** *patient* 260

pacientemente *patiently* 257

el **padre** *father* 36

los **padres** *parents (mother and father)* 10

el **padrino** *godfather* 36

pagar *to pay* 164

pagar con tarjeta *to pay by credit card* 164

pagar en efectivo *to pay in cash* 164

la **página** *page* 45

la **página web** *website* 35

el **país** *country* 45

el **paisaje** *landscape* 72

el **pájaro** *bird* 22

la **palabra** *word* 31
el **palacio** *palace* 68
la **palmera** *palm tree* 279
la **pampa** *the pampas* 435
el **pan** *bread* 192
el/la **panadero(a)** *baker* 190
panameño(a) *Panamanian* 70
la **pandereta** *tambourine* 105
el **pantalón** *pants* 149
el **pantalón corto** *shorts* 140
los **pantalones** *pants* 9
los **pantalones cortos** *shorts* 135
la **papa** *potato* 9
el **papá** *dad, father* 67
las **papas fritas** *French fries* 10
el **papel** *(piece of) paper* 313
la **papelería** *stationery store* 156
el **paquete** *package* 200
para *to* 8 *for* 14
Para mí... *In my opinion ...* 344
para qué *what for* 62
la **parada de autobús** *bus stop* 296
paraguayo(a) *Paraguayan* 382
el **paraíso** *paradise* 397
parar(se) *to stop* 317
parecido(a) *similar* 47
la **pared** *wall* 86
la **pareja** *pair* 33
el/la **pariente** *relative* 190
el **parque** *park* 112
el **párrafo** *paragraph* 48
la **parte** *part* 1
el/la **participante** *participant* 121
participar *to take part* 64
el **participio** *participle* 246
la **particularidad** *peculiarity* 383
el/la **partidario(a)** *supporter* 436
el **partido** *game, match* 75
el **partido de baloncesto** *basketball game* 14
pasado mañana *the day after tomorrow* 410
el/la **pasajero(a)** *passenger* 304
Pásame..., por favor. *Could you pass me ..., please?* 188
el **pasaporte** *passport* 21
pasar *to happen* 41 *to spend* 47 *to pass* 188 *to come in* 398
pasar la aspiradora *to vacuum* 91
pasear *to go for a walk* 364
el **paseo** *walk* 123 *ride* 293
el **pasillo** *hallway* 88 *aisle* 304
la **pasión** *passion* 124
el **paso** *step* 78 *passage* 436

el **paso de cebra** *crosswalk* 112
la **pasta** *pasta* 192
la **pasta de dientes** *toothpaste* 252
el **pastel** *cake* 211
la **pastilla** *pill, tablet* 260
patinar *to skate* 268
el **patio** *courtyard* 91
el **patrimonio** *heritage* 91
Patrimonio de la Humanidad *World Heritage* 91
el **pavo** *turkey* 215
el/la **payaso(a)** *clown* 153
el **peatón** *pedestrian* 112
el **pecho** *chest* 244
peculiar *peculiar* 33
el **pedal** *pedal* 310
pedir (irreg. **i, i**) *to order* 8 *to ask for* 18
peinarse *to comb one's hair* 252
pelar *to peel* 208
la **película** *movie* 14
peligroso(a) *dangerous* 25
pelirrojo(a) *red-haired* 44
el **pelo** *hair* 15
la **pelota** *ball* 372
la **peluquería** *hair salon* 156
la **península** *peninsula* 278
la **península Ibérica** *Iberian Peninsula* 278
pensar (irreg. **ie**) *to think* 18
pensativo(a) *pensive* 280
el/la **peor** *worst* 402
peor *worse* 54
el **pepino** *cucumber* 267
pequeño(a) *small* 40 *little* 67
la **pera** *pear* 192
la **percha** *hanger* 320
perder (irreg. **ie**) *to lose* 152
perder el autobús *to miss the bus* 296
perderse (irreg. **ie**) *to get lost* 21
Perdón./Perdona. *Excuse me.* 240
Perdone. *Excuse me.* 240
perezoso(a) *lazy* 44
perfectamente *perfectly* 351
perfecto(a) *perfect* 168
¡Perfecto! *Great!* 138
el **perfil** *profile* 67
el **perfume** *perfume* 279
la **perfumería** *perfume store* 156
el **periódico** *newspaper* 92
el/la **periodista** *journalist* 153
el **periodo** *period* 215

perjudicial *damaging* 437
permitir *to allow* 426
pero *but* 2
el **perro** *dog* 337
perseguir (irreg. **i, i**) *to pursue* 55
la **persona** *person* 1
el **personaje** *character* 31 *celebrity* 63
personal *personal* 36
la **personalidad** *personality* 1
pertenecer (irreg.) *to belong* 87
peruano(a) *Peruvian* 174
pesar *to weigh* 44
el **pescado** *fish* 192
el/la **pescador(a)** *fisherman/ woman* 429
pesimista *pessimistic* 44
el **peso** *weight* 45 *peso* 320
la **pestaña** *eyelash* 244
el **petróleo** *oil* 321
el **pez** *fish* 423
el **piano** *piano* 389
picante *hot (spicy)* 216
picar *to chop* 206 *to itch* 260
el **pico** *peak* 371
el **pie** *foot* 244
la **piel** *skin* 25
Pienso que... *I think ...* 344
la **pierna** *leg* 244
la **pieza** *item, piece* 95
el **pijama** *pajamas* 140
el/la **piloto** *pilot* 303
la **pimienta** *pepper (spice)* 208
el **pimiento** *pepper (vegetable)* 234
pintar *to paint* 15
pintarse *to put makeup on* 252
pintarse los labios *to put lipstick on* 252
el/la **pintor(a)** *painter* 356
la **pintura** *painting* 242 *paint* 367
la **piña** *pineapple* 192
¡pío! *peep!* 427
la **pirámide** *pyramid* 214
el/la **pirata** *pirate* 83
pisar *to press* 310
la **piscina** *swimming pool* 15
el **piso** *floor, story* 87
la **pista** *clue* 162
la **pizarra** *chalkboard* 2
la **pizza** *pizza* 8
la **pizzería** *pizzeria* 383
el **plan** *plan* 59
la **plancha** *iron* 88
planchar *to iron* 88
planear *to plan* 59

próximo(a) next 181

el **próximo año** next year 410

el **próximo mes** next month 410

el **proyecto** project 70

prudente careful, prudent 313

publicado(a) posted 40

público(a) public 261

el **pueblo** people 43 town, village 69

¿Puede(s) ayudarme? Can you help me? 240

¿Puede(s) darme…? Can I borrow …? 188

¿Puede(s) pasarme…? Can you pass me …? 188

la **puerta** door 8 gate 296

el **puerto** port 400

puertorriqueño(a) Puerto Rican 122

pues… er … 123 well 138 then 357

el **puesto** stall 165

la **pulsera** bracelet 140

el **punto** point 376

el **punto de encuentro** meeting point 355

la **puntuación** punctuation 79

que that 19 who 25 than 54

qué what 3

¡Qué casualidad! What a coincidence! 324

¡Qué emoción! How exciting! 398

¡Qué maravilla! It's wonderful! 32

¿Qué opinas? What do you think? 84

¿Qué tal? How are you doing? 5

¿Qué tal…? How's…? 2

¿Qué tal se encuentra/te encuentras? How are you feeling? 240

¿Qué tal si…? Why don't we/you…? 292

¿Qué te parece? What do you think? 84

¡Qué va! Not at all!, No way! 344

¡Qué vergüenza! How embarrassing! 147

quedar to be left 321

quedar bien/mal to fit well/badly 164

quedar grande/pequeño(a) to be too big/too small 164

quedarse to stay 121

querer (irreg.) to want 18

Querido(a)… Dear … 147

la **quesadilla** quesadilla (a griddled tortilla with filling) 214

el **queso** cheese 192

quien whom 37

quién(es) who 2

la **Química** chemistry (subject) 348

el **quiosco** kiosk 156

¡quiquiriquí! cock-a-doodle-do! 427

quitar to remove 169 to take away 187

quitarse to take off 431

quizás maybe 249

la **raíz** stem 1

rallado(a) grated 190

la **rana** frog 22

rápidamente quickly 254

rápido quickly, fast 108

¡Rápido! Quick! 102

rápido(a) fast 21

la **raqueta** racket 372

rara vez seldom 16

raro(a) strange 147

el **rasgo** trait 1

el **rasgo físico** physical trait 48

la **raza** race 71

real real 64 royal 87

realista realist 280

realizar to perform, to carry out 245

realmente in fact 71

las **rebajas** sales 170

la **recepción** reception 320

el/la **recepcionista** receptionist 320

la **receta** recipe 187 prescription 263

recibir to receive 12

el **reciclaje** recycling 431

recoger to collect 172

recogido(a) compiled 53 tied back 280

la **recomendación** recommendation 14

recomendado(a) recommended 193

recomendar (irreg. **ie**) to recommend 266

reconocer (irreg.) to recognize 86

recopilar to gather 125

recordar (irreg. **ue**) to remember 18

recorrer to go around 155

el **recuerdo** souvenir 21 memories 301

el **recurso natural** natural resource 95

los **recursos** resources 281

la **red** web 41 network 305 net 372

referirse a (irreg. **ie, i**) to refer to 55 to mean 406

reflejar to show 425

el **reflejo** reflection 176

reflexivo(a) reflexive 1

reformular to reformulate 125

el **refresco** soda 10

el **refrigerador** refrigerator 104

regalar to give (as a present) 106

el **regalo** present 49

regatear to bargain 165

la **región** region 43

regresar to come back 181

regular regular 1

la **reina** queen 243

reír(se) (irreg. **i**) to laugh 45

la **relación** relationship 36

relacionar to match 19 to relate 43

relajarse to relax 270

el **relámpago** lightning 416

relativo(a) relative 402

la **religión** religion 435

religioso(a) religious 300

relleno(a) filled 222

el **reloj** clock 2 watch 140

remar to row 398

el **remate de cabeza** header 376

el **remedio** remedy 260

el **repaso** review 26

el **repelente de mosquitos** insect repellent 422

repetir (irreg. **i, i**) to repeat 18

la **réplica** replica 93

el **reportaje fotográfico** illustrated feature 239

el/la **reportero(a)** reporter 316

el/la **representante** exponent 55

representar to perform 41 to represent 51

representativo(a) representative 123

la **reproducción** reproduction 247

el **reptil** reptile 423

el **requisito** *requirement* 351

el **rescate** *ransom* 87

la **reserva** *reserve* 71 *reservation* 306

reservar *to book* 27

el **resfriado** *cold* 14

la **residencia** *residence* 253

la **resina** *resin* 95

resolver (irreg.) *to solve* 69

respecto a *regarding* 269

respetar *to respect* 313

el **respeto** *respect* 219

respetuoso(a) *respectful* 313

respirar *to breathe* 159

responder *to answer* 62

responsable *responsible* 351

la **respuesta** *answer* 32

el **restaurante** *restaurant* 216

el **resto** *rest* 212

el **resultado** *result* 93

resultar *to seem* 123

el **resumen** *summary* 69

el **reto** *challenge* 381

el **retraso** *delay* 304

el **retrato** *portrait* 87

reunirse *to meet* 239

la **revista** *magazine* 156

la **revolución** *revolution* 207

el **rey** *king* 249

rico(a) *rich* 43 *delicious* 273

la **rima** *rhyme* 69

el **rincón** *corner* 72

el **río** *river* 400

rioplatense *from River Plate* 383

la **riqueza** *richness* 71

la **risa** *laugh* 55

el **ritmo** *rhythm* 71

el **rito** *rite* 279

ritual *ritual* 176

la **rivalidad** *rivalry* 373

el **roble** *oak* 20

la **roca** *rock* 120

rodeado(a) *surrounded* 433

la **rodilla** *knee* 244

rojo(a) *red* 148

los **romanos** *Romans* 279

romper (irreg.) *to break* 94

la **ropa** *clothes* 1

la **ropa de caballero** *menswear* 144

la **ropa deportiva** *sportswear* 182

rosado(a) *pink* 148

el **rostro** *face* 41

la **rotación** *rotation* 407

roto(a) *broken* 246

rubio(a) *blond(e)* 44

la **rueda** *wheel* 312

el **ruido** *noise* 315

las **ruinas** *ruins* 72

el **rumano** *Romanian (language)* 279

la **ruta** *route* 199

la **rutina** *routine* 16

S

el **sábado** *Saturday* 8

saber (irreg.) *to know* 24

el **sabor** *taste* 179

saborear *to taste* 15

sacar *to take out* 93 *to take* 145 *to get* 272

sacar dinero *to take out money* 320

sacudir el polvo *to dust* 88

sagrado(a) *holy* 72

la **sal** *salt* 208

la **sala** *living room* 88 *room* 253

la **sala de computación** *computer lab* 348

salado(a) *salty* 216

la **salida** *exit* 65 *access* 174

salir (irreg.) *to go out* 121 *to come out* 161 *to leave* 296

el **salmón** *salmon* 192

el **salón** *living room* 391

el **salón de clase** *classroom* 3

la **salsa** *salsa* 123 *sauce* 187

la **salsa de tomate** *tomato sauce* 208

saltar *to jump* 279

el **salto de agua** *waterfall* 303

la **salud** *health* 260

saludable *healthy* 1

saludar *to greet* 245

saludarse *to greet each other* 245

el **saludo** *greeting* 1

salvadoreño(a) *Salvadoran* 70

salvaje *wild* 424

salvar *to save* 429

la **samba** *samba* 407

el **sancocho** *soup of beef, vegetables and green bananas* 323

la **sandalia** *sandal* 140

la **sandía** *watermelon* 192

el **sándwich** *sandwich* 9

sanitario(a) *health (adjective)* 261

el **saqueo** *looting* 332

la **sartén** *frying pan* 208

se *himself, herself, itself, themselves* 16

el **secador** *hair dryer* 252

la **secadora** *clothes dryer* 104

secar *to dry* 103

secarse *to dry (one's hands, face, hair)* 252

la **sección** *department* 170 *section* 183

seco(a) *dry* 435

el/la **secretario(a)** *secretary* 360

el **secreto** *secret* 214

secreto(a) *secret* 189

la **secuencia** *sequence* 385

secundario(a) *secondary* 66

la **sed** *thirst* 3

la **sede** *seat (venue)* 174

seguir (irreg. **i, i**) *to follow* 14 *to keep* 375

seguir recto *to keep walking straight ahead* 20

seguir una dieta equilibrada *to have a balanced diet* 268

según *according to* 53 *depending on* 278

según se dice... *apparently ...* 422

segundo(a) *second* 61

el **segundo plato** *entrée* 222

seguramente *probably* 351

seguro(a) *sure* 317

seleccionar *to select* 59

la **selva** *jungle* 400

el **semáforo** *stoplight* 112

la **semana** *week* 19

la **semana pasada** *last week* 143

la **semana que viene** *next week* 109

sembrar (irreg. **ie**) *to plant* 199

la **semejanza** *similarity* 38

la **semilla** *seed* 195

sencillamente *simply* 384

el **senderismo** *hiking* 372

el/la **senderista** *hiker* 371

sentado(a) *sitting* 114

sentarse (irreg. **ie**) *to sit* 127

el **sentido** *direction* 407

sentimental *sentimental* 365

el **sentimiento** *feeling* 50

sentir (irreg. **ie, i**) *to feel* 90 *to be sorry* 366

sentirse (irreg. **ie, i**) *to feel* 166

la **señal** *sign* 112 *signal* 311 *tone (on phone)* 361

la **señal de pare** *stop sign* 112

el **señor**   *gentleman 9 Mr. 37 man 46*

la **señora**   *Mrs. 4 lady 6 madam 112*

separado(a)   *apart 248*

septiembre   *September 40*

séptimo(a)   *seventh 70*

la **sequía**   *drought 424*

ser (irreg.)   *to be 1*

la **serenata**   *serenade 83*

la **serie**   *series 343*

serio(a)   *serious 44*

la **serpiente**   *snake 34*

el **servicio**   *service 112*

la **servilleta**   *napkin 216*

servir (irreg. **i, i**)   *to serve 18*

si   *if 34 whether 36*

sí   *yes 13*

Sí, claro.   *Yes, of course. 344*

siempre   *always 5*

la **siesta**   *siesta, nap 255*

el **siglo**   *century 43*

el **significado**   *meaning 322*

significar   *to mean 71*

siguiente   *following 14*

la **silla**   *chair 8*

el **sillón**   *armchair 96*

la **silueta**   *silhouette, outline 41*

simbólico(a)   *symbolic 37*

el **símbolo**   *symbol 251*

similar   *similar 35*

simpático(a)   *nice 2*

simplemente   *simply 315*

sin   *without 70*

sin embargo   *however 219*

sincero(a)   *sincere 44*

singular   *singular 202*

sino   *but 319*

el **síntoma**   *symptom 1*

sísmico(a)   *seismic 419*

el **sistema**   *system 45*

el **sitio**   *place 266*

la **situación**   *situation 141 location 174*

situado(a)   *located 70*

situar   *to place 227*

situarse   *to be located 419*

sobre   *about 31 above 89 on 94*

sobre todo   *mainly 367*

el/la **sobrino(a)**   *nephew/niece 36*

sociable   *sociable 124*

social   *social 51*

la **sociedad**   *society 383*

la **sociedad protectora de animales**   *society for the prevention of cruelty to animals 361*

el/la **socorrista**   *lifeguard 356*

el **sofá**   *sofa 96*

sofisticado(a)   *sophisticated 171*

el **sol**   *sun 25*

solar   *sun (adjective) 25*

sólido(a)   *solid 191*

solo   *only 14*

solo(a)   *alone, on one's own 19 single 245*

soltero(a)   *single 36*

la **solución**   *solution 283*

el **sombrero**   *hat 140*

el **sombrero hongo**   *derby 175*

sonar   *to sound 331*

la **sonatina**   *sonatina 55*

el **sonido**   *noise 316 sound 331*

la **sonrisa**   *smile 19*

la **sopa**   *soup 186*

la **sopa de letras**   *wordsearch 279*

soportar   *to stand, to bear 362*

el **sorbete**   *sorbet 137*

sorprendente   *surprising 153*

sorprender   *to surprise 366*

sorprenderse   *to be surprised 311*

sorprendido(a)   *surprised 52*

la **sorpresa**   *surprise 82*

el **sorteo**   *draw 274*

soso(a)   *tasteless 216*

el **sótano**   *basement 88*

su, sus   *his, her, its, their 8*

suave   *soft 146 mild 257 gentle 280*

subir   *to go up 13 to climb 159 to get on 303 to get in 315 to rise 442*

subjetivo(a)   *subjective 281*

el **subjuntivo**   *subjunctive 358*

sucio(a)   *dirty 89*

la **sudadera**   *sweatshirt 140*

sudar   *to sweat 252*

el **suroeste**   *southwest 408*

suelen/sueles...   *they/you usually ... 13*

el **sueño**   *sleepiness 3 dream 118*

la **suerte**   *luck 228*

el **suéter**   *sweater 140*

sufrir   *to suffer 159*

la **sugerencia**   *suggestion 203*

sugerir (irreg. **ie, i**)   *to suggest 220*

la **superficie**   *surface 407 area 428*

el **superlativo**   *superlative 54*

el **supermercado**   *supermarket 156*

suponer (irreg.)   *to constitute 376*

el **sur**   *south 408*

el **sureste**   *southeast 408*

el **surf**   *surfing 404*

el **suroeste**   *southwest 408*

el **suspiro**   *sigh 55*

sustentar   *to support 177*

el **susto**   *fright 361*

suyo(a)   *his, her, your, their 38*

el/la **suyo(a)**   *his, hers, yours, theirs 225*

el **tabasco**   *tabasco 198*

la **tabla**   *table 51*

el **tablero**   *board 131*

tacaño(a)   *stingy 44*

el **taco**   *taco 187*

el **talento**   *talent 369*

la **talla**   *size 148*

tallado(a)   *sculpted 251*

también   *also 3*

el **tambor**   *drum 71*

tampoco   *neither, not ... either 99*

tan   *as 54 so 97*

el **tango**   *tango 362*

el **tanque de gasolina**   *gas tank 312*

tanto(a)   *so much 322*

tanto como   *as much as 54*

tantos(as)   *so many 35*

tapar   *to cover 122*

el **tapón**   *plug 436*

tardar   *to take (time) 422*

tarde   *late 17*

la **tarde**   *afternoon 160*

la **tarea**   *task 33 chore 88 homework 129*

la **tarifa**   *price 296*

la **tarjeta de crédito**   *credit card 164*

la **tarjeta de embarque**   *boarding pass 304*

el **tarro**   *jar 200*

el **taxi**   *taxi 110*

la **taza**   *cup 190*

te   *yourself 16 (to) you (informal) 106*

el **té**   *tea 145*

Te toca a ti.   *It's your turn. 375*

el **teatro**   *theater 116*

el/la **técnico(a) informático(a)**   *computer technician 356*

el **tejado**   *roof 88*

el **tejido**   *fabric 171*

tejido(a)   *knitted 157*

el/la **telefonista**   *operator 356*

el **teléfono**   *telephone* 13

la **telenovela**   *soap opera* 343

la **televisión**   *television* 13

el **televisor**   *television set* 8

el **tema**   *theme* 105 *topic* 274

la **temperatura**   *temperature* 416

la **temporada**   *season* 271

temporal   *time (adjective)* 150

temprano   *early* 17

el **tenedor**   *fork* 216

tener (irreg.)   *to have* 3

tener barba   *to have a beard* 44

tener bigote   *to have a moustache* 42

tener cuidado   *to be careful* 254

tener hambre   *to be hungry* 211

tener náuseas   *to feel sick/ nauseous* 159

tener sed   *to be thirsty* 211

tener sueño   *to be sleepy* 2

el **tenis**   *tennis* 372

los **tenis**   *tennis shoes* 9

la **teoría**   *theory* 53

tercer(o)(a)   *third* 163

las **termas**   *hot springs* 415

la **terminación**   *ending* 90

terminar   *to end, to finish* 46

el **termómetro**   *thermometer* 416

la **terraza**   *terrace* 324

el **terremoto**   *earthquake* 416

el **terreno**   *plot of land* 407

terrestre   *land (adjective)* 174

terrible   *terrible* 316

el **territorio**   *territory* 71

la **tesis**   *thesis* 437

el **tesoro**   *treasure* 203

textil   *textile (adjective)* 171

el **textil**   *textile* 157

el **texto**   *text* 47

la **tía**   *aunt* 4

el **tiempo**   *time* 47 *tense* 162 *weather* 211

el **tiempo libre**   *leisure time* 1

la **tienda**   *store* 12

la **tienda de alimentación**   *grocery store* 121

la **tienda de artesanía**   *handicrafts store* 156

la **tienda de bisutería**   *costume jewelry store* 156

la **tienda de comestibles**   *grocery store* 112

la **tienda de deportes**   *sports store* 156

la **tienda de disfraces**   *costume shop* 156

la **tienda de música**   *music store* 156

la **tienda de regalos**   *gift shop* 156

la **tienda de ropa**   *clothing store* 156

Tienes razón.   *You're right.* 344

la **tierra**   *land* 71

la **Tierra**   *Earth* 407

tierra adentro   *inland* 224

las **tijeras**   *scissors* 252

tímido(a)   *shy* 5

el **tío**   *uncle* 4

típico(a)   *typical* 8

el **tipo**   *kind, type* 111

la **tira cómica**   *comic strip* 315

tirar   *to throw* 313

la **tirolina**   *zip line* 59

titularse   *to be titled* 281

el **título**   *title* 249

la **toalla**   *towel* 320

el **tobillo**   *ankle* 244

tocar   *to touch* 15 *to play* 68

tocar a la puerta   *to knock on the door* 152

tocar la guitarra   *to play the guitar* 364

todavía   *yet* 14 *still* 139

todo   *everything* 25

todo(a)   *entire, whole* 21 *all* 109

todos(as)   *every, all* 7 *all of* 12 *everyone* 13

todos los días   *every day* 16

tomar   *to take (medicine, photo, drink, taxi)* 14 *to take, to seize* 291

tomar apuntes   *to take notes* 348

tomar el sol   *to sunbathe* 364

el **tomate**   *tomato* 192

la **tontería**   *silly thing* 384

la **tormenta**   *storm* 416

el **tornado**   *tornado* 416

el **torneo**   *tournament* 376

el **toro**   *bull* 258

la **torre**   *tower* 266

la **torta**   *cake* 220 *pancake* 331

la **tortilla**   *tortilla* 193 *omelet* 193

la **tortuga marina**   *turtle* 422

la **tos**   *cough* 15

toser   *to cough* 260

tostar (irreg. **ue**)   *to roast* 325

total   *total* 183

totalmente   *totally* 43

trabajador(a)   *hardworking* 44

trabajar   *to work* 7

la **tradición**   *tradition* 72

tradicional   *traditional* 72

traducir (irreg.)   *to translate* 384

traer (irreg.)   *to bring* 24

el **tráfico**   *traffic* 112

el **traje**   *suit* 140

el **traje de baño**   *swimsuit* 140

la **tranquilidad**   *calm, peace* 425

tranquilo(a)   *calm* 52

Tranquilo(a).   *Don't you worry.* 50

transcurrir   *to take place* 390

transformar   *to change* 107

transformarse en   *to become* 90

transportar   *to carry* 176

el **transporte**   *transportation* 1

la **travesía**   *journey* 42

el **tren**   *train* 304

el **trigo**   *wheat* 193

triple   *triple* 324

triste   *sad* 52

tropical   *tropical* 71

el **trozo**   *piece* 206

tú   *you* 2

tu, tus   *your* 21

la **tuna**   *musical group made up of university students* 102

el **túnel**   *tunnel* 215

el **tuno**   *university student who is a member of a tuna* 102

el **turismo**   *tourism* 25

el **turismo a pie**   *sightseeing (walking)* 20

el **turismo rural**   *rural tourism* 319

el/la **turista**   *tourist* 119

turístico(a)   *tourist (adjective)* 119

turquesa   *turquoise* 124

tuyo(a)   *your* 38

el/la **tuyo(a)**   *yours* 62

la **ubicación**   *location* 409

último(a)   *last* 150

un, una   *a, an* 6

Un abrazo.   *Best wishes, Love, (in letters)* 5

¡Un momento!   *Just a minute!* 377

Un saludo.   *Best wishes.* 45

el **uncu**   *traditional Andean garment* 176

único(a)   *only* 77 *unique* 101

la **unidad**   *unit* 28

la **unión**   *union* 382

unir   *to unite* 436

la **universidad**   *university* 102

uno(a)   *one* 11

unos(as)   *some* 6

urbanístico(a)   *urban* 113

las **urgencias** *emergency* 261

uruguayo(a) *Uruguayan* 357

usar *to use* 15

el **uso** *use* 194

usted *you* 4

ustedes *you* 4

el **utensilio** *utensil* 208

útil *useful* 32

utilizar *to use* 55

la **uva** *grape* 192

la **vaca** *cow* 424

las **vacaciones** *vacation* 25

vaciar *to empty* 332

vacío(a) *empty* 121

la **vacuna** *vaccine* 339

vacunarse *to get vaccinated* 339

vago(a) *vague* 55

el **vagón** *car (of a train)* 304

la **vainilla** *vanilla* 212

valer (irreg.) *to cost* 167

valioso(a) *valuable* 167

el **valle** *valley* 400

el **vallenato** *Colombian popular dance* 331

el **valor** *value* 177

la **valoración** *judgment* 374

el **vals** *waltz* 331

variado(a) *varied* 171

la **variedad** *variety* 59

varios(as) *several* 7

el **vasco** *Basque (language)* 279

el **vaso** *glass* 216

el/la **vecino(a)** *neighbor* 124

la **vegetación** *vegetation* 71

vegetal *vegetable (adjective)* 176

vegetariano(a) *vegetarian* 193

la **vela** *candle* 191

la **velocidad** *speed* 335

vencer (irreg.) *to win* 153 *to beat* 376

la **venda** *bandage* 260

el/la **vendedor(a)** *seller* 12 *salesperson* 351

vender *to sell* 12

venezolano(a) *Venezuelan* 303

venir (irreg.) *to come* 21

la **ventaja** *advantage* 59

la **ventana** *window* 86

la **ventanilla** *window* 312

ver (irreg.) *to see, to watch* 15

el **veraneo** *summer vacation* 280

el **verano** *summer* 9

verbal *verbal* 181

el **verbo** *verb* 1

la **verdad** *truth* 45

… **¿verdad?** … *isn't it?/don't you?/etc.* 84

verdadero(a) *true* 153

verde *green* 148

la **verdura** *vegetable* 192

la **versión** *version* 247

el **verso** *line (of poetry)* 69

el **vestido** *dress* 8

la **vestimenta** *clothing* 176

vestir (irreg. **i, i**) *to dress* 18

vestirse (irreg. **i, i**) *to get dressed* 16

el/la **veterinario(a)** *veterinarian* 354

la **vía** *means* 227 *train track* 304

viajar *to travel* 20

el **viaje** *trip* 20 *journey* 59

el/la **viajero(a)** *traveler* 296

la **victoria** *win* 153

la **vicuña** *vicuña* 176

la **vida** *life* 37

el **video** *video* 27

el **videojuego** *videogame* 14

viejo(a) *old* 49

el **viernes** *Friday* 253

el **vinagre** *vinegar* 208

el **violín** *violin* 71

virgen *virgin (adjective)* 433

el **virreinato** *viceroyalty* 227

el **visado** *visa* 339

la **visión global** *overall view* 435

la **visita** *visit* 211

el/la **visitante** *visitor* 111

visitar *to visit* 296

la **vista** *view* 319

vital *vital* 376

la **vitamina** *vitamin* 266

vivir *to live* 8

el **vocabulario** *vocabulary* 1

la **vocal** *vowel* 90

el **volante** *steering wheel* 312

volar (irreg. **ue**) *to fly* 18

el **volcán** *volcano* 35

volcánico(a) *volcanic* 35

el **voleibol** *volleyball* 372

el **volumen** *volume* 303

el/la **voluntario(a)** *volunteer* 159

volver (irreg.) *to return* 18 *to come back* 19

vosotros(as) *you* 4

la **votación** *voting* 69

la **voz** *voice* 357

el **vuelo** *flight* 297

el **vuelo directo** *direct flight* 304

la **vuelta** *turn* 302

vuestro(a) *your* 38

el/la **vuestro(a)** *yours* 38

y *and* 1

ya *now* 129 *already* 146

ya no *not any more* 14

el **yacimiento** *deposit* 95

la **yema** *yolk* 190

yo *I* 2

el **yogur** *yogurt* 192

la **yuca** *cassava* 331

la **zanahoria** *carrot* 192

la **zapatería** *shoe store* 156

la **zapatilla** *slipper* 140

el **zapato** *shoe* 8

la **zona** *zone* 35

el **zoológico** *zoo* 112

GLOSARIO INGLÉS-ESPAÑOL

Belizean *beliceño(a)* 70

to **belong** *pertenecer (irreg.)* 87

below zero *bajo cero* 416

belt *el cinturón* 315

bench *el banco* 112

to **benefit** *beneficiar* 436

beside *al lado de* 22

best *el/la mejor* 21

Best wishes, *Un abrazo.* 5 *Un saludo.* 45

better *mejor* 8

between *entre* 38

bicycle *la bicicleta* 15

big *grande* 7 *gran* 20

big game *el clásico* 345

biggest *el/la mayor* 122

bike *la moto* 357

bill *el billete* 164 *la factura* 320

biologist *el/la biólogo(a)* 175

biology (subject) *la Biología* 348

biosphere *la biosfera* 71

bird *el pájaro* 22 *el ave* 423

birthday *el cumpleaños* 60

birthplace *el lugar de nacimiento* 60

bitter *amargo(a)* 216

black *negro(a)* 148

block *la cuadra* 112

blond(e) *rubio(a)* 44

blouse *la blusa* 89

blue *azul* 148

board *el tablero* 131

boarding pass *la tarjeta de embarque* 304

boat *el barco* 20 *la lancha* 423

body *el cuerpo* 14

to **boil** *cocer (irreg. ue), hervir (irreg. ie, i)* 208

boiled *cocido(a), hervido(a)* 216

Bolivian *boliviano(a)* 160

bonfire *la hoguera* 279

book *el libro* 2

to **book** *reservar* 27

bookcase *la estantería* 9

bookstore *la librería* 156

boot *la bota* 138

border *la frontera* 382

to **border on** *limitar con* 70

bored *(estar) aburrido(a)* 52

boring *(ser) aburrido(a)* 13

botanic *botánico(a)* 411

both *ambos(as)* 330

to **bother** *molestar* 362

bottle *la botella* 200

bottom *el fondo* 301

bowl *el bol* 208

box *el cuadro* 73 *la caja* 200

boy *el chico* 2

boyfriend *el novio* 57

bracelet *la pulsera* 140

brake *el freno* 312

to **brake** *frenar* 312

bread *el pan* 192

breaded *empanado(a)* 216

to **break** *romper (irreg.)* 94

breakfast *el desayuno* 250

to **breathe** *respirar* 159

breeze *la brisa* 280

brick (adjective) *de ladrillo* 88

brief *breve* 277

bright *brillante* 171

to **bring** *traer (irreg.)* 24 *llevar* 87

British *británico(a)* 70

brochure *el folleto* 296

broken *roto(a)* 246

brother *el hermano* 36

brown *marrón* 43 *de color café* 148

brunet/brunette *moreno(a)* 2

to **brush** *cepillarse* 252

budget *el presupuesto* 365

to **build** *construir (irreg.)* 403

building *el edificio* 89 *la construcción* 91

bull *el toro* 258

bullring *la plaza de toros* 259

bus *el autobús* 21 *la buseta, el camión, el colectivo, la guagua* 315

bus station *la estación de autobuses* 296

bus stop *la parada de autobús* 296

busy *atareado(a)* 90 *ocupado(a)* 109

but *pero* 2 *sino* 319

butter *la mantequilla* 192

to **buy** *comprar* 12

by *en* 20 *por* 40 *junto a* 145

by turns *por turnos* 87

C

cacao *el cacao* 198

cacao tree *el cacaotero* 203

cacao-growing *cacaotero(a)* 199

café *el café* 112

cafeteria *la cafetería, el comedor* 348

cake *el pastel* 211 *la torta* 220

to **call** *llamar* 13

calm (adjective) *tranquilo(a)* 52 *en calma* 280

calm *la tranquilidad* 425

camelid *el camélido* 149

camera *la cámara* 34

campground *el cámping* 179

can *la lata, el bote* 200

can *poder (irreg. ue, u)* 18

Can I borrow ...? *¿Me da(s)...? ¿Puede(s) darme...?* 188

Can you help me? *¿Me ayuda(s)?* 240

Can you help me? *¿Puede(s) ayudarme?* 240

Can you pass me ...? *¿Me pasas...?* 188 *¿Puedes pasarme...?* 188

Canadian *canadiense* 46

canal *el canal* 70

candidate *el/la candidato(a)* 19

candle *la vela* 191

candy *los dulces* 127

cane *la caña* 71

canyon *el cañón* 400

cap *la gorra* 140 *el gorro* 141

cape *la capa* 105

capital city *la capital* 20

car *el carro* 13 *el coche* 21

car (of a train) *el vagón* 304

careful *cuidadoso(a)* 254 *prudente* 313

carefully *cuidadosamente* 250

Caribbean *caribeño(a)* 124

carnival *el carnaval* 154

carrot *la zanahoria* 192

to **carry** *llevar* 26 *transportar* 176

carry-on luggage *el equipaje de mano* 304

to **carry out** *realizar* 245

case *el caso* 32

cash register *la caja* 164

cashier *el/la cajero(a)* 164

cassava *la yuca* 331

casserole dish *la cazuela* 208

castle *el castillo* 119

casual *informal* 182

cat *el gato* 52

Catalan (language) *el catalán* 247

category *la categoría* 274

cathedral *la catedral* 115

cause *la causa* 332

to **cause** *producir (irreg.)* 139 *originar* 333 *provocar* 376

to **fill**   *llenar* 203

filled   *relleno(a)* 222

finally   *finalmente* 70 *por fin* 136 *por último* 229

to **find**   *encontrar (irreg. ue)* 30 *localizar* 266

to **find out**   *descubrir (irreg.)* 246

finger   *el dedo (de la mano)* 244

to **finish**   *terminar* 46

fire   *el fuego* 419

firefighter   *el/la bombero(a)* 356

fireplace   *la chimenea* 127

first   *primer(o)(a)* 1

first class   *la primera clase* 304

fish   *el pescado* 192 *el pez* 423

fisherman/woman   *el/la pescador(a)* 429

to **fit well/badly**   *quedar bien/mal* 164

to **fix**   *arreglar* 109

fixed   *establecido(a)* 311

flag   *la bandera* 2

flat   *aplastado(a)* 193

flea market   *el mercado de pulga* 165

fleshy   *carnoso(a)* 195

flight   *el vuelo* 297

flight attendant   *el/la auxiliar de vuelo* 304

flood   *la inundación* 431

floor   *la planta* 8 *el piso* 87

floor plan   *el plano* 101

flora   *la flora* 71

flour   *la harina* 190

flower   *la flor* 22

flu   *la gripe* 260

flute   *la flauta* 71

to **fly**   *volar (irreg. ue)* 18

folder   *la carpeta* 129

folk (adjective)   *folclórico(a)* 155

folklore   *el folclore* 51

to **follow**   *seguir (irreg. i, i)* 14

following   *siguiente* 14

food   *la comida* 1 *el alimento* 192

foot   *el pie* 244

football   *el fútbol americano* 372

footwear   *el calzado* 138

for   *por* 8 *para* 14 *durante* 119

for dessert   *de postre* 8

for example   *por ejemplo* 71

for sale   *en venta* 100

to **forbid**   *prohibir* 360

forecast   *la previsión, el pronóstico* 419 *la predicción* 420

forehead   *la frente* 244

forest   *el bosque* 400

forest fire   *el incendio forestal* 424

to **forget**   *olvidar* 220

fork   *el tenedor* 216

form   *la forma* 63

to **form**   *formar* 402

formal   *formal* 202

formality   *la formalidad* 218

formation   *la formación* 246

former player   *el/la exjugador(a)* 376

fortress   *el alcázar* 82 *la fortaleza* 120

fortunately   *por suerte* 169 *por fortuna* 380

fossil   *el fósil* 94

fossilized   *fosilizado(a)* 95

founded   *fundado(a)* 82

fountain   *la fuente* 91

to **frame**   *enmarcar* 280

free   *libre* 122

freezer   *el congelador* 104

French (language)   *el francés* 122

French (nationality)   *francés(a)* 401

French fries   *las papas fritas* 10

frequency   *la frecuencia* 1

frequent   *frecuente* 254

frequently   *frecuentemente* 254

fresh   *fresco(a)* 216

fresh air   *el aire puro* 20

Friday   *el viernes* 253

fried   *frito(a)* 216

friend   *el/la amigo(a)* 3

fright   *el susto* 361

frightened   *asustado(a)* 391

frog   *la rana* 22

from   *de* 36 *desde* 65 *a partir de* 95

front   *la fachada* 89

frozen   *helado(a)* 435

fruit   *la fruta* 10 *el fruto* 195

frustrated   *frustrado(a)* 52

to **fry**   *freír (irreg.)* 208

frying pan   *la sartén* 208

full   *lleno(a)* 89

fun   *divertido(a)* 44

function   *la función* 15

fundamental   *fundamental* 209

funny   *divertido(a)* 32 *gracioso(a)* 44

furious   *furioso(a)* 52

furnace   *la caldera de calefacción* 104

furniture   *los muebles* 96

further   *más allá* 280

fusion   *la fusión* 71

future   *el futuro* 359

to **gain**   *adquirir (irreg. ie)* 367

Galician (language)   *el gallego* 279

gallon   *el galón* 313

game   *el juego* 70 *el partido* 75

garage   *el garaje* 13

garbage   *la basura* 93

garden   *el jardín* 88

garden vegetables   *las hortalizas* 192

garlic   *el ajo* 192

garment   *la prenda* 141

gas   *la gasolina* 312

gas pedal   *el acelerador* 312

gas station   *la gasolinera* 312

gas tank   *el tanque de gasolina* 312

gate   *la puerta* 296

to **gather**   *obtener (irreg.)* 61 *recopilar* 125

gaucho   *el gaucho* 383

gaze   *la mirada* 280

gear   *la marcha* 310

gel   *el gel* 252

generally   *generalmente* 46

generous   *generoso(a)* 44

gentle   *suave* 280

gentleman   *el señor* 9

genuine   *auténtico(a)* 145

geographic   *geográfico(a)* 434

geography (subject)   *la Geografía* 348

German (language)   *el alemán* 246

German (nationality)   *alemán(a)* 46

gesture   *el gesto* 245

to **get**   *conseguir (irreg. i, i)* 166 *sacar* 272

to **get along well/badly**   *llevarse bien/mal* 36

to **get angry**   *enojarse* 77

to **get away**   *escapar(se)* 43

to **get bored**   *aburrirse* 14

to **get dressed**   *vestirse (irreg. i, i)* 16

to **get in**   *subir (a)* 315

to **get lost**   *perderse (irreg. ie)* 21

to **get married**   *casarse* 61

to **get off**   *bajar (de)* 311

to **get on** *subir (a)* 303
to **get ready** *prepararse* 142 *arreglarse* 252
to **get sick** *enfermar* 268
to **get the wrong ...** *equivocarse de...* 329
to **get up** *levantarse* 16
to **get used to** *acostumbrarse a* 159
to **get vaccinated** *vacunarse* 339
to **get washed** *lavarse* 252
giant *el gigante* 30
gift shop *la tienda de regalos* 156
girl *la chica* 36 *la muchacha* 280
girlfriend *la novia* 57
to **give** *dar (irreg.)* 83 *impartir* 349
to **give** (as a present) *regalar* 106
to **give a prize** *premiar* 51
to **give a ticket** *poner una multa* 312
giving *la entrega* 108
glacier *el glaciar* 139
glass *el vaso* 216
glasses *las gafas* 44
global *global* 73
global warming *el calentamiento global* 139
glove *el guante* 372
to **go** *ir (irreg.)* 24 *acudir* 261
to **go to a concert** *ir a un concierto* 364
to **go to an exhibit** *ir a una exposición* 364
to **go around** *recorrer* 155
to **go camping** *hacer cámping* 25 *ir de cámping* 325
to **go down** *bajar* 127
to **go for a swim** *bañarse* 308 *darse un baño* 414
to **go for a walk** *pasear* 364
to **go in** *entrar* 114
Go on! *¡Anímate!* 274
to **go out** *salir (irreg.)* 121
to **go through** *atravesar (irreg. ie)* 139
to **go to bed** *acostarse (irreg. ue)* 16
to **go to the movies** *ir al cine* 364
to **go to the theater** *ir al teatro* 364
to **go up** *subir* 13
to **go with** *acompañar* 51
goal *el objetivo* 376
god/goddess *el/la dios(a)* 53
godfather *el padrino* 36
godmother *la madrina* 36
gold *el oro* 87
gold (adjective) *dorado(a)* 148
golden *dorado(a)* 148

goldsmithing *la orfebrería* 299
golf *el golf* 372
good *buen* 48 *bueno(a)* 216
Good idea! *¡Estupendo!* 292
Good luck! *¡Buena suerte!* 136
good morning *buenos días* 2
goodbye *la despedida* 2
government *el gobierno* 174
grade *la nota* 272
gradually *gradualmente* 159
grains *los cereales* 192
gram *el gramo* 190
grammar *la gramática* 1
granddaughter *la nieta* 36
grandfather/grandmother *el/la abuelo(a)* 36
grandparents *los abuelos* 37
grandson *el nieto* 36
grape *la uva* 192
grated *rallado(a)* 190
gray *gris* 148
great *gran* 59 *fenomenal* 292
Great! *¡Perfecto!* 138 *¡Estupendo!* 292
Greek *griego(a)* 203
green *verde* 148
to **greet** *saludar* 245
to **greet each other** *saludarse* 245
greeting *el saludo* 1
grilled *a la plancha* 216
to **grind** *moler (irreg. ue)* 325
grocery store *la tienda de alimentación* 121 *el colmado* 124
group *el grupo* 43
to **grow** *cultivar* 300
guacamole *el guacamole* 228
Guarani *el guaraní* 346
Guatemalan *guatemalteco(a)* 70
to **guess** *adivinar* 49
guest *el/la invitado(a)* 97 *el/la huésped* 320
guide *el/la guía* 139
guys (form of address) *muchachos* 198
gym *el gimnasio* 372

H

habit *el hábito* 1 *la costumbre* 298
habitual *habitual* 1
hair *el pelo* 15
hair dryer *el secador* 252

hair salon *la peluquería* 156
hairbrush *el cepillo* 252
half *la mitad* 406
hallway *el pasillo* 88
hand *la mano* 244
hand luggage *el equipaje de mano* 304
handicrafts *la artesanía* 154
handicrafts store *la tienda de artesanía* 156
to **hang** *colgar (irreg. ue)* 99
hanger *la percha* 320
to **happen** *pasar* 41 *ocurrir* 43
happily *alegremente* 254
happy *contento(a)* 56 *feliz* 254
hard *difícil* 5 *duro(a)* 175
hardworking *trabajador(a)* 44
harp *el arpa* 331
harvest *la cosecha* 199
haste *la prisa* 254
hat *el sombrero* 140
to **have** *tener (irreg.)* 3 *poseer (irreg.)* 428
to **have a balanced diet** *seguir una dieta equilibrada* 268
to **have a beard** *tener barba* 44
to **have a moustache** *tener bigote* 42
to **have a picnic** *hacer picnic* 364
to **have breakfast** *desayunar* 10
to **have dinner** *cenar* 159
to **have lunch** *comer* 8 *almorzar (irreg. ue)* 142
hazelnut *la avellana* 195
he *él* 4
He/She/It can't possibly ... *Es imposible que...* 374
head *la cabeza* 14
header *el remate de cabeza* 376
headlight *el faro* 312
health *la salud* 260
health (adjective) *sanitario(a)* 261
health care *la atención sanitaria* 261
healthy *saludable* 1
to **hear** *oír (irreg.)* 90
heart *el corazón* 120
to **heat** *calentar (irreg. ie)* 108
height *la altura* 45
help *la ayuda* 97
to **help** *ayudar* 69
hemisphere *el hemisferio* 174
hen *la gallina* 424
her *su, sus* 8 *suyo(a)(os)(as)* 38
(to) her *le* 106

here *aquí* 9

heritage *el patrimonio* 91

hero *el héroe* 87

hers *el/la/los/las suyo(a)(os)(as)* 38

herself *se* 16

hidden *escondido(a)* 239

to hide *ocultar* 426

high *elevado(a)* 159

highest *máximo(a)* 55

high-speed train *el AVE* 266

highway *la carretera* 305

hiker *el/la senderista* 371

hiking *el senderismo* 372

hill *el cerro* 162 *la colina* 400

(to) him *le* 106

himself *se* 16

to hire *contratar* 427

his *su, sus* 8 *suyo(a)(os)(as), el/la/los/las suyo(a)(os)(as)* 38

Hispanic *hispano(a)* 61

historic *histórico(a)* 118

history (subject) *la Historia* 348

hobby *la afición* 364

to hold *celebrar* 83

holy *sagrado(a)* 72

home *la casa* 8

homework *la tarea* 129

Honduran *hondureño(a)* 70

hope *la ilusión* 55

horizon *el horizonte* 280

horrible *horrible* 374

horse *el caballo* 424

hospitable *hospitalario(a)* 124

hospital *el hospital* 258

hot *caliente* 216

hot (spicy) *picante* 216

hot springs *los baños termales* 431

hot springs *las aguas termales* 59 *las termas* 415

hotel *el hotel* 320

hour *la hora* 161

house *la casa* 88

how *cómo* 2

How are you? *¿Cómo está(s)?* 2

How are you doing? *¿Qué tal?* 5

How are you feeling? *¿Qué tal se encuentra/te encuentras?* 240

How do you do? *Encantado(a).* 2

How do you feel? *¿Cómo te sientes/se siente?* 240

How embarrassing! *¡Qué vergüenza!* 147

How exciting! *¡Qué emoción!* 398

how many *cuántos(as)* 37

how much *cuánto(a)* 45

How much is it? *¿Cuánto cuesta?* 8

however *sin embargo* 219

How's ...? *¿Qué tal...?* 2

to hug *abrazar* 374

huge *enorme* 34

human *humano(a)* 14

humid *húmedo(a)* 435

hummingbird *el colibrí* 324

hunger *el hambre* 3

to hurry *darse prisa* 42

to hurt *hacer daño* 138 *doler (irreg. ue)* 260

husband *el esposo* 36

hydroelectric power station *la central hidroeléctrica* 382

hygiene *la higiene* 252

I *yo* 2

I agree. *Estoy de acuerdo.* 344

I disagree. *No estoy de acuerdo.* 344

I don't know ... *No sé...* 292

I hope ... *Ojalá...* 343

I/he/we love ... *me/le/nos encanta...* 84

I think ... *Creo/Pienso que...* 344

(the) Iberian Peninsula *la península Ibérica* 278

ice *el hielo* 416

ice cream *el helado* 10

I'd love to but ... *Es que...* 292

ID number *el número de identidad* 60

idea *la idea* 73

ideal *ideal* 19

to identify *identificar* 1

if *si* 34

ill *mal, enfermo(a)* 14

illness *la enfermedad* 14

illogical *ilógico(a)* 213

to illustrate *ilustrar* 315

illustrated feature *el reportaje fotográfico* 239

illustration *la ilustración* 66

I'm sure ... *Estoy seguro(a) de que...* 374

image *la imagen* 102

imaginary *imaginario(a)* 407

to imagine *imaginar* 39

immaterial *inmaterial* 363

immigrant *el/la inmigrante* 367

impact *el impacto* 399

impatient *impaciente* 44

imperative *el imperativo* 202

imperfect *el imperfecto* 298

impersonal *impersonal* 270

importance *la importancia* 177

important *importante* 37

impossible *imposible* 34

impression *la impresión* 7

impressive *impresionante* 307

to improve *mejorar* 381

in *en* 3 *de* 16 *dentro de* 88

in a while *en un rato* 410

in fact *realmente* 71

in front of *delante de* 22 *frente a* 127

in general *en general* 61 *por lo general* 253

in half an hour *en media hora* 410

in love *enamorado(a)* 52

In my opinion ... *Para mí, En mi opinión...* 344

in particular *en particular* 175

in the end *al final* 136

in the evening *por la noche* 160

in the past *antiguamente* 176

Inca *inca* 174

to include *incluir (irreg.)* 225

incomplete *incompleto(a)* 188

to incorporate *incorporar* 175

to increase *aumentar* 303

incredible *increíble* 20

indefinites *los indefinidos* 194

independence *la independencia* 135

independent *autónomo(a)* 253

index card *la ficha* 131

to indicate *indicar* 167

indigenous *indígena* 43 *autóctono(a)* 411

indirect *indirecto(a)* 106

industry *la industria* 171

inference *la inferencia* 177

infinitive *el infinitivo* 229

influence *la influencia* 71

to influence *influir (irreg.)* 175 *dejar huella en* 383

to inform *informar* 291

informal *informal* 202

information *la información* 20

information desk *el mostrador de información* 20

informative *informativo(a)* 333

ingredient *el ingrediente* 189

legacy   la herencia 184
legend   la leyenda 34
legumes   las legumbres 192
leisure   el ocio 1
leisure time   el tiempo libre 1
lemon   el limón 145
length   la longitud 139
lentil   la lenteja 192
less   menos 54 menor 271
Let's go!   ¡Adelante! 377
letter   la carta 45 la letra 279
lettuce   la lechuga 192
level   el nivel 163
to **liberate**   liberar 87
librarian   el/la bibliotecario(a) 356
library   la biblioteca 112
to **lie**   mentir (irreg. ie, i) 90
life   la vida 37
life jacket   el chaleco salvavidas 304
lifeguard   el/la socorrista 356
to **lift weights**   levantar pesas 372
light (adjective)   ligero(a) 233
light   la luz 97
to **light**   encender (irreg. ie) 279
light colors   los colores claros 148
lightning   el relámpago 416
like   como 47 igual que 106
to **like**   gustar 1
likes   los gustos 1
line   la línea 69
line (of poetry)   el verso 69
linguistic   lingüístico(a) 47
lip   el labio 244
liquid   líquido(a) 191
list   la lista 48
to **listen**   escuchar 14
liter   el litro 200
literary   literario(a) 55
literature (subject)   la Literatura 348
little   poco 10   pequeño(a) 67 poco(a) 194
to **live**   vivir 8
lively   alegre 42 animado(a) 428
living room   la sala 88 el salón 391
llama   la llama 137
to **load the dishwasher**   cargar el lavaplatos 88
local   local 64
to **locate**   localizar 266
located   situado(a) 70

location   la situación 174 la localización 338 la ubicación 409
logical   lógico(a) 77
long   largo(a) 21
to **look**   mirar 135
to **look after**   cuidar 274
to **look at**   mirar 306
to **look for**   buscar 31
to **look up**   consultar 296
loose-fitting   ancho(a) 149
looting   el saqueo 332
to **lose**   perder (irreg. ie) 152
love   el amor 55
Love, (in letters)   Un abrazo. 5
to **love**   amar 102 encantar 366
loved   amado(a) 103
lovely   lindo(a) 57
lover   el/la amante 428
luck   la suerte 228
luggage   el equipaje 20
lunch   el almuerzo 8
lute   el laúd 105

M

machine   el aparato 27 la máquina 318
madam   la señora 112
magazine   la revista 156
magic   mágico(a) 34
magnificent   magnífico(a) 308
main   principal 53
main character   el/la protagonista 365
main square   la plaza de armas 115
mainly   principalmente 157 sobre todo 367
majority   la mayoría 47
to **make**   hacer (irreg.) 14 elaborar 176
to **make easy**   facilitar 436
to **make up**   componer (irreg.) 286 inventar 385
makeup   el maquillaje 252
mambo   el mambo 124
man   el hombre 7 el señor 46
to **manage to make**   lograr hacer 325
manager   el/la director(a) 324
mangrove swamp   el manglar 71
manual   el manual 310
manufacture   la elaboración 176
to **manufacture**   fabricar 141

many   muchos(as) 194 numerosos(as) 355
many times   muchas veces 16
map   el mapa 296
maracas   las maracas 331
marathon   el maratón 181
March   marzo 316
mariachi   el mariachi 103
marimba   la marimba 71
marine (adjective)   marino(a) 404
marital status   el estado civil 36
to **mark**   marcar 407
marker   el marcador 150
market   el mercado 139
married   casado(a) 36
marvel   la maravilla 404
marvelous   maravilloso(a) 50
masculine   masculino(a) 38
mask   la máscara 155
masterpiece   la obra maestra 155
match   el partido 75
to **match**   relacionar 19 combinar con 138
material   el material 126
mathematics (subject)   las Matemáticas 348
to **matter**   importar 168
May   mayo 60
Mayan   maya 30
maybe   quizás 249
mayonnaise   la mayonesa 208
(to) me   me 106
meal   la comida 192
to **mean**   significar 71 referirse a (irreg. ie, i) 406
meaning   el significado 322
means   la vía 227
means of transportation   el medio de transporte 291
to **measure**   medir (irreg. i, i) 18
measurement   la medida 45
meat   la carne 192
mechanic   el/la mecánico(a) 356
medicine (drug)   el medicamento 14
medicine (science)   la Medicina 357
to **meditate**   meditar 268
to **meet**   encontrarse (irreg. ue) 43 reunirse 239
meeting point   el punto de encuentro 355
melancholic   melancólico(a) 125
melon   el melón 192
melting   el deshielo 139

memorable   *memorable* 405
memories   *los recuerdos* 301
memory   *la memoria* 122
menswear   *la ropa de caballero* 144
to **mention**   *mencionar* 116
menu   *la carta* 9
meow!   *¡miau!* 427
merchandise   *las mercancías* 157
merengue   *el merengue* 123
message   *el mensaje* 66
metaphor   *la metáfora* 281
meter   *el metro* 45
method   *el método* 205
metric   *métrico(a)* 45
metropolitan   *metropolitano(a)* 355
Mexican   *mexicano(a)* 226
microwave   *el microondas* 104
Middle Ages   *la Edad Media* 105
mild   *suave* 257
mile   *la milla* 45
milk   *la leche* 192
million   *el millón* 47
mine   *la mina* 162
mine   *el/la/los/las mío(a)(os)(as)* 38
mineral   *el mineral* 163
mineral water   *el agua mineral* 188
mining (adjective)   *minero(a)* 163
minute   *el minuto* 102
mirror   *el espejo* 96
Miskitos   *los misquitos* 71
to **miss the bus**   *perder el autobús* 296
mission   *la misión* 31
mistake   *el error* 196
to **mix**   *mezclar* 208
mixture   *la mezcla, la fusión* 71
model (example)   *el modelo* 3
model (person)   *el/la modelo* 281
moderate   *moderado(a)* 269
modern   *moderno(a)* 149
modernism   *el Modernismo* 55
modernist   *modernista* 55
mom   *la mamá* 38
moment   *el momento* 255
monarch butterfly   *la mariposa monarca* 429
monastery   *el monasterio* 276
Monday   *el lunes* 253
money   *el dinero* 164
monk   *el monje* 147
monkey   *el mono* 424
monument   *el monumento* 91
mood (in grammar)   *el modo* 358
moon   *la luna* 72

more   *más* 32
more than   *más de* 95
morning   *la mañana* 16
mosquito   *el mosquito* 83
most   *la mayor parte* 278
mother   *la madre* 36 *la mamá* 38
motif   *el motivo* 157
motorcycle   *la motocicleta* 357
motto   *el lema* 425
mount   *el monte* 403
mountain   *la montaña* 400
mountain climber   *el/la alpinista, el/la montañero(a)* 371
mountain climbing   *el alpinismo* 372
mountain range   *la cordillera* 71
mountain sickness   *el mal de altura* 159
mountainous   *montañoso(a)* 70
moustache   *el bigote* 42
mouth   *la boca* 244
to **move closer**   *acercarse* 302
to **move forward**   *avanzar* 131
movement   *el movimiento* 24
movie   *la película* 14
movie theater   *el cine* 364
Mr.   *don* (before first name) 82 *el señor* 37
Mrs.   *la señora* 4
much   *mucho* 10
mud   *el barro* 53
multicolored   *multicolor* 176
multiple   *múltiple* 157
municipal   *municipal* 378
museum   *el museo* 20
music   *la música* 14
music store   *la tienda de música* 156
musical (adjective)   *musical* 111
musical   *el musical* 407
musician   *el/la músico(a)* 31
must   *deber* 270
mustard   *la mostaza* 208
my   *mi, mis* 2
myself   *me* 16
mysterious   *misterioso(a)* 342
mystery   *el misterio* 332
myth   *el mito* 332
mythical   *mítico(a)* 295

Nahuatl   *náhuatl* 71
nail polish   *el esmalte (de uñas)* 252
name   *el nombre* 19

nap   *la siesta* 255
nape (of the neck)   *la nuca* 280
napkin   *la servilleta* 216
narrative   *narrativo(a)* 385
narrow   *estrecho(a)* 70
national   *nacional* 29
nationality   *la nacionalidad* 46
native   *el/la indígena* 51
native (adjective)   *nativo(a)* 47
native to   *originario(a) de* 209
natural   *natural* 59
natural resource   *el recurso natural* 95
nature   *la naturaleza* 20
navigator   *el/la navegante* 87
navy   *la marina* 87
near   *cerca de* 22
nearby   *cercano(a)* 139
nearly   *cerca de* 422
necessary   *necesario(a)* 20
neck   *el cuello* 244
necklace   *el collar* 140
need   *la necesidad* 273
to **need**   *necesitar* 27
negative   *negativo(a)* 63
neighbor   *el/la vecino(a)* 124
neighborhood   *el barrio* 112
neither   *tampoco* 99
nephew   *el sobrino* 36
nervous   *nervioso(a)* 52
nest   *el nido* 429
net   *la red* 372
network   *la red* 305
neuter   *neutro(a)* 128
never   *nunca* 16
new   *nuevo(a)* 5
news   *la noticia* 264
newspaper   *el periódico* 92 *la gaceta* 153 *el diario* 376
next (adverb)   *a continuación* 206
next (adjective)   *próximo(a)* 181
next month   *el mes que viene, el próximo mes* 410
next to   *al lado de* 22 *junto a* 299
next week   *la semana que viene* 109
next year   *el próximo año* 181
Nicaraguan   *nicaragüense* 51
nice   *simpático(a)* 2 *bonito(a)* 84
Nice to meet you.   *Encantado(a).* 2
niece   *la sobrina* 36
night   *la noche* 279
nightclub   *la discoteca* 368
nightstand   *la mesita de noche* 96

no   *no* 8 *ninguno(a), ningún* 194
No way!   *¡Qué va!* 344
nobody   *nadie* 25
noise   *el ruido* 315 *el sonido* 316
none   *ningún, ninguno(a)* 194
normal   *normal* 131
normally   *normalmente* 27
north   *el norte* 408
northeast   *el noreste* 408
northwest   *el noroeste* 408
nose   *la nariz* 244
(not) any   *ninguno(a), ningún* 194
not any more   *ya no* 14
not at all   *nada* 10
Not at all.   *¡Qué va!, En absoluto.* 344
not ... either   *tampoco* 99
not much   *poco* 10
note   *la nota* 56
notebook   *el cuaderno* 2
nothing   *nada* 34
to **notice**   *fijarse en* 86   *apreciar* 401
noun   *el nombre* 6
November   *noviembre* 169
now   *ahora* 60 *ya* 129
nowadays   *actualmente* 171
number   *el número* 37
nurse   *el/la enfermero(a)* 14
nurse's office   *la enfermería* 14
nuts   *los frutos secos* 195

oak   *el roble* 20
object   *el objeto* 1
objective (adjective)   *objetivo(a)* 281
objective   *el objetivo* 376
obligation   *la obligación* 270
obsession   *la obsesión* 332
obstacle   *el obstáculo* 436
Obviously ...   *Es evidente que...* 374
occasionally   *ocasionalmente* 272
to **occupy**   *ocupar* 87
ocean   *el océano* 400
October   *octubre* 144
odd   *curioso(a)* 201
of   *de* 1
of course   *claro* 41 *desde luego, por supuesto* 344
to **offer**   *ofrecer (irreg.)* 190

offering   *la ofrenda* 295
office   *la oficina* 58
office worker   *el/la oficinista* 59
official   *oficial* 226
often   *a menudo* 301
oil   *el aceite* 208 *el petróleo* 321
old   *mayor* 2 *antiguo(a)* 35 *viejo(a)* 49
old part of town   *el casco viejo* 401
older   *mayor* 67
olive oil   *el aceite de oliva* 267
olive tree   *el olivo* 279
omelet   *la tortilla* 193
on   *en* 13 *encima de* 22 *sobre* 94
on a visit   *de visita* 203
on one's own   *solo(a)* 19
on the other hand   *en cambio* 382
on the outskirts   *en las afueras* 112
on top of   *encima de* 22
one   *uno(a)* 11   *algún, alguno(a) (os)(as)* 194
one week/two days/ ... ago   *hace una semana/dos días/...* 150
on-going   *en desarrollo* 314
one-way ticket   *el boleto sencillo* 304
onion   *la cebolla* 192
only   *solo* 14 *único(a)* 77
onomatopoeia   *la onomatopeya* 427
to **open**   *abrir (irreg.)* 12 *inaugurar* 297
open-air   *al aire libre* 165
opened   *abierto* 246
opening   *la apertura* 376
opera   *la ópera* 379
operator   *el/la telefonista* 356
opponent   *el/la antagonista* 385
opportunity   *la oportunidad* 92
optimistic   *optimista* 44
option   *la opción* 21
or   *o* 49
oral   *oral* 155
orange   *la naranja* 190
orange (color)   *anaranjado(a)* 148
orange blossom   *el azahar* 190
orange tree   *el naranjo* 279
orchid   *la orquídea* 331
order   *el orden* 77 *el mandato* 218 *la orden* 270
to **order**   *pedir (irreg. i, i)* 8 *ordenar* 109

organize   *organizar* 64
organized   *organizado(a)* 77
origin   *el origen* 35
original   *original* 154
originally   *originalmente* 207
ornament   *el adorno* 95
other   *otro(a)* 35
ounce   *la onza* 286
our   *nuestro(a)* 38
ours   *el/la nuestro(a)* 38
ourselves   *nos* 16
out sick   *ausente por enfermedad* 14
outline   *la silueta* 41
outside   *fuera (de)* 88
outskirts   *las afueras* 112
oven   *el horno* 104
overall view   *la visión global* 435
own   *propio(a)* 69
owner   *el/la dueño(a)* 121 *el/la propietario(a)* 329

pack   *el envase* 263
to **pack**   *preparar* 143 *envasar* 263 *hacer el equipaje* 296
package   *el paquete* 200
to **package**   *envasar* 263
page   *la página* 45
pain   *el dolor* 260
paint   *la pintura* 367
to **paint**   *pintar* 15
painter   *el/la pintor(a)* 356
painting   *el cuadro* 96 *la pintura* 242
pair   *la pareja* 33
pajamas   *el pijama* 140
palace   *el palacio* 68
palm tree   *la palmera* 279
(the) pampas   *la pampa* 435
Panamanian   *panameño(a)* 70
pancake   *la torta* 331
pantry   *la despensa* 88
pants   *los pantalones* 9 *el pantalón* 149
paper   *el papel* 313
parade   *el desfile* 149
paradise   *el paraíso* 397
paragraph   *el párrafo* 48 *el apartado* 333
Paraguayan   *paraguayo(a)* 382
parents (mother and father)   *los padres* 10

to **remove** *quitar* 169

to **rent** *alquilar* 394

to **repeat** *repetir (irreg. i, i)* 18

replica *la réplica* 93

report *el boletín* 442

reporter *el/la reportero(a)* 316

to **represent** *representar* 51

representative *representativo(a)* 123

reproduction *la reproducción* 247

reptile *el reptil* 423

requirement *el requisito* 351

to **research** *investigar* 83

researcher *el/la investigador(a)* 332

reservation *la reserva* 306

reserve *la reserva* 71

residence *la residencia* 253

resin *la resina* 95

resources *los recursos* 281

respect *el respeto* 219

to **respect** *respetar* 313

respectful *respetuoso(a)* 313

responsible *responsable* 351

rest *el resto* 212 *el descanso* 255 *los/las demás* 385

to **rest** *descansar* 14

restaurant *el restaurante* 216

restrooms *los aseos* 348

result *el resultado* 93

to **return** *volver (irreg.)* 18

revenue *los ingresos* 319

reverse *la marcha atrás* 310

review *el repaso* 26

revolution *la revolución* 207

rhyme *la rima* 69

rhythm *el ritmo* 71

ribbon *la cinta* 105

rice *el arroz* 192

rich *rico(a)* 43

richness *la riqueza* 71

riddle *la adivinanza* 209

ride *el paseo* 293

to **ride** *montar* 58

to **ride a bicycle** *montar en bici* 364

to **ride a horse** *montar a caballo* 364

to **ride a skateboard** *montar en monopatín* 364

rind *la cáscara* 190

ring *el anillo* 140

ripe *maduro(a)* 228

to **rise** *subir* 442

rite *el rito* 279

ritual *ritual* 176

rivalry *la rivalidad* 373

river *el río* 400

road *la calle* 20 *la carretera* 305

to **roast** *asar* 208 *tostar (irreg. ue)* 325

roasted *asado(a)* 216

robe *la bata* 140

rock *la roca* 120

Romance language *la lengua romance* 279

Romanian (language) *el rumano* 279

Romans *los romanos* 279

roof *el tejado* 88

room *la habitación* 27 *el cuarto* 92 *la sala* 253

rooster *el gallo* 424

rotation *la rotación* 407

round (of matches) *la jornada* 376

round-trip ticket *el boleto de ida y vuelta* 304

route *la ruta* 199

routine *la rutina* 16

to **row** *remar* 398

royal *real* 87

rug *la alfombra* 96

ruins *las ruinas* 72

to **run** *correr* 146 *dirigir* 318

rural tourism *el turismo rural* 319

Russian salad *la ensaladilla* 9

sad *triste* 52

sailor *el/la marinero(a)* 367

salad *la ensalada* 9

sales *las rebajas* 170

salesclerk *el/la dependiente(a)* 164

salesperson *el/la vendedor(a)* 351

salmon *el salmón* 192

salsa *la salsa* 123

salt *la sal* 208

salty *salado(a)* 216

Salvadoran *salvadoreño(a)* 70

samba *la samba* 407

same *mismo(a)* 150 *igual* 150

sandal *la sandalia* 140

sandwich *el sándwich* 9

Saturday *el sábado* 8

sauce *la salsa* 187

to **save** *salvar* 429

to **save energy** *ahorrar energía* 424

to **say** *decir (irreg.)* 90

to **say goodbye** *despedirse (irreg. i, i)* 166

scales *la balanza* 85

scarf *la bufanda* 140

scene *la escena* 117

schedule *el horario* 296

school *la escuela* 112

school (adjective) *escolar* 403

science (subject) *las Ciencias* 14

scientific *científico(a)* 203

scissors *las tijeras* 252

script *el guión* 169

sculpted *tallado(a)* 251

sculpture *la escultura* 280

sea *el mar* 400

sea (adjective) *marino(a)* 404

season *la temporada* 271

seasoning *los condimentos* 208

seat *la sede* 174 *el asiento* 304

seat belt *el cinturón de seguridad* 312

second *segundo(a)* 61

secondary *secundario(a)* 66

secret *el secreto* 214

secret (adjective) *secreto(a)* 189

secretary *el/la secretario(a)* 360

section *la sección* 183

to **see** *ver (irreg.)* 15 *apreciar* 401

See you. *Hasta la vista.* 2

See you later. *Hasta luego.* 2

See you soon. *Hasta pronto.* 2

See you tomorrow. *Hasta mañana.* 2

seed *la semilla* 195 *el grano* 198

to **seem** *resultar* 123

seismic *sísmico(a)* 419

to **seize** *tomar* 291

seldom *rara vez* 16

to **select** *seleccionar* 59

self-assessment *la autoevaluación* 79

to **sell** *vender* 12

seller *el/la vendedor(a)* 12

to **send** *enviar* 40 *mandar* 118

sentence *la oración* 43 *la frase* 79

sentimental *sentimental* 365

September *septiembre* 40

sequence *la secuencia* 385

serenade *la serenata* 83

series *la serie* 343

serious *serio(a)* 44

to **serve** *servir (irreg. i, i)* 18

service *el servicio* 112

to **set up** *instalar* 165

setting *el marco* 385

seventh *séptimo(a)* 70

several *varios(as)* 7 *diversos(as)* 243

to **shake hands** *estrechar la mano* 245

shampoo *el champú* 252

shape *la figura* 157

to **shave** *afeitarse* 252

she *ella* 4

sheep *la oveja* 424

shelf *el estante* 96

shellfish *el marisco* 192

ship *el barco* 20

shirt *la camisa* 98

shoe *el zapato* 8

shoe store *la zapatería* 156

to **shop** *hacer la compra* 200

shopping *las compras* 164

shopping *de compras* 8

shopping list *la lista de la compra* 200

shopping mall *el centro comercial* 8

short *bajo(a)* 5 *corto(a)* 42

shorts *los pantalones cortos* 135 *el pantalón corto* 140

shot *la inyección* 260

shoulder *el hombro* 244

to **shout** *gritar* 314

show *el espectáculo* 160

to **show** *enseñar* 97 *mostrar (irreg. ue)* 101 *reflejar* 425

shrimp *el camarón* 192

shy *tímido(a)* 5

siblings *los hermanos* 36

sick *enfermo(a)* 14

sidewalk *la acera* 112

siesta *la siesta* 255

sigh *el suspiro* 55

sightseeing (walking) *el turismo a pie* 20

sign *el cartel* 12 *señal* 112 *muestra* 157

signal *la señal* 311

silhouette *la silueta* 41

silly thing *la tontería* 384

silver *la plata* 137

silver (adjective) *plateado(a)* 148

silversmithing *la orfebrería* 299

similar *similar* 35 *parecido(a)* 47

similarity *la semejanza* 38

simply *simplemente* 315

sencillamente 384

since *desde* 47

sincere *sincero(a)* 44

Sincerely yours. *Atentamente.* 19

to **sing** *cantar* 15

singer *el/la cantante* 356

single *soltero(a)* 36 *solo(a)* 245

single room *la habitación sencilla* 320

singular *singular* 202

sink *el lavabo* 8

sister *la hermana* 36

to **sit** *sentarse (irreg. ie)* 127

sitting *sentado(a)* 114

situation *la situación* 141

size *la talla* 148

to **skate** *patinar* 268

to **ski** *esquiar* 375

skiing *el esquí* 372

skin *la piel* 25

skirt *la falda* 141 *la pollera* 171

skis *los esquís* 372

skull *el cráneo* 251

sky *el cielo* 55

slave *el/la esclavo(a)* 43

to **sleep** *dormir (irreg. ue, u)* 25

sleepiness *el sueño* 3

slide *la diapositiva* 381

slipper *la zapatilla* 140

slogan *el eslogan* 205

slow *lento(a)* 254

slowly *despacio, lentamente* 254

small *pequeño(a)* 40

small village *la aldea* 403

smell *el olor* 325

to **smell** *oler (irreg.)* 15

smile *la sonrisa* 19

smiley *el emoticono* 53

snake *la serpiente* 34

to **sneeze** *estornudar* 260

snow *la nieve* 416

to **snow** *nevar (irreg. ie)* 416

so *así que* 20 *más* 42 *tan* 97

so many *tantos(as)* 35

so much *tanto(a)* 322

soap *el jabón* 252

soap opera *la telenovela* 343

soccer *el fútbol* 372

soccer player *el/la futbolista* 45

sociable *sociable* 124

social *social* 51

society *la sociedad* 383

sock *el calcetín* 138

soda *el refresco* 10

sofa *el sofá* 96

soft *suave* 146

solid *sólido(a)* 191

solution *la solución* 283

to **solve** *resolver (irreg.)* 69

some *unos(as)* 6 *algún, alguno(a)(os)(as)* 194

someone *alguien* 321

something *algo* 8

son *el hijo* 36

song *la canción* 51

soon *pronto* 107

sophisticated *sofisticado(a)* 171

sorbet *el sorbete* 137

sound *el sonido* 331

to **sound** *sonar* 331

to **sound like** *imitar* 243

soup *la sopa* 186

sour *agrio(a)* 216

south *el sur* 408

southeast *el sureste* 408

Southern Ocean *el océano Glacial Antártico* 400

southwest *el suroeste* 408

souvenir *el recuerdo* 21

spa *el balneario* 274

spaghetti *los espaguetis* 233

Spanish (subject) *el Español* 2

Spanish (language) *el español* 38 *el castellano* 247

Spanish (nationality) *español(a)* 46

Spanish American *hispanoamericano(a)* 105

Spanish-speaking *hispanohablante* 219

to **speak** *hablar* 13

speaker *el/la hablante* 226

special *especial* 124

specially *especialmente* 245

specials (on a menu) *el menú del día* 216

specialty *la especialidad* 223

specific *específico(a)* 125 *determinado(a)* 165

spectacular *espectacular* 118

spectator *el/la espectador(a)* 280

speech bubble *el bocadillo* 41

speed *la velocidad* 335

spelling *la ortografía* 79

to **spend** (time) *pasar* 47

spice *la especia* 215

spider *la araña* 422

spinach *las espinacas* 192

spontaneous *espontáneo(a)* 44

spoon *la cuchara* 216

spoonful *la cucharada* 190

sport *el deporte* 1

sports store *la tienda de deportes* 156

sportsman *el deportista* 254

sportswear *la ropa deportiva* 182

sportswoman *la deportista* 254

spread out *extendido(a)* 72

spring *la primavera* 211

spy *el/la espía* 385

square *la plaza* 112 *la casilla* 131 *el cuadrado* 157

square (adjective) *cuadrado(a)* 176

stage *el escenario* 379 *la etapa* 394

stairs *la escalera* 13

stall *el puesto* 165

to **stand** *soportar* 362

to **stand in line** *hacer cola/fila* 200

star *la estrella* 345

to **start** (a car) *arrancar* 312

state *el estado* 21

statement *la afirmación* 67

stationery store *la papelería* 156

statistics *la estadística* 269

stay *la estancia* 121

to **stay** *quedarse* 121 *alojarse* 253 *mantenerse (irreg.)* 376

to **stay healthy** *mantenerse sano(a)* 268

steering wheel *el volante* 312

stem *la raíz* 1

step *el paso* 78

stereo *el equipo de música* 104

still *todavía* 139

stingy *tacaño(a)* 44

stomach *el estómago* 14

stone (adjective) *de piedra* 88

stone-paved *empedrado(a)* 123

to **stop** *parar(se)* 317 *dejar de* 431

stop sign *la señal de pare* 112

stoplight *el semáforo* 112

stopover *la escala* 304

store *la tienda* 12 *el comercio* 355

storm *la tormenta* 416

story *la planta* 8 *el cuento, la historia* 35 *el piso* 87 *la narración* 322

stove *la estufa* 104

strange *extraño(a)* 84 *raro(a)* 147

strategy *la estrategia* 73

strawberry *la fresa* 192

street *la calle* 20

street (adjective) *callejero(a)* 51

street map *el plano* 130

street market *el mercadillo* 165

striped *de rayas* 148

strong *fuerte* 44

structure *la estructura* 73

student *el/la estudiante* 2 *el/la alumno(a)* 212

student (adjective) *estudiantil* 251

studies *los estudios* 347

studious *estudioso(a)* 44

to **study** *estudiar* 54

style *el estilo* 91

subject (school) *la asignatura* 348

subjective *subjetivo(a)* 281

subjunctive *el subjuntivo* 358

subway *el metro* 21

success *el éxito* 365

such as *como* 40

suddenly *de repente* 315 *de pronto* 316

to **suffer** *sufrir* 159

sugar *el azúcar* 208

to **suggest** *sugerir (irreg. ie, i)* 220

suggestion *la sugerencia* 203

suit *el traje* 140

suitcase *la maleta* 20

summary *el resumen* 69

summer *el verano* 9

summer vacation *el veraneo* 280

sun *el sol* 25

sun (adjective) *solar* 25

to **sunbathe** *tomar el sol* 364

sunblock *el filtro solar* 25

Sunday *el domingo* 13

sunglasses *las gafas de sol* 140

superlative *el superlativo* 54

supermarket *el supermercado* 156

to **support** *sustentar* 177

supporter *el/la aficionado(a)* 376 *el/la partidario(a)* 436

sure *seguro(a)* 317

surface *la superficie* 407

surfing *el surf* 404

surgeon *el/la cirujano(a)* 356

surname *el apellido* 60

surprise *la sorpresa* 82

to **surprise** *sorprender* 366

surprised *sorprendido(a)* 52

surprising *sorprendente* 153

surrounded *rodeado(a)* 433

survey *la encuesta* 37

to **sweat** *sudar* 252

sweater *el suéter* 140

sweatshirt *la sudadera* 140

to **sweep** *barrer* 13

sweet (adjective) *dulce* 216

to **swim** *nadar* 15

swimming pool *la piscina* 15

swimsuit *el traje de baño* 140

symbol *el símbolo* 251

symbolic *simbólico(a)* 37

symptom *el síntoma* 1

system *el sistema* 45

T

tabasco *el tabasco* 198

table *la mesa* 8 *la tabla* 51

tablecloth *el mantel* 216

tablet *la pastilla* 261

taco *el taco* 187

tag *la etiqueta* 164

to **take** *tomar* 14 *sacar* 145 *llevar* 208 *tardar* 422

to **take a bath** *bañarse* 252

to **take a photo of** *fotografiar* 35

to **take a shower** *ducharse* 252

to **take an exam** *hacer un examen* 348

to **take away** *quitar* 187 *llevarse* 301

to **take care of** *cuidar* 14

to **take notes** *tomar apuntes* 348

to **take off** *despegar* 304 *quitarse* 431

to **take out** *sacar* 93

to **take out money** *sacar dinero* 320

to **take part** *intervenir (irreg.)* 51 *participar* 64

to **take place** *transcurrir* 390

to **take up** *ocupar* 122

talent *el talento* 369

to **talk** *conversar* 124

tall *alto(a)* 44

tambourine *la pandereta* 105

tango *el tango* 362

task *la tarea* 33

taste *el sabor* 179

to **taste** *saborear* 15 *probar (irreg. ue)* 198

tasteless *soso(a)* 216

taxi *el taxi* 110

tea *el té* 145

teacher *el/la profesor(a)* 2

team *el equipo* 19

telephone *el teléfono* 13

telephone conversation   la conversación telefónica 352
television   la televisión 13
television set   el televisor 8
to tell   contar (irreg. ue) 64 narrar 314 enseñar 312
temperature   la temperatura 416
tennis   el tenis 372
tennis shoes   los tenis 9
tense (of verb)   el tiempo 162
terrace   la terraza 324
terrible   terrible 316
terrific   fenomenal 292
territory   el territorio 71
text   el texto 47
textile   el textil 157
textile (adjective)   textil 171
than   que 54
thank you   gracias 39
that   que 19
that (at a distance)   ese, esa, eso 114
that (far away)   aquel, aquella, aquello 114
that one (at a distance)   ese, esa 114
that one (far away)   aquel, aquella 114
That's not true.   No es cierto/verdad. 344
That's true.   Es cierto/verdad. 344
that's why   por eso 428
the (singular)   el, la 2
the (plural)   los, las 1
the day after tomorrow   pasado mañana 410
the day before yesterday   anteayer 150
theater   el teatro 116
their   su, sus 8 suyo(a)(os)(as) 38
theirs   el/la/los/las suyo(a)(os)(as) 38
(to) them   les 106
theme   el tema 105
themselves   se 16
then   después 14 luego 48 entonces 69 pues 357
theory   la teoría 53
there   allí 20 ahí 22
there is/there are   hay 22
thermometer   el termómetro 416
these   estos, estas 114
thesis   la tesis 437
they   ellos(as) 4
they/you usually …   suelen/sueles… 13

thick   grueso(a) 176
thin   delgado(a) 2 ligero(a) 280
thing   la cosa 6
to think   pensar (irreg. ie) 18 opinar 84
third   tercer(o)(a) 163
thirst   la sed 3
this   este, esta, esto 114
this afternoon   esta tarde 410
this morning   esta mañana 410
this one   este, esta 114
this way   así 89
those (at a distance)   esos, esas 114
those (far away)   aquellos, aquellas 38
throat   la garganta 260
through   a través de 280
to throw   arrojar 295 tirar 313
Thursday   el jueves 349
ticket   el boleto 20
tidy   ordenado(a) 357
to tidy up   ordenar 13
tie   la corbata 140
to tie   empatar 372
tied back   recogido(a) 280
tile   el azulejo 91
time   la hora 15 el tiempo 47
time (adjective)   temporal 150
tip   la propina 216
tired   cansado(a) 2
title   el título 249
to   para 8 a 21
to the left   a la izquierda 22
to the right   a la derecha 22
today   hoy 5
toe   el dedo (del pie) 244
together   juntos(as) 40
together with   junto con 347
toilet   el inodoro 9
toiletries bag   el neceser 256
tomato   el tomate 192
tomato sauce   la salsa de tomate 208
tomorrow   mañana 67
tomorrow night   mañana por la noche 391
tone (on phone)   la señal 361
tonight   esta noche 410
too (before adjective)   demasiado 194
too many   demasiados(as) 194
too much   demasiado(a) 194 demasiado 195
tooth (in general)   el diente 244
tooth (molar)   la muela 261

toothpaste   la pasta de dientes 252
top   máximo(a) 55
topic   el tema 274
tornado   el tornado 416
tortilla   tortilla 193 omelet 193
total   total 183
totally   totalmente 43
to touch   tocar 15
tourism   el turismo 25
tourist   el/la turista 119
tourist (adjective)   turístico(a) 119
tourist class   la clase turista 304
tourist development   el complejo turístico 403
tourist guide book   la guía turística 20
tournament   el torneo 376
towards   hacia 412
towel   la toalla 320
tower   la torre 266
town   el pueblo 69
tradition   la tradición 72
traditional   tradicional 72
traffic   el tráfico 112
train   el tren 304
to train   entrenar 377
train platform   el andén 304
train station   la estación de tren 304
train track   la vía 304
trait   el rasgo 1
transit   el movimiento 297
to translate   traducir (irreg.) 384
transportation   el transporte 1
to travel   viajar 20
travel agency   la agencia de viajes 296
travel agent   el/la agente de viajes 296
traveler   el/la viajero(a) 296
tray   la bandeja 208
treasure   el tesoro 203
tree   el árbol 20
trip   el viaje 20
triple   triple 324
tropical   tropical 71
true   verdadero(a) 153
Truly yours.   Atentamente. 19
truth   la verdad 45
to try   intentar 291
to try clothes on   probarse ropa 164
T-shirt   la camiseta 140
Tuesday   el martes 349
tuna   el atún 192

tunnel el túnel 215

turkey el pavo 215

turn la vuelta 302

to **turn into** convertir (irreg. ie, i) 166

to **turn right/left** doblar a la derecha/a la izquierda 20

turquoise turquesa 124

turtle la tortuga marina 422

twin mellizo(a) 47

type el tipo 111 el género 123

typical típico(a) 8 propio(a) 71

uncle el tío 4

uncomfortable incómodo(a) 148

under debajo de 22

to **understand** entender (irreg. ie) 18 comprender 435

unforeseen inesperado(a) 315

unforgettable inolvidable 221

unfortunately desafortunadamente 163 desgraciadamente 404

union la unión 382

unique único(a) 101

unit la unidad 28

to **unite** unir 436

university la universidad 102

university student el/la estudiante universitario(a) 105

unknown desconocido(a) 332

to **unload the dishwasher** descargar el lavaplatos 88

unpleasant antipático(a) 4

untidy desordenado(a) 89

up arriba 214

to **upset** molestar 362

upstairs arriba 391

urban urbanístico(a) 113

Uruguayan uruguayo(a) 357

(to) us nos 106

use el uso 194

to **use** usar 15 utilizar 55 emplear 105

to **use for** destinar a 305

useful útil 32 práctico(a) 339

uses (of medicine) las indicaciones 263

usually habitualmente 104

utensil el utensilio 208

vacation las vacaciones 25

vaccine la vacuna 339

vacuum (cleaner) la aspiradora 91

to **vacuum** pasar la aspiradora 91

vague vago(a) 55

valley el valle 400

valuable valioso(a) 167

value el valor 177

valued apreciado(a) 171

vanilla la vainilla 212

varied variado(a) 171

variety la variedad 59

vase el florero 96

vegetable (adjective) vegetal 176

vegetable la verdura 192

vegetarian vegetariano(a) 193

vegetation la vegetación 71

Venezuelan venezolano(a) 303

verb el verbo 1

verbal verbal 181

version la versión 247

very muy 2

veterinarian el/la veterinario(a) 354

viceroyalty el virreinato 227

vicuña la vicuña 176

video el video 27

videogame el videojuego 14

view la vista 319

viewer el/la espectador(a) 280

viewpoint el mirador 370

village el pueblo 69

vinegar el vinagre 208

violin el violín 71

virgin (adjective) virgen 433

visa el visado 339

visit la visita 211

to **visit** visitar 296

visitor el/la visitante 111

vital vital 376

vitamin la vitamina 266

vocabulary el vocabulario 1

voice la voz 357

volcanic volcánico(a) 35

volcano el volcán 35

volleyball el voleibol 372

volume el volumen 303

volunteer el/la voluntario(a) 159

voting la votación 69

vowel la vocal 90

waist la cintura 244

to **wait** esperar 45

waiter/waitress el/la mesero(a) 216

to **wake up** despertarse (irreg. ie) 16

walk el paseo 123

to **walk** caminar 21 andar (irreg.) 175

wall la pared 86

walnut la nuez 195

waltz el vals 331

to **want** querer (irreg.) 18

wardrobe el armario 8

warm cálido(a) 149

warning la advertencia 263

to **wash** lavar 13

to **wash up** lavarse 252

washing machine la lavadora 104

watch el reloj 140

to **watch** ver (irreg.) 15 observar 407

water el agua 14

waterfall la catarata 302 el salto de agua 303 la cascada 400

watermelon la sandía 192

wavy ondulado(a) 280

way la forma, la manera 21 el modo 175 el camino 227

we nosotros(as) 4

weak débil 14

to **wear** llevar 9

to **wear glasses** llevar gafas 44

weather el tiempo 211

weather (adjective) meteorológico(a) 419

web la red 41

website la página web 35

wedding la boda 179

wedding (adjective) matrimonial 176

Wednesday el miércoles 349

week la semana 19

weekend el fin de semana 17

to **weigh** pesar 44

weight el peso 45

welcome bienvenido(a) 2

well bien 8 pues 138

well-known conocido(a) 123

west el oeste 408

what qué 3 lo que 20

what a coincidence! ¡qué casualidad! 324

Y

Z

ÍNDICE GRAMATICAL

hoy   410; see also *temporal expressions with the future; expressing plans and intentions*

 I

identifying people and things   6; see also *articles; nouns*

-ido   246; see also *verbs, past participle, regular verbs*

imperfect tense   298; see also *verbs, temporal expressions with the imperfect; verbs, imperfect tense, regular verbs, irregular verbs*

importante   374; *adjectives;* see also *expressing doubt and making value statements*

increíble   374; *adjectives;* see also *expressing doubt and making value statements*

indefinites   194; ningún, ninguno(a), algún, alguno(a)(os)(as), poco(a)(os)(as), mucho(a)(os)(as), todo(a)(os)(as), demasiado(a)(os)(as); see also *expressing quantity*

indirect object   106; see also *indirect object pronouns*

indirect object pronouns   106; me, te, le, nos, os, les, se

interrogative words   62; qué, cuál(es), quién(es), cuánto(a), cuántos(as), dónde, cuándo, cómo, por qué, para qué, adónde, de dónde

ir   24, 158, 202, 210, 218, 298, 374; "ir a" + infinitive 410, 418; see also *verbs, commands, affirmative informal commands in singular, irregular verbs; affirmative formal commands, irregular verbs; negative commands, irregular verbs; verbs, present tense, irregular verbs; verbs, preterite tense, irregular verbs; verbs, imperfect tense, irregular verbs; verbs, present tense subjunctive, irregular verbs*

ir a + *place*   24; see also a; ir; *expressing movement*

-ir verbs   12; see also *verbs, present tense, regular verbs;* abrir

-ísimo(a)(os)(as)   54; see also *superlative*

izquierda de, a la   22; see also *expressing location and existence*

 J

jugar   366; see also *verbs, present tense subjunctive, stem-changing verbs*

 L

lado de, al   22; see also *expressing location and existence*

lavarse   16; see also *reflexive pronuns; expressing daily routines; verbs, reflexive verbs*

le, les   106; see also *indirect object pronouns*

leer   90, 246; see also *verbs, present progressive; verbs, present participle;* -yendo; *verbs, past participle;* -eído

lejos de   22; see also *expressing location and existence*

levantarse   16; see also *reflexive pronouns; expressing daily routines; verbs, reflexive verbs*

llegar   142, 374; see also *verbs, preterite tense, irregular "yo" form verbs (car > qué, gar > gué, zar > cé); verbs, present tense subjunctive, spelling-changing verbs*

lo, la, los, las   98; see also *direct object pronouns*

luego   410; see also *temporal expressions with the future; expressing plans and intentions*

lunes que viene, el   410; see also *temporal expressions with the future; expressing plans and intentions*

 M

malo   374; see also *adjectives; expressing doubt and making value statements*

mañana   410; see also *temporal expressions with the future; expressing plans and intentions*

mañana, esta   410; see also *temporal expressions with the future; expressing plans and intentions*

mañana, por la   410; see also *temporal expressions with the future; expressing plans and intentions*

maquillar   246; see also *verbs, past participle, regular verbs*

maquillarse   16; see also *reflexive pronouns; verbs, reflexive verbs*

más + adjetivo + que   54; see also *comparison*

me   16; see also *direct object pronouns; indirect object pronouns; reflexive pronouns; verbs, reflexive verbs;* gustar

media hora, en   410; see also *temporal expressions with the future; expressing plans and intentions*

medir   18, 166; see also *verbs, present tense, stem-changing verbs (e > i); verbs, preterite tense, stem-changing verbs (e > i)*

mejor   402; see also *adjectives; comparison*

menos + adjetivo + que   54; see also *comparison*

-mente   254; see also *adverbs ending in -mente*

mentir   90, 166; see also *verbs, present participle, stem-changing verbs (e > i); verbs, preterite tense, stem-changing verbs (e > i)*

mes pasado, el   150; see also *temporal expressions with the past tense*

mes que viene, el   410; see also *temporal expressions with the future; expressing plans and intentions*

mi(s)   38; see also *expressing possession; nouns, agreement, noun + possessive adjective; possessive adjectives, placement*

mientras   314; see also *verbs, imperfect tense*

mío(a)(os)(as)   38; see also *expressing possession; nouns, agreement, noun + possessive adjective; possessive adjectives, placement; possessive pronouns*

molestar   366; see also *expressing feelings and emotions;* gustar

morir   90, 246; see also *verbs, present participle, stem-changing verbs (o > u); verbs, past participle, irregular verbs*

muchas veces   16, 298; see also *adverbs of frequency; expressing frequency; temporal expressions with the imperfect*

CRÉDITOS FOTOGRÁFICOS (TEACHER'S EDITION)

Cubierta F. Waldhaeusl/ARCO/A. G. E. FOTOSTOCK; Michael S. Lewis/GETTY IMAGES SALES SPAIN; I. Preysler/Atrezzo: Helen Chelton; ISTOCKPHOTO; **Contracubierta** GARCÍA-PELAYO/Juancho/MUSEU PICASSO, BARCELONA; Hauke Dressler/A. G. E. FOTOSTOCK; Marcos Brindicci/REUTERS/CORDON PRESS; Ken Gillham/GETTY IMAGES SALES SPAIN; **T1** I. Preysler/Atrezzo: Helen Chelton; **T4** Adam Woolfitt/ A. G. E. FOTOSTOCK; I. Preysler/Atrezzo: Helen Chelton; **T5** Jacques Jangoux/A. G. E. FOTOSTOCK; **T7** I. Preysler/Atrezzo: Helen Chelton; Javier Larrea/A. G. E. FOTOSTOCK; **T8** I. Preysler/Atrezzo: Helen Chelton; SEIS x SEIS; **T9** C. Díez Polanco; FUNDACIÓN SANTILLANA; I. Preysler/Atrezzo: Helen Chelton; ISTOCKPHOTO; **T11** I. Preysler/Atrezzo: Helen Chelton; **T15** I. Preysler/Atrezzo: Helen Chelton; SERIDEC PHOTOIMAGENES CD; The Art Archive/Museo Nacional de Historia Guatemala City/Gianni Dagli Orti/The Picture Desk Limited; **T16** I. Preysler/Atrezzo: Helen Chelton; **T18** Amos Morgan/A. G. E. FOTOSTOCK; **T22** I. Preysler/Atrezzo: Helen Chelton. **T23** I. Preysler/ Atrezzo: Helen Chelton; ARCHIVO SANTILLANA

CRÉDITOS FOTOGRÁFICOS (STUDENT BOOK)

Cubierta: 001 F. Waldhaeusl/ ARCO/A. G. E. FOTOSTOCK; Michael S. Lewis/GETTY IMAGES SALES SPAIN; I. PREYSLER/ATREZZO: HELEN CHELTON; ISTOCKPHOTO; **Contracubierta: 001** GARCÍA-PELAYO/Juancho/MUSEU PICASSO, BARCELONA; Hauke Dressler/A. G. E. FOTOSTOCK; Marcos Brindicci/ REUTERS/CORDON PRESS; Ken Gillham/GETTY IMAGES SALES SPAIN; **I** I. PREYSLER/ATREZZO: HELEN CHELTON **IV** I. PREYSLER/ATREZZO: HELEN CHELTON; S. Jiménez; ISTOCKPHOTO **V** F. Morera; Gavin Hellier/GETTY IMAGES SALES SPAIN; I. PREYSLER/ ATREZZO: HELEN CHELTON **VI** J. C. Muñoz; Jenny & Tony Enderby, José Fuste Raga/A. G. E. FOTOSTOCK **X** Photos.com Plus/GETTY IMAGES SALES SPAIN **XI** C. Díez Polanco; Sergio Pitamitz/A. G. E. FOTOSTOCK; EFE; Image Source/FOTONONSTOP; I. PREYSLER/ATREZZO: HELEN CHELTON; SEIS X SEIS **XII** F. Waldhaeusl/ ARCO/A. G. E. FOTOSTOCK **XVIII** C. Díez Polanco; ARCO/F. Gierth, Michele Falzone, Sylvain Grandadam/A. G. E. FOTOSTOCK; EFE; I. PREYSLER/ATREZZO: HELEN CHELTON; SEIS X SEIS **XIV** Bill Bachmann/A. G. E. FOTOSTOCK **XV** C. Díez Polanco; José Enrique Molina/A. G. E. FOTOSTOCK; EFE; Photos.com Plus/GETTY IMAGES SALES SPAIN; I. PREYSLER/ATREZZO: HELEN CHELTON; SEIS X SEIS **XVI** Photos.com Plus/GETTY IMAGES SALES SPAIN **XVII** C. Díez Polanco; G. Aldana; Buddy Mays/ CORBIS/ CORDON PRESS; EFE; I. PREYSLER/ATREZZO: HELEN CHELTON; ISTOCKPHOTO; SEIS X SEIS **XVIII** J. Lucas **XIX** C. Díez Polanco; M. Sánchez; Joseph Sohm/A. G. E. FOTOSTOCK; EFE; I. PREYSLER/ATREZZO: HELEN CHELTON; SEIS X SEIS **XX** Heeb Christian/A. G. E. FOTOSTOCK **XXI** C. Díez Polanco; EFE; Ethel Davis/GETTY IMAGES SALES SPAIN; I. PREYSLER/ATREZZO: HELEN CHELTON; ISTOCKPHOTO; SEIS X SEIS **XXII** DEA/PUBBLI AER FOTO/A. G. E. FOTOSTOCK **XXIII** C. Díez Polanco; Chad Ehlers, Ximena Griscti/A. G. E. FOTOSTOCK; EFE; I. PREYSLER/ ATREZZO: HELEN CHELTON; ISTOCKPHOTO; SEIS X SEIS **XXIV** Hauke Dressler/A. G. E. FOTOSTOCK **XXV** C. Díez Polanco; J. C. Muñoz; Manfred Gottschalk, Stuart Pearce/A. G. E. FOTOSTOCK; EFE; I. PREYSLER/ATREZZO: HELEN CHELTON; SEIS X SEIS; **000** I. PREYSLER/ATREZZO: HELEN CHELTON **002** Prats i Camps; Comstock/GETTY IMAGES SALES SPAIN; I. PREYSLER/ATREZZO: HELEN CHELTON; ISTOCKPHOTO **003** J. Jaime; Sony Computer Entertainment Inc.; I. PREYSLER/ATREZZO: HELEN CHELTON; ISTOCKPHOTO **005** F. Morera; J. Jaime; SERIDEC PHOTOIMAGE-NES CD; A. G. E. FOTOSTOCK; Gavin Hellier/GETTY IMAGES SALES SPAIN; I. PREYSLER/ATREZZO: HELEN CHELTON; ISTOCKPHOTO **007** Prats i Camps; COMSTOCK; ISTOCKPHOTO **008** Prats i Camps; I. PREYSLER/ATREZZO: HELEN CHELTON **009** Prats i Camps; Photos.com Plus/GETTY IMAGES SALES SPAIN; AbleStock.com/HIGHRES PRESS STOCK; ISTOCKPHOTO **011** J. Jaime; Prats i Camps; AbleStock.com/HIGHRES PRESS STOCK; I. PREYSLER/ATREZZO: HELEN CHELTON; ISTOCKPHOTO **012** AbleStock.com/HIGHRES PRESS STOCK **013** J. Jaime; Prats i Camps; COMSTOCK; AbleStock.com/HIGHRES PRESS STOCK **014** J. Jaime; Prats i Camps; I. PREYSLER/ATREZZO: HELEN CHELTON **015** A. Prieto/AGENCIA ESTUDIO SAN SIMÓN; AbleStock.com/HIGHRES PRESS STOCK **016** C. Pérez; Photos.com Plus/GETTY IMAGES SALES SPAIN **017** Prats i Camps **019** D. Serra; J. Jaime; Prats i Camps; Cafetería Alverán, Boadilla del Monte/I. PREYSLER/ATREZZO: HELEN CHELTON **020** J. M.ª Escudero; I. PREYSLER/ATREZZO: HELEN CHELTON; ISTOCKPHOTO **021** I. PREYSLER/ATREZZO: HELEN CHELTON **025** Johanna Hanno/A. G. E. FOTOSTOCK; FOTONONSTOP; AbleStock.com/HIGHRES PRESS STOCK **026** J. Jaime; Franco Pizzochero, Science Photo Library/A. G. E. FOTOSTOCK; Photos.com Plus/GETTY IMAGES SALES SPAIN; AbleStock.com/HIGHRES PRESS STOCK; ISTOCKPHOTO **027** A. Viñas; J. Jaime; SERIDEC PHOTOIMAGENES CD; Ken Cavanagh/A. G. E. FOTOSTOCK; AbleStock.com/HIGHRES PRESS STOCK; I. PREYSLER/ATREZZO: HELEN CHELTON; ISTOCKPHOTO **028** Philippe Michel/A. G. E. FOTOSTOCK; Wendy Connett/GETTY IMAGES SALES SPAIN **029** Krauel; Margie Politzer/A. G. E. FOTOSTOCK **030** C. Díez Polanco; Image Source/FOTONONSTOP; I. PREYSLER/ATREZZO: HELEN CHELTON **031** C. Díez Polanco; Image Source/FOTONONSTOP; Photos.com Plus/GETTY IMAGES SALES SPAIN; I. PREYSLER/ATREZZO: HELEN CHELTON **032** Prats i Camps; COMSTOCK; I. PREYSLER/ATREZZO: HELEN CHELTON **033** Liane Cary, Margie Politzer, Philippe Michel/ A. G. E. FOTOSTOCK; Wendy Connett/GETTY IMAGES SALES SPAIN; I. PREYSLER/ATREZZO: HELEN CHELTON **034** VolcanoDiscovery/Tom Pfeiffer, Wendy Connett/GETTY IMAGES SALES SPAIN; I. PREYSLER/ATREZZO: HELEN CHELTON **035** C. Díez Polanco; PureStock/A. G. E. FOTOSTOCK; I. PREYSLER/ATREZZO: HELEN CHELTON **036** Prats i Camps; I. PREYSLER/ATREZZO: HELEN CHELTON **037** GARCÍA-PELAYO/ Juancho; I. PREYSLER/ATREZZO: HELEN CHELTON **039** Prats i Camps; Photos.com Plus/GETTY IMAGES SALES SPAIN; I. PREYSLER/ATREZZO: HELEN CHELTON; ISTOCKPHOTO **040** I. PREYSLER/ATREZZO: HELEN CHELTON **041** Prats i Camps; Wendy Connett/GETTY IMAGES SALES SPAIN; I. PREYSLER/ATREZZO: HELEN CHELTON **042** Alberto Paredes, Dennis MacDonald, Richard Cummins/A. G. E. FOTOSTOCK; I. PREYS-LER/ATREZZO: HELEN CHELTON **043** Adalberto Ríos Szalay, Alberto Paredes/A. G. E. FOTOSTOCK; AbleStock.com/HIGHRES PRESS STOCK; I. PREYSLER/ATREZZO: HELEN CHELTON **044** Prats i Camps; SERIDEC PHOTOIMAGENES CD; Photos.com Plus/GETTY IMAGES SALES SPAIN; AbleStock.com/HIGHRES PRESS STOCK; I. PREYSLER/ATREZZO: HELEN CHELTON; ISTOCKPHOTO **045** ISTOCKPHOTO **046** A. Prieto/AGENCIA ESTUDIO SAN SIMÓN **047** C. Díez Polanco; J. L. Pelaez, Inc/A. G. E. FOTOSTOCK **048** S. Enríquez; AbleStock.com/HIGHRES PRESS STOCK; ISTOCKPHOTO **049** Prats i Camps; Philippe Michel/A. G. E. FOTOSTOCK **050** Jane Sweeney, Stefano Paterna/A. G. E. FOTOSTOCK; I. PREYS-LER/ATREZZO: HELEN CHELTON **051** In Pictures/Barry Lewis/CORBIS/CORDON PRESS; I. PREYSLER/ATREZZO: HELEN CHELTON **053** A. Castellanos/MUSEO NACIONAL DE HISTORIA Y ANTROPOLOGÍA, MÉXICO; AbleStock.com/HIGHRES PRESS STOCK; ISTOCKPHOTO **054** I. PREYSLER/ATREZZO: HELEN CHELTON **055** BIBLIOTECA NACIONAL DE ESPAÑA/Laboratorio Biblioteca Nacional; SERIDEC PHOTOIMAGE-NES CD; Photos.com Plus/GETTY IMAGES SALES SPAIN; AbleStock.com/HIGHRES PRESS STOCK **056** I. PREYSLER/ATREZZO: HELEN CHELTON **057** C. Pérez; Richard Cummins/A. G. E. FOTOSTOCK; I. PREYSLER/ATREZZO: HELEN CHELTON **058** Liane Cary/A. G. E. FOTOSTOCK; I. PREYSLER/ATREZZO: HELEN CHELTON; ISTOCKPHOTO **059** True North Images/A. G. E. FOTOSTOCK; I. PREYSLER/ATREZZO: HELEN CHELTON **060** S. Enríquez **061** Prats i Camps; Photos.com Plus/GETTY IMAGES SALES SPAIN **062** ISTOCKPHOTO **063** I. PREYSLER/ATREZZO: HELEN CHELTON **064** Prats i Camps; FOTONONSTOP **065** Nik Wheeler, CuboImages/Robert Harding/Marco Simoni/ CORBIS/CORDON;I. PREYSLER/ ATREZZO: HELEN CHELTON **067** Juniors Bildarchiv/A. G. E. FOTOSTOCK **068** John Coletti, Philippe Michel/A. G. E. FOTOSTOCK; Wendy Connett/ GETTY IMAGES SALES SPAIN; I. PREYSLER/ATREZZO: HELEN CHELTON **069** I. PREYSLER/ATREZZO: HELEN CHELTON **070** AbleStock.com/ HIGHRES PRESS STOCK **071** Sergio Pitamitz/A. G. E. FOTOSTOCK; Edgar Romero/ AFP PHOTO/GETTY IMAGES SALES SPAIN **072** C. Díez Polanco **073** SEIS X SEIS **075** Prats i Camps **077** Krauel; FOTONONSTOP **078** The Bridgeman Art Library/INDEX **079** Prats i Camps **080** G. R. Richardson, Sylvain Grandadam/A. G. E. FOTOSTOCK **081** Katja Kreder/A. G. E. FOTOSTOCK **082** Angelo Cavalli/A. G. E. FOTOSTOCK; Reinhard Eisele/ CORBIS/CORDON PRESS; I. PREYSLER/ATREZZO: HELEN CHELTON **083** Reinhard Eisele/ CORBIS/CORDON PRESS; Photos.com Plus/GETTY IMAGES SALES SPAIN; I. PREYSLER/ATREZZO: HELEN CHELTON **084** Prats i Camps; S. Enríquez; COMSTOCK; AbleStock.com/HIGHRES PRESS STOCK; I. PREYSLER/ATREZZO: HELEN CHELTON **085** J. Jaime/Francisco Arribas; Prats i Camps; I. PREYSLER/ATREZZO: HELEN CHELTON; ISTOCKPHOTO **086** C. Díez Polanco; Palladium/A. G. E. FOTOSTOCK; Alamy Images/ACI AGENCIA DE FOTOGRAFÍA; I. PREYSLER/ATREZZO: HELEN CHELTON **087** GARCÍA-PELAYO/Juancho/BIBLIOTECA NACIONAL DE ESPAÑA; I. PREYSLER/ATREZZO: HELEN CHELTON **088** Prats i Camps; SERIDEC PHOTOIMAGENES CD; DIGITAL BANK; AbleStock.com/HIGHRES PRESS STOCK; I. PREYSLER/ATREZZO: HELEN CHELTON **089** Álvaro Leiva/A. G. E. FOTOSTOCK; ISTOCKPHOTO **090** I. PREYSLER/ATREZZO: HELEN CHELTON **091** Daniele Schneider/FOTONONSTOP **092** I. PREYSLER/ATREZZO: HELEN CHELTON **093** Álvaro Leiva/A. G. E. FOTOSTOCK;